EUROPE IN OUR TIME

A HISTORY 1945–1992

Walter Laqueur

PENGUIN BOOKS

PENGUIN BOOKS
Published by the Penguin Group
Penguin Books USA Inc.,
375 Hudson Street, New York, New York 10014, U.S.A.
Penguin Books Ltd, 27 Wrights Lane, London W8 5TZ, England
Penguin Books Australia Ltd, Ringwood, Victoria, Australia
Penguin Books Canada Ltd, 10 Alcorn Avenue,
Toronto, Ontario, Canada M4V 3B2
Penguin Books (N.Z.) Ltd, 182–190 Wairau Road,
Auckland 10, New Zealand

Penguin Books Ltd, Registered Offices:
Harmondsworth, Middlesex, England

First published in the United States of America by
Viking Penguin, a division of Penguin Books USA Inc., 1992
Published in Penguin Books 1993

3 5 7 9 10 8 6 4

THE LIBRARY OF CONGRESS HAS CATALOGED THE HARDCOVER AS FOLLOWS:
Laqueur, Walter.
Europe in our time : a history, 1945–1992 / Walter Laqueur.
p.   cm.
Includes index.
ISBN 0-670-83507-2 (hc.)
ISBN 0 14 01.3969 9 (pbk.)
1. Europe—History—1945–   I. Title.
D1051.L28   1992
940.5—dc20   91-16752

Printed in the United States of America
Set in Sabon and Centaur
Designed by Ann Gold

PREFACE

The end of the Second World War was the closing of one of the most unhappy chapters in the long history of the continent. For many years after 1945 the countries of Europe had to live with its consequences. It took less time than most had assumed to rebuild the cities and the industries, but even after the various economic miracles had taken place, the continent was still divided, with thousands of nuclear arms and strong conventional forces deployed on both sides of the iron curtain.*

Only now can it be said with assurance that the postwar age has finally come to an end. The late 1980s witnessed a new era of reform in the Soviet Union, and in 1989 the communist regimes in Eastern Europe collapsed. At the same time the magical year 1992 came and went, which should have resulted in a single common market, comprising more than three hundred million people. It is far too early even to speculate about the political and social consequences of 1992, which may well be less far-reaching, in the short run, than widely assumed. But it is not too early to state that the agenda of European politics has decisively changed and that it is no longer dominated by the consequences of Hitler's and Stalin's crimes five decades ago.

The end of the postwar age is not the end of history, nor is it the end of conflicts and crises, but European concerns are certainly

---

* The term was not invented by either Goebbels or Churchill, as commonly believed. The first use I have seen was in Ethel Snowden, *Through Bolshevik Russia*, New York–London, 1920: "We were behind the 'iron curtain' at last!" (p. 32).

v

now very different from what they were. Those who saw the Berlin wall coming down in November 1989 could truly say (and perhaps with even greater justification) what Goethe had noted on the occasion of the battle of Valmy (1792): "From this place and this time forth commences a new era in world history and you can all say that you were present at its birth." There is always some doubt with regard to periodization in history, but seldom have the parameters been as obvious as in this specific case.

Less than fifty years have passed since the guns fell silent and the air raids ceased in Europe, and it is difficult now to imagine the extent of the suffering, the destruction, and the hopelessness prevailing at the time. True, Victory Day was celebrated everywhere, but on the day after, only the bravest spirits could see light at the end of the tunnel, as far as the prospects for a revival of Europe were concerned. It was not just the amount of material destruction, but the absence of hope. Fortunately, perhaps, only a very few people gave much thought in 1945 to the future of their country, let alone the continent. The overwhelming majority were wholly preoccupied with such prosaic issues as getting food and shelter for the next day or week.

Most of those who were concerned with Europe's future were in a state of shock and despair; there were excellent reasons for their pessimism, and not just because Europe had lost its pre-eminent place in the world. The relative decline of Europe was a long, drawn-out process that had begun much earlier as a consequence of political, economic, social, and, last but not least, demographic processes.

When I attended geography classes in the early 1930s, my teachers and textbooks told me that London, Berlin, and Paris, together with New York, were the biggest cities in the world. By 1980 these had been long overtaken by Mexico City, Cairo, Peking, São Paulo, and Bombay. Berlin was divided, but even a reunited Berlin has fewer inhabitants than Seoul and Tientsin. Paris is now less populous than Bogotá, Madras, and Mukden (now known as Shenyang). The global scale has radically changed during my own lifetime, and demographers tell us that by the year 2000 cities such as Kinshasa (a sleepy village called Léopoldville in the 1930s), Nagoya, Pusan, and Ahmedabad— of which even the star pupils of 1931 had not heard—may well have over five million inhabitants. Few Europeans are disturbed because their main cities have not grown at the rate of Calcutta, for they are only too aware of the price that would have been paid.

The European continent is aging. The statisticians have established that it takes 2.1 children per mother for the general population to remain steady. But the fertility rate in Britain is 1.85, in France 1.81, in West Germany 1.40, in Spain and Italy 1.30. The birthrate in North Africa and in Turkey, on the other hand, is three times higher; there is massive endemic unemployment in these parts.

The crisis facing Europe in 1945 arose not because it had lost its dominating position but because the survival of the continent was at stake. As the result of two world wars—called European civil wars by some observers—and of fascist aggressive tyranny and nationalist passions running wild, Europe had become politically impotent and was on the verge of economic collapse. It is worth recalling that not so long ago it appeared uncertain whether European agriculture would be able to provide the minimum needed to prevent starvation. The prospects for industry appeared equally dismal, and the greatest worry of the financiers was the "dollar gap"—the strength of the dollar and the weakness of the main European currencies. Eastern Europe was incorporated in all but name in the Soviet empire. Germany had ceased to exist as a unit; the small and middle-sized states of Western Europe were incapable of defending themselves, and seemed no longer viable, politically as well as economically.

Further, the continent displayed all the signs of cultural exhaustion. Admittedly, Europe had been declared dead many times during the preceding thousand years. Prophets had been announcing for centuries that the old continent had reached the stage of senescence, and that its societies were in an advanced stage of corruption. Though the message of *finis Europae* had been proclaimed many times, there was in 1945 more reason than ever to predict the continent's impending demise.

But, whatever the philosophers were saying, the people of Europe had no intention of disappearing from the historical scene. Ironically, it was the external threat that gave the first spur to European recovery. Had Stalin been satisfied with turning Eastern Europe into a mere Soviet sphere of influence, it is doubtful whether Western Europe would have rallied, whether there would have been a Marshall Plan, the OEEC, and the treaty of Brussels, which ultimately led to NATO (the North Atlantic Treaty Organization). Stalin's policy of recasting Eastern Europe in the Soviet mold was a double mistake: it did not add to Soviet security, and it galvanized the rest of Europe.

The economies of Western Europe would have been rebuilt in any case, but it would have taken much longer, nor is it certain whether inter-European cooperation would have made similar progress. As Jean Monnet once said: "The crises are the great federators," and postwar Europe certainly faced a major crisis of survival.

The Soviet Union quite likely never intended to invade Western Europe, as many feared at the time. But it is also true that a vacuum of power in Western Europe would have constituted a permanent temptation to the superpower in the East, with its formidable military power headed by a leadership that knew neither scruples nor internal divisions. Fear of Russia was probably the single most important cause generating greater willingness in Europe to cooperate, but it was not, of course, the only such factor. Another was the need to integrate West Germany into the European community so as to make war impossible, to prevent a recurrence of the horrible events of the 1930s and '40s.

For the Germans such a scheme had also much to recommend it. It was the best, perhaps the only, way to rejoin European and world politics on equal terms. The Germans also understood, as did the other West Europeans, the great advantage of a common, greater market: lasting progress could not be sustained simply by relying on the goodwill and the farsightedness of Europeans of the first hour such as Robert Schuman, Henri Spaak, or Adenauer; a supranational element, however inconspicuous, was needed. To quote again Jean Monnet: "Nothing is possible without men, nothing is lasting without institutions." Thus, soon after the war the first touches were put to a common European home.

The history of Europe in the postwar period is untidy. It often defies generalization, because it is the history not of one continent but of many countries. There are common threads and continent-wide trends, but there were even more disparate elements and national peculiarities: while one country went left, another turned right; while one prospered, another faced serious social and economic difficulties. If European cooperation made progress, it was agonizingly slow, and national politics reasserted themselves all along.

German economic recovery gathered speed with the merger of its three Western zones and, above all, the all-important currency reform of June 1948. The German boom was interrupted by the recession caused by the Korean War, but this was also true with regard to the rest of Europe. It was, however, of short duration, and by 1960 the German economic recovery was not only an established fact but the envy of Europe and the rest of the world. France and Italy, after some uncertain beginnings, witnessed strong economic growth in the mid-1950s; and Spain followed still later. Britain faced a severe postwar economic crisis (1947–48), and its development during the subsequent two decades was much less striking than that of its European neighbors.

By and large, the immediate economic consequences of the war had been overcome within a very short time. By late 1950 European output was already 30 to 35 percent higher than during the prewar years. By the 1960s the continent was far more prosperous than ever before, and the boom continued, making it the longest and most striking in European history.

When Stalin died in 1953, there was widespread belief that another turning point in the history of the continent had been reached. Yet relations between the two blocs did not improve as dramatically as many had hoped. In retrospect, it is more than doubtful whether there were any "missed opportunities." Stalin's heirs had no wish to loosen their hold over Eastern Europe; on the contrary, they were not even willing to tolerate more liberal communist regimes, as Hungary (in 1956) and Czechoslovakia (in 1968) found out to their detriment. The self-confidence of Khrushchev, and later of Brezhnev and his crew, was still unbroken. They were convinced that the communist system worked reasonably well, and that it would prevail in the competition with the West. There seemed to them no reason to reform it, let alone carry out radical change.

Decolonization made rapid progress after the war. Holland was the first to lose its colonial empire, Britain gave up India in 1947, and the rest of its empire during the years after; Algeria and the other formerly French possessions had gained their independence by 1962, followed by Portugal's African colonies in the 1970s. In some instances the transfer of power was relatively smooth; in other cases independence was preceded (or followed) by a great deal of violence. But as far as the formerly imperial powers were concerned, the consequences of decolonization were hardly shattering. Though there had been dire warnings that the loss of raw materials and markets would be fatal to the metropolis, Europe prospered as never before.

Toward the end of the 1960s, close observers of the European

scene detected the first signs of a malaise. It was not easy to describe
the manifestations and even more difficult to analyze their causes. In
Britain, the roots were clearly in large part economic: sterling had to
be devaluated in 1967, taxes were increased, wages and government
expenditures frozen. In France, the student unrest in 1968 turned
almost overnight into mass protest, and de Gaulle's rule, seemingly
invincible, appeared suddenly very vulnerable indeed. Nationwide
strikes and terrorist attacks undermined Italian society.

The movement toward European unity seemed to have run out
of steam. De Gaulle had been a convert to the European idea, but his
interest was limited to economic cooperation, and he did all he could
to keep Britain out of the European Community. Britain had stayed
aloof in the beginning. By the time it applied for membership, de
Gaulle exercised his right of veto. Only after he had left the scene
was Britain, together with Ireland and Denmark, admitted (1973).
Norway had narrowly rejected membership in a plebiscite, but there,
too, public opinion began to change in the 1980s.

As the six became the nine, it was widely hoped that the Community would get a second wind, but this did not happen, at least
not right away. National egotism prevailed over supranational aspirations; the member states quarreled about regional and agricultural
surpluses, and about the introduction of a European monetary system.
Since the member nations were preoccupied with recurrent budgetary
crises, the concept of a common European policy remained largely a
dream. Centrifugal forces seemed to prevail on all levels: in 1966
France had taken its military forces out of NATO, U.S. bases had to
be removed from France, and the NATO council was transferred from
Paris to Brussels. When Leo Tindemans, the Belgian statesman, wrote
a report about the state of Europe in 1976, he compared Europe to
a house half finished and without a roof: unless completed, it would,
exposed to the rain and the storm, sooner or later collapse. The
Tindemans report, though widely praised, was quickly forgotten and
had no influence on the conduct of European policies.

After years of an unprecedented boom, the European economies
began to stagnate; the first oil shock of 1973 and the second shock
toward the end of the decade triggered a recession. More worrisome
was the lack of solidarity and concerted action shown by the European
countries in these years of adversity. The instinctive reaction was to
play it "each for himself" rather than to consult and coordinate pol-

icies. The deeper problem of Europe was not economic but a curious case of *abulia* (utter listlessness)—a concept coined by nineteenth-century psychiatrists denoting a loss or lack of will for no obvious reasons. The optimism of the 1950s and 1960s had given way to a pessimism for which it was difficult to find "objective reasons." Compared with the problems facing the United States at the time, not to mention the enormous difficulties confronting the third world, the problems of the European countries seemed almost trivial. There was a strange discrepancy between their economic strength and their political and military impotence. Perhaps it had to do with the exaggerated hopes attached to détente. In 1972 the advent of a golden age was announced in the capitals of Europe: the conflicts of the postwar era had come to an end, a turning point in world affairs had been reached, peace had descended on the world.

This euphoria lasted for a year or two before it emerged that peace had not yet descended, that neither the global conflict nor regional tensions had ended. A vague but persistent feeling evolved that the democracies had become ungovernable. There was talk about a new, tragic period of social and political regression, and of the possibility that the whole European system might crumble.

Monsieur Giscard d'Estaing, the French president at the time, thought: "The world is unhappy. It is unhappy because it does not know where it is going, and because it guessed that, should it know, it would be to discover that it is going toward catastrophe." Shortly before leaving office in 1974, Chancellor Willy Brandt reportedly told some of his confidants that Western Europe had only twenty or thirty years of democracy left; after that it would sink, engineless and rudderless, into the surrounding sea of dictatorship.

Fortunately, Mr. Brandt's pessimism was not borne out by events, not even in the short run. In 1973 the colonels in Greece were overthrown, in 1975 the Portuguese dictatorship was defeated, and in 1976 Spain had its first freely elected government in forty years.

The dire predictions of Giscard and Brandt did not reflect merely personal despondency. This was the time when the terms "Englanditis," "Hollanditis," and "Finlandization" gained currency, describing various aspects of the European malaise that affected domestic and foreign policy. A few years later fear became fashionable in West Germany and some other European countries. Articles and speeches compared the world's situation with that of 1914: the world was sliding into a catastrophe, owing mainly to American adventurism, personified by President Reagan.

A great many reasons have been adduced to explain the European crisis of the seventies and early eighties, including the weakness of a political system unable to resist the conflicting demands of various sections of society, or the growing confrontation between the urge for greater freedom and the need for more order. The postwar period had witnessed a steady erosion of authority, partly as a consequence of, and in deliberate reaction against, the evil-doings of the fascist dictatorships of the 1930s. The anti-authoritarian urge was not only intelligible but in many respects admirable, and it corresponded with a deep-seated human longing for freedom. But increasingly it interfered with the effective conduct of the affairs of state.

The old idea that the survival of a free society depended on the civic virtues of its members, on accepting that there could be no rights without duties, was widely considered outmoded. Such abdication of responsibility reflected a state of intellectual anarchy, and intellectual anarchy, as Comte once observed, was the main factor behind all the great political and moral crises.

Lastly, there was anti-Americanism, fueled by NATO's decision in 1979 to install intermediate nuclear weapons in Western Europe. This provoked a violent reaction, not only among the left, but also among the churches and other sectors of society. The roots of anti-American feeling, however, went much deeper. Why should Europe have to depend on the American defense umbrella forty years after the end of the war? European strength in manpower and material resources was at least as great as America's; its GNP was much greater than the Soviet bloc's.

But with all its manpower, resources, and prosperity, Europe's willingness to spend on defense was strictly limited, and furthermore Europe was still disunited. Hence the humiliating dependence on the United States—the fear of "decoupling," on the one hand (that is, of an American withdrawal from Europe), and, on the other, apprehension that Washington would somehow involve Europe in a conflict with the Soviet bloc that was not in the continent's best interest. In the final analysis, Europe's problem of the 1970s was not the intractability of the issues but the absence of the qualities needed to confront them.

As the 1970s drew to a close, the state of Europe seemed dismal, her outlook at best uncertain. But then, slowly at first, the mood again began to change from pessimism to a new optimism. Why? It is as difficult to explain the euphoria of the late 1980s as it is the apocalyptic fears of the 1970s.

Such changes in historical mood are not unprecedented. France toward the end of the nineteenth century is a classic example. The general feeling at the time among the educated classes was that the country was on the way to total ruin. A great many causes were given, such as alcoholism, the low birthrate, the growth of atheism and pacifism, pornography, general cultural decadence, and whatnot. But around 1905 pessimism quickly went out of fashion, and patriotism, sports, and a heroic life-style became the new preoccupation. The underlying so-called objective factors had not changed: Frenchmen and women were drinking as much as before, and neither church attendance nor the birthrate had increased significantly.

The change in the European mood was equally inexplicable, except perhaps with reference to the fact that the economic situation improved around 1980–85 in most European countries. But a GNP growth rate of 2, 3, even 4 percent was hardly sufficient to explain the transition from dark pessimism to buoyant optimism. Furthermore, certain major social problems, such as unemployment and the presence of substantial immigrant communities, were hardly affected by the economic upturn. Was it perhaps the appearance on the scene of a new generation, with its own ideas and ideals? But the difference between the young Europeans of the 1980s and those twenty years earlier was not that enormous: if in the 1960s there had been a trend toward political radicalism, the inclination in the 1980s was toward radical ecological concerns.

Two major trends gave fresh impetus, directly and indirectly, to the European revival. One was the new acceleration of the movement toward European unity, the other the stunning developments in the Soviet Union and Eastern Europe. In late 1969 an EEC summit conference in The Hague had decided that European economic and monetary union ought to be completed by 1980. Simultaneously it was agreed that foreign policy, too, should be coordinated (the D'Avignon report of 1970). In fact, most recommendations and resolutions remained a dead letter. The existing European institutions, such as the

Council, the Parliament, and the Court of Justice continued to function, but they were of no great consequence. The EEC expanded, but
the accession of Greece, Spain, and Portugal did not bring European
unity any nearer. Mrs. Thatcher's main preoccupation was to defend
the British treasury against European agricultural interests; why
should Britain underwrite European agricultural overproduction just
because the French and other governments were unable or unwilling
to apply pressure on their domestic lobbies and bring prices down?
When the colorful Mr. Papandreou was prime minister of Greece, his
main concern was to keep Turkey out; the future of Europe did not
figure highly on his agenda.

In this dismal situation it was to the credit of the French—and
of individual Frenchmen in Brussels—that they infused new ideas and
energy into the European somnolence. The initiative began at the
Fontainebleau summit in 1984, continued at the Milan meeting the
year after, and brought about the "Single European Act" (SEA) in
1986. This stated that the Community should aim by 1992 at a
genuine internal market without frontiers in which the free movements
of goods, persons, services, and capital was ensured. This radical
departure meant amending the treaty of Rome (the basic document
of European cooperation), it meant a unified European monetary
system, and it meant European social legislation. Nor would a single
currency be possible without a central European bank.

The new initiative implied giving far more power to the existing
European institutions and creating new ones. As Jacques Delors, the
French president of the EEC, told the European Parliament in June
1988, the embryo of a European government might have to develop
in the 1990s, and the Community would be responsible for some 80
percent of economic and social legislation. Such predictions provoked
a nationalist backlash among some governments, and as German unity
came under way and the East European countries moved closer to
the West, it seemed more than likely that the timetable for economic
and political unification would have to be revised.

That the fences between Western and Eastern Europe had come
down was a matter of great joy, but it also meant that the obstacles
to integration had grown immeasurably. The process of European
economic, social, and political unification may last well into the third
millennium, progress may be slow, and setbacks are virtually certain.
But the general trend has been set. So much integration has already

taken place on the economic level that the movement toward a supranational Community can be slowed but probably no longer permanently blocked.

The other major event of truly enormous significance was the
victory of the reform party in the Soviet Union after 1985 and the
de-Sovietization of Eastern Europe. That the communist system was
no longer working had been no secret. In some East European countries, such as Poland, a crisis had arisen well before Gorbachev came
to power. But Poland was not the Soviet Union, nor was Hungary,
and the great majority of Russia-watchers assumed that the ruling
stratum in the Soviet Union together with its stalwart allies, East
Germany and Czechoslovakia, would hang on to power for another
decade and perhaps longer. True, the economic situation was going
from bad to worse, and the communist systems were steadily falling
behind the West. But this alone might not have provoked the great
crisis of 1989–90. In the end, the loss of confidence and hope among
rulers and ruled alike was more decisive than the empty store shelves.
Few people were actually starving in the Soviet Union, but even fewer
believed anymore in the system and its doctrine.

The gradual dismantling of the apparatus of repression in Eastern Europe opened the way to a better future—to freedom, peace,
and prosperity. It also opened the door to the common European
home invoked by Gorbachev and others. And finally it liquidated the
postwar political order that had divided the continent and been the
cause over the decades of so much unhappiness and tension.

If the analyst of contemporary Europe had finished his account
on January 1, 1990—a fitting date in many respects—it would have
been only natural for him to share in the general euphoria and to end
his account by welcoming the golden age that had at long last come.
There had been so many false dawns, so many disappointments in
Europe's recent history, that a little excess optimism would have been
perfectly justified.

But history neither begins nor ends at some specific date, and
both the saddest and the most joyous events may have altogether
unforeseen consequences. Nineteen eighty-nine was an enormous victory for the cause of freedom. The overthrow of a tyranny creates
the preconditions to the emergence of a free society, but it provides
no guarantee that this is bound to happen. The difficulties that will
face the successor states of the Soviet Union and the countries of

Eastern Europe in the years ahead are truly staggering. Paraphrasing
Nikolai Chernichevsky, the Russian writer, it can be said that the
road to European unity is not the Champs-Elysées, a straight bou-
levard, with the Arc de Triomphe in sight from the very beginning.
Equally, the road to freedom in Russia is not the Nevsky Prospekt—
there will be obstacles and long detours, and the final aim may well
disappear from sight at times. The jubilations in Bonn, New York,
and elsewhere in 1988–89 about the victory of democracy in the Soviet
Union were, as subsequent events have shown, at the very least,
premature.

If this study were to deal with Europe during the Napoleonic
age, it would be incongruous to end the introduction on a personal
note. But it covers a period through which the author has lived, it
deals with a continent reasonably well known to him, and he even
had the privilege on occasion to watch some of the dramatis personae
from up close. Such proximity has its advantages as well as its pitfalls.
For someone living through the frustrations as well as the achievements of the postwar age, it was not always easy to keep the detachment that may come naturally to the historian dealing with distant
events.

I have been commenting on postwar trends in Europe all my
adult life. My first systematic attempt to describe and analyze them
was *Europe Since Hitler,* which I finished writing in 1969. I felt
relatively optimistic then about the prospects for greater collaboration
within Western Europe and for improved relations between East and
West. But the 1970s brought little to sustain such optimism, and as
I tried to summarize the lessons of that decade (*A Continent Astray,*
1979), the conclusions were critical, probably even too bitter. Europe
seemed in a stupor, almost all the promise had vanished, and a political
decline had set in, the end of which was not in sight. My observations
were probably not unfair, but at times anger tended to becloud my
judgment concerning the wider perspectives.

Since then another decade has come and gone, and the balance
has been redressed. It was a decade of important, and largely unforeseen, events. It also brought the end of the postwar era in sight,
and as a result it was bound to affect our whole perspective on this
period. In Hegelian terms, the 1980s were the synthesis to the thesis
and antithesis provided by the two previous stages since 1945. Or,

at the very least, they brought a tide in the affairs of Europe which (as we have known since Shakespeare), taken at its flood, leads on to fortune; whereas "omitted, all the voyage of their life is bound in shallows and in miseries."

Washington, May 1991

CONTENTS

Preface   V

PART ONE: POSTWAR

Europe Divided   3
The New Balance of Power: The European Vacuum   12
The Heritage of Fascism: The Purge of Collaborators   22
From War to Peace   30
     Britain: Labour in Power   31
     France Liberated   39
     Italy Divided   45
     The Smaller Countries   51
     Stalin's Last Years   55
     The Sovietization of Eastern Europe   67
     German Twilight   76
The Breakdown of the Wartime Alliance   88
The Origins of the Cold War   105
Toward European Cooperation   116
Christian Democracy and Democratic Socialism   126
The Rise of European Communism   144
Russia After Stalin   149

PART TWO: ECONOMIC MIRACLE

The Economic State of Europe in 1945   167
The Recovery of European Industry   182

The Surge of European Agriculture   188
The Transport Revolution   192
The Expansion of European Trade   196
France: Modernization and Its Discontents   200
The German *Wirtschaftswunder*   205
Italy: From Uncertain Beginnings to Stormy Growth   208
Britain: Stop-Go   212
Economic Development in the Rest of Europe   216
The Soviet Economy   220
The Industrialization of Eastern Europe   227
The Welfare State Emerges   231
Health and Housing   240
Prosperity and the New Consumerism   246
Leisure for All   249
The New Social Structures   253
Trade Unions: Power and Weakness   258
The New Managerial Class   261

PART THREE: EUROPEAN CULTURE: THE POSTWAR SCENE

Postwar Blues   267

PART FOUR: CONSOLIDATION 1955–72

The Two Blocs   293
False Dawn at Geneva   298
Rebellion in Eastern Europe   301
West-East Negotiations 1956–61   309
The Berlin Crisis   316
La France Seule   323
European Cooperation: New Initiatives   328
The Cuban Crisis   333
Polycentrism in Eastern Europe   338
1968: The Year of the Students' Revolt   345
The Invasion of Czechoslovakia   354

Britain: From Churchill to Heath 362
France: The Coming of the Fifth Republic 370
Germany: Adenauer and After 375
Italy: Opening to the Left 381
Spain: The End of the Franco Era 385
Benelux and Scandinavia 388
Austria and Switzerland 393
Greece 395
The Soviet Union: Khrushchev and His Successors 397
Eastern Europe: Between Conformity and Independence 404

PART FIVE: THE END OF THE POSTWAR ERA: WESTERN EUROPE

The European Economy 1970–90 415
Social Forces: Old and New 435
  Ecology and the Greens 435
  Separatism and the National Minorities 441
  Guest Workers and New Immigrants 444
  Terrorism 446
Germany: From the Great Coalition to Reunification 449
Holland and Belgium 461
Britain: The Thatcherite Revolution 465
France Since de Gaulle 474
Italy: Domestic Crisis and Recovery 488
Spain After Franco 493
Scandinavia: Between National Concerns
  and European Cooperation 499

PART SIX: THE END OF THE POSTWAR ERA: THE SOVIET UNION AND EASTERN EUROPE

The Soviet Union Under Brezhnev and Gorbachev:
  Decline and Reform 507
Stagnation in Eastern Europe 529
The East European Revolution 550

Epilogue   567
Bibliography   571
Index   587

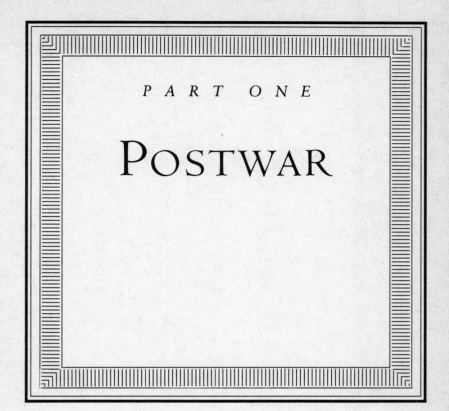

PART ONE

POSTWAR

EUROPE DIVIDED

The Second World War ended in Europe with the surrender of the Germans on May 7, 1945. The document was signed in Rheims by Field Marshal Jodl on behalf of the Wehrmacht and by Lieutenant General Bedell Smith on behalf of the American and British forces, with French and Russian officers as witnesses. Later on there was a similar ceremony in Berlin between the Russians and Germans, and all hostilities ceased on May 8. The longest and most destructive war in modern history was over. A Frenchwoman, Micheline Maurel, who had been an inmate of a concentration camp, describes the unreality of the first hours of freedom: "I passed the whole day in a sort of paralysing ecstasy. I tried to persuade myself that I was free. I tried to write a poem. But I never got further than: Free, free, free at last. Freedom as yet did not mean much to me. . . ." For the millions of soldiers this was the end of the road. The Russians, who had fought their way after initial defeats through half of Europe, from Stalingrad to Berlin. The Western armies which had advanced from the Normandy beachheads the year before. Soon they would be demobilized, return home, rejoin their families, and resume their peacetime occupations. For millions of German soldiers it was the beginning of the long road to captivity.

Most of France, Belgium, and Italy, and almost all of Eastern Europe had been liberated well before May 1945. When the armistice was signed, Nazi rule was limited to a small section of Germany, to Norway, Denmark, and parts of Czechoslovakia. The Third Reich, which its leader had predicted would last a thousand years, was at the end of its tether. "Do you want total war?" Dr. Goebbels had asked in 1943. Now there was total defeat.

The Allied leaders exchanged messages of congratulation. Stalin cabled Churchill: "This historic victory has been achieved by the joint struggle of the Soviet, British, and American armies for the liberation of Europe." Churchill, in a victory broadcast that evening, told the British people: "I wish I could tell you tonight that all our toils and troubles are over." But it was Victory Day only in Europe; the Japanese were still fighting, and even though the end in the Pacific was now in sight, it was already clear that there could be no relaxation in the efforts to tackle the tremendous problems of the postwar world facing victors and vanquished alike.

On that long-awaited day of victory, few people chose to think of the challenges and problems of the future. In London there were floodlights for the first time after six years of blackout; everyone was cheerful, happy, and orderly; not a single drunk was to be seen or heard. Big Ben was floodlit, so were the Clock Tower, Speaker's Corner, County Hall, the Horse Guards, the Lake in Saint James's Park, and Buckingham Palace. There was the joyous roar of the crowds, songs, and fireworks. In Moscow the news was received at 2:00 A.M. "I looked out of the window," Ilya Ehrenburg wrote; "almost everywhere there were lights in the windows—people were staying awake. Everyone embraced everyone else, someone sobbed aloud. At 4 am Gorky Street was thronged." There were salvos from a thousand guns. There was great joy and deep sadness. "That evening," writes a Russian, "there could not have been a single table in the Soviet Union where those gathering round it were not conscious of an empty place." On the afternoon of the 8th, General de Gaulle went to the Arc de Triomphe. The place was very full; after the general had saluted the Tomb of the Unknown Soldier, the human torrent broke through the barriers. But, with all the demonstrations, the official speeches, the sound of church bells, and the artillery salvos, the rejoicing of the people was grave and measured: "*Comme ils sont obscurs, les lendemains de la France!*"

The German reaction was one of stupor and apathy. There had been fears that the young soldiers would not surrender, that fanatical partisan and guerrilla units would fight on. But nothing of the sort happened; the last act of the Gotterdämmerung, the twilight of the Nordic gods, had already taken place, and no one wanted to prolong the agony. Hitler had committed suicide a few days before in his bunker; Mussolini had been caught trying to escape and was hanged by partisans; their dreams of power had been buried with them. Germany was utterly exhausted. Hitler had said that, if Germany did not win the war, it would be a sign of weakness, of inferiority, and the country might as well perish. His death wish was almost coming true.

There were parades, laughter, and dancing in the streets all over Europe on Victory Day, but on the morning after, Europeans began to take stock of the consequences of the war. It was a horrifying balance, enough to fill with despair even the staunchest hearts. Not since the seventeenth century had a war in Europe been fought so ferociously and caused so much destruction. Peace had now returned, but many felt, like the poet at the end of the Thirty Years War, that it was the peace of a churchyard. It had come too late. Not a few feared that Europe would never again rise from the ashes. Europe had not fully recovered from the terrible bloodbath of the First World War and its ravages; but now, in retrospect, that war seemed almost insignificant. There had been eight million victims in 1914–18; now there were four times as many. France with 620,000 victims and Britain with 260,000 had suffered less in the second war, but the loss of life in Central and Eastern Europe was enormous. Poland had lost more than 20 percent of its total population (including the millions of Jews murdered), and Yugoslavia 10 percent. Soviet losses were estimated between twenty and thirty million, German (again including civilian losses) at more than five million. Even a small country like Greece had suffered grievously.

Material losses, too, were incomparably greater than during the First World War. Large parts of Europe had been directly affected: Poland and Russia, Yugoslavia and Greece, Italy and northern France, Belgium and Holland, and, in the last stages, Germany. There had been massive air raids; both Russians and Germans had in their retreat followed a scorched-earth policy. Hardly a major city in Europe had escaped altogether unscathed; some, such as Warsaw, had been destroyed to such an extent that it was uncertain whether they could be rebuilt. In 1935 Hitler had said that ten years later no one would be able to recognize Berlin. His prophecy had come true, though not in the sense intended. Some thought it would take fifteen years to clear away the rubble in the former German capital; others were less

optimistic. The coastal and northern regions of France had been rav-
aged during the last year of the war, and immense damage had been
done in cities like Boulogne, Le Havre, Rouen, and Brest. Parts of
Holland had been inundated—the Walcheren had been flooded, and
the land area south of the Zuyder Sea had been submerged. In Italy,
Naples, Milan, and Turin, centers of industry and commerce, had
suffered badly; Pisa, Verona, and Lyons, Budapest and Leningrad,
Kiev and Cracow, and many other cities were partly destroyed. All
visitors to Central Europe reported a feeling of unreality: lunar land-
scapes dotted with enormous heaps of rubble and bomb craters, deserted and stinking ruins that had once been business centers and
residential areas. To find housing for the survivors was the most urgent
problem, but in Germany about a quarter of all houses were uninhabitable, and almost as many in Poland, Greece, Yugoslavia, and
the European part of the Soviet Union. Many more had been damaged.
The problem was particularly acute in the cities. In Düsseldorf 93
percent of all houses were thought to be uninhabitable. In the American zone of Germany 81 percent of all houses had been destroyed
or damaged. In the German-occupied parts of the Soviet Union the
homes of six million families had been destroyed, leaving about
twenty-five million people without shelter.

The specter of famine appeared all over Europe. During the early
stages of the war farming had prospered, but later on, with the loss
of manpower and the lack of machinery, fertilizers, and seed, harvests
were severely reduced and there were heavy losses in livestock; the
situation deteriorated further as the result of a severe drought in 1945.
The harvest of cereal crops in continental Europe (excluding the Soviet
Union) fell from a prewar average of fifty-nine million tons to thirty-
one million. In France, normally a rich agricultural country, the crop
of food grains had fallen by more than half. Denmark had not suffered
much material damage, but it could not resume food deliveries to its
regular customers, such as Germany and Britain, because these were
now unable to pay. All over Europe strict food rationing was in force,
and in most places the rations were now smaller than in wartime. A
year after the end of the war, it was estimated that about one hundred
million people in Europe were being fed at a level of fifteen hundred
calories a day or less. One thousand five hundred calories or less is
recommended for reducing weight; it is not an ideal level of nutrition
for those doing heavy physical work or for growing children, or in

general for people who have been underfed for years. But even this level could not always be maintained; the authorities in the American and British zones of Germany had to cut the rations in 1946 to nine hundred to a thousand calories. There were desperate food shortages in the Soviet Union; he who lost his ration book faced starvation.

Those living in the destroyed cities lacked clothes, shoes, domestic equipment, and tools. As winter approached, fuel became a matter of life and death. Coal production had fallen drastically all over the continent; it was now only 42 percent of the prewar level. The Ruhr coal industry was producing only twenty-five thousand tons a day, compared with four hundred thousand before the war. But even if larger supplies had been available, there would have been no way of transporting them to where they were needed most. Perhaps the gravest result of the war in the sense of material damage was the destruction of the network of communications on which Europe depended: 740 out of 958 important bridges in the American and British zones of Germany had been destroyed; France had only 35 percent of its railway locomotives left and about the same share of its merchant fleet. In Holland all bridges on the north of the Leopold Canal were destroyed, completely paralyzing the main Dutch and Belgian canal system for six months. Northern France and western Germany traditionally depended on inland waterways for bulk transport, but these, too, were now out of action. Many ports could not be used: Toulon was blocked by the French ships that had been scuttled there; Calais, Boulogne, Bordeaux, and Dunkirk were paralyzed. For many months after the liberation, there was only one adequate bridge across the Rhine (at Nijmegen), only one across the Elbe (in Hamburg). In Germany railway transport had virtually come to a standstill, and it took many months to get the trains moving again. The experts now realized, as one of them reported, that the bombing of cities had not created as much distress and dislocation as the destruction of the vital rail and water routes.

Even now it is impossible to establish with any degree of accuracy to what extent industry was still working at the end of the war; in the prevailing chaos, statistics did not receive top priority. It was perhaps at 35 percent of the prewar level in France, higher in the neutral countries and those that had not suffered greatly (like Denmark and Czechoslovakia), but much lower in Germany, Austria, and Greece. The few reliable figures speak for themselves: pig-iron output in 1946 in the countries that now make up the EEC (France, Germany, Italy, and Benelux) was less than a third of the 1938 figure, crude steel output about a third. But 1938 had not been a very good year; in most European countries the depression had not been completely overcome. In France, for instance, industrial production in 1938 was more than 20 percent below the level of 1929. Throughout the continent the financial system had been disrupted, with consequent inflation. The amount of money in circulation in Germany was seven times as high as in 1938. Prices in France during the war had increased fourfold. In Hungary and Greece the currency collapsed. Soon after the war, Belgium and Norway had to devalue and to reform their currencies immediately to ward off a similar fate. In short, the European economy in 1945 had ceased to be viable; the continent was faced with economic collapse, hunger, and disease. Before recovery and reconstruction could even be contemplated, massive first aid and disaster relief were needed. This was supplied by UNRRA, the United Nations Relief and Rehabilitation Administration, financed mainly by the United States, which provided food, raw materials, and equipment, and helped to install essential services in Italy, Yugoslavia, Greece, Austria, Czechoslovakia, Poland, and parts of the Soviet Union. UNRRA by its charter was to assist only those peoples who had opposed the Axis; in Germany supplies were provided directly by the occupying powers. Whole countries were now living on charity, and to say that economic prospects were uncertain would have been a gross understatement in the summer of 1945. There seemed to be no prospects.

Those who ought to have planned for these postwar emergencies were doubly mistaken in their assumptions; they underrated the gravity of the economic crisis, and they were not aware of how desperately acute it really was, how close Europe stood to collapse. But once they did realize this, they became far too pessimistic about the long-term chances for European recovery. The various economic blueprints prepared in Washington and London during the last year of the war make strange reading today. The problems facing the planners after the defeat of Germany were of a very different order of magnitude from what they had imagined: the loans they thought would be sufficient to cover Europe's immediate postwar needs were but a drop in a seemingly bottomless bucket. Yet, once the experts understood how near to collapse Europe really was, the tendency was to underrate national resilience and to exaggerate the permanence of the damage that had been caused. In parts of Europe, paralysis was almost total, but already, after a few months, some visitors found that, though industrial production had come to a standstill, under the debris equipment was often intact; only 15 to 20 percent in the heavily bombed Ruhr area was damaged beyond repair. Two decades later, when the economists tried to explain the astonishing economic revival in Europe, some of them belatedly reached the conclusion that the war years had not been wholly years of economic waste, but a time when productive capacity expanded, in Britain and in Germany alike. Many plants had been bombed or destroyed or (in Germany) dismantled, but even so fixed assets in German industry in 1946 were higher than they had been ten years before.

The preconditions for a spectacular recovery existed in 1945 but were hidden beneath the surface; not even the most sanguine expected rapid economic expansion. It was difficult not to be overwhelmed by the extent of the catastrophe, which, after all, was not only, and not mainly, economic in character. The psychological shock seemed to have created a state of general paralysis.

Before the First World War, Europe had indisputably been the dominant factor in world politics; it had the strongest armies, it was the world's banker; 83 percent of all the world's investments were made by the three leading European powers—Britain, France, and Germany. America may have been the first industrial power in the world, but its interests in world politics and world trade were still limited. Although there were stirrings of revolt, on the whole European colonial rule was still undisputed. Before 1914 London, Paris, and Berlin had been the cultural centers of the world, and few scientific discoveries of importance had been made outside Europe. The general feeling was one of optimism; even those critical of the social order were aware of the steady improvement that had taken place over the years.

The First World War put an end to all this; its consequences—the postwar economic crisis, the victory of Bolshevism and the rise of fascism—contained, moreover, the seeds of another war. America's position was immensely strengthened, and eventually also Russia's, but both these powers were almost totally absorbed in their domestic problems; their global ambitions and the ability to pursue them were limited. The Second World War brought a profound change. The eclipse of the Axis powers, the occupation of Germany and Italy, put an end to their dreams of world domination. But Britain and France were almost equally weakened. To survive, Britain had to sell about one-third of her overseas assets. At the end of the war, her annual income from overseas investment was less than half that before the war; the merchant fleet was reduced to three-quarters of its prewar size, and only 2 percent of British industry was producing for export. To win the war, Britain had had to incur large debts, and its currency had been undermined. Although a victor, Britain in 1945 was as poor as most other European nations, and her people were certainly no better fed. Since her economy depended on the import of two-thirds of the food required and the bulk of her raw materials, and since she was now unable to pay for these imports, her prospects seemed very bleak indeed. Even the strictest controls and rationing, which remained in force for some years after the war, seemed unlikely to be of much help in the long run.

The situation was more hopeful in France, which was less dependent on imports. But it was hopeful only potentially, in a long-term view. Torn by internal convulsions and unsure of herself, the country had to grapple for many years with economic difficulties and inflation, with structural social problems, and with political instability at home and complications abroad. Like England, Belgium, and Holland, France was soon to lose its colonial empire. The economic effects of decolonization were less than anticipated; those who in the past had argued that Europe could not exist without colonies were proved mistaken. France tried to resist the rising tide of Asian and African nationalism, and became involved in colonial wars before realizing that the time had come to cut her losses. But this was because French prestige was involved; from an economic point of view, the French colonies were a dead loss.

Above all, the self-confidence of the European powers had collapsed. Many now realized (to quote Paul Valéry) that there had been nothing more stupid in history than the competition between the European states, and that European politics had not matched European thought in depth and quality; the radiance and staying power of its civilization had been destroyed by its internal squabbles. The political future of Europe was now decided between Washington and Moscow; its economy faced ruin but for massive American aid. Europe's cultural predominance had been undermined by the exodus to

America of many scholars from Germany in the thirties, by the stifling of cultural life and scientific research by the totalitarian powers, and by the ravages of war. True, the war had given fresh impetus to discoveries and to technological advance in many fields, but only the richest countries could now afford to engage in research, which had become steadily more expensive. American universities succeeded to the position once held by European institutes of higher learning, and New York became more important than any European capital as a center of literature, music, and the arts.

This loss of self-confidence certainly did not extend to the Soviet Union. Its position had been enormously strengthened as a result of the war. Hitler had attacked Russia in June 1941 to "save Europe from Bolshevism," to destroy it, or at least to drive it into Asia, where he thought it belonged. As one outcome of the war, Soviet troops were now one hundred miles from the Rhine, and occupying the whole of Eastern Europe and most of the Balkans. The Soviet Union had not only successfully resisted the German onslaught, it had now emerged as the strongest military power in Europe. Communists had taken a prominent part in the resistance movements in most Nazi-occupied countries, and there was a good deal of sympathy for the Soviet Union. In the years immediately after the war, the prospects of a victory for communist parties in Western and Central Europe seemed brighter than ever before. But the problems of economic reconstruction facing the Soviet Union were no less formidable than those in the West. Industrial and agricultural production in 1945 was considerably below the prewar level; the western regions were in ruins; many millions had been killed. With all its military might, Russia in 1945 was still a desperately poor country. It was clear that healing the wounds and rebuilding the national economy was a gigantic task that would take many years and demand a colossal effort.

THE NEW BALANCE
OF POWER:
THE EUROPEAN VACUUM

The political map of Europe, or, to be precise, of Central and Eastern Europe, was radically changed. Several countries disappeared; others, which had ceased to exist, such as Poland, Austria, and Yugoslavia, were now restored. The greatest gains by far were made by the Soviet Union; it reoccupied the three Baltic states (Lithuania, Latvia, and Estonia) which it had first seized in 1940; it annexed most of East Prussia, it took the Petsamo district and part of the Karelian Isthmus from Finland, acquired the sub-Carpathian region from Czechoslovakia, Bessarabia and parts of the Bukovina from Rumania. In September 1939, on the basis of the pact with Germany, the Soviet Union had occupied eastern Poland. This territory had been lost during the war, but was reoccupied in 1944 and now remained firmly in Soviet hands. Poland was compensated by large stretches of formerly German areas up to the Oder-Neisse Line. These were the major changes—the others were comparatively insignificant: France, of course, recovered Alsace-Lorraine, Yugoslavia received part of Venezia Giulia, Rumania had to surrender southern Dobrudja to Bulgaria. There were minor border rectifications elsewhere, and the future of the industrially important Saar region was left in abeyance for a number of years. Elsewhere, the prewar frontiers were re-established. All this, of course, occurred only gradually. The peace treaties with Italy, Rumania, Bulgaria, Hungary, and Finland were not signed until 1947, the treaty with Austria in 1955—and about Germany there was no agreement at all between the Allies, and consequently no treaty.

Of all the changes, those concerning Poland were the most far-reaching. The country, as defined by its frontiers, was moved bodily more than two hundred miles to the west. The Western Allies had agreed in principle at the wartime conferences that Poland should be compensated in the west for its losses in the east—but the solution envisaged by Washington and London was less far-reaching than the one carried out by the Russians. There was a genuine conflict of interests: from the Russian point of view, it was only fair to let Germany compensate Poland for the eastern territories Poland had to cede to Russia; this also served Russia's purpose, since it meant that the new Poland would have to lean heavily on Moscow for protection against the Germans, who would not easily accept the loss of such a large part of their territory. From the Western point of view, the Polish advance into what had once been Germany went too far. It created immense problems for the administration of Germany, such as the uprooting of many millions of Germans now driven from their homes and the creation of an enormous new refugee problem. The territorial changes were moreover bound to be a source of perpetual political unrest in the heart of Europe. At Potsdam the Western powers reluctantly accepted the new *de facto* frontier and left the final boundaries of Poland to be determined at the peace settlement which was never held.

Germany (and Austria) were divided into zones of occupation, as had been agreed before the end of the war. The Russians were in control of the eastern provinces: Saxony, Thuringia, Brandenburg, and Mecklenburg; the British took over part of the Rhineland, the Ruhr, Lower Saxony, and North Germany. The American and French zones were in South Germany. Berlin, wholly within the Russian zone, was almost divided into four sectors. These frontiers did not exactly correspond to the armistice lines; the Americans and the British had reached positions farther to the east, and had stopped their advance toward Berlin only in order to allow the Russians to capture the former German capital. But the wartime alliance was still in effect, and, in accordance with decisions previously reached, the Western armies retreated from their forward positions once the Russians had arrived.

There was a great difference between the way the map of Europe was redrawn in the peace treaties of 1919, and its redivision after the Second World War. In 1919 there was a great deal of haggling about territorial issues, ethnic and language frontiers, and so forth. An effort was made to ascertain the wishes of the population directly affected, even though in the end some of the decisions taken were clearly unjust and in violation of the declared principle of self-determination. After the Second World War, ethnic considerations hardly counted; no one bothered to find out what the local populations wanted; the balance of power, the West-East relations, were the overriding consideration. Once it had emerged that the Soviet Union would have the decisive influence all over Eastern Europe, it was of little importance for the world at large whether the border between Poland and Czechoslovakia or between Hungary and Rumania followed the ethnic or any other line. The Soviet Union usually saw to it that these conflicts were rapidly solved. This is not to say that a solution of territorial disputes not based on ethnic considerations was necessarily unjust and cynical. The ethnic map of Eastern Europe and the Balkans was such that simply tracing new frontiers could not always restore justice. Both Rumania and Hungary had good claims on Transylvania, a region that had several times changed hands. But the Hungarian settlers were in the eastern part of Transylvania, the one farthest from the Hungarian border, whereas the regions nearer to Hungary were largely settled by Rumanians. Only by some form of compromise—or, alternatively, by the establishment of a large number of mini-states—could justice have been done. Ethnic considerations, in any case, were not the only ones that mattered; there were geographic and economic factors to be considered, not to mention the part played by the respective countries in the war. When Czech and Hungarian interests clashed, Jan Masaryk, Prague's foreign minister, asked: "Who won this war—Hungary or the United Nations?" Hungary and Rumania had both been on the losing side; after the war they quarreled about certain territories, but the Rumanian government was at the time more acceptable to Moscow, and so Bucharest got a better deal than it would have obtained a year or two later, when Hungary was already much more closely linked with the Soviet Union. Again, a case could be made for restoring the South Tyrol to Austria. This had been lost to Italy in 1919 and was still predominantly Austrian in character; but Italy had to cede some territory to Yugoslavia—a claim strongly backed by the Soviet Union, for Tito had not yet quarreled with Moscow. In these circumstances, and since Austria lacked a strong backer among the powers, the Western Allies thought Italy should not be pressed too hard, and it was allowed to keep South Tyrol.

All together some forty or fifty million people were expelled from their homes and became refugees, the greatest migration Europe had known since the Völkerwanderung fifteen hundred years earlier. There were millions of prisoners of war and forced laborers brought to Hitler's Reich between 1940 and 1944 who began to stream back once hostilities ceased. Some six million of these displaced persons were counted in Germany when the war ended; three months later two-thirds of them had been repatriated, but at the same time an even bigger wave of new refugees began to arrive, and migration continued in almost every direction. Some had been uprooted for the second or third time: 250,000 Finns living in Soviet Karelia had taken refuge in Finland at the time of the first Russo-Finnish war in 1939, returning to their homes when Finland recovered Karelia in 1941. Ethnic Germans (Volksdeutsche) living in Eastern Europe, some since the thirteenth century, had been evacuated by the Nazis in 1939–40 and brought to Germany; they were resettled in Poland after 1941, only to be evacuated again when the tide of war turned. Some ten million Germans fled from the German provinces east of the Oder-Neisse Line and from Czechoslovakia and Hungary, mostly into West Germany. There was also a substantial internal migration from the Soviet zone to West Germany, which continued right up to the erection of the Berlin Wall in 1961. There were in addition hundreds of thousands of Poles, including 160,000 in General Anders' army, Ukrainians and Latvians, who found themselves at the end of the war far from their homeland and who, for political reasons, could not or would not go back. There was also the movement of many thousands of Jews, the remnant of their people, the former inmates of death camps and ghettos who wanted to leave a continent that had become a slaughterhouse and cemetery for their communities and families.

Agreements were signed between the Soviet Union, Yugoslavia, Rumania, Czechoslovakia, and Hungary about the exchange of minorities following the redrawing of the political map. As a result, there were further migration waves in Eastern Europe: hundreds of thousands of Poles from the regions now transferred to the Soviet Union streamed to the newly acquired western territories: peasants from eastern Galicia were settled in Pomerania and Silesia, the University of Lwów was transferred to Breslau, now renamed Wrocław. The northern regions of Czechoslovakia, formerly inhabited by more than three million Sudeten Germans, were now taken over by Czechs and Slovaks. In the Soviet Union "suspected" minorities such as the

Volga Germans, the Crimean Tartars, and several Caucasian peoples
had been expelled beyond the Urals during the war; some of them
were permitted to return in the 1950s. The tribulations of the Soviet
prisoners of war in Germany did not end with their repatriation in
1945; almost all were immediately sent to forced-labor camps in the
far north and far east of the U.S.S.R. They joined several millions of
Soviet citizens, politically undesirable elements or just suspects, in
camps whose very existence was staunchly denied by Western communists. After Stalin's death in 1953 most of these camps were gradually dissolved and the survivors released.

As the result of these migrations, the ethnic map of Central and
Eastern Europe was redrawn. About a thousand years of German
history, of steady colonization in the East, was erased; so was the
eastward movement of Poles and Lithuanians, which had lasted several centuries. It was replaced by a Russian westward drive. The new
Germany found itself saddled with a refugee problem on an unprecedented scale: more than ten million newcomers. The presence of
these millions in Europe was to be a heavy burden for the host countries for many years; a large proportion of them were either very old
or very young, but even those able to work found it difficult to assimilate the new cultural and social milieu, and in many cases to learn
a new language. Relatively few migrated overseas, mainly to America
and Australia.

There had been nothing like it since the Huguenots were expelled
from France in the seventeenth century, except perhaps the exchange
of populations between Turkey and Greece after the First World War.
But this was on a far smaller scale, and it happened on the border of
Europe and Asia and was largely ignored at the time. With all its
ravages, the First World War had not caused a total breakdown of
the conventional standards of civilization, which included the understanding that the civilian population was not to be killed off or uprooted. The Second World War, on the other hand, had witnessed
barbarities on an unprecedented scale; after several years of Nazi rule
in Europe, the expulsion of millions of civilians after the war passed
almost without notice. There were protests on practical grounds: the
British and Americans—now responsible for West Germany, in which
millions of refugees were dumped—were unable to cope with the
problem. But protests against the very principle of expelling people
from their homes were few, and they carried little weight against the

background of Auschwitz and the hecatombs of victims throughout Central and Eastern Europe. The new political map reflected the new balance of power. The shift in world politics had started in the early nineteenth century with the development of modern means of communication: the steamship, the railway network, the telegraph. The European system was gradually giving way to a world system, but all that seemed to happen at first was the transformation of the balance of power in Europe into a balance embracing the whole world, as one writer has put it. The ultimate decisions were still taken in Europe. The Second World War brought the Russians into the heart of Europe; Eastern Europe and most of the Balkans were now under Soviet domination. Western and Southern Europe as well as Germany were now almost totally dependent on American help. The European peoples were paying a heavy price for their internecine quarrels.

The First World War had broken out as a result of the tension between Russia and Austria in the Balkans, of the nationalist passions that were running high in Europe, and of a breakdown in diplomacy. German militarism, vanity, and arrogance had played a baneful role, but one could not in fairness apportion all the blame (as was done in the Versailles Peace Treaty) to Germany and its allies. All the big and many of the small European powers had territorial claims and colonial ambitions, but the influence of the lunatic fringe consciously working for war was limited. Not one major European power had deliberately provoked the war; they had maneuvered themselves into a situation from which followed a war that most people thought would be both brief and not very destructive.

The First World War was not inevitable, but the Second could not have been prevented once Hitler had seized power in Germany. The origins and the character of this movement and of fascism in general have been discussed for a long time and at great length. Fascist and semifascist movements emerged in the 1920s in several European countries; wherever they came to power, they distinguished themselves by the leadership principle, the suppression of all democratic freedoms, rabid nationalist propaganda, and, in most cases, an aggressive foreign policy. The rise of fascism had more than one cause; there was the patriotic fever stirred up by what many Germans regarded as the unjust peace treaty of 1919, the resentment of the "havenots" (Italy, Germany) against the "plutocrats" (Britain, France), the economic and social consequences of the great depression, the fear of Bolshevism, the breakdown of liberalism, and the impotence of the Social Democratic parties. It is doubtful whether Italian fascism by itself would have provoked a new world war, not because it was opposed to war, but simply because it was not strong enough. Left to his own resources, Mussolini was not capable of engaging in anything more ambitious than another colonial war on the Abyssinian scale. It took the triumph of Nazism in Germany in 1933 to make a new war almost a foregone conclusion. Nazism was not only more aggressive than other European fascist movements, it also had the most far-reaching aspirations, and it had (or so it seemed to its leaders) the ability to challenge the whole world. From the day he came to power, Hitler was firmly resolved to rearm Germany, and he worked methodically not merely for the extension of German Lebensraum but for a new war. The Western powers tried to appease him with territorial concessions, by promising economic help and colonies. But Hitler wanted German hegemony in Europe, and he was aware that this aim could not be attained by peaceful means. He prepared, therefore, systematically and relentlessly, for a war that he was sure he would win and which he imagined would lead to a "New Order" in Europe. After his early easy successes, he threw all caution to the winds and tackled at the same time the British Empire, the Soviet Union, and the United States, all this on the basis of a racial doctrine that, unlike communist ideology, had no universal appeal but, on the contrary, regarded all other peoples as in various degrees inferior. In the future world order, as the Nazi leaders saw it, Germany would have satellites but no real allies. Hitler's early victories made the enterprise seem much less hopeless than it appears in retrospect; in these victories the element of surprise played an important role, and so did the shortsightedness and weakness of Hitler's enemies. In early 1942 he seemed very near to attaining his aims; after so many striking victories, German military power appeared irresistible. At the height of Germany's triumph, Hitler's New Order extended all over mainland Europe. Spain and Portugal were not involved in the war, and Sweden and Switzerland had stayed neutral, but the rest of the continent was in his hands; Soviet power had been pushed back to Moscow, the Volga, and the Caucasus. As an attempt to unite Europe under German leadership, the Second World War was in some respects reminiscent of the Napoleonic campaigns, but Napoleon waged war against governments, not peoples. In the wake of his victories, some of the achievements of the French Revolution were transplanted to other European lands. The benefits, if any, that the peoples of Europe derived from German occupation were purely incidental, such as factories established to increase German industrial output in areas beyond the range of Allied bombers and the roads built to improve communications with the front. What did these count against the suffering of the peoples, the atrocities committed by the occupiers, the general humiliation, the profound hatred of Nazism and the Germans?

During the long nights of the war, people all over Europe pondered the causes of the war and the reasons for the defeat. That Nazism was unprecedented in its cruelty no one doubted, but how to explain the quick and total defeat of France and the other European countries? What were the lessons to be drawn for the postwar world? The old ruling classes had failed; if so, how to ensure that the old system (and the "old gang") would not make a comeback after the end of the hostilities? This mood was by no means limited to the occupied countries. It was equally strongly developed in England, which shared the general disgust with the past; after the war, there would have to be a more just, more democratic society. Already the First World War had caused a minor social revolution, affecting, for instance, the status of women. If women had taken such an active part in the war effort, they could clearly no longer be refused the right to vote. During the Second World War, many barriers of caste and convention had fallen. Millions of soldiers had seen foreign countries and had drawn comparisons with their own way of life at home. Their horizon had broadened, their expectations increased. They would be less easily satisfied in future. Some of the resistance movements developed fairly clear and detailed programs for the postwar world, others remained vague. But there was a common denominator in the emphasis on sweeping change, the abolition of class privileges, and the full restoration of freedom. Communists all over Europe profited from the new mood. Their unfortunate record during the years of the German-Soviet pact was forgotten, whereas the prominent role they had later played in the resistance movements was vividly remembered. Communist policy after June 21, 1941, had coincided with the national interests of the occupied European countries, and the communists had made the most of it. The "bourgeois" parties were usually loosely connected factions, whereas the communist organizations

were far more tightly knit and therefore in a much better position to
survive suppression and resume their activities under the occupation.
The Soviet Union had gained tremendous prestige after the tide of
war had turned. The communists had always preached the superiority
of Soviet society, and all their predictions seemed to have come true.
Communist influence was stronger in Western than in Eastern and
Central Europe, partly because communist traditions there were more
deeply rooted, partly because Western Europe was not exposed to
direct contacts with the Soviet Union at the end of the war. Pro-Soviet
enthusiasm in Europe usually grew with distance.

The war brought to the fore new policies and new men. Who
would have believed in the spring of 1940 that ten years later a little-
known brigadier general named de Gaulle and two obscure teachers
named Bidault and Mollet would be among the central political figures
in France? That two retired gentlemen, Adenauer and de Gasperi,
living respectively near Cologne and in Vatican City, would emerge
as the new leaders of their countries, inaugurating a new era in the
history of Germany and Italy? Einar Gerhardsen, who was to be
Norwegian prime minister for sixteen years after the war, worked as
an unskilled laborer during the German occupation, repairing roads;
Kurt Schumacher, leader of the German socialists; Léon Blum, once
and future prime minister of France; Novotny, the future Czech prime
minister; and Cyrankiewicz, the future Polish prime minister, were
all in German prisons or concentration camps. Some of the old leaders
had escaped to London, and the communists to Moscow; they now
returned with the Allied armies. But even among the communists,
where the question of succession was not usually decided by election,
there were many new faces in addition to the long-established leaders
of the Communist International such as Dimitrov, Rákosi, and Gottwald, who seized power in Bulgaria, Hungary, and Czechoslovakia.
There were those who had risen from the ranks and who had not
been to Moscow during the war, men like Gomułka, Rajk, Kádár,
and Tito. In Moscow they were suspect from the very beginning, but
they were the representatives of a new generation of communists, and
Moscow could not do without them altogether.

Up to 1939 there had been a traditional equilibrium in Europe.
War had broken out because one country, Germany, tried to upset
that balance, annexing more and more neighboring territories in an
attempt to establish its hegemony over the whole of Europe. The end

of the war brought the downfall and the complete destruction of Nazism. But in the process the traditional balance of power in Europe was also destroyed. Britain, France, and the other European countries were greatly weakened. The Berlin-Rome Axis had been defeated owing to the military efforts of the new superpowers, America and the Soviet Union. Russia, as the result of the war, advanced far into the heart of Europe, and the old prewar alliances between France and Eastern Europe were replaced by a much closer association between the new "popular democracies" and the Soviet Union. Britain, France, Germany, and Italy were for years to become dependent on American assistance. The old European equilibrium was replaced by the global balance of power between America and Russia. Europe paid a terrible price for its disunity: its division into so many nation-states with conflicting interests.

The fate of the continent was now being decided in Moscow and Washington. The eclipse of the old world seemed complete.

THE HERITAGE OF
FASCISM: THE PURGE
OF COLLABORATORS

One immediate problem facing the victors was how to deal with those who had unleashed the war and brought untold suffering to Europe. The cry to punish the losers had been heard after many a war; in 1918 there was a general demand to hang the Kaiser. But the Second World War had not been fought in accordance with established rules. Nazism had not merely been out to defeat the military forces of its opponents; it had sought to enslave and, in some cases, to destroy the civilian population. The German leaders were guilty, not only of the preparation of aggressive war, but also of war crimes (first used as a term in international law in 1906) and of crimes against humanity. The Allies formally agreed in July 1945 to prosecute and punish the main war criminals.

They soon realized the complications involved in this task. It was easy enough to establish the identity of the main war criminals, but what about the many others, lower down in the hierarchy, who had been instrumental in carrying out their policies? What to do with the rank-and-file members of organizations such as the fascist parties and the storm troopers? Were they all to be punished, and if so by whom and in what way? The demand for punishment received fresh impetus in the Allied countries after the discovery of the extermination camps during the last weeks of the war. It seemed a matter of elementary justice, and at the same time a precondition for rebuilding a new Germany, that those responsible should answer for their crimes. But the Nazi Party in Germany had counted eight million members; it included most of the higher civil servants, almost the whole business and intellectual elite. How could a new Germany (or Austria or Italy) be built without the active cooperation of these men and women? Moreover, it soon appeared that de-Nazification alone was not sufficient; it would be necessary to re-educate millions of people. But who would be in charge of this operation? The Allied armies had been trained to win a war, not to take up legal or educational assignments. It seemed inevitable that the Germans and the other peoples concerned should take an active part in purging their own ranks.

De-Nazification and the treatment of Nazi collaborators varied greatly from country to country. The Americans and the British tackled it in a slow but methodical way: in the British zone more than two million cases had been examined when de-Nazification ended in 1948. The Russians and the French were more inclined to concentrate on the main criminals and to let the small fry escape punishment. Nor were they as particular in their choice of instruments to build the new Germany. Stalin distrusted the Germans, but he was willing to try out men who, regardless of their political past, would carry out instructions. In some countries the purges were short and violent. In France thousands of fascists and suspected collaborators were lynched at the time of the liberation on the basis of death sentences pronounced by self-appointed courts.

Within a year or two, the purge was virtually over in these countries, whereas in Germany, where it had got under way only slowly, it went on for many years. It took a long time to find some of the criminals, and even longer to locate the surviving witnesses and the evidence. One of the most important trials, against the Auschwitz personnel, did not begin until 1963. The Maidanek trial began in 1975; the verdict was delivered six years later. The trial of Klaus Barbie, the slaughterer of Lyons, took place in 1987.

The severity of the purge varied as well. In Belgium some 634,000 cases were opened after the liberation, an enormous figure for a country with 8 million inhabitants; eventually only some 87,000 were brought to trial, of whom 77,000 were sentenced. In Austria, where Nazism had been far more deeply rooted and much more widespread, only about 9,000 people were brought to trial, and there were only 35 death sentences. Among those who administered justice and among the police, there were few who had not been associated with Nazism in one form or another. Frequently they were inclined to let those charged escape with nominal punishment. In Italy and France, on the other hand, the purge was sometimes used by individuals as a welcome occasion to settle accounts with political or personal enemies. Austrian justice was perverted on more than one occasion by a conspiracy of silence; no one had seen or heard evil. In the Netherlands about 150,000–200,000 men and women were detailed after the war as suspected collaborators; determining that someone had dined in public with a German or subscribed to a collaborationist journal was sufficient reason for lodging charges. In Germany, and particularly in Austria, on the other hand, the mere fact that someone had been a high Gestapo official was not sufficient reason to bring him to trial, unless specific crimes could be proved against him. It was argued that he had after all only carried out instructions.

The question of obeying orders played a central role in the most famous of all war-crime cases—the Nuremberg trial of twenty-four major German war criminals, which was opened in August 1945 and went on for over a year. Among them were the main surviving Nazi leaders, such as Goering, Ribbentrop the foreign minister, Rosenberg the ideologist, army commanders such as Keitel and Jodl, and Admiral Doenitz. Hundreds of people took part in the preparation of the trial, and the typewritten records cover more than five million pages. Many Germans were at first inclined to regard the trial as a travesty of justice, but the sheer weight of evidence had a considerable impact. Millions of innocent people had been murdered, and the account had to be settled. One of the Nuremberg defendants, Hans Frank, former governor-general of Poland, said that "a thousand years shall pass and this guilt of Germany will not be erased." Others remained defiant to the end. When Julius Streicher, the leading Jew-baiter, mounted the steps of the gallows, his last words were "*Heil Hitler.*" Hermann Goering, for many years the second-most-influential man in Nazi Germany, described himself as essentially a man of peace and committed suicide a few hours before he was to be executed. Most of the accused were neither defiant nor repentant; they had not really known what was going on, and anyway they had obeyed orders. In the Third Reich, they said, it was only the word of the Fuehrer that had counted. Ten of the Nuremberg defendants were sentenced to death and executed; three were acquitted; the rest received prison terms of varying length. From 1966 Rudolf Hess was the only inmate of Spandau Prison. He died there in 1987, aged ninety-one.

The Nuremberg verdict concerned not only individuals; entire organizations were found guilty of crimes against humanity.

The trial has been criticized, and not only in Germany, for a variety of reasons. The list of the accused was to a certain extent arbitrary; in the dock, alongside the most powerful political and military figures was a radio commentator, and in one case a son was substituted for the father. The defendants were assisted by counsel, but not all the evidence could be introduced. When discussing German aggression against Poland in 1939, the lawyers could not mention the secret protocol under which Poland was divided between Germany and the Soviet Union. There were more basic misgivings: the accused had been charged with violations of international law, but such law was binding only on states, not on individuals; individuals, it was maintained, could be brought to justice only under the laws of their own country, not on the basis of a new order established after a war.

There were serious inconsistencies in the Nuremberg trial which caused much concern to legal experts whose main preoccupation was with international law rather than political necessities. But what other course was open? The crimes committed by the National Socialists were in many ways unprecedented, and it would have been unthinkable not to punish the perpetrators simply because there were no legal precedents. This was imperfect justice, but there was no alternative.

Many other trials followed, of army leaders charged with war crimes (such as von Manstein), of the running economic enterprises that had employed slave labor or been in other ways actively involved in Hitler's policy of aggression (I. G. Farben, Flick, Krupp), of senior officials of the German Foreign Ministry, and, of course, of those in charge of police and other special units involved in the Final Solution, the murder of five million Jews. These trials went on for many years. Some of the main criminals disappeared without trace, re-emerging after a few years in another country. Some had stayed behind, but the evidence against them was almost impossible to assemble; their victims were dead and their accomplices unlikely to break silence. Yet the German legal machine, whatever its other shortcomings, worked with great persistence and thoroughness. Once a case had been opened, it was not easily given up. Originally it had been decided that twenty years would be sufficient to complete investigations and trials, but in 1965 thousands of cases were still unfinished, and it was decided, against considerable opposition, to prolong the term.

De-Nazification was not an unqualified success; not infrequently a lowly official was severely punished while his superior got away scot free or with a mere fine. There were other anomalies which strengthened the belief of many Germans that in the Nuremberg and subsequent trials justice had not been done; the victors had simply taken their revenge. The full horrors of the extermination camps were brought home to the public only as a result of the trials of the late fifties (including the famous Eichmann trial), and it was then that the majority of Germans accepted the facts and tried, each in his fashion, to come to terms with the past. Eichmann, who had been in charge of the Gestapo department dealing with the Final Solution, escaped to Latin America after the war. He was traced and kidnapped by the Israelis and brought to trial in Jerusalem. These revelations had a profound impact on the younger generation, who refused to accept the arguments so often used by their elders that they had not known, and that in any case in a totalitarian regime there was no way of resisting the state. The moral issues became a subject of wide public debate, preoccupying writers and theologians as well as ordinary citizens.

It was up to the German people to confront its own past. Re-education by the Allies was bound to remain a dead letter. The Western Allies had decided—to quote one of the directives—that "Germany will not be occupied for the purpose of liberation but as a defeated enemy nation." Fraternization was strictly forbidden in the early days, even with the not-too-numerous Germans who had been active opponents of the regime and had suffered for it. Yet the Allies soon realized that to run the essential services they had to employ specialists and administrators most of whom had been in one way or another connected with Nazism. Later on, when an independent German administration emerged, first on a local basis and then statewide, there was a fairly high percentage of former members of the Nazi Party among those in key positions. True, no leading Nazi could hope to re-enter German political life, but rank-and-file members or fellow travelers usually regarded their past as a youthful aberration; they had long ago shed their Nazi beliefs. Some sincerely tried to make amends. But the very fact that such people were permitted to take up key positions in public life so soon after the downfall of the Third Reich aroused much distrust outside Germany.

The other European countries faced similar problems on a lesser scale. In Eastern Europe and in the occupied sections of Russia there had been no major quislings. There the Germans had not looked for collaborators as they had in Western Europe; they imposed their own direct control over what they regarded as racial inferiors. There had been low-level collaboration, thousands had volunteered to take part in the Final Solution, but no political or intellectual leaders were compromised; there was no native Nazi movement whose members had to be prosecuted. Hungary and Rumania were exceptions, but even there the purge did not constitute a major problem. In Italy the repression of fascism was violent but short-lived. Special courts established after the liberation dealt with the cases of high-ranking and politically active fascists; those who had merely been rank-and-file members found it relatively easy to re-enter political life or to resume their professional careers. Of the eight hundred thousand civil servants, many of whom had been members of the Fascist Party, no more than a few hundred were removed from their posts. There were only a few major trials, the most important of military leaders like Roatta (who escaped in the middle of his trial) and Graziani. Some fascists, or suspected fascists, were lynched or sentenced to death by partisan tribunals during the first weeks after the liberation of northern Italy, where Mussolini made his last stand in 1944–45. Their exact number is not known. The official figure of "1,732 murders and disappearances" is probably too low; the numbers given by neofascists are grossly exaggerated. After the amnesty of October 1946, only three or four thousand former fascists or war criminals remained in prison.

Italy and Austria were by far the most lenient in their treatment of fascism and National Socialism. Since so many citizens had been involved, it was thought that only the most prominent could be eliminated from public life. But there were other reasons as well: Mussolini had not been able to establish a fully totalitarian regime in Italy; its language had been extreme, its practice less so. Neither the army nor the state administration had been completely penetrated by fascism, and there were many leading intellectual figures who had not belonged to the party. The regime had not been noted for its humanitarian character, but it had killed far fewer of its opponents than Hitler's. In contrast to Nazism, there had been in fascism a comic-opera element which found its expression during the liberation. When the partisans took over a village or a small town, the Casa del Popolo became the new communist (or socialist) headquarters; there were violent scenes, but the few prominent fascists usually escaped, while the rest simply denied having belonged to the blackshirts. The scene was repeated all over Italy.

The French purge was much more radical. According to the official figures, there were 170,000 cases, resulting in 120,000 sentences, including 4,785 death sentences, of which almost 2,000 were carried out. But these figures do not tell the whole story; according to official estimates, some 4,500 collaborators were killed by partisans during or after the liberation; unofficial sources give considerably higher figures. These summary executions were particularly numerous in the Midi, the partisan stronghold. Those affected were usually local police chiefs or Gestapo agents who had collaborated with the occupiers and caused the death of Frenchmen, but there were also cases of political and private vengeance. Later on the purge became systematic. The most famous trials were those of Pétain and Laval, the Vichy head of state and foreign minister respectively. Laval was condemned to death and executed; Pétain, in view of his advanced age, was imprisoned.

Among those executed there were writers and journalists, but some of the main pillars of the Vichy regime were not even brought to trial. A well-known admiral (Estava) was given a long prison term, but his superior, whose instructions he had carried out, had meanwhile been reintegrated into the French army. Many observers thought that Laval, whatever his crimes, should have been given a fuller chance to defend himself. In a few cases it appeared that the record of the judge or the public prosecutor during the occupation was no better than that of the accused. There had been relatively few active resisters, in contrast to the truly staggering number of those who after the liberation claimed to have resisted from the first hour. Feelings of guilt were widespread, and at least some of those brought to trial in 1945 had to serve as scapegoats for the collective bad conscience of their compatriots.

In France more death sentences were imposed than elsewhere, but the other liberated countries took the purge no less seriously. More than 150,000 arrests were made in Holland, and eighteen thousand in Norway, where collaboration had been rare. In these two countries, as well as in Belgium and Denmark, the purge was more systematic than in France and Italy: thousands were deprived of their civil rights and banned from pursuing their professions. Leading writers, like Hamsun and Charles Maurras, were also arrested, but their lives were spared on the ground of their advanced age and diminished responsibility. Some of the leading collaborators and Nazi agents, such as the Belgian Degrelle and the Croat dictator Ante Pavelic, escaped and were not apprehended. Pavelic died in Madrid in 1959; Degrelle was last spotted in Spain's Costa del Sol in 1988.

No one was completely satisfied with the way the purge was carried out. In some ways it went too far, in others it was not radical enough. But conditions were still far from normal: the war was just over; the new governments were faced with a great many urgent tasks; their authority was not yet firmly established. Everyone agreed that Nazism had to be eradicated and the collaborators had to be punished, but in the prevailing circumstances, and with passions still running high, no one could expect exemplary justice.

FROM WAR TO PEACE

Political developments throughout Western Europe followed certain common patterns. Immediately after the war, there was a marked trend toward the left. In France and Italy the communists polled more votes than ever before, and for the first time they were represented in government. In 1945, too, the Labour Party came to power in one of the greatest political landslides in recent British history. There were communists in the first postwar governments of Belgium, Denmark, and most of the German *Länder;* in Norway the merger between the Labor and Communist parties was mooted, but the idea was abandoned. Monarchy was under heavy fire: in Italy, after a referendum, it had to go; in Greece and Belgium it just survived, but only after concessions had been made to make it more palatable. The right wing was everywhere on the retreat; the extreme right had been compromised through collaboration with Nazism, and the moderate conservatives, too, were identified with the old order that had suffered defeat and which few wanted restored. In the given economic situation there was little scope for the traditional advocates of laissez-faire liberalism; planning and the demand for nationalization had many powerful supporters. There was considerable pressure for sweeping reforms in politics and society; in Italy this was the famous *vento del nord* (the north wind), northern Italy having been the scene of most of the fighting between fascists and antifascists toward the end of the war. The mood did not last: within two or three years, the center parties had established their ascendancy on the continent and the communists were again in opposition. In Britain, too, Labour was voted out of office in 1951. Partly it was the result of the stabilization of conditions generally, and of economic improvement. The communists did not always play their cards well: in Belgium, and on a much larger scale in Greece, they had made a frontal attack on the government immediately after the end of the war and had been defeated. International relations also had a considerable impact; as the Cold War developed and the Stalinist era reached its height, European communists had to pursue extreme policies which left them in almost complete isolation. But this split was not widely foreseen in 1945, and it is to the immediate postwar period that we must now turn.

BRITAIN: LABOUR IN POWER

Since the critical days of 1940, Britain had been ruled by a coalition government, dominated by the Tories, but with Labour having considerable influence. The two parties were agreed that after the war new elections should be held, and so in May 1945 the wartime coalition was replaced by a caretaker government. In the general elections of July 1945, Labour gained a sweeping victory, a majority of 145, over all other parties. There was general admiration for Churchill the great war leader, but Churchill was also the leader of the Conservative Party, identified with the old England of dole queues and hunger marches, slums and millions of unemployed. Churchill's election call to "leave these socialist dreamers to their Utopias of nightmares" left his listeners unmoved. There was a general urge for radical change, for greater social justice. The wartime government had in some ways taken account of these aspirations; it had paved the road to the welfare state by sponsoring the Beveridge Report on the extension of social services after the war. But Churchill and the other Conservatives strongly doubted whether a country facing bankruptcy could afford these benefits. Although they were worried about the revolution of expectations that had taken place during the war, their doubts, justified or not, were very much out of line with the national mood, as the election results proved; sections of the middle class and much of the white-collar vote went over to Labour. Of the 393 Labour members of Parliament, 253 had been elected for the first time. A whole new generation was now entering politics: the wartime captains and majors, many young teachers, lawyers, and civil servants, among them Hugh Gaitskell (1906–63) and Harold Wilson, two future leaders of the party.

The Labour Party differed in essential respects from the continental socialist parties. It was gradualist in inspiration, not revolutionary; pragmatic in its approach; and it united in its ranks people of various political persuasions, such as liberals, Christian Socialists, and a few orthodox Marxists. This was perhaps not conducive to doctrinal clarity, but it made Labour a people's party, unlike either the Social Democratic or the communist parties on the continent, whose social bases were narrower. Parochial rather than internationalist in its outlook, it had never played a very active part in the international socialist movement. To the revolutionaries it was a typical reformist party, drab, lacking direction and perspective, aiming at piecemeal change and ultimately a welfare state, not at a real socialist society. But with all this the Labour Party enjoyed considerable prestige abroad. Other parties had perhaps more sophisticated programs, but the Labour Party was the one example of a movement trying in its policy to combine democracy, parliamentary action, and social justice. The continental Social Democrats had been less successful, while the communists preached a socialism without democracy which was not attractive to the West European working class with its deep-rooted democratic traditions and its instinctive opposition to dictatorship of any sort.

The great problem facing the Labour Party in 1945 was to build a welfare state in a nearly bankrupt country. Direct war damage was comparatively small, but for more than five years the great majority of the adult population had either been in uniform or worked in war industries or other unproductive enterprises. Britain had always been basically a poor country; without significant sources of raw material (other than coal), it had made its living by its industrial skill and its position as a center of world trade and finance. For its livelihood it had to rely largely on imports of food and raw materials, but as a result of the war it had become far more difficult to pay for these imports: Britain's income from foreign investments was now only a fraction of what it had been. The inescapable conclusion was that Britain would have to "export or die." But how to export, unless there was sufficient money to pay for the raw materials in the first place? The gold and dollar reserves were down to about 450 million pounds sterling against an external debt of 3.5 billion pounds accumulated during the war. It was a vicious circle, and a major American loan was needed to save the country from insolvency. Eventually, a loan of 1.1 billion pounds was arranged with the United States; "No comparable credit in time of peace has ever been given before," said Lord Keynes, who had negotiated it. But this was no more than first aid, a massive injection, a "springboard not a sofa" (in Churchill's words). The same problem, the dollar shortage, was to recur time and time again in the following years.

The new Labour government, unlike the parliamentary group of the party, included few new faces; the average age of the ministers was over sixty; they had all been in politics for many years. Its inner core were men of considerable strength and experience. Initially there were doubts whether Clement Attlee (1883–1967) was the best man to be prime minister; quiet, self-effacing, avoiding all histrionics, he was in many respects the very antithesis of Churchill. Instead of the flamboyant gestures and the rolling, memorable phrases, the public was now treated to short factual statements, lacking sparkle or inspiration. Attlee, one of his contemporaries said, was such a modest man because there was so much he had to be modest about. But he had a great deal of common sense; he was tough in his own quiet way, and was probably better equipped to cope with the problems of the postwar world than Churchill or any other leader inside the Labour Party. He had the strong support of Ernest Bevin (1881–1951), who had been appointed, somewhat surprisingly, foreign secretary. Bevin, representing the trade-union element in the party, had been one of its main pillars for many years, serving in the wartime coalition as minister of labor. He tackled his new assignment with great enthusiasm. Relations with Washington were traditionally cordial, and he was certain that ties with Russia would be equally friendly: "Left would be able to speak to Left"; they had after all a common language. On Britain's other postwar problems, such as India and Palestine, he envisaged compromise solutions; these could be reached, given a minimum of reason and goodwill.

Bevin soon realized that Britain's overseas problems were much less tractable than he had thought, that the Russians usually did not speak the same language, and that there was no meeting of minds even when they did. He came under heavy criticism from the left wing of the party for not pursuing a "socialist foreign policy." But what scope was there for a socialist foreign policy in the postwar world dominated by America, the bulwark of capitalism, and Russia, which, though socialist in name, pursued a foreign policy that had surprisingly little in common with the ideals of British left-wingers? It began to dawn on many of them that there was far less freedom of action for that "third force" between America and Russia which they had so often discussed.

Herbert Morrison (1888–1965) acted as foreign secretary after Bevin's death, but during most of the Labour government's span he devoted his time to domestic affairs. He had been the leader of London's socialists for many years and done much to reform the London County Council. Like Bevin, he did not have the benefit of a higher education and distrusted intellectuals in politics; he believed they lacked a sense of reality. At the 1946 Labour Party conference he said: "The government has gone as far left as is consistent with sound reason and national interest."

The left wing was represented in the Cabinet by Sir Stafford Cripps (1889–1952) and Aneurin Bevan (1897–1960), the former as president of the Board of Trade and subsequently chancellor of the exchequer, the latter as minister of health, responsible for establishing Britain's National Health Service. It would be difficult to imagine two political figures more dissimilar in character and background: Cripps an eminent lawyer, rich and impeccably upper-middle-class, a vegetarian and teetotaler, austere, even Spartan, in his whole way of life. A man of very powerful intellect, he notably lacked the common touch; in the past he had often quarreled with his party, whose policy he considered insufficiently radical. A devout Christian and a lay preacher, he had advocated close collaboration with the communists in the 1930s, and as a result had been temporarily excluded from the party. Bevan, a miner's son from Wales, had worked in the pits as a boy. He once wrote that he hated the Tory Party with a deep burning hatred; his "lower than vermin" speech (referring to the Conservatives) probably cost his party hundreds of thousands of votes. A man of great vitality and passion and a brilliant speaker, he combined a belief in fundamentalist socialism with considerable personal charm, diplomatic talent, and an ability to win over reluctant opponents to his schemes. This he showed in his dealings with Britain's general medical practitioners, deeply distrustful of the new health scheme. For all his left-wing militancy, he had few illusions about the character and aims of Stalinism, and during the Berlin blockade he was one of the leading hawks in the Cabinet when the question of breaking the blockade was discussed. Unlike Cripps, he did not despise the good things in life. With his comparatively early death, the left wing in the Labour Party lost its one leader of stature.

These, then, were the men who set out in August 1945 to build a new Britain. Within less than a year, they had introduced seventy-five bills, a giant program of nationalization and of social service. In December 1945 the Bank of England was nationalized, and, later, civil air transport. The coal industry was nationalized in 1946–47, as were public transport, electricity and gas, the railways, road haulage, and the steel industry. (Road haulage and steel were denationalized by the Conservative government that replaced Labour.) The main National Insurance bill became law in 1946. Compulsory and universal in its scope, it insured the whole adult population for sickness, unemployment, and retirement benefits; there were widow pensions, maternity and death grants. In the same year, medicine was nationalized—a somewhat crude but accurate term, for under the National Health Service free medical services were provided for all. It cost far more than originally anticipated: within a year after it had become law, more than five million pairs of spectacles had been issued and almost two hundred million free prescriptions filled. The National Health Service became the second-largest item in Britain's expenditure, exceeding 500 million pounds a year. The British quickly became accustomed to free medicine; there were controversies as to how to run the service, but the principle was universally accepted. The National Health Service was in many ways a symbol of Labour's postwar reforms; long overdue, they were exceedingly difficult to finance. The Labour government tried at one and the same time, in the words of John Strachey:

—to eliminate gross want from the population;
—to eliminate the major economic hazards of working-class life—unemployment, sickness, old age;
—to endow the family by children's allowances;
—to undertake both in the public and private sector a massive programme of investment, amounting to a general re-equipment of sections of British industry and absorbing over 20 per cent of the national income;
—to build 200,000 houses a year, year after year;

—to raise the school leaving age;
—to raise the volume of British exports to over 170 per cent of
their prewar volume;
—to maintain a rearmament programme of some £1,500m a year.

Such a program strained the resources of an impoverished country to the utmost.

Nineteen forty-five and 1946 were hard years for Britain. The hope had been expressed during the war that "things would not be the same again," but in fact many old worries continued to beset the country; life certainly did not become any easier. The ugliness of the big cities, the poor food in the restaurants, and the limited selection of goods in the shops depressed both natives and foreign visitors. In some respects, control and rationing became even stricter in this postwar period of austerity.

Housing, too, was a major problem. A White Paper published in 1944 stated that 758,000 new houses would have to be built; it seemed an enormous figure at the time, but the fact soon emerged that even this was quite insufficient. When the government failed to provide flats and houses, some militant groups decided in favor of self-help: squatters invaded empty houses and blocks of flats and, often for days, refused to move until alternative accommodation was found. Army camps were converted for civilian use, hardly a desirable solution. The squatters' movement succeeded in dramatizing the plight of many people, and compelled the government to give high priority to new housing schemes and to ban temporarily all nonessential building.

The transition to a peacetime economy was hampered by many obstacles. Productivity was low, and there was an increasing number of labor disputes. Raw materials, even coal, were in short supply. These difficulties reached a climax during the winter of 1946–47, the most severe winter of the century, with massive snowfalls which disrupted the whole life of a country unprepared for near-arctic conditions. Transport stopped; power stations were now and again closed down for lack of fuel; electricity was drastically cut. The acute fuel crisis came on top of the permanent convertibility crisis, and as a result two million workers were without employment. Electric fires were banned for many hours during the day; there was no greyhound racing; and even television, just outgrowing its infancy, was drastically cut. The old "Keep left" and "Let us face the future" programs of 1945 vintage seemed inappropriate in this national emergency, which lasted for many weeks. In March 1947 the snows came back, and when everyone thought that the worst was over, the flood waters hit Britain. There was great gloom and a tendency to make the government responsible for natural catastrophes over which they clearly had no control: "Starve with Strachey and Shiver with Shinwell" became the new slogan, referring to the ministers of food and fuel respectively. When Mr. Shinwell argued that the crisis was really a blessing in disguise, the reaction of the public was not too friendly even though, in retrospect, Shinwell was not far from the mark. Only as a result of this acute crisis did many people begin to realize what they were up against. During the previous eighteen months they had been preoccupied with remembrance of things past or dreams of the future, oblivious of the stark realities of the present. After the winter of 1946–47, no one could doubt any longer that postwar recovery would be an uphill struggle and that, short of a major effort, Britain would hardly find its place in the postwar world. The great wave of enthusiasm began to ebb, and many early illusions were shattered.

These illusions had not been limited to domestic issues, for there had also been a great deal of wishful thinking on world affairs. "Particularly when the Labour Party is in office, foreign policy becomes the last refuge of Utopianism," in Denis Healey's words. Few people were prepared for the postwar confrontation with communism; when British troops had been used against communist partisans in Greece, not only the left had been up in arms; public opinion, including the *Times* and most of the press, had protested. Communism, it was generally thought, was after all only a radical democratic and social reform movement. It had some unlovely aspects but, all things considered, was eminently suited for countries that lacked a democratic tradition of long standing. This belief persisted for several years after the end of the war; Orwell's *Animal Farm* was read by many when it appeared in 1945 as an amusing fairy tale that had no bearing on contemporary issues. The reports on forced-labor camps in Stalin's Russia were dismissed as slanderous fabrications. It was thought to be the Western statesmen's fault if they failed to get along with Stalin and his representatives; had they shown more friendship and sympathy, most of the difficulties could have been removed. Churchill said in a famous speech in Fulton in March 1946:

From Stettin on the Baltic to Trieste on the Adriatic, an iron
curtain has descended across the continent. Behind that line lie
all the capitals of the ancient states of central and eastern Europe—Warsaw, Berlin, Prague, Vienna, Budapest, Belgrade, Bucharest and Sofia. . . . From what I have seen of our Russian
friends and allies during the war I am convinced that there is
nothing they admire so much as strength and nothing for which
they have less respect than military weakness.

This was, of course, a mere statement of fact, but Churchill was
bitterly attacked for it; had he not advocated intervention in Russia
back in 1918? Was he not responsible for the growing tension between
West and East? There was mounting evidence during 1946 and 1947
that Soviet policy was perhaps not as altruistic and peaceful as many
had believed, but a real change in public opinion came only in 1948,
after the communist takeover in Prague, the Berlin blockade, and the
excommunication of Tito by Moscow. If a staunch communist like
Tito could not get along with Stalin, even the Labour left wing was
willing to admit that there was perhaps a grain of truth after all in
Ernest Bevin's complaints about the Russians.

The determination of the early postwar period not to rest until
social justice prevailed in Britain evaporated as the formidable obstacles to radical change were more fully understood. In later years
there has been a tendency to belittle the achievements of 1945–47:
"The nationalisation of half a dozen major industries, the construction
of an all-in system of social security and a free health service, and the
tentative application of planning to the national economy—the
achievement of these reforms seemed to have exchanged the content
of British socialism," as Richard Crossman said. But these reforms
carried out in a few years were a major social achievement, and they
initiated a long-term shift of political power and influence. It was not
a dramatic revolution, and its effects were not immediately visible.
The results certainly fell short of expectations, but, all things considered, it was a substantial achievement with far-reaching consequences,
and it served as a model for many other countries in the postwar
world.

FRANCE LIBERATED

Soon after the fall of France in June 1940, leaflets were published, signed by a virtually unknown brigadier general: "France has lost a battle, it has not lost the war." It was the beginning of the Free French movement, which in France's darkest hour carried on the struggle. "*Honneur et patrie, voici la France!*" In 1940 it seemed a hopeless venture; four years later General Charles de Gaulle returned to Paris and became the head of the provisional French government. The history of the Fourth Republic thus begins on June 18, 1940, with de Gaulle's first broadcast from London.

De Gaulle was born in Lille in 1890 and chose the career of a professional army officer. He fought in the First World War and commanded an armored division in 1940. In the years between, he developed interesting new concepts about the army of the future and the role of the tank forces. In June 1940, at the time of the defeat, he was serving as secretary of state for the army in Paul Reynaud's government. He was not at all widely known, and no one assumed at the time that his desertion (for his refusal to return to France from London was technically desertion) was to inaugurate a new chapter in the history of France. The policies of de Gaulle, one of the most striking figures in the history of postwar Europe, evoked mixed reactions from the very beginning. Frenchmen and foreigners alike have been repelled by his colossal egocentricity and his dictatorial and capricious style even when he was at his best. But everyone agreed that there has been no one quite like him in recent French—or European—history. What he said on one occasion about the Jews applies to himself with even greater justice: he was absolutely sure of himself and domineering. De Gaulle was totally convinced that he had a historical mission to save France, to restore its honor and dignity, to make it again a great nation. Everything else had to be subordinated to this belief; it was always *la France seule,* and he her only legitimate representative; "*J'étais la France,*" he wrote later; politicians, parties, and the Allies existed for him only in relation to his own image of eternal France and his mission on her behalf. It was an outdated, romantic vision, but it was of considerable relevance at a time when there was no leadership and when many other Frenchmen despaired.

In London in 1940 a few followers gathered around him: Cassin,

Maurice Schumann, Pleven, Soustelle, Palewski, Raymond Aron. Little known then, the names were to recur frequently in the annals of the Fourth and Fifth republics. The political and social character of the Free French movement was vague: de Gaulle was impeccably bourgeois and Catholic, tending toward traditional right-wing attitudes, certainly not a fervent republican. He took a poor view of the *république des camarades* whose corruption had contributed so much to the 1940 debacle. His style was authoritarian; he never pretended to be a democrat or a socialist. Yet his movement, setting itself in deliberate opposition to Vichy, was driven by the very logic of events toward a rapprochement with the left and left-of-center groups that were its natural allies. Gradually most of the resistance groups that had been organized in France accepted his leadership, and some of their representatives joined him in London.

The years of exile were unhappy ones for the general. The British and the Americans gave him help, but refused to treat him as an equal; in their eyes he was a deserving French patriot, but his claims to be recognized *de facto* and *de jure* as head of the French government in exile were not taken seriously. He was ordered around by the Allies: to make a trip, to give a speech on a certain day, to be silent on another. It was a galling experience, and his self-esteem was deeply wounded; as a result he behaved more imperiously than ever, refusing to compromise, regarding himself as the whole authority for all decisions concerning the future of France. Churchill and Roosevelt found him quite insufferable.

After the landing in North Africa in November 1942, the center of the French political scene shifted from London to Algiers, where, in the following year, a Consultative Assembly was established. For a little while the future of the Free French movement seemed in the balance; Giraud, a higher-ranking general than de Gaulle who had escaped from a German prison camp, staked his claim to be the leader of all Free French forces. But de Gaulle's position had already become so strong that the Allied leaders, albeit somewhat reluctantly, had to opt for him. De Gaulle now had around him a group of distinguished advisers, some of them well-known politicians such as Vincent Auriol, Pierre Cot, Henri Queuille, others as yet relatively unknown: Pierre Mendès-France and Jean Monnet. The communists, too, were represented, and three days before the Allied landings in Normandy a provisional government was established in Algiers. Its aims, other than the liberation of France, were not made very clear. In de Gaulle's many speeches the vision of a future France always figures prominently but, the idea of French grandeur apart, no one had a clear notion of what kind of regime the general envisaged. Was it to be a parliamentary democracy more or less on the pattern of the Third Republic? This seemed unlikely in view of the general criticism leveled against its shortcomings. The future of France depended, of course, to a considerable extent on the changes that had been taking place inside France.

The various local resistance groups inside the country had joined forces in May 1943 in a national council (CNR—Conseil National de la Résistance). All political groups were represented in the CNR, which was headed by Georges Bidault, then a left-wing Catholic. The communists had at first kept out of the resistance movement, but with Hitler's attack on the Soviet Union in June 1941 the "imperialist" war (as they had called it) turned into a patriotic, antifascist war from the Soviet point of view, and they joined it wholeheartedly. Because of their devotion and their superior organization, they soon gained a dominant position within the main partisan group, the FFI (Forces Françaises de l'Intérieur). There was tension between them and other resistance movements, and the communist attempts to seize all key positions and to impose their will on other groups aroused suspicions. But the situation in France did not resemble that in Greece or Yugoslavia, and the country was spared a civil war. An attempt was made to work out a common political program, in the Charter of the CNR. It was not clearly defined, but the general trend was obvious: opposing "economic and financial feudalism," the program called for the nationalization of some of the key industries and services and stressed the need for a plan. It stood for the establishment of "true economic and social democracy," the introduction of comprehensive social services, the principle of merit as the only criterion in education. It was very much an expression of the general demand for sweeping changes in the postwar world, *"la révolution par la loi,"* in the words of Bidault.

On August 25, 1944, de Gaulle returned to Paris. The general's path along the Champs-Elysées turned into a moving demonstration; Parisians gave him a hero's welcome amid scenes of mass enthusiasm. France was free again! French flags, the Cross of Lorraine, the symbol of French patriotism, and portraits of de Gaulle appeared now in every window, replacing the picture of the old marshal of Vichy, who, with the remnants of his government, had escaped to Germany. A fortnight later a new government was constituted. De Gaulle refused to proclaim a new republic, as his advisers had suggested. He argued that he had represented France all along, that continuity had been preserved. It was typical of the man and his style. The government was a mixture of the old and the new France. The twenty-two members, of whom thirteen represented political parties, included most of the men who were to play leading roles in the annals of the Fourth Republic: Bidault, Mendès-France, René Mayer, Pleven, Teitgen, Lacoste, and de Menthon. There were also two communists, one of them, Tillon, a well-known partisan leader.

The new government faced a number of most urgent tasks. The war against Germany had not yet been won; not even the whole of France had been liberated. France was expected to make a real contribution to the war effort in the last phase of the struggle. Eventually a million Frenchmen were enlisted, but more than twice that number of forced laborers and prisoners of war were still in German camps. The economic situation had gone from bad to worse; the output of coal, to give but one example, was down to a fraction of the level of 1938. There was no shortage of food in the provinces, but communication between town and country had broken down. For Christmas 1944 Parisians could buy apples but little else; even bread was in short supply.

Politically, the country was on the brink of anarchy; outside Paris the decisions of the central government were largely ignored. Partisan leaders and local chieftains effectively ruled large parts of France. De Gaulle began to tour the country almost immediately after his return to restore the authority of the central government. In October 1944 the "Patriotic Guards" (the self-appointed local militia) were dissolved and the central organs of administration and security took over. Financial problems were pressing, and inflation was severe. Mendès-France wanted to apply drastic measures and to introduce a regime of austerity: to block bank accounts, to tax illicit profits, to devalue the currency, as had recently been done in Belgium. René Pleven, his main antagonist, proposed easier remedies, such as floating a loan instead of introducing stringent controls. De Gaulle and the Cabinet opted for Pleven's policy, whereupon Mendès-France resigned in April 1945. In later years many realized that opting for

Pleven's policy was a fateful mistake, for the failure to apply drastic measures at that turning point was to bedevil the French economy for a long time to come.

France also faced crises in some of its overseas territories: Indochina, Syria, and Lebanon. The country had still to regain its status as a big power; much to de Gaulle's chagrin, France had not been represented at the conferences of Yalta and Potsdam. The general put most of the blame on the West, and snubbed the new American and British ambassadors, singling out for favorable attention Bogomolov, the Soviet ambassador, thus establishing a pattern that he was to follow for many years. But the Russians were not particularly forthcoming; when de Gaulle went to Moscow in January 1945, Stalin, too, had found him a very difficult interlocutor. Since France was no longer in Stalin's eyes a country of great consequence, de Gaulle and his ministers were largely ignored.

It was de Gaulle's ambition to take a position in world affairs somewhere in between the Anglo-Saxons and the Russians, but the time was not yet ripe for such grand designs. The general was not greatly interested in economic affairs, even though these had to be given priority in the early postwar period. The average Frenchman did not want to hear about a policy of grandeur; the general admitted as much in his memoirs: "Which are the immediate preoccupations of Frenchmen? The majority above all wants to survive!" Problems of supply and transport and the reorganization of agriculture and industry figured high on the list of priorities. Electricity was down to half the prewar output; rationing, unlike that in Britain, was very badly organized. Most of the newspapers were given new names and new editors. Some of the reforms contemplated during the war were now carried out. In December 1944 the coal mines were nationalized, and, shortly after, the four biggest banks, Air France, and certain large factories, such as the Renault motor works. In some cases the decision on what was to be nationalized was made dependent on the behavior of the owners during the occupation.

Considerable shifts had taken place in French political life. Some of the leaders of the Third Republic, such as Herriot, Léon Blum, and Paul Reynaud, were still in German prisons. None of them was held in high esteem, even though they had suffered during the occupation; only Léon Blum was again to play a leading part in French politics. The communists were now the strongest party, with some nine hundred thousand members. Their dubious behavior during the first two years of the war was forgotten. Thorez, their leader, returned from his Moscow exile and became a minister of state. The communists had an almost unassailable position in some parts of France, and could probably have seized power if they had so wanted in the anarchy of the first months after the liberation. But the wartime alliance was still in force, and the communists were not encouraged by Moscow to pursue such revolutionary aims. Their ambition, on the contrary, was now to be part of the government coalition and to be accepted by the other political parties. De Gaulle distrusted them because of their dependence on Moscow's guidance, but he could not ignore them. Though the socialists did not in principle reject cooperation with them, they were not particularly enthusiastic either. They were afraid of being swallowed up by the communists, with their much-superior monolithic organization; events in Eastern Europe, and in particular the fate of the socialist parties behind the Iron Curtain, seemed to justify their suspicions. Léon Blum had written during the war that, without socialism, democracy was imperfect; without democracy, socialism was helpless. The communists certainly demonstrated that a nondemocratic party was not necessarily helpless, but their ruthless efficiency did not make them any more attractive. Soon most of the goodwill and the wartime solidarity disappeared and gave place to bitter strife on the left.

Meanwhile, the socialists were preoccupied with putting their own house in order, and the leadership was gradually taken over by new men. Some of their traditional working-class support had passed to the communists, but the socialists, who in October 1945 obtained 24 percent of the vote (in comparison with the 26 percent of the communists), still had their proletarian base in the country and also considerable support among white-collar workers and the intelligentsia. The MRP was a new party; its leaders were left-of-center Catholics like Georges Bidault (1899–1983), but much of its support came from regions that had been traditionally conservative (Normandy, Alsace, Brittany). There was no strong right-wing party at the time except for a group of "Independents," and millions of conservative votes went for that reason to the MRP. The Radical Socialist Party, the main pillar of the Third Republic, was now only a shadow of its former self, polling 6 percent of the total. It was, moreover, a house divided, for there was nothing in common between the left-

wing planned economy advocated by Mendès-France (1907–82) and
the old-fashioned laissez-faire liberalism such as proposed by René
Mayer. De Gaulle had no organized political support during these
early days. The old socialist and radical leaders refused to work under
him, objecting to his dictatorial style. The communists demanded key
positions in the Cabinet, such as foreign affairs, defense, and domestic
affairs, which he refused to give them; he offered them five other
posts, which were not acceptable to them. In October 1945 a referendum was held on the character of the new Consultative Assembly
to be elected. The results at first sight seemed to reinforce de Gaulle's
position; there was to be no return to the anarchy of the Third Republic. But the unanimity was more apparent than real. The three
parties that claimed to be the legitimate heirs of the resistance (communists, socialists, MRP) polled 75 percent of the vote and elected
de Gaulle head of the new government. But they wanted strict limitations of his power. Relations between the government and the Assembly were strained; the general had been deeply offended by the
demand made by a socialist parliamentarian to reduce the military
budget by 20 percent. On January 20, 1946, he called a Cabinet
meeting; appearing in full uniform and without any forewarning, he
told his ministers that he had decided to resign. The transition from
war to peace was over; the political parties, he said, could now assume
full responsibility for affairs of state; de Gaulle was no longer needed.

In his heart the general did not, of course, feel so optimistic
about the ability of the political parties. He was in fact not at all
happy about the way things had turned out. He was fairly certain
that the parties would fail again, as they had in the Third Republic,
and that his hour was still to come. But for the time being he had to
concede defeat. The first chapter in the history of postwar France had
been closed with the rejection of the war leader by the politicians.

ITALY DIVIDED

Italy, like France, faced a revolutionary situation at the end of the
war. Its liberation took place in several stages: after the setbacks of
the Axis in North Africa, the Allied powers had invaded Italy in July
1943. On July 25 of that year, much to everyone's surprise, the Fascist
Grand Council deposed Mussolini, who was arrested shortly after-

ward. A new government was established under Marshal Badoglio which, while ostensibly continuing the fight on Germany's side, wanted to end the war as soon as possible. Italy, unlike Germany or the Soviet Union, had never blossomed into full totalitarianism, for opposition to the supreme leader still existed. Mussolini had weakened the position of the court, the army, the church, and the bureaucracy, but he had not crushed them; at a time of crisis, his enemies made common cause and overthrew his regime.

The Germans were taken unawares by the sudden turn of events, and it took them a few weeks to react. During August they moved troops into Italy, and on September 9 reoccupied Rome. Badoglio had started negotiations with the Allies, but progress was slow, and not until September 8 did Italy decide to surrender. In the middle of the "forty-five days" (as this curious interlude came to be called), the Germans disarmed some sixty Italian divisions, rescued Mussolini from his prison, and occupied most of Italy. The Allies, reacting slowly to the challenge that had suddenly arisen, could not match the German performance. By September, Italy was divided in two, the agricultural south, from which the Allies were slowly advancing, and the industrial North, occupied by the Germans, in which Mussolini established a new, more radical, fascist regime, the Republic of Salo. Mussolini intended to learn from past mistakes; his appeal was now mainly directed to the "common people." The Duce and his assistants fulminated against the plutocrats, the aristocracy, and the military leaders who had betrayed him.

In the south, meanwhile, political life was resumed. It appeared, again to everyone's surprise, that the nucleus of the leading parties had somehow managed to survive twenty years of fascist suppression; they were all revived within a few weeks. Even their old leaders were still present, men in their seventies and eighties like Croce, Orlando, Nitti, Bonomi, Don Sturzo, and Sforza, anxiously waiting for their turn to re-enter politics. There was in many ways more continuity in Italian political life than in other European countries that had suffered years of dictatorship. The partisan movement's inspiration was overwhelmingly communist and socialist, but these units were mainly active in the north. By the time the north was liberated, a new political structure had been established in central and southern Italy, traditionally more conservative in its attitude, which could not easily be dislodged.

Badoglio's government was replaced by one headed by Bonomi (1873–1951), who had been a socialist before the First World War but had subsequently moved to the right. Under him, three major and three minor parties participated in the coalition. The strongest was the Christian Democratic Party, not unnaturally, in which the clergy still played such an important role. It united in its ranks people of very different political persuasions, from the moderate left to the far right; its leadership was, on the whole, more to the left than its rank and file. The socialists, the oldest of all surviving parties, were heirs to a great tradition, but all too often they showed poor judgment, an inability to take decisions in a critical situation, and they gradually lost influence to their rivals on the right and left. They soon split into a left wing (under Nenni), which for many years favored close collaboration with the communists, and a right wing, which opposed it. The communists had managed to preserve their cadres even under fascism; they had been very active in the resistance and now reaped the fruits of their perseverance. In Togliatti they had a leader of considerable stature, an excellent tactician who helped to make his party the strongest of all European communist parties outside the Soviet bloc. It had four hundred thousand members in early 1945; later this figure passed the two-million mark. Of the smaller parties, only the Action Party deserves mention, for it was the one attempt to infuse a new element into Italian politics. Under the name Giustizia e Libertà it had developed among antifascist émigrés in Paris as a small activist democratic-socialist group of intellectuals, dissatisfied with the record of the established parties, whose failures had led to the victory of Mussolini. The Action Party took a leading part in the resistance, and after Bonomi's resignation in June 1945, their leader, Parri, became prime minister. But even though the Action Party had a strong position among the intelligentsia, it had no influence on the trade unions or other working-class institutions; it lacked both the political know-how and the resources of the Christian Democrats and the communists, and failed to gain a mass basis.

The future of the monarchy was one of the main issues facing the country. It had been traditionally opposed by the left, and was further compromised by its collaboration with the fascist regime. The ranks of Christian Democrats and of the liberals were divided. Even in the eyes of erstwhile supporters, the monarchy had now become a liability. The Socialist and Action parties opposed the king; the communists were in principle against the monarchy but announced their willingness to compromise and to postpone a decision. The situation was further complicated by the conflicting attitudes of the occupying powers: American policy was that King Emmanuel III ought to go, while Churchill wanted to keep him. Meanwhile, the king had resigned in favor of his son, Umberto II. But the problem persisted. In a general referendum on June 2, 1946, 54 percent of all Italians voted for a republic. Support for the monarchy was unexpectedly strong, especially in the south, where a majority of voters continued to favor it. Others were no doubt influenced by a speech of the Pope (Pius XII), who, in a radio broadcast on the eve of the election, had called all Italians "to choose between the supporters and the enemies of Christian civilization." But his intervention did not decisively affect the outcome either: Umberto II left for Portugal, and the House of Savoy ceased to rule Italy.

Other political issues were not tackled in the same decisive way. Bonomi's government was weak in almost every respect; it neglected to purge fascist elements, and did little to promote economic reconstruction. A great many hopes had been put on the purer, juster, and more democratic society that was to be built after the overthrow of fascism. But liberation came as an anticlimax. Although the fascist tyranny disappeared, the realization of the dreams of yesteryear seemed as remote as ever. The whole atmosphere of 1945—the inefficiency, cynicism, corruption, and hopelessness—have been realistically described in the novels of Pavone, Moravia, and others, and in the films of the period; they provide a more vivid picture than any historical account. As in France, there was great dissatisfaction, especially among the left and the resistance, about the way Italian politics were drifting. In May and June 1945 there had perhaps been a chance for them to seize power; effective control, after all, was in many places in the hands of the partisans or local militias that had been organized under communist or left-wing-socialist leadership. But there was also the warning example of the Greek civil war. The communists knew that the British and American armies would have intervened against any attempt to seize power by force. They opted therefore for democratic action within the newly established political framework. There was some "direct action" in the industrial field as factories in northern Italy were taken by the workers, who assumed control by means of factory councils. The old owners had often collaborated with fascism, and the former managers had disappeared or were turned out. But these attempts to establish workers' control did not last long either. The factory councils did not prove efficient, productivity was low and still falling, and the Allied powers threatened to cut off raw materials unless normal conditions were restored.

In June 1945 Parri, the leader of the Action Party, headed the only radical government in Italian postwar history. It was received with enthusiasm by the former members of the resistance movement, who hoped it would at last cope with the problems that Bonomi had been so slow to tackle. Parri devised a scheme that favored medium and small industrial enterprises in preference to the big firms. He also intended to introduce other economic and financial reforms, such as a more efficient income tax, that would have brought about structural changes in the country's economy. Measures like these naturally provoked the opposition of vested interests, which, recovering from the shock of 1944–45, rallied in defense of their cause. Parri was in many ways a tragic figure, a man of "unquestioned integrity and lofty aspirations, and with a conscience tempered by long suffering," in the words of H. Stuart Hughes. Scrupulous to a fault, he lacked practical political experience and the ability to take quick decisions. But the defeat of his government was due in the last resort not to personal shortcomings but to the weakness of his party. The Action Party was after all a minority group that had never really sought to become a mass party. The situation facing it in 1945 was not exactly promising; there were many signs of anarchy and general disintegration; separatist movements had sprung up in Sicily and other parts of the country; there was growing unemployment, a weakening of the authority of the central government, and a breakdown in public order, since the police had almost ceased to function. At the same time, major foreign political decisions had to be taken. In Parri's Cabinet all parties were represented, but the Liberals and the Christian Democrats largely sabotaged his policy, which they considered far too radical. The communist attitude was little better; they exploited the situation to strengthen their own position throughout the country. Parri fell in December, after six months in office. On resigning, he said at a press conference that the "fifth column" inside his government, having "systematically undermined his position, was now preparing to restore to power those political and social forces that had formed the basis of the fascist regime." It was not, of course, a return to fascism, but the re-emergence of the forces that stood for tradition and order; it was also the end of the dreams about radical social and political change in postwar Italy.

The fall of the Parri government inaugurated the rule of the Christian Democratic Party. De Gasperi, its leader, headed a government in which at first communists and socialists were also represented. A man of great personal integrity and considerable stamina, gentle and conciliatory in his approach, he combined shrewdness with an extraordinary firmness of purpose. Gradually he outmaneuvered the socialists and communists, and as the authority of the state was slowly re-established throughout the country, the economic situation improved. The socialists split, and the communists eventually found themselves in isolation. When their press attacked de Gasperi, the prime minister used the opportunity to resign and form a new Cabinet in May 1947, from which the communists found themselves excluded for the first time since the war. They threatened to react violently, but their hour had passed with the ebbing of the revolutionary enthusiasm of May-June 1945. The Christian Democrats were now by far the biggest political party—polling 48 percent of the total vote in the elections of 1948. De Gasperi proudly introduced his new coalition as a "government of rebirth and salvation." In Scelba he had a capable minister of the interior who thwarted the attempts of the communists and the left-wing socialists to attain their aims by extraparliamentary means, such as riots and other disorders. From now on, decision-making was in the hands of the Christian Democrats, divided into a left and right wing, and to a lesser extent to the small parties that were their coalition partners. The communists and the left-wing socialists were out in the wilderness.

The Italian economy was in poor shape at the end of the war. Industrial output was down to one-quarter of the prewar figure; the output of electric energy, usually a good indicator, was only 30 percent of that of 1941. But war damage was not as extensive as had at first appeared. Italian industry, concentrated for the most part in the north, had suffered comparatively little; its productive capacity had been reduced by only 5 to 10 percent. The fall in production was mainly due to the general dislocation, transport difficulties, the lack of foreign exchange, and the consequent inability to buy foreign raw materials. Galloping inflation was another major impediment on the road to economic recovery; the amount of money in circulation in 1946 was twenty times as great as in 1938. A currency reform and a project for a tax on property were hotly debated but, as in France, ultimately defeated. As a result, economic recovery was slowed down, an inflationary spiral developed, and Italy became the last major European country to benefit from the great economic boom of the 1950s.

The pattern of postwar developments in Italy resembles in some respects that of France: there was a rapid succession of Cabinets, and in both countries strong communist parties emerged that, after 1947, were no longer represented in the government coalitions. But in some ways the parallel with Germany is even closer. In both countries, after a transitional period, political power passed firmly into the hands of Christian Democratic parties. These provided reasonably effective leadership, and their position became virtually unassailable for many years. The close identification of the communists with the Soviet Union, at first a source of strength, gradually became a liability. Most Italians wanted a government capable of tackling the urgent economic problems; political issues played a minor role. It was difficult to work up violent passions against de Gasperi and Adenauer, and absurd to compare them with Mussolini and Hitler. But the failure to carry out radical reforms in 1945 perpetuated deep internal divisions. A large part of the population was not just pushed into opposition; it found itself outside the political system.

THE SMALLER COUNTRIES

The problems faced in 1945 by governments and political parties all over Europe were, broadly speaking, similar: the transition from war to peace, the purge of collaborators in the occupied countries, the reintroduction of democratic institutions, the challenge of communism, and the reconstruction of the national economies. In some countries the transition was smoother than in others; Belgium had suffered much less than neighboring Holland during the last phase of the war, and its economic situation was much better in 1945–46. But economic well-being did not necessarily imply political stability. Belgium was plagued by internal dissension. The old conflict between the French-speaking Walloons, radical in politics, anticlerical, and gravitating toward France, and the Catholic and conservative Flemings reappeared, the former accusing the latter of insufficient zeal in resisting the Germans. The position of the king was a major bone of contention; he was criticized for staying behind in 1940 and above all for contracting a second marriage at a time of national misfortune; this was considered frivolous by many of his subjects. The country was evenly divided on the issue, and eventually the king abdicated in favor of his son Baudouin. But the struggle dragged on for a long time and poisoned relations between the parties.

Holland faced problems of a different sort. The revolt in the Dutch East Indies spread within weeks after Japan's surrender, and the Dutch government found little support in Washington and London for its attempts to reimpose control. There was a widespread belief—quite mistaken, as later appeared—that without Indonesia the Dutch economy would collapse. There were internal difficulties, too; the political parties did not find it easy to adjust themselves to the postwar climate. Most enterprising were the Dutch Social Democrats, who decided to transform their party into a labor movement, more or less on the British model. They gained considerable influence and were to play an important part in Dutch postwar history.

Denmark and Norway had suffered less than Holland during the war, and the transition to peace (and a peace economy) was relatively brief, involving no major complications. In Denmark both king and government had stayed behind, having been caught by the unexpected German attack, but their behavior during the occupation was beyond reproach, and though some of the resistance leaders were co-opted into the government, the political parties were able to pick up the threads where they had left them in 1940. The Norwegian king and government had been in exile in London and returned soon after the end of the war. The Norwegian merchant fleet, the country's greatest economic asset, had been severely reduced by wartime operations, and a major effort was needed to rebuild it. In domestic politics the Social Democrats were still, as in Denmark, the strongest party. During the occupation, the communists had won many new adherents, but this was not to be a lasting achievement. The Norwegian Socialist Party, traditionally one of the most radical in Europe, still had a much wider electoral appeal. The Norwegian communists, moreover, had committed the mistake of not joining the general resistance movement, but had established their own separate group. Once the war was over, they found themselves deprived of all political influence.

Whereas the occupied countries faced many common problems after the liberation, conditions in those that had been neutral varied greatly. Sweden and Switzerland, even Spain and Turkey had lived in fear of invasion, and much of their effort had been devoted to national defense. Their political structure differed enormously: Sweden had a Social Democratic government, Switzerland was predominantly liberal in an old-fashioned way, Spain was ruled by a right-wing military dictatorship, and the definition of the Turkish system presented difficulties even to the most seasoned political observer—a relatively enlightened dictatorship gradually transformed itself into a democracy of sorts.

There were few recriminations on the part of the Allies against Sweden and Switzerland; they had been exposed to a real threat and could not have behaved very differently toward the Germans. Inside these countries, however, not everyone took such a lenient view. Had not the spirit of compromise been carried too far? Had it really been necessary to turn back the thousands of refugees who had knocked on their doors before and during the war? Had not some circles inside the country adjusted themselves by embracing quasi-Nazi views? The general inclination was to let bygones be bygones, but some thought that these disturbing questions should not be brushed aside, and they were indeed to occupy many Swedes and Swiss for years to come. There were no second thoughts about the wisdom of having stayed neutral; it was a question of how to interpret neutrality. Switzerland decided after the war not to join the newly founded United Nations because this might divert the country from its time-honored neutrality.

Spain, on the other hand, was severely criticized. General Franco (1891–1975) had cooperated closely with Hitler and Mussolini, and a division of Spanish volunteers had participated in the war in the East. But when it came to the decisive question whether Spain should join the war on Germany's side, the Caudillo had balked. After three years of destructive civil war that had cost hundreds of thousands of lives, the country was not strong enough. Nevertheless, the general feeling in the West in 1945 was that the Franco regime, a remnant of the fascist thirties, should be ostracized. Spain was excluded from the United Nations, and France shut its border with Spain in February 1946 and kept it closed for two years. The United Nations frequently discussed sanctions against Spain, and at one stage many states withdrew their diplomatic representatives from Madrid. But the decisive impulse for the overthrow of the regime had to come from within, and this failed to materialize. There was much grumbling inside Spain about the economic stagnation, a social policy that favored the rich, the corruption of the bureaucracy, and the dominant position of the church. But the opposition was itself a house divided, and after the terrible bloodletting of 1936–39 political apathy was widespread. Franco was bad, but a new civil war would be worse. However objectionable the regime might be, keeping about a quarter of a million of its subjects under police surveillance, it was neither fair nor correct to define the regime as full-fledged fascist in the accepted sense. The hold of the Falange, the Spanish fascist party, was not remotely comparable to that of the fascist parties of Germany and Italy; after 1946 its importance steadily declined, whereas the influence of the army and the church became stronger. In March 1947 Spain received a new constitution, which in some respects was quite unprecedented: it was to be a monarchy without a king, with General Franco as permanent head of state. Visitors to Spain at the end of the war were struck by the strangely non-European character of the country; one of them defined it as a detached portion of Latin America. Spanish politics, too, like those of neighboring Portugal, resembled the military regimes of certain Latin American countries.

It seemed even less certain whether Turkey should be considered part of Europe. Once the war had ended, the country found itself under considerable pressure; the Soviet Union renewed its old demand for control over the Black Sea Straits, and for good measure also pressed for the cession of some border provinces. Turkey in 1945 was still a backward agricultural country with a one-party system. In the 1920s and '30s far-reaching social reforms aimed at modernization had been introduced, but Kemal Atatürk, the father of modern Turkey, had died in 1938, and though his successors had not on the whole deviated from the basic tenets of Kemalism, this movement had lost much of its momentum. Leading politicians, such as Menderes and Bayar, split away from the Kemalist People's Party and founded their own group, the Democratic Party, which in the elections of 1950 gained a crushing victory over its opponents and was to rule the country for the next decade.

Visitors to Europe soon after the end of the war were also struck by the fact that, almost immediately after the fighting was over, the various nation-states, big and small, retreated into their own shells, and that domestic affairs became far more important than foreign policies. It seemed an anachronism: how could these small, separate units survive in the postwar world? There were, of course, well-known historical reasons: the nation-state had always been for most people the natural entity; "Europe" was a vague concept for all but a few statesmen and intellectuals. And yet perceptive observers also sensed that there was a movement in the opposite direction: a recognition of common political interests, the understanding that economic recovery in Europe would succeed only if it was based on close cooperation. In addition, there was the growing danger from the East. It is easy to belittle this danger in retrospect; the acquisitive appetite of the Soviet Union was after all not unlimited, nor was Russia strong enough in 1945 to pursue a policy of aggression beyond the lines that had been agreed upon in Yalta and Potsdam. But the Russians had allies in the West, and it is not certain that, but for the resolute resistance of the nations of Western, Central, and Southern Europe, some would not have succumbed. The fate of Eastern Europe was there for all to see. The Soviet Union, the great hope of the resistance movement during the war, had become the main danger, and this, too, made Europe close its ranks.

STALIN'S LAST YEARS

Stalin was at the height of his power at the end of the Second World War. Soviet forces had occupied Eastern Europe and most of the Balkans. In the Far East, Russia had taken revenge for its defeat by Japan forty years earlier, a fact that Stalin did not fail to recall. Most of the long-held aims of Russian foreign policy had been achieved; it seemed only a question of time before Russia would control the Dardanelles and gain a permanent foothold in the Middle East. This was not the result of some great design. Before the war Stalin had followed an isolationist policy ("socialism in one country"), since the country was not strong enough to pursue a more militant course. But the end of the war opened new opportunities to extend the borders of the Soviet Union and to promote the cause of communism, and Stalin grasped them with both hands.

The Soviet Union emerged from the war as one of the two superpowers, but it was still much weaker than the United States, which had suffered hardly at all. The ferocious onslaught of the German armies, and the Russian defeats of 1941–42, had left deep wounds. About twenty million Soviet citizens had been killed or had died of starvation and exposure. Entire cities—Kharkov, Kiev, Minsk—had to be rebuilt; Leningrad, the former capital, besieged by the Germans for two years, was a mere shadow of the beautiful and active city it had once been. Absolute priority was given to the rebuilding of the national economy as the occupied territories were liberated. Even so, steel production was only half the prewar level as the war ended, and agricultural output was down to 60 percent. The great decline in production was caused not only by enemy action. Though the Germans never reached the oil fields of Baku, production there, too, was halved during the war. The general dislocation, the lack of skilled workers, of transport, of food and shelter, affected output in every area. Soviet citizens had not exactly been spoiled before the war; they had been accustomed to many privations and had put up with conditions that were unthinkable elsewhere in Europe. But the postwar years were the darkest, most difficult period in recent Russian history.

Great changes had taken place in the Soviet economy. Whole industries had been transferred to the east during the war, but only half of them returned after 1945, consequent upon the decision to industrialize Siberia and Soviet Central Asia. Russians had to work even harder than before the war; the forty-hour week introduced in certain branches of industry in 1937 had long been abolished. Food rations were pitifully small. Workers were not permitted to move from one job to another; they were tied to their place of work like serfs in feudal Europe. The food supply did not improve, for both 1946 and 1947 were years of drought; the ravages of the war quite apart, Soviet agriculture had not yet recovered from the terrible setback it had suffered during collectivization in the late twenties and early thirties. Even in 1953 there were fewer cattle in Russia than twenty-five years earlier. There were not enough tractors and agricultural machines; the peasants had to sow and harvest by hand, and sometimes even to put themselves to harness. Russia had a socialist planning system, and in theory it should have been possible to prevent inflation, but the ruble rapidly lost its purchasing power, and in 1947 a currency reform had to be carried out.

There was more abject poverty in Russia than in war-ravaged

Europe. To soldiers in the Soviet occupation army, even postwar Germany seemed almost a paradise as far as housing, food, consumer goods, and living standards in general were concerned. A giant effort was made to rebuild the national economy, with the stress, as before the war, on heavy industry. The rate of recovery was most impressive; by the end of 1945 the production of coal was almost 90 percent of the prewar level, of oil 62 percent, of steel 67 percent. Not much advance was made in 1946, a year of economic reorganization and conversion, when there were power shortages and other bottlenecks. But by the end of the following year, 1947, Russian industry had reached the prewar level, and in 1950 it exceeded it by 40 percent. It had been widely believed that the war had set back the Soviet economy by several decades, but in fact its growth was retarded by only a few years. Enormous power stations were established in Kuibyshev, Stalingrad, and elsewhere; the Volga-Don Canal was built; giant new industrial concerns, such as the Zaporozh steel plant, were established, and others greatly expanded. The coal mines were mechanized, and new oil fields developed beyond the Volga and in the Urals. A new five-year plan was adopted in 1946, to be fulfilled in less than five years. In a speech in February 1946, Stalin had announced that in fifteen years the Soviet Union would produce five hundred million tons of coal and sixty million tons of steel and oil. These seemed almost fantastic figures, outstripping in some respects the United States. But all the targets were achieved, some in considerably less time.

The Soviet Union did not accomplish this single-handed. During the first postwar years, Russia received help from the West, and extracted raw materials at nominal prices from its new satellites in Eastern Europe. Two million German prisoners of war constituted a welcome addition to the labor force. Goods and equipment to the value of many billions of dollars were shipped to Russia from Germany, Manchuria, and other places in lieu of reparations. Without this the recovery of the Soviet economy would not have made such rapid progress, but in the last resort it was the great efforts of the Soviet people that made the economic recovery possible.

Much of the postwar planning was misdirected. There was Stalin's giant project of afforestation to prevent erosion; fifteen million acres of trees were to be planted, but the scheme was abandoned after the death of the dictator. During the war a relatively liberal policy had been pursued in agriculture; the peasants had been permitted to devote much of their time to the cultivation of their small private plots (which had imperceptibly grown in size). After the war, especially after 1950, much stricter controls were introduced. According to a plan mooted by Khrushchev, the number of *kolkhozy* (the collective agricultural settlements) was reduced by merging several small units into one agricultural town (*agrogorod*). It was assumed that as a result a more efficient unit would emerge and, incidentally, political control would become easier. In 1947 there had been 250,000 *kolkhozy*; by the end of 1950 only 125,000 were left; by 1952 their number was reduced to 94,000. Some of them were relatively affluent, especially those on rich soil or those producing technical crops such as cotton. But the great majority were very poor, and their members lived in extremely primitive conditions. When the peasants grew old, their families had to take care of them; unlike the workers and employees in the cities, they were not eligible for old-age pensions. The migration from the countryside to the cities continued; the labor force in agriculture in 1950 was about 10 percent smaller than before the war.

During the war years, everything had been subordinated to the war effort, and the general political climate was relatively liberal—certainly in comparison with the purges, the trials, the constant indoctrination, and the strict orthodoxy of the 1930s. The emphasis had been on patriotism and the fatherland; the traditional heroes of Russian history—from Alexander Nevsky to Suvorov and Kutuzov—made a spectacular comeback. The Communist International had been dissolved while the persecution of the Russian Orthodox Church had ceased, and it was permitted to contribute to the war effort. In the army, dual control was abolished; the political commissars had only an advisory function. The composition of the ruling elite, the Communist Party, had changed; it counted 3.4 million members on the eve of the war, almost six million when it ended. Every other party member in 1946 had joined during the war; these new members, and most of the Russian citizens, had great expectations for postwar Russia. There was a general conviction that things would not be the same again, that the bureaucrats and the apparatchiki would lose their power, that the squalor, the injustices, and the inhumanity would give way to more humane conditions, that no one would now have to fear the notorious knock on the door in the early hours of the morning.

The great sacrifices, it was argued, could not have been in vain; the superhuman efforts that had been demanded of the Russian people would have to be rewarded. During the war Soviet citizens had become accustomed to greater freedom; soldiers on the eve of a battle in which many of them would undoubtedly be killed were no longer intimidated by the secret police. Millions of Russian soldiers had been abroad during and after the war, and their experiences were not likely to be forgotten. Would they react like the Decembrists, the young officers who under the impact of their experience in France in 1814–15 had engaged in a revolutionary conspiracy? The authorities thought there was a real danger that foreign political and cultural ideas would infiltrate the Soviet Union and act as a revolutionary ferment, an element of decomposition within the established order. Against this strict measures were taken; indoctrination was strengthened, and controls were made much more severe. There were additional reasons for this policy: the Soviet Union had acquired at the end of the war a great many territories and millions of new citizens. These included the following:

	SQ. MILES	POPULATION (1945)
Lithuania	24,000	3.0 million
Latvia	20,000	2.0 "
Estonia	18,000	1.1 "
Eastern Poland	68,000	10.0 "
Bessarabia and Bukovina	19,000	3.7 "
Moldavia	13,000	2.2 "
East Prussia	3,500	0.4 "
Carpatho-Russia	5,000	0.8 "
Karelia	16,000	0.5 "
Petsamo	4,000	0.004 "
Tannu Tuva	64,000	0.06 "
Kurile Islands	4,000	0.004 "
Southern Sakhalin	14,000	0.4 "

The gains in territory amounted to an area larger than Spain and Portugal together, and there were millions of new citizens who had to be re-educated. In the areas that had been temporarily occupied by the Germans, millions of Soviet citizens had collaborated with the enemy—they had now to be punished. Some of the smaller nationalities—or, to be precise, those which had survived the rigors of the transfer—had been resettled in the Soviet east. Stalin would probably have taken similar measures against the Ukrainians, except (as one of his assistants later remarked) that there were so many of them. All indications in 1946 pointed to the return of the prewar political orthodoxy and the terrorization of the population. A Soviet history textbook of the Khrushchev period summarized developments on the domestic scene:

> The Stalin personality cult took deep root after the war. It tainted all aspects of party work, and the work of its central bodies. The Leninist principles of collective leadership went by the board. Only one plenary meeting of the Central Committee was held in postwar years, and no party congress was convened, although none had been held for fourteen years. In the circumstances, many fundamental questions of party policy were not given deep enough study, and the solutions took no account of what the party membership thought. Mostly, decisions were taken by Stalin on his own.
>
> In the ideological field the Stalin cult created a rift between theory and practice. The collective thought of the party was ignored. Stalin thought no one but he was qualified to deal with matters of theory. The words of Marx, Engels, and Lenin were, in effect, relegated to relative obscurity. No written works of any worth appeared in the fields of political economy, philosophy, and history. [*A Short History of the U.S.S.R.*, pt. II, p. 270 (Moscow: Academy of Sciences of the U.S.S.R., 1965).]

This is a severe indictment, but it still omits many essential aspects of Stalinism. Although it mentions that Stalin did not consult the party on his decisions, it does not comment on the character of his decisions. It notes some of his misdeeds vis-à-vis the Communist Party, but not with regard to the country at large. Above all, it explains the whole phenomenon as a freak, purely accidental, a temporary aberration from the canons of Bolshevism, the result of the negative character traits of one single man. But Bolshevism is founded *inter alia* on the belief in historical laws, and the question arises therefore whether the Stalin phenomenon was accidental or inevitable. This was a disturbing question. Communism, as everyone in Russia knew, was the dictatorship of the proletariat. The proletariat would be in power until such time as a classless society would emerge, when the state with its repressive function would no longer be needed. But the dictatorship of the proletariat had always meant, in practice, the absolute rule of a handful of people, and from them power had passed into the hands of one man. Stalin concentrated more power in his hands than any ruler in modern history, and he had been deified like the pharaohs of ancient Egypt. There were, in other words, striking contradictions between official theory and practice, between the task the country was asked to fulfill and the political system under which its two hundred million inhabitants were forced to exist. Stalin was convinced that the people were far too backward to be given more freedom; they needed iron discipline and a hard taskmaster. All this, however unpleasant, would have been easier to digest, for Russians and foreigners alike, had it been stated in so many words. Instead, official propaganda maintained that the Soviet Union was the happiest and freest country in the whole world.

These postwar shocks did not come as a total surprise, for many political observers, including some leading socialists, had from the beginning of the revolution given warning that dictatorship was not a political system that could be adopted and discarded at will. Once chosen, it would have a lasting impact on the state and on society; it would not be a "transient phenomenon." Rosa Luxemburg had predicted with astonishing foresight that the dictatorship of the working class would gradually turn into the dictatorship over the working class—first by a small group of people, and ultimately by one man, firmly convinced that he knew what was best for the party and the people at large. But it was not just a question of Stalin's style; there were elements of madness in many of his actions. Some could no doubt be explained in rational terms. The breakneck speed of economic development (and the price that had to be paid for it), and the exclusive stress on heavy industry, were attacked by some and defended by others; these were issues of legitimate controversy. Other policies were not merely wrong and self-defeating but plainly irrational: the purges and mass arrests, for instance, which struck down Stalin's closest collaborators. Toward the end of his life, these irrational measures became more and more frequent. Some reflected the corruption through total power of the supreme leader who had lost touch with realities; some can be explained as the result of progressive paranoia and other manifestations of mental disease. Whatever the explanation, the political system that emerged in postwar Russia was

very different from the "higher form of democracy" that successive generations of Russian revolutionaries had dreamed about and
fought for.

Stalin was in his middle sixties when the war ended, and he had
been in power for more than fifteen years. All opposition, even all
potential opposition, had been eliminated long before. A prodigious
worker, he ran the country practically single-handed; morbidly suspicious of rivals, he delegated authority as little as possible and played
off his lieutenants against one another. While professing great belief
in mankind in general, he despised human beings and was convinced
that without him the country and the communist system would go
under. He was a firm believer in the revolution from above, the imposition of policies by decree, and distrusted any spontaneous movement from below. In the 1920s he had opted for "socialism in one
country" because he realized that, other reasons apart, Russia was
simply not strong enough to pursue a policy of world revolution. But
in 1945 he was presented with the great opportunity, which he could
not let pass, to impose the Soviet system on the countries of Eastern
Europe and the Balkans. Systematically he proceeded to export his
political system to Poland, Hungary, Rumania, and other countries.
There was hardly any pretense that the people of those countries
wanted to adopt Stalinism; it was simply the inexorable course of
history, with him, Stalin, as the instrument of providence.

Stalin's lieutenants, the members of the Politburo and the Central
Committee Secretariat, obeyed the Boss (as they called him) unquestioningly. Any deviation, however slight, would not just have cost
them their jobs; their very lives would have been in danger. The Old
Bolsheviks, who had made the revolution in 1917, had disappeared
in the trials and purges of the 1930s. Only a handful now remained.
Kalinin (1875–1946), the titular head of state, was a peasant by origin
and had been a metalworker in his youth. He had supported Stalin
in his fight for power in the twenties and was rewarded by a post
that was purely honorific. Two other survivors of the pre-Soviet period
were the faithful Molotov and Voroshilov, marshal of the Soviet
Union. Molotov (1890–1986) was second only to Stalin; for ten years
(1939–49), and again after Stalin's death, he served as foreign minister. A Bolshevik fundamentalist, he unflinchingly carried out all
orders; his belief in Stalin's wisdom was not shaken even after he was
virtually eliminated from the leadership in 1949, or after his wife was

arrested. Voroshilov (1881–1969) had been a Red Army leader in the early days, but his record during the war was less than brilliant. He, too, was now a mere figurehead. Far more powerful were the younger members of the Politburo—Beria, Zhdanov, Malenkov, and Khrushchev. Beria, like Stalin a Georgian by origin, was head of the secret police, a state within the state, with a standing army of several hundred thousand. Beria's empire embraced not only all the normal secret-police functions, but also activities as diverse as irrigation and agricultural projects (on which the inmates of the labor camps were employed), the state archives, nuclear research, etc. In theory, the secret police were subject to the instructions of both the government and the Communist Party. In practice, they were omnipotent, and even the highest functionaries of party and state trembled when they had to face Beria's acolytes. Beria was subsequently made responsible for all the evils of the "cult of personality." Andrei Zhdanov (1896–1948) was one of the central figures in the early postwar period, secretary of the party Central Committee, and the supreme authority (next to Stalin) on all ideological issues. He also played an important role in the coordination of the activities of communist parties outside the Soviet Union. Malenkov, the youngest member of the Politburo, had risen very quickly after 1939 and was for a while the main contender for power after Stalin's death. His field was party organization, but he also had a close interest in the management of industry. Khrushchev (1894–1971) rose to the top more slowly; for many years he was a leading party-organizer in Moscow and the Ukraine. Of peasant origin, he had worked in his youth as a locksmith in the Donets region. Like so many of his generation in the higher echelons of the party, he was an all-round man, dealing in the course of his work with problems in the spheres, among many others, of agriculture and industry. Of the rest, Kaganovich should be mentioned; he was an old comrade-in-arms of Stalin, but his position in the leadership was gradually declining. There was also Bulganin, the perfect bureaucrat, chairman of the State Bank, minister of defense, chairman of the Moscow City Council, another all-rounder. Last but not least, Mikoyan (1895–1978), the wily Armenian who was to outlast them all, a specialist in foreign and internal trade and in his later years, by sheer staying power, an "elder statesman." As these lines are written, Kaganovich, born in 1893, is the only member of Stalin's entourage still alive.

While the dictator was alive, there hardly seemed to be any differences between the men around Stalin; they all acted as his instruments and spoke with one voice. Only after his death did it appear that they had personalities and policies of their own. During Stalin's lifetime there was a great deal of jockeying for position and infighting, but it was next to impossible to explain such internal warfare in terms of political or ideological differences. Usually it was a struggle for power, and the issues involved hardly ever concerned basic principles. Bitter fighting took place between the Zhdanov and the Malenkov factions. Malenkov had gained considerable power during the war through his department of cadres, which was in charge of all appointments and nominations. Zhdanov, who resented the success of the upstart and disliked some of his policies, managed to reduce his rival's influence immediately after the war. But in 1947, when Zhdanov fell ill, Malenkov launched a counteroffensive, and after Zhdanov's death succeeded in ousting most of his rival's followers from their positions. As in medieval Europe, everyone in the hierarchy owed his position to someone else—*nul homme sans seigneur*. When the seigneur fell from grace his protégé, too, was in grave danger, unless of course he managed in good time to transfer his loyalties to a new master. Thus, when Malenkov's star was in eclipse, his protégé Professor Alexandrov, head of the important propaganda department (agitprop), was deposed, only to return to grace a few years later, when Malenkov's star shone brighter again, and to disappear finally into oblivion when his master lost his position in the party leadership. Zhdanov's followers were in even more serious trouble after the death of their boss; the whole Leningrad party leadership, men like Kuznetsov and Rodionov (who was also chairman of the Russian Republic's Council of Ministers), were sentenced to death on trumped-up charges. This "Leningrad affair" was kept secret at the time, though it involved Voznesensky, a member of the supreme party body, the Politburo, who was executed. All this was carried out in complete secrecy; from one day to the next, a member of the Politburo had become an "unperson." Purges went on throughout the entire country; in some places, in the course of one year up to 25 percent of the local leaders were deposed. Sometimes this only meant transfer to another party job; if there was any purpose behind these changes (which is by no means certain), it was perhaps to prevent the bureaucratization of Soviet life. If so, it was not very successful, for the system itself presupposed the existence of a gigantic bureaucratic machine, and changing the bureaucrats from time to time did not have a profound effect on the essence of the system.

Originally the Communist Party had been a group of like-minded intellectuals and professional revolutionaries with a sprinkling of working-class members. As a state party, it became more and more "white-collar" in character; everybody in a leading position in society had to belong to the party, whose vast army of professional organizers constituted its backbone. The position of the party was not undisputed: the political commissars had to give way to professional officers in the army and to a new breed of technocrats in industry and agriculture. With Pervukhin and Saburov, representatives of this stratum entered the top party leadership. They were faithful communists; in education and mental makeup they did not differ from the regional party secretary. But by assuming responsibility for the national economy, they developed certain specific characteristics and, as a group, common interests; their influence was to grow in subsequent years. Mention has been made of the unlimited powers enjoyed by the secret police, in theory an instrument of party and state, but in practice totally independent, an authority against which there was no appeal. In one sphere, however, party activities were greatly strengthened after the end of the war: propaganda became much more concentrated, ideological control grew far stricter, and the heresy hunts, which had been discontinued during the war, were renewed. Great stress was put on education; the number of students in higher educational institutions grew from eight hundred thousand before the war to 1.2 million in 1946. A Higher Party School and an Academy of Social Sciences were established in 1946. In the postwar intellectual climate, their main assignment was to popularize the works of Stalin.

Party propaganda put heavy emphasis on Russian superiority to the West, not just during the Soviet period, but all throughout history. Claims were put forward to many Russian "firsts" in science, technology, and most other fields of human cultural endeavor, including the invention of the telephone, the automobile, and the airplane. Many writers, composers, philosophers, and painters came under fire for "slavishly imitating Western patterns," and "cosmopolitanism" became one of the main sins. Others were condemned for having produced work that was not sufficiently optimistic in mood; it was not enough to be a communist or to accept communist ideology in principle; the party line had to be reflected down to the last detail. This campaign of total regimentation of the arts and sciences was initiated by Andrei Zhdanov, but it was not the personal whim of one Soviet leader; in fact, it gained further momentum after Zhdanov's death. The ideological line was laid down in a number of party decrees in 1946 concerning the performance of two literary magazines (one of which, *Leningrad,* was closed down) and the state of Soviet music. Evgeni Varga, a leading economist, was severely criticized for having suggested that within the next ten years or so a major economic crisis in the West was not a foregone conclusion, that, on the contrary, a new boom was not inconceivable. He even suggested that the ruling classes in the West might make certain concessions to the workers; and he thought it not impossible that they would give up their colonies. Such views were emphatically rejected, for they were incompatible with Stalin's policy, which was based on the assumption that an armed conflict between capitalism and communism was sooner or later inevitable.

No field, no aspect of life in the Soviet Union was exempt from control, and the results were usually disastrous. In genetics, the Lysenko school, which denied the laws of traditional genetics, took over, only to be denounced in later years as a group of charlatans and forgers. The Soviet cinema (to provide another illustration) had produced interesting films in the 1920s, some of which had won world acclaim. After the end of the war, filmmakers had to conform strictly to the new canon, but, hard as they tried, they could not satisfy the authorities. As a result, the number of films released steadily dropped, until in the year before Stalin's death it reached the all-time low of five (compared with the hundreds of films released each year not only in the United States, but also in Japan and India). Conditions in other fields were similar: Einstein and Freud were bitterly denounced as spokesmen of imperialism and reaction, and a leading Soviet writer said in a solemn and widely publicized statement that if a jackal could write he would do so like Sartre and T. S. Eliot.

Russia had always been a country of contrasts, but in the postwar period the contradictions became more glaring than ever. Economic recovery was impressive. The nation as a whole, though still desperately poor, was growing richer each year, but the individual standard of life hardly improved. The average Russian family still lived in one room; food was scarce, clothing and other necessities of daily life difficult to obtain and substandard. More and more Soviet citizens were acquiring a higher education, yet at the same time ideological control became more rigid and severe than ever before. According to the official doctrine, the regime was the freest, most democratic on earth, yet the individual had no political rights and was quite helpless vis-à-vis the authorities. The all-pervasive, absurd, and mendacious propaganda was an insult to the intelligence and the maturity of Soviet citizens. According to official doctrine, proletarian internationalism remained the great lodestar of Soviet policy, domestic and foreign. But in fact the country was deliberately isolated from the outside world; all foreign influence, however innocuous, was denounced. A country in which industrialization and the general educational level were making rapid strides was run like a kindergarten presided over by strict disciplinarians. Marxism-Leninism preached the unity of theory and practice, but in reality theory and practice became more and more divorced from each other. The war had given rise to great hopes in the Soviet Union; the postwar era was a period of even greater disappointments.

THE SOVIETIZATION OF EASTERN EUROPE

All Eastern Europe and the Balkans with the exception of Greece, Albania, and Yugoslavia were in Soviet occupation as the war ended, and all the countries in the area, again with the exception of Greece, became, to use the official term, "popular democracies," or, as less kind observers put it, Soviet satellites. Political developments in these countries during the first postwar decade were very similar, and it became the custom to regard them as a unit. But, apart from belonging to the Soviet sphere of influence and being subjected to the same treatment after 1945, there were considerable differences that should not be ignored. The Poles, Czechs, Serbs, and Bulgarians were "brother Slavs"; the Hungarians, Rumanians, and East Germans were not. Most of the peoples in this area had lived for centuries under foreign rule, and attained national independence only during the nineteenth century or after the First World War. They were all intensely nationalist in spirit and, with the exception of Czechoslovakia, preponderantly agrarian in character. But their agrarian structure was unsound; much of the land was in the hands of comparatively few families, while the great majority of peasants had little or no land. There had been sporadic agrarian reforms after 1918 in some countries, but in Hungary and Poland this problem was far from being solved. There were substantial national minorities: the presence of millions of Ukrainians and Jews in Poland, of Germans and Hungarians in Czechoslovakia, the coexistence of Serbs, Croats, and other peoples in Yugoslavia, to name but a few, gave rise to severe political and social problems. There were no major armed conflicts among the countries of Eastern Europe and the Balkans between the two world wars, but neither was there much goodwill, and most had territorial claims with regard to one or several neighboring countries. Twenty years is a short time by which to judge the performance of any country, but the interim balance was not encouraging. Only Czechoslovakia, traditionally the most advanced country of Eastern Europe, provided reasonably efficient government, tackled successfully its social and economic problems, and did not depart from parliamentary democracy. In the history of the other countries, democratic regimes were only brief interludes; for most of the time power was in the hands of a small oligarchy which ruled with the help of the army. In Hungary governments were fairly stable; in other countries there were frequent violent overturns.

The incapacity of the ruling classes of these countries to manage their domestic affairs reasonably efficiently, and above all their inability to join forces, was a basic source of weakness. For, from a geopolitical point of view, their situation was precarious; they were situated between superior and much more powerful forces, Germany to the west and the Soviet Union to the east. They had attained independence at a time when these neighbors had been temporarily weakened. Once the two powers recovered their strength, the future of the smaller nations of Eastern Europe was again in the balance. During the Nazi era, all of Eastern Europe passed under German control. Some countries were occupied (Poland, Czechoslovakia, Yugoslavia); others became cobelligerents on Germany's side (Hungary and Rumania). Bulgaria, though an ally of Germany, managed to stay out of the war against Russia. In Yugoslavia and Albania major resistance movements emerged, a fact that was to be of great relevance in the postwar world, for these countries showed more independence than those of their neighbors, who owed their liberation entirely to the Red Army. There were resistance groups in Poland, too, but for geographical and other reasons these never attained the same importance as in Yugoslavia. In other East European countries there was little or no resistance, either because the population was by and large pro-German and anti-Russian, or because it was apathetic and in any case geographical conditions did not favor guerrilla warfare.

The occupation of Eastern Europe and the Balkans by the Soviet army took place between the summer of 1944 and the spring of 1945. It is never easy to keep an occupying army from committing excesses, and the commanders of the Red Army did not try very hard. After years of bitter fighting and much suffering, the struggle had at last moved beyond the borders of the Soviet Union; it seemed unrealistic to expect the veterans of many battles to behave with exemplary discipline. The excesses did not last very long, nor were they organized, but there was a great deal of violence: civilians were shot, women were raped, looting and plundering were an everyday occurrence. Such incidents were more frequent in the former enemy countries, but Poland, Yugoslavia, and Czechoslovakia were not spared, and the age-old feeling of superiority among the Poles and other East European peoples vis-à-vis their eastern neighbors received fresh fuel: the Russians, they said, were still part of Asia; European civilization had not yet reached them.

Poland and Yugoslavia were the countries hardest hit by the ravages of the war. Six million Polish citizens had been killed, half of them Jews; Yugoslavia, a smaller country, lost about two million. Damage to Yugoslav industry was estimated at one-third of its prewar value. Damage in Poland was even more extensive. In 1945 almost half its arable land was left uncultivated, and agricultural output was down to 38 percent of the prewar level. A million farms were left without horses, and there were, of course, no tractors. Above all, the communication system had broken down almost completely. Hungary and Rumania had suffered less, and they had many resources: Hungary's industry was second only to Czechoslovakia's in Eastern Europe, and it had always exported much of its agricultural produce. Rumania had oil fields and also a considerable agricultural surplus. But the economic outlook in these countries in 1945 was in some ways even bleaker than in Poland and Yugoslavia. The former was compensated for its losses by the East German territories, and both Yugoslavia and Poland received substantial help from UNRRA. Hungary and Rumania, as former enemy nations, did not get such assistance; on the contrary, they had to pay reparations, $300 million in each case, mainly to the Soviet Union. The Hungarian currency collapsed; in August 1946 the dollar was worth 29.667 million pengös, and a new currency, the forint, had to be introduced. Rumania, largely dependent on its agricultural crops, suffered disastrous droughts in 1946 and 1947. Bulgaria and Czechoslovakia, on the other hand, were comparatively little affected by the war; their economic difficulties stemmed from the general dislocation of the postwar period, the breakdown in trade and communications between them and their neighbors.

Political developments in East European countries after 1945 followed a very similar pattern. At first, all-party coalitions were established from which only the fascist and extreme right-wing parties were excluded. These gave way after a year or two to new coalitions, in which the communists obtained all the commanding positions while their partners were reduced to the status of mere satellites. Eventually these "popular fronts" were replaced by one-party communist regimes. But the process did not stop at this point, for the purges continued inside the communist parties. The first victims were party leaders accused of "national-communist" deviations (such as Rajk in Hungary, Gomułka in Poland, Patrascanu in Rumania, and Traicho Kostov in Bulgaria). After this heresy had been stamped out, other targets were chosen, and as the purge continued the pattern became more and more obscure. It turned into a struggle between various communist factions in which ideological attitudes or even the degree of loyalty to Moscow no longer played a decisive role.

There were local variations. In Yugoslavia and Albania the communists had seized power without outside help, and the prewar democratic parties were weak or nonexistent. There was therefore no need for real or bogus coalition governments, and power was in communist hands from the very beginning, the few noncommunists having been removed in the summer of 1945. The purges, too, were of varying intensity in the different countries. But, except for Yugoslavia, political developments in all of them were so strikingly similar that most observers at the time came to believe that they followed not only an agreed pattern but also a timetable that had been fixed in advance. This, in retrospect, appears less certain. There was no doubt agreement about the ultimate aim and, broadly speaking, about the interim phases. The communists knew that cooperation with noncommunist parties was not to last forever, that the socialist parties were to be taken over or, if not, crushed. They were well aware what key positions they needed and what techniques should be used in preparation for the takeover. But there is no reason to believe that a strict timetable ever existed, or that there were instructions concerning, for instance, the duration of the quasi-democratic phase before the ultimate seizure of power. Such decisions were taken more or less spontaneously, and usually depended on a great many factors. The Bulgarian communists seized full power in 1945; their Czechoslovak comrades could have done so with equal ease at the same time but preferred to wait almost three years.

There had been a strong Communist Party in prewar Czechoslovakia, and it was no great surprise, therefore, that in the first free elections in that country (in May 1946) it polled slightly more than a third of the total. Elsewhere, communist parties had before the war been illegal and numerically very weak, counting at most a few hundred or a few thousand members. Their growth in the postwar period was favored above all by the presence of Soviet troops. In Bulgaria there was also a strong traditional pro-Russian sentiment; in Yugoslavia the partisans under Tito had gained much popularity as the patriotic force par excellence; their fight against the enemy had attracted sympathizers from all sections of the population, including the peasants. By and large, however, the communists were still a tiny minority at the end of the war, and ethnically many of them belonged to minority groups. This had a direct influence on their policy—for instance, with regard to collaborators and ex-fascists. The purge among these elements was on the whole less severe than in Western Europe. The leaders were usually eliminated, but the rank and file were not punished, and many of them found their way subsequently into the Hungarian and Rumanian communist parties. In Rumania and Bulgaria, the communists did not immediately abolish the monarchy. King Michael of Rumania was forced to abdicate only in December 1947, three years after the Soviet occupation; King Simon II of Bulgaria, aged nine, went into exile in September 1946. General Kimon Georgiev was prime minister of Bulgaria for more than two years, even though the communists had fought this "military fascist" in the twenties and thirties. In Rumania the communists collaborated with Tatarescu, who had been a right-of-center prime minister before the war. Pasecki, a profascist youth leader in prewar Poland, became one of the communists' most trusted allies after 1945. They preferred right-wing leaders willing to cooperate to socialists reluctant to do so, for the latter were potentially dangerous rivals. They knew that ultimately the outcome of the struggle depended on seizing control of the secret police, the army, the radio, the press, and the Ministry of the Interior. Aware of their lack of mass support, the communists advocated whenever possible postponement of elections, because, as they argued, conditions were not yet ripe. Wherever free elections took place, the results were not encouraging from the communist point of view. In Hungary in November 1945 the Smallholders Party polled almost four times as many votes as the communists; in Berlin in October 1946 the communist vote (despite massive Soviet support) was below 20 percent—less, in fact, than they had polled before Hitler came to power.

The communist parties proceeded cautiously with their program of social change. Firms formerly owned by Germans were immediately taken over by the authorities, but otherwise there was little change during the first year after liberation. During 1946 most banks, insurance companies, iron and steel foundries, mining, and some other industries were nationalized, and many big factories were taken over by the state. In Poland, for instance, this applied to all factories employing more than two hundred workers. In Hungary and Czechoslovakia nationalization at first proceeded very slowly; banks and most of the retail trade in Hungary were not taken over by the state until 1948.

There were differences in the speed of land reform. Whereas the very big estates in Rumania had already been distributed as the result of agrarian reform after the First World War, the opponents of land reform in Hungary had prevented it, arguing that, since Hungary was mainly producing wheat, the preservation of large units was an economic necessity. Less than 1 percent of the landowners in Hungary owned almost half the land; there were, on the other hand, hundreds of thousands of landless peasants. In 1945 all Hungarian political parties agreed that agrarian reform was to be tackled immediately. The polarization of land tenure was less extreme in the other East European countries, and the redistribution of property was made easier as a result of the acquisition of new territories (in Poland) and the expulsion of three million Germans from Czechoslovakia. But from the communist point of view agrarian reform was merely the first step toward the collectivization of agriculture on the Soviet model. At first they pursued this aim slowly and cautiously. There was not enough machinery to make collectivization a success, and the Russian example had shown that undue haste in this respect could have disastrous consequences. In 1946 some countries began to experiment on a limited scale with agricultural cooperatives that were voluntary in character. The first decisions about the forced collectivization of agriculture were not taken until the summer of 1948.

The communists were fully aware that radical change could be introduced only after they were themselves firmly entrenched politically. This aim, the consolidation of their political influence, they pursued relentlessly and with much less restraint. They did not, however, attack their rivals frontally but used what Rákosi, the Hungarian leader, later called the "salami technique," gradually undermining the positions of their competitors. Some of the leaders of the parties opposing them were won over by bribes or flattery; those who did not yield to this treatment were threatened with violence or arrested and silenced. Some were removed on the pretext that they were not acceptable to the occupying power; others were arrested on trumped-up charges. In Poland, Hungary, and Rumania, the "peasant parties" were the communists' main rivals, because they had a far broader mass basis. The Polish communists benefited from the reluctance of their rivals to join the provisional government established in July 1945. Mikolajczyk, leader of the Peasant Party, was then in London; by the time he reached Poland, the communists had seized most key positions. When the Peasant Party resumed its activities, the communists, already firmly entrenched in the police, constantly disrupted its work and harassed and arrested its local leaders, banned its meetings, and ultimately manipulated the elections in such a way that Mikolajczyk, fearing for his life, fled from Poland in October 1947.

In Hungary the communists were at first in a weaker position, since some of the key offices, such as the prime-ministership, were not in their hands. The Smallholders Party, as the elections had shown, was by far the strongest political group. They were, in fact, entitled to form a government without communist participation, but were willing to compromise, demanding only that the party secretary, Bela Kovacs, should become minister of the interior. Faced with this demand, Rakosi threatened that his party would refuse to join the coalition. He implied that as a result the occupying power would install a government of its choice. The Smallholders retreated and made it possible for the communists, in the course of two years, to destroy a party far bigger than their own, by applying various forms of repression and terror. The communists agreed to collaborate only with those noncommunist politicians who were willing to accept their leadership; others were dismissed from their posts or arrested. The usual charge against them was that they had made their party a "haven for fascists and reactionaries." Thus the Smallholders lost all power; Bela Kovacs, the party secretary and most dynamic leader, was arrested in February 1947, and his party colleagues in the government, still nominally constituting the majority, were unable to obtain his release. In Poland and Hungary the socialist parties were taken over by the communists (in 1947 and 1948, respectively) after all the socialists who opposed the merger had been excluded from membership. The same happened to the smaller and less influential Rumanian Socialist Party under Titel Petrescu in 1946, and a similar pattern was followed in Czechoslovakia in 1948. In Rumania there was open Soviet intervention: Vyshinsky, the Soviet representative, demanded in March 1945 the dismissal of the prime minister, General Radescu; he was to be replaced by Petru Groza, a wealthy landowner who had no specific policy of his own and was willing to serve under the communists. The Peasant Party and the other oppositionists were persecuted; their leaders, Maniu and Michalace, were arrested in June 1947 and given life sentences. In Bulgaria the transition to full communist rule was the most rapid of all. Dr. Dimitrov, the leftist leader of the Peasant Party, was forced to resign, and his party was taken over by the communists even before the war had ended. The technique they applied was simple and effective: they delegated several hundred of their members to join the Peasant Party; by various manipulations, these elected themselves local leaders, deposed the central leadership (Petkov and Lulchev), and then decided to merge with the communists. The Social Democrats were silenced in May 1945, when the police seized their newspapers and transferred them to the communists. Several opposition leaders courageously continued to speak up in Parliament; some of them were subsequently even asked to join the government, for the transition had been carried out (the Russians thought) in indecent haste. This they refused to do, and it would hardly have affected the final outcome of the unequal struggle even if they had. In August 1947 Nikolai Petkov was sentenced to death, and the communists announced that they would no longer tolerate opposition. In Yugoslavia some opposition leaders were arrested in 1945–46, but repression on the whole was less severe, simply because the communist hold on the country was much stronger from the very beginning. The partisan army had emerged victorious from the war, and there was no need to go through all the formalities and niceties of coalition and national front; there was no scope for the opposition parties. In Czechoslovakia, on the other hand, the coalition functioned comparatively well for the first two years after the war. The police and the army were in communist hands, but the political parties under President Beneš (whose willingness to collaborate with Moscow was above suspicion) were on the whole in agreement with the policy to be followed. There was a tug-of-war in Slovakia, and also inside the Social Democratic Party, between procommunist elements and advocates of an independent line, but the confrontation came to a head only during the second half of 1947. The first two postwar years were the happiest in the history of the Czech Republic; they were years of relative economic prosperity and political freedom, and it was hoped that the country would escape the trend toward dictatorship which was already so marked elsewhere in Eastern Europe.

East European politics were decided in Moscow, but the Soviet leaders hoped to give these countries at least the appearance of an independent existence. The idea of annexing them like the Baltic countries or eastern Poland was rejected for the time being. Stalin strongly resisted any plan for a merger between the satellites. When Marshal Tito (1892–1980) and the Bulgarian Dimitrov (1882–1949), the former secretary of the Communist International, discussed the possibility of a Balkan Union in 1946, they were sharply rebuked by the Russians, who advised them that even a customs union was unnecessary; Moscow clearly preferred to deal with its clients separately rather than as a group.

The Soviet Union derived substantial economic benefit from Eastern Europe, extracting reparations from Hungary, Rumania, and East Germany. The other countries were forced to sell much of their produce to Russia well under world market prices and to buy Soviet goods at artificially high prices. This, combined with the behavior of Soviet troops during the occupation, the unpopularity of communism in general, and the inevitable clash between communism and the church, made the task of the local communists very difficult, hard as they tried to pursue popular policies. They displayed great energy in tackling social reforms and economic reconstruction, and remarkable skill in crushing all opposition.

By 1947 the prewar level of industrial production was attained, though agriculture was still lagging behind. Most countries had adopted short-term plans, usually for a period of three years, to cope with the immediate economic problems. In their various enterprises the communists showed great initiative and resourcefulness; their political know-how was vastly superior to that of their rivals. They had a clear concept of political power, how to obtain and how to use it, and they had no scruples in dealing with their rivals. In some countries communism was more popular than in others; there was less resistance in Yugoslavia, Bulgaria, and Czechoslovakia than in Poland, Hungary, and Rumania. But everywhere communists were a minority, and there was no reason to assume that they would ever get majority support in a democratic way. Therefore, a regime of coercion and terror was inevitable. Ultimately, the East European communists, with all their drive and other accomplishments, were dependent on Soviet help; sometimes the presence of the Red Army sufficed as deterrent; on other occasions direct intervention was called for. It was in the last resort not the general secretary of the party or the prime minister who ruled, but the Soviet ambassador, whose position was, broadly speaking, similar to that of a Roman proconsul. Once it had been decided that Eastern Europe was to belong to the Soviet sphere of influence, direct involvement on Moscow's part was inescapable; any withdrawal of Soviet troops, or a policy of noninterference in the satellite countries would have caused the downfall of most of these governments within a very short time. And this is what eventually came to pass (in 1989) when it appeared that the East European governments could no longer count on Soviet military intervention when needed.

GERMAN TWILIGHT

What remained of Germany was at first divided into five parts, the four occupation zones and Berlin, itself subdivided into four sectors. The three Western zones, which subsequently became the Federal

Republic of Germany (Bundesrepublik Deutschland) had about forty-seven million inhabitants, the Eastern zone and the Eastern sector of Berlin about eighteen million. Every fifth inhabitant of West Germany was a refugee; more than eight million had fled from East Prussia, Silesia, and Czechoslovakia. There was, in addition, a steady stream of refugees from the Soviet zone to the West, about two million between 1945 and 1952. This continued until the building of the Berlin Wall in August 1961 made such escape impossible. East Germany was the only European country whose population decreased between 1945 and 1960.

There was no active political life in Germany in the immediate postwar period. There were still hundreds of thousands of prisoners of war, and many in the Federal Republic itself were debarred from playing an active part in politics because of their Nazi past. In the general chaos of 1945–46, the finding of shelter and sufficient food had a far higher priority than politics. There was no time to ponder the past, and little inclination to think about the future. The responsibility for the administration of Germany rested wholly with the occupying powers. Political parties were re-established in the Soviet zone almost immediately after the end of the war, in August 1945 in the British zone, in September in the American zone, and lastly, in December, in the French zone. But since the country was then run at every level by the occupation authorities, it was not at all clear what role these parties would play. The communists in East Germany had a head start: a plane from Moscow with Ulbricht (1893–1973) and other German communist leaders landed in Berlin even before the fighting had ended. Within a short time, they established the nucleus of a party organization; backed by the authority of the occupation army, they soon welded it into an instrument of political power. In their first manifestos they stressed that it was the task of their party to fight for democracy and to uproot the remnants of Nazism; "communism" and "revolution" did not figure in these appeals. The presence of the Soviet army made it possible to impose from above, by decree, all the changes that were deemed necessary; there was no need to appeal to the revolutionary impulses of the masses. Walter Ulbricht was the central figure among the East German leaders, and he remained at the helm for more than two decades. A typical apparatchik of the Stalin period, he was neither a popular charismatic leader, nor an outstanding speaker or ideologist; but he had the reputation of a capable organizer and an energetic party boss of the new style; above all, his loyalty to the Russians was never in question. The other parties that were allowed in the Soviet zone after the war had at first far more popular backing than the communists, as far as can be established from the results of local elections, but the Russians did not want them to play an important political role and they gradually faded away, leading a mere shadow existence.

Three major parties emerged in the Western zones: the Social Democrats (SPD), the Christian Democrats (CDU), and the Liberals (FDP). The SPD was the oldest German party; during the last years of Wilhelmian Germany and for much of the Weimar period, it had also been the strongest. But it hardly ever had a commensurate influence on German politics, for its appeal was by and large restricted to the working class. Although it represented the views and interests of a strong minority, it had never been able to attract other sections and to become a truly national party. When in government, the Social Democrats had always needed coalition partners to rule; they were never in a position to carry out their own political program, for which, they thought, the time was not yet ripe. Their belief in democracy and order was deeply rooted, and they lacked a sense for political power; even in 1918 they had not known how to exercise it. The idea of a revolution, though still an essential part of their ideological program, seemed altogether unreal, and the Soviet example had acted as a further deterrent. How could a socialist and democratic society be established if the majority of the population was not yet in favor of it? The party had crumbled in 1933, unable to put up a determined resistance to Hitler; some of its leaders were discredited by their performance in the Weimar Republic, others had died. There was still a fairly strong Social Democratic tradition in certain parts of Germany, above all in the big cities, but unlike the communists the Social Democrats did not enjoy the active support of any occupying power. On the contrary, the Western Allies were deeply distrustful of the new party leader, Dr. Kurt Schumacher (1895–1952), an invalid of the First World War, who had spent almost the entire Nazi era in prisons and concentration camps. Schumacher, a man of high principles and inflexible character, was convinced that the socialists' readiness to compromise had been one of the main reasons for their past defeats. Under Schumacher these mistakes were not to be repeated. The party was to combine a radical socialist program (including the

nationalization of big industrial enterprises and banks) with resistance
to communist encroachments and a firm, sometimes intransigent, line
vis-à-vis the occupying powers.

The Christian Democratic Union, the other big all-German
party, advocated at its first conference, in December 1945, a federal
structure for the new Germany as a form of protection against the
excessive powers that would otherwise be wielded by the central
authorities. Catholic influence was very strong in this party, but it
was not a mere revival of the Catholic Center Party, one of the big
parties of the Weimar Republic. There was a new readiness to cross
the barriers between the confessions. Nor would the political prospects of a party exclusively Catholic in character have been very
bright, for, though the predominantly Protestant regions of East Germany had been lost, and though the Catholics were traditionally much
better organized than the Protestants, they did not constitute a majority in the Bundesrepublik. In its first manifestos the new party
stressed its socialist beliefs, a socialism that opposed the class struggle
and emphasized "social responsibility." "Socialism" in the program
of the CDU gradually gave way to "solidarity" and later, after the
economic situation had improved, to a policy oriented toward a free-
market economy and laissez-faire liberalism. Such a program was by
no means unpopular. Germany had lived for many years under a
system of restrictions and controls, regimented by a network of state
regulations. The Nazi Party, after all, had also claimed to be socialist
in character. Policies that promised little or no state interference had
had a good chance of being accepted, provided, of course, that they
were also effective in terms of stability and economic progress. Of
the early Christian Democratic leaders, only Konrad Adenauer (1876–
1967) was to play a central part in German politics. A former burgomaster of Cologne, a devout Catholic, and a Rhinelander by origin,
he became the undisputed leader of his party, and later of West Germany. He disliked the Prussian tradition that had been so deeply
ingrained in modern German history and believed in close cooperation
with the Western powers, above all in a reconciliation with France,
the "hereditary enemy." He was convinced that a large dose of parliamentary democracy would not be healthy for Germany; in his view,
it had helped to destroy the Weimar Republic. Adenauer's style of
work was paternalistic, if not authoritarian. He was neither a great
thinker nor a great statesman in the traditional sense, but over the

years his resolution, shrewdness, and persistence won the "old man"—he was nearly eighty-seven when he reluctantly resigned—the grudging admiration of even his adversaries.

The Free Democratic Party, which also came into being in 1945, was a curious amalgam of South German radicals and right-of-center nationalists from the North. One of their early leaders, Theodor Heuss (1884–1963), became West Germany's first president. For more than a decade they cooperated with the CDU in the central government, but they never gained sufficient popular support to play an important, independent role in German politics. In the first elections after the war they polled approximately 10 percent of the vote (about as much as the communists), and this was to remain their share for the next fifteen years, until, in the 1960s, the party suffered a further decline. The electoral system adopted in the new Germany was a composite of proportional representation and the British system, and the smaller parties complained that it was unjust, favoring the two big parties. The legislators had been influenced by the bitter experience of the Weimar Republic, with its proliferation of small parties, in which workable and stable majorities had been exceedingly rare.

The real political revival took place in the Western zones in 1947–48, as the parties consolidated their positions and gradually received greater freedom of action from the occupation authorities. In the Soviet zone, too, party politics began to play a bigger role, but it was the policy of one party only. The communist leaders were aware that they needed a broader mass basis to carry out their policies. They could, of course, count on the Russians, but complete identification with the occupation authorities was a mixed blessing. The harsh Soviet line during the first two years, the seizure of so much property, including factories, livestock, and art treasures, caused inevitably a great deal of hardship and antagonized not only the middle classes but also most workers and peasants. The disappointing results of the local elections in the Soviet zone in the winter of 1945–46 eventually induced the communists to drop all democratic pretenses. This involved the creation of a party of a "new type," truly Bolshevik in character, and the elimination of all other independent political forces. The turn of the Social Democrats came first. They were systematically harassed, and their leaders were arrested, while rank-and-file militants lost their jobs or their ration cards. Social Democratic offices and newspapers were "spontaneously" attacked by "angry workers." After only a few weeks, these strong-arm tactics showed results: in February 1946 Schumacher recommended the dissolution of all SPD organizations in East Germany, since the communists had made it impossible for the socialists to function there. Otto Grotewohl (1894–1964), the SPD leader in the zone, was at that time equally bitter about communist tactics, but gradually persuaded himself that there was still hope of saving the Social Democratic movement in the East, provided they cooperated closely with the communists. This policy was highly unpopular with the party activists; despite the terror, 82 percent of Berlin's Social Democrats voted against a merger with the communists; only 12 percent were in favor of it. But the opponents of "working-class unity," as the communists called them, could not in the long run resist the pressure exerted by the occupation authorities and the police. Their organizations were smashed, and Grotewohl, with a handful of supporters, carried the day. In April 1946 the first conference of the "Socialist Unity Party" (SED) took place, and from then on it was plain sailing; the Social Democrats were absorbed in the new Communist Party. The "bourgeois parties" had received more than half the vote in the Eastern zone elections of 1946, but they offered no serious challenge to the well-organized communists; soon they differed from the communists only in name, and those among their leaders who were unwilling to follow the lure of the SED were forced to resign or arrested. As a result of these developments in East Germany, the influence of the Communist Party in West Germany dwindled into insignificance. Social Democrats, Christian Democrats, and Liberals were alarmed about the fate of their comrades in the East, and a militant anticommunism spread in their parties.

The gradual imposition of a communist dictatorship in East Germany during the winter of 1945–46 also brought about a change in the policy of the Western occupying powers. At first they had been reluctant to do anything that could offend the Soviet Union. But the Russians did not reciprocate, and strongly resented any criticism, however mild, let alone interference with their policy in East Germany. Gradually the Americans and the British began to retaliate, and coordinated their policy without paying undue attention to Soviet wishes and complaints. In January 1947 the American and British zones were merged into one economic unit. The French had at first opposed any step toward German reunification, but when their efforts to persuade the Russians to modify their policy failed, they, too, changed their line, and from the summer of 1947 on, the three Western powers generally followed a common policy. De-Nazification ended, the last prisoners of war were released, and a central German government came into being, at first in the form of a Supreme Economic Council. The German political parties and their leaders were given an increasing share in running the country, foreign affairs and defense remaining in the early years the prerogative of the occupying powers. But a new economic plan was adopted, and many of the restrictions on German industrial production were removed, step by step. In June 1948 a drastic currency reform was carried out: ten old marks were (to simplify somewhat a highly complex operation) exchanged for one new mark. A calculated risk was taken with the decision to reintroduce the free play of supply and demand, the mechanism of a market economy. Rationing continued for a few essential goods, such as bread, milk, coal, and electricity. It was not at all certain whether a country that had been impoverished to such an extent would have the necessary resources to increase production and to expose itself to the cold winds of the market without catastrophic results, but the gamble paid off: the reform succeeded better than even the most optimistic had dared to hope. At first prices rose and unemployment increased, but both were brought under control and gave way to stability and full employment. Almost overnight, shops were again full of goods that had not been seen for years; production rose by 50 percent within six months, and in the following year it increased by an additional 25 percent. Great energies were released by the reform: it was a most spectacular turning point in postwar German history, the beginning of the "economic miracle" of the fifties. The reform paved the way for the subsequent triumph of the CDU, which was given the credit for these successes.

The Soviet Union had opposed the currency reform, which it regarded, not without justification, as a further important step toward the unification of the three Western zones. Two months before the reform, Marshal Sokolovsky had left the Allied Control Council in protest, adjourning its session *sine die*. Three years after the end of the war, this marked the end of formal Allied cooperation in Germany.

The Soviet Union then decided to bring pressure on the West in Berlin, at the point where it was weakest. During the night of June 23, 1948, all land traffic from the West to Berlin was stopped; the former German capital, almost entirely dependent on food and fuel supplies from the West, was to be starved into submission. Berlin had long been a thorn in the flesh of the Soviet authorities: a communist stronghold in the Weimar Republic, it had now become a symbol of resistance to the imposition of communist rule. The leader of the Social Democrats in Berlin, the strongest party by far, was Professor Ernst Reuter (1889–1953). Reuter had been a well-known communist after the First World War, but had subsequently resigned from the party, which did not endear him to the Soviets and his former comrades. He was the soul of the resistance, and the Soviet authorities did their best to obstruct his election as chief burgomaster. Berlin was an island, and it was also the one remaining hole in the curtain, through which many refugees from the East escaped every day. The Allies faced a difficult dilemma. To supply Berlin by air was not only an unprecedented logistic operation; it was bound to be extremely costly, as well as risky from a military point of view: what if a military confrontation with the Russians ensued? But public opinion in the West, under the fresh impression of the overthrow of democracy in Czechoslovakia, was all in favor of making a stand. General Lucius Clay (1897–1978), the American commander-in-chief, wrote at the time that, if Berlin fell to the Russians, the whole of Germany would follow, and then the whole of Europe would become part of the new Soviet empire. An "air bridge" was improvised, and eventually worked with clocklike precision. In the course of two hundred thousand flights, West Berlin was supplied with almost 1.5 million tons of goods, including nine hundred thousand tons of coal. The Soviet authorities had clearly underrated the resourcefulness and determination of the West. They realized too late that the only way to stop the Western planes was to attack them, but this would have led to armed conflict, and probably to all-out war. After a few months, Stalin decided that the risks involved were too heavy, and he began a slow retreat. On May 12, 1949, after more than three hundred days, the blockade was lifted. Berliners celebrated; the general feeling was that at least in one place the Soviet advance had been halted.

The reintegration of West Germany proceeded rapidly after 1949. Membership in the OEEC (the Marshall Plan) in 1948 was the first step toward independence and foreign recognition. In April 1951 West Germany became a member of the newly founded European Coal and Steel Community, and one month later it joined the Council of Europe. In July 1951 the state of war between Germany and the Western Allies was officially ended; a similar agreement with the Soviet Union was not signed until 1955. There was no formal peace treaty, for the former Allies could no longer agree on essential questions. In 1951 West Germany appointed its first foreign minister (Adenauer) and its diplomatic representatives. With the treaties of Paris (1954), the occupation status was ended and the Allied control authorities were abolished; Western troops were to remain stationed in Germany on the basis of new agreements. Germany's own contribution toward the defense of the West was discussed for a number of years. The German Parliament, against strong internal opposition, favored the incorporation of German units in a West European defense scheme. This project had first been proposed in 1950 by René Pleven, the French prime minister, to prevent the revival of a separate, national Germany army. But Pleven's plan was rejected in 1954 by the French Parliament, and Germany instead joined NATO (the North Atlantic Treaty Organization) in October 1954. In 1955 Theodor Blank became the first German minister of defense. When the Six decided to join forces in 1957, it was taken for granted that Germany would be a founding member.

These were the main stages in the re-emergence of West Germany on the European scene in the fifties. The country rapidly moved into second place in the list of the world's trading nations; its political influence was by no means equal to its economic power, but it was clear that Germany would not remain a power vacuum for any length of time. The Cold War hastened the process of reintegration, which in the eyes of some Germans went in fact too fast. The Social Democrats opposed both entry into the Council of Europe and the creation of a new German army: "*Ohne mich*" ("Without Me") was a popular slogan in the early and middle fifties. But a majority of Germans did not think this practical politics, and they accepted, albeit without great enthusiasm, the German military contribution within NATO. The general elections of 1953 showed that the CDU had improved its position; it now polled 45 percent of the total vote, whereas the Social Democrats had fallen back to 29 percent.

There was genuine enthusiasm for the European idea in Germany during the fifties. Hitler, too, had advocated a united Europe, and a few Germans may have regarded the new European idea as a convenient backdoor channel for establishing German hegemony over the old continent. However, most Germans realized, as did a majority of Frenchmen and Italians, that in a shrinking world a divided Europe had become too small a unit, and that everyone would benefit from closer cooperation. The stability of German politics in the fifties can be explained only against the background of the country's astonishing economic recovery, but the economic miracle in its turn was possible only because of the political stability. The recovery took several years to gather momentum after the currency reform had created the preconditions. Although there had been a surprising increase in industrial output in 1949, there was more than 9-percent unemployment in 1950, and Germany had an unfavorable balance of payments until 1951. The statistics of industrial production indicate that growth was uninterrupted and steady:

WEST GERMAN INDUSTRIAL PRODUCTION (1958 = 100)

1948	27	1953	67	1957	97
1949	39	1954	74	1958	100
1950	49	1955	86	1959	107
1951	58	1956	92	1960	119
1952	61				

The gross national product (GNP) increased threefold between 1950 and 1964, faster than in any other European country, though not as fast as in Japan. All together, industrial output increased sixfold between 1949 and 1964. There had been nothing comparable in German history; those who had predicted the downfall of capitalism in Central Europe were confounded; the gains exceeded even the most sanguine dreams of the optimists. In retrospect, a great many reasons can be adduced to explain the miracle. Germans had been underfed for many years, they did not have proper housing and clothing, millions wanted cars and all the new machinery that made the chores of daily life less of a burden. The result was an enormous consumer demand, and many new industries had to be established to satisfy it. The chemical industry in particular mushroomed, and the electrical and textile industries, traditionally located in Berlin and central Germany, had to be rebuilt in the West. Even the millions of refugees proved to be an economic asset, for without a substantial labor force there could have been no miracle. In 1960 unemployment had fallen to less than 1 percent, and for everyone who wanted a job there were seven places to be filled; in addition, more than a million foreign workers had found employment in Germany. It has been claimed that the recovery would not have been possible without the initial help given to Germany under the Marshall Plan, $1.5 billion between 1948 and 1952. But Britain and France received even bigger sums, and the Marshall Plan alone does not suffice as an explanation for the boom. The fact that world trade recovered much more quickly after the Second than after the First World War was probably more decisive in Germany's spectacular recovery.

While West Germany became to all intents and purposes part of the Western political, economic, and military system, East Germany was accepted as a full-fledged "popular democracy" in the East. In the elections of October 1950, 99.7 percent of all votes were in favor of the government. Developments in East Germany followed a pattern that had been established elsewhere in Eastern Europe: First the non-communist parties were smashed, then the communist leadership was purged of obstreperous and undesirable elements, a process which lasted until well after Stalin's death in 1953. Agriculture was collectivized, though at a slower rate than in neighboring countries. In many ways, the tasks facing the East German leaders were more difficult than those confronting the other satellites. For the citizens of East Germany continued to be aware of events in the other, bigger part of Germany, and though they could not give vent to their feelings in free elections, they voted with their feet. In one month alone (March 1953) fifty-eight thousand left their homes and escaped to the West. Some were attracted by the fleshpots of West Germany; others found the lack of freedom in their own zone intolerable. Young people were struck by the contrast between ideology and realities. The leaders were well aware of their unpopularity, but there was little they could do to counteract the attractions of West Germany. There was, on top of it all, a severe economic crisis in 1952–53: Russia continued to extract goods on a massive scale, and there was no Marshall Plan for East Germany to assist it in its postwar takeoff. In June 1953 a strike of East Berlin construction workers sparked off a mass revolt which, but for the intervention of Soviet armed forces, would have swept away the regime. This crisis acted as a warning sign; even though it was not followed by liberalization in the political field, a determined effort was made by the authorities to improve the standard of living. Reparations to the Soviet Union ceased, and within the next ten years

East Germany became the second-biggest industrial power within the communist bloc in Europe. The efforts to win genuine political support for the regime by making East Germany a showcase demonstrating the advantages of its communist society over the other part of Germany were less successful. Gradually the population resigned itself to the *status quo* as the feeling grew that they would have to live with it for a long time and that accommodation with the regime was unavoidable. After 1953 the danger of an overthrow of the East German regime from within had passed. But the communist rulers were more ambitious; they wanted to win, or at least to hold their own, in peaceful competition with the Federal Republic. This uphill struggle continued for eight more years, until, with the building of the Berlin Wall in 1961, they admitted that they had failed.

THE BREAKDOWN
OF THE WARTIME
ALLIANCE

The rift between the Allies developed even before the war ended. To some observers this breakup of the wartime alliance was inexplicable, the result of misunderstandings perhaps, or of diplomatic failure. Surely the alliance would have lasted had the leaders only shown more goodwill and imagination, had they been less influenced by suspicion and narrow egotism. Such an appraisal ignored the deep differences between Soviet and Western society and political life; it took for granted that America, Britain, and the Soviet Union had more or less the same war aims, the same concept of a postwar world, or at least that their divergent aims were somehow compatible. It also ignored the prehistory of the war. The Soviet Union had not entered the war because Britain was in mortal danger and Hitler about to establish Nazi rule all over Europe. Up to June 21, 1941, the Soviet Union had cooperated with Germany and bitterly attacked "Western imperialism"; the changes in its policy came only as a result of the German invasion. America had been committed even before Pearl Harbor, but it did not become a belligerent until it was attacked. What held the wartime alliance was the common peril; there was no valid reason to assume that it would outlast the war, and it was not surprising that the first strains began to appear soon after the tide of the war turned. The more the German and Japanese armies were weakened, the less the Allies needed one another, the more acute became the struggle for power in the postwar world. Hitler's last hope was that the Allies would fall out. His wish was realized, but he was mistaken in assuming that the split would occur in time to save his regime. Although the origins of the Cold War lie in the last year of war, it developed real momentum only after the defeat of Germany and Japan.

The differences between the Allies manifested themselves in disagreement about the future of Poland and later of Germany, about territorial changes, reparations, and the government of occupied (or liberated) countries. The settlement of these problems would have been difficult enough between big powers of similar character and structure; the peace treaties after the First World War had not, after all, been easily achieved. The differences between the Soviet Union and the Western Allies were of course far more deeply rooted than the differences that came to light in 1919. They did not even speak the same language, unless it was a matter of straightforward geographical fact or economic figures. When they decided on the "democratic transformation" of a certain country, America and Britain took it for granted that this referred to parliamentary Western-style democracy, whereas for Moscow this was Stalinism. Western-style democracy meant a restoration of capitalism, which was unacceptable to Stalin, certainly as far as his own sphere of influence was concerned, for capitalism and fascism, according to Soviet doctrine, were birds of a feather. The Western Allies put great stress on free elections in the liberated countries. For the Soviet Union this was an imperialist ruse, because such elections were bound to bring anti-Soviet elements to power, since neither the Soviet Union nor communism was popular in Eastern Europe and the Balkans; the workers and peasants in these countries were not aware of their real class interests. A lengthy period of political retraining and indoctrination was therefore necessary, and, above all, a social revolution imposed from above. This, as the Russians saw it, was the historical necessity; "bourgeois democracy" and free elections were mere red herrings.

During the latter part of the war, many exchanges took place between Washington, London, and Moscow about the future of Central and Eastern Europe and the Balkans. London displayed much more activity than Washington; it was still America's declared policy to get out of Europe as quickly as possible after the end of the war. In May 1944 Winston Churchill suggested a deal to Stalin according to which Rumania would be part of Russia's sphere of influence, while Greece would be under British control. The Russians agreed, but only on condition that the scheme also received President Roosevelt's blessing. The American administration was far from enthusiastic, however. The whole scheme smacked too much of old-fashioned imperialism. During a visit to Moscow in October 1944, Churchill resumed this discussion with Stalin: Why should we be at cross-purposes in small ways? How would it do for you to have a 90-percent predominance in Rumania, for us to have a 90-percent say in Greece, and go fifty-fifty about Yugoslavia? For good measure, Churchill added on a sheet of paper: "Bulgaria 75:25, Hungary 50:50." Stalin took out his blue pencil, made a large tick on it, and handed it back: "It was all settled in no more time than it takes to sit down." Churchill had some pangs of conscience and asked: "Might it not be thought rather cynical if it seemed we had disposed of these issues, so fateful to millions of people, in such an off hand manner? Let us burn the paper." "No, you keep it," said Stalin.

This scene has often been recalled. The agreement that was reached regulated for a while the status of Greece and Rumania, but it did not form the basis of postwar policy. The United States, opposing the idea of spheres of influence, had submitted at Yalta a Declaration on Liberated Europe which, though somewhat vague in the first place, and further watered down by the Russians, established the principle of joint responsibility between the three parties. The Declaration mentioned the right of all peoples to choose the form of government under which they wanted to live, and the restoration of sovereign rights and self-government to those who had been forcibly deprived of them by the aggressors. More specifically, the three governments promised to establish conditions of internal peace, to carry out emergency measures for the relief of distressed peoples, and to form interim governmental authorities broadly representative of all democratic elements; they also promised free elections as soon as possible. It was an admirable document, but quite oblivious of the military and political facts of life, and therefore doomed from the outset. It ignored the fact that in the countries liberated by the Red Army the Soviet Union would inevitably have the decisive say.

The conflict first came to a head over Poland, the main bone of contention between the Allies during the last year of war. The Soviet Union had made it clear from the very beginning that it aimed to regain all its territories, including those it had acquired as the result of the German-Soviet pact of 1939—i.e., eastern Poland. Britain had accepted this position in principle and had tried without much success to persuade the Polish government-in-exile (in London) to accept the

Soviet demand on the understanding that the new Poland would be compensated in the West. America was not in principle opposed to the idea but suggested that discussion of territorial settlements should be left to the peace conference. During 1941 and 1942, while Poland was still occupied by the Germans, the issue was largely academic, but with the advance of the Red Army in 1943 the question of Polish-Soviet relations became suddenly acute. A major crisis developed after the German announcement that the graves of some fourteen thousand Polish officers had been found near the village of Katyn. They had been prisoners of the Russians and were apparently killed in 1940. The Soviet Union immediately denied this as an infernal lie, designed to sow distrust among the Allies. Since the Germans had committed so many atrocities, it seemed at the time more than likely that they were also responsible for the Katyn massacre. But against this was the evidence that the fourteen thousand had disappeared well before the Germans invaded Russia. In the circumstances, the Polish government asked the International Red Cross to verify the German allegations, very much against Churchill's advice. He had told them: "If they are dead, nothing you can do will bring them back." The Soviet government immediately broke off relations with the Polish government-in-exile. Subsequent investigations have left no doubt that for once the German allegations were correct: the Polish officers had been killed by the Soviet secret police. In April 1990 the Soviet Union officially admitted it.

In the meetings with his allies, Stalin always stressed that the Soviet Union would not be satisfied with anything less than a friendly Polish government. Poland had been part of the *cordon sanitaire* established around Russia; twice in a generation Russia had been attacked by the Germans through Poland. The Russian complaints about the anti-Soviet attitude of the Polish government in London were not groundless, but the Poles' distrust of their eastern neighbors was deeply rooted in history, and recent events had done nothing to weaken it. For centuries Russia had made common cause with Germany in suppressing Poland; for more than a century the country had been divided between these two and Austria, and it had regained independence only in 1918. In 1939, immediately after the German attack, Poland was invaded by the Russians according to a prearranged plan; the friendship between Russia and Germany had been cemented in blood, Molotov said at the time—Polish blood. Nor had subsequent events reassured the Poles; the Polish soldiers held captive in the Soviet Union had been kept in prison camps until well after the invasion of 1941. Inside Poland a resistance army had been active, but the Russians did everything in their power to weaken it. On August 1, 1944, this Polish Home Army had risen against the Germans, while the Red Army was shelling the suburbs of the Polish capital. Hitler sent five divisions to suppress the rising, but the Soviet army neither helped the Polish insurgents nor cooperated with the Western Allies in providing assistance. Within a few weeks, the Germans had defeated the Home Army and destroyed Warsaw. The Russians washed their hands of the whole affair. They wanted to have nothing to do with an adventure about which, they said, they had not been consulted, but the Poles claimed that the communist radio station in Warsaw had called on the people of Warsaw to rise. Stalin knew that most Poles loathed the Russians and that, especially among the Polish elite, there was no willingness to collaborate with the Soviet Union.

The Western Allies, like Russia, wanted governments to be established in the liberated countries that would be friendly toward them and their political system. But for Stalin the only friend that could be trusted was a totally dependent agent, a satellite; any other kind of government was suspect. Stalin made occasional exceptions, as in Finland, which he thought a hard nut to crack. Finland also had the advantage that, from a geopolitical point of view, the country was less important than Russia's western neighbors. The absence of loyal communist supporters in a country such as Poland made it all the more vital to establish from the very beginning governments dominated by people on whom Moscow could really depend. But such governments could be set up only against the will of the great majority of the population.

The Russians appointed a communist government for Poland (the Lublin government) when their troops crossed the old frontiers, whereas the Western Allies continued to recognize the London government-in-exile, with which the Soviet Union had broken off relations. Churchill and Roosevelt tried hard to reach a compromise, to establish a united Polish government on the basis of a merger of the London and Lublin groups. When Stalin met Roosevelt and Churchill in February 1945, the future of Poland was discussed at almost every session. Russia was in the stronger position, for, as the Allied leaders were meeting, most of Poland was already occupied by the Red Army, which in its pursuit of the Germans had reached the Oder and was only about forty miles from Berlin. It was against this background that the Allied leaders tried to work out solutions for postwar Europe.

When the Big Three met at Yalta, Franklin Roosevelt had just been re-elected, the first American president to be elected for a fourth term. His first years in office, and above all the New Deal, had been the subject of bitter conflict and internal strife. But in 1944 there were no major controversies in American policy, either domestic or foreign; the immediate task was to win the war—"to finish the job and bring the boys home." Roosevelt had a superb feeling for domestic politics; his experience in foreign affairs was more limited. In his dealings he revealed a mixture of cleverness and naïveté, and even in retrospect it is not always easy to establish where one began and the other ended. He hoped that cooperation with Russia would continue after the war; he had a hunch (he said) that Stalin would cooperate. He dealt with him (and the Soviet Union in general) as he would have treated a dissenting faction within the Democratic Party, hoping that from the usual give-and-take that constitutes American politics a reasonable compromise would emerge. Roosevelt was not in good health at the time of the conference: "At this critical time Roosevelt's health and strength had faded," Churchill wrote later. To a much greater extent than Churchill and Stalin, he was influenced by his advisers. Among them were some who had direct experience in dealing with the Russians and who advocated a tougher line—Averell Harriman, the American ambassador in Moscow; his deputy, George Kennan; and General John R. Deane, the military attaché in Moscow. There were also some policy advisers from Washington, and the counsel of the secretaries of state, Edward Stettinius (1900–1949) and James Byrnes (1879–1972), of General George Marshall (1880–1959), and of Henry Stimson (1867–1950), secretary of war, was against toughness; the war had to be won, and America was not in a position to impose its wishes about the future of territories that were already occupied by the Russians. Other advisers, such as Harry Hopkins and Joseph Davies, a former American ambassador to Moscow, went even further. Davies, as appears from his Moscow diary, wholeheartedly supported all of Stalin's policies, including even the Moscow trials. He believed that the Soviet leaders were at bottom moved by altruistic impulses, and that it was their primary aim to promote peace and the brotherhood of man. These beliefs, though not perhaps in such an extreme form, were by and large shared by public opinion in the United States during the war. Criticism of Russia and of Stalin's regime was thought to be in bad taste. Russia, after all, was an ally, fighting heroically against the common enemy. Stalin's victories seemed to justify all his policies in the past, however harsh and cruel. It was widely assumed that postwar Russia, united under a great and benevolent leader and no longer threatened by external enemies, would be the natural ally of the United States in shaping the "one world" of which Roosevelt's presidential rival Wendell Willkie had written. At the same time, there was a great deal of suspicion of Churchill and British policy: Churchill's proposals were thought to embody outworn and reactionary concepts such as the balance of power, or to have been designed to further traditional British imperialist interests. Roosevelt was convinced that Stalin was not an imperialist, and some of his advisers told him that Churchill was more concerned with maintaining Britain's position in Europe than with preserving peace. The president genuinely believed in the United Nations as the chosen instrument to regulate the problems of the postwar world, and in personal diplomacy, not power politics. These attitudes were praiseworthy, but they ignored both the basic character of Stalin's regime and the political realities of Eastern Europe. During the last weeks of the war, when Soviet demands increased, Washington and London drew closer, but at the Yalta Conference Roosevelt was still very much concerned not to "gang up" with Churchill against Stalin. Without American support, Britain could not achieve much in resisting Soviet political and territorial demands in Eastern Europe.

Winston Churchill, who had been in politics longer than the other two war leaders, was now at the apex of his career. Unlike Roosevelt's, his interest in domestic affairs and party politics was limited, and his ability in this field not outstanding. His heart was in world affairs and in the conduct of the war. Not all his enterprises had been crowned with success; if his political life had ended in 1938, the verdict of history would have been that Churchill was a gifted amateur, flamboyant and full of energy and ideas, but deficient in judgment, a conservative statesman basically rooted in the eighteenth, not the twentieth century. He had realized earlier and more acutely than other British leaders the dangers of Hitlerism, and when the hour of trial came he was ready to lead his country, giving fresh courage to its people at a time of great peril. Under his leadership, Britain continued the fight against seemingly overwhelming odds. His personal prestige as a war leader was tremendous, so much so that many tended to forget that the country he represented was no longer the great power it had been in the past.

Churchill's position at Yalta was not an easy one. Britain had gone to war as a result of the German attack on Poland, to which it had pledged its support. It could not stand idly by while the European balance of power was being destroyed by Hitler's aggression. But at the end of the war Poland's independence was again in danger, and Russian power constituted a threat more formidable than Hitler. Churchill's understanding of the motives of Soviet politics was unsophisticated; he had never read Marx or Lenin and relied on his own instinct. For him it was simply a big-power conflict; questions of ideology hardly came in. But he realized much earlier than the Americans and the European left what the Russian advance into Europe meant: the whole of Eastern Europe and the Balkans would be swallowed up and become part of the new Russian empire, and no one could be certain that the Soviet advance would stop at the line that had been agreed upon, for Europe in its then state of weakness was hardly in a position to resist. New dictatorships and police states would be set up, and it was not to this end that the war had been fought. From the Americans Churchill could not at first expect much help; Roosevelt was still convinced that Stalin did not want annexations and that they would work together for stability and peace. There was no way to influence Stalin but friendly persuasion.

Stalin, too, was at the height of his power at the end of the war. But his power, unlike that of Churchill and Roosevelt, was unlimited; it was not to be challenged in an election. The war had done a great deal to refurbish Stalin's image both in the outside world and among his own people. He had usurped power in the 1920s and relentlessly destroyed all opposition. In some respects he pursued the policies outlined by Lenin, building socialism, as he understood it, in one country. Agriculture was collectivized, and industry built up at breakneck speed. The society and the regime, with its grotesque cult of the leader, its permanent purges, were a mixture of rationality and madness, just as Stalin himself combined sincere ideological conviction, cynicism, and unlimited personal ambition. But most of the negative aspects of Stalinism were forgotten in 1945. It seemed that his policies had been wholly justified, for he had prepared his country for the great onslaught he had predicted would one day come, and under his leadership the Soviet people had resisted and destroyed the invader. That many of his policies, both before and during the war, had gravely weakened Russia's ability to defend itself was forgotten in the hour of triumph.

There were few doubts in the West about Stalin's greatness. In a speech at Yalta, Churchill declared that "we regard Marshal Stalin's life as most precious to the hopes and hearts of all of us," and a little later, in a speech in the House of Commons, "I know of no government which stands to its obligations . . . more solidly than the Russian Soviet government." There was a certain guilty feeling in the West about the absence of a "second front" before June 1944. Few people recalled what Stalin's attitude had been in 1940, when an invasion of Britain seemed imminent. Enormous quantities of war materiel and food had been shipped to Russia from the United States under the Lend-Lease Act, including almost 15,000 planes, 7,000 tanks, 52,000 jeeps, and 376,000 trucks. Yet to Western public opinion all this seemed woefully insufficient. Only the Western experts stationed in Moscow knew that Soviet newspapers had not been permitted to mention these deliveries.

There was much potential friction, but it did not come out in the open until after the Yalta Conference, which was in many ways the high tide of Allied cooperation. There it was resolved that Poland's eastern frontiers would roughly follow the Curzon Line, as the Russians had demanded. Since the British and the Americans opposed the Oder-Neisse Line, it was decided to postpone a final settlement of Poland's western borders until the peace conference. The communist Polish government was to be enlarged and become fully representative, pledged to hold free and unfettered elections. The Western powers interpreted this as the establishment of a new, democratic government, whereas the Soviets maintained that only a few noncommunists would be co-opted, and these only on condition that they accept Poland's new frontiers as defined at Yalta, which few noncommunist Poles did. Stalin found the Western insistence on a democratic regime for Poland irritating; the Soviet Union, after all, had not been given the opportunity to share control in liberated Italy or in Greece, where Britain faced a strong left-wing resistance movement opposed to the return of the monarchy. The Western Allies regarded these territories as their own preserve; with what right were they meddling in East European affairs? The Western powers were in a better tactical position; they could be reasonably certain that from free elections democratic governments would emerge. The Russians, on the other hand, knew that Polish or Rumanian communists would not have stood a chance in elections, and this strictly limited their freedom of maneuver.

A great many topics were discussed at Yalta, such as Russia's entry into the war against Japan, the organization of the United Nations (at Russian insistence, the permanent members of the Security Council were given the right of veto), German reparations (a figure of $20 billion was mentioned by the Russians), and French participation in the occupation of Germany. Some questions were left open, but on most issues agreement was reached. This did not mean much, for it still remained to be seen how the agreements would be interpreted and carried out.

The complications began almost the moment the conference was over. In Rumania a communist-controlled government was appointed following a Soviet ultimatum. In Poland, Marshal Zhukov (1896–1974) invited sixteen leaders of the Polish Home Army to lunch to discuss ways and means of cooperating in the war against Germany. At the end of the lunch they were arrested, to reappear only in a show trial in Moscow and to be sentenced to lengthy prison terms for alleged sabotage. On May 4, Churchill wrote his foreign secretary that the "terrible things which had happened during the Soviet advance clearly showed the kind of domination the Russians intended to impose." The Russians, meanwhile, complained that the Western Allies were negotiating with the Germans behind their back, and they were greatly offended when the Lend-Lease agreement was abruptly ended a few days after the war. The honeymoon between the Allies was drawing to a close.

Roosevelt died on April 12, 1945. During the last months he had been tired, anxious to avoid further argument. Harry Truman, his successor, had little experience in foreign affairs and thought it wise to continue Roosevelt's policies, at least until he was more firmly in the saddle. He sent Harry Hopkins (1890–1946), Roosevelt's close confidant, to Moscow in an attempt to settle the disputes that had arisen. Upon his return, Hopkins reported complete success, but his optimism was not justified, as soon appeared. Truman had asked

Churchill to "forget the old power politics," but the new American president himself was not permitted to forget power politics for very long.

The Allied conference scheduled to deal with the most urgent postwar problems was convened in Potsdam during the second half of July 1945. It was the first time that Harry Truman represented the United States; in the middle of the conference Attlee and Bevin were to replace Churchill and Eden after Labour's election victory. The discussions ranged over a wide field, from Poland and Spain to Greece and Libya. But the most important topic was the future of Germany. Various schemes had been drawn up during the war to ensure that Germany would never again be a danger to its neighbors and to the world at large. In 1944, at the time of the Yalta Conference, everyone seemed to agree that Germany should be broken up into a number of small states. But by the time Germany surrendered, both Russia and the Western Allies had reached the conclusion that these schemes were not workable, and in any case not desirable. Germany was to be treated as one economic unit; there was to be decentralization, but not dismemberment. In the economic field a similar change of mind had taken place. In 1944 the Americans had produced a plan for the pastoralization of Germany. The reasoning behind it was that, if the Germans did not have the potential to produce arms, they would not be in a position to wage war. This, the so-called Morgenthau Plan, did not, however, become official policy; it had been based on the assumption that it would be exceedingly difficult to keep Germany down, whereas, once Germany had capitulated, it appeared that it was far weaker than the Allies had imagined; the real problem was to keep it from complete collapse. Soviet views, too, had changed. The official line had been violently anti-German up to 1945, but after that there was a marked shift. Ilya Ehrenburg, the most outstanding propagandist of the anti-German line, was officially rebuked, and as the Russians entered Berlin, banners were displayed with a recent Stalin quotation to the effect that Hitlers come and go but the German people remains. There were also economic considerations: the Russians were pressing for very heavy reparations, and they realized that it would be impossible to extract them unless German industry could be set to work.

The Potsdam Conference was in agreement about a number of principles: that Germany should be disarmed and demilitarized, that the Nazi Party should be dissolved, that it should be brought home to the German people that they had suffered total military defeat and could not escape responsibility for what they had brought upon themselves; that all war criminals should be brought to judgment, and that political life should be reconstructed on a democratic basis; that all democratic parties should be encouraged, and education and the legal system reorganized; and that for the time being there should be no central German government, the Allies being responsible for those central departments (such as finance, transport, etc.) that would have to be established.

There was no difficulty in drawing up such a statement of intent; the real test was in carrying out these agreed policies, for a "democratic party" still meant different things to Stalin and the Western Allies. Two problems provoked much dissension from the very beginning: the frontiers of the new Germany, and the question of reparations. America and Britain agreed to Soviet annexation of part of East Prussia, but they thought that Polish territorial claims went too far. How could the many million Germans expelled from these territories be resettled in a much smaller and poorer Germany? The Oder-Neisse Line served as a basis for discussion, but there was an eastern and a western Neisse, about a hundred kilometers apart; the Americans, as a last concession, were willing to accept the former, whereas the Russians and Poles would not budge from the latter. In the end, the West gave way, as before at Yalta. The Poles were to retain control of the occupied territories, though the final border would be settled only in the German peace treaty. Poles and Russians had much reason to be satisfied with the outcome of the conference.

Everyone agreed that the Allied control authorities were to ensure—to quote the official formula—"the production of goods and services essential to maintain in Germany average living standards not exceeding the average of other European countries." But on reparations there was no end of haggling. The Russians argued that the sum of $20 billion had been agreed upon at Yalta, of which they were to get half. The Western leaders replied that this had merely been a basis for discussion. They recalled that unrealistic demands for reparations after the First World War had been the source of much misfortune to victors and vanquished alike. They also argued that the annexation of a sizable part of German territory by Russia and Poland constituted reparation for war damage. They objected to fixing an overall figure for reparations, but it was in principle agreed, after long haggling, that the Russians would be entitled not only to reparations extracted from their own zone, but also to 25 percent of industrial equipment from the Western zones, since it was not thought necessary to maintain Germany's postwar economy on the level previously envisaged.

In the course of the Potsdam Conference, the Russians complained about the civil war in Greece and demanded the inclusion of the progressive forces in that country in the government. Much to everyone's surprise, Russia also declared an interest in Tangier and in the former Italian colonies, suggesting at one stage Soviet trusteeship for Libya. This clearly worried the Western statesmen. Russian territorial demands in Poland, Germany, Rumania, or Czechoslovakia could be explained with reference to the Soviet wish to strengthen its defenses, but a strategic position in Africa was obviously not a defensive measure. Moscow also demanded the annexation of two Turkish provinces and pressed for control over the Black Sea Straits; it was intolerable that Turkey should have a "hand on Russia's throat." Western suspicions began to increase. Was there no end to Russian demands? The admiration for Russian achievements was dimmed by fear of Soviet ruthlessness and power, and by the realization that Moscow's supporters in the West would, if they could, destroy free governments everywhere. The Potsdam Conference reached a number of decisions with regard to the future administration of Germany, but most of them were ambiguous and self-contradictory; the conference as a whole was not a success, for the spirit behind these accords was no longer one of implicit trust. The wartime alliance was in the process of disintegration. Some of the agreements were a dead letter from the beginning; others were soon to be disregarded. The whole political climate was rapidly changing.

The conferences of Yalta and Potsdam have been, in retrospect, the subject of much criticism. At the time, the decisions were on the whole welcomed, but only a few months later, when the full details became known, and with the change in the political climate, there were bitter attacks on the Western leaders, and on Roosevelt in particular. The charge was that they had been outsmarted by Moscow, had failed to foresee that the Russians would turn against the West after the war. America had been in a position to speak the only language the Russians understood—the language of power—yet Roosevelt and his advisers had surrendered to Stalin all along the line. Later, after the Cold War had abated, a revisionist school of thought argued that the Cold War was the natural outcome of American policy. The alliance would have remained intact had Washington been even more forthcoming, had it not indirectly used the A-bomb as a threat, and had it not given the Russians any ground for suspicion. Stalin was told at Potsdam by Truman that a new weapon with an immense power of destruction had just been tried out, but he was not surprised, for he had received the information from his own sources well before.

The West did not negotiate from a position of strength at Yalta, as far as Eastern Europe was concerned. Roosevelt, as already noted, was very ill at the time; a more vigorous American president, one with fewer illusions about Russia, the United Nations, and the post-war world in general, would have been more alert to the dangers ahead. It is likely that some mistakes would not have been committed; the West could have insisted, for instance, on a land bridge to Berlin. But the territories in dispute were occupied by Soviet forces, and in such circumstances it is unlikely that more forceful language would have greatly impressed the Russians. Opinion at home in the United States was anxious for an early withdrawal from Europe, and shortly after the end of hostilities the troops themselves began to clamor for even quicker demobilization than envisaged in Roosevelt's undertaking to withdraw the army within two years. In the circumstances, America was not in a good position to pursue a tough policy (unless atomic threats were indeed to be employed, which was unthinkable). More use could have been made of economic leverage and of the Soviet need for continued American help. In January 1945 the Soviet Union had applied for a $6-billion loan; later on, the Russian insistence on reparations was further evidence of its need for economic assistance. However, in Stalin's view Russia was in fact doing America a favor by asking for a loan; as he saw it, the American economy would face a postwar slump unless demand was artificially created. Roosevelt (and then Truman) should have had a clear reparations policy and should have used economic aid as a diplomatic instrument in negotiating with Stalin. But, however badly it needed economic aid, there is no reason to assume that the Soviet Union would have been persuaded by such means, no matter how substantial the scale, to desist from annexations and from imposing its will on the countries of Eastern Europe. Had America opposed the Oder-Neisse Line more strongly at Potsdam, the border between East Germany and Poland would have run some sixty miles to the east, but this would have hardly constituted a basic change affecting the overall balance of power.

In short, greater Western toughness at Yalta and Potsdam would have hastened the outbreak of the Cold War, but it could not have been prevented once Europe had become a power vacuum. America was committed not to become involved in European politics and to withdraw its army, while Britain alone was too weak to resist Soviet pressure. In these circumstances, the Soviet advance to the west was only natural: politics, like nature, abhors a vacuum. Averell Harriman, ambassador to Moscow, had realized in 1944 that, if the Soviet right to penetrate her immediate neighbors in order to safeguard Russian security was accepted, the penetration of the next immediate neighbors would follow with equal logic. The real question was how far the Soviet Union would expand and how difficult, or how easy, the process of digesting its immediate neighbors would prove to be.

Stalin deeply distrusted the Western leaders, despite their professions of friendship and sympathy. Even before Yalta he told Djilas: "Churchill is the kind who, if you don't watch him, will slip a kopek out of your pocket. . . . Roosevelt is not like that. He dips in his hands only for bigger coins." Roosevelt, of all people, had done nothing to merit such suspicion. But Stalin distrusted everyone, and there was no good reason to be less suspicious of Westerners than of his own subjects. There is no proof that he deliberately decided at a certain stage to turn against his allies regardless of consequences. He would no doubt have preferred to continue receiving Western economic aid, but it was even more important that his political and territorial demands be accepted. It soon appeared that he could not attain both aims; the more extreme his demands, the more resistance they provoked. One thing led to another, and within a few months the wartime alliance had collapsed.

All this would probably have happened even if it had merely been a traditional conflict between big powers pursuing their opposed interests. But the Soviet Union was not just another state; it had an ideology and a social system sharply differing from those of the West, and it was doctrinally committed to assist the victory of communism all over the globe. As long as capitalism and socialism existed, "we cannot live in peace, one or the other will triumph," Lenin had declared. More than two decades had passed since those lines had been written, and the Soviet Union under Stalin had undergone important changes. The messianic mission was no longer so acutely felt, and ideological motivation in Soviet foreign policy had certainly lessened over the years. But the totalitarian state that had developed still had a dynamism of its own; it was impossible to understand the mainsprings of Soviet policy while ignoring this essential feature of its character. Russia was not a traditional nation-state, not a "static" great power; it did not pursue realpolitik as the West understood it.

Protestant and Catholic rulers in Europe had agreed after the Reformation on the principle that the religion professed by the individual should depend on his place of residence: *Cuius regio, eius religio*. Could an arrangement on similar lines have worked in postwar Europe? Stalin seems to have thought so; he said on one occasion that this war was different from previous ones in that the occupying power was imposing its social system on the countries under its control. He did not interfere in Greece in 1944–45; the revolutionary party in Athens could expect no help from Moscow, for the Russians regarded Greece as outside their sphere of interest. But it is doubtful whether any such arrangements would have worked in Central Europe, even if America had accepted the principle of spheres of interest. Communism was ideologically committed to renew the struggle against "Western imperialism" once the war ended, as Jacques Duclos, the French communist leader, had written in April 1945. The renewal of the contest could have been delayed but not indefinitely postponed. In Stalin's eyes, the Western proposals to establish governments that were friendly to the Soviet Union and yet representative of all the democratic elements in the countries were a mere trick, a new attempt at capitalism encirclement. Only communists were acceptable to him, and among the communists only those handpicked by him could be trusted. Suspicions and misunderstanding played a certain part in the outbreak of the Cold War, but underlying these suspicions there were real conflicts of interest. Collaboration with the West after 1945 would have involved the liberalization of Stalin's regime and the opening of the Soviet Union to all kinds of undesirable foreign influences. Such a policy was contrary to Stalin's principles, to his entire attitude and outlook. During the war, when his country was threatened, certain concessions had to be made, but the continuation of such policies

in peacetime would have endangered the very existence of the Soviet
state. It seems most unlikely in retrospect whether any Western
concessions could have induced Stalin in the long run to act against
his best interests. His political system was based on a state-of-siege
mentality; the sacrifices he demanded from his people could be justified only with reference to the unrelenting hostility of the capitalist
wolves and sharks waiting for the opportunity to attack the Soviet
Union. This system needed tension, not relaxation, in its relations
with the outside world.

THE ORIGINS OF
THE COLD WAR

Three years after the end of the war, Europe's main economic wounds had been healed; industrial and agricultural output had almost reached prewar levels. (There were notable exceptions: Italy's recovery was seriously lagging behind, and in Germany it had hardly begun.) The significance of the achievement should not, however, be overrated, for the thirties had been years of depression, and regaining the level of 1938 was not in itself a reason for congratulation. There were, moreover, serious difficulties that had not existed before the war: Europe was not earning enough dollars to pay for its imports, and without this a lasting recovery seemed well nigh impossible. Some put the blame on the mistaken economic and financial policies of the respective governments, while others claimed that it was, in fact, a structural crisis, for Europe's place in the world had radically changed. Nor was it certain whether Europe still had the will and the ability to regain its old prosperity and influence. "What is Europe now?" Churchill wrote in 1947. "A rubble heap, a charnel house, a breeding ground of pestilence and hate." He was not alone in his pessimism.

Within a year after the end of the war, the Soviet Union accused its former allies of fascist aggression, imperialist expansion, and preparing a new world war. On the other hand, many people in the West felt, to quote again Churchill's famous speech at Fulton in March 1946, that the police governments established in Eastern Europe did not represent the liberated Europe they had fought for, nor did such a Europe contain the essentials of peace. Many came to believe with President Truman that, unless Russia was met with a strong hand

and an iron fist, another world war would be in the making. It seemed only normal that the former Allies did not see eye to eye on many problems, and that there were clashes of opinion and interest. But who had expected that within two years after the end of hostilities Europe would be divided into two implacably hostile camps, and that there would be widespread fear of a new world war?

Western policy during the immediate postwar period has been severely criticized from opposed points of view. Around 1950 the general opinion was that Western policy toward the Soviet Union had been too credulous and soft. A decade later, some critics argued that, on the contrary, the West had not shown enough goodwill, that there had been hysteria and a tendency to overrate both Soviet hostility and Soviet power. Stalinist Russia, they argued, was basically a conservative country in search of security, but with no desire to expand beyond its natural borders. Western statesmen, and the general public in Europe and America, had come to believe during the war in an image of Russia that had little in common with Soviet realities. Since the Soviet Union was an ally in the struggle against Hitler, any criticism of its internal regime was thought to harm the war effort. By 1946 most people were less ready to show much consideration, as it became more and more obvious that Stalin's tyranny had not mellowed.

In 1946 the Greek civil war was resumed from bases beyond Greece's border. The Soviet Union refused to withdraw from Persia and put growing pressure on Turkey. All opposition was gradually eliminated in Eastern Europe and the Balkans, while the Soviet Union's efforts to impose its political system on its zone of Germany became more intense. At the foreign ministers' meetings throughout 1946–47, little progress was achieved toward a lasting peace settlement. The Soviet stand became more and more adamant, despite constant, often pathetic Western attempts to reach compromises and to allay Soviet suspicions. In 1947 and 1948 the situation deteriorated further. The democratic regime was overthrown in Czechoslovakia, which became a full-fledged satellite; the Berlin blockade was imposed; the Soviet Union refused to cooperate with the West in the new projects for the economic recovery of Europe that had been mooted (such as the Marshall Plan), and in the attempts to establish international control of nuclear weapons. The communist parties of Western Europe, above all those of France and Italy, preached the violent overthrow of governments that, they claimed, had sold out to American monopoly capitalism. Nineteen forty-eight saw the first meeting of the Cominform, a new organization that in some ways resembled the Communist International, which had been dissolved during the war. The Western communists were criticized on this occasion for having in the past put too much emphasis on parliamentary activities; from now on their opposition would have to be far more militant. Strikes and widespread disorders occurred that summer all over Europe. There was in all probability no concerted, detailed plan behind these actions, but more and more people in the West came to believe that there was a growing Soviet threat that could be averted only by a firm stand and the application of counterforce. Suddenly the West felt cheated, and in this rude awakening many wartime illusions were shattered and there was an inclination to overdramatize the conflict, to attribute to Stalin and the other communist leaders not only satanic cunning and evil but also relentless and unlimited territorial ambitions. Having ignored communist ideology for many years, the West now betrayed a growing inclination to take strictly at face value all theoretical writings about world revolution and the coming inevitable conflict. There was a tendency to view largely in military terms a struggle that was essentially political in nature. But it is also true that Europe in 1947–48 was neither stable nor prosperous; not much initiative and force would have been needed by a resolute minority to impose its will. Democracy in Czechoslovakia had after all been overthrown, and there were disturbing reports from Finland and other countries. The language of communist leaders was violent; perhaps they did not mean all they said, but one could certainly not afford to ignore their pronouncements and predictions.

America was certainly unprepared for political warfare; it lacked the experience and the organizational weapons. There were "Russian" parties, some big, some smaller, in all European countries, but there was no corresponding "American" party. Above all, the West lacked a common political philosophy, the purpose and single-mindedness needed for sustained political warfare. Zhdanov, the ideologist of the Cominform, was the first to popularize the idea of the existence of two hostile camps in Europe and the world. But Western Europe was in fact anything but a "camp"; rent by deep internal divisions, it contained conservative, liberal, Catholic, and socialist forces, as well

as many others. The only unifying tie was the common threat and
the wish not to succumb to it. At the height of the Cold War, the
slogan "liberating" Eastern Europe gained some currency in the West,
but there was little thought and even less conviction behind it; the
posture of the West was essentially defensive; it had little to oppose
to the dynamic, aggressive policy of the Soviet Union and the communist parties. There were foolish speeches on the part of Western
leaders which perhaps aggravated relations with the Soviet Union,
and some of the fears were quite irrational. But more often Western
actions came as an answer, usually belated, to a Soviet challenge.
These answers deepened the mutual distrust, for once the West had
begun to suspect Soviet motives there was a tendency to dismiss out
of hand all Soviet initiatives, even if they might have helped to reduce
tension. There were such moves even at the height of the Cold War:
Soviet policy was not always consistent. After a barrage of anti-
Western propaganda and action, there usually came a proposal of a
more conciliatory nature, such as Stalin's suggestion in 1952 concerning free elections in a neutral Germany. Perhaps there was a
feeling in the Kremlin that things had gone too far. But after their
bitter disappointment of 1945–47, there was little inclination in the
West to take up these Soviet initiatives. In its essential orientation,
Soviet strategy was immovable; "We shall never get out of Germany,"
Stalin told Kardelj, the Yugoslav foreign minister, in 1948. Western
statesmen were to regret in later years that they had failed to probe
sufficiently the more conciliatory Soviet proposals, if only because
these omissions contributed to the emergence of the myth of the "lost
opportunities."

The Cold War created a far greater degree of European unity
than had been thought possible, and it also brought about lasting
American involvement in European affairs. These developments were
highly undesirable from the Soviet point of view, and to that extent
Soviet policy between 1946 and 1949 can be said to have failed.
Soviet influence in Europe was no longer expanding; the borders were
frozen, and a stalemate prevailed in international relations. Even
France, hitherto reluctant to make common cause with the "Anglo-
Saxons," changed its course and began to cooperate in the economic
and political field, and to coordinate its military efforts. From now
on it was clear that the map of Europe could be changed only as the
result of a major war. While the Soviets talked about such a war as

an eschatological certainty, their policy remained cautious. In Berlin in 1949 the Soviet leadership retreated after it had encountered resolute resistance. Aggression in Korea in 1950 is more difficult to explain; it was probably thought that a local conflict in the Far East did not involve the risk of global war; the extent of Soviet involvement in the preparation of this attack was, in any case, not fully known. Soviet suspicion of the West was often self-defeating; Western proposals from which it would have benefited, and which involved hardly any political risks, were rejected, such as the American invitations in 1946–47 for economic cooperation. To a certain extent this may have been deliberate, in view of the built-in need for tension in the Stalinist system. But there was an extra cutting edge in its hostility that cannot be explained with reference to domestic needs and traditional deep-seated suspicions. The Soviet attitude toward Germany had been much more friendly during the two years preceding Hitler's attack than after the war. Was it only because the Soviet Union felt more threatened in 1939 than in 1947? There is no obvious explanation. In 1949 the first Soviet nuclear bomb was exploded, but the implications of warfare in the nuclear age dawned only gradually on the Kremlin; Stalin was too old and inflexible by then to revise his policy, and he continued to pursue his aims with an intransigence mitigated only by his native caution. He genuinely believed that communism as he envisaged it could not coexist in the long run with governments and societies of a different character. He did not want to settle conflicts with the outside world; on the contrary, he deliberately sharpened them. At the same time, he did not draw the ultimate conclusions from his own theories. The contradictions of Stalinism were partly inherent in the system, but the tortuous personality of the supreme leader certainly added further complications. As the Hungarian Marxist philosopher Georg Lukacs later wrote:

[The] epoch which ended with Stalin's death was not consistent . . . and this of necessity, for the fundamental axiom of Stalin's policy—the inherent need for a constant sharpening of conflicts—determined not only the internal affairs of the Soviet Union, but also involved the perspective of a third world war. Fortunately Stalin did not go right to the end in drawing conclusions from his doctrine; hence his policy also included elements of a recognition of the new epoch; but only elements.

The contradictions of American policy were of a different character. The general trend after the war was to withdraw and to cut
commitments in Europe as soon and as much as possible. In April,
at the foreign ministers' conference in London, Secretary of State
Byrnes (1879–1972) had suggested the withdrawal of all Allied troops
from the continent, but he encountered stubborn resistance from Molotov, who also rejected a draft treaty on Germany and made it known
that Russia was in no hurry to conclude such a treaty. Molotov refused
to discuss Austria, and showed no interest in a twenty-five-year agreement to keep Germany disarmed. In the following months, the American line hardened; in a speech at Stuttgart in September, Byrnes
declared that "as long as there will be an occupying army in Germany,
America will be part of it."

It was not any single event that had caused America to change
its policy. Throughout 1946 there was still much goodwill toward
Russia in Washington, and a somewhat naïve belief that all the misunderstandings could be sorted out in direct talks at the highest level.
Even Truman seems to have believed that "Old Joe" was basically a
decent fellow, a reasonable man at heart, with whom one could do
business but for the unfortunate fact that every so often he was the
prisoner of the Politburo. Churchill's Fulton speech was not at all
well received in the United States, and those few who, like James
Forrestal, demanded a tougher line toward Russia were isolated. Such
leading Americans as Bedell Smith (1895–1961) and General Marshall
were still in favor of moderation, as were elder statesmen like Cordell
Hull (1871–1955). Their change of mind came only in 1947, when
they realized after endless talks with the Russians that "one cannot
reach agreement with the Russians about Germany" (Bedell Smith),
and that the Russians were "coldly determined to exploit the present
state of Europe to propagate communism" (General Marshall). The
Soviets' refusal to withdraw their troops from Iran seemed a minor
disagreement at the time; in any case, they left after a few months.
Soviet territorial demands on Turkey were not followed up by action,
but the support given to the insurgents in Greece was more serious.
During the first phase of the civil war, in 1944–45, Stalin had loyally
observed the agreement with Churchill according to which Greece
was part of the British sphere of influence; the Greek communists
received no help in their armed struggle against the government. The
decision to renew the civil war was made in May 1946; it cannot

have been taken without Soviet knowledge and, in all probability, Soviet support. It was a deliberate decision, not a case of automatic escalation, and it was bound to lead to a major crisis.

The Soviet leaders from Stalin on down were firmly convinced that Europe would not recover from the war, and that, above all, America would be faced within two or three years with a major economic crisis on the scale of the great depression. This was the most important underlying assumption of Soviet policy; it gave Moscow a confidence that would have been otherwise inexplicable in the light of American nuclear superiority. The great crisis of the capitalist world seemed inevitable, but constant pressure had to be maintained to hasten its downfall.

These predictions seemed to be confirmed when Bevin informed Washington in February 1947 that Britain could no longer assist Greece and Turkey economically or militarily. Truman asked Congress for $400 million for economic and military aid to these countries. "The free peoples of the world look to us for support," Truman said. "It must be the policy of the United States to support them resisting subjugation by armed minorities or by outside pressure primarily through economic and financial help." The Truman Doctrine was followed four months later by General Marshall's commencement speech at Harvard: "Our policy is not directed against any country or doctrine but against hunger, poverty, desperation and chaos. The initiative must come from Europe." Russian and Eastern Europe were not excluded from the Marshall Plan, but they decided, for reasons to be discussed below, not to participate. This, in June 1947, was the real turning point; collaboration between West and East was at an end, and Europe was finally split.

It has been argued that the Truman Doctrine made it impossible for the Russians to adhere to the Marshall Plan, that they might have cooperated but for the American promise of military assistance to certain European countries. According to this view, America should have provided economic help to Europe but refrained from giving military help even to countries badly needing it. However, financial schemes would hardly have deterred the Russians. Economic aid is not of much help to countries directly threatened with armed intervention; Greece's priorities in 1946–47 were of a different order.

Washington's decision to take a leading role in European politics was not taken at once, and it was reached with reluctance. For the first two years after the war, Britain was almost alone in resisting Soviet pressure in Central Europe, while America still believed in a policy of concessions. The change in Washington's policy came with the progressive disillusionment of the American representatives who were dealing with the Russians. They had hoped that at least on Germany there would be agreement; instead it now became the main battlefield of the Cold War. The Soviets wanted $10 billion in reparations from Germany, to be extracted largely from the zones occupied by the West. But the German economy was at a very low ebb, running only at a fraction of its former capacity. America was forced to provide massive help almost from the beginning of the occupation to prevent a complete collapse. The Russian demand meant, in effect, that America would have to pay even more, for without such an infusion German industry would not be able to deliver goods to Russia. This America was unwilling to do unconditionally; it insisted that the Russians remove the barriers they had erected between their zone and the others, cease their campaign of terror against noncommunist political leaders, and put an end to the arrests and the kidnappings. In Soviet eyes this was intolerable interference in their internal affairs.

Public opinion also played an important part in the change in American policy. Suddenly the American press woke up to the fact that Russia was still a dictatorship, a police regime which feared and repressed all internal opposition, as a *New York Times* correspondent put it after his return from the Soviet capital in July 1946. These reports should not have come as a surprise, because the state of affairs described was not exactly new, but they did come as a shock, precisely because the public was so little prepared for them. There were signs of hysteria and histrionics, as well as "threats of blustering or superfluous gestures of outward toughness," against which George Kennan warned in a famous article on "The Sources of Soviet Conduct" (*Foreign Affairs*, July 1947). Kennan, a leading American diplomat with considerable Soviet experience, suggested that the main aim of Soviet policy was to "make sure that it has filled every nook and cranny available to it in the basin of world power." It was applying constant pressure in that direction, but there was no evidence that the goal must be reached at any given time. On the contrary, if Soviet policy found unassailable barriers in its path, it accepted them philosophically and accommodated itself to them. Mr. Kennan advocated a long-term Western policy of containment, the "adroit and vigilant

application of counter-force at a series of constantly shifting geographical and political points, corresponding to the shifts and ma-
noeuvres of Soviet policy." In the long run, Kennan predicted, the
Soviet regime would either break up or mellow, for no messianic
movement could face frustrations indefinitely without adjusting itself
in one way or another to the logic of that state of affairs.

Critics of the containment doctrine argued that America was
not strong enough to contain the Soviet Union on a global scale, that
the American counterforce would ultimately consist of a "heteroge-
neous array of satellites, clients, dependents and puppets" (as Walter
Lippmann put it), that it ignored legitimate Soviet interests and fears.
There was a tendency among Western observers to overrate the extent
of Soviet fears and the need to reassure Moscow. As subsequent events
were to show, the assumptions underlying containment were correct;
eventually it brought about the Soviet retreat from Eastern Central
Europe.

In Europe containment became official American policy in practice, if not in name, after the Prague coup and the Berlin blockade,
and the United States began to rearm on a massive scale. Washington
had decided to impress on Stalin that there were to be no changes in
the *status quo* in Europe. The Russians accepted the fact; the foreign
ministers who had held a series of increasingly fruitless conferences
in 1948 and 1949 stopped meeting. Any further discussion seemed
pointless; they were not to assemble again until the year after Stalin's
death.

The two parts of Europe were now hermetically sealed off from
each other, with Berlin as the only hole in the curtain. Thousands
streamed through it every week, mostly East Germans, all in one
direction. There was no physical contact between West and East.
Trade had dwindled to a minimum, and there was of course no tourism in either direction. Western books and newspapers were banned
in the East; radio stations continued their propaganda contest in the
air, but the Western stations were heavily jammed. The Eastern-bloc
countries were shaken by deep internal convulsions; communist leaders disappeared overnight, and it was not at all clear whether their
successors were more firmly in the saddle. There seemed to be no
purpose in trying to negotiate with Stalin's satellites, for their dependence on Moscow was by now total. The situation inside the Kremlin,
too, was far from stable, and indications of a new major purge became

more numerous. Stalin's position seemed secure enough, but no one
else's. Suddenly, in the middle of all the guessing about Soviet policies,
which had become more and more unpredictable, there came on
March 6, 1953, the news of Stalin's death following a stroke six days
earlier.

Stalin was seventy-three and had been in indifferent health for
a number of years, but the news of his death was still unexpected.
Never in modern history had one man cast such a giant shadow, over
his own country and the world at large. His own subjects had certainly
grown accustomed over the years to the idea that somehow the "father
of the peoples" was immortal, that for better or worse he would be
with them forever. In their first message his successors spoke of "confusion," and there were reports from Moscow about tears and mourn-
ing. But many people all over the world breathed more freely.

Stalin's death aroused great expectations; imperceptibly at first,
a thaw set in. It did not yet herald the end of the Cold War; the
changes in both foreign and domestic policy were less drastic and
took longer than many had at first expected. But with his death a
whole epoch of Soviet history came to an end. When the new Soviet
leaders re-examined Stalin's foreign policy, they found that both sides
had kept in Europe what they already had before the Cold War started.
In an overall view, Stalin was certainly not the winner in Europe, for
balanced against the consolidation of the Soviet empire there was
NATO and, more important, the new spirit of European cooperation,
which but for the Soviet challenge would have remained a dead letter.
There was the defection of Yugoslavia, not weighing very heavily in
the global scales but disturbing in its implications for the future: if
one communist country could successfully defy the communist metropolis, there was the danger that the example would spread. For all
its immediate successes, Stalin's policy contained the seeds of destruction of the new Soviet empire. But it took more than three decades
for anyone to realize how disastrous his policy had been.

The claim that a more rational Western policy could have averted
the Cold War can be made only if one ignores some essential factors:
the intransigence of communist ideology in the postwar period, the
dynamics of Stalinism and totalitarian societies in general, and Stalin's
paranoia. Soviet policy was a mixture of realpolitik and persecution
mania, of rational and irrational factors. Toward the end of his life,
to quote Khrushchev, "Stalin's persecution mania reached unbeliev-

able dimensions." The basic difference between the West and the Soviet Union could not have been resolved by gestures and declarations, however forthcoming, on the part of the West. The Cold War could have been avoided only if the Soviet Union had not been possessed by the idea of the infallibility of its own doctrine: As Arthur Schlesinger wrote in *Foreign Affairs* in October 1967, "These convictions transformed an impasse between national states into a religious war, a tragedy of possibility into one of necessity."

TOWARD EUROPEAN COOPERATION

The movement for European unity was given a decisive impetus in the postwar period as a result of the coup in Prague in 1948 and the outbreak of the Korean War in 1950. The European idea had been advocated by philosophers and statesmen for centuries, although for them military considerations had not been overriding. As far back as 1650, William Penn had called for the establishment of a European parliament; the Abbé Saint-Pierre, Cardinal Alberoni, and others had formulated similar plans during the seventeenth century. Romantics (like Novalis) had evoked in their writings the good old days when the whole of Christian Europe had been one nation; unromantic statesmen like Napoleon had unsuccessfully attempted to unite Europe by force. In the twentieth century, the Pan-European movement had explained in detail the great benefits that would accrue to all if Europe were to unite, and Briand had tried to inaugurate a policy of little steps toward the same end. Hitler had attempted in his own way to unite Europe under German hegemony, and there had been many expressions of European solidarity among the various anti-Nazi resistance movements during the war.

The idea of a European federation thus had many adherents on the left and right alike when the war ended. They were at one in the belief that, after the destruction wrought by two European civil wars, the continent could be rebuilt only by a common effort. Beyond the disputes that kept them apart, the European nations had many ideas and interests, ambitions and sentiments in common. There was also the growing conviction that in the modern world, especially in the economic field, the small nation-state as an independent unit was no longer viable. Winston Churchill, in a speech in Zurich in September 1946, had talked about the need for a new initiative to help this turbulent and mighty continent take its rightful place with other groupings, and help shape the destinies of men. Europe at present was little more than a plaything of outside powers; united, it could overcome all its internal difficulties and again be a great power in the world.

The first major initiative toward European unity came in the economic field, as the result of the threatened breakdown of the British and French economies in 1947. In his famous Harvard speech, General Marshall, anticipating de Gaulle, talked about the need for European cooperation up to the Urals, and of the necessity for a common program of recovery. A four-year plan of American aid, such as was envisaged, and the creation of a common European market would again make the old continent viable and relieve America of the burden of permanent economic support. The Organization for European Economic Cooperation (OEEC) was established to act as a framework for these projects. It included seventeen European nations; America at first stayed out, but later became an associate and eventually a full member. The aims of this body were limited: to close the dollar gap and to liberalize European trade. These purposes were achieved within a remarkably short period without undue difficulty. Trade between the European nations doubled within six years, a favorable balance of trade helped to close the dollar gap, and the GNP of most European countries increased at a remarkably steady rate each year. When American aid came to an end, the advantages of OEEC were obvious to all, and it was decided not to abolish the organization. But there was already a rift between the maximalists, who wanted to enlarge its scope and saw it as a mere beginning, and the minimalists, who pleaded special circumstances and difficulties and opposed any such initiative. British leaders argued that their country, while welcoming European cooperation, had close ties with the Commonwealth and was interested not merely in European trade but equally in a revival of world trade. For that reason, Britain wanted to pursue a flexible policy and opposed a European customs union—the next logical step in the development of OEEC. By 1950 it was clear that little further progress would be made by OEEC. The original impetus had petered out, and a new initiative was needed to give fresh momentum to the more ambitious aims of the European federalists.

Meanwhile, on a similar contingency basis, the first steps had been taken toward strengthening European defense. The idea that there should be some form of Atlantic union backed by America and the British Commonwealth was pressed by British and Canadian leaders, whereas the French from the beginning put greater stress on the European character of such a scheme and also emphasized the need for closer political collaboration within the framework of a European assembly. But the prospects for cooperation in the military field were not as good as the chances for economic union, nor was there any reason to assume Europe would be able to defend itself without American help within the foreseeable future. American benevolence and good wishes were not enough; the United States would have not only to join a European defense organization but to take the leading part in it. Such "entangling alliances" had been anathema to American policymakers from the early days of the Republic, and the decision to establish NATO signified a revolution in American foreign policy. From the outset, Europe's military weakness and inability to defend itself without foreign assistance shaped the character of the treaty; it was an Atlantic, not a European alliance, and this gave rise to doubts and criticism. Was it not a mere abstraction, an alliance of limited scope and duration in which the divergent interests of the member states would always be a divisive factor? America was a global power with many interests in various parts of the world. Could it be taken for granted that Europe would always receive top priority? Would America be ready to go to war and risk using nuclear weapons in response to a limited Soviet offensive in Europe? These arguments were countered by the NATO planners, who were developing a "forward strategy" aimed at defending Europe as far to the east as possible.

The groundwork for NATO was laid in Brussels in 1948, and the treaty was signed in April 1949; its headquarters were established in Paris. In addition to the United States and Canada, the following countries joined the organization: the Benelux countries, Britain, Norway, Iceland, Denmark (but not Sweden!), Greece, Turkey (in 1952), Italy, West Germany, France, and Portugal. In the early days of NATO, the main emphasis was on rather loose joint defense planning and the re-equipment of European armies with American arms. The real test, the unification of command and the integration of forces, came later, after the question of German participation had been solved, following much heart-searching and a real crisis.

The joint economic and military measures taken during the late forties were on a strictly *ad hoc* basis, designed to cope with immediate dangers and problems. These steps did not, however, satisfy the advocates of political unity who, meeting in The Hague in May 1948, decided to establish a permanent European assembly, the Council of Europe, in Strasbourg. Strictly unofficial, this 130-member body was consultative in character; its meetings were mainly devoted to the discussion of human rights and cultural relations, and it had, of course, no power to enforce its resolutions.

Among economic planners and businessmen on the continent, the conviction was growing that a new initiative was needed to advance beyond OEEC. A lasting solution to Europe's difficulties would be found only within a common market which would coordinate fiscal and monetary policies and promote large-scale, low-cost production and a substantial rise in productivity.

The initiative for a first scheme along these lines was taken by the French in May 1950; they envisaged a coal-and-steel pool between France and Germany under a common authority. This was the Schuman Plan, and its authors saw it as the first step toward a common European economic system. It was a mere pilot scheme, but it concerned one of the continent's key industries, accounting for about a quarter of the total trade of the six countries that were eventually to constitute "Little Europe." It was "the first expression of the Europe that is being born," in the words of Jean Monnet (1888–1979), who was the real spiritual father of the project. At the beginning the plan encountered predictable opposition: the British argued that it was not compatible with their Commonwealth links, Labour saw it as a big-business conspiracy, and Harold Macmillan maintained that "our people will not hand on to any supranational authority the right to close our pits or our steel works." Inside Germany and France, too, there was resistance on both the left and the right; the communists appeared as the true defenders of the national interest that had been betrayed by Schuman, Adenauer, and de Gasperi. De Gaulle and his movement, then in opposition, were on principle against any curtailment of French sovereignty; the German Social Democrats said they were in favor of real European unity—not the "Europe Inc." of the tycoons of heavy industry. But, despite all opposition, the Common Coal and Steel Market came into being in 1953, and within the next five years proved itself an outstanding success. Steel production rose by 42 percent, trade between the six member countries flourished, there were no political or economic ill effects. This had a profound influence on the early opponents of the Common Market; the lesson that industrial production among the Six increased more than twice as fast as in Britain between 1950 and 1955, and almost three times as fast between 1955 and 1960, was not lost on them. De Gaulle and the German and Italian Social Democrats came to accept the Common Market, and even the West European communists were eventually compelled to modify their opposition, despite all Lenin's warnings against the perils of the Capitalist United States of Europe.

After the Schuman Plan had been accepted, a further initiative was undertaken by the Benelux countries which suggested the elimination of tariffs and the coordination of monetary policies. Other proposals concerned the establishment of a European atomic pool to meet future power shortages. At conferences in Messina in 1955 and in Rome in 1957, it was decided to found a European market, and to establish an atomic pool (Euratom). The new European Economic Community (EEC) had certain escape clauses which reassured de Gaulle; with its emphasis on economic integration, it went beyond a mere customs union but fell short of complete economic union. Its main purpose was to bring about continuous and balanced expansion, to foster a high level of employment and raise the standard of living, to stabilize prices, and to prevent lack of equilibrium in the balance of payments. These aims were to be accomplished in three preliminary stages, each lasting four years.

The EEC came into being on January 1, 1958. The founding members were France, Germany, Italy, Holland, Belgium, and Luxembourg. Headed by a nine-member commission ("to be chosen for their general competence and of indisputable independence"), it was based on a quasi-federal structure independent of governments and private interests—a European Parliament, a Council of Ministers, a Central Commission, and a Court of Justice. These organs were to supervise the EEC and the many other agencies that were formed in its wake (the European Social Fund, the Economic and Social Committee, the Overseas Development Fund, the European Investment Bank, the Transport Committee, etc.). The founding document, known as the Rome Treaty, envisaged immediate tariff-cutting and the total abolition of customs barriers by 1967. External tariffs were to be retained, and this became one of the main targets of criticism by nonmembers. But the tariffs were usually lower than in the past: almost nonexistent in the case of raw materials, less than 6 percent for finished goods, 13–17 percent for capital equipment. On the whole, the Common Market contributed toward a general liberalization of international trade; it did not simply replace the old nation-state protectionism by a new European bloc surrounded by high tariff walls.

Within five years of its foundation, EEC, covering a total population of 165 million, emerged as the world's greatest trading power, the biggest exporter and buyer of raw materials. It was the second-largest importer, and its steel production was second only to that of the United States; total industrial production of the Six increased by 70 percent between 1950 and 1960. These impressive achievements were not just the result of pooling resources (as some argued), or liberalizing trade, and trusting the free play of market mechanisms and unregulated competition. Most of the inspiration behind the Common Market was provided by French experts (Monnet, the father of the Schuman Plan; Robert Marjolin; Etienne Hirsch; Pierre Uri; and the Belgian Jean Rey) who believed in *dirigisme,* in economic and social planning. They realized from the outset that not all branches of the European economy were viable; even the most fervent believers in laissez-faire liberalism were forced to admit that, in order to survive, agriculture had to be centrally planned. Big business viewed the activities of the planners with misgivings; in its view, the Eurocrats in Brussels had far too much power. The laissez-faire enthusiasts did not necessarily oppose the new common ethos and community spirit and the informal consultations between organizations and individuals on every level, but they did not agree with the social goals set by the Eurocrats in Brussels. On the part of the governments, too, there was suspicion that the supranational authority was becoming too strong and independent, that a new technocratic elite was developing whose prime allegiance was to Europe, not to their country of origin. There was every reason to assume that the importance and scope of centralized European decisionmaking was likely to increase even more in the years to come. Almost from the beginning, there were conflicts of interest between public (European) and private (business) planning.

In part these were due to structural differences, for industry in France (to give one illustration) was nationalized to a larger extent than in Germany. Such conflicts did not, however, make cooperation impossible, as the Benelux example had shown. Within its closely integrated structure, Holland had put much more stress on a planned economy than Belgium without causing lasting damage to collaboration between the two countries.

There were from the beginning considerable strains and stresses in the new European community, but there was also a welcome fresh spirit, a much-needed dynamism, and the first stirrings of a new European patriotism. Though frontiers remained, they seemed to shrink in importance; small placards were to be seen saying: "Another border but still Europe." The new Europe seemed big enough to accommodate both specialists and conservatives, and even de Gaulle, the opponent of a closely linked federal union, came to accept the new structure as an "imposing confederation." The one real crisis facing EEC was the result of its very success: Britain and the other European countries that had at first opposed the project came to realize their mistake and belatedly asked to be admitted. The dissension among EEC members on this issue belongs to a later chapter of European history.

The efforts to achieve closer integration were less successful in the military field. Following the outbreak of the Korean War, America began to press again for a European integrated force under a centralized command with the inclusion of German units. But the impact of Korea was less strongly felt in Europe than in America, and there were still deep fears of revival of German militarism. The French countered American pressure with a plan of their own, which provided for small national contingents in a unified European army. There was to be a common budget, and of course supranational control. The basic assumption in this, the Pleven Plan for a European Defense Community (EDC), was that within NATO control over German remilitarization would be inadequate, and that more than a coalition of the old type was needed. The American reaction was at first cool: Washington was not certain whether the Pleven Plan was just a maneuver to delay German inclusion in NATO, or whether it was sincerely meant as a workable solution to a difficult problem. After initial hesitation, America decided to accept EDC, and by the spring of 1953 six European governments had signed the treaty, which then had to be ratified by their parliaments. The project was defeated in the very country in which it had originated. Mendès-France, then French prime minister, demanded a lower level of supranational control and integration than at first envisaged. But even this modification did not appease the French critics, who were opposed to any limitations affecting the French army but refused to grant any such right to the German forces. The French demands were mutually exclusive, and so, in a dramatic vote on August 30, 1954, Gaullists joining forces with the communists defeated the scheme. Soon after this setback, Britain made a fresh proposal, reviving an old project providing for direct German membership in NATO. To allay French fears, provisions were made for tying German units closely into the NATO structure, and the British also promised to keep their forces (the British army of the Rhine) on the continent for an unlimited period to counterbalance the effects of German remilitarization. The reaction in Paris was not enthusiastic, but it was realized that a second French vote against European military integration would simply result in Germany's admission to NATO in conditions that would be even less desirable from the French point of view. The French Parliament reluctantly ratified the new scheme in October 1954. NATO and Western defense were strengthened, but only after the defeat of the idea of a specifically European defense community.

NATO had been founded to deter an outright Soviet attack on Western Europe. This aim was achieved, although the resolution passed at a meeting in Lisbon in 1952, providing for a military force of no fewer than ninety-six divisions, proved to be too ambitious and was never realized. After Stalin's death, as the immediate danger of a Soviet invasion decreased, there were first signs of disintegration of the alliance; the United States was still preoccupied with Korea, and England and France were deeply involved in the Middle East and in Indochina and Algeria, respectively. In the early years of NATO, American nuclear supremacy remained the chief deterrent, but this state of affairs was highly unsatisfactory from the European point of view. Only the United States would decide in what circumstances a nuclear response to an attack on Europe was necessary. There was much concern in Europe about the future, for sooner or later a nuclear balance between West and East would be reached, and it was not at all clear how to prepare for the defense of Europe in these changed conditions. In France, and among some circles in other European countries, new approaches to European defense were advocated to make the continent less dependent on America. All these schemes were based on the assumption that Europe would be able to provide adequate conventional forces and, ultimately, a separate West European nuclear system. Not every threat against Western Europe could be met with the massive retaliation of the Rapid Deployment Force that Dulles had announced. If not, how were the threats below this level to be met? Britain decided to develop its own nuclear armory, and France its *force de frappe;* West Germany wanted the United States to surrender its exclusive control of NATO's nuclear arsenal. These conflicting demands, the failure to stop atomic proliferation, and the inability to establish a strong, independent European defense force caused a deep crisis in NATO in the early sixties. In the early discussions about European defense, German rearmament had been the main bone of contention; it was widely feared that a new European military alliance would be dominated by West Germany. These fears were psychologically only too intelligible, but they ignored the changed world situation. Germany, after the total defeat of 1945, was not in a mood to engage in big-power politics, and, more important, it was no longer in a position to do so; the dimensions of the international scene had radically changed.

Despite the astonishing economic recovery, the interim balance sheet of the movement for European unity drawn in the late fifties was therefore bound to be disappointing to the federalists. A large measure of cooperation between the West European governments had been achieved, but the federalists wanted unity, not just collaboration. The staying power of nationalism was stronger; vested interests and particularist positions were more deeply rooted than had been assumed. Britain, which preferred not to become too closely entangled in European affairs, was the main culprit during the early stage; once Britain had succeeded in enlisting American support for the defense of Europe, it lost interest in the other schemes for European unity. Conservatives and Labour alike greatly overrated the strength of Commonwealth ties, and their estimate of Britain's political, economic, and military potential in the postwar world was far too complacent. There was the traditional distrust of Frenchmen, Germans, and other continentals; the few advocates of European unity in Britain in the early fifties faced an uphill struggle, for the idea had far less appeal there than on the continent. There was an almost general belief that, by the circumstances of geography and historical tradition alike, Britain was not really part of Europe. Hugh Gaitskell believed it; so did, many years later, Mrs. Thatcher. By the time a majority of British statesmen (and public opinion) had, after a delay of ten years, reluctantly reached the conclusion that, at least in the economic field, Britain's future lay with Europe, the gates of the new Europe had been closed to them. France under de Gaulle had emerged as the leading force in EEC, and used its veto to keep Britain out of the European Community. De Gaulle now replaced Britain as the main obstacle to European unity. Driven by a conception of world affairs that was antiquated in character and dictated solely by French national interests (as the general interpreted them), he pursued a policy that was inherently contradictory: he wanted to lessen Europe's dependence on America, but he intended to keep out of his scheme half of Europe, and furthermore opposed attempts to make the Community a more closely knit unit. By the late fifties the original impetus of the European idea had run out. The new institutions went on functioning on their own momentum, some of the old rivalries had been buried, and the economic map of the continent had greatly changed. But the achievements still fell woefully short of the dreams of the federalists, who regarded it as at best a transitional stage toward the realization of a far more ambitious goal.

CHRISTIAN DEMOCRACY
AND DEMOCRATIC
SOCIALISM

There were certain common features in political developments throughout postwar Europe: the weakness of democratic socialism, the retreat of communism after 1948, and the emergence of strong Christian Democratic parties. The history of the French and Italian communist parties is in many respects similar, and there are interesting parallels in the rise of Christian Democracy in West Germany and in Italy. It is tempting to single out these common features and to ignore others that do not fit into the picture. The Christian Democratic movements in Germany and Italy were incomparably stronger than the French MRP, which after a promising start lost much of its influence when Gaullism appeared on the scene. There was no parallel to Gaullism in other European countries. The German Christian Democrats faced an easier task than their Italian colleagues; they were less dependent on their allies, their party had greater internal cohesion, and they had a prime minister who was their undisputed leader for fourteen years. In Italy within the same period, de Gasperi was followed by Pella, Fanfani, Scelba, Segni, Zolli, again Fanfani, again Segni, Tambroni, again Fanfani, Leone, and Moro; some of these leaders represented the left wing of the party, others the right or center.

The emergence of Christian Democracy as a leading political force was no doubt the most important new factor in postwar European politics. There had been confessional parties in various European countries before, such as the German Zentrum, the Austrian People's Party, the Belgian Catholic Party, or Gil Robles' Acción Popular in Spain. They had been on the whole right-wing in orientation, their appeal based on a vague religiosity: they represented conservative and ecclesiastical interests, whereas postwar Christian Democracy took great pains to stress that it stood for something essentially new, that it had no connection with political formations that had existed in the past. Only the Catholic People's Party in Holland continued to emphasize its confessional aspect; the others dissociated themselves from this tradition and were moreover far more independent of ecclesiastical control than their predecessors; left-wing Catholic trends were not uncommon in France and Italy. The prewar Christian parties had been antisocialist and antiliberal in inspiration, a response to anticlericalism and laicism; this was their main *raison d'être*. Postwar Christian Democracy was a much more complex phenomenon: it had genuinely accepted democracy and carried out some important economic reforms. De Gasperi once said that the Christian Democrats were not fighting communism's economic program. They had the support of various social classes, including a substantial working-class and peasant basis; their "class character" defied ready-made explanations.

Christian Democracy in Italy was in the tradition of Don Luigi Sturzo's Popular Party of the early twenties—a lay party with left-of-center tendencies, which after the rise of fascism had been unceremoniously dropped by the Vatican. The party, as it emerged in 1944, consisted of a strong conservative wing, tending toward "authoritarian democracy," represented by Catholic Action leaders such as Gedda and Lombardo. The left wing included Catholic trade-unionists who wanted to transform their movement into a genuine labor party; Gronchi, who later became president of the Republic; and Fanfani, who stood for an independent Italian foreign policy, gravitating occasionally toward neutralism. Under Segni, prime minister from 1955 to 1957, important political and social reforms were carried out. De Gasperi, who was forced to resign in 1953 and died a year later, was of the center, masterly at playing off left and right against each other. He had won in the 1948 election, and again in 1953, at a time of high international tension when communism seemed the overriding danger, but he strongly resisted pressure from the right wing of his own party to pursue conservative and strictly confessional policies. He refused to cooperate with the monarchists, who had emerged as a sizable force in the elections, and preferred a coalition with the small center parties, though this involved him in almost permanent bargaining with his partners and laid him open to constant attacks from both the left and the right within the coalition. After de Gasperi's death, both the left and the right wings of the Christian Democrats attempted, without lasting success, to control the party and the government; the center tried equally unsuccessfully to find a formula (as de Gasperi had done) that would be acceptable to the whole party, and if possible also to potential coalition partners. With short interruptions, this internal tug-of-war lasted for many years and often paralyzed the party. The great economic upsurge that began in the middle fifties and the consequent prosperity were only to a small extent the result of government initiative and direction (such as the Vanoni Plan); it developed its own momentum despite the instability and defeatism of political life. Originally pledged to radical reform, the Christian Democrats became, at most, a party of gradualism. With all their shortcomings and apparent failures, they succeeded in clinging to power because of the split within the left. During the 1950s they provided that bare minimum of political stability which made the transformation of the Italian economy possible, and eventually had far-reaching repercussions on the structure of society.

The French Mouvement Républicain Populaire (MRP) was at first the only new political party of the Fourth Republic. Its ideological origins can be traced to Marc Sangnier's left-wing Catholic Le Sillon; its organizational predecessor was the small Jeune République, a left-of-center group in the Third Republic which, to its great credit, had almost without exception opposed Pétain in 1940. But essentially it was a new movement, having been conceived in the days of the resistance. Among its leaders, Georges Bidault had been secretary of the General Council of the resistance movement and Maurice Schumann, de Menthon, Pierre Teitgen, and others among its leading figures also played an important part in the resistance. From the early days of the Fourth Republic and up to its very end, the party played a key role in French politics. It was represented in most cabinets; Bidault was prime minister in 1946 and again in 1949–50, and Robert Schuman headed the government in 1947–48. Between them, these two monopolized the Foreign Ministry during the Fourth Republic, an almost constant fixture in an otherwise rapidly fluctuating system.

The MRP was at first a party of the left trying, as one of its members put it, to reconcile the traditions of 1789 with Christian thought. During the early years of the Republic, it voted in favor of the nationalization of key branches of the national economy. It was MRP policy to favor nationalization wherever business was a public service, or where private finance threatened the independence of the state, or where private initiative simply did not function. Until January 1946 the MRP collaborated closely with de Gaulle; it was strongly opposed to the polarization in world politics represented by the Cold War and tried to act as a "third force," first between the communists and their enemies, and later between de Gaulle and his adversaries. The MRP was by no means opposed in principle to collaborating with the communists; it wanted good relations with the Soviet Union, and it was only with considerable reluctance, and as the result of heavy communist attacks, that it changed its position in 1947–48. Yet, despite the left-wing orientation of many of its leaders, support for the MRP came largely from the regions of France that were traditionally conservative. In 1946 the MRP received 26 percent of the vote, but when de Gaulle made his first bid for power in the following year, the moderates shifted their support and the party suffered heavy losses, including about 60 percent of its share in Paris. By 1951 its vote had been halved, and it never recovered from this setback. The party continued to exist, but it gradually ceased to be a leading force in French politics; at the time of the Algerian war, it was further weakened by the secession of Bidault and other advocates of French Algeria.

The decline of the MRP was the result of more than a single cause. Though France was much more Catholic than West Germany, the church there had far less influence in politics than in Germany, let alone in Italy. In the Third Republic it had been exceedingly difficult for a practicing Catholic to play a leading role in politics; it certainly did not help in terms of electoral appeal. In the Fourth Republic anticlericalism was much weaker, which made it easier for a confessional party to function. But at the same time the need for the existence of such a party had lessened; its left-wing supporters could as well vote socialist, its right wing join the moderates or the Gaullists, as indeed many of them subsequently did.

Nineteen forty-seven was the year of de Gaulle. The general had resigned the year before in disgust with the parties and the whole political system. He wanted to liberate the country from the stranglehold of the parties, as he declared in a series of speeches, asserting that Parliament had ceased to be representative of the will of the nation and demanding a change in the constitution. His speeches were made at a time of economic and political crisis, and they met with a warm response.

In April 1947 de Gaulle announced the formation of the Rassemblement du Peuple Français (RPF), which was to be a national movement, not just another political party. In the municipal elections of October 1947 it received about 40 percent of the total vote. For de Gaulle, this was only a beginning; ultimately the RPF was to embrace the whole nation. De Gaulle's foreign political orientation was at that time anti-European and critical of American policy, which he thought far too lenient toward Germany. He had encountered American opposition when demanding the detachment of the Rhineland from Germany. Subsequently he modified his attitude toward Germany; his ultimate ambition was to bring Western Europe under French leadership, and this could not be realized against German opposition.

The success of the RPF was startling; in a few months, with hardly any financial backing, a great party machine came into existence. Big business continued to support the traditional right, regarding Gaullism as radical and irresponsible. The general had to rely mainly on the enthusiasm of his early collaborators from the days of London and Algiers, who now, again, constituted the backbone of his movement. His electoral success was most marked in Normandy and Brittany on the one hand, and Alsace-Lorraine on the other, the east and the west of France, but there was also substantial support in Paris, Lyons, and Bordeaux. Within a year the RPF had become a seemingly irresistible force; within another year stagnation set in, and then decline. De Gaulle had promised a great deal, and then inexplicably shied away from taking the next step. One of his closest collaborators complained that "the General told us to go to the Rubicon—and to take out our fishing rods." A coup d'état seemed in the cards, but de Gaulle, despite his contempt for the parties, hesitated to disregard altogether the rules of the parliamentary game. It was not simply a failure of nerve at a decisive moment; time, as the general realized, was not yet ripe, the crisis not deep enough. The communist disorders of 1947 were suppressed by Jules Moch, the socialist minister of the interior; the economic situation slowly improved after 1949, and prices were stabilized. De Gaulle's warnings against European unity ("Do not abandon your soldiers, do not give up your sovereignty"), his anti-British tirades, his invocation of the treaty with the Soviet Union fell on deaf ears; the "European" policy of the parties of the center and the moderate left had a wider appeal. The RPF had no press of its own to spread its message, and, above all, there was not yet a television network, which was to play such a decisive part in de Gaulle's second bid for power, ten years later.

The RPF lost much of its support in 1952 as the conservative electorate began again to vote for the traditional right-wing groups. By 1953 there were only ten Gaullist councilors left in the Paris municipality, compared with fifty-two in 1947. There was also internal dissension. In March 1952 the Gaullist right wing in Parliament defied party discipline and voted for the new Pinay government and its program of economic stabilization. In December 1952 Jacques Soustelle, one of de Gaulle's most faithful followers, was asked by the president of the Republic to form a new government, but there was not even a remote chance of success; since the RPF had deliberately isolated itself, no one wanted to cooperate with it. Realizing this, the Gaullists decided not to persevere in sterile opposition; they participated in the subsequent governments of Laniel, Mendès-France, and Edgar Faure. Stage by stage, the RPF was drawn into the parliamentary game, and became a political party like all the others, much to the disgust of General de Gaulle. At a press conference in July 1955, he announced for the second time his retirement from public life. He did not exclude a comeback altogether, but, he added prophetically, it would be only after an unusual shock. De Gaulle retired to his house at Colombey-les-deux-Eglises to write the second part of his autobiography, one of the most powerful, most interesting, and also most idiosyncratic political documents of our time. He maintained contact with some of the leading figures of the Fourth Republic during his weekly visits to Paris, which became almost a ritual. Soustelle, Michel Debré, Jacques Chaban-Delmas, and his other lieutenants continued to play a part of some importance in French politics, while de Gaulle himself was biding his time. Toward the end of 1954, the latent unrest in Algeria turned into open rebellion. When de Gaulle retired, this had been only a small cloud on a distant horizon; it took three more years for the crisis to deepen and the "unusual shock" to which he had alluded to arise.

Between 1948 and 1958 France had nineteen different governments; their short-lived character and lack of initiative (*immobilisme*)

became proverbial. They included both advocates and opponents of
EDC, those who pressed for more active warfare in Algeria and those
who were against it. A new mass movement mushroomed for a little
while on the extreme right: Poujadism, a mixture of right-wing and
populist elements. The refusal to pay taxes became the declared policy
of certain sections of the population. A "Weimar situation" threatened
the Fourth Republic; the antidemocratic left and right increased in
strength, and the center was paralyzed. The socialists, the MRP, even
the Independents of the right split on such issues as EDC, Indochina,
and above all Algeria. The Laniel government was broken by Dien
Bien Phu, the military disaster in Indochina which led to the French
decision to abandon its position there. This was followed by one of
the few outstanding postwar governments, that of Pierre Mendès-
France. Formally a Radical Democrat, Mendès-France pursued a policy well to the left of his party and eventually established his own
group in Parliament. Lacking de Gaulle's charisma, he had few political friends; his appeal to reason, his decisive economic policy, his
courage, and his new dynamic style ("*gouverner c'est choisir*") won
him the grudging respect even of his adversaries, but his government
could not be a lasting success; though the country needed strong
leadership, it was far too divided internally to tolerate that. During
his eight months of office, Mendès-France liquidated the Indochinese
war and granted autonomy to Tunisia, thus removing two of the main
sources of weakness in foreign politics. But he was defeated by the
domestic imbroglio and the growing Algerian crisis, and those who
followed him sank deeper into the quagmire with every step.

France at the time seemed to face well-nigh-insurmountable
structural difficulties: industry was stagnating, agriculture was antiquated, there was no economic justification for the existence of the
vast army of small shopkeepers, and the whole system of distribution
was cumbersome and wasteful. The housing situation in the drab and
neglected cities was disastrous. The most enthusiastic tourist found
little to admire but museums and old monuments. In this atmosphere
of apathy and despair, France, in the eyes of friends and enemies alike,
seemed doomed. Yet below the surface there was an imperceptible
turn for the better. The population figures, which had remained static
for a long time, suddenly took an upward turn. French industry expanded as many new factories were set up and the existing ones were
modernized. France became the country of the fastest trains and the

most advanced cars in Europe. By 1957 the industrial output was 46 percent higher than in 1949, and agricultural production, too, had risen by a quarter. The construction of new buildings more than trebled between 1951 and 1957; new suburbs came into being; the French cities were given a new look. Great economic schemes were tackled in North Africa, with the emphasis on investment in minerals and natural gas. Though the country was plagued by recurrent fiscal and foreign-trade crises which seriously impeded its growth, the economic outlook was far more promising by 1958 than at the beginning of the decade. Economic progress—as in Italy—seemed to have its own laws and momentum, irrespective of the political immobilism. Though not all sections of the population benefited equally from the boom, what was astonishing was that a country deeply permeated by *incivisme*, lacking cohesion, self-confidence, and faith, made any progress at all. Not only the outside world but the French themselves were slow to realize what great progress they were making.

The contrast between France and Germany in the 1950s was glaring. There was perhaps too much stability on the other side of the Rhine; the hold of the Christian Democrats (CDU) was never seriously in danger. For almost fifteen years, up to his resignation in 1963, the party and the country were led by Konrad Adenauer, the imprint of whose rule was felt in every aspect of German politics. Under him Germany recovered from the deep wounds caused by the war and established close ties with the Western world. Adenauer had the self-confidence of a man whose formative years had been spent in a world less subject to uncertainties and self-doubt, the pre-1914 world. Like de Gaulle and Churchill (with whom otherwise he had little in common), he regarded economics as a necessary evil, and left it largely to Ludwig Erhard (1897–1977), the main protagonist of a socialist market economy. By instinct and conviction alike, Adenauer was a conservative, and this corresponded well with the prevailing mood of the nation: "No experiments!" But Adenauer had also learned his lesson from the bitter experience of the Weimar Republic. He knew about the limits of liberalism and realized that there could be no stability without social security, that the great majority of the population had to share in the prosperity. Gross earnings almost trebled in West Germany between 1950 and 1962, while the cost-of-living index between 1950 and 1959 rose only from 100 to 121, in contrast to a rise from 100 to 147 in England, and from 100 to 167 in France. The advocates of a "people's capitalism" drew fresh courage from the substantial increase in the number of shareholders; the number of cars increased eightfold during the decade. The German countryside was gradually transformed as agriculture was thoroughly mechanized. By 1960 the distance between town and country had shrunk; there were excellent shops and modern houses even in the smallest villages, and of course electricity and telephones. The refugees from the East, many millions of them, were quickly integrated; the attempt to establish a separate refugee movement was not a success, and was eventually abandoned. An ambitious housing program was successfully carried out. These and other achievements created a feeling of self-satisfaction in which there was little scope for radical politics of either left- or right-wing inspiration. The neo-Nazis showed some activity in Lower Saxony, but their local successes in the early fifties were a flash in the pan. Communist influence decreased steadily after 1947; the banning of the Communist Party in 1956 by the Constitutional Court seemed unwise and unnecessary in the circumstances.

There was not much change in German politics in the 1950s, and certainly very little excitement. From time to time the Liberals (FDP) quarreled with their senior coalition partners and threatened to withdraw. The CDU polled 45 percent of the total vote in the elections of 1953—a great achievement, but not sufficient to allow it to rule the country single-handed. There was dissension within the CDU between its left and right wings, and also, to a certain extent, between its various regional organizations. Franz Josef Strauss (1915–1989), the leader of the party in Bavaria, attained Cabinet rank at the comparatively early age of thirty-eight; a stormy career as minister of defense was suddenly cut short in a flurry of charges and countercharges, but he made a comeback in the coalition government of the late sixties. Gerhard Schroeder (1910–90), a lawyer from Silesia, was another pillar of the conservative trend in the party; he was in turn minister of the interior, foreign minister, and eventually minister of defense. Although Adenauer's anti-Nazi record was above reproach, he was less than scrupulous in the choice of his closest collaborators; there could be but one opinion about the career of men like Theodor Oberländer and Hans Globke in the Nazi era, but the former was dropped only after protests from all sides, and Globke, a lawyer who had provided the official interpretation to the anti-

Semitic Nuremberg laws of 1935, remained for years the chancellor's close associate and confidant, despite heavy pressure. The motive for such stubbornness was Adenauer's feeling of loyalty to his associates, certainly not anti-Semitism. For it was mainly owing to the personal intervention of the chancellor that the Bundestag approved in 1953 the law on compensation for Israel and individual Jews who had suffered from Hitler's policies. Israel alone received loans and goods totaling $715 million over a period of twelve years. Communist East Germany refused to pay any restitution, claiming that since Nazism had been uprooted in the German Democratic Republic there was no need to make amends. The East German communists refused as a matter of principle to accept responsibility for anything that happened before 1945; according to them, only a tiny minority, not wide sections of the German people, had been involved in Nazi crimes. A change in East German policy did not come until 1990.

In a difficult period of German history, Adenauer provided much-needed stability and prudent leadership. One of his most important contributions was the reconciliation with France and the close collaboration that ensued after centuries of bitter enmity. Paul-Henri Spaak (1899–1972), the Belgian prime minister, himself a great fighter for the European idea, wrote of Adenauer: "Without him no Coal and Steel Pool, no Common Market, and no Euratom. Without him the dream of a United Europe would not have become a reality." Yet, with all this, the effects of fifteen years of Adenauer's rule were not all positive. The more ambitious plans for social reform were not carried out; there were strong conservative trends in German society, gravitating not toward Nazism but more in the tradition of Wilhelmian Germany, which many still remembered with some nostalgia as the "good old times." Far too little attention was paid to the expansion of education, and the introduction of confessionalism in the schools created major problems. Adenauer's foreign policy was often criticized for its rigidity—not always fairly, for until 1953 no opportunities existed to be missed in relations with Russia and the Eastern bloc. After Stalin's death a more elastic German policy toward the East would probably have done some good; at the very least it would have silenced the government's critics. Adenauer firmly believed that one day communism would crumble from within, or that, at any rate, the growing pressure of China on Russia would force the Soviet Union to modify its policy toward Europe. As a German patriot, he regretted the division of Germany and the loss of its eastern territories; as a Rhinelander and a Catholic, he was oriented toward the West and showed less concern for reunification than many of his colleagues or critics. But was there ever a real chance that the two Germanies would be reunited? When the foreign ministers of the Big Four met in Berlin in January 1954, their points of view did not seem to differ widely; both sides professed to be, in principle, in favor of reunification. Molotov demanded the withdrawal of Allied troops even before the elections that would decide about Germany's future, and he insisted that the reunified Germany should remain neutral. Eden, on the other hand, suggested that the Allied troops should be withdrawn only after the elections, and that an independent German state should be free to enter (or to renounce) any international pacts and obligations. It has been maintained that the year 1955 was a turning point; with the gradual political and military integration of West Germany into the Atlantic alliance, the door to German unity was closed. But even before that date there was no real prospect for reunification except on terms unacceptable to the great majority of Germans. Khrushchev clarified the Soviet attitude by his insistence on the "political and social achievements" of East Germany, the DDR, which he said would have to be maintained in future, and by his opposition to any "mechanical reunion" of the two parts of Germany, which had developed in opposite directions. When Christian Pineau, the French foreign minister, inquired in Moscow in May 1956 about the chances for German reunification, he was told quite candidly that "we prefer seventeen million Germans under our influence to seventy million Germans even if they are neutral."

The general European trend toward the right also affected Britain, for in 1951 the Conservatives returned to power. After the initial wave of reforms, the Labour Party showed signs of exhaustion; after 1948 it displayed little initiative or leadership. When the Labour lead over the Tories was whittled down to a mere seventeen in the elections of 1950, the Attlee government preferred to eschew any controversial policies. The party was weakened by the resignation of some of its principal leaders: Bevin, seriously ill, retired in 1950, Aneurin Bevan and other spokesmen of the left wing resigned from the government the year after, following cuts in the social services. In 1951 Attlee called for new elections, from which the Conservatives emerged with a majority of twenty-six over Labour; this majority increased to sixty-seven in 1955 and to 107 in 1959. Churchill became prime minister for the second time in 1951; he was replaced in April 1955 by Anthony Eden (1897–1977), who after the Suez disaster gave way to Harold Macmillan (1894–1986). The Conservative Party was lucky to come to power at a time when the worst postwar shortages were over; the Labour Party had begun to abolish rationing and controls, which were so unpopular, and the Tories found themselves in the fortunate position of being able to finish the job. They denationalized the steel industry but were careful not to touch the structure of the welfare state, which, within a very few years, had gained general approval. Any attempt to tamper with these services would have meant courting political disaster. The Tories, in fact, spent more on social services than Labour; the Attlee government had built two hundred thousand houses a year; subsequent Tory governments provided three hundred thousand. The country was able to afford these social policies, it was thought, in view of the small but steady economic growth, which gathered further momentum during the late fifties and early sixties. By and large, however, economic expansion in Britain was slower than in any other major European country. "Export or Die" had been the slogan after the war; exports did increase substantially, but imports grew even faster. As a result, the balance of payments was negative every year (with the exception of 1958). Britain constantly needed fresh loans, and there was a permanent danger of devaluation.

On the surface all seemed well. That the country was living beyond its means was only slowly realized. The years of austerity were over; Britain seemed to be sharing in the general European boom. There was a great deal of new building and reconstruction; new suburbs sprang up; people were far better dressed and nourished than in the immediate postwar period. The capital regained its status and became "swinging London." The social services were a source of envy in most other European nations; they included free education at all levels. But despite the mild boom Britain did not keep pace with Europe; it spent much less on hospitals, roads, and reconstruction than most continental countries.

Britain still had a great many international obligations in the early fifties. The defense budget was a heavy burden on the impoverished nation, even though India, Ceylon, and Burma had become independent in 1948, and Ghana and Malaya in 1957. Eventually almost all former British colonies and protectorates attained independence; the emergence of a multiracial Commonwealth was a source of pride. But it was not readily obvious whether the new Commonwealth would still be a major factor in world affairs. Goodwill alone was not sufficient to keep it a going concern: the economic interests of Britain and the former colonies frequently clashed. The underdeveloped countries of Asia and Africa needed economic assistance which the metropolis could not always provide. Immigration from Africa and Asia to Britain, not very substantial by world standards, gradually became a major problem, for Britain was already densely populated; unlike Canada or Australia, it could not easily absorb immigrants.

Britain was still compelled to allocate considerable sums to defense, in view of the continued British presence in parts of Asia and Africa. Conscription ceased only in 1960. Meanwhile, an independent nuclear deterrent had been developed: an experimental A-bomb was exploded in 1953, an H-bomb four years later. The Commonwealth declined in importance from year to year, but both major parties were still far from enthusiastic about closer ties with Europe. Hugh Gaitskell, who had succeeded Clement Attlee as leader of the Labour Party in 1955, was as emphatic in this respect as the Tories. Gaitskell and the Labour Party opposed the Suez expedition in 1956, which came as the answer to the nationalization of the Suez Canal Company by Colonel Nasser. Indifferently planned and badly executed, the operation encountered opposition all over the world. The Suez setbacks, though they caused the downfall of Anthony Eden, did not seriously weaken the position of the Conservative Party, but they did demonstrate that Britain had ceased to be a world power.

Britain in the 1950s presented a confusing picture, to Englishmen and foreigners alike. There was full employment and a steady improvement in the standard of living. Harold Macmillan's slogan of 1957, that the British "had never had it so good," was more than propaganda. And yet Britain was falling behind; partly this was an inevitable process, given the absence of natural resources and the need to import food and most raw materials. But few political leaders had sufficient courage to state bluntly that the country could not continue to live on borrowed money and that a greater national effort had to be made. Productivity was low; not much imagination and drive were shown by industrial managers or the trade unions, which often fought modernization tooth and nail. There was "inflation without expansion and inadequate investment in the wrong industries," to quote F. Paish. In some ways the malaise went even deeper: the welfare state had not brought real equality of opportunity, and there was less social mobility than in other industrialized countries; large sections of the intelligentsia were estranged; a sense of frustration and a narrowing of horizons was beginning to be felt at a time when most other European countries were in the middle of a great upsurge. It was a creeping malaise: Britain did not face a major, acute crisis, and yet there was nothing like the buoyancy, the confidence, and the excitement that were felt on the continent. The explanation that the loss of the empire was the real cause of the decline is unconvincing; there was no direct relationship. France, Holland, and other European countries had overcome similar experiences without a major shock; their prosperity had not been affected by the loss of their overseas possessions. More difficult perhaps for Britain were the political and psychological consequences, the need to find a more modest place in the postwar world. To adjust itself to a new role in Europe was a painful process, and there was a great deal of instinctive resistance among the left and right alike to facing unpleasant facts.

EUROPEAN SOCIALISM

European socialism was in a state of decline in the 1950s. The Italian Socialist Party split, and the French party was in full retreat. The continental socialist parties were heirs to a proud tradition; founded in the last third of the nineteenth century, they were all, in contrast to the British Labour Party, Marxist in inspiration, though for several decades there had been a growing discrepancy between their orthodox revolutionary theory and their revisionist practice. They did not reap lasting benefit from the great left-wing upsurge of 1945, which enhanced communist influence far more than theirs. The Cold War was bound to damage the cause of socialism, for, as far as public opinion was concerned, socialism and communism were birds of a feather. Although communism in France and Italy succeeded in keeping its working-class basis, the growing opposition to communism among the rest of the population caused a swing to the right. Nor did it help that Stalin's crimes were committed, according to the official version, in the cause of "peace and socialism."

The socialist parties of France and Italy suffered from a lack of vitality. In 1945 the French party had polled almost a quarter of the vote (23 percent); in 1946 its share had fallen to 18 percent; in 1962 it was reduced to a mere 12.6 percent. In 1946 it had 354,000 members, but by 1960 only 60,000 were left. It became a party of aged officials, teachers, traditional laicists—left-of-center in character, pro-European, but with no clear political or social program. When Léon Blum (1872–1950), the prewar leader of the party, returned from his German prison, he was aware that French socialism had to discard its more outdated elements; the emphasis was now to be on freedom and human rights, not on the class struggle. It was to be a popular radical party, not a proletarian one. But Blum was too old and tired to provide the necessary guidance, and the younger party leaders were absorbed in quarrels about current political issues (such as French colonial policy, in Vietnam and Algeria); no one had the time or the inclination to re-examine basic ideological issues. The left wing of 1945 (Guy Mollet) soon moved to the right, whereas the reformers of 1945 (André Philip and Daniel Mayer) found themselves on the left of the party or even outside it. The defection of the PSU (Unified Socialist Party) in 1960 further weakened the socialists, who had been discredited by their participation in so many short-lived and ineffectual governments of the Fourth Republic.

The Italian Socialist Party was perhaps the most radical and, in a Marxist sense, fundamentalist of all European socialist movements: antimilitarism and anticlericalism were central planks in its program. Its general outlook had been shaped by the fascist experience and, after 1944, by the narrowly reactionary policy pursued by the Italian upper class. In the thirties and during the war, the party had favored a popular front with the communists. Pietro Nenni, its leader, was willing to continue to cooperate with his allies even after the outbreak of the Cold War, but there was growing opposition from within; in January 1947 Giuseppe Saragat left the party, and with him half its parliamentary deputies and a substantial number of the rank and file. The split drove Pietro Nenni into even closer collaboration with the communists, whereas the Saragat wing (the Social Democrats) took part in the government from 1948 to 1951, and again in 1958. Nenni was too clever a politician, and too much of a socialist and a democrat, to be entirely happy with his status as a fellow traveler. After Stalin's death, and in particular after the Hungarian uprising, his party re-

gained its indepe... ence and sought to re-establish its ties with the
Saragat wing. It ...o began to accept the important changes that were
taking place ...ly during the fifties; while not joining the government, it pr... support for left-of-center coalitions from the outside.
Both win... lian socialism had better leadership than the French
move... its decline was less pronounced during the fifties and
sixt... oth countries the communists were firmly entrenched
...orking-class party, and neither socialist party could
...ormer position.

...est of Europe, as in Britain, socialism maintained its
...tside France and Italy, communism was no serious rival,
...ialists retained their position as the main party of the left.
...eir great strength, but, being so closely identified with one
...cial class, they could not hope to appeal to others with
...cess. There were narrow limits to the growth of their influ-
...the Austrian Socialist Party, one of the strongest on the conti-
...ent, with almost seven hundred thousand members, polled 44 percent
of the total vote in the elections of 1945—and exactly the same percentage in 1962. The Dutch party polled 28 percent in 1946, and
again 28 percent in 1963. The figures for the Swiss Social Democrats
were 26 percent in 1947 and 26 percent in 1963. Even in West Germany, the Social Democrats did not succeed in making substantial
inroads into the middle-class vote, and electoral fluctuations were
therefore comparatively small. Since the numerical share of the working class in the general population did not grow, what hope was there
for a decisive socialist advance in Europe? There was, of course, the
example of the Labour Party, but it seemed doubtful whether its
formula could be applied on the continent. The European socialist
parties, trying to compromise between doctrinaire extremism and a
"sell-out of basic principles," all too often fell between two stools.
They neglected their socialist heritage: not a single socialist party in
Europe managed to maintain an effective press and publishing house.
There was little interest in politics beyond the current issues facing
the parties, the general feeling being that in modern industrial society
theory was no longer relevant.

In the late fifties all continental socialist parties reached the
conclusion that much of the old doctrinal ballast had to be jettisoned.
The German Social Democrats in their Godesberg Program (1959)
decided to transform themselves into a party of the whole people,

with the emphasis on freedom, the rights of the in*vidual, and social*
justice, rather than class interests; the class struggle *to be replaced*
by a progressive incomes policy. The party even expr*willingness*
to accept the principle of a free-market economy—prov*ided*
that there was real competition, not monopolistic rule. *ourse*
party likewise stressed freedom and social justice in its n*an*
of 1958, and the Dutch Partij van de Arbeid, which ha*d*
itself immediately after the war on the British Labour Party,
its 1959 program the far-reaching changes that had taken
capitalism and decided to concentrate on constructive efforts
the existing social framework. In the same year the Swiss Social L
ocrats, too, rejected many traditional Marxist principles. Europ
socialism at last ceased to be revolutionary in theory as well
practice.

All these changes were clearly long overdue, for, if capitalism
had changed, so had the character of the working class. After the
coming of the welfare state, few workers were likely to respond to
appeals to mount the barricades. But the implications of the changes
had to be carefully considered. What exactly was the policy of a radical
democratic party of the left going to be? If it accepted, broadly speaking, the existing economic and social setup, could it hope to persuade
the electorate that it was able to run the country more efficiently than
the advocates of free enterprise? If the stress was to be on economic
and social planning, in contrast to the blind laws of supply and demand, what exactly were to be the social priorities? At the turn of
the century, many on the left had feared that the socialist leaders
would be corrupted if they joined a bourgeois coalition government.
Sixty years later, on the contrary, the main fear was that the socialist
leaders would grow old and sour in opposition and that, as a result,
they would lack experience to provide effective national leadership if
their hour ever came. These assumptions were groundless, as later
appeared. The German Social Democrats had acquired during the
fifties a great deal of experience in ruling some of the *Länder,* including
Lower Saxony, Hesse, Berlin, and Hamburg. The Social Democratic
parties of Scandinavia were the governing parties, and the Dutch and
Belgian Social Democrats, too, participated in many coalition governments throughout the fifties. The Austrian party shared power with
the Christian People's Party on the basis of a complicated agreement
allocating all public offices according to a rigid proportional system.

All these parties retained the support of the majority of the working class, and they tried, though not always with conspicuous success, to surmount in the elections the "40-percent hurdle," which they regarded as a precondition for the extension of their influence beyond their traditional social basis.

THE RISE OF
EUROPEAN COMMUNISM

After Hitler's attack on Russia, European communism had taken a leading part in the resistance movement and had attracted many new followers. This, and the Soviet military victory, had made communism respectable all over the continent. In 1945 the communists faced little competition. Most of the prewar parties had been discredited because they had failed to resist the German occupation. Those with a resistance record equal to the communists were in a less favorable position because they were organizationally weaker; they had been less well prepared for conspiratorial work under the German occupation, and after 1945 they had difficulties in adapting themselves quickly to the new order that was emerging. Even in Holland, Belgium, and the Scandinavian countries, where communism had traditionally been weak, it was now a force to be reckoned with. The Dutch party's central newspaper had a circulation of a quarter of a million, and the Danish and Swedish parties gained substantially in the elections of 1945. In Belgium the communists felt sufficiently strong to challenge the authority of the government shortly after it returned from London in November 1944; there were demonstrations and eventually a concerted attempt to overthrow the government. But the communists had overestimated their own strength and ignored in their calculations the presence of Allied troops; their insurrection was suppressed within two days.

Communist advances were most striking in France and Italy. The French party counted eight hundred thousand members soon after the end of the war, and Italian communism emerged as the biggest political force in all the major cities except Milan, which remained for some years a socialist stronghold. At the time of the liberation, large sections of southern France and northern Italy were in the hands of communist partisan units; these were reluctant to disband and to hand over power to the representatives of the central government. But this was, on the whole, a rearguard action on the part of local chieftains; the party line did not envisage an armed insurrection while the war was still on. The exceptions were Belgium and Greece, but the challenge of the Belgian communists was easily defeated, and the Greeks (EAM) feared that they could not hold out against the British troops stationed in the country. After the first round of the civil war was over, they decided to sign an armistice agreement with the government.

In most countries the communists joined the national coalition governments that were formed after the liberation, while their partisan units (such as the French FFI) were absorbed into the regular armies. It was general communist policy in 1945 to press for close collaboration with the Social Democrats and other left-of-center parties. Their program was by no means particularly radical in character; they did not at first oppose the monarchy in Italy, even if this meant that the socialists appeared more radical; their aim was to extend their influence through the coalition. These moderate policies paid handsome dividends. In the elections of 1946 and 1947, they strengthened their position in France and Italy at the expense of the socialists. The turning point came in April and May 1947, for, with the hardening of the Soviet line and the communist takeover in Eastern Europe, the West European communists had to fall in line and, as a result, found themselves in growing isolation.

After 1948 communism was in opposition throughout Europe; the case of Iceland, where the communists remained part of the government coalition, was a mere curiosity. The "hard course" of the Cominform excluded collaboration with noncommunist forces, and in the circumstances the "peace campaign," designed to attract noncommunists, carried little conviction. The West European communists found it increasingly difficult to combine their continued presence in coalition governments with the more radical policies prescribed by Moscow. In France they decided to support a major strike in one of the chief nationalized industries. This left Paul Ramadier, the socialist prime minister, with no alternative but to exclude them from his government. It is not certain that the action had been planned by the communists; the Renault strike had in fact been instigated by "ultra-left" elements, but once the majority of workers had joined it, the communists felt duty bound to support it. In Italy the communists decided in May 1947 that de Gasperi's new economic program was unacceptable, and they, too, left the coalition. If the communist exodus had been unplanned, their subsequent actions were certainly coordinated. In October–November 1947 large-scale strikes broke out in France and Italy. French mines were occupied by strikers led by the communists, there were mass demonstrations, and an open challenge was thrown out to the French and Italian governments. After some initial hesitation, Moch and Scelba, the respective ministers of the interior, were given full powers to deal with the emergency, and they suppressed the disorders without undue difficulty. In Greece the communist forces had decided even earlier (in March 1946) to renew the armed struggle. The situation was now more promising from their point of view, because the British troops had been withdrawn and the neighboring communist countries were bound to give them full support. The first guerrilla activities were highly successful, and in 1947 it was decided to proceed with the second stage of the insurrection. When large-scale fighting developed, Greece appealed for UN aid in view of the open assistance given to the communists from across the border. However, the UN could do little but investigate the complaints and register them. Not until 1948 did the tide begin to turn against the communists. Support from Yugoslavia ceased. Under the Truman Doctrine, America extended help to the Greek army, and once America was involved, Stalin became skeptical about the prospects for the whole venture. A government offensive in the Grammos Mountains in 1949 routed the communist forces and ended a civil war that had caused much loss of life, forty-five thousand killed, and enormous material damage, and had delayed the recovery of the country for many years.

The East European purges had their parallels in the West: old leaders of French communism such as André Marty, Charles Tillon, and Auguste Lecoeur were branded traitors overnight. After Tito's excommunication, Aksel Larsen, the Danish party chief, and Peder Furubotn, the Norwegian leader, were expelled, and a similar fate befell prominent communists in West Germany and Greece (Jeorjios Siantos, General Markos, Nikos Zachariadis) and the illegal Spanish party. Communist influence in Germany and in all the smaller European countries rapidly dwindled. The Belgian party, which had polled 14 percent of the total vote in 1946, was left with less than a third of that figure in the 1960s. Even in France and Italy, where communism on the whole managed to keep its position, the party press lost most of its readers, and party membership also declined.

In view of the shocks and convulsions in Eastern Europe during Stalin's last years, the decline in communist influence in the West was less surprising than the fact that its eclipse was by no means total. Part of the reason was that the main trade-union organizations were firmly under communist control, while the reports of the noncommunist press about the Soviet Union and Eastern Europe were *a priori* branded as lies and falsifications. When, after Stalin's death, it could no longer be denied that these accounts had been substantially correct, the communist leaders promised that, past mistakes having been corrected, there would be no recurrence of what was euphemistically called the "cult of the individual." Many intellectuals left the party after Khrushchev's revelations in 1956 and as a result of the events in Hungary; a few had already dissociated themselves at the time of the anti-Tito campaigns. But the rank and file was much less affected by events in distant countries. Communism in France and Italy was more than just a political party; it was a faith and a way of life. The prosperity of the fifties raised standards of living, but it also made the injustices of the social system appear in an even more glaring light. The *condition prolétarienne* had by no means altogether disappeared in France; in Italy there was still massive tax evasion on the part of the rich, land was unequally distributed, and poverty in the south was disappearing only very slowly. Hundreds of thousands of Frenchmen and Italians belonged to communist social clubs and trade unions, read communist newspapers and literature, watched communist films; even their social life proceeded often within the framework of a closed system. Their dreams of a better social order did not conflict with the harsh realities of communism in practice, as was the case in Eastern Europe. By the end of the fifties, there were no doubt more genuine believers in communism left in Western than in Eastern Europe. Western communism gradually dissociated itself from Stalinism, a process that began earlier and went further in Italy than in France. But the admission that mistakes had been committed no more induced the rank-and-file communist to leave the party than a religious believer to give up his faith because some church dignitaries had misbehaved.

Communism in France and Italy had a far greater staying power than generally anticipated. Partly, no doubt, this was the force of inertia; political movements often continue to flourish for a long time after the conditions that produced them have disappeared. The communist parties of France and Italy at any rate maintained their influence on more than a quarter of the electorate in the two countries. The revolutionary élan lessened as the working class itself underwent important changes and became more "bourgeois" in character. The communists could still count on a substantial vote in the elections and mobilize the masses for occasional mass demonstrations, though on a declining scale and less frequently. They still had powerful political machines at their disposal, but not for revolutionary action. Was the history of Social Democracy to repeat itself? Gradually West European communism began to show "revisionist" symptoms; the gulf between revolutionary theory and reformist practice grew steadily wider.

RUSSIA AFTER STALIN

The Nineteenth Congress of the Communist Party of the Soviet Union (CPSU) opened in Moscow in October 1952. According to the party statutes, such a congress was to be convened every three years; in fact it had not met for thirteen years, since 1939. This contravention of the statutes was not perhaps of great consequence, for the congress, far from being the supreme party authority, had long ceased to have any real influence on Soviet politics. But it was certainly indicative of the many anomalies in Soviet life, of the discrepancy between theory and practice. Stalin systematically ignored the rules he had himself helped to establish.

Great social changes had taken place since he had consolidated his power in the late 1920s; the working class now constituted more than a quarter of the population, and every fifth Russian belonged to what was somewhat sweepingly defined as the "technical intelligentsia." The country was run by a huge, centralized state apparatus, a giant bureaucracy which to all intents and purposes constituted a new class. All major decisions, and many that were not important, affecting all parts of the Soviet Union, however distant, were taken in Moscow. This lack of local initiative seriously impeded the country's development. Nor was there much stability at the center: Stalin was apparently convinced that the party and government leadership needed a violent shakeup from time to time. At the Nineteenth Congress Malenkov played the central role, and it was generally believed that he was now the heir apparent. Molotov and Mikoyan, though still members of the Presidium (as the Politburo had been renamed), had in 1949 ceased to be minister of foreign affairs and foreign trade, respectively. They seemed to be the first candidates for a new purge. Klim Voroshilov, another old associate, was thought by Stalin to be a British agent, and even Lavrenti Beria, head of the all-powerful secret police, was charged soon after the congress with gross neglect of duty. Stalin was firmly convinced that he himself was absolutely indispensable. We have it on the authority of one of his successors that he told his inner circle in 1952: "You are as blind as kittens. . . . What would you do without me? You do not know your enemies!"

The Nineteenth Party Congress did not come to grips with the serious problems and imbalances facing the country. It changed the name of the party ("Bolshevik" was dropped) but did not provide new guidance. The discrepancy between heavy industry and the other branches of the national economy was to continue; the compulsory deliveries of agricultural products at nominal prices were to be maintained. Soviet foreign policy was to remain as rigid as before; it regarded the "popular democracies" as satellites, not partners, and the rest of the world as one hostile reactionary bloc. In one of his last published tracts, Stalin had written that a war was more likely to break out between capitalist countries than between them and the Soviet Union.

During the last year of Stalin's life, there was a sense of approaching crisis; economic difficulties were becoming more acute, and no more windfalls like the German reparations could be expected, while China's demands for economic assistance became more comprehensive and insistent. Official figures about production in heavy industry were most impressive, but they exaggerated the real progress that had been made. The living standards of the bulk of the population had hardly risen. The cult of production at any price had become an intolerable burden for the economy, with its exclusive stress on quantity and almost total neglect of quality and social need. Goods were often shoddy, could not be used, or had to be discarded after a short time. As planning became more and more rigid, commodities were produced without any regard for the laws of supply and demand. The question whether a factory (or a whole branch of industry or agriculture) was economically viable was hardly ever asked. Russia's industrial recovery since the war had made great strides, but there was so little coordination with other branches of the economy that the imbalances threatened the entire further progress of the country.

Immediately after the congress, there was a further hardening in the political line and a number of indications that a new major purge on the scale of events in 1936–38 was being prepared. On January 13, 1953, the Soviet press announced that a conspiracy had been discovered: a group of prominent physicians (most of them of Jewish origin) had been responsible for the death of several Soviet leaders (such as Andrei Zhdanov and Shcherbakov) and were now plotting, on behalf of foreign espionage agencies, to murder Soviet marshals and other leading figures of the regime. From that day on, there was a crescendo of attacks on such poisoners, spies, vermin, animals in human shape, obviously directed not primarily against these underlings but their (as yet unnamed) sponsors inside the country. There were constant calls for more vigilance; denunciations of individuals and of entire categories of people became a daily occurrence. A great fear again spread throughout the Soviet Union, for everyone who remembered 1936 realized that the present accusations were merely the prelude to a much wider wave of repression, which could ultimately affect millions of people. These purges were self-generating, as previous experience and the recent trials in the satellite countries had shown; each wave of arrests led to fresh accusations. Stalin's basic intention was to get rid of the party leaders and replace them with "new and inexperienced people," as Khrushchev later asserted. But the incipient purge had also a strongly anti-Semitic character; there was apparently a plan to deport all persons of Jewish origin to the Arctic region or some other remote area of the Soviet Union. Other nationalities, too, were suspect; it was later said that Stalin did not envisage the deportation of the Ukrainians only because there were too many of them.

In the middle of this gathering storm, on the morning of March 6, 1953, Stalin's death was reported. The circumstances have given rise to much speculation; a great many people in the Soviet Union, including almost the entire party leadership, had every reason to feel threatened by the coming purge. There were rumors that certain Soviet leaders had in some way precipitated the demise of the ailing dictator, but no real evidence to this effect has come to light. Stalin's funeral was a great state occasion, but in comparison with the pomp and circumstance that had marked his seventieth birthday, the speeches and the articles in the press were restrained and sober. The new leaders were already preoccupied with the division of power among themselves. Certain important policy decisions had been taken even before the funeral; the Presidium, which with its twenty-five members was far too unwieldy to be the supreme decisionmaking body, was reduced to a membership of ten; Stalin's private Secretariat was dissolved; it had been in practice the most important political institution in Soviet political life, though neither the constitution nor the party program had provided for its existence and it had hardly ever been mentioned in print. The purge was immediately stopped, and the arrested doctors were released; some were no longer alive. A little later an amnesty was proclaimed: all prisoners serving sentences of less than five years were to be released. This effectively excluded political prisoners, whose turn came during the next two years. There were the first admissions, albeit incidental and halfhearted, that "individual officials had committed arbitrary and illegal acts." De-Stalinization, however modest, thus started even before the funeral orations had been presented. A whole epoch in the history of the Soviet Union had come to an end with the death of the dictator.

The transition from one-man rule to government by a small committee (or "collective leadership," as it was officially called) was not altogether smooth. Among the ten men who now shaped Soviet policy there were a great many conflicting ambitions, much mutual distrust, and also some real disagreements about the policies to be pursued. The tug-of-war between individuals and groups led to frequent changes in the Presidium until, four years after Stalin's death, collective leadership again gave way to one-man rule. Georgi Malenkov was both head of the Soviet government and general secretary of the CPSU for a few days after Stalin's death, but his colleagues, deeply apprehensive that one of them would concentrate too much power in his hands, soon forced him to resign his party job. Vyacheslav Molotov and Anastas Mikoyan made a comeback as ministers of foreign affairs and foreign trade, respectively; Nikolai Bulganin (1895–1975) became minister of defense. Beria was again in charge of the various police, secret-police, and intelligence services; parts of his empire had been removed from his control under Stalin. Nikita Khrushchev became general secretary of the party in September 1953; but since, under Stalin, the importance of the party had been substantially reduced, not much attention was paid to this appointment at the time.

Beria (1899–1953) was the first member of the Presidium to fall victim to the bitter internal struggle. On July 10, 1953, it was announced that he had been unmasked as a capitalist agent; the name of this traitor was to be accursed forever. Six months later a brief report appeared in the Soviet press that he and six accomplices had recently been executed. Beria, the most powerful man in the Soviet Union, the "faithful disciple and close associate" of his late country-man, one of the three orators at Stalin's funeral, thus overnight became an unperson. His political record was frightful; he had been respon-sible for the arrest and execution of millions of Soviet citizens between 1938 and 1953. It is unlikely, however, that his colleagues, all of them hardened Stalinists, decided to eliminate him in a sudden fit of moral indignation or because they were afraid that he would rein-troduce orthodox Stalinism. There were signs, on the contrary, that after Stalin's death Beria was one of the chief advocates of a liberal course; he seems to have suggested a compromise with the West concerning the future of Germany. His colleagues feared the concen-tration of too much power in his hands, and they decided, with the help of some army commanders, to nip this danger in the bud.

With Beria's fall, the quarrels in the party leadership moved to a different plane. There were policy differences; Molotov, unbending, inflexible, Stalin's most faithful assistant, stood for the continuation of traditional policies, while Malenkov was more acutely aware that change had become necessary. The current five-year plan, which en-visaged a rise in production of 50 percent, was going badly, and agricultural output per head was still little higher than in tsarist times. Malenkov proposed to remedy the disproportion between investment in heavy industry and in the rest of the national economy, and to take urgent measures to raise the standard of living by spending more on light industry, housing, etc. He faced strong opposition on the part of his colleagues, and after about a year his reforms were severely curtailed in scope. In foreign policy, too, he stood for a more con-ciliatory approach. In a speech in March 1954 he warned that a third world war would mean the end of world civilization. Again he was disavowed and had to retreat; six weeks later he declared that a new world war would merely bring about the end of capitalism.

During the second half of 1954 it became evident that Malen-kov's position was in jeopardy, and in February 1955 he had to resign as chairman of the Council of Ministers, to be replaced by Nikolai Bulganin. There had been a heated policy debate in the Kremlin, but it would be unwise to overrate the ideological element in this conflict.

In both the economic field and foreign affairs, the policies of those who succeeded Malenkov differed little from those he had wanted to pursue. This was particularly evident in foreign policy. Feelers were again put out to the West suggesting discussion of some of the major outstanding problems in Europe. In July, Bulganin met Eisenhower, Eden, and Mollet in Geneva, arousing great hopes for a general reconciliation and a speedy settlement of unresolved questions. The new "spirit of Geneva" became something of a symbol. This general optimism proved to be unfounded. The new Soviet willingness to enter into discussions with the West did not necessarily imply a readiness to retreat from the old position, and the talks were inconclusive. Agreement on the Austrian peace treaty in February remained the only positive achievement of the year 1955.

There were fresh initiatives in Soviet policy in other parts of the globe. The importance of the third world and the opportunity to enhance Soviet influence in these regions gradually dawned on the Kremlin, and measures were taken to establish closer links with African and Asian countries. The arms deal with Egypt in the spring of 1955 opened a new era in the relations between the Soviet Union and the Arab world; the visit of Bulganin and Khrushchev to New Delhi in November 1955 paved the way for closer ties with India. Efforts were made to mend fences within the communist camp; attacks on the "traitor and Judas" Tito and his "fascist regime" ceased, and a high-ranking Soviet delegation, including Khrushchev, visited Belgrade in May 1955. In a speech at the Belgrade airport, Khrushchev said: "We sincerely regret what happened and resolutely reject the things that occurred." The accusations against the Yugoslav leaders had been fabricated by Beria, the "enemy of the people." Molotov opposed the reconciliation with Tito, but he was outvoted; the majority of the Soviet Presidium agreed that it was high time to bury the hatchet. Yugoslavia continued to insist on its independence, whereas Soviet criticism of the "Yugoslav road to communism" by no means ceased in 1955. The most painful and embarrassing manifestations of the breach were removed, even though this implied a vindication of Tito's policy and a loss of face on the part of the Soviet leadership.

Nikita Sergeyevich Khrushchev had not been among the main contenders for the succession while Stalin was alive, and he remained in the background during the first months after his death. Gradually, however, the position of the new general secretary of the party increased in importance and strength as the CPSU regained much of the influence it had lost in Stalin's last years. Inside the party, many key positions were filled with Khrushchev's personal appointees. His name appeared more and more often in the press and on the radio; after Malenkov's fall, he was the most influential member of the Presidium. Not all his suggestions were accepted by his colleagues. Khrushchev, who took a particular interest in agriculture, proposed to solve the permanent crisis in the production of food and livestock by drastically expanding the cultivated area, mainly in Kazakhstan and western Siberia (the "virgin-lands" scheme) and by extending the area under corn. But these schemes were criticized and partly rejected at the time, to be given top priority only several years later, after Khrushchev had broken the opposition in the Presidium and emerged as the undisputed leader.

There were dramatic changes in the intellectual climate after Stalin's death: Pomerantsev's essay on the need for sincerity in literature appeared, as did Ehrenburg's novel *The Thaw,* which gave its name to the whole period. Not everyone welcomed these stirrings, and the first skirmishes between "liberals" and "conservatives" took place. It was not a clear, decisive break with the legacy of Stalinism; the habits of the period of the "cult of the individual" had become too deeply ingrained. Above all, those who succeeded Stalin had without exception made their political career under him; they were his nominees and close comrades-in-arms, and they could not dissociate themselves entirely from him without committing political suicide. They tried to eliminate some of the blatantly irrational and unnecessary features of the old regime, to rationalize and modernize it while keeping most of its essentials. This policy, which continued for many years, involved the Soviet leadership in many contradictions and inconsistencies. How much of the truth about the Stalin era could be safely divulged? Khrushchev at the Twentieth Party Congress in 1956 made a first attempt to shed some light on the most recent period of Soviet history, but he did so in a report that was not published for more than three decades; soon the campaign of de-Stalinization was halted, and those who had gone too far in revealing the truth were sharply called to order. Nor was it easy to find a new political equilibrium after Stalin's death. Collective leadership did not function too well; the principle itself was not yet firmly rooted, for one-man rule (*edinonachalie*) had been the norm for a long time and had become deeply ingrained at every level of Soviet society. Those who had believed that Stalin's death would inaugurate a new era of real inner-party democracy and the gradual liberalization of the regime came to realize before long that it would be, at best, a protracted and painful process, and that it would by no means follow a straight course.

Political developments in the people's democracies during Stalin's last years followed the Soviet pattern. Their policies were more and more closely coordinated with (and controlled by) the Kremlin. National deviations from the established norms, the "national roads to communism," became anathema; the Soviet experience was to serve as the great example by which all these countries were to be guided. They all adopted five- or six-year plans to develop industrial production; collectivization in agriculture was put on the agenda; the noncommunist parties that had come into being after the war were dissolved or lost their independence. The armies, the secret police, architecture and literature, every aspect of life was closely modeled on the Soviet pattern. But despite the effort to attain uniformity there were still differences in the speed with which the process of Stalinization proceeded. Bulgaria was quickest in emulating the Soviet Union and the most extreme; Poland and Rumania in some respects lagged behind; communism had even less mass support there than in the other East European countries. The Polish and Rumanian leaders were no doubt aware that the policies they were following were bound to promote disaffection among large sections of the population, and they tried to achieve their aims without arousing excessive antagonism. Thus, whereas 92 percent of Bulgaria's agriculture had been collectivized by the end of the fifties, the figure for Poland was only 15.

The political climate in the people's democracies during the late Stalin period was one of cynicism, servility, and moral corruption. In the Soviet Union indoctrination had already lasted for more than three decades, and a great part of the population had gradually come to accept at least part of the official doctrine. Eastern Europe, on the other hand, was more exposed to external influences, and few people outside the middle and higher echelons of the party were well disposed toward communist policies. In the Soviet Union communism had a strong patriotic, even nationalistic appeal: the revolution had been carried out (partly at least) against outside enemies; it had made

Russia a great industrial and military power. Communism in Eastern Europe was a foreign importation, not an indigenous product. In the eyes of a Polish, a Hungarian, or a Rumanian patriot, even the achievements of the native communist regimes were no reason for pride. The geographical proximity and the military predominance of the Soviet Union made for caution and obedience, but they did not make East Europeans sincere friends and loyal supporters of Russia.

The Czech coup and the break with Yugoslavia, both in 1948, were the most important milestones on the road to satellization.

The Czechoslovak Communist Party had emerged in the relatively free elections of 1946 as the country's strongest force. But communist domination was by no means total; the police, for instance, were in communist hands, but the minister of justice, a noncommunist, often refused to sanction their activities, or even countermanded their orders. The noncommunist parties, which in 1945–46 had been satisfied with playing second fiddle, gradually asserted themselves. There was reason to doubt whether in new elections the communists would be able to repeat their 1946 victory. They had a small majority in Parliament and shared the government with the Social Democrats led by Zdenek Fierlinger. But among the socialists there was growing opposition to Fierlinger's policy, which had made their party virtually indistinguishable from the communists'. In November 1947, by a majority decision, Fierlinger was removed from the party executive. As a result, the communists feared they would be outvoted and their position would be seriously weakened. They had been criticized all along by Moscow and other communist parties for their lack of revolutionary zeal, their "exaggerated willingness" to cooperate with bourgeois parties within the National Front coalition. A decision was taken to put an end to "formal democracy" and to bring Czechoslovakia into line with the other East European countries. The party organized mass demonstrations, and on February 25, 1948, took over completely. President Edward Beneš, ailing and unwilling to offend the Russians, felt in no position to resist the communist demand for full power. There were threats that the Soviet-army units stationed in the country would be used unless the communist demands were accepted forthwith. The noncommunist parties were dissolved or taken over by the communists, and their leaders arrested; Jan Masaryk, the foreign minister, was found dead on the pavement out-

side his office. There was no resistance; Klement Gottwald, the communist leader who succeeded Beneš in June 1948, is reported to have
said that it was "like cutting butter with a sharp knife."

Soviet policies in Yugoslavia were far less successful. Of all the
East European communist leaders, Tito (Josip Broz) (1892–1980) was
the only one who had come to power by his own efforts, not through
Soviet help, and his party had a broad popular basis. From the very
beginning this put him in a special position, and made it possible for
Yugoslavia to adopt a more independent policy vis-à-vis the Soviet
Union. In 1945–46 the Yugoslavs represented the left, militant wing
within the communist camp; they were disappointed at not getting
stronger Soviet support for their territorial claims (in Trieste); there
were also complaints about Russian "great-power chauvinism" and
Soviet sabotage of Yugoslavia's economic plans. After much friction
between Yugoslav-army leaders and the Soviet military mission in
Belgrade, the Russian advisers were withdrawn in March 1948. A
letter sent by the CPSU to the Yugoslav leadership contained threats
and bitter complaints: Tito was compared to Trotsky and at the same
time attacked as a nationalist; there was no democracy inside the
Yugoslav party, and Tito was accused of trying to liquidate the CPY;
Yugoslavia had been liberated, and the Yugoslav party had come to
power only following the advance of the Soviet army; Tito and his
colleagues should therefore behave with greater propriety and mod-
esty. The conflict between Moscow and Belgrade did not concern
basic Marxist-Leninist principles, even though references to communist doctrine figured prominently in the correspondence. It was the
direct result of the Soviet attempt to impose full control, as in other
East European countries. Stalin clearly misjudged the situation; according to Khrushchev, he believed he had only to lift his little finger
to overthrow Tito. But even a massive Soviet campaign lasting several
years was not sufficient to dislodge Tito, who decided to fight once
he realized that there was no room for compromise.

On June 28, 1948, the CPY was expelled from the Cominform
and the quarrel became public. The Soviet Union brought every kind
of pressure to bear except direct military intervention to overthrow
Tito and the Yugoslav leadership. All the satellites attacked Belgrade;
all economic agreements were broken; an attempt was made to starve
Yugoslavia into submission. There was an unprecedented propaganda

campaign against Tito and his colleagues, but only a handful of Yugoslav-party leaders heeded Stalin's appeal; the great majority rallied around Tito. The attacks helped to make the regime more popular inside the country, for Tito now appeared as the champion of Yugoslav national independence against foreign encroachments. During the following years, Yugoslavia gradually developed its own brand of socialism: great emphasis was put on decentralization, workers councils were established in 1950 to run the factories, and attempts were made to limit the privileges of the new elite. The arrest of Milovan Djilas, one of Tito's closest associates in the early days, who maintained that democratization in Yugoslavia had not gone far enough and that a new class had come into being, showed that there were limits to Tito's liberalism. But compared with the satellites, Yugoslavia was a shining example of democracy; it remained independent in both foreign and domestic policy, and for many on the European left it was a beacon of hope during a dark period. From the Soviet point of view, the failure to overthrow the "Tito clique" was a serious setback which boded ill for the future. In the global balance of power Yugoslavia hardly counted, but the self-assertion of a small country against Soviet control was a matter of grave concern. Once one communist party had successfully defied the Soviet leadership, there was the danger that insubordination would spread; it was the beginning of the end of the monolithic character of world communism.

The split between the Soviet Union and Yugoslavia precipitated mass purges and a series of show trials throughout Eastern Europe, but it was certainly not the only cause; such trials were an inherent part of the Stalinist system. First came the trial of Laszlo Rajk, the Hungarian minister of the interior, and some other, less prominent Hungarian leaders in September 1949. Rajk was accused of having been an informer and a police spy throughout his political career, an employee of Dulles and of Aleksandar Rankovic, the Yugoslav minister of the interior. Rajk duly admitted all these charges as well as many others, equally fantastic, and was executed. Next was Traicho Kostov, the Bulgarian deputy prime minister and a great hero of the party from the underground days. The charges were roughly the same as in the case of Rajk, but Kostov, hardened against torture in the prisons of prewar Bulgaria, in open court unexpectedly withdrew his confession, to the great consternation of those who were stage-managing his trial. In Czechoslovakia the purge began in 1949–50 and reached its climax with the November 1951 trial of Rudolf Slansky, former party secretary; Vlado Clementis, former foreign minister; and others. Slansky had been a faithful Stalinist, and his admission of guilt was even less convincing than that of the other communist leaders in Eastern Europe. He and his colleagues were accused of being foreign intelligence agents, of engaging in financial speculation, and (an innovation) of being Zionists: there were openly anti-Semitic overtones in this trial. It was common knowledge that Slansky, a Jew by origin, had been an implacable enemy of Zionism throughout his life. As the trials went on, the charges became more and more grotesque, but the accused continued to incriminate themselves; sometimes they were also denounced by their wives and children.

The outside world watched these proceedings with amazement and horror, unable to understand what pressure could have induced the accused to admit charges that were so manifestly absurd. In Rumania, Ana Pauker and Vasile Luca, two of the most prominent party leaders, fell victim to the purge in May 1952; Patrascanu, a former party secretary, was executed in April 1954; in Poland, Władisłav Gomułka, Marian Spychalski, and Zenon Kliszko were arrested in 1949. In East Germany, Paul Merker was ousted from the leadership in 1950, and Wilhelm Zaisser and Rudolf Herrnstadt after the workers' revolt of June 1953. These are just a few of the more outstanding among the many who were purged, arrested, or executed. All together some 550,000 party members were purged in Czechoslovakia, 300,000 in Poland and East Germany, and only slightly fewer in the other satellite countries. For a rank-and-file party member this usually meant no more than that he was likely to experience difficulties in daily life and perhaps to lose his job. But the more highly placed the victim, the more dangerous were the consequences. It is impossible to find a common denominator for the trials. In some cases internal intrigues and the struggle for power played a major role; there is little doubt that for Rákosi, Rajk was a dangerous rival, and Vulko Chervenkov, the Bulgarian leader, for similar reasons wanted to remove Kostov. It is more difficult to explain the particularly savage character of the Prague trial entirely in terms of dissension among the Czech leadership; Soviet pressure apparently played a major part. The Polish party leadership, though it arrested Gomułka and his associates, resisted Soviet demands for a show trial. The trials and purges have been explained with reference to historical traditions, and political and psychological mechanisms. It has been argued that the Stalinist system was based on the application of terror, and that recurrent trials and purges were needed to spread fear among the population. There is some truth in all these explanations, yet in the last resort motivation was irrational. There probably was no master plan, and many events defy explanation to this day.

The last years of the Stalin era, in Eastern Europe as in the Soviet Union, were a period of remarkable industrial expansion, but the costs of production were inordinately high, and living standards actually declined. Shortages in almost all fields of the national economy affected the consumer and imperiled future economic growth. Some countries were affected more than others: Hungary in 1953 was on the verge of an economic catastrophe, whereas the situation in neighboring Czechoslovakia was less critical. Following the lead given by Malenkov after Stalin's death, all the "people's democracies" adjusted their economic policy, and there were also certain changes in the political sphere. In Hungary the "New Course" went considerably beyond the limits set by Moscow: Rákosi had to give up the prime-ministership, and Imre Nagy, a "Muscovite" like Matyas Rákosi but far more liberal and democratic in his outlook, introduced economic and political reforms. The development of heavy industry was no longer regarded as an end in itself; many political prisoners were freed, and the whole atmosphere became markedly freer. Nagy became very popular among the masses, but for that very reason antagonized the old leadership. After Malenkov's fall, Imre Nagy, too, had to go, and at the end of 1955 was excluded from the party. The Stalinist leaders made a comeback, even if they could not recover all the positions they had lost. The great and growing discontent among workers and peasants, and above all among the younger generation and the students, could no longer be contained, and, the year after, it led to a major explosion.

There were signs of growing discontent in East Germany and Czechoslovakia, such as the revolt of June 17, 1953, in East Berlin and the big strike in the Czech town of Pilsen. Both governments took urgent measures to improve living conditions but opposed political reform. Klement Gottwald, the leader of Czech communism, died in 1953, but Antonin Zapotocki, and in particular Antonin Novotny, who subsequently emerged as the central figure in the regime, were typical products of the Stalinist era. Poland and Rumania were the last East European countries to introduce the New Course. They had been slightly less affected than the other satellites by the trials and other tribulations of the late Stalin period. Bołeslav Bierut, the leader of the Polish party, had to give up the post of prime minister in 1954; in December of that year the minister of public security had to step down after sensational revelations about the practices of the secret police had been made by a high Polish official who had defected to the West. The first reforms were purely economic in character, but the opposition movement soon gathered momentum. The Communist Party, whose membership had decreased over a number of years, found itself isolated from a population profoundly anticommunist, while inside the party there was growing opposition to the leadership. In Poland and Hungary a prerevolutionary situation existed in 1955, and as events during the next year were to show, only minor impulses were needed to spark an explosion.

Stalin's policy in his East European empire had effected enormous political, social, and economic changes. With the exception of Yugoslavia, all the countries became part of a monolithic bloc. Their policy, their economy, their military forces were closely integrated under Soviet leadership and strict control. Comecon (the Council for Mutual Economic Assistance) was established in Warsaw in January 1949 as an East European counterweight to the Marshall Plan, and the Warsaw Pact (signed in 1955) was the military answer to NATO. But this was only official recognition of the existing state of affairs. The Soviet Union under Stalin interfered in the internal affairs of its satellites without any hesitation, at every level and in every field. His successors showed more tact in their dealings with the East European capitals, though there were limits to their restraint, as events in Budapest in 1956 were to prove.

The Stalinist practice of centralization and strict control contained the seeds of its own destruction. These policies were deeply offensive to intensely nationalist peoples, and on occasion they antagonized even the communist leadership. Although no communist leader wanted to reverse the social order, the idea of a national communism, free from outside interference, more democratic and humane in character, gained some open adherents and many more tacit sympathizers. National communism did not necessarily mean the gradual emergence of a more liberal regime, but it opened the door to the many changes that were to take place all over Eastern Europe during the next decade.

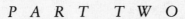

PART TWO

ECONOMIC
MIRACLE

THE ECONOMIC STATE
OF EUROPE IN 1945

Western Europe, occupying only 3 percent of the world's land surface, contained in 1960 about 9 percent of the population of the globe. It produced one-quarter of the world's industrial output, accounted for 40 percent of the world's trade, and was thus the world's greatest market. Europe's postwar growth was spectacular; few observers had assumed at the end of the war that Europe would so quickly recover from its wounds. The prewar history of Europe did not augur well for the prospects of quick growth. Summarizing Europe's position at the end of the 1930s, a Swedish economist wrote that it presented a picture of half-finished transformation in relation to technological change and the new developments in the international market. Many factors resisted change: obsolete equipment, restrictive practices by governments, management, and workers alike. Productivity in agriculture was low, many industries were stagnating, and widespread unemployment kept national output and income down: as Svennilson said, "Europe was suffering from the arteriosclerosis of an old-established, heavily capitalized economic system, inflexible in relation to violent economic change." The Second World War caused enormous ravages and paralyzed economic activity; it is estimated that nearly a year after liberation French and Belgian industries were running at only 20–35 percent of their prewar level and that German production was even lower. Britain, which had suffered less direct damage than the continent, reached the prewar level of production in 1946, but in most European countries the situation seemed far less promising; in that year steel production in Western Europe, to provide but one illustration, was only half what it had been in 1939. There were acute food shortages, and high priority was given to means to avert the danger of starvation. Encouraging progress was made in 1945 and 1946, but then came the great setback of 1947, when disastrous climatic conditions caused havoc and destroyed much of the agricultural crop. After that catastrophic year the situation gradually improved, as more fertilizers became available. Britain had been the first to mechanize its agriculture; the continent followed during the 1950s.

Industrial recovery, too, made rapid progress. In 1948 the industries of France and of most other European countries (except Germany) were already producing more than before the war. Recovery after the First World War, too, had been rapid, but many still remembered how this impetus had petered out after a few years and was followed by long period of stagnation and decline. Would history repeat itself? The difficulties seemed overwhelming. As a result of the unsatisfied demand of the long years of war, there was tremendous inflationary pressure. All European governments faced this danger, while the balance of trade with the United States grew steadily worse and resulted in a grave "dollar gap." More than ever before, Europe was dependent on exports, but to restore its position as an industrial manufacturer it had to acquire new equipment and raw materials, and for these it was not able to pay. This balance-of-payments deficit was bridged only by very substantial American grants and, after 1947, by the Marshall Plan. Marshall aid was the blood transfusion that "sustained the weakening European economies and gave them strength to work their own recovery," in the words of the OEEC's "Economic Progress and Problems of Western Europe" (June 1951). From the end of 1947 to June 1950, about $9.4 billion was made available to the countries most in need. The effects in terms of economic progress were startling: total output of goods and services during those three years rose by 25 percent, and during the second half of 1950 European output was already running 30 to 35 percent above the prewar level. In certain key industries the advance was even more striking: steel production increased by 70 percent between 1947 and 1950, cement by 80 percent, vehicles by 150 percent, and refined oil products by 200 percent. Exports rose by 91 percent, and Europe seemed well on the way to recovery, when in the early summer of 1950 the Korean War broke out and put in jeopardy many of these achievements. It caused raw-material shortages, rising prices, and new inflationary pressures. Devaluation had made European goods more competitive on the world's markets and helped to close the dollar gap, but with the outbreak of the war the prices of raw materials skyrocketed, profoundly affecting the terms of trade. At the same time it became necessary to strengthen Europe's defenses; defense expenditure in 1950 absorbed a considerable part of the productive resources of Europe, and the volume of goods available for civilian consumption had to be drastically reduced. Since some European countries—such as Germany, Austria, and Greece—had made only a very imperfect recovery, and since a large part of Europe's imports was still financed by American loans, prospects again seemed very bleak indeed. Yet the outbreak of the Korean War, it appears in retrospect, interrupted Europe's recovery only briefly. The re-equipment of industry and agriculture continued; structural unemployment and the dollar gap gradually disappeared. Each country had a separate national plan to speed up recovery; France's Monnet Plan was the most famous of them. These plans had much to recommend them; they were all aimed at a rapid expansion of the national economy and of exports. But there was one fatal flaw: there was no attempt to coordinate; on the contrary, there was a great deal of overlapping. It was soon realized that all European countries were bound to suffer unless customs barriers were broken down and trade was liberalized, unless the European economy became far more integrated than it had been before the war. The Schuman Plan was the precursor of the later and more ambitious plans for West European economic union. European planners regarded the recovery of the immediate postwar period merely as a first step toward a greater goal; it was gratifying that the European economy had so quickly reached prewar levels, but it was not forgotten that Europe in the 1930s had not exactly been a prosperous continent. Production in many countries had, in fact, been lower in 1938 than ten years earlier. With a growing population, Europe needed a long period of continuous growth. The *Economic Survey of Europe* published in 1951 predicted a growth in industrial production of 40–60 percent up to the end of the decade. But these targets were already reached by the middle of the decade, and the upward swing still continued to gather momentum. By 1964 Europe's industrial output was more than two and a half times as great as in 1938.

Economists agree that it is impossible to find a historical precedent for the extended period of prosperity enjoyed by Europe during the fifties and sixties: As Angus Maddison said, "In continental Europe the decade of the 1950s was brilliant, with growth of output and consumption investment and employment surpassing any recorded historical experience and the rhythm of development virtually uninterrupted by recession." Andrew Shonfield has noted that the growth of production was extremely rapid, that there was no halt or reversal in the advance, and that the benefits of the new prosperity were very widely diffused. Michael Postan observed that the ever-mounting affluence was the unique feature of the postwar economy; also remarkable and unexpected was the fact that the economic growth was so powerfully propelled by public sentiment and policies. The following table indicates the percentage of average yearly growth in the gross domestic product* of the main European countries between 1948 and 1963:

Austria	5.8	Italy	6.0
Belgium	3.2	Norway	3.5
Denmark	3.6	Sweden	3.4
France	4.6	Switzerland	3.4
Germany	7.6	United Kingdom	2.5
Holland	4.7		

At the beginning of the postwar period, the rate of growth in Germany, Austria, and Greece was lagging behind the others, because their economies had been more severely affected by the war. For the same reason, their rate of development during the middle and late fifties was faster than that of the other countries. In Italy, too, after a sluggish start, the rate of development gathered momentum during the late fifties. In 1959 Italy was producing 64 percent more than at the beginning of the decade; between 1959 and 1961 the annual rate of growth was 7.5 percent. The expansion of production in France, the Netherlands, Switzerland, and Spain was near the European average, from 45 to 50 percent, between the beginning and the end of the decade. In these countries growth accelerated toward the end of the decade and in the early sixties. Even the mature economies of

---

* The gross national product, GNP, is the total sum of goods and services produced, the finished goods delivered to final purchasers. The gross domestic product, GDP, is the same minus the income received from abroad.

Sweden and Switzerland, which had been least affected by the war, attained a rate of growth of 6 percent or more in 1964. Production in Britain and Belgium rose more slowly; in Britain it was only 21 percent higher at the end of the decade, in Belgium 26 percent. But the rate of growth in Belgium quickened during the early sixties, and in Britain, too, there was a belated, fitful advance. Whereas Germany had topped the list of the fast-growing economies during the fifties, a different picture emerged during the sixties:

GNP ANNUAL AVERAGE RATE OF INCREASE 1960–65

Italy	5.1	Britain	3.3
France	5.1	Japan	9.6
Germany	4.8	United States	4.5

The postwar growth of the European economy was first interrupted by the outbreak of the Korean War and then slowed down by the recession of 1957–58. The causes of this second slump were more complex than those of the earlier setback. Several European countries—notably France, Britain, Belgium, and Denmark—had adopted restrictive measures to lessen the pressure on their currencies, which had increased as the result of an adverse balance of payments. The slowing down of the rate of growth was deliberate and envisaged as a temporary measure. The recessions of the fifties were of short duration and had no lasting effects; even during the slump years 1952 and 1958, European production rose by approximately 2 percent. The recessions of the 1960s were more serious in character: economic growth in France was slowed down in 1963–65, Italy went through a crisis in 1963–64, and the German economic miracle came to a halt in 1966–67. Nineteen sixty-four had been an excellent year in most European countries, with a rise in industrial output of 7 percent; in some the advance was even more substantial, but the poor showing of Italy (0.3 percent) affected the general picture. Nineteen sixty-seven, on the other hand, was a year of crisis: in Britain, West Germany, and Austria industrial production actually fell, and the average European gain was only 1.2 percent. There was a new upsurge in the early 1970s, to be followed by an acute recession in 1972–73. European productivity, which had averaged 5.5 percent in the 1950s and 1960s, fell to about 2 percent in the 1970s, to pick up significantly only in the mid-1980s. These trends and their causes will be discussed later on in the present survey.

The stormy development of Europe's economy during the two decades after the war has certain unique features. Never in its history, not even before the First World War, had industrial Europe made such striking advances. Even the sluggish performance of the British economy was in excess of Britain's development before 1914, let alone her economic record between the two wars. This performance provided economists with much food for thought. The Marxists among them (but not only they) had for many years predicted the demise of capitalism, which, they argued, had long exhausted its historical role. In their view, capitalist economy, as the crisis of 1929 and the slump of the 1930s had shown, had become incapable of acting as an agent of economic development. That the "capitalist economies" of Europe had acquired a new lease on life and made greater progress than ever before seemed to belie these assumptions. American neo-Marxists maintained that the postwar boom was essentially military in character, with defense expenditure as the stabilizing factor. Such arguments were hardly relevant to developments in Europe. There is no straightforward formula to explain the boom after the Second World War. The European governments had on the whole digested the lesson of the great prewar depression and were able to maintain high levels of purchasing power and thus to stimulate demand by the application of Keynesian techniques—manipulating taxation, monetary policy, spending, and borrowing. The customs barriers between the countries were reduced; the Common Market and EFTA, its rival organization, provided large markets and thus stimulated economic activity. There was a much higher degree of collaboration between industries in various countries than before, and Europe thus enjoyed some of the advantages from which America alone had benefited in the past. The great business concerns, such as Unilever, ICI, the German chemical concerns, and the German, Italian, and French car manufacturers (to name but a few), could plan and produce more cheaply and rationally, and invest more in research. At the same time the European economy had become far more planned and less capitalist (in the laissez-faire sense) than in the past. The coal mines in Britain and France had been nationalized; the production of electricity was entirely in the hands of the state in Italy and Britain, and largely so in France and Germany as well. So were air transport, the railways, and to a lesser extent sea transport (80 percent in Italy, 37 percent in France). About 40 percent of the Italian and French banks were

INDUSTRIAL PRODUCTION IN EASTERN EUROPE (1958 = 100)

	1938	1948	1953	1959	1962	1965
Bulgaria	11	22	55	121	170	238
Czechoslovakia	31	44	64	112	143	159
East Germany	38	27	66	112	137	159
Hungary	28	38	84	111	149	177
Poland	16	28	61	109	145	182
Rumania	25	22	63	110	168	243
Yugoslavia	29	43	53	113	150	217
U.S.S.R.	23	40	58	111	146	184

state-owned; 60 percent of the Italian iron and steel industries and the same percentage of the French aircraft industry (to give a few more examples) had been nationalized. The part played by the state in the national economy was thus infinitely more important than in the past, but these changes in ownership were not in themselves sufficient to explain the great postwar boom. West Germany, which adopted liberal economic policies, made as much progress as Italy and France, which put more emphasis on planning and state ownership. An influential school of economists (W. A. Lewis, Kindleberger) has argued that the rapid advance of Europe's economy was connected with the availability of a large supply of labor, stemming from a high rate of natural population increase, from immigration, from the presence of unemployed workers, or from transfers from agriculture to industry; with the exhaustion of Europe's excess supply of labor, the rates of economic growth fell: instead of an annual increase of 6–8 percent, a yearly growth of 2–4 percent became more common. This was a plausible explanation: Europe had large idle capacities both in manpower and equipment after the war; once these resources were put to good use, an unprecedented economic expansion ensued. Some of these factors were not likely to recur, and hence the gradual decline in the rate of growth in the sixties. But other factors also contributed to the boom: greater productivity, technical innovation, the expansion of world trade, and even psychological considerations such as increased self-confidence on the part of industrialists, bankers, and economic planners.

Economic recovery in the Soviet Union also made rapid strides after the war. The output of coal in 1952 was twice what it had been in 1945; the production of steel, oil, and electricity almost trebled during the same period. Stalin and his assistants were convinced that the performance of the Soviet economy was greatly superior to that of the "capitalist world" because it was planned, because there was no unemployment, and because its resources would always be fully used. During the 1930s, at the time of the great recession in the West, the Soviet economy had indeed forged ahead, and the country had become the second industrial power in the world. According to official (but untrue) statistics, the Soviet national income grew for decades by a steady 8–10 percent per year; industrial output in 1963 was said to be forty-four times as large as in the late 1920s. The aim of catching up with and overtaking America had first been announced in the early 1930s; Khrushchev declared in the 1950s that the target would be achieved in 1970. But the official figures of the Stalin era have always been, justifiably, suspect, and there could be no doubt that Soviet standards of living were, even in the 1960s, substantially lower than those in the West. They were, in fact, inferior to the level reached by some of the countries of Eastern Europe. And although the Soviet economy continued to advance, its rate of growth declined. Considerable progress was made during the 1950s: the Soviet GNP was 36 percent of the American in 1957, and reached the 50-percent mark five years later. At that time it seemed to have a good chance of overtaking America within a decade or two if the same rate of growth continued. After 1962 progress became slower, whereas America, emerging from the recession of the early sixties, moved ahead faster. By 1968 the Soviet GNP was still only half that of America. When, many years later, in the late 1980s, some more or less truthful statistics were published for the first time under glasnost, it appeared that the Soviet GNP was considerably less than half that of the United States. In other words, Soviet economic achievements had been grossly exaggerated since the 1930s, and it is difficult even now to differentiate between propaganda, fantasies, and real achievements. The Soviet economic planners focused on the race with the United States, apparently ignoring the fact that economic growth in some West European countries, and particularly in Japan, was actually faster than in the United States.

The Soviet economy, like that of Western Europe, suffered from various imbalances, albeit of a different character. Under Stalin it had been the basic rule of economic policy to give priority to heavy industry at the expense of agriculture, light industry, and consumer goods in general. The development of Soviet industry, with its strong emphasis on heavy industry and armaments, had spectacular results, but these were achieved at a high price, both from the political and the economic point of view. This growth entailed severe repression and a great deal of human suffering; it meant resisting the increasing demand for a better standard of living. It also involved a great deal of waste. A high percentage of the goods produced were of such low quality they were unusable. These imbalances became even more pronounced during the last years of Stalin's rule, and his successors faced almost immediately the urgent necessity of reorganizing Soviet industry and agriculture. Heavy industry continued to receive priority, but far more resources were now devoted to agriculture, to housing, and to articles of mass consumption. Substantial progress was made in all these fields, and there was a marked rise in the standard of living—not comparable to Western Europe's but certainly impressive in comparison with the Stalin era. In the 1960s further economic reforms were carried out, albeit halfheartedly, mainly to decentralize the economy and to make individual industries and factories more profitable, and greater attention was paid to productivity.

Economic development in the communist countries of Eastern Europe followed in broad outline the same course as in the Soviet Union. The rapid increase in industrial production in the fifties was followed by stagnation and decline in the early sixties, and a shortlived upsurge in the late sixties. The emphasis in all these countries was on heavy industry; all faced considerable difficulties in the agricultural field. Between 1960 and 1963 agricultural production in East Germany, Hungary, and Czechoslovakia was actually lower than it had been before the war. The less industrialized countries—Bulgaria, Yugoslavia, and Rumania—developed the most rapidly, whereas Poland, East Germany, Czechoslovakia, and Hungary, starting at a higher level, did not make equally striking progress. All these countries had a great many obstacles to overcome: the aftereffects of the destruction of the war, reparations extracted by the Soviet Union, unfavorable trade agreements with their senior partner, and the severe dislocation caused by the collectivization of agriculture. Considering all these adverse factors, their progress was impressive, but it was not remotely equal to West European economic growth. The following table indicates the percentage of growth in the GNP of various European countries between 1938 and 1964.

West Germany	220	Rumania	118
Holland	152	Poland	115
Bulgaria	147	Greece	97
France	135	Hungary	84
Italy	132	Czechoslovakia	84

In absolute terms, the gross national product of Poland was the largest in Eastern Europe in 1964, followed by East Germany and Czechoslovakia. The total GNP of all six East European countries was bigger than that of France but smaller than West Germany.

In broad outline, there were certain similarities in the postwar development of Western and Eastern Europe: economic progress was quicker than at any previous period during the history of the continent; in both West and East there was a decline in the rate of growth toward the end of the second postwar decade. The most striking developments were the industrialization of the less developed countries of Eastern and Southern Europe, and the all-round progress and consequent rise in living standards in the industrial countries. There were also enormous qualitative changes. Housing conditions improved, working hours were reduced, and educational facilities were spread more widely than ever before. The peoples of Europe were better fed and better clothed, unemployment had virtually disappeared by the middle fifties, and there was a great and growing demand for labor. Hundreds of thousands of workers from Southern and Southeastern Europe migrated to Germany, France, and Switzerland to find more highly paid employment than in their native countries. Comprehensive social-security schemes providing medical care, pensions for the aged, unemployment benefits, and many other grants and services were adopted almost everywhere. Great changes took place in technology, and with the growing specialization a much higher degree of technical knowledge became necessary for industrial workers and farmers. The unskilled laborer gave way to the skilled or semiskilled worker, the peasant to the agricultural specialist. The growing prosperity caused far-reaching social changes. Many sociologists maintained that the manual workers were gradually absorbed into the middle classes. Marxists, on the other hand, argued, that despite the improvements, social injustice and poverty continued to exist, and they rejected the findings of social scientists according to which the embourgeoisement of the worker was already an established fact. But no one was likely to dispute that, twenty years after the Second World War, the European worker had more to lose than his chains.

The population of Western Europe (the OECD countries in Europe) was 264 million in 1940; twenty-five years later it was 320 million. In the 1930s no demographer had expected such a rapid increase.* Population had grown steadily up to the First World War despite substantial emigration overseas, but had stagnated after 1918. Fertility declined by almost half between 1900 and 1940 in Britain, Germany, Scandinavia, and Switzerland, and the trend in other countries was only slightly less marked. Since the death rate also fell substantially during this period, the age composition of the population became very different from what it had been in the past: Europe became preponderantly middle-aged. In the 1930s this trend became even more pronounced; in Belgium, Sweden, and Britain the number of births and deaths was about even; in France and Ireland there was an absolute decline, because there were more deaths than births. Most demographers predicted that this decline would continue and even gather momentum throughout Western and Northern Europe; no one envisaged the 12-percent increase in Western Europe that actually took place between 1940 and 1955. The postwar European baby boom was smaller than the American, and after 1955 the birthrate again fell. But the overall growth of population nevertheless proceeded at a higher rate than between the wars, as a result partly of the decline in infant mortality, partly of the fall in the death rate. Particularly striking was the upward swing in France, once the most populous European country, where the population had hardly increased for almost a century. French postwar governments introduced generous family allowances, and the migration of several hundred thousand Frenchmen from North Africa further helped to change the outlook in a country that had been for a long time the classical example of "race suicide." Holland had always had one of the highest birthrates in west Europe; its population doubled between 1900 and 1958, and there was a similar striking increase in Switzerland, whereas in neigh-

---

* In relative terms, Europe's portion of the world population has been steadily declining. The population of Western and Eastern Europe taken together account now (1990) for 16 percent of the total, but according to the demographers' predictions, it will be only 10 percent in the year 2025.

POPULATION (IN THOUSANDS)

	1950	1966	1990
Austria	6,900	7,300	7,700
Belgium	8,600	9,500	9,900
Czechoslovakia	12,300	14,200	
France	41,700	49,400	56,000
West Germany	n.a.	59,600	60,900
Hungary	9,300	10,100	10,500
Italy	46,300	51,900	57,400
Netherlands	10,100	12,400	14,800
Poland	24,800	31,600	38,100
Rumania	16,300	19,100	
Spain	27,800	31,800	39,400
Sweden	7,000	7,800	8,500
Switzerland	4,600	6,000	6,700
United Kingdom	50,000	54,900	57,400
Yugoslavia	16,300	19,700	
Soviet Union	180,000	227,000	291,000

boring Austria it remained as before—much below the European average.

While the birthrate rose in almost all the developed European countries, there was a striking decline in Southern and Eastern Europe as the result of industrialization and urbanization. The total population of Eastern Europe, not counting the Soviet Union, increased between 1950 and 1964 from 106 to 120 million, although the birthrate fell from 21 to 13 in Hungary, from 26 to 15 in Rumania, and from 30 to 17 in Poland. Significantly, the only country in which the birthrate remained as before the Second World War was Albania (about 37–38), the least developed of all. The population of the Soviet Union grew to approximately 227 million—282 million in 1987, while the birthrate fell from 26 to 19. The process of urbanization in the Soviet Union was more marked than in any other major European country; the number of city dwellers more than doubled between 1939 and 1946; in some of the larger cities it has trebled or quadrupled during the last forty years.

The population growth and the emergence of huge conurbations posed a great many problems to the planners. The density of population in Western Europe is four times as high as in the United States. The industrial and commercial heartland of Europe—Belgium and Britain, parts of West Germany, and northern Italy—were gradually transformed into urban areas with hardly any agriculture, and it

POPULATION OF MAJOR SOVIET CITIES

	1926	1959	1986
Baku	453,300	968,000	1,722,000
Dnepropetrovsk	236,700	658,000	1,116,000
Donetsk	174,200	701,000	1,081,000
Gorky (Nizhni Novgorod)	222,300	942,000	1,409,000
Kazan	179,000	643,000	1,057,000
Kharkov	417,300	930,000	1,567,000
Kiev	513,600	1,101,000	2,495,000
Kuibyshev (Samara)	175,600	806,000	1,267,000
Leningrad	1,690,000	3,300,000	5,000,000
Minsk	134,800	509,000	1,510,000
Moscow	2,029,400	5,032,000	8,714,000
Odessa	420,800	667,000	1,132,000
Ufa	98,000	546,000	1,077,000
Perm (Molotov)	119,700	628,000	1,065,000
Rostov	308,100	597,000	1,000,000
Sverdlovsk	140,300	777,000	1,315,000
Tbilisi	294,000	694,000	1,174,000
Volgograd (Stalingrad)	151,400	591,000	1,000,000
Voronezh	121,600	454,000	860,000
Yerevan	64,600	509,000	1,148,000
Zaporozhe	55,700	435,000	863,000

seemed likely that the congestion in these parts would become even greater as internal migration continued from the agricultural regions to areas offering greater economic opportunities. All over Europe the proportion of the population engaged in industry continued to rise, but the tertiary sector, the services, increased even more. Before 1914 almost half of Western Europe's working population had been employed in agriculture (including fishing and forestry). By the 1930s only one-third was so employed, and by 1955 the farming population represented only 24 percent of the total. The trend continued during the fifties and sixties; by 1965 only 17 percent of the Common Market population was engaged in agriculture (25 percent in Italy, 18 percent in France, 6 percent in Belgium—in Britain it was no more than 3 percent). By the late 1980s less than 10 percent in Italy, 7 percent in France, and 2.5 percent in Belgium were employed in agriculture. In most South European countries agriculture was still the occupation of 40 percent or more of the population, but there, too, the trend toward industry and the services was unmistakable. In Spain two out of three workers had been employed in agriculture in 1910; but in the early 1950s the share of agriculture had fallen to less than 50 percent, and by 1966 it was less than 33 percent. In 1985 it was no more than 15 percent. In Eastern Europe the process was equally marked. In all these areas, agriculture had been dominant before the Second World War. After 1945 the number of those engaged in industry rose rapidly, though agriculture continued to employ a relatively high percentage of the working population even in the industrialized countries of Eastern Europe (Czechoslovakia, East Germany, and the U.S.S.R.). The degree of industrialization was usually an indication of prosperity. There were exceptions: in Denmark, which boasts a highly developed and profitable agriculture, the percentage of those employed in agriculture is almost six times as high as in Britain, but its per-capita income is higher. Among the major European nations, the exodus from agriculture was most pronounced in Germany and France; between 1955 and the late sixties there was a further decline of about 20 percent in the agricultural-labor force of Western Europe, but there was still overemployment in agriculture, and the Common Market experts have demanded a further reduction of the agricultural-labor force by five to eight million during the next decade. Political, economic, and cultural life had been concentrated in the big cities of Europe even when the great majority of the population still lived and worked in the countryside. With the industrial revolution there was a constant stream to the towns, at times becoming a torrent; by the middle of the twentieth century Europe had become, to all intents and purposes, an urban continent.

There was more or less full employment in Western Europe during the postwar reconstruction period, despite certain ups and downs during the 1960s. The situation changed, however, in the 1970s, partly as the result of economic stagnation but also as a consequence of increasing automation. Even during a relatively prosperous year such as 1989, more than 16 percent of the working population of Italy and Spain were unemployed, as were 9.5, 8, and 6 percent in France, West Germany, and Britain respectively. In some ways these figures convey an exaggerated picture, for they included people who had registered as unemployed but did not really look for work. They also included students who had just graduated but had not yet looked for jobs for any length of time, and other such categories. In some respects, however, the state of affairs was worse than the figures indicate. Unemployment was higher in certain areas and age groups than in others. It was considerably higher among young people than among older ones, and in economically declining regions such as the north of England, the Ruhr, and the old heavy-industry locations in northern France and Belgium. That unemployment was a social and political as much as an economic evil was manifest, for instance, in the growth of right-wing groups that attacked foreign workers, who were perceived to deprive local workers not only of jobs but of housing and other services. State and local authorities as well as employers' associations and trade unions gradually realized that, with the progress of automation, unemployment was there to stay, and that various new schemes, such as work sharing and a shortening of the work week, had to be envisaged to alleviate it.

THE RECOVERY OF
EUROPEAN INDUSTRY

Europe had been the industrial center of the world up to the end of the nineteenth century; the United States caught up with the old continent during the First World War, and the Soviet Union reached the West European level of heavy-industry output in the late 1950s. Europe, with 15 percent of the world's population, continued, however, to be the world's greatest market; about 40 percent of the world's GNP is still produced in the European continent (including the U.S.S.R.).

At the same time basic structural changes took place within industry. Coal and iron had been the traditional backbone of industrial development, and their importance during the industrial revolution in the nineteenth and early twentieth centuries was paramount. Great political as well as economic influence was attributed to the giants of heavy industry: the names of Krupp, Mannesmann, Thyssen, Schneider-Creusot, Vickers, and Skoda became symbols of the political-economic-military establishments, and their importance, even if often exaggerated, was during that period very substantial indeed. After 1945 the situation changed: coal was gradually displaced by oil and other fuels; the value of German steel production in the early 1960s was only two-thirds that of the chemical industry; Krupp fell to sixteenth place in the list of Europe's industrial giants. Of all the major industrial enterprises that had been family property, only one—Thyssen—did not change hands and became a public company.

The eclipse of coal mining was felt all over Europe. Coal had been the fuel par excellence of the industrial revolution; it had no rival as a source of energy. Before the First World War, Europe had exported considerable quantities of coal to other parts of the world, but after 1918, with growing domestic energy demands, a shortage developed. Europe's coal reserves are limited, and coal mining became more expensive as deeper and less profitable seams had to be worked, and as a result Europe's supply pattern of sources of energy began to change rapidly. At first considerable quantities of coal were still imported, mainly from the United States, but from the early fifties the import of crude oil and refined petroleum products increased every year. Crude-oil imports, which had been a mere 17 million tons in 1929, rose to 450 million in 1967. As more and more unprofitable pits were closed down, the output of British coal mining, the most important in Europe, fell steadily; having reached its peak before 1914, when yearly output was about 300 million tons, it had fallen in 1964 to 196 million, in 1967 there was a further decline to 175 million, and in the late 1980s it was a mere 100 million. In 1966 oil supplied 51 percent of the Common Market countries' energy demands. This spectacular rise became possible as the result of the discovery of vast oil resources, mainly in the Middle East, in the 1940s and '50s; but oil was also discovered in the North Sea. This dependence created new problems. Although oil was very much cheaper than coal, there was the danger that in a political crisis the supply would be stopped; this happened during the Suez crisis in 1956 and again during the Arab-Israeli war in 1967. The European countries tried to counteract the effects of these stoppages by storing several months' supply and by gradually developing other sources of energy, particularly natural gas and nuclear power; substantial quantities of natural gas were found in the Soviet Union but also in Holland and other West European countries. The development of nuclear power, mainly as a source of generating electricity, took longer than had originally been expected because of the high cost of technological progress, but eventually it came to play a significant role in most countries of Western and Eastern Europe.

The coal-mining industry had its defenders, despite the high cost of production. While the critics argued that coal had ceased to be an industry and become a giant social-insurance scheme requiring vast government subsidies, its advocates maintained that it was dangerous from both a political and an economic point of view to neglect coal mining altogether. The retraining of miners, too, presented major problems, especially in West Germany and Britain. In West Germany about 15 percent of the mining-labor force changed their occupation between 1960 and 1963, but not everyone was able or willing to move to a new place and to look for a new job.

Industrial development in Eastern Europe at first followed a somewhat different pattern. Coal production in the Soviet Union almost trebled between 1948 and 1965, increasing from 150 million tons to 427 million. It rose to 578 million tons in 1965 and 751 million in 1986. The production of oil increased tenfold to 309 million tons in 1968. Yet domestic demand rose even faster, and the problem was most acutely felt in the communist countries of Eastern Europe, which, in contrast to the Soviet Union, had no sizable indigenous oil supplies. The Soviet Union, which had begun in the fifties to export considerable quantities of oil to Western Europe and was also Eastern Europe's sole supplier, might thus face a shortage in the future. It therefore began to take an interest in the import of natural gas from Iran and Afghanistan. Fuel demand in Eastern Europe was kept low in the 1950s, but with industrial expansion and the increase in road transport the relative importance of coal began to decline, and the planners, aware that coal made for a high-cost industry, were looking for alternative sources of energy. With some delay, Eastern Europe thus followed the example of the West.

Western Europe's share of world oil-refining capacity rose from 4 percent before the war to over 20 percent in 1960 with the erection of giant refineries in Rotterdam, Southampton, and Hamburg. The petrochemical industry made great strides, above all in France, and the network of pipelines was greatly expanded in the sixties. The German chemical industry had been traditionally strongest; I. G. Farben had monopolized the field to such an extent that the Allies thought it safer to dissolve this firm at the end of the war. Yet so rapid was the progress of the industry that by the sixties each one of the three successor firms (Hoechst, Bayer, and BASF) produced more than the old I. G. Farben. The output of the European chemical industry trebled between 1950 and 1960; Britain was again overtaken by Germany, while the French and Italian industries, which had started the race well behind these two leaders, developed at an even faster rate than Germany. In all these countries there was a tendency toward the amalgamation of enterprises, partly as the result of stiff competition, partly to meet the need to devote a larger share of capital to research than in any other industry. In Italy, RNI joined forces with Montedison and emerged as the largest single firm on the continent. Only the very largest units could survive the stiff competition unless, like the Belgian firm Solvay, they decided to limit their range of products; the biggest firms, such as Bayer, produced no fewer than twelve thousand different items, most of which had not been known before the war; and there were many new synthetic products which replaced natural fibers, metals, wood, and glass, and others in the petrochemical and pharmaceutical industries. In the Soviet Union the growing importance of the chemical industry was recognized with some delay; preference in investment had always been given to iron and steel. Under Khrushchev an effort was made to correct this disproportion, but it was not easy to catch up with the advance that had meanwhile been made in the West. By 1966 less than 6 percent of the industrial production of the U.S.S.R. originated in the chemical industry, whereas the percentage was twice as high in the developed industrial nations of the West.

The European chemical industries had to compete not only among themselves but also against the giant American concerns such as Du Pont which spearheaded the American economic invasion of Europe. The European industries lacked not know-how and labor but capital to finance their programs of research, innovation, and expansion. American firms succeeded in gaining a foothold in the continental chemical industry above all owing to their greater financial strength. The European chemical industry had been centered in northeastern England (ICI) and in the Rhineland and the Ruhr before the war, but in the fifties and sixties new locations were added: the Maas River, where Shell and ICI established enormous plants, Lyons, and northern and southern Italy.

The postwar growth of the European automobile industry was comparable only to the development of the chemical industry. It had begun to establish itself before the First World War and reached maturity in the twenties and thirties, but its early successes were dwarfed by the development after 1950. Germany emerged in the sixties as the largest producer of motor vehicles, with a yearly output of slightly less than three million passenger cars, whereas Britain and France produced between 1.5 and two million cars each. The Italian industry, too, grew quickly from small beginnings, topping the one-million mark in 1963. Germany was the biggest exporter; in 1961 one million German cars were sold abroad, more than two hundred thousand in the United States alone. Yet inside Europe the share of Volkswagen, the most successful postwar car, declined, whereas Fiat and the French cars advanced during the sixties. By the late 1980s Italy, France, and Britain each produced about two million units annually, whereas the Spanish industry, which had developed quickly in the 1980s, sold almost one million—slightly less than the Japanese share—in the European market. The location of the European car industry has hardly changed. In Britain it is still concentrated in Birmingham and Coventry, Oxford, Luton, and Dagenham. Three of the four major French firms are located in and around Paris, and Fiat's two main factories are in Turin. The one major new development was the emergence of Volkswagen in Wolfsburg, a new town not far from Hanover that owes its existence entirely to the car industry.

The postwar history of the European aircraft industry is less happy. Britain and France developed their commercial jet liners, such as the Caravelle and the Comet, but with the appearance of larger, faster, and above all far more expensive aircraft, neither the French industry, largely state-owned, nor the two British groups (Hawker and BAC), could go on competing with the great American firms.

The European engineering industries had mixed fortunes during the two decades after 1945. The producers of textile, mining, and railway equipment did not fare too well on the whole. Britain, which had been the world's leading shipbuilder, lost out to Japan, which became the world's major producer, accounting for nearly half the total new world tonnage by the end of the sixties, and was also overtaken by Germany. In the Soviet Union great stress was put on the production of machine tools, which became one of Russia's main articles of export. The fastest-developing branch all over Europe was the electrical industry, and more particularly electronics. The main discoveries that paved the way for development of the electronics industry were made before 1914, and television was well established by the 1930s. But the techniques of automation were perfected only with the development of radar and of servomotors during the Second World War. Big American firms like IBM took an immediate lead in the new field of computers, but the phenomenal growth of some European producers, such as the Italian Olivetti and the French Machines Bull and Thomson-Brandt, should also be registered. The biggest European electrical companies were, as before the war, German, British, and Dutch (Siemens, English Electric, and Philips). Philips concentrated on radio, television, and domestic appliances, while the German firms put more stress on the production of heavy equipment (turbines, transformers, etc.).

The overall picture of industrial development in Europe was thus one of intense development and, despite occasional crises and setbacks, of unprecedented prosperity. Western Europe made more rapid progress than the United States, and its living standards were far in advance of the Soviet Union and Eastern Europe.

THE SURGE OF
EUROPEAN AGRICULTURE

During the two decades after the Second World War, country life all over Europe changed out of recognition; technological innovation profoundly affected agriculture, and the traditional peasant village all but disappeared. The number of tractors in use had been fairly negligible before 1945 except in the Soviet Union and Britain; between 1950 and 1962 it increased from 350,000 to 2.6 million in the Common Market countries alone. The use of fertilizers grew by over 85 percent between the 1930s and 1959, and as a result of these and other improvements, productivity in agriculture doubled in France and West Germany between the early fifties and the middle sixties; a shrinking labor force produced far more food than in the prewar years.

The recovery from the ravages of war proceeded at first relatively slowly; it has been estimated that at the end of the war the level of agricultural production was only about two-thirds what it had been before, and in Germany, Austria, and Greece it was still lower. Agricultural yields surpassed the prewar level only in 1949–50 (again with the exception of Germany, Austria, and Greece), and the recovery in the output of livestock products took longer.

As the men returned to the farms, and as investment in agriculture rose, the wartime shortages were overcome. By 1957 agricultural output in Western Europe was about 35 percent higher than twenty years earlier, and it continued to increase steadily. Livestock farming in Britain expanded, while in Denmark there were again more pigs, and in Ireland more cattle, than people. Great progress was made in animal breeding by the introduction of industrial methods, selective breeding, and artificial insemination; battery production increased the output of poultry and eggs. Agricultural education improved all over the continent; better strains of seed were used, and the widespread application of fertilizers and pesticides contributed to the rapid growth in agricultural output.

By the middle sixties the countries of Western Europe, with the exception of Britain, produced over 95 percent of their cereal requirements, almost all the meat they needed, and more than their domestic consumption of potatoes, sugar, and vegetables. There was a glut of milk and butter, and the Common Market countries had to adopt emergency measures to cope with this surplus and to give subsidies to farmers to switch from milk to meat production. The Malthusians, who had predicted for so long that the growth of population would soon outstrip the production of food, were clearly proved wrong.

European agriculture is one of high yields but also of high cost; by and large it is still one of Europe's biggest industries, contributing between 5 and 20 percent of the national income in the countries of Southern Europe, 5 percent in Denmark and Italy, between 1.5 and 5 percent in most other West European countries. France is Western Europe's leading agricultural exporter, the granary of the Common Market and also the chief supplier of meat and sugar, whereas Britain and West Germany are the chief importers of food. The agricultural-labor force of Europe has steadily declined and is at present only about one-third of the prewar level. This decline would have proceeded even more rapidly but for the protectionist policies of most European governments.

The rising standards of life in the cities attracted a great many farmers, especially those of the younger generation. The problem facing most European governments was to speed up structural change and rationalization in agriculture while preventing a mass exodus from the countryside, which would have led to the total collapse of rural society. For a variety of reasons, such as balance-of-payments considerations, but also political expediency, it was necessary to offer the farmers prices high enough to give them incomes comparable to those obtainable in the towns. At the same time it was counterproductive to give such support to backward farms, which puts a premium on efficiency.

Farming subsidies were the decisive factor in bringing about the dramatic increase in food production, but this progress was achieved at a high cost; it slowed down overall economic growth and caused inflationary increases in wages and prices, and the bill for the state subsidies had to be footed above all by the low-income consumer. The question posed to many European countries was: why produce locally what could be bought cheaper elsewhere? From a purely economic point of view there was no convincing case to justify the continuation of subsidies, but political considerations (as well as sentimental reasons) played an important part in the decision to maintain them. The erosion of the peasant economy, the desertion of the countryside, dependence on the import of cheap food from outside were feared, and it became the policy of most European governments to arrest the decline of peasant agriculture despite the high financial and social costs involved.

The liberalization of agricultural trade and the adoption of a common European agricultural policy proved to be an uphill struggle, for there were conflicts of interest between the exporting countries, eager to boost their sales, and those with a less competitive agriculture. It was official French policy to protect agriculture from American and Canadian imports, but at the same time to lower tariffs sufficiently inside Europe so that French agriculture could establish itself as the chief provider of agricultural produce for its neighbors. However, other countries also followed a protectionist policy, even Denmark, which had the most competitive agriculture of all.

The members of the European Community were committed to a common agricultural policy and to liberalizing trade in agricultural products, yet the negotiations between the member states dragged on for many years and ran into untold difficulties and crises. The member states were willing to make a great many concessions on condition that the social and economic structure of their respective agricultural systems was not affected. But the whole point was that structural changes were inevitable to bring about a more rational division of labor in Europe and a common policy.

After protracted negotiations, agreement was reached, as the result of what was called a deal between German industry and French agriculture, on a common policy of fixing farm prices as of July 1, 1967. Reductions of agricultural prices were involved which led to violent demonstrations on the part of French, German, and Belgian farmers. Since the politicians could not ignore the pressure exerted by the powerful agricultural lobby, it was clear that the coordination and rationalization of European agriculture would proceed only at a slow rate. There were other negative aspects: the new Common Market agricultural policy replaced national protectionism by its European counterpart; while promoting trade between the countries of Europe, it reduced world trade by excluding overseas producers such as the United States, Australia, Canada—not to mention the developing countries of the third world. Of all the aspects of European integration, agriculture proved the most complex, and the one most difficult to tackle.

THE TRANSPORT
REVOLUTION

Europe's spectacular industrial and agricultural recovery and its postwar boom would not have been possible without a corresponding expansion in transport. During the war, communications all over Europe had been severely damaged, but the repair work was accomplished more quickly than anyone thought possible in 1945.

The railway network of the United Kingdom (thirty thousand kilometers) had hardly been affected by the war, and those of France and Germany (forty thousand and thirty-five thousand kilometers, respectively) were quickly restored. European railways now had to accommodate a far greater volume of traffic than before; both freight and passenger transport was 60 percent higher in 1957 than in the last year before the war. During the next decade, between 1957 and 1966, progress was much slower, ranging from 15 to 20 percent in Western Europe, as railways met increasing competition from other means of transport (in Britain the volume of freight carried by rail actually declined during this period).

The total length of the railway network began to decrease as uneconomical lines were shut down. The loss caused by wartime destruction had delayed the modernization of the European railway system. Even the countries that made most progress in the use of diesel locomotives and electrification (such as Switzerland) were often forced by their respective governments to operate at unremunerative rates so as to stimulate tourism and commerce. By the middle sixties the nationalized railways of Germany, France, and Britain had to be supported by their respective governments to the tune of $400–800 million per year, and even the Swiss federal railways, which had operated during the fifties at a substantial profit, were running at a loss. But as the roads of Europe became more and more congested, it was clear that the railway age was by no means over and that, irrespective of financial considerations, no country could afford to neglect its railway system.

The merchant fleets of Europe, totaling 37 million registered tons (not counting oil tankers) in 1948, more than doubled in size during the subsequent two decades. The Greek fleet expanded from 1.2 million tons to 7 million, the Norwegian from 4 to 16 million, and the Soviet fleet from 2 to 9 million tons. The British fleet, 18 million tons in 1948, developed at a much slower rate; it counted 21 million tons in 1966. By 1987 the Greek fleet—or, to be precise, the vessels registered as Greek—had expanded to 51 million in tonnage, the Norwegian to 14 million, the Soviet fleet to 28 million, whereas the British had shrunk to 16.8 million. The increase in the number of oil tankers, on the other hand, proceeded all over Europe very quickly, and, with the growing import of Middle Eastern oil, mammoth tankers of over 100,000 (and even 200,000) tons entered service.

The most far-reaching advance revolutionizing the whole transport system took place in the air and on the highways of Europe. Between 1948 and 1965 the volume of airline business (passenger kilometers flown) increased roughly tenfold, and it has continued to rise. Big shiny airports were built in the vicinity of all large cities, very much in contrast to the primitive, ramshackle constructions during the early, "heroic" days of civil aviation. Almost all European airlines were nationalized and enjoyed a near monopoly, with the result that air fares in Western Europe were considerably higher than in the United States (and, incidentally, the Soviet Union).

Transatlantic travel, on the other hand, was considerably cheaper. In 1958, for the first time, more people crossed the Atlantic by air than by sea, and after that sea travel gradually became the preserve of the wealthy tourist—more leisurely but also more expensive than the seven-hour air route. Air transport on shorter routes inside Europe faced difficulties of a different character: congestion in the air and on the ground and the growing distance between airports and cities. The flying time between Paris and London airports was approximately forty-five minutes in the 1960s, much less than in the prewar days, but this increase in speed was offset by congestion on

CAR OWNERSHIP IN EUROPE
(IN MILLIONS)

	1948	1965	1988
France	1.5	9.6	21.0
West Germany	0.2	9.0	26.0
Netherlands	0.08	1.2	5.0
Italy	0.2	5.4	22.3
United Kingdom	2.0	9.0	16.4

the ground; it took as much time, if not more, to reach the center of London or Paris from their respective airports, despite all the technological progress. Delivery of mail, especially over short distances— to give another illustration—also became slower. Fifty years earlier there had been several daily deliveries in most European cities; this was reduced to one or two deliveries a day by the 1960s. As a result, a new industry came into being in the 1980s—private mail delivery.

The motor vehicle had appeared on the inadequate roads of Europe before the First World War, but ownership of cars remained for a long time restricted to a relatively small section of the population, because of high prices and maintenance costs. During the war many cars and trucks had been destroyed and few new ones were built except for military use. In 1948 there were in Western Europe five million cars in use, not counting 2.7 million passenger trucks. By 1957 the number of trucks had doubled and the number of cars trebled. In 1965 the number of cars on the roads of Europe had again trebled, reaching a total of forty-four million. In 1982 it was more than a hundred million.

Road transport was far less developed in the communist countries. Poland, for example, had only about 250,000 cars in 1965 (3.1 million in 1987), less than a tenth of the far less populous Benelux countries. In the sixties Eastern Europe began to make efforts to catch up with the West; in 1966 the Soviet Union signed an agreement with Fiat for an annual production of six hundred thousand cars.

The automobile helped to solve some problems, but it created many others. It made for much greater mobility; millions of blue- and white-collar workers streamed by car every day into London and Paris, Turin and Milan. In Germany and England it was not unknown for many thousands to travel fifty miles or more to their place of work, and in the Paris region more than two million had to make a journey lasting on the average one hour and twenty minutes. With millions more cars in use every year, it seemed that the total paralysis of the roads and cities of Europe, constructed in the pre-automobile age, was only a question of time. The Germans, in the Nazi era, had been the first to build roads of a new type, the Autobahnen. This work was continued, but by 1967 there was less than four thousand kilometers of these multilane motorways. Italy was second, with less than half (including the famous Autostrada del Sole leading from Milan to Naples), followed by Britain, France, and Holland. There was an ambitious program for the construction of further European superhighways across the borders, but the number of cars on the densely populated continent increased even faster, and the rush hour in the metropolitan area became a nightmare for drivers and planners alike.

THE EXPANSION OF
EUROPEAN TRADE

In 1960 Western Europe's share of world trade was almost 40 percent; the Eastern bloc, including the U.S.S.R., accounted for another 12 percent. These figures need to be amplified, for more than half of this trade was between the various European countries, which were one another's best customers. But what remained was still impressive, exceeding the total foreign trade of the United States. It is of some interest to compare these figures with the state of affairs in the late 1980s. In the years that had passed there had been yet another tremendous expansion in world trade; new major exporters had appeared, mainly in the Far East, which had not figured at all in 1960. However, the share of Europe in world trade had hardly changed. West Germany exported more than both the United States and Japan, and though America was the single largest importer of goods, it nevertheless imported considerably less than the combined import of the EEC. The combined exports of France and Italy were larger than those of Japan; those of Holland were as great as those of the Soviet Union.

Before 1914 Europe had been the world's main banker, deriving substantial revenues from its annual $30 billion of investments; these fell after the First World War, but Europe's dependence on world trade, its role as the workshop of the world, was not affected. It had to import food and raw materials and to pay for them by exporting capital goods. Britain, the leading trading nation in the nineteenth century, lost its position, regained it temporarily in the 1930s, but was again overtaken by America after the Second World War, and also by West Germany in 1959. Germany led the postwar European expansion; its trade with foreign countries increased every year between 1948 and 1962 by an average of 16 percent. European trade increased faster than world trade, and this despite the fact that the continent's dependence on the import of food and raw materials (with the exception of crude oil) decreased as it became almost self-sufficient in agricultural produce, and as many raw materials were replaced by synthetic fibers and plastics.

Britain remained the leading European market for the import of food and raw materials, but its pattern of exports changed radically: before 1914 it had exported coal and textiles; after 1945 their share decreased to about 5 percent and the electrical and car industries became the main exporters. The expansion of British foreign trade was much less striking than that of the other European countries (about 2 percent a year on average between 1948 and 1962), partly as the result of internal economic difficulties, partly because of Britain's exclusion from the Common Market, which during the 1950s became the biggest trading unit in the world.

In the early postwar period Britain showed marked reluctance to abandon its ties with the Commonwealth, its most important traditional export market. But the Commonwealth countries meanwhile pursued industrialization programs of their own, and Britain's share in their trade decreased throughout the fifties and sixties while its trade relations with the Common Market countries increased from year to year. Britain sought admission to EEC, and when this was vetoed by the French, EFTA, the European Free Trade Association, consisting of Britain, the Scandinavian countries, Portugal, Switzerland, and Austria, was established in 1960 under British leadership. Though EFTA made a contribution toward the further liberalization of trade in Europe, it was very much an *ad hoc* creation, lacking the political rationale and the wider economic and social aims of the Common Market. Three EFTA members—Britain, Austria, and Switzerland—in fact traded more with the Common Market countries than with their own free-trade associates. EFTA was generally regarded as a temporary stage on the road to a further merger of all European countries into one common market.

As Europe's economic recovery got under way, there were two major obstacles impeding the expansion of trade: the high tariffs imposed by many European countries during the interwar period (and by some even before 1914) and the chronic shortage of dollars, which had become the main international payment medium. There was general agreement that trade should be expanded: GATT (the General Agreement on Tariffs and Trade), founded in 1947, pursued this aim; the Marshall Plan and, in the 1960s, the Kennedy Round were designed to achieve similar objectives. The Common Market envisaged in 1956 a twelve-to-fifteen-year period for the reduction of customs duties and quantitative restrictions. By 1965 customs were down to one-fifth of the 1957 level, and total abolition was envisaged for 1970. Within eight years these measures resulted in an increase of trade among the Common Market countries of about 240 percent, whereas their trade with outside countries expanded by about 100 percent.

The postwar dollar shortage was overcome mainly by Marshall aid, but European discrimination against American imports continued till 1956, and restrictions on capital movements remained in force in most European countries up to 1958. During the 1950s Europe's financial strength substantially increased; its dollar and gold reserves rose from $10 billion in 1950 to about $30 billion in 1964. The "dollar era" thus ended in the 1960s. American government aid to Europe had been discontinued in the late 1950s, and by 1963 more private European money was invested in the United States than vice versa.

Certain long-term trends emerge from an examination of the pattern of Europe's postwar trade. The liberalization of trade had highly beneficial effects; it promoted economic growth and a rational division of labor between European countries, and, through the pooling of resources, made it possible to tackle major projects that would have been out of reach for any single country. Foreign trade was of paramount importance for nations such as Germany and Belgium, where domestic demand alone would not have been sufficient to sustain a high level of economic activity; every sixth worker in German industry was working for export.

The general trend was toward more trade between the various European countries and a lessening of economic ties with the rest of the world. Trade with the Soviet bloc increased but was not of great importance to either EEC or EFTA. This inward-looking character—excepting trade with the U.S.—of the Common Market (and of Europe in general) was widely criticized, mainly because of its impact on outside countries. But Europeans have argued that the trend was a natural one, corresponding to local needs, and that heavy reliance on trade with non-Europeans made the continent too vulnerable to the effects and repercussions of political and economic crises in distant parts of the world.

FRANCE:
MODERNIZATION AND
ITS DISCONTENTS

Postwar economic developments in the various European countries were very similar in some respects and totally different in others. We must turn at this point, therefore, from a broad survey of the common trends to a discussion of specific conditions in the major European countries.

France experienced a boom which was totally unexpected. Not even the most optimistic would have predicted in 1945 an upsurge of this magnitude. France had been the museum of Europe, the country in which nothing ever changed. After 1934 the number of deaths exceeded the number of births. Following the Second World War this trend was suddenly reversed: between 1938 and 1967 the population grew by nine million, from forty-one to fifty million, more than it had grown during the preceding hundred years. The country was unevenly populated; Paris and the north had most of the industry and in consequence a relatively high living standard; the southwest, on the other hand, had lost one-third of its population during the last seventy years. Brittany and the Massif Central were also underdeveloped regions.

Except for iron ore and bauxite, France had few natural resources favoring the development of its industry. It was less industrialized than Britain and West Germany; in 1936, 37 percent of all Frenchmen were still employed in agriculture. Most of the farms in the south and west were too small to be economically viable. Even in industry the small- or medium-size family business was the most common; 60 percent of all industrial enterprises and 90 percent of the retail trade fell into this category as France entered the 1960s. The general mood during the postwar period was far from optimistic, and new initiatives encountered much hostility. The mistaken economic policies of the early postwar French governments, especially their refusal to accept the Mendès-France plan (providing for currency reform and the taxation of war profits), resulted in inflation, the flight of French capital abroad, and a general climate of instability. In these unpromising circumstances Jean Monnet, the father of the plan, and a few of his colleagues maintained that the alternative facing France was modernization or decline: there was no hope that the country could somehow muddle through by adopting half-measures.

In January 1946 an office for overall economic planning was created under the first de Gaulle government, which was to have a growing impact on the development of the French economy. In some respects there had always been more state intervention in the economy in France than in the other European countries, because of its bureaucratic and highly centralized system of administration. But the idea of planning had won new adherents in the years of the resistance, when many had pondered the deeper reasons for France's decline before 1940. The French plan, unlike the Soviet, did not prescribe detailed goals, nor did the planners have the power to compel an enterprise to pursue a certain course of action. It simply provided an indication of the likely (and desirable) overall development during the years to come, but under a number of able directors (Jean Monnet, 1946–52; Etienne Hirsch, 1952–59; Pierre Masse, 1959–65), the planners, with government help, did indirectly influence the course of economic development through the nationalized industries, and by directing credit investment and extending (or withdrawing) tax rebates. The French economy, it was said, had been ruled in the past by the proverbial "two hundred families"; after the war there was no doubt that the balance of power had shifted, for the opinion of a few dozen high government officials mattered far more than the views of all the private captains of industry.

By 1954 a great deal of progress had been made; industrial production, to give but one indication, was 50 percent higher than before the war. The French steel industry had been completely modernized, and the electrical industry had doubled its output. Prototypes of modern cars and aircraft were developed, and the French railway system was about to become the fastest and most efficient in Europe. But progress was limited to these sectors of the economy; the rest continued to stagnate. There was little new construction, and Paris and the other major cities continued to decay. The peasants had no use for the fifty thousand tractors offered by the plan; they wanted to stick to their traditional methods. Despite the stabilization program of the governments of Henri Queuille and René Mayer, prices continued to rise and tax morale remained low. Yet, with all this, the Fourth Republic did increase its gross national product at an average rate of 5 percent a year, a most creditable achievement, the fruits of which were to be reaped by de Gaulle's regime.

Contrary to popular belief, economic advance during the troubled years 1948–58 was greater than during the Gaullist decade (1958–68). Inflation continued in the Fifth Republic at a steady 3–6 percent per year, whereas during the Fourth Republic there had been, on the whole, stability except for the increases (of 12–15 percent) in 1951, 1952, and 1958. It was fortunate for France that the devaluation of 1958 just preceded the 1959 upsurge in world trade; devaluation made French exports more competitive, and they increased in volume by 30 percent within one year. As a result, France's gold reserves grew substantially; the percentage of its GNP that went to exports (16) was as high as that of Britain and Germany, but the percentage of imports (11) was considerably lower, giving France greater self-sufficiency in food and raw materials.

The Gaullists (and many other circles inside France) had been at first strongly opposed to the Common Market; they realized only gradually that France would benefit from European integration more than any other country: French sales to the other EEC countries accounted for 22 percent of its total foreign sales in 1958; ten years later the percentage was 41. French agriculture, in a poor state before 1958, was saved by the Common Market; 18 percent of French agricultural exports went to EEC countries in 1958, more than 50 percent in 1968. Another factor that greatly contributed to French prosperity was, ironically enough, the influx of American capital, about which, for obvious political reasons, the Gaullist regime had mixed feelings.

Four years of economic progress followed after the Gaullists took power in 1958; the GNP grew between 4 and 7 percent per year, and the investment rate was 22 percent of the GNP. The index of per-capita GNP showed a rise from 100 (in 1958) to 126 in 1964, compared with 136 in Italy, 131 in Germany, and 119 in Britain over the same period. Even if the achievements were not equal to those made by Germany and Italy, the most ardent optimists would hardly have anticipated that the output of electrical current, 20 million kilowatts in 1937, would rise more than fivefold to 105 million in 1966, or that the output of steel would go up from 8 million to 19.6 million tons; 34,000 tons of aluminum had been produced in France in 1927, 363,000 in 1966; the production of cement increased from 4 million tons to 23 million tons. In 1937 ships of a total registered tonnage of 27,000 had been built in French docks; in 1966, 430,000.

A new spirit of optimism and confidence prevailed. New industries were established in the underdeveloped regions of the country, and the modernization of agriculture made rapid strides. In view of its successes, the French plan was widely studied abroad; French industrial management, the intellectual infrastructure of its economy, became a source of envy, and French produce gained a high reputation for quality.

There were, admittedly, many shadows. In 1964 and 1965 the French economy stagnated, followed by a fitful upsurge in 1966–67. Total output in 1967 grew by more than 4 percent, but most of this was the result of good harvests, whereas industrial output increased by only 2 percent. France was still the West European country in which industry absorbed the smallest proportion of total manpower, the only country in which the share of employment in manufacturing had actually declined. It was also the only European country that had not solved its housing problem; few new hospitals and schools were built, despite the acute need and the great backlog; not one new school had been built in Paris between the wars. Rising land-prices acted as a further brake on new construction, and there was no clear central housing policy; old tenants benefited from low controlled rents, whereas for younger married couples and workers changing their jobs it was almost impossible to find new homes. French industrial development was held back by the absence of large units comparable to the great firms of Britain, Holland, or West Germany, and by the relatively small allocations to research and development. Many argued that the country was living beyond its means, and that the billions earmarked for de Gaulle's *force de frappe* would have been better employed for other purposes. The big traditional industries, now na-

COST OF LIVING INDICES

	GERMANY	FRANCE	ITALY	BRITAIN	HOLLAND
1958	100	100	100	100	100
1962	108	119	109	112	106
1965	118	132	130	125	122

tionalized, such as coal, steel, and the railways, were overexpanded and showed large deficits. The performance of the new industries was more impressive, but the social climate was far from satisfactory, as the big strikes of May-June 1968 were to show. There were almost half a million unemployed in France in 1968; twenty years later it was more than four times that large. The cost of living was rising faster than in any other major European country. Consumer prices were about 45 percent higher in 1968 than in 1958—the fastest increase in the Common Market countries. All this contributed to a feeling of malaise, and it explains the dissatisfaction experienced in France despite the great progress in industrial expansion and modernization.

THE GERMAN
WIRTSCHAFTSWUNDER

The early phases of West Germany's postwar economic development up to the currency reform of 1948 have been described earlier in the present book. The first indication of what later became known as the economic miracle (the *Wirtschaftswunder*) appeared in 1949–50, when the volume of foreign trade doubled within one year. But the starting point had been so low that it was perhaps even more remarkable that trade rose by 75 percent the year after, and trebled between 1954 and 1964. Industrial production in West Germany increased sixfold between 1948 and 1964, while the level of unemployment fell from 8 or 9 percent in 1949–52 to less than 1 percent in 1961, and to an all-time low of 0.4 percent in 1965. At that time there were six jobs for every person unemployed, and hundreds of thousands of foreign workers (mainly from Italy, Spain, Greece, Turkey, and Yugoslavia) were needed to keep the rapidly expanding German economy going.

German economic policy differed greatly from that pursued in France. There was no overall plan; Erhard and the other neoliberal architects of the miracle were firm believers in the free play of the market forces, of supply and demand. It was not a rigid, nineteenth-century laissez-faire liberalism: they were well aware that state intervention was necessary from time to time, as in 1950, when building was encouraged at a time of slackness, or in 1951, when temporary import restrictions were imposed, and again after 1955, when the rediscount rate was raised to prevent the boom from getting out of hand. The success of Erhard's social market economy (*soziale Marktwirtschaft*) was infectious; even the Social Democrats accepted the principle: competition as far as possible, planning as far as necessary.

German agriculture had been sheltered for generations behind a high protective tariff; it was backward and quite incapable of competing with the neighboring countries, let alone overseas exporters. Subsidies were continued after the war, and agriculture was relieved of direct taxation, with the intention of giving it a respite in which to modernize and become competitive. The wider use of fertilizers was promoted, and the number of tractors in use increased from 138,000 in 1950 to 1.164 million in 1965. As a result of these and other measures, productivity in agriculture in 1964 was two and a half times that in 1950, while the number of those it employed fell from five to three million. The German village within a decade changed its face. Barely recognizable to the visitor who had known it before the war, it had become virtually indistinguishable from the suburb of a big town; there were the same fashions and consumer goods, as many cars and television antennas. The idiocy of rural life of which Marx had written was a thing of the past.

The achievements of the German miracle are impressive but not unique. Italy and Austria made as much progress, and the Japanese performance was even more spectacular. What surprised most observers was that such striking progress was made within such a short time after total defeat. The restrictions imposed by the Allies on German economic development and the dismantling of factories continued well into the early fifties, but by 1958 Germany was already so prosperous that its currency could be made fully convertible. The problems arising from the influx of ten million expellees from the East were thought to be well nigh insoluble, yet within a few years the great majority had been absorbed. At the end of the war many German cities were in ruins, but between 1948 and 1964 eight million dwelling units were constructed, and after 1953 half a million units annually, a higher rate per capita than in any other Western country.

What were the mainsprings of the "German miracle"? Above all, no doubt, German know-how, the presence of millions of skilled workers, and a great industrial tradition. The destruction during the war of so many factories made a radical new beginning possible; the newest machinery was used, and efforts were concentrated on the most promising branches of industry. Germany's success in expanding foreign trade has been mentioned; there was also a very substantial domestic demand for consumer goods that had been suppressed since the great depression. Germany had to spend much less on its defense than its neighbors, and up to the late fifties little if any development aid was extended to the Afro-Asian countries.

The postwar boom was unprecedented in German history. During the seventeen years before the First World War, a period of continuous progress, a rate of growth of 5 percent was exceeded only once; but during the first seventeen years after the Second World War such a rate was achieved no fewer than nine times, and in three years it exceeded 10 percent. Toward the end of the fifties the boom seemed to become uncontrollable; a great deal of foreign capital streamed into Germany, and the government was seriously worried about a possible overheating of the economy. It tried to check the influx of capital by lowering the interest rate and (in 1961) altering the exchange rate of the German mark.

After 1962 the rate of growth slackened; demand slowed, and there were increased labor shortages. In the European growth league Germany was overtaken in the sixties by many countries that had lagged behind during the fifties, and in 1966 it was hit by a real economic recession. There had been some indications of this during the previous year. Under the impact of the crisis, industrial production in 1966 rose only by 1 percent over 1965. In February 1967 there were almost seven hundred thousand unemployed, and many industrial enterprises, including Volkswagen, the symbol of the postwar boom, temporarily introduced a shorter working week. This in its turn had grave psychological effects: a public that had been accustomed to uninterrupted economic growth over a longer period was totally unprepared for a recession, and there were manifestations of near hysteria. According to a public-opinion poll taken at the time, most citizens feared that a crisis of the magnitude of 1929 was just around the corner. German self-confidence was not yet deeply rooted, despite all the achievements of the miracle—the modernization of industry, the fact that it had one of the most stable currencies in the world, and that of the major countries it was least affected by strikes.

In the event, the German economy recovered quickly from the minirecession of the 1960s, German exports continued to rise and the economy again became the envy of the other European countries.

ITALY: FROM
UNCERTAIN BEGINNINGS
TO STORMY GROWTH

Postwar economic developments in Italy and in Germany were similar in some respects, although the "Italian miracle" began later and lasted longer than the German. There were other important differences: Italy as a whole was not a highly developed industrial country; its output before the Second World War had been only about one-third that of Germany. Up to 1956 more Italians were employed in agriculture than in industry.

Like Germany, Italy emerged from the war with an economy that had been severely damaged; industrial output was only one-fifth of what it had been in 1938, and agricultural production was slightly more than half. By 1948 Italian industry had again reached the prewar level, but the recovery of agriculture took a little longer. Inflation was the main problem during the early postwar years, though eventually Einaudi's policy was as successful as Erhard's in Germany. The situation began to ease after 1950, and in 1956 the Italian lira became partly convertible. Italian industry made tremendous strides during the 1950s and accelerated even further during the early 1960s.

In the early sixties Italy made more rapid progress than any other major country in the world, including the Soviet Union and even Japan. This advance was all the more striking in view of Italy's basic poverty; the country lacks raw materials for industrial development and is a major importer of food. The most impressive industrial progress was made in the production of cars and office machinery, and in the electrical industry; by 1967 every third refrigerator produced in Europe was of Italian origin. Existing factories expanded and new ones were established; the steel plant erected in

INDEX OF INDUSTRIAL PRODUCTION

1948	63	1961	200
1953	100	1963	241
1958	142	1966	285

Taranto in the backward south was among the most modern in the world. Italians belied their *dolce far niente* reputation and emerged as the most hardworking and inventive European people. Productivity rose steeply—between 1961 and 1963 alone it went up by about 30 percent.

Tourism brought a growing stream of visitors into the country (twenty-seven million by 1966). Since they mostly came during certain periods and congregated in certain districts, the natives of Rome, Venice, and above all the coastal resorts found themselves at times outnumbered by the millions of tourists from the North.

Italian workers used to walk to their factories in the years after the war or get there by bicycle. In a famous postwar film the disaster that befell a family when the bicycle was stolen was given dramatic expression. In 1960 one out of twenty-one Italians was the owner of a car; by 1968, one out of seven; In 1986 almost one out of two. Italians had about as many telephones and television sets per thousand inhabitants as the French. The standard of living in northern Italy in the sixties approached that of its most highly industrialized neighbors on the continent; there was hardly any difference between Milan or Turin and metropolitan centers in France or Germany. The backwardness of southern Italy continued to have a marked effect on the general picture; 36 percent of the total population lived in the south, but they accounted for less than 25 percent of the national income, despite years of effort to develop the south, also called the Mezzogiorno, large-scale investment and development projects. The gulf between north and south widened further during the fifties and sixties, and there was a mass migration from southern Italy to the northern towns (and to Germany and France); entire villages were left without men, and in some places only the older generation remained. Not all were easily employable: in the 1951 census, five million Italians were found to be illiterate, and many more semiliterate. The effects of centuries of neglect could not be repaired in a few years.

Between 1959 and 1961 Italy's economy grew at such a fast rate (about 7.5 percent per year) that the government, fearing inflation, took measures to curtail both domestic consumption and investment. The rate of growth fell to 4.8 percent in 1963 and to about 3 percent in 1964–65, but rose again to 5.5 percent in 1965–67. While other European countries complained about stagnation, Italy forged ahead: its exports increased by a further 60 percent between 1964 and 1967. As a late starter, Italy could avoid many of the mistakes of the older industrial nations; unlike Britain and Germany, it was not burdened by outdated coal mines and still plants. The textile industry was one of the weaker links in the Italian economy, but the situation was not dissimilar in other European countries.

Italy, some foreign critics have claimed, could outsell its rivals because wages were for a long time considerably lower. There was also a substantial and apparently intractable residue of unemployment—almost 7 percent of the total labor force, 1.4 million, in 1961. Even during the boom years of the late sixties, the number of unemployed hovered around the one-million mark. There was, however, no deliberate policy to maintain an "industrial reserve army" to keep wages down. On the contrary, wages went up substantially during the sixties and in northern Italy were nearly on a par with the neighboring countries. Italian unemployment was largely a social problem; the migration of the agricultural laborers from the south into the cities of the north continued without interruption. During 1968 half a million such newcomers were counted, and they all too often lacked the skills needed for industrial employment.

The Italian *miracolo economico* received less publicity than the German *Wirtschaftswunder*, but in its overall effects it was even more impressive. As in Germany and in France, the achievement tended to overshadow the shortcomings; Italian agriculture, subdivided into diminutive holdings, had not shared equally in the general boom, not enough schools and new roads had been built, and not enough money was spent on higher education and research. Capital supply was exceedingly limited, and even the most substantial Italian firms (such as Olivetti) found themselves at one time or another on the brink of collapse and in need of state support. Fiat, Italy's largest enterprise, was an exception. It had developed in particularly favorable circumstances behind high protective tariffs in the fascist era. For many years it had a virtual monopoly on the domestic market. Fiat put the years of high protection to good use, and by the 1950s had become a very efficient and competitive producer. Whereas many Italian industrialists were at first fearful of the implications of the Common Market, the owners and managers of Fiat had no such doubts, and subsequent events justified their optimism.

By the middle sixties about 20–30 percent of Italy's industry, including 60 percent of its steel production, was controlled by the government. Of the nine biggest companies five were state-owned (Montecatini-Edison, IRI, ENI, Finsider, and Finmeccanica), and only four were in private hands (Fiat, Pirelli, Olivetti, and Suia Viscosa). Within the framework of the state corporations there was a wide scope for empire builders, like Mattei: ENI was established to produce hydrocarbons and exploit natural gas, but under Mattei's rule it became a giant holding company, owning, *inter alia,* the daily *Il Giorno* of Milan (Fiat owned *La Stampa* in Turin) and a corporation engaged in motel construction.

BRITAIN: STOP-GO

The performance of Britain's economy in the first postwar decades has entered the annals of history as a tale of woe, of constant balance-of-payments crises, of overspending and living on credit. The U.S. loan was exhausted in 1948, and in the following year the pound was devalued from $4.03 to $2.80. The outbreak of the Korean War made a new rearmament program necessary; defense expenditure rose from 6 to 10 percent of the national income, and the building program and other reconstruction projects had to be cut to meet the bill. There were further balance-of-payments crises in 1955, 1957, 1961, and 1967–68. In 1967 the pound was again under heavy pressure, and only another devaluation and massive foreign intervention saved sterling from collapse.

The crises in the British balance of payments and the consequent fluctuations in the economy recurred so frequently and proved so difficult to overcome that in the end they came to be regarded, in Postan's words, "not only as painful affliction but also as a symptom of an organic malaise of the British body economic." Up to the 1950s both Germany and France had a living standard considerably lower than that of the United Kingdom, but in the sixties Britain was overtaken by its two rivals. This decline had begun well before 1945. In 1880 Britain, Germany, and the United States were each producing about one million tons of steel; in 1913 Britain produced eight million, Germany seventeen million, and the United States thirty-one million. But it was only a relative decline: Britain's GNP grew between 1948 and 1962 by 2.5 percent a year (3.5 percent between 1947 and 1950, 3.3 percent between 1960 and 1965), which compares favorably with any other period in modern British history (1.7 percent between 1870 and 1913, 2.2 percent between 1924 and 1937). The rise in the standard of living was on an unprecedented scale, and Mr. Macmillan's famous slogan of the 1959 election campaign, "You've never had it so good," was quite correct, strictly speaking. Britain did not stagnate; it simply advanced at a slower rate than the other major countries. Its share in world trade fell steadily during the postwar period—from 21.3 percent in 1951 to 19 percent in 1956. Two and a half percentage points (as Andrew Shonfield has pointed out) may not seem very much, but this was in fact equivalent to $1 billion of export earnings.

Various reasons have been adduced to explain Britain's relative decline after 1945. It has been argued that the welfare state became too expensive, that the state took too large a proportion of the national income, and that direct taxation was too high. But in France the state took an even larger proportion, and taxation in both Germany and France was higher than in Britain and almost as high in the United States. It is also asserted that Britain did not spend enough on research and development, and as a result fell behind the other countries, but a comparison of the figures shows that Britain spent more on R & D than any other European country, and, in proportion to the GNP, almost as much as the United States. Yet another school of thought has maintained that the poor British investment performance has been the root of the evil. The figures seem irrefutable in this respect; Britain was indeed at the bottom of the league:

	INVESTMENT RATIOS 1955–64 %	GROSS SAVINGS AS % OF DISPOSABLE INCOME 1964
Japan	28.2	25.2
Germany	23.7	13.1
France	19.2	12.8
Sweden	22.8	10.2
U.S.A.	17.1	10.1
Britain	15.8	7.7

When confronted with a crisis during the postwar period, it seemed to be the policy of the British government to cut investment first. The decline of the British shipbuilding industry might serve as an illustration. Britain had many advantages at the end of the war to enable it to recover its leading position in this field—well-equipped yards, a highly skilled labor force, and a full order book. But the owners were reluctant to invest in new productive capacity, with the result that tonnage built fell from 1.2 million in 1949 to 1 million in 1965, while tonnage built in Japan increased from 0.1 to 5 million during the same period.

A great deal of responsibility falls on British trade unions and management. Wages have consistently risen faster than output and productivity. There was a 20-percent wage increase in real terms between 1951 and 1958, and a further 30-percent increase between 1958 and 1964. Under Stafford Cripps the trade unions accepted a wage freeze on the understanding that the government would hold down the price level; ever since, the union leaders have regarded such policies with great distrust and more often than not have refused to collaborate with the government. As a result, British products became so expensive that they were not competitive on world markets. Much damage to the economy was done by the antiquated structure of the trade-union movement (the existence of six hundred unions compared with sixteen in West Germany), with their guild-and-craft-union mentality and their unending internecine fights about who should do what job. Frequently the work of many thousands of workers was paralyzed by the action of a few hundred craftsmen striking for their own factional interest. There were wildcat strikes over whether the tea break should be at ten or eleven o'clock; nowhere did people go on strike on such frivolous grounds as in Britain. It was not so much the militancy of the trade unions that caused the disruption as their inability to think in modern terms, to adjust their outlook to the changes in technology and organization.

Management bore an equal share of responsibility. Britain had been the pioneer of the industrial revolution, but the tradition of inventiveness and initiative seemed to have exhausted itself. The level of managerial know-how was low, and there was not much interest in learning new methods; everyone talked about the need to export, but the efforts were often amateurish and the after-sales service provided inferior to that of other trading nations. In an interesting study, Professor Dunning has shown that within the British economy the section under American control has consistently yielded 50 percent more return than British firms, because of lower administrative costs, better salesmanship, high productivity, and greater capital intensity.

The economic malaise was partly due to wrong policy decisions taken at the top or, equally often, to indecision. By 1949 Labour had exhausted its ideas on how to run the economy; important branches had been nationalized, but 80 percent of the total was still in private hands, and to that sector the party had no lead to give. The Conservatives were at first luckier. When they came to power in 1951, it was possible to dismantle many of the wartime restrictions. Between 1952 and 1954 prices of raw materials went down by 25 percent, which meant a substantial reduction in Britain's import bill. But after the boom of 1952–54 there were again several years of stagnation. Labour and Conservative alike were opposed to joining Europe; they "knew in their bones" (as Anthony Eden said in 1952) that they could not join a European federation. Hugh Gaitskell, the new leader of the Labour Party, was hardly less emphatic. Meanwhile, Germany and Italy increased their exports six times as fast as Britain, and Macmillan and Harold Wilson reluctantly reached the conclusion that there was no alternative to joining the Common Market.

It would be unfair (and unhistorical) to ignore the objective circumstances that aggravated the British malaise. As a result of the war, Britain had lost most of its prewar income from overseas and found itself saddled with growing debts. Its financial and defense obligations overseas, and the remaining imperial commitments, constituted a heavy burden. It was clear that the country could not shoulder this burden indefinitely, but it was not at all easy to find immediate solutions: Britain could not opt out of history and could not change basic geographical facts. More densely populated than France, Italy, or West Germany, it needed to import more raw materials and foodstuffs than its continental neighbors and rivals.

No single factor, but a combination of circumstances, caused Britain's postwar difficulties. It was a constant vicious circle: the growth of the economy was held back by deflationary policies which were adopted to combat rising prices and inflation. Most other European countries, too, had recourse to a "stop-go" policy, but much less often, and they made greater progress between the stops. Successive British governments applied various measures to deal with the recurring crises: devaluation, cuts in defense spending, import controls, and export incentives. But these were palliatives; the main problems remained: to increase efficiency, to improve organization, to invest more wisely, and, generally speaking, to make the most of resources.

ECONOMIC
DEVELOPMENT IN
THE REST OF EUROPE

A striking feature of Europe after the war was the great similarity in the economic development of the small countries.

Between 1954 and 1964 industrial output doubled in Holland, Sweden, and Austria, countries that had little in common. On a different level, economic development took much the same course in Spain and Greece. These two countries faced similar problems, such as the need to find capital for investment in industry; their GNP grew in the sixties at about the same high rate (7–8 percent). In 1964 per-capita income in Spain was $570, in Greece $590. There were trends common to all European countries irrespective of their past history, geographical position, and economic structure.

Spain had stagnated for centuries. The consequences of the civil war of 1936–39 had paralyzed its economy for two decades, but a change began to be felt in the late fifties, after Spain joined the United Nations and expanded its foreign trade. The rigid economic regulations were abolished, and the country was exposed to the fresh wind of the free market; the government tried by trial and error to modernize the economic structure. There was also progress in Spanish agriculture; average output went up by one-third in the decade after 1956. Following substantial French, German, and American investment in Spanish industry, there was a marked upswing in industrial production after 1958, and the GNP grew at a faster rate than even the Italian. But since the starting point had been so low, there remained a great deal of leeway to be made up: even after a decade of boom, per-capita income in Spain was only one-third that of the Scandinavian countries. Tourism was an important source of income; it developed rapidly in the late fifties and sixties as Spain overtook France, and, with seventeen million visitors in 1966, it took second place in Europe, after Italy.

The boom in Greece had started a few years earlier than in Spain; the devaluation of the drachma had given a powerful stimulus to economic recovery. Between 1953 and 1963 the GNP grew at an average rate of 6.3 percent; in 1966 it reached 8 percent; but the country was still predominantly agrarian, and the value of industrial output did not exceed that of agriculture until 1965. Inflation and political instability jeopardized the development in the sixties. The merchant fleet was a powerful economic asset, and though the influx of tourists was not on the same scale as in Spain, the flow of visitors continued to grow from year to year and represented in 1964 about 13 percent of the value of exports.

Both Holland and Belgium had suffered greatly during the war, and their recovery was at first slow. The two countries were hit by a recession in 1958, but Holland recovered more quickly and, generally speaking, made quicker progress. Its GNP grew at an average rate of 5.4 percent per year between 1958 and 1966. The Belgian advance had been among the most sluggish on the continent in the fifties (2.7 percent), but it gathered speed in the early sixties (3.6 percent). Belgium had always been more industrial in character, and it was more heavily affected by the general European crisis in the coal industry and heavy metallurgy. Agriculture, however, provided more than 80 percent of domestic consumption, thus reducing the import bill. Both countries lost their empires in Africa and Southeast Asia after the war, but this had surprisingly little effect on their economic development; on the contrary, Holland forged ahead more quickly than ever before, extending its chemical and electrical industries and improving its agriculture.

Switzerland was one of the few European countries that had been only indirectly affected by the war. No recovery schemes were necessary. Its postwar economic development proceeded at a slow and uneventful rate, but toward the late fifties, in the wake of the general European boom, its progress quickened, resulting in an average yearly increase of 6 percent in the GNP between 1958 and 1964. This sudden spurt caused rising prices and inflation, as in other parts of Europe, and the Swiss government adopted a stabilization program in 1964 to slow down the expansion.

The Austrian boom lasted even longer; there was a steady annual growth of almost 6 percent in the GNP between 1953 and 1964, but Austria had started at a considerably lower level than Switzerland. The country suffered, moreover, from a lack of capital to promote industrialization, and its excision from the Common Market had a detrimental effect on its economic development. Twenty-two percent of Austria's industry had been nationalized, including 60 percent of all big enterprises. There was a marked shift during the fifties from agriculture to industry; industrial output doubled between 1938 and 1954, and again between 1954 and 1965.

Sweden, like Switzerland, had emerged unscathed from the war. And, like that of Switzerland, its growth during the fifties was steady but unexciting; between 1958 and 1964 it gathered speed and reached an average yearly increase in the GNP of 5.1 percent. Also like Switzerland, it faced a shortage of labor and had to adopt restrictive measures in 1964 to prevent the boom from getting out of hand. Sweden's industry was high-cost and highly specialized, but famous for its quality products; it exported about half of its industrial output and succeeded in doubling its exports between 1955 and 1965. Despite the lack of important natural resources, it attained the highest living standard in Europe, and one of the highest in the world.

Neighboring Denmark and Norway are dissimilar in their economic structure. The former has a highly developed agriculture, whereas in the latter the merchant and fishing fleets are of paramount importance. Both participated in the general boom that lasted from 1958 to 1963 in Denmark and to 1964 in Norway. Danish attempts to curb the inflationary pressures offer an interesting illustration of the effects of a stop-go policy; its GNP rose by 0.8 percent in 1963, by 7.4 in 1964, by 4.7 in 1965. The country experienced difficulties in finding export markets for its agricultural produce because of its exclusion from the Common Market, and there was a deliberate shift toward investment in industry.

The pattern that emerges in all these smaller European countries is consistent: the postwar recovery was followed by years of comparatively slow growth in the fifties, but toward the end of the decade the movement gathered momentum, and there followed a boom of five to seven years' duration. Since the middle sixties this development has again slowed down. Seen in a wider context, the postwar era was a period of unprecedented economic prosperity for all European countries, although considerable differences continued to prevail between them—the per-capita GNP was still almost ten times higher in Sweden than in Turkey—and there were also great differences within the various countries, such as the disparity between northern and southern Italy.

PER-CAPITA GNP IN U.S. $

	1965	1966	1990
Austria	1,270	1,380	19,140
Belgium	1,780	1,910	17,500
Denmark	2,100	2,320	23,700
France	1,920	2,250(1967)	19,200
W. Germany	1,900	2,400(1967)	22,900
Greece	590(1964)	690	
Holland	1,550	1,670	
Iceland	2,470	2,850	
Ireland	920	1,010	10,000
Italy	1,100	1,350(1967)	16,300
Norway	1,880	2,020	25,300
Portugal	420	430	4,900
Spain	570(1964)	770	10,400
Sweden	2,500	2,730	25,000
Switzerland	2,330	2,480	31,500
Turkey	250	290	1,500
United Kingdom	1,810	2,050(1967)	16,300
United States	3,560	3,840	22,200

THE SOVIET ECONOMY

The Soviet economy recovered quickly from the destruction of war. Steel production, which had reached 18 million tons in 1940, was down to 12 million in 1945, but climbed to 34 million in 1952, the year before Stalin's death. The figures for coal are 166 million tons in 1940, 149 million at the end of the war, and 300 million in 1952. The recovery in the output of crude oil was even more spectacular: 31 million tons in 1940, 19 million in 1945, and 199 million in 1952. Progress in agriculture was much less impressive, because of a number of adverse harvests, and especially as the result of the low priority accorded to agriculture in the Soviet economy.

Under Stalin the economic system was geared to the attainment of certain strategically important goals in certain key industries, to the detriment of everything else. It was to all intents and purposes a war economy, even in days of peace. It imposed the tightest controls, concentrated all available resources on the development of heavy industry, and severely restricted occupational mobility. The political price that had to be paid was a ruthless dictatorship, constant purges, terrorism, and forced-labor camps, with millions of inmates, as an institutionalized part of the regime. It succeeded in keeping consumption low and maintaining a high rate of investment; the whole system was based on the exploitation of agriculture, which provided the surplus for capital formation. From 1928 to 1955 gross investment grew twice as fast as the GNP, and three times as fast as consumption. Russia under Stalin provided (to quote Harry Schwartz) a classic case of forced rapid industrialization. "Tens of millions of Russians were transferred from agriculture to industrial and other non-farm occupations. A massive transfusion of scientific and technical knowledge from abroad was injected into Soviet society, producing a large cadre of skilled workers and a substantial technological elite of scientists." Stalin expanded the range of Soviet industrial production and raised the physical volume enormously; under him Russia became the world's second industrial power. Measured in these terms, his rule was no doubt a great success.

It is not at all certain, however, that this was the only road open to the Soviet Union; other countries made greater progress during the postwar period without paying such a terrible price in human suffering. While Soviet heavy industry mushroomed and the armed forces were given the highest priority, the standard of living remained among the lowest in Europe. Stalinist economists argued that the concentration on heavy industry created the preconditions for all-round economic development and thus eventually for a general rise in the standard of living. But these predictions were only half fulfilled; the standard of life did rise, but less quickly than in most other Western nations. In the major European nations real wages more than doubled between 1950 and 1966; in the Soviet Union they increased only by 83 percent, according to official figures which are open to some doubt; they should have risen much faster, since the starting point in the Soviet Union was so much lower.

Great demographic changes have taken place during the last thirty years. The population of the Soviet Union grew from 170 million in 1939 to 234 million in 1970. The growth was even quicker in the Asian regions of the country than in European Russia, the result partly of deportations or population transfers, partly of a high birthrate. Russia was predominantly agrarian; even by the late 1960s about 36 percent of the population was still employed on the land, though the percentage was falling. Urbanization made steady progress, but in the year Stalin died the majority of Soviet citizens still lived in the countryside, and only in 1961 did city dwellers for the first time outnumber the rural population. The birthrate declined from twenty-six per thousand in 1958 to eighteen per thousand in 1966, and in the same period the natural population increase fell from eighteen to fourteen per thousand.

Stalin's successors tried to tackle the urgent problems facing them. They believed, like Stalin, that priority should be given to heavy industry, but they realized that the national economy as a whole was bound to suffer if the disproportion between heavy industry and agriculture remained too pronounced. The failure of agriculture under Stalin was concealed by spurious statistics; in 1952, for instance, the grain yield was officially stated to have been about 125 million tons, whereas the real harvest was only 90 million, as Khrushchev revealed six years later. After Stalin's death, a major effort was made to improve the food supply by cultivating the virgin lands of western Siberia and Kazakhstan, by paying higher prices to the *kolkhoz* farmers, and by lifting some of the restrictions affecting work on their private plots. The 1953 harvest was a disaster—82 million tons, less than the yield in tsarist Russia in 1913—and 1954 was not a much better year. After that the results of the new policy were increasingly felt: 127 million tons were harvested in 1956, 141 million in 1958, and a record harvest, admittedly in very favorable climatic conditions, of 170 million in 1966–67. In between there were setbacks, and the Soviet Union was forced to import wheat from Canada and other countries. In other fields achievements were even less striking: the number of cattle in 1966 was 93 million compared with 60 million in tsarist Russia; there were 137 million sheep and goats (as against 121 million before the First World War), while the number of pigs had almost trebled. Meat production consequently grew at a slow rate, from 8 million tons (average in 1946–50) to 10.8 million in 1966. This in turn affected the cost of living; in January 1962 the retail price of meat went up by 30 percent.

Malenkov, in a speech not long after Stalin's death, had promised "an abundance of food for the people and of raw materials for consumer-goods industries in the next two or three years." But this would have meant a radical shift in priorities, the investment of far more capital in consumer goods and agriculture. This policy, the "new course," encountered stiff resistance from other Soviet leaders, who demanded priority for heavy industry and for the requirements of the army. In the contest between guns (or, to be precise, rockets) and butter, most of the old leaders opted for continuity in economic policy, and Malenkov's proposals were defeated. Nevertheless, his initiative had not been altogether in vain, for some of his suggestions were adopted by his successors; important reforms continued in both industry and agriculture after his downfall. The virgin-lands program got under way, the Machine-Tractor Stations were disbanded, minimum wages were raised, and there were changes in industrial organization: twenty-five ministries were abolished as part of a drive to combat overcentralization. More attention was paid to urban housing: construction completed in 1958 was twice as high as that in 1955. Altogether the output of Soviet industry and agriculture in 1958 was thought to be more than a third above that of 1954.

Economic growth during this period was impressive, but toward the end of the fifties there was growing evidence of a slowdown; in 1957 the sixth five-year plan had to be scrapped as a new dispute over the allocation of resources developed. The Soviet leadership was overcommitted; it tried to accomplish too much in too many directions at the same time. It attempted to match the military-space program of the United States, even though the resources at its disposal were much more limited; it had opted for large-scale investment in new industrial plant and equipment; and the returns from farming in the virgin lands proved to be disappointing after the first, successful harvests. The rate of growth fell as defense spending increased by one-third between 1959 and 1963. In absolute terms, the key industries continued to make great progress even after 1958.

Steel output rose from 54 million tons in 1958 to 84 million in 1964; oil production doubled (113 million tons to 225 million), as did the output of electricity and cement (33 million tons to 63 million). Soviet steel production in 1963 was greater than that of Britain, France, and West Germany combined, and equaled 80 percent of American production; in 1968 it reached 85 percent of the United States'. But industrial growth as a whole was less impressive, and the Soviet leaders were troubled by the declining rate of development, from 13 percent in 1954 to 10 percent in 1958 and 7.5 percent in 1964. The decline in the rate of growth of the gross national product was even more marked. It had been 10 percent in 1958, when the Soviet GNP was said to be about 44 percent of the American. This was a considerable advance over 1950 (32 percent) and 1955 (36 percent), but in 1961 it fell to 6.5 percent, in 1962 and 1963 it did not exceed 3 percent, and though there was a recovery in 1964 (7–8 percent), progress during the years following was again less striking.

At the Twenty-first Congress of the Communist Party, Khrushchev had declared that by 1970 the Soviet Union would outproduce the United States not merely in absolute terms but also on a per-capita basis. These boasts were soon forgotten; two days after Khrushchev's fall in 1964, *Pravda* editorially denounced the style of the deposed leader, his "harebrained scheming, immature conclusions, hasty decisions, and actions divorced from reality." The Soviet workers and peasants had been promised lower prices, a shorter work week, and, generally speaking, a much higher standard of living, but the price index of food was actually higher in 1964 than at the beginning of the Khrushchev period, and the production of textiles (to give another example) had increased only slightly. The goals of the seven-year plan (1959–65) had to be revised in view of continuing imbalances—steel and machinery construction made faster progress than anticipated, but other industries, and above all agriculture, were again lagging behind. The virgin lands had produced a good harvest in 1958 but failed to equal, let alone exceed, their performance thereafter. The economy was suffering from an acute capital shortage, and the somewhat halfhearted attempts to obtain loans from the West bore little fruit. Fulfillment of the seven-year plan was further impeded by additional increases in military spending between 1961 and 1963, which in a critical period withdrew important resources in manpower and materials from the national economy.

In 1957 the country was subdivided into a number of large economic units (the *sovnarkhozy*) to make for more effective economic planning and to lessen the effect of the dead hand of a centralized bureaucracy. This new emphasis on regionalism was not, however, successful, for within the framework of the Soviet economic system the coordination of the overall plan was possible only on the basis of information available nowhere but in Moscow. Khrushchev's successors therefore returned to the centralized ministerial planning system. These gropings for a new form of organization reflected the general feeling that the existing planning and control techniques were unsuited for an economic system that was becoming year by year more diverse and sophisticated. The innovators were given some scope for experimentation, but the reforms did not go very deep. A great many unsolved questions remained, above all the problem of striking a viable balance between plan and market: "What should be the role of the political leadership and of the central planners? Should prices be allowed to fluctuate in response to supply and demand? If they are so allowed, then how would the state exercise control over the economy?" as Alec Nove posed the question. Western observers sometimes tended to overrate the political effect of the economic reforms.

It remains to be noted that some East European countries were less cautious than the Soviet Union in applying the new ideas: in 1967 about 30 percent of all prices in Hungary were determined by market forces rather than by the plan; in the Soviet Union the percentage was probably nearer 5.

Khrushchev's downfall was partly connected with the setbacks of the Soviet economy in 1962–63. In one of his last speeches before that event, he argued in a spirit of self-criticism that even large allocations of capital would fail to have the desired effect if the investments were spread over an enormous number of projects. His successors faced the same dilemma. They said they regarded the development of heavy industry as of foremost importance, but they also demanded an instant improvement in agriculture. They promised higher living standards but at the same time announced higher military spending. Agriculture was initially given high priority, but after the good harvests of 1966–67 investment in agriculture was again reduced. Money incomes were increased, and the rate of consumer-goods production, which had steadily decreased during the last two decades, went up again in 1966–67.

SOVIET GROWTH

CAPITAL-GOODS INDUSTRIES		NONDURABLE CONSUMER GOODS
	PERCENTAGE	
1951–55	12.4	10.0
1956–60	13.0	6.9
1961–65	11.3	4.8

But consumer demand was not even remotely satisfied; though retail sales went up by 36 percent between 1961 and 1966, personal savings rose during the same period almost six times as fast. The burden of defense expenditure became heavier from year to year; it rose from about 9 billion rubles in 1960 to almost 17 billion in 1968. These were the official figures; the real cost of the competition with America in the field of rocketry and nuclear weapons was probably even higher. At the same time, the rate of investment in the national economy fell sharply; in the 1960s it was little more than half of what it had been in the previous decade. As far as quantity was concerned, achievements were still impressive; according to the official statistics, the

Soviet Union had a higher GNP per capita than Italy and Japan. But hardly anyone familiar with conditions in these countries would maintain that the standard of living of the average Soviet citizen was equal (let alone superior) to that of the average Italian or Japanese. By 1990 it was probably lower than in Portugal—and declining.

THE INDUSTRIALIZATION
OF EASTERN EUROPE

For the first decade after the Second World War the economic development of the communist countries of Eastern Europe closely followed the Soviet pattern, but there was greater diversity after 1955. During the immediate postwar period, following the communist takeover, industry was nationalized and the first measures to collectivize agriculture were carried out. The economies of Eastern Europe were exploited to speed up the recovery of the Soviet economy: Moscow exacted its tribute from some of its satellites in the form of reparations; elsewhere joint companies were set up, giving the Soviet Union a dominating position. Russia insisted that the people's democracies direct their foreign trade toward Moscow. One of the instruments for coordinating the economic activities of the Soviet Union and its allies was the Council for Mutual Economic Assistance (CMEA or Comecon), established in January 1949. It was not an alliance between equals: the Soviet exports of raw materials and machinery were well above world-market prices, whereas the people's democracies were forced to sell their goods to Russia cheaply. Industrial progress was nevertheless made in Eastern Europe, though at an appalling price. The industrial output in East Germany and Czechoslovakia almost doubled between 1948 and 1955, and in the less industrialized countries, starting from a lower level, it rose even faster. According to official figures, the national income in Bulgaria and Rumania rose between 1950 and 1955 at the rate of 12 and 14 percent a year respectively, and in Yugoslavia even faster, a performance never again repeated by any other East European country. How meaningful these and similar figures really are, no one can say;

there is no doubt that the foundations of industrialization were laid during that period in the less developed countries, but the imbalances of Stalinism were even more palpable there than in the Soviet Union, particularly the dislocation in agriculture following collectivization and the effects of heavy spending on defense. After Stalin's death, Malenkov's new course was adopted for a little while in Eastern Europe as well as in the Soviet Union. Wages were increased, prices and taxes cut; investment in heavy industry was temporarily reduced, agricultural production boosted. An attempt was made to reduce the dangerous economic tensions that had developed, but in some countries these reforms did not come in time. There was unrest in East Germany and Czechoslovakia, and on a far more dangerous scale in Poland and Hungary. The Soviet Union was forced to reconsider its whole relationship with the popular democracies, and the grosser forms of exploitation ceased. In some instances Moscow had to come to the help of its allies by extending credits, canceling debts, and taking other emergency measures.

Under Khrushchev the policy of economic integration of the Soviet bloc was pursued, and the East European countries became even more dependent on Moscow for deliveries of raw materials required for their industrialization programs. There was more diversity: Poland was in no hurry to collectivize its agriculture, and in Hungary in 1958 there were only half as many collective farms as in 1956. All over the Soviet bloc the rate of growth was lower during the second half of the fifties than before; in Rumania and East Germany it was only half the rate of the early fifties. During 1960–65, again following the Soviet pattern, it fell even further, except in Rumania. In Czechoslovakia and Hungary these were years of virtual standstill. The average yearly growth of the GNP in Czechoslovakia during 1961–65 was 1.3 percent; nowhere in the Eastern bloc did it exceed 5 percent. After 1965 most East European countries recovered from the crisis, and economic progress quickened again.

The industrially backward countries of Eastern Europe made much faster progress than East Germany and Czechoslovakia. The disparity in their rates of growth became significant in particular during the second decade, after they had overcome initial difficulties (such as balance-of-payments problems). Agricultural production, on the other hand, was lagging behind in all of them; the situation was most favorable in Rumania and Poland, but in Czechoslovakia, East Ger-

	INDEX OF INDUSTRIAL PRODUCTION 1938 = 100 (1964)	INDEX OF AGRICULTURAL PRODUCTION 1938 = 100 (1960–63 AVERAGE)	PER-CAPITA GNP 1964 U.S. $
Bulgaria	625	111	690
Rumania	498	129	680
Poland	370	132	890
Hungary	314	98	1,020
Czechoslovakia	242	92	1,470
East Germany	208	80	1,400

many, and Hungary average output was below the prewar yield. (The index of agricultural production in France and Italy, for example, was 151 and 147 respectively, compared with the last prewar year.) Since most East European countries were still predominantly agrarian in structure, the stagnation in agriculture depressed the economic performance as a whole. Despite all the industrialization efforts, per-capita income in Bulgaria and Rumania in the middle sixties was not substantially higher than in Greece. Twenty years after the end of the war, per-capita income in the more developed Comecon countries was still twice as high as in Bulgaria and Rumania, and per-capita income in the industrialized countries of Western Europe was still almost twice as high as in Czechoslovakia and East Germany, and more than twice that of Hungary. Two bumper harvests in succession and a speed-up in the production of consumer goods in 1966–68 accounted for a marked rise in income per head in most East European countries, but as it subsequently appeared this recovery did not constitute the beginning of a long-term trend.

Comecon was the arena of much dissension between the Soviet Union and its junior partners. With the secession of China from the bloc, which incidentally also had economic consequences, and the spread of polycentrism, political and economic nationalism asserted itself. There were few difficulties with East Germany and Bulgaria, in view of their political dependence on the Soviet Union; three-quarters of Bulgarian trade was with Russia and the other bloc countries, and East Germany remained not only Russia's most faithful ally but also its most important trading partner. Among the others, however, there were many complaints; Rumania was in open rebellion, maintaining that the internal division of labor decided upon by Comecon was detrimental to its economic interest and impeded its industrial development. Czechoslovakia, Hungary, and Poland argued that they had to pay prices considerably above world-market prices for Soviet raw materials, while for their part the Russians contended that the products they bought from Eastern Europe were not up to world-market quality, and that, in any case, world-market prices were not appropriate as a yardstick in trade relations between socialist countries; Moscow was firmly opposed to any attempts by its allies to attract Western capital and technological expertise. On the other hand, it insisted that Eastern Europe together with the Soviet Union provide military and industrial equipment, sometimes free of charge and always on special terms, to Egypt, India, and other Asian and African countries, usually in the pursuit of Soviet foreign-policy objectives. Such Soviet demands were not necessarily in the best interests of the East European countries, and a great deal of ideological, political, and even military pressure was needed to overcome their lack of enthusiasm. Certain concessions had to be made by the Soviet Union; Hungary and Czechoslovakia were permitted to introduce economic reforms (less emphasis on heavy industry, increased incentives, more stress on market forces) that went beyond those adopted in the Soviet Union. Rumania as well as Poland, Hungary, and Czechoslovakia expanded their trade with the noncommunist world up to 40–45 percent.

THE WELFARE
STATE EMERGES

Profound changes have affected almost all aspects of European social life since the end of the Second World War. This was a new age of social reforms, and although some of them had been initiated well before the First World War, their full impact was felt only after 1945, when the social-security services expanded in new directions and became far more comprehensive. The welfare state removed some of the most oppressive features of early industrial society, but it could not, as some had apparently hoped, effect a radical transformation of the human condition. Poverty was not stamped out except in the most advanced countries of Northern Europe; the hardships and pains of sickness and old age were alleviated but did not disappear. Although the welfare state made people healthier, it did not necessarily make them happier. On the contrary, once material deprivation became less acute, other forms of suffering were more intensely felt: the boredom and anonymity of life in the big cities, or, to use the catchword of the sixties, alienation. The figures for drug addiction, suicide, and juvenile crime climbed steadily higher. But if the impact of the welfare state on the human condition was not as deep as some had expected, there was no doubt about the material benefits. The terrible insecurity which had for so long haunted so many all over Europe disappeared as it became generally accepted that no one should starve, that everyone had a right to shelter, and that lack of money should not stand in the way of health. True, not everyone benefited from these reforms in equal measure; some of the provisions were inadequate (such as old-age pensions in many countries), and some categories of people were unaccountably left out altogether. Measured by the standards of an ideal society, the postwar changes were highly inadequate, at best a few steps in the right direction; but compared with conditions in the past and with the present state of affairs in other parts of the world, they were a tremendous achievement, probably the greatest social advance in many centuries.

There was a marked increase in mobility between the classes; the old elites in some countries were still firmly entrenched in strongholds such as the foreign service and the officer corps. But a new meritocracy gained most of the key positions in the higher civil service and in business; the haute bourgeoisie was no longer secure even in its control of the conservative parties of Western Europe. Progressive taxation narrowed the gap between the highest and lowest incomes, but businessmen still succeeded in amassing great fortunes and sometimes even in evading the increasingly stiff death duties. But with growing prosperity and more equal opportunity in education, the marks distinguishing the classes from one another became much less pronounced; the old proverb, "clothes maketh man" lost significance as it became more and more difficult to "place" a man or woman according to his or her attire; even the cars people drove were no longer a reliable guide to their class status.

The postwar world produced the mixed economy and the welfare state; it also witnessed the emergence of the "permissive society." The war of 1914–18 had seen the first great break with the morals and manners of the nineteenth century, and the new freedom had been widely celebrated in the early twenties in the capitals of Western Europe. But this movement had affected only a relatively small layer of society. The moral code of the nineteenth century, though severely shaken and often tacitly ignored, was outwardly still very much in evidence. The changes that took place after the Second World War were deeper and more far-reaching than those between the wars: church attendance dropped all over Europe, all authority was questioned, sexual freedom spread to an extent unknown before, and by the late sixties the academic youth of Europe was everywhere up in arms against the "establishment." Even before the revolt of the students, a great deal of restlessness had been felt among working-class youth; European newspapers during the fifties were full of the exploits of the teddy boys (in England), the *Halbstarke* (in Germany), the *blousons noirs* (in France), the *gamberros* (in Spain), not to mention

the *khooligans* of communist Europe. Youth movements, both inchoate and organized, had been part of the European scene in one
form or another almost without interruption since the Romantic age;
the idea of a youth culture, the concept of the revolt of the younger
generation, of the class struggle in school and university, had been
widely discussed in Central Europe even before the First World War.
But at that time parents, teachers, and other authorities had not considered even for a moment abdicating what they regarded as their
natural responsibilities toward the young generation; "law and order"
was then not a slogan, it was the self-evident foundation of society.
After the Second World War the self-confidence of the older generation had been severely shaken, and as a result there was much greater
readiness to take the ideas of young people seriously and to accept
their demands. But this did not necessarily satisfy a movement often
devoid of rational and clearly formulated programs; protest was above
all a biological necessity (as it had been throughout history), the urge
for self-assertion was stronger than the desire to carry out any specific
reform.

The student-power movement was certainly more spectacular
than the struggle for the full emancipation of the weaker sex. By 1945
women had attained almost complete legal equality, even if in Switzerland they did not have the right to vote, and although certain dis-
criminatory provisions with regard to property rights still persisted
in many countries. Women entered many professions that had been
virtually closed to them before, and many more of them now received
a higher education. But the limits of social, as distinct from legal,
emancipation also became more obvious. The principle of equal pay
for equal work was not accepted in practice in most European countries, and many leading positions in the economy and in public life
remained, as before, closed to women. The situation in Eastern Europe
was basically the same. True, they had made great progress in various
professions; there were, to give one illustration, more women than
men physicians in the Soviet Union. But no women rose to key positions in the Communist Party or the state apparatus. A few women
politicians, such as Ana Pauker in Rumania, had played a prominent
part in the first years after the war, but they did not last long. The
politburos of the various East European communist parties were as
much a male preserve as the traditional London clubs. The social

emancipation of women had made more progress in Scandinavia than in any other part of Europe, and it was these countries that were also the pioneers of the new sexual freedom.

Legislation in this respect became more liberal, sex education in schools was no longer opposed, and as far as public opinion was concerned premarital sexual intercourse was accepted in theory as well as in practice. Books, plays, and movies faced more lenient censors than in any other period in modern history; subjects that had formerly been taboo were now freely discussed; the underground presses of Europe went out of business, for hard-core pornography was widely published and in some places openly traded. The contraceptive pill was freely obtainable by the middle sixties in many countries (not, however, in the Soviet Union) and this, too, contributed toward a profound change in sexual mores. In Britain there were six times as many divorces in 1966 as in 1938; the divorce rate was very high in the immediate postwar period, fell during the fifties, but increased again in the sixties. It was higher in most East European countries (Hungary, Rumania, and the Soviet Union) than in the West, and higher in Denmark and Sweden than in Britain and Benelux. Couples married at an earlier age, and with increasing longevity they could look forward to a married life that would last almost twice as long as fifty years earlier.

The permissive society modified its attitude toward crime and punishment. Juvenile crime and acts of violence against persons increased, but in some other respects there was a fall in the crime rate: 1,200 adults out of 100,000 had been sentenced by German courts in 1900; 1,190 in 1930; but only 780 (not counting traffic offenders) in 1960. As the social roots of crime were better understood, and as new theories about the possible influence of genetic factors were discussed, there was more emphasis on rehabilitation than on punishment. The prison regime became more liberal, and capital punishment had been abolished by the middle sixties by all countries except those of Eastern Europe, France, Greece, and Spain. This liberal trend was, however, by no means undisputed; it was usually advocated by a relatively small section of intellectuals, whereas society as a whole was less inclined to initiate progressive social experiments. As the negative features of the new liberalism were more palpably felt, many claimed that too much in this direction had been done too fast. The police forces and the courts usually took a more conservative attitude toward the treatment of criminals than the reformers who were dealing with the problems from a distance.

In the Soviet Union the repressive effects of the Stalin era were all-pervasive. Social services were far less comprehensive than in any developed capitalist country; the principle of free education was no longer adhered to as tuition fees were reintroduced in the universities and the upper grades of secondary schools. Divorce was made difficult, and abortion was virtually abolished. Although the Soviet Union enjoyed the reputation among Western progressives as the country with the most highly developed social services, and Western conservatives were convinced that sexual license in communist society was without precedent or parallel, the real situation was very different indeed. After 1956 more liberal attitudes prevailed; old-age pensions and other benefits were increased, school and university fees were abolished, and the restrictions on divorce and abortion partly rescinded. But this liberalism had narrow limits: the manifestations of the new sexual freedom in the capitalist world were emphatically rejected prior to glasnost, and Soviet literature, cinema, and plays remained the cleanest (in the Victorian sense) on the continent; the official Soviet attitude toward psychoanalysis was no more lenient than that of the Vatican.

Many postwar fashions were ephemeral, but there is no doubt that a great deal of qualitative change had taken place in European social life, that the social policies pursued had resulted in a society that was in many respects totally different from any previous one. The welfare state was something essentially new, and it is to this concept and its practical aspects that we shall turn next.

Germany in the age of Bismarck had been the pioneer of social legislation such as compulsory insurance, old-age pensions, and health insurance. Other European countries, following the German example, had introduced similar legislation for the protection of industrial workers well before the First World War. France and Belgium had been the first to grant family allowances; Russia, and Germany under Hitler, gave special assistance to mothers bearing more than the average number of children. But most of these prewar schemes were rudimentary and selective; they were designed to give a minimum of security to the very poorest, but the concept of public assistance at the time was not far removed from the charity schemes of the Victorian era. The principle of equality of opportunity was not yet generally accepted, nor was the idea that society had certain duties toward all of its members.

The social reforms carried out all over Europe after the Second World War seemed at first to be only an extension of the legislation of earlier years, even though their character was much more systematic and they went much further than all previous schemes. West European expenditure on social services quadrupled between 1930 and 1957; in Sweden it was six times higher in the latter year, in France seven, in Italy fourteen. Taken separately, the new measures were merely a continuation of a policy inaugurated decades before, but they also had a profound cumulative effect, gradually giving birth to the welfare state.

Social-welfare schemes varied greatly from country to country in scope, in their priorities, and in the way they were financed and administered. The highly industrialized countries had more comprehensive services; the poor countries of Southern Europe (except Italy) introduced social legislation only later, and the services they offered were much inferior to those of Britain and Sweden, which were the most comprehensive. West Germany and Belgium now provide old-age pensions that are among the most liberal, and France offers the highest family allowances and sizable health benefits. Social security in Britain is operated by the state, whereas many services in Scandinavia, such as unemployment insurance and the health service (except in Sweden), are run by nongovernmental bodies. In Germany, France, and Italy cooperative insurance agencies play an important role, and some of the insurance programs were until recently financed almost entirely by contributions of employers and employees; state contributions have only recently become a factor of importance. In the communist states of Eastern Europe the trade unions have traditionally played the central role in administering the social services.

The various insurance schemes had originally been sponsored to assist the industrial working class and were extended only much later to the self-employed. By 1960 almost the whole population of Britain and Sweden was covered by the health service, and the great majority of citizens in France, Germany, and Italy (85, 87, and 88 percent, respectively). In the Soviet Union, too, most social services were extended after 1965 to cover the peasants, hitherto largely excluded from these benefits. Free medical care was provided in the

1950s to all insured persons in Britain, Italy, Germany, Spain, and a number of smaller countries, whereas in France, the Scandinavian countries, Belgium, and Switzerland sick persons had to make a contribution, usually ranging from 10 to 25 percent of the cost. In France and Belgium it was customary to pay directly but to claim a refund later. Health benefits varied greatly; in Germany, for instance, they were about 20 percent (for the first six weeks) in West Germany. Old-age pensions were paid to men in most countries at the age of sixty-five (sixty for women); in France and Italy the retirement age was sixty (fifty-five for women in Italy), whereas in Sweden it was sixty-seven and in Norway seventy. Old-age pensions in France and Britain were low, approximately $40 per month for a man over sixty-five after forty years of work; they were twice as high in Italy, where, however, fewer people qualified for the benefits. Family allowances also varied greatly from country to country. In Scandinavia the scheme extended to all residents: elsewhere it was restricted mainly to wage earners. In many places the rate per child increased up to the third or fourth child; in some it was constant irrespective of the size of the family. In some European countries those allowances were paid for children up to the age of fourteen, in others up to twenty-one, and there were striking differences in the level of allowances: a family with three children received almost $60 per month in France (in 1964), but only $24 in Italy and only about $10 in Britain. All European countries with the exception of Portugal also had maternity allowances, and a few provided additional benefits ranging from marriage grants (Belgium, Spain, Switzerland) to home-furnishing loans for young couples and low-cost holidays for housewives (Sweden).

Equality in educational opportunity has been one of the basic features of the welfare-state concept; higher education is now free or available at nominal charges in all West and North European countries. In 1953 more than 70 percent of the students in Britain received state grants; subsequently grants were extended to all students without exception. In France, too, public education is free at all levels; some German *Länder* demand a fee of about $150 per year, while others (such as Hesse) have abolished tuition fees altogether. In Scandinavia and Holland tuition is either free or financed by state loans to be repaid over a period of five to ten years. These reforms involved growing state expenditure on education; while national income rose quickly, the proportion of the GNP spent on education increased even faster: from 2.7 to 4.2 percent in Sweden between 1938 and 1956, and at approximately the same rate in Britain.

Friedrich Engels, writing on the housing question, maintained that there were already enough houses in existence to provide the working class with room and healthy living accommodation. Similarly, later advocates of the welfare state underrated the cost of the services they envisaged. In 1967 almost 17 percent of the German GNP was spent on social services; 14–15 percent in France, Sweden, Belgium, Italy, and Holland; 11 percent in Britain and Denmark; 10 percent in Switzerland and the Soviet Union. By the late 1980s the major European countries spent 40–50 percent or more of their GNP on social protection (old-age, unemployment, and family allowances but not the health service). The United Kingdom (25 percent) was at the lower end of the scale. Different means were used to raise this money. In Scandinavia, as in Britain, the state contributes the main share of welfare and pension funds, in contrast to 18 percent of the total cost in West Germany (in 1963), 11 percent in Italy, and 6 percent in France and the Netherlands. In Britain employers contribute less than 20 percent of the cost, whereas in France and Italy they contribute about two-thirds of the social-security bill. Before the Second World War Germany and Britain had been leading the rest of Europe by a great margin in per-capita expenditure on social security; after 1945 the picture began to change.

PER-CAPITA SOCIAL SECURITY EXPENDITURE
IN DOLLARS AT 1954 PRICES

	1930	1957
Belgium	12	148
France	17	136
Germany	54	132
Holland	10	56
Italy	5	54
Sweden	22	135
Switzerland	24	96
United Kingdom	59	93

As public outlays continued to rise year by year, there was growing criticism of some of the provisions of the welfare state. According to these arguments, reforms had gone too far, making the individual utterly dependent on the state and destroying every urge toward self-help. Critics in Britain suggested that those who wanted to contract out of the National Health Service should be encouraged to do so, and that more scope should be given to private initiative in education. They argued that the burden on the state was too heavy, that growing expenditure for social services had raised taxation to such an extent that there was little incentive for the individual to exert himself for his own good and that of society. But these critics were a minority; most citizens enjoyed the benefits of the welfare state and took them for granted. A radical reduction in the social services was politically impossible, for the great majority would have resisted it tooth and nail.

HEALTH AND HOUSING

Advances in medical knowledge and the greater availability of
health services to entire populations have resulted in a significant improvement in the state of health of the peoples of
Europe. The average life expectancy in Switzerland around the turn
of the century was fifty years; it is now well over seventy. In Spain
during the same period it has risen from thirty-four to seventy years.
Infant mortality, twenty-seven out of a thousand in 1900, fell to
twenty in Austria fifty years later and decreased from thirteen to 1.4
in the Netherlands. There was a dramatic decline in epidemic diseases
following the discovery of new, powerful drugs; tuberculosis, for
instance, ceased to be one of the main killers. Though little progress
was made in curing mental diseases, a whole arsenal of new medi-
cations made it much easier to control these illnesses and to reduce
the number of those permanently hospitalized. Cancer, on the other
hand, was on the increase; and with rising life expectancy there was
also a higher incidence of diseases of the heart and the nervous system.

There was also a steady rise in deaths from traffic accidents.
Between 1948 and 1956 their number doubled in Germany, Norway,
and the Netherlands; in France, Italy, and Spain the number more
than trebled.

Greater attention than before was paid to preventive medicine,
to health in schools and industry, to the purification of water and air.
The number of practicing physicians doubled, roughly speaking, between the late 1920s and 1960; there was one physician for every
700 residents of Switzerland (481 in 1981!), but only one for 1,700
Finns, with other European countries somewhere in between these

extremes. Some interesting differences existed in health care among European countries, but how significant were they? Though Italy had almost twice as many doctors as France, France had almost twice as many nurses; the life expectancy in both countries was roughly the same. The number of dentists increased even faster during this period, and 80 percent more hospital beds were available. West European expenditure on medical care was almost four times as high in the 1950s as during the decade before the war, but a higher share of the total was devoted to the ancillary medical services. Expenditure on the health services in Britain remained fairly stable, at 4 percent of the GNP, between 1950 and 1960, but steeply increased in later years. By 1990 the figure had risen to 12.5 percent, and in the other major European countries the share was slightly higher. France and West Germany spent 14 and 18 percent, respectively, for their health services.

The improvement in the state of public health during the postwar period was striking throughout Europe, but, as in most other fields, expectations rose even faster than achievements. There were still serious shortcomings, and few medical experts would have agreed even after several decades of continuous progress that the situation in this respect was really satisfactory.

Whole stretches of Europe were in ruins as the Second World War ended. Some countries had been more affected by the destruction than others. Whereas 20–25 percent of all houses in Germany and Greece had been totally destroyed by military action, only 6–7 percent in France and Britain were destroyed; big cities naturally fared worse than the countryside in this respect. Europe's housing situation had been far from satisfactory even before the war; urban construction had been interrupted during the First World War and had again come to a standstill during the great depression.

The prewar cities of Europe were essentially a product of the nineteenth century: houses of brick and stone solidly built, meant to last at least a hundred years. With the rapid growth of the urban population, many of them had become overcrowded, and most of them were ugly; large tracts of monotonous rows of buildings had degenerated into slums within a decade or two. In France and Belgium at the end of the war only every other house had running water— only every third in Italy, Spain, and Austria. Only one house in ten in these countries had a fixed bath, versus one out of three in highly developed countries such as Germany and Sweden. The housing situation in Britain, the Scandinavian countries, Belgium, and Switzerland was on the whole better than in the rest of the continent, certainly as far as space was concerned, but even there housing did not meet minimum standards of safety and health, let alone of comfort; 20–30 percent of the buildings in many British cities had been declared unfit before 1939. The state of affairs had further deteriorated during the war, when no major repairs could be undertaken.

In this critical situation, all European governments had to give priority to housing construction, allocating on the average 3–5 percent of their GNP for the purpose. By 1950 the number of houses in Western Europe was already higher than before the war. In Eastern Europe, on the other hand, where the shortage was even more acute, little new building was carried out during the first postwar decade. During the 1950s there was further substantial progress in Western Europe; the number of houses, roughly speaking, doubled. Construction in a good year in the sixties was more than half a million units in West Germany, four hundred thousand in France and Italy, almost four hundred thousand in Britain, almost three hundred thousand in Spain. There were also extensive programs of slum clearance, so that the real increase in accommodations was smaller than indicated by these impressive figures.

The quality of building was low during the immediate postwar period, when utility standards prevailed; afterward, during the late fifties, the new flats and houses became more spacious and more pleasing to the eye. Greater attention was paid to layout and individual design, to landscaping and community amenities. It was by no means easy to achieve the goals that had been set. The building industry was on the whole inefficient and conservative in outlook, consisting mostly of small firms. The methods of building had changed little since the nineteenth century, and in view of the seasonal fluctuation in building activity it was difficult to attract and keep a sufficient labor force. During the second postwar decade rationalization and mechanization of building processes made considerable progress, and with it the production of prefabricated houses, concrete-panel construction, and the standardization of materials, components, and fixtures. To boost housing Britain had established a Ministry of Town and Country Planning even before the end of the war; ministers of housing were also appointed in Spain and several other countries. Modern technology and a more imaginative approach made for comfortable and aesthetically pleasing living, but not necessarily for cheaper houses and flats. The rising cost of building was another problem that could be solved only by massive state subsidies.

Generalizations are difficult, for standards of housing differ greatly between countries (and between town and country) in accordance with social and climatic conditions. Tradition also played its part. In Britain and Holland city dwellers have a preference for houses, whereas elsewhere on the continent there has been for a long time a preference for flats. Owner occupancy is everywhere greater in the rural than in the urban areas. The price of land had gone up in all European cities; if the cost of an average-size house was not much less than $3,000 in Southern Europe in the late 1950s, it was likely to be almost three times as high in Central and Northern Europe. Such prices put new houses out of reach of the great majority of the population and made state assistance imperative. There was little speculative building during the first five years after the war; rents were controlled in most European countries, and because of the progress of inflation the landlord's outlay on repairs was usually higher than his income from rent.

There was little incentive for private initiative in building, and most of Europe's new postwar housing was state-supported by means of tax reliefs (West Germany), loans at low interest rates (Switzerland, France, and other countries), direct initiative by the local authorities (Britain), or special benefits accorded to housing cooperatives (Scandinavia, Holland, Austria). Later on, with growing prosperity, the share of private building increased; mortgages in most countries were available at 5–8 percent interest for a period of ten to twenty-five years. Switzerland was an exception; money there was available on more favorable terms, and as a result 90 percent of the new buildings were privately financed.

Sweden, Switzerland, and West Germany were among the countries that made most progress in housing, but Britain was still in the lead in the average number of rooms per person; around 1960 this number was 1.5 in Britain, 1.1 in West Germany, 1.0 in France, 0.9 in Italy. There are no comparable statistics for the Soviet Union, but it is known that only after 1956 was a major effort made to alleviate the acute housing shortage; construction almost trebled between 1953 and 1960, and more than two million units were built in 1965. Housing conditions had been abysmally bad during the Stalin era; there is reason to believe that even a decade after Stalin's death, after a major building effort, the urban population in the Soviet Union had only just as much space per capita at its disposal as before the revolution. The average Soviet family lived in a single room, and it had to share a kitchen and other amenities with its neighbors; it spent a lower percentage of its budget (less than 4 percent) on rent, fuel, and light than a family in the West, but, given the inferior standard of housing, such comparisons are not very meaningful. To combat overcrowding, strict regulations were introduced in the Stalin era to restrict the influx of new residents into Moscow and other cities. The decrees of 1957 which stressed the gravity of the situation and accorded higher priority to urban housing brought certain improvements. During the sixties Soviet families in urban areas were able to move into two- or three-room flats, according to the size of the family. Even so, the targets of the plans were never reached, the quality of the new buildings was inferior, and the standard of Soviet housing is still much below that in Western countries. Meanwhile, private initiative through cooperative housing is encouraged, and the share of owner-occupied houses and flats is as high as in some West European countries. The housing situation in Eastern Europe was on the whole slightly better than in the Soviet Union, but still much below West European standards. There were 1,572 rooms per thousand inhabitants in Belgium in 1961, compared with 832 in East Germany, 666 in Hungary, 580 in Poland, and 545 in Bulgaria. Building cooperatives have been encouraged, following the Soviet example; prospective buyers have to make down payments of between 15 percent (Poland) and 40 percent (Russia) of the price and borrow the rest of the money from the banks, such loans being granted for ten to fifteen years. In the more prosperous East European countries, notably East Germany and Czechoslovakia, the quality of building has markedly improved since the middle fifties.

The design of new housing has also greatly improved throughout Europe; there has been a general orientation toward sunlight, space between high buildings, and efforts made to avoid monotony and uniformity. The idea of new garden cities first appeared in Germany and England toward the end of the nineteenth century. These concepts received fresh impetus with the Abercrombie Plan adopted in Britain during the Second World War, which provided for several new cities to be established within a radius of sixty miles from London in order to disperse the population in the most heavily congested areas. There were similar plans for satellite towns around Paris, and five new cities have been built in the Ruhr. Near Stockholm two new cities, Vallingby and Hoegernaestaden, have developed since 1945; these have been in most ways the most successful of Europe's new towns. Speculative building has been instrumental in building a new middle-class suburb near Paris (Paris II) promising to "introduce a new quality into urban life." Interesting and on the whole successful experiments were undertaken in Berlin; the Hansa Viertel represents a unique but not unharmonious mixture of styles, each building being designed by a different architect. Walter Gropius was in charge of the building of new residential areas in the north and the southeast of the city.

In comparison with the state of affairs before the war, the housing situation in Europe has greatly improved. Nowhere has the problem been entirely solved, partly as the result of rising costs, but also in consequence of higher standards and expectations. What was considered adequate housing in 1918 is now no longer acceptable. At the earlier date only a tiny percentage of houses and flats in Britain had central heating; now it is considered essential by most house buyers. Rents in the center and "desirable areas" of European cities (Paris, London, Rome, Geneva, and Zurich being the most flagrant cases) have skyrocketed; cheaper housing is usually available in the outlying suburbs, but the growing distance between these new residential districts and the places of employment now presents an increasingly difficult problem.

PROSPERITY AND
THE NEW
CONSUMERISM

Throughout the nineteenth century Britain had enjoyed far higher living standards than the continent; it had been estimated that around 1870 per-capita GNP in Germany, France, Denmark, Sweden, and Belgium was only two-thirds that of the United Kingdom, and in the other European countries even less. Between 1870 and 1913 per-capita GNP in Britain rose by more than 80 percent, between 1913 and 1955 by almost 70 percent, and in the subsequent decade by about 50 percent. But in the other countries just mentioned it rose even faster; all had overtaken Britain by 1980. With growing prosperity, important changes took place in consumption patterns. Europeans were not just consuming more of almost everything; there were far-reaching qualitative changes.

Food has been traditionally the largest single factor in private consumption; it is estimated that one hundred years ago about 65 percent of private expenditure in Germany went on food, drink, and tobacco, but that by 1965 this had fallen to 36 percent. A similar trend could be observed throughout Europe; the corresponding figures for the developed countries of Western and Northern Europe were in the range of 32–42 percent, but considerably higher in the South of the continent. In 1990 it was 17–22 percent in the United Kingdom, France, and West Germany, slightly higher in Italy and Spain, and 35–40 percent in the poorest countries, such as Portugal and Turkey. Eating habits have always varied according to national (and local) traditions; many of these have remained unchanged, but the consumption of cereals has declined all over Europe in comparison with the prewar period, and so has the consumption of potatoes everywhere except in Italy, where they have never been a major item. The consumption of meat and fish, or sugar, milk, and eggs, on the other hand, has risen rapidly, and so has the calorie intake in general, from 2,800 in France in 1950 to 2,940 by the end of the decade, and from 2,300 in Italy to 2,750. The main nutritional problem of Western Europe in the 1960s was that people ate too much rather than too little, and in the most prosperous countries a slight decline in the calorie intake could already be detected. Italians and Belgians were still the greatest bread eaters in Europe, the Belgians and the French ate more meat than the others, the Dutch were drinking more milk than anyone else, and the Italians came first in the consumption of fresh fruit. The consumption of wine in Italy rose from 84 liters a year before the war to 95 in the sixties, but fell in France (where mortality from alcoholism had been fairly high) from 138 to 116 liters within one decade. Expenditure on alcohol was roughly the same in the various European countries, accounting for 5–7 percent of the total budget, but there were marked variations in prices. The same amount of money bought more than three times the quantity of alcohol in France and Southern Europe as in Britain. Per-capita expenditure on tobacco was still roughly 4 percent of personal consumption throughout Western Europe in the late 1960s, the Dutch, Danish, Swiss, Belgians, and British being the heaviest smokers. The discovery of the connection between lung cancer and cigarette smoking caused a drop in cigarette smoking in the sixties, and higher taxation also acted as a brake; the share of taxes in the retail price of a packet of cigarettes was 75 percent in Britain in 1955, and it has increased since.

That Northern Europe spends more on fuel and light than the South is self-explanatory; more significant is the general postwar rise in spending on household durables. The number of telephones, television sets, and radios, like that of refrigerators and cars, has become the usual yardstick of the statistician for measuring the standard of living. It is not always a reliable one: Denmark (to give but one example), with a standard of living roughly equal to that of West Germany, had in the 1960s twice as many telephones per head, and France, with a higher standard of living than most, had only half as many per head as Germany. Broadly speaking, expenditure on household appliances has risen faster than on any other item in the household budget; the use of washing machines, refrigerators, and vacuum cleaners, which before the Second World War was restricted to a small section of the population, spread during the fifties and sixties to the low-income groups: European kitchens became mechanized as more women went out to work and as domestic help was no longer freely available. The price of many of these appliances remained fairly high, but the widespread availability of installment plans brought these commodities within the range of the great majority of the population. Canned, tinned, deep-frozen, and precooked foods increased in both volume and variety, ranging from frozen orange juice to instant coffee. "Do-it-yourself" operations became of growing importance; for some it was a hobby, for others a necessity, since there were now so few artisans who could be called upon to undertake repair work. Europeans were better dressed in the postwar period although they spent relatively less on clothing; the share of this item in the personal budget in France fell from 14.5 percent in the late twenties to 11 percent in the middle sixties, from 14 to 12 percent in Belgium, and from 13 to 11 percent in Britain. The most important new feature in this field was the growing use of synthetic fibers, the production of which quadrupled between 1960 and 1966.

The new design for living, especially the new products, had a marked egalitarian effect; the same kinds of furniture and appliances were often found in flats and housing projects all over Western and Northern Europe, especially among the younger generation, regardless of their class status. The deproletarization of the working class made rapid strides in both Western and Eastern Europe, despite the great differences in income, and middle-class attitudes gradually extended far beyond the traditional confines of this class.

LEISURE FOR ALL

Leisure, idleness, activities undertaken as an end in themselves, have usually been the preserve of a happy few, the aristocracy and those with great inherited wealth. As the workweek contracted and as physical work became less strenuous, leisure in the developed industrial societies became for the first time an inherent part of the new way of life. It is true that the change came slowly; there was no dramatic, sudden decrease in the time spent at work. The workweek had been forty-eight hours in most European countries before the Second World War and fell to forty-two to forty-four hours in the 1950s. France, which had introduced a forty-hour week in the 1930s, was the one major exception, but this was more apparent than real, for it represented the legal minimum and most French employees were only too eager to work overtime. But there was more time at the disposal of the individual as the number of paid holidays increased and vacations became longer. By 1955 there were twenty-nine days of paid holidays a year in Sweden, including vacation and paid statutory holidays, and twenty-eight in Germany and Italy; in the 1960s their number had risen to thirty-two to thirty-five in these countries. Rising productivity and the introduction of more sophisticated machinery reduced the physical effort needed at work, and increased output. This made it possible to get both more pay (and hence more goods) and more leisure. With the introduction of still more modern equipment and with automatic methods, especially in the growth industries, it was predicted that the workweek would in the not-too-distant future shrink to four days, and ultimately to less.

By upbringing and education, men and women were prepared

over the ages to be useful members of society, but very few knew other than by instinct how to spend their free time in the most enjoyable way. They needed to relearn what previous generations had mastered to a high degree: how to transform free time into genuine leisure. Greater leisure offered many opportunities; some took up or further developed hobbies ranging from stamp collecting to bird watching, from sailing and camping to cultivating small gardens. A minority preferred strenuous activities such as mountaineering; the majority stuck to less exacting pastimes, like watching television, playing bingo, or attending ball games. In Britain in 1990 an estimated five million people, mainly women, played bingo in commercial bingo halls. On average, those aged over four years spent more than twenty-five hours a week watching television—slightly less than the year before. Though the general standard of European television was higher than that of the big American networks, there were many complaints about declining levels. The do-it-yourself industry prospered; car and photography fans devoted much time, and frequently invested a great deal of money, in the pursuit of their hobbies. Others joined adult-education courses ranging in scope from the study of languages to folk dancing, the collection of antiques, or the emulation of Grandma Moses. The number of radio hams, of members of rifle clubs, and of many other associations and clubs increased; the news-stands offered an almost unlimited variety of periodicals devoted to every hobby and pastime. There was a steady increase in the attendance of concerts, plays, operas, the ballet, and exhibitions, and the number of amateur artists and those making music at home also went up substantially.

More leisure did not by itself assure greater happiness and the full development of the faculties of individual members of society; there was also growing boredom and a feeling of emptiness. Leisure, like work, had its discontents, and men and women had to be retrained to seek fulfillment in their free time. Authoritarian regimes tried to provide organized leisure activities, as fascist Italy had done with its *dopo lavoro* schemes and Nazi Germany with *Kraft durch Freude*. In the West the negative aspects of mass culture, propagated and magnified by advertising, induced many to spend their time in activities that, though certainly an end in themselves, were neither enjoyable nor profitable.

These were the birth pangs of the new *civilisation de loisir*. With

all its problems, few doubted its tremendous advantages and possibilities. Concerning the benefits of tourism there was little dispute. It
was almost always rewarding, it helped to broaden the horizon of
millions of people, and in some ways it contributed to better understanding between men and women of different nations.

Mass tourism was virtually unknown before the Second World
War. Biarritz, Baden-Baden, and a few other watering places and
some Italian and Swiss resorts had had their influx of visitors for over
a century; some thousands of wandering scholars and artisans had
ventured outside their native countries; but the great majority of
Europeans had no more thought of traveling abroad than of visiting
another planet. The great change in this respect came with growing
prosperity, and above all with the greater mobility provided by the
automobile, chartered flights, and package tours. By the middle fifties,
thirty million tourists were crossing European frontiers every year,
and in 1966 their number exceeded a hundred million. Domestic
tourism, needless to say, was even more extensive; it is estimated that
in any year during the sixties three out of four Swedes and almost
every other German and Frenchman took a holiday outside his usual
place of residence. But most of the glamour was attached to foreign
tourism, and its economic importance for many countries was of the
highest order. During the months of July and August the highways
of Europe, the railway stations, and the airports were scenes of mass
migration the like of which had never been witnessed in human history. Governments promoted the stream of tourists by making it much
easier to cross frontiers: visas between most European countries were
gradually abolished, and by 1960 there was only the most perfunctory
border control. Enterprising businessmen cashed in on the tourist
boom, organizing group travel at a fraction of the price individual
travelers would have to pay. Hotels, motels, and camping sites mushroomed all over Europe, catering to all tastes and purses. Nineteen
sixty-seven was declared International Tourist Year, and the travel-
agency prospectuses grew in size and scope with each season; they
covered international congresses of every possible description, festivals, exhibitions, *sons-et-lumières*, pilgrimages, safaris in Africa,
cheap excursions for music lovers, bachelors, senior citizens, and children. The number of visitors from other continents was relatively
small, but that, too, increased steeply. Half a million Americans had
come to Europe in 1955; by 1960 their number had trebled, and there

was a growing stream of visitors from Japan, Australia, and other distant places. Few Europeans other than immigrants went to the United States before the Second World War; in 1966, 562,000 took the trip across the Atlantic.

The average European tourist spent less on his foreign holiday in this age of mass tourism than the well-to-do traveler in earlier periods; many of the visits that appeared in the statistics were day trips with no economic benefit for the host country but for the occasional cup of tea or coffee and the purchase of some souvenirs. At one stage or another, Britain and France were forced to introduce severe currency restrictions on money spent on holidays abroad, and President Johnson called on his countrymen to spend their holidays in their native country to combat a persistent adverse balance of payments. Despite these restrictions, foreign tourism became an economic factor of ever-growing importance. In 1986 Spain, with $10 billion, was the leading earner of foreign tourist receipts, closely followed by Italy ($9.8 billion) and France ($9.7 billion). Switzerland earned $4.2 billion and Austria $6.0 billion, more than 5 percent of the GNP.

Eastern Europe, which had been hermetically sealed off to foreign tourists during the Stalin era, gradually opened its borders during the late fifties. Czechoslovakia had 2.7 million foreign visitors, Hungary 1.6 million in 1966, and Rumania attracted hundreds of thousands of tourists to the Black Sea shores. Few Western visitors went to the Soviet Union, although the Black Sea coast and the Caucasus were great tourist attractions. Russia was still a faraway country for most Europeans, and there were still too many restrictions on free movement; though tourist facilities had been greatly expanded, they were, all other considerations apart, not remotely sufficient to absorb a mass invasion, as in Spain, Italy, or even Yugoslavia.

THE NEW SOCIAL
STRUCTURES

The political and economic changes that have taken place in Europe since 1939 have deeply affected the nature of European society. There is, however, no unanimity about the significance of these developments, for long-term social trends are usually more difficult to assess and interpret than economic developments. Orthodox Marxists, with their traditional emphasis on the (relative) pauperization of the working class, on the capitalists' rising profits, and on the sharpening class struggle, question whether there has been qualitative change. They had predicted the impending demise of the capitalist system and were unprepared for a long period of accelerated economic growth and visibly rising living standards. They had always put their hopes on the industrial working class as the main agent of social revolution, but with rapid technological change this class ceased to expand in the most developed countries. Though there were more jobs each year, they were not necessarily for manual workers; the decline in the number of coal miners, for instance, has already been noted. Insufficient militancy among the workers had previously been explained as the result of general logical backwardness, an inadequate class consciousness, and the presence of a "labor aristocracy." These traditional explanations were found wanting in the postwar world; the changes in vocabulary of the critics of society betrayed an awareness of social change, as the "establishment" and the "military-industrial complex" replaced the "ruling class," and the stress on the proletarian character of the revolutionary movement gradually diminished. The non-Marxists, on the other hand, emphasized that the character of the ownership of the means of production had radically

changed since the heyday of laissez-faire capitalism, that economics
was now mixed, that a new class of managers had emerged, that the
tertiary (service) sector of the economy had grown much faster as an
employer of labor than had industry, that class differences had become
blurred, and that everywhere the state engaged in the redistribution
of the national income by means of progressive taxation and the
welfare state. In between the two extremes, the total rejection of the
established order and its more or less unqualified acceptance, there
was a whole gamut of opinions.

About the statistical facts there was little dispute. Fewer Europeans were employed in agriculture every year; the industrial labor
force was not expanding in the most developed countries; in Britain,
Belgium, and Switzerland 46–47 percent of the labor force was engaged in industrial production in 1910. In West Germany its share
(including mining, construction, etc.) was 48 percent in 1950 and
remained at that level during the fifties and sixties. But since then the
industrial labor force has been shrinking, with a corresponding rise
of those employed in the service sector. The percentage of women in
the labor force rose in most European countries between 1945 and
the middle sixties; it was the highest in the Soviet Union, Sweden,
and Austria (50–60 percent), much lower, but increasing, in the Mediterranean countries (20–35 percent), and decreasing in Norway and
France. The percentage of the self-employed declined in most countries, from 32 percent in West Germany in 1950 to less than 20 percent
in 1964. The tertiary sector, the service industries, increased at the
most rapid rate. International comparisons are difficult, since statistical definitions vary from country to country. In the more advanced
European countries, one-third or more of the total labor force is now
engaged in providing various services, and the proportion is still rising.
With technological progress there was a growing demand for skilled
and semiskilled workers, and the number of salaried employees in
industry rose twice as fast as that of wage earners.

A consistently high rate of employment has been one of the main
features of European postwar economic development. There was unemployment in the early postwar period; more than 1.5 million unemployed were counted in Germany and Italy in 1950. Italy, and to
a lesser extent Belgium, were plagued during the fifties by a persistent
unemployment problem, but almost all other European countries had
by 1955 reached full or overfull employment. In 1964 Ireland still

had an unemployment quota exceeding 3 percent, but in Italy it had fallen to 2.4 percent, and in Germany that year there were sixteen unemployed for every hundred vacancies. There were fluctuations: the recession of 1966 caused a temporary increase in unemployment, but within a few months it fell again, and by late 1967 it was well below the full-employment rate of 2 percent in France and West Germany.

Another category of employees, the guest workers, became a factor of vital importance in the national economy of many European countries. There had been such migrants even before the First World War: Polish agricultural laborers, for instance, went for the harvest to East Germany, and thousands of Polish miners went temporarily or permanently to work in the coal mines of northern France. But the migration in the fifties and sixties was of a different magnitude. In Switzerland entire branches of the national economy, such as the building industry, were taken over by the Italians; in 1958 about 17 percent of the labor force was thought to be of foreign origin; ten years later their share had doubled, and this despite the efforts of the Swiss government to combat the danger of *Überfremdung* and to reduce the number of foreign workers by 10 percent. West Germany and France attached millions of foreign workers, many of them permanent, and hundreds of thousands of immigrants from the Commonwealth had settled in Britain. The guest workers in Germany came mainly from Turkey and Southern Europe. The guest workers in France came above all from North Africa, and those in England from the Caribbean, India, and Pakistan. The presence of the "guest workers" was an economic necessity, but socially and politically it created major problems. There were language difficulties, they did not always enjoy equal social benefits, and during a recession they were likely to be the first dismissed. They took over entire quarters and suburbs in European cities, and there was friction with the local population. When Enoch Powell, a British Conservative leader, asked for voluntary repatriation in 1968, he had the leadership of the political parties and the whole establishment against him, but public opinion in the areas affected was largely on his side. The government of the day adopted stringent measures to restrict further immigration, which meant in some cases that holders of British passports were prevented from entering Britain.

The outward manifestations of rising living standards were all

too obvious, but not all classes and groups of people benefited from
the general prosperity to the same extent. Average living standards
do not indicate the contrast between rich and poor, or between the
urban and the rural population. Although the following figures are
indicative of the general trend, they leave a great many questions
unanswered. Real wages increased between 1953 and 1965 by approximately 36 percent in the United Kingdom, by 58 percent in
France, 80 percent in Italy, and 100 percent in West Germany. In
absolute terms, wages were highest in 1964 in the Scandinavian countries ($1.25–$1.40 per hour as compared with $2.00 in the United
States). In West Germany, the Netherlands, and Switzerland the
hourly wage was at the time roughly $1.00, but in France only 75
cents and in Italy 60 cents. Real hourly wages in West Germany in
1948 had been about as high as in 1914, 35 cents, but they trebled
during the next fifteen years. Since then the wage level has tended to
become more uniform in the major European countries. Wages in
light industries (textiles, food, shoes) have been consistently below
the average, whereas printers, miners, and those employed in the
growth industries were paid the highest wages. The wages of unskilled
workers increased faster than those of their skilled and semiskilled
colleagues. Wages rose faster than prices, which were relatively stable
in the fifties; between 1955 and 1960 they rose by a mere 7–9 percent
in West Germany and Italy, whereas in France they increased by 35
percent in the same period. During the next five years the general
trend was much more uniform; West European prices rose by 20
percent, with Germany and France slightly below the average, and
the Italian figure up to 24 percent.

This constant rise in real wages was the result of a steady increase
in productivity. Within Europe there were substantial differences, with
the most developed industrial countries in the lead. Europe suffered
from certain obvious disadvantages in comparison with America: a
low level of investment, a limited market with its corollary of small-
scale production and insufficient allocations for scientific and technological research. Nevertheless, all European countries witnessed an
unprecedented rise in labor productivity in the 1950s, partly as a
result of technological improvement but mainly because of more efficient use of machinery and of the labor force.

Despite this remarkable progress, the feeling grew in Europe that
there was a dangerous technology gap and that the old continent was

GROWTH OF LABOR PRODUCTIVITY 1949–59

(Compound Annual Percentage of Growth)

West Germany	5.7	Holland	3.6
Italy	4.8	Sweden	2.9
Austria	4.8	Belgium	2.7
France	4.3	United States	2.0
Spain	4.3	United Kingdom	1.8
Switzerland	3.7		

falling behind the Far East. The gap was clearly noticeable in the most modern (and most promising) fields of advanced technology, such as automation and electronics. America spent more than any European country on research and development (between 3 and 3.5 percent of its GNP) in the 1960s, compared with 2.2 in Britain, roughly 1.3–1.6 in France and Germany, and less than 1 percent in Italy. There are no reliable figures for Russia, but Soviet expenditure was believed to be between 2 and 3 percent. Superior working conditions and higher salaries attracted European scientists and technologists to the United States; during the late fifties it was only a small flow, about thirteen hundred persons between 1956 and 1961, but these included some of the most promising young graduates, who had decided to join MIT, Caltech, or private industry. Their number increased in the sixties and eventually affected between 10 and 20 percent of the science and technology graduates in Switzerland, Holland, the Scandinavian countries, and also in Britain.

TRADE UNIONS:
POWER AND WEAKNESS

European trade unions have for over a century played an important role in defending the rights of the working class. After protracted struggles, they gained universal recognition. By 1945 the struggle had been won, and they became a powerful force on the social scene, whether supporting the government or in opposition, although at times public opinion was antagonized. In the eyes of revolutionaries, the trade-union leaders were reformists, defenders of the establishment who had given up the struggle for a radical transformation of society; all they wanted were better conditions for their members within the present social order. In the view of the nonsocialist critics, the ossified trade-union bureaucracy, with its shortsighted, bigoted approach, constituted the major obstacle to modernization, invariably putting the factional interests of their members above those of society as a whole.

In the European trade-union movement the communists had two strong bases, the French CGT (which before 1940 had been close to the socialists), with 1.5 million members, and the Italian CGIL, with 3.5 million members. These two were the strongest trade-union movements in France and Italy. They had, however, to compete with sizable minority groups (CFTD and CGT/FO in France, and CISL and UIL in Italy) which were under socialist and Christian Democratic influences, respectively. The British Trade Union Congress (TUC), close to the Labour Party, had about eight million members and was thus the strongest union movement in Europe; the German DGB followed with about 6.5 million members (1967). The communist trade-union movements belonged to the Soviet-controlled WFTU (International

Confederation of Free Trade Unions). But these parent bodies exerted only a limited degree of control; the communist unions, for instance, did not approve the Soviet invasion of Czechoslovakia in 1968, much to the chagrin of the Soviet sponsors of the WFTU. The communist unions of Western Europe displayed a great deal of militancy but were not really preparing for social revolution, as shown by the stabilizing role played by the French CGT in the dramatic events of May–June 1968. Although France and Italy had a high incidence of strikes (higher in Italy than in France), this had its roots in the general social climate of these countries, not in the beliefs and activities of union leaders. Strikes in England, which were only slightly less frequent than in France, had a more disruptive effect on the economy, because so many of them were unofficial in character. In the British union movement the archaic concept of the craft union still prevailed and there were still hundreds of small unions, whereas in the United States, West Germany, and many other countries, workers were organized in big industrial units, such as the IG Metall in West Germany, uniting all workers in a given industry regardless of their job in the factory. British trade-unionism was plagued by demarcation disputes (who should do what in a factory), and frequently a minor quarrel between two small unions paralyzed a whole industry. There were some mass strikes in other European countries (for instance, in Denmark in 1965, in Belgium and Sweden in 1966), but on the whole there was not much social unrest in the small European countries and even less in West Germany, where strikes were virtually unknown—though strike threats were not. The German union leaders were no less tough than their colleagues in France, Italy, and Britain, and they were more successful in getting higher wages and better working conditions for their members; they were more aware that modernization was inevitable and took a more positive attitude toward the introduction of automation in industry. Some of their colleagues in Britain and France, on the other hand, fought tooth and nail for the survival of crafts and methods of work that were antiquated and clearly wasteful. The Germans realized earlier that they had to adapt themselves to technological progress, and decided to run their own retraining schemes for their members.

Trade-union leaders attained a much higher status than ever before: in Britain they were knighted; in Germany even the radicals among them became members of the supervisory councils of leading enterprises; in France and Italy their views were listened to with attention by the leaders of the state. But at the same time the limits of trade-union power had become much clearer. The membership was not on the whole interested in political demonstrations. Their attitude toward the unions was utilitarian; they needed unions to defend their interests and to improve their conditions, but not as the chosen instrument to carry out their political demands. From the 1970s onward, the number of workers organized in unions began to shrink in most European countries, for a variety of reasons. The number of manual workers declined, and the unions were less successful in organizing those employed in the service sectors. Certain industries with a militant tradition (such as the mine workers) were affected more than others; British miners found out to their detriment that strikes were pointless at a time when many pits were closed down because they were no longer economical. Generally speaking, during the 1980s there was relatively little working-class militancy, or, at any rate the unions exercised their influence through means other than mass strikes.

THE NEW
MANAGERIAL CLASS

James Burnham, in a book widely read during the Second World War, had drawn attention to the political implications of the emergence of a new class, the managers, who, he predicted, would gradually gain control over politics and the economy in both the communist and the Western worlds. In their extreme form, these predictions have not materialized; the technocrats' influence has certainly grown, but they are running neither the Soviet Union nor the leading Western countries. Economic decision-making in France as in Britain, in Germany as in Italy, has passed from the traditional nineteenth-century patron or *Unternehmer* to the high civil servants in collaboration with the managers controlling all but a few big companies. These managers are employees—they do not own the companies they represent—but ownership itself has become far more complex, with the family business giving way to the anonymous company.

This was one of the new trends cutting across existing class divisions; whether it had a basic effect on the social structure, except for providing greater mobility, is still open to doubt. The managers are not, strictly speaking, a "new class," certainly not in the classic Marxist concept of class, but since so much power has been concentrated in their hands, it seemed that a re-examination of the whole issue of the legal ownership of the means of production and its political significance was overdue. In a similar way, the higher ranks of the civil service have gained a great deal of power, independent of class interests and pressure groups, however influential. This trend became even more pronounced as socialist governments came to power and whole industries were nationalized. No one in his right mind was likely to argue that class interests no longer mattered, but the whole issue had become far more complex. This applied not only to the new breed of managers and civil servants, but equally to Churchill and de Gaulle, primarily concerned with the greatness of their native countries; they subordinated economic and social considerations to this overriding concern.

In the Soviet Union, as in the West, important changes took place in the social structure, but not always in the direction foreseen by the founding fathers of the regime. The Soviet Union remains committed to the ideal of a classless society, the means of production are not privately owned, and capitalism has not been restored, even though left-wing critics of Russian communism have long predicted it. There is still a great deal of social mobility, and the favored social groups have no firm tenure or security. At the same time there are enormous differences in status, income, and above all political power, not to mention the existence of "social economy." Various theories, such as the concept of "bureaucratic collectivism," have been applied to interpret the growing divergence between theory and reality. For in reality, though everyone was equal, some were clearly far more equal than others, with an income-tax maximum of 13 percent, virtually no death duty, and growing emphasis on rank, insignia, hierarchy, and social differentiation. Political power is in the hands of a small ruling elite consisting of high party, government, and military officials; in the selection of these officials and in the shaping of the policies they pursue, the average Soviet citizen has little if any say. Under Stalin the trend toward social stratification was particularly marked; the old tsarist system of uniforms and ranks returned with a vengeance. After Stalin's death Khrushchev tried to do away with the extremes of inequality. At this point, as far as the goal of social equality is concerned, the Soviet Union ranks somewhere in the middle of the European scale; differences in income and status are clearly more pronounced there than in the Scandinavian countries, while the welfare services are less developed. On the other hand, Soviet society is obviously more egalitarian than the societies of Southern Europe with their extremes of incomes and property. Some observers have argued that with growing prosperity the distortions of the communist ideal would gradually disappear and the ruling elite would fade away. But these predictions were not borne out by events.

More than any other European country, the Soviet Union seems to be subject to Roberto Michel's "iron law of oligarchy"; instead of "withering away," the state has become omnipresent and omnipotent. This is very much in contrast to Lenin's expectations: he wrote that, so long as the state existed, a Marxist had no right to speak of freedom.

In Western Europe the general development has been on the whole toward greater equality; wages and salaries have risen every-where, whereas income from property (interest, profits, rents) has fallen in Britain from 33 percent before the war to 26 percent of the national income, in Germany from 39 percent in 1950 to 30 percent in 1963. These figures are only roughly approximate; millionaires, too, earn salaries, and workers and peasants, on the other hand, also have incomes from savings and rents (it has been estimated that in Britain the working class accounts for two-thirds of all personal savings). All industrialized European countries have introduced income policies to ensure a fairer distribution of income and property. These measures have, however, been more successful in achieving an equitable distribution of earned income than of property. It was estimated that, in Britain in 1960, 5 percent of the population still owned about 75 percent of the total personal wealth, and there were still many ways and means of accumulating great wealth, and loopholes for evading death duties. In 1990 the top 10 percent of adults in Britain still owned 54 percent of the marketable wealth. The concentration of personal property is decreasing, though slowly, as taxation gradually takes its toll. The redistribution of the national product of Europe in favor of the lower income groups has been more marked since 1945 than during any other period since the nineteenth century, but the continuing existence of so much unearned income and property has been a source of much resentment. Trade-unionists have not as a rule taken kindly to the suggestion that they should pursue a policy of wage restraint while other (unearned) income was not affected by such restrictions.

Social goals in Europe after the Second World War have differed from those in America; there has been less public squalor in the midst of less private affluence. The welfare state has softened class divisions in European society, but it has not done away with them; so far it has achieved only a modest redistribution of income. Though social services have brought greater economic and social equality, there has been an inclination to belittle their effect; social reform came not in the wake of a great revolution but as the result of blueprints and administrative decisions. It came without sound and fury; there was no bloodshed, and no great passions were aroused. There was no great wave of idealism and anticlimax such as usually happens in a revolution. For these reasons the postwar social reforms have not gripped the imagination of the masses; they were welcomed and taken for granted, but they did not arouse much enthusiasm. In the long run, however, it is not the commotion that counts but the enduring results, and in this perspective the European welfare state, with all its imperfections and limitations, compares favorably with the more spectacular and radical attempts to transform society in the twentieth century.

PART THREE

EUROPEAN CULTURE:
The Postwar Scene

POSTWAR BLUES

Philosophers and poets pondered the idea of Europe during the darkest hours of the war and Nazi oppression. By 1945 little was left of intellectual Europe: many universities were in ruins; leading scientists, writers, and artists had perished. After Hitler's rise to power there had been a large-scale exodus from Germany, and later on, to a lesser extent, from France and Italy, Austria and Hungary: writers and physicists, sociologists and art historians, painters and composers settled in the New World and made important contributions to the development of their disciplines and of intellectual life in general in the United States. In some Nazi-occupied countries, such as Poland, the intelligentsia had been systematically exterminated. In the German universities entire disciplines, such as sociology and psychology, had been suppressed, while others had been confined to a mere shadow existence. In Italy the hand of the dictatorship had been less heavy on cultural life; it had not invariably opposed modern art, and an intellectual opponent of the regime like Croce had been left more or less in peace. But the climate of the dictatorship had not been congenial to the muses. Germany, Italy, and the occupied countries had been cut off for years from current trends in the outside world; a new generation had grown up in cultural isolation. Soviet Russia under Stalin had become a cultural wasteland, and the worst was yet to come.

No one doubted that it would take a long time to overcome the cultural ravages of fascism, Stalinism, and war. The terror and the war had been an experience that had profoundly affected all those who had lived through them. Perhaps that would act as a powerful stimulus to a new cultural revival. But the experience had been too negative, the destruction too extensive. What inspiration could satirists draw from Auschwitz? As the war ended, the shadow of mass destruction hung heavily over mankind. As one of the characters in Max Frisch's *The Chinese Wall* said: "A slight whim on the part of the man on the throne, a nervous breakdown, a touch of neurosis, a flame struck by his madness, a moment of impatience on account of indigestion—and the jig is up. Everything! A cloud of yellow or brown ashes boiling up towards the heavens in the shape of a mushroom, a dirty cauliflower—and the rest is silence, radio-active silence."

The prevailing mood as the last gun fell silent was one of anguish and helplessness. Human nature had been revealed in its basest aspects, and there was no certainty that there would not be an even more murderous repeat performance. But the hangover was not felt equally strongly in all countries; it did not hit them at exactly the same time, and it did not manifest itself everywhere in the same way. There had always been common European currents and fashions transcending national borders, but no country was quite like another, and alongside similarities there were profound differences.

The economic, social, and moral climate of France after the liberation was one of impotence and despair. As Michel Crozier said, "Everything seemed destined for failure in a country torn and disoriented, convinced that its future did not depend on itself." But within this general prostration there was an intense and enthusiastic intellectual life whose exponents enjoyed a very wide audience; their dramatic differences of opinion were treated as events of national importance: "They were prepared to involve themselves in politics, or at least in social criticism; they felt they were endowed with a mission and they sought by all available means to take part in action."

Fifteen years later a totally different situation prevailed. Optimism had returned following the great economic advance, and the people as a whole had regained confidence in a society that no longer seemed doomed. But intellectual life had lost its fervor and distinction.

The mood in Britain after 1945 was optimistic, but there were few outstanding intellectual leaders, and they certainly did not have a wide audience. The wave of protest in England came only ten years later; it was born neither of cosmic despair nor of Orwell's dire forebodings. Orwell had written after the war that "Since about 1930 the world had given no reason for optimism whatsoever. Nothing in sight except a welter of lies, cruelty, hatred and ignorance . . ." The protest of the angry young men had its roots in the boredom of the welfare state, the dissatisfaction with a far too rigid class structure, the disgust with the "shiny barbarism" of mass culture.

In West Germany, following the experience of Nazi rule and the postwar dislocation and uncertainties, it took a long time for any intellectual movement to develop. The literary avant-garde and some of the students constituted themselves a protest movement, but this became an event of national importance only in the middle sixties, when student demonstrations hit the headlines. Some of the sources of this movement were specifically German, such as the protest against the conservative tendencies in society, the complacency about the economic miracle. Others were part of the general European mood of boredom and the feeling of impotence: whatever the literary intelligentsia said or did, however shocking or revolutionary, it somehow seemed not to matter.

In Italy the intellectual climate resembled that of France in some respects but not in others, and the situation in countries that had been spared the ravages of war was again quite different. Sociologists noted a progressive Americanization of European mass culture, but on a higher level of intellectual endeavor differences between Europe and America, and also often between the various European countries, became more marked.

All over Europe the distance between the "two cultures" widened. In science tremendous advances had been made during the war years which were now applied to civilian use: atomic energy, jet propulsion, radar, antibiotics. In medicine whole groups of new drugs for dealing with infectious and mental diseases came on the market; tuberculosis, once a dreaded killer, was all but stamped out. This was the beginning of a new era of organ transplants, cardiac pacemakers, and cryosurgery. The biochemists established new fields such as molecular biology in their search for the secrets of the genetic code (DNA). Biological manipulation, for so long the preserve of science fiction, seemed now a distinct possibility. In other fields, such as space travel, science fiction was overtaken by the rapid advance of science: the invention of semiconductors in 1948, of integrated circuits and lasers, the development of guidance and control systems and of data processing generated a new technological revolution. The role of the computer was compared to that of the steam engine in the nineteenth

century; moreover, it was likely to match or simulate many of man's
intellectual capacities. Many of these new discoveries were made in
Europe. It was a time of tremendous excitement among scientists and
technologists; entirely new vistas opened up, and they found themselves out of step with the mood of the literary intelligentsia. National
frontiers mattered so much less to the physicist than to the writer or
poet; he was less addicted to pessimism and *Weltschmerz* and, incidentally, less to anti-Americanism.

Economists, sociologists, and political scientists were in demand
as advisers and consultants to government commissions, traveling
abroad on behalf of national and international organizations, providing guidance to private business and public bodies. In various ways
the critics of society were integrated, drawn into "the system." Many
of them felt that, with the old passions spent, the end of ideology was
in sight. This left the literary intelligentsia, the writers and poets, the
theologians and philosophers, as the only ones to fulfill what they
thought of as the real mission of the intellectual: to be an outsider,
to undertake a comprehensive critique of society, radically to reject
existing conditions, and to appeal to the conscience of mankind. This
function they fulfilled with all the verve they could muster, but also
all the traditional fondness for broad generalizations and the same
contempt for hard facts that Tocqueville had noted a century earlier
when writing about the *hommes de lettres* in the age of the French
Revolution.

The story of the postwar-European *Zeitgeist* is largely the story
of the moods and frustrations of the literary intelligentsia. The decay
of prewar Europe as they saw it was now even more advanced; everything had become, as Moravia said, an imbroglio of lies. In the new
philosophy being was without reason, without cause, without necessity. If human existence was unintelligible, so, very often, was the
new art: the new drama concentrated on the more painful aspects of
life, and conversation became often altogether unintelligible, an "absurd noise." Anxieties and obsessions, crime and guilt, sickness and
insanity, torture and the collapse of morals became the central topics
of the contemporary novel, the avant-garde play and film. To describe
them was thought to have a cathartic effect, to be the best cure. In
this general reaction against nineteenth-century optimism, even theologians preached that religion was torment, not peace; malady, not
health; it did not mark the road to salvation but revealed the whole

problematic character of existence. This was not a comforting picture, and the politics of the men of letters were, not surprisingly, those of radical protest. The protest did not always follow from their philosophy, for despair does not necessarily breed activism. The protest was the expression of a mood, not a logical conclusion.

How deep was this postwar despair? In part, no doubt, it was a fashionable and highly marketable *Weltschmerz*. As material conditions improved and the economic miracle got under way, the public seemed positively to relish the joyless plays, novels, and films. In part it was genuine, especially during the early postwar years. There is a world of difference between the stark horror and pessimism of that time and the fashionable *ennui*, and *noia* of the late fifties. But the despair of the man of letters had more specific origins: he realized with bewilderment that his universe had become an unsolvable mystery; the separation of culture and scientific knowledge had become almost complete in a world of progressive specialization. The scientists had made tremendous progress and gained great prestige as a class. To what comparable achievements could poets and composers point, or philosophers and theologians? It was only too tempting in this situation to question the value of scientific advance: what good was it to mankind if so much of it was devoted to inventing and perfecting means to destroy civilization and human life? The man of letters and the artist felt isolated in this absurd world. The radical departures from tradition in modern art were rejected by a public that preferred the Beatles to stochastic music, *My Fair Lady* to both the theatre of the absurd and kitchen-sink drama, and Brigitte Bardot to Ingmar Bergman. The marital affairs of Queen Soraya and Queen Fabiola, not to mention Aly Khan, continued to preoccupy the millions, the ideas of Lukacs and Ernst Bloch only a few thousand. The revolutionaries were now talking in a language that only the avant-garde could understand. "Alienation" became the favorite and often misused catchword of the literary intelligentsia, which refused to look for a place in a world that seemed both hopeless and senseless. A great many prophets of doom raised their voices and found an enthusiastic public.

The widening of the gulf between the intellectuals and the rest of society, the radical protest against the "establishment," the increasing distance between the man of letters and the artistic avant-garde on the one hand, and the social and natural scientist on the other, were phenomena common to many countries as the capitals of Europe moved nearer to one another. Before the Second World War a trip abroad was considered a luxury, a preserve of the affluent. By the early sixties it had become almost the exception to find high-school graduates who had not visited one or more foreign countries, often for a lengthy period. National frontiers mattered less than at any time in the past. German philosophy triumphed in France after the war; Kafka and Brecht were discovered in Paris and London; Italian films had a profound impact on the cinema throughout the continent. Music and theatre festivals at Salzburg, Bayreuth, and Edinburgh brought leading composers and critics together each year. Boulez found more congenial surroundings for his work in West Germany; Stockhausen was equally at home in France or Germany. The Italian composers Berio and Nono were fêted in England as much as in their native country. Among the pioneers of the new style in French painting, Hartung and Wols were German by origin, de Stael and Lanskoy Russian; Zak was Polish, Vasarely Hungarian, Michaux Belgian. Crosscurrents and cross-fertilization could be observed in every field: successful novels were translated into foreign languages within a few weeks; hit songs spread within days to the farthest corner of Europe. Movies and TV programs steeped in local color were shown all over the continent; millions of Czech citizens watched with bated breath the incredible adventures of that improbable German hero of the Wild West, Old Shatterhand; millions of Poles followed with breathless tension the successes and failures of Dr. Finlay, the Scots country physician. The impact of American civilization was felt even in France, which jealously guarded its cultural independence. It is impossible to explain French postwar literature without reference to Faulkner and Hemingway, and by 1960 the French language itself had been so corrupted that there was an outcry against that new bastard lingo, "Franglais." It was not, of course, one-way traffic, for every European intellectual current and fashion, from existentialism to the miniskirt, was eagerly absorbed in the United States.

Some of these currents were mere seven-day wonders; others had a lasting effect. Psychoanalysis profoundly influenced European thought. The significance of the work of Sigmund Freud, who died in 1939, had been realized before the war by a small circle of devoted followers in Germany; in his native Austria he was virtually ignored; there were a handful of disciples in other European countries, but academic psychiatry had rejected psychoanalysis, and few others had anything but a vague notion about the superego, transference, and the Oedipus complex. During the Nazi era, psychoanalysis was banned as a ferment of decomposition; in the Soviet Union and postwar Eastern Europe, it was considered a counterrevolutionary trend, and the Catholic church, too, vehemently denounced it. The prospects of psychoanalysis at the time seemed very dim indeed, yet after the war, having become firmly rooted in the United States, it was rediscovered in Europe and enjoyed a great revival. Its impact in the medical field was not so strong as its indirect influence on education, literature, and the arts.

More pervasive still was the impact of Marxism. There had been Marxist parties in Europe for almost a century, some of them fairly strong; but among the intelligentsia Marxism had not made great strides before 1945, except perhaps in Weimar Germany and among some East European and Viennese intellectuals. This changed after the war: many French and Italian intellectuals were attracted by Marxist ideas; the prewar polemics between little groups of cognoscenti about class consciousness, imperialism, and dialectics of nature were rediscovered and eagerly refought. Even among the British, the traditional empiricists and enemies of philosophical speculation, Marxism found some fervent advocates. As a rule it was not Marxism in its simplified Russian form, which in the European context seemed too crude and unsophisticated; nor was it the traditional orthodox Marxism of Karl Kautsky, which was too pedantic and uninspiring. European intellectuals were more interested in the ideas of the young Marx on alienation than in his economic doctrines. Lenin and Stalin were less eagerly studied than the intellectual deviationists such as the Italian Gramsci or the German Karl Korsch. Lukacs, the Hungarian communist who had quarreled with the Russians in the 1920s about the function of class consciousness, had a remarkable revival after the war; so, within more modest limits, did Ernst Bloch, who on a Marxist basis had developed a nonmaterialist philosophy of hope. In France and Italy native schools of Marxist thought developed, much of it devoted to the exegesis of the master rather than to innovation. Even nonconformist Marxists such as Lucien Goldmann or Althusser did not venture far beyond the ideas that had their origins in Germany, Holland, and Austria between the two world wars. At the end of the fifties the interest in Marxism abated somewhat; the new radicalism of the sixties had different sources. The war in Vietnam acted as a catalyst for a protest movement that was more often anarchist, pacifist, or utopian-socialist than Marxist in character. The new rebels had few illusions about the role of the proletariat as an agent of revolution; the workers, they maintained, had been corrupted by the welfare state and absorbed into neocapitalist society; fresh impulses toward radical change could emanate only from among the young, especially the students, and their natural allies, the "damned of the earth," the downtrodden, exploited masses of the underdeveloped countries. The new revolutionary movement of the sixties was elitist and antiliberal in character, and though it did not reject the Marxist heritage altogether, its real roots were not dissimilar to those of earlier youth movements in Europe, before and after the First World War—romantic protest against society and its conventions, in which cultural pessimism and boredom were mixed with an awakened social conscience. In part the new youth movement was rational and political in character, in part an irrational manifestation of the new malaise of postindustrial society.

THE GREAT CONFRONTATION

The great confrontation among intellectuals in the late forties and fifties was between communism and its critics. It is not easy in retrospect to understand its intensity or the passion that went into it. The popularity of communism was mainly due, as Georges Bernanos said, to the shortcomings of Western societies and the moral default of those who should have stood for spiritual values; young intellectuals became communists in the same way that young priests and young nobles in the eighteenth century had been enraptured by the Social Contract and Jean-Jacques Rousseau. They were disturbed by the injustices of Western society; the direct impact of the Soviet Union (of which hardly anyone had firsthand knowledge) was relatively slight. In France and Italy communism appeared as the legitimate heir of the resistance movement, the one most likely to realize its dreams and aspirations. Guilt feelings played an important role: among those in Italy who had been fascist fellow travelers as young men, or those in France who had refrained from active involvement in the resistance, many now became zealous converts to communism. Their position was not enviable as the Cold War unfolded: the communist intellectuals had to defend the policies of Stalinism, which became progressively more irrational and indefensible. Communism was then in its most belligerent mood and became more and more isolated. At one stage or another, every single communist intellectual was bound to have doubts about the infallibility of the party, but many hesitated for a long time to express any critical view, because they felt that by voicing doubts they would not merely put themselves outside the party but in fact join the class enemy, reaction and fascism. Robert Debreuilh in Simone de Beauvoir's *Mandarins* knew about the existence of forced-labor camps in the Soviet Union but refused to talk or write about them; it would be "tantamount to working against mankind." This, then, was the typical dilemma of the fellow-traveling intellectual of the late 1940s: whatever its current difficulties, communism was not only basically true, it was also the wave of the future.

There was a great deal of confusion and fear among all classes of the population after the Prague coup and the outbreak of the Korean War, when Soviet occupation of Western Europe seemed a distinct possibility. Communists in France and Italy at that time dominated the writers' and artists' associations, calling on fellow artists and writers not merely to protest against American aggression in Korea, or to sign manifestos for world peace, but to condemn "Judas" Tito and the many other wreckers and criminals who were so suddenly and implausibly uncovered in the socialist countries of the East. This was the age of big cultural congresses (Wrocław in 1948, Paris and Prague in 1949); Fadeyev, addressing the Wrocław Congress of Intellectuals, declared, "If hyenas could use fountain pens and jackals could use typewriters they would write like T. S. Eliot." The World Peace Council claimed 550 million signatures to its appeal—not all, admittedly, intellectuals: Picasso and Joliot-Curie, Neruda and Laxness, Yves Montand, Gérard Philippe, Simone Signoret, and the dean of Canterbury were among the many enthusiastic supporters.

The communist campaign was bound to provoke resistance among some sections of the intelligentsia. It was not likely to clash with believing Christians, for with them it had no common language. Right-wing intellectuals, with a few exceptions, had been discredited during the war. The countermovement originated among left-wing intellectuals, not a few of them ex-communists. David Rousset, who with Sartre and Camus had helped to found a new left-wing party in

Paris, appealed in November 1949 to all former fellow deportees to
Nazi Germany to support an investigation into conditions in Soviet
concentration camps. The communist reaction was predictable, but
Sartre and many other fellow travelers also turned against Rousset:
"With whom are you—with the people of the Soviet Union, building
a new society, or with their enemies?" But more and more intellectuals
began to raise their voices in defense of freedom of culture, and rival
cultural congresses were arranged. The communist leadership in the
writers' and artists' associations was challenged; new literary magazines came into being. Each fresh wave of repression in the East caused
new defections among the procommunist intellectuals. The Soviet
campaign against Tito, the trials and death sentences in Eastern Europe, the increasing repression during Stalin's last years made it more
and more difficult for an intellectual to defend communism with an
untroubled conscience. After Hungary, and especially after Khrushchev's famous "secret speech," it became obvious who had been
right, in the quarrels between communist and anticommunist intellectuals during the first decade after the war, about the real situation
in the Soviet Union.

Aggressive Stalinism was a greater threat to the cultural values
of the West than Franco or Salazar, and it demanded more foresight
and also more courage to stand up and be counted at that time of
peril than to stay neutral. In later years critics claimed that the Stalinist
danger had been mythical and that the Cold War had been largely
the creation of the intellectual Cold Warriors who had strayed from
the real vocation of the intellectual, which was to be a critic of his
own society and an enemy of his government; by betraying their true
mission the intellectuals defending cultural freedom had committed
a new *trahison des clercs*. The anti-Stalinist intellectuals were not
easily forgiven for being right.

After 1956 the thaw set in, and within narrow limits cultural
exchanges between West and East got under way. These cultural
exchanges had a considerable impact on the younger generation in
the Soviet Union, and even more in the popular democracies, which
were more receptive to European ideas. Beyond the official condem-
nations, many Soviet intellectuals remained acutely aware of their
European heritage; they wanted to be part of Europe and to be accepted in the West as well as in their own country. The intelligentsia
in the Soviet Union and Eastern Europe fostered revolutionary ideas

and thus came into conflict with the conservative elements in communist society, above all in the party leadership, which, correctly from their point of view, regarded criticism by the intellectuals as a menace undermining their authority.

A new upsurge of Marxist and para-Marxist ideology took place in West Germany, and to a lesser degree in Britain and some of the smaller European countries, following the student unrest in the late 1960s. A new generation of intellectuals discovered for itself ideas that had sprouted in Germany in the 1920s; for more than a decade these were the trendsetters in the universities. But, as always, it was not a universal trend. In Italy, and in particular in France, the 1970s witnessed growing criticism of Marxism; even before Sartre died, he had been half forgotten and his status as the guru of a generation was largely taken over by his great antagonist, the skeptical liberal Raymond Aron. The publication of Solzhenitsyn's Gulag trilogy had an enormous impact and helped to bring about the ideological turnabout. But dozens of books on the Stalinist camps and the terror had been published for many years before without having a remotely similar impact. Obviously, the time was ripe for a reaction against the late 1940s, when the extreme left had been the undisputed vanguard in France and Italy. In West Germany and Britain there had been no such left-wing upsurge until two decades later. In the 1980s neo-Marxism showed clear signs of exhaustion all over Europe, with yesterday's insiders becoming outsiders again. This was clearly connected with the ebbing fortunes of the regimes in the Soviet Union and Eastern Europe. Radicals on the left found new preoccupations and outlets, among which ecological problems figured most prominently.

No survey of postwar intellectual developments would be complete without mentioning, however briefly, the reforms in the Protestant and Catholic churches. This refers, for instance, to the liturgical movement among the Protestants and the political engagement of leading churchmen in the peace movement and other causes of the left. Perhaps even more dramatic were the changes introduced by Pope John XXIII (Angelo Roncalli), who convoked an Ecumenical Council (1962–65) to revolutionize the social teachings of the church. True, Pope John's successor did not share his reformist zeal, and the changes were slowed down. But even in its later, conservative phase the Catholic church committed itself to active participation in politics;

it played a crucial role in the events in Poland, as in certain third-world countries.

THE KNOWLEDGE REVOLUTION

Common to all countries was a knowledge revolution which manifested itself in almost every field. This refers to school reform with the aim of democratization, and a veritable explosion in higher education. Many universities expanded tenfold or more with classes swelling to enormous sizes. New universities came into being in the 1950s and 1960s; by 1990 they had firmly established themselves—from East Anglia and Brighton to Nanterre, Konstanz, and farther east and south.

After 1945 the paperback revolution and the long-playing record brought literature and music to the masses as never before; later on, records were replaced first by cassettes and still later by compact discs—all within the lifetime of one generation. The age of the computer dawned, profoundly affecting not only the economy but also science and entertainment. Television made for a passive, consumers' culture with many problematical implications. But it is also true that the number of scientists now alive is greater than that of all scientists that have ever lived over the centuries. Similarly, more people are now writing, painting, composing, and performing music than ever before.

The role of science and technology became even more crucial for society and the state. In Britain, France, West Germany, and other countries, ministries of science and technology were established and a significant part of the national product was devoted to scientific research. While in the United States government-financed research declined, that of the EEC almost doubled between 1965 and 1981. Yet the cost of research, especially in the nuclear field and in space, increased so rapidly that, even in cooperation, Europe was in danger of falling behind the United States and also Japan.

Compared with the natural sciences, the humanities seemed to stagnate, but this was not a specifically European development. There was an infinite variety of philosophical schools which had little in common with one another—neither the subjects they addressed nor the language they used. Sociology and political science greatly expanded after the war, but it is difficult to point to any specific European contribution, even though their cradle had been in Germany and France, in Britain and Italy. In the Soviet Union and Eastern Europe these disciplines had virtually ceased to exist under Stalinism. They were given some modest latitude during the first thaw (1955–64) and only under glasnost did they begin to come into their own.

In the West, interest in history continued undiminished; contemporary history became a legitimate topic of research in the postwar period, and social history attracted more practitioners (though not necessarily readers) than the more traditional branches such as diplomatic history. But the great controversies of the time—such as the German historians' dispute on the outbreak of World War I, and later on, in the 1980s, the argument about Nazism—still concerned political history.

In economics as in sociology, the center of gravity moved after 1945 from Europe to the United States. But the basic ideas on which postwar economic thought came to rest had emerged in Britain and in smaller European countries such as Austria and Sweden during the previous decades. Those who developed them further were often European émigrés. This refers as much to liberal doctrine (Hajek, von Mises) as to neo-Marxism. Keynesianism, which argued that the main purpose of a national economy was to provide full employment and that inflation and rising prices were not (as orthodox economists believed) an unmitigated disaster, had much influence after the war, though more in the academic world than in government. In the 1950s there was a shift away from economic theory to the application of new techniques such as econometrics and input-output analysis. Keynesianism seemed less and less relevant, because it could be said that "we are all Keynesians," including Mrs. Thatcher: even under her government, public spending continued to rise most of the time.

A history of European culture in the twentieth century has not been written, and it is unlikely that it ever will be written, for the simple reason that it would have to cover far too much ground and that there are not enough common themes.

If, nevertheless, such a cultural history is written, one of the important early chapters ought to focus on French existentialism. Intellectually, France in the years after the war was undoubtedly the most exciting country in Europe, and existentialism emerged as the philosophy of the day.

Jean-Paul Sartre, its high priest, was forty when the war ended.
He had studied German philosophy before the war and was profoundly influenced by Husserl and Heidegger. A philosophy at the
same time pessimistic and activist, existentialism maintained that man
was essentially what he made of himself, and that his existence preceded his essence. The world was not by itself intelligible; it was up
to man (and man alone) to choose a meaning for his life, and for the
world in general. There was no room for religion or any other me-
taphysical scheme, in this philosophy; in Sartre's view, God and Reason had disappeared from the world in the twentieth century. His
philosophy was one of freedom and choice, leading man beyond despair; it was to save mankind from the basic absurdity of life and the
lack of purpose by engagement and the cult of action. Under the
impact of the war and the influence of Marxism, existentialism stood
for the radical transformation of bourgeois society—indeed, for revolution in Europe as elsewhere.

The politics of existentialism has been discussed in countless
articles, philosophical tracts, and even novels and plays; in retrospect,
Sartre's influence as a playwright was considerably greater than as a
political philosopher. Sartre and his friends were usually less interested
in the real facts and merits of a case than in the "correct position"
to be taken by the intellectuals, and this led them into situations they
were later to regret.

However, existentialism, increasingly fragmented, by no means
had the scene all to itself; the left-wing Catholics, on the basis of a
Weltanschauung quite different from Sartre's, reached conclusions
remarkably similar to his. They thought little of Western civilization
in its present state and bitterly opposed the established order. They
tried never to oppose the Communist Party, which was for them the
progressive force par excellence and the motor of history.

This lasted for a decade, and then a new movement, anti-
ideological and antimetaphysical in character, gathered ground. The
leading philosophers and writers no longer claimed to have immediate
messages for the troubled world. Political and social messages were
increasingly ignored, the problems of the human condition dismissed.
Whereas in the early postwar years the position of the Communist
Party had been almost unassailable among the intellectuals, by 1965
not many of the erstwhile enthusiasts remained, and yet another
twenty years later a party very much reduced in size and influence

had few intellectuals left in its ranks. If in the exciting early postwar years the doctrine of universal responsibility had been heatedly discussed in the coffeehouses of the *rive gauche,* positivism, hard concrete facts, figured far more prominently in the intellectual discourse twenty-five years later, and structuralism began to take over many positions in which existentialism had reigned supreme.

The general mood in Italy was in some respects similar to that in France—a moral hangover, the feeling that there had been a massive *trahison des clercs* under fascism and that, as a result, Italy was in a state of disarray. Many prominent Italian intellectuals turned to the extreme left as a delayed reaction against fascism; many had a bad conscience for having accommodated themselves with the Mussolini regime. In addition, there was a general feeling that the upper classes had actively cooperated with fascism and the church had not behaved much better. But, unlike in France, there were no new philosophies; neorealism permeated the work of the writers and the filmmakers. Such early postwar films as *Rome—Open City* and *The Bicycle Thief* were successful far beyond the border of Italy, portraying the fear, the poverty, and the weakness of Italy during the last year of war and after the liberation.

After 1950 subtle changes took place. The partisan leader and hero gradually disappeared, and though there was still revulsion against upper-class moral corruption (*La Dolce Vita*), despair about the lower-middle-class way of life and the emptiness of small-town life were equally often the main theme. Literature became less political and more literary, the positive heroes more contemplative, even passive. Much of Italian culture was deliberately regional in character, in the absence of a single cultural center as in France and England. Italian cultural life in the 1960s and 1970s presented a contradictory picture of somnolence and vitality, even hyperactivity, of provincialism and great openness to outside influences. The latest French avant-garde novels and Soviet poems became known earlier in Italy than in other countries, but the creative tension of the early postwar years disappeared.

The cultural scene in Britain was quite different from the continental: there was little cosmic despair or abstract activism. True, the intelligentsia had become far more politically active during the war. But there seemed to be much less reason for pessimism in postwar Britain than on the continent, despite the immediate deprivations and the austerity. The young intellectuals frequently found their place in the Labour movement, which dominated the British political scene in the early postwar period and effected important social and economic changes. Ideological controversies in the French style seemed quite pointless in the circumstances. Nor is it possible to point to any outstanding trend, group, or movement in the early postwar age; neither T. S. Eliot nor E. M. Forster, neither Evelyn Waugh nor George Orwell regarded himself as the head of a school or as a guru. True, in the 1950s, when the immediate hopes connected with a Labour victory had faded, there was a strong trend toward apathy on the one hand, and on the other a great deal of anger among the young generation. Between 1954 and 1956 *Lucky Jim, Look Back in Anger,* and *Room at the Top* were published, clearly expressing a certain common mood, a wish to break certain taboos. And yet, with all the private and public frustration and boredom, it took not many years for the angry young men to make their peace with the world.

True, the banner of radicalism was subsequently taken up by a yet younger generation defying the establishment with their songs (the Beatles), their journals (*Private Eye*), and the antinuclear marches. Anti-Americanism became *de rigueur* in some circles, and a New Left discovered somewhat belatedly Lukacs, Gramsci, and Ernst Bloch. But there was also a general upsurge in cultural activity: much of the art trade moved from Paris to London; there was more interest than ever in concerts, operas, and the ballet; and the London theatrical scene witnessed the end of cultural provincialism. Traditionally, British cultural life had been largely concentrated in the capital, but with the opening of many redbrick universities there was a substantial change in the pattern. A new wave of radicalism among the intellectuals took place as the ruling Tory Party turned right under Mrs. Thatcher. The prime minister clearly preferred successful businessmen to ineffectual dons, and the intellectuals retaliated in kind.

Before 1933 the position of Germany in many sciences, in literature, and in the arts had been pre-eminent, but the anticultural policy of Nazism had caused irreversible damage. True, the German universities reopened their gates soon after the end of the war, books were published, plays and concerts performed, movies released. But years were to pass until West Germany was to overcome, at least in part, the effects of the missing years. First to gain recognition were the proponents of contemporary music (which had been banned altogether under Hitler) and to some extent also the playwrights. The award of Nobel prizes to German scientists in the 1970s and 1980s tended to show that Germany had again caught up with other centers of modern science.

Among the literary intelligentsia it was difficult at first to detect specific trends and schools of thought. After a decade many intellectuals began to put themselves into deliberate opposition to a society that, they claimed, was smug, conservative, dishonest, devoid of cultural values. In later years there appeared also a fairly strong admixture of anti-Americanism in the fashionable literary circles and among the filmmakers: these views also gained considerable influence in the universities. "Society" reacted by declaring the *littérateurs* irresponsible, purely destructive in their criticism, uninformed about the basic facts of social, economic, and political life. While the writers went on castigating the "lies of bourgeois society," their critics claimed that many of the new films, plays, and novels on political subjects were merely a travesty of reality. These controversies raged until the 1980s, when the polarization became less pronounced and the general climate somewhat more moderate. In any case, these stirrings had been limited to certain circles, and they had been part of a general European—indeed, global—trend. Forty-five years after the end of the war the German cultural balance-sheet was still disappointing compared with the achievements of the late nineteenth and early twentieth centuries, when Germany had been the *Kulturnation* par excellence. But these days had gone forever; if measured by more modest yardsticks and viewed against the German catastrophe under Hitler, postwar developments were not unpromising.

One of the cardinal issues affecting European cultural life was the breakdown in communication between the avant-garde and the general public. There had always been tension between the avant-garde and mass culture, nor was this a specifically European phenomenon. However, after the Second World War the distance between the preoccupation of the few and the taste of the many became greater than ever, especially in music and the plastic arts, but also to a certain extent in the theatre and the cinema. On the other hand, the postwar revolution in literature and architecture was less sweeping. These issues are philosophical and aesthetic in essence and cannot be discussed in the present context in view of their complexity. Suffice it to say that, whereas certain postwar fashions such as the theatre of the

absurd appealed to a wider public, at least for a while, most of the
modern trends in painting, sculpture, and also music did not have a
wide and lasting impact. They came under fire not so much because
of their daring experimentation, but because of their sterility, their
solipsism and lack of any attempt to communicate with the "consumer." Visitors to museums and galleries still preferred the old masters, even if these did not express the spirit of the age, and the same
was true, *mutatis mutandis,* with regard to recent music. While music
festivals in Bayreuth, Edinburgh, and Salzburg attracted many thousands each year, few conductors wanted to venture beyond Mahler
and Debussy, nor was there any strong demand from the public for
contemporary composers.

The controversies concerning the repertoire of the theatres were
on similar lines. Some contemporary plays in the 1960s seemed to be
based on the assumption that (as one critic put it) a prostitute or a
criminal was *a priori* more honest and more interesting than other
people, not merely that life was senseless and without any redeeming
features at all, but that love, ideals, honesty, heroism, kindness, the
spirit of sacrifice, optimism belonged to mass culture, were mere
"kitsch." The public reacted by queuing during two decades for tickets
for *The Mousetrap,* Agatha Christie's play. The leading theatres increasingly depended on state grants, and their directors had the unenviable task of striking a judicious balance between the popular
and the esoteric, the classic and the modern, the generally accepted
and the new and unfamiliar.

In the 1930s the position of the theatre had been threatened by
the cinema; after the war the cinema felt the pinch as the result of
the rapid progress of television. Between 1957 and 1963 one-third of
all British cinemas went out of business and were converted into
bowling alleys and bingo halls; the same trend was visible in other
European countries. As the production of movies became much more
costly, the number of new films declined, and though one could think
of some outstanding productions, the quality did not on the whole
compare favorably with the great prewar movies.

The full impact of television was only gradually felt. Television
was launched in England in June 1946 with 1,750 subscribers; in
West Germany in 1952 with 1,500. Saturation point was not reached
until the 1970s. Television drew audiences much larger than the other
mass media, and for longer periods, and had, therefore, a greater

impact on the public. This was also true vis-à-vis politics, as reflected in the impact of West German television on East Germany, that of Austrian television on her neighbors, and the struggle for Soviet television between conservatives and progressives.

The cultural influence of television was problematical. The main task of the new medium was light entertainment, frequently catering to the lowest common denominator. Though the general level of European television was superior to that of the American networks, the aversion of many intellectuals to the "idiot box," which propagated not only new heroes but something akin to a new way of life, was by no means splenetic. Competition between state-funded networks and commercial programs did not solve these problems: television largely set the national agenda, it had an important impact on the national leadership, it standardized and stultified cultural values. Television opened new horizons, but it also greatly contributed to the trend toward a less active and spontaneous culture, and this at a time when there was much more time for leisure pursuits than ever before.

THE SOVIET UNION

During the war many Soviet intellectuals had dreamed about a relaxation of political controls and greater cultural freedom. The years after brought bitter disappointment. A series of decrees was issued beginning in 1946 affecting eventually every aspect of cultural life, providing strictest regimentation. This policy became known as Zhdanovism, having been sponsored by one of the leading members of the Politburo, but it expressed, of course, the wish of the supreme leader and all his acolytes. Zhdanov died in 1948, but the policy he had inaugurated gathered even greater momentum after his death. Culture had not just to be partisan, it had to adhere to the party line in every little detail. The great watchword of the time was "socialist realism," but this did not mean that Soviet writers or painters had to depict reality truthfully—their supreme command was to embellish it. Soviet historians, philosophers, and economists had to quote Marx, Lenin, and above all Stalin as often as possible. Many books and essays written during this period were little more than a series of quotations from the "classics," loosely strung together. Novels, plays, and poems had to deliver a constructive message; heroes had to be positive, larger than life; real conflicts were taboo, for, according to official doctrine, they had disappeared from Soviet society; the only conflicts that still existed were between the good and the better. In these circumstances there was no room either for tragedy or for humor, and least of all for lyricism. Truly great artists were bitterly attacked and were no longer published, exhibited, or performed.

On top of the intolerable controls, certain new elements of cultural policy were introduced. This refers above all to the principle of Russian exclusivity and superiority and the concerted attack against "rootless cosmopolitans"—mainly but not exclusively Jewish writers, scientists, and artists. Many of them lost their jobs, and some also their lives. Whole disciplines, such as genetics, ceased to exist, and the number of movies released during the last years of Stalin's life declined to almost zero.

A gradual improvement took place after the death of the dictator. Slow at first, the "thaw" gathered momentum after 1956. True, two steps forward were usually followed by one backward step, and by about 1960 the outer limits of the new freedom had been reached. Still, during the thaw the gulf between official slogans and realities was reduced, and most of the writers and artists suppressed in the postwar era were again permitted to publish. Subjects that had previously been taboo were discussed in books, on stage, and on screen. Two parties emerged—some young and not-so-young liberals striving for greater cultural freedom, and a neo-Stalinism (anti-intellectualism and anti-Westernism with an admixture of chauvinism) which firmly believed that too much democracy would lead to the ruin of the country. Khrushchev was a liberating influence in various ways in Soviet politics, but he sympathized with the conservatives' view on cultural policy. Khrushchev made it repeatedly clear that he would not stand for the publication of "rubbish"—literature and art that were "ideologically harmful." Thus, even under Stalin's successors, every work of art had to have a message that had to conform with the party line.

The narrow limits of the new freedom were shown in the cases of Boris Pasternak and Alexander Solzhenitsyn. One of the greatest masters of the Russian language, Pasternak was awarded the Nobel Prize in 1958 for his novel *Doctor Zhivago*, published in Italy (but not in the Soviet Union) the year before. Pasternak was forced to reject the Nobel Prize and was attacked in the Soviet media in the most violent terms as a degenerate and a traitor to his country. Yet *Doctor Zhivago* was by no means an anti-Soviet novel, merely unpolitical; when it was eventually permitted to appear, thirty years later, most critics found it difficult to understand why at one time it had scandalized the political establishment.

In contrast to Solzhenitsyn, Pasternak was at least not expelled from his native country. Solzhenitsyn's *One Day in the Life of Ivan Denisovich* was not merely a literary event but a political sensation—the first description of life in a forced-labor camp. He, too, was awarded the Nobel Prize (in 1970) and attacked at home for distorting reality and for indulging a "pathological preoccupation with marginal aspects of Soviet life." The censorship refused to pass his next major novel, and eventually he was expelled from the Soviet Union, a fate he shared with a growing number of Soviet writers, painters, composers, filmmakers, ballet dancers, and musicians.

Exile, no doubt, was evidence of great progress since the Stalin era, when these men and women would have found themselves, at the very least, in the Gulag. But it also meant that no work of art critical of the party line could appear, that art must not be "modernistic" and that, generally speaking, the party had no desire to give up its function as ultimate arbiter on all things cultural. True, some of the works of some of Stalin's victims, such as Babel and Mandelstam, or even émigrés like Ivan Bunin could be published after 1960. But there was by no means full rehabilitation for them. In fact, after Khrushchev's fall, cultural controls were again tightened. De-Stalinization in history was discontinued; authors of samizdat fiction were arrested and sent to labor camps. Liberal editors were removed from their positions; bulldozers were sent to destroy open-air exhibitions of paintings that had not been officially sanctioned. True, some disciplines were more tightly controlled than others. Worst of all fared the "party sciences" (philosophy, history, economics, etc.). But even the natural sciences, which were less severely controlled, suffered great and lasting damage as the result of both political and bureaucratic interference.

Soviet cultural life was still largely cut off from the rest of the world; much creative endeavor was frustrated and stifled. Soviet writers, artists, and scientists were in no way inferior to their colleagues in the West, but they often lacked the opportunity to display their talent. Although a great creative potential existed, much of it was submerged under official restrictions. This state of affairs did not begin to change until glasnost, in the late 1980s.

A radical cultural reorientation had taken place in Eastern Europe after 1945, following the Soviet occupation and the emergence of communist governments. The intellectuals were expected to become communists, or at least to pay lip service to the new cause; they also had to embrace its specifically Russian elements, which caused additional resentment even among the left-wing intelligentsia. The new rulers distrusted the intelligentsia, and not without reason; as subsequently emerged, the rebellious intellectuals were very much behind the national upsurges that took place in Poland and Hungary in the 1950s and in Czechoslovakia in 1967–68.

However, the *Gleichschaltung* during the first postwar decade was followed by a period of greater cultural freedom than in the Soviet Union. Except for Rumania and Bulgaria, and in part also East Germany, cultural relations with the West were renewed; lip service still had to be paid to Soviet ideology, but there was a general reorientation toward the West, coupled with a reawakening of national themes. Whereas until about 1955 there had been little differences between the cultural policies of the various East European countries, such differences became quite pronounced thereafter.

The most dramatic changes took place in Poland in the 1950s, when Gomułka at first welcomed the support of the intelligentsia against the diehard Stalinists, only to turn against his erstwhile allies later on. Polish intellectuals were freer to visit the West than those from other East European countries, Western books and newspapers circulated more freely in Poland than elsewhere, and the Catholics were given a freer hand than any other church in the East to publish. Thus, with all the ups and downs on the political scene, cultural freedom made steady if unspectacular progress over the years, and by the 1970s and 1980s, despite all the setbacks, there was infinitely more freedom in Poland than in the Soviet Union.

This was very much in contrast to Czechoslovakia, where the military intervention of 1968 led to two decades of brutal cultural repression. The leading liberal intellectuals lost their jobs and all possibility of working in their profession. They played a leading role in the underground struggle against the authorities, which was symbolically recognized by the election of the playwright Vaclav Havel as the new president of a free Czechoslovakia in 1989. There was cultural repression in Hungary, too, after the clampdown of 1956, but it never went as far as in Prague. Kádár showed more tolerance than his Czech colleagues, and an uneasy compromise was reached with the intelligentsia; a "gray zone" of cultural activity came into being, disfavored by the authorities but not really banned.

Throughout the 1970s and 1980s the intellectuals achieved some more freedom of maneuver; Hungary was far from being a happy country, but it seemed almost heaven to the sorely tried intellectuals of East Germany. True, at one time it appeared as if the East German intelligentsia, despite their opposition to Ulbricht and Honecker, came to identify themselves to some extent with the new state, partly because they were critical of the negative features of life in West Germany, but also because they seemed to be proud of their own achievements, having recovered from the ravages of war and become the most prosperous country of the East European bloc. But a heavy price had to be paid for the new conformism; culturally East Germany became a desert with only a few oases. Once part of one of the world's cultural centers, East Germany became an East European backwater. During the 1970s and 1980s leading writers and artists, mainly of the younger generation, emigrated to West Germany; their exodus predated the great migration from East to West of 1989–90. The communist authorities seemed not to mind; the intellectuals were troublemakers and in any case easily replaceable. Culture seemed not to figure high among their priorities.

In the other East European countries there were widely different degrees of cultural freedom. In Yugoslavia party and state opposed what they considered "reactionary ideas," and individual heretics such as the erstwhile Politburo member Milovan Djilas spent many years in prison. However, gradually the cultural controls were relaxed and links with the West no longer obstructed. Rumania moved to national communism early on, but this was not accompanied by greater cultural freedom. On the contrary, right up to Ceausescu's fall in 1989, it remained one of the most repressive regimes in this as in other respects. Lastly, Albania remained under its Stalinist rulers the most backward of the East European countries, and also the most radical in orientation. It was the only regime in Europe, perhaps in the whole world, in which the constitution announced that religion had been officially abolished.

Thus intellectual life in Eastern Europe after Stalin's death followed a pattern that differed to a considerable degree from country to country. Intellectuals played an important role in the movement toward greater political freedom which eventually led to the revolutionary events of 1989. Their part was more decisive in some countries than in others, but everywhere they contributed to the advent of the day when the shackles were finally broken.

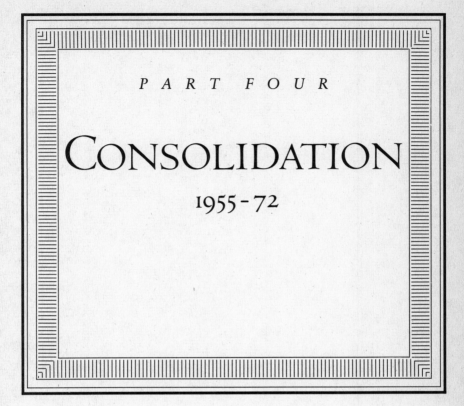

PART FOUR

CONSOLIDATION

1955-72

THE TWO BLOCS

Stalin's death and the gradual disappearance of the worst features of his regime gave rise to high hopes in the West: the end of the Cold War was believed to be at hand; a new era of détente and peaceful coexistence seemed to have dawned over a continent torn by bitter strife. Such optimism was only natural: the international climate was bound to improve after reaching its nadir in 1951–52. But the optimism prevailing at the time in the Western capitals was not altogether warranted; to a certain extent it was based on a misjudgment of the motives of Soviet policy, on the mistaken belief that Cold War and peaceful coexistence were mutually exclusive policies, whereas in fact they were only different aspects of Soviet foreign policy. The new rulers of Russia resented many of Stalin's methods; they wanted, within limits, an improvement in relations with the West, and above all with the third world. They had a more realistic understanding than Stalin of the consequences of a nuclear war, and wanted therefore to reach an agreement on the banning of the use of nuclear weapons. But they were still Stalin's disciples, good communists and Soviet patriots, feeling in their bones that their regime was not secure so long as communism had not prevailed all over the world. They felt acutely threatened by the spread of Western ideas to the "popular democracies" and ultimately to the Soviet Union. It was not at all clear whether they could afford to pursue a policy of peaceful coexistence without jeopardizing their whole system. Militarily the Soviet Union had little to fear, and even though its economic performance was lagging behind Western Europe's, there was steady improvement. Since only a handful of Soviet and East European citizens had the opportunity to compare Western and communist living standards at first hand, economic discontent did not constitute a major problem. The demand for more political freedom presented a more serious challenge. To resist this with any effect, the Soviet rulers had constantly to stress (and to exaggerate) the dangers allegedly facing the socialist camp from outside. Such an approach, however necessary for the survival of the regime, limited from the very beginning the scope of a rapprochement with the West. There was room for agreement on specific topics, but there could be no peaceful coexistence in the realm of ideas, as Soviet leaders frequently emphasized, and this in the last resort made a real détente impossible.

It is unlikely that the concept of world revolution has played a central role in Soviet political and strategic thought since the early 1920s. Under Stalin, Soviet foreign policy was directed to the acquisition and consolidation of spheres of interest, and his successors pursued basically the same line. This at first sight seemed a reassuring development from the Western point of view, for it created the precondition for a détente based on a division of spheres of influences as practiced at Yalta and Potsdam. But the Soviet Union was still the leader of the communist camp; it could not simply abdicate from this role, and the growing conflict with China made it altogether impossible for Russia to follow a policy based only on national interest. The West based its policy on *status quo* thinking; the Soviet leaders could not do so, for it would have fatally undermined the legitimacy of their rule. Soviet communism had little appeal in Europe beyond the borders of the Soviet state, but this did not make the Soviet leaders lose interest in the outside world. The Soviet positions in Poland, East Germany, Czechoslovakia, and Hungary were, they argued, necessary guarantees for the security of the Soviet state. But were the achievements of socialism in the "popular democracies" safe without yet another *cordon sanitaire* beyond the Iron Curtain—a neutral Germany, for instance? These aspirations clashed head-on with the desire of the European peoples to remain independent. Soviet troops had advanced into the heart of Europe; they were now stationed 150 miles from the French border, three hundred from the English Channel. Any further advance would have given them total domination of the continent. It is unlikely that at any time after the war Soviet leaders actively contemplated a march on the Channel. It is not so certain that they would have missed the opportunity, had it arisen, to acquire a dominating position in Western Europe.

Military considerations played a central role in the political negotiations of the fifties and sixties, and they ought to be at least briefly discussed. "Massive retaliation" was the official American strategy during the middle fifties, the threat to use the American nuclear arsenal to repel even a local Soviet attack. Russia could not at the time threaten the American continent, but Western Europe was to all intents and purposes a Soviet hostage. In October 1957 the first sputnik was launched, and at about the same time the Soviet Union began to develop its first intercontinental ballistic missiles (ICBMs). In Europe there was growing skepticism about the massive-retaliation doctrine; would America in a real crisis be willing to sacrifice American cities for the sake of Berlin, or even Paris and London? Would not undue reliance on nuclear bombs eventually lead to defeatism? For, while a general war was ruled out, local military action by the Soviet Union was certainly not, and there was no known way to counter it but by matching it in conventional strength. France and Britain had their own modest nuclear programs, but their conventional forces were inadequate, and Western Europe could not be defended without American help. France and Britain, Germany and Italy had mobilized millions of soldiers in the First and Second World Wars, but in the postwar world they found it increasingly difficult to make even the modest military effort needed to contribute their share to the defense of Europe. Britain and France had imperial commitments; even after these had been liquidated, the military position of the West in Europe did not substantially improve, and NATO was permanently under strength. There was a striking incongruence between Western Europe's economic performance and its military importance, which restricted its freedom of action and ultimately its political influence. It had, for instance, a much greater stake in the Middle East than the United States, in view of its dependence on oil supplies from the Persian Gulf and North Africa, but because of its military weakness and the absence of a common policy, it was incapable of defending its interests there and was practically reduced to the role of passive onlooker in the struggle between the Soviet Union and the United States for influence in the Middle East.

Painfully aware of their own weakness, many Western observers tended in the late fifties and early sixties to overrate Soviet military strength. The Kremlin, needless to say, did nothing to dispel these fears. Its nuclear arsenal was at the time much smaller than commonly assumed; it began to catch up with America only in 1966, while its conventional strength in Europe was probably only half of the 175 divisions with which it was generally credited. But even if Russia's real military strength was not as formidable as commonly assumed, it kept the initiative in foreign policy, trying to force the West out of Berlin and attempting to establish missile bases in Cuba. Once their bluff was called by President Kennedy, the Soviet leaders retreated, and the West made a more realistic appraisal of Soviet strength. Moscow's foreign-policy makers showed greater circumspection during the subsequent years, stressing in their speeches the great destruction that would be caused in a future war; hitherto they had been reluctant to deal with the subject. They accused the Chinese of reckless adventurism: Peking, they said, wanted to push America and Russia over the brink, believing that with the elimination of its two main rivals the road would be clear for the Chinese to dominate the world. But how, Khrushchev asked, could a real Marxist possibly argue that nuclear war was a paper tiger? Did the Chinese really think that bombs recognized class distinctions? Drawing the lessons of Cuba and Berlin, the Soviet leaders decided to acquire greater military mobility by developing their naval and air forces. By 1968 it was generally assumed that the Soviet Union would soon achieve strategic parity with the West, if that concept still had any meaning in the age of overkill.

The great expectations of 1955 ("the spirit of Geneva") faded quickly as the meeting of heads of states and foreign ministers failed to produce any tangible results, and the invasion of Hungary seemed to quash all hope of an understanding. This was followed by several minor crises and, in 1959, by a fresh upsurge of optimism following Khrushchev's visit to the United States. A new freeze was the result of the failure of the Paris summit in 1960. The Cuban missile crisis, however, cleared the air for a new détente, which gave birth to the Nuclear Test Ban Treaty of August 1963. Khrushchev's successors seemed a little less enthusiastic about friendly relations with the West, but they did not radically reverse his policy. It was the general belief in the Western capitals between 1963 and 1968 that the "Europeanization of Russia" was an inevitable process. Yet developments inside Russia lent no support to this optimistic assessment, and the invasion of Czechoslovakia created new fears among Russia's neighbors. If, according to the Brezhnev doctrine of 1968, the Soviet Union was entitled to interfere in the affairs of its East European allies, what was there to prevent it from giving military support in favorable circumstances to its partisans in the noncommunist world? It was not at all certain that new sources of conflict would not develop. The peoples of Eastern Europe had not become reconciled to Soviet interference, and their striving for more freedom and national independence was from time to time bound to upset tall calculations.

FALSE DAWN AT
GENEVA

S oon after Stalin's death the idea of a summit meeting was mooted as the most likely way to break the deadlock between the two blocs. Stalin's successors wanted a détente, but the new collective leadership needed time to agree on the form and substance of an approach. The idea of a summit meeting, to be followed by a conference of foreign ministers, had originated in the Western capitals; it was welcomed by Marshal Bulganin, the then head of the Soviet government, once the struggle for power in the Politburo had come to a temporary halt. At his meeting with Eisenhower, Eden, and Faure in Geneva in November 1955, the main topics on the agenda were Germany and control of nuclear weapons. Briefly, the Soviet aim was the removal of American bases from Europe, which it regarded as the main military danger; it was also Soviet policy to prevent, or at any rate to postpone, German rearmament. The Western powers, on the other hand, put the stress on the German question: without the re-unification of Germany, they claimed, there would be no lasting peace in Europe. They were convinced that without the presence of American forces, and short of a substantial German contribution to NATO, Western Europe would be unable to resist Soviet political and military pressure. But the Russians had lost what little enthusiasm they had had previously for the idea of German reunification; they wanted a neutral Germany and were opposed to free all-German elections, which would have resulted in a certain communist defeat. On the other hand, they took the initiative with a sweeping proposal for an unconditional ban on all nuclear devices. The Western powers were not eager to discuss this, being only too aware of Soviet superiority in conventional military strength, and since the Soviet blueprint made no provision for international inspection, they had no difficulty finding fault with it. To the Soviets the idea of foreign observers' snooping around their military installations was utterly repugnant; they wanted to rest the unconditional ban on mutual trust. But the trust did not exist, and any such arrangement would have put the West at a clear disadvantage, for in the Soviet Union it would have been relatively easy to produce bombs and to hide them, whereas it was almost impossible to do so in the open Western societies. President Eisenhower then suggested the "Open Sky" plan as a possible solution to the question of inspection, but this was not acceptable to Moscow. The Geneva meeting and the subsequent foreign ministers' conference ended with the participants—in the words of a British observer—still looking at each other across the Great Divide.

The meetings were not, however, a total loss, for they reflected greater willingness than before to look for common ground. The Soviet Union certainly showed greater readiness to normalize its relations with some of its European neighbors, notably Yugoslavia, Austria, and Finland. Khrushchev's visit to Belgrade in 1955 and Tito's mission to Moscow the following year signified the end of the bitter feud that had raged after Yugoslavia's expulsion from the Cominform. The Kremlin recognized in principle the existence of different roads to socialism, and though Soviet-Yugoslav relations were by no means undisturbed in the subsequent years, Tito's right to pursue an independent policy was by and large acknowledged. A new serious crisis arose, however, in 1968, with the reassertion of Soviet military power throughout Eastern Europe; Yugoslavia felt itself directly threatened. Soviet willingness to conclude a peace treaty with Austria (the Staatsvertrag) ended a deadlock of almost ten years during which it had been Moscow's policy to maintain that the Austrian question could be considered only in the general context of the German problem. Suddenly the Soviet position changed: Austria undertook not to allow military bases on its territory and not to join alliances, whereupon the Soviet Union withdrew its forces and Austria regained full political independence.

Some Western observers, greatly encouraged by this development, thought that the Austrian treaty could serve as a model for Germany. But this was an unrealistic assumption. Germany was the great prize to be won in the cold war. Its strategic position made it most unlikely that it could ever be neutralized. Chancellor Adenauer was as little inclined as the Russian leaders to make any substantial concessions. He was convinced that Moscow would have gradually to modify its attitude toward West Germany; in his eyes the Soviet Union was a colossus with feet of clay which would weaken, if not disintegrate, as a result of its internal contradictions and the growing pressure exerted by the "Yellow Peril." The changes inside the country after Stalin's death reinforced his belief; when a Soviet invitation to visit Moscow was extended to him in June 1955, he accepted, though with notable lack of enthusiasm, perhaps mainly to satisfy his domestic critics, who had argued all along that no opportunity to reach an agreement with Russia should be missed. The Soviet Union wanted normal relations with West Germany but was unwilling to pay a high price. Although Adenauer's visit to Moscow led to a restoration of normal diplomatic and trade ties between the two countries, there was no basic change in Soviet-German relations. This remained the only visit of a German head of government to the Soviet Union since the war, and the one tangible result was the return of the last German prisoners of war from the Soviet camps. Some of Adenauer's critics later maintained that the old chancellor was not flexible enough in his approach to the Soviet Union; there was a real chance for a new rapprochement with Russia, perhaps even a new Rapallo. But Rapallo, the often invoked symbol of the pro-Russian orientation in Germany in the early years after the First World War, had been a gesture, a demonstration, rather than a consistent policy. The Soviet leaders certainly would have liked to detach West Germany from the Western alliance, but they had little to offer in exchange.

Adenauer's visit to Moscow thus failed to bring a solution of the German problem any nearer; it continued to be the most important single issue in West-East relations in Europe. With the sudden outbreak of rebellions in Eastern Europe, the Russians concentrated on reasserting their hold over their own camp. This was clearly not the time for new initiatives in international relations, and Western public opinion, which followed with great sympathy the stirrings in Russia's former satellites, would hardly have been receptive to any new Soviet moves. For the time being, further top-level negotiations were ruled out.

REBELLION IN
EASTERN EUROPE

Boiling point was reached first in Poland. The economic and social consequences of Stalinism had given rise to intolerable tensions in all walks of life, and as political controls were slightly relaxed under the "New Course" there was open talk about the shortcomings of the communist regime. The party leadership was deeply split; Bierut, Moscow's man, who had been both prime minister and first secretary of the party, died suddenly during a visit to Moscow in the summer of 1956. Ochab, whom the Russians wanted as his successor, was a middle-of-the-roader; opposed to liberal reforms, he was nevertheless willing to compromise, realizing that the country could no longer be ruled with Stalinist methods. The diehards in the leadership, the so-called Natolin group, on the other hand, were firmly opposed to any basic change; they were willing to call on the Soviet army, if necessary, to suppress the reform movement. But these men were isolated; the masses were prepared to fight rather than to endure the tyranny any longer. The spirit of rebellion was infectious: in an act of open defiance, the Polish party leadership refused to reelect to the Politburo Rokossovski, the Soviet marshal, who had been appointed by Moscow to function as Polish war minister. The security police, having been purged of its Stalinist high command, was unwilling to support the Natolin group. The diehards could count on Pax, a noncommunist Catholic organization headed by Piasecki, a prewar leader of a profascist organization, who after his arrest by the Soviet secret police in 1944 had thrown in his lot with the Russians. But Pax, too, was a small isolated group, ostracized by the great majority of Polish Catholics.

Even though the liberals were a minority in the party leadership, the middle-of-the-roaders were willing to enter into a tactical alliance with them, and they had the support of the overwhelming majority of the rank and file of the party. Students and writers played a leading role in giving expression to the discontent of the masses; Adam Wazyk, in his widely read and discussed "Poem for Adults," castigated the failures and shortcomings, which everyone knew but no one had dared to condemn hitherto. *Po Prostu,* a student newspaper, suddenly gained great popularity by spearheading the fight for freedom. There were mass meetings and demonstrations in the streets of Warsaw and other Polish cities; everything indicated that the point of explosion was near.

It was in this critical situation that Gomułka's candidacy for the highest party post was first mooted and found an overwhelming response. When the Eighth Party Plenum convened on October 19, 1956, the main points on the agenda were to co-opt Gomułka and three of his political supporters to the Central Committee, and to nominate him to the position of first secretary of the party. Władisław Gomułka, a member of the Communist Party since 1926, did not have many allies among the leaders of the party. He was respected for his personal integrity, but his modest intellectual gifts and certain deficiencies and traits of character did not make him an eminently suitable candidate for the position. In the eyes of many Poles, however, he symbolized in 1956 the resistance to Soviet domination. He had fought in the underground during the war but was removed from the party leadership in 1949 and subsequently arrested as a "national deviationist." Released from prison in late 1954, he was not at first fully rehabilitated. Gomulka rejected the offer of some minor post, for he was convinced that in view of the split in the party leadership and the critical situation in the country his return to a key position was merely a question of time. For the rank-and-file party member Gomułka was the savior, the man of the hour, and the anticommunists—i.e., the majority of the population—regarded him as the lesser evil in comparison with the Bierut-Mine faction, which had ruled Poland since 1945.

The Soviet leaders were greatly worried about the turn events had taken in Warsaw, and on the day the critical party plenum opened they arrived unannounced in the Polish capital. There were bitter recriminations: Khrushchev, Molotov, and their colleagues accused the Polish Politburo of anti-Soviet propaganda and of many other sins in the communist calendar. But the Poles stood their ground against all attempts to interfere in their internal affairs. There were mass demonstrations in favor of Gomułka, and the Soviet leaders must have realized within a very short time that the suppression of the "Polish October" could be effected only through massive military intervention. Gomułka assured the Soviet leaders that Poland would remain a loyal member of the communist bloc and continue to support Soviet foreign and defense policies. He resisted the growing popular demand for the withdrawal of the Soviet troops from Poland. Very reluctantly the visitors gave their blessing to the new Polish leadership. It is not at all certain that they would not have opposed Gomułka's rise to power more actively but for the turn events had taken in Hungary. Moscow preferred to deal with one emergency at a time, and the situation in Warsaw seemed harmless enough in comparison with the rapidly unfolding crisis in Hungary. Gomułka and his supporters ousted the Stalinist clique from the Politburo and proclaimed their own "Polish road" to socialism. The tremendous wave of political activity all over Poland, on the crest of which they had seized power, was soon arrested. After the takeover Gomułka did all he could to regain control over political life. The Polish people were told that they had to be satisfied with the gains that had been achieved: Poland's geographical situation, between the Soviet Union and communist East Germany, narrowly circumscribed its freedom of action. That Poland had acquired substantial territories that had formerly belonged to Germany also made the alliance with Russia a political necessity. Anti-Russian feeling had been in the past as strong as anti-German in Poland, but with the change in the European balance of power, Soviet paramountcy had to be accepted; the new official Polish ideology based itself on anti-Germanism as its main component.

Gomulka was widely praised at the time for providing responsible leadership, sparing his country a civil war and Soviet intervention. While making concessions to the Russians, he was able to secure for Poland a greater measure of freedom than enjoyed by any other communist country at the time. He induced the Soviet leaders to cancel the Polish debts, and as a result of this and other measures the economic situation of the country began slowly to improve. He did not press for the collectivization of agriculture (this was the one really unique feature of the "Polish road"), and sought a *modus vivendi* with the church, which was more influential in Poland than in any other East European country. The concessions made to the intellectuals were gradually withdrawn. *Po Prostu,* the journal that had played such a central role in the struggle against the Stalinists, was suppressed in October 1957. Leading Polish intellectuals left the Communist Party in protest against the reimposition of cultural controls. They had mistakenly expected that the new regime would follow a radically different course, even though Gomułka had made it clear from the very beginning that he was opposed to both dogmatism (Stalinism) and revisionism—i.e., the demand for more freedom. The great hopes raised by October thus slowly faded away: Poland still remained for some years the freest "popular democracy," and the East German leaders were worried that the "destructive influence" of Polish ideas would contaminate the younger generation in their country. But Gomułka gave full and loyal support to the Russians, even against Tito, and the Soviet leaders had no reason subsequently to regret the approval given him in 1956.

As hope gave way to disillusionment and cynicism in Poland, the new leadership became isolated. There had been only a brief encounter between the Polish *pays réel* and *pays légal* during the critical days of October. But since Gomułka was in effective control of the army and the security forces, and since the public had become more and more apathetic, there was no scope for an active opposition movement. The intellectuals were in opposition to the regime, but, lacking mass support, they made little impact on the public at large. Within a decade after October, the Gomułka regime, once the most liberal and progressive by East European standards, was to become a pillar of orthodoxy in the communist camp.

Communism in Hungary did not succeed in enlisting mass support during the early years of its rule. Imposed on the country by the Soviet army, the Communist Party barely managed to cling to power. Its economic policy resulted in a considerable lowering of living standards and the disaffection of the great majority of the population. There was no active opposition to the regime because of the terror, but once the fear lessened a revolutionary situation was bound to arise. The revelations about the crimes of the Stalin era at the Soviet Communist Party congress in 1956 weakened the self-confidence of the old leadership. The most discredited members of the government, such as Rákosi, were dropped in July 1956, and some minor concessions were made to popular opinion: it was the classical example of a bad government making halfhearted attempts to reform itself in order to weather a coming storm. Instead of appeasing the masses, this policy gave a powerful impetus to the opposition movement. The intellectuals and the students demanded freedom of criticism, while old party members now released from prison insisted on basic policy changes such as the democratization of political life and the removal of all old Stalinists. The ferment in Poland also had a great impact on developments in Hungary; during the second half of October the revolutionary agitation reached its climax. On the 23rd all political meetings and demonstrations were banned, and when this order was defied, the AVH (secret police) opened fire on the crowds. In protest the workers joined the struggle, revolutionary committees were set up throughout Hungary, and the troops that were sent to defend the regime refused to obey and fraternized with the rebels. In desperation the Hungarian government called on the Soviet troops stationed in the country to intervene, but the Russians were not prepared at this stage for an effective military operation against the insurgents. The revolutionary movement spread like wildfire, the supporters of the old regime disappeared overnight, freedom of speech was restored, and the borders of Hungary were opened for the first time in a decade.

The Hungarian government and Communist Party were still led at that stage by Rákosi's closest collaborators, such as Gero, who made a belated attempt to reassert their authority in the face of the rising protest movement. These diehards were opposed to the return to power of Imre Nagy, who symbolized liberal communism in the eyes of most Hungarians. Nagy had been prime minister in 1954, was dismissed and purged the year after, and was restored to party membership only in October 1956. Within a few days events in Hungary moved much faster and much further than in Poland. The Stalinists did succeed in containing the revolution; Nagy became head of a coalition government in which some of the traditional parties, such as the Smallholders, were also represented. To some observers this seemed the beginning of a return to a democratic multiparty system. In his negotiations with Moscow, Nagy demanded the withdrawal of the Soviet troops, Hungary's release from the Warsaw Pact, and recognition of its neutral status between East and West. Such manifestations of independence by a former satellite were of course quite unacceptable to the Kremlin and only hastened the decision to invade Hungary.

A great many explanations have been provided for the success of the Poles and the failure of the Hungarians in 1956. Nagy, to be sure, did not always act decisively, nor did he receive much help from his own supporters; the insurgents did not lay down their arms even after the Stalinists had been routed, and the ultimative demand for Hungary's neutralization was a bad tactical move. But even with the benefit of hindsight it is difficult to see how Nagy could have acted differently. The revolutionary movement in Hungary was more intense than in Poland, but it did not have sufficient time to organize itself and to work out a clear policy. The old party leadership had resisted the movement for reform up to the last moment, thus making a revolutionary outburst inevitable.

The international situation, the involvement of Britain and France in the Suez operation, may have further contributed to the Soviet decision to intervene; it certainly made the suppression of the Hungarian revolution easier as far as world opinion was concerned. But events in Czechoslovakia twelve years later showed that not too much importance should be attributed to these factors; even if liberal communism had been far more restrained, even if Nagy had been more cautious and if the demand for leaving the Warsaw Pact had not been advanced, the Soviet leaders would in all probability still have opted in favor of military intervention. World public opinion does not count for much in Moscow's eyes if basic Soviet interests are involved. Nor was the Soviet Union impressed by Hungary's call for help to the United Nations, and the support for Hungary given by Peking, Belgrade, and Warsaw was purely platonic.

Hungarian resistance continued for a few days after the attack by Soviet tanks on November 4, but it was a fight against overwhelming odds; having admitted defeat, the Hungarian government sought asylum in the Yugoslav embassy in Budapest. The military battle had been easily won by the Soviet forces, but the political aim of the intervention was more difficult to attain. The Stalinist old guard could not be called upon to form a new government; middle-of-the-road collaborationists were needed, able and willing to work with the Soviet Union for the "normalization" of the situation. They found such a man in the person of János Kádár, an old communist who in background and orientation had much in common with Gomułka. One of the few party leaders of working-class origin, he had not been in the Soviet Union during the war and had been arrested and imprisoned during the purge of the early fifties. In 1956 he was one of the leading liberal communists; as such he joined the Nagy government, and he was not even among those who opposed the decision to renounce the Warsaw Pact. Then, suddenly, within a few hours, he changed sides, declared that counterrevolutionary forces were taking advantage of Nagy's weakness, and established a countergovernment, which appealed for Soviet intervention to give legitimacy to the invasion. Kádár's sudden change of heart has not been satisfactorily explained to this day; it has been said that he had been chosen by the Soviet leaders to be Rákosi's successor well before the revolution, but that the uprising had interfered with the orderly execution of the plan.

The task facing Kádár after the suppression of the uprising was not an enviable one. Having been carried to power by the Soviet troops, he lost all popular support. In the eyes of all but a handful of his compatriots, he was a quisling who had sold his country to the Russians. Kádár governed by martial law; the rule of the political police was restored; strikes were suppressed by mass arrests; leading writers were given long prison sentences. Nagy and the members of his government left the Yugoslav embassy, having been promised that nothing untoward would happen to them, only to be arrested outside the building. They were tried in secret, and only much later did it become known that several of them, including Nagy, had been executed.

The Soviet invasion and the ensuing counterrevolution caused a wave of indignation all over Europe. Passions were running high, and for some months it seemed as if the Soviet invasion had destroyed forever the chance of a rapprochement between the East and West, and that it also marked a great divide in the history of the communist camp. Cynical observers predicted that Hungary would soon be forgotten, and subsequent events proved them right. The invasion did not have a great impact outside Western Europe; most Asian and Middle Eastern countries in the United Nations abstained from voting for the withdrawal of the Soviet troops. A few West European communists left their parties in protest, but the communist camp soon recovered its balance, and the Soviet decision to invade Hungary was universally accepted. After a suitable interval, Western statesmen resumed their contacts with Moscow; as far as they were concerned, this had been an internal affair within the Soviet sphere of interest; the idea of responding to the appeal for help by the Nagy government had never been seriously considered, since no one wanted to risk a world war for Hungary. The 180,000 Hungarians who left the country after the Soviet invasion were welcomed in the West and received much sympathy; after a few months they, too, were forgotten.

A comparison between Kádár and Gomułka shows many parallels in their early careers but wide divergences in their policies after 1956. Gomułka came to power on a wave of resistance to Moscow, whereas Kádár was imposed on his country by the Soviet army. The circumstances under which Kádár gained power could hardly have been less auspicious, but ten years later Hungary was beyond doubt the freer country. While Gomułka had steadily moved toward the reimposition of tight controls and the suppression of all democratic stirrings, Kádár had followed a more liberal policy, removing the leading Stalinists from their posts, deideologizing daily life, concentrating on economic development and the raising of living standards. After 1963 those Czech, East German, and Polish communists who wanted more freedom began to look to Budapest, for Hungary went further than other communist countries in its opening to the West and in its economic reforms. Kádár's government, which at first had been among the most vulnerable in Eastern Europe, gradually became one of the more stable regimes. This was not necessarily an indication of its popularity, but, on the contrary, as many observers have pointed out, a sign of growing public apathy. After the heroic struggle of 1956, more and more Hungarians understood that in view of their geopolitical position there was no hope that real independence would be restored to their country in the near future: the Soviet Union would not give up its hold. The realization of these basic facts made for despair and cynicism but also for the reluctant acceptance of a state of affairs that was not likely to change in the foreseeable future. The revolutionary spirit exhausted itself and gave way to a mood of *attentisme*. Kádár's regime did not succeed in appeasing the Hungarian people, let alone in infusing any enthusiasm among them, but it managed to neutralize public opinion in the country, which was no mean achievement after the defeat and bloodletting of 1956.

WEST-EAST
NEGOTIATIONS
1956–61

fter the failure of the summit meeting in 1955 and the East
European and Suez crises, there was an interval in negotiations
between Moscow and the West. Bulganin resumed his correspondence with Eisenhower in March 1957, suggesting a new approach to a nuclear test ban in the form of a moratorium on tests for
two or three years under the control of an international commission.
In October 1957 a new plan for a demilitarized zone in Central Europe
was submitted by Adam Rapacki, Poland's foreign minister, no doubt
with the Soviet Union's blessing. In the meantime, NATO forces in
Europe had been equipped with tactical nuclear weapons, and the
disarmament problem assumed ever-growing urgency. Experts from
West and East met in Geneva in July 1958 in the first of a series of
conferences to deal with ways of controlling nuclear tests and measures to prevent surprise attacks. These negotiations lasted more than
five years; they covered both policy issues and technical problems
such as the establishment of observer posts and the composition of
the commission that was to supervise the control system. The West
favored a neutral chairman, but the Russians, who had developed an
intense dislike for Dag Hammarskjöld, the Swedish secretary general
of the United Nations, maintained that only nations could be neutral,
not individuals. After protracted debates and countless blueprints that
were submitted, discussed, and rejected, the ice was suddenly broken
in August 1963 and a nuclear-test-ban agreement signed, not because
the experts had at long last found an ingenious formula, but as the
result of a change of heart in the Kremlin.

The year 1958 began with several promising Soviet moves designed to reduce international tension, but it ended with a Soviet ultimatum on Berlin which precipitated a new and exceedingly serious world crisis. In January 1958 Bulganin had suggested a new summit conference; the Western leaders, with the failure of 1955 still fresh in their minds, insisted that this be preceded by a foreign ministers' meeting to establish whether there was sufficient common ground for the success of a summit meeting. Following up its peace offensive, the Soviet government announced in March the unilateral suspension of nuclear tests for the duration of six months. The impact of this move on the West was smaller than expected, for the announcement had come, as Eisenhower pointed out in his reply to Bulganin, just after Moscow had completed a series of tests of unprecedented intensity. Dissatisfied with the lack of progress, and under new pressure to regain the foreign-policy initiative, the Kremlin veered in the autumn to a more militant line. Khrushchev, who had become the chief Soviet spokesman, made it known in November that the situation in West Berlin was a serious and acute threat to peace that could no longer be tolerated, and announced that the Soviet Union would hand over its functions in West Berlin to the East German government at the end of six months; it was willing to accept either the demilitarization of West Berlin or a solution within a general German peace treaty, but it was not ready to put up any longer with the *status quo*. The Soviet Union had frequently pressed for a change in the *status quo* in Central Europe, but this was the first time that the demand came in the form of an ultimatum.

The small Western garrisons in Berlin did not of course constitute a military threat to the Eastern bloc. Politically, the existence of a Western island in the middle of East Germany was no doubt a constant irritant for the communists. It was an anomaly, but so was the division of Germany, which the Russians did not question. Berlin was also the weakest point in the Western pact system, and the Soviet decision to concentrate pressure there was only natural, given the premises of Soviet foreign policy. Militarily, the Western powers could not defend Berlin against an attack, and it must have seemed doubtful whether they would be willing to risk a wider conflagration for the sake of the former German capital. Not a few people in Western Europe and also in the United States were in favor of a retreat from Berlin, if only a face-saving formula could be found. The Germans, they argued, had after all provoked the war and lost it; wasn't it only fair that they should pay this price, too? The Western position in West Berlin, they argued, was untenable, and if a lasting understanding could be bought at the price of surrendering Berlin, wasn't it advisable to explore the Soviet proposal? This in brief was the basic dilemma facing Eisenhower, and later on Kennedy. Eventually America decided against a retreat: whereas the surrender of Berlin would have been a severe blow to West Germany and a grave setback for the whole Western alliance, there was no certainty that it would have brought détente with the Soviet leaders any nearer. It was more probable that a Western retreat from Berlin would have encouraged the Soviet Union to apply political and military pressure in other trouble spots in the hope that the Western leaders would show as little resistance else-where. After the building of the wall in 1961, the Berlin crisis faded for several years to the background. For the Soviet leaders the risks of brinkmanship were too high; they, and the East Germans, contin-ued to lodge protests and warnings from time to time, but there was no attempt to dislodge the Western powers by force. They were con-fident that in view of its isolation the Western position in Berlin would gradually wither away.

Among the factors that may have induced Khrushchev to de-escalate the Berlin conflict, relations with China were probably paramount. After 1959 this conflict came to preoccupy the Soviet leadership more and more, and it was clear from the beginning that the danger from the East was not just political and ideological in character. Soviet attempts to change the *status quo* in Central Europe were also counterproductive, inasmuch as they impressed on the United States the need to increase and improve its defenses. These rearmament programs became more expensive every year for all con-cerned, but the Soviet economy, with a much smaller GNP than the United States, felt the strain even more acutely. Soviet foreign policy blew hot and cold alternately between 1958 and 1962; this confused Western observers no end, but there was probably less deliberate intent in it than was commonly assumed at the time. There were conflicting domestic and foreign pressures on the Soviet leaders, their priorities changed from time to time, and Khrushchev's mercurial temperament no doubt also contributed to the sudden changes.

Nineteen fifty-nine was a year of great optimism, of constant coming and going between the world's capitals in anticipation of another summit meeting, which was to break the stalemate. Richard

Nixon, then American vice-president, visited the Soviet capital, as did Harold Macmillan, the British prime minister. Among the visitors to Washington were Kozlov and Mikoyan, two senior members of the Soviet Politburo. In September, Khrushchev himself went for the first time to the bastion of capitalism, and at Camp David had several long talks with President Eisenhower. The atmosphere was cordial, but not much substance emerged from these conversations. Khrushchev could obviously not discuss with Eisenhower his difficulties with Mao, nor was he free to make any suggestions about an atom-free zone in Asia. He ridiculed the rumors about the differences between Moscow and Peking: he and Mao were good friends, he said; the two nations would always stand together in any international dispute. Eisenhower, on the other hand, had to take into consideration the views of his European allies about Germany and Berlin. Both West Germany and France were opposed to raising the Berlin issue. De Gaulle was in fact more reluctant to give the American president any mandate to speak on behalf of the West, and he had grave doubts about the uses of a summit meeting. Khrushchev withdrew his ultimative demand for a settlement on Berlin, suggesting a new scheme for complete disarmament within a period of four years. Soon after his return to Moscow, he announced substantial cuts in the Soviet armed forces. The road seemed clear for a new summit meeting, which, it was decided, should take place in Paris in May 1960.

The prelude to the Paris meeting was highly inauspicious: on the eve of the meeting, on May 1, a U-2 high-altitude American spy plane was shot down over Soviet territory; the American government, instead of denying all knowledge (as is customary in such cases), tried to defend its action, and a few days later the president himself accepted full responsibility for the incident. With this the summit meeting was doomed; Khrushchev declared immediately after his arrival in Paris that he would walk out unless the president apologized, punished those responsible, and promised to discontinue the flights. The flights were stopped; with the development of earth satellites, such missions had become obsolete and unnecessary. But Eisenhower would not apologize. And so, after a few days, amid bitter recriminations, the conference ended in total failure, and Khrushchev withdrew the invitation for a visit to Moscow which he had extended to Eisenhower the year before.

The U-2 affair was, to put it mildly, clumsily handled by the

Americans, but such flights had been routine for a number of years, and since the Soviet leaders were no doubt aware of them, it seemed that the incident was for Khrushchev merely a pretext to back out of the conference. What, then, was his real reason? Since his meeting with Eisenhower at Camp David, the Chinese had officially declared that any international agreement (including one on disarmament) arrived at in their absence would not be binding to them. As a result, Khrushchev's hands were tied; he could not negotiate with the West without sacrificing the unity of the communist camp. In the Soviet Politburo, too, there seem to have been doubts about the wisdom of another summit meeting. At Camp David there had been distinct hopes that the West would make concessions over Germany and Berlin. The British government was inclined to look for a compromise with the Russians, and Eisenhower himself had admitted on one occasion that the situation in Berlin was "abnormal." But during the succeeding months the Western position on Germany again hardened; it was realized in the Western capitals that they were about to strike a bad bargain. The Russians had little to offer in exchange: East Germany was no longer expendable, and the Soviet Union would not withdraw its forces from the DDR or from the other East European countries. For Moscow the situation had suddenly become unpromising, and Khrushchev was now very angry at America and President Eisenhower personally, whom he had previously described to the Soviet people as a man of "wise statesmanship, courage and will power." This anger was real enough; Khrushchev's whole design for a détente with the West, his patient work over many months, was now in ruins. Another year was to pass before he resumed the dialogue with the new American president. But the meeting with Kennedy in Vienna in June 1961 was very different in spirit from the talks at Camp David. The political barometer had fallen; the Soviet delegates had walked out of the Geneva disarmament conference, and at the United Nations, banging his shoe, Khrushchev had reminded his listeners that Russia had nuclear weapons and rockets.

Russia was sure of its strength, he said; it no longer feared an American attack. On Berlin, he presented Kennedy with a new ultimatum: he would sign a separate peace treaty with East Germany by the end of the year if no German treaty was forthcoming. Khrushchev was out to frighten Kennedy; the new American president gained the impression that the Soviet leaders were willing to risk a nuclear war to get their way on Germany. The underlying Soviet assumption was that counsel was still divided in Washington about the advisability of a showdown with Russia over Berlin, and that fears within the Atlantic alliance, in particular in Britain and Italy, made for a greater readiness to accept Soviet demands. The Soviet threats were not, however, altogether convincing, for Moscow's relations with China were deteriorating steadily, the Soviet hold over the communist bloc was loosening, and there was no certainty that a world crisis would help restore the unity of the camp and reassert Soviet leadership. Above all, Khrushchev misjudged the American mood. The Americans were not to be pushed out of Berlin, out of Germany, and ultimately out of Europe under pressure; threats made them angry, less inclined to meet the Russians halfway. The Vienna meeting ended in disagreement all along the line, and the American president left in a somber mood. He said that he had realized on that occasion that words like "war," "peace," "aggression," "justice," "democracy," and "popular will," had very different meanings in the West and the East. Kennedy was determined to act with great caution, but above all the meeting had impressed on him the need for firmness in his dealings with the Russians.

The most striking feature of West-East relations during the fifties and early sixties is that throughout the whole period the initiative remained with the Soviet Union. The Soviet leaders pursued a dynamic policy even in unfavorable conditions; they initiated new moves, unleashed crises, published ultimatums, if necessary made sudden concessions even when the situation on the domestic front or within the communist camp was far from stable. Western statesmen, by contrast, seemed lackadaisical, even lethargic; they sometimes reacted with vigor to Soviet moves, but seldom took any major initiative. Secretary of State John Foster Dulles had a consistent foreign-policy concept, but it was better suited to the period before 1956 than to the years following, when European politics again came into flux. Kennedy's advisers developed a grand design which foundered quickly. The American leaders had to take into account the wishes and dislikes of their European allies to a far larger extent than Moscow considered the desires of its clients, and this, too, greatly hampered their freedom of action. Europe's inability to develop a common foreign policy was the main stumbling block; national interests had again proved stronger than common European or Atlantic policies that had, in principle, been agreed upon. Nor is it certain that a more dynamic, purposeful, and adaptable Western foreign policy would have been able to prevail over Soviet resistance. Moscow was firmly resolved not to accept any solution of the German question contrary to its own interests, and since these were diametrically opposed to those of the West, there was little room for new initiatives and diplomatic maneuvers. It is doubtful, therefore, whether any opportunities were missed by the West.

The position of Western leaders was weakened moreover by the emergence of a substantial domestic opposition unwilling to give them the benefit of doubt in the confrontation with the Soviet bloc. In these circles it was widely believed that the Cold War had ended with Stalin's death, and that defense spending could therefore be substantially reduced. As the years passed, a new generation of thinkers appeared who maintained that the West bore most of the responsibility for the deterioration of relations with Stalin's Russia in 1945–48, while others claimed that the Cold War was a convenient myth conjured up by the military-industrial complex to suppress popular liberation movements all over the world. In this new climate of opinion, the Cold War seemed both an unwanted distraction from domestic policies and a bore, and there was a growing number of people who thought that if ignored it would disappear.

THE BERLIN CRISIS

The German issue continued to overshadow all other European problems even after the Cold War had abated. The Russians regarded Germany as the key in the struggle for Europe, and their spokesmen labored the issue relentlessly; Germany was the main danger to world peace, a hotbed of militarism and fascism, and a military and political danger to the Soviet Union, as well as to all its neighbors in the West and the East. This Soviet policy aroused a great deal of bewilderment in the West, where, fifteen years after the end of the war, Germany was still on probation in the eyes of many and there was much criticism of Adenauer and his successors, but no one familiar with the German situation would have argued that Germany was again about to become fascist, or that West Germany constituted a military threat to anyone in Europe. The Soviet leaders were not known as men given to hysteria, and there was no reason to doubt that they were fully aware of the real situation in Germany and their own crushing military superiority. As a result, more and more Western observers reached the conclusion that the Soviet leaders were deliberately exaggerating the German danger so as to strengthen their own position in both Western and Eastern Europe. As a means of political warfare it had much to recommend it: there was envy of the German economic miracle and a great deal of political uneasiness among Germany's Western neighbors. Poland and Czechoslovakia had been occupied by the Nazi armies during the war; both, but especially Poland, had suffered greatly, and memories of those years were still alive. Since the West German government had not yet formally recognized

the territorial changes that had taken place in Eastern Europe after
the war, there was still the fear that it might one day claim what it
had lost in 1945. A close alliance with Russia seemed the only guarantee for Poland to keep what it had acquired. There was a great deal
of unreality in all the polemics about the Oder-Neisse Line, because
as a result of the division of Germany this was now East Germany's,
not West Germany's frontier, and it was not of the slightest practical
consequence whether or not West Germany recognized it. But with
nationalist passions running high, Polish and, to a lesser extent, Czech
fears were an important political factor, and the Soviet Union did its
best to keep them alive and to impress on its allies that they would
be no match for West German revanchism without constant Soviet
protection. By not officially recognizing the territorial changes of
1945, West Germany thus played into Moscow's hands.

The Soviet approach toward Germany was not, however, wholly
Machiavellian. The defeat of the Russian army in the 1914–18 war,
and the near defeat in 1941–42, had left deep traces in the Russian
consciousness. Propagandist considerations apart, and although the
Soviet Union had become a superpower while Germany was virtually
defenseless, there was an inbuilt tendency to magnify the German
danger. In the Soviet view, NATO without Germany was not a serious
adversary; with Germany it was a factor that could not be ignored.
The maximum aim of Soviet policy in Europe was therefore to detach
Germany from the Western alliance. On three occasions—in 1952,
in 1955, and again in 1964—attempts were made to open a dialogue
with Bonn. It is not entirely clear how serious Stalin was in 1952,
but it is almost impossible to believe that he would have agreed to
dismantle the communist regime in East Germany, and short of this
there was no hope for German reunification. In 1955 the Soviet leaders
were simply probing German intentions but did not make any substantial promises, and in 1964 Khrushchev was overthrown before
he could enter into serious negotiations. These three overtures apart,
it was Soviet policy to isolate Germany, to prevent German rearmament, and to thwart systematically all hopes for German reunification. Long-term aims were also attributed to this policy, for it was
likely to result in a growing feeling of frustration inside Germany,
which would eventually undermine the democratic character of government. It could lead to the growth of extremist movements either

on the left or, more probably, on the right, which would be more inclined to leave the Western alliance and to make a deal with the Soviet Union.

Germany's Eastern policy was not very effective in counteracting Soviet designs. The refugee organizations bitterly opposed any official declaration concerning the lost territories, which would have contributed toward a reconciliation with Poland and Czechoslovakia. Both the leaders of the CDU and the Social Democrats were deeply reluctant to antagonize potential voters among these circles. A new initiative to improve relations with Eastern Europe was taken only in 1969, following the electoral victory of the Social Democrats that year. Even the great coalition that came into being in 1966 inexcusably failed to take decisive action in this direction.

Germany's freedom of action in Eastern Europe was narrowly circumscribed by the Hallstein Doctrine, formulated in December 1955, which made known to all neutral and nonaligned countries that West Germany would regard diplomatic recognition of East Germany as an unfriendly act, interpreted as accepting the division of the country. The thesis that East Germany was not a sovereign state and that West Germany alone had the right to represent Germany (*Alleinvertretung*) greatly complicated Germany's position, for, whatever the lawyers said about the continued juridical unity of Germany as a state, *de facto* there were now two countries in existence, and West Germany found it increasingly difficult to induce other countries to ignore the DDR. The Hallstein Doctrine meant that for many years West Germany could have no diplomatic representation in the capitals of Eastern Europe, for the communist regimes naturally recognized East Berlin. Bonn also exposed itself to various kinds of blackmail in Asia, Africa, and the Middle East as a result of clinging to the doctrine long after it had outlived its usefulness. The Hallstein Doctrine was never officially dropped but gradually ignored: West Germany had excepted the Soviet Union right from the beginning, and in 1966 it declared its willingness to have diplomatic ties with all East European countries.

With Adenauer's resignation there were gradual changes in Germany's Eastern policy. Bonn began to pay more attention to relations with its Eastern neighbors: representatives of Krupp and other leading German firms were frequent visitors to their capitals, and official German trade missions were established in Prague, Bucharest, and

Budapest. There was a great deal of bridge building, even though the skeptics kept arguing that trade could never be a substitute for a clear policy. There was a gradual change also with regard to East Germany, a greater tendency to accept the *status quo* in the DDR and to help make it more human. A policy of "little steps" toward normalization was mooted by one school of thought, expecting a change for the better through a gradual rapprochement (*Wandel durch Annäherung*), and it was argued that Germany should concentrate its efforts on the popular democracies, since for the time being there was little hope of inducing the Soviet Union to change its policy vis-à-vis Germany. On the other hand, there was the view that the road to Eastern Europe ran via Moscow, and that all attempts to bypass the Soviet Union were doomed to failure.

For many years Bonn was criticized, and not altogether without reason, for the inertia of its Eastern policy and its unwillingness to adopt the Western policy of détente vis-à-vis the communist camp. At last there came a change: in 1967 it was announced that the Munich Pact of 1938 was considered by Germany null and void, and various proposals were made for a reduction of both Western and Eastern armed forces in Germany. Bonn also expressed its wish to sign a treaty with the Soviet Union and all other East European countries renouncing the use or threat of force (*Gewaltverzicht*). It was largely the Protestant churches and the Social Democrats who brought about the change in the political climate inside Germany which made this reorientation in its Eastern policy possible.

The initiative of 1967–68 was warmly welcomed in Western capitals but not in Moscow, Warsaw, or East Berlin. There Bonn's initiative was violently denounced as an act of political aggression that increased international tension, and it was later thought to have contributed largely to the Soviet decision to invade Czechoslovakia.

It is one of the great ironies of contemporary history that the West German "opening to the East," demanded by its allies and by liberal opinion inside the country, had such negative consequences. If the West Germans had not left the decision to modify their Eastern policy so late, the communist governments would have been compelled to look for other, much less plausible pretexts to intervene in the affairs of their allies.

During the late fifties and early sixties Berlin was the focus of West-East tension in Europe. After the division of Germany, West

Germany had treated it as one of its *Länder,* though young Berliners were not obliged to serve in the German army, and there were several other important exceptions designed to pacify the Russians. East Germany, on the other hand, treated Berlin as part of the Soviet zone and, in violation of the city's four-power status, established its capital there. Since 1947 the communists had disputed the legal rights of the Western powers to have a garrison in West Berlin and insisted on its demilitarization and neutralization. The Soviet ultimatum of November 1958 demanded the end of the occupation status of West Berlin and the implicit recognition by the Western powers of the East German government. It was, as Philip Windsor has pointed out, not a sudden departure from Soviet policy, and it did not yet hold the threat of a separate peace treaty with East Germany. This new element was introduced by Khrushchev later, when it emerged that the Western allies were unwilling to make any substantial concessions.

Soviet pressure was stepped up during the second half of 1960 and reached its climax in the early summer of the following year. In July, in a speech at the Moscow Military Academy, Khrushchev announced that, in view of increasing international tension, all manpower reductions in the Soviet armed forces would be suspended and the Soviet military budget increased by one-third. The NATO council meeting a few days later made it clear that the West would not give up its position in Berlin; the French were the most outspoken in their refusal to consider a recognition of the DDR. Ulbricht, the East German leader, had promised the Western allies certain guarantees if West Berlin became neutral, but at the same time told his fellow Germans that with the conclusion of a separate peace treaty his government would exercise sovereignty over West Berlin as well. On July 16 John McCloy, a former American high commissioner in Germany, arrived in Moscow as President Kennedy's personal envoy, but from his talks with Khrushchev no hope for an agreement emerged; an Italian attempt to negotiate was no more successful. Then, during the first week of August, Khrushchev began to act. At a meeting of the Warsaw Pact countries it was decided to close the frontier between East and West Berlin. This was a risky step, but the Soviet leadership no doubt felt itself compelled to take action: having insisted for so long that the Berlin problem had to be solved, they had at last to show some progress. For East Germany it was indeed a real emergency. The DDR was meant to be the showcase of socialist achievements for the whole of Germany, yet, far from attracting the West Germans, it lost each week many thousands of its citizens who preferred the freedom (or the fleshpots) of the West. During the last week of July 1961 ten thousand East German refugees appeared in the West Berlin reception centers, and on one single day, August 7, 1961, more than two thousand registered. This was not just a matter of loss of prestige for the DDR; unless the stream of refugees was stopped, the whole East German economy was likely to be paralyzed. On two different occasions, in June and July 1961, Ulbricht had still declared that there was no intention to close the border and to build a wall. But the communist leadership was now a prisoner of its own escalation of the Berlin crisis; the more pressure it applied, the more it swelled the stream of refugees, for everyone sensed that it might be the last opportunity to escape.

During the night of August 13, units of the East German army closed all crossings from East Berlin to the West, and in the subsequent days a wall was built along the Soviet sector. This was in violation of the four-power status, which provided free access to all parts of the city, and it came as a great shock to West Berliners and West Germans. There was an immediate outcry for countermeasures: surely the West would not remain inactive in the face of such a flagrant violation of international law? Dean Rusk, the American secretary of state, condemned the building of the wall, and other Western spokesmen denounced it also in no uncertain terms. Lyndon Johnson, then vice-president, was dispatched to Bonn and Berlin and, trying to reassure the Germans, declared that the communists would fail in the long run because they had put themselves against the forces of history. But the Germans in their present mood were not satisfied with references to the distant future; as the news was received of the circumstances, in which East Germans had found their death while trying to cross the border, the general excitement reached a climax. The Western powers were not, however, prepared for military counteraction; they had contingency plans for a Soviet–East German takeover of the whole city, but not for cutting off the Eastern part of the city. According to the Western concept, East Berlin was part of the Soviet sphere of influence, within which the communists had full freedom of action. They were not willing to risk a military clash; only when faced several days later with new threats, such as interference with air transport and American patrols in East Berlin, did they react with greater firmness, announcing that any act of aggression would be resisted. Khrushchev and Ulbricht were not willing to escalate the crisis any further; the idea of a separate peace treaty was dropped for the time being, and tension was gradually permitted to die down.

The communist leaders had every reason to be satisfied with the outcome of the crisis. They had not achieved all they wanted, but the building of the wall contributed decisively to the consolidation of the East German regime; the official explanation given out by East Berlin (that the wall had to be erected to prevent the infiltration of Western diversionists) was hardly meant to be believed, and from a propagandist point of view the wall was not exactly the pride of Ulbricht's regime. But the long-term political gain was substantial. The refugee stream was halted; only a few daring spirits succeeded, at great risk, in crossing into the West after August 13. The East German government overcame the economic problems caused by the mass exodus and grew far more self-confident and assured. In West Germany, on the other hand, the seeds of distrust vis-à-vis its Western partners were sown; if America was incapable of resisting Soviet encroachments in Berlin, would it be willing to defend West Germany against an all-out attack? President Kennedy in a speech in November reiterated his support for German reunification on the basis of self-determination; during a visit to Berlin he declared to great acclaim, "We are all Berliners." But confidence in America was shaken, and not a few Germans were now more willing than before to ponder the implications of Gaullism.

LA FRANCE SEULE

General de Gaulle came to power for the second time in 1958, and it soon appeared that he had his own concept of Europe, on which he was not willing to compromise. The general, never an admirer of the "Anglo-Saxons," had been deeply hurt by their behavior toward him during the war years. A proud man, he had not forgotten the snubs and the slights, real and imaginary, to which he had been exposed in exile. But it was not of course simply a matter of personal resentment; de Gaulle stood uncompromisingly for French self-interest, and he was convinced that there was little common ground between his country and Britain and America. His concept of international politics was essentially eighteenth-century in inspiration; ideology played little if any part in it. For this reason he was not likely to be impressed by the alleged Soviet threat, and the need for Atlantic or European unity appeared much less urgent to him than to his contemporaries. Such an outlook was intriguing, if only because it was so different from everyone else's, and many foreigners admired the general's utter self-confidence in a world of uncertainties, his Olympian calm, his majestic style. His views on many topics were so out-of-date and irrelevant that they seemed occasionally ultramodern. De Gaulle put much of the blame for the ills of contemporary Europe on the decisions taken at Yalta and Potsdam, partly because France had not been represented there, partly because these conferences had perpetuated the division of Europe into two rigid power blocs, and the intrusion of the two non-European superpowers. He had no sympathy with the attempts to create European political unity, and initially he was also opposed to the Common Market. The blueprints of the Eurocrats were for him flights of fancy in the style of the *Arabian Nights,* and he compared their work for a European federation to the efforts to create Volapük, the artificial language. About the advantages of economic cooperation he later changed his mind; all European countries had derived great benefits from it, and none more than France. But he was not willing to be party to the various political and military unification schemes.

His differences with the Americans emerged clearly when he met Secretary of State Dulles soon after having again become president of the Republic. This was more than a dispute about a specific line of policy; it was a basic conflict. The Americans regarded France as a European power in the same sense as Germany or Italy, whereas in de Gaulle's eyes France's place was with the world powers. To underline his disagreement with the Americans and to stress France's independence, de Gaulle gave instructions in March 1959 to withdraw from NATO Mediterranean Command all French naval units that had been assigned to it. Since these were few in number, the decision was of no great consequence; it was, as so often with de Gaulle, the gesture that mattered. His decision also established a new pattern, often to be repeated in subsequent years. De Gaulle opposed the American schemes for the defense of Europe partly because he doubted Washington's capacity to lead the alliance, in view of its inexperience and lack of vision, but also because American national interests were not identical with those of Europe. De Gaulle foresaw some of the basic problems of the balance of terror: no one could know when or how one or the other of the great nuclear powers would use its weapons. It seemed, as the 1950s drew to their close, that all the concepts about the defense of France and of Europe and even a third world war that had been considered basic at the inception of NATO were already out-of-date. The alliance of the free world, the reciprocal commitments of Europe and the United States, could not in the long run preserve European security unless (to quote de Gaulle) there existed in the Old World "a bastion of power and prosperity of the same order as that which the United States constitutes in the New World."

De Gaulle was touching on a real dilemma. The doubts he expressed about the future of the American commitment in Europe were real, and so was the necessity to strengthen the old continent's capacity to defend itself. Unfortunately, de Gaulle contributed little toward this aim; on the contrary, he seemed fairly resolved to sabotage all such attempts. Europe, as he conceived it, included both Western and Eastern Europe ("Europe to the Urals"), for the European countries, despite all ideological differences, had more in common with one another than with America and Russia; England would perhaps one day become part of Europe, but it was not yet ready to be admitted. This was a grand design, but since it ignored the power realities of the 1960s it was bound to fail. Europe, as de Gaulle envisaged it, was to be a loose federation of independent states ("*L'Europe des patries,*" as he was misquoted); the attempts to establish a supranational "High Authority," acting on majority decisions, he thought premature if not utopian; the sovereign state was still the basic unit and could not be expected to surrender any of its prerogatives. For this reason he insisted on a French nuclear deterrent, however diminutive, and he despised the British for having virtually signed theirs away at Nassau in 1963.

De Gaulle's European policy was based on close cooperation with Germany. He loyally supported Germany against Soviet and East European pressure, but expected in return German concurrence with his own European projects. The other Common Market countries he hardly ever bothered to consult; the new Europe he envisaged was to be based on the Paris-Bonn axis, with West Germany, as befitting, taking a back seat. It was not a policy likely to endear him to many Europeans. French defense policy was based on the correct assumption that there could be no real independence, let alone big-power status, without a nuclear deterrent. For this reason de Gaulle needed his *force de frappe,* and he persevered against much domestic opposition and Washington's refusal to help him. He insisted on the project despite the great cost and its very limited military value.

The American political and military schemes, developed during the 1960s, found in de Gaulle an implacable foe. He regarded them as hardly veiled attempts to subjugate Europe, and he was firmly resolved not to be an American satellite. America, to be sure, talked about partnership, but had never clearly defined it. Instead the United States evolved half-baked projects such as the ill-starred MLF—a scheme for establishing multilateral, seaborne mixed-manned nuclear forces, a supranational and therefore, in de Gaulle's eyes, artificial creation. France's foreign policy veered more and more toward a neutral position. In 1965 it left SEATO, the Southeast Asian equivalent of NATO, and it ceased to participate in NATO's European maneuvers. In March 1966 de Gaulle announced that French forces would be withdrawn from the treaty organization, and French officers from NATO Command, and the headquarters of the organization was accordingly transferred from Paris to Brussels. The alliance was not to be dissolved, but as far as France was concerned it was to be put on ice. As a result of this show of independence vis-à-vis America, France's prestige soared in the uncommitted countries, and de Gaulle was given a cordial reception in the Soviet Union in June 1966; previously the Soviet leaders had viewed the Paris-Bonn axis with undisguised hostility. Kosygin returned the visit in December 1966, and again there was a warm welcome and many professions of friendship. But, as some of de Gaulle's critics had predicted, the newly acquired prestige was largely spurious. Once the banquets, the speeches, and the rest of the pomp and circumstance were over, some minor cultural and economic agreements were all there was to show. De Gaulle became accustomed, as one of his critics noted, to playing a game of poker without cards. There was a great deal of unreality in so many of his initiatives; his whole policy was based on the assumption that there was a stable balance of power and that France would in any case be defended in an emergency by the Western alliance. He deliberately ignored the fact that not much would have remained of the balance of power had other Western countries behaved in a similar way.

Official Washington showed surprising patience about de Gaulle's attempt to undermine American influence in various parts of the world, and the French assault on American monetary policies and the dollar. This Gaullist opposition helped draw attention to some of the main weaknesses of America's grand strategy. The French suggestions for disengagement in Europe were not all devoid of merit, and the general's approach to world politics, however quaint and antiquated, had a consistency and sometimes a grandeur which commanded the respect even of his bitterest enemies. But it totally failed to present any realistic alternatives, for it overrated French strength and Europe's capacity to defend itself without America's help. The reckoning came in the summer of 1968, when the student revolt demonstrated how brittle Gaullist rule was. The uncertainty created by the domestic unrest led to the near collapse of the franc; the monetary crisis showed that France was in immediate need of massive foreign help, especially from West Germany and the United States. The Soviet invasion of Czechoslovakia and the change in the balance of power in the Mediterranean revealed that French foreign and defense policies had been based on mistaken assumptions.

EUROPEAN
COOPERATION:
NEW INITIATIVES

The efforts to create a European supranational political authority had failed in 1954; France was at the time preoccupied with the war in Vietnam, and the other countries concerned in the initiative were not really willing to give up their sovereignty. The realities of the nation-state proved stronger than the seemingly abstract concept of a united Europe. But the endeavor to establish a Common Market and free-trade zone in Europe continued. West Germany, Italy, France, and Benelux joined forces to establish a new European community on January 1, 1958. During the first decade of its existence the chief problems confronting the Six were whether any European states other than the founding members should also be admitted, and how much freedom of action should be given to the administration of the Common Market, headed at the time by a West German, Professor Walter Hallstein. The two main decisionmaking organs in the Community were the Council of Ministers and the Commission. The former was composed of the foreign ministers of the respective countries, representing the national interests, with a voting system that gave more votes to the big countries than to the small. In the Commission, on the other hand, the permanent, supranational element prevailed, the Eurocrats representing the common interests of the organization.

The existence of the Commission and its powers was a source of great annoyance to de Gaulle; the abdication of sovereign rights was a dangerous deviation from his concept of a "Europe of the fatherlands." De Gaulle's hostility was partly shared by Professor Erhard, Adenauer's successor, who, while favoring close European cooperation, was also critical of the Commission's attempts to enlarge its sphere of influence. In 1965 de Gaulle forced a showdown; the Community was immersed at the time in difficult negotiations about its agricultural policies. France did not accept the proposals worked out by the Commission and suddenly presented it with an ultimatum: unless a solution acceptable to France was adopted within a given period, France would withdraw and boycott further meetings of the Community. Although the issue at stake, agricultural financing, was certainly important for France, de Gaulle's real aim was to prevent any further strengthening of the Commission and to forestall any possibility that France would in future be outvoted by its partners. At a press conference he made his position abundantly clear: when the Treaty of Rome had been negotiated, France had been weak, its partners had taken advantage of this weakness, and as a result certain mistakes had been made that had to be corrected. France, needless to say, was not alone among the Six in fighting for its national interests, but no other did it so relentlessly and with so little consideration for its partners. De Gaulle's point of view was strictly utilitarian; the overriding consideration was always the extent to which France was likely to profit from its collaboration with the Community. The patience of France's partners was wearing thin; they had too often been angered by de Gaulle's cavalier attitude, and there was no willingness to give in to the French ultimatum. Even the Germans had serious misgivings; their delegation at the time was headed by Foreign Minister Schroeder, who was not one of de Gaulle's admirers. France faced the possibility that the majority would use its absence to invite Britain to fill the vacant chair. At this stage de Gaulle decided to compromise, and the French delegates returned to Brussels. They had to make some concessions but succeeded nevertheless in weakening the Commission and tilting the balance of power within the Community: all really important issues were to be decided in future by the foreign ministers. The dangerous trend toward supranationalism had again been checked.

The economic success of the Community compelled its critics to reconsider their attitudes toward it. The Soviet Union and the East European governments had asserted that the Common Market was bound to fail in view of the inexorable competition between the capitalist countries described by Lenin many years before. This thesis had to be modified in light of the achievements of the Common Market, and the communist theoreticians soon found a new explanation: the collective interest of neocapitalism was after all stronger than the divisive trends among its components.

The European countries who had stayed out or were left out when the Common Market was founded had second thoughts, too. EFTA, the European Free Trade Association, founded in the summer of 1960, was much less ambitious and comprehensive than the Community; it did not, for instance, aim at the coordination of the foreign trade of its member states, nor did it want to establish common economic, financial, and social policies. Having missed the opportunity to take the initiative for a European Common Market in the early fifties, Britain reluctantly reached the conclusion that EFTA could be only a temporary stage on the road toward closer integration. The Macmillan government announced in July 1961 that it wanted to initiate negotiations with the Six about joining the Common Market. It applied officially soon after, and so did Sweden, Switzerland, and Austria. In the first postwar decade most Labour leaders had been convinced that the Treaty of Rome was a mere trade agreement, designed to prevent the adoption of socialist policies on the continent, whereas most Conservatives resented (as did General de Gaulle) its political implications—the fact that it was meant to be the eventual basis of a supranational political institution that would involve the abdication of British sovereignty in some fields. The idea that foreigners would have a decisive say in shaping British domestic and foreign policies was quite intolerable to most Englishmen. But gradually the political and economic climate began to change. The limitations of Britain's postwar role and the loosening of the ties with the Commonwealth became more obvious, and the European idea kindled the imagination of many British public figures. This enthusiasm was not, of course, altogether disinterested; the economic success of the Six was the main attraction and persuaded many that it would be easier to solve Britain's own difficulties within the wider European framework. It was equally true, however, as Macmillan told de Gaulle during a visit to Paris, that Britain had been genuinely converted and that it now looked to a European future. There were major stumbling blocks: Britain wanted safeguards for the protection of its special interests, such as agriculture and the ties with Commonwealth countries (in particular Canada, Australia, and New Zealand), and there was the future of EFTA to be considered. Britain did not want to desert the Seven without reaching an agreement about the other EFTA members that wanted to join the Common Market. The British representatives made it clear that they were not suggesting a basic modification of the Treaty of Rome. Nevertheless, their insistence on conditions was a mistake; it would have been wiser to apply without any preconditions, for from inside the Community they would have been able to influence Common Market policies. But in view of French opposition it is unlikely that even an unconditional application would have been more successful. The negotiations dragged out for a long time and finally broke down after General de Gaulle's famous press conference in January 1963 at which he announced that Britain was not yet ready to join the Community. This declaration greatly annoyed the other members of the Community, who were more favorably disposed, and who, in addition, had not been consulted by the French. De Gaulle had not initially opposed the British application, for he assumed that Britain was not serious about joining. Only when he realized that there had been a real change of heart in London did he come out squarely against the British initiative. His basic public argument was that Britain, by tradition and by political and economic interest, was not really part of Europe. The general's vision of Europe was essentially Carolingian, and he deeply distrusted a country that was far too close to the United States for his taste, almost an American "Trojan horse." De Gaulle wanted to keep the Community small; "interdependence" and "integration" were words without meaning for him. One day, he said, Europe would be an imposing confederation, but meanwhile he did all he could to torpedo the federative efforts. In the last resort, de Gaulle was not worried by Britain's different cultural traditions or political interests but by the fact that it would have constituted a serious rival to French leadership of the Community.

All other members of the Common Market were in favor of Britain's entry, but they were powerless to overcome the French veto. Erhard, Schroeder, and Brandt did not regard the French-German alliance as an end in itself, but they could not, or would not, stand up to de Gaulle. Though Adenauer and Kiesinger were Francophiles, they, too, had misgivings about de Gaulle's policy and would have preferred a European Community including Britain. However, faced with a French ultimatum, they gave in, for a Europe without France was unthinkable.

Prime Minister Wilson again tried to break the deadlock in 1966–67 by reapplying for membership without any preconditions. But the Labour government was no more successful than its Conservative predecessor: the general would not budge. Britain then suggested, without much success, various other schemes to circumvent French opposition, such as a technological union and new approaches to European defense. Meanwhile, groups of continental "Europeans" considered ways and means to achieve closer political union: Jean Monnet's European action committee, and Spaak, the Belgian foreign minister, submitted various plans; other schemes were prepared by official and semiofficial German and French bodies (such as the Fouchet Committee). But these attempts to pick up the threads of 1954 were in vain; after long and fruitless discussions, all the projects had to be shelved.

If Western Europe remained politically impotent despite its spectacular economic recovery, this was to a great extent the responsibility of the old man in the Elysée, with his colossal vanity and his policy of grand gestures, who wanted for his country a role far above its real strength. It was only after he had disappeared from the political scene (in 1970–71) that new initiatives could be taken to bring about a great measure of unity in Western Europe.

THE CUBAN CRISIS

The Cuban crisis was the watershed that marked the end of an acute phase in the Cold War and opened a new era of détente. It is not quite clear what induced Khrushchev in the summer of 1962 to establish rocket bases in Cuba. It is unlikely that it was meant to act as a deterrent, defending Cuba against an American invasion. Perhaps the Soviet leaders intended to use the bases for bargaining with the Americans; perhaps Khrushchev hoped to extract a high price for their withdrawal, such as an American retreat from Berlin or at least from Turkey. On October 14 firm evidence was received in Washington of the establishment of launching pads, and on October 22 President Kennedy made his first announcement. It was, as a Soviet commentator put it at the time, the most dangerous week since the Second World War, and it ended with a Soviet defeat and a setback for Khrushchev, who had been personally responsible for what even the Chinese hard-liners called a dangerous policy. Moscow had clearly underrated American resolution; the crisis made the Soviet leaders aware of American superiority in arms systems, and compelled them to re-examine their strategy. Russia clearly needed a breathing space to catch up with American ICBM strength, and it had to improve its strategic mobility. The Soviet leaders had also to reconsider their policy vis-à-vis China: Chinese attacks were no longer restricted to specific aspects of Soviet policy; they exceeded in vigor and bitterness anything that had ever emanated from the West. In a conversation with Japanese socialists, Mao declared in August 1964 that the Soviet regime was imperialist, that it had annexed parts of Rumania, Poland, and East Germany, driving out the local inhabitants. Mao said that he was willing not to press the Mongolian issue for the moment, but justice demanded that Moscow immediately return the Kurile Islands to Japan. The Chinese comrades, in other words, had moved far beyond Mr. Dulles in their attitude toward the Soviet Union.

There was a curious parallelism between the two superpowers, with America bogged down in Vietnam, incapable of winning a war against a much weaker enemy, and the Soviet Union seemingly powerless to prevent the disintegration of the communist bloc. Neither superpower seemed able to impose its will upon its centrifugal European allies, despite economic and military superiority. It was, as subsequent events were to show, a false symmetry, but this was barely noticed in the West at the time. There was clearly no immediate military danger to Western Europe, and the Soviet Union had obviously given up hope that the Western communist parties would be able to seize power in the foreseeable future. Khrushchev was overthrown in October 1964, but his successors seemed determined to continue, in broad outline, his foreign policy. France made it known on every possible occasion that the identity of interests with the other Western powers had shrunk even more. As the Soviet threat diminished, General de Gaulle saw the emergence of a new European balance of power: Western Europe alone would soon be able to act as a counterforce to the Soviet Union.

Similar separatist trends evolved in other European countries and developed into a general NATO crisis. American strategy planners, with their changing ideas about deterrence and flexible response, faced increasing skepticism in Europe. America wanted to withdraw part of its forces from Europe and urged the European governments to improve their mobilization system and strengthen their conventional forces. Those in Europe who wanted to get rid of American bases but still insisted on the American umbrella in case of an attack, seemed not to mind if NATO were greatly weakened, or even dissolved, but at the same time they were reluctant to increase their own defense spending: in fact, they wanted the best of both worlds. The Vietnam War was unpopular in Europe from the beginning and became even more so; it was the rallying point of the opposition forces among the younger generation.

The decline of NATO was highly gratifying from the Soviet point of view, but its effects on communist Europe were definitely not. Nor were developments in the third world encouraging: In 1966 Kwame Nkrumah, one of Moscow's great friends in Africa, was overthrown in Ghana. Indonesian communism all but disappeared, and in 1967 Egypt and Syria, Moscow's allies in the Middle East, suffered a major defeat. In Greece a revolutionary situation had existed for some time, but before the left could exploit it a right-wing military dictatorship was established. Taken separately, these incidents hardly mattered; seen in a wider perspective, they seemed to constitute a dangerous shift in the global balance of power: "imperialism" seemed everywhere on the offensive, and the tide was running against the communists. Inside Russia there were gradual changes: Khrushchev's style had annoyed his colleagues and it played an important part in his downfall, but there were also policy differences. Khrushchev, they thought, had gone too far in "appeasing" the West; in his later years he even seemed to have envisaged a deal with West Germany shortly before he was overthrown. He had not given sufficient support to the Soviet army command for its plans, and this policy, too, was reversed after his downfall. Defense spending rose substantially after 1965. De-Stalinization was gradually discontinued, and stricter controls were reimposed. This in turn had direct repercussions on Soviet foreign policy, since a tough domestic policy could not be maintained for long without influencing Russia's relations with the outside world—not because the Soviet leaders had remained ideological antics but (in the words of Richard Lowenthal) because the distrust with which a despotic regime watches the people under its rule is inevitably projected onto the outside world, preventing a genuine solution of major issues in dispute and a genuine agreement on its place in the world.

The discussion about military policy during the years of the détente reflected the policy dilemmas facing the Kremlin. It remained the supreme Soviet aim to achieve strategic parity with America and ultimately superiority: the years of détente were put to good use in this respect. But at the same time there was growing awareness in Moscow that the scientific-technological revolution made it necessary to re-examine the question of war as an instrument of policy. According to their Chinese opponents, the Soviet leaders had retreated from Lenin's (and Clausewitz's) teaching that war was a continuation of politics; they had "gone soft" and been awed into "capitulationism" toward the West through fear of nuclear war. The Soviet leaders certainly wanted to avoid the dangers of a major military conflict, and they were also aware that small wars could easily escalate into big ones. To that extent the détente was from the Soviet point of view not just a tactical temporary retreat made in order to catch up with American nuclear capability; the basic dilemmas of a major confrontation were likely to persist even after the Soviet Union attained parity or military superiority.

Brezhnev and Kosygin accepted the statement of the military lobby that the all-round strengthening of the armed forces had been neglected under Khrushchev, and decided to reallocate resources. The military budget went up by 5 percent in 1966 and by 8 percent the year after. These were the published figures; there is reason to believe that the real increases were higher. In 1965–66 a small Soviet fleet was stationed in the eastern Mediterranean and subsequently expanded. The Soviet leaders justified these measures by referring to the worsening world situation and to the increasingly aggressive character of "imperialism." At a conference of European communist parties in Karlovy Vary in Czechoslovakia, the militant spirit found expression in resolutions describing the United States as the most aggressive imperialist power, aiming at world domination. The removal of American bases from Europe and the American Sixth Fleet from the Mediterranean was described as the most urgent aim in the political field. At the same time, a campaign for a new system of European collective security was launched. This scheme, as the Soviet Union envisaged it, accepted the territorial *status quo* in Europe and made provision for replacing NATO and the Warsaw Pact with a comprehensive security system to be guaranteed by all European states, and by the Soviet Union and the United States. From the Western point of view the project had several fatal flaws; it did not, for instance, affect the bilateral agreements between the communist states: the Soviet army could still remain on the Elbe while the Americans would have to withdraw from Europe with the dissolution of NATO. The scheme would have given official sanction to Soviet hegemony in Europe; nevertheless, some West European governments were willing to consider the Soviet proposals as a basis for discussion. The Middle Eastern war in 1967 and the Czechoslovak crisis of 1968 interrupted this dialogue.

One faction in the Soviet leadership had for some time advocated a more militant line in both domestic and foreign policy, and its influence grew as a result of the new setbacks. Kosygin went to the United States in June 1967, but his talks with President Johnson at Glassboro were inconclusive. The old understanding between Moscow and Washington to avoid any direct confrontation continued in force, but the Soviet Union was no more able to help America to extricate itself from the Vietnam morass than the United States was able to assist Russia in the Middle East. Washington still wanted to improve relations with the Soviet Union; Lyndon Johnson was almost pathetically eager to visit Moscow during the last months of his presidency and to have a summit meeting with the Soviet leaders. General political considerations apart, Johnson no doubt wanted to refurbish his image as a peace president, which had been badly damaged in Vietnam. But the Russians in 1967–68 were no longer in the mood to oblige; the spirit of détente and cooperation had all but vanished.

In Western Europe, too, there was growing pessimism as 1967 drew to its close. The Vietnam War had raised grave doubts about American priorities. It had always been taken for granted that Europe was uppermost in American priorities as regards the contest with Russia. With American military power and political interest so heavily engaged in Southeast Asia, the defense of Europe suffered, and the balance of power on the continent was bound to be affected. Fortunately from the West European point of view, Moscow did not show much vigor in exploiting the American weakness; moreover, the unexpected crises in the Middle East and Eastern Europe played havoc with Soviet plans. But it was unlikely that the Soviet leaders would remain inactive for long. The détente, as subsequent events were to show, had not solved any problems, nor had the conflict become less bitter. Although the acute danger of war had disappeared, so had Western hopes for peaceful coexistence. There remained deep uneasiness about the shape of things to come.

POLYCENTRISM
IN EASTERN EUROPE

Disarray and confusion were not limited to the Western camp: under Stalin the communist system had been monolithic; ten years after his death it appeared irrevocably split, the once-solid bloc a battlefield for ideological supremacy and political leadership. The differences between the various communist countries and parties seemed in some ways even more irreconcilable than West-East tensions, because each believed itself to be the sole possessor of the means of grace, because each thought it was more authentically Marxist-Leninist, and because each believed its sense of mission was so much more acute.

Throughout the Stalin era there had been but one major split: Tito had defied the Kremlin and had never recanted. There was a reconciliation between Moscow and Belgrade in 1955–56, but, having tasted freedom, the Yugoslavs insisted on maintaining their independent status. National communism was contained by the Soviet leadership in Poland in 1956 and suppressed in Hungary, but the unfolding conflict with China was a problem of a different magnitude.

Many reasons have been advanced for the rift between the two communist superpowers between 1958 and 1963, including Soviet unwillingness to help China with its nuclear program, Chinese complaints about insufficient Soviet economic assistance, and ideological divergences. The Chinese leaders were opposed to Khrushchev's de-Stalinization and his "revisionist" approach in both domestic and foreign affairs; they were not supported by Moscow in their dispute with India; and they had never renounced their claims to a number of territories in the Far East seized by the Russians in the nineteenth century. The conflict was not over the correct ideological interpretation of Marx and Lenin but over national interests, autonomy, and big-power aspirations. Russian and Chinese quarreled because they were dissimilar in national character, heirs to a markedly different cultural and social inheritance and because their political and economic interests diverged. The fact that Peking claimed to be closer to Leninist orthodoxy was of no great significance; in 1956 the Chinese had taken a more liberal view on some issues than their Soviet comrades. When Tito quarreled with Stalin in 1948, the Yugoslavs had been to the "left" of the world communist movement; ten years later they were to its "right." The ideological orientation changed; the insistence on the right to autonomy remained. The terms "left" and "right" lost their relevance in the context of communist intrabloc relations.

Attempts to patch up the differences between Moscow and Peking were made; the conference of the eighty-one communist parties in Moscow in 1960 worked out what Lenin would have called a rotten compromise—"a confusion of incompatible political formulas," as one observer put it—which could only lead to the continuation of polemics, with both sides stressing their own part of the document until the inevitable happened and the polemics came into the open. Soviet experts were withdrawn from China; political, military, and economic cooperation between the two countries came to a standstill, and day by day the propaganda warfare reached new heights of vituperation. Peking accused Moscow of splitting the world communist movement, while the Soviet Union tried to mobilize international support to isolate the Chinese. But adequate support was not forthcoming; some parties openly sympathized with Peking, and others, although not identifying themselves with Chinese policies, were opposed in principle to excommunication because, as Palmiero Togliatti, the Italian leader, put it in 1964, "this contained the danger of a resurgence of authoritarian and sectarian methods of leadership in the individual parties." The view gained ground that a central direction for the world movement, formerly essential, was now a thing of the past. Polycentrism (a term coined by Togliatti in June 1956) was, in other words, not a deviation but a necessary new stage corresponding to the new situation in the communist movement, a new development in its doctrine and its changing structure. From the Far East polycentrism spread to Eastern Europe. Albania, the smallest communist country, was the next to defy the Soviet Union. Its leaders were among the very few who had been brought to power not with the help of the Russians but through their own exertions at the end of a long partisan war. Albania had no common border with the Soviet Union, and there was little likelihood that its neighbors would agree among themselves to take common action against it. Tirana and Belgrade had been in bitter conflict since the late forties; this was outwardly ideological in character, since Albania was more Stalinist than Stalin, and continued to be so even after the dictator's death. The deeper, underlying causes were easier to understand against the background of traditional Balkan rivalries; they concerned territorial questions and the fate of the Albanian minority in the Kosmet region of Yugoslavia. Whereas relations between Moscow and Belgrade were strained, Albania remained a faithful member of the Soviet camp, but with the reconciliation between the two, it became restive and, in 1960–61, openly defiant. There was nothing in common between Tirana and Peking except their hostility to Soviet policies. Albania desperately needed a protector and found one in Chairman Mao, becoming in the process China's bridgehead in Europe. The political, military, and economic importance of the Peking-Tirana axis was not overwhelming; its most interesting feature was the powerful radio transmitter, broadcasting day and night bitter attacks on the American imperialists and their "number-one assistants," the Soviet revisionists.

Rumania was next in line to dissociate itself from Soviet policies. This country, like Albania, had been a faithful member of the bloc, but with the erosion of Soviet controls the Rumanian desire for a more independent policy collided with Moscow's centralizing plans. The dispute was initially economic in character: Rumania opposed the Soviet-sponsored Comecon initiative to coordinate more closely economic relations between Russia and its East European clients, fearing that the new division of labor insisted upon by Moscow would greatly impede, if not completely frustrate, its own industrialization program. Much to Khrushchev's chagrin, the Rumanian leaders succeeded in thwarting his schemes and gradually adopted a more independent foreign political line. In 1964–65 Rumania was (to quote Adam Ulam) the only state in the world that could boast of the following combination of achievements: she was an ally of the Soviet Union, a friend of China, and the communist state whose diplomatic and commercial relations with the West had improved and expanded.

The prime minister visited Peking and Paris; he and the new party leader Ceausescu admonished the Soviet and Chinese comrades to settle their dispute and at the same time expressed doubts whether the Warsaw treaty was still necessary. In 1967 Rumania was the only communist country, with the exception of Cuba, not to break off relations with Israel. Its independent course was, however, largely restricted to its foreign policy; desatellization progressed much more quickly than de-Stalinization; the party and the police remained in firm control, and Rumania was by no means in the forefront of the liberal forces within the communist camp.

The Sino-Soviet split caused a great deal of disarray in European communism, although there were not many open defections. The East European states remained faithful to the Soviet line, but there were misgivings about the policy followed by Khrushchev and his successors. Poland and Hungary, for instance, favored a more conciliatory attitude. In Western Europe the divisive tendencies were reinforced by differences of opinion on other topical issues, of which the Common Market was one. The initial communist attitude had been one of total rejection, but as the economic benefits of the European Community became manifest there was greater readiness to accept the new economic framework and to work for political and social change from within. It was by no means true that European communism had become Social Democratic in inspiration, as some of its left-wing critics maintained. But as Soviet control over the camp weakened, European political traditions began to reassert themselves, and the communist parties realized that it had been a mistake to copy Soviet policies slavishly and to apply them in countries with different political traditions. According to the Leninist theory of revolution, it was impossible to take over the bourgeois state from within. The West European communists did not deny the validity of this contention for countries lacking democratic traditions, and they interpreted the historical role of Stalinism in this light. But they were no longer willing to accept such generalizations as binding on all countries irrespective of the degree of their political, social, and economic development. The communist parties of Britain and Holland, of Sweden and Austria and Switzerland, and even the Spanish and Greek parties in exile, all criticized Soviet policy at the time of the Czechoslovak crisis in 1968. This was not a sudden eruption, nor were these parties willing to draw far-reaching conclusions, but it certainly reflected the ferment that had begun to work years before. The basic issue was whether the world communist movement should have a center and accept its discipline. Moscow insisted on its leading role as deriving both from its great revolutionary experience and from its power, but many communist parties dissented, stressing that the Soviet experience had negative as well as positive aspects, and that Soviet power had on occasion been misused. The general secretary of the Spanish Communist Party declared ruefully in November 1968 that, although a certain détente had been achieved in the Cold War, acute tension, a kind of new Cold War, had developed in the communist camp: "It is sad to see that when the words 'socialist commonwealth' are spoken they do not refer to the commonwealth which the fourteen states [where communist parties are in power] should form, but only to five states [the Soviet Union and her four allies who invaded Czechoslovakia]. It would seem as if the socialist commonwealth were a piece of cloth inexorably shrinking."

At its conferences in 1957 and 1960 the world communist movement adopted resolutions affirming the socialist principles of completely equal rights, respect for territorial integrity and national independence, and nonintervention in one another's domestic affairs. These were unrealistic resolutions, given the unequal distribution of power within the communist camp and the fact that these principles had never been adhered to in the past. But in the past at least the pretense of equality and nonintervention had been maintained. The new leaders did not have Stalin's authority, and the decision taken by his successors to drop appearances was bound to provoke resistance. Moscow could still rely on certain sections of the movement to back the Soviet Union, partly out of self-interest, partly out of fear, but it could no longer command the respect and admiration of millions of revolutionaries outside the Soviet Union; the invasion was in fact tantamount to abdicating all ideological legitimacy.

Polycentrism was the result of national differences whose existence the communist leaders had always in theory admitted, and for which they had made allowances in their tactics. But in practice substantial differences in approach were always discouraged, if not roundly condemned. Yugoslav observers, who have had more time than others to ponder these questions, have stated in their theoretical writings that communism is not a magic formula that will do away with conflicts and contradictions. Edvard Kardelj has drawn attention to a point first made many years before by the Social Democratic critics of Bolshevism—that the starting point of each country on its road to socialism is of paramount importance for its subsequent development. If the starting point was very low, it was more than likely that political backwardness would be perpetuated, and even canonized as part of the great heritage of the past. One neo-Marxist school of thought in the West asserted, on the other hand, that it was all a question of productive forces, and interpreted the development of world communism from Stalin to Khrushchev and beyond in terms of improving living standards that would more or less automatically lead toward more freedom. There was, no doubt, a grain of truth in this argument; that the Chinese found their supporters mainly in the more backward areas of the world, with Albania as their only European bastion, was hardly altogether accidental.

The economic progress made in the Soviet Union or East Germany in the fifties and sixties found no reflection in the political character of these regimes. "Economic determinists" apart, opinion in the West ranged from the prophets of an inevitable clash among communist powers to those who denied the very possibility of conflict on the ground that, since all communists agreed on essentials, any dispute among them could be of a tactical nature only. The late Franz Borkenau was virtually alone in predicting, shortly after the Chinese communists came to power, that a conflict between Moscow and Peking was inevitable, because totalitarian regimes were bound to extend their absolute control as far as they could; the unity of the communist camp could be based only on domination, not on equality, and discord was bound to arise. To this "law" of totalitarian rule another might be added—that there is no room at the top for more than one man, or one small group of men.

To many outsiders the dispute between Khrushchev and Mao, between Tito and Hoxha, between Togliatti and Thorez, seemed perhaps trifling. A Hindu might at the time have reached similar conclusions with regard to the quarrel between Luther and Leo X. There was in theory no reason why communists should not coexist on the basis of mutual toleration despite differences of opinion; but tolerance is a state of mind notably absent from missionary movements, and from their own point of view the communists rightly feared it: a slackening of the dynamism of the world movement, of its revolutionary zeal and fervor, would have incalculable consequences. If factions were officially recognized on the international level, it would not be long before similar factions were established in each communist regime and party. The unity of the regime would be disrupted, real party democracy would be restored, and the communist parties would gradually become the same as other parties—for, obviously, there could be no iron discipline at home if anarchy became the rule within the world movement. This would have been the end of communism as known during the first half of the century; communist parties would have continued to exist—radical, even revolutionary, in character— but they would have shed the heritage of tyranny. The Soviet leaders, and with them the Poles, the East Germans, and the Bulgarians, were firmly resolved to contain the danger.

1968: THE YEAR OF
THE STUDENTS' REVOLT

All the discussions about détente and its long-range consequences were based on one assumption that seemed safe enough at the time: that the internal situation was everywhere reasonably stable, unlikely to undergo sudden and violent change in the foreseeable future. The fifties and the early sixties had been the quiet years; the *status quo* was rarely questioned; there were strikes, but their aim was not the overthrow of the system. Students were apolitical and almost suspiciously quiet; the revolutionary impetus had faded away. Political observers noted the "end of ideology," and forecast the arrival of the technocratic society. There was convergence in the political thought of left and right; differences of opinion persisted about priorities and about ways and means, but the consensus was wider than in any previous period. Suddenly, to everyone's astonishment, the assumptions about the exhaustion of political ideas were challenged by a wave of student revolt which affected the whole of Europe in 1967–68. It should perhaps not have come as a complete surprise, for Europe had a tradition of youth revolt, and the conflict between the generations had often assumed a political character. Students had played a leading role both in the Russian revolutionary movement and in the early phases of European fascism. There had been signs in the late fifties indicating a growing spirit of revolt among the young generation—the Aldermaston marches in Britain advocating nuclear disarmament, the French movement in support of Algerian independence, and the prominent part played by students and young intellectuals in all the revolutionary movements in Eastern Europe. Later on, resistance to the Vietnam War spread from America to

Europe and became the main force of political activity among the young generation, but it was not regarded as a serious challenge to any Western government. In Latin America or Turkey students have succeeded in overthrowing governments, but no one believed that this could happen in the open societies of the West. It was generally assumed among the older generation that the negative lessons of the 1930s and the world war, European revolution and counterrevolution, and the sacrifices they entailed were still so fresh in memory that no one would risk similar disasters by propagating a policy of violent change. This ignored the simple fact that a new generation had grown up for which all these experiences, Stalin and Hitler alike, had little meaning, and for whom history started around 1960. This could be observed most clearly in France, where many small sects on the extreme left were preaching violence, *groupuscules* consisting of Trotskyites (of various persuasions), Maoists, Castroists-Guevarists, anarchists, and others engaged in hairsplitting disputes about revolutionary tactics. They seemed to have been relegated to Trotsky's famous "dustbin of history"; few expected that they would receive a new lease on life not as the result of an "objective revolutionary situation" but with the advent of a new generation willing to give extremist politics a new chance.

After several years of growing political activity and radicalism among French students, the first major confrontation occurred in November 1967 with the strike of sociology teachers and students at the new University of Nanterre, near Paris. In February 1968 Paris students struck, demanding the removal of restrictions on movement between boys' and girls' hostels, and Molotov cocktails were thrown at some buildings, taken as symbols of the capitalist system, by members of a small ultraradical group of *enragés*. Meanwhile, the leadership of UNEF, the national students' union, had passed into the hands of a militant group; Cohn-Bendit, Sauvageot, and Geismar first achieved prominence during those hectic weeks. There was growing unrest, but it seemed to be confined to the universities and to concern their internal affairs. There was no sign of a national crisis when Prime Minister Pompidou left on an official visit to Teheran in early May, yet within a few days the situation changed completely. Student demonstrations and attempts to take over university buildings were broken up by the police; dozens of students were injured, and others arrested. This in turn led to bigger demonstrations and more intensive police repression. The police, unaccustomed to street fighting on this scale, behaved with unnecessary violence; according to a poll taken during this period, four-fifths of the population of Paris sympathized with the student-protest movement, which, it was commonly believed, concerned long-overdue university reforms. Cohn-Bendit and his comrades seemed suddenly to have found a mass basis for their cause. They thought that by deliberately provoking police violence they would be able to show up the real, brutal face of the regime and its repressive character. Within the next few days it became clear that they were not really interested in reforming what most of them thought was long past reform; they stood for the destruction of the old university and regarded education, rightly from their point of view, as a marginal problem. Revolution was now the real issue. The rebels from Nanterre and the Sorbonne had the support of the teachers' federation, which declared a sympathy strike; the left-wing Catholic trade-unionists (CFDT) and many intellectuals also rallied to their side. On May 13 hundreds of thousands of Parisians demonstrated against the Gaullist regime; all over France action committees came into being; the workers joined the general movement, against the advice of the Communist and Socialist parties and the CGT. Student soviets were established in most universities. The state of high tension, of revolutionary expectation, was reminiscent of the atmosphere in Petrograd in 1917. Michel Butor and Nathalie Sarraute stormed the Society of the Men of Letters; footballers, television stars, and even young rabbis joined the cultural revolution. On May 13 the Sorbonne was occupied by the students; four days later ten million workers were striking, and on the 18th de Gaulle returned posthaste from his state visit to Bucharest. What had started as a happening had turned into the most serious challenge his regime had ever faced.

There was no revolutionary situation in France in the early summer of 1968, but there was certainly a great deal of discontent and restlessness. The paternalism of the Gaullist regime, its empty phrases, its social and economic failures, the mandarinism still dominating academic life, and a great many other negative aspects of French society had antagonized wide sections of the French people. The economic situation was, everything considered, not worse than in most countries, and, compared with Spain, not to mention Eastern Europe, France was still a haven of freedom. But many Frenchmen were not in a mood to engage in such comparisons; what mattered to them was that they had a great many grievances and that their expectations had not been fulfilled. This reaction came as a great shock to leading Gaullists, and de Gaulle was disgusted; "Reforms yes—bed-wetting no," the general is said to have declared soon after his return. By that time the leaders of the political opposition—the communists, the socialists, Mendès-France, and Mitterrand—had joined the revolutionary bandwagon, and it seemed doubtful whether the Gaullist regime would survive. Authority was breaking down everywhere; the reins of government, central and local, appeared to be slipping; the bourgeoisie seemed paralyzed by fear. The general himself appeared to have lost heart as the crisis reached its climax during the last days of May. The government negotiated with the CGT and reached agreement, conceding substantial wage increases to industrial workers. Much to everyone's surprise, the agreement was turned down by the rank and file, and thus the deadlock was complete. On May 29 de Gaulle left Paris for an unknown destination, and there were rumors that he was about to resign. He went in fact to Baden-Baden to consult the general commanding French troops in West Germany. Having assured himself of this general's loyalty, he returned to the capital in fighting spirit. In a very brief television appearance the next afternoon he announced that, having a mandate from the people, he would not resign. The National Assembly would be dissolved and new elections held on June 23. De Gaulle also called for civic action everywhere and at once, in defense of the Republic against the threat of communist dictatorship. Within minutes a million supporters shouting "*La France aux français*" and singing "La Marseillaise" filled the streets of Paris in a march on the Place de la Concorde. The minister of the interior telephoned all regional prefects, asking for firm and immediate measures to put down any disturbances. It took only a few hours for the antirevolutionary party to regain confidence, while all vigor seemed to have gone out of the left. Gradually the workers evacuated the factories and the students left the colleges they had seized. The ultraradical student groups were outlawed, and the communists, accused by the general quite undeservedly of having plotted revolution, retreated everywhere. The June elections brought victory to the party of order while all left-wing parties lost votes. Within the left there were bitter mutual recriminations, directed above all against Cohn-Bendit and his comrades, who with their ultraradical slogans, their adventurism, and their thoughtless violence had antagonized wide sections of the public, which had in the beginning sympathized with their cause. Yet many felt that Gaullism's victory was hollow; the student movement had only too effectively revealed its weakness. It seemed doubtful that it would overcome this blow to its prestige; the financial crisis six months after the May events showed that the repercussions were by no means over.

The events in France gave encouragement to the student movement in many other countries, but nowhere else did student revolt trigger a mass movement; its impact, despite the great publicity it received, was on the whole limited to the universities. The German student movement spearheaded by the socialist SDS had its traditional stronghold in West Berlin, the freest and most progressive of all West German universities. In its early stages its demands mainly concerned *Mitbestimmung,* codetermination, but leadership of the movement, as in France, soon passed into the hands of the most radical sections: the moment their demands were granted, they presented new ones, until study in some faculties came to a standstill. There was also a growing tendency to engage in street fighting. In June 1967 Berlin students demonstrated against the shah of Iran, then on a visit to the former German capital. In the course of the riots that ensued, one student was shot by the police; he became the martyr of the movement, which as a result of this incident gained many new adherents. In February 1968 the radical student groups launched a major campaign against Axel Springer, head of Germany's biggest newspaper concern. Springer's newspapers were violently hostile to the student movement and everything it stood for. This campaign had the support of many liberals who thought that the concentration of so many newspapers in the hands of one press lord was a danger to democracy. Other SDS initiatives were less successful; the attempt to engage in revolutionary violence met determined resistance in a country in which the consequences of the politics of violence were still well remembered. In Berlin the student movement had more to fear from the irate population than from the police; in view of Berlin's exposed position, the students' antics were regarded by most of its citizens as a real danger to its freedom.

The German student movement was the most highly ideological in character; students of theology, sociology, and literature produced many books and pamphlets to prove that the old order was corrupt to the core, and that only total rejection of neocapitalism (or "late capitalism," as others called it) would open a road to a better world. Some gravitated toward Soviet communism, but the majority drew their inspiration from revolutionary movements in the third world. In some respects it was an almost uncanny repeat performance of the noble-savage fashion that had swept Europe two centuries earlier. With all their rejections of modern social science, the rebels had become hopelessly enmeshed in the philosophical and sociological jargon of the day, and many of them were quite unable to express themselves clearly and precisely. For this reason, if for no other, they found it difficult to communicate with those sections of the population who had not been fortunate enough to read Marcuse, Bloch, Adorno, and other masters of contemporary thought. Rudi Dutschke, the most prominent leader of the movement, was shot and badly wounded by a mad youngster; there were fresh demonstrations, and an attempt was made, not too successfully, to put the blame on Springer and the Bonn government. The public response was not encouraging, and as a result the center of the rebels' activities was transferred back to the universities, where their position was incomparably stronger.

The Italian student movement first gained prominence in April–May 1966, when several big demonstrations were staged in Rome, ending in riots. The second and bigger wave of youth revolt lasted from November 1967 to the following summer and spread throughout Italy. The students demanded higher grants and better facilities in the universities, but, as in the other European countries, their protests turned into a revolt against bourgeois society *tout court*. In Spain students were in the forefront of the struggle for the overthrow of Franco's dictatorship. A poll carried out in 1963 had shown that 77 percent of them were not interested in politics, but in the following years radicalization made quick progress. Demonstrations in open defiance of the authorities began in February 1965; Barcelona University was first closed in April 1966, and by the spring of 1968 the movement had affected all Spain. The political impact of the student movement in Britain was in comparison much more limited. On various occasions students seized university buildings, and many of their demands for university reform were accepted. But, with the exception of the demonstration in October 1968 against the war in Vietnam, they did not succeed in mobilizing substantial public support for their wider political aims.

The student movement made itself heard and seen at one time

or another in most European countries, even in Eastern Europe, where it faced a totally different political situation, described elsewhere in the present study. About the mainsprings of the movement in the West there was general agreement: the number of students had trebled or even quadrupled since the war, there was overcrowding, and facilities were often quite inadequate. The internal structure of the universities was antiquated, too much of the medieval mumbo-jumbo still persisted, the administration and/or the professors ruled autocratically, and the students' demand for some form of codetermination was by no means unreasonable. It was surely no coincidence that almost all the leaders of the extreme groups were students of sociology and political science, of theology and philosophy. These fields were in a state of crisis which was reflected in the private frustration of the students who had failed to receive an answer to the questions preoccupying them. It was only natural that a young generation should turn against its predecessor, confident that it would have done much better. On an even deeper level, there was dissatisfaction with the modern consumer society and a chiliastic urge in the tradition of the messianic hopes of former ages.

However, there remain many question marks about the cultural and political aims of the movement that, in view of its diffuse and inchoate character, are all the more difficult to answer. There were from the very beginning doubts about the genuine seriousness of the movement; the element of "happening," of histrionics, the acting out of fantasies, was strongly marked. There was a great deal of talk about revolution, but no one seemed to want to seize power. Perhaps it was an act of self-preservation on the part of the student leaders, who were dimly aware that in a postrevolutionary dictatorship power would not have remained for long in their hands. "Liberation" was the main slogan, but it was liberty only for like-minded people; the chief enemy of the young rebel of the sixties was not the fascist or the Stalinist, not even the conservative, but the liberal, with his all-pervasive, repressive tolerance. The movement claimed to be rationalist in character, a "second enlightenment"; yet there was much evidence of the opposite—the uncritical acceptance of myths, the rejection of historical experience (for history showed so clearly the limits of revolutionary movements). The movement put everything in question, but questioning its own basic beliefs was taboo. In its ideology it tried to combine incompatible ingredients, such as utopianism and decadence, freedom and dictatorship, Marcuse's one-dimensional pessimism and Mao's revolutionary optimism. The adulation of some of its heroes was reminiscent of the cult of certain film stars.

Some of the more farsighted leaders of the movement realized that the power in the advanced countries was so solid, and the means of repression at its disposal were so manifold, that the attempt to wrest power from its hands was hopeless. The whole system was so deeply rooted that it seemed doubtful whether basic changes could be effected even in the unlikely event of a successful revolution. Hence the great hopes attached to the revolution in the third world; there, as Frantz Fanon claimed, a new beginning, radically different from the decaying West, was still possible. Only gradually did it dawn on them that the third-world revolutions had little if any guidance to offer advanced societies facing totally different problems. But if it was impossible to overthrow the established order in the advanced countries of the West, there was certainly a good chance of paralyzing it. Life there had become fantastically complex, and for that reason more vulnerable than ever before. If a few strategically placed obstacles could bring traffic to a standstill in a big town during the rush hour, could not a few determined revolutionaries through their actions paralyze not just the universities but public life in general? Society had become very tolerant. Its adversaries had more to fear from the blandishments of the television companies than from police repression, for they were given a free run of the media of mass communication. The more extreme their views, the more publicity they were likely to receive. Yet in the long run society was bound to defend itself against anarchy, not because it was the victim of ideological manipulation but because the great majority of the population had an interest in the maintenance of law and order and had no trust in a future society engineered by the Dutschkes, Cohn-Bendits, and Tariq Alis. But they were not greatly worried by the possibility of a right-wing, authoritarian reaction, for they hoped that this would only exacerbate the crisis and that their cause would benefit therefrom.

The central dilemma confronting the revolutionary youth movement was that their demand for absolute freedom collided with complex political-economic realities limiting freedom and democracy. Their quarrel was not just with neocapitalism but with modern social systems in general, for they all contained strong elements of repression. Despite its radical political demands, the European revolutionary movement of the sixties was, as in America, basically motivated by cultural discontent. It rejected alike the emptiness of mass culture and the higher idiocies of intellectual fashions; the charge leveled against it, that it lacked positive content, was therefore largely irrelevant. It was romantic in inspiration, and romantic movements are always based on a mood rather than a program. It could act in given situations as a catalyst of the general discontent that in periods of prolonged peace seems to be inherent in human existence. The revolutionary movement could provoke a "confrontation" with the system; it could in certain conditions seriously weaken it. But it had no alternative to offer, and it was therefore, in the last resort, bound to be a failure. At the time, these events were widely regarded as a turning point in the history of postwar Europe. Twenty years later they seemed to have been no more than a fascinating interlude. European politics have not been revolutionized; in Britain and West Germany conservative governments were still, or again, in power. The same was true with regard to Italy; only in France did the socialists constitute the government, but their policies were far from those envisaged by the revolutionaries of 1968. Twenty years later the student leaders of 1968 were now professional men and women approaching middle age. Many of them had joined established political parties, others had found a new home in the ecological movements, which had their origins in part in 1968. New generations of students showed little interest in the ideas that had once inspired Dutschke, Cohn-Bendit, and Tariq Ali. True, reforms had been carried out in the universities, but these most probably would have come in any case. Many intellectuals still, or again, tended to the left, but this had been the case before 1968 as well.

THE INVASION OF
CZECHOSLOVAKIA

The communist seizure of power in Prague in February 1948 was a turning point in Europe's postwar history; twenty years later the Soviet invasion of Czechoslovakia had a similarly profound effect on European politics. Czechoslovakia is the one East European communist country with democratic traditions, and it has been oriented toward the West during most of its recent history, an orientation that was not incompatible with feelings of Slav solidarity. Although the Western tradition was firmly suppressed after 1948, it had not been altogether uprooted, and it re-emerged with the relaxation of political controls in the early sixties. Czechoslovakia was one of the last communist countries to engage in de-Stalinization, but the process was halted midway; "liberalization" was permitted to proceed much further in the economic field than in political and cultural life. The thaw of 1961–62 was followed by a refreeze. The progressive cultural periodicals were either discontinued or put under strict political control. There was general disillusionment with communism, and this in a country in which the party had once been highly popular. Writers and students continued to maintain that, since there had been no basic change in the structure of the political system, there were no guarantees that the "mistakes of the past" (to use the official euphemism) would not be repeated. The economic situation was going from bad to worse, and among the Slovaks there was growing resentment of the Prague leadership, which accused them of separatism instead of showing understanding for their specific problems. Power rested in the hands of Antonin Novotny, for many years first secretary of the party and at the same time president of the Republic, who had been deeply implicated in the crimes of the Stalin era. Student demonstrations in Prague in November 1967 concerning living conditions in student hostels were brutally suppressed by the police and thus triggered a wide sympathy movement. By itself the student protest would have remained as ineffective as the demonstrations of Warsaw students in the spring of 1965, but it coincided with an acute crisis in the party leadership; the "liberals," supported by the Slovaks, had a majority in the Central Committee, and they used the opportunity for an all-out attack on the constant violation of internal party democracy by the Novotny faction. Novotny and the conservatives were relieved of their functions in early January 1968, and a new leadership established under Alexander Dubček, formerly first secretary of the Slovak party. Their declared political program was the democratization of public life—"so that every honest citizen believing in socialism and the unity of the country feels that he is being useful and counts for something," as Dubček said. The new action program published in April stated that socialism must provide "for a fuller assertion of the personality than any bourgeois democracy." The new course had wide popular support; it was accompanied by the demand that the National Assembly, which for so many years had been a mere rubber stamp, should decide important political issues, and that the crimes of the fifties should be thoroughly investigated and those responsible for them punished. The censors themselves suggested the abolition of censorship in March, and a freedom of expression prevailed, unprecedented in any communist regime. There was no intention to retreat from socialist principles in industry and agriculture, but economic reforms (such as decentralization) were to be promoted more vigorously than in the past. While trying to expand trade links with the West, the new leaders repeatedly declared that the basic orientation of Czechoslovak foreign policy was toward the Soviet Union; there was no intention of leaving Comecon or the Warsaw Pact. Addressing the Central Committee on April 1, 1968, Dubček stated: "We must continue to build up our army . . . as a firm link in the alliance of the Warsaw Pact armies."

There was no reason to doubt these professions of loyalty, yet the new Czech leaders encountered hostility among their communist allies almost from the beginning. Without at first directly attacking them, the Soviet press began to suggest that the internal situation in Czechoslovakia was very serious, because "antisocial elements," behind a screen of democratization and liberalization, were advocating a "return to the bourgeois republic of Masaryk and Beneš." Gomułka, the Polish leader, was no doubt much displeased by the slogan shouted by Warsaw demonstrators: "We want a Polish Dubček." But the leading voice in the hostile chorus was taken by the East Germans, who claimed that imperialism was trying to detach Czechoslovakia, against the wishes of its people, from the Eastern bloc by means of "ideological subversion." They were the first to accuse the Czech leaders of not opposing this process and in some ways of assisting it. The East German leaders feared that the new Czechoslovak leadership would establish diplomatic relations and expand economic ties with West Germany, and thus weaken East Germany's position in world affairs and even inside the communist bloc. They feared still more that the call for "socialism in freedom," if not suppressed, would soon reverberate in their own country. The Soviet attitude was one of extreme displeasure, but officially, at any rate, it was still one of noninterference in Czechoslovakia's internal affairs. By early May, however, a high-ranking Soviet officer was reported for the first time to have suggested military intervention to assist loyal Czech comrades in their struggle against the antisocialist elements. During May, Moscow clearly became more concerned; the free public debate developing in Czechoslovakia suggested to them that the Prague leadership was losing its grip. The disclosures about the crimes of the Stalin era were, moreover, extremely embarrassing, since they involved Soviet officials. Above all, the purge was beginning to reach those elements in the party, the army, and the secret police on which the Kremlin had been able to count in the past.

Liberalization in Czechoslovakia coincided with a marked hardening in Soviet policies, both domestic and foreign, and it was therefore all the more provocative from the Soviet point of view. Facing the separatist tendencies in so many communist countries, with Albania now firmly arrayed in the Chinese camp and Rumania moving toward independence in its foreign policy, the Soviet leadership found it imperative to take immediate action against the further disintegration of their camp. Czechoslovakia's deviation must have appeared to Moscow far more dangerous than Rumanian separatism, for Rumania had no common border with any Western country. Besides, domestic liberalization had been no more marked in Rumania than in the other bloc countries, whereas the new spirit of freedom in

Prague was bound to be infectious, to spread to other East European countries, and eventually perhaps to infiltrate the Soviet Union itself, undermining the existing political system. The repeated accusations concerning the growing influence of "antisocialist elements" in Czechoslovakia were untrue, and those responsible for making them knew it; but the Soviet leaders, Gomułka, and Ulbricht were no doubt correct in claiming that events in Czechoslovakia constituted a real danger—not to socialism, but to the men at the helm in Moscow, Warsaw, and East Berlin.

A decision was taken, probably in late May, to bring to an end the Czechoslovak experiment of "socialism in freedom." There were reports of Soviet troop movements in Poland, and during the second half of May, Marshal Grechko visited Prague, announcing that Warsaw Pact command-staff exercises would be held in Czechoslovakia in June. Repeated assurances by the Czech leaders of their firm friendship and alliance with the Soviet Union did nothing to allay Soviet distrust; Moscow had decided that the process of democratization was to be stopped, and this could be effected only by a change in the leadership. The Russians, needless to say, would have greatly preferred to achieve their aim peacefully, by political pressure rather than a full-scale military invasion. It was clear that military action would not involve any major risk, in view of the understanding with America about the division of spheres of influence, and it could be taken for granted that the West would refrain from action, as it had done during the Hungarian crisis of 1956. But it was also certain that the decision to occupy Czechoslovakia would deepen the rift in the communist camp and was also bound to alarm the West. For a number of years Moscow had tried, not unsuccessfully, to persuade the European members of NATO that there was no Soviet threat and that the continued existence of the Atlantic alliance was the main obstacle to a real détente and a lasting peace. Given the disagreements among its West European members, their indecision, and other disruptive forces, there had been a reasonable hope that this line would be successful. Now Soviet military intervention would reawaken old fears, undo much of the Soviet diplomatic spadework, and give NATO a new lease on life.

The Soviet, Polish, and East German propaganda campaign against Czechoslovak reform policies was intensified during June and July. Brezhnev and Kosygin referred on various occasions to the par-

allel between Hungary in 1956 and Czechoslovakia in 1965. In mid-
July the leaders of the communist countries, excluding Rumania and
Czechoslovakia, met in Warsaw to discuss the danger of "Czech revisionism," informing Prague at the same time that they had no intention of interfering in its internal matters, which, they said, would
violate the principle of respect for independence and equality in relations between socialist countries. But this principle, they added, was
not sacrosanct, for Czechoslovakia was now in danger of being torn
from the socialist community, and such a situation was completely
unacceptable. Various means were used to intimidate the Czech leadership: an anti-Semitic campaign was launched against the few Jews
in leading positions in Prague, to prove that revisionism was a Jewish
disease. This stratagem had worked in Poland, but Czechoslovakia
did not have the same strong anti-Semitic traditions: the allegation
was too absurd to be believed. Later on, *agents provocateurs* went
to work, planting arms caches (which were said to belong to German
revanchists) and using other techniques similar to those applied by
the Nazis before their occupation of Czechoslovakia in 1938–39. To
intimidate the Czechs and Slovaks, the Warsaw Pact troops that had
held maneuvers in Czechoslovakia were not withdrawn from the
country until August 3. Meanwhile, the Soviet, Polish, and East German press emphasized the danger of massive West German intervention and "international counterrevolution." When this did not help,
the Prague leaders were summoned to a meeting with the Soviet Politburo (only two of its members had been left behind) at the border
village of Cierna nad-Tisou. Again they did not budge. Dubček was
willing to give the Russians specific assurances about their legitimate
defense interests, but he rejected all imputations of "counterrevolution" and refused to discuss the Soviet demand for a purge of some
of the country's progressive leaders. Several days later yet another
meeting with the Eastern-bloc leaders (except the Rumanians) took
place in Bratislava.

The two gatherings did nothing to solve the basic conflict. The
Soviets did not withdraw their ultimatum; they had not succeeded in
driving a wedge between the Prague leaders; on the contrary, national
unity in Czechoslovakia was stronger now than before. This made
the experiment all the more dangerous from Moscow's point of view,
and the propaganda campaign against it was stepped up. Moscow
asserted that there was a witch hunt against loyal, pro-Soviet workers,

and that the Prague revisionists were not carrying out the Cierna and Bratislava resolutions. In Moscow, the visits to Prague of Marshal Tito and Ceausescu, the Rumanian leader, in mid-August raised the specter of a revisionist bloc, a new "Little Entente," and the Soviet Presidium decided, apparently between August 10 and 17, that, since other methods of pressure had failed, the military occupation of Czechoslovakia was now to proceed. How deep differences of opinion in the Kremlin went is not known, though some Soviet leaders undoubtedly had more misgivings than others. It was clear that a high price would have to be paid. Many foreign communist parties, including some of the most influential, like the French and the Italian, had expressed support for Dubček and warned Moscow against the invasion. There was a real dilemma, but, weighing the alternatives, there could be no doubt in the minds of the Soviet leaders. The continuation of the new course endangered the existence of all the conservative regimes in the bloc, whereas the propaganda setback caused by the invasion would not be lasting; after a few months, world public opinion was bound to forget, and so would the dissenting communist parties. It had been that way after the suppression of the Hungarian revolt in 1956, and there was no reason to assume that the pattern would not repeat itself.

To give more plausibility and legitimacy to their invasion on August 21, plans were made for the establishment of a quisling government in Prague which was to ask the fraternal Soviet people and their allies to give them military assistance against internal and external enemies. It is not known what went wrong in the political preparation of the invasion, but when the Soviet troops entered Czechoslovakia their generals seemed to have no clear political directives. In the Security Council, Moscow at first claimed that the invitation came from the Czechoslovak government, but in fact the Soviets found no one willing to collaborate with them; they arrested Dubček, Cernik, Smrkovsky, and the other leaders, but Svoboda, the president, refused to dismiss and replace them. When Svoboda rejected the demand for the appointment of a new leadership handed to him by the Soviet ambassador, the scene shifted to Moscow. Svoboda, together with several potential collaborators, was invited to meet the Soviet Presidium, but he insisted on the presence of the arrested leaders. On their arrival, after being in the hands of the Soviet political police, they were neither physically nor psychologically in the best condition to stand up to Brezhnev, who is reported to have threatened their country and them personally with the direst consequences if they failed to comply with Soviet demands. With one dissenting voice, they accepted the Soviet ultimatum: Soviet troops were to be stationed for an indefinite period on Czechoslovak soil, censorship was to be restored, the "notorious rehabilitation campaign" was to be discontinued, the economic reforms were to be watered down. Generally speaking, coercion was again to replace popular consent as the basis of communist rule. True, the Russians paid lip service to the reform program, with which, they said, they did not want to interfere; nor were they anxious to restore Novotny to power; he was too discredited to fulfill any useful purpose. They assumed, not without reason, that they would gradually be able to replace Dubček and the other progressives with more pliant leaders, and that eventually the new middle-of-the-roaders, under Soviet pressure and to ensure their own political survival, would suppress "revisionism" altogether. Gomułka had acted that way after 1956, and there was every reason to assume that events in Prague would follow a similar course.

The occupation of Czechoslovakia came as a great relief in Warsaw and East Berlin; troops from both countries took part in the military operation. The participation of German troops was not, to put it cautiously, in good taste; but, then, Ulbricht and his colleagues had never been bashful men. Although Hungarian units also took part, Budapest clearly felt ill-at-ease; memories of 1956 lingered on. The Soviet leaders, for want of more convincing arguments, claimed that history would justify their action, but meanwhile Chou En-lai, the Chinese prime minister, called the invasion the most barefaced example of fascist power politics. The Albanians spoke about "fascist aggression"; the Yugoslavs expressed extreme concern about the "illegal occupation" of Czechoslovakia and mobilized their army; the Rumanian leaders called it a "flagrant violation of the national sovereignty of a socialist country."

The Soviet action was sharply condemned in the Western capitals, but the policy of the governments remained one of studious noninterference. As far as they were concerned, this was a purely internal affair between the Soviet Union and one of its allies. In Washington and Paris official circles played down the long-term consequences of the Soviet invasion. President Johnson continued to talk about a summit meeting, since the East-West détente had priority in his eyes. Michel Debré, the French foreign minister, thought it unwise to close a road simply because an accident had taken place. In the United Nations the Arab governments and some Asian countries opposed any condemnation of the Soviet action. For their part, the Soviet leaders, soon after the immediate storm had subsided, launched a new diplomatic offensive aimed at persuading the West that the events in Czechoslovakia were not an obstacle to a normalization of relations between West and East. It seemed as if they had after all been correct in assuming that the international repercussions of the occupation would be shortlived and not very profound. But in fact they underrated the long-term effects of the invasion, which was bound to be a turning point in European postwar history. The military balance, to be sure, had hardly been changed; the number of Soviet troops stationed in Czechoslovakia was relatively small and did not constitute a major danger for the West. But most of the Western assumptions underlying the détente had been disproved, and this in the long run could not remain without consequences. It had been believed that as a result of the détente the era of bipolarity would come to an end (if it was not already over), that the centrifugal, disintegrative trends in both blocs would gradually lead to the shaping of a new European political system. De Gaulle and others were convinced that the Soviet threat to the West had diminished, if not altogether disappeared, and that consequently there was a good chance for the reunification of Europe-to-the-Vistula, if not to the Urals. It had been assumed that, as a result of the gradual Europeanization of the Soviet bloc, Russia would be willing to grant its allies a larger degree of freedom and independence—provided, of course, that its elementary security interests were not affected.

The invasion put an end to the hopes for gradual change in Eastern Europe: it now appeared that the initiative for any basic change in the character of the communist regime could come from Moscow only. There were no indications that such a change could reasonably be expected in the foreseeable future. The events of 1968 meant that Soviet hostility toward political systems different from its own had not abated and that, barring totally unforeseen circumstances, the Cold War would continue for an indefinite period.

BRITAIN:
FROM CHURCHILL
TO HEATH

The Conservatives replaced Labour as Britain's ruling party in 1951 and remained in power for the next thirteen years. Labour was still basically the party of the working class, while the Tories, broadly speaking, represented the upper and middle classes. The socialist program envisaged the nationalization of the key sectors of the national economy, while the Conservatives, at least in theory, stood for economic freedom, minimal state intervention, and the defense of the traditional ideas of Toryism. (The Liberals still polled several million votes but, under the British electoral system, had ceased to play an important role; their representation in Parliament was reduced to less than a dozen.) The doctrinal position of Conservatives and Labour seemed diametrically opposed, but in practice there was a great deal of common ground on issues of vital national importance, such as foreign policy and defense, while the harsh realities of Britain's financial situation reduced the number of economic choices open to Labour and Conservatives alike ("Butskellism"). The more farsighted Conservative leaders realized that their party had to adapt itself to the welfare state if it was to maintain its position in British political life. They did not abolish or reduce the social services that had been introduced by Labour, and of the nationalized industries only road transport and steel were denationalized by Churchill after his comeback in 1951 (steel was again nationalized when Labour returned to power in the sixties). The Tory government built more houses than Labour, and Macmillan's "wind of change" speech indicated that the Conservatives had accepted the loss of empire, with all its consequences. The leadership of the party was passing steadily from mem-

bers of the aristocracy to representatives of the middle class; Eton
and Harrow old boys still predominated in the Tory cabinets, but
graduates of Oxford and Cambridge constituted an almost equally
high percentage of Labour's front bench.

Churchill suffered a stroke when in office; his illness was kept
secret at the time, but in April 1955 he had to retire. Anthony Eden,
who succeeded him, had been intimately involved for many years in
the conduct of British foreign policy; his experience in other branches
of government was limited. He had been expected to replace Churchill
one day, and his selection came as no surprise. Ironically, it was in
his own field of specialization, foreign affairs, that Eden failed; but
for Colonel Nasser's nationalization of the Suez Canal and the inept
way Eden handled the ensuing crisis, his government might have lasted
many more years. As tension mounted, Eden showed lack of judgment
and, more surprising in an Englishman of his background, a lack of
sangfroid. At the height of the crisis he suffered a breakdown and
was replaced by Harold Macmillan, who had a great deal of political
experience in both the domestic and foreign fields; in the twenties
and thirties he had been one of the chief spokesmen of progressive
Toryism. Under his leadership the Conservatives survived the humiliation of Suez without major ill effects.

Britain's main problems in the years following were domestic in
character, and in this respect Macmillan's government was by no
means a brilliant success. The rapid turnover at the Treasury (Thor-
neycroft, Selwyn Lloyd, Heathcoat Amory et al.) was an indication
of the continuing financial difficulties. But there was fitful economic
progress, and though the spirit of Britain during the late fifties was
not one of buoyant optimism, a feeling of confidence returned after
the economic setbacks of the late forties and the political shocks of
the middle fifties had been overcome. The small Conservative majority
of 1951 rose at the elections of 1955 and increased again in 1959:
the position of the Tories seemed almost unassailable. But if the standard of living had risen, expectations had grown even faster; the
British people became increasingly weary of heavy taxation, wage
freezes, higher bank rates and mortgage charges. The Conservative
leadership showed signs of fatigue, and the feeling spread that Labour
ought to be given another chance. The Profumo scandal and several
other incidents further damaged the prestige of the Macmillan government, and the prime minister, sensing that public opinion (includ-

ing important segments of his own party) was turning against him, decided to resign in October 1963. This was about one year before the next general election was due, and Sir Alec Douglas-Home's Cabinet had therefore the character of a caretaker government. Douglas-Home was a High Tory and had been a member of the House of Lords, an unlikely choice for prime minister in the twentieth century. But the policies he followed hardly differed from those of his predecessor, which again showed that the freedom of maneuver of both prime minister and governing party had become very limited indeed. Douglas-Home had been the candidate of a small but influential group within the Conservative Party for whom Butler (the leader who had been thought most likely to replace Macmillan) was too radical and therefore unreliable. Douglas-Home's election caused a great deal of resentment inside the party, and the demand gained ground that the succession should in future be decided by open democratic vote. In these inauspicious conditions Douglas-Home did surprisingly well, and though his party was defeated in the elections of October 1964, Labour returned to power with a majority of only thirteen seats over the Tories.

Labour had been in a state of profound internal crisis throughout the 1950s. After the resignation of Attlee, the mantle of the leader passed to Hugh Gaitskell, an economist by training, an Oxford don, and a wartime civil servant. Gaitskell's personal integrity was widely respected, and his intellectual competence, especially in his own field, was beyond doubt. But he lacked dynamism and the charisma of a born leader capable of inspiring his followers and winning new supporters to his cause. Above all, he had to face bitter opposition inside the party, for Labour was virtually split during most of these years, and the fundamentalist left attacked the leadership for allegedly betraying socialist principles. The left stood for full nationalization and a strictly controlled economy, and for neutrality and disarmament in foreign affairs. The difficulty with the left-wing program was not so much its extremism as its unreal character: a political program, however extreme, has a chance of eventually succeeding if it is attuned to political realities and exigencies; that of the Labour left was not, for Britain's economic difficulties could not be cured by the medicines suggested by these circles. Although almost everyone in Britain preferred peace to war, and friendship with all nations to tension and crisis, praiseworthy sentiments are not sufficient to resolve interna-

tional conflicts. The nuclear disarmers went each Easter on their Aldermaston protest march; the Labour Party conference regularly voted
each year to abolish nuclear arms; and anti-Americanism made some
headway in the country. Unilateralism had its attractions, but was it
practical politics for a party in power? When Labour was again called
on to form a government, yesterday's rebels soon found themselves
pursuing the very policies they had denounced not long before, and
they in turn came under attack from a new generation of radical
critics.

These battles lasted for several years, and in the end, under
Gaitskell's patient leadership, the party slowly closed its ranks, realizing that it would be condemned to stay in the political wilderness
forever unless it ceased its internal strife. Then, with better prospects
in sight, Gaitskell suddenly died. The two main candidates for the
succession were George Brown, an indefatigable, highly extroverted,
and somewhat erratic party stalwart of working-class background,
and Harold Wilson, like Gaitskell an economist by training, a former
Oxford don, and a wartime civil servant. Wilson at an early age had
been president of the Board of Trade but, together with other left-
wing ministers, had resigned in protest against some of the government's policies.

Wilson showed greater tactical skill than Gaitskell; his decision
to dissolve Parliament early in 1966 resulted in a much larger majority
for Labour and thus provided a secure basis for carrying out the
Labour Party election program. But soon the government was overtaken by a series of economic emergencies, and within two years it
had lost its popular support, while Wilson's personal prestige declined
even more sharply. The government seemed to totter from one disaster
to another—the devaluation of sterling in November 1967 was only
one of a series of major blows. Even the most secure Labour seats
were no longer safe in the by-elections of 1967 and 1968; much of
the blame was put on the prime minister personally; Wilson, his many
critics argued, had not made the full seriousness of the latent economic
crisis known to the people and seemed incapable of acting decisively
at the right time. Though much of this criticism was justified, it was
an oversimplification to put all the blame on the prime minister and
his entourage: Britain's difficulties were largely structural. Both the
City of London, with its periodical jitters provoking unnecessary monetary crises, and the trade-union leadership, with its unwillingness to

cooperate in the modernization and streamlining of Britain's economy, bore a heavy share of responsibility. The resignation of Frank
Cousins, head of the largest trade union, was typical of the lack of
support for the government from within its own ranks. But it would
be invidious to single out individual culprits: no government could
have worked wonders while the country failed to earn its way in the
world.

The Conservatives would have been even more successful in
making political capital of Labour's weakness but for the dissension
of their own ranks. The leadership had passed after Douglas-Home's
resignation to Edward Heath, who led his party to victory in June
1970. Within the party there were wide-ranging differences of opinion
on such issues as immigration, Rhodesia, the social services, and incomes policy. Some imaginative measures had been taken by the Tories when in government to cope with the economic situation, such
as the establishment of the National Economic Development Council
in 1961, in which business, trade unions, and government cooperated
in shaping economic policy. Unfortunately, this new body did not
gain the influence it was hoped it would acquire. The establishment
of a National Incomes Council was also envisaged, but failed to come
into being because the trade unions refused to participate.

Foreign affairs played a comparatively minor part in Britain's
crisis. The decolonization of the empire continued as Ghana and
Nigeria gained independence in the fifties. They were followed by the
East African countries. Malaya (1957) and Singapore (1959). The
West Indian Federation, established in 1958, foundered in 1962. More
serious from Britain's point of view was the breakdown of the Central
African Federation in 1963, for it led, two years later, to the Rhodesian
crisis. The majority of white settlers refused to surrender their position
to the Africans, claiming that such a policy would lead to a state of
chaos similar to the situation in the Congo. The British government
applied economic sanctions in accordance with UN resolutions, but
the African countries, now Britain's Commonwealth partners, demanded in addition the use of force against the Rhodesian prime
minister, Ian Smith, and his regime. There was little popular sympathy
in Britain for military action, and the Wilson government tried to
steer a middle course between the two extremes as the Rhodesian
issue came to play temporarily a role out of all proportion to its
intrinsic importance in British politics. Elsewhere, the transfer of

power presented fewer difficulties: Malta became independent in 1964, and also British Guyana, the last African colonies, and, after a prolonged struggle and civil war, Aden. Despite strong Spanish pressure, Britain was not willing to surrender Gibraltar. In Cyprus and South Arabia the British exodus was followed by bitter internal strife; the consequences of the British decision to leave the Persian Gulf will not be clear for years to come. The Commonwealth prime ministers continued to meet from time to time, but these were social occasions rather than events of great political consequences. There was reluctance to sever ancient ties altogether, and it was thought that the old framework could still be of some limited use. But membership in the Commonwealth in these conditions had almost lost its meaning; there were exchanges of opinion but no binding decisions.

Britain's foreign and defense policy had to be modified in the postwar era in the light of the country's diminished resources and reduced status in the world. It was a complicated and often painful adjustment; military positions east of Suez were gradually given up, and the army on the Rhine was reduced. Conscription was abolished, and a small professional army was entrusted with the defense of Britain and its shrinking commitments abroad. Britain produced its own nuclear devices but did not have the financial strength to compete with the United States and the Soviet Union in the missile race. The construction of Britain's own rocket, Blue Streak, had to be given up in 1960 because it proved too costly. The common Anglo-American project for the production of Skybolt rockets was also discontinued, and Britain became almost entirely dependent on the Polaris submarine and American rockets and aircraft to give even token credibility to her deterrent.

Successive governments showed in their foreign policy a great deal of caution and notable reluctance to engage independently in any major initiative. Such prudence was in marked contrast to de Gaulle's striking but ultimately futile ventures. Conservatives and Labour shared the conviction that reason should prevail in world affairs and violence should not be used to solve conflicts. There was much willingness to mediate between East and West, North and South; to look for a compromise was the recommendation to all antagonists. The Americans, some Englishmen argued, had the power and the money but lacked the experience to act wisely in complicated international situations, and they would therefore benefit from British advice. But the special relationship between London and Washington, which had existed during the Second World War and had lingered on during the decade after, faded away. American foreign policy lacked resolution rather than advice, of which there was more than enough, and the Soviet Union preferred to talk to Washington directly without intermediaries. Macmillan's visit to Moscow and Wilson's more frequent trips were therefore of no great political consequence, nor did the often heralded expansion of British trade with the Soviet Union ever materialize, though individual British firms no doubt benefited from trading with the Soviet Union.

Unlike the United States, Britain had established diplomatic links with China, but the hope of improving relations with Peking and exerting a moderating influence was not realized. British diplomats and journalists were harassed and kept under house arrest in China, and London could do little to alleviate their lot or effect their release. The Foreign Office tried to improve relations with individual communist countries, but since their freedom of action was strictly limited, the immediate value of these contacts was not great. The attitude of the communist countries certainly did not give much encouragement to the British left, and sympathies for the third world also began to fade. Nehru had died, and not much remained of the spirit of Bandung. The record of Sukarno and Nkrumah, of Nasser and Ben Bella, did not inspire much enthusiasm, and Mao's policy made sense only to the staunchest believers in his cause. Castro, Che Guevara, and Ho Chi Minh still had their admirers in some circles, but these were distant idols, hardly of much relevance to the conduct of British policy.

The belief of sections of the British establishment in its historical mission of playing Greeks to the Washington Romans had a parallel in the conviction of the radical left that socialist movements abroad were expecting British moral guidance. Such assumptions contained a grain of truth, for there existed a traditional reservoir of goodwill toward Britain in Europe as well as in other parts of the world. These hidden assets are not to be belittled, but they did not make it any easier for British policymakers (and the British people in general) to come to terms with their new, vastly reduced status in the world. This was the main challenge facing Britain in the fifties and sixties—not an easy one to meet, in view of Britain's leading role in the past and the inclination to hanker after lost power and splendor. Feelings of resentment vis-à-vis the United States and West Germany were more pronounced, however, among the literary intelligentsia than among other sections of the population. There was bound to be a great deal of dissatisfaction in this difficult period of transition; sometimes it found expression in unexpected directions, such as the resurgence of nationalist and separatist movements in Scotland and Wales and the revival of religious strife in Ulster. If Labour had not done well, there was no certainty that the Tories would have done any better. Some critics put the blame for Britain's malaise on the people as a whole ("suicide of a nation"), but less alarmist observers, too, wrote with growing concern about the consequences of inefficiency and the fact that the country, despite all warnings, was still living beyond its means. There were frequent complaints about the absence of a common national purpose and the general preoccupation with individual (or sectional) material interests. This feeling of malaise, combined with political frustration and economic stagnation, caused a great deal of heart-searching. The world success of the Beatles, the exploits of Sir Francis Chichester sailing the oceans in his *Gipsy Moth,* and stories in American news magazines about swinging London were not sufficient to dispel the mood of dejection.

FRANCE: THE COMING OF THE FIFTH REPUBLIC

As government followed government in rapid succession in the middle fifties, France seemed to be heading toward the brink of disaster. Since no single political party had a majority, all governments were coalitions and thus carried in themselves from the beginning the seeds of dissolution. There was growing anger among Frenchmen of all classes about a system of parties and politicians that was unable to provide a minimum of political stability. Economic progress was more substantial than appeared at first sight, but inflation deprived many Frenchmen of its fruits. The state of affairs was somewhat reminiscent of Germany before 1933: the Fourth Republic was steadily losing the last shreds of its authority, until in the end hardly anyone was willing to lift a finger in its defense. The extremes gained ground: the communists and, on the other hand, the Poujadists, a right-wing populist group, who at the general elections of 1956 obtained at their first attempt fifty seats in Parliament. Together, the two could effectively block most initiatives of the democratic center.

The colonial wars were the greatest immediate danger to the survival of democracy in France. The Mendès-France government had liquidated the bloody and protracted war in Indochina; Tunisia became independent in 1956, and even before that, in 1955, the Moroccan imbroglio had been settled by permitting the sultan to return to his country from exile. Algeria was the greatest problem of all; the insurrection there had broken out in November 1954, only a short while after the end of the war in Indochina. When the revolt began, fewer than fifty thousand French soldiers were stationed in Algeria; in two years that figure was doubled, and later it increased to 350,000.

The French army had to withdraw part of its contingent from NATO to cope with the attacks carried out by the Algerian Liberation Movement (FLN). Government after government (headed by Edgar Faure, Félix Gaillard, Guy Mollet, and Bourges-Maunoury) was unable to bring to a successful conclusion a war that was fought with increasing bitterness on both sides. France was deeply split on the issue; at first a majority of Frenchmen were strongly opposed to a retreat from Algeria, for, unlike Indochina or Morocco, this was not a colony but a part of metropolitan France and, incidentally, also the home of one million Frenchmen.

As the FLN received substantial support from neighboring African and Arab countries, the French army felt increasingly frustrated in its military actions and "pacification" program. Its commanders claimed that their hands were tied and that they did not receive full support from the Paris politicians. The army had the enthusiastic backing of the local French population and of individual French leaders such as Bidault, the former head of the MRP, and Soustelle, de Gaulle's former lieutenant, who bitterly opposed any retreat from "Algérie Française." As the war entered its fourth year, there was a shift in public opinion, and more and more Frenchmen admitted that there would have to be a negotiated peace. The right and the Pieds Noirs (the French Algerians), on the other hand, were determined not to surrender the Algerian position, and prepared for a war to the bitter end. Terrorist acts became a daily occurrence in both Algeria and metropolitan France, with the OAS (Organisation de l'Armée Secrète) leading the fight against "defeatists and traitors." When Pierre Pflimlin, believed to favor a negotiated settlement, was asked to form a new government in May 1958, tension reached a climax. On May 13, the French army in Algeria was in open revolt; in Corsica local "committees of public safety" were established in defiance of government authority.

In this acute crisis many eyes turned to de Gaulle; his leadership alone seemed acceptable to a majority of Frenchmen and thus a guarantee against the outbreak of civil war. De Gaulle accepted the call on condition that he be given a free hand to deal with the emergency; he was not willing to share power with parties and politicians. His views on Algeria were by no means clear, and he did little to clarify them. The army expected him to give them full support to continue the war; General Salan, the commander-in-chief in Algeria, had proclaimed de Gaulle chief of state even before the politicians in Paris had made up their minds. But de Gaulle seems to have been skeptical about the chances for military victory and was willing to make major concessions to the FLN. His main efforts were at first directed toward strengthening his own position. He ruled by decree; the political parties were not suppressed, but they lost effective power. Under the new constitution, the president had the right to appoint the prime minister and to dissolve Parliament, and effective control over defense and foreign policy was in his hands. He was directly elected by the people for a period of seven years, and made repeated use of a popular referendum, thus further reducing the importance of Parliament. When the deputies opposed the appointment of Georges Pompidou, de Gaulle's candidate, as prime minister, the president simply ignored the decision and reappointed him the following day. Some of his governments were composed of Gaullists in combination with leaders of other groups (Guy Mollet, Giscard d'Estaing), but the key positions were always in the hands of his own faithful followers: Michel Debré, Georges Pompidou, and Couve de Murville could be relied upon to carry out unquestioningly the general's instructions. Before 1968 the Gaullists never obtained an absolute majority of votes, but they were the strongest party, and the new electoral system provided them with a safe parliamentary base. The new constitution had been welcomed by 29 percent of all Frenchmen in a plebiscite in September 1958; there was every reason to believe that the Fifth Republic had a firmer and more secure basis than its predecessor.

The Algerian problem had not yet been solved, however; the war continued while various schemes to give Algeria greater autonomy or semi-independence were elaborated, discussed, and rejected. Although these plans did not satisfy the FLN, they infuriated the protagonists of Algérie Française. In January 1960 the French army in Algeria rebelled when General Massu, one of its heroes, was recalled by de Gaulle. A more serious showdown came in April 1961, when a number of generals (Salan, Jouhaud, Challe, and Zeller) openly defied the general. By that time, however, public opinion in France was solidly behind de Gaulle; it seemed hopeless to continue the war, and the acts of terrorism carried out by the OAS in metropolitan France did not endear their perpetrators to the population at large. The insurgents might have succeeded in overthrowing an old-style Cabinet and dictating their policy to the country, but de Gaulle, who did not fail to appear in a general's uniform in his effective television appearances, was a much more formidable antagonist, and in the face of resolute resistance the rebellion quickly collapsed. De Gaulle's Algerian policy received the support of 90 percent of all Frenchmen in a referendum in 1962, and the army, albeit somewhat reluctantly, followed suit.

Negotiations with the FLN in Evian (in Switzerland) dragged on for a long time, but in March 1962 agreement was at last reached. Algeria became independent; most of the French Algerians migrated to France and were absorbed without much difficulty in its political and economic life; the dire predictions about a fascist backlash did not materialize.

At the end of the Algerian war, de Gaulle was at the height of his power. For the first time in many years, France had a homogeneous government providing effective leadership. It was not a democratic regime by the standards of the Third or Fourth Republic, but the negative experience of parliamentary government with its shortcomings and abuses was still fresh in everyone's mind, and the Gaullist slogans of stability, tradition, and progress thus fell on welcoming ears. The economy continued to improve after the devaluation of the franc in 1958; in this respect de Gaulle was reaping the fruits of the initiatives undertaken by his predecessors. There was opposition among the center groups against Gaullist foreign and domestic policies, but Lecanuet, the leader of these forces, polled only 15 percent of the vote in 1964, in comparison with de Gaulle's 44 percent and the 31 percent given to Mitterrand, who represented the left-wing Federation. But behind the outward façade of stability a slow process of erosion of the Gaullist regime was setting in. The general's main interest was focused on defense and foreign policy. His anti-NATO line and blocking of Britain's entry into the EEC were criticized by many Frenchmen. Even among de Gaulle's own followers, some failed to see any purpose in his foreign policy; others, shocked by the growing cost of an independent French deterrent, began to regard it as a mere waste of money. The dictatorial style, the grand gestures that bore so little relation to France's present needs, irritated a growing number of young Frenchmen. In 1967 the first signs of an incipient crisis could be detected; in the parliamentary elections of March 1967 the Gaullist share of the vote fell to 38 percent. Separatist trends were reported from Brittany; there was growing student unrest and increasing dissatisfaction among the working class. The economy had recovered in 1966–67 from the crisis of 1963 (and the measures taken by the government to combat it), but the stabilization program and the price freeze were only partly successful, and real wages grew only slowly. It became increasingly obvious that the achievements of the government were lagging sadly behind its promises. *Paris s'ennuyait:* impatience grew, and with it unwillingness to put up much longer with the general's paternalistic regime.

The events of May–June 1968 have been described above: they were part of a general European trend, but, to almost everyone's surprise, they found their most acute and dramatic manifestation in the European country that was believed to be more stable than the rest. Although de Gaulle once more defeated his challengers, the shortcomings of his regime had become only too manifest. The Gaullist government did not find it at all easy to cope with the economic consequences of the *évènements*. The general's idiosyncratic style and splenetic utterances, his disregard for his own ministers, as shown in his handling of the Israeli arms embargo, became a source of embarrassment to his own party. There was, in short, a growing feeling in 1969 that he had outlasted his usefulness, and his decision to withdraw from the political scene was welcomed by a majority of Frenchmen. His place in history will be debated for a long time. Probably no other Frenchman would have been able to liquidate the war in Algeria as he did, and it was his great merit to have provided a period of stability after the uncertainties of the Fourth Republic. Under his leadership France had recovered, but the whole political regime was tied up with his own person. By clinging to power too long, de Gaulle put in question the achievements of the earlier years of his rule.

GERMANY:
ADENAUER AND AFTER

Though the German question preoccupied the chancelleries of Europe and America, German domestic affairs were a model of tranquillity. The Adenauer years were uneventful; there were no striking gains, other than economic, and no great crises. The old chancellor was averse to experimenting in either foreign or domestic policy; he believed in guided democracy, Germany's political history in his own lifetime having taught him the dangers of excessive freedom. In the German postwar Basic Law (Grundgesetz) an effort was made not to repeat the mistakes of the Weimar Republic. The electoral system put a premium on stability, favoring the two big parties, the Christian Democrats (CDU) and the Social Democrats (SPD). The Liberals (FDP) were all along a poor third, and the other parties either failed to overcome the 5-percent hurdle for representation in Parliament, or counted for little even if they did. Adenauer was bitterly attacked by his critics for lack of imagination, the paternalistic attitude toward his own countrymen, the invariable pro-Western attitude which prevented any rapprochement with the East. Adenauer believed that Germany needed a long time to recover its equilibrium. The fifties were a period of political stagnation which provoked boredom rather than dissent; it alienated the intellectuals, not the working class. This *immobilisme* certainly helped to perpetuate the division of the country, and Germany's faithful adherence to the Atlantic alliance limited its freedom of maneuver in foreign affairs.

On the credit side of the balance sheet was the fact that millions of refugees from the East were absorbed, that the century-old enmity with France was buried, that the new German army (Bundeswehr), unlike its predecessors (Reichswehr and Wehrmacht), was firmly integrated into the democratic order and no longer the breeding ground for dangerous dictatorial tendencies. Adenauer's policy corresponded in many ways to the German postwar mood, with "Above all no experiments!" as its first commandment.

Adenauer's policy, despite its lack of inspiration and excitement, had a great deal of popular support. In the general elections of 1957 the CDU received for the first time an absolute majority—270 seats in the Bundestag out of a total of 497, with 169 for the SPD and 41 for the Liberals. Four years later the first signs of a decline in CDU fortunes appeared, stemming perhaps not so much from any major failure on the part of the government as from the feeling that new men and new ideas were needed. In the elections of 1961 the share of the CDU declined to 45 percent, whereas the Social Democratic poll rose to 36 percent. The Christian Democrats, while still the biggest party, had again to look for outside support to form a coalition, and thus to lay themselves open (as they saw it) to political blackmail. The elections of 1961 thus foreshadowed the end of the Adenauer era.

The success of the chancellor's rule during the 1950s had a profound impact on German society and should be measured not only by the extent of electoral support given to his party; the changes that took place in SPD policy were another outcome of Adenauer's successes. Up to the late fifties the Social Democrats had toyed with neutralism and, in theory at least, continued to put the emphasis on the class struggle and a radical socialist policy, including a far-reaching nationalization program. In 1958–59 the party leadership realized that, in view of the unchanging Soviet and East German hostility, neutralism was no longer a practical proposition, and in their new (Godesberg) program they undertook a drastic revision of their domestic policy. The party of the working class was to be transformed into a broad popular movement appealing to all sections of the population. Under the leadership of Willy Brandt and Herbert Wehner, formerly a leading communist and therefore particularly disliked by his ex-comrades, the party made a major effort to win the confidence of those sections of German society that in the past had rejected Social Democracy as dangerous and irresponsible. In this way the SPD laid itself open to attacks from the left, especially from the younger generation and the intellectuals. But these radical forces, though militant and highly vocal, constituted a small minority, whereas support by at least part of the middle class was essential for any electoral break-through, as the SPD victory in 1969 showed.

The president of the Republic played a much less important role in the postwar German political system than in the Weimar period. He served as a symbol, giving legitimacy to the system, but had little influence on shaping current policies. Theodor Heuss, a highly cultured South German of impeccable liberal background, admirably fulfilled this task and was re-elected for a second term; the election of Heinrich Lübke in 1959 was one of Adenauer's less successful schemes; Lübke, a ponderous North German, gradually became the butt of much sarcasm as the result of maladroit gestures and speeches, and he was further discredited when it appeared that his political past during the Nazi era had not been so blameless as was at first thought. Franz Josef Strauss, the South German leader of the Christian Democrats, was at the center of another political storm. Greatly annoyed by often unfair attacks in *Der Spiegel,* an influential news magazine, the then minister of defense gave instructions for the arrest of some of its correspondents on suspicion of betraying military secrets. This high-handed action aroused great indignation; those arrested had to be quickly released, and Strauss's political career seemed at an end. But with his political base in Munich still intact the Bavarian leader, one of the most talented political figures and certainly the most dynamic to have emerged in the fifties, spent a few years mending his fences and eventually returned to Bonn as the holder of a key economic portfolio in the Great Coalition of 1966. Ludwig Erhard, vice-chancellor under Adenauer, was the most popular figure in the CDU government; the portly architect of the economic miracle embodied for many Germans stability and prosperity. His critics called him a "rubber lion," doubting his capacity to act decisively in a time of crisis. Adenauer tried to sabotage Erhard's election as his successor, and after Erhard had been elected in April 1963 by the CDU despite the retiring chancellor's opposition, Adenauer continued his attacks.

Erhard remained chancellor for a little over three years, and his reign was, broadly speaking, as uneventful as that of his predecessor. The new chancellor was less enthusiastic than Adenauer about de Gaulle's European policies, and would have preferred to see Britain join the Common Market; he was also somewhat more conciliatory toward the Soviet Union. But he lacked the firmness to stand up to de Gaulle, and as Bonn's options in Eastern Europe continued to be limited, there was no substantial advance toward a rapprochement with the East. There were indications of an economic recession in 1965 as domestic orders leveled off, and the growth rate during 1966 fell to a mere 3 percent. The recession was not the result of any major mistake or miscalculation on Erhard's part; it was common to almost all European countries. But, having been accustomed to uninterrupted economic growth since the end of the wars, the Germans took it much harder than the others, and consequently it had wider political repercussions. The confidence so recently gained disappeared almost overnight, and Erhard became the first victim of the changing mood. In October 1966 the Liberals withdrew from the coalition, giving as their official reason their opposition to Erhard's budget, which provided for tax increases. Their decision reflected the loss of confidence, sometimes bordering on near hysteria, which affected wide sections of the people, not excluding Erhard's own party. Faced with growing opposition inside the CDU, Erhard resigned in November 1966 and was replaced by Kurt Kiesinger, who was to head the first Great Coalition in the history of postwar Germany.

Kiesinger, Swabian by origin, had made his name in local politics; he was a firm believer in the alliance with France and, like Erhard, a Protestant. Willy Brandt became vice-chancellor and foreign minister; Schroeder, who had been a member of most governments since the early fifties, was appointed minister of defense, while Strauss and the Social Democrat Schiller were made responsible for economic affairs; Herbert Wehner and Gustav Heinemann, who became president three years later, were other leading Social Democrats to join the Cabinet. The CDU had opted for the Great Coalition in view of the gravity of the economic crisis. Aware of the decreasing popularity of their party, they wanted to share responsibility. For the Social Democrats the decision to enter the government was not an easy one, and a substantial number disagreed, arguing that, by accepting responsibility for dealing with a crisis that was not of their making, the Social Democrats were tying their own hands and in the long run were bound to suffer a reverse. The party leadership, on the other hand, was convinced that the opportunity was too good to be allowed to pass; it was their only chance of demonstrating that the Social Democrats had a constructive contribution to make and could be entrusted with the management of the affairs of state.

The Great Coalition quickly overcame the economic crisis but failed to make use of its authority in foreign policy. It had been argued for a long time that neither CDU nor SPD could afford to recognize the Oder-Neisse Line for fear of the influence of the refugee organizations and electoral setbacks. The Great Coalition offered a unique opportunity to break out of this vicious circle, but it was not taken. Only after the Social Democrats formed a government with Brandt as chancellor was new initiative taken (the *Ostpolitik*) to improve Germany's relations with its Eastern neighbors.

As the immediate crisis passed, an increasing number of critics argued that a strong opposition was needed for the functioning of a healthy democracy; the Free Democrats were hardly equipped to fulfill this task. There was a distinct danger that the radical forces on right and left would exploit the situation. The rise of the right-wing NPD, led by Adolf von Thadden, raised the ghost of the Nazi Party. The NPD did comparatively well in the traditional strongholds of National Socialism—Lower Saxony, Franconia, parts of Hesse—polling between 5 and 10 percent in local elections. Its support was mainly in small towns among the middle-aged lower-middle classes, but it also had some backing in other age groups and social strata. It was fundamentally a negative phenomenon, reflecting a variety of discontents and representing a reassertion of the nationalist spirit in Germany.

Though many former Nazis belonged to the NPD, its ideological orientation was closer to the pre-1933 conservatives than to the Hitler movement, and it certainly lacked the dynamic character of National Socialism. On the extreme left, the German Communist Party became legal again in 1968 under a new name (DKP), but it attracted even fewer followers than the NPD. More striking were the activities of the various antiparliamentary factions on the extreme left (APO), most of them militants of the student movements. These groups, too, were small in number, but their strategic concentration in the big cities, and their constant attempts to provoke the authorities and the establishment, attracted an enormous amount of publicity. Their ideological beliefs were a curious mixture of Marxism with strong utopian-anarchist elements and ideas that had traditionally been a preserve of the extreme right (elitism, *Kulturpessimismus,* the cult of violence, opposition to liberalism and "repressive tolerance"). Their activities had a considerable impact on life in the universities but hardly affected national politics, apart from provoking a great deal of hostility and probably quite unwarranted fear.

Two decades after the end of the war, Germany had regained an uneasy equilibrium but not yet its self-confidence; the longing for stability at almost any price was still very strong, and there was an inclination to magnify every crisis, political or economic.

ITALY: OPENING
TO THE LEFT

Christian Democracy remained the leading force in Italian as in German politics, throughout the postwar era. But the Democrazia Cristiana (DC), with a smaller electoral basis than the German CDU, could not always provide stable government. After Alcide de Gasperi had left the political scene it lacked a leader whose authority was accepted unquestioningly by the whole party. In the ten years after de Gasperi's death there were no fewer than twelve governments; a certain measure of stability returned only with the installation of the first Aldo Moro government in December 1963. Influential sections of the DC made great efforts to establish an opening to the left (*apertura a sinistra*), trying to induce the Nenni socialists to give up their alliance with the communists and join the government coalition. They needed additional parliamentary support, for in the elections of 1953 they and the small parties supporting them failed to obtain an absolute majority. The right wing (Giuseppe Pella and others) regarded the proposed opening with deep misgivings, opposing in principle any major concession to the left. In 1955 it seemed for a moment that the *apertura* would come into being despite their opposition; Giovanni Gronchi, a left-wing Christian Democrat, was elected president of the Republic with the votes of both socialists and communists. A year after, following the revelations made by Khrushchev at the Twentieth Congress of the Soviet Communist Party, Nenni decided to dissociate himself from the communists and to renew his collaboration with the Saragat group, which had split away several years earlier. But this policy did not find sufficient support in Nenni's own party; the veteran socialist leader was outvoted in 1957 by left-wing opponents, and the *apertura* was dropped for the time being.

Scelba and Segni headed uneasy coalition governments in which both the Saragat socialists and the right-of-center liberals participated. These were followed by Zolli's caretaker government from May 1957 to July 1958; it was based on the DC alone and thus depended on parliamentary support from parties outside the government. In the elections of May 1958 the Christian Democrats improved their position, but with 42 percent of the total vote they were still dependent on the backing of at least two of the smaller parties. The communists, who had not yet fully recovered from the shock of the invasion of Hungary, polled 22 percent; the Nenni socialists improved their position, with 14 percent of the total; and the Saragat group was a poor fourth, with little more than 4 percent. After the elections Fanfani formed a government, with Saragat's help, but it lasted only six months; a dynamic and highly ambitious leader belonging to the DC left wing, Fanfani antagonized a great many influential people within his own party. Saragat, on the other hand, was afraid that his party's participation in a minority government would further weaken its position. Subsequent cabinets (Segni, Fernando Tambroni, and again Amintore Fanfani) were drawn exclusively from the ranks of the DC; their dependence on outside support and the constant changes ruled out any consistent policy. There was a prolonged crisis in 1960, when the liberals decided no longer to support the DC. In March 1962 Saragat's Social Democrats and the small Republican Party joined yet another Cabinet headed by Fanfani. The Social Democrats urged the Christian Democrats to make another effort to gain Nenni's support. Conditions seemed auspicious, for in the Vatican, too, the idea of an *apertura* had won new adherents. Moro, the party secretary, was no less eager to establish a left-center coalition, but for a long time there was little progress, because Nenni was still the captive of the opponents within his own party of any such cooperation. Only after many setbacks were his views accepted, at a party congress in December 1963. The socialists then joined the Moro Cabinet (with Nenni as deputy prime minister), while Nenni's left-wing opponents broke away and established their own organization (Partito Socialista Italiano di Unità Proletaria). Nenni and Saragat again joined forces in 1966, almost twenty years after their ways had first parted.

Throughout all these years there was hardly any change in the internal balance of power. The share of the Christian Democrats fell to 38 percent in the elections of 1963, and increased a little, to 39 percent, four years later. The communists progressed from 25 to 27 percent in 1968, but the United Socialist Party (PSU) did less well than anticipated, obtaining only 14.5 percent of the total.

Italy's economic progress continued throughout this period, despite constant government crises and reshuffles, and the DC received some credit for these achievements. At the same time there was widespread dissatisfaction with administrative inefficiency and many complaints about corruption and nepotism. The continuing great influence of the clergy also caused resentment and indirectly affected the DC. Despite greater prosperity, the number of strikes increased, reflecting growing working-class unrest. The operation of Italian democracy was far from perfect; the rule of the apparatus and of the party secretaries provoked much criticism; Italy, it was argued, was a partitocracy, its structure more appropriate to neofeudalism than to a modern democratic state.

The Italian Communist Party was well placed to profit from the political malaise. More than any other West European communist party it showed initiative and tactical skill, as, for instance, by dissociating itself on occasion from Soviet policy or even criticizing it openly. Togliatti, in his testament, had gone further than other communist leaders in condemning Stalinism; Luigi Longo, his successor, followed a somewhat more orthodox policy. Italian communists remained in the forefront of the liberal forces in the camp of world communism, as shown by their opposition to the Soviet invasion of Czechoslovakia. But the transformation of the PCI into a "normal" radical-socialist and democratic party, as had been predicted by some observers in the 1950s, still seemed a distant prospect.

Successive Italian governments were strong advocates of a détente in international politics, and Fanfani in particular occasionally toyed with neutralist policies. But there were few illusions in Rome about Italy's role in the world; it was clear that, even in North Africa and the Middle East, the traditional spheres of Italian interest, there was only limited scope for an independent Italian policy. The dispute over Trieste and Venezia Giulia having been settled in 1954 in agreement with Belgrade, the problem of South Tyrol (Alto Adige) came to the fore. This region had been part of Austria before 1919; of its 380,000 inhabitants, about 220,000 were German-speaking. They resented the lack of cultural autonomy and the encouragement given by the government to the migration of Italians into the area, thus further weakening the position of the Tyrolese. As the demands of the South Tyrolese met no response, extremists among them launched a campaign that caused tension between the Austrian government and the Italians.

SPAIN: THE END OF
THE FRANCO ERA

General Franco, whose days seemed to be numbered at the end of the Second World War, continued to rule Spain for another quarter of a century. The country's economy stagnated, wages were abysmally low, social services almost nonexistent; less than 1 percent of the budget was allocated to education, but the regime nevertheless succeeded in suppressing all political opposition. The economic situation slowly improved in the later fifties and the sixties; American credits and French and German investments acted as a spur to industrialization, and the rapidly growing influx of millions of tourists constituted another major source of income. Above all, Spain needed social reform: of six and a half million peasant holdings, five million were of one hectare or less, while nine thousand big land-owners each held a hundred thousand hectares or more. Social inequality in the towns, too, was more marked than in any other European country. The government, however, showed no intention of tackling these problems. Official complacency was criticized without much effect by the more farsighted sections of the Catholic church. There were widespread strikes in Catalonia and in the Basque country in 1951, and again in 1956–57, when unrest also affected Madrid. The strike movement in April and May 1962 began in the Asturian mines and quickly spread to other parts of the country; it had the tacit support of "Catholic Action." The government had to give in to some of the strikers' demands; the Caudillo complained bitterly that the Catholic lay groups had been taken over by the communists. Ferment among workers, university students, and the separatists, in Catalonia and the Basque country, continued throughout the sixties, until in January 1969 a state of emergency was proclaimed to enable the government to cope with this increasingly serious challenge to its rule.

The main weakness of the opposition was its internal division: the monarchists did not see eye to eye with one another, the democratic left (Democratic Union) competed with Gil Robles' right-wing front, and no one wished to cooperate with the communists. The government tried to appease its opponents by making certain concessions: the military courts were abolished in 1963, and a new press law was introduced that gave the Spanish press somewhat greater freedom than before; the workers received the right to strike, albeit narrowly circumscribed, and greater tolerance was shown to the minority religions. In 1969 the teaching of the Basque language was at last permitted in state schools. The Organic Law of 1966 provided for the division of executive powers between the head of state and Parliament, and for the free election of one hundred (out of the six hundred) members of Parliament; two representatives were to be elected from each province. Political parties were still banned but, compared with the situation in the early postwar years, these reforms marked a great advance. The law was approved in a plebiscite by 96 percent of the population.

Spain was at the time still a kingdom without a king, since General Franco was opposed to the restoration of the monarchy in his lifetime. Within the monarchist camp the Carlists fought the Bourbons, with the government preferring the latter. The Carlist candidate was expelled from Spain by the government in December 1968. The Bourbons were divided into supporters of the more liberal Don Juan, the Pretender (the younger son of Alfonso XIII, the last king of Spain), and those who backed Don Juan Carlos, his son. The church, the Falange, and the army were the traditional pillars of Franco's regime, and the Caudillo maintained himself in power by playing off one against another. But these forces, too, were troubled by infighting; there was a generational conflict in both church and army; the younger officers wanted both the modernization of the regime and quicker promotion, and the younger clergy did not wish to be closely identified with the regime. The Falange, fascist in inspiration, had not succeeded in putting its own imprint on Spanish politics and society. It had gradually been eased out of the government, though some of its leaders kept key positions in the provinces and the state-sponsored trade unions. A minority within the Falange moved toward the left; the majority was engaged in defending the positions it had gained in the forties and fifties. Both the Catholic hierarchy and the anticlerical Falange were opposed to the powerful Catholic Opus Dei movement. Opus Dei had the support of many younger economists and technocrats—the ministers of commerce and finance belonged to this group—whereas the bishops were fearful of its modernist zeal and pro-European enthusiasm. The Falange, on the other hand, stood for a corporative state and opposed the "liberal-capitalist spirit" of Opus Dei, which, they claimed, undermined the foundation of the regime. The official state-sponsored trade unions were challenged by workers' associations (*comisiones obreras*) that had developed in illegality and gradually attained considerable influence. The battle for the recognition of these organizations, as well as the independent student associations, became after 1965 the focus of the struggle between government and opposition. Basque nationalism also intensified its fight against the Franco regime; after the assassination of the police chief of San Sebastián in August 1968, a state of emergency was declared which lasted many months.

General Franco was more successful in his foreign policy. As the danger of a United Nations boycott passed, many countries established normal relations with Madrid. Whereas the Fourth Republic had closed the border with Spain, de Gaulle sought to have closer links with Franco; Couve de Murville, the French foreign minister, went to Madrid in 1964, and in January 1969 Michel Debré went on a similar mission to the Spanish capital. Franco maintained close relations with Castro's Cuba, notwithstanding the ideological gulf between the two regimes and the fact that he thereby incurred American displeasure.

BENELUX AND
SCANDINAVIA

The Netherlands lost their colonial empire after the Second World War; West Irian, their last major possession in Southeast Asia, was given up in 1962. Decolonization was a great psychological shock, but neither Holland's economy nor its domestic policy was greatly affected. The socialists (Partij van de Arbeid) and the Catholic People's Party, each polling fairly regularly about 30 percent of the vote at consecutive general elections, formed a coalition under Willem Drees, the socialist leader, which lasted until 1958, when the conservative parties (which included the two Protestant parties, the Christian Historical Union, and the Antirevolution Party) replaced the socialists in the government. Relations between the parties had been poisoned as a result of the prolonged crisis of 1956, when it took almost four months to form a new government. The main cause of the malaise in Dutch politics was the deep-rooted confessionalism which permeated all aspects of Dutch society; schools and hospitals, even radio stations, and almost all other associations were strictly divided on confessional lines. To surmount this division became the main task of Dutch politics, but the vested interests were not easily overcome, and no party could find a remedy.

The socialists returned to power for a short time within a coalition government in 1965–66. Both they and the Catholics lost votes in the general election of 1967; the socialists were weakened by the defection of a pacifist, anti-NATO group, while a radical faction split away from the Catholic People's Party in 1968. A new element on the political scene appeared with the Farmers' Party, founded in 1959, and the Amsterdam Provos, predating by a few years the upsurge of the European New Left, added color and excitement, if not many constructive political ideas, to Dutch political life.

Internal dissension in Belgium, complicated by the national conflict between Flemish and Walloons, was far more bitter than in Holland. The Flamands had been defeated in their bid for the return of King Leopold III, and they felt their national identity endangered by the steady encroachment of the French language. The Walloons, on the other hand, complained about economic discrimination; many of them supported the Socialist Party. The socialists, under the leadership of Camille Huysmans, Spaak, and Van Acker, were represented in all the early postwar governments but were ousted in 1949, when the Christian Socialists, having gained almost 48 percent of the total vote, took over. The socialists returned to power in 1954 and tried to push through a new school-and-language law, which caused a great deal of trouble, reminiscent of the German *Kulturkampf* in the late nineteenth century, culminating in street demonstrations and disturbances. After years of struggle, a spirit of compromise prevailed; the Christian Social Party (CVP) under Gaston Eyskens, replaced the socialists in 1958, but formed a coalition with them in April 1961, which tried to find a solution to the language dispute by freezing the linguistic borders, dividing the country into four main regions, and granting these a large measure of cultural autonomy. This policy, intended to put Flemish fears at rest, did not, however, have the desired result: the Liberals opposed it, and with the quarrel about the character of Louvain University, which later spread to Brussels, the conflict became more bitter than ever. Both the socialists and the Christian Social Party suffered substantial losses in the elections of 1967, while the Liberals made considerable gains. Belgium was the country in which a general strike had first taken place; another such strike, in 1960, showed that there was again much dissatisfaction among the industrial working class. The country's economic progress was less than that of its neighbors. Heavy industry and, in particular, the coal mines faced difficult problems of adjustment in the postwar period.

The Eyskens government decided in 1958 to give independence to the Congo, but since under Belgian rule little had been done to educate a native elite that would be capable of running a country, decolonization soon ran into trouble. The mutiny of the black troops, Lumumba's murder, the secession of Katanga and other provinces, and the ill-fated Belgian intervention in Katanga were stages in the disintegration of Belgium's former colony. It took years to overcome a crisis that in its early phases could certainly have been halted. However, as Brussels gained new importance as a European center, the seat of both the Common Market headquarters and NATO, as well as other international organizations such as Euratom, some of the old spirit of confidence returned to the country.

The Nordic Council, established in 1951, provided a framework for close cooperation on all levels between the Scandinavian countries. There were of course limits to such coordination in foreign policy: Finland was exposed to direct Soviet pressure and had to refrain from any political moves likely to irritate Moscow. Norway and Denmark, which had been victims of Nazi aggression during the war, opted for collective security by joining NATO. Sweden, which had remained neutral, decided not to join any power bloc. All the Scandinavian countries made great economic progress, and considerable advances on the road to the complete welfare state, with Finland, the poorest country, in each case lagging behind; all except Finland were monarchies, and in all (again except Finland) the Social Democrats played a leading role; in Sweden they were in power without interruption throughout the whole postwar period.

Finland had not shared the fate of the East European countries and had not been incorporated into the Soviet Union, though Russia clearly regarded it as part of its own sphere of influence. The Soviet leaders distrusted the Finnish Social Democrats and insisted on keeping them out of the government. Their chosen instruments were Juho Paasikivi, president of Finland until 1956, and after that Urho Kekkonen, also a leader of the Agrarian Party. To ensure Kekkonen's election, Moscow openly intervened in 1956 in Finnish politics, as it did on several occasions during the postwar period. At a time of crisis the Russians usually referred to the provision for joint consultations in the Soviet-Finnish defense treaty, which meant in practice the right to send troops into Finland. The Finnish Communist Party was fairly strong, polling around 20 percent in most elections, but since its abortive attempt to stage a coup d'état in 1948 the democratic parties, except Kekkonen's Agrarians and the Simonites, a breakaway group from the Social Democrats, refused to cooperate with them. Since the Russians, on the other hand, insisted until 1966 on keeping the Social Democrats out of the government, Finnish politics became very complicated, and it was almost impossible to find a stable government majority; there were no fewer than twenty-five different cabinets between the end of the war and 1966.

Sweden, by contrast, was a model of stability. The Social Democrats under Prime Minister Erlander dominated its politics throughout the whole postwar period. The Swedish communists, one of the most liberal communist parties in Europe, were too few to have any decisive impact on national policies; the center parties, among whom the Liberals were the strongest, seemed more than once near the verge of success, but the Social Democrats always mustered enough strength in the decisive tests. They suffered losses in the elections of 1956 but improved their position in 1958 and 1960. There were fresh signs in the sixties of a decline of Social Democratic influence, but the center parties suffered a fresh setback in the elections of 1968: unlike the socialists in Norway, who had been ousted in 1955 after many years in power, the Swedish Social Democrats increased their vote, a reflection of their success in economic and social policy; Sweden became in the postwar era both the richest and the most egalitarian European country. It was also a laboratory for the observation of some of the side effects of the welfare state. Boredom, as Schopenhauer noted, is an evil not to be taken lightly. In addition to Sweden's noninvolvement in power blocs, there was a strong neutralist undercurrent in public sentiment, not confined to the Social Democrats; there was much sympathy for victims of tyranny, especially in faraway countries. Swedish policy toward Germany before 1945 and vis-à-vis the Soviet Union after the Second World War had been more restrained.

In Denmark, too, the Social Democrats were the leading political force; their share in the elections throughout the postwar period remained more or less steady at 40 percent, with only minor fluctuations. Under Hans Hedtoft, Hans Hansen, Viggo Kampman, and Jens Krag, they were represented in almost all postwar governments, either alone or in cooperation with other parties; they were in opposition between 1950 and 1953, when they were replaced by the liberal Peasant Party (Venstre). An interesting phenomenon without parallel at the time in any other European country was the emergence of the Socialist People's Party, founded by Aksel Larsen, in 1958. Larsen, the former leader of Danish communism, having been excommunicated by Moscow, established his own political group, drawing votes away from the Social Democrats and all but annihilating the official Communist Party. His group polled 11 percent of the vote in the 1966 elections and became overnight an important factor in Danish politics, since the Social Democrats, lacking a working majority, badly needed his support. Larsen's party took a neutralist, radical-socialist line, but its success faltered as radicals and moderates within its ranks began to fight one another. The Danish economy showed signs of strains after 1966; following sterling, the kroner also had to be devalued. Economic problems contributed to the fall of the Social Democratic government; after the elections of 1968 it was replaced by a coalition of the center groups under the leadership of Hilmar Baunsgaard, head of the Radical Venstre, which had seceded from the Venstre.

Norway had been more severely affected than either Sweden or Denmark by the war, and most of the efforts during the first postwar decade were devoted to economic reconstruction. Once this task was successfully accomplished, under the leadership of the Social Democrats headed by Einar Gerhardsen, and the groundwork had been laid for a welfare state on the Swedish pattern, the party's fortunes began to decline. It was also weakened by the defection of a left-wing group, the pacifist Socialist People's Party. In 1965 the socialists were forced into opposition, following the formation of a new government by the four center parties.

AUSTRIA AND
SWITZERLAND

For twenty years Austria was ruled by a coalition of the Christian Social Party and Social Democrats, the two parties that virtually monopolized Austrian politics. Between the two world wars they had bitterly fought each other, but the experience of the Nazi Anschluss had made them discover common ground. After the country had regained its independent status in 1945, the leaders of both parties realized that, in view of Austria's exposed position, concessions on both sides were imperative to prevent fresh disasters. An elaborate and slightly ridiculous system was evolved by which all official positions from top to bottom were distributed between nominees of the two parties in fixed proportions. The system was cumbersome and often wasteful, but it worked with some success until 1966, when, following a crisis among the socialists and a small shift in the balance of power, the Christian Social Party felt strong enough to terminate the coalition. The party, ably led during the postwar period by Figl and Raab, Gorbach and Klaus, took great care not to deviate to any major extent in its foreign or domestic policy from the broad lines established during the long years of coalition. As in Germany, following a swing of the political pendulum the Social Democrats (under Kreisky) came to power a few years later.

There were few, if any, changes in Swiss domestic policies. The position of the leading parties, the Freisinn (liberals), the Social Democrats, and the Conservatives, remained unchanged. In pursuance of its traditional neutrality, Switzerland did not join the United Nations, though it was represented in several organizations sponsored by the UN, such as UNESCO. In view of the underlying political character of the Common Market, Switzerland could not join this organization either but decided to participate in EFTA. The Swiss policy of neutrality had evolved in an age in which it could be assumed that all sides would respect it. In the Second World War, however, Switzerland escaped occupation largely by good luck and by its readiness to defend itself. The implications were not lost on Swiss citizens, and the principle of neutrality was questioned after 1945; in these changed political conditions, greater stress than ever before was put on national defense.

GREECE

From the end of the civil war until 1955 Greece was ruled by a conservative government under Papagos. This was succeeded by a coalition of center and right-wing forces led by Konstantinos Karamanlis, who, after a great deal of electoral maneuvering and manipulation, received a small majority. The position of the ruling coalition was weakened by the Cyprus conflict, the unpopularity of the royal family and the army command, and such incidents as the assassination of the left-wing deputy Lambrakis by right-wing elements. In the 1963 elections George Papandreou's Progressive Center Union (EPEK) received more votes than Karamanlis's ERE. Since Papandreou did not, however, have an absolute majority but would have been dependent on the support of EDA (a communist-front organization), he called for new elections in 1964, in which his group obtained an absolute majority. The conservative forces were bitterly opposed to EPEK, which they accused, quite unfairly, of "communist leanings"; the army command feared that Papandreou would subject them to a political purge and prevailed on the king to refuse to head the Ministry of Defense with the leader of the liberals. Papandreou in response mobilized the masses against the court and the right-wing forces. To forestall yet another electoral victory by the liberals, a group of officers carried out a coup d'état in April 1967 and established a right-wing military dictatorship. Most politicians were removed from positions of influence; some were arrested, others escaped abroad. King Constantine II tried without success to curb some of the excesses of the new regime, but after the failure in December 1967 of a highly amateurish countercoup, he, too, went into exile. Civil liberties ceased to exist in the very country in which the term "democracy" had been coined.

THE SOVIET UNION: KHRUSHCHEV AND HIS SUCCESSORS

After Stalin's death, political power in the Soviet Union passed into the hands of a small group of his closest associates. With Beria's arrest and execution, and after the fall of Malenkov, Nikita Sergeevich Khrushchev emerged as the strongest contender for power. He had been less in the limelight than most other members of the Presidium but, once he was elected first secretary of the party in September 1953, his faction became strongly entrenched in the party apparatus. Khrushchev in turn was overthrown in 1964, but those whom he had ousted remained in the political wilderness. He was replaced by new men, who had not yet reached front rank in Stalin's lifetime. After 1953 some of the worst excesses of the Stalinist system ceased, but many basic features remained, and hopes for radical change and a far greater measure of freedom did not materialize. Although Khrushchev favored de-Stalinization within limits, after his fall this policy was gradually abandoned. His appointment as first party secretary did not at first attract much attention, for in Stalin's time the party had lost much of its earlier influence. But within a few years Khrushchev gained control of the Central Committee, and many regional key positions were also in the hands of his appointees. At the same time the party as a political factor greatly increased in importance, as Stalin's private apparatus was dissolved and as the secret police were brought under the control of the party leadership.

Khrushchev gave the key speech at the Communist Party's Twentieth Congress in 1956; though unpublished in the Soviet Union, this speech was of momentous importance, for it was the first time that a Soviet leader had openly talked about the crimes of the Stalin era.

Everyone had known about them, but it had been unthinkable to mention these things in public; Stalin had been the party, and the party had always been right. Khrushchev's revelations were highly selective: he mentioned only the Stalinists who had been wronged by Stalin, not his political opponents within the party, let alone his non-communist victims. Moreover, Khrushchev put all the blame on certain negative traits in Stalin's character, which was at best a superficial explanation for a highly complex phenomenon. The deeper causes of Stalinism he did not touch, nor did he suggest any remedies that would make a recurrence impossible. What Khrushchev told his comrades and fellow countrymen was, in fact, that Stalin had been a bungler, and during his later years a madman with criminal tendencies, but that the new leaders were good men and could be trusted.

The secret speech came as a profound shock. Not just the conservative elements in the party, men like Molotov, but also many in the middle and lower ranks, were bitterly opposed to the new policy. Although they, too, were critical of certain aspects of Stalinism, they did not question the system as such, and they feared that by disavowing Stalin Khrushchev was undermining the very legitimacy of Soviet rule. For, once the principle of infallibility was given up, his successors, and indeed everyone from top to bottom in the line of command, was likely to be criticized in future, and this was bound to put into question the whole political system.

While antagonizing his rivals in the Soviet leadership, Khrushchev at the same time weakened their position, for his speech caused a great deal of heart-searching within the party vis-à-vis its own past, and gave further impetus to the release of Stalin's surviving victims from prison and labor camps. Since Khrushchev's rivals in the Presidium had been more deeply involved than he himself in the purges and terror, they were put on the defensive: they could not get rid of him without turning back the wheels of history, and this, in view of the general mood in the party, seemed well nigh impossible after the Twentieth Congress. Molotov lost his job to Shepilov, one of Khrushchev's men, and as the result of the great confrontation in the Presidium in June 1957 the entire old guard was routed. The "anti-party group," as it was called after its defeat, consisted of Molotov, Kaganovich, Malenkov, Bulganin, and Voroshilov, as well as Saburov and Pervukhin, the economic experts. They were all opposed to Khrushchev's economic policy and had many other grievances as well.

Since they had a majority in the Presidium, their victory, and the replacement of Khrushchev by Molotov, had seemed a foregone conclusion. But Khrushchev fought back, mobilizing the Central Committee, in which his supporters were in the majority. The Central Committee was in theory the highest policymaking body, but it had largely been ignored by the leaders in the past; the reassertion of its authority constituted a significant shift in the internal balance of power. Some of Khrushchev's rivals were immediately dropped; others, such as Bulganin and Voroshilov, were ousted later on. They were all disgraced, but there were no arrests or executions; the victims of the purge were shifted to minor positions outside Moscow: Molotov, for instance, became Soviet ambassador to Mongolia.

This was the end of collective leadership; after June 1957 Khrushchev could pursue without hindrance his reforms, such as the abolition of the Machine-Tractor Stations in agriculture and the establishment of *sovnarkhozy*, regional economic councils, as the basic unit in the national economy. By 1959, when the Twenty-first Party Congress was held, the Soviet Union was again ruled by one man, though Khrushchev was subject to far more constraints than Stalin. The congress was called to adopt the seven-year plan; according to Khrushchev, the country was now entering a new phase, in which material abundance, and with it communism, was at last within reach. To achieve this, Khrushchev demanded greater stress on agriculture and light industry. But although output in Soviet agriculture rose by 50 percent between Stalin's death and 1959, there was only a small increase thereafter, and this in turn had a direct impact on food supplies and the standard of living.

Khrushchev's foreign policy was not an outstanding success either; the building of rocket-launching sites and the transfer to Cuba of a substantial nuclear arsenal were considered a reckless adventure even by the Chinese hawks. After the confrontation with America, Khrushchev changed his line and became a protagonist of peaceful coexistence. His cuts in military spending antagonized the powerful military lobby. The attitude to Germany became more threatening than ever, yet toward the end of his reign Khrushchev seemed inclined to seek a rapprochement with Bonn. He quarreled with Nasser but subsequently made him a "Hero of the Soviet Union" without consulting the Presidium; he also made major loans and arms shipments available to Egypt. Relations with China deteriorated during the Khrushchev era, and there were further defections from the Soviet camp as the battle for hegemony over world communism reached a new climax.

The intellectuals found at times a powerful though inconsistent ally in Khrushchev in their struggle for greater cultural freedom; Khrushchev personally read Solzhenitsyn's book on life in Soviet labor camps and authorized its publication. This was an important breakthrough, for it opened the way to a whole new literature dealing with aspects of the past that had hitherto been taboo. Such liberalism had its limits. Khrushchev warned the intellectuals that he would not hesitate to have them shot if they overstepped the boundaries and endangered (as the Hungarian writers had done) the very foundations of the regime. On other occasions he behaved in an almost incredibly boorish manner, denouncing all modern influences in the arts, including film and music, and unleashing a minor witch hunt against the perpetrators of avant-garde art. De-Stalinization, too, followed a curiously inconsistent pattern. Many, but by no means all, of Stalin's victims were rehabilitated, most of them posthumously; the Twenty-second Party Congress, in October 1961, brought further revelations and gave a powerful fresh impetus to this movement. Symbolically, Stalin's remains were removed from the mausoleum in the Red Square and reburied at the Kremlin wall. Yet every now and then the movement was reversed, and those who had gone too far in their condemnation of the "cult of the individual" were severely reprimanded. Like postwar Germany, the Soviet Union faced a major problem in coming to terms with its own past, but since the country had not been defeated in the war, and many of the old leaders were still in power, the inhibitions and the vested interests militating against any radical change were far more powerful than in Germany.

The main topic of the Twenty-second Congress was the adoption of a new party program envisaging in some detail the transition to communism. The state would finally wither away and be replaced by various public and communal organizations; the party, however, would still retain its central role in Soviet society. Soviet citizens were promised a radiant future. There was a boastful streak in Khrushchev's personality, and the fact that so many of his promises had not come true did not deter him from making fresh predictions. In June 1957 he had declared that the Soviet Union would within four years overtake America in the production of meat, butter, and milk.

In 1961 he announced that Soviet productivity would rise to the American level by 1970, which meant of course that the country would be outproducing the United States, since Russia was more populous. These and similar pronouncements did not go down very well in the Soviet Union, for everyone knew that they were unrealistic. Among the intelligentsia there was a great deal of contempt for the leader, who was regarded as little better than an uneducated, uncouth *muzhik*. Popular reaction, too, was often negative. A great purveyor of anecdotes, Khrushchev himself became the butt of many jokes, but not a few of those who had ridiculed him came to regret it later on.

Everything considered, the Khrushchev years were not bad ones for Russia: considerable economic progress was made, and, above all, there was reason to believe that gradually more freedom would be allowed. The intellectuals in particular were to look back in later years with nostalgia to the relative cultural freedom of Khrushchev's rule. The cult of Khrushchev, whose seventieth birthday in 1964 was made an occasion of official rejoicing, was mild and relatively harmless. With all his weaknesses and inconsistencies, Khrushchev was an agent of freedom and progress in Soviet postwar history. He attacked Stalin, though he would not and could not attack the system that had produced Stalin. But in comparison with that of his successors his record shines brightly.

Most of the Stalinist old guard were eliminated under Khrushchev, and though some of their policies were rehabilitated after his fall in 1964, none of them made a political comeback: they were too old and discredited, and their seats were taken by new men. Mikoyan, who was on good terms with Khrushchev, survived his fall but was bowed out in 1966, more or less gracefully, and Voroshilov and Shvernik, too, became honorary pensioners and disappeared from the political scene. Suslov, who had the reputation of being an ideologist, remained a member of the inner circle, but Brezhnev and Kosygin rose more rapidly, and until a stroke put an end to his public career in 1963, Frol Kozlov seemed the Soviet leader most likely to succeed Khrushchev. Brezhnev had won his spurs as a party organizer, whereas Kosygin's career had been in the economic field. Podgorny and Shelest also came to the fore; the former was a protégé of Khrushchev who survived the fall of his protector and became president of the Soviet Union; the second was, like Kozlov and Brezhnev, a conservative and a hard-liner. Perhaps most significant was the rise of younger party

leaders such as Polyansky (born on the day of the October Revolution), Voronov, Mazurov, Shelepin, and Semichastny. The last two
named had been leaders of the Komsomol, the Soviet youth organization, who were subsequently given leading positions in the political
police. These men, together with a few others, constituted the top
leadership in the early sixties, and it was their decision to depose
Khrushchev in October 1964.

Khrushchev's prestige had suffered as the result of the Cuban
defeat; there was resentment among the military men as well as the
party apparatchiki: Khrushchev's attempt to divide the Communist
Party into an industrial and an agricultural branch was obviously
impractical and was soon abandoned. Above all, there was dissatisfaction with his arbitrary style of work, which caused much irritation
and impatience and contributed to his downfall. The conspirators
made use of Khrushchev's absence on holiday to proclaim Brezhnev
first party secretary and Kosygin head of the Soviet government. On
October 16, 1964, it was announced that Comrade Khrushchev had
resigned because of his "advanced age and deteriorating health." Soon
the attacks on him began; he was made responsible for all the economic shortcomings and other failures in Soviet foreign and domestic
policy. After a while the attacks ceased, and he, too, became an
unperson, like so many other Soviet leaders before him.

Leonid Brezhnev and Aleksei Kosygin, the leading spirits in the
new team, did not make any drastic policy changes. Domestic policies
were pursued more or less as before—indeed, the absence of any new
ideas and initiatives was perhaps the most significant feature of the
post-Khrushchev era; there seemed to be no definite policy and no
clear purpose. De-Stalinization was gradually stopped; there was no
further rehabilitation of Stalin's victims. In April 1965 Brezhnev gave
the signal for the rehabilitation of Stalin and Zhdanov, and their
policies were again praised. There was some further economic decentralization, but care was taken not to engage in any radical reform.
The Twenty-third Party Congress in 1966 brought no surprises either;
the Soviet regime went on existing by its own momentum, as it were:
some leaders were promoted and others lost ground, there was a slow
but steady rise in the standard of living, and the country gathered
strength in the military field. But politically it was now weaker than
ever before in its history—a conservative society with a superstructure
of revolutionary phraseology. The appeal of Soviet communism was

almost nonexistent beyond its own borders; it could reassert its authority, as in Czechoslovakia, only by force of arms.

Soviet foreign policy became more similar in character to that of Ivan Kalita and Ivan the Terrible than of Lenin. The handling of neither the Middle Eastern crisis in 1967 nor the Czech crisis the year after inspired much confidence in the new leadership. The political weakness, the many conflicts inside the Soviet bloc and within the Soviet Union, were not conducive to a policy of détente with the West, even though the Soviet leaders wanted to prevent major military confrontation with the United States. At least some among them seemed to believe that the rot which had afflicted the communist world in the sixties had to be stopped and Soviet military strength reasserted. But there were obvious limits to Soviet action in Central Europe, for any intervention in Germany was bound to lead to a head-on collision with NATO.

On the home front, there was no danger of an immediate crisis; intellectual ferment was easily suppressed by arrests and stiff prison sentences, as in the Sinyavsky-Daniel case. There were manifestations of dissatisfaction and criticism among the intelligentsia, but a censorship far more severe than in tsarist times and a well-functioning secret police prevented all but the most courageous spirits from openly voicing dissent. There were indications of the continued existence of national antagonisms between the peoples of the U.S.S.R., but these, too, were seemingly kept well under control. The long-term prospects were less reassuring: the erosion of the official ideology created problems for which no solution was in sight. A generation earlier, millions of communists had genuinely believed in the truth of their doctrine and in Stalin's infallible wisdom. Now official communist ideology was no longer taken seriously except by those officially entrusted with the propagation of the faith and by the poor in spirit. Soviet communism had set out with greater hopes and ambitions; it had wanted to build a richer, freer, and more progressive society than any previous one in history, to be a beam of light to all the oppressed throughout the world. These dreams had certainly not come true. Russia's place in the world had become stronger, and its military power was impressive; a new society had been created; but it inspired little enthusiasm.

EASTERN EUROPE:
BETWEEN CONFORMITY
AND INDEPENDENCE

EAST GERMANY

Throughout the postwar period East Germany remained the Soviet Union's faithful client. While the other East European countries showed signs of independence in varying degrees, East Germany after the suppression of the revolt of 1953 gave little cause for Soviet complaints. The presence of twenty Soviet divisions, first as an occupying force, later under the provision of the Warsaw Pact, effectively guaranteed the *status quo*. As far as the East German leadership was concerned, loyalty to the Soviet Union was genuine: Walter Ulbricht and his colleagues needed Soviet protection more than any other communist regime in Eastern Europe, both because of the inferior position of the DDR vis-à-vis West Germany, and because of the unpopularity of their rule. For these reasons they could not afford to make any substantial concessions to the people, and their regime remained the most orthodox in Eastern Europe. They were perturbed by the "liberal excesses" of the Khrushchev era, and banned certain books published in the U.S.S.R. in the early sixties. The same phenomenon was to recur in the age of glasnost twenty years later. There was continuity in the political leadership: for twenty-five years Ulbricht remained at the helm, and though there were frequent changes under him, including defections to the West and suicides, his own position was never seriously threatened. The prewar communist generation was gradually replaced by younger men who had not been involved in the political storms of the twenties and thirties. In 1971 Ulbricht retired and Erich Honecker succeeded him. Technocrats such as Ewald, Jarowinsky, and Mittag were not without success in running the economy. During the fifties the DDR had not been able to keep pace with the rapid development of the West German economy, and the propaganda about the advantages of the socialist planned system had sounded hollow. After 1962, and in particular after the Sixth Party Congress in 1963, the SED (Socialist Unity Party) adopted a more flexible economic policy. Within the next five years the DDR became the country with the highest living standard in Comecon, and its industry the best developed outside the Soviet Union.

Only after many years would it emerge that the achievements were more apparent than real.

The building of the Berlin Wall in 1961 closed the escape route to the West and, together with the establishment of a sizable standing army (the National People's Army), stabilized the position of the regime. The most difficult task of the East German leaders was to inculcate a feeling of separate national identity in their subjects, most of whom still believed that the division of Germany was artificial and would not last. The leadership, on the other hand, stressed on every occasion that West Germany was not merely a foreign country but the main enemy, that the division would be lasting—unless communism came to power in West Germany. At first they found it difficult to oppose openly the movement for German reunification, but since the West Germans refused to deal with them they could, in fact, champion the cause of German unity without being seriously challenged. In the sixties a less rigid policy was adopted in Bonn, which greatly alarmed the East Germans, who regarded it as far more dangerous than the earlier boycott. As a result, they became more intransigent, and the demand for German unity disappeared from their political program.

The government tried to gain diplomatic recognition throughout the world and to combat West Germany's claim to be Germany's representative. It achieved some success in the third world, though major countries such as Egypt and India, heavily indebted to the Soviet bloc though they were, were reluctant to grant East Berlin diplomatic recognition. Ulbricht's visit to Belgrade in 1966 was intended to improve relations with the nonorthodox forces in the communist world. The democratic revival in Czechoslovakia in 1968 awakened old fears in East Germany, and Ulbricht was reported to have been among those who brought pressure on the Soviet leaders in favor of intervention. Young people in East Germany, Ulbricht said during a visit to Czechoslovakia in 1968, were not engaged in revolutionary, destructive activities; they were singing merry songs.

POLAND

The great promise of the Polish October (1956) was followed by long years of bitter disappointment. Some of the worst economic bottlenecks were overcome as the Soviet government extended aid to Warsaw and as American credits were made available. About 80 percent of the agricultural cooperatives established during the Stalin era were dissolved after 1956, and this had in the short run a beneficial influence on output. But agriculture remained backward; the distance between town and country did not diminish. For many years Poland continued to have a passive foreign-trade balance, and the zloty remained one of Eastern Europe's weakest currencies. The tension with the Catholic church did not abate; Cardinal Wyszinski was permitted to visit Rome, but the Polish bishops were severely attacked by the Warsaw government when, together with the German bishops, they appealed in 1966 for an effort to overcome national antagonisms with a spirit of goodwill. Any such attempt at reconciliation with "German revanchism" was anathema to Władisław Gomułka and the other Polish leaders. Enmity toward Germany was a pillar of Polish policy; any attempt to reduce tension was even more dangerous than questioning communism. Influential circles in the Polish leadership also tried to make anti-Semitism ("anti-Zionism") part of official Polish ideology. Jews had always been numerous and prominent in the communist movement in Poland, and some of them had been in leading positions in the early years of the regime. After Stalin's death, most Jewish communists joined the liberals, whereas the "Partisans," headed by General Moczar, following a national communist line, tried to remove them from the party. They argued that Jews were not trustworthy; having spent the war years abroad, and having entered Poland in 1944 with the Red Army, they were little better than foreign agents. The Partisans deliberately exaggerated the part of the Jews in Polish politics; there were only about thirty thousand of them left in Poland after the war, and Moczar used the issue as a stratagem against his rivals, the Gomułka faction, in the struggle for power. This open recrudescence of anti-Semitism culminated in a wholesale rewriting of history; according to the new official version, Poles had helped the Jews during the Nazi occupation but the Jews had brought the disaster upon themselves by collaborating with the enemy. A commission for the supervision of Jews and of anti-Jewish propaganda was established; it was abolished in December 1968, following the unfavorable publicity these activities attracted abroad. In March 1968 students demonstrated in Warsaw for more freedom and a more independent, more national policy. The government, greatly disturbed by the ferment in neighboring Czechoslovakia, undertook severe reprisals, and a major purge ensued. Many leading figures in Polish intellectual life, and not a few in politics, were dismissed from their posts; the majority were of Jewish origin, and they were all branded as "Zionists." The Moczar group used the opportunity for a major onslaught on the Gomułka faction, which, it claimed, had shown a lamentable lack of toughness all along vis-à-vis Poland's enemies. Gomułka was pushed onto the defensive; at one time his political survival seemed in question, but eventually he outmaneuvered his opponents, no doubt mainly because the Partisans were somewhat suspect in the eyes of the Russians. The exalted anti-Germanism and anti-Semitism would have passed, but their whole approach was basically nationalist, and there was reason to fear that sooner or later they would turn also against Russia in the time-honored Polish tradition. Eventually, in 1970, Gomułka and his closest collaborators were overthrown following widespread manifestations of working-class protest.

Poland in the sixties was a deeply unhappy country, despite the improvement in the economic situation since the early fifties and notwithstanding the fact that some of the worst social inequalities had disappeared. But, more than in the neighboring countries, the communist regime had failed to grow roots in Poland, and few believers in the cause of communism were left even within the ranks of the party. Communism remained in power because no other regime would have been acceptable to the Soviet Union. Such a situation vitiated Poles' deep-seated longing to reassert their national identity and to live in freedom; it was bound to lead to cynicism and frustration.

HUNGARY

While Soviet troops continued to be stationed in Hungary, the Kádár government pursued a relatively liberal course after the suppression of the popular uprising of 1956. Some of the country's leading writers were released from prison under the 1960 amnesty. János Kádár and his government were among Khrushchev's closest supporters; they fought both left-wing and right-wing deviations. The exclusion from the Communist Party of Rákosi and Gero in 1962 was meant to reassure the population that there would be no return to the bad old days of Stalinism. In its foreign policy, too, Hungary tried to steer a moderate course; its relations with Yugoslavia were fairly cordial, and though it had to participate in the invasion of Czechoslovakia in 1968, it did so without conviction and with a minimum of fanfare. Most of the government's efforts were concentrated on the economy. After experiencing difficulties in agriculture and several years of stagnation in industry, there was a new upswing as the economic reform program got under way. Under their program, first adopted in 1965, productivity was increased, foreign trade with both West and East expanded, and investment steered toward the most profitable sectors. The previous planning system was largely abolished; firms were judged on the basis of their profitability, and the income of both managers and workers was tied to productivity.

Hungary went further with its economic reforms than any other East European communist country except Yugoslavia. This gave rise to misgivings among its conservative neighbors, including the Soviet Union, which feared that sweeping economic reforms would in the long run stimulate the demand for more political freedom.

CZECHOSLOVAKIA

For a decade after Stalin's death, Czechoslovakia remained the least changed of all his satellites. The big Gottwald monument, symbol of the old era, was not removed from one of Prague's central squares until 1961, and very reluctantly at that. Political conservatism was paralleled by economic stagnation and gave rise to much popular discontent. Czechoslovakia had been industrially the most developed country in Eastern Europe, and the one with the closest ties to the West; the isolation imposed on it was as acutely felt as the wretched economic situation. There were internal conflicts in the party leadership, culminating in 1962 in the arrest of Rudolf Barak, a former minister of state security. In this struggle for power, ideological considerations did not play a major part, and there was little hope for a substantial improvement. When the Communist Party had seized power in 1948, it had had a mass following, in sharp contrast to Poland and Hungary; large sections of the working class and many intellectuals were among its supporters. Fifteen years later, communist militancy had given way to disillusionment and despair, which pervaded even the higher ranks of the party and government apparatus. Communism had been tried and, as was now admitted, had been a failure.

Under Prime Minister Lenart an economic reform program was launched in 1966 along the lines proposed by Professor Ota Sik, a leading economist. This project provided, as in Hungary, for changes in the system of planning, and a larger output of consumer goods. But, given the deteriorating economic situation, the success of the scheme depended on substantial Russian credits, which Prague failed to obtain despite all efforts and remonstrances. Czechoslovakia wanted closer political and economic relations with Eastern Europe, and these links were vetoed by Moscow. The developments leading to the rise of Dubček and the Soviet invasion have been described: the military occupation of the country proceeded smoothly, but the political solution of the crisis desired by Russia proved more difficult than in Hungary in 1956. Direct military rule by the Soviet occupation forces was not desirable, for political reasons; gradually the conservatives returned and ousted the progressives. Although it strengthened the Soviet hold over Czechoslovakia and removed the danger of defection, the Soviet policy had consequences that could easily be foreseen: deep frustration, which sooner or later would again cause an acute crisis.

RUMANIA

Rumania was among Stalin's most faithful satellites; measured by economic performance, it was among the least successful. After the arrest and purge of Ana Pauker and Vasile Luca, who had led the party during the Stalin era, Gheorghe Gheorgiu Dej emerged as the outstanding figure in the country. Together with his closest assistants Chivu Stoica and Gheorghe Apostol, he was in effective control of party and state up to the time of his death in March 1965. The Russian occupation forces left Rumania in 1958. Earlier, Bucharest had been released from paying reparations to Russia, which removed a serious obstacle to her economic recovery. The mixed Soviet-Rumanian companies for the exploitation of the country's natural wealth were also dissolved, much to Bucharest's relief. The withdrawal of the Russian troops gave a great boost to the self-confidence of the leaders, who gradually became more independent in their foreign and economic policy. The domestic scene was hardly affected by the new course. In 1960 they adopted a program envisaging the further rapid development of heavy industry; this brought them into conflict with the industrially developed Comecon countries, which had other plans for the division of labor in Eastern Europe. The Sino-Soviet dispute made an opening for more freedom of maneuver than ever before, and Gheorgiu Dej was not slow to make the most of it. Cultural relations with the Soviet Union were reduced to a minimum, and the Rumanian press published open attacks on Soviet historians for having belittled the role of the Rumanian people in the struggle against Nazism and for justifying the annexation of Bessarabia by Russia in 1812 as a progressive step. Bessarabia had been returned to Rumania in 1918, but again seized by the Soviet Union in 1945, and it remained an explosive issue. In April 1964 the Central Committee of the Rumanian party adopted a resolution stressing the equal, independent, and sovereign character of each socialist state; this was tantamount to a Rumanian Declaration of Independence. There were complaints in the East European capitals that the Rumanians were no longer fulfilling their obligations under the Warsaw treaty, which gave rise to a great deal of mutual recrimination.

When Nicolae Ceausescu succeeded Gheorgiu Dej, there was no question that he would pursue policies similar to those of his predecessor. Ceausescu, the son of a peasant and a prewar member of the communist youth movement, was co-opted to the Politburo at the early age of thirty-seven, and quickly asserted himself against his rivals of the old guard; the most serious competitor, Alexandru Draghici, formerly minister of internal security, was deposed in April 1968, and the other members of the anti-Ceausescu group had publicly to recant. Ceausescu's policy resembled in some respects that followed by Khrushchev. By reopening the trials and purges of the Stalin era, by rehabilitating Patrascanu, a former secretary of the party who had been executed in 1954, and Luca, he implicated the party old guard and incidentally also Gheorgiu Dej, and reinforced his own position. It was a difficult balancing act: Ceausescu welcomed the nationalist revival on the domestic scene but did not want to lose control over it. He wanted to pursue an independent line in foreign affairs but was aware that he could defy the Soviet Union only up to a certain point. Bucharest approved the Czechoslovak democratic revival in 1968 and condemned the Soviet invasion, perhaps more because it welcomed a strengthening of the communist club of independents than out of sympathy for what was happening in Prague. Faced with a stern Soviet warning and the possible danger of Soviet military intervention under the guise of Warsaw Pact maneuvers, Ceausescu had to retreat from his exposed position.

PART FIVE

THE END OF THE OF THE POSTWAR ERA:

Western Europe

THE EUROPEAN
ECONOMY 1970–90

CRISIS AND RECOVERY

The years from 1950 to 1973 were the golden age of the European economy. Never before had there been such a long period of sustained growth. Inflation was under control—and there was virtually full employment. What were the causes of the slowdown and the subsequent recession? At the time there was a tendency to attribute most of the blame to the oil shock of 1973–74, the dramatic increase of energy prices in the wake of the Arab-Israeli war. The price of oil rose fourfold in one year, and there was a similar increase in the price of other raw materials, which severely affected the many countries largely dependent on cheap energy. Thus the German rate of growth, which had been about 5 percent in the 1960s, was only half that figure in the 1970s, and the same was true with regard to Italy. The British economy had developed more sluggishly, with an annual growth of 2.6 percent; it decreased to 1.2 percent in 1979. The same year, virtually no growth was registered in countries such as France and Denmark.

The period of 1950–73 had witnessed low inflation, as little as 2.7 percent in West Germany and between 4 and 5 percent in France, the U.K., Italy, and most other West European countries. But in the 1970s Italy and the United Kingdom registered 16-percent inflation, and even in West Germany, where anti-inflationary policies were most effective, the rate doubled. Unemployment had been less than 3 percent in all major and most minor European countries; in West Germany it was a mere 1 percent. By 1981 the U.K., Belgium, Spain, and other countries had two-digit unemployment. By 1989 unemployment in Britain had decreased, but in Spain it was still 15 percent, and in France and Italy, too, it was still above the 10-percent mark. The total number of unemployed in Western Europe doubled between 1970 and 1980, and by the middle 1980s it had increased again, to almost 20 million. Some regions, such as the north of England and the south of Spain, suffered in particular, because of outdated industries which were no longer competitive and had to be closed. Even in Germany, the country of the economic miracle, the decline of the coal-and-steel industry caused grave social problems in the Ruhr, and the same was true with regard to Belgium and northern France.

Although the oil shock triggered the recession, a multitude of other factors were also involved. To begin with, the European recession was part of a wider, worldwide crisis, a general slackening of demand. Some of its causes were "objective": economic development in the Western world had always been cyclical. Furthermore, some of the specific circumstances that had favored the postwar boom, such as the rebuilding of destroyed cities and industries, no longer applied. Last but not least, the breakup of the Bretton Woods system, the introduction of flexible exchange rates, and the consequent devaluation in many countries introduced a factor of major uncertainty which had not existed before. All currencies became subject to sudden fluctuations, and this did not contribute to business confidence. Even the mighty deutschmark, considered the strongest currency in Europe (bar the Swiss franc), had its instants of weakness. In late 1980 a leading French economic magazine announced that the fall of the mark signaled the end of an era, and there was even talk of an international rescue operation in its behalf. This sudden decline was probably the result of the second oil shock, as a result of which inflation in France, Britain, and Italy rose to 15–20 percent, and well above this in some smaller countries.

However, the second oil shock was much more quickly overcome than the first, as the result of various schemes scheduled to save energy. Furthermore, OPEC proved to be incapable of keeping prices high, and successful anti-inflationary policies were adopted in most European countries. By 1986 inflation rates were down to one-quarter of what they had been in 1980, and Germany even showed a negative inflation rate. These disinflationary policies were achieved without major damage to overall economic growth, though, as has been mentioned, there was a negative impact on the labor market.

Toward the late 1980s there was again a palpable rise in consumer prices (8 percent in Sweden and the U.K.), but most major economies, such as the German and the French, succeeded in keeping it down to 2.5–3.5 percent.

Stated in the broadest terms, the European economy went through two periods of recession (1973–74 and 1979–83) after an era of unprecedented growth. The growth rates in the good years of the seventies and eighties were lower than they had been in the fifties and sixties, but this, for a variety of reasons, was only to be expected. Inflation receded during the 1980s, and financial stability on the whole increased. Turbulence on the stock exchanges had no lasting impact on the economy, as some feared.

Perhaps most striking was the advance made in the 1980s by Britain and some of the smaller European countries. Britain's economic performance in the sixties and seventies had been poor, but beginning in 1981 there was an uninterrupted period of substantial growth—second only to Japan's. The British GNP rose by 4 percent in 1987 and 5 percent the year after. Nevertheless, seen in longer perspective, such growth was sporadic, and the British economy was overtaken during the postwar period not only by West Germany's and France's, but eventually also by Italy's. Remarkable progress was achieved by some of the smaller European economies, such as Spain (with a growth rate of 5.5 percent in 1987), which considerably benefited from joining the EEC in 1986. Norway and Finland also showed striking results. Of the major economies, France and West Germany, after sluggish growth during the early years of the decade, showed progress well above expectations during the late 1980s.

Thus the 1980s were on the whole a story of progress and achievement, certainly in comparison with the previous decade. Before we turn to specific issues and countries, attention should be drawn to certain weaknesses and dangers accompanying these positive developments. Unemployment remained relatively high. If it decreased from 12.6 percent in the U.K. in 1983 to 6 percent in 1989, it rose during the same period in France from 8 to 10 percent and in Italy from 10 to 11 percent, remaining static in West Germany at 8 percent. Other clouds on the horizon were considerable budget deficits in some countries, such as Italy, high (and rising) wage costs limiting the ability of certain countries to compete in the world markets, and a declining rate of investment. Above all, there was the continuing European dependence on Middle Eastern oil, and the danger that political and military developments in this unstable area would trigger a third oil shock, potentially more dangerous than the previous two.

The case of Sweden, one of Europe's most affluent countries, serves as an example of Europe's vulnerability. Unemployment was virtually nonexistent in Sweden, and the GNP rose by 3 percent in 1987 and 2 percent in 1989. But since wages rose in the same time by more than 10 percent annually, and even higher indirect taxes were needed to cover social expenditure, an acutely critical situation ensued in 1990.

The history of European agriculture in the 1970s and 1980s is the story of grave problems caused by an abundance of food production and the need to regulate it. The exodus from the countryside continued but, because of rapid progress in the technology of both agriculture and animal husbandry and also because of greater capital investment, the output continued to grow rapidly. Between 1970 and 1986 the export of agricultural products from Western Europe grew sixfold. As an exporter, Western Europe became a major competitor for the U.S., Canada, and Australia—accounting, for instance, for half the world's exports of dairy products.

Whereas the main problem facing European agriculture in the immediate postwar period was to feed the hungry continent, over-production, in stark contrast, was the main concern of farmers and policymakers alike in the 1970s and 1980s. At the same time, agriculture has come under attack by the environmentalists (for the destruction of wildlife resulting from the use of pesticides and herbicides), and increasing concern has been voiced by the medical profession concerning the effects of animal-fat consumption on the human organism (heart disease).

The common agricultural policy of the EEC was to guarantee supplies, to stabilize markets, and to ensure reasonable prices for consumers. Whereas there was virtual agreement on the former targets, the problem of finding an equitable price level proved virtually insoluble, and caused constant friction within the community as the food-importing countries (such as the U.K.) had to support the higher prices demanded by European farmers. At the same time the main food-producing countries overseas complained about European protectionism.

The growth of surpluses, increased by the accession to the EEC of Spain, Greece, and Portugal and the decline in meat and dairy-product consumption, caused ever-increasing financial pressures. Price support for agriculture rose sevenfold between the early 1970s and 1988. Various committee reports were drafted, discussed, and in part adopted; eventually it was decided to introduce a system of quotas instead of price cuts. There are no easy answers to the question of agricultural prices and surpluses, and these problems became even more acute when there was a general crisis of the EEC budget in the late 1980s. The Common Agricultural Policy will, no doubt, figure high on the agenda of Europe well beyond 1992.

Industrial development in the market economies of Europe by and large followed the pattern of the economy in general. Industrial growth was affected by the two recessions of the 1970s, to recover again in the 1980s, albeit at a slower rate than before. The real problem of European industry was its relatively slow adaptation to new technologies, and the slow rate of industrial revival. Hence the frequent references to the "technology gap" and "relative economic decline." If there has been growth in Western (as distinct from Southern) Europe, it has more often come in the service sector than in the traditional industries, many of which were in a state of decline. This refers not only to the traditional "heavy industry" (iron and steel) but also to the textile industry and substantial parts of the food-and-drink industry. Europe lost out to Japan in the field of cameras, radios, and most electronic equipment; it remained fairly strong in mechanical engineering, chemicals, cars and trucks, and electrical engineering.

On the positive side of the ledger was the deregulation in the major industrial countries, which assisted industrial development during the 1980s. The gradual creation of an internal European market, the abolition of tariff and nontariff barriers, and, generally speaking, growing European cooperation also had a beneficial effect. True, not all the cooperative ventures were crowned with success—the failure of Euratom was an outstanding example. While industrial research and development have increased more substantially in Europe than in the United States, Western Europe has been lagging behind its major rivals in such key industries as telecommunications and office equipment. Even West Germany, in many ways the leading force in Europe as far as innovative technology is concerned, has not been able to make significant progress in these fields.

ENERGY

The question of energy supplies has always been of crucial importance for Europe. But only after the Middle Eastern war of 1973 did it emerge how important the supply was, when oil supplies were interrupted and an embargo was put on supplies to certain countries. Europe had become increasingly dependent on the supply of oil during the 1960s, yet there was no common European energy policy. As a result, European reaction in 1973 was a sad example of disunity; far from showing solidarity, each European country tried to get the best deal it could in direct negotiations with the oil producers. Ironically, the countries on which a boycott had been imposed (Germany and the Netherlands) fared better than the others.

Seen in retrospect, the oil shock had some salutary effects. This was not so much because of the emergence of a common European energy policy, for progress in that respect was limited and painfully slow. But the individual states introduced measures to reduce their dependence on imports by saving on consumption and by developing alternative sources of energy. Consequently, imports substantially decreased after 1973, and again after the new price increases of 1980. However, there was a recurrent pattern—whenever oil prices went down, complacency set in and the reliance on imported oil tended to grow. Oil, after all, had undoubted advantages in comparison with coal (half of which had to be imported, too), and also in comparison with atomic energy, considered unsafe by many. As a result of such complacency, there was always the danger that an ambitious Middle Eastern dictator could become the arbiter of European economic growth. The Kuwait crisis of 1990–91 and the decline in Soviet oil output were warning signs that could not be ignored.

While France and Belgium continued their nuclear policy, other countries slowed down their nuclear construction program or, like the Swedes, decided to close down their reactors at some future date. On the other hand, a lessening of dependence occurred because of the decline in the traditional heavy industries, which had been among the main consumers of energy. Perhaps even more important was the impact of oil production in the North Sea since the late 1970s. The existence of North Sea oil fields had been known (or suspected) for a long time. But the cost of extracting the oil was relatively high, and only with the increase of the OPEC prices did development in the North Sea become a practical proposition. Although the dependence on imported fuels continued to be high, and a great deal remained to be done to use energy more efficiently, import dependence at the end of the 1980s was far more widespread among a variety of sources of energy, so as to reduce the effects of future shocks.

The most important achievement of the European Community was not in promoting industry or agriculture or energy but in the gradual establishment of what had been the original aim—a common (or, as it later came to be called, internal) market. The abolition of direct tariff barriers in the 1960s had been a crucial step forward. But by no means did it lead to the free movement of goods or the disappearance of restrictions, qualitative or quantitative. The fragmentation of the national economies largely continued, and with it the survival of uncompetitive industries and of low productivity. A new impetus to the establishment of an internal market was given only with the report of the Delors Committee in 1985. (For many years a leading official, Jacques Delors served in 1990 as president of the European Communities).

The report aimed at the removal of all physical, technical, and fiscal barriers, and thus the establishment of a single European market. It argued that everyone in Europe would benefit from the economies of scale; a market of 320 million people could successfully compete with the U.S. and Japan; resources would be used more effectively, and duplication would be prevented. Although the community spent about as much on research as did Japan, the splitting of European research budgets meant not only that the wheel was reinvented several times over (as one official report put it) but that many large projects could not be undertaken by any single member country. A subsequent study (the Cecchini report) argued that the savings accruing from the removal of barriers would amount to 5 percent of the GDP. This included the direct savings accruing from the removal of border controls, as well as the far greater savings from cooperation and rationalization in European industry.

Although the Single Europe Act was passed by all parliaments in 1987, and this led immediately to a new upsurge of European ventures such as RACE (telecommunications) and BRITTE (use of advanced technologies), there was also a great deal of skepticism and hesitancy, largely from the outside. Thus it was feared that U.S. and Japanese imports would be discriminated against by the use of all kinds of standards, that preference would still be given to goods produced in Europe, and that, as one commentator put it, Europe's standards "would match Japan's for opacity and fiddliness." In the third world and the (former) communist countries, fears were voiced that the new, united Europe would be inward-looking, that it would be "fortress Europe" rather than a major pillar of the liberalization of trade.

But there was also opposition from the inside, above all by Mrs. Thatcher's government in Britain, but also by some of the South European countries, fearful that they would not be able to compete with Germany and France on an equal footing. Mrs. Thatcher, forever fearful (like de Gaulle before her) of an "interventionist bureaucracy" in Brussels, warned against the "suppression of nationhood" and the concentration of most power at the center of a European conglomerate. "Willing and active cooperation between sovereign states is the best way to build a successful European community," she said in a speech at Bruges in September 1988.

Mrs. Thatcher's opposition was not shared by all members of her government, let alone by British business, nor even the Labour Party. More widespread were the doubts voiced that the internal market was no panacea, that it would at best establish the preconditions for a new expansion and harmonization of European economic activity. But there was no certainty that European governments, business, and the nations would make use of the new opportunities and match the dynamism and vitality of their main competitors outside Europe. The horse could be taken to the water, but it could not be compelled to drink.

So far we have been dealing with the European economy as an entity. But great differences existed between the various European countries; furthermore, not all of Western Europe belonged to EEC. Per-capita income in the Scandinavian countries, after all, was many times higher than in Greece and Portugal. Nor have we been dealing with trends in Eastern Europe, which followed quite different lines.

West Germany, which had emerged by the early 1970s as the strongest European economy, had overcome the oil shock and the ensuing recession with less difficulty than most of her neighbors. As far as investment, inflation, productivity, and above all foreign trade were concerned, Germany's lead increased during the 1970s. However, in 1980–81 the German economy showed sudden signs of weakness; the current-account deficit grew; it seemed as if German competitiveness had suddenly plummeted, perhaps mainly as the result of rising labor costs. And since the country depended more than any other major economic power on exports, a climate of doom and gloom spread. Industrial restructuring was needed, to create higher export surpluses. Would the country be able to achieve this aim? By early 1985 almost 10 percent of the work force was unemployed. However, it soon appeared that the worst fears were misplaced; the economy picked up again because of the growth in world demand, wage moderation at home, and a number of other factors.

If growth had been a mere 1–2 percent between 1982 and 1986, it was close to 4 percent during the years after. The unemployment rate remained fairly high, at 6.5–8 percent, partly as the result of the presence of guest workers and the new arrivals from East Germany and Eastern Europe; but inflation fell from 3.5 percent in the beginning of the decade to 1–3 percent in the subsequent years. With its huge trade surpluses in the late 1980s, Germany seemed a great success story.

Then, quite suddenly, the dramatic events in East Germany opened a new era, which had considerable promise in the long run but presented great difficulties in the short and medium range.

FRANCE

Developments in France up to the early 1970s have been described as the "thirty glorious years," in the words of Jean Fourastié, the noted economic historian. But then France was hit by the recession; growth halved, inflation doubled, and unemployment quadrupled. An attempt was made by Raymond Barre to bring some order into the plans to stop the downward slide. This aimed at both liberalizing the economy and maintaining a strong currency. He succeeded in maintaining the exchange rate, but inflation and unemployment remained impervious to government policies, and there was a worrying decline in investment.

This, broadly speaking, was the general situation when the socialists came to power in 1981. Their policy was to reflate the economy by increasing wages, reducing the workweek (so as to increase employment by job sharing), and nationalizing some of the largest corporations (including Pechiney, Rhône Poulenc, Thomson and Saint-Gobain), as well as all major banks. This policy proved to be a disaster as far as the economic performance of the country was concerned. Within two years an almost complete reversal had to be carried out under a new watchword—"modernization." The new measures, aiming at the restructuring of the economy and a "third industrial revolution," did not begin to yield fruit until 1985–86, when there was a general upswing in the European economy. The French GNP grew by more than 3 percent in 1988 and remained at the same level during the year after. But unemployment still remained steady (at 9–10 percent), and though exports substantially expanded, so did imports, resulting in a negative trade balance. Investment began to increase again, and a general consensus was reached about the economic policy between the socialists and the liberal-conservative forces, something like "Butskellism" in Britain thirty years earlier. The guidelines of the Chirac government (1986) were, broadly speaking, also those of the socialist Rocard government which succeeded it.

BRITAIN

Nowhere had relative economic decline been so pronounced as in the U.K. Whereas in 1900 about one-third of global exports came from Britain, this had declined to one-thirteenth by the early 1980s. At the same time, and not unconnected with this phenomenon, per-capita income in Britain was overtaken by that of many other developed countries. Investment remained low in the 1970s, the inflation rate soared, and at the same time there was a very substantial increase in unemployment. While the top tax rate on earned income in Britain was 83 percent (98 percent on unearned income), tax receipts in the country were, in fact, lower than in the other West European countries, simply because the tax base was too narrow. A great many reasons have been adduced to explain the spread of "Englanditis," such as excessive government spending, terms-of-trade imbalances, excessive union power, the rigid stratification of British society, and so on. Some of these will be discussed later on, but there was no single cause of the British decline. Neither the Conservatives (1970–74) nor, even less, Labour (1974–79) succeeded in coming to terms with the English disease, and toward the end of the 1970s it seemed that Britain was no longer capable of competing on the world markets. From 1979 to 1982 British manufactured output declined by 15 percent, and unemployment rose from 5 to 13 percent.

Against many predictions, Mrs. Thatcher's monetarist policy succeeded in turning the British economy around. There were seven years of strong growth; inflation went down to 4.5–6 percent, unemployment decreased to 6 percent. The GNP annually rose by 4 percent or more in 1985–88, among the highest rates in Europe. The reason for the success was above all a substantial increase in productivity, and the power of the unions was broken; they had insisted on massive state support for outdated industries and opposed the introduction of new technologies.

A price had to be paid for the recovery of the British economy; any visitor to the United Kingdom in the 1980s immediately realized the unevenness of prosperity—the discrepancy, for instance, between the prosperous south and the lamentable situation in the Midlands and the north. But, by and large, Mrs. Thatcher's government was successful up to 1988–89 in managing to get the economy going again. On the other hand, many of the traditional weaknesses persisted even in her time, such as the rates of saving and investment, which remained relatively low. After the seven good years, the economy showed signs of "overheating," the external deficit and inflation rose again. GNP growth declined as the government tried to limit the increase in domestic demand so as to divert output to export. By 1990 Britain was in the midst of an economic downturn.

ITALY

Italy suffered from the recession in the 1970s as much as the other European countries. Productivity and investment fell, and unemployment rose. The fall in profits was dramatic; credits became very difficult to obtain. There was a recovery in 1978–79, which manifested itself in a recovery in Italian exports. Then came the second oil shock, which caused record inflation and a new recession in 1981–83. But this time productivity increased even during the recession, and the recovery was remarkable—growth rates of 3.5–4 percent were registered toward the end of the 1980s. On the debit side, there were high budget deficits and, as in Britain, very substantial regional differences. If in northern Italy employment was almost full, there was a 21-percent rate of unemployment in the south. According to the economists, half of the trade deficit was due to the Mezzogiorno. Grants were still extended to obsolete sectors of the economy. Seen in retrospect, the attempts of the central government over a period of forty years to bring about basic change in the south of the country had not been successful.

OTHER WEST EUROPEAN COUNTRIES

The fortunes of the smaller West European countries' economies cannot be analyzed here in detail. Most of them followed the same general pattern: recession in the 1970s, recovery during the 1980s.

This was true with regard to Belgium which was in dire straits in view of the prevalence of old, outdated heavy industries; its GNP grew by 4 percent toward the end of 1980s, even though unemployment remained high. The Dutch pattern was similar in both respects; Holland had, however, a low inflation rate.

Among the Scandinavian countries, Denmark fared worst and Norway best. Denmark showed negative growth when all other economies were booming (1988); high social costs had to be covered at a time when the country found it difficult to compete in the world markets. The misfortunes of Sweden in the 1980s have been mentioned elsewhere. Norway, once the poorest Scandinavian country, became one of the richest in the 1980s, mainly because of the income from North Sea oil. Its per-capita income exceeded that of West Germany and France in the late 1980s. The Norwegian growth rate was 3.5–4 percent over many years. However, with the decline of oil prices between 1986 and 1990, growth slowed down and inflation increased. Finland also fared well, even though it depended heavily on imports of raw materials; its growth rate was consistently over the European average; inflation remained low, and unemployment likewise.

This leaves Spain, which went through a very difficult period in the 1970s, partly because of its great dependence on imported oil, but also because of its antiquated agriculture. Its industries were largely outdated, and its banking system was ineffective. By 1977 inflation ran at 25 percent. But the Spanish government undertook ambitious reforms, heavily investing in energy and the restructuring of industry; agriculture, too, recovered, growing at the rate of 5 percent per annum in the early 1980s, and at a still higher rate during the subsequent years. The new policies showed results after 1986, when Spain joined the EEC. Inflation fell to 4.8 percent in 1988, the GNP grew by 5 percent, and Spain attracted more foreign investments than any other European country. But unemployment remained high, about 15 percent, even though (as in Italy) a certain portion of the unemployed worked, in fact, in the sizable second ("black") sector of the economy. But, with all the achievements of modernization, Spanish productivity was still at least 20 percent below the European average. Spain had limited time to catch up, and it was also clear that the great boom of the eighties would not last forever.

THE SOVIET UNION
AND EASTERN EUROPE

No mention has been made so far of developments in the Soviet Union and Eastern Europe. Yet it was precisely in these countries that the economic situation became most critical and ultimately turned into a major political crisis. According to the official Soviet version, up to 1986 the overall economic trends were highly satisfactory; even according to many Western experts, there was no reason for immediate worry. Even though growth was slowing down, it was still quite respectable by international standards; in any case, most mature economies were developing more slowly than those that had just "taken off."

According to official Soviet sources (with Western experts' estimates in parentheses), the Soviet economy had shown an annual rate of growth of 11 percent (7 percent) in the 1950s, and this had declined to 7 percent (3 percent) during 1969–72.

Some Western specialists pointed to potential sources of danger back in the early 1970s. They stressed, above all, the decline in productivity. There had been major progress in the 1950s, because the

Soviets had seemingly unlimited reserves of manpower. Almost every year some 2 percent joined the industrial labor force, and there was no shortage of capital for investment in industry. But during the 1960s productivity fell, because the reserves shrunk. Furthermore, the situation in Soviet agriculture was altogether unsatisfactory; this had been evident in the Khrushchev era; though agriculture improved a little during the late 1960s, it deteriorated again later. Since 25 percent of the Soviet GNP was still derived from agriculture in 1969 (in contrast to 3–5 percent in the developed industrial countries), Soviet overall economic performance was bound to be directly affected by this failure.

Two other circumstances ought to be mentioned. In the 1950s most of the investment had gone into traditional heavy industries. But the development of the "new industries," above all the chemical field and electronics, coincided with a tightening of investment. There was much talk about the new scientific-technological revolution (NTR being the Russian abbreviation), but little action.

Lastly, the high cost of the arms race. The Soviet Union spent three times as much per capita for this purpose as the U.S., or more, though it could ill afford it. Still, the overall picture seemed encouraging. According to official figures, the Soviet GNP had risen by 1972 to 66 percent (52 percent) of the American, and industrial output was 75 percent (60–65 percent); again, the figures in parentheses are those given by Western experts. As it subsequently appeared, both sets of figures were grossly exaggerated.

The ninth five-year plan ended in 1975–76, and the targets set for the tenth showed that the Soviet leadership regarded the adverse trends as structural, unlikely to disappear soon; the targets for the new plan were considerably more modest. But even these modest aims were not fulfilled. Growth declined to 2.5–3 percent, and during the last two years of the plan they were even lower, 1–1.5 percent. For the first time in the history of the Soviet Union, growth was considerably slower than in most "capitalist" countries. True, the Soviet terms of trade improved as the Soviet Union looked like an important supplier of oil and natural gas on the world market. On the other hand, productivity continued to decline, and the situation of the Soviet consumer also deteriorated. If greater preference had been given to consumption goods in the ninth plan, this was not so in the tenth.

Substantial grain imports came from the U.S., Canada, and Argentina to compensate for the shortfall in Soviet agriculture.

When Brezhnev died, it appeared that the aims of the eleventh five-year plan had not remotely been attained, and that the attempts to make Soviet agriculture (which suffered four bad harvests in succession) more productive had been an even greater failure, despite the hundreds of billions of rubles that had been invested.

Soviet industry had grown as the result of pouring in extensive resources; once this practice stopped, progress ceased. The attempts to achieve intensive growth failed: productivity remained low or even decreased, the machinery became more and more outdated, and the whole infrastructure, including transport, deteriorated.

It had always been difficult to form a more or less realistic picture of the true state of affairs in the Soviet economy, given the dearth of figures and the fact that those published could not be trusted. Statistics became even rarer in the late 1970s, and for good reason. Only under glasnost did it emerge that, far from achieving a growth rate of 2.2 percent in 1979 and 2.6 percent in 1982, the Soviet economy had actually been experiencing negative growth for a number of years.

In 1982 about three-quarters of the industrial plan was fulfilled, and under Andropov there was a shortlived upsurge, mainly because of the introduction of stricter disciplinary measures and the "new-broom effect." But this had little impact on the quality of the output. The Soviet Union produced several times as many shoes and tractors (to give but two examples) as the U.S., but these were of inferior quality, so they either could not be used or broke down after a short time. Thus quantity *per se* was not at all indicative of the economic performance.

There was no change in policy under the shortlived Chernenko government. It is not even clear to what extent the leadership was aware of the seriousness of the situation. It could well be that the incomplete and often false figures produced by the statisticians misled not only the Soviet people and the outside world but also the leaders in the Kremlin.

Thus, when Gorbachev came to power in early 1985, the performance of the Soviet system manifested itself in a number of paradoxes, to quote a semiofficial American summary:

It was the world's largest producer of energy but used two to three times more energy per unit of economic output than the leading industrial countries.

It was the world's largest producer of wheat, but 20 percent of the crop was lost from field to mill because of inadequate transportation and storage.

It was one of the world's most populous nations but found itself short of labor, partly because of low productivity (according to "Gorbachev's Economic Plans," study papers submitted to the Joint Economic Committee of the Congress of the United States, 1987). To this one ought to add that the state had a large budget deficit, that inflation was widespread and substantial, that there had been little investment in the 1970s and 1980s—all of which had never been admitted before glasnost. Furthermore, the Soviet expenditure on defense, in terms of percentage of the GNP, however one measured it, was considerably higher than even hawkish Western observers had assumed.

Gorbachev was the first Soviet leader in many a year who openly admitted the dangerous state of affairs and called for radical reform. There had been a blueprint to carry out certain changes in the mid-1960s sponsored by Kosygin, but it largely remained on paper. Gorbachev's early official pronouncements did not yet betray a feeling of alarm, and the goals of the twelfth five-year plan (1986–90) were unrealistically high. But as the months passed and the situation deteriorated all along the line, the statements of leading spokesmen admitted that the country was not just on the verge of a crisis but moving toward disaster.

Two additional factors reduced government revenue. One was the decline in oil prices on the world market between 1985 and 1990; oil had become the main Soviet foreign-currency earner. The other was the anti-alcoholic campaign started early in the Gorbachev period. The social price of vodka consumption was unacceptably high. But it was also true that the government had derived many billions of rubles from its monopoly on this drink.

What were the steps suggested by the proponents of economic reform? Above all, the broadening of private and cooperative initiative in agriculture and also in industry, a drastic reduction of bureaucratic interference and *khozraschet,* the demand that enterprises had to be self-financing and to show a profit.

These proposals were criticized by the radical reformers for not going far enough. They argued that the Soviet economic system was basically flawed and that tinkering with it would not produce significant results. The "administrative command system" had to be replaced by the market; the emphasis had to be on incentives; subsidies had to be cut or abolished even if it resulted in temporary hardship such as unemployment or a decline in the standard of living.

The conservatives and neo-Stalinists, on the other hand, criticized the reform for going too far, for straying from Marxism-Leninism and social justice and introducing capitalist methods ill-suited to the Russian tradition. They claimed that even if a system of this kind was more efficient it would not work in the Soviet Union, since the Russian people were more interested in spiritual values than in material goods.

If the Soviet economy had grown by 3.5 percent in 1986, progress in the year that followed was no more than 1.5 percent, and in 1988–91 there was a decline, partly because of the continuing failure in agriculture, but also because of increasing difficulties in industry.

Supplies were disrupted as a result of an inefficient transport system, of accidents such as Chernobyl and the Armenian earthquake, but also as a result of the outdated machinery used and the opposition on the part of the bureaucracy, which sabotaged decentralization. Last but not least, militant workers protested against rising prices and deteriorating supplies of consumer goods. Popular dissatisfaction was fueled by the great profits allegedly made by the new cooperatives that had been legalized, above all in the service sector. For five years the government hesitated to take the plunge in their campaign toward radical change, for fear that perestroika would become even less popular and lead to major political unrest.

In many respects, the pattern of development in Eastern Europe followed the Soviet development: a failure to introduce reforms, and slow decline in the 1970s turning into rapid decline in the 1980s and ultimately into an acute crisis. However, the signs of danger were perceived in Eastern Europe earlier than in the Soviet Union.

Heavy East European borrowing in the West in the 1970s and the inability to service the loans led to insolvency and an acute crisis of confidence. On the other hand, certain East European countries went further than the Soviet Union in toying with various alternative schemes for "market socialism." Although East Germany and Czechoslovakia, after some halfhearted attempts to modernize their economies, returned around 1980 toward centralistic practices,

Yugoslavia, and later also Hungary and Poland, tried to find new economic mechanisms and levers to rationalize their economies. This included a greater emphasis on material incentives. Some more freedom was given to small enterprises. There were also moves toward the elimination of rigid planning, with some decisionmaking on the local level, the relaxation of the state foreign-trade monopoly, and a rudimentary form of *khozraschet*. These reforms showed modest success from the consumers' point of view, first in Yugoslavia and later in Hungary. But they made no difference to the Polish economy.

Eventually, stagnation prevailed in Hungary and galloping inflation in Yugoslavia. East Germany and Czechoslovakia followed their own traditional methods; foreign observers tended to overrate their relative success. In actual fact, real growth in both countries had been small after 1975; both had low hard-currency earnings, experienced major shortages of energy and labor, and caused enormous ecological damage in their territory. But for massive direct West German support for the DDR, the myth of East Germany as a major industrial power would not have persisted so long.

Rumania under Ceausescu pursued its own idiosyncratic policy, which caused shortages and misery in almost every field. Despite constant shortages in agriculture, food was diverted for export (as in the Soviet Union in the early 1930s), and imports were severely cut in order to pay back the external debt at almost any price.

When 1989, the year of miracles, approached, the general deterioration of the East European economies quickened, partly as a result of economic factors, but also because of strikes and political unrest. Comecon (CMEA) virtually ceased to exist, as the various economies drifted apart (and closer to Western Europe) and as the Soviet market shrank. Major reforms were at long last introduced in Eastern Europe, but it was clear that the economic policies of the new noncommunist governments would not show striking successes in the near future. On the contrary, economic recovery (which included a cut in subsidies) was bound to lead at least temporarily to more acute suffering, such as unemployment and a falling standard of living. Hence the call for Western economic aid on a massive scale, something akin to a new Marshall Plan. But, unlike East Germany, the other East European economies had no wealthy relations committed to come to their help. And even in East Germany there were bound to be difficult years ahead on the road to a basic recovery.

COMPARATIVE STATISTICAL TABLES

GNP (1990)
(IN $BILLION)

France	990
W. Germany	1.125
U.K.	800
Eire	30
Netherlands	240
Switzerland	180
Austria	126
Belgium	160
Spain	340
Portugal	41
Greece	53
Italy	820
Sweden	180
Finland	104
Denmark	108
Norway	91

GROWTH OF REAL GNP
(IN PERCENTAGES)

	1970	1975	1980	1985	1989
U.S.A.	−0.3	−1.3	−0.2	3.4	2.6
Japan	10.8	2.7	4.3	4.9	5.2
W. Germany	5.1	−1.4	1.5	1.9	3.9
France	5.7	−0.3	1.6	1.9	3.6
Italy	5.3	−2.7	4.2	2.6	3.0
U.K.	2.2	−0.9	−2.3	3.7	2.1
Belgium	5.5	−1.4	4.1	0.9	4.3(1988)
Denmark	2.0	−0.7	−0.4	4.3	0.4(1988)
Greece	8.0	6.1	1.8	3.1	4.0(1988)
Netherlands	2.5	−0.5	1.1	2.6	3.3
Norway	2.0	4.2	4.2	5.3	2.3(1988)
Spain	4.1	0.5	1.2	2.3	5.0(1988)
Sweden	6.7	2.7	1.4	2.2	1.9
Switzerland	6.4	−7.3	4.6	4.1	2.8

GROWTH OF REAL
EXPORTS OF GOODS
AND SERVICES
(IN PERCENTAGES)

	1970	1975	1980	1985	1988
U.S.A.	8.1	−3.5	9.1	−1.2	17.6
Japan	17.0	0.7	17.7	5.6	8.1
W. Germany	6.5	−6.7	5.3	6.8	5.8
France	16.3	−1.7	2.7	1.9	6.7
Italy	6.0	1.6	−8.7	3.9	5.9
U.K.	5.2	−2.8	0.0	5.9	0.7

GROWTH OF CONSUMER
PRICES
(IN PERCENTAGES)

	1970	1975	1980	1985	1989
U.S.A.	5.8	9.1	13.5	3.5	5.9
Japan	7.7	11.8	7.7	2.0	3.6
W. Germany	3.4	6.0	5.5	2.0	2.8
France	5.2	11.8	13.6	5.8	3.4
Italy	5.0	17.0	21.2	9.2	6.1
U.K.	6.4	24.2	18.0	6.1	7.5

UNEMPLOYMENT RATES
(IN PERCENTAGES)

	1970	1975	1980	1985	1989	1991
U.S.A.	5.0	8.3	7.2	7.2	5.5	6.8
Japan	1.2	1.9	2.0	2.6	2.1	2.0
W. Germany	0.6	4.0	3.3	8.3	7.4	6.1
France	2.5	4.2	6.3	10.2	9.4	9.2
Italy	5.4	5.9	7.7	10.2	10.9	9.6
U.K.	2.4	3.6	6.1	11.6	5.3	7.0

SOCIAL FORCES:
OLD AND NEW

ECOLOGY AND THE GREENS

The most interesting new political force to emerge in Europe in the 1970s was the Green parties. The problems to which these parties addressed themselves transcended political boundaries by far. The idea that man had stupidly and often criminally ignored the needs of nature goes far back into history; the term "ecology" (*Ökologie*) had been coined more than a hundred years earlier by the German natural philosopher Ernst Haeckel, the founder of something akin to a religion of nature. The realization that the treasures of nature were finite, that the stormy and uncontrolled growth of modern industry had alienated man from nature and had caused irreparable harm (the term often used was *Raubwirtschaft*—"exploitative economy") went back even further. Antipollution legislation had been passed sporadically as early as the middle of the last century in various European countries and, on a regional basis, as early as the Middle Ages.

But, on the whole, awareness of the issues involved was limited to fringe and cultish groups, more often of the right than the left: the German youth movement of the first third of the twentieth century, various sun-worshipping and vegetarian groups (both Hitler and Himmler were practicing vegetarians), and various vitalist and holistic sects. Ecological ideas were propagated among the left by populist thinkers advocating life in agricultural communes. But similar ideas also appeared on the right, such as the British Green Shirts, the (Canadian) Social Credit movement, and the German Artamanen. The

ideas figured in the novels of Knut Hamsun, sundry blood-and-soil
German writers, and, in a different form, the stories of Tolkien and
Henry Williamson.

Ecology became a political force only in the 1970s, partly as a
result of the energy crisis, partly because of the increasingly severe
damage caused to the environment by air and water pollution. The
air of wide sections of Europe had become unpleasant and unhealthy
to breathe, thanks to nitrogen and sulfuric emissions from cars, factories, and powerplants, to acid rain, and to radiation. The water had
become unsafe to drink; many rivers and lakes were, in fact, biolog-
ically dead, and in wide stretches it was unsafe even to swim. Perhaps
most dramatic was the damage caused to the forests of Europe. Generations of poets had been singing the praise of these forests; generations of tourists had walked under these trees for relaxation and
enjoyment. Yet by 1980 word had got around that the forests were
dying and much of the wildlife was disappearing; this was above all
in the Alpine region and in Eastern Europe, but to some degree no
country was exempted.

It was reported from Poland and Czechoslovakia that about a
quarter of the forests were dead or dying (figures that probably erred
on the low side); the figures for West Germany and Finland were even
higher. At the same time it became known that Europe's main rivers,
such as the Danube, the Rhine, the Vistula, and the Volga, were so
polluted that much of the water was not even suitable for industrial
use. The North Sea, the Baltic, and, above all, the Mediterranean were
so polluted by phosphate, nitrogen, and dangerous metals that they
constituted a major health hazard; some of main lakes in the Soviet
Union had deteriorated beyond salvage. If the situation was bad in
Western Europe, it was much worse in the East, with sulfur-dioxide
emissions four times higher in East Germany and Czechoslovakia than
in the West, with water and air pollution also much higher.

The importance and urgency of ecological concerns quickly penetrated public consciousness. The political parties adopted programs
aimed at introducing new standards for the protection of the environment. In most countries environment ministries were set up, and
1987 was declared "European year of the environment." The Chernobyl disaster in 1986 as well as other major mishaps, such as the
toxic emission into the Rhine at Basel in 1987, added impetus to the
ecological awareness.

If, nevertheless, specific Green parties evolved, the reason was that these were usually based on a variety of causes not necessarily connected with the environment, such as support for women's liberation, pacifism, guest workers, and exile seekers. Most of these Green movements came into being in the 1970s, sharing some of the traditional beliefs of the left but opposing others. All began their activities on a local basis, then extended their work to districts and provinces; eventually they became parties on a national scale. Most successful were the German Greens, who began as citizens' initiative groups, became a political party in 1979, and entered Parliament for the first time in 1983. Four years later they had forty-two representatives in the Bundestag, and on a regional level, such as in Hesse and West Berlin, they became part of the ruling coalition. They were also quite successful in Sweden (with twenty deputies in Parliament in 1988), and in Switzerland and Austria (where they received about 5 percent of the total). But even in countries where they failed to enter Parliament (such as Britain and France) they became a force to reckon with on the local level. In East Germany and Czechoslovakia, countries severely affected by environmental damage, ecological groups played a role of some significance in the events that led to the overthrow of the communist regimes in 1989.

Demonstrations against pollution took place in the Cracow, Wrocław, Szceczin, and Poznań regions during the 1980s. In Czechoslovakia, Charter 77 made the growing environmental crisis one of the main planks of its program, publishing classified internal government reports on the subject. In Hungary the Danube Circle mobilized the public against various projects envisaged by the Budapest and Prague governments which would have caused a further deterioration in the situation. The Czech manifesto was entitled "Let the People Breathe"; the East German was called "Chernobyl Is Everywhere." However, the East German Greens also directed their propaganda against the power plants working on bitumen, which had caused more or less permanent pollution in the south of the DDR. In Rumania, President Ceausescu's plan in 1988–89 to destroy hundreds of villages in Transylvania fueled the opposition to his rule and caused an international outcry.

In the Soviet Union opposition against the rerouting of Siberian rivers and protests against the pollution of Lake Baikal became major political issues. Frequently these causes were adopted by the Russian right, but ecological issues also played a major role in the emergence of national movements in the Baltic States and Armenia.

In the mid-1980s some observers predicted that the growth of the Green parties would continue and that they would eventually replace the major established parties, because their program seemed so much more relevant to current concerns. But these predictions did not materialize, for a number of reasons. In West Germany the Greens became involved in unending debates between "Realos" and "Fundis" (fundamentalists), and their movement stagnated. Their potential social basis (the so-called new social movements) was too narrow; among university students the Greens scored high, but there was no corresponding progress in working-class neighborhoods—or, indeed, in agricultural regions.

The Green movement in the German-language countries had its origins largely in the antinuclear movement of the early 1980s. But as détente between the superpowers and arms control made dramatic progress toward the end of the decade, the age of the mass demonstrations passed, and with it an important part of the Greens' political *raison d'être*. Present-day Green parties are uneasy coalitions of orthodox ecologists, people dissatisfied for one reason or another with existing parties, new rightists as well as former Maoists, regional nationalists (such as Basque and Bretons), and Trotskyite "entryists," hoping to gain supporters for their own causes, as well as all kinds of faddists and sectarians, including even ideologists of a new paganism. Some of them (the Realos) are willing to work within the existing system—but they are in danger of being absorbed by the system. The fundamentalists show no willingness to make compromises or to cooperate with other political forces, and they tend to maneuver themselves, therefore, into political isolation and, ultimately, irrelevance. Thus the early leaders of the German Greens in West and East, such as Petra Kelly and Rudolf Bahro, Otto Schily and General Bastian, found themselves eventually outside the movement to which they had devoted so much of their time and energy.

In France, as in Germany, growing awareness of ecological concerns dates back to the revolutionary upsurge of the late 1960s. So does governmental response; France was one of the first European governments to appoint an environment minister (who later called his office *le ministère de l'impossible*). The French movement was mainly based on opposition to the growing use of nuclear energy for civilian purpose. However, unlike in other West European countries, the threat of nuclear war was never taken very seriously in France. The ecological movement was also handicapped by the traditional factional strife among the French left, in which some of the most influential environmentalists did not want to become involved. When in power, the socialists disappointed the Greens, because they more or less continued the pronuclear policy of their predecessors, nor had the ecologists a clear option for providing alternative energy sources. They came to find their allies mainly in regional groups, particularly in the west and east of France, where there was substantial opposition against the building of new nuclear plants.

It has been the historical merit of the environmentalists to dramatize the effects of pollution, to stress the need for the protection and conservation of natural resources, and to make people think about the limits of growth. Some of these problems have in the meantime been solved, others have not and will not be in the foreseeable future, nor is there unanimity among the scientists as to the cause of the damage—ranging from the death of the North Sea seals to the dying of the forests. The EEC have been engaged since 1972 in pursuing environmental policies, including legislation on water pollution and noise levels. Even before, in the 1960s, a transnational agreement aimed at reducing the pollution of the river Rhine had given tangible results, and air pollution in the United Kingdom during the 1980s was reduced by more than 20 percent. Some Mediterranean beaches have been cleaned up, and according to some sources there has been significant improvement in the degree of pollution of the North Sea, whereas the situation in the Baltic is far less satisfactory.

There is full agreement among the experts that the ozone layer has to be protected, and that the disposal of toxic waste should be regulated by international agreement. But in other respects solutions are more controversial. The dying of the forest was obviously the result of exposure to heavy pollutants over a long time. But more trees were uprooted by the winter storms of 1989–90, and there were, furthermore, additional complicating factors. The chemical impact of acidification is not so easy to explain as initially assumed. Other scientists maintain that, even if the interaction of pollutants has not yet been satisfactorily explained, it does not follow that one can wait with drastic actions until such explanations will exist. On the contrary, it would be advisable to restrict all pollutants, even those less toxic, to be on the safe side.

Although there has been merit in the critique of the Greens concerning the primitive belief in unrestrained growth underlying both capitalism and socialism of a bygone age, their own political economy has not been persuasive. The ideal society as envisaged by the ecologists would be heavily based on a back-to-the-land movement, on an agriculture based on something like Maoist communes producing organic food. They believe in egalitarianism and self-sufficiency; they oppose consumerism and trade (except within "bioregions") and, to a large extent, both the old-fashioned industries and modern technologies. However, quite apart from the fact that societies built along these lines have little attraction for many people, they would not be in a position to feed and clothe five billion people.

During the 1980s there was growing willingness in the richer and more developed European countries to invest in reducing environmental damage, particularly in the energy and chemical industries. Investments for this purpose in West Germany grew from 30 billion deutschmarks in 1983 to 50 billion six years later. However, not all countries showed such willingness; thus the British government refused to invest 3 billion over ten years in the adjustments necessary to reduce emissions in the power plants that were thought to be responsible for causing pollution in Scandinavia. The British claimed that it had not been proved that these investments would have the desired effect.

East European countries, such as East Germany, refused to make such investments because they could not afford them. According to the then-prevailing ideology, production was thought to be far more important than the preservation of the environment. However, even before 1989 popular pressure prevented the execution of various major projects that would have caused considerable further damage. Thus, with or without the pressure of environmental lobbies, parties, or movements, considerable progress has been made between 1975 and 1990 to save the environment and to reclaim some of the damage. At the same time international cooperation has been as yet quite insufficient, the means invested too small considering the magnitude of the challenges, and advance too slow.

SEPARATISM AND THE
NATIONAL MINORITIES

The new Europe that emerged in 1945 was ethnically more homogenous than before, as a result of the redrawing of frontiers and the transfer of population. However, given Europe's history, total homogeneity was neither possible nor desirable. Yugoslavia, Switzerland, and Belgium are obvious examples of states constituted by more than one nation. Elsewhere in Europe ethnic nations had a certain degree of autonomy but did not aspire to full independence or were refused full autonomy by the central authorities. During the first two postwar decades the nationalism of these "nations without a state" did not play a major political role, but there was a distinct change in the 1970s and 1980s.

Various explanations can be adduced for this reassertion of nationalist demands. One was the growing democratization of Europe, with political freedom making headway in Spain, Yugoslavia, and the Soviet Union. National awareness had, of course, existed before among—to mention but a few examples—the Basques, the Slovenes, and the Azerbaijani. But under Franco, Tito, and the preglasnost Soviet regime, short shrift would have been made (and, when needed, was made) whenever these minorities overstepped the narrow boundaries of regional autonomy. Elsewhere in Western Europe the reassertion of minority nationalism was part of a general process for which economic as well as cultural motives could be adduced.

National tensions have existed throughout history wherever ethnic groups have cohabited in the same city or region, even in Switzerland (the Jura conflict) and the Scandinavian countries. Some of these conflicts were more or less peacefully contained, such as those in the Alto Adige (South Tyrol) region in Italy and in Sardinia. Elsewhere, as in Belgium, the *arrangement communautaire* has been less successful, with frequent crises though virtually no use of violence. In extreme cases, tension led to terrorist campaigns, as in Northern Ireland and Euzkadi (the Basque region of northern Spain). In both these cases nationalist aspirations go back for a long time, but the acute phase of rebellion was reached in the early 1970s. Although the extremists among the Basques and the Irish Catholics constituted only a minority among a minority, their armed attack created serious problems for the central governments. Violent separatism raises several interesting questions. One concerns the palpable difference between their official doctrine (which was internationalist and left-wing) and their true motivation and their actions, which were based on an exclusive nationalism.

Nor is it readily obvious why other nationalities, such as the Catalan, which could point to similar complaints against the central government, tried to reach their targets using political rather than terrorist means. Perhaps a relatively small group like the Basques felt under stronger pressure than the more numerous Catalans, because they feared that time was against them, that their culture and way of life would be submerged by the influx of Spanish immigrants into their native region.

In the case of Scottish nationalism there was general resentment against rule from afar. As the general economic and social situation in England deteriorated, the demand for "devolution" became stronger; the discovery of substantial oil fields off the shores of Scotland was not unconnected with the upsurge of Scottish nationalism. In the general elections of 1974 the Scottish nationalists scored 30 percent of the total vote; at a special referendum in 1979, 32 percent of the voters opted for devolution. In the elections since then, the Scottish nationalists have not done remotely as well. Neither Breton nor Corsican regional nationalism is a new phenomenon, but both had a revival in the 1970s. Underdevelopment and the dissatisfaction of the farmers played an important role, and there was also some terrorist activity, albeit on a small scale.

In some of the most acute cases of national strife in Europe, poverty and underdevelopment also played a significant role, with Northern Ireland as an obvious example. Elsewhere, traditional religious tensions were a factor of importance; again Northern Ireland comes to mind, but also the Muslim Albanians in Kosovo. However, the Basques were as good Catholics as their Spanish neighbors; furthermore, the Basque region was among the most prosperous and developed in Spain. Attempts to explain the struggle waged by militant national minorities with reference to one or two specific reasons are bound to be misleading; even if correct in one or two cases, they are irrelevant in others.

Nor is it readily obvious why governments succeed in solving, or at least assuaging, conflict in some cases but not in others. Effective dictatorships are in a position to suppress open manifestations of conflict by means of brutal repression; they can solve it, for instance, by massive population transfer. But as Europe became gradually more democratic, such means were ruled out. As a result, violent separatist action continued. Thus, over a period of twenty years there were more than two thousand victims in Northern Ireland, more than three-quarters of whom were civilians, not combatants. Nevertheless, and despite attempts to carry terrorist operations to England, these actions did not seriously disrupt the fabric of society.

In fact, there has been a gradual decline in the number of victims in Northern Ireland since the mid-1970s. More serious politically were national tensions in Eastern Europe. Ceausescu's repression of the Hungarian minority contributed to his downfall. In Yugoslavia the revolt of the ethnic Albanians, but also the resistance of Croats and Slovenes against the dominant Serbian element, greatly contributed to the destabilization of Yugoslav politics in the late 1980s.

Lastly, the Soviet Union. As political reform got under way, separatist movements gathered strength and, as in the case of the three Baltic States, demanded independence. However, whereas in Lithuania the autochthonous population constituted a clear majority, the position of Latvians and Estonians in their own country had greatly weakened over the years, and the economy of the Baltic countries, furthermore, was orientated vis-à-vis the Soviet Union. Separatist movements came into being in the western Ukraine and Moldavia (formerly Bessarabia), but in both cases resentment against "alien" rule was clearer than ideas as to the political future of these areas.

National conflicts in the Caucasus date back for centuries; thus the civil-war-like conditions in 1988–91, the exodus of the Azerbaidjani from Armenia, and of Armenians and Russians from Azerbaidjan, did not come as a bolt out of the blue. Riots in Central Asia, the demands of the Crimea Tartars and the Volga Germans (both groups had been deported to Central Asia during the Second World War), and also an increase in anti-Semitism among Russian right-wing circles contributed to the general ferment in the Soviet Union.

There are many varieties of ethnic conflict in contemporary Europe. In some instances such strife has been contained; in others, given the multiethnic map of Europe's population, it is unlikely that satisfactory solutions will ever be found—justice to one group would inevitably mean injustice to another. It is possible that some of the regional nationalisms will achieve some of their aspirations in a more closely integrated Europe. But it would be unrealistic to consider a united Europe a panacea for the often contradictory demands of so many groups.

GUEST WORKERS
AND NEW IMMIGRANTS

Traditional tensions between ethnic groups quite apart, there appeared yet another form of social and political conflict with the arrival of millions of "guest workers." As the West European economy prospered, there was an acute labor shortage, which brought about a major influx of workers from abroad—frequently from overseas. Although the arrival of seasonal workers was not a novelty in Europe, many of the newcomers from the West Indies, North Africa, and Turkey, areas with high unemployment, had no intention of returning to their native countries. They complained, frequently not without reason, that they were paid lower wages, and that they encountered all kinds of political, social, and cultural discrimination. At the same time there was among them an unwillingness to return to their countries of origin, nor did they want to assimilate with their countries of adoption, as had been the norm among immigrant waves in the past.

As unemployment in Western Europe steeply increased after the "oil shock" of 1973, most West European governments took measures to stop immigration of foreign labor and to provide various inducements for "guest workers" to leave. Figures concerning migrant labor in Europe are unreliable, since there is a considerable number of illegals; in Italy, for instance, they are believed to outnumber legal foreign residents. In Switzerland foreign workers constitute some 17 percent of the total labor force; in Germany they are about 10 percent. In France the number of "guest workers" probably fell between 1975 and 1985; in Britain new legislation has restricted the number of arrivals but could not significantly reduce the number of those already present.

The total number of foreign workers in Europe was estimated at between fifteen and eighteen million in the 1980s. However, mere figures do not convey a realistic idea of the extent and severity of the social and political tensions. These immigrants are concentrated in certain regions, such as London and the West Midlands, Paris, the Rhône Alps, and Provence–Côte d'Azur. In West Germany, Frankfurt's population is about one-quarter foreign; in Munich and Stuttgart's they constitute not much less than 20 percent. Furthermore, there are concentrations within these concentrations: whole residential quarters of Berlin, London, Paris, and other cities were predominantly settled by recent arrivals from overseas.

Since the birthrate among the new immigrants was significantly higher than that of the native citizens, problems of schooling and housing added to the prevailing tension and mutual hostility. Even though many of the newcomers were occupied in badly paid jobs which the locals were unwilling to accept, both in industry and the service sectors (the health services in France and West Germany largely depend on the presence of foreign nurses), there has been increasing pressure to limit and reduce the foreign element. New political parties of the right have exploited the complaints of the local population about the "foreign invasion"—Le Pen's National Front and the West German Republican Party were but two manifestations of this backlash.

The situation was aggravated because the West European countries are densely populated, because since the early 1970s unemployment has become endemic, and because other kinds of immigration have continued all along. Thus France, following the loss of its North African territories, had absorbed more than a million Frenchmen, and West Germany, following the great postwar migration, had accepted during the 1970s and 1980s an equal number of expatriates from Eastern Europe and hundreds of thousands from the DDR. Lastly, there was a substantial number of political-asylum seekers from overseas countries such as Pakistan, Sri Lanka, and Bangladesh—two hundred thousand in the peak year 1986—who claimed to be persecuted in their country of origin. The claim of some of them was no doubt correct, but the majority came in search of a better life and higher living standards. No one could fairly blame them, but their aspirations happened to collide with the rights of the residents of the densely populated subcontinent of Western Europe.

TERRORISM

The exploits of small terrorist groups of extreme left- and right-wing persuasion, of militant nationalists from Europe and abroad, preoccupied European public opinion and the governments to an extraordinary degree. Mention has been made of the two most significant separatist groups, the Basques and the IRA. But there was also a great deal of domestic terrorism in Western Europe, especially during the 1970s, the heyday of groups such as the Italian Red Brigades and the West German Baader-Meinhof gang. Public opinion tended to take the activities of these groups more seriously than they deserved, and democratic authorities found it difficult to cope with an enemy who did not observe the rules of the democratic game but engaged in indiscriminate murder.

The fascination of terrorism was in its dramatic and unpredictable character: nobody knew where the next blow would fall. But fascination was one thing, political effect another; seen in this light, terrorism was quite ineffectual. After a few years of hectic activity the left-wing groups in Italy and West Germany were broken. In Turkey the clash of violent gangs from the extreme left and right had led to a civil-war climate in 1978–79. Yet, the moment a military dictatorship took over, terrorism virtually ceased. The new regime was criticized for its harsh and indiscriminate measures, but this was of little comfort to the terrorists. The Turkish example proved what should have been clear well before: terrorism could in optimal conditions achieve the (temporary) overthrow of a democratic order, but since terrorism could flourish only in a democratic regime, the terrorists were digging their own graves by provoking an antidemocratic backlash which invariably brought about the effective suppression of terrorism.

Left- and right-wing terrorism in Europe died down in the 1980s, even though individual terrorist acts continued, such as the attempt on the life of the Pope, against German industrialists, bankers, and an occasional high government official. Despite a certain amount of international collaboration, the terrorist groups realized that there was virtually no chance to destabilize, as they had hoped, democratically elected governments; against effective dictatorships, terrorist groups stood no chance in any case. Furthermore, Soviet support for "movements of national liberation," which had been given freely earlier on, was restricted after 1982–83.

The separatist-nationalist groups, as has been mentioned before, showed greater staying power, partly because they had broader public support, but also because they received assistance from bases across the border (such as in Ireland). A problem of a different kind for European governments was constituted by the incidents of transnational terrorism such as the assassination of Turkish diplomats by the Armenian Asala, and the attacks against Jewish, American, and other targets by extremist Palestinian groups.

Lastly, and most ominously, there were not a few cases of statesponsored terrorism, mainly by groups acting on behalf of Iran, Libya, and Syria. These attacks were chiefly directed against political émigrés from these countries, but on occasion also against American and other Western targets, including civil aviation, with sometimes heavy losses. When the West European governments apprehended and sentenced the terrorists involved in these operations, their sponsors would retaliate by taking hostages or by engaging in other forms of attacks. Some of them, such as Iran and the Qaddafi government, claimed that they had a perfect right to "carry out death sentences" against their enemies outside their national boundaries, or the "enemies of Islam," as in the case of Salman Rushdie, the writer of Indian origin. Syria proceeded more cautiously; there were no open claims, and the connections between the terrorists and their paymasters and arms suppliers were difficult to prove.

The reaction of many West European governments was less than steadfast; there was always the hope that deported terrorists would not return. Such appeasement helped to prolong the terrorist campaigns, and in a few cases may have been responsible for major terrorist outrages. Nevertheless, there was an overall decline in the frequency of terrorist attacks, in particular after the U.S. air attack against Libya.

This attack was widely condemned in Europe at the time; nevertheless, it had a sobering effect on the more active practitioners of state terrorism. There was the growing realization that open defiance of international law would bring them into isolation, which they could ill afford, and that secret support for terrorist operations in Europe would not remain secret for long. Thus it became known after the overthrow of the communist regimes in Eastern Europe that throughout the 1970s and 1980s national and international terrorists had been given asylum as well as other assistance in East Germany, Czechoslovakia, Hungary, and probably other countries as well. Despite the loss of these sponsors there was no reason to assume that terrorism, even if in the long run ineffective, would die out altogether.

GERMANY: FROM THE GREAT COALITION TO REUNIFICATION

The story of Germany during the postwar period was of pivotal importance for Europe, not because of any dramatic events which shook the nation prior to 1989, not even because West Germany was the most populous country in Western Europe and its economy the strongest. Germany was important, above all, because of its geopolitical position: the Cold War had broken out primarily because of Germany; without Germany, Western Europe could not be defended; and as relations between the superpowers improved, it was again in Germany that the results could be seen first.

In the later 1960s Germany had been ruled for the first and only time in its postwar history by a coalition of the two biggest parties, the Christian Democrats (CDU) and the Social Democrats (SPD). This grand coalition came to an end after the elections of 1969, not because of any sudden political earthquake (the CDU lost two percentage points, the SPD gained three) but because the Liberals (FDP), who had earlier on collaborated with the CDU, decided to switch sides. Thus the SPD came to power for the first time in four decades, and it was to rule the country for the next thirteen years. Its leader, Willy Brandt, had been a popular mayor of West Berlin, and his main attention, not unnaturally, was focused on relations with the East. His interest in economics was limited; he left the management of the national economy to capable experts such as Karl Schiller, Alex Möller, and later Helmut Schmidt. Brandt's main efforts were devoted to *Ostpolitik*—the normalization of relations with the DDR, and the improvement of ties with the Soviet Union and the other East European countries.

The negotiations lasted a number of years and were exceedingly complicated; West Germany had to give up its earlier demand to represent the whole of Germany in the international arena (*Allein-anspruch*). It is unlikely that the negotiations would have led to success in 1971–72 except that they coincided with the general trend toward détente in world politics. Since both Washington and Moscow were interested in the reduction of tensions, the West German initiative led to an agreement, and the various treaties were eventually approved by an overwhelming majority in West Germany. Ulbricht, the veteran East German leader, who proved to be a major obstacle on the road to an understanding, had to resign following Soviet pressure.

Willy Brandt deservedly received the Nobel Prize for his efforts, but the immediate effect of the treaties was less significant than some Germans had hoped and others had feared. The Soviet media at regular intervals continued to conjure up the danger of "German revanchism." As for West German links with East Germany, the cynics were claiming: "Before we had no relations, and now we have bad relations." Personal meetings between Brandt (and later Helmut Schmidt) and the East German leaders such as Willy Stoph and Erich Honecker had no tangible results, except some minor humanitarian alleviations in the lot of the East German population. It became easier for elderly people from the East to visit their relations in the West. In response to West German economic help, including direct payments, thousands of political prisoners were released and permitted to emigrate from the East.

On the West German domestic front, perhaps the most important initiatives came in the field of social services (including a new pension-reform act), law (the legalization of abortion), and education. New universities were founded, and radical reforms introduced in elementary education. Partly under the impact of the students' rebellion in 1967–69, "antielitist reforms" were promulgated which had unfortunate effects, causing a substantial decline in educational standards. Since the *Länder* had, however, a decisive influence in this respect, the state of affairs greatly varied from region to region, and in subsequent years many of the most obvious mistakes were repaired on the local level.

By and large the record of the government was favorably assessed by public opinion. In the elections of 1972 the Christian Democrats lost another percentage point, while the Social Democrats gained three; with almost 46 percent of the total, they emerged for the first time as the strongest party in the land. Much had to do with Brandt's personality and the international recognition he had gained.

However, soon after the elections, the popularity of the chancellor began to wane. The economic situation worsened as the result of the first oil shock: inflation and unemployment went up. This led to bickering between the coalition partners and growing ferment inside the Social Democratic Party as to the correct policy to be followed. An increasingly strong left wing (including the Jusos, the Young Socialists) were pressing for radical economic and social change so as to bring about a decisive shift in the economic as well as the political balance of power. Doubts were voiced more and more loudly about Brandt's competence as a leader. His critics inside the party, which included a majority of the senior figures, charged him with being distant and lazy at a time when the public wanted to feel the presence of a strong leader.

In May 1974 Chancellor Brandt resigned after it had been established that Günter Guillaume, one of his closest aides, had been an East German spy. Helmut Schmidt, who had wanted the job for a long time, succeeded him, and Walter Scheel, the Liberal leader and architect of the alliance, was elected president the same year. Genscher, another Liberal, became both party leader and the new foreign minister, positions he was to hold throughout the 1980s. Schmidt, more pragmatic, less hesitant, and less given to moods than his predecessor, had fewer enemies than Brandt but also fewer friends, especially in his own party. Helmut was a right-of-center Social Democrat, and this at a time when the left wing was getting increasingly stronger.

Brandt never turned his back on the Western alliance; he understood that, without the American presence, his *Ostpolitik* would never succeed. Nevertheless, under his leadership German foreign policy tended to be more amenable to Soviet concerns; Brandt assumed that sooner rather than later the U.S. presence in Europe would be reduced, or perhaps altogether ended. Schmidt, while supporting *Ostpolitik,* was a more committed Atlanticist, having served as minister of defense in earlier years. But he, too, had grave doubts about the quality of American leadership under Carter, as well as under Reagan, and he missed few opportunities to provide advice, even if such advice had not been asked for.

Schmidt's task at home was not enviable; there were no more Nobel prizes to be won in German politics. The effects of the recession of the late 1970s became acutely felt, albeit later in Germany than in other European countries, and new tensions appeared in the alliance with the Liberals. The image of the SPD as the responsible party was damaged by the extreme demands of the left wing, which were impossible to realize during a recession and which merely provided grist for the mills of the conservatives. In the elections of 1976 the CDU re-emerged as the strongest party. The ruling alliance polled just enough votes to scrape through.

Helmut Schmidt has entered the annals of recent German history as a staunch fighter for economic stabilization, resisting wage inflation (and inflationary growth) and chaos on the international money markets. Schmidt played a leading role at a series of international economic summits which took place—from Rambouillet (1976) to Ottawa (Montebello, 1981)—in which he successfully struggled against protectionism. In his foreign policy Schmidt tried to prevent a further deterioration of relations between the two superpowers; as he saw it, there was no reason that détente should not continue. At the same time, more than other German politicians, he understood the importance of deterrence as the basis for détente: the Western alliance had to be predictable and reliable. For this reason he believed that the introduction of new Soviet arms (the SS-20 missiles) made a Western response imperative. Above all, he worked for a close relationship with France, having discovered a great deal in common with Giscard d'Estaing, the conservative-liberal French president, whereas he had little respect for the leaders of the British Labour Party.

No mention has been made so far of yet another problem that confronted the German governments of the 1970s—terrorism. As in many other parts of Europe at the time, small groups of terrorists engaged in killing political enemies or even committed quite indiscriminate murders. Although the militants involved were no more than a handful, their activities preoccupied not only the media but also the government for many months. It should have been obvious that no democratic government could possibly provide protection to all its citizens against such attacks, and that in any case, however tragic the results, terrorism was bound to remain politically irrelevant. But these basic truths took years to percolate, and in the meantime the public was very much agitated, demanding drastic action, and political polarization set in. A minority, mainly of intellectuals, argued that there must have been "objective" political and social reasons driving the terrorists to acts of despair, and that unless the alleged social roots of terrorism were tackled, it could not be eradicated. The majority, on the other hand, demanded the application of strict law-and-order measures. The government tried to steer a middle course between these extremes.

Given the specific vulnerability of the German electorate vis-à-vis political and economic shocks, and the traditional longing for strong government, it may seem surprising in retrospect that the extreme right wing did not gain more influence during these years of uncertainty. But since the eclipse of the NPD in the late 1960s (they had not managed to enter Parliament in 1969) and the rise of the Republicans in the late 1980s, the extreme right was absorbed by the CDU, just as the extreme left (and the Greens) were more or less integrated in the SPD. While Franz Josef Strauss was alive, any right-wing group found it next to impossible to establish a presence right of the CDU. Perhaps the most talented politician of his time, a man with a volcanic temperament, Strauss was immensely popular in his native Bavaria. But north of the Main his mere name provoked great antagonism, so that all his attempts to attain the very highest office in the land were doomed. He was suspected of dictatorial, antidemocratic ambitions, of aspiring to a position similar to that of de Gaulle. In reality, he was a conservative populist, not dogmatic, but far more adaptable to changing realities than, for instance, Konrad Adenauer. Thus, toward the end of his life, with all his anticommunist convictions, he became one of the staunchest advocates of a rapprochement with the Soviet Union and the DDR, and devoted a considerable amount of his time to pushing through major grants and credits for the East.

All was not well inside the FDP, the junior partner in the coalition. The party had moved somewhat to the left over the years, but the differences between the Liberals and the SPD were growing nevertheless. With regard to foreign policy, there was more or less unanimity. But as the SPD left wing grew in influence, and as it turned increasingly against Schmidt, the FDP began to fear both for its principles and its survival. On past occasions it had not always been easy to overcome the 5-percent hurdle (the minimum fixed in the constitution for representation in Parliament), and the Liberal leaders were justly apprehensive that, if the FDP's image as the party of the center, of responsibility and moderation, was adversely affected, it would be crushed between the stronger power blocs to its left and its right.

Thus Helmut Schmidt faced increasing trouble on several fronts. His own party turned against NATO strategy, such as the double-track decision, and began to veer increasingly toward a barely veiled neutralism. In 1979 Schmidt had succeeded for the last time in persuading his colleagues to accept a compromise: the INF (intermediate nuclear forces) were to be deployed in West Germany—but only if other European countries would do the same—and, in any case, strong emphasis was to be given to arms-control negotiations with Moscow. After 1979 a growing section of the SPD turned toward unilateralism and the peace movement, arguing that the Soviet deployment of the SS-20 was purely defensive and that no Western reaction was called for.

Schmidt undertook valiant efforts to save détente. He visited the various Eastern bloc countries, including the DDR, and invited Brezhnev to Bonn. He also signed a major steel-pipe deal with the Soviet Union. The Soviets were to pay for the deliveries by supplying oil and natural gas, and the economic help for the DDR was increased. But the international climate, especially after the Soviet invasion of Afghanistan, was averse to such efforts. The DDR leadership under Honecker showed increasing confidence, even arrogance, in its dealings with Bonn. In retrospect, it is interesting to note that, whereas all West German parties tended to overrate the popularity of the East German regime and its achievements, the Social Democrats did so more than the others. In the 1980s they began to cooperate with the SED, the East German state party, even in the ideological field, not for tactical reasons but out of a genuine belief that the DDR was there to stay and that a rapprochement with the political order in the other part of Germany was inevitable.

However, the immediate causes of the crisis that eventually brought down Schmidt were domestic and economic in character. In 1979 the first signs of an economic downturn could be detected, and during the subsequent two years there was a further deterioration. Not since the mid-1950s had there been such a high rate of unemployment. At the very time when the junior partners in the alliance demanded no further increases in social spending (so as to encourage industry to start reinvesting), Schmidt's own party passed resolutions insisting on such spending—as well as higher taxes for industry and greater power for the unions. There was sniping against Schmidt from the left, especially on the part of Willy Brandt, who may have recalled that, when his own government had been in trouble, Schmidt had not shown great loyalty either. The government coalition began to unravel on the local level first in Berlin, then in Hamburg, where the Social Democrats lost their absolute majority as the result of the emergence of a Green party.

In September 1982 Schmidt put the question of confidence to the Bundestag and narrowly lost, an outcome that cannot have come as a surprise to him. Within six months new elections took place, resulting in a clear CDU victory (48 percent), and an equally clear setback for the Social Democrats (38 percent). The Liberals, regarded by many as turncoats, just barely scraped through, and so did, for the first time, the Greens. The SPD had fought the campaign under Hans Jochen Vogel, who became head of the Social Democrats in opposition. The new CDU government was led by Helmut Kohl, aged fifty-two at the time, an uncharismatic but shrewd and effective politician who had worked his way up through local politics in his native Rhineland.

When the CDU returned to power, it faced daunting tasks on the economic front, since the world was in the middle of an economic recession. But signs of a recovery could already be detected: Germany's oil-import costs fell within the next four years to less than half; current-account surplus (that is, the revenues derived from exports) rose from $3 billion in 1982 to $29 billion in 1986 and continued to rise to new record heights ($50 billion and more) during the years after. Inflation, which had been over 6 percent in 1981, decreased to minus 1 percent in 1986. In brief, by 1985–86 Germany was again in the middle of a boom, partly because of general global trends, partly because of tough and unpopular decisions taken by the Kohl government, but also because of the policy of Helmut Schmidt, which bore fruit only after his resignation.

Among the unpopular measures taken by Kohl were cutting 5 percent in unemployment benefits, reducing maternity leave, and making loans to students dependent on a means test. All this was intended to reduce the government's financial deficit, an objective that was achieved by 1985—thanks perhaps more to the general global upswing than to the actual savings achieved at home. Chancellor Kohl had the support of the unions in his economic policy. They did not press wage demands while the going was tough; real wages did not rise in 1982–84, and only minimally in the subsequent years. As the economic situation improved toward the end of the decade, it seemed only natural that the workers would more strongly press their demands to participate in the boom.

But the greatest trials confronted the government on the home front, and they were connected with the wave of *Angst* which suddenly engulfed the country. Enormous demonstrations took place, the largest in Bonn in October 1983 with more than three hundred thousand participants, most of them young, protesting against the deployment of new missiles in Germany. It was not just a protest against a specific move in the arms race, which had now lasted for more than three decades. The great fear was fueled by a genuine belief that the two superpowers were on a collision course, that this was mainly America's fault, and that Germany, to survive, must opt out of the Western alliance. The apocalyptic mood went back to the 1960s, when Karl Jaspers, not a man of the left but a distinguished philosopher, wrote a book in which he proved beyond any reasonable doubt that the situation in Germany resembled the state of affairs on the eve of Hitler's takeover. Soon after, Günter Grass, the famous writer, a moderate in politics, wrote that there was "no more hope left," and Günther Gauss, a Social Democratic intellectual and diplomat, made it known that a nuclear war was inevitable within the next ten or fifteen years. Heinrich Böll proclaimed that it was an "international honor" that the number of those willing to serve in the Bundeswehr, the West German army, decreased every year.

The German intellectuals, or in any case many among them, were unhappy not only with America, but perhaps even more so with their own country—the crass materialism of German society, the imperfections of the German political system. The radicalization of the 1960s and 1970s was accompanied and intensified by the discovery of Marxism, and this at the very time when Marxism was discarded as irrelevant to the problems of modern society in both West (France) and East. There was a cult of third-world regimes, such as the Chinese and even the North Koreans, and the overthrow of the shah of Iran was welcomed with great enthusiasm and the firm belief that such a reactionary regime could only be succeeded by a freer and more humane one. This radicalization also affected the churches, the Protestant perhaps more than the Catholic. According to their spokesmen, the church had to take an equidistant position, not only between the two power blocs but also between their ideologies. For real freedom did not exist in the West; the freedom of the liberal state was not Christian freedom: the old idea of a German *Sonderweg*, a third road between West and East, reappeared in new garb.

What caused this radicalization? Was it the reaction against the "Cold War consensus" of the 1950s, or the result of some specific shock? But there was no Vietnam or Watergate in Germany, only some minor scandals concerning the financing of political parties, and these happened when radicalization had neared its end. Or was it perhaps the manifestation of a bad (historical) conscience? Since the record of the German intellectuals vis-à-vis Nazism had not been impressive, there was perhaps a need to show (with forty years' delay) that a new generation of intellectuals had learned to resist the totalitarian encroachment of the state, of imperialism and militarism. Having shown excessive admiration for, and blind faith in, authority, German intellectuals now wished to do away with all authority. There was an all-or-nothing syndrome: since the system was not perfect, it was worthless.

In brief, German intellectuals felt a great deal of discontent during the 1970s. But how important were the intellectuals politically? The majority of the population continued to vote for parties of the center and the right. Even though the Social Democrats had moved to the left while in opposition, the intellectual trendsetters found it difficult to regard the SPD as their spiritual home. Their influence was exerted indirectly—through the media rather than the political parties, and also through their impact on the young. The Greens were essentially a movement of the younger generation. Their appearance on the political scene caused puzzlement and suspicion among Germany's neighbors. Germany's Western allies had come to regard the country as moderate and reliable; the sudden manifestation, sometimes quite hysterical, of *Angst* made them doubt whether Germany could still be relied upon. On various occasions in their history, the Germans had been given to fits of aggression; now the aggression seemed to be directed inward.

But if there were fears with regard to Germany's unpredictability, they were largely unwarranted. As the nuclear war did not materialize but as, on the contrary, a new Soviet leadership conceded that it had been a mistake to deploy the SS-20 and thus to provoke the West; as the communist regimes in Eastern Europe collapsed and Western economies flourished, there was a palpable change of mood in Germany. The young radicals of the late 1960s were succeeded by a still younger generation, which did not share the political conviction of their predecessors, and new intellectual fashions replaced the old ones. Even patriotism again became fashionable in some circles. There were not a few in the Bundesrepublik who said that they liked the DDR because certain specific German qualities had been better preserved there than in the West. Such views, alas, were not shared, as it was soon to appear, by a majority of East Germans, who voted with their feet the moment the wall came down.

Nevertheless, the outcome of the elections in January 1987 was not at all good from the point of view of the CDU; it lost more than 4 points in comparison with the previous elections. But the Social Democrats, though they emerged as the strongest party, were also weakened, thanks to the advent of the Greens. For several years an internal debate had raged among the Social Democrats as to whether the party should cooperate with, and ultimately perhaps integrate, the Greens. One wing, headed by Willy Brandt, argued that close cooperation was essential; others opposed it because such a course of action would have caused the loss of support of many traditional Social Democratic voters, especially among the working class, without necessarily gaining a new basis from among the "new social movements."

Brandt and his supporters tended to overrate the prospects of the Greens. Having reached a certain level of support, they failed to expand further but began to decline. Pacifism, the original inspiration of the party, became of less importance as relations between the two superpowers improved and new arms control agreements were signed. The Greens had established for themselves a niche on the German political scene, even though a relatively small one, by gaining the support of special-interest groups, such as the radical feminists. Thus the Social Democrats found it necessary to enter regional coalitions with them so as to obtain a working majority—as happened, for instance, in West Berlin.

The CDU fared even less well in regional elections such as in Lower Saxony and the Rhineland, and the fact that the Social Democrats did not gain much either offered small comfort. While the economy was performing well, various social issues became of growing political importance. The CDU was instrumental in pushing through social-welfare reforms (as in the health service) that, though inevitable, were not popular. Animosity against guest workers and asylum seekers was growing, and this led to the spectacular growth of the new Republican Party on the far right. Founded in 1983 and led by a Bavarian journalist (and erstwhile SS officer) named Schönhuber, the party gained more than 7 percent in the elections to the European Parliament in 1989. Predominantly based in South Germany, it scored as much as 14 percent in Bavaria, doing much less well in the North.

The Republicans opposed giving the right of vote to foreigners, even those who had resided in Germany for a number of years. They were the proponents of an extreme nationalism, demanding that preference should always be given to German interests. The long-term prospects of the Republicans were no greater than those of the Greens. But since many of their voters had previously supported the CDU, their defection did some harm to the Christian Democrats.

Other factors were also involved in the weakening of the CDU. The leftward slide of the Social Democrats had gradually been contained, and something like an internal consensus had been reached among the Social Democrats after the years of infighting. Though the Christian Democratic leadership seemed competent enough, they did not exude brilliance, new ideas, or dynamism; the Social Democrats frequently had the better public speakers.

Above all, there was the boredom factor. The feeling seemed to gain ground among the public that the CDU had had its chance for many years, and time had come to see new faces in Bonn.

Television did not dictate the outcome of elections, but it still had an indirect influence, as the events in East Germany in 1989 had shown; that millions of East Germans had been watching Western TV for years helped to undermine the Honecker regime.

In West Germany, too, television played an important part in setting the national agenda, and there was no denying that in the media the left had considerably more supporters than the CDU. Thus the outcome of the elections in the DDR was welcomed with something less than boundless enthusiasm by West German television. While Mrs. Thatcher was successful in her policies, media opposition had no effect on her popularity. But once she began to slip, media exposure magnified her failures. The situation in West Germany was quite similar.

This, in broadest outline, was the situation in West Germany when, quite unexpectedly, the storm broke in the DDR, totally changing the political landscape. Events in East Germany will be discussed in some detail where they belong, in the general context of the East European revolution of 1989. The breakdown of the East German regime led inevitably to the reunification of Germany in October 1990. Reunification created major economic and social problems in the short and probably also the medium range, but also considerable opportunities in the long run. Whereas the political prospects of the Christian Democrats had appeared dim in 1988, they improved considerably within the following two years, partly because reunification was carried out under the leadership of Chancellor Kohl and his collaborators, but also because the experience of forty years induced many citizens of the DDR to reject not only communism but every kind of socialism. As a result of unification, Germany emerged as the strongest country in Europe; it is too early even to speculate about the consequences of this development for relations between Germany and her neighbors and the internal European balance of power.

HOLLAND AND
BELGIUM

Both Holland and Belgium, albeit for different reasons, went through serious crises in the late 1960s and 1970s. In Holland a process akin to a cultural revolution took place; Belgium underwent an economic depression combined with the aggravation of tension between the Flamands and the Walloons.

The deeper reasons for the Dutch malaise were rooted in large part in the rigidity of the country's social structures, the strict religious divisions in political and cultural life, and, generally speaking, the heavy burden of tradition, making change and innovation very difficult indeed.

Then, in 1964–65, a period of tension set in which manifested itself on various levels. Students occupied the university and the Rijksmuseum; Poujadist farmers abducted the minister of agriculture; squatters appeared all over the place. Amsterdam, the city of almost obsessive cleanliness, of sobriety and quiet patriotism, turned into one of the main centers of hippiedom and drugs. The Dutch churches radically revised their theology and became very active in politics, favoring a neutralist foreign-policy orientation. The Dutch Labor Party (PvdA) was all but taken over by the New Left. At the same time there was a palpable deterioration in the economic situation, manifesting itself above all in a substantial growth in unemployment. A visitor to Amsterdam in the 1970s, whatever his political sympathies, was bound to reach the conclusion that Holland was a troubled country, even though little fighting occurred in the streets and no one was killed. Economically, Holland was saved during this difficult period by the rapidly increasing revenues from natural gas. But most of these revenues went into consumption rather than investment; the standard of living of individuals did not decline, but the economy was weakened.

In Dutch political life, Christian Democrats and Social Democrats have been for a long time about equal in strength. The Christian Democrats were originally a Protestant party but have absorbed strong Catholic elements in the postwar period. The Liberals were the third traditional Dutch party, but in the 1960s several new parties appeared on the scene. Whatever the merits of these new groups, the result was that it became increasingly difficult to put together government coalitions, usually headed by a Christian Democratic prime minister. Thus it took five months to form a new government in 1972–73, and almost seven in 1977. The coalitions were either center-right, as in 1986–88, or center-left, as after 1988.

During the 1970s the opinion prevailed among the more pessimistic observers of the Dutch scene that Holland was gradually sliding into a state of not-so-happy permissiveness bordering on anarchy. But the worsening economic situation had a sobering effect. After 1979 successive governments came to see it as their main task to reduce public-sector spending and combat inflation. This approach was, broadly speaking, successful. The economy began to recover steadily after 1983; unemployment, too, decreased, even though it remained relatively high. Simultaneously, there was a swing in public opinion: extreme permissiveness became outmoded, and there was a growing demand to "clear up the cities." If, to give but one example, a mere 25 percent of the population had been in favor of retaining capital punishment in the late 1960s, this turned into a majority in favor by 1988. If in the 1970s anti-NATO sentiment had been running high, political concerns and fears changed in the 1980s as the danger of a collision between the two blocs disappeared. Ecological apprehensions figured high on the Dutch agenda; there was a growing demand to limit immigration, and also the fear that "Brussels"—that is to say the EEC—would have undue political influence on Dutch domestic affairs after 1992.

Whatever the dangers facing the Dutch in the 1970s, they seemed puny in comparison with the threats confronting the Belgians. A multitude of political parties made Dutch politics barely manageable, but this trend was even more pronounced in Belgium. Eight or ten political parties were represented in the Dutch parliament, eleven in the Belgian. The very survival of the Belgian state was threatened by the growing tension between the two main communities. The French-speaking Walloons concentrated mainly in the south had traditionally been better off than the predominantly rural Flamands in the north. They had dominated the political life for a long time, but the trend was reversed in the postwar period. Mining and the old heavy industries became a drag on the Belgian economy; the more modern industries developed in the Flemish regions. The Flemish asserted themselves with much vigor in social and cultural life; the language issue increasingly divided the country and changed the political scene. The traditional parties, above all the Christian Socialists and the Social Democrats, split according to linguistic lines. Among the Walloons, the Social Democrats are stronger, whereas among the Flemish, the Christian Socialists have considerably more influence; the Liberals are more or less equally divided.

Attempts were made to reduce the tension by strengthening the federal character (regionalization) of the country, giving more autonomy to the two communities. To this end, the constitution was amended twice (in 1971 and in 1980), and in 1989 a special new status was worked out for Brussels, which had become the most important single bone of contention. However, these measures had only a limited effect; whereas Switzerland had, by and large successfully, solved its language problems, passions in Belgium continued to run high. The issues at stake concerned not only the language of tuition at a certain university, admittedly a major issue in a small country, but also (in one famous case) whether polling stations for elections in a small town should be set up in a local school or in civil-defense trucks sent by the central government. That an issue of this kind should become a matter of national concern appeared laughable to outsiders, but in the Belgian context it turned into a major political problem.

As in Holland, the proliferation of parties made it difficult to set up and maintain coalition governments. Although Belgian governments have been headed for a long time by the same leaders (such as Wilfried Martens and Gaston Eyskens), there have been frequent resignations and government crises. In 1987–88 Belgium was without a government for six months. Fortunately, the political crisis had little effect on the economic situation. It took Belgium longer than other European countries to emerge from the stagnation of the 1970s, and by 1983 the unemployment rate was still 14 percent (down to 8 percent in 1991), but a strong recovery had set in by 1986, with annual growth of 2–5 percent during the years after, and a low inflation rate.

That the headquarters of the European Community was located in Brussels, and the increasing importance of the EEC, also added, albeit indirectly, to the importance of Belgium.

BRITAIN: THE THATCHERITE REVOLUTION

The history of Britain in the 1970s was by and large a seemingly unending sequence of misfortunes. Although the first two post-war decades had witnessed steady growth and the emergence of a welfare state, it was also true that the country was gradually falling behind the other major European countries; by the 1980s the British GNP was smaller than the Italian. The Labour government under Harold Wilson had all kinds of plans to reform the economy, but the country's weak financial position resulted in the devaluation of sterling (1967), and the increasing power of the unions strictly limited the freedom of action of the government. Eventually, Wilson found himself isolated in his Cabinet, and Labour lost the elections in June 1970, merely six years after it had returned to office.

Edward Heath, who became the new prime minister, had been the leader of the Tories for only a short time, and he had never been popular among many fellow conservatives, who gave him the nick-name "the grocer." But the fact that he had not attended Eton or Harrow and had not seen military service in one of the elite regiments was probably not the decisive factor in the final analysis; the doubts about his ability to lead party and country went deeper. His successor, after all, was the daughter of a grocer, and her origins in Grantham, Lincolnshire, had been even more modest. The misfortune of the Tory government in 1970 was that, although it came to power with radical slogans, such as the intention "to change the history of the nation," it did not stay the course, but capitulated after less than two years in the face of a major strike wave. The government's record in foreign affairs was considerably better: it led the country into Europe, despite the vehement resistance of the great majority of both the Labour Party and some Tories as well.

It was under Heath that the Irish troubles flared up again, and they escalated in 1972–74; British military forces were originally sent to Ulster to protect Catholics from Protestant mobs, but within a short time they found themselves under siege by the "Provisionals" and later also by the traditional IRA. But Northern Ireland remained a sideshow; the decisive front was at home. The miners easily defeated the Heath government, compelling it to retreat from its economic policy. In 1973, as a result of another miners' strike, a three-day workweek had to be imposed in British industry, and in early 1974 they brought down the Tories. Heath fought the elections under the slogan "Who rules Britain?" But the response of the electorate was equivocal. There was no overall majority for either party, and another general election became necessary toward the end of 1974 in which Labour emerged with a small but workable majority.

Heath was deposed as leader of the party a year later and replaced by the woman who had served under him as secretary of education. Would it have been possible to resist the onslaught of the miners? Most politicians—left, right, and center—agreed that some key unions were far too powerful, and that they had a near stranglehold on the economy of the country. They resisted innovation tooth and nail. British industry had stagnated since 1964, but substantial wage demands continued all the same and were acceded to. As a result, British industry became still less competitive, and inflation soared. Furthermore, the militant unions were unpopular even among the left, because their main concern was not social justice for the working class but maximum earnings for their members. The Tories, however, long known as the party of class privilege, were not in a good position to speak on behalf of the nation; it is doubtful whether they could have mustered sufficient public support. The public was fed up with the militants—but not as much as ten years later, when Margaret Thatcher defeated the unions.

Harold Wilson, who once again became prime minister, faced an extraordinarily difficult task, for the 1970s were a period of worldwide recession, quite apart from the specifically British crisis. Thus unemployment reached the one-million mark and continued to rise, the pound came under such pressure that Dennis Healey, the chancellor of the exchequer, was compelled to apply to the International Monetary Fund for help. The IMF insisted on cuts in government expenditure, which, in turn, provoked the ire of the unions and also of the more radical sections of the Labour Party. Labour had steadily moved to the left during the previous decade, which brought the party on a collision course with the government, which had insisted on a maximum 5-percent pay rise (in 1978), whereas Labour had rejected this policy. It is easy to understand why Wilson, increasingly frustrated, resigned as prime minister, to be succeeded by James Callaghan, and why Home Secretary Roy Jenkins accepted an invitation to become president of the EEC Commission.

Callaghan, in his sixties at the time, came from an impeccable working-class background and had been a union official in addition. He performed well as prime minister—better, according to his colleagues, than previously as foreign secretary, home secretary, and chancellor of the exchequer. But in the final analysis there was little he could achieve in an economic situation that went from bad to worse. Like Wilson, he had little support from his own party.

A growing number of Labourites, headed by Tony Benn, were firmly convinced that all the economic ills stemmed from the lack of socialist vigor on the part of the leadership; these ills could easily be cured by sweeping nationalization of industries, banks, and the economy in general. The left wing of the Labour Party gradually prevailed over the center and the right wing, but it was a Pyrrhic victory. The left-wingers failed to realize that their electoral basis (manual labor) was shrinking. True, the Labour Party was more "proletarian" in its composition than the other European socialist parties, but as the proletariat declined in numbers so did the percentage of voters attracted by the Labour Party.

Furthermore, experience over the decades had shown that about one-third of the working class tended to give its vote to the Conservatives, and the more radical the Labour Party's policy, the higher the Tory vote. As Eric Hobsbawm, the unorthodox communist intellectual, put it with irrefutable logic: "If people don't vote Labor, there can be no Labor government. . . ." It could well have been that the Labour militants, among whom there were not a few Trotskyites who had infiltrated the party, felt more comfortable in opposition than in seeing their ideals sullied by constant compromises with unpleasant realities. This was true as much of foreign policy (Britain's membership in NATO, its possession of nuclear weapons, etc.) as of domestic problems.

Between 1972 and 1976 sterling fell by 40 percent in comparison with other countries, and credit is due to Callaghan, Healey, and the others who refused to admit defeat in a seemingly hopeless situation. There were faint signs of improvement toward the end of the decade: the rate of inflation was halved and fell to 13 percent in 1976, the strike waves abated, foreign investment in Britain increased as North Sea oil came onstream. But unemployment remained high and productivity low, and there was always the danger that inflation would again accelerate with the next downturn in the business cycle. Furthermore, government spending continued to exceed revenue.

The country cheerfully continued to live beyond its means, and the outside world increasingly referred to "Englanditis," pitying once-proud Albion which had turned into the "sick man of Europe." As the state of affairs deteriorated, pressure for greater autonomy and even separation was growing in Scotland and Wales. The "social contract," the uneasy and reluctant understanding between the Labour government and the unions, finally broke down in the "winter of discontent" 1978–79. A "Day of Action" inaugurated six weeks of strikes, wholly uncoordinated and frequently against the wish of the union leadership. As a result, essential services came to a standstill, in parts of the country sick people were turned away from hospitals, the dead were not buried, and in at least one case schoolchildren were denounced as strike breakers because they had taken sandwiches to school rather than go hungry when the employees who normally provided school meals were on strike. The impression was gaining ground that the country was rapidly gliding toward chaos, and the Labour Party was not to recover from the harm caused for a decade.

The winter of discontent opened the way for Mrs. Thatcher. In the elections of May 1979 the Conservatives had a clear majority. But even this was only the beginning; the real extent of Labour's decline could be measured only in the elections of 1983, when Labour attracted a mere 28 percent of the vote, with 26 percent for the Liberal-SDP Alliance. It was not that there had been a sudden overwhelming swing to the Tories, who still did not gain the majority of the popular vote; the Labour movement had merely driven itself into near isolation.

When Margaret Thatcher came to power in 1979, she was not yet a national figure. Her experience in national politics on the highest level was limited, and the problems facing her government were daunting. The number of unemployed was soon to reach two million; an inflation rate of 18 percent was forecast; the lending rate was 17 percent. The City of London did not think highly of the capacity of the new prime minister to bring about a lasting improvement in the economic situation. But Mrs. Thatcher thrived on adversity; she was a leader of strong convictions and iron nerves and, unlike most of her predecessors, never afraid of taking unpopular measures. She was a fervent believer in economic liberalism as formulated by Hayek, Friedman, and the monetarists; in many respects she was not a conservative of the old school. She had recognized (like most others) that the welfare state had become too expensive and that raising taxes was not the answer to remedy the situation. (The same was true, of course, to a greater or lesser extent, for all European countries.) As she saw it, leading branches of the economy had to be privatized and the powers of the unions restricted; above all, the rate of public spending had to be reduced. She told the Conservative leadership that the years of decline "brought on ourselves by self-deception and self-inflicted wounds" were over. The cardinal sin had been Heath's U-turn in 1972—once a policy had been decided upon, it had to be carried through, irrespective of public furor and the doubts and wavering of the "wets" in the Tory ranks. The experts had told her that British enterprise was doomed, but she was going to show them how defeatist, how wrong they were.

Luck, as the saying goes, favored the bold. From 1981 on, Britain witnessed eight years of uninterrupted growth. By the late 1980s Britain's inflation rate was less than West Germany's and France's (let alone Italy's and Spain's). The growth rate was 4–5 percent, the envy of the rest of Europe; inflation, which had been almost 22 percent when Mrs. Thatcher came to power, was down to 3.7 percent by 1983. Most Britons had never had it so good (to use Macmillan's famous phrase of almost thirty years earlier), and this explains the unprecedented three consecutive electoral victories.

By 1990, when she resigned under pressure generated inside her own party, Mrs. Thatcher had been longer in power than any other British prime minister in modern history. She did not flinch when riots broke out in British cities such as Liverpool and London (1981);

she defeated without much difficulty the railway strike of 1982 and the miners' strike of 1984. She sent the navy in 1982 to defend the Falkland Island against an Argentinian invasion, even though most other Europeans thought that fighting a war was no longer befitting a Western nation.

In all these endeavors she was successful, and she gradually acquired a reputation for invincibility. The "wets" and the intellectuals were sputtering with rage at her reactionary policies. But public opinion supported her, because she had succeeded at turning the economy around. By 1986 no more articles appeared analyzing the roots of Englanditis; on the contrary, treatises were written to probe the mainsprings of the "British miracle."

So much for the sunny side of Thatcherism. A closer look showed that her achievement was neither complete nor consistent, and that without a great deal of luck she would not have been able to stay the course. Industrial output fell during her first years in power, and unemployment doubled to 2.5 million in 1983, to reach 3.4 million in 1986. Only after that date did a dramatic decline in unemployment set in. Mrs. Thatcher was saved, broadly speaking, during her first term in office by the steadily increasing tax revenues accruing from North Sea oil, by the sudden national solidarity produced by the Falkland conflict, and, last but not least, by the disarray in the ranks of the opposition.

In late 1980 James Callaghan had resigned as leader of the Labour opposition, to be succeeded by Michael Foot, a gifted writer and orator, and a darling of the left wing in the 1940s, but now well past his prime and not an effective party leader. While he was head of the party, there was an exodus of some senior Labour politicians (the "gang of four"—including David Owen and Roy Jenkins) who had lost hope that the Labour Party could be saved from the suicidal policies of the radicals who had gradually gained the upper hand and were now dictating its course of action. They formed the Social Democratic Party (SDP), which soon established an alliance with the Liberals, who for some time under their leader David Steel had moved leftward. In the elections of 1983 this coalition came close to overtaking Labour in the popular vote. In October 1983 another radical, Neil Kinnock, was chosen to succeed Michael Foot.

Thatcher managed to break the power of the unions, partly because of their great unpopularity but also because the more radical among them were, in fact, quite vulnerable, fighting a lost cause. Thus the miners protested against the impending closure of pits that had become uneconomical. One could sympathize with their plight, but it was clear that under any conceivable economic system, capitalist or communist, work in these pits had to come to an end. It was equally obvious that the vehement action of printers against the introduction of revolutionary new technologies was doomed.

The high tide of Thatcherism was between 1985 and 1989, when even her bitter critics were paying grudging respect to the prime minister. She had shifted the agenda in British politics; like Reagan, she had been winning hearts and minds in the battle of ideas. The idea that nationalization was a panacea was no longer taken seriously, and, on a higher level of economic sophistication, the days of Keynesianism were numbered.

But in other respects Mrs. Thatcher's record, considering what she had wanted to achieve, was less impressive. She had wanted to cut down drastically on the bureaucracy and public spending. Yet, in actual fact, nothing of the sort did occur; the welfare state was there to stay, and no political party was in a position to make truly radical cuts without risking total electoral defeat. If nationalization was no cure, there was also a feeling that privatization had gone too far under Thatcher (for instance, with regard to the water resources) and that, generally speaking, the social contrasts between rich and poor (and between northern England and the south) had risen dangerously. Rightly or wrongly, Thatcher gained the reputation of being unfeeling, lacking charity and compassion for those many who through no fault of their own had not partaken of the new prosperity. She was respected for her toughness but never really loved. Her style was found grating by many; she gained the reputation of an excellent surgeon in an emergency but not of a healer of old wounds, not a national leader of vision and wisdom.

For much of the time the "Iron Lady" acted as her own foreign minister, and frequently she showed a sure touch. There was the special relationship with President Reagan, a leading member of her fan club; important U.S. help (mainly intelligence) was extended to Britain during the Falkland war. Britain reciprocated by staunchly supporting Washington on various occasions—such as at the time of the U.S. air strike at Tripoli, when there was a pained outcry from all other European capitals. She was a reasonably good European until, in the late 1980s, she began to pick quarrels with the EEC bureaucracy in Brussels, making it known that she was opposed to greater European cooperation in the political field. But she was also quite popular in the Soviet Union, having been among the first to declare that Mr. Gorbachev was a leader with whom one could do business.

In May 1989 Mrs. Thatcher celebrated the tenth anniversary of her ascent to power. It should have been a joyous occasion, not just because she had stayed in office for so long, establishing a new record. With the exception of Winston Churchill, it is difficult to think of a British political leader whose personality had made a similar impact on the fate of the country.

But in actual fact neither Mrs. Thatcher nor her party was in the right mood to celebrate. The outcome of the June 1989 elections confirmed a trend that had prevailed for some time—Labour was overtaking the Conservatives; the country was turning against the party in power. Subsequent by-elections and opinion polls showed even more clearly how unpopular Tory politics had become. To some extent it was a reaction against specific measures, such as the poll tax, the privatization of water and electricity, and doubtful reforms in the health service, but the real reasons went considerably deeper. There was, to begin with, a widespread feeling of boredom, the conviction that the incumbent had accomplished her task, that she had run out of ideas, and that the time had come to give another party a chance. Neither Adenauer nor de Gaulle had escaped the consequences of this historical syndrome. It came therefore as no great surprise that Mrs. Thatcher was ousted toward the end of 1990; she was succeeded as prime minister by John Major, who had served under her.

The economic situation began to deteriorate in 1988; inflation had risen again to 8 percent (9 percent the year after); the trade deficit was much too high for comfort. To combat these trends, the interest rate had been raised to 15 percent, and output growth had slowed. Perhaps more important, the Labour Party, for years in hopeless disarray, had recovered and, following the collapse of the Liberal-SDP alliance, re-emerged as the only effective antagonist to the government. Paradoxically, the moderate Labour leadership was helped in its recovery by the Conservatives, who had defeated the radical unions and the militant local Labour councils, which had been increasingly dominated by all kinds of sectarians and eccentrics, a caricature of the "new social movements," united mainly in their desire to spend freely for all kinds of improbable causes. Neil Kinnock had been considered initially by many a political lightweight, but he brought about a near revolution: Labour retreated from its commitment, last proclaimed in 1987, to unilateral disarmament. The party affirmed not only its loyalty to Europe (at a time when Mrs. Thatcher switched to anti-Europeanism) but even to NATO. It made known that when in power Labour would no longer support compulsory union membership (the "closed shop"), and that, though it would revoke some of Mrs. Thatcher's legislation, this would by no means apply to all the changes she had introduced. It was a tribute to Thatcherism even in decline: the mood of the country had changed to such an extent in the 1980s that a return to the *status quo ante* had become unthinkable.

In the new Labour program, published in May 1990, readers had to strain their eyes to discover the very term "socialism" just once. Needless to say, not all Labourites had been converted to the idea of a truly popular party; some muttered "betrayal," and it was far from certain whether the new reasonableness would survive once Labour regained power. In retrospect, there was no doubt among friends and foes alike: other European leaders had come and gone, but the 1980s had been the Thatcher decade. If additional proof was needed, it was provided by the elections in spring 1992. Despite the dismal economic situation, Labor did not succeed in replacing the Tories as the leading party.

FRANCE SINCE
DE GAULLE

The de Gaulle era ended suddenly and unexpectedly. The general had called a referendum on regional reform in April 1969, even though the need for such a snap election was not readily obvious. When it appeared that he had been narrowly defeated (by a million votes), he announced his immediate resignation in the briefest of communiqués. Ten years earlier he would have fought back, but the general had visibly aged and become more pessimistic. Perhaps he had not overcome the shock of the events of 1968, when the Paris students' revolt had triggered mass demonstrations that had almost overthrown his regime. De Gaulle died eighteen months later in his country retreat, Colombey-les-Deux-Eglises.

His successor, Georges Pompidou, was aged fifty-eight at the time, a politician who was not meant to be de Gaulle's heir, even though he had served him for six years as prime minister. A *bon vivant* and a lover of literature rather than a passionate politician, Pompidou was suspect to the orthodox Gaullists, and they were correct in believing that in mentality he was not one of them. But he did exceedingly well in the presidential elections of June 1969, polling more votes than de Gaulle in 1965, and he appeased the Gaullists by appointing Jacques Chaban-Delmas as his prime minister. Chaban-Delmas, a man of charm and dynamism, had played a prominent part in the wartime resistance. He was close to the mainstream of Gaullism, and also more eager to engage in social and economic reform than the new president. Pompidou was more inclined to believe that France's ills stemmed from her poverty and backwardness, and that economic progress would provide the answer to most of her problems.

Pompidou was a shrewd politician and, appearances notwith-standing, could be as ruthless as his predecessor. Without much fan-fare, he did away with some of the extravagances of Gaullism. The franc was devalued to make the French economy more competitive. Some of de Gaulle's more costly prestige projects were discontinued. The veto of Britain's entry to the EEC was dropped, and though France did not rejoin NATO, it moved toward greater cooperation.

In other respects, there were narrow limits beyond which Pompidou could not move. Thus he could not restrain his foreign minister, Michel Jobert, who, playing up to domestic xenophobia, gave higher priority to annoying France's friends and allies than to improving relations with them. Pompidou was willing to placate the workers through some form of participation (*contrats du progrès*), but he opposed basic economic and administrative reform, and he feared major changes in the educational system as much as in local government. The bitter experience of his successors proved that these fears were not unfounded.

During its first three years the reputation of the Pompidou regime soared on a wave of success, and domestic as well as foreign observers predicted a glorious future for France. Economic progress continued, the left was split, and the regime faced no major challenges. But even before the full effects of the economic recession of 1973 were felt, public support began to ebb. Increasingly there was talk about the shortcomings, the aimlessness and weakness of the regime. Chaban Delmas had to resign because of some differences of opinion with the income-tax authorities concerning his personal declarations. He was replaced by Pierre Messmer, a loyal and well-meaning but colorless personality. Meanwhile, the left, having agreed on a common program, gathered strength, whereas in the government camp there were increasing signs of tiredness and internal divisions. Pompidou's grave illness further weakened the resolution of his government at a time when it was most needed. It engaged in conflicting half-measures, trying to combat inflation without affecting economic growth. It attempted to stem the rise of prices without much success and floated the franc without visible benefit to the economy.

The country sank into an economic recession, and the political consequences soon followed. In the elections of 1973 the left made substantial progress, polling 46 percent of the total vote. It emerged once again that France was divided into two camps of more or less equal strength. As the left moved toward unity and the right toward division, and as the party in power was blamed for the deteriorating economic situation, the ruling coalition's base of power continued to shrink. Giscard d'Estaing, who became president after Pompidou's death in April 1974, scraped through by a mere three hundred thousand votes.

Economic grievances apart, the basic complaints against Pompidou's administration and that of his successor focused on the absence of change, and this at a time when the demand for reform was no longer limited to revolutionaries of the left. France, it was widely argued, was a "blocked society"; it was ruled by a bureaucracy, octopuslike (*tentaculaire*), ineffective, and out of touch with the people. Technocracy, it was said, was no answer to the social and political ills, and most people had no feeling of active participation. The rigid social structures did not correspond with the exigencies of a modern society. The government did not dare to do away with the archaic procedures, prerogatives, and privileges, sometimes of medieval origin, of small groups in society.

Such complaints were by no means groundless; it was also true that differences in income were greater in France than in almost any other advanced industrial society, and that taxation was often ineffective. When Giscard tried to push through a modern capital-gains tax, he encountered stiff resistance from the rich. The French right, which had never been distinguished for the depth of its social conscience, was clearly in no mood for concessions; as a result, the latent social conflicts became even more acute. Lastly, there was the growing conviction that successive governments sold on economic growth had neglected the quality of life. This criticism was exaggerated, but again it was the perception that counted, and the perception gave rise to ecological concerns that became a major issue in French politics.

This, then, was one side of the picture, and it is easy to forget that there was another side. France had made progress during the preceding two decades over and above the expectations of even the most sanguine observers. It had become a modern country. For the first time some of its key industries were able to compete on the world markets; its agriculture had become far more productive; the average Frenchman was much better off in 1975 than in 1955. Social mobility had increased, and, with all the criticism of the bureaucracy, there was no denying that the leading French *cadres* were as good as any in Europe. Within a relatively short time France had acquired a system of social services equal to that of her neighbors. Those advocating radical and immediate change too often forgot that, with all the popular complaints and demands, French society was still essentially conservative—its heart on the left but its purse (or checkbook) on the right. There was an inclination to ignore the instinctive opposition, not just among the very wealthy, to any radical changes in their daily habits, customs, and way of life. In short, though a majority of Frenchmen were in favor of reform, there was no enthusiasm at all for radical change. Confusion was not a monopoly of the government; the opposition also combined mutually exclusive demands in its program.

Giscard tried to introduce a new style, partly on the Kennedy pattern, and there was a great deal of idealistic speechmaking during the early days of his rule about a new society and a new democracy. But the new president, neither earthy politician nor charismatic leader, never quite managed to display the common touch, and found the going rough from the very beginning. To the Gaullists he was even more suspect than his predecessor. While Jacques Chirac served as his prime minister, criticism was muted, but when Chirac was replaced by Raymond Barre, an economics professor, the right as well as the old Gaullists (who still formed the core of the government coalition) were up in arms, and only fear of a socialist victory prevented a total breakdown. The left had made considerable gains in the local elections of 1976, and in the municipal elections the following year it obtained some 52 percent of the vote. Their progress seemed irresistible, their seizure of power only a matter of time. Of Giscard's many promised reforms, only some materialized in the end. The right to vote was given to young people over the age of eighteen; similar reforms had been made by the British Labour government in the late sixties and in West Germany in 1970. There were concessions to the environmentalists and to those pressing for educational reform. But in the economic field the pressures were such that the government could do little but cope with the most urgent problems. It did not use the opportunity to carry out far-reaching reforms, which, precisely at a time of crisis, might have found popular support.

The recession reached its climax in late 1975. Industrial production had fallen by more than 10 percent during the preceding year, price controls were no longer effective, and more than a million

Frenchmen were out of work. Then improvement set in; Chirac had been replaced by Raymond Barre, a Sorbonne economics professor (Giscard called him the best French economist) whose "plan" was at least in part successful; inflation did not further increase, even though the franc still was under pressure. Economic growth was renewed, and the government deficit was reduced, even though unemployment still proved intractable. As in Germany, there was no major industrial unrest, but the educational reforms were strongly disliked by the students.

There were no more major political initiatives of the kind that had been so dear to the heart of de Gaulle. Giscard showed some activity in the third world; he demonstrated greater friendliness toward the Soviet Union and Eastern Europe than either his predecessor or his successors; above all, he gave strong support to European cooperation. In close collaboration with Helmut Schmidt, he was instrumental in making both the Council of Europe and the European Parliament institutions of some importance. These moves were followed with much suspicion by the Gaullists, with their traditional aversion to any move likely to detract from French sovereignty. Some optimistic observers tended to detect in France during the Giscard era the birth of a new civic spirit, of trust and cooperation, and a decrease of old tensions and conflicts between the classes. But there was also much of the old inertia, suspicion, and the traditional deep-seated negativism, the lack of positive involvement in public affairs. French morale, in short, remained fairly low, and even France's admirers thought that the country would improve only as the result either of a gradual process over a long time or (less likely) following some unpleasant shock therapy.

The elections of 1978 did not provide a shock of this kind, since it soon appeared that the left was less united than it had appeared earlier on. The French voting pattern again showed considerable consistency. *Il faut que ça se change* had been the slogan of the left, but it emerged that, with all the grumbling, popular dissatisfaction was less deep-seated than had been assumed. In any case, widespread distrust of the communists (and the dependence of the socialists on the PCF) was still a major obstacle on the road to a victory of the left.

As Giscard's incumbency approached its end, the pollsters made it known that, with all its shortcomings, the ruling coalition, and above all Giscard personally, stood a good chance to continue to rule France. The first round of the elections to the presidency (April 1981) seemed to bear out these predictions. But the second round brought a reversal: Mitterrand won more convincingly than Giscard seven years earlier, and in the general elections that followed, the socialists emerged as the strongest party by far, with 38 percent of the total.

The victory of the left was in considerable part the merit of François Mitterrand, who for many years in the wilderness had worked with patience and a considerable Machiavellian talent for a union of the forces of the left. Born in 1916, the son of a railway-station master, he was a socialist by neither origin nor early training. Serving in the French army during the war, he was taken prisoner but escaped, and he became the youngest minister in the Ramadier government soon after the war. During the years that followed he represented a small left-of-center (but not socialist) group in Parliament, and served frequently as minister. In the public eye he became very much identified with the weaknesses and the ultimate impotence of the Fourth Republic. After de Gaulle's return to power, Mitterrand was among the politicians for whom the general had no use, and it was at this stage that Mitterrand became actively involved in socialist politics. He ran against de Gaulle, and later against Giscard, and did surprisingly well. But in French politics, as elsewhere, there were no prizes for losers.

In the final analysis, Mitterrand succeeded as a figure of political integration because of his very pragmatism (or ambiguities). He was sufficiently middle-class by background and outlook to attract middle-class voters of the center. At the same time the communists found him more acceptable as a partner than the more orthodox socialists, whose outlook had been shaped by the age-old rivalry with communism. Mitterrand was not regarded as a statesman of genius or great vision, nor did he exude the charisma of the born leader. But there was only limited demand for leadership of this kind in the post–de Gaulle era. He happened to be a man of considerable common sense and a very accomplished tactician whose whole way of thinking seemed to be closer to the heart of average Frenchmen than that of his rivals.

True, Mitterrand would still have failed in the end but for the changes that took place inside the left during the 1970s—more specifically, the steady decline of the communists. The PCF had emerged after the Second World War as the leading party of the left, polling fairly regularly a quarter of the total, thus passing by far the socialists, who seemed in a process of irreversible decline, reaching the nadir of their fortunes in the 1960s: Gaston Deferre, the official candidate of the Socialist Party, polled no more than 5 percent in the elections of 1969.

But even if the old Socialist Party was discredited and split, there existed a reservoir of goodwill and support in France for a left-wing movement outside the Communist Party. When Mitterrand took over the leadership of the Socialist Party in 1971 as a result of a compli-cated, internal coup, the balance between the two parties began to change—slowly at first, with greater speed thereafter. Mitterrand, a man of considerable self-confidence, did not hesitate to collaborate with the communists in an effort to achieve a united front based on a common program. Nor was he deterred by the frequent communist betrayals, such as in 1977, when the PCF suddenly, and without any convincing reason, turned against its partner, giving notice that all the agreements that had been reached with so much effort were null and void. Mitterrand was confident that in the long run the com-munists would suffer more from this turn of events than the socialists, that the PCF needed him more than he needed them, and that even from a position of relative weakness he would be able to outmaneuver them, just as he had earlier outmaneuvered the old Socialist Party leadership. His confidence was borne out by subsequent events: The rapid decline of the communists began in 1978, when the party still attracted 20 percent of the total vote. In the elections of 1981, after Mitterrand's victory, they polled only 16 percent, and in 1986 a mere 9.7 percent. Even though they slightly improved their position on subsequent occasions, mainly because of their superior organizational strength, the party that had for years been the strongest in France lost more than half of their voters within less than a decade. If they still kept some of their regional working-class strongholds, the de-fection of the intellectuals was near total.

The victory of the left in 1981 caused a great deal of enthusiasm among those who had been excluded from power for so long. Among the new men (including four communists who would disappear after a few years without leaving a trace) there was the feeling that they had a mandate to carry out radical reforms. This included the na-tionalization of nine industrial groups, including the steel industry, space, and armaments, as well as electronics, thirty-six banks, and leading insurance companies. Public opinion was at first by no means opposed to nationalization; among the socialist leadership, the more orthodox wing, such as Pierre Mauroy, the new prime minister, supported full nationalization, whereas a minority (including Delors and Rocard, the leading economic experts) recommended state control, less expensive and cumbersome. But the view of the orthodox prevailed, and the nationalization law was passed in early 1982. The new government also raised minimum wages and family allocations and reduced the workweek.

All these measures were in accordance with the party program, and in principle few opposed them. But there were doubts from the very beginning about paying for the new social benefits; at a time of considerable economic growth it might have been possible to cover the cost at least in part, but what if the economy stagnated or declined? Within a year of their coming to power, this was precisely the situation faced by the socialists. There was a general decline in confidence, partly caused by the nationalization program. French exports fell substantially, industrial production stagnated, a policy of deflation euphemistically called *rigueur* ("austerity") had to be adopted, and the dreams of 1981 gave way to the disenchantment of 1983. The municipal elections that year showed a substantial decline in support for the left, and this trend continued during the following year.

That a new government had meanwhile been formed by Mauroy made little difference. Despite changes in economic policy, unemployment continued to increase and inflation remained higher than in other developed countries, as did the budgetary deficit. In brief, whereas the other European countries emerged from the recession, France did not. The political repercussions were therefore predictable: in the elections to the European Parliament (June 1984), the socialists polled a mere 20 percent (compared with 38 percent three years earlier); the communists, with 11.2 percent, were almost overtaken by the National Front (10.9 percent), the new force on the extreme right.

The decline in socialist popularity was not only rooted in the poor economic performance of the country; some of its social and political reforms were equally controversial. Thus the socialists engaged in a widespread purge of the state-owned media, and there was great public resistance to the Savary bill, scheduled to abolish private education. Almost a million citizens of Paris demonstrated in March 1984 against a law that had aroused the ire of some because of its anticlerical character and antagonized others because they believed that it would bring about a general decline in educational standards and a state monopoly over the schools. A second demonstration (in June 1984) brought an even larger crowd to the streets. The law had to be watered down and was eventually dropped.

Mauroy, who had been preoccupied for many months trying vainly to steer the education law through Parliament—to the detriment of other, at least equally important issues—resigned and was succeeded by Laurent Fabius, at thirty-eight years of age the youngest French prime minister for a very long time. He was a wealthy young man about town, the product of France's best schools (the Ecole Normale and ENA), yet he had thrown in his lot with the Socialist Party, and more particularly with Mitterrand, serving as his *chef du cabinet*. He had made his reputation as a man of the left inside the party, but his convictions mellowed rather quickly; his reputation when he was appointed was that of a dynamic leader rather than a radical, an intelligent man, but a little too smooth for the taste of some. Some of the old ministers left the Cabinet; others were shifted or remained in their posts.

When Fabius tried to reintroduce a degree of private enterprise into the economy and to limit the power of the bureaucracy (under the cloak of "modernization"), resistance inside the Socialist Party was limited; a more sober spirit had prevailed after the lost illusions of 1981. Nevertheless, the "new-broom effect" did not last long; Fabius did not create the impression of a forceful leader, and the assessment of those who had claimed all along that "Mitterrand had appointed himself prime minister" seemed to be borne out by events. The handling of minor crises, such as the rebellion in New Caledonia (one of the few remaining French dependencies in the Pacific) and the sinking of the *Greenpeace* (which led to the resignation of Charles Hernu, minister of defense), further weakened his position, which was also undermined by his surprisingly weak performance in a television duel with Jacques Chirac (in October 1985).

True, the overall French economic situation began to improve in 1985, but the socialists benefited only to a limited extent from this trend. They performed much better than in the elections to the European Parliament (obtaining 31 percent of the total, compared with

20 percent), but the communists did worse than the National Front (9.7 percent as against 9.8 percent), and the united right attracted 42 percent. One of the main reasons for the defeat was that the socialists were widely believed to have been weak on law and order; this referred both to their seeming inability to deal with the acts of terror committed by Middle Eastern extremists in France, and also to their perceived reluctance to limit foreign immigration. France had 4.5 million legal immigrants by the late 1980s, some 8 percent of the population. Thirty thousand new foreigners arrived each year to join their families, and in addition there was a sizable amount of illegal immigration; ten thousand were caught in 1989, but many thousands probably were not. The outcome of the elections of 1986 meant that France now had a socialist president and a right-of-center parliamentary majority. Though a situation of this kind was by no means uncommon in the United States, it had never happened before in France. In the event, however, the *cohabitation,* which lasted for two years, did not work too badly. Relations between Mitterrand and Prime Minister Chirac were anything but close, but a broad understanding emerged. While Mitterrand would have a decisive say on foreign policy and defense, he would but seldom actively interfere in domestic policy. Sections of the right (including Raymond Barre) would have preferred confrontation to cohabitation, with the aim of forcing Mitterrand out before his incumbency ended. But this would have involved basic constitutional change, and it is not certain whether it would have had the support of the electorate. A strong presidency, after all, had been de Gaulle's basic idea, and his heirs could not therefore easily weaken the institution, even though they resented Mitterrand's misuse of his power—as they saw it.

The Chirac government pushed through Parliament several re-privatization bills (including Elf-Aquitaine and Saint-Gobain, as well as two major banks, Parisbas and Suez), and the socialists decided not to fight a last-ditch battle in view of their negative experience with their nationalization policy. However, Chirac's government soon ran into difficulties that in some respects—such as educational reform—resembled those of its predecessors. Since the socialist economic program had in previous years become more and more centrist and moderate, it was not easy for the moderates of the right to take a position clearly distinct from that of the moderates of the left. In view of a far-reaching consensus between left and right, the electorate was called upon to decide which camp was more likely to carry out this consensus policy.

Giscard was too remote to generate enthusiasm among the public. Barre, on the other hand, was trusted, but only within the field of his specialization. Though Chirac did have political experience, he had frequently changed his opinions—less elegantly than Mitterrand—and there was a residue of distrust with regard to his judgment. In the presidential elections of 1988 Chirac was a clear loser. Even though a majority of the French were inclined to the right rather than the left, a significant percentage of right-wing voters (including some of the National Front) preferred Mitterrand to Chirac. Making use of the divisions on the right, Mitterrand called for new parliamentary elections, and though the socialists did not score as well as in 1981 in terms of seats in Parliament, they were still in a position to form a new government under Michel Rocard.

Rocard (yet another graduate of the ENA, like Laurent Fabius and Chirac) was the most gifted politician in the Socialist Party next to Mitterrand, and he had on various occasions been his rival for the leadership, which did not endear him to the president. However, of all the socialist leaders he was the most popular among the nonsocialists. Whatever Mitterrand's personal predilections, he had little choice but to appoint Rocard, given the dependence of the socialists on outside support (Fabius became president of the National Assembly). Rocard's reformist policy in 1988–91 faced, in fact, more resistance from inside his party than from the right. But since under his leadership economic growth was satisfactory (3 percent or more in 1988–90), whereas inflation was kept low (2.5–3 percent), his political position remained stronger than could have been expected, considering that the socialists could not rely on a solid basis of support in Parliament. Eventually, Rocard was forced to resign by Mitterrand (May 1991).

During the 1970s and 1980s important changes took place in the French political landscape, reflecting deeper economic, social, and ideological developments among the public. This refers, on the one hand, to the decline of the agricultural population and of manual labor, not to mention the emergence of a subproletariat consisting mainly of foreign workers. It also refers to the more or less constant rise in the standard of living, and a greater egalitarianism, less perhaps in income discrepancy than in the equality of chances.

The Communist Party adjusted itself less well than all others to these trends, and as a result suffered most. Its erstwhile sources of strength—its Marxist orthodoxy, its unquestioning orientation toward the working class and the Soviet Union—caused its growing isolation. Unlike the Italian Communist Party, it did not consider in time a widening of its social base, let alone Social Democratization or liberalization. Nor, given the tensions between French and North African workers, could it make substantial progress among the so-called subproletariat. While, according to public-opinion polls, resentment toward foreign workers was not higher in 1990 than it had been a decade earlier, it remained a major factor in French politics. A majority of Frenchmen resented the presence of so many foreigners. Without this, the rise of Jean Le Pen's National Front would be inexplicable. This party had polled a mere 0.75 percent in the presidential elections of 1981, but more than 14 percent in the presidential elections of 1988, truly a political earthquake, as its leader said. (The number of foreigners in France had risen from 1.4 million to more than four million between 1954 and 1974.)

In France, as in West Germany and in Britain, concentrations of foreign immigrants were far greater in some parts of the country than in others. They were strongest in Paris and its suburbs as well as the south (Provence and Rhône-Alpes, including Marseilles, Nice, and Toulon). There were also substantial congregations in the east (Alsace-Lorraine), but virtually none in the west (Bretagne, Normandie). Whereas the immigration law of 1981 had favored the reunification of families and normalized the status of the *"sans papier,"* more recent laws have favored stringent controls, including administrative expulsion of the illegal immigrants. The parties of the right refused to cooperate with Le Pen's movement except on the local level, but their attitude toward foreign immigrants became more hostile over the years, and their demands for more government action more vociferous.

In view of the increasingly open anti-Semitism of the National Front, its racist character cannot be seriously disputed. However, it is also true that much of the antagonism against the North Africans was sociocultural. Whereas earlier immigrant waves (such as the Poles and Belgians) had been integrated in French social life without much difficulty, the North Africans frequently showed no wish to conform. On the contrary, many of them insisted on keeping their language,

customs, and traditional way of life. With the tide of Muslim fun-
damentalism running high, the insistence on religious and social habits, sometimes in clear contravention of the law of the land, was bound
to create tension with the host nation.

The National Front did not do so well in the elections after the
presidential vote of 1988, but it still polled regularly 9–10 percent of
the total, more in certain areas. Unlike Poujadism in the 1950s, its
public base seemed secure, and it was not likely to disappear soon
from the French political scene.

No mention has been made so far of French foreign and defense
policy in the 1970s and 1980s. Broadly speaking, there were no startling new departures: French relations with the U.S. were better than
under de Gaulle; attempts were made to improve links with the East,
even though expectations as to Mr. Gorbachev's reforms were less
sanguine in Paris than in Bonn. France became involved in a minor
war (helping Chad to repel Qaddafi's invasion), which it successfully
concluded. Above all, France was drawn more and more into the
network of European political and social initiatives. Public-opinion
polls showed that the country that had once shown the most reluctance vis-à-vis European political unity has more recently demonstrated a more positive attitude than its neighbors with regard to the
emergence of a European government. As for defense, there was more
of a consensus in France than in the other major European countries.

In 1990 the revolutionaries of 1968 were middle-aged men and
women; if they were trying to draw a balance sheet of the two decades
that had passed since, the results were mixed. The most trusted if not
the most popular politician of the period was not one of their own
generation but Mitterrand, who had professed, politically speaking,
several religions during his life, whose personality had been formed
in the prewar period, and whose first ministerial appointment dated
back to 1946. Alarmists would point in 1990 to growing social tensions, what with the presence of three million unemployed but, above
all, in view of the growing skepticism among the public with regard
to the traditional virtues, the ideals, and above all the political institutions of the Republic.

Political parties were mistrusted, and one in three Frenchmen
refused (or found it impossible) to define himself (or herself) as either
left- or right-wing. For two hundred years it had been generally agreed
that the left was the party of political and social justice, and the right

the party of patriotism and pragmatism. But this division had become questionable since the Second World War: there had been nothing particularly patriotic about Vichy, whereas the left had learned from bitter experience that idealism and dreams were not always a good guide toward economic success and social progress. Those pointing to the alleged greater harmony that had prevailed in French society before 1968 or prior to the world wars tended to forget that the general mood had been anything but positive during these earlier periods, when there had been a veritable flood of books and manifestos entitled *Finis Galliae*.

During the 1970s the purchasing power of the workers had risen annually by about 5 percent, and by not much less in the late 1980s, which explains the relative social peace prevailing in this period. During the same time the gross inequalities between classes and groups had been slowly reduced. There was still a great deal of dissatisfaction, but also less emigration from France than from any other comparable European country. The clouds on the political and social horizons were there for all to see. Unlike the adverse demographic trends and the seemingly innate defeatism of previous ages, however, the problems confronting the French people toward the end of the century seemed tractable. There have been violent eruptions in French society in the past, and they are possible even now. But it could be safely predicted that if these were to occur again, they would be rooted in unpredictable changes in the national mood rather than in "objective," measurable, economic or social trends. As the prestige of the ruling Socialists and Mitterrand's personal prestige declined sharply in 1991–92 the French right received fresh impetus. This would have been even more strongly felt but for the divisions on the right with Le Pen's extremist National Front making the most of the ethnic conflicts between Frenchmen and immigrant North Africans.

ITALY: DOMESTIC CRISIS AND RECOVERY

In 1991 Italy's fiftieth postwar government was installed, a record by European and probably all other standards. Yet this extreme political instability had no fatal consequences as far as Italian society and economics were concerned. After some years of major turbulence in the 1970s, the 1980s were, by and large, a period of calm and steady progress. The changes on top occurred within a small group of Christian Democrat politicians such as Mariano Rumor and Aldo Moro, Emilio Colombo, Ciriaco de Mita, and Amintore Fanfani, all of whom repeatedly headed governments. Perhaps the most outstanding example was Giulio Andreotti, who had been prime minister six times—the 1991 coalition was the eighth he headed—and served as minister in twenty-eight of them. The only significant interruption occurred when Bettino Craxi, the socialist leader, headed the government for three years in a row, but again with Christian Democratic support.

All governments in postwar Italy have been dominated by the Christian Democrats, or at the very least survived with their assistance. The communists were not considered acceptable partners until the 1980s, and the other parties were too small to provide an alternative. Craxi, the socialist leader since 1974, tried to emulate the French example; his strategy was to surpass the communists, who for decades had dominated the left-wing scene. But the Italian Communist Party was far less sectarian than the French. In fact, during the late 1970s and early 1980s it seemed for a while that they, in turn, might overtake the Christian Democrats: in the European elections of 1984 they came out on top.

They had gained new prestige as the champions of Eurocommunism, well before democratic reform became fashionable under Gorbachev. But the Christian Democrats recovered from their temporary eclipse, and in the elections of 1987 they again polled 34 percent, whereas the communists fell back to 26 percent, even though they continued to shed their Leninist ballast. By 1990 they were discussing whether to change their name (they did so in 1991) and to apply to membership in the Socialist International. The majority of their members felt that they had become a Social Democratic party in all but name, and why not take the last, logical step? A militant minority continued to press for more radical politics. The socialists did make some progress all along, but not sufficiently to participate in the political process from a position of strength; they were still, by and large, the junior partner.

Forty-five years of Christian Democratic rule raised doubts among some observers as to how deeply democracy was rooted in Italian life. But in actual fact Italian democracy did not fatally suffer, even though the main opposition party was never given the chance to form a government on the national level. This for two reasons: The Christian Democrats were fully aware that they could not rule the country while on a confrontation course with the communists and the trade unions. Hence their willingness to make concessions, such as introducing the Workers' Statute in the 1970s and, generally speaking, the policy of the "historical compromise." Furthermore, communists had the chance to rule many districts, cities, and communes, not only in northern Italy, where their influence was strongest, but temporarily also in Rome and Naples. Much as the church and many Christian Democrats resented it, the ruling party could not prevent the passing of a new and more liberal divorce law in 1974. Thus there were obvious limits to Christian Democratic power.

Mention has been made of the political convulsions of the 1970s, which coincided with a general economic crisis. Italy was perhaps even more dependent than other European countries upon energy imports, and it suffered more from the oil shocks. This was the period of mass strikes, unrest in the universities, and, for a number of years, the emergence of the Red Brigades and other terrorist gangs. Violence escalated, public figures were maimed or assassinated, and in 1978 Aldo Moro, former prime minister, was kidnapped and murdered.

The state and its security organs seemed powerless facing this violent onslaught, and there were dire prophecies about the impending collapse of Italian society.

Yet the fears, it soon appeared, were unfounded. Paradoxically, the murder of Moro, whose sympathy had been center-left, caused a backlash, as a result of which the terrorists were defeated without much difficulty. The call for stronger measures united right and left, and once the terrorists had to face the full power of the state (and a more sophisticated counterterrorist strategy), their fate was sealed. It soon transpired that the real threat facing the country was not the attacks inspired by sociology lecturers and lapsed theologians, but ordinary crime (which continued to spread at an alarming rate) and also our old acquaintance the Mafia, often declared dead but always re-emerging as a potent factor in southern Italian life. In the 1980s it extended its activity to northern Italy.

Mention has been made of Italy's economic difficulties in the late 1970s, when inflation reached 22 percent and unemployment was among Europe's highest. In view of these signs of weakness, it came as a surprise that in the next decade Italy overtook Britain in GNP and per-capita income. Though Italy's progress in the 1980s was substantial, it was not higher than in Thatcher's Britain. If there was a sudden quantum leap, this had largely to do with a new approach in national bookkeeping: in the past Italian statisticians had always ignored the "second economy," which, in fact, accounted for 20 percent or even more of the national product. Italy's progress, as a communist elder statesman (Amendola) once put it, was remarkable: it had changed in thirty years—that is to say, from about 1955 to 1985—more than in the preceding two thousand.

But progress was uneven, and some of its concomitants were anything but positive—above all, the great social and economic discrepancies between north and south. Whereas 35 percent of Italians lived in the south, only 24 percent of the GNP was generated there. For decades Rome had tried to spur economic development in the Mezzogiorno by massive allocations, but without striking success except for some pockets in the southeast. Unemployment in Calabria and other southern regions was still more than twice as high as in the north. The south seemed a bottomless pit, and gradually resistance in the north crystallized. In the elections of 1990 antisouthern leagues first appeared in Lombardy and other northern districts, making significant gains scoring up to 20 percent of the poll. Since the southern birthrate is much higher than in northern Italy (where it is less than 10 per thousand, the lowest in Europe), there seems to be an imminent threat of a further influx of southerners on top of the immigration of the 1950s and 1960s, which had generated social and cultural tensions that had not yet been overcome. Combined with the influx of third-world illegal immigrants, mainly from North Africa, this gave rise, perhaps for the first time in Italian history, to a strong anti-alien sentiment, similar in character to the mood in France, which could no longer be ignored by the central government and the major political parties.

Italy, as so often in the past, continues to be a country of paradoxes. Though enormous progress has been achieved on many fronts, the general mood has frequently been one of self-doubt, even despair. Italy is poor in natural resources; it has to import much of the food it consumes, as well as the energy it requires, which is a heavy burden on the country's trade balance. Some of the country's economic problems are self-inflicted, such as constant overspending: the debt of the public sector is almost as high as America's. Italy has only a very few big corporations, a drawback in international competition, yet investment in the south has mainly been directed toward big companies (including declining industries such as steel) rather than smaller companies based on local products—which would have been the appropriate strategy in this specific instance.

In the sociopolitical sphere, the lack of principled policies, the internal splits and intrigues, have been at the bottom of popular skepticism vis-à-vis all political parties as well as the authority of the state. The abolition of secret voting in Parliament in 1988 was hailed by many as a near-revolutionary act, since it made it difficult for parliamentarians to vote against their own party at critical moments, a practice that had been quite common in the past. The decline of communist influence has been noted, but the same was true with regard to the Catholic church. Critics pointed to the increasing generation gap and the weakening of family ties, which had acted as an important social stabilizer through the ages. The list of woes could easily be prolonged: it included a school-and-university system deficient in many respects, a health service functioning with difficulty, and frequent strikes in the public sector, which made communication and transport difficult and risky.

Yet, with all this disorganization, Italy has by no means lapsed into anarchy; life has continued even if governments were rapidly succeeding one another—or if, for long stretches of time, Italy was without a government altogether. Despite the inferior level of public medicine, Italians have been relatively healthy; despite mediocre schools and poor universities, generations of talented professionals and outstanding intellectuals have emerged; and, with all her economic difficulties, Italy has prospered no less than other parts of Europe, showing a remarkable spirit of innovation. It has been a recurring *miracolo* for which there is no obvious answer. Italy has been the classical country of individualism; Italians have traditionally expected (and received) less from the state than other Europeans, and adjusted their behavior accordingly. This, perhaps, could be part of the answer to the riddle.

Spanish working-class immigration, the Basque population constitutes only a minority in the Basque homeland (Euzkadi) in northwestern Spain. Within the Basque community the separatists constitute only a minority; the legal wing of ETA, Herri Batasuna, never had more than four or five deputies elected to the Cortes (and one in the European Parliament). Its politics are a curious mixture of Leninist and ecological phraseology with an extremely chauvinist, quasi-fascist mentality. Although their demands for political and cultural autonomy were justified, their attempt to impose their domination over the majority of non-Basque residents had, of course, to be resisted by the central government.

Violent attacks continued against the police as well as civilians, French as much as Spanish and foreign tourists. Nor did ETA except Basque citizens who disagreed with them. From time to time the government would enter negotiations with ETA (as in 1988) and a temporary cease-fire would come into force. But invariably the talks would break down, and the terrorist attacks were renewed. ETA received some outside help, especially on the part of Algeria and Libya. But such assistance from abroad certainly does not explain the exceptional fanaticism shown by a relatively small nationalist group divided, moreover, into several factions.

Political and economic developments in Spain since Franco's death have been positive beyond the wildest dreams of inveterate optimists. The country has not relapsed, as many feared, into chaos and yet another civil war. On the contrary, democratic institutions took root, and leaders and public alike have shown an astonishing degree of political maturity and moderation. Economic progress has been spectacular: during 1987–90 Spain was again on the top of the European growth league at 4–5 percent, with inflation well under control. True, there were clouds on the economic horizon, such as the worsening of trade accounts and stagnant receipts from tourism. Above all there was the high rate of unemployment, with about half of the unemployed under twenty-four years of age and government efforts to reduce youth unemployment failing to succeed.

The general strike of 1988 reflected a social ferment which the party in power could ignore only at its risk. The socialists had given much-needed stability to the country during a critical period. To the outside world it still presented a common front. Felipe González was unanimously re-elected its leader in 1988. But inside the party, and among the local federations, there was growing conflict, and the relations between PSOE and UGT remained tense. Like all political parties that had been in power for many years, the socialists showed signs of wear and tear by the end of the decade.

SCANDINAVIA: BETWEEN NATIONAL CONCERNS AND EUROPEAN COOPERATION

Hardly affected by foreign political threats, important social and economic changes took place in Scandinavia during the 1970s and 1980s. All the Northern countries had been pioneers of social welfare, enjoyed the highest living standard, and had exemplary human-rights records. There was a great deal of cooperation between them on many levels, as codified in the treaty of cooperation of 1962. However, since that date not much further progress had been made toward a Nordic Union. What did change was the internal economic balance. Traditionally, Sweden and Denmark had been among the most prosperous countries, whereas Norway and Finland had been relatively poor, at least by Scandinavian standards. However, during the 1970s and 1980s Norway caught up with its eastern and southern neighbors, mainly because of the revenues from offshore oil after 1973. Finland also made steady progress, whereas the Danish economy stagnated; Sweden, too, ran into growing economic and social troubles in the 1980s.

In all four Northern countries strong Social Democratic parties have played a leading role, whereas the nonsocialist parties were divided. Social Democrats have ruled Norway with short interruptions from 1963 to 1981 and again from 1986 to 1989; in Sweden they have been in power from 1933 to 1976, and again since 1982. In Finland they were represented in virtually every Cabinet since the Second World War; in Denmark, Social Democrats headed all governments from 1953 to 1982 with only one short interruption. Some of these Social Democratic parties were originally quite radical, but they became reformist during the postwar period, transforming themselves from working-class parties into popular mass movements trying to appeal to all sections of the population.

Danish political life was dominated for a long time by four traditional major parties, but in the elections of 1973 new groups achieved a breakthrough. Most notorious among them was the Progressive Party, which polled some 10 percent of the total; its main demand was major cuts in taxation. Denmark has been plagued by unemployment and an inflation rate that at one time reached 20 percent (it was 9 percent in 1989). The Conservative leader Poul Schlüter, whose party has been in power with short interruptions since 1982, had the unenviable task of pushing through a policy of wage restraint and price control, at a time when citizens of Denmark were already paying a higher income-tax rate than any other country. The Danish economy had grown by an average modest 1.5 percent throughout the 1970s and 1980s, but toward the late 1980s (specifically in 1987 and 1988), when the rest of Europe prospered, Denmark showed signs of weakness and further declined—to recover slightly in 1989–90.

Schlüter's government consisted of three nonsocialist parties— the Conservatives, Liberals, and Radical Liberals—and had a very narrow majority. The situation was further complicated by the fact that some elements of this coalition were opposed to NATO; Denmark's membership again became a matter of topical controversy, though this specific bone of contention lost much of its divisiveness with the new détente in Europe after 1987.

Norway has been the most successful Scandinavian country during the last two decades. Up to 1986 the government treasury showed a yearly surplus, and the main problems facing it were the results of overheating, of too-rapid growth.

As in Denmark, the socialists and nonsocialists are more or less evenly balanced. The Conservatives increased their share from 17 percent to 30 percent between 1973 and 1985, but mainly at the expense of the other center parties. ("Conservative" in the Scandinavian context means a liberal party of the center, not of the right.) Radicalism did appear in Norway, as in Denmark, in the shape of the populist Progress Party, which in 1989 polled 13 percent of the total, the closest to a landslide in this country's politics. As in Denmark, the main complaints of the Progress Party concerned income tax, but it also put considerable emphasis on stricter controls on

emigration. Norwegians had decided in 1970 against joining the EEC
for fear that the specific character of the country would be affected.
For the same reasons, there was even greater aversion to immigration,
though the numbers involved were small. The Norwegian boom was
mainly the result of the North Sea oil and gas revenues, but it was
clear that this source of income was finite, and the question arose
what would happen to the mainland economy thereafter. Traditionally, there had not been much industry in Norway, and successive
governments tried to establish a stronger industrial base—for instance,
by developing an engineering industry. Nevertheless, unemployment
increased toward the end of the 1980s, and there were major strikes
in 1988, for the first time in recent Norwegian history. With all this,
the economic situation again improved during the years after; if Norway continued to face serious problems with regard to its more distant
future, the immediate prospects were better than those of almost all
other European countries.

The other Scandinavian success story at least up to 1991 has
been that of Finland, which in many respects is more surprising, since
there was no sudden major windfall as in the case of Norway's oil.
Finland had most often been the poorest of the Scandinavian countries; its political system was unstable, with eight parties represented
in Parliament and more contesting the elections. The average duration
of a Finnish government after 1945 had been little more than a year.
Furthermore, there was for many years strong indirect pressure on
the part of the Soviet Union: a Finnish president or prime minister
could not be elected unless he had been vetted by the Kremlin. Thus
the old leadership of the Social Democrats was debarred for many
years after 1945 from playing an important role in Finnish politics,
and when Harri Holkeri became prime minister in 1987, it was the
first time that the Soviets had accepted a member of the Conservative
Party in this position. There have been few significant changes in the
internal political balance except the split (between Eurocommunists
and Stalinists) and decline of the communists, who up to the 1970s
were a significant factor in Finnish politics, with 20 percent or more
of the total. In the 1980s their share decreased to less than 10 percent,
and their influence in Finnish policy declined accordingly.

During the 1960s and 1970s the issue of Finlandization was a
matter of some agitation, both inside Finland and abroad. "Finlandization" was a synonym for "self-censorship." Though officially Fin-

land was a neutral country, it was tacitly understood that there was a special Soviet-Finnish relationship, and the Finnish leadership did everything in its power not to irritate the Russians and in some respects even to anticipate their wishes. Given Finland's size and geographical location, such a policy could be justified: Finland had to be silent, while other, more distant nations could speak up without fear.

With all this, Finland had, of course, infinitely more freedom than even Poland or Hungary. What irritated many Westerners—and also some thoughtful Finns—was the denial on the part of some Finnish leaders that Finlandization existed, and the allegation that it was an invention on the part of ignorant or malevolent foreigners. It emerged in later years that Finlandization had in fact gone even further than suspected. Thus leading politicians of the Center Party had conspired with the Soviets in 1982 to prevent the election of the Social Democrat Mauno Koivisto as president of the country. But by that time Finlandization was on the decline; Koivisto was elected, and re-elected four years later. Not all Finnish leaders had shared the conviction that Finlandization was vital for the existence of the country; the best-known proponent of this line was Urho Kekkonen, and there were also some Social Democratic leaders who went well beyond what was necessary to appease the Russians. But Kekkonen died in 1981, and during the 1980s relations between the two countries became more normal, largely, no doubt, because of the Soviet preoccupation with other, more urgent political issues. At the same time there has been a substantial decline in Soviet-Finnish trade.

Most Finnish governments in recent years have been based on a coalition between Social Democrats and Conservatives. Economic growth was substantial throughout the 1970s and 1980s, foreign investment in Finland increased, and there was hardly any unemployment. On the debit side, growth was unbalanced; imports grew more quickly than exports, which was at least in part the consequence of the declining competiveness of Finnish industry.

Lastly, Sweden. The country has been ruled for more than forty years by Social Democrats, who attracted fairly consistently 40–45 percent of the electorate. Between 1976 and 1982 the nonsocialist parties formed a coalition government, but the socialists returned to power in 1982. Since they had no absolute majority, they had to rely on support by the communists (5 percent) and/or the Ecologists, who also received 5 percent in the last elections.

The Swedish model of a welfare state ("from cradle to grave") has been widely admired all over the world, but though Sweden's social services are indeed admirable, the country has found it increasingly difficult to afford them. Some of the traditional industries, such as steel and shipbuilding, have collapsed. Swedish competitiveness has declined, despite a 16-percent devaluation of the krona in 1986. At the same time economic growth has been modest (1.9 percent in the 1980s) and wage increases have been rapid and substantial. Strikes have become far more frequent, and labor morale is low, with growing absenteeism, especially among younger workers. The people have become accustomed to believing that the state will take care of all their needs, and Stockholm has probably the highest density of Porsches in the world, but the savings rate is among the lowest, and productivity is declining. The shortages in services and housing have increased; rent control makes it unprofitable to build new houses, and the state is no longer in a position to maintain day-care centers for about one-third of the children in need of it. The Swedish model of social justice has gone too far in the direction of egalitarianism. Although Sweden has virtually liquidated unemployment, this, in turn, has triggered widespread strikes affecting schools, banks, and local government.

Prime Minister Olof Palme was assassinated in 1986 in mysterious circumstances; his successor, Ingvar Carlsson, introduced in 1990 both a wage-and-price freeze and a two-year ban on strikes, which was widely resented as a violation of the citizens' basic rights. Sweden remains one of the world's richest countries on a per-capita basis, but Swedish society is no longer an undisputed model for the rest of the world. The problems that have appeared over the last decade will not be solved easily and quickly.

More than fifty years of Social Democratic rule came to an end as the result of the elections of September 1991. But it was also the end of Swedish consensus politics. A majority of Swedes were dissatisfied with the kind of state and society that had emerged over the decades. But they could not agree on alternative models, and since the opposition was deeply split, a long period of disunity and political struggle seemed in the offing.

PART SIX

THE END OF THE OF THE POSTWAR ERA:
The Soviet Union and Eastern Europe

THE SOVIET UNION UNDER BREZHNEV AND GORBACHEV: DECLINE AND REFORM

Leonid Brezhnev had been one of the conspirators who engineered the overthrow of Khrushchev in 1964. No one had thought of him as an obvious candidate for the highest position in party and state; nevertheless, he soon emerged as the supreme leader. He had fewer enemies than the others, and he was not thought to be of the stuff stern dictators are made of. Those who elected him thought of him as an interim appointment, yet such were his tactical skill and his staying power that he remained in office up to the day of his death, more than eighteen years later, despite a long decline in his mental and physical faculties.

He had belonged to the Central Committee and even to the Politburo (as an alternate member) under Stalin, having earned his spurs in the Ukraine and Moldavia. He was not an Old Bolshevik in the Spartan mold, or a fanatical ideologist, but an extrovert and a firm believer in the live-and-let-live principle, especially with regard to the *nomenklatura*, the party leadership and state bureaucracy. In many respects he personified better than anyone else the qualities expected in a communist leader of the post-Stalin era. He was an inveterate optimist, and as he grew older he preferred not to be bothered with unpleasant facts. His device was "no experimentation," and he abolished some of the more extravagant or ludicrous reforms that had been carried out under Khrushchev. He also firmly believed in the "stability of the cadres"; leading communists were replaced only in cases of gross disloyalty and incompetence.

Such an approach was bound to endear him to the official class: the fact that a district party secretary or the head of a big factory

showed only mediocre capacity or was corrupt was not in itself enough
to bring about his demotion. Brezhnev reasoned, perhaps not without
justification, that one never knew whether a change might not be for
the worse. As in China, the turnover in the party leadership was small
and a gerontocracy gradually emerged; by the 1970s the average age
of members of the Central Committee was sixty-three, and in the
Politburo eventually considerably higher.

Brezhnev belonged to the generation that had lived through the
forced industrialization of the 1930s, the collectivization of agriculture and the mass purges, the war, and the difficult years of reconstruction. Surely he, and those around him, deserved the good things
in life as conditions became easier in the 1960s and 1970s. The secretary general of the CPSU collected expensive cars—a Rolls-Royce,
a Mercedes, a Cadillac—but he also liked to see others enjoy themselves. He accepted an unprecedented number of Lenin orders, enjoying a Brezhnev cult in the course of which he became *post factum*
even a great military leader. However, in contrast to Stalin, no one
took him very seriously. He made himself head of state as well as
marshal of the Soviet Union. He was a vain man but not an egoist;
the *nomenklatura* had never had it so good.

Under his regime, the Brezhnev doctrine (never to give up territory that had been conquered) became state dogma; Soviet troops
invaded Czechoslovakia and Afghanistan. But the heyday of détente
also occurred in his reign. All in all, it was a period of unprecedented
calm and, if one believed the official statistics, also a time of substantial, steady growth. According to these pronouncements, enormous progress was achieved in virtually every field. In Krasnoyarsk,
the biggest electricity plant was built and the biggest gas pipeline was
constructed, as was BAM, the Baikal-Amur railway line, three thousand kilometers long, the "construction of the century." Thousands
of new factories were completed during the 1970s; the GNP allegedly
grew by 63 percent, productivity in industry by 56 percent. The Tyumen oil and natural-gas fields were developed, the output of commodities of mass consumption almost doubled, and medical and
educational services improved.

A new, more democratic constitution was adopted in 1977;
according to official reports, at least 140 million people had actively
participated in the debates preceding it. The official media claimed it
was an exciting period of heroic work, of growing communist con-

sciousness, of the steady progress of Soviet political, economic, and military power. At last "developed socialism" had dawned, and even foreign observers gave the Brezhnev regime excellent marks—at least up to the late 1970s.

True, from inside the country the state of affairs appeared much less rosy; rates of growth and productivity were steadily declining. Kosygin, the second man in the Politburo and also prime minister, pressed for economic reform, aiming at decentralization, greater incentives, tying wages to output and prices to demand. But Kosygin was a sourpuss and probably (as Brezhnev saw it) exaggerated the gravity of the situation. Kosygin's initiative was quietly sabotaged by the bureaucracy, a fact that seems not to have caused Brezhnev any sleepless nights.

The party, the army, and the KGB kept and strengthened their positions as pillars of the regime. The lot of the lower echelons of the party and state bureaucracy also improved. New orders and awards were established, such as the Order of October, of Friendship of the Peoples, of Workers' Glory. Brezhnev helped himself to as many of them as feasible, and in the end he was a hero of the Soviet Union four times over, not to mention the Lenin Prize for Literature for his autobiography, a work of monumental insignificance, which, needless to say, had not been written by him.

But the masses also benefited to a modest extent. Virtually every family received a television set and a refrigerator. There was some bread and a lot of circuses: the celebration of the fiftieth anniversary of the October Revolution (1967), Lenin's hundredth birthday (1970), and, above all, the Moscow Olympic Games (1980). Some dissidents made unpleasant noises, and a growing number of writers and artists, such as Alexander Solzhenitsyn, were exiled or sent to a prison camp. Stalin and most of his lackeys, such as Voroshilov, were partly rehabilitated; shortly before his death Molotov, Stalin's shadow, was readmitted to the Communist Party. The cultural policy of the regime was markedly less liberal than that of Khrushchev, who had not been a paragon of cultural freedom either. But not that many people cared about the fate of the editorial board of *Novy Mir* or of academician Sakharov. That 107 million Russians were rehoused during the seventies was a matter of greater interest.

Skeptical and even downright pessimistic views became more frequent, both inside the Soviet Union and among Western observers, toward the end of the Brezhnev era. The loss of vigor and direction on the part of the Soviet leadership was no longer a secret and became a cause of concern to even the strongest sympathizers with the regime.

From the revelations during the age of glasnost it became known that between 1979 and 1982 the economy virtually stood still or even declined, that life expectancy decreased and infant mortality rose, that alcohol sales tripled, that the agricultural policy was an unmitigated disaster, that working conditions became worse and lines longer, that the quality of goods produced was often abysmal. Neither the tenth nor the eleventh five-year plan (1976–84) was fulfilled, and the standard of living of most strata of the population actually deteriorated. But the worst was not the stagnation in output and productivity or the failure of living standards to improve. It was the loss of morale among people, the loss of interest in work, the corruption and abuse of power among officials.

By the late 1970s the feeling was gaining ground that the system was failing, that there was something radically wrong with it, and that a further deterioration seemed inevitable. As one outside observer put it at the time: "The new Soviet man has turned pessimist."

What caused this change of mood in the Soviet Union, and when exactly did it occur? According to one expert (Timothy Colton) there was still a feeling of euphoria when Brezhnev's seventieth birthday was celebrated in 1976, a feeling that great things had been achieved and that yet greater achievements were around the corner. Other observers had detected an undertone of deep pessimism well before 1976, and the works of the village writers—such as Abramov, Shukshin, Rasputin, and Belov, to name but a few—were certainly anything but hopeful about the state of the country. The crop failure of 1975 should have been a last warning sign; a close observer noted that middle-class pessimism was, in fact, palpably felt even before the agricultural disaster. The working class, by and large, had never quite shared the optimism of the middle class, because most of its members had never benefited from the privileges and rewards of those included in Stalin's "big deal."

Economic dissatisfaction certainly played an important role in the growth of pessimism. But it was of even greater significance that the erstwhile high expectations for a better future were not fulfilled. It had been promised under Khrushchev that in the very near future Soviet society would catch up with and overtake the West. As long as Soviet society was virtually sealed off from outside information, Soviet citizens were not in a position to compare their own lot with the situation in the developed Western countries or Japan. But gradually information percolated which persuaded Soviet citizens that, far from catching up, their system was falling behind—and this at a time when consumerism, the possession of material goods for which the term *veshism* was coined, had become a central concern of Soviet society.

Other reasons for the growing pessimism had little or nothing to do with the economic situation. Communism had envisaged not just a tremendous growth in industrial and agricultural output; it had promised the emergence of a new type of *Homo sovieticus*. A new man and woman had indeed emerged, but there was little enthusiasm about the result.

The agonizing question "What has become of us?" was asked by Vasili Shukshin, one of the most gifted of the younger writers (and also a producer and an actor), and it was echoed through the Soviet Union. There was the general feeling that not only had the quality of life deteriorated but also the relationship between human beings. Elementary solidarity seemed on the way out, as did compassion. People appeared no longer to care about one another. All that mattered was money and connections with the right people. Culturally, the 1970s were a desert.

Despite their advanced age and their isolation from the people, Brezhnev and his colleagues were not entirely unaware of the growing malaise facing the country over the incompetence of the central planners, the shortages of metal and fuel, the disasters in agriculture, the do-nothing attitude of officials in high places and low who never fulfilled plans, falsified statistics, and merely paid lip service to instructions from above. In two speeches in 1978 and 1979 Brezhnev cajoled and threatened the bureaucracy, and, as usual, everyone agreed and promised to mend his ways. Again, as customary, nothing happened.

Nepotism and corruption continued to spread; the local party secretaries ruled the country like nineteenth-century viceroys, and so did the leaders in the Central Asian and Caucasian republics. When Brezhnev or other leading members of the Politburo came for a visit, there would be a royal welcome with red carpets, impressive ceremonies, and many presents. Tremendous achievements in all fields would be reported, many of them pure fantasy or grossly exaggerated. Mafia-like organizations spread which, in cooperation with the local administrations, more or less officially collected protection money.

Many of these shortcomings might have been accepted had there been the feeling that the leadership was still in command, that the members of the Politburo were men of vigor as well as vision and a sense of direction. But there was no evidence of either vigor or wisdom; "developed socialism," the official definition of the late Brezhnev era, became a synonym for senility on top and apathy among the masses. The public appearances of the leaders became less and less frequent, their speeches shorter and more tired. It was embarrassing to watch tottering old men being helped to their seats on state occasions. For years the feeling was spreading that something ought to be done to rejuvenate and invigorate the leadership. But the impatient younger people were not in a position to do so. The system had developed in such a way that nothing could be done until finally nature took its course: Kosygin died in 1980; Mikhail Suslov, the chief ideologist, in January 1982; and Brezhnev in November of that year. He was succeeded by Yuri Andropov, who had headed the KGB for fifteen years.

Andropov looked like a professional man—a lawyer, perhaps, or a physician—going on in years, dignified, and slightly world-weary. He had acquired, for reasons that are not entirely clear, the reputation of an intellectual and a closet liberal, more outside the Soviet Union than in Russia. He was reasonably well educated, certainly in comparison with most of his colleagues in the Politburo. However, one would look in vain in his speeches and articles for interesting new ideas or depth of analysis. Perhaps he had these qualities, but if so, he knew well how to hide them. The characteristics that made his rise to high office possible were those of a seasoned apparatchik and a loyal administrator rather than an original thinker and a creative innovator. During the last two years of Brezhnev's life a number of scandals occurred affecting members of his family. There is reason to assume that the KGB, then under Andropov, helped to make these scandals known, so as to undermine the position of the general secretary and his supporters. When Andropov, in his eulogy for Brezhnev on Red Square, talked about the heavy loss to the party—nay, to all mankind—of the glorious son of the fatherland, the outstanding leader of the Communist Party and the Soviet state, there was little conviction behind it.

Like the other leaders of the party, Andropov lived sheltered from the harsh realities of Soviet life. Neither he nor his wife had to queue in front of shops, nor was he dependent on the care provided by the Soviet health services for ordinary mortals. But, thanks to his job, he was in a unique position to know the real state of the Union, not the one reported in speeches on state occasions or in the columns of *Pravda*. Over the years the KGB had supplied him with a steady stream of information, not only about the White House and American military preparations but about growing apathy, cynicism, and corruption nearer home. It was Andropov's tragedy that he was probably better aware than anyone else in the Soviet Union that the situation was going from bad to worse, but that, because of his orthodox party training and mental makeup, he was unable to envisage truly radical change.

When he came to power, he was an elderly man in indifferent health. During the fourteen months he directed affairs of state, no change for the better could be registered in domestic affairs, and in foreign policy there was a marked deterioration in the situation. Soviet foreign-policy makers showed no initiative; there were only truculent gestures which led to Soviet self-isolation.

Andropov tried to consolidate his position by ousting some of the old Brezhnevites and bringing in his own people. But those he picked, such as Gaidar Aliev from Baku and Grigori Romanov from Leningrad, were less than outstanding choices, reflecting badly on his judgment. His speeches were cautious, almost timid, and though he freely admitted that in some respects the state of affairs was unsatisfactory, there was no sense of particular urgency. He did order systematic police raids in Moscow and elsewhere to harass black- and gray-marketeers and to find out whether officials were visiting dentists or bathhouses during working hours. But these practices were so unpopular that they had to be discontinued after a while.

Measures against corruption were tightened, and also against dissidents. He called for the intensification of ideological warfare and on a few occasions was shown on television mixing with Moscow factory workers. But he lacked the common touch; there was nothing natural, spontaneous, or easy in these appearances, and in no way did they enhance his stature. It was a period of quarter-measures, of decisions adopted but not carried out, and thus not essentially different from the late Brezhnev era.

True, he was the first Soviet leader to admit that he did not have the answers to all problems, and he made suggestions that, though not novel in any way, were sensible and were later picked up by Gorbachev, specifically the need for a new system of management and planning. He even hinted occasionally that it might be desirable to take the public more into the confidence of the party. In his last speech, addressing the Central Committee in June 1983, a word that was later to figure so often was first mentioned—"glasnost."

Ill for a long time, Andropov died on February 9, 1984, and was succeeded by Konstantin Chernenko. A native of Siberia, he had met Brezhnev in 1950 and attached himself to this rising star, becoming his confidant and *chef de cabinet*. Chernenko was a singularly unfortunate choice, quite apart from the fact that the new leader was unknown in the country. After a few appearances in public when the cruel TV cameras and microphones focused on him, the embarrassment became acute. Here was another Soviet leader who had no *gravitas*, exuded no charisma, stumbled through his speeches, showed no signs of dynamism and creativity, who seemed only half alive, a figurehead rather than a forceful leader.

He was, in brief, a nonentity, a typical middle-echelon apparatchik who in his prime would probably have acquitted himself as a competent organization man. But Chernenko's (and Russia's) misfortune was that he came to power when he was long past his prime, beset by various maladies, and when, on the other hand, there was growing disenchantment and impatience among the Soviet people. Within a few years they had watched three leaders go through a process of physical and intellectual decline, and they craved a leader strong and intelligent enough to tackle at long last the growing problems facing the country.

Who had been responsible for Chernenko's election in the first place? He was a stopgap candidate; one of the younger members of the Politburo would have been a more obvious choice. But the Politburo was divided between the old Brezhnevites and the followers of the late Andropov, and the younger members were also at loggerheads. Chernenko personified the maintenance of the *status quo,* and for this reason he had the support of the Brezhnevites, afraid of losing their jobs. Furthermore, many bureaucrats feared the inevitable shakeup that was bound to follow the appointment of a new and more vigorous leader. The underworld was also relieved, because the harassment by the security organs ceased.

There were few personal or political changes under Chernenko except for the ouster or demotion of some Andropov appointees. On his seventy-fourth birthday Chernenko got his fourth Order of Lenin. The Russian nationalists who had been bothered by Andropov's Leninism also breathed more freely, because they believed that Chernenko, a native of Siberia, was at heart one of them. It is impossible to say whether this was a correct assumption, for during much of the year when he was in office Chernenko was not able to carry out his functions, resting in the Crimea or hospitalized near Moscow.

There was the pretense that he was running the country, and in September he made, in fact, several public appearances, addressing the Soviet Writers' Union, advising them to stay closer to the people and to carry out the instructions of the party.

For much of this time Gorbachev, the youngest member of the Politburo, presided over the meetings of the leading party and state organs, and on occasion he was even referred to as "our second general secretary," an office that did not constitutionally exist. Gorbachev enjoyed the support of the main kingmakers: Gromyko, the veteran foreign policy maker, and Ustinov, who had for many years presided over the mighty defense industries. But Ustinov, another septuagenarian, died in December 1984, and the Romanov-Grishin coalition in the Politburo tried hard to block Gorbachev's promotion.

Following a last tug-of-war, Gorbachev emerged as the most likely successor in the weeks before Chernenko's death in March 1985. He was elected by a narrow margin and gave the usual eulogy addressing the Central Committee, praising his predecessor as an outstanding leader of party and state. But it was a very short eulogy, two or three minutes only; the rest of the speech concentrated on the main issues confronting the party—perestroika, a decisive turn in the economy, *uskorenie* (acceleration), democratization, and glasnost, the concept that was to play a central role in Soviet policies during the years to come.

Mikhail Sergeevich Gorbachev was born in 1931 in Privolnoe, a village near Stavropol in the North Caucasus, a third-generation communist. Following graduation from a local school, he worked for a while as a combine-harvester operator, and at an astonishingly young age he received the Order of the Red Banner for services in agriculture. At nineteen he went to Moscow to study law; there he met Raisa, his future wife.

A lucky star was shining over his career. First he served as secretary of the local communist youth organization, later as district secretary for propaganda, eventually as first secretary in one of the most important agricultural regions of the country. In 1978 he became a secretary of the Central Committee, which meant his transfer to Moscow. In 1979 he was made a candidate member of the Politburo, and just one year later a full member. As the most junior member, he was given the least popular task, agriculture, and this at a time when Soviet agriculture was in a state of permanent crisis despite the enormous investments that had been made. An assignment of this kind was high-risk, almost an invitation to disaster, and it is a sign of Gorbachev's adroitness and luck to have survived politically. Luck—because he was saved by the death of Brezhnev, who, not without reason, became the scapegoat for the ill-fated food program of the 1970s. Furthermore, the harvest of 1983 was better than that of previous years, and as new members joined the Politburo, Gorbachev could free himself from the burdensome appointment. He began to travel abroad and made an excellent impression on his Western interlocutors.

Gorbachev's first appearances in 1985 did not yet herald the advent of important changes. In his speeches he focused on the great Soviet achievements, and he did not even use the term "reform," let alone "radical reform," prior to the Twenty-seventh Party Congress, in February 1986. The new general secretary was moving with great care; only after his main adversaries had been removed from the Politburo did he feel free to stress that perestroika was indeed tantamount to radical change. There was certainly a change in Gorbachev's thinking during the second half of 1986, and even more so during the two following years. Perhaps he realized only gradually the full extent of the crisis facing the Soviet Union. And he also understood that, unless he got the economy moving again, economic decline would affect all aspects of Soviet life: the shortages would become even more critical, and the quality of life and the social services would deteriorate still further.

Certain measures could be taken with relative ease without

touching the roots of the system, such as imposing stricter labor discipline and threatening the bureaucrats with loss of jobs or privileges (the "new-broom effect"). But experience had shown that these measures worked only for a limited time, acting as a minor palliative. Real change could be effected only by dismantling the old system, which no longer worked—that is to say, scrapping the old, cumbersome planning apparatus, giving much freer rein to private initiative; in brief, letting the market mechanism take over.

Most economists agreed on the measures that had to be taken, even though not on the speed with which they should be introduced. But most party secretaries told Gorbachev that the results would be so painful during the interim period (unemployment and the rise in prices following the abolition of state subsidies) that radical reforms were politically unacceptable, except perhaps with great caution and over a longish period. Only in 1990, after long and bitter debates, were decisions taken to do away at some future date with most of the state subsidies for some basic commodities.

These decisions did not go far enough, as far as the radicals were concerned; they argued that only decisive measures could forestall a disaster. But they went too far for the taste of the conservatives, who argued all along that such changes would enrich a thin layer of exploiters and speculators, whereas the lot of the broad masses of people would worsen. They pointed to the fact that by 1990 the quality of some goods had greatly improved but the prices on the open market were such that only a small part of the population could afford them.

During the first five years there was a great deal of talk about perestroika; some 140,000 cooperatives were in existence by 1989, but mainly in the fields of trade, consumer goods and services; the situation in industry and agriculture was not substantially affected. On the contrary, partial liberalization tended to aggravate the distortions in the economy, thus adding to popular discontent. Most conservatives and virtually all radicals agreed that the old *kolkhoz*-and-state-farm system had failed, and that Soviet farmers should be able to rent land and work it without the traditional, strict state-control system. But few farmers made use of the new opportunities. They were not certain whether the new arrangements would last, or whether they would again be abolished as they had at the end of the NEP (the New Economic Policy) in the late 1920s, when agriculture had been collectivized. Furthermore, Soviet farmers lacked capital and essential equipment, and the local bureaucracy was far from helpful in creating conditions in which the new-style farms stood a real chance to succeed.

Reform was more striking in the political field, and above all in Soviet culture, in the widest sense of the term. The main milestones in the process were the Nineteenth Party Conference in June–July 1988 and, more important, the elections to the Congress of People's Deputies and its first sessions (March–June 1989). The 1990 abolition of paragraph six in the Soviet constitution should also be mentioned in this context; it had given official sanction to the monopoly of Communist Party rule in Soviet political life. The party conference passed a resolution according to which the rule of law would be anchored in the constitution and become the norm of life; the legal rights of the individual would be guaranteed and protected. This involved major changes in the legislative system. The rubber-stamp Supreme Soviet, which had met in the past on rare occasions only to acclaim the leadership and to confirm their policy, changed out of recognition.

It was replaced by a Congress of People's Deputies of 2,250 members; for the first time in many decades, more than one candidate was competing for seats in the elections. The first elections were far from free by accepted democratic standards, since there were no political parties and many candidates were appointed by the Communist Party and its satellite organization; in fact, 88 percent of those elected were members of the Communist Party. But it was also true that many candidates contesting the elections (and winning seats) were far from desirable from the Communist Party point of view. Thus, in the country's largest electoral district (Moscow), Boris Eltsin celebrated a runaway victory, even though he had been removed the year before from his position as the capital's first party secretary. He went on to be elected chairman of the Supreme Soviet of the Russian Republic (RSFSR). Other prominent delegates included Andrei Sakharov, Nobel Prize winner and the most prominent Soviet human-rights advocate. His death in December 1989 was a great loss to the cause of reform and to the country. He had been released by Gorbachev from his Gorky exile in 1986; together with other outspoken critics of the regime, he established a parliamentary faction, the Interregional Group. That there was a strong trend toward the opposition appeared even more clearly in the local elections of 1990, when radical reformers carried cities such as Moscow, Leningrad, and Sverdlovsk. Since the Congress of People's Deputies was too large to cope with day-to-day activities, a smaller body, the new Supreme Soviet, with some 450 members, assumed this function.

In September 1988 Gorbachev was elected president of the Soviet Union by the Parliament, not in direct elections. The next year, the President's Council came into being, a relatively small group of advisers, including economists and writers, whose exact function was not entirely clear, except that some of the power of both Politburo and Council of Ministers was diverted to this new body.

There were considerable changes in the constitution of the supreme party organs. Thus in early 1989 some ninety-eight members and candidate members of the Central Committee collectively resigned for reasons of age. However, even after these changes Gorbachev could not count on a reform-minded majority in the Central Committee, and still less in the Politburo, where his only firm allies were Eduard Shevardnadze, the foreign minister, and Alexander Yakovlev, the exponent of the radical trend in the leadership and therefore the butt of many attacks by conservatives and neo-Stalinists.

The conservatives, headed initially by Egor Ligachev, were opposed to what they regarded as too quick and drastic a retreat from Leninist norms. They were not in principle opposed to economic reform, but they favored gradualism, and they believed that glasnost had gone too far: the country, as they saw it, was bound to become ungovernable. The opposition to the glasnost course was even more pronounced further down in the party leadership. It sounds its classic expression in a famous open letter by a Leningrad teacher, Nina Andreeva ("I cannot sacrifice principles"—March 1988). The principles that Mrs. Andreeva did not want to sacrifice were, broadly speaking, Stalinism suitably adjusted to present-day conditions, with a strong admixture of xenophobia, anti-Westernism, and anti-Semitism. She strongly attacked the de-Stalinization campaign, which had gathered unprecedented momentum, and charged those responsible for it with betrayal and leading the country to ruin. This was an open declaration of war against glasnost, perestroika, and the reform policy in general, and it was rebutted in the media. Yet Mrs. Andreeva's views were shared, at least to some extent, by sections of the population, more in some regions of the country than in others.

The opponents of the reform course were strange bedfellows: some were old-style Russian nationalists, hankering back to the good old days before 1917. Others, on the contrary, were unregenerated Stalinists, who sincerely believed that the much-maligned "father of the peoples" had been, in fact, the greatest leader in Soviet history, a farsighted patriot. His mistakes, if any, had been insignificant compared with his momentous achievements. These two segments of the opposition had not initially much in common, but something akin to an ideological confluence took place: The Stalinists gradually dropped their Leninist and internationalist doctrines and largely converted to Russian nationalism. The conservatives, at the same time, embraced populist, quasi-egalitarian views on socioeconomic issues. What held them together in the final analysis was the perception of a common enemy—the reform movement, which, as they saw it, wanted to turn the Soviet Union into a Western-style, liberal-democratic society, jettisoning traditional Russian values in the process, introducing Western mass culture, and thus bringing about the social and moral as well as the political ruin of Great Russia.

The re-emergence of a "Russian party" under glasnost should not have come as a surprise. The victory of Marxism in 1917 had been considered at one time as the final triumph of Westernism in the struggle for the Russian soul. But as Marxism-Leninism was tried and found wanting, "Westernism" became the main culprit, and internationalism gave way to a new wave of Russian patriotism. Seen in the context of seventy years of Soviet history, the right-wing reaction against the "left-wing excesses" of the 1920s and 1930s was almost inevitable. The backlash tended to become extreme with the emergence of groups such as Pamyat ("Memory"), which had an ideology rooted in the Black Hundred gangs of the late tsarist period and enriched by such Nazi doctrines as the belief in the omnipotent conspiracies and the all-pervasive, satanic activities of *zhidomasonstvo*—Jews and Freemasons.

This was the ugly face of glasnost, and it found supporters not only among the most backward sections of the population but also among the intelligentsia. However, the majority of the intellectuals, and a great many other people in addition, were attracted by the new spirit of freedom ushered in by the reform movement. It is not at all certain that Gorbachev and his advisers had aimed from the beginning at a cultural revolution; his early speeches certainly did not point in this direction. But gradually the belief seems to have gained ground among the leading reformers that changes in society and the economy would not be forthcoming unless there were basic changes in society, greater honesty, and more freedom of thought and expression.

This meant, above all, confronting the Soviet past, not just the Brezhnevite period of stagnation (*zastoi*) but *a fortiori* Stalinism and eventually even Lenin and his policies. In 1986 Gorbachev still argued that the very term "Stalinism" was an invention of "our enemies"— i.e., anti-Soviet circles. Merely a year later the anti-Stalin campaign was in full swing. Many books that had been suppressed for a long time were published, and though the revelations were less than sensational for Western observers of the Soviet scene, the effect was shattering inside the Soviet Union.

Ultimately, this turned into self-criticism: Obviously, the enormous crimes had not been committed by a single individual. Stalin had prevailed in the struggle for power because his approach and mentality had greatly appealed to a large number of his subjects. The "cult" had been ridiculous, but the majority had sincerely believed in not only the wisdom but also the goodness of J. V. Stalin. He had found millions of all-too-willing helpers. To explain the sources of this phenomenon one had to go back well beyond Stalin, to the weakness of the democratic tradition in Russian history on the one hand, and the antidemocratic character of the October Revolution and of Leninism on the other. Such confrontation with the past was very painful for many Russian nationalists and Leninists, who claimed either that Stalinism had not been so bad after all, or, alternatively, that it was a perversion of Leninism and that, in any case, it had been part of a far wider phenomenon of the 1930s, "from Madrid to Shanghai," in no way specifically Russian, but imported from abroad and executed largely by aliens.

Glasnost meant confronting the past, but it was even more crucial to come to terms with the present state of affairs. This was impossible without honestly analyzing the many failures in the economy and social life. For the first time in many decades, articles appeared and speeches were made admitting the whole extent of failures in economic performance. This meant telling the truth about crime (including the existence of organized crime on a large scale), of poverty, of the unsatisfactory state of the health service (including a decline in life expectancy), of alcoholism, the drug scene, and prostitution.

All other countries faced similar problems, but only in the Soviet Union had their presence been denied earlier on, and the revelations were therefore all the more shattering. The quality of life in the Soviet Union was reassessed and found greatly wanting, not just with regard to economic factors but, far more important, concerning the low level of manners and morality. Where did all the frustration, the spite and the anger among the people come from? Once upon a time kindness, generosity, the capacity for friendship had been among the outstanding characteristics of the Russian people. Why had these traits become so rare? Why had people become so hard, distrustful, and unfeeling? Was it just the harsh living conditions, the unending standing in line, generating anger and envy, or did the political system breed simulation and suspicion? But living conditions had been even worse for most people in the last century. There was a growing feeling that somehow, sometime, Russian history had taken a wrong turn and that, as a result, many of the old virtues had disappeared.

Up to 1987 the way the Soviet Union had solved its national problems had been advertised as a model for all mankind. The outward picture was one of cooperation and harmony, even though experts had long suspected that under the surface there was not much love lost between the nations of the Soviet Union, and even less between them and the dominant nation, the Russians. The ferment had existed before but, for a variety of reasons, only seldom manifested itself openly. Police repression was one of these reasons; the toleration of corruption as an integral way of life, particularly in Central Asia, another. There were yet other causes, such as the demographic upsurge in Central Asia and the infectious rise of nationalist-religious trends in the Middle East.

Furthermore, officially sanctioned Russian nationalism was increasingly bound to provoke similar trends in the non-Russian republics. Russian pressures for cultural assimilation collided with a trend toward national assertion among virtually all major and many minor non-Russian ethnic groups. The economic situation, especially in Central Asia, was bad, and did not improve; many years of monoculture had exhausted the soil and the water resources. Unemployment, open and hidden, had become a constant feature.

All in all, it appeared that the impact of decades of communist indoctrination had been far more superficial than even the skeptics had assumed. The basic structure of society had not changed that much since the prerevolutionary days; belonging to a clan was of far greater significance than membership in the party. Religious customs and quasi-religious traditions were unbroken, and a new nationalism was rearing its head.

The first indication that all was not well appeared following the Alma-Ata riots (December 1986). Subsequently the Nagorno-Karabakh crisis between Armenia and Azerbaidjan led to virtual civil war and to Soviet military intervention in Baku. In April 1989 Soviet army units opened fire on a mass demonstration in Tbilisi, the Georgian capital; in June of that year there were major clashes in Fergana, and, in 1990, also in other Central Asian cities, such as Osh. Though initially directed against a Turkish minority (the Meschetians), the Fergana massacres gradually turned against local Russians. A Russian mass exodus ensued from Central Asia as well as from Azerbaidjan.

In the meantime (throughout 1989), all three Baltic States had denounced the forcible, and hence illegal, incorporation of their countries into the Soviet Union under the Molotov-Ribbentrop pact. Their solemn declaration of independence from Moscow was, not surprisingly, rejected by the Kremlin, and led to countermeasures. In Lithuania there was a clear native majority (some 85 percent), but a great many Russians had migrated to Latvia after 1945, and there had always been a strong Russian ethnic presence in Estonia. Not all Russians in the Baltic countries opposed the separatist trends, but most of them did, which caused further complications, both in the internal affairs of these countries and in relations with Moscow.

Although the right of secession had always been guaranteed on a theoretical level in the Soviet constitution, it had been quite unthinkable that any republic would actually exercise this right. There was no question that, even in Gorbachev's liberal era, the central government would gladly accede to such demands. The Kremlin maintained that secession was not ruled out in principle, but only after at least two-thirds of the population had voted for it, and after a cooling-off period lasting several years.

No mention has been made of the many other national problems confronting the Soviet Union, such as the demands of the Ukrainian nationalists, the Russian-Germans, and the Tartars for the restoration of their national republics, which had been liquidated under Stalin during the Second World War. But in these territories (in the Volga region and the Crimea, respectively) newcomers had settled for decades. In the absence of any real prospect for a satisfactory solution, many Russian-Germans opted for leaving the Soviet Union, as did many Jews in view of the rise of anti-Semitism and the fear that they could not count on the help of the government.

As so many nationalities voiced complaints and reasserted their historical demands, it was only natural that the Russians, too, should appear among those claiming that they had been exploited all along, had earned no gratitude, and therefore wanted at long last to be masters in their own house. Their spokesmen demanded an end to the subventions annually paid to other republics; they wanted to have their own television, academy of science, Communist Party, trade unions, encyclopedia, and so on. Some of these complaints were justified, others not: it was next to impossible to figure out whether Russia had been exploited by the rest of the Union, or vice versa. In any case, many of the republics had been forcibly occupied by the Russians rather than joined them of their own free will.

Lenin had once called tsarist Russia "the prison of the peoples," and his definition was widely repeated as greater freedom prevailed throughout the Soviet Union. It was not always a fair statement of the state of affairs; in not a few instances, national hatred was not even primarily directed against the Russians, as in the case of Armenia and Azerbaidjan, Kirgizia and Uzbekistan. Without military intervention from the center, the door would have been opened to carnage on a massive scale. Nor is it feasible in the modern world for all nationalities to attain full sovereignty. It was ironic that so many Soviet republics should ask for their own currency at the very time that Western Europe was moving to a common currency. Some of the demands raised by the nationalists could not possibly be fulfilled, because justice to one group would have meant injustice to another. It was unrealistic to expect from the Soviet leadership Solomonic decisions satisfying all the claimants. But they could have considered a new order of national coexistence inside the Soviet Union, granting a larger degree of freedom to its components on a truly federal basis. Their failure to do so in good time was a tragic, possibly a fatal error of omission.

Soviet foreign policy underwent far-reaching and sometimes sudden changes during the Brezhnev era. The pendulum swung from the cordial atmosphere of the détente summits in the early 1970s to a climate of confrontation in the early 1980s. A substantial improvement in relations with the West occurred only as a result of the "New Thinking" under Gorbachev. Détente had produced not only climatic changes but also SALT I, as well as closer political and economic relations between the two blocs, with the Helsinki agreement on human rights as the last major achievement. However, even by 1974–75 it was clear that the great expectations that had been attached in the West to a rapprochement with the Soviet Union would not be fulfilled. There were manifold reasons. To a considerable extent, Western expectations had been quite unrealistic, based on the mistaken assumption that under Brezhnev there had been a radical change in Soviet outlook and intentions. Therefore, the realization that the Soviet Union continued to build up its armed forces with undiminished vigor came as a surprise and a shock, as did the fact that Soviet policies in the third world, culminating in the invasion of Afghanistan (1980), were offensive in character and could not possibly be explained with reference to legitimate Soviet defense interests.

Soviet-American relations deteriorated under President Carter; the emphasis on human rights caused offense in Moscow. At the same time the great expectations that had been attached by both sides to the expansion of trade were not fulfilled, not so much out of ill will as because of the incompatibility of the two systems and the economic weakness of the Soviet Union, and in view of the fact that the ruble was not convertible, an insurmountable hurdle on the road to closer economic relations.

By 1981 Soviet spokesmen had ceased to mention détente, except as a historical memory, and instead the brink-of-war theme appeared in Soviet propaganda. Even earlier, in 1976, President Ford had dissociated himself from the term "détente." Soviet attitudes toward the West became particularly hostile in the Reagan period. Partly it was the result of Reagan's rhetoric (communism as the "focus of evil in the modern world" and as a "bizarre chapter in human history"). But far more decisive was the military modernization which had been inaugurated by the Reagan administration. Between 1968 and 1977 Soviet military spending (in constant terms) had risen from $101 billion to $130 billion, whereas U.S. military expenditures fell from $130 billion to $96 billion. Under Reagan the trend was reversed; the Soviet Union had maneuvered itself into an arms race which it could not possibly afford at a time of a growing domestic crisis.

Facing an unyielding opponent in Washington, one should have

expected a determined Soviet effort to split the NATO alliance, trying
to prevent the deployment of missiles in Western Europe. However,
neither Soviet promises nor Soviet threats proved to be effective, and
the German Bundestag voted the deployment of the Euromissiles in
November 1983, as did other European countries. There was no
progress at the MBFR (Mutual Balanced Force Reduction) talks in
Vienna, no improvement in relations with China, and the Kremlin
continued to pour money into all kinds of third-world adventures
(with Cuba and East Germany as their main proxies), which gave
them few if any returns. The war in Afghanistan did not go well; in
brief, Soviet foreign policy during the stagnation period under Gromyko could show very little to its credit. Even relations with the
European communist parties became more distant during the age of
Eurocommunism; the camp was hopelessly split, and attempts to
restore unity were not undertaken any longer.

The only hope nursed in Moscow was that the Reagan administration would not last forever. However, the laws of biology applied
also in Moscow, and as it turned out, Reagan was still in office to
negotiate in 1986–88—with Brezhnev's and Andropov's successor—
far-reaching agreements to remove some of the major bones of contention between the two countries.

There had been signals indicating a Soviet wish to resume negotiations with the West even before Gorbachev's election. But they
were halfhearted, and it was only in 1987 that a dramatic change in
the general atmosphere did take place. In this respect as in others,
the Gorbachev administration showed readiness to reconsider many
of the basic tenets underlying Soviet foreign policy in the past. This
process of reconsideration, which became known under the name
"New Thinking," did not go quite so far as in domestic affairs: Soviet
national interests were re-examined and modified but not necessarily
given up. Still, it was an important new departure which made Gorbachev more popular in Western capitals than in his own country. It
was realized in Moscow that the era of negativism and the policy of
boycott had led the country into an impasse, that the Soviet Union
was in no danger of being attacked, and that, on the other hand, a
policy of conquests, direct or indirect, was no longer feasible. The
acceptance of these basic truths led to the Soviet exodus from Afghanistan and, more important yet, nonintervention in Eastern Europe
as the crisis broke in 1989. The Soviet leaders confirmed the principle

of "free choice" and nonaggression, even if it meant the emergence of noncommunist governments in Prague, Warsaw, Budapest, and East Berlin.

It is difficult to exaggerate the significance of this change in Soviet policy, which spelled the end of Stalin's postwar order in Central and Eastern Europe. At the same time efforts to normalize relations with China continued, and Soviet activities in the third world became much less ambitious and more realistic. But most Soviet efforts were directed toward closer collaboration with the United States and the building of a "common European home." There was no intention in the Kremlin to engage in unilateral disarmament, partly because the armed forces were still a powerful lobby but also because of the innate conviction of the Soviet leaders that they must not neglect the defense of their country. However, cuts were made and basic strategies reexamined: previously no one had dared to resist the demands of the army command as far as budgetary allocations and the distribution of resources were concerned.

No one outside the Kremlin could say for certain whether Soviet defense spending had been at the rate of 12–14 percent of the GNP, or twice as high, as others claimed. But there was general agreement that it had been much too high and that a backward economy could not afford an enormously expensive high-technology defense establishment. Even if the military command did not like it, most civilian leaders had been converted by 1990 to the idea that peaceful coexistence had become inevitable, that war could no longer be a rational means of policy, and that national security was not guaranteed by the size of the military arsenal. In brief, relations with the outside world were no longer dictated by ideological ambitions and paranoiac fears. Conflicts were likely to persist, but there was a good chance that they were about to become as normal as interstate relations in other parts of the world.

The important changes that took place in Soviet foreign policy created much goodwill and even enthusiasm in the West, and they were widely welcomed inside the Soviet Union. But for the great majority of Soviet citizens domestic problems figured far more prominently. As perestroika ran out of steam in 1990, the economic situation became even more critical, and no solution seemed in sight for the conflicting demands of the major peoples and nationalities constituting the Soviet Union. By autumn 1990, Gorbachev had thrown in his lot with the conservative elements, and his erstwhile liberal supporters such as Yakovlev and Shevardnadze had resigned or been forced out of the leadership. Very little remained of the initial reformist impetus which had made Gorbachev so popular both in his own country and in the West. The upbeat mood of the early days of glasnost vanished and was replaced by pessimistic predictions. Even those who believed they detected light at the end of the tunnel felt that salvation was not certain and, in any case, not near.

True, the cause of democratic reform in Russia received a fresh impetus as the result of the coup that failed in August 1991. It had been staged by leading figures from within the Communist Party, the army and the KGB. But a high price had to be paid. It was the end of Communism in the USSR and meant the virtual disintegration of the old Soviet Union. All republics and many nationalities were staking their claims for independence, and many of these demands included the seeds of future conflicts; the viability of the secessionist entities emerging from the chaos was often doubtful. The period of transition to a new, lasting order was likely to be troubled and prolonged.

STAGNATION IN
EASTERN EUROPE

S oon after the end of the war Stalin had said in conversation with Milovan Djilas, then a young Yugoslav communist leader, that upon the countries under the control of the victorious powers the social (and political) system of their masters would be imposed. The basic concept was not new; the principle *cujus regio, eius religio* had been underlying the peace treaties during the Reformation.

The first two postwar decades bore out Stalin's predictions. True, Finland was not compelled to become a "people's democracy," and Stalin did not militarily intervene when Yugoslavia chose its own road to communism. But within a decade the process of Sovietization of Eastern Europe and the Balkans was completed, and by the 1960s it appeared to most observers that this process was irreversible. The socioeconomic system that had emerged was less than a full success, and the sporadic rebellions in Eastern Europe showed that political support for the ruling communist parties was far from unanimous. Still, Soviet control over Eastern Europe seemed complete. It was codified in the Brezhnev doctrine (of limited sovereignty), which maintained that Moscow would not surrender any of the positions that had been gained as the result of the Second World War.

If, nevertheless, palpable differences began to evolve in political style and economic organization between the "popular democracies," these concessions were rooted not in Soviet weakness but, on the contrary, in the conviction that some more latitude could be granted, precisely because the Soviet position was strong and unassailable. The socioeconomic difficulties deepened and became endemic in the late 1970s, as they did in the Soviet Union. But even by 1985 no one would have dared to predict that the days of communist rule were numbered.

In retrospect, it can be argued that the battle for the hearts and minds of the peoples of Eastern Europe had in fact been lost as early as the 1950s. But at the time such a claim would have appeared quite outlandish, in view of the seemingly immensely powerful communist parties, with their millions of members and their elaborate apparatus of propaganda and repression, not to mention the presence of hundreds of thousands of Soviet soldiers. Only after 1985, with the dawn of the Gorbachev era in the Soviet Union, did the future of the East European communist regimes begin to appear insecure. But Gorbachev himself could not know at the time how far the changes triggered under his rule would ultimately go.

The rulers of the East European countries in the 1970s were members of one age cohort—Ceausescu, Edward Gierek, Honecker, Todor Zhivkov, Gustav Husák, and Kádár were all born between 1911 and 1918. With the exception of Gierek, they continued to be in power in the 1980s, when they all reached biblical age. The composition of the East European leadership thus closely resembled the Brezhnev regime and its immediate successors, which also consisted of septuagenarians. Elderly people, they tended to be out of touch not only with the younger generation but with the general mood of the country. This is not to say that younger leaders would have tackled the growing problems more successfully, but merely to note that those in power were not even aware of the problems and no attempt was made at serious reform. For if (as they thought) the state of affairs was more or less normal, why engage in dubious changes?

There were marked differences between the repressive style of leadership of the Czech communists or the Ceausescu family in Rumania and the mildly reformist rule of Kádár, who abhorred any "cult of the individual" and believed that all Hungarians who did not actively oppose his rule were at least potential allies. But even the more repressive regimes did not show an excess of cruelty as under Stalin—there were no trumped-up political trials, political enemies were not liquidated except perhaps in Bulgaria or Albania, and there were few severe prison sentences. In Poland (after 1976) and in Hungary dissident groups were allowed to develop even though their freedom of action was very limited; in East Germany opponents were frequently permitted to leave for the West. The East European leaders seem to have genuinely believed that their position was secure. If the economic growth rates were palpably decreasing from the late 1970s on, the full extent of the failure was kept from the leadership, because everyone faked production figures, so that in the end even the secret police was no longer in a position to know the true state of affairs. Only in Poland could the inability of the state to service the foreign loans and credits that had been taken during the 1970s not possibly be ignored. Poland's economic plight triggered the ten-year crisis that led to the collapse first of the Communist Party and ultimately of the military dictatorship.

But the leadership in the other East European countries could still comfort itself that their indebtedness was less, and if there were economic difficulties, the capitalist countries, too, were facing such problems at the time. Similar arguments were adduced with regard to insufficient collaboration between the communist countries. If economic and military cooperation was far from complete, one could always point to similar problems afflicting NATO, EEC, and other Western institutions.

The Brezhnev leadership had no intention of dropping its East European allies, even though the tangible gains accruing from the Soviet presence in Eastern Europe were less and less obvious. The Soviet Union certainly lost money in Eastern Europe, beginning with the energy crisis of the 1970s. The Soviets had to supply oil and other raw materials at prices lower than on the world market; the Comecon (CMEA) countries were paying back, more often than not, in industrial products of low quality. The Soviet leaders must have been aware in 1985 that neither Poles nor Hungarians nor Rumanians nor Yugoslavs were any more amiably disposed toward them than in 1945, and they could not even be certain of the loyalty of the Czechs or the Bulgarians.

This left the East Germans, who needed the Warsaw Pact more than the others, for without Soviet backing the very survival of the regime might have been in question. But there was not much love lost even between East Berlin and the Kremlin, in view of the conviction of many East Germans that their regime had been more effective in building communism than that of their senior partner; such feelings were bound to create resentment among the Soviets. There must have been at the very least the suspicion in Moscow that the population was far more drawn to Western Europe than to the East, whether because of the irresistible pull of the capitalist fleshpots or because of the feeling that, in contrast to the Russians, they were part of the European civilization by historical and cultural tradition as much as by choice.

The one major consideration that prevented a loosening of the ties between the Soviet Union and the East European countries was strategic-military. The East European countries served as a glacis, a buffer zone, at a time when political relations between the two blocs were tense and a military conflict could not be entirely ruled out, at least by the military planners. Once relations between the Soviet Union and the West were to improve, once it became clear that a military collision in Europe was not just unlikely but quite unthinkable, the case in favor of the Soviet–East European alliance was bound to become very weak indeed. A new leadership in Moscow would, of course, have preferred if the socialist structures in these countries had become so deeply rooted that they could survive without Soviet intervention. But if this was not the case after decades of great efforts, there was less and less willingness to launch periodic military invasions (as in Hungary and Czechoslovakia) to save the regimes.

POLAND

The chain of events that led to the overthrow of the communist regime in Poland in 1989 began almost twenty years earlier. The economic situation in the country under Gomułka had been steadily deteriorating in the 1960s, and the attempts by the regime to gain time by playing out various domestic political forces against one another (the seemingly satisfied workers against the rebellious intellectuals in 1968) proved to be ultimately futile. The hold of the government rested on the maintenance of low prices for staple foods. When this was no longer possible, the government's position crumbled. The announcement, a few weeks before Christmas 1970, that meat prices would be raised by 36 percent led to mass demonstrations and strikes. The killing of striking ("counterrevolutionary") workers only discredited the regime further.

In January 1971 Edward Gierek was appointed the new first secretary of the party; he took a conciliatory line vis-à-vis the workers and promised a new pragmatic policy, unencumbered by ideological fetters. Born of a Polish family in France, Gierek had been a member of the Politburo, albeit not a prominent one, for a number of years.

During the next four or five years the promises of the new leaders were borne out to a considerable extent. Gierek gained the support of the Catholic church through his policy of concessions; his domestic policy was less harsh than Gomułka's before him. Above all, he went all-out for economic growth—Polish industrial-growth rates were almost as high as the Japanese. Coal production reached two hundred million tons annually; shipbuilding, the electric and car industries, and agriculture made significant progress. However, this stormy quantitative growth was largely based on credits from abroad, which went into industries for whose products there was declining demand on the world markets. Thus huge steelworks were built at a time when all over the world steel capacities were being reduced. The food situation again became critical in 1976, following two bad harvests; grain and other staple foods had to be imported from abroad. When the government tried to increase food prices, it encountered stiff resistance and, mindful of the events of 1970, hastily retreated.

By 1976 the Gierek experiment had run out of steam; Poland, the tenth-strongest industrial nation in the world, was the first communist regime to be bankrupt, unable to pay its debtors. Inside Poland the domestic opposition gathered strength; the Catholic church called the leadership to defend the workers' interests; various trade-union and intellectual groups (such as KOR) emerged. Significantly, for the first time in Polish postwar history a coalition of oppositionist forces evolved, which, in 1980, gave birth to "Solidarity." A great psychological uplift was given to the opposition by the election in October 1978 of Karol Wojtyla as the new Pope (John Paul II). He visited his native country the following year and was given an unprecedented welcome.

Thus the stage was set for a new major confrontation between rulers and ruled, and in the end it mattered little that the Gierek regime tried to appease the workers whereas Gomułka had chosen brutal repression. Again it was the attempt of the government to increase meat prices that brought about an acute crisis, with the militant Gdańsk shipyards in the forefront of the struggle headed by Lech Wałesa, an electrician who was the leader of Solidarity. Strikes spread rapidly all over Poland; within a few months Solidarity, the alternative trade-union movement, had ten million members, which is to say that the majority of Poland's working population had joined it. The Gierek government negotiated with the strikers, and an agreement was reached according to which food supplies would be guaranteed, a five-day week introduced, and far-reaching political and economic reforms carried out. Gierek resigned soon after and was replaced by Stanisław Kania, a veteran apparatchik who tried hard but unsuccessfully to gain a minimum of popular support and confidence.

The next eighteen months were a period of near chaos. The agreement between the government and Solidarity (the "new social contract") remained largely a dead letter, partly because the economy could not afford it, but also because the bureaucracy sabotaged substantial reform. If the political system became more liberal and a hitherto unheard-of degree of freedom prevailed (including almost free elections to the Communist Party congress), this was not the result of a deliberate policy but the outcome of the increasing weakness of party and state. All along, the economic situation was deteriorating; the national income in 1982 was 25 percent lower than it had been in 1978—not a particularly good year.

It was clear that the uneasy coexistence between Solidarity and the Communist Party (by now subject to internal splits) could not continue for long. Soviet concern steadily mounted: the longer the Polish crisis lasted, the more threatening seemed the danger of infection. At one stage, toward the end of 1980, a Soviet invasion appears to have been considered, but was dismissed at the time. While negotiations continued for many months between the Communist Party and the increasingly bitter and frustrated Solidarity, General Wojciech Jaruzelski (who had taken over from Kania) was planning a coup. It took place on December 13, 1981, and with surprising ease a military dictatorship was established. Most opposition leaders were arrested, and Solidarity ceased to be a serious threat to the authorities. However, it soon emerged that the new government was in no way prepared to confront the basic problems that had faced Polish society since the 1960s. If Solidarity was virtually extinct, so was the Communist Party; many key positions in the administration were taken by military officers, for want of party officials who had the very minimum of competence and loyalty.

The new government consisted of officers and civilians who believed, rightly or wrongly, that the only alternative to their autocratic rule was foreign intervention; their communist convictions (if any) were neither deeply rooted nor consistent. If this was a communist regime, it was of a type never envisaged by Marxist-Leninist thinkers. Even the leading party organs, such as the Politburo, were no longer of great importance; it was in actual fact a traditional military dictatorship. Despite its appeal to patriotism, the Jaruzelski regime failed to bring about a reconciliation with the people; the workers remained sullenly hostile, most of the intelligentsia was actively opposed, and the peasants were in any case against a regime that had systematically neglected them.

Thus economic stagnation continued, and though the state-of-war legislation was eventually abolished, the regime came in no way closer to true normalization. Jaruzelski, to be sure, unlike his predecessors, had never made extravagant promises, but represented his regime as a bitter necessity—a bulwark against anarchy. The regime was even willing to concede a major role to the Catholic church in Polish society in exchange for toleration by the clergy. When Gorbachev became the new Soviet leader, Jaruzelski welcomed both the Soviet reform program and the prospect that Poland might gain a greater measure of independence. A Polish reform program providing autonomy, self-financing, and self-management was introduced but remained largely cosmetic. The bureaucracy did not collaborate, and the people failed to believe in either the competence or the good intentions of the government. In a referendum carried out in December 1987, only a minority (46 percent) voted for the government.

Thus, by 1988, the situation came to resemble the state of affairs during the late Gierek period: sporadic strikes, acute dissatisfaction among the masses, and the growing danger of a new explosion. Jaruzelski favored a policy of political concessions. A few opposition newspapers were legalized; more important, new attempts were made to draw the Solidarity leadership into something akin to a (junior) partnership to face the unfolding crisis. Lech Wałesa met on various occasions with General Kiszczak, minister of the interior; this in turn led to roundtable talks that resulted in the legalization of Solidarity and its various branches, as well as free parliamentary elections in June 1989—the first such elections in the history of Poland for many years, and the first free elections in Eastern Europe for four decades.

They resulted in an overwhelming victory for the opposition which took over the reins of government. Lech Wałesa, the Solidarity leader, became president of Poland in December 1990.

The transition toward democracy in Poland was as bumpy as elsewhere in Eastern Europe. Too many political parties came into being, governments changed every few months, the economic reforms had painful consequences. Being ethnically homogenous, Poland was not plagued by inner national conflicts. But it escaped few of the other difficulties besetting the countries of Eastern Europe on their road from Communism to a new social and political order.

HUNGARY

During the 1970s and 1980s Hungary was often described in the West as the happiest country in the Eastern bloc, a consumers' paradise, the country of "goulash communism" and *enrichissez-vous*. In fact, Hungarian prosperity, as it subsequently appeared, was modest, and political freedom narrowly limited. But in comparison with the sadder state of affairs in other communist countries, it understandably looked like a shining example. There was also political continuity: For thirty-two years the regime was headed by János Kádár, an old communist who had spent seven years of his life in prison—half under the old regime, half under Rákosi, Stalin's man in Budapest. Trained as a typewriter repairman, he had never worked in his profession; his style of work was quite different from that of other contemporary communist leaders. A modest man, he detested the cult of leadership which was the fashion under Brezhnev, Ceausescu, even Tito. His main assignment, as he saw it, was to heal the wounds of 1956 and, after this goal had been achieved, to give as much economic freedom as possible inside the bloc. This is the story of the so-called NEM (New Economic Mechanism), which was inaugurated in 1968 and proceeded in two stages. The first wave of reforms lasted from 1968 to 1973. Afterward there followed a retreat, as the result of both domestic and external pressures.

But a second reform age dawned in 1978 and lasted to the mid-1980s, when it appeared that reforms no longer worked and when the Hungarian economy had been engulfed in the general crisis in

Eastern Europe. No one could say for certain what the NEM was. It meant (among other things) greater freedom for small enterprises; many people were holding two or even three jobs, professional cooperatives were permitted long before they came into existence in the Soviet Union, cooperatives of up to thirty persons were allowed to form within state enterprises, the "gray" economy was legalized, and the black market often ignored. There was not much interference in Hungarian agriculture, and as a result it did relatively well; one-third of the produce came from the private sector. In the later stages of the reforms something like a market came into being in Hungary, and employees in agriculture and industry could elect their managers. Hungarians could travel almost freely abroad and were even permitted to work there—up to five years.

All this helped to create a new middle class in everything but name. Budapest's supermarkets showed a more ample supply of goods, and there were more private cars in its streets than in other East European capitals. But there were also many workers who could not hold a second job or plot of land or open a little shop. They were resentful about inflation and growing income differentials. Something akin to an old-fashioned class struggle developed, with the lower-income recipients claiming that the new system was creating (and perpetuating) inequality. Although the authorities raised the income of the neediest, this was not sufficient to solve the problem. Hungary's communist neighbors, including the Soviet Union, were also showing disquiet about the "excessive liberalism" practiced by Kádár.

There followed several years of "retrenchment," but Kádár succeeded in outmaneuvering his orthodox Marxist critics at home and in reassuring his Soviet friends that decentralization and a little competition were politically quite harmless. Why oppose them if they contributed to the popularity of the regime? After all, even more people were employed in private firms in East Germany and Poland. Brezhnev gave his blessing, and a new, more far-reaching set of reforms was carried out, including the breakup of some large state enterprises. However, this second reform era, though welcomed by most of the population, failed to give startling results. Throughout the 1980s there was little if any economic growth, and even the not wholly reliable official statistics revealed some years of negative growth. Again according to official reports, the living standard of one-third of the population actually declined. Import controls were introduced in 1982, and state subsidies to many unprofitable enterprises were cut. But inflation still continued to rise after 1985.

What had gone wrong? Hungary had received very substantial credits from the West and favorable trade terms during the 1970s. In 1989 its foreign debt was $20 billion; its foreign indebtedness was higher on a per-capita basis than that of any other East European country. Many of the credits had been invested, as in Poland, in unproductive enterprises. Furthermore, it appeared that the economic system was basically flawed and that the Kádár reforms, welcome as they were, amounted to mere tinkering; structural change was excluded. As the Kádár era drew to its close, it became clear that, as in the Soviet Union, economic inefficiency quite apart, the social cost of the system had been unacceptably high. The ecological situation was bad and deteriorating, the life expectancy of males was declining, the whole infrastructure was woefully inadequate—new subscribers to the telephone service had to wait thirteen years.

In its foreign policy Hungary followed, albeit reluctantly, the Soviet lead. But the true sympathies of the Hungarians were with Western Europe, and relations with Austria were close all along. If Hungary had an enemy, it was Ceausescu, who brutally repressed the Hungarian minority in Transylvania. Relations with Czechoslovakia were also far from cordial. Once the crisis broke, Hungary was the first East European country to express the wish to join the European Community.

After Gorbachev's rise to power in 1985, it might have been possible to carry out more radical change in Hungary, and some communist leaders, such as Pozsgay, Nyers, and Bihari, favored such a course of action. But it would have been too little and too late. In any case, Kádár and the majority of the party leadership, having been discredited as a result of their failures, were no longer in real command. With the crisis becoming more and more severe, Kádár (who had originally wanted to stay on for a few more years) was forced to resign in May 1988 and was replaced by Karoly Grosz, an old apparatchik, who had the reputation of a reasonably able leader and good communicator, but who, as it was soon to appear, was quite incapable of dealing with the heritage bequeathed to him.

Hungary was in the forefront of political liberalization before the flood that washed away the Communist Party. From 1985 on the party had proclaimed pluralism, at least as an ideal; in all elections there had to be more than one candidate. Even earlier, unorthodox Marxists and other thinkers of the left (such as Agnes Heller and Hegedus of the older generation and György Konrád of the younger) had been given more freedom than dissenters in other East European countries. The authorities probably believed that dissenters of the left hardly constituted a danger to the survival of the regime. But it is also true that the Social Democratic wing inside the communist leadership genuinely wanted a democratization of political life. Without the spadework done by reformists such as Pozsgay the transition to democracy in Hungary would not have been as smooth and peaceful as it eventually was. This is their historical merit; it was the tragedy of these communists that, by the time they had a free hand to carry out their reforms, the regime had been discredited to such an extent that the question dividing public opinion was no longer whether socialism should be discarded but how quickly and radically this could be safely done.

EAST GERMANY
AND CZECHOSLOVAKIA

If the communist regimes in Poland and Hungary engaged in political and economic reform in the 1970s and 1980s, partly of their own volition but also because of growing domestic pressures, the same two decades brought no change in either East Germany or Czechoslovakia. These were the years of stagnation, as in the Soviet Union, even if outwardly the general impression was one of stability and a certain prosperity. Gustav Husák's position in Prague seemed unassailable; he was replaced in 1987 by Milos Jakes but mainly, no doubt, for reasons of age; there were no significant differences of opinion between them. Erich Honecker came to power in 1971, replacing Walter Ulbricht, and he stayed on to the bitter end eighteen years later. Of working-class origin, born in the Saar region, he had joined the Communist Party even before Hitler's rise and spent many years in a concentration camp. Later, he was for a long time head of the FDJ, the East German youth organization.

The economic situation in both countries seemed to be relatively satisfactory; true, growth had been much faster prior to 1975 than in the years after. But industrial output still continued to grow, and according to official U.S. figures, in 1989 per-capita income in East Germany was more than $12,000, higher than the $10,000 in Czechoslovakia. If correct, this would have been considerably more than in Spain or Israel, almost as high as in Italy and the United Kingdom. Had these figures been correct, the upheaval in 1989–90 would have been quite incomprehensible. True, the East European revolution occurred not only because of economic shortcomings, but the economic failures certainly did play an important role. It is difficult to understand, even in retrospect, why economic performance was given so much more stress in the West than the political stability of these two countries. Partly, no doubt, it was the misleading effect of the official statistics, which before 1989 grossly exaggerated the achievements of the regimes everywhere in the communist bloc. Any East German or Czechoslovak citizen knew that his standard of living was not three-quarters that of West Germany or France, but much lower; whatever his nominal wages, there was little he could buy.

Still, of all the East European countries East Germany was the most prosperous, and the capital, East Berlin, was something like a show window for the "really existing socialism," a slogan that came to haunt East European communism during the years after. Yet even the most superficial analysis in the 1980s tended to show that the country had huge deficits in its foreign trade and a growing indebtedness. The rate of investment was steadily declining; investments were made in ambitious projects which this little country could ill afford. Industries were overmanned, a huge bureaucracy impeded production, and the concentration on lignite as a source of energy caused the pollution of air and water to a degree unprecedented in Europe, except perhaps in Czechoslovakia and southwestern Poland.

Generally speaking, the prevailing economic system always put the emphasis on quantity rather than quality. As a result, achieving the plan was invariably the sole criterion for efficiency. Whether the product was useful, whether it could be exported, whether there was a demand for it—these were not decisive issues at all. Increase in productivity figured high on the government's list of priorities. Yet, according to West German assessments, productivity in the West was about twice as high as in the East; far from catching up, East Germany was falling behind in the 1980s.

As in the Soviet Union, the East German budget allocated enormous subventions to keep the price of staple foods low. There were further subventions to keep rents low, but the quality of housing was inferior and deteriorating every year, since there were no funds for repair work. Visitors to East Germany in the 1980s who ventured outside the capital would find not just single buildings but whole quarters in historical cities in an advanced state of decay and ruin. Lastly, there was a constant decline in the whole infrastructure (roads, rails, telecommunication) which directly affected the economic output. True, there were social services which functioned tolerably well, such as education and help for working mothers. But a comparatively well-educated labor force was bound to feel doubly frustrated confronting a system that made work unnecessarily unpleasant, complicated, unrewarding, and, in the final analysis, unproductive.

All power was, in theory at least, in the hands of the East German state party, the SED, with its more than two million members (the number of Czech communists was about equal; in more populous Poland, communist membership exceeded three million). In actual fact, the rank-and-file party member had not the slightest influence on policymaking, which was in the hands of a handful of elderly Politburo members. These gerontocrats preached the old ideals of social justice but in reality enjoyed innumerable privileges and a standard of living infinitely higher than that of the average citizen. Ideologically they (like their Czech colleagues) were hardliners, even though some concessions were made in the 1980s to German (and Prussian) nationalism. But, by and large, there was strong resistance to any innovation in this as in all other fields. The only time the East German leaders diverged from the Soviet model was after 1987, when they showed distinct coolness toward the Gorbachev reforms. As Kurt Hager, a member of the Politburo, put it: Just because your neighbor refurbishes his apartment, there is no cogent reason to follow his example. The East German leadership was both arrogant and out of touch with the mood of the people, a potentially fatal mixture in political behavior. When, in the summer of 1989, Moscow sent a highly placed emissary (Falin, who had been ambassador to Germany) to warn the East Berlin comrades that all was not well below the calm surface in their country, the East German Politburo assured the Kremlin that everything was under control and that no help would be needed. A few months later they were out of office, many of them under arrest.

Their arrogance manifested itself in their attitude toward Bonn. Without direct and indirect West German financial help, the economic situation would have been catastrophic. But, far from showing a conciliatory attitude toward the other, bigger, and more powerful part of Germany, the DDR did all it could to carry through a policy of *Abgrenzung*—that is to say, of distancing itself and of heaping up petty obstacles, making contacts between the two Germanys more difficult.

Cultural and political exchanges between the two Germanys were kept to a minimum. The East Berlin Politburo could not interfere with West German radio and television, the cumulative impact of which was underrated by them. They seem to have believed that the population had been so thoroughly indoctrinated that the propaganda of the "class enemy" would not fall on fertile ground. For the same reason, relatively many East German intellectuals were permitted to leave for the West, apparently on the assumption that poets, actors, or painters were not essential to the smooth functioning of society and that others could always be found to replace them. Between 1984 and 1988 some 150,000 citizens left the DDR (350,000 in 1989). The fact that among them were not a few sons and daughters of the *nomenklatura,* even of the supreme leadership, seems not to have caused sleepless nights to members of the Politburo.

If the leadership was showing any liberal inclination at all, it was in its relationship with the churches—much in contrast with the Czech communists, who showed no interest in reaching a *modus vivendi* with the church. The East German Protestant church received more freedom of action than previously, which seemed harmless enough, because in the past it had not shown much courage in its relationship with the party. But in the 1980s Protestant churches began to make more aggressive use of the new freedom, however limited. The opposition groups that were mainly instrumental in ultimately bringing down the SED regime had begun their struggle for ecological causes, pacifism, and human rights under the umbrella of the Protestant church.

Montesquieu once wrote, Happy the country that has no history. Czechoslovakia virtually had no history between 1969 and 1989, but no one would have thought of it as a happy country. Unlike in Hungary after 1956, no attempt was made at national reconciliation. On the contrary, repression was massive and brutal. One-third of the old party membership was "purged"; leading intellectuals were sent to the coal mines, made to work as street sweepers and in similar capacities. The political leadership tried to freeze the country—ideologically as well as socially and economically.

During these two decades Czechoslovakia was a gray, joyless country; there were no mass demonstrations against the regime, but this was the result of apathy rather than public support. Among the intelligentsia there was bitter opposition (Charter 77), but its activities were effectively suppressed by the authorities, who would have taken even more severe measures except for their wish not to cause too much offense in the West. At the same time the awareness of the intolerable situation grew among the population, as did the courage to stand up and be counted. Originally 242 individuals had signed Charter 77, the manifesto of the opposition; by 1989, despite arrests and political trials, the number had risen to 1,575. Furthermore, new opposition groups had come into being, ranging from a group of reform communists (*obroda*) to pacifists, ecologists, and the "Democratic Initiative." Whereas the East German government made occasional concessions to a more liberal cultural policy, in Czechoslovakia even jazz bands were persecuted as enemies of the regime. Whereas the East German rulers could point to the outstanding achievements of their swimmers and athletes and interpret them as the manifestations of "real socialism," the Czechs could not even point to their excellent tennis players, male and female, for these had defected to the West. The tutelage and repression, in short, were more and more perceived as acutely intolerable, and this in a country that, in contrast to other East European nations, had a strong democratic tradition. Given such a state of affairs, it seems in retrospect all the more surprising that, when the revolution eventually came, it was virtually bloodless, despite the enormous anger that had accumulated.

On its road toward a more normal economic and political system Czechoslovakia faced all the problems its neighbors did. President Vaclav Havel's initially great authority was not sufficient to maintain the territorial integrity of the country. Many Slovaks insisted on a measure of sovereignty that was unacceptable to most Czechs, and these tensions eventually led to a final division between the two parts. The Czechs opted for democracy and a Western-style economic system; leading Slovaks preferred an economy that was largely state controlled. The breakdown of the old republic established by Masaryk in 1918–19 was more than the personal tragedy of Vaclav Havel, it was the end of a historical era, in line with the general trend toward separatism in Eastern Europe.

RUMANIA AND BULGARIA

Rumania and Bulgaria were the two communist countries in which the regimes were last to come under attack. The opposition was weakest there, not because of the popularity of the leaders but as a result of repression. This common feature apart, developments in Bulgaria and Rumania had followed different lines. Bulgaria had modeled itself most closely on the Soviet pattern; Rumania had distanced itself furthest, especially in its foreign policy. Rumania was the only Warsaw Pact country to oppose the invasion of Czechoslovakia in 1968. The year before, it had been the first to establish diplomatic relations with West Germany, and it was the only communist country not to sever relations with Israel in 1967. On many occasions Rumania went out of its way to stress its independence, up to the point of implying that Bessarabia (Moldavia) historically belonged to Rumania, and that Bucharest had not accepted the Soviet annexation after the Second World War.

Rumanian cultural policy was unabashedly nationalist, but it was also Stalinist in its rigidity and all-pervasiveness. Stalinist was also the cult of the leader, the *conducatore,* the unending, ridiculously excessive praise heaped on him. Whereas Stalin had always taken great pains to keep members of his family far from the levers of power and out of the limelight, Ceausescu established a new model for leadership of rule—not by the Central Committee of the party, not by the Politburo, but through the family: his wife, Elena; his three brothers; his son Nicu; and even more distant relations. He assumed, no doubt correctly, that he could usually rely on his clan, whereas the loyalty of outsiders would always be questionable.

Ceausescu's economic policy was highly ambitious and lacked a sense of reality. Throughout the 1970s the growth rate of the country was 6–9 percent annually, according to official statistics, and the investment rate up to 30 percent. Yet at the end of this period Rumania was still among Europe's poorest countries, with shortages everywhere and daily power cuts even in the capital. Ceausescu decided to invest heavily in the petrochemical products, and this when oil had to be imported at a high price, since Rumania's own output and reserves were dwindling. Toward the end of his reign he decided to reduce the fifteen thousand existing villages to seven thousand. This would have meant the disappearance of some fifteen hundred Hungarian villages in the northwest of the country, a prospect that greatly added to national tensions. Whereas other communist countries were at least partly aware of the growing economic difficulties, Ceausescu seems to have been blissfully unaware, and he opposed all reforms. He insisted that foreign loans be repaid within a number of years, irrespective of the suffering caused as a result. State control was pervasive and covered all spheres of social and individual life. Not only was abortion illegal; women had to undergo mandatory medical examinations to determine whether they had violated the law.

Under Ceausescu, Rumania became isolated from both West and East. Relations with the Soviet Union and the other communist countries were cool; with the U.S., Western Europe, and China they deteriorated. In the late 1960s and early 1970s he did have many well-wishers in the West who regarded him as a man of courage and independent views, perhaps another Tito. But these illusions gradually faded. In 1987 Ceausescu voluntarily surrendered "most-favored-nation status," aware that in view of Rumania's dismal record on human rights the regime would fail the test.

Until a few years before his death, Ceausescu was a man of enormous energy, of cunning and unlimited self-confidence. He knew exactly how far he could go in provoking the Soviet Union. He was excellent at playing off his underlings against one another, and his secret police was the envy of other dictators. But for the general breakdown of other communist regimes and the "echo effect" of revolutions, his regime might well have lasted several more years.

In comparison with Rumania, Bulgaria was almost a success story. Todor Zhivkov stayed in power from 1959 to November 1989. Under his rule, a predominantly agrarian country became largely urbanized and industrialized. With its nine million inhabitants a much smaller country than Rumania, Bulgaria's economic planning was less ambitious, and fewer mistakes were committed. Some of the products of the new electric and electronic industries were exported to the Eastern bloc, even though they could hardly compete on the world markets. In contrast to Rumania, the Bulgarian leadership discussed economic reforms all along, and on occasion resolutions on far-reaching change were adopted—as in 1987, when Zhivkov announced his own perestroika, which went considerably further than the Soviet original. But the reforms usually remained a dead letter, except perhaps the modest decentralization carried out in the 1970s.

After years of relatively high growth, the situation deteriorated in the late 1970s. Nineteen seventy-seven and 1980 were years of negative growth. At first it was believed that these were mere temporary setbacks, but from 1984 on there could no longer be doubts about the massive deterioration in the situation. Bad harvests and negative trade balances led to shortages, power cuts, and a general decline in the standard of living. Bulgaria's indebtedness was $7.5 billion, not an enormous sum by international standards, but still a major factor in view of its small foreign trade with non-Comecon countries.

At the same time national tensions came to the fore, above all the attempt to force the cultural assimilation of the Muslim minority (some 10 percent of the population), which led to demonstrations, riots, and the exodus of three hundred thousand Muslims to Turkey. Fifty thousand of them subsequently returned, because they found living conditions in Turkey unacceptable. Zhivkov's Muslim policy was not unpopular among the population. But it showed that, as in Yugoslavia and the Soviet Union, Muslim minorities, more than all others, proved resistant to modern secular civilization in all forms, and that communism was no more capable than Western societies of coping with Islamic religious nationalism.

Unlike most other communist leaders, Zhivkov had not been averse to promote younger leaders to the highest party organs. But even inside the party there was growing dissatisfaction with the prevailing outdated style and doctrine. In view of the traditional cultural proximity with Russia, the Gorbachev example had a more direct impact on Bulgaria than elsewhere in the Eastern bloc. The Moscow liberal newspapers and periodicals found nowhere more avid readers than in Sofia and Plovdiv. Thus the stage was set for the emergence of a strong opposition movement.

YUGOSLAVIA AFTER TITO

Many East European countries have been threatened by national strife, but only in one case, Yugoslavia, was the very existence of the country put into question. From the beginning—that is to say, since the peace treaties after the First World War—Yugoslavia was derided by her enemies as an artificial creation. It consisted of six republics and two autonomous provinces. There was no undisputed "dominant state nation" as in the Soviet Union; the most numerous, the Serbs, counted less than 40 percent of the total. Historically and culturally there was nothing in common between the areas that had been part of the Austro-Hungarian Empire (Slovenia and Croatia) and those that had belonged for centuries to the Ottoman Empire. The Croatians were Catholics, the Serbians orthodox Christians, and there was a substantial Muslim minority in Bosnia and Kosovo.

During the Second World War the components of Yugoslavia had frequently found themselves in opposite camps. Furthermore, the republics were by no means homogeneous but contained sizable national minorities. What held Yugoslavia together after the war was, firstly, the outside danger: whatever their internal differences, the great majority of Yugoslavs had no desire to become part of the Soviet empire. Secondly, the person of Tito, the national hero, acted as an integrative figure. Thirdly, and of lesser importance, the Yugoslav army tried to maintain throughout all postwar crises its image as the defender of Yugoslav unity against all enemies, from outside and within. Lastly, there was reasonable doubt whether the various components of the country would be viable, independent states if the country disintegrated. But such realistic considerations have seldom deterred separatists from pursuing their demands.

The danger of outside invasion seemed acute as the result of the invasion of Czechoslovakia; the threat lingered on throughout the 1970s but virtually disappeared in the 1980s. Tito died in 1980, and not a few observers predicted that Yugoslavia would disintegrate within a year or two. (Most other leaders of the partisan generation had predeceased him—except Djilas, who was in opposition.) The dire predictions did not materialize, at least not immediately. But it is also true that the process of slow decomposition and growing tension which had begun during Tito's lifetime and continued during the 1980s confronted the country with immense difficulties.

There were enormous regional differences in the Yugoslav economy, especially between the relatively developed north and the much more backward parts of the country. The overall situation was lamentable, even though Yugoslavia had gone considerably further in its economic reforms than other communist countries (worker self-management, the introduction of a marketlike mechanism). Substantial Western credits—amounting to $20 billion by 1985—had not brought about radical change in the situation. On the contrary, the heavy burden of repayment of interest caused further deterioration. By the early 1980s inflation ran at 30 percent; in early 1990 it had reached 2,000 percent. As the result of drastic cuts in the public sector, it was reduced to 160 percent by the end of 1990. The dinar had become the first communist convertible currency in Eastern Europe, but the unemployment level was between 15 and 20 percent. Mitigating factors were Western tourism and the influx of hard currency among the one million Yugoslav workers employed abroad. Like its neighboring countries, Yugoslavia was compelled to introduce cuts in supplies and an austerity regime.

Bad as it was, the economic situation was a less acute threat than the growing separatist movements. There had been a major Croatian crisis in 1971; some of the separatist leaders had been arrested, only to re-emerge in 1990 with even stronger popular support. The Serbs made concessions toward the other nations; a political arrangement in 1984 provided for a truly collective leadership; the president of each republic was to serve as chairman of the Yugoslav federation for one year. The Serbs were reluctant to make concessions of this kind vis-à-vis the Albanians in the Kosovo area, for this region was considered part of the historical Serbian heartland; the Muslims had been settled there later on, by the Ottoman rulers. But the Albanians showed growing militancy and made life for the local Serbs uncomfortable—comparable to the situation of Russians in Azerbaidjan or Central Asia. Albanian pressure and the separatist trends in the other republics brought about a Serbian backlash; complaints of reverse discrimination and the "Slobodan Milosevic phenomenon"—the emergence of a national-communist leader in the late 1980s, preaching stronger Serbian self-assertion since the conciliatory approach had failed.

Under Tito, Yugoslavia had played a prominent role in world affairs as a leader of the nonaligned movement. But in the 1970s the Cubans appearing in a nonaligned, neutralist pose, had out-maneuvered the Yugoslavs; once the Cubans had been discredited, the "Bandung movement" ceased to be a factor of political importance. On the credit side, Yugoslavia's liberal migration and cultural policy should be mentioned; there was far more freedom in this respect than in the other East European countries. But this was not sufficient to stem the separatist tide, and thus, albeit for different reasons, the year 1990 brought a major political crisis for Yugoslavia as much as for its neighbors.

ALBANIA

Albania is the smallest East European country and also the most backward and isolated. It was not, therefore, surprising that its Stalinist political system should persevere long after such systems had disappeared elsewhere. Albania's was a curious mixture of primitive communism and nationalism in which clannishness played a crucial role. Albania had broken first with Yugoslavia, later with the Soviet Union, and ultimately (in 1978) with its only remaining protector, China. Since no one was particularly interested in this poor, mountainous country, the eccentricities of its leaders were more or less ignored. Enver Hoxha ruled the country from 1944 to 1985, when his chosen successor, Ramiz Alia, took over; Alia was slightly more inclined toward economic reform. In the meantime, Mehmet Shehu, prime minister for twenty-seven years, had been shot at Hoxha's behest (1981), reportedly at a Politburo meeting. Not much was known in the outside world about events inside Albania; what became known did not whet the appetite for more. Eventually, the repercussions of the East European revolution of 1989 percolated to Albania, despite all the precautionary measures that had been taken to isolate the country from the outside world. In mid-1990 the first major anti-government demonstrations took place in Tiranë. They spread despite the political reforms introduced by President (and supreme party leader) Ramiz Alia. By early 1991 Albania was in a state of chaos with thousands of citizens escaping abroad.

THE EAST EUROPEAN
REVOLUTION

Nineteen eighty-nine was the *annus mirabilis* which swept away the East European communist regimes after four decades of oppression. The great majority of the citizens of these countries had never been able to take part in democratic elections, nor could they voice their opinions freely. Millions of East Germans had been forbidden to see their relations and friends on the other side of the wall; millions all over Eastern Europe had lived in fear of the omnipresent secret police. In Poland and Hungary the progress of liberation had begun before 1989; in East Germany it began during the summer and lasted for several months; in Czechoslovakia and Rumania the revolution was wholly spontaneous and toppled the regime in a few days.

All over Eastern Europe millions demonstrated their great joy and jubilation. True, everywhere enormous difficulties were looming ahead, and in some countries, such as Rumania and Bulgaria, victory over the old regime was far from complete. But life in Eastern Europe had been so miserable, except for a happy few, that a few days of jubilation unencumbered by fears about the future seemed only natural. Soon enough the daily routine would again confront the East Europeans, the necessity to liquidate the heritage of the past and to build their economic and social life anew. Few doubted that it would be a long, painful process, that many deprivations were still ahead, that setbacks were quite likely, and that success in the struggle for a better life would be uncertain for a long time to come.

The breakdown of the communist regimes came almost like a

bolt from the blue. Most American and West European diplomats, editorial writers, and academic experts were firmly convinced that an East European revolution was just not in the cards. Many people in Eastern Europe and many well-wishers elsewhere had never given up hope. But the flame of liberty had not burned brightly, and outsiders had (rightly) assumed that radical change would come only as the result of a breakdown in the center—that is to say, in the Soviet Union—at the end of a longish process and following the united struggle of yesterday's "people's democracies."

There was such change in Moscow after Gorbachev's rise to power. But its extent had not been tested, and no one could say for certain whether the new regime in the Soviet Union, however liberal at home, would not again invade Eastern Europe to keep its positions there. All this could be found out only by trial and error, and it was a dangerous game to explore.

Furthermore, the communist regimes in Eastern Europe, perhaps with the exception of Poland, seemed as yet firmly entrenched. The majority of them were headed by elderly people, but there was no lack of younger careerists waiting to be adopted by the Politburo and slip into their shoes.

How often in the postwar period had attempts been made to challenge the establishment, and it had ended always in defeat. But 1989 was not 1956 or 1968. After forty-five years of communist rule there was a history of accumulated failure. The old self-confidence no longer prevailed among the communist leadership, and there was also the "echo effect" which has already been mentioned: once the onslaught against tyranny had been successful in one country, revolutionary uprisings tended to be infectious, as in 1848 and in other past situations. In all East European capitals but one, the old leadership capitulated without offering serious resistance. Only in Rumania was the powerful *siguranza* fighting back, but even there the outcome was not seriously in doubt.

The revolutionaries of 1989 were a mixed lot. Some reform communists were among them, and many anticommunists, practicing Christians, students, workers, members of persecuted national minorities, and also people who had never before taken an active part in politics. Within a few weeks their ways would again part, but they were united in the belief that there would be no future for any of them if the old order was not defeated.

THE BEGINNING OF THE END

First on the road to freedom, as so often in the past, were the Poles. Even in 1986 there were clear indications that the Jaruzelski government was faltering. The economic situation continued to deteriorate, and in December of that year a new austerity regime was introduced. Even before, in September, there had been a general amnesty for the opponents of the regime. Despite extensive strikes, Jerzy Urban, the government spokesman, continued to declare that Solidarity was dead, but this opinion was by no means shared by his superiors. The question that divided them was whether they should negotiate with Solidarity. Eventually, the proponents of such talks gained the upper hand, and the roundtable conversations got under way in February 1989.

Within a relatively short time, agreement was reached between the government and the opposition; the former accepted (partly) free elections, the latter promised to support the unpopular economic policy of the regime. According to this agreement, the opposition was to get some 40 percent of the seats in Parliament, and the government promised that the elections thereafter (1993) would be truly free. However, so overwhelming was the Solidarity victory in the June 1989 election that it was propelled much earlier into power than it had expected—or was prepared for.

Having given up the party leadership, Jaruzelski stayed on as president of Poland; he was elected by just one vote thanks to the abstention of the Solidarity representatives, who knew that the Kremlin would not yet accept one from their ranks. However, Tadeusz Mazowiecki, a longtime Catholic Solidarity member, became the new prime minister in September. The communists retained the ministries of defense and the interior, but all other key positions were now in the hands of their opponents. Poland thus had the first noncommunist government in Eastern Europe for forty years.

True, in facing the grim economic realities and the need to deal with them, Solidarity was almost immediately faced with internal fissures. But the communists were even more dispirited and split. In January 1990 the party dissolved itself, or, to be precise, transformed itself into a Social Democratic party. Wałesa, the Solidarity leader, decided at first not to enter government; he tried to lead the movement from the outside. Solidarity, as he saw it, should be both government and opposition at the same time. Paradoxically, the rapidly worsening economic crisis, manifesting itself in growing inflation and unemployment, prevented a total break among yesterday's opponents of the communist regime.

Solidarity had, broadly speaking, a blueprint—the Balcerowicz plan—to introduce a market economy. But this involved painful measures, such as the abolition of state subsidies, the closing of unprofitable enterprises, and the stabilization of the currency. There was no certainty that even a united Poland would succeed in the transition to a viable economy. It was clear, beyond any shadow of doubt, that a split leadership would land the country in total economic disaster. This grim state of affairs, perhaps more than any other consideration, imposed unity, at least during the most critical period. There were, moreover, foreign-policy challenges, such as the impending reunification of Germany, which also had a cohesive effect.

Solidarity had greater political credit than any other movement in modern Polish history. But the credit was not unlimited; unless it remained united, unless it could show within a few years that it was able to handle the economic situation more competently than its predecessors, its days would be numbered, and the democratic revival would be remembered as a short, inconclusive interval in Polish history.

HUNGARY CUTS LOOSE

In May 1988 Karoly Grosz had succeeded János Kádár as the leader of the Hungarian Communist Party. He was not opposed to substantial economic reform but wanted a minimum of political change. Ten, even five years earlier this approach might have worked, at least for a while. But the pulse of history had immeasurably quickened, and when Grosz entered office, he did not even have the support of his own party, in which the influence of the reformers was steadily growing. As in Poland, the Communist Party agreed on the radical transformation of Hungary's political life, aiming at a multiparty system within the next four or five years. It accepted that in this new system the Communist Party would no longer play the leading role. Again as in Poland, events proceeded much faster than had been assumed. During the spring and late summer of 1989 there was a radical reassessment of party doctrine and history. In a moving ceremony in June 1989 attended by tens of thousands, the party leadership paid homage to Imre Nagy, the erstwhile leader who had been executed after the failure of the uprising of 1956. The same month, Grosz was joined by three reform communists, but this collective leadership lasted only until October. At that stage the Communist Party decided by a great majority to dissolve itself and (as in Poland and East Germany) to transform itself into a socialist party. A small faction opted for continued existence as a Marxist party.

In the meantime, Parliament had begun to play a far more active role in the political life of the country, passing a great many new laws and even a new constitution. New political parties developed, above all the Alliance of Free Democrats and the Democratic Forum. The Forum was a right-of-center, strongly patriotic group, with mass support in both the countryside and the major cities. Though strongly anticommunist, it favored the gradual and cautious liquidation of the old economic and social order, in contrast to the Free Democrats, which had many intellectuals among its leaders and stood for a radical break with past structures. The mood in the country favored the former rather than the latter, for anticommunism was matched by fear of an unchartered future.

Hungary's internal change during 1989 was also reflected in its foreign policy. President Bush was given a warm welcome in Budapest in July 1989, even though he could promise Hungary much less help than had been hoped for. Diplomatic relations were re-established with Israel and South Korea, and the tension with Rumania reached a new climax because of the persecution of the Hungarian minority in Rumania and the exodus of tens of thousands of them.

The election campaign in 1990 had been acrimonious, but the two leading parties showed a willingness to collaborate in its aftermath. The victorious Democratic Forum gave their vote to the election of Göncz, a Free Democrat, as head of Parliament and acting president of Hungary. He had been an active member of the national revolt in 1956 and was given a life sentence at the time. The Free Democrats, on the other hand, promised their support for much of the legislation proposed by the Democratic Forum.

BLOODLESS REVOLUTION

Change in East Germany and Czechoslovakia came much more suddenly than in Poland and Hungary; the decision fell in the streets, not in party headquarters or conference halls. During July and August 1989 thousands of (mainly young) East Germans invaded the West Germany embassies in Budapest, Prague, and Warsaw, asking for asylum. After initially hesitating, the Hungarians agreed in September to let them out to the West. The Czechs and the Poles followed their example. The East German authorities foolishly demanded that the trains from Prague and Warsaw pass DDR territory—which triggered new demonstrations and magnified the political damage that had been done.

From this date on, the stream of East Germans escaping to the West did not abate, and it continued even after Honecker had resigned. During the first week of November no fewer than fifty thousand left, and during the early months of 1990 it was two thousand a day on the average. The West German regional authorities were overwhelmed by the influx and did nothing to encourage the newcomers. They received no special assistance and were housed in conditions considerably worse than in their native country. Yet such was the despair, and so high were the hopes for a better life in the West, that even these difficulties hardly had an impact on the stream of new settlers.

Those who decided to stay in the DDR did not do so because they had great sympathy with the Honecker regime. The election of May 1989, with the usual 99-percent approval rate of the government, had been an obvious fraud and had caused much anger. The East Berlin Politburo's support for the Tiananmen Square massacre had added fuel, and even Gorbachev's visit to East Berlin had not brought about any change in the public mood. Leipzig (later renamed Hero City) became the main scene of protest demonstrations against the regime. Every Monday evening, after church service in the Nikolai Kirche, there were demonstrations, growing in numbers each week. In September only a few hundred participated, but on October 2 about ten thousand congregated, on October 9 seventy thousand, on October 16 two hundred thousand. On November 17 half a million were marching in Berlin. In the beginning the state security service (Stasi) tried to break up the march and to arrest the leaders. But once tens of thousands were in the streets, the police were no longer able to cope with resistance of this magnitude. There was still the possibility of applying the Chinese approach, and at one stage the order to shoot seems to have been given by Honecker, but it was ignored on the local level.

The turning point came on October 6 and 7, when great celebrations were scheduled to take part all over the DDR on the occasion of the fortieth anniversary of the foundation of the communist regime. The festivities began with the usual parades, but toward evening protest demonstrations were reported from all over the country. Four days later the Politburo announced its readiness to open a dialogue with the opposition, a gesture that, naturally, came far too late.

On October 17 Honecker resigned and handed over to Egon Krenz, a younger and more adaptable member of the Politburo. But, hard as Krenz tried, the time for half-measures had passed; by November 8 both the Politburo and the government resigned *in toto*. Krenz lasted only a few weeks in office.

Hans Modrow, former mayor of Dresden and one of the very few SED leaders held in almost general respect, became the prime minister who was to steer the country through the difficult period up to the elections of March 1990. Even a few days prior to his appointment, it was decided to abolish the travel restrictions and orders were given to open the wall at various points, including the Brandenburg Gate. From the evening of November 9 on, millions of East Germans streamed to West Berlin and West Germany, and considerable numbers of West Germans moved in the opposite direction.

There was an outbreak of joy such as Germany had not known in her history. Official and unofficial receptions took place; orchestras were playing in the streets; institutions, churches, theatres, and shops were kept open all hours as the citizens of the DDR, many for the first time in their lives, made use of the right to travel hitherto denied to them. On November 12 the mayors of West and East Berlin met at the Potsdamer Platz (which in a past age had been the center of town) and decided on various cooperative measures: the reunification of Germany got under way on the administrative level.

It is difficult to describe the emotions among the people during the days after the hated wall had come down. For a few days all the deprivations, the accumulated fear and hate of more than a generation, seemed forgotten. All that mattered was the new freedom and dreams of a brilliant future. Within a few weeks, by necessity, a more sober mood was to prevail.

Not only was the DDR a poor country in comparison with the other part of Germany; it was doubtful whether through its own efforts, without massive infusions of capital, it would succeed in turning the economy around. "German unity" became the new slogan; it is difficult to establish to what extent this longing for the common fatherland stemmed from "pure" patriotism, and to what degree it was rooted in dire economic necessity. A majority of East Germans had reached the conclusion that the DDR had no future as an independent state. The demand for Germany unity, as quickly and completely as possible, had enormous support in East Germany; it was much less popular among Germany's neighbors, above all in the East. Germany's Western allies, after some initial hesitation, accepted it as inevitable. But in Poland and the Soviet Union guarantees were demanded, concerning the borders of a united Germany and also its status between the two great military blocs.

At the same time there was disappointment among East German intellectuals, including those who had been in the forefront of the struggle against the tyranny before October 1989. They opposed a mass exodus and feared that the option of so many of their fellow citizens for the West German way of life was rooted not so much in the appeal of the West German democratic institutions as in the magnetic attractions of the fleshpots of the West.

In December 1989 daily roundtable discussions got under way in East Berlin in which the SED, its former bloc parties (such as the East CDU), and the new opposition groups, including the New Forum and Democracy Now, met to deal with the main problems facing the country. This referred to the dismantling of the dictatorship and its tools of repression and propaganda, and the functioning of the economy, which was in even poorer shape following the mass exodus than before.

The election campaign was short and sharp; leading politicians from the West took a prominent part in it. The opposition groups, which had originally spearheaded the struggle in Leipzig and elsewhere, did not have much of a chance, because of their inexperience, their lack of resources, and the multitude of factions contesting the election. The East German Social Democrats seemed to stand a much better chance, largely because the SED was discredited, as were its "bourgeois" satellites. The SPD, on the other hand, had been forced to dissolve early on by the communists and was not therefore compromised because of collaborating with the old regime. But in the event the CDU and other right-of-center forces gained a great victory, with 48 percent of the vote; Lothar de Maizière became the new prime minister. Paradoxically, the SPD did worst in the predominantly working-class regions of Saxony and Thuringia, the historical heartland of German Social Democracy. In other parts of the DDR, the Social Democrats and the SED, which, like all other East European communist parties, had transformed itself into a Party for Democratic Socialism (PDS), under the leadership of Klaus Gysi, achieved somewhat better results (16 percent for the PDS compared with 21 percent for the Social Democrats).

All throughout the spring of 1990 negotiations between East Berlin and Bonn continued. The main topic at hand was the economic help to be extended to the DDR, the measures to be taken to achieve the integration of the East German economy, and, above all, the rate of exchange between the two marks. Thus, quite inevitably, the manifestations of great joy and national solidarity that had been so characteristic during October and November 1989 gave way to doubts about the future and haggling about topics such as old-age pensions. The recognition that the country still faced an acutely critical situation impelled most parties, including the East German Social Democrats, to enter a grand-coalition government. Reunification took place in October 1990, and there were all-German elections in December of that year.

REVOLUTION IN PRAGUE

If the fall of the East German regime had taken a few weeks, in Czechoslovakia it merely took a few days, and the revolution was equally gentle—no blood was shed. The decisive date was November 17, 1989, when a demonstration called to commemorate the fiftieth anniversary of the execution of nine Czech students and the closing of all Czech universities by the German occupiers turned into a protest march against the regime. Some fifty thousand citizens, most of them students, participated in the march, which was brutally suppressed by the police; many were arrested, seventy-one injured, and, according to rumor, several were killed. There had been demonstrations in Prague earlier on, but never had so many dared to participate; events in East Germany, Poland, and Czechoslovakia obviously had a direct impact. Several members of the Politburo immediately realized that the application of force on such a massive scale had been a fatal mistake and expressed regret. But the accumulated tension had risen so much that an explosion would have occurred, in any case, sooner or later.

Students constituted the bulk of participants in the early demonstrations, as did actors of the Prague theatres and other artists. A general strike was called for November 27; there was, however, no certainty at first whether workers in industry and the services would follow this appeal. On previous occasions the intelligentsia had been more or less isolated in its oppositionist activities, and the party leadership therefore made a determined effort to keep the support of the workers. But these efforts were no more successful than the many appeals and speeches over television; the great majority of the population had long ago lost faith in party and government, and their passivity now turned into militancy: they wanted political change as quickly as possible.

On November 20 a civic forum was established to coordinate opposition activities, and from this date on, giant demonstrations took place daily. The communist youth organization distanced itself from the party leadership, as did the small "bloc" parties, which had been permitted to exist since 1948 yet had never before played any active political role. Journalists no longer submitted their manuscripts to the censorship but openly expressed their support for the opposition. When the Prague Communist Party district secretary tried to appeal to the workers in the capital's biggest factory, CKD, on November 23, a huge choir replied, "We are not children—resign!" All this on television, watched by millions of people. Power had slipped out of the hands of the party leadership.

On the evening of November 24 Jakes, the first party secretary, announced the collective resignation of the Politburo. Two days later a special party conference took place; in the new Central Committee only four of the 140 former members were represented. For a few days it was not clear who would succeed President Husák, but eventually Vaclav Havel, the playwright and one of the most outstanding figures of Charter 77, was elected; Alexander Dubček resumed the function from which he had been ousted after the Soviet invasion in 1968—that of president of the Parliament. Jan Carnogurski became vice-president (also in control of the secret police); Jiri Dienstbier, foreign minister. Only a few weeks earlier Carnogurski had been in prison, Dienstbier had worked as a stoker, Havel was in semihiding between arrests, and Dubček (like Havel and the others) had been contemptuously dismissed by the spokesmen of the old regime as a "zero" and a "has-been."

Events in Prague proceeded with breakneck speed. In a speech addressing a crowd of two hundred thousand, Havel said, "One day the historians will call these days extraordinary." If anything, this was an understatement. The Czechoslovak revolution was unique in that there was not even much verbal violence, let alone arrests. Though the opposition had not been well organized, it was probably the most disciplined, mature, and humane revolution of all times, still more surprising in view of the decades of suppression. The revolution was in the tradition of the Czech enlightenment and of Masaryk; it was, in many ways, a protest against violence.

In the end, the communist leadership was infected by the mood of the people, and, following the example of Warsaw, Budapest, and East Berlin, it abdicated. So thorough had been their failure and consequent loss of self-confidence that the old saying seemed no longer to apply—that ruling classes never abdicate voluntarily.

CEAUSESCU'S FALL

Of all the East European rulers, Nicolae Ceausescu felt most secure in the saddle. He was unhappy about the Soviet reforms and the political changes in the neighboring countries, but Rumania was effectively isolated from the rest of the world, and Ceausescu therefore saw no reason to cancel a visit of state to Iran during the second half of December 1989. Yet it was precisely during these days that the popular anger, accumulated over a long time, reached its climax.

When Ceausescu returned from Teheran, he called a mass demonstration, assuming that he would as usual again receive full support. However, whereas on past such occasions there had been long ovations honoring the great leader, this time there were only hostile shouts, much to Ceausescu's evident discomfort. The next day (December 22) he gave orders to the army to open fire on the demonstrators. But the orders were disobeyed. Milea, the minister of defense, committed suicide or was killed.

This was the end of the dictatorship. Ceausescu and his wife tried to escape but were apprehended. On December 25 they were condemned to death by a military tribunal and immediately executed. All this happened with great haste, and there was criticism later on: why had there not been due process of law? Against this it was argued that the security police, which, unlike the army, continued to fight, might have liberated the dictator, in an attempt to re-establish the old regime. Fighting did indeed continue for almost a week, and there were hundreds of victims, but during the last days of December the National Salvation Front was firmly established.

What triggered off the Rumanian revolution, and who were its leaders? It is impossible to provide a clear answer, even with the benefit of hindsight, for there were no leaders. The persecution of a popular Hungarian pastor in Timişoara triggered a local demonstration on December 17, which was suppressed by the local security forces. There were many victims, and rumor magnified the extent of the bloodbath that had taken place. There were demonstrations of solidarity with Timişoara in Bucharest and other cities of Rumania. Many thousands escaped over the Hungarian border, the "Rumanian story" dominated world radio and television, and for a little while even foreign intervention seemed possible.

There had all along been a number of men and women critical of Ceausescu's rule, such as the human-rights activist Dorina Cornea and former communist officials such as Ion Iliescu (who became president of the National Salvation Front), Silvio Brucan (former Rumanian envoy to the United Nations and the U.S.), and Petru Roman, the youngest of the group, a professor of mechanical engineering.

In the weeks after the fall of the old regime some of Rumania's traditional parties re-emerged, such as the National Liberals, the Peasant Party, and the Social Democrats. But in addition some sixty or seventy other political groups tried to assert themselves. In Rumania, unlike other East European countries, there was a growing feeling that the revolution had turned sour, or that it had been hijacked by the National Salvation Front, the leaders of which had all been in the service of the old regime. There were strikes, new demonstrations, and clashes. The National Salvation Front leaders emphatically denied the accusations that they were continuing a more streamlined version of Ceausescu's policies. They referred to hostile demonstrators as a "bunch of thugs and vagabonds" who were not motivated by the desire to build a democratic regime in the country.

The National Salvation Front won an overwhelming victory in the general elections that took place in May 1990, but accusations and counteraccusations continued. Change in Bucharest was not remotely so radical and clearcut as in Warsaw, Prague, and Budapest.

BULGARIA

Bulgaria was the only Eastern-bloc country that experienced an old-style "revolution from above"—that is to say, a coup carried out by members of the Politburo against the man who had ruled Bulgaria for thirty-five years. On November 10, 1989, a meeting of the Central Committee took place and Todor Zhivkov listened, evidently much to his surprise, to his own resignation, read out by his colleagues. They also used the opportunity to thank him for his past services to party and country. He was succeeded by Peter Mladenov, who had been foreign minister in the old regime; the following February, Andrei Lukyanov became prime minister. On December 8 the new party leadership had second thoughts about Zhivkov's past merits; he and his son and some of his close collaborators were subjected to severe criticism and, a few days later, excluded from the party.

A small opposition had existed in Bulgaria for some time; on the eve of Zhivkov's resignation some four thousand people had participated in a demonstration in Sofia. But these groups—Glasnost, Eco-Glasnost, and Podkrepa (an unofficial trade union)—were not remotely strong enough to overthrow the old leadership. Such a move could come only from inside the Politburo. The anti-Zhivkov faction consisted of younger men who had reached the conclusion that some kind of reform was needed to forestall more serious conflict, and since Zhivkov, almost eighty years of age, showed no readiness to resign, he was removed. They had no desire to carry out far-reaching political reforms; they wanted to prevent radical change—above all to maintain the political monopoly of the Communist Party even though the role of Parliament was reactivated. They had to make some concessions to the popular demands, and this opened the door to the growth of the opposition movement. Sofia's Southern Park turned into something like Speaker's Corner in London's Hyde Park, and in subsequent demonstrations tens of thousands of residents of the capital participated.

In the first free elections, which took place in Bulgaria in June 1990, the Socialist Party (formerly the communists) received 47 percent of the vote but a majority of seats in the Parliament, which enabled them to hold on to power. They had done much less well in Sofia and the other major cities but retained their position, for the time being, thanks to the strong hold of the party apparatus in the countryside. However, the party now had a majority of the urban intelligentsia as well as other sections of the population in opposition to its rule; as in Rumania, the political struggle for liberation was bound to continue. Thus Peter Mladenov as president was forced to resign and was replaced by a leader of the opposition. A new generation of leaders emerged such as Zhelyu Zhelev and Dimitar Popov; in January 1991 Zhivkov was put on trial on charges of corruption.

FERMENT IN YUGOSLAVIA

Political change in Yugoslavia, unlike in other East European countries, had occurred well before 1989; some reforms had taken place in Tito's life, some thereafter. Nevertheless, the country was affected by the general turbulence in Eastern Europe, and this opened a critical stage in Yugoslav history. The riots in the Kosovo region continued; in Montenegro the party leadership was overthrown, following popular pressure. Above all, tensions between Serbia and the other republics became more intense: Slovenia announced that it would leave the Yugoslav federation, and in Croatia, following the elections of March 1990, the anti-Serbian faction gained the upper hand. Slovenia and Croatia virtually opted for a market economy and a multiparty system. (The federal government, in the meantime, had promised pluralism, though not yet a multiparty system.) Serbia, too, had advocated far-reaching reforms, but these had largely remained a dead letter.

Milosevic, the Serbian prime minister, was attacked by the heads of the other republics for trying to reimpose a centralist system on the Yugoslav federation; he was also accused of populist and even neo-Stalinist tactics. It is difficult to say what his real inspiration was; probably he was above all a Serbian nationalist. Milosevic had initially been quite popular in his native republic. But during 1989 the opposition to his leadership grew in Belgrade as much as in Zagreb and Ljubljana. There were strikes, and threats of even bigger strikes, and various new political groups in Belgrade spoke out for political pluralism. These included a new Democratic Party as well as the Movement for Democratic Renewal (which largely consisted of members, or former members, of the Socialist Youth Alliance) as well as intellectual ginger groups such as the Serbian Writers' Association.

Mention has been made of the separatist tendencies among the non-Serbians. Milosevic's policy was bound to backfire and to undermine the very survival of the Yugoslav federation: The Slovenes expressed support for the Kosovo Albanians (with whom they had otherwise little in common), and the Croats sympathized with the Slovenian policy of asserting their own sovereignty. Serbia had initially threatened that it would break economic and political ties with Slovenia, but the Slovenians were not intimidated and accepted the challenge. With the victory of the Croatian nationalists (the United Croatian Opposition) under Franjo Tudjman, who had spent years in prison, the isolation of Belgrade became even more pronounced.

This political struggle took place against the background of a severe economic crisis. The country had moved far away from even the relatively liberal style of communism practiced in Tito's last years. Within a few months in 1991 Yugoslavia fell apart. First Slovenia seceded, soon after Croatia declared its independence. The Serbian leadership under Milosevic resisted this move and substantial sections of Croatia were seized by the old Yugoslav army which was under Serbian command as well as by Serbian partisans from among the Serbian minority in Croatia. But the bloodiest fighting took place when Bosnia-Herzegovina declared its independence in 1992. The fighting for Sarajevo not only demanded thousands of victims, it became a major issue in European and world politics. The reluctance of the new Europe to impose a solution is understandable in light of the great complexity of the situation in these components of the former Yugoslav state. At the same time, it pointed to the limits of the power of the new Europe that had neither the political will nor the instruments to act as a force of order in its borderlands. In these circumstances there was every reason to assume that national conflicts would continue to dominate Balkan politics as they had in earlier centuries.

The East European revolution of 1989 ought to be viewed as the end of a period, during which the Soviet Union attempted to impose an alien political and social system on unwilling peoples from the Baltic to the Aegean. The events that took place in 1989 and the year after more or less liquidated the structures that had been established during the postwar period, and wherever the demolition work had not been carried out in full, it was probably only a question of time until it would be completed. But if the revolution of 1989 was one of hope, it was also rooted in despair, opening the way into an uncertain future.

Eastern Europe had always been the poorer part of the continent; its experiments with democracy had been, at best, inconclusive. It had been divided by national strife; the tensions in the Balkan States had continued throughout the nineteenth and early twentieth centuries. Many such unsolved (and sometimes insoluble) issues were bound to re-emerge as political freedom returned to these parts. Many East Europeans wanted to rejoin Europe as they regained their liberty. But, with all the sympathy for European ways, they had never been part of Europe, such as it was, in the past. Nor was it at all clear whether economic and political structures that worked reasonably well in Western Europe could be transplanted to the East. Certainly it was not just a matter of promulgating new democratic constitutions; the East European constitutions after the First World War had been exemplary, yet within less than a decade only Czechoslovakia had an effective parliamentary democracy.

Few East Europeans believed that Thatcherism had a future in Eastern Europe; almost all of them preferred a market system which sustained at the same time a welfare state on the Scandinavian (or French or West German) model. But these welfare states had become possible only on the basis of a high level of economic development and prosperity, which did not exist in Eastern Europe—and was not likely to prevail for a long time to come. Even in East Germany, which had better prospects than the others, there was bound to be a difficult transition period.

Thus, on the day after tyranny had been vanquished in Eastern

Europe, it became clear that the road to freedom and the pursuit of happiness would be long, arduous, with probably not a few setbacks ahead. The painful process of rebuilding the economy was still to begin. Tyranny had been defeated, but political freedom was not yet secure.

EPILOGUE

It was the general consensus in Europe in 1945 that the recovery would take a long time, involve enormous efforts, and that, even if all went well, Europe's place in the world would never be the same again. These assumptions proved to be correct inasmuch as the great colonial empires disintegrated; in any case they would have vanished sooner or later. In most other respects, the pessimism of 1945 has not been borne out by subsequent events. But the fact that Europe was not doomed was only slowly realized; there was a deep-seated conviction that Europe was ruined forever. Around 1960 and for years after, Sartre and Frantz Fanon were by no means the only thinkers to predict that Europe was in a state of advanced decay, that it was dying in convulsions, that there was no room for foolish hopes. Such pessimism was not limited to novelists and essayists: *An Introduction to Contemporary History* (1964), an influential work by the historian Geoffrey Barraclough, argued that for various reasons Europe was steadily losing ground. In fact, one of the chapters was entitled "The Dwarfing of Europe." It was said that new regional blocs were emerging in Africa and Asia of far greater importance than poor old Europe, which was confronted, moreover, with an enormous ideological challenge by Marxism-Leninism for which, quite probably, it had no answer.

Three decades later it seems clear that the major cultural impulses and political initiatives expected from the Third World have not as yet emerged, and that the attraction of Marxism-Leninism has proved to be much less formidable than had been assumed.

If there was a feeling that a new age had dawned, it had mainly to do with the fact that "dwarfed Europe" had somehow gotten a second wind, that it had made astonishing economic progress, that the cold war in Europe had been overcome, and that the spirit of freedom had reawakened in Eastern Europe. Europe had become again a "partner in world leadership," to quote President Bush, speaking in 1990.

The decades since 1945 have witnessed not only economic recovery but political reconciliation, first between traditional enemies such as France and Germany, and subsequently between the Soviet Union and Western Europe. The very idea that a war could take place in Western Europe became unthinkable in the 1950s and 1960s as the countries drew closer together and increasingly cooperated.

There was initially less optimism as far as relations between West and East were concerned, even though there had been a certain lessening of tensions since Stalin's day. But the Soviet armed forces had invaded Hungary in 1956 and Czechoslovakia in 1968, and until the middle 1980s it seemed doubtful whether they would ever give up their hold on Eastern Europe, however unpopular the Communist regimes. It was only after Gorbachev's rise to power that Soviet domestic and foreign policies were submitted to radical revision. This resulted in the collapse of the DDR, the emergence of democratic (or at the very least, more democratic) regimes in Eastern Europe, and an increasing belief in "our common European home." Even a few years earlier these developments had appeared quite impossible. But Western Europe with its prosperity and its free institutions acted like a magnet on its neighbors in the East without even being aware of its magnetic influence or of the inherent weakness of its neighbors to the east.

Could the European reconciliation have taken place earlier on? Probably not, for it is doubtful whether greater diplomatic concessions on the part of the West would have had much effect: events in the East had to run their course, the learning process in these countries could not be shortened, and it had to be based on their own political and economic experience, not on persuasion on the part of outsiders.

The history of postwar Europe, unlike many other periods in the history of the continent, reads almost like a Hollywood movie of the old-fashioned kind, with all kinds of tensions and conflict but a strikingly happy ending. But history has no end and the historian knows that there is an almost unlimited number of possibilities that things may take a wrong turn. It is conceivable that decreasing conflict between states could lead to increasing tension inside societies, with all kinds of virulent nationalism playing a destructive role and the fabric of society weakened by any number of factors for which there may be no discernible "objective" causes. The great achievements of the cause of freedom in Eastern Europe and the former Soviet Union are not yet deeply anchored; it will probably be a long time before they can be taken for granted. There may be setbacks in the movement toward greater European collaboration. Events in Eastern Europe in 1990–91 came as an anticlimax after the high expectations of 1988–89.

Europe now has an EEC flag, as well as an anthem and emblem (though most Europeans may not be aware of this). There are a European passport and a European driving license. But it would be unrealistic to expect a common European defense and foreign policy in the near future. National interests and traditions militate against integration in these fields. It is obvious that without substantial progress toward a common defense and foreign policy European unity will be, at best, incomplete in a world in which Europe faces not only friends and well-wishers. Influential circles continue to oppose further political integration, and national parliaments are reluctant to delegate more power to a European parliament.

Europe has become a civilian superpower, and it would be a factor of paramount importance in a world by and large free of violence and in which military power no longer counts. But such a stage in the development of mankind has not yet been reached. The performance of Europe at times of world crisis has been less than inspiring; its inability to act during the Persian Gulf crisis was additional evidence. Its leaders have not acted decisively or in unison; Europe is not yet equipped to deal with a crisis in which more than economic power is involved. To this extent uncertainties remain with regard to the future of Europe; they will disappear only when the continent becomes strong and united enough to defend both its values and its interests without outside help, and this could be a long time ahead.

In Eastern Europe and the former Soviet Union, the economic situation in this era of transition was worse than it had been for decades. The centrifugal separatist forces have become much stronger; not surprisingly, democratization and the weakening of central power coincided. While these trends were only natural, it is also true that they created uncertainties and grave dangers, ranging from the Balkanization of Eastern Europe to the reimposition of dictatorial rule.

It is unfortunately only too easy to think of the many obstacles and pitfalls still ahead. But the historian's preoccupation is with the past, and seen in this light Western Europe's recovery since the Second World War has been remarkable, well beyond the expectations of inveterate optimists. Was it hard work, or luck, or the growing realization that an internally divided continent had no future? Or was it a mixture of these and other factors? It is too early to provide more than tentative answers for questions that will preoccupy historians for a long time to come. With regard to the Soviet Union and Eastern Europe, only the very courageous (and foolhardy) will provide a historical balance sheet with any degree of certainty. It is easy to see what political, social, and economic systems have failed. It is impossible as yet to say what will succeed them.

BIBLIOGRAPHY

WORKS OF REFERENCE

Basic Statistics of the Community, Brussels (annually).
C. Cook and J. Paxton: *European Political Facts*, London 1965.
Europa Yearbook, London (annually).
A. Grosser (ed.): *Les pays de l'Europe occidentale* (Paris, annually 1979–).
R. Mayne (ed.): *Handbooks to the Modern World: Western Europe*, London 1986.
L. L. Paklons: *European Bibliography*, Bruges 1964.
J. Paxton: *A Dictionary of European Communities*, London 1982.
H. Pehrson and H. Wulff: *The European Bibliography*, Leyden 1965.
United Nations: *Statistical Yearbook* (annually).

GENERAL WORKS: POSTWAR

R. Aron: *The Century of Total War*, New York 1964.
J. Becker (ed.): *Power in Europe 1945–50*, Berlin 1986.
N. Beloff: *Europe and the Europeans*, London 1957
J. Freymond: *Western Europe Since the War*, London 1964.
S. R. Graubard (ed.): *A New Europe*, New York 1964.
M. J. Hogan: *The Marshall Plan*, London 1987.
R. Mayne: *Post War*, London 1983.
R. Mayne (ed.): *The Recovery of Europe*, London 1973.
A. Sampson: *The New Europeans*, London 1968.
H. Seton Watson: *Neither War nor Peace*, London 1960.

YALTA, POTSDAM, THE BEGINNING OF THE COLD WAR

T. H. Anderson: *The United States, Great Britain and the Cold War 1944–47*, New York 1981.

L. E. Davis: *The Cold War Begins*, Princeton 1974.

M. Dockrill: *The Cold War 1945–63*, Atlantic Highlands, N.J., 1988.

H. Feis: *Between War and Peace: The Potsdam Conference*, New York 1960.

D. F. Fleming: *The Cold War and Its Origins*, Garden City, N.Y., 1961.

A. Fontaine: *Histoire de la Guerre Froide*, Paris 1967.

J. Gaddis, *Strategies of Containment*, New York 1982.

F. J. Harbutt: *The Iron Curtain*, Oxford 1986.

M. F. Hertz: *Beginnings of the Cold War*, Bloomington, Ind., 1986.

J. Laloy: *Yalta—Yesterday, Today, Tomorrow*, New York 1988.

V. Mastny: *Russia's Road to the Cold War*, New York 1979.

W. H. McNeill, *America, Britain and Russia: Their Cooperation and Conflict 1941–46*, London 1953.

V. Rothwell: *Britain and the Cold War*, London 1982.

H. Thomas: *Armed Truce: The Beginnings of the Cold War*, London 1986.

C. Wilmot: *The Struggle for Europe*, London 1953.

WAR CRIME TRIALS AND POSTWAR PURGES

R. Aron: *Histoire de la libération de la France*, Paris 1958.

R. E. Conot: *Justice at Nuremberg*, New York 1983.

E. Davidson: *The Trial of the Germans*, New York 1967.

C. Fitzgibbon: *Denazification*, London 1969.

H. L. Mason: *The Purge of Dutch Quislings*, London 1956.

L. Noguères: *La Haute Cour de la libération 1944–1949*, Paris 1965.

P. Novick: *The Resistance Versus Vichy*, New York 1986.

Les Procès de la collaboration (verbatim reports of the trials of Pétain, Laval, Maurras, de Binon, and others), Paris n.d.

P. Serant: *Les Vaincus de la libération*, Paris 1964.

B. Smith: *The Road to Nuremberg*, New York 1981.

A. and J. Tusa: *The Nuremberg Trial*, New York 1984.

DIPLOMATIC MEMOIRS, BIOGRAPHIES

D. Acheson: *Present at the Creation*, New York 1969.

C. Bohlen: *Witness to History*, New York 1973.

A. Bullock: *Ernest Bevin*, 3 vols., London 1960–83.

J. Byrnes: *Speaking Frankly*, New York 1947.

W. Churchill: *The Second World War*, vol. VI, London 1953.

J. Ciechanowski: *Defeat in Victory*, New York 1947.

C. de Gaulle: *Mémoires d'espoir*, 2 vols., Paris 1970–71.

M. Gilbert: *Winston Churchill: Never Despair*, Boston 1988.

A. Horne: *H. Macmillan*, 2 vols., New York 1989.

C. Hull: *The Memoirs of Cordell Hull*, New York 1948.

R. R. James: *Anthony Eden: A Biography*, New York 1987.

G. Kennan: *Memoirs*, 2 vols., New York 1967, 1972.

S. Mikolajczyk: *The Rape of Poland*, London 1948.

R. Marjolin: *Architect of European Unity*, London 1989.

J. Monnet: *Mémoires*, Paris 1978.

H. P. Schwarz: *Adenauer: Der Aufstieg*, Stuttgart 1986.

H. S. Truman: *Years of Decision*, New York 1955.

GREAT BRITAIN AFTER THE WAR

D. E. Ashford: *Policy and Policies in Britain*, London 1981.

C. R. Attlee: *As It Happened*, London 1954.

C. Barnett: *The Pride and the Fall*, London 1987.

C. J. A. Bartlett: *A History of Postwar Britain*, London 1977.

S. H. Beer: *Britain Against Herself*, New York 1982.

J. Beveridge: *Beveridge and His Plan*, London 1954.

P. Calvocoressi: *The British Experience 1945–75*, London 1978.

J. Campbell: *Aneurin Bevan*, New York 1987.

R. H. S. Crossman (ed.): *New Fabian Essays*, London 1954.

H. Dalton: *High Tide and After*, London 1962.

W. R. Louis and R. Owen: *Suez 1956*, New York 1989.

R. B. McCallum and A. Readman: *The British Elections of 1945*, London 1947.

K. O. Morgan: *Labor in Power 1945–51*, Oxford 1984.

H. Morrison: *An Autobiography*, London 1961.

H. Pelling: *A Short History of the Labour Party*, London 1976.

M. Sissons and P. French: *An Age of Austerity*, London 1963.

A. Sked and C. Cook: *Post-War Britain*, London 1984.

E. Watkins: *The Cautious Revolution*, London 1952.

C. M. Woodhouse: *British Foreign Policy Since the Second World War*, London 1962.

FRANCE

R. Aron: *Immuable et changeante: de la IVe à la Ve République*, Paris 1959.

J. Barsalou: *La Mal Aimée: Histoire de la IVe République*, Paris 1964.

J. Chapsal: *La Vie politique en France depuis 1940*, Paris 1966.

M. Duverger: *Les Partis politiques*, Paris 1960.

J. Fauvet: *La IVe République*, Paris 1960.

E. Furniss: *France: The Troubled Ally*, New York 1955.

C. Gavin: *Liberated France*, New York 1955.

F. Goguel and A. Grosser: *La Politique en France*, Paris 1964.

S. Hoffmann (ed.): *In Search of France*, New York 1963.

J. Lacouture: *De Gaulle*, vols. 2 and 3, Paris 1986.

M. Larkin: *France Since the Popular Front*, Oxford 1988.

H. Luethy: *France Against Herself*, London 1955.

R. Macridis: *French Politics in Transition*, Cambridge 1975.

H. Michel: *Les Courants de la pensée de la Résistance*, Paris 1962.

J. P. Rioux: *The Fourth Republic*, Cambridge 1987.

A. Siegfried: *De la IIIe à la IVe République*, Paris 1956.

D. Thomson: *Democracy in France*, London 1958.

A. Werth: *France 1940–1955*, London 1956.

P. Williams: *Politics in Post-War France*, London 1965.

ITALY

G. Andreotti: *De Gasperi e suo tempo*, Rome 1956, 1977.

G. Andreotti: *Diari 1976–79*, Milan 1981.

A. Battaglia et al.: *Dieci anni dopo*, Bari 1955.

I. Bonomi: *Diario di un anno*, Milan 1947.

J. Earle: *Italy in the 1970s*, Newton Abbot 1975.

M. Grindrod: *The New Italy*, London 1947.

J. Haycraft: *Italian Labyrinth*, London 1985.

N. Kogan: *A Political History of Postwar Italy*, New York 1983.

J. La Palombara: *Democracy Italian Style*, New Haven 1987.

G. Mammarella: *Italy After Fascism*, Montreal 1964.

G. Pasquino: *Istituzioni, partiti, lobbies*, Bari 1988.

D. Sassoon: *Contemporary Italy*, London 1986.

WEST GERMANY

K. Adenauer: *Memoirs*, 2 vols., London 1966, 1968.

F. R. Alleman: *Bonn ist nicht Weimar*, Köln 1956.

R. Altmann: *Das Erbe Adenauers*, Stuttgart 1960.

M. Balfour: *West Germany: A Contemporary History*, London 1982.

D. L. Bark and D. R. Gress: *A History of West Germany*, 2 vols., Oxford 1989.

K. Boelling: *Republic in Suspense*, London 1964.

W. Brandt: *Begegnungen und Einsichten*, Hamburg 1976.

H. Dollinger: *Deutschland unter den Besatzungsmächten*, München 1967.

T. Ellwein: *Das Regierungssystem der Bundesregierung Deutschland*, Opladen 1977.

T. Ellwein and W. Bruder: *Die Bundesrepublik Deutschland*, Freiburg 1984.

F. Erler: *Democracy in Germany*, London 1965.

T. Eschenburg: *Jahre der Besatzung 1945–49*, Stuttgart 1983.

T. Eschenburg: *Staat und Gesellschaft in Deutschland*, Stuttgart 1956.

H. Grebing (ed.): *Die Nachkriegsentwicklung in Westdeutschland*, Stuttgart 1980.

W. Grewe: *Deutsche Aussenpolitik der Nachkriegszeit*, Stuttgart 1960.

A. Grosser: *Geschichte Deutschlands seit 1945*, Stuttgart 1974.

T. Heuss: *Aufzeichnungen 1945–47*, Tübingen 1966.

K. Hildebrand, *Von Erhard zur grossen Koalition*, Wiesbaden 1984.

R. Hiscocks: *The Adenauer Era*, London 1966.

R. Loewenthal and H. P. Schwarz: *Die zweite Republik*, Stuttgart 1974.

P. Merkl: *The Origins of the West German Republic*, New York 1965.

R. Morgan: *The United States and West Germany*, London 1974.

W. E. Paterson and G. Smith: *The West German Model*, London 1981.

G. Pridham: *Christian Democracy in West Germany*, New York 1977.

H. P. Schwarz: *Die Aera Adenauer 1949–1957*, Wiesbaden 1981.

H. P. Schwarz: *Die Aera Adenauer 1957–1963*, vol. II, Wiesbaden 1983.

H. P. Schwarz: *Vom Reich zur Bundesrepublik Deutschlands*, Wiesbaden 1967.

G. Stolper: *Deutsche Wirtschaftsgeschichte seit 1870*, Tübingen 1964.

F. J. Strauss: *The Grand Design*, New York 1965.

EASTERN EUROPE

R. R. Betts (ed.): *Central and South East Europe, 1945–48*, London 1950.

J. F. Brown: *Eastern Europe and Communist Rule*, Durham, N.C., 1988.

Z. Brzezinski: *The Soviet Bloc: Unity and Conflict*, New York 1961.

F. Fejto: *Histoire des démocraties populaires*, Paris 1969.

S. Fischer-Galati: *Eastern Europe in the 1980s*, New York 1981.

S. Fischer-Galati (ed.): *Rumania*, New York 1957.

E. Halperin: *The Triumphant Heretic*, London 1958.

P. Johnson: *Redesigning the Communist Economy*, Boulder 1989.

M. Kaser and M. C. Radice: *The Economic History of Eastern Europe*, Oxford 1987.

J. Korbel: *The Communist Subversion of Czechoslovakia*, Princeton 1959.

W. Markert (ed.): *Polen*, Köln 1959.

N. Panov: *Albania*, London 1989.

H. Renner: *History of Czechoslovakia Since 1945*, London 1989.

H. Roos: *A History of Modern Poland*, London 1966.

J. Rothschild: *Return to Diversity*, New York 1989.

J. Rupnik: *The Other Europe*, London 1988.

D. Rusinow, *The Yugoslav Experiment*, Berkeley 1968.

H. Seton Watson: *The East European Revolution*, London 1950.

E. Taborski: *Communism in Czechoslovakia 1948–56*, Princeton 1961.

A. Ulam: *Titoism and the Cominform*, Cambridge, Mass., 1952.

F. A. Vali: *Rift and Revolution in Hungary*, Cambridge, Mass., 1961.

P. Zinner (ed.): *National Communism and Popular Revolt in Eastern Europe*, New York 1956.

COLD WAR, DÉTENTE, WEST-EAST RELATIONS

R. Aron: *The Great Debate*, New York 1965.

C. Bell: *Negotiations from Strength*, New York 1963.

A. Buchan: *NATO in the 1960s*, London 1965.

A. Buchan and P. Windsor: *Arms and Stability in Europe*, London 1963.

W. Bull: *The Control of the Arms Race*, London 1965.

H. B. Cleveland: *The Atlantic Idea and Its European Rivals*, New York 1967.

A. Cottrell and J. Dougherty: *The Politics of the Atlantic Alliance*, New York 1964.

L. Freedman: *The Evolution of Nuclear Strategy*, London 1981.

J. Freymond: *Western Europe Since the War*, London 1964.

P. Hassner: *Change and Security in Europe*, London 1968.

Die Internationale Politik: Jahrbücher der deutschen Gesellschaft für auswärtige Politik (annually 1961).

K. Kaiser et al.: *Amerika und Westeuropa*, Stuttgart 1979.

H. Kissinger: *The Troubled Partnership*, New York 1966.

J. Kraft: *The Grand Design*, New York 1962.

W. La Feber: *America, Russia and the Cold War*, Princeton 1973.

J. Laloy: *Entre guerre et paix*, Paris 1966.

W. Laqueur and L. Labedz: *Polycentrism*, Cambridge, Mass., 1962.

R. Maddox: *The New Left and the Origins of the Cold War*, New York 1976.

P. Mosely: *The Kremlin and World Politics*, New York 1960.

R. Osgood: *NATO and the Entangling Alliance*, New York 1962.

J. L. Richardson: *Germany and the Atlantic Alliance*, Cambridge 1966.

P. Seabury: *The Rise and Decline of the Cold War*, New York 1967.

H. Seton Watson: *The End of Alliance*, London 1964.

G. H. Snyder: *Deterrence and Defense*, New York 1963.

T. W. Stanley: *NATO in Transition*, New York 1965.

T. W. Wolfe: *Soviet Strategy at the Crossroads*, Cambridge 1965.

UNITED EUROPE 1945–1970

E. Benoit: *Europe at Sixes and Sevens*, London 1961.

M. Camps: *The European Market and American Policy*, London 1956.

M. J. Hogan: *The Marshall Plan: America, Britain and the Reconstruction of Western Europe*, Cambridge 1987.

Lord Ismay, *NATO: The First Five Years*, London 1954.

U. W. Kitzinger: *The Challenge of the Common Market*, London 1962.

G. Lichtheim: *The New Europe*, London 1963.

J. Lodge (ed.): *European Union*, London 1986.

R. Mayne: *The Community of Europe*, London 1962.

A. Milward: *The Reconstruction of Western Europe 1945–51*, Berkeley 1984.

R. Price: *The Political Future of the European Community*, London 1962.

R. Price (ed.): *The Dynamics of European Union*, London 1987.

O. Riste (ed.): *Western Security: The Formative Years*, Oslo 1985.

H. A. Schmitt: *The Path to European Unity*, London 1962.

F. de la Serre: *La Grande Bretagne et la Communauté Européenne*, Paris 1987.

H. K. Smith: *The State of Europe*, New York 1949.

G. L. Weil: *A Handbook of the EEC*, London 1965.

T. H. White: *Fire in the Ashes*, New York 1953.

A. J. Zurcher: *The Struggle to Unite Europe*, New York 1958.

COMMUNISM IN WESTERN EUROPE

R. Aron: *The Opium of the Intellectuals*, London 1957.

E. Bettiza: *Il comunismo europeo*, Milan 1978.

D. M. Blackmer and S. G. Tarrow: *Communism in Italy and France*, New York 1976.

F. Borkenau: *European Communism*, London 1953.

S. Carrillo: *Eurocomunismo y estado*, Madrid 1977.

D. Caute: *Communism and the French Intellectuals*, London 1964.

M. Einaudi: *Communism in Western Europe*, New York 1951.

J. Elleinstein: *Le P.C.*, Paris 1976.

J. Fauvet: *Histoire du parti communiste française*, 2 vols., Paris 1964–65.

G. Galli: *Istoria di partitio comunista italiano*, Milan 1975.

W. Griffith (ed.): *Communism in Europe*, Cambridge 1964.

E. J. Hobsbawm and G. Napolitano (eds.): *The Italian Road to Socialism*, London 1977.

D. G. Kousoulas: *Revolution and Defeat: The Story of the Greek Communist Party*, London 1965.

L. Labedz (ed.): *Revisionism*, Cambridge, Mass., 1963.

A. Laurens and T. Pfister: *Les Nouveaux Communistes*, Paris 1973.

B. Lazitch: *Les Partis communistes d'Europe 1919–55*, Paris 1956.

G. Lichtheim: *Marxism in Modern France*, New York 1966.

G. Mammarella: *Il partito comunista italiano 1945–75*, Florence 1976.

C. Micaud: *Communism and the French Left*, New York 1963.

N. McInnes: *The Communist Parties of Western Europe*, London 1973.

K. Middlemas: *Power and the Party*, London 1980.

A. Ronchey: *Accade in Italia 1968–77*, Rome 1977.

A. Rossi: *Physiologie du parti communiste française*, Paris 1948.

J. Semprun: *Autobiografia de Frederic Sanchez*, Barcelona 1978.

P. Spriano: *Storia del partito comunista italiano*, 5 vols., Torino 1975.

R. Tierski: *French Communism 1920–1972*, New York 1974.

N. Wood: *Communism and the British Intellectuals*, London 1957.

C. M. Woodhouse: *Apple of Discord*, London 1948.

SOVIET UNION 1945–70

A. Avtorkhanov: *Stalin and the Soviet Communist Party*, New York 1959.

R. Conquest: *Power and Politics in the USSR*, London 1962.

D. Dallin: *Soviet Foreign Policy After Stalin*, New Haven 1961.

I. Deutscher: *Stalin*, London 1966.

M. Djilas: *The New Class*, New York 1957.

J. Erickson: *The Soviet High Command*, London 1962.

M. Fainsod: *How Russia Is Ruled*, Cambridge, Mass., 1965.

W. Hahn: *Postwar Soviet Politics*, Ithaca, N.Y., 1982.

G. Hosking: *The First Socialist Society*, Cambridge, Mass., 1985.

M. Heller and A. M. Nekrich: *Utopia in Power*, New York 1981.

N. Khrushchev: *Khrushchev Remembers*, Boston 1970.

W. Laqueur: *Stalin*, New York 1990.

W. Leonhard: *The Kremlin Since Stalin*, New York 1962.

M. McCauley (ed.): *Khrushchev and Khrushchevism*, London 1987.

R. A. Medvedev: *Khrushchev*, Oxford 1962.

R. A. Medvedev: *Let History Judge*, New York 1989.

B. Meissner: *Sowjet Russland zwischen Revolution und Restauration*, Köln 1956.

A. Nove: *An Economic History of the USSR*, London 1972.

R. W. Pethybridge: *A History of Post-War Russia*, London 1966.

A. D. Sakharov: *A. D. Sakharov Speaks*, London 1974.

L. Schapiro: *The Communist Party of the Soviet Union*, London 1960.

H. Seton Watson: *From Lenin to Malenkov*, London 1954.

M. Tatu: *Power in the Kremlin*, Paris and London 1969.

R. C. Tucker (ed.): *Stalinism*, New York 1977.
A. Ulam: *Expansion and Coexistence*, New York 1974.
A. Ulam: *Stalin*, New York 1973.
G. R. Urban (ed.): *Stalinism*, London 1982.
B. D. Wolfe: *Communist Totalitarianism*, New York 1961.

EAST GERMANY

G. Castellan: *DDR-Allemagne de L'Est*, Paris 1985.
D. Childs: *The G.D.R.: Moscow's German Ally*, London 1983.
S. Doernberg: *Die Geburt eines neuen Deutschland 1945–49*, Berlin 1959.
H. Duhnke: *Stalinismus in Deutschland: Die Geschichte der sowjetischen Besatzungszone*, Köln 1955.
C. J. Friedrich (ed.): *The Soviet Zone of Germany*, New York 1956.
P. Nettl: *The Eastern Zone and Soviet Policy in Germany 1945–50*, New York 1951.
E. Richert: *Das zweite Deutschland*, Frankfurt 1964.
C. Stern: *Porträt einer bolschewistischen Partei*, Köln 1957.
C. Stern: *Ulbricht*, Köln 1963.
H. Weber: *Die DDR 1945–1986*, München 1986.

ECONOMICS AND SOCIAL TRENDS

D. H. Aldcroft: *The European Economy 1914–1970*, London 1978.
P. Alpert: *Twentieth Century Economic History of Western Europe*, New York 1967.
A. Boltho: *The European Economy: Growth and Crisis*, Oxford 1982.
A. Bramwell: *Ecology in the 20th Century*, London 1989.
R. Dahrendorf: *Europa's Economy in Crisis*, New York 1982.
J. F. Dewhurst et al.: *Europe's Needs and Resources*, New York 1961.
M. Emerson: *Europe's Stagflation*, Oxford 1984.
R. Hudson and J. Lewis: *Uneven Development in Southern Europe*, London 1985.
C. P. Kindleberger: *Europe's Postwar Growth*, Cambridge 1967.
D. S. Landes (ed.): *European Union*, Lexington, Ky., 1983.
A. Maddison: *Economic Growth in the West*, New York 1964.
M. J. Miller: *Foreign Workers in Western Europe*, New York 1981.
OECD: *Economic Country Surveys* (annually).
A. Pierre (ed.): *Unemployment and Growth in the Western Economies*, New York 1984.
M. Postan: *An Economic History of Western Europe*, London 1967.
A. Shonfield: *Modern Capitalism*, London 1967.

United Nations: *Some Factors in Economic Growth in Europe During the 1950s*, New York 1964.

United Nations Economic Survey of Europe (annually) 1948–.

A. M. Williams: *The West European Economy*, London 1987.

GERMANY AND THE BERLIN CRISIS

W. Brandt: *The Ordeal of Coexistence*, London 1963.

H. von Brentano: *Germany and Europe*, London 1964.

N. Gelb: *The Berlin Wall*, New York 1987.

W. Grewe: *Rückblenden 1976–1951*, Berlin 1979.

H. Herzfeld: *Berlin in der Weltpolitik*, Berlin and New York 1973.

D. Mahnke: *Berlin im geteilten Deutschland*, Berlin 1972.

J. Mander: *Berlin: Hostage for the West*, London 1962.

G. McDermott: *Berlin: Success of a Mission*, London 1963.

D. Prowe: *Berlin: Weltstadt in Krisen*, Berlin 1973.

J. L. Richardson: *Germany and the Atlantic Alliance*, New York 1966.

A. Riklin: *Das Berlin Problem*, Köln 1964.

J. M. Schick: *The Berlin Crisis 1958–1962*, Philadelphia 1971.

J. E. Smith: *The Defense of Berlin*, New York 1966.

H. Speier: *Divided Berlin*, New York 1961.

W. Stoetzle: *Kennedy und Adenauer in der Berlin Krise*, Bonn 1973.

F. J. Strauss: *The Grand Design*, London 1965.

F. A. Vali: *The Quest for a United Germany*, New York 1967.

P. Windsor: *City on Leave: A History of Berlin 1945–62*, London 1963.

GAULLISM

E. Ashcroft: *De Gaulle*, London 1962.

H. Beuve Mery: *Onze Ans de règne*, Paris 1974.

J. Charlot: *La Phénomène gaulliste*, Paris 1970.

M. Couve de Murville: *Une Politique étrangère 1958–69*, Paris 1971.

M. Ferro: *De Gaulle et l'Amérique*, Paris 1973.

S. Friedlaender (ed.): *La Politique extérieure du Général de Gaulle*, Paris 1985.

P. de la Gorce: *De Gaulle entre deux mondes*, Paris 1964.

G. Gozard: *De Gaulle face à l'Europe*, Paris 1976.

O. Guichard: *Mon Général*, Paris 1980.

J. Lacouture: *De Gaulle*, vol. 3 *Le Souverain*, Paris 1986.

B. Ledwidge: *De Gaulle et les américains*, Paris 1984.

R. Macridis: *De Gaulle: Implacable Ally*, New York 1966.

R. Massip: *De Gaulle et l'Europe*, Paris 1963.

L. Noël: *Comprendre de Gaulle*, Paris 1973.
R. Rémond: *La Retour du de Gaulle*, Paris 1985.
D. Schoenbrun: *The Three Lives of Charles de Gaulle*, New York 1966.
J. Touchard: *Le Gaullisme 1940–1969*, Paris 1978.
J. M. Tournoux: *La Tragédie du général*, Paris 1967.

DÉTENTE, NATIONAL SECURITY, ARMS CONTROL

J. Alford and K. Hunt: *Europe in the Western Alliance*, New York 1988.
R. Aron: *The Great Debate*, New York 1965.
N. Brown: *Arms Without Europe*, London 1967.
A. Buchan and P. Windsor: *Arms and Stability in Europe*, London 1963.
H. Bull: *The Control of the Arms Race*, London 1965.
B. Burrows and G. Edwards: *The Defense of Western Europe*, London 1982.
L. Freedman: *The Troubled Alliance*, London 1983.
E. Fursdon: *The European Defence Community*, London 1980.
A. Grosser: *The Western Alliance*, London 1980.
P. Hassner: *Chance and Security in Europe*, New York 1967.
S. Hoffmann: *Gulliver's Troubles*, New York 1986.
J. Laloy: *Entre guerre et paix*, Paris 1966.
G. Liska: *Europe Ascendant*, New York 1964.
M. Smith: *Western Europe and the United States*, London 1984.
T. W. Stanley: *Europe in Transition*, New York 1965.
G. R. Urban (ed.): *Detente*, London 1976.
T. W. Wolfe: *Soviet Strategy at the Crossroads*, New York 1965.
J. H. Wyllie: *European Security in the Nuclear Age*, Oxford 1986.

REVOLUTION 1968, THE NEW SOCIAL MOVEMENTS

T. Ali: *New Revolutionaries*, London 1969.
A. Bramwell: *Ecology in the 20th Century*, London 1989.
K. W. Brand (ed.): *Neue soziale Bewegungen*, Opladen 1982.
A. Cockburn and R. Blackburn: *Student Power*, London 1969.
D. Cohn Bendit: *Obsolete Communism*, London 1968.
L. Feuer: *The Conflict of Generations*, New York 1969.
A. Gorz: *Ecologie et liberté*, Paris 1977.
W. Hulsberg: *The German Greens*, London 1988.
R. Jungk: *Menschenleben*, Munich 1983.
M. Langner: *Die Grünen auf dem Prüfstand*, Bergisch Gladbach 1987.
W. Laqueur: *The Age of Terrorism*, Boston 1987.
S. M. Lipset: *Student Politics*, New York 1967.
F. Müller-Rommel (ed.): *New Politics in Western Europe*, Boulder 1989.

T. Nairn: *The Beginning of the End*, London 1968.
D. Nelkin and M. Pollak: *The Atom Besieged*, Cambridge 1981.
L. F. Push (ed.): *Feminismus*, Frankfurt 1983.
N. Ryschkowsky: *Die linke Linke*, München 1968.
E. K. Scheuch: *Die Widertäufer der Wohlstandsgesellschaft*, Köln 1968.
P. Seale and M. Conville: *French Revolution*, London 1968.
A. Touraine: *L'après Socialisme*, Paris 1980.
A. Touraine: *Le Mouvement de mai*, Paris 1968.

THE ECONOMY IN CONTEMPORARY EUROPE

A. Boltho (ed.): *The European Economy*, Oxford 1982.
F. Caron: *An Economic History of Modern France*, New York 1980.
H. D. Clout: *Regional Development in Western Europe*, Chichester 1981.
A. F. Freris: *The Greek Economy in the Twentieth Century*, London 1986.
R. T. Griffith: *The Economy and Politics of the Netherlands Since 1945*, The Hague 1980.
P. Hall and D. Hay: *Growth Centres in the European Urban System*, London 1980.
K. Hardach: *The Political Economy of Germany in the Twentieth Century*, London 1985.
J. Harrison: *The Spanish Economy in the Twentieth Century*, London 1985.
U. Himmelstrand (ed.): *Beyond Welfare Capitalism*, London 1981.
F. Hodne: *The Norwegian Economy 1920–1980*, London 1983.
E. Hoernel and J. E. Vahlne: *The Multinationals: The Swedish Case*, London 1986.
G. D. Holmes and P. D. Fawcett: *The Contemporary French Economy*, London 1983.
J. R. Hough: *The French Economy*, London 1982.
R. King: *The Industrial Geography of Italy*, London 1986.
R. King: *Italy*, London 1987.
J. Klatzmann: *L'Agriculture française*, Paris 1978.
S. Pollard: *The Development of the British Economy 1914–1982*, London 1983.
D. I. Scargill: *Urban France*, London 1983.
A. H. Smith: *The Planned Economies of Eastern Europe*, London 1982.
E. Owen Smith: *The West German Economy*, London 1983.
A. M. Williams: *Western European Economy*, London 1987.

RIGHT-WING EXTREMISM

J. Algazy: *La Tentation néofasciste en France*, Paris 1984.

G. Bartsch: *Revolution von Rechts?*, Freiburg 1975.

K. von Beyme (ed.): *Right-Wing Extremism in Western Europe*, London 1988.

A. Chebel D'Appollonia: *L'Extrème Droit en France: De Maurras à Le Pen*, Brussels 1988.

P. Dudek: *Jugendliche Rechtsextremisten*, Köln 1985.

P. Dudek and H. G. Jaschke: *Entstehung des Rechtsradikalismus in der Bundesrepublik*, Opladen 1984.

M. Feit: *Die neue Rechte in der Bundesrepublik*, Frankfurt 1987.

F. Ferraresi: *La destra radicale*, Milan 1987.

H. Herb et al.: *Der neue Rechtsextremismus*, Lohra 1980.

J. Lorien et al.: *Le Système Le Pen*, Brussels 1986.

N. Mayer: *Le Front National à découvert*, Paris 1989.

L. Niethammer: *Angepasster Faschismus*, Frankfurt 1969.

P. Rosenbaum: *Neofaschismus in Italien*, Frankfurt 1975.

A. Silbermann and J. Schöps: *Antisemitismus nach dem Holokaust*, Köln 1986.

J. Tussel and J. Aviles: *La derecha española contemporánea*, Madrid 1986.

M. Walker: *The National Front*, Glasgow 1978.

P. Wilkinson: *The New Fascists*, London 1981.

EASTERN EUROPE AND THE SOVIET UNION
FROM BREZHNEV TO GORBACHEV

J. D. Bell: *The Bulgarian Communist Party*, Stanford 1986.

S. Bialer: *The Soviet Paradox*, New York 1981.

J. F. Brown: *Eastern Europe and Communist Rule*, Durham, N.C., 1988.

Z. Brzezinski: *The Grand Failure*, New York 1989.

S. Cohen: *Rethinking the Soviet Experience*, New York 1985.

T. Colton: *The Dilemma of Reform in the Soviet Union*, New York 1986.

R. Conquest: *The Last Empire*, Stanford 1986.

J. Dunlop: *The New Russian Nationalism*, New York 1985.

M. Frankland: *The Sixth Continent*, London 1987.

T. Garton Ash: *We the People: The Revolution of '89*, London 1990.

C. Gati: *The Bloc that Failed*, Bloomington, Ind., 1990.

C. Gati: *Hungary and the Soviet Bloc*, Durham, N.C., 1986.

M. Goldman: *Gorbachev's Challenge*, New York 1987.

W. Griffith (ed.): *Central and Eastern Europe*, Boulder 1989.

J. Hacker: *Der Ostblock*, Baden-Baden 1983.

P. Johnson: *Redesigning the Communist Economy*, New York 1989.

A. Knight: *The KGB*, London 1988.

V. Kusin: *From Dubček to Charter 77*, New York 1978.

W. Laqueur: *The Long Road to Freedom*, New York 1989.

P. Lendvai: *Hungary: The Art of Survival*, London 1988.

M. McCauley: *The G.D.R. Since 1945*, London 1984.

R. Medvedev: *Let History Judge*, New York 1989.

O. Narkiewicz: *Eastern Europe*, London 1986.

A. Nove: *An Economic History of the USSR*, London 1982.

T. Rakowska-Harmstone (ed.): *Communism in Eastern Europe*, Blooming-ton, Ind., 1984.

H. Renner: *History of Czechoslovakia Since 1945*, Boston 1989.

J. Rupnik: *The Other Europe*, New York 1989.

N. Shafir: *Romania*, London 1985.

G. Simon: *Nationalismus und Nationalitätenproblem in der Sowjetunion*, Baden-Baden 1986.

N. Stone and E. Strouhal: *Czechoslovakia: Crossroads and Crisis*, New York 1989.

M. Walker: *The Walking Giant*, New York 1987.

SOCIALISM IN EUROPE

R. Abs: *Histoire du parti socialiste belge*, Brussels 1979.

G. Braunthal: *The West German Social Democrats*, Boulder 1983.

L. Covatta et al.: *Storia del partito socialista*, Milan 1979.

E. Jacobs: *European Trade Unionism*, London 1973.

N. Nugent and D. Lowe: *The Left in France*, London 1982.

W. E. Paterson and I. Campbell: *Social Democracy in Post-War Europe*, London 1974.

W. E. Paterson and E. H. Thomas (eds.): *The Future of Social-Democracy*, Oxford 1986.

J. Rovan: *Geschichte der deutschen Sozialdemokratie*, Frankfurt 1980.

WEST GERMANY IN THE 1970S AND 1980S

Allensbacher Jahrbuch der Demoskopie 1978–83, Wien 1983.

S. Aust: *Der Baader Meinhof Komplex*, Hamburg 1986.

A. Baring: *Machtwechsel*, Stuttgart 1982.

W. Brandt: *Begegnungen und Einsichten*, Zürich 1978.

F. Fuerstenberg: *Die Sozialstruktur der Bundesrepublik Deutschland*, Opladen 1978.

G. Gaus: *Wo Deutschland liegt*, Hamburg 1983.

J. Gross: *Unsere letzten Jahre*, Stuttgart 1980.

H. Haftendorn: *Sicherheit und Entspannung*, Baden-Baden 1983.

A. Hillgruber: *Deutsche Geschichte von 1945–82*, Berlin 1984.

E. Jesse: *Die Demokratie der Bundesrepublik Deutschland*, Berlin 1984.

W. Kaltefleiter: *Parteien im Umbruch*, Düsseldorff 1984.

G. Langguth: *Protestbewegung*, Köln 1983.

H. Schmidt: *Der Kurs heisst Frieden*, Düsseldorff 1979.

E. Schulz: *Die deutsche Nation in Europa*, Bonn 1982.

G. Schweigler: *Grundlagen der aussenpolitischen Orientierung*, Baden-Baden 1985.

WESTERN EUROPE: THE LAST TWO DECADES

J. Ardagh: *The New France*, London 1977.

D. E. Ashford: *Policy and Politics in Britain*, London 1981.

F. Borella: *Les Partis politiques en Europe*, Paris 1984.

R. Carr and J. I. Fusi: *Spain: Dictatorship to Democracy*, London 1981.

R. Clogg: *Parties and Elections in Greece*, London 1987.

T. E. Derry: *A History of Scandinavia*, London 1979.

H. Ehrmann: *Politics in France*, New York 1976.

J. Fitzmaurice: *The Politics of Belgium*, London 1983.

W. Hanrieder: *Germany, America, Europe*, New Haven 1989.

J. Haycraft: *Italian Labyrinth*, London 1985.

M. Holmes: *Thatcherism*, New York 1989.

P. Jenkins: *Mrs. Thatcher's Revolution*, London 1989.

D. Kavanagh: *Thatcherism and British Politics*, Oxford 1989.

G. Kurian (ed.): *The Benelux Countries*, New York 1989.

G. Kurian (ed.): *Scandinavia*, New York 1989

R. E. McIrvin: *The Christian Democratic Parties of Western Europe*, London 1979.

J. Miller: *Foreign Workers in Western Europe*, London 1981.

R. Morodo: *La transición política*, Madrid 1988.

E. Mujal Leon: *Communism and Political Change in Spain*, Bloomington, Ind., 1983.

P. Preston (ed.): *Spain in Crisis*, London 1976.

P. Preston: *The Triumph of Democracy in Spain*, London 1986.

P. Riddell: *The Thatcher Decade*, New York 1989.

G. Ross et al. (eds.): *The Mitterrand Experiment*, Oxford 1987.

M. Smith: *Western Europe and the United States*, London 1984.

H. Young: *The Iron Lady*, New York 1989.

SOCIAL CONDITIONS 1970–90

S. Acquaviva et al.: *Social Structures in Italy*, London 1976.

M. Childs: *Sweden: The Middle Way on Trial*, New Haven 1980.

P. Flora (ed.): *Growth to Limit: The Western European Welfare States Since World War II*, 5 vols., Berlin 1986–88.

D. Haley: *Contemporary France*, London 1984.

A. H. Halsey: *Change in British Society*, Oxford 1988.

H. Kellenbenz (ed.): *Handbuch der europäischen Wirtschafts und Sozialgeschichte*, vol. 5 Stuttgart 1987.

J. Krejci: *Social Structure in Divided Germany*, London 1976.

P. Léon: *Histoire économique et sociale du monde*, vol. 6, Paris 1977.

E. Lupri: *The Changing Position of Women in Family and Society*, Leiden 1984.

A. Marwick: *British Society Since 1945*, London 1982.

J. Salt and J. Clout (eds.): *Migration in Postwar Europe*, Oxford 1976.

F. Tipton and R. Aldrich: *An Economic Social History of Europe from 1939 to the Present*, Baltimore 1987.

United Nations: *Demographic Yearbook*.

INDEX

Abercrombie Plan, 244–45
Abgrenzung, 542
abortion, 235, 450, 544
abulia, xi
acid rain, 436
Action Party (Italy), 47, 49, 127
Aden, 367
Adenauer, Konrad, viii, 20, 51, 84,
    119, 316, 318, 453, 472
  assessment of, 79–80, 133, 135
  background of, 79
  ex-Nazis associated with, 134–35
  foreign policy of, 135, 300, 331,
    375
German reunification and, 136, 375
  popular support for, 376
adult-education courses, 250
Afghanistan, 184, 454, 508, 525, 526
Africa, 138, 154, 567
  decolonization and, ix, 10, 137,
    217, 366–67
  see also North Africa
Agrarian Party (Finland), 390
agriculture, 188–91
  in Belgium, 178, 179, 190, 217
  in Bulgaria, 156
  central planning of, 121
  collectivization of, 58, 73, 86, 95,
    156, 228, 303, 406, 518
  Common Market policy on, 190–
    191, 329, 330, 418–19
  in Czechoslovakia, 175, 180
  in Denmark, 180, 188, 189, 190,
    218

in Eastern Europe, 228–29
in East Germany, 175, 180
at end of World War II, 6, 11, 68,
    69, 70, 168, 188
environmental and health concerns
    and, 418
failure feared for, vii
in France, 6, 132, 133, 179, 188,
    189, 190, 200, 202, 229, 476
in Great Britain, 168, 178, 179,
    188, 189
in Hungary, 175, 228, 408
in Italy, 178, 179, 189, 208, 210,
    229
mechanization of, 168, 188–89,
    205
in Netherlands, 217
overproduction in, xiv, 189, 418
in Poland, 69, 156, 303, 406, 533
in Rumania, 70, 432
in Soviet Union, 56, 58, 95, 155,
    175, 180, 188, 220, 221, 222,
    224, 399, 428–29, 430, 432,
    510, 516, 517–18
in Spain, 179–80, 216, 427
subsidies for, 189–90, 205, 419
trade in, 189–91, 197, 429, 432
in West Germany, 134, 178, 180,
    188, 189, 190, 205
work force in, 179–80, 189, 200,
    221, 254
agrogorod, 58
aircraft industry, 186
Air France, 43

airline business, 193
Albania, 67, 68, 530
    birthrate in, 178
    China and, 343, 356, 549
    Communist takeover of, 70
    Czech invasion opposed by, 360
    political upheaval in, 549
    as Stalinist holdout, 289, 339–40,
        549
Alberoni, Giulio, Cardinal, 116
alcohol, alcoholism, 247, 430, 521
Aldermaston marches, 345, 365
Afonso XIII, King of Spain, 386
Algeria, ix, 123, 129, 131, 132, 345,
    370–73
Ali, Tariq, 352, 353
Alia, Ramiz, 549
Alianza Popular (Spain), 495, 496
Aliev, Gaidar, 513
Alliance of Free Democrats (Hun-
    gary), 554
Alto Adige (South Tyrol), 383–84,
    441
Amsterdam, 461
Amsterdam Provos, 388
Anders, Wladyslaw, 15
Andreeva, Nina, 519
Andreotti, Giulio, 488
Andropov, Yuri, 429, 512–14
Animal Farm (Orwell), 37
Anschluss, 393
anti-Americanism, xii, 282, 365, 447
Antirevolution Party (Netherlands),
    388
anti-Semitism, 135, 151, 160, 358,
    406–7, 443, 485, 520
apertura a sinistra, 381–82
Apostol, Gheorghe, 410
Arab-Israeli war (1967), 183, 335,
    336
Arabs, 361
Argentina, 429, 470
Armenia, 438, 443, 447, 523, 524
arms control talks, 106, 293, 298–
    99, 309–15, 454, 525, 526
Aron, Raymond, 40, 277
Artamanen, 435
Asala, 447
Asia, 138, 154, 361, 567

rising nationalism in, 10
Atatürk, Kemal, 54
atomic energy, 183, 420, 439
atomic weapons:
    China's development of, 338
    European deployment of, v, xii,
        123–24, 295, 452, 454, 456,
        458, 526
    France and, 124, 203, 325
    Great Britain and, 124, 138, 325,
        367, 468
    protests against, 345, 365, 438,
        456
    Soviet development of, 109, 225,
        296
    as U.S. threat, 101, 123, 295
    see also arms control talks
Attlee, Clement, 33, 98, 136, 137,
    138, 364
audio technology, 278
Auriol, Vincent, 40
Auschwitz, 17, 23
Australia, 138, 191, 252, 330
Austria, 17, 91, 110, 154, 188, 197,
    267, 538
    Anschluss and, 393
    coalition government of, 393
    Common Market and, 218, 330
    de-Nazification in, 22, 23–24, 27
    economy of, 169, 170, 171, 205,
        216, 218
    at end of World War II, 7, 8, 13
    housing in, 241, 243
    infant mortality in, 240
    Italy's border dispute with, 383–
        384, 441
    labor force in, 254
    politics in, 437
    postwar borders of, 12
    Soviet relations with, 299
    tourism in, 252
Austro-Hungarian Empire, 547
Autobahnen, 195
automobile industry, 185–86,
    209
automobiles:
    deaths caused by, 240
    ownership of, 194–95, 537
    pollution and, 436

Autostrada del Sole, 195
Azerbaijan, 441, 443, 523, 524

Baader-Meinhof gang, 446
Baden-Baden, 251
Badoglio, Pietro, 46, 47
Bahro, Rudolf, 438
Baikal, Lake, 437
Baikal–Amur railway, 508
Baku oil fields, 56
Balkan States, 68, 106, 565
  ethnic minorities of, 14
  independence movements in, 523
  proposed union of, 75
  Soviet domination of, 17, 55, 62,
    67, 69, 75, 95, 529
  see also specific countries
Baltic Sea, 436, 439
Baltic States:
  economies of, 443
  national movements in, 438, 443
  see also Estonia; Latvia; Lithuania
"Bandung movement," 549
banking systems, xiv, 43, 72, 79,
  172, 481
Bank of England, 35
Barak, Rudolf, 409
Barbie, Klaus, 23
Barcelona University, 350
Barraclough, Geoffrey, 567
Barre, Raymond, 423, 477, 483
BASF, 184
Basic Law, 375
Basques, 385, 387, 441, 442, 446,
  494, 496–97
Bastian, General, 438
Batasuna, Herri, 497
Baudouin, King of Belgium, 52
Bayer, 184, 185
Beatles, 282, 369
Beauvoir, Simone de, 275
Belgium, 120, 198, 247, 259
  agriculture in, 178, 179, 190,
    217
  birthdate in, 177
  decolonization by, 217, 389–90
  de-Nazification in, 23, 28
  economy of, 171, 178, 179, 181,

217, 246, 389, 426, 461, 463–
  464
  at end of World War II, 3, 5, 7, 8,
    51, 167
  Flamand-Walloon conflict in, 51–
    52, 389, 441, 461, 463
  housing in, 241, 242, 244
  labor force in, 254
  labor movement in, 389
  nuclear power policy of, 420
  politics in, 30, 31, 51–52, 462–63
  social reform in, 235, 236, 237,
    238
Benelux, 8, 118, 120, 122, 234
  automobiles in, 194
  Common Market and, 8, 120, 328
  see also Netherlands
Beneš, Edvard, 75, 157, 356
Benn, Tony, 467
Beria, Lavrenti, 63, 150, 152–53,
  154, 397
Berlin, at end of World War II, 5–6,
  13, 72, 76–77, 101
Berlin, West, 245, 445, 455
Berlin blockade (1948), 34–35, 38,
  82–83, 106, 113
Berlin crisis (1958), 310–11
Berlin crisis (1961), 296, 319–22
Berlin wall:
  building of, 15, 77, 87, 311, 321–
    322, 405
  collapse of, v–vi, 458
Bernanos, Georges, 274
Bessarabia (Moldavia), 410, 443,
  544
Bevan, Aneurin, 34–35, 136
Beveridge Report, 31
Bevin, Ernest, 33, 34, 38, 98, 111,
  136
Biarritz, 251
Bicycle Thief, The, 281
Bidault, Georges, 20, 41, 42, 44, 128,
  129, 371
Bierut, Boleslav, 301
birthrates:
  in Albania, 178
  in Belgium, 177
  in France, vii, 177
  in Great Britain, vii, 177

birthrates (*cont.*)
  in Hungary, 178
  in Ireland, 177
  in Italy, vii, 491
  of migrant workers, 445
  in North Africa, vii
  in Poland, 178
  in Rumania, 178
  in Scandinavia, 177
  in Soviet Union, 178, 221
  in Spain, vii
  in Sweden, 177
  in Switzerland, 177
  in Turkey, vii
  in West Germany, vii, 177
Black Sea, 252
Black Sea Straits, 54, 100
Blank, Theodor, 84
Bloch, Ernst, 273, 282
blousons noirs, 232
Blue Streak rocket, 367
Blum, Léon, 20, 43, 140
Böll, Heinrich, 456
Bolshevism, 60
Borkenau, Franz, 343
Bourbons, 386
Brandt, Willy, xi, 331, 376, 378,
    449, 450–51, 455, 458
Bretton Woods system, 416
Brezhnev, Leonid, ix, 336, 357, 360,
    401, 402, 429, 454, 507–12,
    514, 516, 530, 536, 537
Brezhnev doctrine, 297, 508, 529
bridges, World War II destruction
    of, 7
British Guyana, 367
Brittany, 373, 442
BRITTE, 422
Brown, George, 365
Brucan, Silvio, 561
Brussels:
  Common Market headquarters in,
    121, 390, 464
  NATO headquarters in, x, 326,
    390
Brussels, treaty of, vii
Bulganin, N. A., 63, 152, 153, 154,
    298, 309, 310, 398, 399
Bulgaria, 67, 68, 288, 530

agriculture in, 156
Communist takeover of, 71, 74,
    76, 90
democratization of, 544, 545–46,
    562–63
economy of, 175, 227, 229, 545
at end of World War II, 12, 70
ethnic tensions in, 546
housing in, 244
Sovietization of, 156
Bundesrepublik Deutschland, *see* Ger-
    many, Federal Republic of
Bundeswehr, 375–76
Bunin, Ivan, 287
"bureaucratic collectivism," 262
Burma, 137
Burnham, James, 261
Bush, George, 554, 568
Butor, Michael, 347
"Butskellism," 362, 424
Byrnes, James, 93, 110

Callaghan, James, 467, 468, 470
Camus, Albert, 275
Canada, 118, 138, 191, 222, 330,
    429
cancer, 240, 247
capital-gains tax, 476
capital punishment, 234, 462
Carlists, 386
Carlsson, Ingvar, 503
Carnogursky, Jan, 560
Carrillo, Santiago, 496
Carter, Jimmy, 451, 525
Castro, Fidel, 387
Catalonia, 385, 442, 495, 496
"Catholic Action," 385
Catholic Center Party (Weimar Ger-
    many), 79
Catholic Church, 273, 457, 462, 466,
    491
  in France, 129
  left wing of, 280
  national separatist movements and,
    442
  Opus Dei movement of, 387
  in Poland, 278, 288, 301, 304,
    406, 535

reform in, 277
in Spain, 385, 386, 387
in Yugoslavia, 547
see also churches
Catholic People's Party (Netherlands), 127, 388
Caucasus, 252, 443, 511
CDU, *see* Christian Democratic Union
Ceausescu, Elena, 544, 561
Ceausescu, Nicolae, 289, 341, 359, 410–11, 432, 437, 443, 530, 536, 538, 544–45, 560–61
Ceausescu, Nicu, 544
Cecchini report, 421
censorship, 355, 360, 403, 405, 494, 559
Center Democratic Union (UCD) (Spain), 495
Center Party (Finland), 502
Central African Federation, 366
Central Asia, 443, 511, 522–23
Ceylon, 137
Chaban-Delmas, Jacques, 131, 474, 475
Chad, 486
Charter 77, 437, 543, 560
chemical industry, 182, 184–85, 217, 428
Chernenko, Konstantin, 429, 514–15
Chernichevsky, Nikolai, xvi
Chernobyl, 431, 436
"Chernobyl Is Everywhere," 437
Chervenkov, Vulko, 160
Chichester, Sir Francis, 369
China, People's Republic of, 356, 508, 555
  Great Britain and, 368
  Soviet Union and, 135, 150, 229, 294, 296, 311–14, 333–34, 335, 338–39, 341, 343, 399, 410, 526, 527
Chinese Wall, The (Frisch), 268
Chirac, Jacques, 424, 477, 478, 482, 483–84
Chou En-lai, 360
Christian Democratic parties, 126–128, 142, 258
  class character of, 127

confessional parties compared with, 126–27
  rise of, 126
Christian Democratic Party (Belgium), 463
Christian Democratic Party (France), 126
Christian Democratic Party (Italy), 47, 49, 50, 51, 126, 127–28, 381–83, 488–89
Christian Democratic Party (Netherlands), 462
Christian Democratic Union (CDU) (West Germany), 51, 78, 80, 81, 375
  declines of, 376, 450–51
  dissension in, 134, 377, 378
  electoral victories of, 82, 84, 133, 452, 455
  founding of, 79
  in Great Coalition, 318, 378–79, 449, 451, 455
  philosophy of, 79
  rightists absorbed by, 453
  social reforms by, 459
Christian Historical Union (Netherlands), 388
Chrisitan People's Party (Austria), 142
Christian Socialist Party (Belgium), 389
Christian Social Party (Austria), 393
Christian Social Party (CVP) (Belgium), 389
churches:
  communism opposed by, 75–76
  political involvement of, xii, 54, 79, 107, 127, 461, 462
  see also Catholic Church; Christian Democratic parties; Protestant Church
Churchill, Sir Winston, 33, 40, 48, 91, 98, 102, 105, 133, 262, 472
  at end of World War II, 4, 31, 94–95
  European unification supported by, 117
  "iron curtain" speech of, v*n*, 37–38, 105, 110

Churchill, Sir Winston (*cont.*)
  in postwar Allied negotiations, 89–
    97
  retirement of, 363
  second prime ministerial term of,
    137, 362–63
  Stalin's territorial deal with, 89–
    90, 110
civil service, 261–62
Clay, Lucius, 83
Clementis, Vlado, 160
clothing, 248
coal industry, 7, 32, 35, 36, 42, 43,
    57, 172, 173, 182–84, 197, 220,
    416, 533
Cohn-Bendit, Daniel, 346, 347, 348,
    352, 353
Cold War, 105–15, 129, 139, 293–
    297
  Czech invasion and, 361
  ending of, 527
  European communists and, 31,
    275, 276
  as myth, 315
  origins of, 2, 88–89, 102, 114–15
  as outcome of U.S. policy, 101,
    105–8, 114–15, 456
  Soviet territorial demands and,
    106–7, 110
  Stalin's death and, 293, 315
  U.S.–European relations and, 108,
    111–12
  West German–European relations
    and, 84
  West Germany as prize in, 299–
    300, 449
Colombo, Emilio, 488
Colton, Timothy, 510
Comecon (Council for Mutual Eco-
    nomic Assistance), 162, 227,
    229, 355, 432
Cominform, 10, 145, 158, 299
Common Agricultural Policy, 419
Common Coal and Steel Market, 120
Common Market, 211, 328–32, 341,
    390, 462, 501
  agricultural policy of, 190–91,
    329, 330, 418–19
  Commission of, 328–29
  Council of Ministers of, 120, 328

  founding of, 120–21, 328
  France and, xiv, 122, 197, 202,
    323–24, 328–32, 373, 475
  Great Britain and, xiv, 122, 125,
    197, 215, 329–32, 377, 422,
    472, 475
  headquarters of, 121, 390, 464
  members of, xiv, 8, 120, 122, 197,
    328, 330, 417, 419, 427, 495–
    496
  1969 summit of, xiii
  1984 summit of, xiv
  North-South split in, 422
  as political institution, 330
  Single European Act of, xiv
  Switzerland and, 394
  symbols of, 569
  trade and, xiv, 121, 172, 191,
    196–99, 202
Commonwealth, 117–18, 119, 124,
    138, 197, 330, 366, 367
communism, Communist parties,
    144–48
  collapse of, v, xiii, xiv, xv, 76,
    447–48, 458, 526–27, 550–51
  in Denmark, 30
  Eastern European ascendency of,
    70–76
  in Indonesia, 335
  in labor movement, 258–59
  polycentrism and, 338–44
  postwar influence of, 19–20, 30–
    31, 32, 106–7, 144–48, 274–
    278, 280–81
  Soviet Union and, 44, 51, 70, 74,
    75–76, 145
  see also specific countries
Communist International, 20, 58
Communist Party (Belgium), 144,
    145, 147
Communist Party (Bulgaria), 562,
    563
Communist Party (Czechoslovakia),
    71, 157, 354, 355, 409, 541,
    559
Communist Party (Denmark), 144,
    391
Communist Party (East Germany),
    77–78, 81, 86, 405, 539, 541,
    554, 558

Communist Party (Finland), 390
Communist Party (France), 30, 40,
    41, 43–45, 139, 141, 144–48,
    347, 359, 370, 478, 479–80,
    483, 485, 488
Communist Party (Greece), 110, 145,
    341
Communist Party (Hungary), 304–5,
    408, 538, 553–54
Communist Party (Iceland), 145
Communist Party (Italy), 46, 47–48,
    50–51, 139, 141, 144–48, 359,
    383, 485, 488–89, 491
Communist Party (Netherlands), 144,
    341
Communist Party (Norway), 30, 52
Communist Party (Poland), 162,
    301–4, 307, 308, 534, 541,
    554
Communist Party (Rumania), 410
Communist Party (Soviet Union), 58,
    60, 63, 65, 149, 152, 155, 158,
    397, 400, 402, 509, 518
Communist Party (Spain), 146, 341,
    342, 385–86, 495
Communist Party (Sweden), 391
Communist Party (West Germany),
    30, 51, 80, 81, 134, 379
Communist Party (Yugoslavia), 158–
    159
computers, 186, 269–70
Comte, Auguste, xii
confessional parties, 126–27
Congo, Belgian, 389–90
Congress, U.S., Joint Economic Com-
    mittee of, 430
Conseil National de la Résistance
    (CNR), 41
Conservative Party (Denmark), 500
Conservative Party (Finland), 501,
    502
Conservative Party (Great Britain),
    34, 369, 425, 472
    Common Market and, 330, 332
    defeats of, 31, 466
    denationalization by, 35, 137
    dissension in, 364, 366
    foreign policy of, 124, 138, 362,
        363, 367–69, 465–66
    nature of, 31, 362–63

power regained by, 136–37, 215,
        362, 363, 468
    rightward swing of, 282
Conservative Party (Norway), 500
Conservative Party (Switzerland), 393
Constantine II, King of Greece, 396
Consultative Assembly (France),
    40, 45
consumer trends, 246–48
containment doctrine, 112–13
Continent Astray, A (Laqueur), xvi
contraceptives, 234
contrats du progrès, 475
Convergencia i Unio (Catalonia), 496
Cornea, Dorina, 561
Corsica, 442
cost of living indices, 204
Cot, Pierre, 40
Council for Mutual Economic Assis-
    tance (CMEA) (Comecon), 162,
    227, 229, 355, 432
Council of Europe, xii–xiv, 83–84,
    119, 478
Couve de Murville, Maurice, 372,
    387
Craxi, Bettino, 488
crime, 231, 234–35, 490, 521
Crimea Tartars, 443, 523
Cripps, Sir Stafford, 34, 35, 214
Croats, 68, 443, 547, 548, 564
Crossman, Richard, 38
Crozier, Michel, 268
Cuba, 341, 387, 526, 549
Cuban missile crisis, 296, 333, 399
cultural congresses, 275
culture, postwar developments in,
    267–74, 278–85
currencies, see monetary systems
Curzon Line, 96
Cyprus, 367, 395
Czechoslovakia, xv, 3, 7, 8, 15, 67,
    160, 316, 318, 407, 408–9,
    538, 565
    agriculture in, 175, 180
    Communist takeover of, 38, 71,
        75, 76, 83, 106, 107, 113, 116,
        157–58, 275, 354, 409
    democratic history of, 68, 354
    demonstration of, 543, 550, 558–
        560

Czechoslovakia (*cont.*)
   economy of, 70, 72, 161–62, 175,
      176, 180, 227, 228–29, 230,
      408–9, 431–32, 539–40
   ethnic minorities of, 68, 72, 354
   Havel's election in, 288, 559–60
   housing in, 244
   liberalization in, 354–56, 409
   pollution in, 436
   postwar borders of, 12, 14
   social unrest in, 228, 288, 408–9,
      437
   Soviet invasion of, ix, 259, 288,
      296–97, 306, 319, 327, 336,
      341, 354–61, 383, 403, 405–6,
      408, 409, 411, 508, 544, 568
   terrorists supported by, 448
   tourism in, 252

Danube Circle, 437
Danube River, 436
Davies, Joseph, 93
D'Avignon report, xiii
DDR, *see* German Democratic
   Republic
Deane, John R., 93
Debré, Michel, 131, 361, 372, 387
Decembrists, 59
Declaration on Liberated Europe, 90
decolonization:
   by Belgium, 217, 389–90
   economic effects of, ix, 138, 217,
      373, 388, 445
   by France, ix, 10, 131–32, 370–
      373, 445
   by Great Britain, ix, 33, 137–38,
      362
   by Netherlands, ix, 52, 217, 388
   by Portugal, ix
defense spending, 169, 172, 212, 315
   in Eastern Europe, 228, 230
   in France, 203
   in Great Britain, 138, 215
   in Soviet Union, 221, 223, 225,
      320, 335, 336, 399, 428, 525,
      527
   in Switzerland, 394
   in U.S., 525
   in West Germany, 207
Deferre, Gaston, 480

deflation, 481
de Gasperi, Alcide, 20, 50, 51, 119,
   127, 128, 146, 381
de Gaulle, Charles, 20, 133, 201,
   202, 262, 323–27, 361, 367,
   378, 387, 453, 472, 483
   Algerian War and, 371–73
   background of, 39
   character of, 39, 40, 43, 132, 323
   death of, 474
   European unification and, 117,
      119, 122, 125, 130–31, 323–
      324, 325, 328–32, 334, 422
   French liberation politics and, 4,
      39–45
   1968 student unrest and, x, 326–
      327, 347–49, 474
   postwar rise to power of, 129–30
   resignations of, 45, 129, 131, 474
   second term of office of, 323–27,
      371–74, 479
Degrelle, Léon, 29
Delors, Jacques, xiv, 421, 481
Delors Committee, 421
Democracy Now (East Germany),
   557
Democratic Forum (Hungary), 554
Democratic Party (Turkey), 54
Democratic Party (Yugoslavia), 564
"democratic transformation," 89
Democratic Union Party (Spain), 386
de-Nazification, 22–29
   differing approaches to, 23–24,
      26–28
   international law and, 25
   obeying orders as defense in, 24
   punishment and, 23–24, 25–26,
      27–29
   as revenge, 26
   time taken for, 23
Denmark, 118, 247, 259
   agriculture in, 180, 188, 189, 190,
      218
   de-Nazification in, 28
   economy of, 171, 180, 218, 246,
      392, 415, 426, 499, 500
   at end of World War II, 3, 6, 7
   European Community membership
      of, x
   as NATO member, 390, 500

politics in, 30, 52, 391–92, 499–
    500
social reform in, 234, 238
dentists, 241
depression, Great, 8, 172
détente, 319, 345, 438
    Berlin Crisis and, 311, 313
    as cause for hope, xi, 293
    Czech invasion and, 360–61
    decline of, 524–25
    ideology as block to, 294
    post-missile crisis renewal of, 296,
        335–37
    Soviet–East European alliance and,
        531
    Soviet Union's political weakness
        and, 403
    West Germany and, 450, 452, 454
Dien Bien Phu, 132
Dienstbier, Jiri, 560
"direct action," 48, 49
dirigisme, 121
divorce, 234, 235, 489
Djilas, Milovan, 102, 159, 289, 529,
    547
DKP, see Communist Party (West
    Germany)
Doctor Zhivago, 286–87
Doenitz, Karl, 24
Dolce Vita, La, 281
dollar gap, vii, 117, 168, 169
dopo lavoro, 250
Douglas-Home, Sir Alec, 364, 366
Draghici, Alexandru, 410
Drees, Willem, 388
Dubček, Alexander, 355, 356, 358–
    360, 409, 560
Duclos, Jacques, 103
Dulles, John Foster, 124, 159, 314,
    324, 334
Du Pont, 185
Dutch East Indies, 52
Dutschke, Rudi, 350, 352, 353

Eastern Europe:
    anti-Russian feelings in, 69, 89, 92,
        157, 303
    collapse of communism in, v, xiii,
        xiv, xv, 76, 447–48, 458, 526–
        527, 550–51

cultural developments in, 276,
    288–90
dissidents in, 530
economic and political uncertainty
    in, 564–65
economies of, 227–30, 431–32
ending of postwar era in, 505–65
ethnic minorities of, 67, 68, 71, 72,
    441, 443
housing in, 6, 176, 244
industrialization of, 227–30
intellectual revolt in, 277
Nazi collaboration in, 26–27, 68–
    69, 71
pollution in, 436, 437, 440
polycentrism in, 338–44
population of, 178
purges and trials in, 159–61, 162,
    276, 407, 409, 411, 542–43
rulers of, 530
in Soviet empire, vii, ix, 11, 13, 14,
    17, 57, 62, 67–76, 88–89, 95,
    101–2, 106, 156–63, 227–30,
    294, 297, 299–308, 313, 404–
    411, 529–32, 551, 568
Soviet SS-20 missiles in, 452, 454,
    458
student-power movement in, 351
as terrorist haven, 447–48
tourism in, 252
Western European trade with,
    198–99
youth movements of, 233
see also specific countries
Ecologist Party (Sweden), 502
ecology movements, xiii, 353, 435–
    440, 462
Economic Survey of Europe, 169
Ecumenical Council, 277
Eden, Sir Anthony, 98, 136, 137,
    138, 154, 215, 298, 363
edinonachalie, 156
education, 65, 67, 235, 237–38, 450,
    475, 477, 481–82
EEC (European Economic Commu-
    nity), see Common Market
EFTA (European Free Trade Associa-
    tion), 172, 197, 198, 330–31,
    394
Egypt, 154, 230, 335, 399, 405

Ehrenburg, Ilya, 4, 98, 155
Eichmann, Adolf, 26
Eisenhower, Dwight D., 154, 298,
    299, 309, 310, 311, 312, 313
electricity, production of, 172, 173,
    201, 203
electronics industry, 186–87, 428
Eliot, T. S., 275, 282
Emmanuel III, King of Italy, 48
energy policy, 420–21
Engels, Friedrich, 238
engineering industries, 186
"Englanditis," xi, 424–25, 468, 470
ENI, 211
Erhard, Ludwig, 133, 205, 208, 328,
    331, 377–78
Estonia, 12, 443, 523
ETA (Basque group), 496–97
Euratom (atomic pool), 120, 390,
    419
Eurocommunism, 496
Eurocrats, 121, 324
Europe:
    consolidation of, 291–411
    decline of, vi–vii
    democratization of, 441, 443
    economies of, 165, 264
    industrial development in, 182–87
    nation-states of, 54–55
    population of, 177n, 182
    postwar border and ethnic move-
       ments in, 12–17, 441
    postwar cultural developments in,
       267–74, 278–85
    postwar politics of, 1–163
    pre–World War I dominance of, 9
    separatism and national minorities
       in, 441–44
    West Germany's relationship with,
       84, 449, 460
    as world's largest market, 182
    World War II refugee problem in,
       13, 14–16, 53
    see also Balkan States; Eastern Eu-
       rope; Western Europe; specific
       countries
European Coal and Steel Community,
    83
European Council, see Council of
    Europe

European Court of Justice, xiii–xiv,
    120
European Defense Community
    (EDC), 122, 132
European Economic Community
    (EEC), see Common Market
European Free Trade Association
    (EFTA), 172, 197, 198, 330–31,
    394
European Parliament, xiii–xiv, 120,
    459, 478, 481, 482–83, 497
European unification, 116–25
    Czech invasion and, 361
    defense and, 118–19, 122
    economics of, 116–17, 120
    historical proposals for, 116
    movement for, 84–85, 116
    national egotism and, x, 124
    resistance to, 119–20, 422
    timetable for, xiv–xvi
    see also Common Market
"European year of the environment,"
    436
Europe Since Hitler (Laqueur), xv,
    494n
Euzkadi, 441, 497
existentialism, 272, 279–80
extermination camps, 26
Eyskens, Gaston, 389, 463

Fabius, Laurent, 482, 484
Falange (Spain), 54, 386–87, 494
Falkland Islands, 470, 471
family allowances, 235, 237, 238,
    481
Fanfani, Amintore, 382, 383, 488
Fanon, Frantz, 352, 567
Farmer's Party (Netherlands), 388
fascism, 9, 17–18, 45–46, 54, 250,
    267, 281, 494
Fascist Grand Council (Italy), 45
Faure, Edgar, 298, 371
FDP, see Liberal Party (West
    Germany)
Fiat, 186, 194, 210–11
Fierlinger, Zdenek, 157
film industry, 66, 284, 286
Final Solution, 5, 25, 26, 27
Finland, 240
    economy of, 417, 426, 499, 501

politics in, 107, 390–91
pollution in, 436
postwar borders of, 12, 15
Soviet Union and, 92, 299, 390,
    501–2, 529
Finlandization, xi, 501–2
First World War, *see* World War I
Flamands, 51–52, 389, 461, 463
Flick, Friedrich, 25
FLN (Front de Libération National),
    371, 372, 373
food consumption trends, 246–48
food rationing, 6–7, 43, 56, 82, 137
Foot, Michael, 470
force de frappe, 124, 203, 325
Forces Françaises de l'Intérieur
    (FFI), 41
Ford, Gerald R., 525
Foreign Affairs, 112, 115
forests, pollution's effect on, 436
Forrestal, James, 110
Forster, E. M., 282
Fouchet Committee, 332
Fourastié, Jean, 423
Fraga, Manuel, 495
France, xiv, 9, 17, 19, 39–45, 48,
    51, 53, 86, 108, 118, 120, 135,
    232, 240, 248, 267, 295, 306,
    312, 323–27, 334, 370–74, 375,
    452, 568
  agriculture in, 6, 132, 133, 179,
      188, 189, 190, 200, 202, 229,
      476
  alcoholism in, 247
  birthrate in, vii, 177
  cohabitation government of, 483
  Common Market and, xiv, 122,
      197, 202, 323–24, 328–32,
      373, 475
  culture in, 272
  decolonization by, ix, 10, 131–32,
      370–73, 445
  defense spending in, 203
  de-Nazification in, 23, 28
  East Germany and, 320
  ecological movement of, 438–39
  economy of, ix, 42–43, 117, 130,
      132–33, 168, 169, 170, 171,
      172–73, 176, 179, 180, 181,
      200–4, 212, 246, 256, 257, 261,

370, 373, 415, 416, 417, 423–
    424, 474–87
  at end of World War II, 3, 5, 6, 7,
      10, 21, 167
  environmental ministry of, 438
  European unification and, 119–20,
      122, 125, 373
  Fifth Republic of, 323–27, 372–74
  foreign policy of, 43, 373, 387,
      475, 486
  foreign workers in, 176, 444–45,
      484–85
  Fourth Republic of, 42, 370, 372,
      373, 479
  historical changes of mood in, xiii,
      268
  housing in, 132, 203, 241, 242,
      243, 245
  immigration into, 483, 484–85,
      491
  industrial development in, 8, 184,
      185–86, 200–4, 476
  labor force in, 176, 254, 255
  labor movement in, 146, 258–59,
      260
  liberation of, 39
  NATO withdrawal of, x, 324, 326,
      371, 373, 475
  1968 political unrest in, x, 259,
      326–27, 346–49, 373–74
  nuclear power policy of, 420
  occupied Germany and, 13, 23, 79,
      81–82, 97
  politics in, 129–32, 274, 275,
      277, 437, 438–39, 474–
      87
  postwar borders of, 12
  social reform in, 234, 235, 236,
      237, 238, 476–77, 487
  Soviet Union and, 43, 312, 326,
      478, 486
  terrorism in, 483
  Third Republic of, 41, 43, 44, 45
  tourism and, 251, 252
  trade by, 196, 202
  transportation in, 7, 172, 192, 193,
      195, 201–2
  U.S. and, 323, 324, 326, 327, 331,
      486
  workweek in, 249, 424

Franco, Francisco, 53–54, 350, 385–
    387, 441, 493–94, 495
Frank, Hans, 24
Frankfurt, 445
Free Democratic Party (West Ger-
    many), 80
Free French movement, 39–40
Freemasons, 520
Freisinn (Switzerland), 393
French Revolution, 19
Freud, Sigmund, 272
Frisch, Max, 268
Front de Libération National (FLN),
    371, 372, 373
Fundis, 438
Furubotn, Peder, 146

Gaillard, Félix, 371
Gaitskell, Hugh, 32, 125, 138, 215,
    364, 365
gamberros, 232
garden cities, 244–45
Gaullism, 126, 130–31, 322, 474–75
Gauss, Günther, 456
General Agreement on Tariffs and
    Trade (GATT), 198
genetics, 66, 269, 286
Geneva summit (1955), 298–99
Georgiev, Kimon, 71
Gerhardsen, Einar, 20, 392
German Democratic Republic (East
    Germany), xv, 67, 135, 161–62,
    288, 304, 313, 404–6, 565
  agriculture in, 175, 180
  army of, 405
  Communist takeover of, 77–78,
    80–82, 86
  culture of, 289
  Czech invasion and, 356–58, 360,
    406
  democratization of, 541–42, 550,
    554, 555–58, 568
  dissidents in, 530
  economy of, 86–87, 175, 176,
    180, 227, 228–29, 322, 405,
    431–32, 539–40, 557
  escapees from, 83, 86, 113, 404
  housing in, 244
  migrant workers in, 255

  pollution in, 436, 440
  social interest in, 228, 437, 438
  Soviet Union and, 404, 526, 531,
    541
  terrorists supported by, 448
  West Germany and, 135, 316–19,
    375, 378, 404, 405, 432, 445,
    449–50, 451, 454, 542
German reunification:
  Adenauer's lack of interest in, 136
  date of, 558
  East Germany's position on, 405,
    557
  economics of, 423, 460
  European unification and, xiv
  Soviet Union and, 317, 557
  Western support for, 298, 322, 451
German-Soviet pact (Molotov-
    Ribbentrop pact), 90, 523
Germany, Federal Republic of (West),
    120, 178, 214, 232, 240, 353,
    368, 375–80, 449–60, 544
  agriculture in, 134, 178, 180, 188,
    189, 190, 205
  army of, 375–76
  birthrate in, vii, 177
  as Cold War prize, 299–300, 449
  Common Market and, 8, 120, 328,
    329, 377
  defense spending in, 207
  de Gaulle and, 325, 327, 377–78
  East Germany and, 135, 316–19,
    375, 378, 404, 405, 432, 445,
    449–50, 451, 454, 542
  economy of, viii–ix, 82, 84–86,
    105, 133–34, 171, 173, 176,
    178, 180, 181, 203, 205–7, 208,
    212, 246, 256, 261, 263, 376,
    378, 415, 416, 417, 422–23,
    449, 452, 454–56
  establishment of, 76–84
  Europe's relationship with, 84,
    449, 460
  foreign policy of, 135, 300, 331,
    375–80, 449–50, 452, 454
  foreign workers in, 85–86, 176,
    205, 423, 444–45, 459
  Great Coalition government of,
    318, 378–79, 449, 451, 455

housing in, 134, 205, 242, 243
industrial development in, 182,
    183–84, 185–87, 203, 205
intellectual movements of, 269,
    456–57
labor force in, 254
labor movement in, 214, 258–59
migrant workers in, 85–86, 176,
    205, 255
NATO and, 84, 118–19, 122–23,
    298, 317, 403, 453
paid holiday time in, 249
period of fear in, xi–xii, 456, 457
politics in, 51, 133–36, 277, 378–
    379, 437, 438, 449–60
pollution in, 436, 440
refugees in, 134, 445
social reform in, 236, 237, 238,
    450, 459, 477
Soviet Union and, 298, 299–300,
    312, 315, 316–23, 335, 377,
    399, 403, 449, 454
student-power movement in, 349–
    350, 450
technological development in, 419–
    420
terrorism in, 446, 452–53
tourism and, 251
transportation in, 7, 192, 194–95
Germany, Imperial, 9, 17, 78, 91,
    135, 235
Germany, Nazi, 3, 17–18, 46, 135,
    235, 250, 267, 282–83, 358,
    494
Germany, occupied, 4–5, 6, 7, 9, 10,
    89, 97, 106, 110, 167
    borders of, 12, 316–17
    de-Nazification in, 22, 23, 24–26,
        82
    economy of, 169
    political parties reestablished in,
        77–81
    population of, 77
    postwar refugees in, 15, 16, 77
    Potsdam Conference and, 98–100
    zones of, 13, 76–77
Germany, Weimar Republic of, 78,
    79, 83, 133, 273, 375
Gestapo, 24, 26, 28

Gewaltverzicht, 319
Ghana, 137, 335, 366
Gheorgiu Dej, Gheorghe, 410, 411
Gibraltar, 367
Gierek, Edward, 530, 532–34
Gypsy Moth, 369
Giscard d'Estaing, Valéry, xi, 372,
    452
Giustizia e Libertà, 47
glasnost, 235, 279, 288, 404, 429,
    510, 513, 515, 519, 521, 528
Gleichschaltung, 288
Globke, Hans, 134–35
Godesberg Program, 141, 376
Goebbels, Joseph, vn, 4
Goering, Hermann, 24
Goethe, Johann Wolfgang von, vi
Goldmann, Lucien, 273
Gomułka, Władysław, 20, 70, 160,
    161, 288, 302–4, 307, 308, 356,
    357, 360, 406–7
Göncz, Arpad, 554
González, Felipe, 495, 496, 497–98
Gorbachev, Mikhail, xv, 429, 472,
    486, 489, 513, 515–19, 520,
    525, 527–28, 530, 538, 568
Gorbachev, Raisa, 516
"Gorbachev's Economic Plans," 430
Gottwald, Klement, 20, 158, 162
Grass, Günter, 456
Graziani, Rodolfo, 27
Great Britain, xiv, 9, 30, 31–38, 43,
    118, 178, 232, 247, 250, 295,
    306, 353, 362–69
    agriculture in, 168, 178, 179, 188,
        189
    birthrate in, vii, 177
    Common Market and, xiv, 122,
        125, 197, 215, 329–32, 373,
        377, 422, 472, 475
    decolonization by, ix, 33, 137–38,
        362
    defense spending in, 138, 215
    economy of, ix, x, 32–33, 36, 117,
        137, 138–39, 167, 171, 172,
        178, 179, 180, 181, 203, 212–
        215, 246, 256, 257, 263, 363,
        365–66, 415, 416, 417, 424–
        425, 465–73

Great Britain (*cont.*)
  at end of World War II, 5, 6, 7, 9,
    10, 21, 32, 36
  European unification and, 119,
    124–25, 215, 323, 325
  foreign debt of, 32–33, 137
  foreign policy of, 33–34, 37–38,
    362, 363, 364–69, 465–66, 468
  foreign workers in, 444–45
  housing in, 36, 137, 242, 243, 244,
    245, 362
  immigration into, 138, 366, 444
  industrial development in, 183–84,
    185–86, 203
  labor force in, 254, 255, 256
  labor movement in, 214, 258, 259,
    260, 365–66, 425, 465, 466,
    467, 468, 470–71, 472–73
  nationalist and separatist move-
    ments in, 369, 441, 442, 443,
    468
  occupied Germany and, 13, 16, 23,
    81–82, 98–100
  politics in, 31–38, 136–38, 277,
    437, 465–73
  pollution in, 439, 440
  postwar culture of, 281–82
  postwar mood of, 268–69
  postwar relations of Soviet Union
    and U.S. with, 88–104
  social reform in, 234, 236, 237,
    238, 239
  tourism and, 252
  transportation in, 172, 192, 193,
    195
  U.S. aid to, 33, 86, 212, 471
  U.S. relations with, 367–68
  see also Conservative Party (Great
    Britain); Labour Party (Great
    Britain)
Greece; xi, xiv, 16, 37, 41, 48, 67,
  100, 118, 188, 205, 234
  British control of, 88–89, 96, 103,
    110, 111
  Common Market and, xiv, 419
  economy of, 169, 170, 216, 217,
    422
  at end of World War II, 5, 6, 7, 8
  merchant fleet of, 193, 217

  military dictatorship in, 335, 395–
    396
  postwar politics in, 30, 31, 106,
    110–11, 146, 395
  Turkey and, xiv, 16
Green parties, 435–40
  of Austria, 437
  of East Germany, 437, 438
  electoral success of, 437, 455
  ideals of, 440
  social concerns of, 437, 458
  stagnation of, 438
  of Sweden, 437
  as uneasy coalitions, 438
  of West Germany, 437, 438, 453,
    455, 457, 458, 459
Grechko, Andrei, 357
Greenpeace, 482
Green Shirts, 435
Gromyko, Andrei, 515
Gronchi, Giovanni, 381
Gropius, Walter, 245
gross domestic product (GDP), definition of, 170*n*
gross national product (GNP), xii,
    xiii, 117, 175–76
  of Austria, 218
  of Belgium, 426
  of Czechoslovakia, 176, 228
  definition of, 170*n*
  of Denmark, 218, 246
  of Eastern Europe, 228, 229
  of East Germany, 176
  of Europe, 182, 219, 433
  of France, 176, 202–3, 246, 424
  of Great Britain, 203, 212–13,
    246, 417, 425, 465, 490
  of Greece, 216, 217
  growth rates of, 170–71, 176,
    202–3, 216, 219, 246, 433
  of Italy, 203, 490
  of Japan, 85, 174
  of Poland, 176
  of Soviet Union, 174, 223, 226,
    311, 428, 508
  of Spain, 216, 427
  of Sweden, 218, 219, 246, 418
  of Switzerland, 217
  of U.S., 174

of West Germany, 85, 170, 171, 176, 203, 246
gross savings, 213
Grosz, Karoly, 538, 554
Grotewohl, Otto, 81
Groza, Petru, 74
Grundgesetz, 375
guest workers, *see* migrant workers
Guillaume, Günter, 451
Guyana, British, 367
Gysi, Klaus, 558

Haeckel, Ernst, 435
Hager, Kurt, 541
Halbstarke, 232
Hallstein, Walter, 328
Hallstein Doctrine, 318
Hamburg, 455
Hammarskjöld, Dag, 309
Hamsun, Knut, 436
Hansen, Hans, 391
Harriman, Averell, 93, 102
Havel, Vaclav, 288, 559–60
Healey, Denis, 37, 466–67, 468
health care, 34, 236–37, 239, 240–241
heart disease, 240, 418
Heath, Edward, 366, 465, 466, 469
Hedtoft, Hans, 391
Heidegger, Martin, 280
Heinemann, Gustav, 378
Hernu, Charles, 482
Herrnstadt, Rudolf, 160
Hess, Rudolf, 24
Heuss, Theodor, 80, 377
highway systems, 195
Himmler, Heinrich, 435
Hirsch, Etienne, 121, 201
Hitler, Adolf, 5, 11, 17, 18, 41, 51, 53, 78, 84, 88, 92, 116, 283, 435
hobbies, 250
Hobsbawm, Eric, 467
Hoechst, 184
Hoegernaestaden, 245
Holkeri, Harri, 501
Holland, *see* Netherlands
"Hollanditis," xi

Honecker, Erich, 289, 404, 450, 454, 459, 530, 539, 555, 556
Hopkins, Harry, 93, 97
household appliances, 247–48
housing, 132, 241–45
  in Belgium, 241, 242, 244
  city planning and, 244–45
  cost of, 243, 245
  in Eastern Europe, 6, 176, 244
  in East Germany, 541
  at end of World War II, 6, 36, 57, 77, 85, 241
  Engels on, 238
  in France, 132, 203, 241, 242, 243, 245
  government programs for, 36, 134, 137, 203, 206, 223, 242
  in Great Britain, 36, 137, 242, 243, 244, 245, 362
  in Italy, 241, 242, 243
  in Soviet Union, 57, 223, 243–44
  in West Germany, 134, 206, 242, 243
Hoxha, Enver, 549
Hughes, H. Stuart, 49
Hull, Cordell, 110
humanities, 278–79
Hungary, xv, 67, 234, 267, 341, 400, 536–39
  agriculture in, 175, 228, 408
  birthrate in, 178
  Communist takeover of, 72, 73–74, 76, 90
  Czech invasion and, 360
  democratization of, 538–39, 550, 553–54
  dissidents in, 530, 539
  economy of, 72, 161, 175, 225, 228, 230, 408, 432, 536–38
  at end of World War II, 8, 15, 27, 69, 70
  ethnic minorities of, 68
  foreign policy of, 408, 538, 554
  housing in, 244
  New Course in, 161
  New Economic Mechanism of, 536–37
  1956 revolution in, ix, 276, 338, 358, 359

Hungary (*cont.*)
political stability of, 68
postwar borders of, 14
social unrest in, 228, 288, 289,
303, 304–5, 437
Soviet invasion of, 303, 304–8,
382, 408, 409, 568
terrorists supported by, 448
tourism in, 252
Husák, Gustav, 530, 539, 559
Husserl, Edmund, 280
Huysmans, Camille, 389

ICBMs (intercontinental ballistic missiles), 295, 333
Iceland, 118
ICI, 185
I.G. Farben, 25, 184
IG Metall, 259
Iliescu, Ion, 561
India, ix, 33, 137, 154, 230, 338,
405
Indochina, 43, 123, 132, 370, 371
Indonesia, 52, 335
industry:
at end of World War II, 7–9, 11,
50, 56, 69
in 1970s and 1980s, 419–20, 429
recovery of, 182–87
infant mortality, 240, 510
inflation, 415–17, 434
agricultural subsidies and, 190
in Belgium, 464
in Denmark, 218, 500
in Finland, 426
in France, 42, 201, 202, 204, 370,
415, 416, 417, 423, 481
in Great Britain, 138–39, 415,
416, 417, 424, 425, 466, 468,
469
in Greece, 217
in Hungary, 537–38
in Italy, 50–51, 209, 415, 416
in Keynesian economic theory, 279
Korean War and, 168–69
in Netherlands, 426, 462
in Norway, 426
oil shocks and, 416, 425, 451
in Poland, 533
postwar, 168

in Soviet Union, 56, 82, 430, 431,
517
in Spain, 427, 497
in Switzerland, 217
in West Germany, 415, 416, 417,
423, 452, 455
in Yugoslavia, 432, 548
intercontinental ballistic missiles
(ICBMs), 295, 333
intermediate nuclear forces (INF),
454
International Confederation of Free
Trade Unions (WFTU), 258–59
international law, 25
International Monetary Fund (IMF),
467
International Red Cross, 91
*Introduction to Contemporary His-
tory, An* (Barraclough), 567
investment ratios, 213
Iran (Persia), 106, 184, 447
Ireland, Northern, 369, 441, 442,
443, 446, 447, 466
Ireland, Republic of, x, 177, 188,
254–55
Irish Republican Army (IRA), 446,
466
iron curtain:
Churchill's reference to, 38
first reference to, vn
"iron law of oligarchy," 263
Islam, 442, 486, 546, 548
Israel, 135, 341, 374, 544, 554
Italy, 45–51, 96, 118, 120, 205, 215,
240, 241, 246, 247, 269, 286,
295, 381–84, 488–92
agriculture in, 178, 179, 189, 208,
210, 229
Austria's border dispute with,
383–84, 441
birthrate in, vii, 177, 491
coalition governments of, 381–84
Common Market and, 8, 120, 211,
328
as country of paradoxes, 491–92
culture of, 281
de-Nazification in, 22, 23, 27
economy of, ix, 105, 133, 170,
171, 173, 178, 179, 180, 203,
205, 208–11, 256, 257, 261,

383, 415, 416, 417–18, 425–26,
    488, 489, 490
  at end of World War II, 3, 5, 6, 8,
    10
  fascism in, 17–18, 45–46, 54, 250,
    267, 281, 494
  foreign policy of, 383–84
  foreign workers in, 444
  housing in, 241, 242, 243
  immigration into, 491
  industrial development in, 184,
    185–86, 209
  labor movement in, 146, 258–60
  liberation of, 45–48
  paid holiday time in, 249
  politics of, 30, 48–51, 274, 275,
    277, 485, 488–89
  postwar borders of, 14
  "second economy" of, 490
  social reform in, 236, 237, 238,
    489
  social unrest in, x
  student-power movement in, 350
  terrorism in, 446, 489–90
  tourism in, 251, 252

Jakes, Milos, 539, 559
Japan, 196, 252, 278, 334, 421
  economy of, 417
  industrial development in, 186,
    205, 214, 419
  in World War II, 4, 97
Jaruzelski, Wojciech, 534–35, 552
Jaspers, Karl, 456
Jenkins, Roy, 467, 470
Jeune République, 128
Jews, 39
  Final Solution and, 5, 25, 26, 27,
    69
  in Poland, 5, 68, 69, 358, 406–7
  as postwar refugees, 15
  in Soviet Union, 286
  see also anti-Semitism
Jobert, Michel, 475
Jodl, Alfred, 3, 24
John Paul II, Pope, 533
Johnson, Lyndon B., 252, 321, 337,
    360
John XXIII, Pope, 277

Juan Carlos de Borbón, 386, 494
Jura conflict, 441
Jusos (Young Socialists), 451

Kádár, János, 20, 289, 306–8, 408,
    430, 536, 537–38, 553
Kaganovich, L. M., 63, 398
Kalinin, M. I., 62
Kampman, Viggo, 391
Kania, Stanisław, 534
Karamanlis, Konstantinos, 395
Kardelj, Edvard, 108, 342–43
Katyn masscre, 91
Kautsky, Karl, 273
Keitel, Wilhelm, 24
Kekkonen, Urho, 390, 502
Kelly, Petra, 438
Kennan, George, 93, 112–13
Kennedy, John F., 296, 311, 313,
    314, 320, 322, 333, 477
Kennedy Round, 198
Keynes, John Maynard, Lord, 33
Keynesianism, 279, 471
KGB, 509, 572
khooligans, 233
khozraschet, 432
Khrushchev, Nikita, ix, 58, 114–15,
    136, 147, 151, 154, 158, 174,
    185, 221, 262, 299, 302, 340,
    381, 397–402, 408, 411
  assessment of, 401
  background of, 63
  Berlin Crisis and, 320–22
  boasts by 400–1, 510
  Cuban missile crisis and, 333, 399
  cultural policy of, 286, 287, 400,
    509
  downfall of, 223–24, 225, 287,
    317, 334, 335, 397, 402, 507
  general secretary, appointment as,
    152, 154–55, 397
  reforms by, 397, 399
  Stalin revelations by, 276, 397–98
  U.S. negotiations with, 310–15
Kiesinger, Kurt, 331, 378
Kinnock, Neil, 470, 473
Kirgizia, 524
Kliszko, Zenon, 160
Kohl, Helmut, 455–56, 460
Koivisto, Mauno, 502

Kolkhozy, 58, 222, 517
Komsomol, 402
Korea, Republic of (South), 554
Korean War, viii, 109, 116, 122, 123, 168–69, 275
Korsch, Karl, 273
Kosovo, 442, 548, 563, 564
Kostov, Traicho, 70, 159–60
Kosygin, Aleksei, 336, 337, 357, 401, 402, 430, 509, 512
Kovacs, Bela, 73, 74
Kozlov, Frol, 312, 401
Kraft durch Freude, 250
Krag, Jens, 391
Kreisky, Bruno, 393
Krenz, Egon, 555
Krupp, 25, 182, 318
Kulturkampf, 389
Kulturpessimismus, 379
Kurile Islands, 334
Kuwait, 420

labor force:
  in agriculture, 179–80, 189, 200, 221, 254
  in industry, 254, 428, 430
  migrant workers in, 85–86, 176, 181, 205, 255
  self-employment in, 254
  in service industries, 179, 254
  women in, 248, 254
labor movement, 258–60, 263
  in Belgium, 389
  communists and, 258–59
  declining militancy of, 260
  "direct action" by, 48–49
  in East Germany, 86
  in France, 146, 258–59, 260
  in Great Britain, 214, 258, 259, 260, 365–66, 425, 466, 467, 468, 470–71, 472–73
  in Italy, 146, 258–60
  modernization and, 259, 365–66, 425, 466
  in Netherlands, 52
  in Norway, 501
  rising status of, 259–60
  in Spain, 387, 494, 497
  in Sweden, 503
  in West Germany, 214, 258–59

Labor Party (Netherlands), 142, 388, 461
Labor Party (Norway), 30
Labour Party (Great Britain), 98, 119, 124, 139, 141, 214–15, 258, 282, 330, 332, 369, 422, 425, 452, 472, 477
  defeats of, 136–37, 362, 465, 468
  foreign policy of, 33–34, 37–38, 362, 364–65, 367, 466, 473
  leading figures of, 32, 33–35, 467
  nationalization and social programs of, 35–37, 362, 364, 467
  nature of, 32, 362
  power regained by, 364, 466
  rise to power of, 30, 31
land reform, in Eastern Europe, 72–73
Larsen, Aksel, 146, 391–92
Latin America, 54, 346
Latvia, 12, 443, 523
Laval, Pierre, 28
Lebanon, 43
Lecoeur, Auguste, 146
leisure activities, 249–52
Lend-Lease Act (1941), 96, 97
Lenin, V. I., 95, 103, 120, 263, 273, 285, 329, 335, 339, 521, 524
Leningrad, 56
Leningrad, 66
"Leningrad affair," 64
Leopold III, King of Belgium, 389
Le Pen, Jean, 445, 485
"Let the People Breathe," 437
Lewis, W. A., 173
Liberal Party (Belgium), 389, 463
Liberal Party (Denmark), 500
Liberal Party (Great Britain), 362
Liberal Party (Italy), 49
Liberal Party (Netherlands), 462
Liberal Party (Sweden), 391
Liberal Party (FDP) (West Germany), 78, 81, 134, 375, 376, 449, 451, 453–54
Libya, 100, 447, 471, 486
life expectancy, 240, 241, 510, 521, 538
Ligachev, Egor, 519
Lippmann, Walter, 113
literacy, 209

Lithuania, 12, 443, 523
London, 4, 244–45, 445, 469
Longo, Luigi, 383
Louvain University, 389
Lowenthal, Richard, 335
Lübke, Heinrich, 377
Luca, Vasile, 160, 410
Lukacs, Georg, 109, 273, 282
Lukyanov, Andrei, 562
Luxembourg, 120
    see also Benelux
Luxemburg, Rosa, 61
Lysenko school of genetics, 66

McCloy, John, 320
Macmillan, Harold, 137, 138, 213,
    215, 312, 330, 362, 363–64,
    368, 469
Maddison, Angus, 170
Mafia, 490
Maidanek, 23
mail delivery, 194
Maizière, Lothar de, 558
Major, John, 472
Malaya, 137, 366
Malenkov, G. M., 63, 64, 149, 152,
    153, 154, 155, 222, 228, 397,
    398
Malta, 367
Mandarins (Beauvoir), 275
managerial class, 261–62
Mao Tse-tung, 312, 333–34, 340,
    343, 352, 368
Marcuse, Herbert, 352
Marjolin, Robert, 121
"market socialism," 431
marriage grants, 237
Marshall, George, 93, 110, 111, 117
Marshall Plan, vii, 83, 86, 106, 111,
    117, 119, 168, 198
Martens, Wilfierd, 463
Marty, André, 146
Marx, Karl, 205, 273, 285, 339
Marxism, 273–74, 277, 379, 456
Masaryk, Jan, 14, 157–58, 356,
    560
Masse, Pierre, 201
maternity allowances, 237
Maurel, Micheline, 3
Mauroy, Pierre, 481, 482

Maurras, Charles, 29
Mayer, Daniel, 140
Mayer, René, 42, 45, 202
Mazowiecki, Tadeusz, 552
media, 66, 278, 284–85, 286, 459–
    460
medical care, 34, 236–37, 239, 240–
    241
Mediterranean Sea, pollution in, 436,
    439
Memory (Pamyat), 520
Mendès-France, Pierre, 40, 42, 45,
    123, 131, 132, 348, 370
Mendès-France plan, 201
mental diseases, 240
merchant fleets, 193, 217, 218
Merker, Paul, 160
Messmer, Pierre, 475
Michael, King of Rumania, 71
Michel, Roberto, 263
Middle East, 55, 123, 183, 193, 295,
    333, 336, 367, 383, 418, 522
migrant workers, 85–86, 176, 181,
    205, 255, 423, 437, 444–45,
    459, 484–85
Mikolajczyk, Stanislaw, 73
Mikoyan, Anastas, 63, 149, 152,
    312, 401
Mita, Ciriaco de, 488
Mitbestimmung, 349
Mitterrand, François, 348, 373, 479,
    480, 482, 483, 484, 486
Mladenov, Peter, 562, 563
MLF (Multi-Lateral Force), 325
Moch, Jules, 130, 146
Moczar, General, 406–7
Modrow, Hans, 556
Moldavia (Bessarabia), 410, 443,
    544
Möller, Alex, 449
Mollet, Guy, 20, 140, 154, 371,
    372
Molotov, V. M., 62–63, 91, 110,
    136, 149, 152, 153, 302, 398,
    399, 509
Molotov-Ribbentrop pact (German-
    Soviet pact), 90, 523
monarchies, decline of, 30, 47–48,
    71
monetarists, 469

monetary systems:
  in Belgium, 171
  in Denmark, 171, 392
  devaluations of, 169, 171, 202,
    217, 365, 373, 392, 416, 465,
    468, 475, 503
  at end of World War II, 8, 10,
    50–51
  flexible exchange rates for, 416
  in France, 171, 201, 202, 326,
    373, 423, 475
  in Great Britain, 137, 171, 212,
    215, 365, 466–67, 468
  in Greece, 217
  in Hungary, 70
  in Italy, 208
  in Poland, 406
  in Soviet Union, 56
  in Sweden, 503
  in Switzerland, 416
  tourism and, 252
  unification of, xiv, 120
  in West Germany, viii, 82, 205,
    207, 416, 452
  of Yugoslavia, 548
Monnet, Jean, viii, 40, 119, 121,
  201, 332
Monnet Plan, 169
Montedison, 184–85
Moravia, Alberto, 270
Morgenthau Plan, 98
Moro, Aldo, 381, 382, 488, 489–90
Morocco, 370, 371
Morrison, Herbert, 34
Mousetrap, The (Christie), 284
Mouvement Républicain Populaire
  (MRP) (France), 44, 45, 126,
  128–29, 132
Movement for Democratic Renewal
  (Yugoslavia), 564
Multi-Lateral Force (MLF), 325
Munich, 445
Munich Pact, 319
Mussolini, Benito, 5, 18, 27, 45–46,
  51, 53
Mutual Balanced Force Reduction
  talks, 526

Nagy, Imre, 161, 305–6, 307, 308,
  554

Napoleon I, Emperor of France, 18–
  19, 116
Nasser, Gamal Abdel, 138, 363, 368,
  399
National Democratic Party (NPD)
  (West Germany), 379, 453
National Economic Development
  Council (Great Britain), 366
National Front (France), 445, 481,
  483, 484, 485–86
National Health Service (Great Britain), 34, 239
nationalization:
  civil service and, 261–62
  in Eastern Europe, 72
  in France, 43, 122, 129, 172–73,
    424, 480–81, 483
  in Great Britain, 35, 137, 172,
    215, 362, 364, 467, 471
  in Italy, 211
  in Netherlands, 122
  of transportation, 193–94
  in West Germany, 79, 122, 376
National Liberal Party (Rumania),
  561
National People's Army (East Germany), 405
National Salvation Front (Rumania),
  561
nation-states, 54–55
"nations without a state," 441
NATO, see North Atlantic Treaty
  Organization
natural gas, 133, 183, 184, 428, 454,
  461
Nenni, Pietro, 140, 381, 382
neo-Nazis, 134
neo-Stalinism, 286
Netherlands, 120, 195, 196, 247,
  257, 420
  coalition governments of, 462
  confessionalism in, 388
  cultural unrest in, 461–62
  decolonization by, ix, 52, 217,
    388
  de-Nazification in, 24, 28
  economy of, 170, 217, 256, 388,
    426, 461–62
  at end of World War II, 5, 6, 7,
    51, 52

industrial development in, 183,
186–87, 203, 216
infant mortality in, 240
population growth in, 177
social reform in, 237, 238
see also Benelux
New Caledonia, 482
New Course, 161, 162, 301
New Deal, 93
New Economic Policy, 517–18
New Forum (East Germany), 557
New York, N.Y., cultural predominance of, 11
New York Times, 112
New Zealand, 330
Nigeria, 366
Nixon, Richard, M., 311–12
Nkrumah, Kwame, 335
Nobel Prize:
of Brandt, 450
of German scientists, 283
of Pasternak, 286
of Sakharov, 518
of Solzhenitsyn, 287
nomenklatura, 507, 508, 542
Nordic Council, 390
North Africa, vii, 40, 133, 177, 295,
383, 445, 491
North Atlantic Treaty Organization
(NATO) vii, 114, 320, 334, 336,
357, 388, 462, 468, 473, 500
atomic weapons and, v, xii, 123–
124, 295
establishment of, 118–19
European nuclear weapons installations by, xii, 309, 526
France's withdrawal from, x, 324,
326, 371, 373, 475
headquarters of, x, 326, 390
members of, 118, 390, 496
military weakness of, 295
West Germany as member of, 84,
118–19, 122–23, 298, 317, 403,
453
North Sea:
oil industry in, 183, 421, 426, 442,
468, 470
pollution in, 436, 439
Norway, 118, 237, 240
currency reform in, 8

de-Nazification in, 28
economy of, 218, 392, 417, 426,
500–1
at end of World War II, 3, 392
European Community membership
and, x, 501
immigration into, 501
labor force in, 254
merchant fleet of, 193
as NATO member, 390
politics in, 30, 52, 499, 500–1
Nove, Alec, 224
Novotny, Antonin, 20, 162, 354–55,
360
Novy Mir, 509
NPD (National Democratic Party)
(West Germany), 379, 453
nuclear power, 183, 420, 439
Nuclear Test Ban Treaty (1963), 296,
309
nuclear weapons, see atomic weapons
Nuremberg laws, 135
Nuremberg trials, 24–25, 26

OAS (Organisation de l'Armée Secrète), 371
Oberländer, Theodor, 134
obroda, 543
Oder-Neisse Line, 96, 99, 102, 317,
379
"Ohne mich," 84
oil industry, 197, 227, 430, 455
in Middle East, 183, 193
in North Sea, 183, 421, 426, 442,
468, 470, 501
in Soviet Union, 56, 57, 173, 184,
223, 428, 454, 508
oil shocks:
economic effects of, x, 415, 416,
418, 422–23, 425, 451, 489,
495
fear of, 418
first, x, 415, 416, 420, 422–23,
444
second, x, 416, 418, 425
oil tankers, 193
One Day in the Life of Ivan Denisovich (Solzhenitsyn), 287
"Open Sky" plan, 299
Opus Dei movement, 387

Organisation de l'Armée Secrète
    (OAS), 371
Organization for European Economic
    Cooperation (OEEC), *see* Mar-
    shall Plan
Organization of Petroleum Exporting
    Countries (OPEC), 416, 421
Orwell, George, 37, 268–69, 282
Ostpolitik, 379, 449, 451
Ottoman Empire, 547
Owen, David, 470
ozone destruction, 439

Paasikivi, Juho, 390
Paish, F., 139
Palestine, 33
Palestinian groups, 447
Palme, Olof, 503
Pamyat (Memory), 520
Papandreou, Andreas, xiv
Papandreou, George, 395
Paris, 245, 445, 485
Paris summit (1960), 296, 312–13
Partido Popular (Spain), 496
Partij van de Arbeid (Netherlands),
    142, 388, 461
Partito Socialista Italiano di Unità
    Proletaria, 382
Party for Democratic Socialism (East
    Germany), 558
Pasternak, Boris, 286–87
Pauker, Ana, 160, 233, 410
Pavelic, Ante, 29
Pax, 301
Peasant Party (Bulgaria), 74
Peasant Party (Denmark), 391–92
Peasant Party (Poland), 73
Peasant Party (Rumania), 74, 561
Pella, Giuseppe, 381
Penn, William, 16
"people's capitalism," 134
People's Party (Turkey), 54
perestroika, 431, 515, 516–21, 527–
    528, 546
Persia (Iran), 106, 184, 447
Persian Gulf, 295, 367, 569
Pétain, Henri Philippe, 28, 128
Petkov, Nikolai, 74, 75
Petrescu, Titel, 74
petrochemical industry, 184, 185

Pflimlin, Pierre, 371
pharmaceutical industry, 185
Philip, André, 140
physicians, 240–41
Pieds Noirs, 371
Pineau, Christian, 136
Pius XII, Pope, 48
Pleven, René, 40, 42–43, 84
Pleven, Plan, 122–23
Podgorny, Nikolai, 401
"Poem for Adults" (Wazyk), 302
Poland, xv, 318, 341, 406–7
    agriculture in, 69, 156, 303, 406,
        533
    Allied negotiations on, 89, 90–93,
        95, 96
    automobiles in, 194
    birthrate in, 178
    Catholic Church in, 278, 288, 301,
        304, 406, 535
    communist takeover of, 73, 74, 76
    Czech invasion and, 356–58, 360
    democratization of, 531, 532–36,
        550, 552–53, 554
    dissidents in, 530
    economy of, 72, 175, 176, 228–
        229, 230, 406, 407, 432, 530,
        532–33, 535, 553
    at end of World War II, 6, 8, 67,
        69, 267
    ethnic minorities of, 68
    historic relations of Germany and
        Russia with, 91, 406, 407
    housing in, 244
    Jews in, 5, 68, 69, 358, 406–7
    Katyn massacre and, 91
    military dictatorship of, 534–35
    Nazi-Soviet division of, 25, 91
    New Course in, 162, 301
    1956 rebellion in, 301–4, 308,
        338, 406
    pollution in, 436
    postwar borders of, 12–13, 96, 99,
        102, 316–17
    social unrest in, 228, 288
    Solidarity movement in, 533–36,
        552–53
    Sovietization of, 156
    World War II casualties in, 5, 69
Polaris submarine, 367

Polish Home Army, 92, 97
Politburo, 62, 63, 110, 149, 298, 313, 358, 507, 508, 512, 516, 519
pollution, 435, 436, 437, 439, 440
polycentrism, in Communist world, 338–44
Pompidou, Georges, 346, 372, 474–476
Popov, Dimitar, 563
Po Prostu, 302, 304
Popular Party (Italy), 127
population growth, vii, 177–79, 200, 221, 445, 491
Portugal, 237
    Common Market and, xiv, 419
    decolonization by, ix
    defeat of dictatorship in, xi
    economy of, 246, 422
    as EFTA member, 197
    as NATO member, 118
    World War II neutrality of, 18
Postan, Michael, 170, 212
Potsdam Conference (1945), 13, 43, 55, 98–102, 294, 323
Poujadism, 132, 370, 461, 486
Powell, Enoch, 255
Pravda, 223, 513
Presidium, 149, 152, 155, 398, 399
Private Eye, 282
productivity gains, 121, 168, 170–171, 256–57
    in Belgium, 171
    in Eastern Europe 173, 175, 229
    in France, 170, 477
    in Great Britain, 171, 425, 468
    in Italy, 170, 210, 426
    in Netherlands, 170
    in Soviet Union, 508, 509
    in Spain, 170
    in Sweden, 170–71, 503
    in Switzerland, 170–71
    in West Germany, 171, 207, 378
Profumo scandal, 363
Progressive Center Union (EPEK) (Greece), 395
Progressive Party (Denmark), 500
Progress Party (Norway), 500
Protestant Church, 79, 277, 319, 388, 456–57, 462, 466, 542, 546
psychoanalysis, 272–73

Qaddafi, Muammar al-, 486
Queuille, Henri, 40, 202

RACE, 422
Radical Liberal Party (Denmark), 500
Radical Socialist Party (France), 44
Radical Venstre (Denmark), 392
railway systems, 7, 172, 192–93, 201–2
Rajk, Laszlo, 20, 70, 159
Rákosi, Matyas, 20, 73–74, 161, 305, 307, 408, 536
Ramadier, Paul, 145
Rankovic, Alexander, 159
Rapacki, Adam, 309
Rapid Deployment Force, 124
Rassemblement du Peuple Français (RPF), 130–31
Raubwirtschaft, 435
Reagan, Ronald, xii, 451, 471, 525, 526
Realos, 438
recessions:
    Korean War and, viii, 171
    of 1950s, viii, 171, 217
    of 1960s, 171, 174, 207, 255, 378
    of 1970s, 171, 415, 419, 423, 425, 426, 452, 475, 477
    of 1980s, 417, 425
    oil shocks and, x, 415, 416, 418, 422–23, 425
Red Brigades, 446, 489
Reischwehr, 376
religion, national separatism and, 442
Renault motor works, 43, 146
Republican Party (Italy), 382
Republican Party (West Germany), 445, 453, 459
research and development, 213, 257, 278, 419, 421
Reuter, Ernst, 83
Rey, Jean, 121
Reynaud, Paul, 39, 43
Rhine River, 436, 439
Rhodesia, 366, 367
Ribbentrop, Joachim von, 24

RNI, 184–85
Robles, Gil, 386
Rocard, Michel, 424, 481, 484
rockets, 367
Rokossovski, Konstantin, 301
Roman, Petru, 561
Romanov, Grigori, 513
Rome, Treaty of, (1957), xiv, 121,
    329, 330, 331
Rome—Open City, 281
Roosevelt, Franklin D., 40,
    102
    character of, 93
    death of, 97
    in postwar Allied negotiations, 89–
    97, 100–1
Rosenberg, Alfred, 24
Rousseau, Jean-Jacques, 274
Rousset, David, 275–76
Rumania, 67, 68, 160, 234, 288,
    289, 409–11
    agriculture in, 70, 432
    birthrate of, 178
    Communist takeover of, 73, 76,
    88–89, 97
    Czech invasion opposed by, 356,
    358, 360, 411, 544
    economy of, 175, 227, 228–29,
    340, 409, 410, 432, 544–45
    at end of World War II, 15, 27,
    69
    ethnic tensions in, 442
    foreign policy of, 544
    independent path taken by, 340–
    341, 356, 544
    New Course in, 162
    political upheaval in, 544, 545,
    550, 551, 560–62
    postwar borders of, 12, 14
    social unrest in, 437
    Sovietization of, 156
    tourism in, 252
Rumor, Mariano, 488
Rushdie, Salman, 447
Rusk, Dean, 321
Russia, Imperial, 410
Russian Orthodox Church, 58

Sakharov, Andrei, 509, 518
"salami technique," 73

Salan, Raoul, 371–72
Salo, Republic of, 46
SALT I, 525
samizdat, 287
Sangnier, Marc, 128
Saragat, Giuseppe, 140, 381–82
Sarraute, Nathalie, 347
Sarte, Jean-Paul, 275, 276, 277, 280,
    567
satellite towns, 245
Scandinavia, 197, 237, 242, 257,
    262, 390–92, 422
    economic balance of, 499
    ethnic tensions in, 441
    Nordic Council of, 390
    pollution in, 440
    see also Denmark; Finland; Nor-
    way; Sweden
Scheel, Walter, 451
Schiller, Karl, 378, 449
Schily, Otto, 438
Schlesinger, Arthur, 115
Schlüter, Poul, 500
Schmidt, Helmut, 449, 450, 451–52,
    454–55
Schroeder, Gerhard, 134, 329, 331,
    378
Schumacher, Kurt, 20, 78, 81
Schuman, Robert, viii, 119, 128
Schumann, Maurice, 40, 128
Schuman Plan, 119–20, 121, 169
Schwartz, Harry, 220
science, postwar advances in, 269–
    270, 278
Scotland, 369, 442, 468
SEATO (Southeast Asia Treaty Orga-
    nization), 325–26
Second World War, *see* World War II
SED, *see* Communist Party (East
    Germany)
Segni, Antonio, 382
Serbian Writers' Association, 564
Serbs, 67, 443, 547, 548, 563–64
service industries, 179, 254, 419, 445
sexual revolution, 234, 235
Shehu, Mehmet, 549
Shell, 185
Shepilov, Dimitri T., 398
Shevardnadze, Eduard, 519, 528
Shinwell, Emanuel, 37

shipbuilding industry, 213–14, 503, 533

Shonfield, Andrew, 170, 213

Short History of the U.S.S.R. A, 60

Shukshin, Vasili, 511

Siantos, Jeorjios, 146

Sik, Ota, 409

Simon II, King of Bulgaria, 71

Simonites, 390

Singapore, 366

Single European Act (SEA), xiv, 421

Sinyavsky–Daniel case, 403

Sixth Fleet (U.S.), 336

Skybolt rocket, 367

Slansky, Rudolf, 160

Slavic peoples, 67

Slovenes, 75, 354, 355, 441, 443, 547, 563, 564

Smallholders Party (Hungary), 72, 73–74

Smith, Walter Bedell, 3, 110

Smith, Ian, 366

Snowden, Ethel, v*n*

Social Credit movement, 435

Social Democratic parties, 18, 32, 343

Social Democratic Party (Austria), 393

Social Democratic Party (Belgium), 463

Social Democratic Party (Bulgaria), 74

Social Democratic Party (Czechoslovakia), 75, 157

Social Democratic Party (Denmark), 52, 391–92

Social Democratic Party (East Germany), 80–81, 557–58

Social Democratic Party (Finland), 390, 501, 502

Social Democratic Party (Great Britain), 468, 470

Social Democratic Party (Italy), 120, 140, 382, 489

Social Democratic Party (Netherlands), 52, 462

Social Democratic Party (Norway), 52, 392

Social Democratic Party (Rumania), 561

Social Democratic Party (Sweden), 53

Social Democratic Party (Switzerland), 141, 142, 393

Social Democratic Party (SPD) (West Germany), 81, 205, 375, 454
  background of, 78
  defeat of, 452, 455
  electoral victories of, 449, 450–51, 458
  European unification and, 119–20
  in Great Coalition, 318, 378–79, 449, 451, 455
  leftists absorbed by, 453, 457, 459
  philosophy of, 141–42

socialism, socialists, 139–43, 258, 261–62
  Cold War and, 139
  "developed," 509, 512
  in Eastern Europe, 71, 74
  electoral popularity of, 140, 142–143
  in France, 44–45, 139, 140, 347, 353, 424, 439, 475–87
  in Great Britain, *see* Labour Party (Great Britain)
  ideologies of, 139, 141–42
  in Italy, 46, 47, 50, 139, 140–41, 145, 381–83
  "market," 431
  in occupied Germany, 79

"socialism in one country," 55, 62

Socialist International, 489

Socialist Party (Austria), 141, 142

Socialist Party (Belgium), 389

Socialist Party (Bulgaria), 563

Socialist Party (Norway), 52

Socialist Party (Rumania), 74

Socialist Party (Spain), 495, 497–98

Socialist People's Party (Norway), 392

Socialist People's Party (Denmark), 391–92

socialist realism, 285–86

Socialist Unity Party, *see* Communist Party (East Germany)

social security, 176, 236

Solidarity, 533–36, 552–53

Solvay, 185

Solzhenitsyn, Alexander, 277, 286–287, 400, 509

Sorbonne, 347
"Sources of Soviet Conduct, The"
    (Kennan), 112
Soustelle, Jacques, 40, 131, 371
Southeast Asia, 217, 288
Southeast Asia Treaty Organization
    (SEATO), 325–26
South Tyrol (Alto Adige), 383–84,
    441
Soviet Union, 41, 46, 55–67, 149–
    163, 257, 273, 329, 397–403,
    507–28
    agriculture in, 56, 58, 95, 155,
        175, 180, 188, 220, 221, 222,
        224, 399, 428–29, 430, 432,
        510, 516, 517–18
    automobiles in, 194
    awards and orders in, 509, 515
    birthrate in, 178, 221
    China and, 135, 150, 229, 294,
        296, 311–14, 333–34, 335,
        338–39, 341, 343, 399, 410,
        526, 527
    collective leadership in, 152, 155–
        156, 399
    Congress of People's Deputies of,
        518, 519
    constitution of, 508
    corruption in, 510, 511–12, 513,
        521, 522
    culture of, 267, 285–88
    Czechoslovakia invaded by, ix,
        259, 288, 296–97, 306, 319,
        327, 336, 341, 354–61, 383,
        403, 405–6, 408, 409, 411, 508,
        544, 568
    defense spending in, 221, 223, 225,
        320, 335, 336, 399, 428, 525,
        527
    de-Stalinization in, 152–55, 287,
        335, 338, 400, 402, 519
    dissidents in, 509, 513
    Eastern Europe in empire of, vii,
        ix, 11, 13, 14, 17, 57, 62, 67–
        76, 88–89, 95, 101–2, 106,
        156–63, 227–30, 294, 297,
        299–308, 313, 404–11, 529–
        532, 551, 568
    East Germany and, 404, 526, 531,
        541

    economic reform in, 430–31, 509,
        517–18
    economy of, 56–58, 61, 66–67,
        150, 173–75, 180, 220–26,
        293–94, 311, 427–32, 508–10,
        521, 527
    education in, 65, 67
    at end of World War II, 5, 6, 7, 8,
        11, 21, 55–58
    energy production and consump-
        tion in, 429–30
    ethnic tension in, 403, 441, 443,
        522–24
    European communist parties and,
        44, 51, 70, 74, 75–76, 145
    "Europeanization of," 296
    Finland and, 92, 299, 390, 501–2,
        529
    forced-labor camps of, 16, 37, 276,
        287
    France and, 43, 312, 326, 478, 486
    German reunification and, 317,
        557
    as gerontocracy, 508, 512
    housing in, 57, 223, 243–44
    Hungary invaded by, 303, 304–8,
        382, 408, 409, 568
    industrial development in, 183,
        184, 185, 223
    Jews in, 286
    Katyn massacre and, 91
    labor force in, 254, 428, 430
    merchant fleet of, 193
    military strength of, 295–96, 298–
        299
    occupied Germany and, 13, 23, 80,
        82–83, 106
    oil industry of, 56, 57, 173, 184,
        223, 428, 454, 508
    pessimism in, 510–11, 528
    Poland and, 301–4, 308
    political and social reform in, v,
        xiii, xv, 224–25, 234, 235, 236,
        238, 279, 288, 515, 516–21
    political weakness of, 402–3
    pollution in, 436, 437–38
    population of, 178, 179
    postwar borders of, 12, 59, 99
    postwar relations of Great Britain
        and U.S. with, 89–104

propaganda claims of, 65, 66, 67
purges and trials in, 61, 62, 150,
    151, 220, 398, 411
Russian nationalism in, 520, 522
secret police of, 63, 65, 91, 150,
    156, 397, 509, 572
social structure of, 262–63
SS-20 missiles of, 452, 454, 458
Stalin-era political climate in, 58–
    67, 149–51, 220
Supreme Soviet of, 519
"suspected" minorities in, 15–16
terrorists supported by, 446–47
tourism and, 252
Turkey's territorial dispute with,
    54, 100, 106, 110
Western European fear of, viii, 55
West Germany and, 298, 299–
    300, 312, 315, 316–23, 335,
    372, 399, 403, 449, 454
World War II reparations paid to,
    70, 75, 86, 89, 97, 98, 99–100,
    101, 112, 175, 227, 410
Soviet–U.S. relations, see Cold War;
    détente
Soviet Writers' Union, 515
sovnarkhozy, 224, 399
soziale Marktwirtschaft, 205
Spaak, Henri, viii, 135, 332, 389
space program, 223, 295
Spain, xiv, 18, 205, 232, 240, 246,
    367, 385–87, 493–98
    agriculture in, 179–80, 216, 427
    Basque separatist movement in,
        385, 387, 441, 442, 446, 494,
        496–97
    birthrate in, vii, 177
    Catholic Church in, 385, 386, 387
    Civil War of, 494
    Common Market and, xiv, 417,
        419, 427, 495–96
    economy of, ix, 170, 179–80,
        216–17, 385, 415–16, 417,
        426–27, 493, 497
    end of Franco's rule in, xi
    foreign policy of, 387
    housing in, 241, 242
    life expectancy in, 240
    as NATO member, 496
    post-Franco politics of, 493–98

postwar politics of, 53–54
social reform in, 234, 237, 385–
    386
student-power movement in, 350
tourism and, 252, 497
World War II neutrality of, 18, 53
SPD, see Social Democratic Party
    (West Germany)
Spiegel, Der, 377
Springer, Axel, 349, 350
Spychalski, Marian, 160
SS-20 missiles, 452, 454,
    458
Staatsvertrag, 299
Stalin, Joseph, vii, ix, 4, 23, 57, 75,
    108, 139, 146, 149, 173, 174,
    175, 262, 273, 276, 285, 286,
    294, 317, 338, 529
    Berlin blockade and, 83
    character of, 60, 61, 62, 95, 103–
        104, 109
    Churchill's territorial deal with,
        89–90, 110
    death of, 16, 86, 114, 123, 135,
        151, 397
    de Gaulle and, 43
    Khrushchev's revelations about,
        276, 397–98
    personality cult of, 60, 63, 95, 155,
        521
    in postwar Allied negotiations, 89–
        99, 101–4
    purges and trials held by, 61, 62,
        150, 151, 220, 398, 411
    reburial of, 400
    rehabilitation of, 402, 509
    Soviet economy under, 220–21
    Tito and, 158, 339
state ownership, see nationalization
Steel, David, 470
steel industry:
    of Common Market, 121
    at end of World War II, 167–68
    of France, 201, 203, 480
    of Great Britain, 137, 212, 362
    of Italy, 172–73, 209
    of Soviet Union, 56, 57, 185, 220,
        223
    of Sweden, 503
    of U.S., 212

steel industry (*cont.*)
　of West Germany, 182, 416
Stettinius, Edward, 93
Stimson, Henry L., 93
Stockholm, 245
Stoica, Chivu, 410
Stoph, Willy, 450
Strachey, John, 35–36, 37
Strauss, Franz Josef, 134, 377, 378,
　453
Streicher, Julius, 24
student-power movement, 233, 345–
　353, 385–86, 461
　cultural and political aims of, 351–
　353
　in France, x, 259, 326–27, 346–
　349, 373–74, 474
　in West Germany, 349–50, 450
Sturzo, Luigi, 127
Stuttgart, 445
Suarez, Adolfo, 495
Suez crisis, 137, 138, 183, 306, 363
Suslov, Mikhail, 401, 512
Svoboda, Ludvik, 359
Sweden, 118, 259
　birthrate in, 177
　Common Market and, 330
　economy of, 170–71, 216, 218,
　　246, 391, 417, 418, 426, 503
　housing in, 242, 243
　labor force in, 254, 503
　nuclear power policy of, 420
　paid holiday time in, 249
　politics in, 391, 437, 499, 502–3
　social reform in, 234, 236, 237,
　　238, 503
　World War II neutrality of, 18, 53,
　　390
Switzerland, 197, 233, 240, 247, 257
　birthrate in, 177
　Common Market and, 330
　defense as priority in, 394
　economy of, 170–71, 217, 256,
　　416
　foreign workers in, 176, 444
　housing in, 242, 243
　labor force in, 176, 254, 255
　life expectancy in, 240
　as multinational state, 441, 463
　neutrality of, 18, 53, 393–94

political parties of, 393
social reform in, 237, 238
tourism in, 251, 252
transportation in, 192–93
Syria, 43, 335, 447

Tambroni, Fernando, 382
Tangier, 100
tariffs, 121, 190, 197–98, 205, 419,
　421
Tartars, 523
taxes:
　capital-gains, 476
　in Denmark, 500
　in France, 213, 476
　in Great Britain, 213, 424, 469,
　　470
　in Italy, 49
　in Norway, 500
　progressive, 232
　in Soviet Union, 262
　in Sweden, 418
　welfare state levels of, 213
　in West Germany, 213, 455
technology gap, 256–57, 419
teddy boys, 232
Teitgen, Pierre, 42, 128
television, 278, 284–85, 459–60
terrorism, 371, 372, 446–48, 452–
　453, 483, 489–90
Thadden, Adolf von, 379
Thatcher, Margaret, 282
　assessment of, 470–73
　background of, 465, 466, 469
　character of, 469–70, 471
　Common Market and, xiv, 125,
　　472
　economic policy of, 279, 425, 469,
　　470, 471
　election of, 466, 468
　labor unions defeated by, 466,
　　470–71
　media and, 459–60
　resignation of, 469
Thaw, The (Ehrenburg), 155
Thorez, Maurice, 44
Through Bolshevik Russia (Snow-
　den), v*n*
Thyssen, 182
Tiananmen Square, 555

Tillon, Charles, 42, 146
Times (London), 37
Tindemans, Leo, x
Tindemans report, x
Tito, Marshal, 14, 20, 38, 71, 75,
    146, 154, 158–59, 275, 276,
    299, 304, 338, 339, 359, 441,
    536, 547–48, 549
tobacco, 247
Tocqueville, Alexis de, 270
Togliatti, Palmiero, 47, 339, 383
Tolkien, J. R. R., 436
tourism, 209, 216–17, 251–52, 385,
    497, 548
toxic waste, 439
trade, 171, 196–99
    agriculture, 189–91, 197, 429, 432
    Eastern Europe–Soviet Union, 57,
        175, 227–30
    Eastern–Western Europe, 198–99,
        230, 408
    by France, 481
    by Great Britain, 196–97, 213,
        215, 368, 424
    growth of, 434
    by Italy, 196, 215, 425
    by Netherlands, 196
    by Soviet Union, 222, 368, 428
    by Spain, 216
    Western European, 120–21, 172,
        189–91, 196–99, 202, 419,
        421–22
    Western Europe–U.S., vii, 117,
        168, 169, 186, 191
    by West Germany, 196–97, 198,
        205, 206, 207, 215, 423
Trade Union Congress (TUC), 258
trade unions, *see* labor movement
trahison des clercs, 276, 281
transportation, 172, 192–95, 201–2
Transylvania, 14, 437, 538
Trieste, 383
Trotsky, Leon, 346
Truman, Harry S.:
    at Potsdam conference, 98, 101
    Roosevelt succeeded by, 97
    Soviet policy of, 105–6, 110
Truman Doctrine, 111, 146
tuberculosis, 240, 269
Tudjman, Franjo, 564

Tunisia, 132, 370
Turkey, 205, 346, 546
    birthrate in, vii
    economy of, 219, 246
    at end of World War II, 54
    Greece and, xiv, 16
    as NATO member, 118
    political violence in, 446
    Soviet Union's territorial dispute
        with, 54, 100, 106, 110
    U.S. aid to, 111
    World War II neutrality of, 53
Tyumen oil and gas fields, 508

Überfremdung, 255
Ukraine, 59–60, 68, 151, 443, 523
Ulam, Adam, 340
Ulbricht, Walter, 77–78, 289, 320,
    321, 322, 357, 360, 404, 405–6,
    450, 539
Ulster, *see* Ireland, Northern
Umberto II, King of Italy, 48
unemployment, vii, 169, 434, 461
    in Belgium, 181, 254, 415–16, 464
    in Denmark, 500
    in Eastern Europe, 176
    in Finland, 426
    in France, 180, 181, 204, 416,
        417, 423, 424, 477–78, 481
    in Great Britain, 36, 180, 181,
        415–16, 417, 424, 425, 466,
        468, 469, 470
    in Italy, 180, 210, 254–55, 416,
        417, 425, 426, 490
    migrant workers and, 444–45
    in Netherlands, 461, 462
    in Norway, 501
    oil shocks and, 451
    in Poland, 553
    in Soviet Union, 174, 431, 517,
        522
    in Spain, 180, 415–16, 427, 496,
        497
    in Sweden, 418, 503
    in West Germany, 82, 85, 180,
        181, 205, 207, 254–55, 416,
        417, 423, 451, 454
    in Yugoslavia, 547
UNESCO, 393

Unified Socialist Party (PSU) (France), 140
United Croatian Opposition, 564
United Nations, 53, 94, 101, 146, 216, 306, 307, 313, 361, 366, 387, 393
  Security Council of, 97
United Nations Relief and Rehabilitation Administration (UNRRA), 8, 69–70
United Socialist Party (Italy), 383
United States:
  adventurism of, xii
  de Gaulle and, 323, 324, 326, 327, 331
  economy of, see gross national product; trade
  European scientists' migration to, 10–11, 257, 267
  France's relations with, 43, 486
  German reunification and, 298, 322, 451
  Great Britain's aid from, 33, 86, 212, 471
  Great Britain's relations with, 367–368
  occupied Germany and, 13, 16, 23, 81–83, 98–100, 110
  postwar relations of Great Britain and Soviet Union with, 88–104
  postwar rise of, 9, 21
  research and development in, 419
  tourism and, 251–52
  UNRRA funded by, 8
  Western European financial aid from, 8, 21
  see also anti-Americanism; Cold War; trade
Unternehmer, 261
Urban, Jerzy, 552
Uri, Pierre, 121
uskorenie, 515
Ustinov, Dimitri F., 515
U-2 affair, 312–13
Uzbekistan, 524

Valéry, Paul, 10
Valmy, battle of, vi
Vanoni Plan, 128
Varga, Evgeni, 66

vegetarians, 435
Venezia Giulia, 383
Venstre (Denmark), 391–92
vento del nord, 30
Versailles Peace Treaty (1919), 17
Vienna summit (1961), 313–14
Vietnam War, 274, 328, 334, 337, 345–46, 350
Vistula River, 436
Vogel, Hans Jochen, 455
Volga-Don Canal, 57
Volga Germans, 443, 523–24
Volga River, 436
Volkswagen, 207
Voroshilov, K. E., 62–63, 150, 398, 399, 401, 509
Voznesensky, N., 64
Vyshinsky, Andrei, 74

wages:
  in Denmark, 500
  in Eastern Europe, 228
  in France, 424, 481
  in Great Britain, 214, 256, 263, 467
  in Italy, 210, 256, 418
  in Soviet Union, 221
  in Spain, 385
  in Sweden, 503
  in West Germany, 423, 452, 456
Wales, 369, 468
Wałesa, Lech, 533–36, 552–53
Walloons, 51–52, 389, 461, 463
Wandel durch Annäherung, 319
war crimes:
  first reference to, 22
  trials for, 24–25, 26
Warsaw, 5
Warsaw Pact, 162, 305, 306, 307, 336, 355, 404, 531
Waugh, Evelyn, 282
Wazyk, Adam, 302
Wehner, Herbert, 376, 378
Wehrmacht, 376
Weimar Republic, 78, 79, 83, 133, 273, 375
welfare state legislation, 35–36, 137, 231–39, 263–64, 362, 390, 391, 392
Western Europe:

Rosamunde Pilcher has had a long and distinguished career as a novelist and short story writer, but it was her phenomenally successful novel, *The Shell Seekers*, that captured the hearts of all who read it, and won her international recognition as one of the best-loved storytellers of our time. Her bestselling novels, *September* and *Coming Home*, were made into television films. *Winter Solstice*, her most recent bestseller, was also made into a television film. She was awarded an O.B.E. for services to literature in 2002 and an honorary Doctor of Laws degree from Dundee University in 2010.

Praise for *Winter Solstice*

'Rosamunde Pilcher's warm spell is charming and utterly convincing'   *Daily Mail*

'An entrancing tale of middle-aged love, broken hearts and teenage angst'   *Daily Express*

'Britain's most under-rated novelist'   *Sunday Times*

'Pilcher's strength is knowing what she can do well and writing about what she knows. She has a way of tapping into the emotional life of her readers and making them care about characters not unlike themselves.'

Daily Telegraph

Also by Rosamunde Pilcher

Sleeping Tiger

Another View

The End of Summer

The Empty House

The Day of the Storm

Wild Mountain Thyme

The Shell Seekers

September

Coming Home

SHORT STORY COLLECTIONS

The Blue Bedroom

Flowers in the Rain

ROSAMUNDE PILCHER

Winter Solstice

HODDER

First published in Great Britain in 2000 by Hodder & Stoughton
An Hachette UK company

This edition 2011

20

Copyright © Rosamunde Pilcher 2000

The right of Rosamunde Pilcher to be identified as the Author
of the Work has been asserted by her in accordance with the
Copyright, Designs and Patents Act 1988.

Part title line drawings by Bill Gregory

All characters in this publication are fictitious and any resemblance to
real persons, living or dead, is purely coincidental.

A CIP catalogue record for this title is
available from the British Library.

ISBN 978 0 340 75248 7

Printed and bound by
CPI Group (UK) Ltd, Croydon, CR0 4YY

Hodder Headline's policy is to use papers that are natural,
renewable and recyclable products and made from wood grown
in sustainable forests. The logging and manufacturing processes are
expected to conform to the environmental regulations
of the country of origin.

Hodder and Stoughton Ltd
A division of Hodder Headline
338 Euston Road
London NW1 3BH

www.hodder.co.uk

ACKNOWLEDGEMENTS

There were times during the writing of this book, when my lack of knowledge on certain aspects precipitated a bad case of writer's block. Therefore, I must thank those who gave liberally of their time and expertise, and helped me get going again.

Willie Thomson, who put me in touch with James Sugden of Johnston's of Elgin, and so got the whole show on the road.

James Sugden, for sharing with me his vast knowledge and experience of the woollen trade.

My neighbour, David Tweedie, for his legal advice.

David Anstice, the clock man of Perthshire.

The Rev Dr James Simpson, for his constant interest and wise guidance.

And finally, Robin, who paid back a debt by digging his mother out of a literary hole.

Elfrida

Elfrida

Before Elfrida Phipps left London for good, and moved to the country, she made a trip to Battersea Dogs Home, and returned with a canine companion. It took a good – and heart-rending – half-hour to find him, but as soon as she saw him, sitting very close to the bars of his kennel and gazing up at her with dark, melting eyes, she knew that he was the one. She did not want a large animal, nor did she relish the idea of a yapping lap-dog. This one was exactly the right size. Dog size.

He had a lot of soft hair, some of which fell over his eyes, ears that could prick or droop, and a triumphant plume of a tail.

His colouring was irregularly patched brown and white. The brown bits were the exact shade of milky cocoa. When asked his ancestry, the kennelmaid said she thought there was border collie there and a bit of bearded collie, as well as a few other unidentified breeds. Elfrida didn't care. She liked the expression on his gentle face.

She left a donation for the Battersea Dogs Home, and

her new companion travelled away with her, sitting in the passenger seat of her old car and gazing from the window in a satisfied fashion, as though this were the life to which he was happy to become accustomed.

The next day, she took him to the local poodle parlour for a cut, shampoo and blow dry. He returned to her fluffy and fresh and smelling sweetly of lemonade. His response to all this sybaritic attention was a show of faithful, grateful and loving devotion. He was a shy, even timid, dog, but brave as well. If the doorbell rang, or he thought he spied an intruder, he barked his head off for a moment, then retreated to his basket or to Elfrida's lap.

It took some time to decide on a name for him, but in the end she christened him Horace.

Elfrida, with a basket in her hand and Horace firmly clipped to the end of his lead, closed the front door of her cottage behind her, walked down the narrow path, through the gate, and set off down the pavement towards the Post Office and General Store.

It was a dull grey afternoon in the middle of October with nothing much to commend about it. The last of autumn's leaves were drifting from trees, an unseasonable wind was too chill for even the most ardent of gardeners to be out and about, the street was deserted and the children not yet out of school. Overhead the sky was low with cloud that shifted steadily yet never seemed to clear. She walked briskly, Horace trotting reluctantly at her heels, knowing that this was his exercise for the day and he had no alternative but to make the best of it.

The village was Dibton in Hampshire, and here

Elfrida had come to live eighteen months ago, leaving London for ever and making for herself a new life. At first she had felt a bit solitary, but now she couldn't imagine living anywhere else. From time to time old acquaintances from her theatre days made the intrepid journey from the city and came to stay with her, sleeping on the lumpy divan in the tiny back bedroom that she called her workroom, which was where she kept her sewing-machine and earned a bit of pin money making elaborate and beautiful cushions for an interior-decorating firm in Sloane Street.

When these friends departed, needing reassurance – 'You're all right, aren't you, Elfrida?' they asked. 'No regrets? You don't want to come back to London? You're happy?' – she had been able to set their minds at rest: 'Of course I am. This is my geriatric bolt-hole. This is where I shall spend the twilight of my years.'

So by now there was a comfortable familiarity about it all. She knew who lived in this house, in that cottage. People called her by her name. 'Morning, Elfrida,' or 'Lovely day, Mrs Phipps.' Some of the inhabitants were commuting families, the man of the house setting out early each morning to catch the fast train to London and returning late in the evening to pick up his car from the station and drive the short distance home. Others had lived here all their lives in small stone houses that had belonged to their fathers and their grandfathers before that. Others were new altogether, inhabiting the council estates that ringed the village and employed by the electronics factory in the neighbouring town. It was all very ordinary, and so undemanding. Just, in fact, what Elfrida needed.

Walking, she passed the pub, newly furbished and now

called the Dibton Coach-house. There were wrought-iron signs and a spacious car park. Further on, she passed the church with its yew trees, lych-gate and a noticeboard fluttering with parish news: a guitar concert, an outing for the mothers'-and-toddlers' group. In the churchyard, a man lit a bonfire and the air was sweet with the scent of toasting leaves. Overhead, rooks cawed. A cat sat on one of the churchyard gateposts, but luckily Horace did not notice him.

The street curved and at the end of it, by the dull bungalow which was the new vicarage, she saw the village shop, flying banners advertising ice-cream, and with newspaper placards propped against the wall. Two or three youths with bicycles hung about its door, and the postman, with his red van, was emptying the post-box.

There were bars over the shop window to stop vandals breaking the glass and stealing the tins of biscuits and arrangements of baked beans that were Mrs Jennings's idea of tasteful decoration. Elfrida put down her basket and tied Horace's lead to one of the bars, and he sat looking resigned. He hated being left on the pavement, at the mercy of the jeering youths, but Mrs Jennings didn't like dogs in her establishment. She said they lifted their legs and were dirty brutes.

Inside, the shop was bright with electricity, low-ceilinged and very warm. Refrigerators and freezers hummed and there was strip-lighting and an up-to-date arrangement of display shelving, which had been installed some months ago, a huge improvement, Mrs Jennings insisted, more like a mini-market. Because of all these barriers, it was difficult to know at first glance who was in the shop and who wasn't, and it was not until Elfrida rounded a corner (Instant Coffee and Teas) that she saw the familiar back view standing by the till and paying his due.

Oscar Blundell. Elfrida was past the age when her heart leaped for joy, but she was always pleased to see Oscar. He had been almost the first person she met when she came to live in Dibton, because she had gone to church one Sunday morning, and after the service the Vicar had stopped her outside the door, his hair on end in the fresh spring breeze and his white cassock blowing like clean washing on a line. He had spoken welcoming words, made a few noises about doing flowers and the Women's Institute, and then, mercifully, was diverted. 'And here's our organist. Oscar Blundell. Not our regular organist, you understand, but a splendid spare wheel in times of trouble.'

And Elfrida turned, and saw the man emerging from the darkness of the interior of the church, walking out into the sunshine to join them. She saw the gentle, amused face, the hooded eyes, the hair that had probably once been fair but was now thickly white. He was as tall as Elfrida, which was unusual. She towered over most men, being five foot eleven and thin as a lath, but Oscar she met eye to eye and liked what she saw there. Because it was Sunday he wore a tweed suit and a pleasing tie, and when they shook hands, his grip had a good feel to it.

She said, 'How clever. To play the organ, I mean. Is it your hobby?'

And he replied, quite seriously, 'No, my job. My life.' And then smiled, which took all pomposity from his words. 'My profession,' he amended.

A day or two later, and Elfrida received a telephone call.

'Hello, Gloria Blundell here. You met my husband

7

last Sunday after church. The organist. Come and have dinner on Thursday. You know where we live. The Grange. Turreted red brick at the end of the village.'

'How very kind. I'd love to.'

'How are you settling in?'

'Slowly.'

'Splendid. See you Thursday, then. About seven thirty.'

'Thank you so much.' But the receiver at the other end of the line had already been replaced. Mrs Blundell, it seemed, was not a lady with time to waste.

The Grange was the largest house in Dibton, approached through hugely pretentious gates up a drive. Somehow none of this fitted in exactly with Oscar Blundell, but it would be interesting to go, to meet his wife and see his background. You never really got to know people properly until you had seen them within the ambience of their own home. Seen their furniture and their books and the manner of their lifestyle.

On Thursday morning she had her hair washed, and the colour given its monthly tweak. The shade was officially called strawberry blonde but sometimes it came out more orange than strawberry. This was one of the times, but Elfrida had more important things to worry about. Clothes were a bit of a problem. In the end she put on a flowered skirt, which reached her ankles, and a long cardigan-type garment in lime green knit. The effect of hair, flowers and cardigan was fairly dazzling, but looking bizarre was one of Elfrida's best ways of boosting her confidence.

She set out on foot, a ten-minute walk, down the village, through the pretentious gates and up the drive. For once, she was dead on time. Never having been to the house before, she did not open the front door and walk in, calling, 'Yoo-hoo,' which was her normal procedure, but found a bell and pressed it. She heard it ring at the back of the house. She waited, gazing about her at well-tended lawns, which looked as though they had just had their first cut of the year. There was the smell of new-cut grass, too, and the damp scent of the cool spring evening.

Footsteps. The door opened. A local lady in a blue dress and a flowered apron, clearly not the mistress of the house. 'Good evening. Mrs Phipps, is it? Come along in, Mrs Blundell won't be a moment, just went upstairs to fix her hair.'

'Am I the first?'

'Yes, but not early. Others'll be here soon. Want me to take your coat?'

'No, I'll keep it on, thank you.' No need to enlarge on this, to explain that the little silk blouse beneath the cardigan had a hole under the sleeve.

'The drawing room—'

But they were interrupted. 'You're Elfrida Phipps . . . I am sorry I wasn't here to greet you . . .' Looking up, Elfrida saw her hostess descending the wide staircase from a balustraded landing. She was a large lady, tall and well-built, dressed in black silk trousers and a loose, embroidered Chinese jacket. She carried a tumbler half full of what looked like whisky and soda.

'. . . I got a bit delayed, and then there was a telephone call. Hello,' she held out her hand, 'Gloria Blundell. Good of you to come.'

She had an open, ruddy face with very blue eyes, and hair that, like Elfrida's, had probably been twinked, but to a more discreet shade of soft blonde.

9

'Good of you to invite me.'

'Come along in by the fire. Thank you, Mrs Muswell, I expect the others will just let themselves in. This way . . .'

Elfrida followed her through into a large room, much panelled in the style of the thirties and with a vast red-brick fireplace where burned a log fire. In front of the hearth was a leather-padded club fender, and the room was furnished with hugely padded and patterned sofas and chairs. The curtains were plum velvet, braided in gold, and the floor was closely carpeted and scattered with thick, richly coloured Persian rugs. Nothing looked old or shabby or faded, and all exuded an air of warmth and a cheerful masculine comfort.

'Have you lived here long?' Elfrida asked, trying not to appear too inquisitive.

'Five years. The place was left to me by an old uncle. Always adored it, used to come here as a child.' She dumped her glass on a handy table and went to hurl another enormous log on to the fire. 'I can't tell you the state it was in, everything threadbare and moth-eaten, so I had to have a really good refurbish. Made a new kitchen as well, and a couple of extra bathrooms.'

'Where did you live before?'

'Oh, London. I had a house in Elm Park Gardens.' She picked up her glass, had a restoring swallow, then set it down again. She smiled. 'My dressing drink. I have to have a little boost before parties. What would you like? Sherry? Gin and tonic? Yes, it was a good place to be and marvellously spacious. And Oscar's church, St Biddulph's where he was organist, was only ten minutes or so away. I suppose we'd have stayed there for ever, but my old bachelor uncle was gathered, as they say, and the

Grange came to me. And we have this child, Francesca. She's eleven now. I've always thought it better to bring a child up in the country. I don't know what Oscar's doing. He's meant to pour drinks. Probably forgotten about everything and reading a book. And we have other guests to meet you. The McGeareys. He works in the City. And Joan and Tommy Mills. Tommy's a consultant in our hospital at Pedbury. Sorry, did you say sherry or gin and tonic?'

Elfrida said gin and tonic, and watched while Gloria Blundell went to pour her one from the well-provided table at the far end of the room. She also replenished her own glass, with a generous hand for the Scotch.

Returning, 'There. Hope it's strong enough. You like ice? Now, sit down, be comfortable, tell me about your little cottage.'

'Well . . . it's little.'

Gloria laughed. 'Poulton's Row, isn't it? They were built as railway cottages. Are you frightfully cramped?'

'Not really. I haven't got much furniture and Horace and I don't take up much room. Horace is my dog. A mongrel. Not beautiful.'

'I have two pekes, which are, but they bite guests so they're shut in the kitchen with Mrs Muswell. And what made you come to Dibton?'

'I saw the cottage advertised in *The Sunday Times*. There was a photo. It looked rather dear. And not too expensive.'

'I shall have to come and see it. Haven't been inside one of those little houses since I was a child and used to visit the widow of some old station porter. And what do you do?'

'Sorry?'

11

'Garden? Play golf? Good works?'

Elfrida hedged slightly. She knew a forceful woman when she met one. 'I'm trying to get the garden straight, but it's mostly shifting rubbish so far.'

'Do you ride?'

'I've never ridden a horse in my life.'

'Well, that's straightforward anyway. I used to ride when my sons were boys, but that's a long time ago. Francesca's got a little pony, but I'm afraid she's not all that keen.'

'You have sons as well?'

'Oh, yes. Grown-up now and both married.'

'But . . . ?'

'I was married before, you see. Oscar's my second husband.'

'I'm sorry. I didn't realise.'

'Nothing to be sorry about. My son Giles works in Bristol and Crawford has a job in the City. Computers or something, totally beyond me. Of course, we had known Oscar for years. St Biddulph's, Raleigh Square, was our church. He played divinely at my husband's funeral. When we married, everybody was astonished. "That old bachelor," they said. "Do you have any idea what you're taking on?" '

It was all marvellously intriguing. 'Has Oscar always been a musician?' Elfrida asked.

'Always. He was educated at Westminster Abbey choir school, then went on to teach music at Glastonbury College. He was choir-master and organist there for a number of years. And then he retired from teaching, moved to London, got the post at St Biddulph's. I think he'd have continued there until they carried him out feet first, but then my uncle died and fate decreed otherwise.'

Elfrida felt a little sorry for Oscar. 'Did he mind saying goodbye to London?'

'It was a bit like pulling an old tree up by the roots. But, for Francesca's sake, he put a brave face on it. And here he has his music room, and his books and scores, and he does a little private coaching, just to keep his hand in. Music is his life. He loves it when there's an emergency and he can play for morning service in the Dibton church. And, of course, he's always sneaking over to have a little quiet practice all on his own.' Behind Gloria, quietly, the door from the hall had opened. Talking away, she was unaware of this but, realising that Elfrida's attention had strayed, turned now in her chair to peer over her shoulder.

'Oh, there you are, old boy. We were just talking about you.'

All at once, and all together, the other guests arrived, letting themselves in, and filling the house with the sound of their voices. The Blundells went out to welcome them, and for a moment Elfrida was alone. She thought it would be rather nice to go home now, and have a solitary evening mulling over all she had learned, but of course this was not to be. Almost before she could put the shameful thought out of her mind, her hosts were back, their guests surged into the room and the dinner party was on its way.

It was a formal evening, lavish and traditional, with excellent food and a great deal of splendid wine. They ate smoked salmon and a beautifully presented crown of lamb, and there were three puddings, with bowls of thick cream, and then a creamy, blue-veined Stilton. When the port was handed round, Elfrida noticed, with some

13

amusement, that the ladies did not leave the room but stayed with the men, and although she was now on to copious glasses of water, which she poured for herself from a cut-glass jug, she saw that the other women enjoyed their port, and Gloria, perhaps, most of all.

She wondered if Gloria, sitting in state at the head of the table, had slightly overdone her alcoholic intake and if, when the time came for them to get up, she would heave herself to her feet and fall flat on her face. But Gloria was made of tougher stuff, and when Mrs Muswell put her head round the door to say that coffee was ready in the drawing room, she led the way with a steady step out of the dining room and across the hall.

They gathered around the fire but Elfrida, lifting her cup of coffee from the tray, saw through the uncurtained window a sky of deep sapphire blue. Although the spring day had been fitful, with showers and glimpses of sunshine, while they sat over dinner the clouds had dispersed, and a first star hung in the heavens over the top of a distant, budding beech. There was a window-seat and she went to sit on it, cradling the cup and saucer in her hands and watching the stars.

Presently she was joined by Oscar. 'Are you all right?' he asked her.

She turned to look up at him. So busy had he been through dinner, pouring wine, clearing plates, handing round the delectable puddings, that she had scarcely addressed him.

'Of course. Such a lovely evening. And your daffodils will very soon be out.'

'You like gardens?'

'I've not had much experience. But this one looks particularly inviting.'

'Would you like to take a little stroll and be shown around? It's still not quite dark.'

She glanced at the others, settled in the deep chairs around the fire and in full flood of conversation.

'Yes, I would like that, but wouldn't it be rude?'

'Not at all.' He took the cup from her hand and carried it back to the tray. He set it down. 'Elfrida and I are going to have a stroll around the garden.'

'At this hour?' Gloria was astounded. 'It's dark and it's cold.'

'Not so dark. We'll be ten minutes.'

'Right, but make sure the poor girl's got a coat – it's chilly and damp. Don't let him keep you too long, my dear . . .'

'I won't.'

The others went back to their discussion, which was about the iniquitous price of private education. Elfrida and Oscar went out through the door. He closed it quietly behind him, then lifted from a chair a thick leather coat lined with sheepskin. 'It's Gloria's – you can borrow it,' and he draped it gently over Elfrida's shoulders. Then he opened the half-glassed front door and they stepped outside into the chill and purity of the spring evening. Shrubs and borders loomed in the dusk and underfoot the grass was wet with dew.

They walked. At the far end of the lawn was a brick wall, fronted by borders and broken by an archway with an imposing wrought-iron gate. He opened this and they were in a spacious walled garden, neatly divided into geometrical shapes by hedges of box. One quarter was a rose garden, the bushes pruned and richly composted. Clearly, when summer came, there would be something of a display.

15

Faced with professionalism, she felt inadequate. 'Is this all your work?'

'No. I plan but I employ a labourer.'

'I'm not much good at flower names. I've never had a proper garden.'

'My mother was never lost for names. If someone asked her the name of a flower, and she had no idea what it was, she simply said, with much authority, *Inapoticum Forgetanamia*. It nearly always worked.'

'I must remember that.'

Side by side they strolled down the wide, gravelled pathway. He said, 'I hope you didn't feel too distanced at dinner. I'm afraid we're something of a parochial lot.'

'Not at all. I enjoyed every moment. I like to listen.'

'Country life. It teems with intrigue.'

'Do you miss London?'

'From time to time, enormously. Concerts and the opera. My church, St Biddulph's.'

'Are you a religious person?' Elfrida asked, impulsively, then wished that she hadn't. Too soon for such a personal question.

But he remained unfazed. 'I don't know, but I have spent the whole of my life steeped in the sacred music, the liturgies and magnificats of the Anglican Church. And I would find it uncomfortable to live in a world where I had no one to thank.'

'For blessings, you mean?'

'Just so.'

'I understand, but even so I'm not a bit religious. I only went to church that Sunday because I was feeling a bit isolated and I needed the company of other people. I didn't expect the lovely music. And I'd never heard that setting of the *Te Deum* before.'

16

'The organ is a new one, paid for by countless bring-and-buy sales.'

They trod in silence for a moment. Then Elfrida said, 'Do you count that as a blessing? The new organ, I mean.'

He laughed. 'You're like a little dog, worrying a bone. Yes, of course I do.'

'What else?'

He did not immediately reply. She thought of his wife, his enormously comfortable and lavish house; his music room, his friends, his obvious financial security. She thought it would be interesting to know how Oscar had come to marry Gloria. Had he, after years of bachelordom, small boys, meagre salaries and dusty academic rooms, seen, looming in the future, the emptiness of an elderly bachelor's old age and taken the easy way out? The wealthy, forceful widow, the capable hostess, good friend, competent mother. Or perhaps it was she who had done the stalking, and she who had made the decision. Perhaps they had simply fallen madly in love. Whatever, it seemed to work.

The silence lay between them. She said, 'Don't tell me if you'd rather not.'

'I was simply trying to decide how to explain. I married late in life and Gloria already had boys by her previous marriage. For some reason it never occurred to me that I should have a child of my own. When Francesca was born, I was amazed, not simply that she was *there*, a tiny human being, but so beautiful. And familiar. As though I had known her always. A miracle. Now she is eleven and I am still astounded by my good fortune.'

'Is she here, at home?'

17

'No, at a weekly boarding-school. Tomorrow evening I fetch her for the weekend.'

'I would like to meet her.'

'You shall. I like to think that you will be charmed by her. When Gloria inherited this pile of a house, I kicked against leaving London. But for Francesca I went with the tide and complied. Here, she has space and freedom. Trees, the smell of grass. Room to grow. Room for the rabbits and the guinea-pigs and the pony.'

'For me,' said Elfrida, 'the best is birdsong in the morning and big skies.'

'You too, I believe, have also fled from London?'

'Yes. It was time.'

'A wrench?'

'In a way. I'd lived there all my life. From the moment I left school and left home. I was at RADA. I was on the stage, you see. Much to my parents' disapproval. But I didn't mind about disapproval. I never have, really.'

'An actress. I should have known.'

'And a singer too. And a dancer. Revues and big American musicals. I was the one at the back of the chorus line because I was so dreadfully tall. And then years of fortnightly rep, and bit parts on television. Nothing very illustrious.'

'Do you still work?'

'Heavens, no, I gave it up years ago. I married an actor, which was the most dreadful mistake for every sort of reason. And then he went off to America and was never seen again, so I kept myself by doing any sort of job that came my way, and then I got married again. But that wasn't much use either. I don't think I was ever a very good picker.'

'Was number-two husband an actor as well?' His

voice was amused, which was exactly the way Elfrida wanted it to be. She seldom talked about her husbands, and the only way to make disasters bearable was to laugh about them.

'Oh, no, he was in business. Terribly expensive vinyl flooring. One would have thought I would have been marvellously secure and safe, but he had that disagreeable Victorian conviction that if a man feeds and houses his wife, and doles out some sort of a housekeeping allowance, then he has kept his share of the marital bargain.'

'Well,' said Oscar, 'and why not? An old-established tradition, going back for centuries. Only then it was called slavery.'

'How nice that you understand. Turning sixty was one of the best days of my life, because I got my pension book, and knew that I could walk down to the nearest post office and be given money, cash in hand, for doing nothing. I'd never in my life been given something for nothing. It was like a whole new world.'

'Did you have children?'

'No. Never children.'

'You still haven't explained why you moved to this particular village.'

'A need to move on.'

'A big step.'

It was quite dark now. Turning, Elfrida looked back towards the house and saw, through the lacework of the wrought-iron gate, the glow of the drawing-room windows. Somebody had drawn the curtains. She said, 'I haven't talked about it. I haven't told anybody.'

'You don't need to tell me.'

'Perhaps I've talked too much already. Perhaps I drank too much wine at dinner.'

'I don't think so.'

'There was this man. So special, so lovely, so loving, funny and perfect. Another actor, but successful and famous this time and I won't say his name. Brilliant. We lived together for three years in his little house in Barnes, and then he got Parkinson's disease and it took him another two years to die. It was his house. I had to leave. A week after his funeral I saw an advertisement for the cottage in Poulton's Row. In *The Sunday Times*. And the next week I bought it. I have very little money but it wasn't too expensive. I brought my dear dog Horace with me for company, and I have my pension, and I have a little job making cushions for a rather snob interior designer in London. It's not very arduous and it keeps me busy and my head above water. I always liked to sew, and it's good to work with lovely, expensive materials, and each project is different.' It all sounded very trivial. 'I don't know why I'm telling you all this. It's not very interesting.'

'I find it fascinating.'

'I don't see why you should. But you're very kind.' It was too dark now to see into his face, or read the expression in his hooded eyes. 'I think perhaps it's time we went back to the others.'

'Of course.'

'I love your garden. Thank you. Some time I must see it in daylight.'

That was Thursday. The following Sunday morning it rained, not a spring shower but regular rain drumming against the windows of Elfrida's cottage and darkening the tiny rooms so that she was forced to switch on all the lights. After she had put Horace out into the garden for his morning wee, she made a cup of tea and took it back to bed with her, intending to spend the morning warm, comfortable and idle, reading yesterday's newspapers and struggling to finish the crossword.

But just after eleven she was interrupted by the ringing of the front-door bell, a jangling device operated by a hanging chain. The noise it made was like nothing so much as an emergency fire alarm and Elfrida nearly jumped out of her skin. Horace, lying across the foot of the bed, raised himself into a sitting position and let out a couple of barks. This was as much as he was prepared to do in the cause of protecting his mistress: he was of a cowardly nature and not in the habit of snarling or biting intruders.

Astonished, but not alarmed, Elfrida climbed out of bed, pulled on her dressing-gown, tied the sash and made her way down the steep, narrow staircase. The stairs descended into her living room, and the front door opened straight on to the miniature front garden. There she found a small girl, in jeans and sneakers and a dripping anorak. The anorak had no hood, so the child's head was as wet as the coat of a dog that had just enjoyed a good swim. It was auburn hair, braided into plaits, and her face was freckled and rosy from the chill, damp outdoors.

'Mrs Phipps?'

There were bands on her teeth, a mouthful of iron-mongery.

'Yes.'

'I'm Francesca Blundell. My mother said it's such an awful day, would you like to come for lunch? We've got an enormous bit of beef and there's heaps . . .'

21

'But I've only just been to dinner.'

'She said you'd say that.'

'It's terribly kind. As you can see, I'm not dressed yet. I hadn't even thought about lunch.'

'She was going to phone but I said I'd bicycle.'

'You biked?'

'I left it on the pavement. It's all right.' A douche of water from an overflowing gutter missed her by inches.

'I think,' said Elfrida, 'you'd better come in before you drown.'

'Oh, thank you.' Briskly, Francesca accepted the invitation and stepped indoors. Hearing voices, and deciding that it was safe to appear, Horace, with dignity, descended the stairs. Elfrida closed the door. 'This is Horace, my dog.'

'He's sweet. Hello. Mummy's pekes always yap for hours when there's a visitor. Do you mind if I take off my anorak?'

'No, I think it would be a very good idea.'

This Francesca proceeded to do, unzipping it and draping it over the newel post at the bottom of the banister where it dripped on to the floor.

Francesca looked about her. She said, 'I always thought these were the dearest little houses but I've never been inside one of them.' Her eyes were very large and grey, fringed with thick, fair lashes. 'When Mummy said you were living here, I couldn't wait to come and look. That's why I biked. Do you mind?'

'Not a bit. It's all rather cluttered, I'm afraid.'

'I think it's perfect.'

It wasn't, of course. It was cramped and shabby, filled with the few personal bits and pieces Elfrida had brought with her from London: the sagging sofa, the little

Victorian armchair, the brass fender, the battered desk, lamps, worthless pictures and too many books.

'I was going to lay and light a fire as it's such a grey day, but I haven't got round to it yet. Would you like a cup of tea or coffee or something?'

'No, thank you, I've just had a Coke. Where does that door go?'

'Into the kitchen. I'll show you.'

She led the way, opened the wooden door with the latch and pushed it ajar. Her kitchen was no larger than a ship's galley. Here a small Rayburn simmered away, keeping the whole house warm; a wooden dresser was piled with china, a clay sink stood beneath the window, and a wooden table and two chairs filled the remainder of the space. Alongside the window, a stable door led out into the back garden. The top half of the door was glazed in small panes and through it could be seen the flagged yard and the narrow border, which was as far as Elfrida had got in the way of making a flower-bed. Ferns thrust their way between the flags, and a honeysuckle scrambled over the neighbour's wall.

'It's not very inviting on a day like this, but there's just room to sit out in a deck-chair on a summer evening.'

'Oh, but I love it.' Francesca looked about her with a housewifely eye. 'You haven't got a fridge. And you haven't got a washing-machine. And you haven't got a freezer.'

'No, I haven't got a freezer. But I have got a fridge and a washing-machine, I keep them in the shed at the bottom of the yard. And I do all my dishes in the sink because there's no space for a dishwasher.'

'I think Mummy would die if she had to wash dishes.'

'It's not very arduous when you live on your own.'

'I love all your china. Blue and white. It's my favourite.'

'I love it too. None of it matches, but I buy a bit whenever I find something in a junk shop. There's so much now there's scarcely space for it.'

'What's upstairs?'

'The same. Two rooms and a tiny bathroom. The bath is so small I have to hang my legs over the side. There's a bedroom for me and a workroom where I do my sewing. If I have a guest, they have to sleep there, along with the sewing-machine and scraps of material and order books.'

'Daddy told me you made cushions. I think it's all exactly right for one person. And a dog, of course. Like a dolls' house.'

'Have you got a dolls' house?'

'Yes, but I don't play with it any more. I've got animals. A guinea-pig called Happy but he's not very well. I think he'll have to go to the vet. He's got horrible bare patches all over his fur. And I've got rabbits. And a pony.' She wrinkled her nose. 'He's called Prince but he's a bit nappy sometimes. I think I'd better go now. Mummy said I had to muck him out before lunch and it takes ages, specially in the rain. Thank you for letting me see your house.'

'A pleasure. Thank you for bringing that kind invitation.'

'You'll come, won't you?'

'Of course.'

'Will you walk?'

'No, I'll bring my car because of the rain. And if you ask me where I keep my car, I'll tell you. On the road.'

'Is it that old blue Ford Fiesta?'

'It is. And old is the operative word. But I don't mind provided the wheels go round and the engine starts.'

Francesca smiled at this, revealing, unembarrassed, her wired-up teeth. She said, 'I'll see you later, then.' She reached for her anorak, still dripping, pulled on the sodden garment and tossed free her plaits. Elfrida opened the door for her.

'Mummy said a quarter to one.'

'I'll be there, and thank you for coming.'

'I'll come again,' Francesca promised, and Elfrida watched her go splashing down the path and through the gate. A moment later, she was off on her bike with a wave of her hand, pedalling furiously down through the puddles and along the road, out of sight.

Oscar, Gloria and Francesca were Elfrida's first friends. Through them, she met others. Not just the McGeareys and the Millses, but the Foubisters, who were old-established and held the annual church summer fête in the park of their rambling Georgian house. And there was Commander Burton-Jones, RN (Retired), a widower and immensely industrious, labouring in his immaculate garden, chairman of the Public Footpath Association, and principal chorister in the church choir. Commander Burton-Jones ('Bobby's the name') threw racy little drinks parties, and called his bedroom his cabin. Then there were the Dunns, he an immensely wealthy man who had bought and converted the old rectory into a marvel of space and convenience, complete with games room and a covered, heated swimming-pool.

Others, humbler, came into her life one by one, as Elfrida went about her daily business: Mrs Jennings, who ran the village shop and the post office; Mr Hodgkins, who did the rounds once a week with his butcher's van, was a reliable source of news and gossip and held strong political views; Albert Meddows, who answered her advertisement (a postcard stuck up in Mrs Jennings's window) for garden help, and tackled, single-handed, the sad disarray and crooked paving of Elfrida's back garden. The Vicar and his wife invited her to a fork supper, in the course of which it was suggested once more that she join the Women's Institute. Politely declining – she did not enjoy bus trips and had never made a pot of jam in her life – she agreed to involvement with the primary school and ended up producing their annual pantomime at Christmas.

They were all amiable enough and welcoming, but Elfrida found none of them either as interesting or stimulating as the Blundells. Gloria's hospitality was without bounds, and scarcely a week went by when Elfrida was not invited to spend time at the Grange, for a lavish meal or some outdoor occasion like a tennis party (Elfrida did not play tennis but was happy to observe) or a picnic. There were other, more far-flung, occasions; the spring point-to-point at a nearby farm, a visit to a National Trust garden, an evening out at the theatre at Chichester. She had spent Christmas with them, and New Year's Eve, and when she threw her first little party for all her new friends (Albert Meddows having resuscitated her garden, levelled the flagstones, pruned the honeysuckle and painted the shed) it was Oscar who volunteered to be her barman and Gloria who produced copious eats from her own spacious kitchen.

However, there were limits and reservations. There

had to be if Elfrida was not to be absorbed by, and beholden to, the Blundells. From the very first she had recognised Gloria as a forceful woman – with, possibly, a ruthless streak, so determined was she always that things should go her way – and was more than aware of the dangers of such a situation. She had left London to make a life of her own, and knew that it would be only too easy for a single and fairly impoverished female to be swept along (and possibly drowned) in the churning wake of Gloria's social energy.

So, from time to time, Elfrida had learned to step back, to keep to herself, to make excuses. A work over-load, perhaps, or a prior engagement, which could not possibly be broken, with some imagined acquaintance whom Gloria did not know. Every now and then she escaped from the confines of Dibton, packing Horace into the passenger seat of her car and driving far out across country to some other county where she was not known, and where she and Horace could climb a sheep-grazed hill, or follow the path by some dark, flowing stream and find at the end of it a pub full of strangers where she could eat a sandwich and drink coffee and relish her precious solitude.

On such occasions, distanced from Dibton and with perceptions sharpened by a sense of perspective, it became possible to be analytical about her involve-ment with the Blundells and to catalogue her findings, impersonal and detached as a shopping list.

The first was that she liked Oscar immensely; perhaps too much. She was well past the age of romantic love, but companionship was another matter. From their first meeting outside Dibton church, when she had been instantly taken with him, she had come to enjoy his company more and more. Time had not proved that first impression wrong.

But the ice was thin. Elfrida was neither sanctimonious nor a lady with enormously high moral standards; indeed, all the time she lived with him, her dear dead lover had been the husband of another woman. But Elfrida had never met his wife, and the marriage was already on the rocks by the time he and Elfrida found each other, and for this reason she had never been consumed by guilt. On the other hand, there was another and not nearly so harmless scenario, and one that Elfrida had witnessed more than once: that of the single lady, widowed, divorced, or otherwise bereft, being taken under the wing of a loyal girlfriend, only to scarper with the loyal girlfriend's husband. A reprehensible situation and one of which she strongly disapproved.

But in Elfrida's case, it was not about to happen. And she knew that her awareness of danger and her own common sense were her greatest strengths.

Second was that Francesca, at eleven years old, was the daughter whom, if she had ever had a child, Elfrida would have liked to call her own: independent, open and totally straightforward, yet possessed of a sense of the ridiculous that could reduce Elfrida to helpless laughter, and an imagination that was fed by voracious reading of books. Francesca became so absorbed in them that one could go into a room, switch on the television, hold a loud discussion and Francesca would not even raise her head from the page. During the school holidays she frequently turned up at Poulton's Row, to play with Horace or watch Elfrida at her sewing-machine, at the same time asking endless questions about Elfrida's theatrical past, which she clearly found fascinating.

Her relationship with her father was unusually close and very sweet. He was old enough to be her grandfather, but their delight in each other's company went far beyond that of the normal parent and child. From behind his closed music-room door could be heard the two of them playing duets on his piano, and fumbling mistakes brought not recrimination but much laughter. On winter evenings he read aloud to her, the two of them curled up in his huge armchair, and her affection for him was manifested in frequent hugs, thin arms wound about his neck and kisses pressed on the top of his thick white hair.

As for Gloria, Gloria was a man's woman, so closer to her grown-up, married sons than to her lately conceived daughter. Elfrida had met these sons, Giles and Crawford Bellamy, and their pretty, well-dressed wives, when they turned up at the Grange for a weekend or drove down from London for Sunday lunch. Although not twins, they were strangely similar, conventional and opinionated. Elfrida got the impression that neither of the brothers approved of her, but as she didn't much like either of them it was not worth bothering about. Gloria doted on them, which was far more important, and when the time came for them to leave, the boots of their expensive cars loaded down with fresh vegetables and fruit from Gloria's kitchen garden, she would stand, waving them away, like any sentimental mother. It was patently clear that in her eyes neither son could do wrong, and Elfrida was pretty sure that if Gloria had not approved of their chosen brides, then both Daphne and Arabella would have got short shrift.

But Francesca was a different cup of tea. Deeply influenced by Oscar, she went her own way, followed her own interests, and found books and music a good deal more alluring than the local Pony Club gymkhana. Even so, she was never rebellious or sulky and cared for her bad-tempered little pony with good grace and exercised him regularly, riding around the paddock that Gloria had set aside for equestrian activities and taking him on long hacks down the quiet tracks by the little river. Often, on these occasions, Oscar accompanied her, mounted on an ancient sit-up-and-beg bicycle, relic of his schoolmaster days.

Gloria let them be, possibly, Elfrida decided, because Francesca was not that important to her; not as absorbing or fulfilling as her own hectic lifestyle, her parties, her circle of friends. Important, too, was her position as social mentor, and sometimes she reminded Elfrida of a huntsman, blowing his horn for attention and whipping in his hounds.

Only once had Elfrida fallen from grace. It was during a convivial evening at the Foubisters', a dinner party of great formality and style, with candles lit and silver gleaming and an aged butler waiting at table. After dinner, in the long drawing room (rather chilly, for the evening was cool), Oscar had moved to the grand piano to play for them, and after a Chopin etude, had suggested that Elfrida should sing.

She was much embarrassed and taken aback. She had not sung for years, she protested, her voice was hopeless . . .

But old Sir Edwin Foubister added his persuasions. 'Please,' he had said. 'I've always liked a pretty tune.'

So disarming was he that Elfrida found herself hesitating. After all, what did it matter if her voice had lost its youthful timbre, she wobbled on the high notes, and was about to make a fool of herself? At that moment, she caught sight of Gloria's face, florid and set like a bulldog's in an expression of disapproval and dismay. And she knew that Gloria did not want her to sing. Did not want her to stand up with Oscar and entertain the little group. She did not like others to shine, to steal attention, to deflect the conversation away from herself. It was a perception of total clarity and somewhat shocking, as though she had caught Gloria in a state of undress.

In different circumstances Elfrida might have played safe, gracefully declined, made excuses. But she had dined well and drunk delicious wine and, emboldened by this, a tiny flame of self-assertion flickered into life. She had never allowed herself to be bullied, and was not about to start. So she smiled into Gloria's threatening frowns, then turned her head and let the smile rest upon her host. She said, 'If you want, I should like to, very much . . .'

'Splendid.' Like a child, Sir Edwin clapped his hands. 'What a treat.'

And Elfrida stood, and crossed the floor to where Oscar waited for her.

'What will you sing?'

She told him. An old Rodgers and Hart number. 'Do you know it?'

'Of course.'

A chord or two for introduction. It had been a long time. She straightened her shoulders, filled her lungs . . .

I took one look at you,

Her voice had aged to thinness, but she could still hold, truly, the tune.

And then my heart stood still.

And she was all at once consumed by reasonless happiness and felt young again, standing by Oscar, and, with him, filling the room with the music of their youth.

Gloria scarcely spoke for the rest of the evening, but nobody endeavoured to coax her out of her black mood. While they marvelled and congratulated Elfrida on her performance, Gloria drank her brandy. When it was time to leave, Sir Edwin accompanied them out to where Gloria's powerful estate car was parked on the neatly raked gravel. Elfrida bade him goodnight and got into the back of the car but it was Oscar who slipped in behind the wheel, and Gloria was forced to take the passenger seat of her own vehicle.

Heading home, 'How did you enjoy the evening?' Oscar asked his wife.

Gloria replied shortly, 'I have a headache,' and fell silent once more.

Elfrida thought, No wonder, but prudently didn't say it. And that was perhaps the most concerning and sad truth of all. Gloria Blundell, hard-headed and with a stomach like a tin bucket, drank too much. She was never incapable, never hung over. But she drank too much. And Oscar knew it.

Oscar. And now, here he was, in Mrs Jennings's shop on a grey October afternoon, picking up his newspapers and paying for a bag of dog-meal. He wore corduroys, a thick, tweedy-looking sweater and sturdy boots, which seemed to indicate that he had been gardening, remembered these necessary errands, and come.

Mrs Jennings looked up. 'Afternoon, Mrs Phipps.'

With his hand full of change, Oscar turned and saw her. 'Elfrida. Good afternoon.'

She said, 'You must have walked. I didn't see your car.'

'Parked it round the corner. That's it, I think, Mrs Jennings.'

He moved aside to make space for Elfrida, and stood, apparently in no sort of hurry to go. 'We haven't seen you for days. How are you?'

'Oh, surviving. A bit fed up with this weather.'

'Dreadful, isn't it?' Mrs Jennings chipped in. 'Chilly and muggy all at once, doesn't make you feel like doing anything. What have you got there, Mrs Phipps?'

Elfrida unloaded the contents of her basket, so that Mrs Jennings could price them and put it all through her till. A loaf of bread, half a dozen eggs, some bacon and butter, two tins of dog-food and a magazine called *Beautiful Homes.* 'Want me to charge them?'

'If you would, I've left my purse at home.'

Oscar saw the magazine. He said, 'Are you going to go in for some domestic improvements?'

'Probably not, but I find reading about other people's therapeutic. I suppose because I know I haven't got to get my paint pot out. A bit like listening to somebody else cutting the grass.'

Mrs Jennings thought this was very funny. 'Jennings put his mower away back of September. Hates cutting the grass, he does.'

Oscar watched while Elfrida loaded her basket. He said, 'I'll give you a ride home, if you like.'

'I don't mind walking. I've got Horace with me.'

'He's welcome to join us. Thank you, Mrs Jennings, goodbye.'

'Cheerio, Mr Blundell. Regards to the wife.'

Together they emerged from the shop. Outside on the

pavement the youths still loitered. They had been joined by a dubious-looking girl with a cigarette, raven-black hair and a leather skirt that scarcely reached her crotch. Her presence seemed to have galvanised the young men into a pantomime of joshing, insults and meaningless guffaws. Horace, trapped in the middle of such unseemly behaviour, looked miserable. Elfrida untied his lead and he wagged his tail, much relieved. The three of them made their way around the corner and down the narrow lane where Oscar had left his car. She got into the passenger seat, and Horace jumped up and sat on the floor, between her knees, with his head pressed on to her lap. As Oscar joined them, slammed the door, then switched on the ignition, she said, 'I never expect to meet anyone in the shop in the afternoons. Mornings are the social time. That's when you get all the chat.'

'I know. But Gloria's in London and I forgot about the papers.' He turned the car and nosed out into the main street. School for the day was over, and the pavements were busy with a procession of tired, grubby children, trailing satchels and making their way home. The man in the churchyard had got his bonfire going, and grey smoke streamed up into the still, dank air.

'When did Gloria go to London?'

'Yesterday. For some meeting or other. Save the Children, I believe. She took the train. I've got to meet her off the six thirty.'

'Would you like to come back and have a cup of tea with me? Or would you prefer to return to your gardening?'

'How do you know I've been gardening?'

'Clues dropped. Woman's intuition. Mud on your boots.'

He laughed. 'Perfectly correct, Mr Holmes. But I wouldn't say no to a cup of tea. Gardener's perks.'

They passed the pub. Another moment or so and they had reached the lane that ran down the slope towards the railway line, and the terraced cottages that were Poulton's Row. At her gate he drew up and they decanted themselves, Horace, freed of his lead, bounding ahead up the path, and Elfrida, lugging her basket, followed him. She opened the door.

'Don't you ever lock it?' Oscar asked, from behind her.

'Not for a village shopping spree. Anyway, there's little to steal. Come along in, shut the door behind you.' She went through to the kitchen and dumped the basket on the table. 'If you felt very kind, you could put a match to the fire. A day like this needs a bit of cheer.' She filled the kettle at the tap and set it on the stove. Then she took off her jacket, draped it over the back of a chair, and began to assemble a few items of mismatched china.

'Mugs or teacups?'

'Mugs for gardeners.'

'Tea by the fire, or shall we sit in here?'

'I'm always happier with my knees under a table.'

Without much hope, Elfrida opened cake tins. Two were empty. The third contained the heel of a ginger-bread. She put this on the table with a knife. She found milk in the fridge and emptied the carton into a yellow pottery jug. She found the sugar bowl. From the other room could now be heard crackling sounds and the snap of hot twigs. She went to the doorway and stood, leaning against the lintel, observing Oscar. He was placing, with some care, a couple of lumps of coal on the top of his small pyre.

Aware of Elfrida's presence, he straightened, and turned his head to smile at her. 'Blazing nicely. Properly laid, with plenty of kindling. Do you need logs for the winter? I can let you have a load, if you'd like.'

'Where would I store them?'

'We could stack them in the front garden, against the wall.'

'That would be marvellous, if you could spare a few.'

'We've more than enough.' He dusted his hands on his trouser legs and looked about him. 'You know, you have made this little place very charming.'

'It's a muddle, I know. Not enough space. Possessions are a quandary, aren't they! They become part of you and I'm not very good at throwing things away. And there are one or two little bits and pieces I've been carrying about with me for years, dating back to the giddy days when I was on the stage. I was like a snail with its shell on its back. A silk shawl or the odd knick-knack rendered theatrical lodgings a little more bearable.'

'I particularly like your little Staffordshire dogs.'

'They were always part of my luggage, but they're not, actually, a pair.'

'And the little travelling clock.'

'That travelled, too.'

'It appears well-worn.'

'Battered would be nearer the truth. I've had it for years, it was left to me by an elderly godfather. I . . . I have one thing I think might be very valuable, and it's that little picture.'

It hung to one side of the fireplace, and Oscar found his spectacles and put them on, the better to inspect the painting.

'Where did you get this?'

'A present from an actor. We were both in a revival of *Hay Fever* at Chichester, and at the end of the run, he said that he wanted me to have it. A leaving present. He'd picked it up in a junk shop and I don't think paid all that much for it but he was excited because he was sure it was a David Wilkie.'

'Sir David Wilkie?' Oscar frowned. 'A valuable possession. So why did he give it to you?'

But Elfrida would not be drawn. 'To thank me for mending his socks?'

He returned his gaze to the painting. It took up little space, being only about eleven inches by eight, and depicted an elderly couple in eighteenth-century dress sitting at a table on which lay a huge leather Bible. The background was sombre, the man's clothes dark. But the woman wore a canary yellow shawl, and a red dress, and her white bonnet was frilled and ribboned.

'I would say she had dressed for some celebration, wouldn't you?'

'Without doubt. Perhaps, Elfrida, you *should* lock your front door.'

'Perhaps I should.'

'Is it insured?'

'It *is* my insurance. Against a rainy day. When I find myself on the streets with only a couple of plastic bags and Horace at the end of a piece of string, then, and only then, will I think about selling it.'

'A hedge against disaster.' Oscar smiled and took off his spectacles. 'Whatever. It is the manner in which you have put your possessions together that melds into such a pleasing whole. I'm sure you own nothing that you do not think to be beautiful or know to be useful.'

'William Morris.'

'And, perhaps, the measure of good taste.'

'Oscar, you say the nicest things.'

At this moment, from the kitchen, Elfrida's kettle let out a startling toot, which meant that it was boiling. She went to retrieve it. Oscar followed, and watched while she made the tea in a round brown teapot, which she set upon the wooden table.

'If you like builders' tea, you'd better wait for a moment or two. And, if you'd rather, you can have lemon instead of milk. And there's some stale gingerbread.'

'A feast.' Oscar pulled out a chair and settled himself, as though relieved to get the weight off his legs. She sat, too, facing him across the table, and busied herself cutting the gingerbread. She said, 'Oscar, I am going away.'

He did not reply, and she looked up and saw on his face an expression of horrified astonishment.

'For ever?' he asked, fearfully.

'Of course not for ever.'

His relief was evident. 'Thank God for that. What a fright you gave me.'

'I'd never leave Dibton *for ever*. I've told you. This is where I'm going to spend my twilight years. But it's time for a holiday.'

'Are you feeling particularly exhausted?'

'No, but autumn always depresses me. A sort of limbo between summer and Christmas. A dead time. And I'm going to have another birthday soon. Sixty-two. Even more depressing. So, time for a change.'

'Perfectly sensible. It will do you good. Where will you go?'

'To the very end of Cornwall. If you sneeze you're in danger of falling over a cliff into the Atlantic.'

'Cornwall?' Now he was astounded. 'Why Cornwall?'

'Because I have a cousin who lives there. He's called Jeffrey Sutton and he's exactly two years younger than I am. We've always been friends. He's one of those nice people one can telephone without reservation and say, "Can I come and stay?" And you know he'll say yes. And, moreover, sound pleased. So Horace and I will drive down together.'

Oscar shook his head in some bewilderment. 'I never knew that you had a cousin. Or any sort of relation, for that matter.'

'The product of an immaculate conception, you mean?'

'Hardly that. But, admit, it is surprising.'

'I don't think it's surprising at all. Just because I don't rabbit on all the time about my family.' Then Elfrida relented. 'But you're not far wrong. I am a bit denuded. But Jeffrey's a special person and we've always kept in touch.'

'Has he a wife?'

'Actually, he's had two. The first was a pain in the neck. She's called Dodie. I suppose he was charmed by her pretty looks and sweet air of helplessness only to discover, poor man, that he had tied himself to a woman of such self-absorption as to beggar belief. She was, as well, idle and undomestic, and most of Jeffrey's hard-earned salary went on paying the wages of cooks, cleaners, and au pairs in the faint hope of keeping some sort of an establishment going for his two daughters.'

'What happened to the marriage?' Oscar was clearly fascinated.

'He remained constant and enduring, but finally when both the girls were grown, educated and earning, he walked out. There was this girl, Serena, much younger than Jeffrey and perfectly sweet. She was a gardener and ran a nice little business doing flowers for parties and looking after other people's window-boxes. He'd known her for years. When he walked out on his marriage, he walked out on his job as well, wiped the dust of London from the soles of his shoes, and moved, with Serena, as far away from London as he could possibly get. When the very acrimonious divorce was over, he married Serena and almost at once started another little family. A boy and a girl. They live on a shoestring, keeping hens and doing bed and breakfast for summer visitors.'

'Happy ever after?'

'You could say that.'

'What about his daughters? What happened to them?'

'I've rather lost touch. The eldest was called Nicola. She married some man and had a child, I think. She was always dreadfully disagreeable, dissatisfied and perpetually complaining about the unfairness of life. I think she was always terribly jealous of Carrie.'

'Carrie being her sister.'

'Precisely so. And a darling. Jeffrey's nice personality all over again. About ten years ago, when I had to have some female operation – upon which, at this moment, Oscar, I shall not enlarge – she came to take care of me. She stayed for six weeks. I was on my own at the time, living in a grotty little flat in Putney, but she took it all in her stride and we got on like a house on fire.' Elfrida frowned, grappling with mental arithmetic. 'She must be about thirty now. Aged. How time flies.'

'Did she marry?'

'I don't think so. Like I said, I've rather lost touch. Last time I heard, she was working in Austria for some big tour company. You know, being a ski rep and making sure every tourist was in the right hotel. She always loved skiing more than anything. Whatever, I'm sure she's happy. I think your tea will be black enough now.' She poured his mug – it was satisfactorily dark – and gave him a slice of the crumbling gingerbread. 'So, you see, I do have a family, if not a particularly close one.' She smiled at him. 'How about you? Confession time. Do you have any dotty relations you can boast about?'

Oscar put up a hand, and rubbed it over his head. 'I don't know. I suppose I do. But, like you, I haven't much idea where they are or what they're up to.'

'Tell.'

'Well,' thoughtfully, he ate a bit of gingerbread, 'I had a Scottish grandmother. How's that for starters?'

'Hoots toots.'

'She had a great big house in Sutherland, and a certain amount of land, and a farm.'

'A lady of property.'

'I used to spend summer holidays with her, but she died when I was sixteen and I never went back.'

'What was her house called?'

'Corrydale.'

'Was it enormously grand?'

'No. Just enormously comfortable. Huge meals, and gumboots and fishing rods lying around the place. Good smells, of flowers and beeswax polish, and grouse cooking.'

'Oh, delicious. Mouth-watering. I'm sure she was heaven.'

'I don't know about that. But she was totally unpretentious and enormously talented.'

'In what way?'

'I suppose a talent for living. And for music. She was an accomplished pianist. And I mean really accomplished. I think I inherited my small talent from her, and it was she who set me on the road to my chosen career. There was always music at Corrydale. It was part of my life.'

'What else?'

'Sorry?'

'What else did you do?'

'I can scarcely remember. Go out in the evenings and pot rabbits. Fish for trout. Play golf. My grandmother was an avid golfer and she tried to get me going on the links, but I was never a match for her. Then people came to stay and we played tennis, and if it was warm enough, which it mostly wasn't, I might bicycle to the beach and fling myself into the North Sea. At Corrydale, it didn't matter what you did. It was all very relaxed. Good fun.'

'So what happened?'

'My grandmother died. The war was on. My uncle inherited and went to live there.'

'Didn't he invite you for summer holidays?'

'Those days were over. I was sixteen. Into music. Taking examinations. Other interests, other people. A different life.'

'Does he still live there? Your uncle, I mean.'

'No, he lives in London, now, in a mansion flat near the Albert Hall.'

'What's his name?'

'Hector McLellan.'

'Oh, splendid. All kilts and a red beard?'

'Not any more. He's very old.'

'And Corrydale?'

'He made it over to his son, Hughie. My cousin. A feckless fellow, whose one idea was to live a grand life and do things in tremendous style. He filled Corrydale with all his rather degenerate friends, who drank his whisky and behaved badly to the despair of all the respectable old retainers who had worked in the house and on the estate for years. It was all something of a scandal. Then Hughie decided that life north of the border was not for him, so he sold up and scarpered off to Barbados. As far as I know, he's still there, on to his third wife and leading the life of Reilly.'

Elfrida was envious. 'Oh, he *does* sound fascinating.'

'No. Not fascinating. Boringly predictable. We used to put up with each other, but we were never friends.'

'So everything's sold up, and you'll never return?'

'Unlikely.' He leaned back in his chair and crossed his arms. 'Actually, I could go back. When my grandmother died, she left Hughie and me a house between us. But it's been let for years to some old couple. Every quarter I get a trickle of rent, posted from the factor's office. I suppose Hughie gets the same, though it's scarcely enough to pay for a couple of planter's punches.'

'Is it a big house?'

'Not particularly. It's in the middle of the little town. It used to be estate offices, but then it was converted to a dwelling house.'

'How too exciting. I wish I had a house in Scotland.'

'Half a house.'

'Half a house is better than no bread. You could take Francesca for half a holiday.'

'Never thought of it, to be truthful. Never think about the place. I suppose one day Hughie will either offer to buy me out or suggest that I buy him out. But it's not something I worry about. And I prefer not to precipitate any action. The less I have to do with Hughie McLellan the better.'

'I think you're being frightfully feeble.'

'Just keeping a low profile. Now, when are you off?'

'Next Thursday.'

'For how long?'

'A month.'

'Will you send us a postcard?'

'Of course.'

'And let us know when you return?'

'At once.'

'We shall miss you,' said Oscar, and she felt warmed.

The house was called Emblo Cottage. It stood with its granite face to the north wind and the Atlantic, and on this side the windows were small and few and deep-set, with windowsills wide enough for the potted geraniums, scraps of driftwood and the shells Serena loved to collect. Once, it had been part of Emblo, a prosperous dairy farm, and the dwelling of the resident cowman, but the cowman retired and then died, mechanisation took over the milking parlours, agricultural wages soared and the farmer cut his losses and sold the cottage. Since then, it had belonged to three different owners, and had come on the market for the last time just as Jeffrey had made the great decision to cut loose from London, Dodie and his job. He saw the advertisement in *The Times*, got straight into his car, and drove through the night in order to view the property before any other person had time to put in a bid. He found a dank little place, dismally furnished for holiday letting, crouched in an untended garden and set about by stunted sycamores leaning at right angles away from the prevailing wind. But there was a view of the cliffs and the sea, and on the south side a sheltered patch of lawn where wisteria climbed the wall and there still flowered a camellia bush.

He telephoned his bank manager, got a loan and bought the place. When he and Serena moved in, there were birds' nests in the chimneys, old paper peeling from the walls, and a smell of damp and mould that hung over every room. But it didn't matter. They camped in sleeping-bags and opened a bottle of champagne. They were together and they were home.

That had been ten years ago. It had taken two of those years to get the place in order, involving much hard physical labour, dirt, destruction, inconvenience and a succession of plumbers, builders, tilers and stonemasons, who trod around the place in mud-caked boots, boiled up endless cups of tea and indulged in long conversations as to the meaning of life.

From time to time Jeffrey and Serena became exasperated by their slowness and unreliability, but it was impossible not to be beguiled by these amateur philosophers, who seemed to know no sense of hurry, content in the knowledge that tomorrow was another day.

Finally, all was done. The workmen departed, leaving behind them a small, trim, solid stone house, with kitchen and sitting room downstairs and a creaking wooden staircase leading to the upper floor. At the back of the kitchen jutted what had once been a wash-house, slate-floored and airy, and here waterproofs and rubber boots were dumped, and Serena kept her washing-machine and her deep freeze. There was as well a huge clay sink, which Jeffrey had found abandoned in a ditch. Restored, it was constantly in use for washing eggs and mud-caked dogs, and for the buckets of wild flowers Serena loved to pick and arrange in old-fashioned pottery jugs. Upstairs there were three white-painted bedrooms with sloping ceilings, and a small bathroom, which had the best view of all from its window, looking south over the farmer's fields and up the slope of the hill to the moor.

They were not isolated. The farmhouse, with its considerable outbuildings, stood only a hundred yards or so away, so that there was a constant coming and going of traffic up and down the lane and past their gate: tractors, milk lorries and cars, and small children who, dumped by the school bus at the end of the road, walked their way home. The farmer had a family of four, and these children were Ben and Amy's best friends. With them, they rode bicycles, went blackberrying, walked down to the cliffs with haversacks slung from their inadequate shoulders to swim and picnic.

Elfrida had never seen this house, had never been to visit them. But now she was coming, and Jeffrey was filled with an old sensation, almost forgotten, but which he finally acknowledged to himself was excitement.

Elfrida. He was now sixty, and Elfrida was . . . ? Sixty-one, sixty-two? It didn't matter. As a boy, he had always thought the world of her because she was fearless and she made him laugh. As an adolescent, trapped in the inky disciplines of boarding-school, she had been like a light in his life: gloriously attractive, admirably rebellious, fighting parental opposition, and finally going on the stage and becoming an actress. Such determination, bravery and achievement had filled Jeffrey with admiration and devoted attachment. Once or twice she had actually come to his boring school and taken him out for an exeat Saturday or Sunday, and he had boasted about her a little to his friends, and kept her waiting at the ghastly pseudo-Gothic red-brick front door because he wanted others to see her there, sitting in her little red sports car with her dark glasses and her pineapple-coloured hair tied about with a chiffon scarf.

'My cousin. She's in some show or other. In London,' he said, with marvellous casualness, as though it happened to everybody every day. 'They brought it over from New York.'

And finally he would go out to meet her, apologising for lateness, climbing into the tiny bucket seat beside her, being driven away with an impressive roar of the engine and a lot of flying gravel. When he got back to school, he remained determinedly blasé. 'Oh, we just went to the Roadhouse. Had a swim in the pool and a meal.'

He was enormously proud of her and more than a little in love.

But time went by, and they grew up, and lost touch, and made their own lives. Elfrida married some actor or other, and it all fell apart, and then she married another dreary character, and finally ended up with her famously successful lover. All seemed set for lifelong happiness, and then the alliance was stunned by tragedy, his struggle with Parkinson's and eventual death.

The last time Jeffrey had seen Elfrida had been in London, just after she had met this exceptional man, to whom she always referred as Jimbo. 'Not his real name, darling, but my own name for him. I never thought it could be like this. I never thought one could be so close and yet so different from a single human being. He is everything I've never been, and yet I love him more than any person or anything I've ever known.'

'What about your career?' Jeffrey had asked.

'Oh, bugger my career,' Elfrida had said, and collapsed into laughter. He had never seen her so happy, so beautiful, so utterly fulfilled.

His own unhappy marriage was falling to bits, but Elfrida was always there, at the end of the telephone, ringing him up, ready with all sorts of advice, both good and bad, but most important, endlessly sympathetic. Once he took Serena to meet her, and she rang the next evening, and said, 'Jeffrey, darling, she is too sweet ... Cut your losses and concentrate on *her*.'

'What about my daughters?'

'Grown-up and self-supporting. You must think of yourself. Bite the bullet. Don't dither. There's not time. Only one life.'

'Dodie?'

'She'll manage. She'll bleed you white for alimony. She's not going to give up her creature comforts. Let her have the lot and go and be happy.'

Go and be happy. He had done just that.

Five o'clock on a grey October evening. The wind was getting up. He had done the hens, gathered the eggs, shut away the clucking creatures in their small, domestic wooden houses. It was growing dark. Inside Emblo Cottage, Serena had turned on the lights, and small yellow windows glowed out into the dying light. It was a Thursday, the day when the wheelie-bin had to be trundled down the lane in order for the weekly dustbin lorry to empty it in the morning. A wind had got up, blowing in from the sea with an edge to it that tasted and smelled of salt. In this wind, the gorse bushes jigged and rustled along the tops of the hedges. Over its whine, he could hear the water of the stream bubbling its way down the hill and along the edge of the lane. Because it felt cold he went indoors to get a thick jacket. Serena was stirring something at the stove and the children were busy with their homework at the kitchen table.

He said, 'Wheelie-bin.'

'Oh, clever man to remember.'

'Back in five minutes.'

'I shall watch out for Elfrida.'

He trundled the wheelie-bin down the rutted lane and set it in its place on the verge. Across the road was a wooden gate, which led into another farmer's field, and Jeffrey went to lean against this, like any old countryman, felt for his cigarettes, took one and lit it with his old steel lighter. The day was dying. He watched the sky darken, thick with cloud. The sea was the colour of slate, flecked with foam. A rough evening. Breakers boomed at the foot of the cliffs and he could feel the damp of sea mist on his cheeks.

He thought of a poem, once read, long forgotten.

> *My room is a bright glass cabin,*
> *All Cornwall thunders at my door,*
> *And the white ships of winter lie,*
> *In the sea roads of the moor.*

He stayed until his cigarette was finished, then threw away the stub and turned to go home. And, at that moment, saw the headlights approaching from the east, blinking as the road twisted. He leaned against the gate and waited. After a bit an old blue Fiesta appeared, cautiously taking the last narrow bend before the Emblo turning. He knew, instinctively, that it was Elfrida. He stepped into the road, waving his arms, and the car stopped. He opened the door and got in beside her.

He smelt her familiar perfume, the scent she had always used, that was part of her.

He said, 'You mustn't park here. This is the main road. You will be struck by a tractor or a German tour bus. Turn into the lane.'

Which she did, then stopped again.

She said, 'Hello.'

'You made it.'

'Five hours.'

'Found the way?'

'Such a clever map you drew for me.'

'Who's this in the back?'

'Horace, my dog. I told you he had to come.'

'How wonderful that you're here. I kept steeling myself for a telephone call to say that you'd changed your mind.'

'I'd never do that,' Elfrida told him. And then became practical.

'Is this your front drive?'

'It is.'

'Dreadfully narrow, darling.'

'Wide enough.'

'Forward, then.'

He began to laugh. 'Forward.'

She put the car into gear and they lurched up the narrow tunnel that was the lane.

'What sort of a journey did you have?' Jeffrey asked.

'All right. I was a bit nervous. It's years since I've done such a long drive; unknown motorways and thundering lorries I find a little unnerving. This car isn't exactly a Ferrari.'

'Good enough.'

As they approached the cottage, an outside light

came on. Serena, clearly, had heard them grinding up the lane. This light illuminated an open space, backed by a tall granite wall. The road continued towards the distant farm, but Jeffrey said, 'Park here,' so she did. At once two sheepdogs appeared from nowhere, bounding towards them and barking their heads off.

'Not to worry,' Jeffrey assured her, 'they're mine, Tarboy and Findus, and they don't bite.'

'Not even Horace?'

'Least of all Horace.'

They climbed out of the car and let Horace free. There was the usual small skirmish as the three strange dogs met each and circled and sniffed, then Horace disappeared into the thicket of a handy bush and, gratefully, lifted his leg.

Jeffrey was amused. 'What breed is Horace?'

'Unknown. But loyal, troublefree and clean. He can sleep with me. I've brought his basket.'

He opened the boot of her car and heaved out a battered suitcase and a large bulging paper carrier-bag. 'Have you brought your own supplies?'

'That's Horace's food and his bowl and stuff.' From the back seat of the car she hauled his basket and another bulging carrier-bag. Doors were slammed, and Jeffrey led the way up a slate path and around the corner of the house. The wind from the sea pounced upon them, and yellow squares of light, from windows and a half-glassed door, lay upon the cobbles. Jeffrey set down Elfrida's suitcase and opened the door and she went through and into the kitchen. The two children looked up from the table, and Serena turned from the stove and came, aproned and open-armed, to greet them.

'Jeffrey, you actually *found* her. So clever, he went

down with the wheelie-bin and came back with you. What a perfect bit of timing. Did you have a frightful drive? Would you like a cup of tea and something to eat? Oh, and you haven't met the children, have you? Ben. And Amy. This is Elfrida, ducks.'

'We know,' said the boy. 'You've been talking about her for ages.' He was dark and his younger sister blonde. He got up from the table and came to shake hands, his eyes scanning Elfrida's luggage with some interest. He was expecting a present but had been told not to mention this in case none was forthcoming. He had his father's eyes and olive skin, and a thatch of heavy dark hair. Elfrida guessed that in a few years' time, there would be a clutch of broken girlish hearts in the surrounding neighbourhood.

His father came through the door behind Elfrida and dumped the suitcase at the foot of the stairs. 'Hi, Dad.'

'Hi, Ben. Finished your homework?'

'Yep.'

'Good man. And Amy. You done too?'

'I finished mine ages ago,' Amy told him smugly. She was shy. She came to her father and buried her face in his leg, so that all that showed of her was her long flaxen hair, pale as milk, and the faded blue of her dungarees. Elfrida had always known about Ben and Amy but, seeing them now, marvelled that they were actually the children of Jeffrey, although young enough to be his grandchildren. She decided that they were beautiful. But, then, Serena was beautiful in her own individual way. Her hair was as pale as Amy's but twisted up into a chignon and fastened with a tortoiseshell clip. Her eyes were a brilliant blue, and her thin face was dusted with freckles. She wore slender jeans, which made her legs look endless, and a blue pullover, and she had knotted a silk scarf around her neck. Because of the cooking, she had tied the striped apron around her waist, and now made no effort to remove it.

'What's the form?' Jeffrey asked, and Serena told him, 'I'll make a cup of tea for Elfrida if she wants one. Or she can sit by the fire; or go up to her room and unpack; or have a bath. Whatever she wants.'

'When's dinner?'

'Eight, I thought. I'll feed Ben and Amy first.'

Amy emerged from her father's legs. She said, 'Sausages.'

Elfrida frowned. 'Sorry?'

'Sausages for our tea. And mashed potatoes and baked beans.'

'How delicious.'

'But you're having something else. Mum's been making it.'

'Don't tell me, and then it will be a wonderful surprise.'

'It's chicken and mushrooms.'

'*Amy!*' Her brother yelled at her. 'Don't *tell*.'

Elfrida laughed. 'It doesn't matter, I'm sure it will be delicious.'

'Now,' said Serena, raising her voice slightly over the squabblings of her offspring, 'would you like a cup of tea?'

But other treats that had been mentioned were more tempting. 'What I'd really like is to go upstairs and unpack and have a bath. Would that be dreadfully inconvenient?'

'Not a bit. We only have the one bathroom but the children can go in after you. There's plenty of hot water.'

'Bless you. Then that's what I'll do.'

'How about Horace?' Jeffrey asked. 'Does he need to be fed?'

'Yes, of course he does. Are you offering to do it for me? Two scoops of biscuits and half a tin of meat. And a bit of hot water.'

'Is Horace a dog?' asked Ben.

'Well, he's certainly not my husband.'

'Where is he?'

'Outside. Making friends – I hope – with your dogs.'

'I want to go and see . . .'

'I do, too . . .'

'Wait for me . . .'

They were away, out into the dark garden without extra sweaters, gumboots or any wails of protest from their mother. The door was left swinging open, letting in gusts of cold air. Jeffrey went quietly to shut it, then once more picked up Elfrida's suitcase.

'Come,' he said, and led the way up the creaking wooden stairs.

He showed her round, said, 'See you in about an hour. I'll give you a drink,' and left her, closing the door behind him. It had a wooden latch. Elfrida sat on the bed (a double one) and realised, all at once, that she was tired. She yawned enormously, then looked about her at the charming room, minimal to the point of sparseness but marvellously tranquil. A bit like Serena. White walls, white curtains, rush matting on the floor. A pine chest of drawers, draped in white linen and lace. Wooden pegs and a clutch of colourful hangers for a wardrobe. The duvet cover was blue gingham, there were books on the bedside table and new magazines, and a blue pottery mug in which sat a single hydrangea head, blotting-paper pink.

She yawned again. She was here. She had not lost the way, or broken down, or been involved in a fatal accident. And Jeffrey had been out there to meet her at the end of the lane, leaping out from the side of the road like a footpad and waving her to a halt. If he hadn't been so instantly recognisable she might well have been frightened out of her wits, but there could be no mistaking that tall, lanky figure, still lithe and active despite his advancing years and, in all likelihood, kept that way by the company of his youthful wife and little children. Most important, he looked content. He had done the right thing. His life seemed to have worked itself out, which was exactly what she had always wished for him.

After a bit, she got off the bed, unpacked and set about the place her few belongings, turning the simple room into her own. Then she undressed, wrapped herself in her old dressing-gown and went next door to the little bathroom, where she soaked for a little while in a scalding bath. When she got out she had stopped yawning and felt tired no longer but active and cheerful and ready for the evening ahead. She dressed again, in velvet trousers and a silk shirt, gathered up her carpet-bag, which was filled with presents, and went downstairs, feeling like a sailor descending a gangway on to a lower deck. In the kitchen she found the children eating their sausages, while their mother whipped up egg whites in a bowl with an electric beater. As Elfrida appeared she looked up to smile, and said, 'Go and be with Jeffrey – he's in the sitting room. He's lit a fire.'

'Can't I help? I'm not much of a cook, but a dab hand at scouring saucepans.' Serena laughed. 'Not a saucepan to be scoured.'

'Will I see Ben and Amy again?'

'Of course. They'll come and say goodnight after their bath.'

'I had a wonderful bath. Rejuvenating.'

Ben said, 'What does rejuvenating mean?'

'It means make younger,' Serena explained.

'She doesn't look any younger.'

'That's because I'm so old,' Elfrida told him. 'Be sure to come and say goodnight, because I've got something for you . . .' she raised the carpet bag '. . . in here.'

'Can we look now?'

'No, you can look later, by the fire. A bit like Christmas stockings.'

She found Jeffrey in the little sitting room, esconced like any old gentleman by the fire, reading *The Times*. As she appeared, he tossed this aside and rose cautiously to his feet – cautiously because in this room, for some reason, the ceiling was exceptionally low, and Jeffrey was clearly aware of the danger of bashing his head on one of the white-painted beams. He was particularly vulnerable because he was bald, his head burned chestnut brown by the sun, but the remaining hair that circled his collar was still as dark as it had ever been. His eyes were dark, too, laughter lines fanned out over his thin cheeks, and he wore a navy blue sweater with a red bandanna knotted around his neck in lieu of a tie. Elfrida had always had an eye for a good-looking man, and it was gratifying to discover that her cousin Jeffrey was as toothsome as ever.

He said, 'How dashing you look.'

'Clean, at last. Heavenly bath.' She dumped down her carpet-bag, lowered herself into the other armchair and looked about her appreciatively, seeing pictures that were familiar, others that were not. A blazing fire, jugs of dried grasses, family photographs in silver frames, a few pieces of pretty old furniture. There wasn't room for much more. She said, 'You have made an enchanting house here.'

'No credit to me, Elfrida. All Serena. A glass of wine?'

'Delicious, thank you. It's like another world, isn't it, from the way you used to live? The house in Campden Hill, and flogging off to the City every day, and formal entertaining, and knowing all the right people.'

He was on the other side of the room, pouring her wine. He did not immediately reply to her remarks, but seemed to be considering them. Returning, he gave her the wine glass and sat again in his wide-lapped chair. Across the hearthrug, their eyes met.

She said, 'I'm sorry.'

'Why sorry?'

'Tactless. You know I've never thought before I spoke.'

'Not tactless. Just truthful. You're right. Another world and one not mourned. Chasing after money, sending the girls to the right, appallingly expensive schools. Hiring a butler every time we had a dinner party. Redesigning the kitchen because the Harley Wrights on the other side of the square had redesigned theirs and Dodie couldn't stand to be left behind. Perpetually worried about the cash-flow, the state of the stock market, the demands of Lloyds, the possibility of being made redundant. Sometimes I went through the whole night without sleeping. And all about nothing. But I had to walk out to discover that.'

'You're all right now?'

'In what way?'

'I suppose financially.'

'Yes, we're fine. Even keel. We haven't got much but we don't need it.'

'What do you live on? Your hens?'

He began to laugh. 'Scarcely. But they provide an occupation and a tiny income. Bed and breakfast helps in the summer, but we only have one room, which is yours, and the shared bathroom, so we can't charge too much. There's a derelict outbuilding between us and the farm, and from time to time we think of putting in an offer and converting it into an annexe for paying visitors, but it's such an undertaking that we keep putting it off. But Serena still works, doing flowers for weddings and parties and such, and Ben and Amy are getting an excellent education at the local school. To me it's been a revelation, how simply one can live.'

'And happy?'

'Happier than I ever thought possible.'

'And Dodie?'

'She's living in a flat near Hurlingham, very desirable, with a view of the river. Nicola's with her. Nicola's marriage fell to bits, so the two of them are shacked up together, doubtless getting on each other's nerves.'

'And Nicola's child?'

'My granddaughter, Lucy. She's fourteen now. Poor kid, she's living there too. Can't be much fun for her, but there's not much I can do about it. I've tried asking her to come down to us and stay for a bit, but Nicola has labelled me a villain and Serena a witch and refuses to let her visit.'

Elfrida sighed. She could understand perfectly the hopelessness of the situation. She said, 'How about Carrie?'

'Still in Austria or wherever. She's got a good job with a travel company, quite a responsible position.'

'Do you see her?'

'Last time I was in London we had lunch together but our paths seldom cross.'

'Not married?'

'No.'

'Does *she* come here?'

'No, but for the best of reasons. She doesn't want to intrude, to make things awkward for Serena, Ben and Amy. Anyway, she's thirty now, not a child. She leads her own life. If she wants to come to Emblo, she knows she only has to pick up the telephone.' He paused to set down his glass, reach for a cigarette and light it. Elfrida said, 'You haven't given up.'

'No, I haven't given up and don't intend to. Does that offend you?'

'Jeffrey, nothing in all my life has ever offended me. You know that.'

'You look wonderful. How are you?'

'Wonderful, perhaps.'

'Not too lonely?'

'Getting better.'

'It was cruel, what happened to you.'

'Jimbo, you mean? Darling man. It was crueller for him than for me. A slow degeneration of a wonderful, brilliant man. But no regrets, Jeffrey. I know we didn't have very long together, but what we did have was special. Not many people achieve such happiness, even for a year or two.'

'Tell me about your Hampshire hideaway.'

'Dibton. The village is rather ordinary and dull. But somehow that was what I wanted. The house is a tiny railway-worker's cottage, one in a row. All I need.'

'Nice people?'

'Ordinary again. Kind and friendly. I think you could say I've been made welcome. I couldn't stay in London.'

'Any special friends?'

She started telling him about the Foubisters and Bobby Burton-Jones and the Vicar and his wife and the primary school pantomime. She told him about Mrs Jennings and Albert Meddows and the fabulously wealthy Mr Dunn with his indoor swimming-pool and immense conservatory filled with red-hot geraniums and rubber plants.

Finally, she told him about the Blundells. Oscar and Gloria and Francesca. 'They've been truly, enormously kind. Taken me under their wing, one might say. Gloria is wealthy and generous. The two don't always go together, do they? She owns the house they live in. It's called the Grange and is perfectly hideous, but frightfully warm and comfortable. She was married before, so she's got two grown-up married sons, but Francesca is so original and funny and sweet. Gloria is an avid hostess — scarcely a day passes when she isn't organising some party or picnic, or get-together or committee meeting. She's rather horsy and loves gathering a great gang of friends, and setting off for some point-to-point, with a bar in the boot of her car and her pekineses tied to the bumper, barking their heads off at anyone who passes.'

Jeffrey was clearly amused. 'And does Oscar enjoy such occasions?'

'I don't know. But he's a gentle, amiable man . . . a charmer, really . . . and he and Francesca go off together, and put bets on unlikely horses and buy themselves ice-creams.'

'What does he do? Or is he retired?'

'He's a musician. An organist. A pianist. A teacher.'

'How clever of you to find such an interesting couple. They clearly adore you, probably because you've always had the effect of a good strong gust of fresh air.'

But Elfrida voiced her reservations. 'I have to be quite careful and strict with myself. I do not intend to become absorbed.'

'Who wouldn't want to absorb you?'

'You mustn't be partisan.'

'I was always on your side.'

In later years, looking back to those weeks she spent at Emblo, the thing that Elfrida most clearly remembered was the sound of the wind. It blew perpetually, at times shrunken to a lively breeze, at others pounding in from the sea at gale-force strength, assaulting the cliffs, howling down chimneys and rattling doors and windowpanes. After a bit, she became used to its constant presence, but at night it was impossible to ignore, and she would lie in the dark, hearing it sweep in from the Atlantic, stream up across the moor, send the branches of an elderly apple tree tapping like a ghost at her window.

It was – this wind made clear – summer no longer. October moved into November and the nights drew closer every evening. The farmer's cows, his handsome Guernsey dairy herd, trod down from the fields for the morning and evening milking and churned to mud the lane that ran between Emblo and the farmhouse. After the evening milking, they were turned out into the fields again and were adept at seeking shelter in the lea of a wall, or behind a tangle of thicket and gorse.

'Why can't they spend the night indoors?' Elfrida wanted to know.

'They never do. We have no frosts, there's plenty of grass.'

'Poor things.' But she had to admit they looked sleek and happy enough.

The daily routine of the little household took her over, and she slowed herself to its pace. There was always washing to be pegged out, shirts to be ironed, potatoes to be dug, hens to be fed and eggs to be washed. After the first week she realised, with some surprise, that for seven days she had neither read a newspaper nor watched television. The rest of the world could have blown itself to pieces while all Elfrida worried about was whether she could get the sheets off the line before the next shower of rain.

Some evenings she took over the kitchen and cooked supper for Ben and Amy, so that Jeffrey and Serena were able to grab the chance of a dinner out by themselves, or a visit to the nearest cinema. And she taught the children to play rummy, and mesmerised them with stories about the old days when she was in the theatre.

One weekend, the fickle weather turned warm as spring, the wind dropped and the sun shone from a cloudless sky. Determined to make the most of the benevolent day, Serena gathered up the farmer's four youngsters, packed a picnic and they all set out to walk across the fields towards the cliffs, a straggling party, consisting of six children, three adults and three dogs. Amy and Elfrida, side by side, brought up the rear. The footpath crossed stone stiles, and snaked down between gorse and bramble bushes.

Elfrida spied blackberries. 'We should pick them,' she told Amy. 'We could make blackberry jelly.'

But Amy was wiser. 'No, we can't. We can't pick blackberries after the beginning of October because that's when the Cornish witches do wees on them.'

'How extraordinary. How do you know that?'

'Our teacher told us. But she didn't say wees, she said urinated.'

They reached the edge of the cliff and the whole breadth of the ocean was revealed, extravagantly blue and glittering with sunshine. The path trickled on, a precipitous and dangerous-looking descent into a secret cove. It was low tide, so there lay a tiny sickle of sand, and rock pools gleamed like jewels.

With some difficulty they all scrambled down, the dogs bounding fearlessly ahead. On the rocks, Amy left Elfrida and went to join the others on the sand, where Jeffrey had already started everybody digging a mammoth sandcastle and Serena searched for shells and pebbles with which to decorate this edifice.

Now, midday, there was a real warmth in the sun so Elfrida shed her jacket and rolled up the sleeves of her sweater. Rugs, baskets and haversacks had been dumped on a smooth flat rock and she sat beside them, watched the restless sea and felt mesmerised by its sheer size and magnificence. The colours of the water, the clearness were breathtaking: streaks of blue, green, turquoise, purple, all laced and streaked with white surf. A heavy swell was running, and breakers formed far out, moving in and gathering height and weight before finally crashing against the jagged, granite coastline, sending up great fountains of sizzling spray. Overhead the gulls wheeled, and out towards the horizon a small fishing-boat butted its way through the turbulent water.

Staring, bewitched, she lost all sense of time, but after a bit was joined by Serena, come to unpack the picnic. From the haversacks she produced bottles, plastic cups, paper napkins, a bag of apples. As well, there emanated the mouthwatering smell of hot pasties.

Elfrida was amazed. 'Whenever did you make pasties, Serena? They take for ever.'

'I always keep a dozen or so in the deep freeze. The children love them.'

'Me too.'

'I took them out last night. I had a feeling it was going to be a good day. How about a drink? You can have lager or wine. Or lemonade if you're feeling abstemious.'

'Wine would be perfect.'

The bottle was wrapped in a wine cooler and, drunk from a plastic glass, tasted better than any wine had ever tasted before. Elfrida turned back to the sea. She said, 'This is heaven.'

'In the summer we come most weekends. It's easier now that both children can do the walk themselves.'

'What a happy family you are.'

'Yes,' said Serena, and smiled. 'I know. So fortunate. But I do *know* that, Elfrida. I really do. And every day I say thank you.'

From time to time Elfrida left Emblo, and took herself off on her own, driving her little car, leaving Horace behind in the company of Jeffrey's sheepdogs. She found herself amazed that such a small tract of country could be so wild, so remote and yet so varied. The roads, freed of the summer tourist traffic, were narrow and winding, but all she ever met was the occasional bus, butcher's van or tractor. She would cross an empty moor, and the road would slip down into a tiny valley thick with rhododendrons, where enviable gardens were still verdant with hydrangeas and the dangling ballerina blossoms of fuchsia.

One day, she made the trip into the neighbouring town, where she parked her car and walked down into the warren of baffling lanes and alleyways that led to the harbour. On the harbour road were restaurants and gift shops, and many small galleries displaying every kind of art and sculpture. She found a bookshop, went in and took some time in choosing two books for Ben and Amy. So delightful was this that she browsed on and, thinking of Francesca, bought a book for her as well. She found it in the second-hand section: *The Island of Sheep* by John Buchan. She remembered reading it at school, and becoming caught up in the adventure, and knew that it was a story Oscar and Francesca could read together, the two of them squashed into the huge armchair by the flickering log fire.

She had the books wrapped and paid for them, then went out into the street again, continuing on her way. In a craft shop, she found brilliantly patterned hand-knitted sweaters, and chose two: one for Jeffrey and one for Serena. She bought postcards and a bottle of wine and, by now considerably laden, set out once more, walking away from the harbour and into a maze of cobbled streets where washing hung, and window-boxes were brilliant with nasturtiums and pink petunias. Another gallery. Unable to resist, she paused to look in its window, and saw a little abstract painting, its frame bleached like driftwood, with all the colours of Cornwall set into shapes that represented exactly her own impressions and feelings about this ancient land.

Elfrida craved it, not for herself but as a present. She thought that if Jimbo were still alive she would have bought it for him because it was exactly the sort of image he would have loved beyond anything. She imagined giving it to him, bringing it to his house in Barnes where they had been so unimaginably happy together. Watching him strip off the wrappings, watching his face, knowing that his reaction would be one of delight and pleasure . . .

The picture wavered and became watery. She realised that her eyes had filled with tears. She had never cried for Jimbo, simply grieved and mourned privately to herself, and tried to learn to live with the cold loneliness of an existence without him. She had thought that she had achieved this, but it could not be so. She wondered if perhaps she was a woman who could not live without a man, and if this were true then there was nothing she could do about it.

The tears receded. Ridiculous. She was sixty-two, snivelling like a young girl who has lost her lover. But still she stayed, staring at the picture, wanting it. Wanting to share her pleasure. Wanting to give.

The idea occurred to her that she could buy it for Oscar Blundell. But Oscar was not simply Oscar. He was one half of Oscar and Gloria, and Gloria would be bewildered by such a gift. In her head Elfrida could hear Gloria's voice. '*Elfrida!* You can't be serious. It's just a lot of shapes. A child of four could do a better job than that. And which way up is it meant to be? Honestly, Elfrida, you are a hoot. What possessed you to put down good money for a thing like that? You've been robbed.'

No. Not a good idea. Reluctantly, she turned from the window of the gallery and walked on, left the streets behind her and set out on a path that climbed in zigzags to the top of the grass promontory that divided the two beaches. As she climbed, the wind became blustery, and when she reached the shallow summit, she found herself surrounded by ocean and sky, the whole blue curving rim of the horizon. It felt a bit like being at sea. And she came to a bench and sat upon it, huddled in her sheepskin jacket with her packages set about her, like any old pensioner, exhausted by shopping.

But she was not any old pensioner. She was Elfrida. She was here. She had survived, was moving on. But to what? A seagull, scavenging for crusts or some edible picnic titbit, swept down out of the air and landed at her feet. His eyes were cold and acquisitive, and his aggression made her smile. And she found herself longing for company. Specifically for Oscar. She wanted him to be with her, just for a single day, so that when she returned to Dibton, they could talk about the wind and the sea and the gull, and remember and marvel at the magic of a special moment.

Perhaps that was the worst of all. Not having someone to remember things with.

When the day came for Elfrida to return to Dibton, she could scarcely believe that she had been at Emblo for a month, so swiftly had the weeks sped by. They tried to persuade her, of course, to stay. 'You're welcome for as long as you like,' Serena told her, and Elfrida knew she was sincere. 'You've been the best. A lovely mixture of mother, sister and friend. We'll miss you so dreadfully.'

'You're sweet. But no, I must get back. Pick up the thread of life again.'

'You'll come again?'

'Try and stop me.'

She had planned to set off as early as possible, so that she could reach Dibton before darkness fell. At eight in the morning, she was out of doors, and Jeffrey was loading her car. The little family stood about her, and Amy was in tears. 'I don't want you to go. I want you to stay.'

'Guests don't stay for ever, Amy my pet. It's time to leave.'

Horace, too, showed a disloyal reluctance to depart. Every time he was put into the car he jumped out again, and finally had to be dragged by his collar, deposited on the back seat and the door shut behind him. He gazed from the window, his furry face doleful and his dark eyes agonised. 'I think,' Ben observed, 'that he's probably going to cry as well.'

Neither Amy nor Ben was yet dressed and they looked bizarre with padded jackets and gumboots pulled over their pyjamas. When her brother made this remark, Amy's tears welled up once more. Her mother stooped and picked her up and held her on her hip. 'Cheer up, Amy. Horace will be fine once he's on his way.'

'I don't want *anybody* to leave us.'

The parting had gone on for long enough. Elfrida turned to Jeffrey. 'Dear man, thank you a thousand times.' He had not yet shaved, and her cheek grated against the stubble of his dark beard. 'And Serena . . .' A swift kiss, a hand over Amy's flaxen head, and she got firmly in behind the wheel, turned on the ignition and drove off. They stood and waved until the car was lost to view, but she had a pretty good idea that they didn't go back indoors until the little Fiesta had turned out on to the main road, and she and Horace were truly on their way.

Not the time to feel lonely and bereft. The goodbye was not for ever: she could return to Emblo whenever she wanted. In a year, maybe, or sooner. Jeffrey and Serena would always be there, and Ben and Amy. That was the poignant bit: Jeffrey and Serena would remain unchanged, but Ben and Amy would be taller, thinner, fatter; growing street-wise, losing front teeth. She would never know Ben and Amy again as the small children she had come to love during this particular period of their lives. Like the holiday that was over, those children had gone for ever.

To cheer herself up Elfrida looked ahead, in positive fashion, which she had always found a reliable method of dealing with a sense of loss. She was going home to her own little nest, filled with her own possessions. The small and humble refuge she shared with Horace. She would open doors and windows, inspect her garden, put a match to the fire.

Tomorrow, perhaps, she would telephone the Grange and speak to Gloria. And there would be cries of delight that she was back again, and instant summons to come and see them immediately. And when she went Elfrida would take the book with her to give to Francesca. *The Island of Sheep*. I chose it specially, because I loved it so much when I was your age, and I'm sure you'll love it too.

But first, of course, before even reaching Poulton's

Row, Elfrida knew that she must do some shopping. There was no food in the cottage and she had cleaned out the refrigerator before she left. Her first port of call must be Mrs Jennings's mini-market. She began to make a mental list. Bread and milk. Sausages, eggs and butter. Coffee. Biscuits and some tins for Horace. Perhaps some soup for her supper. Something sustaining, like Cullen Skink . . .

Half an hour later, she joined the motorway that led up-country. She switched on her car radio, and settled to the long drive.

The Dibton church clock stood at half past two as she drove into the main street of the village. Outside Mrs Jennings's slouched the usual gang of loutish youths, and a little further on, she spied Bobby Burton-Jones trimming his privet hedge with a pair of shears. Nothing much seemed to have changed, except that most of the trees had shed their leaves and there was a definite wintry feel to the air.

She parked the car, found her bag and went into the shop. It seemed to be empty. She picked up a wire basket and moved up the aisles, taking what she needed from the shelves. Finally she presented herself at the counter, where Mrs Jennings was doing sums on the back of an envelope and had not heard her come in.

But now she looked up, saw Elfrida, laid down her pencil and took off her spectacles. 'Mrs Phipps. Well, what a surprise. Haven't seen you for weeks. Have a good holiday, did you?'

'Wonderful. Just back. Haven't even been home yet, because I had to buy some provisions.' She put the wire basket on the counter and reached for a *Daily Telegraph*. 'You won't believe this but I haven't read a newspaper for a month. To be truthful, I didn't miss it.'

Mrs Jennings made no comment on this. Elfrida looked up and saw that the woman was staring at her, biting her lip and looking much troubled. Elfrida put the newspaper on top of the basket. After a bit, she said, 'Is anything wrong, Mrs Jennings?'

Mrs Jennings said, 'You don't know?'

'Know what?'

'You haven't heard?'

Suddenly Elfrida's mouth was dry. 'No.'

'Mrs Blundell.'

'What about her?'

'She's dead, Mrs Phipps. A car smash at Pudstone roundabout. She was bringing the little girl home from a fireworks party. November the fourth, it was. A great articulated lorry. Heaven knows how it happened. She couldn't have seen it. It was a dreadful night. Pouring with rain.' Elfrida, stunned by shock, said nothing. 'I'm sorry, Mrs Phipps. I thought you might have heard.'

'How could I have heard? I never read a paper. Nobody knew where I was. Nobody knew my address.'

'A tragedy, Mrs Phipps. We couldn't believe it. None of the village could believe it.'

'And Francesca?' She made herself ask the question, dreading the answer.

'She died too, Mrs Phipps. And the two little dogs who were in the back. You couldn't believe the photograph in the paper. That great car, smashed and flattened to bits. They didn't stand a chance. Only good thing was the police said it was instant. They couldn't, any of them, have known a thing.' Mrs Jennings' voice shook a little. She clearly found it almost impossible

71

to speak of what had taken place. 'You hear of things like this happening, but when it happens to folk you know . . .'

'Yes.'

'You've gone white as a sheet, Mrs Phipps. Would you like me to make you a cup of tea? Come into the back shop.'

'No, I'm all right.' Which she was, because she was numb, quite calm and cool, shocked beyond horror. She said, 'A funeral?'

'A couple of days ago. Here in the village. A huge turn-out. A real tribute.'

So she had missed even that chance to mourn and comfort. She said, 'And Oscar? Mr Blundell?'

'Hardly seen him. At the funeral, of course, but not since then. Kept to himself. Poor gentleman. It doesn't bear thinking what he's been through. What he's going through.'

She thought of Francesca laughing and teasing her father, playing duets with him on the piano, curled in his big armchair and reading a book with him. And then blotted the image from her mind, because it was unbearable to remember.

She said, 'Is he at the Grange?'

'Far as I know. The boy's been delivering milk and papers and so forth. Suppose he's just gone into himself. Natural, really. The Vicar went to call, but he didn't even want to see the Vicar. Mrs Muswell goes up to the Grange each day, just like she always did, but she says he just stays in his music room. She leaves a tray for his supper on the kitchen table, but she says most times he doesn't even touch it.'

'Do you think he would see me?'

'I wouldn't know, Mrs Phipps. Except that you and them were always friends.'

'I should have been here.'

'Not your fault, Mrs Phipps.' Someone else had come into the shop. Mrs Jennings put her spectacles on again, in a brave attempt to be businesslike. She said, 'I'll put these things through the till, shall I? It's nice to see you back. We've missed you. I feel I've spoiled your homecoming. I'm sorry.'

'Thank you for telling me. I'm glad it was you and not anybody else.'

She went out of the shop, got back into her car and sat there for a moment, feeling as though the day, her life, had been snapped into two pieces, could never be repaired and would never be the same again. She had moved from the laughter and happiness of Emblo into a place of loss and unthinkable pain. And what upset her most was that she had had no knowledge of the tragedy, no inkling, not a suspicion. For some reason, this made her feel guilty, as though she had reneged on responsibilities, stayed on at Emblo when she should have been here. In Dibton. With Oscar.

After a bit, heavy-hearted, she started up the engine and moved on. Bobby Burton-Jones had finished clipping his hedge and disappeared indoors, which was a relief because she didn't want to stop and talk to anybody. She drove down the main street of the village, passed by her own turning. As the houses thinned out, she came to the great gates of the Grange, the house that had been Gloria's. She turned in, up the drive, and around the curve where the huge cedar tree grew. She saw the elaborate face of the house, and outside the front door, a large black limousine upon the gravel.

She parked a little way off and got out, then saw that behind the wheel of this impressive vehicle there sat a uniformed driver, wearing his cap and reading a newspaper. Hearing her, he glanced up, acknowledged her presence with a nod then went back to his racing results. Clearly he was not expecting conversation. She left him there, went up the steps and through the open doorway into the familiar tiled porch. The half-glassed door was closed, and she did not ring the bell but opened this and went inside.

It was tremendously quiet, but for the tock of the long-case clock, snipping away at the passing seconds. She stood for a little, listening, hoping for comforting domestic sounds from the kitchen, or a thread of music from upstairs. Nothing. The silence was suffocating, like a fog.

To her right, the drawing-room door stood open. She crossed the hall, thick carpets blanketing her footfall, and went through. At first she thought the room was empty and she alone. And then she saw that a man sat in the wing chair by the empty fireplace. Tweed trouser-legs, polished brogues. Not much else was visible.

'Oscar,' she said, softly, and moved forward, to look down at him, and experienced the second stunning shock of that dreadful day. For here was Oscar, aged beyond belief, all at once an old man, bespectacled, wrinkled and hunched in the padded chair, a gnarled hand clenched over the ivory handle of an ebony stick. Instinctively her hand went to her mouth to stop a scream or, perhaps, to conceal her despair.

He looked up at her, and said, 'My word,' and instantly such relief flooded through her that she thought her legs were going to give way. Swiftly, before they did this, she sat with a thump on the padded leather seat of the club fender. They stared at each other. He went on, 'I never heard you coming in. Did you ring a bell? I'm a bit deaf, but I'd have heard the bell. I'd have come to the door ...'

He was not Oscar, aged beyond belief. He was another person, resembling Oscar but not Oscar. Maybe twenty or so years older than Oscar. An old gentleman well into his eighties, and speaking most courteously with a strong Scottish accent. His voice reminded her of a well-loved old doctor, who had looked after her when she was a small child. For some reason this made everything much easier to deal with.

'No,' she told him. 'I didn't ring the bell. I just walked in.'

'You'll forgive me not getting up. I'm a bit stiff and slow these days. Perhaps we should introduce ourselves. I am Hector McLellan. Oscar is my nephew.'

Hector McLellan, who had once owned Corrydale but now lived in London, and whose son Hughie had wiped the dust of Britain from the soles of his shoes and gone to live in Barbados.

She said, 'Oscar told me about you.'

'And you, my dear?'

'Elfrida Phipps. I have a house in the village. I live on my own. Gloria and Oscar were endlessly kind to me. I'm sorry I was so rude when I first came in. I thought you were Oscar, and then, of course, I realised my mistake.'

'Oscar, aged by grief?'

'Yes. I suppose so. You see, I haven't seen Oscar yet. I've been in Cornwall for a month with cousins. I've only just heard about everything from Mrs Jennings in the village shop. I went in to buy bread . . . and things. She told me.'

'Yes. A ghastly accident.'

'What happened?'

The old man shrugged. 'Gloria drove her car on to the roundabout, right into the teeth of this great articulated lorry.'

'You mean, she never saw it?'

'It was very dark. It had started to rain.'

'Mrs Jennings said she'd been to a party with Francesca. Fireworks and such.'

'That's so.'

Elfrida bit her lip. After a little, she said, 'Sometimes at the end of a party, she'd have a strong drink.' And immediately wished she hadn't said such a thing.

But the old man was unfazed. 'I know, my dear. We all knew. Sometimes she overdid it a wee bit. A dram too many at the end of a convivial evening. Hard to say no, perhaps. And then to drive home. Oscar knows this, better than any of us. He is consumed with guilt because he didn't take Francesca to the fireworks party himself. I think it never occurred to him that it was anything more than a children's party, that Gloria wouldn't bring Francesca straight home. But I suppose other parents were there, and it just went on. The rain started just before they set out. And then a momentary lapse of concentration, a confusion of lights, a heavy vehicle, a wet road . . .' He spread his hand in a gesture that said it all. 'Finished. All over. Lives wiped out.'

'I've even missed the funeral.'

'I missed it too. I had a touch of flu, my doctor forbade it. This is my first visit, though of course I wrote my letter of condolence and have been in touch over the

76

telephone. It was while I was speaking to Oscar that I became aware of his situation. So, as soon as I could, I made the journey down from London to talk things through. I am aged, but I am still his uncle. No doubt you saw my car and driver at the door.'

'Yes.' Elfrida frowned. 'You said "his situation". Does that have special meaning?'

'It most certainly does.'

'Am I allowed to be told?'

'No secret, my dear. Gloria has left everything, including this house, to her sons. The day after the funeral they presented themselves and told Oscar he could no longer live here because they intended selling.'

'And where do they imagine he's going to live?'

'They suggested some old folks' home. The Priory, I think it is called. They had brochures for him to read.' He added, with gentle irony, 'They had clearly thought of everything.'

'You mean, they're throwing him out? Into an old folks' home? *Oscar?* They must be mad.'

'No. I don't think they're actually insane, just avaricious and without heart. And they've got two hard wee wives as well, probably pushing from the back line to get every brass farthing they can lay their hands on.'

'Then Oscar must buy another house.'

Hector McLellan lowered his head and regarded Elfrida over the top of his spectacles. He said, 'Oscar is not a man of means.'

'You mean he has no money?'

'A pension, of course, and a little put by, but not enough to buy a decent house at these days' inflated prices.'

'Gloria's sons, Giles and Crawford, must know that.'

Another thought occurred to her. 'And Gloria must have known too. Surely she could have left Oscar *something*. She was so generous, so giving of worldly goods.'

'Maybe she intended to. She was a relatively young woman. In all likelihood it never occurred to her that she would die before Oscar. Or perhaps she simply never got around to making a new will, or even adding a codicil. We shall never know.'

'But he can't go and live in an old folks' home.' The very notion was an affront: Oscar, of all people, bundled in with a lot of incontinent geriatrics, eating milk puddings and being taught to make baskets. Elfrida's vision of an old folks' home was a little fuzzy because she had never been in one. She said firmly, 'I won't let it happen.'

'What will you do?'

'He can come and live with me.' But even as she said it she knew that this was an impractical suggestion. There was scarcely space for one at Poulton's Row, let alone two. And where would she put his grand piano? On the roof, or in the garden shed? 'That's stupid. No, he can't.'

'My notion,' said the old man, 'is that he should move away. This house, this village is too filled with poignant memory. I think he should cut loose. That's why I drove down today to see him. Mrs Muswell gave us lunch. I put forward my suggestion. But he seems unable to make any sort of decision. Doesn't seem to care what happens.'

'Where is he now?'

'He was called to the garden. Some problem with the greenhouse heating system. I said I would wait until he returned, then start back for London. Which is why you found me sitting here in my nephew's chair and looking, doubtless, like an old ghoul.'

'You don't look like an old ghoul, and what was *your* suggestion?'

'That he goes back to Sutherland for a bit. Corrydale, and the wee estate house. Half of it belongs to him anyway, and my Hughie, who is the co-owner, lives in Barbados and is likely to stay there.'

'I thought it was let. The house, I mean. Occupied.'

'No. At the moment, it's standing empty. An elderly couple called Cochrane were living there, but the old man died and the wife has gone to stay with her daughter. I discovered this from our erstwhile factor, Major Billicliffe. He's retired now but he still lives on the Corrydale estate. At the time of Hughie's big sale he bought the forester's house. I gave him a telephone call and we spoke at length. He says the place is in good condition, maybe needs a lick of paint but otherwise sound and dry.'

'Is it furnished?'

'It was a furnished let. There will be no frills, but the essentials of day-to-day living should be there.'

Elfrida thought this over. Sutherland. She imagined it: peat bogs and sheep. Remote as the moon. She said, 'It's a long way for Oscar to go, all on his own.'

'He's known at Corrydale and Creagan. He's family, his grandmother's grandson, my nephew. People are kindly. He will be remembered, even though he's not been back for fifty years.'

'But is he up to such an uprooting? Such upheaval? Why not return to London, and be near the church where he was organist? Wouldn't that be more sensible?'

'A regression. And one haunted, I should think, by memories of his child.'

'Yes, you're right.'

'And, saddest of all, he has abandoned his music. It's as though the best part of him has died.'

'How can I help?'

'That's up to you. A little gentle persuasion, perhaps?'

'I can try.' But she wondered where she was going to find the strength.

They fell silent, gazing sadly at each other. This silence was disturbed by the sound of approaching footsteps, the slow tread of a person crossing the gravel in front of the house. Elfrida raised her head and watched Oscar pass by the long window. All at once she was nervous. She got to her feet. 'He's coming now,' she said.

The front door opened and closed. They waited. A long pause. Then the knob turned, the drawing-room door swung open and he was there, standing, surveying the pair of them across the expanse of the thick carpet. He wore old corduroys and a heavy sweater, knitted and flecked like tweed. His thick white hair fell across his forehead, and he put up a hand to push it aside. She had imagined him diminished, felled by tragedy. But heartbreak is a hidden thing, and Oscar was a private man.

'Elfrida. I knew you had come because I saw your little car.'

She went to meet him, and he took her hands in his own, and leaned forward to kiss her cheek. His lips were icy against her skin. She looked into his eyes. 'Dear Oscar. I'm home again.'

'How long have you been here?'

'About fifteen minutes. I drove up from Cornwall this morning. I went into the shop and Mrs Jennings told me. I hadn't known. I haven't read a newspaper for a month. So I came straight here and walked in on your uncle.'

'I see.' He let go of her hands, and turned to Hector, who sat in his chair and watched their reunion. 'I am sorry I kept you waiting, Hector. There were complications. Something to do with a trip switch. But you have had Elfrida for company.'

'And very pleasant it has been, too. Now, I must be on my way.' Which entailed something of a struggle, the old man leaning on his stick and endeavouring to rise from the chair. Oscar moved forward to lend a hand and, after some effort on both their parts, got his uncle to his feet, supported by his stick, and prepared for departure.

They all moved, at the old gentleman's pace, across the big room and through to the hall. There, Oscar helped him into his old-fashioned overcoat and handed him his aged brown trilby. Hector put this on at a rakish angle.

'It was good of you to come, Hector. I really appreciate it. Splendid to see you.'

'Dear boy. Thank you for lunch. And if you're in town, drop in.'

'Of course.'

'And give thought to my suggestion. It may seem a little drastic, but it would at least give you a breather. You mustn't stay here.' It was then that he remembered something and began groping in the pocket of his overcoat. 'Nearly forgot. Wrote it down for you. Billicliffe's telephone number. All you have to do is give him a ring; he's got the key of your house.' He withdrew from the pocket a scrap of folded paper and handed it over. 'Only thing is,' he added, with a dry twinkle in his rheumy old eyes, 'don't leave it too late in the day. He's inclined to hit the whisky bottle and doesn't make much sense after that.'

But Elfrida was concerned by other, more practical matters. 'How long has the house stood empty?'

'Couple of months. But there's a Mrs Snead who's been going in and out, keeping the place cleaned and aired. Billicliffe arranged that, but I've been paying her wages. Doesn't do to let property disintegrate.'

'You seem,' Elfrida told him, 'to have thought of everything.'

'Haven't much else to think about, these days. Now I must be off. Goodbye, my dear. I have much enjoyed meeting you. I hope, one day, we'll be able to renew our acquaintance.'

'I hope so too. We'll come with you to the car.'

Oscar put a hand beneath Hector's elbow, and they all proceeded out through the front door and down the steps on to the gravel. The afternoon had turned chilly, and a thin rain threatened. The chauffeur, seeing them, got out of the big car, and went round to hold open the door of the passenger seat. With some effort on all sides, Hector was loaded into this and his safety-belt fastened.

'Goodbye, Oscar, dear boy. My thoughts are with you.'

Oscar embraced the old man. 'Thank you again for coming, Hector.'

'I only hope I've been a wee bit of comfort.'

'You have.' He stepped back and closed the door. The car started up. Hector waved a bent old hand, and they stood and watched him go, borne off to London at a suitably dignified pace. They stayed until the car was out of sight, and they could no longer hear the engine.

The ensuing silence was filled by the cawing of rooks. It was cold and damp. Elfrida shivered.

Oscar said, 'Come indoors.'

'Are you sure you don't want me to go as well?'

'No. I don't want you to go. I want you to stay with me.'

'Is Mrs Muswell here?'

'She leaves each day after lunch.'

'Would you like me to make us a cup of tea?'

'I think that would be an excellent idea.'

'May I bring Horace indoors? He's been shut in the car all day.'

'Of course. He's safe now. There are no pekineses to attack him.'

Elfrida thought, Oh, God. She went across the gravel to where her little car was parked and set Horace free. Gratefully he leaped out and shot off across the lawn to a handy laurel bush, beneath which he relieved himself at length. When he was done with this necessary operation, he scratched about for a bit, then returned to them. Oscar stooped and fondled his head, and only then did they all go back into the house. Oscar closed the door behind them and led the way into the kitchen, where it felt comfortingly warm. Gloria's kitchen, large and efficient, from which such copious amounts of delicious food had appeared to sate the appetites of so many relations and friends. Now it was empty, and very neat, and Elfrida saw that Mrs Muswell had left a tray with a single mug, a milk jug and a tin of biscuits on the table. She was clearly doing her best to feed and care for her solitary employer.

She found the kettle, filled it and put it on the Aga to boil. She turned to face Oscar, leaning against the comforting warmth of the stove. She said, 'I wish I was articulate and brilliant at thinking of things to say, but I'm not, Oscar. I'm sorry. I just wish I'd known. I would have come back from Cornwall. I would at least have been at the funeral.'

He had pulled out a chair and sat now at the kitchen table. As she spoke he put his elbows on the table and buried his face in his hands. For a dreadful moment, she thought that he was weeping. She heard herself, rabbiting on, 'For some reason, I never even looked at a newspaper, for the whole month I never read a newspaper. I had no inkling. Until today . . .'

Slowly, he drew his hands from his face, and she saw that he did not weep, but his eyes were filled with an anguish that was almost worse than tears. He said, 'I would have been in touch, but I had no idea where you were.'

'That was because I had no idea that you might need to know.' She took a deep breath. 'Oscar, I *do* know about loss and bereavement. All the time that Jimbo was so ill I knew it was terminal, that he would never recover. But when he died, I found myself quite unprepared for the pain and the terrible emptiness. And I know, too, that what I went through then is simply one tiny fraction of what you are going through now. And there is nothing I can do to help, to ease you.'

'You are here.'

'If you want to talk, I can listen.'

'Not yet.'

'I know. Too early. Too soon.'

'The Vicar called very soon after the accident. Very soon after I had been told that both Gloria and Francesca were dead. He tried to comfort, and mentioned God, and I found myself wondering if he had taken leave of his senses. You asked me once if I was religious, and I don't think I was able to answer your question. I only knew that my music and my work and my choirs meant more to me than any churchly dogma. The *Te Deum*. Do you remember my first dinner party at the Grange, when we strolled around the garden, you said that you had particularly enjoyed a certain setting of the *Te Deum*? The words, and that music, once filled me with a certainty of goodness, and perhaps eternity.

> *"We praise thee, oh Lord. We acknowledge thee to be the Lord.*
>
> *All the earth doth worship thee, the Father Everlasting."*

Thundering away on the organ, pulling out all the stops, hearing the boys' voices soar to the rafters. That was when I truly believed, when I knew a faith that I thought nothing could rock.'

He fell silent. She waited. After a bit, she said, 'And now, Oscar?'

'It was all to do with God. And I cannot believe in a God who would take Francesca away from me. I sent the Vicar home. He departed, I think, in some umbrage.'

Elfrida was sympathetic. 'Poor man.'

'He will survive, no doubt. The kettle's boiling.'

It was a welcome interruption. Elfrida busied herself finding the teapot, the tea, spooning tea, pouring the boiling water. She found another mug for herself, and carried everything over to the table and sat facing Oscar, just as they had sat that day, an eternity ago, before she went to Cornwall, in her little house in Poulton's Row, Oscar with gardening mud on his boots.

'You like builders' tea, don't you?'

'Strong and black.'

She poured her own mug and left the pot to stew. She said, 'Hector told me about your stepsons and the house. About selling it, I mean.'

'They think that I should book into the Priory, a Victorian mansion converted for the benefit of desiccated gentlefolk.'

'You won't go there.'

'I admit, I would rather not.'

'What do you want to do?'

'I would like to be left alone, to lick my wounds. But I can't be left alone *here*, because Giles and Crawford want me out of the way so that they can put the house on the market as soon as possible.'

'Brutes.' She poured his tea, black as ink, and pushed the mug towards him. He reached for the jug, added some milk and drank.

She said, 'Hector McLellan told me his suggestion.'

'I had a suspicion he might have.'

'Is it such a bad idea?'

'Elfrida, it's mad.'

'I don't see why.'

'Then I'll tell you why. Because Sutherland is the other end of the country and I haven't been there for fifty years. For all Hector's optimism, I should not know a single soul. The house will be half empty and hasn't been lived in for weeks. I am not a naturally domesticated animal. I wouldn't know how to start to make it habitable. And who would I turn to?'

'Mrs Snead?'

'Elfrida.'

It was a reproach, but Elfrida persisted. 'Is it very isolated? Your house, I mean.'

'No. It's in the middle of Creagan, the little town.'

It sounded to Elfrida perfectly suitable. 'Is it horrid?' she asked.

'Horrid,' he repeated. 'What words you use. No. It's simply a large, square, undistinguished Victorian dwelling. Not actually ugly, but not blessed with redeeming features. And it has a garden, but that's not much joy in the middle of winter.'

'It won't always be winter.'

'It's just that I can't imagine what the hell I would do with myself.'

'Well, one thing's for sure. You can't stay here, Oscar. And you go into the Priory over my dead body. So you must consider any available alternative. You could come and live with me at Poulton's Row, but as you know there is scarcely space for me and Horace in that little cottage.' Oscar made no comment on this wild suggestion. 'I thought perhaps you'd like to go back to London, but Hector said no.'

'He's right.'

'Scotland,' she mused. 'Sutherland. It would at least be a fresh start.'

'I am sixty-seven and, at the moment, in no shape to start anything. Also, although I can scarcely bear to speak to anyone, I still dread being alone. Solitary. Living alone is the worst. Empty rooms. Even before I married Gloria, there were always colleagues, choristers, schoolboys, a whole world of lively company. My life was full.'

'It can be again.'

'No.'

'Yes, Oscar, it can. Never the same, I know. But you have so much to give people. A generosity of spirit. We mustn't waste it.'

He frowned. 'You said "we".'

'A slip of the tongue. I meant *you*.'

Oscar had finished his tea and the mug stood empty. He reached out for the teapot and poured himself a refill, the tea blacker than ever and singularly unappetising.

'Supposing I went to Scotland. How would I travel so far?'

'There are planes and trains.'

'I would want my car.'

'Then drive. You're in no hurry. Take it in stages . . .'

Elfrida heard her voice drift into silence, and found herself unable to finish her sentence. Because the image of Oscar setting off by himself on such a journey into the unknown filled her with desolation. Gloria should be there beside him to share the driving, Francesca in the back with her computer games and her ingenuous chat. And in the boot of the big car, the two yapping pekes, included in the holiday, along with golf clubs and fishing rods . . .

All gone. Dead. Never again.

He saw her distress, put out his hand and laid it over her own. 'You have to be brave, Elfrida, otherwise I shall go to pieces.'

'I'm trying. But I can't bear it for you.'

'Suppose . . . suppose we discuss your idea. Suppose I went. Drove to Scotland, to Sutherland. If I made that journey, would you come with me?'

She was silenced; could think of nothing to say. She stared into his face, wondering if she had heard aright; if he really had made that extraordinary proposal, or whether, confused by shock and sadness, her imagination had made it all up.

'Come with you?'

'Why not? Is it such a bad idea? To go together? Somehow we'll get there. We shall collect the key from Major Billicliffe, find my house, take possession and spend the winter there.'

'Christmas?'

'No Christmas. Not this year. Would that be so bad? It's so far north that the days will be short and the nights long and dark, and I probably won't be a very lively companion. But by spring, perhaps, I shall be stronger. Time will have passed. Here, as you so clearly stated, I have no future. Giles and Crawford want the house, so I shall let them have it. With all convenient speed.'

'And my house, Oscar? What should I do with my little cottage?'

'Let it. Or shut it up. It will be safe. Your neighbours, I'm sure, will keep an eye on it.'

He meant it. He was asking her to go away with him. He wanted her. Needed her. She, Elfrida. Eccentric, disorganised, not beautiful any longer; even a little raffish. And sixty-two years old.

'Oscar, I'm not sure that I'm that good a bet.'

'You underestimate yourself. Please come, Elfrida. Help me.'

How can I help? she had asked Hector, as they waited for Oscar to return from the glass-houses. And now it was Oscar who had answered the question.

She had been impulsive all her life, made decisions without thought for the future and regretted none of them, however dotty. Looking back, all she regretted were the opportunities missed, either because they had come along at the wrong time or because she had been too timid to grasp them.

She took a deep breath. 'All right. I'll come.'

'Dear girl.'

'I'll come for *you*, Oscar, but I owe it to Gloria as well. I shall never forget her kindness and generosity to a stranger. You and Gloria and Francesca were my first friends when I came to Dibton . . .'

'Go on.'

'I feel ashamed. We've been talking, and this is the first time I've said their names to you. In Cornwall I spoke about you so much. Telling Jeffrey about you all, telling him how good you'd been to me. I went shopping and bought Francesca a book, and I very nearly bought a picture for you and Gloria, but then I thought that Gloria wouldn't really like it.'

'Would I have liked it?'

'I don't know.' A lump had swelled in her throat, and it became difficult to talk. She was crying, and could feel her mouth trembling, but the tears, strangely, were something of a relief, warm and wet, rolling down her cheeks. Old people, she told herself, look dreadful when they cry. She tried to wipe the tears away with her fingers. 'I – I've only been to Scotland once. To Glasgow, ages ago, with a touring company. We had pathetic audiences and it never stopped raining . . .' Fumbling up her sleeve for a handkerchief she found one and blew her nose. '. . . and I couldn't understand a single word anyone said to me.'

'There's Glaswegian for you.'

'It wasn't funny at the time.'

'It's not funny now, but as always you've made me smile.'

'Like a sort of clown?

'No. Not a clown. Just a dear, funny friend.'

Sam

Sam

 At seven o'clock on the first dark Friday morning of December, Sam Howard wheeled his trolley of luggage out into the arrivals hall of Heathrow Airport. Beyond the barrier crowded the usual confusion of people come to meet the plane: elderly couples, youths in trainers, and tired mothers humping toddlers; also uniformed drivers for the VIPs – of which Sam was not one – and unidentified men holding up mysterious notices, written in capitals. MR WILSON was one; and ABDUL AZIZ CONSOLIDATED TRADERS another.

There was nobody to meet Sam. No wife, no driver. No welcome, however tame. He knew that outside the heated terminal building it would be very cold; partly because they had been warned of the temperature in London before the plane landed, but also because everybody was bundled up in padded jackets, gloves, scarves and woollen hats. It had been cold in New York, but a dry crisp cold that stimulated, with a bitter wind blowing up the East river, and all the flags at mastheads flying stiff and square in the teeth of its blast.

His trolley was awkward, laden with two suitcases, a huge American golf-bag and his briefcase. He manoeuvred it towards the automatic exit doors and out into the wet black cold of an English winter morning. There, he joined the queue for taxis. He had only to wait five minutes or so, but that was long enough to freeze the soles of his feet. The taxi was covered, for some reason, in simulated newsprint, and the driver a morose man with a walrus moustache. Sam hoped that he was not a talker. He was not in the mood for conversation.

'Where to, guv?'

'Wandsworth, please. SW seventeen. Fourteen Beauly Road.'

''Op in.'

The driver did not stir himself to help with the luggage, apparently having decided that Sam was young and fit enough to deal with it himself. Accordingly, he humped it aboard, stowed the golf-clubs on the floor, shoved the empty trolley out of the line of trouble and climbed in, slamming the door behind him. The taxi, windscreen wipers going full tilt, trundled forward.

The short wait had chilled him. Sam turned up the collar of his navy blue overcoat and leaned back against the fusty plastic of his seat. He yawned. He felt tired and unclean. He had travelled club with a number of businessmen, but before landing the others had made discreet trips to the lavatory to wash, shave, knot ties and generally freshen themselves up. Probably, poor sods, they had early meetings. He did not have an early meeting and was grateful for this. His first appointment was for Monday at twelve thirty when he had to present himself at White's for lunch with Sir David Swinfield, chairman of Sturrock & Swinfield, and Sam's ultimate boss. Until then, his time was his own.

He yawned again, and ran a hand over the raspy stubble of his chin. Perhaps he *should* have shaved. He would have felt a little less like a vagrant. It occurred to him that he probably looked like one too, dressed as he was in elderly casual clothes: a thick pullover, a pair of worn jeans and boat shoes. His eyes were dry and gritty from lack of sleep, but that was because he had spent the short night reading his book. And his stomach was slightly queasy, but that was doubtless the result of eating a huge meal at two o'clock in the morning, UK time.

The taxi drew up at a red traffic light. Suddenly the driver spoke, flinging the question back over his shoulder.

'Been on 'oliday?'

'No,' Sam told him.

'Fort . . . you know . . . the golf-clubs.'

'No, I haven't been on holiday.'

'On business, then?'

'You could say. I've worked in New York for six years.'

'Blimey. 'Ow do you stand the pace?'

'It's OK. Good. You get used to it.'

Rain streamed down. 'Not much of a mornin' for comin' 'ome.' Green light. They moved forward again.

'No,' Sam agreed. He did not add, And I'm not coming home. Right now, he did not have a home, which seemed to figure with the vagrant image. For the first time in his life, and he was now thirty-nine, he found himself without bricks and mortar to call his own.

Bundled gloomily in his overcoat, cocooned in the back of the taxi, he thought of homes, remembering to the very beginning, Yorkshire and Radley Hill where, an only child, he had been born and brought up. A large, solid, comforting family home, filled with the smell of woodsmoke, spring flowers, and cakes baking. The house was surrounded by four acres of land, and there was a tennis court and a little wood, where on autumn evenings he would stand with his gun, waiting for the pigeons to fly in from the stubble fields. To Radley Hill he had returned from day-school, and then boarding-school, usually with a friend in tow, to spend the holidays. It was a place, comfortable as an old tweed jacket, which he had thought would never change, but of course it did. Because, during his last year at Newcastle University, his mother died, and after that nothing was ever quite the same again.

The family business was a small woollen mill, in a small Yorkshire town. After Newcastle, Sam had intended to spread his wings, perhaps get a job abroad, but with his mother gone he hadn't the heart to abandon his father and, with a degree in engineering under his belt, he went home to Yorkshire, to Radley Hill and the mill. For a few years, father and son boxed along happily together, and business boomed. But then recession hit, and the mill, which specialised in fine worsteds and lightweight tweeds, came up against sophisticated competition from Europe, an influx of imports and a cash-flow problem. At the end of the day, Sturrock & Swinfield, the huge textile conglomerate, based in London, moved in. The little mill was taken over. Sam was given a job under the new umbrella, but his father, too old a dog to learn new tricks, took early retirement. But digging his garden and playing the odd game of golf was not enough to fend off the stress of loneliness, boredom and enforced inactivity, and he died twelve months later of a massive heart-attack.

Radley Hill was left to Sam. After some heart-searching, he put it on the market. It seemed the only sensible thing to do for he was now London-based, still working for Sturrock & Swinfield, and wise to all the ups and downs of fluctuating markets and the business of woollen broking. With the money he got for Radley Hill, he was able to buy his first property, a garden flat in Eel Park Common, so close to the tube station that at night he could hear the rattling of the trains. But it had a scrap of garden that caught the evening sun, and once he had furnished it with some of the smaller stuff from the old house in Yorkshire, it felt familiar and homely. He had been happy there, living a carefree bachelor life, and in memory it was always sunlit and filled with friends. There had been countless impromptu parties when the rooms overflowed and guests ended up sitting on the tiny terrace, and crowded winter weekends when old colleagues from the north came down for rugger matches at Twickenham. And, of course, a number of poignant love affairs.

He was in the throes of one of these when, out of the blue, came a summons from Sir David Swinfield. There, in the prestigious high-rise office, far above the maze of the City of London, Sam was told that he was being transferred to the United States, to New York. The head of the New York office, Mike Passano, had particularly asked for him. It was promotion, responsibility, a rise in salary.

'No reason not to go, Sam?'

New York. He said, 'No, sir,' which was true. No family ties, no wife, no children. Nothing that could not be abandoned. 'No reason.' It was the opportunity for which he had subconsciously yearned ever since university. A new job, a new city, a new country. A new life.

He took the current love affair out to dinner and tried to explain, and she cried a bit and said that, if he wanted, she'd come to New York with him. But he knew that wasn't what he wanted. Feeling a heel, he told her this, and she cried some more, and when it was time to go, he found a taxi for her and put her into it and watched it drive away. He never saw her again.

He was equally ruthless about material possessions. A chunk of his life was over and he had no idea when, if ever, he would return to London. Accordingly, he sold his car and his flat, putting only a few favourite pieces of furniture, pictures and books into store. At the office, he cleared his desk. Someone threw a leaving party, and he was able to say goodbye to all his friends.

'Don't stay too long,' they told him, 'Come back soon.'

But New York waited and, once arrived, he was seduced by all he found. He took to the place like a duck to water, relishing every aspect of the stimulating, cosmopolitan melting-pot that made up the city. Home, there, was a walk-up in Greenwich Village, but after he married Deborah, she persuaded him to move and they ended up in a fancy duplex on East 70th Street. He had always enjoyed the challenge of a new home, new surroundings, doing a bit of painting, shunting furniture around and hanging pictures. But Deborah didn't much want any of the old Greenwich Village stuff in her beautiful new apartment and, anyway, she had engaged the services of an interior designer who would *die* if that sagging old leather sofa was integrated into his string-coloured décor. There were a few spats, but not too many because Sam usually gave in and he was quite happy to have the old leather sofa in his den where he kept his computer and his fax machine. It felt friendly there, and sometimes, at weekends, when Deborah thought he was working overtime, he could lie on the leather sofa and watch football on television.

Homes. East 70th Street had been the last and that, too, had gone. Along with Deborah.

She had never been a moral coward. She told him, face to face, that she was leaving. She was tired of playing second fiddle to Sturrock & Swinfield, tired of being married to a workaholic. There was, of course, another man, and when she told Sam his name he was both appalled and filled with anxiety for her future. He said as much, but Deborah was adamant. It was too late. Her mind was made up. He could not persuade her.

He was furious, but he was hurt too, bewildered and abased. He thought of that old-fashioned word, 'cuckold'. *I am a cuckold. I have been cuckolded.*

And yet, in a way, he understood.

The morning after her departure he walked into the office and was met with covert glances and sympathetic faces. Some colleagues were over-hearty, slapping him chummily on the shoulder, letting him know they were his buddies, there if he needed them.

Others, who had never particularly liked Sam, the Limey, showed signs of snide amusement, resembling cats that had got at the cream. He realised then that probably they had all had a fair idea of what was going on, and Sam, the leading actor in the drama, was the last to know.

During the course of the day Mike Passano appeared,

breezing through the open door and coming to perch on the edge of Sam's desk. For a bit they talked day-to-day business, then Mike said, 'I'm sorry. About Debbie, I mean. Just wanted to let you know.'

'Thanks.'

'It's cold comfort, but at least you haven't got kids to complicate matters.'

'Yeah.'

'If you want to come over for dinner one evening . . .'

'I'm OK, Mike.'

'Right. Well. You can always take a raincheck.'

He soldiered on for six weeks. At the office he found every excuse to stay at his desk long after the others had left, returning late to an empty apartment and no food. Sometimes he stopped off at a bar and had a sandwich and a Scotch. Or two Scotches. For the first time in his life he suffered from insomnia, and during the day found himself pervaded by an unfamiliar restlessness, as though not only his marriage but everything else had gone stale.

Mike Passano said, 'Take a vacation,' but that was the last thing Sam wanted. Instead, slowly, it was borne upon him that he had had enough of New York. He wanted England. He wanted to go home. He wanted misty skies and temperate green fields and warm beer and red buses.

And then one evening, at the nadir of his despair, the telephone rang in the apartment, and it was Sir David Swinfield from London.

'Is this a good time to talk, Sam?'

'As good as any.'

'Hear things aren't running too smoothly for you.'

'Bad news travels fast.'

'Mike Passano told me. Had a word this morning. I'm sorry.'

'Thank you.'

'Do you feel like a change?'

Sam was cautious. 'What did you have in mind?'

'New idea. New project. Right up your street. Might be interesting.'

'Where?'

'UK.'

'You mean leave New York?'

'You've had six years. I'll square it with Mike.'

'Who'd take over?'

'Lowell Oldberg?'

'He's inexperienced.'

'So were you.'

He had to get it right. 'Is this demotion?' Sam asked bluntly.

'No. Just a shunt. Upwards and onwards.' A pause. 'I want you back, Sam. I need you. I think it's time.'

The house in Beauly Road was a semi-detached three-storey Victorian villa, set back from the pavement by a front garden that had been turned into a paved carport. The rest of the quiet residential road was lined on both sides with cars, indication of the affluence of the district. There were trees as well, bare now but which in summer and full leaf would give a country illusion, suggesting a pleasant suburb far from the City of London.

On that black morning it was still dark. As Sam, surrounded by his baggage, paid off the taxi, the front door of the house opened, letting forth a stream of light, and a burly masculine figure appeared. 'Sam.' Semi-prepared for his day in the City, Neil Philip wore the trousers of a business suit and an enveloping navy blue polo-necked sweater. He came down the path and through the gate. 'God, it's good to see you.'

And Sam felt himself swept up into a huge embrace, because Neil had never been a man to be shy about showing emotion. It was a bit like being hugged by a bear. The taxi driver, still expressionless, trundled away, and Neil stooped and scooped up the two enormously heavy suitcases, then charged back towards the open door, leaving Sam to hump the golf-clubs and his briefcase.

'Janey's just getting the kids organised, she'll be down in a moment. Did you have a good flight? Bloody exhausted, probably.' He dumped the suitcases at the foot of the stairs. 'The kettle's on, would you like a cup of coffee?'

'Love one.'

'Come on, then.'

Sam shed his overcoat and draped it over the banister. From upstairs he heard a child's voice complaining about something. A pair of small gumboots and a toy lorry sat side by side on one of the stairs. He followed Neil down the passage into a spacious family kitchen with a skylight and windows over the sink. The curtains were still closed, but overhead he could see the dark clouds, stained with reflected light. There were pine cupboards and a humming fridge, and the table was set for breakfast: a checked tablecloth, packets of cereal, a milk jug, egg cups.

Neil spooned coffee into a jug and poured on boiling water. The delicious, fresh aroma filled the room. 'Do you want something to eat?'

'No, just coffee.'

Sam pulled out a chair and took the weight off

his feet. He could not imagine why he felt so weary, considering that he had been sitting down for at least seven hours. 'You're looking terrific, Neil.'

'Oh, not so bad. Surviving family life.' He found bread and put two slices into an electric toaster. 'You've never seen this house, have you? We bought it a couple of years after you went to New York. Upgrading, Janey called it. And we needed a garden for the children.'

'Remind me.'

'Sorry?'

'Ages. Daisy and Leo. One loses track.'

'Daisy's ten, Leo six. They're wildly excited about you staying. Been talking about it ever since your phone call. How long can you stay?'

'It's not a holiday, Neil. Business. I've been summoned by the chairman. Some new project.'

'Goodbye to New York?'

'For the time being.'

'Sam, I'm so sorry about Deborah and everything.'

'We'll talk about it, but not now. There's too much to say.'

'Let's weave our way down to the pub this evening and you can spill it all out over a pint. But remember, you're welcome here for as long as you like.'

'You're more than kind.'

'It's my nature, old boy, it's my nature.'

The toast popped and Neil removed it from the toaster, then put another couple of slices in. Sam watched him, the neat and precise movements of a large and apparently ungainly man. Neil still had a head of thick dark hair, but there showed a sprinkling of grey. He had put on weight as well, as athletic men tend to do, but otherwise nothing much else seemed to have changed.

Neil Philip was part of Sam's life. They had been friends ever since they met on their first day at boarding-school, two apprehensive new boys feeling their way into the system. Neil was one of the regular visitors at Radley Hill for the holidays, and Sam's mother had ended up calling him her second son. When Sam went to Newcastle, Neil went to Edinburgh University, where he played rugby like a fanatic and spent one brilliant season as fly-half for Scotland. After university, meeting up again in London in the Eel Park Common days, it was as though there had simply been a pause in the conversation. When Neil married Janey, at St Paul's, Knightsbridge, Sam had been their best man. And when Sam married Deborah, in the garden of her grandparents' house in East Hampton, Neil and Janey had flown out to be with him so that Neil could be best man to Sam. Sam was deeply grateful because, otherwise, the bridegroom had been sadly short of family, friends or relations.

Neil poured coffee and put eggs on to boil. From upstairs, voices grew louder, then there were scurrying feet on the stairs and the two children erupted into the kitchen, Daisy dressed in her school uniform and Leo wearing jeans and a pullover. They stood, staring at the stranger.

Sam said, 'Hi.'

They were silent, all at once overcome.

'Say hi back,' Neil told them.

Leo said, 'I fort you'd be wearing a cowboy hat.'

'They don't wear cowboy hats in New York, silly,' his sister squashed him.

'Well, what do they wear?'

'They probably don't wear anything.'

'Who doesn't wear anything?' Janey came through

the door, dressed much as her little son, and her arms were held wide, all ready for her welcome. 'Oh, Sam, it's been too long. It's so heavenly to see you.' He stood, and she hugged and kissed him. 'God, you haven't shaved, you brute.'

'I was too idle.'

'It's been such ages since we saw you. I do hope you can stay for ever. Daisy, you're never going to eat all those Coco Pops, put some of them into Leo's bowl.'

The house was quiet, its owners gone: Neil to his daily grind, Janey to take the children to school. Sam had been shown his bedroom and his bathroom. He had a relaxing bath and shaved, then, bundled into the towel robe he had found on the back of the bathroom door, he fell into bed. It was light now. Through the window he could see the lacy branches of a plane tree. Cars passed, swishing down the road. Far overhead, a jet moved across the sky. He slept.

It rained for most of that weekend, but Monday morning was dry, with even a few clear patches of sky blinking in and out beyond the sailing clouds. After watching a soggy football match on Saturday, organising a long wet walk in Richmond Park on Sunday, and playing a Monopoly marathon after tea-time, Neil inspected the clear morning, said, with faint bitterness, 'Sod's law,' and left for work.

The children were next to go, picked up by a neighbour and taken to school. A Jamaican lady appeared to push the vacuum cleaner around the house, and Janey went off to shop. 'Do you want a key?' she asked Sam. 'I'll be in after four o'clock.'

'In that case, I don't need a key.'

'When will you be *back*?'

'No idea.'

'Well,' she smiled up into his face, gave him a quick kiss, 'good luck.'

Sam was not far behind her, suitably attired for the important occasion, buttoned into his overcoat and armed with an umbrella of Neil's in case of unexpected downpours. He closed the front door on the strains of the cleaning lady singing hymns as she scoured the bath. At twenty-five past twelve he walked up St James's Street, presented himself to the porter at White's and asked for Sir David Swinfield. Sir David was in the bar, he was told, and expecting a guest.

It was three thirty before they emerged from the club, descending the steps to the pavement where Sir David's car and driver waited. Sir David offered a lift, which Sam politely refused. They parted, and he stood and watched as the great black saloon slid out into the stream of traffic and disappeared in the direction of Piccadilly.

Sam turned and set out to walk, at least part of the way, back to Wandsworth. He went by way of Green Park, and Belgrave Square, Sloane Street, and the King's Road. By now, the day had died and the street-lights come on, and shop windows shone and glittered with all the paraphernalia of Christmas decoration and seductive consumerism. He found himself astonished by this: so turned in had he been upon himself that he had forgotten about Christmas. The months, lagging in some respects, had shot past in others. Christmas. He had no idea where he would be for Christmas, and could think of no one who would be expecting a present from him, which was a bleak truth, and brought no credit upon himself.

However, the thought of presents galvanised him into action and he went into a flower shop and bought a huge bouquet of white lilies for Janey; a little further on, he paused at a wine shop, bought cognac and a bottle of champagne for Neil. Burdened, he thought about the children, Daisy and Leo. They should have presents too, but he couldn't think what on earth they would like. He would have to ask them. Having already spent two days in their company, he was pretty sure they would know.

By World's End, he had expended his energy and it had started to rain again. It was now nearly five o'clock and the traffic at its most dense, crawling along at the pace of a snail, but after five minutes or so, he picked up a cab, and gave the driver the address. It took an incredibly long time to get across Wandsworth Bridge, and when they finally trundled up the length of Beauly Road, he saw the lights shining from behind the drawn curtains of number fourteen, and felt welcomed, as though he were coming home.

When he rang the bell, Janey came to let him in. 'There you are. I thought you'd got lost.'

She wore her jeans and a red pullover, and her dark hair was bundled up and fixed with a tortoiseshell clip.

'I've been taking exercise.'

Janey closed the door. 'One would have thought a wet Sunday in Richmond Park might have lasted the week. How did you get on? Lunch with the chairman, I mean.'

'It was all right. I'll tell you but not at this moment.' He handed her the lilies. 'These are for you. A house present for a kind hostess.'

'Thank you. You didn't have to bring me flowers, but I'm glad you did. And lilies. They make the whole house smell like heaven. Come into the kitchen and I'll make you a cup of tea.'

Pausing to take off his coat and hang it up on a peg along with a lot of small overcoats and anoraks, he followed her, hefting the carrier-bag with the bottles. He put the brandy into Neil's wine cupboard and the champagne in the fridge.

'Champagne.' Janey was filling the kettle, plugging it in. 'Does that mean a celebration?'

'Maybe.' He pulled out a chair and sat with his elbows on the table. 'Where are Daisy and Leo?'

'Upstairs, watching television or playing computer games. They're allowed to, once they've done their homework.'

'Delicious smells in this kitchen.'

'It's dinner. I have gloomy news. We have another guest.'

'What's so gloomy about another guest?'

'This one's a pain.'

'Why ask him?'

'I didn't. He asked himself. He's an old acquaintance of my parents, and he's in London on his own and he's at a loose end. He telephoned and sounded pathetic, so I felt I had to invite him. I'm really sorry because I wanted it to be just us three. I've already told Neil. I rang him at the office, and he's livid, but he's going to try to get home a bit early to do the drinks, lay the table and light the fire.'

'I could do all that for you.'

'You're the guest. You have to go and have a shower and a rest and make yourself beautiful.'

'I suppose to impress your unwanted friend.' Janey made a face. 'Come on, what's so gruesome about him?'

She had found a large flowered ewer, filled it with water and was now engaged in arranging her lilies.

'He's not *really* gruesome. Just a bit boring. Likes to be thought of as an old *roué*. When he's around, one instinctively whisks one's behind out of reach of his fingers.'

Sam laughed. 'One of those.'

'You could say so. He's been married three times but he's on his own right now.'

'Where does he come from?'

'I think he was at school with my pa, but now he lives in the Bahamas or Barbados or somewhere. He's been out there for ages.'

'What's he doing in London?'

'Not sure. *En route* for France, I think. He's going to spend Christmas in Nice.'

'He sounds interesting.'

'He isn't. There. Those look lovely. Thank you again. I'll put them, pride of place, in the sitting room.' The kettle boiled and she reached for the teapot. 'I'm longing to hear about today, but I can't concentrate when I'm cooking, and I've still got to make a pudding.'

'It can wait.'

'It was all right, Sam? It was good?'

'Yes. *I* think so.'

'How exciting. I *am* pleased.'

He drank his tea, and then, shooed out of her kitchen by Janey, went upstairs. He found Daisy and Leo in their playroom. They had switched off the television and were sitting at a battered table littered with sheets of paper, which they seemed to be in the process of cutting up. As well as scissors, they had assembled tubes of glue, felt pens, a ball of coloured string and a few scraps of gauzy ribbon. Some form of handcraft was clearly taking place.

They looked up. 'Hello, Sam.'

'Hi. What are you up to?'

'We're making Christmas cards,' Daisy told him importantly. 'My art teacher showed us today, and I'm teaching Leo. You paint glue and then spill glitter and it sticks. But we've got to draw something first.'

'What like?'

'Well, a Christmas tree. Or a stocking. Or a house with lighted windows. The only thing is it's a bit messy, and the glitter gets everywhere. Leo calls it tinkle. Now, Leo, you fold the paper like this, very neatly ... it mustn't be all skew-wiff ...'

It was made obvious that they were in no need of his help. He left them, and went to his room, stripped off his clothes and took a shower.

Have a shower and rest and make yourself beautiful. He had brought *The Times* upstairs with him, and after his shower he put on the towelling robe and collapsed on his bed, intending to read it. But concentration drifted, and he let the paper slip to the floor, and simply lay, staring at the ceiling. Sounds emanated from beyond the closed door. The children's voices; a telephone ringing; Janey's footsteps as she went to answer it. 'Hello,' he heard her say. He caught the mouthwatering smell of dinner being prepared, and later heard taps turned on for the children's bath.

It was a long time since he had been embraced into the bosom of a proper family, felt so cherished and wanted. Investigating this line of thought he realised that Deborah's withdrawal had started months before her announcement that she was leaving, but Sam had been too preoccupied to notice the gradual erosion of their relationship. The break-up of a marriage, he knew, could never be one partner's fault. The other half, one way or another, had to shoulder some part of the blame.

He found himself remembering Radley Hill because the atmosphere of this unremarkable London house, where Neil and Janey were raising their children, brought back secure and comforting memories of the place where Sam had spent his boyhood. Always the welcome, the lighted fire, the scent from the kitchen of delicious, robust food. Boots in the porch, tennis rackets littering the hall, the voices of the youngsters who were his friends; the sound of their footsteps, clattering down the stairs. He wondered if he would ever achieve such a haven of family life. Up to now, in that respect, his efforts had met with failure. He and Deborah might have had children, but she had never been particularly keen on the idea and he was reluctant to force the issue. Which, the way things had turned out, was just as well. But the house in East 70th Street, with just the two of them, had never been more than simply a place to live. True, the living room had been the envy of all their friends, so immaculately decorated in cream and beige, with modern sculptures and cunningly lighted abstracts on the walls. And the kitchen was a marvel of modern convenience, but nothing much had ever emerged from it except a slice of melon or a microwaved pizza. Deborah, partying, preferred to entertain in restaurants.

Radley Hill. Looking back across the frantic, pressurised years of city life – the wheeling and dealing, the late nights, the long days, the smell of subways and car fumes – he remembered Yorkshire, saw the unpretentious solid stone house, the terrace, the lawns, his mother's rose borders. He thought of the little town, where his father's mill stood, where the wind swept aslant the smoke of chimneys, and the river, flowing down from the hills, slipped along between the tree-shaded streets and under curved bridges. The sound of water, running over rocks, was familiar, so much part of life that one simply stopped hearing it. He thought of the surrounding countryside and long Sunday hikes with his father; of fishing in the remote dark tarns that lay cupped in the moors, where the air was cold and clean and the empty spaces pierced with the cry of curlews . . .

Outside, in the street, a car drew up beneath his window. The front door was opened and shut. He heard Janey's voice. 'Neil? Hi, darling.' And he knew that his friend was home.

He heaved himself off the bed, shucked off the towelling robe and proceeded to dress himself in suitable fashion for the evening that lay ahead: pressed chinos, a clean shirt, a navy blue cashmere sweater, no tie; cream socks, polished loafers. He brushed his hair, splashed on a bit of aftershave, went downstairs. The sitting-room door stood open, and he went in and found Neil, in shirt-sleeves, engaged in polishing up some glasses to set out on the drinks table. The room looked festive, prepared for entertaining: magazines and books squared off, cushions fattened, the fire lighted. The lilies Sam had given Janey stood in their jug on a round, polished table, surrounded by an arrangement of Battersea boxes. Their scent, in the warmth, already filled the air. The clock in the middle of the mantelpiece stood at a quarter past seven.

He said, 'Hi.'

Neil turned from his task. 'There you are. Did you have a good kip?'

'I should have been beavering away, helping you.'

'Not at all. Sneaked home early to perform my hostly tasks.'

'I gather we have company for dinner.'

Neil pulled a face. 'Stupid old bugger. Janey should have put him off, but she's got too kind a heart.' He gave a final swipe at the last glass, set it down neatly and tossed the tea-towel aside. 'There, that's it. All done and dusted. Let's have a drink, and sit down for a peaceful moment. I want to hear all about everything before our guest arrives and we have to start listening to him. Scotch? Soda or water? Or on the rocks? You see, I have all the right phraseology, in case you've forgotten how to speak the language.'

'Soda sounds good. Where's Janey?'

'Whipping cream.'

'And the kids?'

'In bed, I hope. Reading books. If not, there'll be trouble.' He poured their drinks, added ice and brought a tumbler over to Sam. Then, with a relieved sigh, he thumped himself down into one of the comfortable chairs that stood at either side of the fire. 'So, tell me, how did the lunch go?'

Sam sat in the opposite chair. 'All right, I suppose.'

'Nothing gruesome? No kindly suggestion of redundancy?'

Sam laughed. It was a good feeling to have someone come straight to the point, to be with a man he had known for most of his life, and from whom he had never had a single secret.

'The very opposite.'

'Really? A new job, then?'

'Yeah.'

'In the States?'

'No. Here. UK.'

'Whereabouts?'

Sam did not answer at once. He took a slug of his drink, cold and crisp and smoky on his tongue, then set down the glass on the low table alongside. 'Ever heard of McTaggart's of Buckly?'

'What – the tweedy people in Sutherland?'

'Yeah, that's right.'

'Well, of course. Any country gentleman worth his salt wears a shooting suit made of Buckly tweed. My father had one, or should I say *has*. Built like a bloody suit of armour.' He chuckled at the thought. 'Don't tell me they're in trouble.'

'Have been. But Sturrock & Swinfield bought them out a few months ago. I'm surprised you didn't pick it up, but perhaps you don't read the *Financial Times*.'

'Every day, but I missed that one. Textiles don't come into my line of business. Extraordinary, McTaggart's going down the drain.' He twisted his mouth into a rueful smile. 'Mind you, probably the eternal lightbulb scenario. Can't expect to make money on a product that lasts for ever.'

'That, of course, was one of their problems. And they never diversified. I suppose they're an old-fashioned set-up and saw no need. But even for the classic tweeds, the market has shrunk. With the great estates sold up and shooting lodges standing empty, there's no longer a call for tweeds for the gamekeepers and the foresters. But they've had other setbacks as well. Old McTaggart died a

114

couple of years ago, and his two sons weren't interested in the business. One was already into computers and the other running a huge garage on the outskirts of Glasgow. They had no desire to return. I suppose life in the far north had lost its appeal.'

'How extraordinary.' Neil let out a sigh. 'Oh, well, I suppose everyone has different aspirations. So what happened then?'

'Well, first the sons did a bit of asset-stripping, selling off all the mill houses, then they put the place on the market. When there wasn't much interest forthcoming, the workforce approached the Local Enterprise Company and together they undertook a management buy-out of the business. Problem is, there's not a bottomless source of employment in that area, as you can well imagine. Anyway, they're all skilled workers, they've been in the trade father and son – weavers, spinners, dyers, you name it.' Sam drained the last drops from his glass. 'So, they were ticking along all right, getting a few new orders, exports to the States, that sort of thing – then, bang, disaster struck. It rained non-stop for two months, the river broke its banks and flooded the mill to the height of a man's head. They lost everything – their stock, their computers, most of the machinery. And that was it. The banks foreclosed, the LEC got their fingers burned and the workforce faced up to a future without employment.'

Neil got to his feet, came over to Sam and took his glass. 'God, that was really hard luck.'

'I know. So, in desperation, they approached Sturrock & Swinfield. David Swinfield carried out a fairly extensive feasibility study on the place and it was duly rescued. The mill's still in a hell of a mess, though. It hasn't been in operation since the flood, and all but three of the workers are laid off.'

Neil handed him his replenished glass. 'So what's your part?'

'I'm to get it back on its feet again. Run the place.'

'Just like that? Straight away?'

'Not quite. Even before the flood, the mill was pretty run-down. Most of the machinery was probably put in at the time of the Ark. It'll be a year before it's all up and going again.'

'I'm surprised that Swinfield's feasibility study showed that there was any financial viability at all in the place. I mean, do you think it's still possible to make something of an industry in such a remote location? To be quite honest, I wonder if it's really worth the hassle.'

'Oh, I think so. Of course, we'll have to diversify, but the name of McTaggart's has terrific goodwill throughout the world. It's worth a hell of a lot if we're to look closer at the luxury markets.'

'What? Not the end of the good old heavyweight thornproofs for "countrywear", surely? That would be tragic. You'll have to keep making those.'

'Of course we will – and tartans too. Those are McTaggart's stock in trade. Tradition. But they'll form only a part of our production. We'll be concentrating more on lighter, more colourful textiles. Jacketing fabrics for the Italian market, for instance. Shawls, scarves, throws, sweaters. You know, the fashion industry. Both expensive and expendable.'

'Cashmere?'

'Of course.'

'So, forays into darkest China are on the cards?'

'David Swinfield already has agents in Manchuria.'

116

'And what about machinery?'

'Probably source it in Switzerland.'

'Which will mean a total retraining programme for the workforce.'

'Yeah, but it'll be carried out on-site by the suppliers' commissioning team. What, unfortunately, it will mean is a reduced workforce.'

Neil was silent, assessing all this. Then he sighed and shook his head, looking a little bemused. 'It sounds exciting, but it's hard to see you settling down to life in a peat bog – after London and then New York. It sounds on a par with being posted as British vice consul to the Andaman Islands. Hardly a leg up.'

'It's what I know about and what I can do.'

'Salary?'

'Upped.'

'Bribery.'

Sam smiled. 'Not at all. Simply a bonus.'

'And what will you do with yourself? Your leisure time, when you're not working flat out on the mill floor, or trying to get books to balance? I hardly think Buckly is going to be a hive of local gaiety. You may well be forced to take up bingo.'

'I shall fish. Remember fishing with my father? And I shall play golf. There are at least five wonderful links in the neighbourhood. I shall join clubs and make friends with old gentlemen in soup-stained pullovers.'

'More likely to be all kitted up by Nick Faldo.'

'Whatever.'

'So you don't feel all this is a bit of a regression?'

'I'm going back to my roots, if that's regressing. And, oddly enough, I relish the prospect of being a troubleshooter. I know about running a small mill, too.

I learned it all from my father. And he truly loved the business. He loved his machines the way other men love their cars. And he used to touch great bales of tweed as though he was caressing them, for the pleasure of feeling the woven wool beneath his fingers. Perhaps I'm the same. I only know I've had enough of marketing. I can't wait to get back to the factory floor, back to the start of it all. Right now, I feel it's exactly what I need.'

Neil eyed him across the hearth. He said, 'Don't be offended, but I am not sure whether your chairman isn't being paternalistic.'

'You mean, because my personal life has fallen apart?'

'Frankly, yes.'

'Don't worry. I asked him the same question over the Stilton. But I'd been earmarked for the Buckly Mill job long before he heard about Deborah.'

'Of course. Silly question, really. Sir David Swinfield didn't get where he is by having a soft heart. When do you go?'

'Soon as possible. But there's a lot of planning and thrashing out to be done before I take off. A meeting's set up for tomorrow morning, with the financial chaps. A time schedule of reinvestment. That sort of thing.'

'Where are you going to live once you get there? I thought you said that the McTaggart sons had sold off all the houses.'

'Yeah, you're right. But that's just a small matter. I'll probably stay in a pub, or rent a house. Never know, I might even shack up with a raven-haired lassie with a turf-roofed cottage.'

Neil laughed. 'And hoots, mon, to you!' He glanced at the clock, shifted his considerable weight in the chair and yawned enormously, running his fingers through his hair. 'Well, all I can say is best of luck, old boy.'

'It just needs a good kick start to get it going again.'

Neil grinned. 'In that case, you'd better buy yourself a decent pair of football boots, because you're going to need them—'

He got no further for, at that moment, the doorbell rang.

Neil said, 'Oh, hell,' set down his glass and got to his feet. 'That'll be the old bore now.'

But before he got any further, they heard the kitchen door open and Janey's swift footsteps pass down the hall. Then, her voice, 'Hello. How are you? How lovely to see you.' She sounded nothing but delighted and Sam thought, not for the first time, what a wonderfully kind girl she was. 'Come along in.' Murmurs of a male voice. 'Oh, chocolates. How kind. I'll have to keep them out of the way of the children. Did you walk from the tube or were you able to get a taxi? Give me your coat, and I'll hang it up. Neil's in here . . .'

The door opened. By now both men were standing, and Neil went forward to greet his guest, who was being ushered into the room by his hostess.

'Hello, there . . .'

'Neil. My word! Good to see you. It's been too long. This is enormously kind of you.'

'Not at all.'

Janey said, 'And look what he's brought me.' She had changed for the evening into black velvet trousers and a white satin shirt, but over these still wore her red and white striped cook's apron. She held up a modest box of After Eight mints. 'Divine chocolates.'

'Just a token. Trying to remember how many years

119

it is since I've seen you both. When was it? A lunch with your parents, Janey. Too long ago.'

Standing with his back to the mantelpiece, Sam eyed the newcomer. He saw a man well into his sixties, but with the bearing and mannerisms of a young blade from forty years ago. He had, probably, been attractive once, in a David Niven-ish way, but now his features were blurred, his cheeks veined and his trim moustache, like his fingers, stained with a lifetime of tobacco. His hair was white, thinning, but worn long on his collar, his eyes gleaming and very pale blue, his face and hands deeply tanned and smudged with age-spots. He wore grey flannel trousers, brown suede shoes, a navy blazer, brass-buttoned, and a blue and white striped shirt. From the high stiff collar streamed a silk tie of great flamboyance, striped in startling shades of red, yellow and peacock green. His wristwatch was gold and there were gold links in the cuffs of his shirt. He had clearly made much effort with his appearance, and smelt strongly of Eau Sauvage.

'Yes, ages,' said Janey. 'It must be seven years. When they were still living in Wiltshire. Now, I must introduce you. This is Sam Howard, who's staying with us for a few days. And, Sam, this is Hughie McLellan.'

'How do you do?'

'Good to meet you.' They shook hands.

'Sam and Neil have been friends for ever, since they were at school.'

'No friend like an old friend. God, the traffic in London is ghastly. Never seen anything so chock-a-block. Took me fifteen minutes to get a taxi.'

'Where are you staying?' Neil asked.

'Oh, my club, of course, but it's not what it was.

Primed the porter, but might just as well have saved myself a gold sovereign. And the trouble.'

'Let me get you a drink, Hughie.'

Hughie visibly brightened. 'Good suggestion.' He glanced at the table upon which stood the bottles and glasses. 'Gin and tonic, if I may.' He patted pockets. 'You don't mind if I smoke, do you, Janey?'

'No. No, of course I don't. There's an ashtray somewhere.' She searched, found one on her desk, emptied it of paperclips and set it down on the table by the sofa.

'Hell, these days nobody smokes. New York is a nightmare. Light up, and a guy comes and shoots you dead.' He had taken from his blazer pocket a silver case, extracted a cigarette and now lit it with a gold lighter. He blew out a cloud of smoke, immediately looked much more relaxed and put out a hand to take his glass from Neil. 'Bless you, dear boy. Happy days.'

'Do you want a drink, Janey?'

'I've got my cook's drink in the kitchen. A glass of wine. Talking of which, Neil, could you come and open a bottle for dinner?'

'Of course. Sorry. I should have done it before. Would you excuse me, Hughie, just for a moment? Sit down, make yourself comfortable. Sam will keep you company . . .'

When they had gone, and the door closed, Hughie proceeded to do as he had been invited. With his drink and his ashtray conveniently to hand, he settled himself in a corner of the sofa, one arm outflung, resting on the deep cushions.

'Charming house, this. Never been here before. Last time I was over, they were still living in Fulham. Known Janey since she was a child. Parents are old friends.'

'She told me. You've come from Barbados, I believe.'

'Yes, I've got a house in Speightstown. Come back to London every now and then, just to keep the old finger on the pulse, check up on my stockbroker, get my hair cut, visit my tailor. Sad thing is, friends are getting a bit thin on the ground; every time I come, some other old mucker has popped his clogs. Sad, really. Still, the truth is we're all getting older.' He stubbed out his cigarette, took another long swig of his gin and tonic and fixed Sam with a speculative eye. 'You're on holiday?'

'You could say that. Just for a few days.'

'What line of business are you in?'

'Wool-broking.' And then, because he did not want to talk about himself, Sam carried on, 'How long have you lived in Barbados?'

'About thirty years. Ran the Beach Club for fifteen of them but chucked it in before I became a raving alcoholic. Before that I had a place in Scotland. It was handed over to me by a parsimonious father who had no intention of paying death duties.'

A mild interest stirred. 'What sort of place?' Sam asked.

'Oh, a sizey estate. Farms, land, that sort of thing. A Victorian pile of a house. Shooting, good fishing.'

'Did you live there full time?'

'Tried to, old boy, but the winters at that latitude are not a joke. And to appreciate life to the full in the back of beyond, it's necessary to have a bit of back-up. It was all very well for one's grandparents, with servants and staff, cooks and keepers slaving away for incredibly modest wages. When I came along, it cost an arm and a leg just to heat the bloody place. Not to say ...' he cocked an eyebrow and gave a sly smile '... not to say that we didn't have a good time. My first wife was a manic hostess, and she made certain that Corrydale was always bulging with house guests. I used to say she had house guests the way other people had mice. Food for an army and drink for a drunken army. Memorable days.' As he talked, recollecting his apparently halcyon past, Hughie fondled his silken tie, stroking it, letting it slip through his fingers. 'Of course, they couldn't last for ever. Then Elaine ran off with a commodity broker, and after that there didn't seem much point soldiering on. As well, half the staff had left, and the bank manager was making disagreeable noises . . .'

Sam listened to all this with a curious mixture of irritation and compassion. Here was a man who had been handed treasure on a silver plate, and squandered the lot. It was hard to be sympathetic, but Hughie's bravura made him a sad character.

'. . . so I sold up and that was it. Moved to Barbados. Best thing I ever did.'

'Sold up. Just like that? Lock, stock and barrel?'

'Well, hardly. The property went in lots. The farm was bought by the sitting tenant, and one or two of the cottages went to faithful old retainers who'd been living in them. What remained – the house, stables, land – was sold to a chain who run country hotels. You know the sort of thing. Fishing available and the odd pot at a pheasant or grouse.'

Hughie knocked back the last of his gin and tonic, then sat gazing thoughtfully at the empty glass.

'Can I get you the other half?' Sam asked.

Hughie brightened. 'What a good idea. Not too much tonic.' Sam took the tumbler from his hand, and Hughie reached once more for his cigarettes.

Fixing the drink, 'How long are you staying in London?'

'As short a time as possible. Flew in about four days ago. Leave on Wednesday. Headed for Nice. I've got an old friend there, Maudie Peabody, perhaps you know her? No? Oh, thank you, old boy. Kind of you. Maudie's an old acquaintance of my early Barbados days. American. Rich as Croesus. Got a divine villa in the hills above Cannes. Spending Christmas with her, and New Year. Then back to Barbados.'

Sam returned to his position by the fire. 'You seem very well organised.'

'Oh, not too bad. Does one's best. Bit lonely now, living on my own. Rather unsuccessful in the marriage stakes. And *that's* bloody expensive. All my ex-wives want a cut of the lolly. What's left of it!'

'Do you have children?'

'No. No children. I had mumps when I was at Eton and that put paid to procreating. Bloody shame, really. I'd have liked kids to look after me in my old age. Truth to tell I'm a bit short of relations. Got my father, but we're only just on speaking terms. He blew a fuse when I sold the place, but there wasn't a mortal thing he could do about it. There's a cousin as well, a dull fellow. Lives in Hampshire. Tried to phone him, but there was no answer.'

'Where does your father live?'

'In solitary and comfortable state in a mansion flat near the Albert Hall. Haven't got in touch yet. Putting it off. Probably drop in on my way back from France. Courtesy visit. We never find much to talk about.'

It was something of a relief to Sam when once more they were joined by Janey and Neil. Janey, apparently done with her cooking, had removed her apron. She looked aglow with pleasure, and came instantly across the room to put her arms around Sam's neck and kiss him soundly. 'Neil's told me. About the new job. I'm thrilled. You don't mind my knowing, do you? So exciting, a real challenge. I'm *really* pleased for you. I can't think of anything more exciting to take on.'

Across her head, Sam caught Neil's eye. Neil looked a bit abashed. 'You didn't mind me telling her?'

'Of course not.' He gave Janey a hug. 'Saved me the trouble.'

'What's this?' Hughie pricked up his ears. 'Am I allowed to be told?'

Janey turned to him. 'It's Sam's new job. He heard today. He's going to the very north of Scotland to restart an old woollen mill.'

'Really?' For the first time Hughie's attention and interest were caught by something and somebody other than himself. 'Scotland, eh? Whereabouts?'

Sam told him. 'Buckly. Sutherland.'

Hughie gaped. 'For God's sake. *Buckly.* Not McTaggart's?'

'You know them?'

'Dear boy, like the back of my hand. Buckly's only a few miles from Corrydale. Used to have all my shooting suits made of Buckly tweed. And Nanny used to knit my shooting stockings with McTaggart's wheeling. Old family firm. Been going for at least a hundred and fifty years. What the hell happened?'

'Old McTaggart died. Sons weren't interested. They ran out of money and were finally finished off by a flood.'

'What a tragic story. Like hearing an old friend has died. And you are going to take over! When do you go north?'

'Soon.'

'Got a place to live?'

'No. All the mill's domestic property has been sold off. I'll camp in a pub, and look around for something to buy.'

Hughie said, 'Interesting.' They all looked at him, but he did not enlarge on this, simply concentrated his attention on carefully stubbing out his cigarette.

At last, 'Why interesting?' asked Janey.

'Because *I* have a house.'

'Where do you have a house?'

'Not Corrydale but Creagan. Even closer to Buckly.'

'Why do you have a house in Creagan?'

'It was the old estate office, and where the factor's family lived. Quite large, solid, Victorian. With a garden at the back. But my grandmother decided it was too far from Corrydale for day-to-day convenience, and she put the factor and his family into more suitable accommodation, within the walls of the park. The old Estate House, she left to me. And to my cousin. We're joint owners.'

Neil frowned. 'So who lives there now?'

'It's standing empty. An old couple called Cochrane have been renting it for the past twenty years, but one has died and the other gone off to live with some relation. To be truthful, one of the reasons I'm in London is to put it on the market. I could do with a bit of the old ready. Tried to ring Oscar – he's the other owner – to talk things over but couldn't get hold of him. He's probably died. Bored himself to death, no doubt.'

Janey ignored this little spurt of malice. She said, 'Would he be willing to sell out his half of the house?'

'Can't imagine why he shouldn't. No earthly use to

him. I have, in fact, a date with Hurst & Fieldmore tomorrow morning, thought I'd sound them out, see if they'd handle a sale.'

'But your cousin . . .'

'Oh, I can square things off with him when I get back from France.'

'So what are you saying, Hughie?'

'That your friend Sam needs a house and I have one for sale. Suit him down to the ground, I should reckon. Short commute to business, close to the shops, championship golf course. No man could ask for more.' He turned his head to look at Neil. 'No harm done, going to cast your eye over the place. We could come to some arrangement. A private deal would suit me very well.'

Sam said, cautiously, 'How much are you asking?'

'Well, there's been no valuation for obvious reasons. But . . .' Hughie dropped his eyes, brushed a little cigarette ash from the knee of his trousers '. . . a hundred and fifty thousand?'

'Between you and your cousin?'

'Exactly so. Seventy-five each.'

'How soon can you get in touch with him?'

'No idea, old boy. He's being elusive. He could be anywhere. But there's no reason why you shouldn't go and have a look at the place.'

'Is there some agent or person I should get in touch with?'

'No need.' Hughie heaved himself sideways and felt in his trouser pocket. From it he withdrew a large, old-fashioned key, attached to a red label upon which was written in capitals, ESTATE HOUSE. He held it up like a trophy.

Janey was amazed. 'Do you carry it with you *all* the time?'

'Stupid girl, of course not. Told you, I was going to see Hurst & Fieldmore tomorrow, was going to hand it over then.'

Sam took the key. 'How do I get in touch with you?'

'Give you my card, old boy. You can fax me in Barbados. And Maudie's telephone number in the South of France, just in case you make a snap decision.'

'I'll certainly look at the house, and thank you. But, of course, nothing can be official without your cousin's approval.'

'Course not. No underhand shenanigans. Everything above board, cut and dried. But, still, a viable proposition.'

There fell another pause. Then Janey said, 'It is the most extraordinary coincidence. I'm sure it's an omen. A marvellous omen. Of everything going right, and everything going well. Shouldn't we celebrate? Sam gave us a bottle of champagne. Why don't we open it, and drink a toast to Sam, McTaggart's, and happy days in his new house?'

'Splendid idea,' said Hughie. 'But if you don't mind, I'd much prefer another gin and tonic.'

Carrie

Carrie

That night, Carrie dreamed of Austria and Oberbeuren. In the dream, the sky was a deep blue and the snow so dazzling that every frozen flake glittered like a jewel. She was skiing. An empty piste. Floating down through the white fields that spread to infinity on either side. There were black pine trees, and the piste ran between these trees, and she was alone. And then, emerging from the pines, she realised that she was not alone, because far ahead she saw another lone skier, a black silhouette, hurtling away from her, down the slope, dancing Kristianas in the snow. She knew that the skier was Andreas, and she wanted him to know that she was there, so that he would wait for her. She called his name. *Andreas. Stop, and let me be with you. Let us ski down together.* She could hear her voice, blown away by the wind, and the sound of her skis on the beaten surface of the piste. *Andreas.* But he was gone. And then she topped a rise and saw that he had heard her call and was waiting, leaning on his sticks, watching for her, his head tipped up, his dark goggles pushed to the top of his head.

He was smiling. White teeth in a deeply tanned face. Perhaps his flight had been just a tease. Andreas. She reached his side and stopped, and only then saw that it was not Andreas at all but another man, with a wolfish grin and eyes hard as grey pebbles. And the sky was not blue any longer but storm dark and she was afraid . . .

The sense of fear awoke her, eyes flying open to the darkness. She could hear the beating of her heart. Disorientated, she saw a strip of uncurtained window, the street lights beyond. Not Austria, not Oberbeuren, but London. Not her pine-scented apartment with the balcony beyond the windows, but Putney, and the spare bedroom of her friends, Sara and David Lumley. Not frosty, starlit skies, but the drip of grey rain. The dream receded. Andreas, who had never been truly hers, was gone. It was all over.

She reached out a hand and found her watch on the bedside table. Six o'clock on a dark early-December morning.

The empty bed felt desolate. She found herself overcome with a physical yearning, a desperate need for Andreas, for him to be here, his smooth, muscular body close to her own. To be back where they both belonged, in the huge carved bed beneath the sloping beams; lovers, bundled in goosedown and bliss. She turned on her side, hugging herself for comfort and warmth. It will be all right. It's like an illness, but I will recover. She closed her eyes, turned her face into the pillow and slept again.

At nine o'clock she awoke once more, and saw that the gloomy winter morning had begun to lighten. By now David and Sara would already have departed for work, and she knew that she was alone in their house. Already she had been here for a week, and in that time had accomplished little; seen nobody, done nothing about finding herself a new job. Sara and David, infinitely understanding, had left her alone, and Carrie's only contact with her family had been to call her father in Cornwall and have a long and comforting conversation with him, lasting almost an hour. 'You will get in touch with your mother, won't you?' he had said, and she had promised that she would, but kept finding good reasons for putting this off. But a week was too long, and she knew that it could be postponed no longer. Today, this very morning, she would telephone Dodie. *Surprise*, she would say, sounding cheerful. *I'm back. Here. In London.*

And there would be astonishment, and explanations and excuses, and then arrangements made for their reunion. She did not dread this, but neither did she much look forward to seeing either her mother or her sister Nicola. She knew that they would have much to tell her and none of it would be good news. However, blood runs thicker than water, and the sooner it was done, and over with, the better.

She got out of bed, pulled on her dressing-gown and went downstairs. The kitchen was neat and shining. Sara was an exemplary housekeeper, despite a full-time job. She had even found time to leave a note for Carrie, propped against the pot plant that stood in the middle of the table.

> *Have a good day. There's bacon in the*
> *fridge and orange juice. David has a late*
> *meeting, but I'll be home usual time.*
> *If you go to Safeway, could you buy a*
> *veg. for supper. Cauliflower will do.*
> *And some Lapsang Souchong teabags.*
> *Love X Sara.*

Carrie boiled a kettle, made coffee, put bread in the toaster. She drank the coffee but didn't eat the toast. The telephone sat on the dresser and looked at her, like a bad conscience. By the time she had drunk three cups of coffee, it was a quarter to ten. Surely even Dodie Sutton would be up and about by now. She reached for the receiver and punched the number. The rain dripped against the window. She heard the ringing tone. She waited.

'Hello.'

'Ma.'

'Who's that?'

'Carrie.'

'*Carrie?* Are you ringing up from Austria?'

'No. London. I'm here. Home.'

'At Ranfurly Road?'

'No. Ranfurly Road's been let for three years. Three months' notice on either side. I'm homeless.'

'Then where are you?'

'In Putney. With friends. Just across the river from you.'

'How long have you been back?'

'About a week. But there's been a lot to do, otherwise I'd have called before.'

'A *week*? Is this a holiday?' Dodie's voice was querulous, as though in some way her daughter had pulled a fast one on her.

'No, not a holiday. I chucked my job in. Decided I'd done it for long enough.'

'I always imagined you were there for good. We haven't seen you for years. What happened?'

'Nothing happened. Just a whim.'

'Will you get another job?'

134

'Have to. Look, Ma, I thought I'd come and see you. Are you going to be in today?'

'I'm in this morning. This afternoon I have to go and play bridge with old Leila Maxwell. She's got cataracts, poor thing, and can scarcely see the cards, but it's the least one can do.'

Carrie persisted. 'How about lunch, then?'

'Here, you mean?'

'I'll take you out if you'd rather.'

'No. I can manage. Soup and pâté or something. Would that be all right?'

'Perfect. How's Nicola?'

'Oh, my dear girl, such dramas.'

Carrie's heart sank. 'Dramas?'

'I think she's gone mad. I'll tell you all about it when you come.' A pause, and then Dodie added, some bright idea having obviously just occurred to her, 'Actually, all this might be rather fortuitous. You coming home, I mean. She'll be back for lunch, but perhaps you could get here a bit earlier and we can have a private chat about it.'

Carrie began to wish that she hadn't telephoned after all. She said, 'And what about Lucy?'

'Lucy's here too. She's got a morning off school, something to do with the boiler being replaced. She's in her room, swotting for some exam or other. She spends most of her time in her room so she won't disturb us.'

'I'd like to see her.'

'Oh, you will, you will. What time will you be here?'

'Eleven thirty? I'll probably walk.'

'Haven't you got a car?'

'Yes, but the exercise will do me no harm.'

'It's a vile day.'

'I'll survive. See you later, then, Ma.'

'I'll expect you.' And Dodie rang off. After a little, Carrie put the receiver down, sat and looked at it for a moment, then found herself laughing. Not from joy, but wryly, because her mother's chill and ambiguous welcome was exactly what she had both dreaded and expected.

It had always been thus. A lack of communication, an antipathy perhaps, that Carrie had come to terms with and learned to accept even before she entered her teens. Being with other families, seeing how they behaved with each other, compounded her perception and, had it not been for the presence of her father, she might well have grown up with no knowledge of loving or being loved.

She had never quite worked out why Jeffrey Sutton married Dodie in the first place. Perhaps because she was pretty, flirtatious and engaging, and as a young woman had the ability to turn herself into exactly the sort of companion any potential husband would wish to spend his life with. Only to discover, too late, that it was all a calculated act. On Dodie's side, in Jeffrey she saw not only an attractive and virile man but security as well, for his job as a City broker was sound, his career climbing steadily, and his colleagues were blessed with the social background Dodie had always craved.

Nicola was their first child, and then, five years later, Carrie appeared. So different were the sisters, so little did they have in common, it seemed that each belonged solely to a single parent. As though Dodie had produced Nicola without co-operation from Jeffrey, and Jeffrey had fathered Carrie, in some miraculous fashion, entirely by himself.

He was her father, her friend, her ally . . . the strong

partner of a marriage that could only be called a misal-
liance. It was Jeffrey who drove his daughters to school,
while their mother lay in bed, sipped China tea and read
novels. Carrie remembered him returning home from
work, the sound of his latch-key in the door, and running downstairs to welcome him because Dodie hadn't
returned from her bridge game and only the au pair
clashed about in the kitchen. Grubby and exhausted after
a demanding day at work, he would dump his briefcase,
shuck himself out of his overcoat and come upstairs to
help with homework or listen to piano practice. It was
Jeffrey who brought fun into family life, always ready with
a spontaneous idea for a picnic, an outing, a holiday. It
was he who had first taken Carrie skiing at Val d'Isère
when she was only ten, to stay in a rented villa and be
part of a cheerful houseparty consisting of two other
families. It was one of the best holidays of Carrie's life,
and the start of a passion that had never left her. Nicola
had turned down the invitation, partly because she was
hopelessly unathletic, but also because she liked being
on her own with Dodie, so that the two of them could
go shopping together and buy new dresses for Nicola to
wear to all the Christmas parties to which she had been
invited and had no intention of missing.

Clothes, boys and parties were Nicola's passionate
interests, and it surprised nobody when she became
engaged, and then married, when she was twenty-one.
The young man in question was called Miles Wesley,
and was all that Dodie had ever dreamed of for her elder
daughter. He had a grandmother called Lady Burfield,
parents with an enviable property in Hampshire, had
been educated at Harrow and held a respectable job with
Hurst & Fieldmore, an old-established property agent

with branches all over the country. Miles was in the head office, in Davies Street, learning the ropes of selling huge sporting estates, grouse moors and tracts of expensive fishing rights. No mother could have wished for more, and Dodie had a lovely time planning a wedding that would be the envy of all her friends and a talking-point for some years to come.

Carrie was not a bridesmaid at this wedding because she refused to be. At fifteen she was tall, lanky and working passionately at her studies, because she wanted, above all else, to get a place at university. Her general appearance was the despair of her mother, who abhorred the worn jeans, heavy boots and baggy T-shirts that Carrie favoured, and nearly fainted away when she brought back from the Oxfam shop a leather jacket that looked like nothing so much as a dead sheep.

When the word bridesmaid was mentioned Carrie made her position instantly clear.

She said, 'No.'

There were terrible rows.

'How can you be so selfish?' Dodie wanted to know.

'Easily.'

'You only have one sister, you could think of her.'

'Look, Ma, I wouldn't do it even for the Queen. I'm five foot nine inches tall, and I'm just not bridesmaid material. I'm not walking down any aisle looking like a great pink taffeta meringue. A complete idiot.'

'You know perfectly well it won't be pink taffeta. Nicola and I have chosen deep rose chiffon.'

'Even worse.'

'You never think of anybody but yourself.'

'This time, that's just what I'm doing. Nicola won't mind. She's got masses of pretty girlfriends just dying to be bridesmaids. Anyway,' Carrie yawned, 'I'm not all that dotty about church weddings.' She found it amusing, sometimes, to wind her mother up a bit. 'Why can't they just nip round the corner to the registry office? Just think of the money you'd save. On the other hand, that would mean no wedding presents and yummy cheques.'

'That is the most unkind thing to say.'

'Just practical.'

Dodie took a deep breath and kept her voice low and even. 'If people wish to give Nicola a cheque for a wedding present then I know it is gratefully received. They have, after all, got to furnish their new flat. Refrigerators, lamps, carpets. Nothing's cheap, you know.'

'Or they could put all that lovely lolly into a special account and use it to pay for the divorce . . .'

Dodie left the room, slamming the door behind her. The subject of bridesmaids was not mentioned again.

Carrie was the first person Jeffrey confided in. She was nineteen now and at Oxford, reading English and philosophy, and relishing every moment of her new life. One Sunday morning, he telephoned from London. 'You doing anything today?'

'Nothing special.'

'I thought I might give you lunch.'

'What a treat.'

'Your mother's with Nicola. Lucy's running a temperature so there was a cry for help. I'll be with you around twelve.'

Carrie was thrilled. 'I'll be ready.'

It was a golden day in October, and when he had collected Carrie from outside her residence he drove her out into the country and stood her lunch at Le

Manoir aux Quat' Saisons. An enormous and expensive treat. After lunch, they wandered into the garden and sat in the benign Indian summer warmth; there was birdsong, and leaves drifted down, like copper pennies, on to the grass.

It was then that he told her about Serena, about meeting her, and seeing her, and falling in love. 'I have known her for five years now. She is young enough to be my daughter, but she means everything to me, and I don't think I can live without her any longer.'

Her father with a lover. Another woman. And Carrie had never had the faintest suspicion. It was hard to come up with something to say.

'Are you shocked, Carrie?'

'Of course I'm not. Just taken unawares.'

'I'm going to leave you all and be with her.' Carrie looked at him, and saw the pain in his dark eyes. 'This is a terrible thing I'm doing to you.'

'No. Just telling me the truth.'

'I would have gone before, taken Serena with me. But I couldn't leave until I felt that both you and Nicola were ...settled, I suppose. Adult. I had to be around while you needed me, while I could still be of use to you. Now it's different. You, I am pretty sure, can stand on your own feet. And Nicola is a married woman with a little girl of her own. I can only hope that she is content. Miles has always seemed a decent sort of chap, if a bit wet. I think she probably runs rings around him, but that's his lookout.'

'Poor man.' She thought of his own marriage to Dodie. She said, 'All these years, have you been very unhappy?'

Jeffrey shook his head. 'No. There have been moments

of great joy, mostly when I was with you. But I'm worn out with keeping up appearances and making the best of things. I'm exhausted by the grind of trying to make enough money, struggling on, working flat out. I need a different life. I need warm love and companionship and laughter, and Dodie is incapable of letting me experience any of these things. As you probably realise, we haven't shared a bed for years. I want a home where friends drop in, sit at the kitchen table and share spaghetti and a bottle of wine. I want to open the front door at the end of a day and hear someone call my name. In the mornings I want to shave, and smell bacon and eggs cooking, and coffee perking. And it's not just the male menopause, it's a deep need that's been simmering for years.'

'I wasn't going to say male menopause.'

'I know you weren't.'

Another family had come out of the hotel into the warm afternoon sunshine. A young mother and father and a little boy. The little boy found a croquet mallet and a ball, and was attempting to hit the ball with the mallet. After three misses, his father came to stand behind him, his hands wrapped around his son's, and show him how.

Carrie said, 'You've done everything you could for us all. No man could have done more. If you feel this way, you must go.'

'What about your mother?'

'She'll be devastated, of course, and her pride will be bruised. But I know she's never put much into your marriage and, perhaps, at the end of the day, she's a person better on her own.' Carrie sighed. 'You have to be realistic, Dad. She'll get a good divorce lawyer and probably take you to the cleaners.'

'I know that. A price I'll have to pay.'

'What about your job?'

'I shall chuck it in.'

'Won't you miss the cut and thrust?'

'No. I've got as high up the ladder as I ever will. And I'm tired of the rat race, and the anxiety and the perpetual driving competition to keep up front. Perhaps I was never a very ambitious animal. And now I'm selfish. Do you think it's wrong, at my great age, to want to be happy?'

'You know what I think.'

For a bit they didn't say anything, simply sat there in silent harmony. Then Jeffrey spoke again. 'This is about *you*, now. There's a trust fund for you – I set it up when you were born. Nicola, too, but hers has mostly gone on that ridiculous wedding. The point is, it's sitting in the bank, breeding a bit of interest, and I think it would be sensible if you cashed it in and used it to buy yourself a house. In London, or somewhere. Property is always a good investment. I like to think of you being independent . . . It's not a great deal of money but it would pay for a fairly modest house. What do you think?'

'I think I like the idea.' Carrie leaned forward and kissed her father's cheek. 'You're sweet. Thank you. We won't lose each other, will we? We'll write letters and faxes and telephone each other, wherever you end up. We'll keep in touch.'

He smiled, and looked less stressed than she had seen him look for a long time. Clearly, he had had a lot on his mind. He said, 'Next Sunday, if I come back to Oxford and bring Serena with me, would you like to meet her?'

'Of course I would. But she mustn't think I'm too important, that I'm ever going to come between you. I don't want to be a reason for Serena to feel guilty or remorseful. This must be where old responsibilities end and your new life begins. Just make sure, this time, that it's all happiness.'

'And you, my darling? What about you? Have you a love in your life?'

'Dozens,' she teased. 'Safety in numbers.'

'No chance of another top-heavy wedding?'

'Not a ghost. Not for years. I have far too many other things to do with my life. And now, on top of everything else, I've got to go and buy myself a house. What a lot of plans we've laid and what a lot of things we've discussed.'

'Don't be too light-hearted. We're in for a traumatic time.'

She took his hand in hers. She said, 'Allies, Dad. Shoulder to shoulder.'

Jeffrey was right. They were in for a traumatic experience, and sounds of resentment and recrimination were to echo for a long time. At the end of the day, though, most people had to agree that Dodie had done very well for herself, and made the best of a sorry situation. As Carrie had foreseen, she let Jeffrey get away with nothing, and ended up with the family house in Campden Hill, her car, most of Jeffrey's worldly goods and much of his money. He contested nothing, and could scarcely have done more to make amends.

As soon as she heard that Carrie had bought herself a small terrace house in Ranfurly Road, Dodie put the Campden Hill house on the market, swearing dramatically that it was too filled with unhappy memories for her to be able to stay there, sold it at a socking profit and moved into a charming old-fashioned apartment in

Fulham, looking south over the river to Putney, with private gardens that marched with Hurlingham.

'My little lonely nest,' she told her friends, sounding both wistful and plucky, and everyone said she was marvellous. In truth she was as content as she had ever been, with her bridge and her little drinkies parties and the unfailing panacea of shopping, returning home with designer bags and boxes stuffed with tissue paper and goodies. With friends, she began to take holidays abroad, cushioned in club class to Paris, or on Mediterranean cruises in immaculately run liners where there was every opportunity to dazzle in a newly acquired wardrobe of clothes. On one of these cruises she met Johnnie Struthers, a retired group captain and a widower. He clearly fancied Dodie, and from time to time, when he was in London, telephoned and took her out to dinner.

She was as happy as she had ever been. And then, seven years after Dodie's own divorce, Nicola Wesley discovered that the mild-mannered Miles was having it off with another woman and grabbed this opportunity to flounce out of a marriage that had become both predictable and boring. She flounced, of course, to her mother and her mother's spacious and pretty apartment. All of which might have been quite fun and companionable, had not Nicola brought with her seven-year-old Lucy, and Dodie knew that her halcyon days were over.

The coffee pot was empty, the dregs of her cup grown cold. Carrie got to her feet, threw the uneaten toast into the bin, rinsed out the pot, put the cup and saucer into the dishwasher. She went upstairs, took a shower, washed her short hair and dressed. Lately she had not bothered too much about how she looked, simply slopped around in old jeans and with no makeup on her face, but this morning she knew that the time had come to take a bit of trouble, if only for Dutch courage.

So, slim camel-coloured trousers, a polo-necked cashmere sweater, polished boots, gold earrings and gold chains around her neck. She sprayed scent, checked her leather shoulder-bag, took her coat from the wardrobe, went downstairs.

The front-door keys lay in a brass bowl on the chest in the hall, alongside a blue bowl of white hyacinths. Over this chest was a long mirror, and as she pulled on her coat and did up the buttons, her reflection gazed back at her. She paused, regarding herself. Saw a tall, slender, dark-haired girl . . . or perhaps, more accurately, a tall, slender, dark-haired woman. After all, soon she would be thirty. Her chestnut-brown hair shone with cleanliness, a lock like a bird's wing swept across her forehead. Her eyes, accentuated by shadow and mascara, were large and dark as coffee, and her face was still tanned from the reflected sunlight of the snowfields. She looked all right. Confident. Not a person to be pitied.

She did up the buttons of the coat, a dark grey loden piped with forest green that had been bought, a year ago, in Vienna. Andreas had been with her, helped to choose the coat, then insisted on paying for it. 'You will wear it for ever,' he told her, 'and you will always look a million dollars.'

It had been a day of bitter cold and thin snow, and when they had bought the coat, they had walked through the streets, arm in arm, to Sacher's and there lunched in some style and . . .

Don't think about it.

She took the keys, punched the alarm and let herself

out of the house; went down the road, then turned into Putney High Street and strode down the busy pavements towards the river. Crossing the bridge, she felt the chill of an east wind, sneaking upriver from the sea. Over the bridge it was only a little way to Farnham Court, the ornate Edwardian block of apartments where, on the fourth floor, Dodie had her flat. She ran up the steps, went in through the heavy main doors, got into the lift and pressed the button. The lift sailed upwards, and finally came to a shuddering halt. She opened the doors with a tremendous clanging sound, crossed the hall and pressed the bell.

Dodie had been waiting for her. She was there almost at once, dealing with the double lock and flinging the door open.

'Carrie!'

She looked much as she had always looked, no older, no thinner, no fatter. Small and trim, with dark, neatly dressed hair flashed with a streak of white that was entirely natural and so enviable. She wore a little cardigan suit, the skirt fashionably short, and court shoes decorated with square gold buckles. A still pretty woman, with apparently everything going for her. Only her mouth gave her away, moulded by the years into an expression of constant discontent. Carrie had always been told that the eyes are the mirror of the soul, but had long ago decided that a person's mouth is the true giveaway of character.

She stepped through the door and Dodie closed it carefully. There were to be no outflung arms then, no hugs, no exclamations of motherly delight.

'Hello, Ma. How are you?' she asked, shedding her coat. 'You're looking marvellous.'

'Thank you, dear. You're looking well, too. So brown. As though you'd just returned from a holiday in the sun. Put your coat on the chair. Do you want coffee or anything?'

'No, I've just finished breakfast.' Now, they kissed, formally, touching cheeks. Dodie's cheek was soft and fragrant. 'I didn't get up till nine.'

'Lovely to have a lie-in. Come along . . .'

She turned and led the way into her sitting room. The clouds on this wintry day parted all at once, and for an instant the room was filled with dazzling winter sunshine. It was a pleasant room, with large windows facing south on to a balcony and, beyond, the view of the river. Alongside it, divided by a double door that always stood open, was Dodie's dining room. Carrie saw the mahogany table, the pretty sideboard, all part of her childhood, from the family house in Campden Hill. There were a great many flowers about the place and the air was heavy with the heady scent of white lilies.

'Where is everybody?' she asked.

'I told you. Lucy's in her room and—'

'Is she not very social?'

'Not noticeably so. She's quite happy there. She's got her desk and her computer and a little television.'

In the white marble fireplace there flickered a small mock-coal electric fire. Dodie settled herself beside this, in her own chair. She had been reading the newspaper when Carrie rang the bell, and now reached for it with a delicate pink-nailed hand, folded it and set it on the coffee table.

Another cloud rolled in and the sunshine was gone.

'It was good of you to come so promptly. I wanted

to tell you about everything, this ridiculous drama that's suddenly blown up.'

'Nicola?'

'She'll be back soon.'

Carrie lowered herself into the chair on the other side of the white sheepskin hearthrug.

'Where's she gone?'

'Travel agent.'

'Is she planning a trip?'

'I think she's gone mad. I said that, didn't I, over the telephone? She's met this man. He's an American. She met him at some party a few weeks ago and they've been seeing each other ever since.'

Carrie thought it sounded quite hopeful, and not at all as though her elder sister had gone mad.

'What sort of American?' she asked cautiously.

'Oh, quite presentable. A businessman. Railways or steel or something. He's based in Cleveland, Ohio, wherever that is. He's called Randall Fischer. And now he's gone back to America and he's invited Nicola to go and spend Christmas with him.'

'In Cleveland, Ohio?'

'No, he's got a place in Florida – apparently he always spends Christmas there.'

It all sounded so reasonable that Carrie could not imagine what the drama was about. 'Is he married?'

'He *says* he's divorced.'

'In that case he probably is. Have you met him?'

'Of course I have. Once or twice she's brought him here for a drink, and one night he took us both out to dinner. To Claridges. He was staying there.'

'In that case he must be loaded.' Carrie frowned. 'Don't you like him, Ma?'

'Oh, he's all right, I suppose. About fifty. Not particularly attractive.'

'Does Nicola think he's attractive?'

'I suppose she does.'

'So what is so dire?'

'I think she's being foolhardy. She really knows nothing about the man.'

'Ma, she's thirty-five. Surely by now she can look after herself, make her own mistakes if she wants to.'

'That's not the point.'

'Then, what is the point? Enlighten me.'

'Don't you see, Carrie? It's Lucy.'

'You mean Lucy is not included in the invitation?'

'She most certainly has been included, but she refuses to go. She says she doesn't want to go to Florida, she won't know anybody, there won't be anything for her to do, and Randall doesn't really want her anyway. He's only asked her because he feels he has to.'

Carrie was sympathetic. 'I see her point. What age is she? Fourteen. She'd probably feel like a fish out of water and, admit it, it's a bit embarrassing watching your own mother in the throes of a love affair.'

A faint flush was creeping up Dodie's neck, a sure sign that she was becoming rattled. She disliked any form of disagreement, and hated being put in a position where she had to argue her point.

'It's such a wonderful opportunity for Lucy. To travel. See another bit of the world.'

'Not if she doesn't want to.'

'But what will she *do*?'

Now, thought Carrie, *we're getting to the nub of the matter.*

'For Christmas, you mean? Stay with you, I suppose.

After all, this seems to be her home for the time being. It's been her home since her parents divorced. Where else would she go?'

Dodie did not at once reply. Instead, restless, she got to her feet, walked away from Carrie and stood at the window, gazing down at the river. Carrie waited. Then her mother turned. 'I can't deal with her on my own. I have a life to lead. I have plans made, invitations ... I may go down to Bournemouth and stay there with the Freemans. They go every year to the Palace Hotel. They've invited me to join them.' Her tone of voice made it perfectly clear that Lucy was not included in this giddy scheme. 'I'm not as young as I was, Carrie. My child-caring days are over. And I'm not going to change my plans for a stubborn little girl.'

No, Carrie thought, I don't suppose for a moment you'd even contemplate such a thing. After a bit, she said, 'What about her father? Miles. Can't she go and spend Christmas with him and his new wife? Or does she never see him now?'

'Oh, yes, she sees him.' Dodie came back to her chair, and sat again, perched forward, tense. 'Every now and then she spends a Sunday with them, but without noticeable enthusiasm.'

'They don't have children, do they?'

'No. And I doubt if they ever will. She's a career woman.' Dodie spoke the words with a curl of her lip. 'Babies won't ever interfere with *her* life.'

'So they wouldn't have Lucy for Christmas?'

'As a matter of fact, in desperation, I telephoned Miles and put the idea to him. I had to do it because Nicola refuses to speak to him or even say his name. But Miles and his wife are going to St Moritz to ski for

Christmas, with a grown-up party. Lucy's never skied and she's hopeless with people she doesn't know. Miles said it was out of the question and she'd just spoil it for everybody.'

Carrie began to feel desperately sorry for the child, slung in limbo between two feuding and unsympathetic parents. She said, trying not to sound too cool, 'In that case, you seem to have come to a deadlock.'

'Nicola is absolutely determined to go to Florida. She can be very selfish, you know. And after all I've done for her . . .'

'Perhaps she just wants to grab the chance of a bit of fun.'

'A bit of fun.' Bitterly, Dodie repeated the words, making them sound almost indecent. Carrie watched her. All at once, it seemed, Dodie did not want to meet her daughter's eyes. She glanced down, fiddled with the cuff of her little jacket, adjusted a gold button. She said, 'That's what I meant when I spoke to you on the telephone. About your abrupt return from Austria coming at a fortuitous time.'

'You mean *me*. *I* take Lucy off your hands.'

Dodie looked up. 'Have you plans laid?'

'Ma, I'm only just back from Austria. I haven't had time to lay a plan. I haven't even got a house, and won't get Ranfurly Road back until the end of February. I'm living out of a suitcase. I'm really not in a position to have someone to stay.'

'I didn't mean that. I thought maybe . . .' she hesitated '. . . your father.'

'Jeffrey?'

'You call him Jeffrey now?'

'I've called him Jeffrey ever since the divorce. He's

151

my father, I know, but he's also Serena's husband and my friend.'

As she spoke their names, Dodie flinched delicately, but Carrie, knowing that she was being cruel, ignored this. 'And I don't think that's a viable idea, either.'

'But he's Lucy's grandfather. Surely . . .'

'Look, Ma. I've already spoken to Jeffrey. I called him the day after I got back. We had a long conversation. We talked about Christmas then, but he's got Serena's brother and his wife and baby coming down to spend the holidays with them. Emblo is going to be bursting full, not an inch for two more people.'

'You could suggest—'

'No. It's not fair on Serena. She can't have us, and she'll be riddled with guilt *because* she can't have us. I'm not going to ask.'

'Oh.' Dodie let out a sigh and sat back in her chair, as though at the end of her tether. She looked like a balloon that has had all the air let out of it, shrunken and suddenly older. 'I really can't go on like this much longer. It's too unsettling. No co-operation from anybody, least of all my own family.'

'But, Ma—'

She did not finish. There came the sound of a key in the lock of the front door, then the door opening and shutting again.

'Nicola's back,' Dodie said, unnecessarily, and she pulled herself together, put a hand to her hair and was sitting, brightly expectant, when Nicola came into the room. Carrie got up and turned to face her sister.

She said, 'Hi.'

'*Carrie!*' Nicola's jaw dropped in astonishment. 'What

on earth are you doing here? I thought you were in Austria.'

'I was,' Carrie told her. 'But I'm back now.'

The sisters eyed each other. They had never been close, never been friends, never shared secrets. And it occurred to Carrie that Nicola, as she matured, was growing to look even more like their mother: the same height, the same neat figure, thick dark hair. The same small, mean-tempered mouth. Put side by side, they could easily have been mistaken for a pair of cross little twins.

Whenever she thought of Nicola, Carrie always had a mental picture of her wearing some little outfit. Skirts and sweaters co-ordinating. Shoes matching handbags, a silken scarf toning exactly with her lipstick. A bit like one of those cardboard cut-out dolls they used to dress in paper outfits with folding tabs to fix them in place: a paper sundress for the beach, a furry-collared coat for a winter walk, a crinoline and poke bonnet for the fancy-dress party. Now, Nicola did not let her down, for there was the immaculately tailored trouser suit beneath a car coat of *faux*-leopard. Her sack bag was of chocolate brown suede and the suede was exactly the same shade as her high-heeled boots.

Nicola laid her handbag on the seat of a chair that stood against the wall. She began to unbutton her fur jacket.

'Back for good?' she asked.

'I don't know. I'll have to see.' Carrie moved forward and gave her sister a kiss, which Nicola, perfunctorily, returned. 'But when did you get home?' She shrugged out of her jacket and tossed it on top of her bag.

'About a week ago. I've been fairly occupied so I didn't ring Ma till this morning.'

'Well, I never did.' She gave Dodie a cold look. 'I suppose Mother's been telling you about all the dramas. Getting you on her side.' Dodie and Nicola were clearly, at this moment, on the worst of terms. Carrie decided that Lucy must have been having a hellish time between the pair of them.

Dodie looked hurt. 'Nicola, that's not fair,' she protested.

'No, but I bet it's true.' Nicola settled herself with a thump in the middle of the sofa. 'Anyway, it's too late now. I've booked my flight. I'm going on the eighteenth of December. For two weeks.'

A pregnant silence followed this defiant announcement. Dodie turned her head away and stared at the flickering electric coals. Disapproval emanated from every bone in her body. Nicola caught Carrie's eye and made a face, as if the two of them were in alliance against their mother. Carrie did not return her glance because, at that moment, she didn't like either of them very much.

But it was no good getting caught up in the on-going row. She said, as evenly as she could, 'There seems to be a problem with Lucy.'

'She was asked to Florida, but she refuses to come with me.'

'I do see her point.'

'Oh, you would.'

'Ma suggested that I look after her for Christmas.'

'You?' Nicola made the word insulting. And then she thought for an instant, and said it again, and this time it didn't sound insulting at all but quite different. A brilliant notion that had not previously occurred to her. *'You.'*

'But I can't.'

'Why not?'

'No house. No home.'

'Ranfurly Road?'

'Still let.'

Dodie now chose to chip into the conversation. 'I thought Carrie might have taken Lucy to stay with your father in Cornwall. But apparently that's out of the question as well.'

'Why?' Nicola demanded.

Carrie told her. 'A dearth of space.'

'And bloody Miles and his bloody wife won't have her, the selfish sods. Excuses, excuses on all sides.' She chewed her thumbnail. 'Anyway, I'm going. I'm going to Florida with Randall, and nobody's going to stop me. I haven't had a holiday for ever, and I'm going.'

Carrie, sympathetic in a way but thinking of Lucy, tried reasoning. 'But, Nicola . . .'

She got no further. Nicola rounded on her. 'It's all very well for you.' Carrie wondered how many thousands of times in her life she had heard that familiar wail. *It's all very well for you.* 'You've never had a family, you don't know what it's like being tied, day in, day out, to a child. Term time and holidays. Keeping Lucy amused, dealing with problems at school. All on your own. As far as I can see, your life has been one long holiday, nothing but skiing and having a good time. Mountains and young people and glühwein parties. And never coming back from Austria. It's years since we set eyes on you. Not a care in the world.'

Carrie, with some difficulty, kept her voice even. 'Nicola, you clearly haven't the faintest idea what I've been doing. My job was public relations officer for a prestigious travel firm, and each morning nine people had to report in to my office. I had a secretary and an apartment of my own, and in high season I very often worked seven days a week. So let's hear a little less about irresponsibility.'

'It's not the same.' Mulish, Nicola stuck to her grudge. 'Not the same as bringing up a child.'

Carrie gave up. 'Look, this isn't getting us any-where.'

Nicola ignored her. 'It's up to you, Mother. You'll have to forget about Bournemouth.'

Dodie, not unnaturally, became incensed. 'I shall do no such thing.'

'You can scarcely leave Lucy here on her own.'

'And why should *I* be the one to make the sacri-fice?'

Suddenly Carrie knew that she could listen to this pointless sniping no longer. The two of them were entrenched, and all the argument in the world was not going to come to any sensible conclusion. 'Do *stop*,' she told them sharply.

Rather surprisingly, they did. After a bit, Nicola said, 'So, have *you* got any bright suggestions, Carrie?'

'I don't know. I only know that we're talking about your daughter, not about a dog that has to go into kennels. If you don't mind, I'd like to go and have a chat with her. She couldn't talk less sense than either her mother or her grandmother.'

'Thank you *very* much.'

'Where's her room?'

'Next to the kitchen.' Nicola gave a jerk of her head. 'At the back.'

Carrie went to the door. As she opened it, her mother

spoke again. 'See if you can persuade her to be a good girl and simply . . . go.'

Carrie did not reply. She went from the room, and closed the door gently behind her.

Lucy

Lucy

Farnham Court had been built at a time when middle-class families were still expected to employ resident servants. Therefore each apartment had been designed with a small and undistinguished room for a housemaid or a hard-worked cook-general. Lucy Wesley, when she came to live with her grandmother after her parents' divorce, had been given this room, and did not really care that it was both cramped and sunless because it was her own.

The window looked out on to the well in the centre of the building, at the bottom of which was a paved courtyard with a few tubs containing shrubs and bulbs that the hall porter was meant to keep trim and watered; there was virtually no view and the window was veiled in folds of white voile. But the walls were yellow, which imparted the illusion of sunlight, and the curtains yellow and white stripes, and Lucy had her bed, piled with teddies, and a large table, with drawers, for doing her homework, and lots of shelves for her huge collection of books. Her computer sat on the table, there were lamps and a small television set, and a sheepskin rug on the blue carpet. When her schoolfriends came to visit they were always loud with envy and admiration, mostly because the space belonged to Lucy only: she didn't have to share it with some tiresome younger sister and the clutter of a sibling's possessions.

It was a very tidy room because Lucy was an extremely tidy person. On the shelves, her books stood in straight, regimented lines, her bed was smooth, her clothes folded. At school, her desk was the same, with pencils sharpened and exercise books squared and neatly stacked. Once a week Mrs Burgess, who came to clean for her grandmother, went through Lucy's room with Hoover and duster and left it smelling strongly of lavender polish, but from time to time, driven by a sort of housewifely compulsion, Lucy cleaned it again herself, polishing the mirror of her dressing-table and the silver frame that held the photograph of her father.

She missed him dreadfully, not simply as a person but because, like a piece of furniture that had lost a leg, with his going all sense of family collapsed, fallen sideways, crooked and useless, and Lucy knew that it was irreparable and would never be the same again. She had been seven years old at the time of her parents' divorce. A bad age (though could there possibly be such a thing as a *good* age?). Still a small child, but old enough to know exactly what was happening. Which was that the fabric of existence had come apart, and that she and her mother were left to put together the detritus of all that remained. They had moved in with Gran, and Lucy had thought for a bit that this was a temporary arrangement, but slowly accepted that it was for good. For some reason, despite disagreements and occasional rows, it seemed to suit both women, and as nobody ever bothered to ask Lucy's opinion, she kept it to herself.

From time to time she saw her father, but his new wife, who was called Marilyn, was wary of involvement, and clearly had no interest in children or stepdaughters, or anything, except her absorbing job, otherwise, surely, she would have had babies of her own by now. She and Miles did not even have a proper house with a garden, but a flat, and it was the sort of flat that if you couldn't be bothered to cook dinner you telephoned and a snacky sort of meal was delivered to the door on a trolley.

Marilyn was certainly not the sort of person one could confide in, and Lucy felt she could no longer confide in her father because of divided loyalties on both their parts. Sometimes she felt that she would burst if she didn't find someone adult to talk to. Her headmistress, Miss Maxwell-Brown, was exactly the sort of person, and had, every now and then in the course of a private interview, intimated quite clearly that if Lucy had something to say then Miss Maxwell-Brown was more than happy to listen. But Lucy's reserve, and that same tiresome loyalty, got in the way. And she was terrified of anybody being sorry for her, as though she were some sort of orphan. So 'No, I'm all right,' she had insisted. 'Really, everything's all right.' And, reluctantly, Miss Maxwell-Brown would let her go.

Now, at a quarter to twelve on a Friday morning, she had finished her homework (it had taken since after breakfast) and was writing in her diary. The diary was fat as a little Bible, leatherbound, and with its own tiny lock and key. It had smooth thick paper that was a pleasure to write upon, and had been a present from Cornwall. 'Happy Christmas, Lucy,' was written upon the flyleaf, 'from Grandfather, Serena, Amy and Ben.'

They never forgot Christmas and birthdays, which was good of them, because Lucy had been a baby when *that* particular marriage broke up, and she had no memory of Jeffrey Sutton, and of course had never met Serena, or Amy or Ben. Sometimes, when life felt really bleak, she lay in bed and wove fantasies about them, about being asked to go and stay and – even less likely – being allowed by Mummy and Gran to make the trip. She planned it all in her mind. A taxi to Paddington and then the train, being met somewhere with a palm tree and a blue sea, and being taken to a house in a wonderful garden, close to a beach perhaps, and where the sea winds would blow in through the open window of her bedroom. And having Ben and Amy would be like having brothers and sisters of her own.

Lucy had kept up the diary ever since the day she had received it. It wasn't so much a diary as a notebook, because there were no dates, just lovely clean pages, which meant that you wrote the date yourself and the day's doings underneath. Sometimes, there was little to record, but other days, if she had been to the cinema or to a concert with the rest of her class, there was quite a lot to remember and she could use up two or three pages. She got a lot of satisfaction out of writing with her best pen on the thick creamy paper. She had a passion for notebooks, paper, pens, the smell of ink, all the tools of writing. Stationery shops were her favourite, and she seldom emerged without a little box of coloured paperclips, a packet of postcards or a new red ink Biro.

She wrote,

Mummy has gone to the travel agent this

*morning. She went right after breakfast. She
and Gran are scarcely speaking to each other
because of Christmas and Bournemouth and
Florida. I wish they would understand how I
would hate Florida. You can't swim all day in
a pool, and I don't like Randall that much, or
ice-cream, or watching videos.*

The diary was better than having nobody to confide in, but a person would be better. She laid down her pen and gazed out at the grey morning beyond the floaty white voile curtains. She thought about Carrie, Mummy's younger sister and a splendid aunt. Carrie would be perfect because she talked to you as though you were a grown-up and yet was always prepared to do exciting and innovative things. Before she disappeared to Austria and never came home again, Carrie had been Lucy's saviour, the giver of special treats, like going to see *La Fille Mal Gardée* at the Opera House, or to Kew on the first warm spring days. Carrie made even the Natural History Museum fun and interesting, and once they had gone down the river together in a boat, all the way to Tower Bridge, and had lunch on board, and all of London, seen from the water, had become a foreign city, unfamiliar, with towers and spires washed in sunlight.

She picked up her pen again.

*I wouldn't have minded spending Christmas
with Dad and Marilyn, but they're going
away to ski. Marilyn says it's a long-standing
engagement. I'm sure Daddy would have put
it off but of course she wouldn't let him. I
don't know what has to be so special about
Christmas anyway, and why everybody makes
such a fuss. Anyway, this afternoon I'm going*

to the pictures with Emma and then back to
tea with her.

While Lucy sat in her bedroom, doing homework and now writing in her diary, beyond the closed door Gran was living her own tidy life. Every now and then during the course of the morning, Lucy had heard the telephone ring then Gran's low voice, chatting away. About an hour ago someone had rung the bell and come to visit, and as Lucy finished her French, she was aware of the soft murmur of conversation from behind the drawing-room doors at the end of the passage. She had no idea who it could be, and did not particularly care. Some boring friend of Gran's. But now she heard the whine of the ascending lift, then the rattle of a latch-key in the front door, and knew that her mother was back from the travel agent.

The awful thing was that, despite Lucy's insistence that she wasn't going to go to Florida, she couldn't be too sure that, in desperation, Mummy would not have booked two flights, and Lucy, willy-nilly, would be dragged along with her. After all, at fourteen, there wasn't much one could do, except sulk for two weeks and loathe every moment of it, and hopefully spoil it all for everybody. She was perfectly capable of all this, and her mother knew that she was, but still, there remained the daunting possibility. She raised her head, like an alert dog, to listen. But the footsteps passed her door and went down the passage towards the sitting room. The door opened and shut. Voices again. She closed her eyes and wished that she could close her ears as well.

Small comfort, but at least the third person, whoever the visitor was, would preclude another row, anyway, for the time being. She waited for what was going to happen

166

next. Which was nothing for about five minutes. And then, once more, the drawing-room door opened and closed, and somebody was approaching. Lucy shut her diary and leaned on it, her head turned to watch the doorknob. Her mother, come to impart the latest news about plans for Florida. Lucy, all at once, felt almost sick with apprehension. But then there was a soft knock, and she knew it wasn't Mummy, because Mummy never knocked, just barged in, invading privacy, whatever Lucy happened to be doing.

At a knock, Miss Maxwell-Brown always called out, 'Come in,' but before she could bring herself to say this, the door opened slowly, and a head came around the edge of it.

'Am I interrupting?' She was smiling. Not her mother. Not Gran. Not some boring acquaintance of Gran's. But . . .

Carrie. Carrie? She'd only just been thinking of Carrie and now she was here, at the door, and not in Austria where Lucy had thought she was, living a glamorous life of skiing holidays and luxury hotels. Carrie. And she used to have long hair, but now it was short and she was very thin and very tanned and just as tall as Lucy remembered.

Carrie. Lucy found herself dumbfounded, without words. A turmoil of mixed emotions. Astonishment and incredulous delight that such a marvellous and unforeseen event was actually taking place. Carrie. She felt the warm blush of sheer pleasure creeping up into her cheeks. Things like this didn't happen very often and she couldn't think of a word to say. Her instinct was to leap to her feet and fling herself into Carrie's arms, but perhaps Carrie would think this dreadfully babyish. Perhaps . . .

Carrie said, 'Don't goggle. It's really me.'

Slowly Lucy got to her feet. She said, 'Goodness.'

Carrie came into the room and closed the door behind her. 'Surprise?'

'Yes. I'd no idea. Have you been here ages?'

'About an hour. Chatting to Ma.'

'No. I mean, in London.'

'A week.'

'I didn't know.'

'Nobody did. Never mind, you know now.' She stooped and planted a kiss on Lucy's cheek. She smelt gorgeous. 'You've grown. Stupid thing to say. I used to bend double to kiss you.' She looked about her. 'What a pretty room. It used to be very gloomy. And how tidy. Have you been giving it a spring-clean?'

'Not this morning. And Gran did it up for me. She let me choose the colours.'

'Perfect. All sunny.' There was a small blue armchair by the bed and Carrie sank into this, long legs stretched out, her neatly booted feet crossed at the ankle. 'Have you been working?'

'Yes. Homework.' Lucy picked up her diary, stowed it away privately in a drawer, then sat again, swivelling her typist's chair round so that she faced her aunt. 'When did you get back?'

'I said. A week ago. I would have let you all know I was coming, but it was all a bit precipitant.'

'How long are you home for?'

'Indefinitely. Chucked the ski job in. At the moment I'm both homeless and unemployed, but it doesn't matter. How's everything with you?'

Lucy shrugged. 'All right.'

'There seems to be a certain crisis looming. Or

168

perhaps it's already loomed. Poor child, you must be wondering what on earth is going to happen next.'

This was in character, and Lucy was grateful. Carrie had always been completely direct, never avoiding awkward questions and coming straight to the point of any dilemma. Suddenly Lucy felt much better and even strong enough to ask, 'Mummy didn't buy *two* air tickets for Florida, did she?'

'Would you have minded?'

'Dreadfully.'

Carrie laughed. 'Don't worry, she's going on her own. So that little battle you've actually won. It must have been something of a fight.'

'Do you think I'm being *really* stupid, not wanting to go with her?'

'No, I think you're absolutely right. You'd be like a sore thumb, a green gooseberry. Much better for Nicola to be on her own. But it does pose problems.'

'You mean, Christmas?'

'No, I don't mean Christmas. I mean you. What do *you* want to do? I bet you anything nobody's even asked you that.'

'Not really.'

'I suggested you went to your father, but apparently he and Marilyn are off to the ski slopes with a lot of their friends.'

'I wouldn't want to go with them. Marilyn doesn't like me much and I've never been skiing, so I don't suppose it would be all that much fun.'

'You haven't got cosy schoolfriends with cosy mothers you'd want to go and be with?'

Lucy felt a bit abashed, because she hadn't. She had schoolfriends, of course, lots of them, but nobody special, nobody with a motherly mother. Emma Forbes was about her closest friend, and *her* mother was the editor of a magazine and always dashing off to meetings. Lucy scarcely knew her, and Emma had to be tremendously independent and organise her own social life with the help of a latch-key and a Swedish au pair. So far, for all their chat and giggles and time spent together, Emma had not even mentioned Christmas.

Carrie was waiting. Her dark eyes watched and were filled with kindness. Lucy said, 'I did think perhaps I could go to Cornwall. To Grandfather. The only thing is that I've never been and I can't even remember him, and I've never met Serena, or Ben or Amy. And Gran's always horrid about him and won't say their names, but I thought perhaps if she didn't have any alternative they might let me go.'

'Would you like that?'

'Yes, I think I would. The only thing is, I've never been . . .' Her voice trailed away. 'And perhaps they wouldn't want me anyway.'

Carrie said, 'I think it's a wonderful idea, and I think one day you should go. But not this Christmas because I spoke to Jeffrey when I got back from Austria and I know they've got a houseful. Their house isn't very big anyway, tiny in fact, and it's going to be stuffed to the gunwales with visitors.'

Hope died. 'Oh, well. It doesn't matter . . .'

'But you should certainly go one day. In the spring, perhaps. They'd love it, and you'd love all of them. We'll have to come up with something else.'

We was significant. 'We?'

'Yes. You and me. Orphans of the storm together. What shall we do?'

'You mean, for Christmas?'

'Of course for Christmas.'

'In London?'

'I think London would be rather dull, don't you? Perhaps we should go away.'

'But where?'

There seemed to be no answer to this. They gazed at each other, then Carrie got to her feet and went to the window, raising the voile curtain and staring down into the cheerless area three floors below. She said, 'I've an idea. I just had it, this moment.' She dropped the curtain, turned, and came to perch on the edge of Lucy's desk. She said, 'Have you ever heard of Elfrida Phipps?'

Lucy shook her head, wondering what was coming next.

'She's heaven. A cousin of Jeffrey's. Your gran could never stand her because she was rather wild and louche and an actress, and always had lots of boyfriends and husbands. They never had what you might call a lot in common and your gran thoroughly disapproved of Elfrida. But I always loved her, and when I was at Oxford I started seeing her again, and we made terrific friends.'

'How old is she?'

'Oh, ancient. Over sixty. But more fun than anyone you ever knew.'

'Where does she live?'

'She used to live in London, but then her . . . well, he wasn't her husband, but she adored him . . . he died and she moved to the country. Once, ages ago, she was ill after an operation, and I stayed with her until she was better. Jeffrey says she's living in a little village in Hampshire. He says the house is weeny, but I'm sure there'd be space for you and me. And if there isn't space Elfrida will make it.

Would that be a good idea, do you think? Shall we give it a try?'

'You and me?'

'And Elfrida.'

'For two weeks?'

'Of course.'

'Would she mind?'

'I'd bet my bottom dollar that she'll jump at it.'

'How will we ask her?'

'I'll ring. I've got her number.'

'Now?'

'No, not now. When I get back to Putney. We don't want the others to know our plans until they're all cut and dried. Then we'll present them as a *fait accompli.*'

'If she *doesn't* have us for Christmas . . . ?'

'We mustn't think so negatively. We must be positive. And at the moment don't say a word. It shall be our secret.' Carrie pushed back the cuff of her cashmere sweater and looked at her watch. 'Heavens, it's nearly one o'clock. I'm starving, aren't you? Your gran said she'd give us soup and pâté, but I'm not sure if that's going to sustain me. Why don't I take all four of us out to lunch? Is there somewhere cheap and cheerful not too far away?'

'There's Rosetti's. It's a five-minute walk.'

'Italian?'

'Spaghetti and stuff.'

'My favourite food. What do you say? Shall we go and round up our mothers and tell them they're in for a treat?'

Lucy remembered Emma. 'I'm going to the cinema this afternoon with a girlfriend. I have to meet her at two thirty.'

'How do you get there?'

'Tube.'

'No problem. We'll have lunch, and then I'll stand you a taxi. You won't be late.'

It was getting better and better. Restaurant lunches and taxis. Lucy wondered if Carrie, returned from Austria, was now rich. She certainly looked rich, in her beautiful clothes and with her shining hair and her glamorous makeup ... just as good as the attenuated models who posed in leather and fur between the glossy pages of Gran's favourite *Vogue*. She felt as though, suddenly, she had walked from a dark and cold corner into a blaze of warm sunshine. All part of being relieved, shed of worry and having Carrie back again, a benevolent presence who was making everything all right. To her horror, emotion caused Lucy's eyes to mist over with ridiculous tears and she felt her face begin to crumple, like a baby's. 'Oh, Carrie ...'

'Hey, don't cry. There's nothing to cry about. We're going to have a great time.' And she opened her arms, and Lucy leaned against her aunt, and pressed her cheek into the soft cashmere of her sweater and smelt her scent again. She was really here. Mercifully, before they could fall, the stupid tears receded and in a moment she was able to find a handkerchief and, lustily, blow her nose. 'I'm sorry.'

'Nothing to be sorry about. Now, wash your face and find a jacket or something. I'll go and break the happy news to the others.'

'Just about lunch?'

'Just about lunch. We won't say a word about our other plans. A secret, between you and me.'

173

She found Dodie in the little kitchen, endeavouring, in a half-hearted sort of way, to organise the promised snack. She had started to lay the table, and was on the point of opening a tin of soup.

Carrie said, 'Don't open it.'

Startled, Dodie turned to face her younger daughter. 'Why not?' She looked out of place in a kitchen, dressed as she was in her neat, formal clothes without a hair out of place. She hadn't even tied on an apron, and held the soup tin at arm's length, as though the opener might bite her.

'Because we're all going out to lunch. My treat. Lucy and I have decided a little self-indulgence is in order. She suggested some place called Rosetti's. Is that all right by you?'

'Well. Yes.' But Dodie still sounded doubtful. 'I thought we'd agreed on soup and pâté. Here.'

'You're quite right. We did. But minds have been changed.'

'It's almost one o'clock. Will we get a table?'

'Why not? Would you like to ring them up? Do you know the number?'

'I think so.'

'Then do that. And keep the can of soup for your supper. Where's Nicola?'

'In the drawing room.'

'Sulking?'

'No. Delighted with herself.'

'Let's make a pact. Over lunch, no word of Florida. Lucy's had enough.'

'Well, I most certainly have.'

Carrie found Nicola deep in an armchair, turning over the pages of the new *Harpers & Queen* that she had bought on her way home from the travel agent. 'Are you planning a new wardrobe for Florida?'

Nicola closed the magazine and dropped it on the floor. 'I know what you think, Carrie, and I don't give a damn.'

'Why should you care? And why shouldn't you go if you want to?'

'Do you really mean that?'

'Anything's better than hanging around here, creating discord and being resentful.'

'Thank you *very* much.'

'Oh, Nicola . . .' Carrie sat on the arm of the sofa. 'Let's call a pax. We're going out for lunch. It'll cheer us up. And we're not going to talk about Florida or Bournemouth or Christmas, or anything.'

'Is this Lucy's idea?'

'No, mine. And I must congratulate you. She's sweet-looking and sweet-natured, which is more than one can say about most fourteen-year-old girls. You've done a good job.'

'Well.' Nicola, with the wind thus taken out of her sails, allowed herself a wry smile. 'Thank you.' And then hastily added, 'But it's not been easy.'

'I don't suppose bringing up children ever is. I wouldn't know. Now, come on, get your skates on. Ma's ringing the restaurant to be sure there's a table for us. And Lucy and I are going to eat great mounds of *carbonara*.'

Over their mother's fireplace was a gold-framed Venetian mirror, which reflected back all the pretty charm of the double room. Nicola stood up and went to inspect herself in this, touching her hair and drawing her little finger across her painted lips. Then, through the mirror, her eyes met Carrie's. She said, 'There is still a problem, though, isn't there?'

'I'll try to find a solution.'

'Carrie, why did you come back from Austria?'

'Oh.' Carrie shrugged. 'A snap decision.'

'Well, whatever the reason, I'm grateful.' Nicola reached for her fur jacket, then spoiled it all by saying. 'At least it takes some of the pressure off me.'

The lunch out proved a good idea. Both Dodie and Nicola relished the restaurant life, and their spirits lifted visibly even as the little party walked the short distance from Farnham Court to Rosetti's. The cold of the grey December day was a good excuse for Dodie to wrap herself in her new black fur-trimmed coat, and as she led the way through the glassed doors and into the warm, delicious-smelling interior of the restaurant, various charming, smiling Italians moved forward to greet her, to relieve her of her coat, to make her feel both pretty and important. The place was not large and a number of diners were already ensconced, but a corner table had been reserved for them. Once they were all sitting, Carrie wasted no time and ordered a round of drinks: gin and tonic for Dodie and Nicola, Coke for Lucy, and a Tio Pepe for herself. Then she chose a bottle of wine to accompany their meal. Relaxed by alcohol, and soothed by the pleasant atmosphere of the little restaurant, tensions gradually loosed off and conversation became, if not sparkling, then reasonably easy.

They had not been together for some years, after all, and there was a great deal of chat and gossip to catch up on. Old friends, old acquaintances, distant relatives. Carrie was told about Dodie's cruises in the

Mediterranean and about one particular Greek island with which she had fallen in love. 'My dream would be to build a little house there.' And Carrie, questioned, told them a bit about Oberbeuren, and the magic of the mountains in summer, when walkers came to stay at the big hotel and the white ski-slopes became green pastures where cattle grazed and cowbells rang out in the glass-clear air.

Dodie and Nicola kept their word, and no mention was made of Christmas, Florida or Bournemouth.

By the time they had finished their coffee, and Carrie was dealing with the bill, it was time for Lucy to go. One of the obliging waiters went out and stood on the cold pavement, with his long white apron flapping in the wind, until he caught the eye of a cruising taxi cab and flagged it down. Carrie gave Lucy some money to pay the fare, and they saw her safely aboard. Perched forward on the seat, she opened the window. 'Carrie, I haven't said thank you. It was a lovely treat.'

'My pleasure. Enjoy the movie. And I'll ring you.'

'Don't let it take too long.'

'Soon as I can. Shan't waste a moment.'

Nicola was more practical. 'Lucy, when will you be home?'

'About seven.'

'Take care.'

'I will.'

The taxi rolled away and they stood and watched it go, then turned and began to stroll back down the pavement in the direction of the river. At the corner of Farnham Road, they paused to say goodbye.

'You've cheered us up no end.' Dodie, warmed by quantities of good food and drink, was prepared to be generous. 'So lovely to have you home again. Keep in touch. Let us know what you plan to do.'

'Yes, of course. 'Bye, Ma.' She dropped a kiss on her mother's cheek. ''Bye, Nicola. Shall I see you before you fly off?'

'Oh, probably, I'll be around. Thanks for the lunch.'

'If I don't see you, have a great time.'

'I have every intention of doing just that.'

They parted. Carrie watched them go, the two ridiculously identical women, each totally bound up in her own affairs and problems. They didn't change. She turned and went on walking, and it wasn't until she was half-way across Putney Bridge, the east wind cold and damp on her cheeks, that she remembered Sara's note on the kitchen table and that she was meant to buy a vegetable for dinner, and a packet of Lapsang Souchong teabags. So, in Putney High Street, she went into a Pakistani grocery and loaded up with cauliflower and leeks, and some tiny new potatoes. She bought the teabags as well, a nutty brown loaf and a couple of bottles of Jacob's Creek wine. The handsome young man behind the till stowed all these into a carrier-bag, and took her money. 'My God,' he remarked, 'this is a cold day and no mistake. You will be grateful to be getting home.'

She agreed, thanked him and went out again. The overcast midwinter afternoon was already sinking into dusk; cars drove with lights on and shop windows spilled bright squares out on to the dank pavements. By the time she had reached the Lumleys' little terrace house Carrie's hands were frozen, and it was quite painful to remove her glove, and struggle with the latch-key. Indoors, she turned on the hall light, dealt with the alarm, and was grateful for the warmth. She went into the kitchen, dumped the carrier bag on the table, and then, still in her coat, filled the kettle and plugged it in. She drew the blue and white checked curtains, and unpacked the groceries, by which time the kettle had boiled and she made a mug of tea. Finally, she took off her coat, draped it over the back of a chair, found her handbag with her address book and settled down by the telephone.

Elfrida Phipps, Poulton's Row, Dibton. Carrie lifted the receiver and punched in the number. She heard the double tone of Elfrida's telephone and waited. She waited for a long time, but there was no reply, and clearly Elfrida had never got around to investing in an answerphone. Perhaps she was out. Carrie gave up, drank her tea, then went upstairs to hang up her coat and change her shoes. Downstairs again, she dealt with the sitting-room curtains, and lit the fire. After that, she returned to the kitchen and had another shot at reaching Elfrida. Once more, no joy. After the third try, by which time Carrie had peeled the potatoes for dinner, cut up the cauliflower, and made a marinade for some chicken breasts, she began to be a little concerned. It was, after all, a long time since they had been in touch. Elfrida had never been a great letter-writer, preferring the telephone, but she had always been *there*. Perhaps, dreadful thought, she had died. This possibility hit Carrie out of the blue, but then common sense got the better of her, and she knew that if anything had happened to Elfrida, Jeffrey would have let her know.

Jeffrey. She would ring her father. Jeffrey would surely know the whereabouts of his cousin. His number at Emblo was one that Carrie knew by heart so she lifted the receiver once more and put through the call. This time she was successful, and he answered almost at once.

179

'Jeffrey Sutton.'

'Jeffrey, it's Carrie.'

'Darling girl. How are you?'

'I'm fine. Cold, though.'

'Isn't it hellish weather? We're almost being blown off the cliff.'

'How are Serena and Ben and Amy?'

'They're well. Serena's taken the car to fetch them from school so I'm sitting in solitary state writing cheques and paying bills. What can I do for you?'

'Have you a moment to talk?'

'How long a moment?'

'Like an hour.'

'For heaven's sake, what's up?'

'I'm looking for Elfrida. I've been ringing the Dibton number, but there's no reply.'

'She's not there.'

'Not *there?*'

'She's in Scotland.'

'What is she doing in Scotland?'

'She went last month. She's been there ever since.'

'Why didn't you tell me when I rang you up last week?'

'There seemed to be other, more important things to talk about. Like you.'

'Yes.' Carrie felt a bit shamefaced. 'Well. I'm sorry.'

'I didn't realise that Elfrida's whereabouts were so important to you.'

'Well, it's important now. Why did she go to Scotland?'

Jeffrey said, 'It's a long story,' and proceeded to tell her.

Listening in some horror to the sorry tale, Carrie

found herself becoming increasingly bewildered. She knew Elfrida very well. Knew her to be kind-hearted and impetuous, without ever much thought for the day ahead. But, even so, it all sounded a bit precipitous.

She said, voicing the first thought that came into her head, 'Is she in love with this man?'

'I don't know, Carrie. I don't really know what's going on. She told me about it over the telephone, and she sounded more distressed than elated.'

'In that case she isn't in love with him. She's just being caring.'

'She told me that he had asked her to go with him, for company and solace, and she'd said yes.'

'What sort of solace, I ask myself.'

'They were leaving the next day, driving, doing the long journey in stages.'

'Whereabouts in Scotland are they?'

'Sutherland. Far north. I've got the address and the telephone number somewhere. I didn't want Elfrida disappearing into the blue without anyone knowing where she was.'

'Has she been touch since she got there?'

'No. I imagine she has other matters to occupy her mind.'

It was all very frustrating. Carrie said, 'Oh, damn.'

'What's that for?'

'I really *wanted* Elfrida. I wanted to get hold of her. To talk to her.'

'Is there some problem?'

'You could say so.'

'With you?'

'No. Not me. Your granddaughter, Lucy Wesley.'

'Explain.'

So then it was Carrie's turn to talk, to try to make clear to her father, in as few words as possible, the hopeless situation that existed at Farnham Court. Nicola taking off to spend Christmas in Florida with her new American boyfriend. Lucy refusing to accompany her. Dodie refusing to be left with Lucy, and instead planning a genteel festive season at the Palace Hotel, Bournemouth. And both Nicola and Dodie refusing to compromise, or give way by a single inch.

'So there's an impasse,' she finished.

'What about Lucy's father?'

'Going skiing. Doesn't want her. It's all so dreadfully unfair, and she's such a nice child, she deserves better. I don't mind taking her on for Christmas, but I haven't got a house or a job or anything, so I thought of Elfrida.'

'You should come to *us*.' Jeffrey sounded agonised with guilt and Carrie hastened to reassure him.

'Jeffrey, we can't possibly come to Emblo. I know there's no space and it's not fair on Serena.'

'Then why don't you ring Elfrida in Scotland? She can only say no, and she'd love a chat. You can hear the whole saga of Mr Blundell from her own lips, and then you'll be far more in the picture than I am.'

Carrie hesitated. 'Doesn't it seem a bit intrusive?'

'I don't think so.'

'I haven't seen Elfrida, or spoken to her, for so long.'

'All the more reason to telephone. Look, don't ring off, I'll find that number and her address. I put it down somewhere . . .'

Carrie hung on. Faint noises could be heard, of drawers being opened and slammed shut, the rustling of papers. It's a stupid idea, she told herself. We can't possibly go so far just to spend Christmas. And then, another voice, *Why not?*

'Carrie?' He was back. 'Got a pencil and paper?' Hastily Carrie scrabbled around, found Sara's shopping list and a Biro stuck in a blue and white mug. 'This is the phone number.' She took it down. 'And this is the address. The Estate House, Creagan, Sutherland.'

'Sounds frightfully grand.'

'I don't think it is.'

'How do you spell Creagan?'

He spelt it out for her.

'Perhaps I should write a letter.' Carrie was beginning to lose her nerve.

'That's feeble. And it'll take too long. Telephone. Right away. Speak to Elfrida. And, Carrie . . .'

'Yes.'

'Send her my love.'

Oscar

Oscar

In midwinter, it was an alien land. Monotone beneath a sky scoured white by the wind. The hills, sweeping down to the coast, were already topped by an icing of snow and the snow merged with the clouds, so that the summits of the hills were lost to view, veiled, blurred, as though already absorbed by the doleful heavens.

It was alien because Oscar did not remember the landscape thus. Always, as a boy, he had come in the summer to visit his grandmother at Corrydale, and in summer, so far north, the afternoons had stretched on and on until ten or eleven o'clock at night, and at bedtime the shadows of trees fell long across golden, sunwashed lawns.

He walked with Horace. He had left the house after lunch, setting out with a stout stick to help him on his way, and insulated against the cold by a fleece-lined jacket, and with an ancient tweed hat pulled low over his brow. His boots were sturdy, built for walking, and once he had traversed the streets of the little town and climbed the hill to the gate above the golf links, he was able to step out at some speed. After a bit he forgot about feeling cold, and was aware of his body, warm beneath all the layers of wool, and the quickened pace of his heartbeat.

Horace bounded cheerfully ahead, and they followed a footpath, high above the links, winding between thickets of gorse. After a mile or so, this path led over a stile and along the track of a disused railway, where once, coming from London, Oscar had chuntered his way into Creagan on the small branch line, with many stops for level crossings and gates to be opened.

The sea lay to his right, beyond the links and the dunes, steel-coloured beneath the winter sky, cheerless; the tide far out. He stopped to listen, and heard the breakers on the beach, driven in by the wind, and the cry of gulls. Observing the gulls, he saw, to his mild surprise, that there were a few hardy golfers out, brightly dressed figures striding down the fairways, hauling their clubs on trolleys behind them. He remembered that when his grandmother played golf she had always employed a caddie, and always the same man, an old reprobate called Sandy, who knew every curve and hazard of fairway and green and advised her accordingly. A good deal of the time Sandy teetered on the verge of drunkenness, but when he caddied for Mrs McLellan, he wore the mien of a sober judge and behaved accordingly.

The old railway track petered out into a thicket of broom, and rounding this stretch, Oscar saw that they had reached the end of the links, the turn of the course and the ninth tee. Now, the next stretch of coastline revealed itself, another wide and shallow bay, an old pier and a cluster of fisher cottages, huddled down, single-storeyed, crouched from the teeth of the wind.

It was then that he heard the voices: a man calling, a murmur of conversation. He turned his head, and saw, below him, a group of four men making their way to the tee. Oscar was instantly wary, fearing that one of them would be Major Billicliffe, that he would be spied and forced into introductions and convivial chat. He stood very still, hoping to render himself invisible, but his fears, thankfully, were ill-founded. Major Billicliffe, tall as a tree and with his skinny shanks draped in tweedy plus-fours, was not one of the group. Instead, Oscar saw the four sturdy figures, bundled up in coloured jackets and waterproof trousers, wearing white golf shoes and long-peaked American caps. Billicliffe would never be so trendy.

Major Billicliffe was the main reason that Oscar had kept a low profile ever since their arrival in Creagan. From time to time, urged by Elfrida, he had nipped across the road to the supermarket to stock up on beer or to buy a loaf of bread, and his daily outing was a trip to the newsagent to pick up *The Times* and the *Telegraph*. On these occasions he kept an eye open, just in case Billicliffe should be bearing down upon him, loud with greeting and invitations to his terrible house.

Elfrida thought Oscar was being feeble. 'He's harmless, Oscar, just a stupid old man. You must be firm if you meet him. Polite but firm.'

'He is a terrifying bore.'

'You can't cower indoors for the rest of your life. It's ridiculous.'

'I am cowering indoors because the weather is inclement, to say the least of it.'

'Rubbish. You spent the whole of Saturday raking leaves in the garden in the pouring rain.'

'Billicliffe can't get into my garden.'

'He could see you over the wall. He's tall enough.'

'Don't even suggest it.'

This walk with Horace was Oscar's first real foray into the countryside, and he had started out because all of a sudden he was restless, filled with nervous energy, and knew a physical need to stretch his legs. Even the prospect of encountering Major Billicliffe did not put him off and, as Elfrida constantly pointed out, he could not spend the rest of his life cowering indoors and ducking behind a sofa every time the front-door bell rang.

It was all very unfortunate. Because Billicliffe, retired factor of Corrydale, was the man who had custody of the key of the Estate House, and calling upon him, to take possession of this key, had been their first priority.

The occasion was not propitious. At the end of a long winter drive from Hampshire, which had taken two days, both Oscar and Elfrida were exhausted. They had travelled by the A1, battling with rain, long-distance lorries and manic car drivers speeding past in the fast lane. Crossing the border into Scotland, climbing Soutra, the rain had turned to sleet, then snow, and conditions had become even more dicey.

Elfrida had suggested stopping once more for a restful night, but Oscar simply wanted to *get* there, so they had pressed on, further and further north. At the summit of Drumochter the snow had been six inches deep and they had crawled along behind the sheltering tailgate of a huge articulated lorry, trusting that if disaster struck, it would at least strike the lorry first.

Darkness fell early, and the final miles were achieved in night-time conditions. As well, Oscar found that his memory failed him, and he became confused by new road systems and bypasses that had been built since his long-ago boyhood visits.

'Why does everything have to change?' he complained pettishly, struggling to read the map by the light of a torch.

'For the better,' Elfrida told him, firmly. 'At least we're not threading our way along a single-track lane.'

Finally, they were crossing the new bridge that spanned the firth.

'In the old days,' Oscar remembered, 'we had to drive over the hills and about five miles inland.'

'You see? Things are better. Where do we go next?'

'We have to turn left, back on to the old road, heading west.'

'Will the old road still be there?'

'If it isn't, we're scuppered.'

But it was there, and in the dark they turned off the fast dual carriageway and set out into the country. By now Elfrida was getting very tired. Finding Billicliffe's house was the final frustrating straw. 'He's in old Ferguson's cottage,' Hector had told Oscar, when asked for instructions and directions. 'Used to be head forester. You remember him. Turn into the main gates and follow your nose. I'll ring Billicliffe and tell him you're coming.'

But somehow, in the darkness, they lost all sense of distance and overshot the main gates. Too late, Oscar saw the sign as it flashed past:

CORRYDALE COUNTRY
HOUSE HOTEL
AA
RAC
★★★★

They had to find a place to turn from which to retrace their steps. This took a long time, and was a muddy farmyard with a ferociously barking dog. Back again, at a snail's pace, and this time they were more successful. Once through the gates Oscar peered around him, trying to find landmarks, but ended up more confused than ever.

'I don't remember any of this,' he complained, sounding as though his amnesia was all Elfrida's fault.

'Things change, Oscar. Things change.'

'I can't see a single bloody house anywhere.'

'Well, we can't drive round in circles for the rest of the night.' Elfrida sounded a little desperate. Oscar hoped she wasn't about to lose her cool: she had been so wonderfully calm for two days and he didn't think he could bear it if she became as despairing as he already felt. 'Are you sure we're on the right road?'

But by now, Oscar wasn't sure. He wasn't sure about anything any longer. He said, sadly, 'Perhaps we're too old for wild-goose chases.'

'Oh, don't be ridiculous, of course we're not. And it's not a wild goose chase, it's a key chase. We've got to get the key. All we have to do is find the stupid cottage.'

Which, in the end, of course they did, quite by chance. They turned left on to a rutted lane that seemed to lead to nowhere, but all at once there was a light shining through naked trees, an open gate and a short driveway, leading to a single small stone house, with a single curtained window lighted from within.

'Is this it?' Elfrida asked, in doubtful tones.

Recognisable. Remembered. Oscar breathed a sigh of relief. 'This,' he told her, 'is it.'

'Thank God for that.'

She turned the car in through the gate, and drew up in front of the small house, the tyres scrunching on pebbly gravel. Their headlights illuminated a rural wooden porchway, a closed door. Elfrida switched off the engine. At once, nearly frightening them both out of their wits, the quiet was ripped apart by a cacophony of deep-throated barking and furious, eerie howls.

Elfrida said, 'For heaven's sake.'

'A dog,' Oscar observed.

'A mastiff. A Rottweiler. A hound. A Baskerville hound. I'm not getting out of this car. I would prefer to keep all my limbs.'

But then there came the sound of a voice, raised in fury, and a slammed door. The barking stopped. In the back seat, poor patient Horace sat up and gazed timidly out of the window. It was clear that he didn't wish to lose a limb either. They waited.

Oscar said, 'We're just going to collect the key and get on our way. No socialising.'

'Whatever you want.'

The door of the cottage was opened. Within shone the dim illumination of a small lobby. A lanky, gangling figure stood there, sagging at the knees in order to peer out beneath the low lintel, and with a hand up to shade his eyes against the glare of the car lights. Elfrida, obligingly, turned them off.

'That you? Blundell? Been waiting . . .'

The sentence was not finished, simply left hanging in the air.

Oscar and Elfrida got out of the car, both stiff and aching with exhaustion. Oscar felt his knees creaking. The outside air was bitterly cold.

'I'm sorry,' he apologised, although indeed they could scarcely have arrived earlier. 'Difficult, driving in the dark. It's all unfamiliar. We've come for the key and then—'

He had been going to say, 'We'll be on our way,' but Major Billicliffe overrode him.

'Of course. Got it here. Come along in. Just going to have a snifter. You'll join me.'

'Well . . .'

'Splendid to see you. Been looking forward. Come in out of the cold.'

He stood aside, holding the door open hospitably, and after a moment's hesitation Oscar capitulated, although all he wanted was no further delay, to complete this hideous journey, get to Creagan and take possession of his house. But it seemed that they were in for a social encounter, with drinks.

'Thank you,' he said weakly, and put out a hand to steer Elfrida in front of him. 'This is my friend, Elfrida Phipps. She came to share the driving with me.'

'Splendid. Splendid. Hell of a long way. Charmed to meet you, ma'am.' He took Elfrida's hand, and for a mad moment Oscar thought he might be about to press a kiss upon it, so courtly and old-world was his manner.

Elfrida said, 'Hello.'

'Now, let's get the door closed and shut the damned cold away. Come along.'

They followed him into a small, low-ceilinged sitting room, where a tiny fire in a tiled grate did little to warm the air. All seemed to be in a state of sad confusion: sagging leather chairs, a wrinkled rug, a carpet covered in dog-hair, ashtrays brimming with pipe ash.

At the back of the room was another door behind which the enraged dog had been shut away. Whines and heavy breathing emanated from beyond, and every now and then there was a thump and a rattle of a latch as, frustrated beyond measure, the imprisoned brute flung its weight against the door.

Elfrida, naturally enough, began to look a bit nervous. 'What kind of dog is it?' she asked.

'Labrador,' Major Billicliffe told her. 'Dear old bitch. Wouldn't hurt a fly.'

Over the fire was a mantelpiece, crowded with an array of objects: tarnished mugs, a golf ball, a clock that had stopped at a quarter past twelve, some dog-eared postcards and invitations, and a leather box in which Major Billicliffe kept his hearing aids. Before doing anything else, he retrieved these, and proceeded to fit them into his huge red ears. Oscar and Elfrida watched, fascinated, while he made a few squeaking adjustments with the tip of his finger. He then turned back to them, wearing an expression of satisfaction, as though a difficult job had been well done.

'That's better. Take them out most of the time. Sometimes forget where I've put 'em. Now, what can I get you?'

He made his way across the room to an old trolley on wheels, laden with bottles and with one or two smeary glasses set out on the bottom shelf. 'Bar's open.'

Oscar longed for a cup of tea, but knew that that

would take much longer to prepare. 'A Scotch would be splendid. Very small. A lot of water.'

'And the lady?'

Elfrida looked a bit nonplussed. She, too, was longing for tea. But she said bravely, 'A sherry?'

'Got some somewhere. Where's the bottle?' He held it up. It contained a very small quantity of liquid. 'Just enough for one.'

Pouring drinks, he talked. Oscar and Elfrida stood by the miserable fire and did not interrupt. ''Fraid the housekeeping's a bit hit and miss these days. Wife died, you know, couple of years ago. Miss her like hell, but what can one do? I've got a female who's meant to come and clean.' Oscar watched him, splashing clumsily about with bottles and jugs, spilling water on the carpet, lifting a glass with a trembling hand. To look at, Major Billicliffe was something of an old wreck, knock-kneed as a horse on its way to the knacker's yard, and with thin stockinged legs that ended in a pair of enormous black, unpolished brogues. His head was bald, sparsely covered with a few strands of grey hair, and his eyes rheumy. His moustache was tobacco-stained, and his yellowed teeth uneven. It was hard to imagine him as a dapper upright officer in any regiment of the British Army.

'Hector rang me and said you'd be coming. Delighted. About time we had a bit of new blood about the place. How is the old boy? Funny we've never met before, you and I, but then it's years ... I've been here since the sixties, came straight out of the Army. Well, not quite. Did a course at Cirencester first, had to qualify. Factor. Not a job any fool can do. Good fishing. The wife found it a bit lonely. Didn't fish. Walked the dogs. The old telly saved her reason.' He had achieved their drinks and now, with a glass in either hand, came shambling over to deliver them. 'The whisky looks a bit pale. Sure that's all right?'

'Perfect,' Oscar lied.

Major Billicliffe returned to the trolley in order to deal with his own thirst, which seemed to require an enormously dark whisky in a small tumbler.

'Ought to be some eats about the place. A crisp. Sit down, make yourselves comfortable.'

'We mustn't be too long.'

'Won't take you five minutes to get to Creagan.' Without much alternative, Oscar and Elfrida perched side by side on a sofa. It stank of dog. Across the hearthrug, Major Billicliffe lowered his tremendous height into the only armchair, his bony knees knobbly beneath the worn tweed of his knickerbockers.

'I'm retired now, of course. Good of Hector to let me buy this cottage, but it was standing empty anyway. And Hughie couldn't have cared less. The days of farm-workers and tied cottages are over. All contractors now. Damned great machinery. Liked working for Hector, but it didn't last long. Hector went, Hughie came, and fairly put the cat amongst the pigeons. Orgies, he used to have in the big house. Bloody orgies. Disgraceful. Set a rotten example. Is that drink all right? Couldn't deal with the feller at all. Parted brass rags, as they say in the Royal Navy, but by then I'd had a bellyful and was ready to go out to grass. Now everything's different. Hughie buggered off to Barbados and sold the place up. Hotel. You probably saw the sign. All plate glass and bathrooms. And the bar prices are daylight robbery. Never go near the place. All that's left of the estate now is the home farm, and young Thomson – his father used to be tenant farmer – bought it when the estate was sold up. Seems to be doing all right. But I never go near the hotel. Told you. Take my pleasures in the golf club. Do you play golf? Quite a jolly little group of us down there. You should join. Put your name up if you like. Short walk from the Estate House. Nice old pair, been living there for years. Cochrane was their name. Then he upped and died and she's gone south to live with her daughter. Lucky for you, perhaps. Then, there's Mrs Snead . . . keeps an eye on the place. Comes and goes. Think Hector pays her a retainer. He never said?'

Oscar nodded.

'Nice woman. Nice woman. Met her in the butcher. Said she'd get the boiler going. Not my responsibility any longer or I'd have popped in for CO's inspection.'

Oscar, feeling desperate, said, 'The key?'

Major Billicliffe frowned, bewildered. 'Sorry?'

'The key. To the Estate House. If you could let me have it, we'll get out of your way.'

'Ah, yes. Got it somewhere.' He knocked back his drink with one expert toss of his elbow, laid down the empty glass and heaved himself to his feet. Across the room once more to an old roll-topped desk, standing open and chaotically untidy. Stooping over this he rootled hopelessly around for a moment or two, feeling into pigeonholes, opening and shutting drawers. At last, 'Eureka,' he exclaimed, and held up a large old-fashioned key, tied to a crumpled label. 'Knew I'd put it somewhere. Get a bit forgetful, these days.'

Oscar and Elfrida finished their meagre drinks and rose firmly to their feet. Oscar took the key from Major Billicliffe's hand. 'Thank you. I am sorry we disturbed you.'

'Didn't disturb me at all. Splendid to have a bit of company. Remember, I'm usually in the club most days. Don't play as much as I used to. Good to have a crack with old chums and you can get a jolly good sandwich in the bar.' They eased their way towards the door. 'You must come and see me again. And perhaps I'll pop in and call at the Estate House. See how you're settling in.'

Elfrida smiled. She said, 'Of course. But don't come *quite* right away. Oscar's not been very well, and we'll need a little time.'

'Of course, of course. But we'll certainly see each other around.'

Now, in the middle of his long walk, Oscar paused to watch the golfers, safe in the knowledge that the dreaded Billicliffe was not one of the four men. They had already positioned themselves, selected clubs, and not wishing to disturb them, or deflect their attention, he stood motionless until the last player had whacked his ball into what appeared to be orbit. The light was already dying, and it occurred to Oscar that they would have to get their skates on if they were to be back in the clubhouse before dark. The golfer stooped to retrieve his tee and, in doing so, caught sight of Oscar.

Across the rolling fairway that lay between them, their eyes met for an instant. The other man raised a hand in greeting, or maybe simply an acknowledgement of Oscar's consideration. Oscar returned his salute. Then the golfer stowed his driver into his bag, picked up the handle of his trolley and set off after his friends. Oscar watched him go, a burly figure in his scarlet jacket and bright blue trousers. He wondered if he was a visitor to Creagan – come, perhaps, from the United States – or a local resident. Moments later he disappeared behind the natural hazard of a gorsy hillock, and Oscar and the dog continued on their way.

He was beginning to feel a bit weary. Below him, between the links and the dunes, he saw the stony track used by the greenkeepers' tractors, which led back to the town. Beyond curved the long sweep of the beach and ahead, in the far distance, he could see, silhouetted against the grey clouds, the random rooftops and the church spire of the town. The effect was sombre as an old etching. It seemed a very long way off, and he wondered if perhaps he had bitten off more than he could chew. But then he spied the small wooden shelter, provided for the convenience of golfers caught in a downpour or needing to take the weight off their feet for a moment or so. As he approached, Oscar saw that it was divided into four segments, giving shelter from any prevailing wind and each furnished with a small wooden bench. He decided to sit for a moment to get his breath, chose the most suitable compartment, and made himself as comfortable as he could.

He thought about the golfers, companionably playing their game, deep into the dusk of a dying afternoon, and knew an envy that was almost resentment. They were together. Friends. Talking, joking, competing. They would have a drink in the clubhouse, part, return to their families. Ordinary men.

He wondered if he would ever be ordinary again.

Once, long ago, as a boy, Oscar had played golf, but never very proficiently. Perhaps he should take it up again, buy himself an expensive set of clubs, with a Big Bertha driver, and astonish everybody, including himself, with a startling prowess at pitch and putt. The prospect, though amusing, did not make him smile. Now, nothing much made him smile.

Grieving. He was still grieving. He had himself often used this innocuous word, writing to friends recently bereaved of wife, parent, even a child. It was a word that covered a multitude of unexperienced emotions. Sympathy was another. 'I send my deepest sympathy and my thoughts are with you,' he would write, sign the letter and duly post it with the knowledge of a necessary task performed to the best of his ability.

He knew now that he had not had an inkling of what he was talking about. Grief was not a state of mind but a physical thing, a void, a deadening blanket of unbearable pain precluding all solace. His only protection, and one that he had built himself, was a palisade of non-communication. Here, in Creagan, he was spared the encounters, the chance meetings with a casual acquaintance. Spared the insult of the Vicar's churchly comfort, the pain of another's embarrassment. The clumsy but well-meant condolences, eyes that did not meet his own.

During his walk he had, as was his custom, observed sky, clouds, hills, birds. Had felt the wind on his cheeks and listened to the thunder of breakers on the shore. He had smelt the sweet strong scent of moss and ling ... all with no reaction, no lift of the spirit, no marvel. No inspiration. No joy. It was a bit like looking at an indifferent painting, a huge landscape painstakingly executed but lacking all soul.

He had always despised self-pity and now, sitting huddled in the small wooden shelter, he fought it like a lion, striving to be positive, to count present blessings. First was the Estate House. The fact that he owned a bit of it and that it stood empty, a timely sanctuary to which he had fled. Second was Elfrida. Her reappearance after her holiday in Cornwall had been of the utmost relief to Oscar. Her companionship had saved his reason, and in her own uncomplicated way she had got him through the blackest times, comforting by simply accepting his limitations. When he fell silent, she left him alone. When he felt compelled to talk, Elfrida listened.

And third was the knowledge that, even if he did not stay for ever in this remote northern community where once he had been a boy, and happy, there was no possibility of return to the house that had been Gloria's. Already her two sons had taken possession of the Grange and put it on the market. In a way Oscar was grateful to them, because their swift and not wholly commendable actions spared him the ordeal of existing in a space haunted by memories of Francesca, and filled only with a cold and numbing silence.

I must go on, he told himself. Move forward, a step at a time. But at sixty-seven, with most of his life behind him, it sometimes seemed impossible to summon the energy. That deadening blanket, compounded of shock and terrible loss, had not only blinded and deafened him but imbued every bone in his body with a dreadful and pervasive fatigue.

'I must go on.' This time he said the words aloud, and Horace, who had been lying at his feet, sat up, looked hopeful and even smiled. He was a very smiley dog. Oscar was grateful for his company. He got to his feet. 'Come on, old chap. Time we headed for home.'

By the time he finally reached the clubhouse it was dark, and Oscar was very tired. He trudged up the right-of-way that led between the fairways and saw the blaze of lights shining out from wide windows behind which figures could be seen, relaxed as though in a friendly pub, sitting at tables, eating sandwiches, doubtless discussing their game. Between the clubhouse and the first tee was a paved forecourt with raised beds that, in summer, would probably sport cheerful clumps of colour: begonias and geraniums. To the side of the clubhouse was the car park, now floodlit from above. A dozen or so vehicles were still standing there, and as Oscar wearily approached he saw a well-worn estate car with its tailgate down. On this a man was perched, in the act of changing his studded golf shoes for a pair of brogues. Oscar recognised the red windcheater and the bright blue weatherproof trousers, but the long-peaked American cap had been removed and cold light shone down upon a head of thick greying hair.

The man tied the last lace and got to his feet. By now Oscar was alongside. For an instant, he hesitated, debating as to whether he should stop and exchange a friendly word. Ask, perhaps, how the game had gone. But even as he wavered the decision was taken out of his hands.

'Hello there. Did you have a good walk?'

Oscar paused, then turned to face him. 'A bit too far, perhaps. I'm out of practice. How did you get along?'

'We gave up on the fifteenth. Chickened out. Too dark and too cold.' He stooped to retrieve his golf shoes, chucked them into the back of the car and slammed the tailgate. 'Not the weather for an enjoyable game.' He came forward. Oscar saw a ruddy countryman's face and a pair of piercingly blue eyes. 'Forgive me, but you're Oscar Blundell.'

Oscar found himself disconcerted by being not only

recognised but identified. He said, 'Yes,' and it sounded like an admission.

'I knew you'd come back to Creagan.' (What else did he know?) 'I've only been here for twenty years, so I never met your grandmother, Mrs McLellan, but I did have the pleasure of a good friendship with Hector. Just for a short while, before he handed Corrydale over to Hughie and went south to live. I'm Peter Kennedy, by the way.' He stuck out a hand, which Oscar took in his own gloved one. 'Welcome to Creagan.'

'Thank you.'

'You must be exhausted. That's a long hike in the teeth of the wind. I'm just going in for a cup of tea. Would you care to join me?'

Oscar was silenced, hesitating, torn by conflicting emotions. It was true. He was bone weary, and the thought of sitting down for a bit in the warmth and indulging in the solace of a restoring and hot cup of tea was a very tempting one. On the other hand, he was not sure if he felt brave enough to go into that brightly lighted and convivial clubhouse. He would perhaps be introduced, have to talk to strangers, answer questions.

But there was something so warm and genuine about his new friend, so disarming and sincere, that he could not bring himself to refuse the invitation outright. Instead he searched for some excuse.

'I have the dog.'

'We'll put him in my car. He'll come to no harm for a little while.'

'I . . .' It had to be said. 'I would prefer not to encounter Major Billicliffe.'

Peter Kennedy's cheerful face creased into an understanding smile. 'Don't worry.' He laid a hand on Oscar's arm. 'He went home five minutes ago. I saw him drive off.'

'You'll think me uncharitable.'

'No, I don't think that. So you'll join me?'

'Yes. Yes, I will. I would like to. Thank you very much.'

'I'm delighted.'

They dealt with Horace, incarcerating him in the back of Peter Kennedy's estate car, along with the shoes and the golf-bag. He gazed at them reproachfully through the back window, but Oscar hardened his heart. 'I won't be long,' he told the dog.

They walked together around the corner of the club-house and up the shallow flight of steps that led to the main door. Peter Kennedy opened this and held it for Oscar to go through into a foyer hectically carpeted and lined with cabinets containing silver trophies and shields. Portraits of former captains glowered down at them. To the right, glassed doors led into the main room, furnished with tables and comfortable chairs, and with a small bar in the corner. As they entered one or two people looked up, but by and large nobody took much notice of them.

'We'll go and sit over there. There's a free table, and we'll be quiet.'

But before they could do this a swing door by the side of the bar flew open, and an elderly waitress appeared. She wore a black skirt and a white blouse, and her white hair was marvellously waved and dressed. Spying them, she was at once all smiles. 'Mr Kennedy, I didn't think we'd be seeing you this evening.'

'Hello, Jessie. Are we too late for a cup of tea?'

'Never too late. You must be frozen, out playing

on a day like this.' Her eyes turned to Oscar, who had removed his tweed hat and was standing there, bundled up in all his layers of coats and sweaters. 'Have you been playing, too?'

'No. Just walking.'

'Jessie, this is Mr Oscar Blundell. He's come to stay at the Estate House.'

'Oh, my, that's who you are! I'd heard you'd moved in but I haven't seen you around. Are you a golfer too?'

'I'm sorry, no.'

'We'll have to rectify that. Now, Mr Kennedy, where do you want to sit?'

But before there was time to tell her an interruption occurred. From across the long room there came a shout, a deep voice ringing out like a clarion, startling everyone, and causing frowns from a group who were crouched around the television. '*Peter!* Come away over and have a word. I haven't seen you for a week or more.'

Peter Kennedy swung round, and Oscar, following his gaze, saw in the far corner a heavily built and aged man sitting in a wheelchair with a tumbler of whisky ready to hand on the table in front of him.

'*Peter!*' He was waving a knotted stick, as though it were possible that he had neither been heard nor seen. 'Come and give me all the news.'

'Would you mind, Oscar, if I left you for a moment? It's old Charlie Beith and I must go and pay my respects.'

'Of course.'

'I'll be just a moment. Jessie will take care of you.' He went, making his way down the length of the room. 'What a great surprise,' he was saying. 'Are you having a day out, Charlie?' And the old man in the wheel-chair greeted him with such delight and affection that

Oscar felt that he was in some way intruding, and turned away.

Jessie took charge. 'Come and sit down and get comfortable. Take your coat off, or you'll not feel the benefit when you go out again. Would you like a scone? And do you prefer Indian or China tea?'

Oscar said. 'I'm sorry, but who is that?'

'Charlie Beith? He's a real character, over ninety, though you'd never know it. Used to farm out at Toshlands, years ago. His grandson's running the place now. He was doing fine till a couple of years ago when he had a stroke. He lives in the old people's home, and Mr Kennedy's a regular visitor. One of his daughters brought him up here this evening, just for a bit of a change and some cheerful company. He's as bright as a button up top.'

'In fact,' Oscar hesitated, 'I didn't mean the old man. I meant Peter Kennedy. I've only just met him, in the car park. He knew my uncle. But I don't know . . .'

'You mean you don't know what he does or who he is? You must be the only soul in Creagan who doesn't. He's our minister. The minister of the church.'

The minister. The Vicar. The Rector. Whatever. The man whose job it was to comfort not only the physically but the emotionally crippled as well. Peter Kennedy's spontaneous friendliness had seemed genuine, but this new knowledge rendered it depressingly suspect. Did he already know why Oscar had returned to Creagan? Had he been told about the ghastly deaths of Oscar's wife and child? And if so, who . . . ?

But I did have the pleasure of a good friendship with Hector.

Had Hector, with only the best of intentions, been

in touch with Peter Kennedy? Explained the situation. Suggested, perhaps, a pastoral visit. Comforting chats; counselling; a gentle urging back to a church in which Oscar no longer believed.

Jessie said, 'Are you all right?'

He looked into her concerned, motherly face. He realised that his own was suffused with heat, his forehead wet with sweat. A heat kindled not by the warm room and his layers of outdoor clothes but an inner turmoil that was frighteningly akin to panic. He knew that he could not stay there or he would suffocate.

With a huge effort, he made himself speak. 'I am sorry. It's very warm. I've just remembered.' His voice sounded unreal, like a voice from another room. 'I promised. I must get home. A telephone call . . .'

'But what about your tea?'

'I'm afraid I can't . . .' Backing off, he tried to apologise again. 'I'm sorry. Please explain to Mr Kennedy. Another time . . .'

He turned away from her and carefully, slowly, made for the door. The plate glass was heavy to open, and swung shut behind him. He crossed the foyer and opened the second set of doors, then stepped out into the bitter air. The cold wind was an assault and he stopped to steady himself, to let the icy air fill his lungs. He could feel the sweat chilling on his brow, and pulled on his old tweed hat. He was all right. He was surviving. All he had to do was get himself home. To be safe. Alone with Elfrida. He went down the steps, crossed over to the car park and retrieved Horace from Peter Kennedy's car. Then he was on his way, walking at a tremendous pace, dragging the dog behind him. Escaping.

Elfrida

Elfrida

In Dibton, the Women's Institute was great on mystery tours. These usually took place on a Saturday afternoon and entailed the ladies being piled into a bus and whirled off to some unknown destination. Quite often, this was a stately home, with gardens to be viewed and a gift shop where they could buy flowered tea-towels, book-marks and packets of home-made fudge. After the shopping, tea would be taken at some local hotel; a proper tea, with fish and chips. Then they would all pile into the bus once more and be driven home.

These outings were very popular.

Spirited so abruptly, by circumstances outwith her control, to the north of Scotland, to Creagan and the Estate House was, Elfrida decided, the mystery tour of all time. From the moment she and Oscar departed from Dibton, she had no idea of what lay in store for her, and there never came an appropriate moment to ask. So precipitant had been their departure, so swift the packing process, and so brief the time for goodbyes, that nitpicking details of their destination lost all importance. They just had to get away.

There were, of course, essential arrangements to be made. Oscar's car had to be serviced and checked and filled with petrol. Oscar saw to that. His stepsons, Giles and Crawford, were informed of his imminent departure, and his bank manager alerted as to his change of address. As for Elfrida, she handed the key of Poulton's Row to her neighbour, with as few explanations as possible, and asked her, as well, to keep an eye on the poor little Ford Fiesta, abandoned on the pavement outside her cottage.

'When will you be back, Mrs Phipps?'

'I've truly no idea. But I'll keep in touch. Here's the car key as well. Use it if you want. It'll do it good.' Rather as though it were an old dog, needing daily exercise. 'I've turned the water off at the mains, and locked all the windows.'

'But where are you going?'

'I think to Scotland.'

Then Oscar had to get in touch with Hector McLellan and put him in the picture, while Elfrida telephoned her cousin Jeffrey in Cornwall and tried to explain to him the circumstances of what she was about to do. She did not make a very good job of this, and it took him some time to get the hang of the situation. When he finally did, however, he only said, 'Good luck,' and once she had given him the address and telephone number of Oscar's house, he let her go and rang off.

Without any clear idea of what sort of clothes she would need, she packed a suitcase with an assortment of garments (warm) and shoes (stout). Then, an ancient, squashy, zipped bag for her most precious things, the possessions that had always travelled everywhere with her. The silk shawl, wrapped around the little painting by Sir David Wilkie; the Staffordshire dogs; her clock; her current piece of tapestry. On top went a few photographs in silver frames and half a dozen books. That was all. Oscar's luggage was scarcely more bulky: a leather holdall, packed by Mrs Muswell, a bulging briefcase and his fishing gear.

'Do you intend to go fishing, Oscar?'

'No idea. But I can't travel to Scotland without my rod. It would be almost sacrilegious.'

There was space for all this in the back of Oscar's Volvo, and still room for Horace, his blanket, his biscuits and his water bowl. Horace, like Elfrida, had no idea what was in store for him but leaped happily into the car and made himself comfortable, clearly relieved that he was not going to be left behind. He did not trust suitcases standing about the place.

'We are travelling light,' Elfrida observed to Oscar, but he was too anxious and distracted to make any comment on her remark.

Instead, he turned away to give last-minute instructions to his loyal Mrs Muswell, who had stood by him all through the dark days, and was now on the doorstep, clearly much distressed, as though at any moment she might burst into tears.

'Mrs Muswell.'

'Send me a postcard,' she told him bravely, but her voice was not steady.

'Of course. Goodbye. Thank you for everything.' And he gave her a quick peck on the cheek, which caused Mrs Muswell to go to pieces. As they drove away from the Grange, Elfrida saw, through the back window, the gallant pinafored figure blowing her nose and wiping her eyes with a handy handkerchief.

'What will become of her?' Elfrida asked, feeling like a traitor.

'Giles has promised he'll see her right. She should have no difficulty in finding a job. She's a marvellous woman.'

After that they stopped talking. Elfrida drove most of the way, only letting Oscar take over when she became dangerously weary. TIREDNESS CAN KILL, roadside signs shouted, at the cars and lorries that streamed north on the A1. TAKE A BREAK. And she would draw the car to the side of the road at the next layby or motorway halt, and change seats with him.

During that first day, he seldom spoke, and she let him be silent and did not even suggest that they listen to Classic FM on the car radio. From time to time they stopped to give Horace a run, stretch their own legs, have something to eat, a cup of tea. The weather was cold and bleak, and darkness fell early, when driving became even more stressful. Because of this, they left the motorway and drove to a small Northumberland town Oscar remembered. There, in the main square, they found an old coaching inn he remembered as well, and it didn't seem to be too modernised or changed. Better still, the management were kindly about Horace and allowed him in, provided he and his blanket stayed upstairs.

On the second morning, as soon as the shops were open, Elfrida walked out into the little town, found a small supermarket and bought provisions for their eventual arrival: a can of soup, bread, butter, bacon and eggs; a packet of coffee, a carton of milk. The man in the shop packed all this into a grocery box for her, and then she spied a bottle of whisky (medicinal?) and bought that too.

The second day's driving was a bit better. Horrible weather, but at least Oscar was more communicative. He eyed the passing fields and farms, pointed out landmarks, gazed warily at the sky and made his own gloomy forecasts. But yet, it was not the time for chatter, for the stream of questions to which she ached to know the answer. What will it be like, Oscar? How big is the Estate House, and will anybody have left it warm, and will there be any hot water? And will it be clean, and will there be sheets? And will people be friendly to us, and will they know you? Or will they shun us?

It was all unimaginable. But, she told herself, grinding in second gear up the slippery slope of Soutra with the windscreen wipers going full tilt and all the world drowned in the whiteness of a sudden sleet storm, this is an adventure.

As a young woman, an actress, she had travelled with touring companies the length and breadth of Britain without ever knowing what awaited at the end of the journey. Her memories of those days were a blur of provincial towns, musty theatres and theatrical lodgings that smelt of boiled cabbage. But she had been young, doing a job she loved, and very happy. Each rattling train journey was a challenge, each grimy theatre a new discovery. A little of that old excitement warmed her now, and she had to remind herself that she was no longer that ardent young girl, but an elderly lady of sixty-two. *At least I am not lonely. Not bored. Or dead.*

The encounter with Major Billicliffe had been the final hurdle. With that accomplished and the key safely in Oscar's pocket, the hard grind of the two-day journey was behind them, and the last few miles were easy, almost carefree. Oscar drove. It was cold, but the snow had ceased, and the dark road ran downhill towards the sea between dense stands of conifer. Elfrida opened her window and heard the soughing of wind in their branches, and smelt pine and a sturdy whiff of salty air. Then the trees fell away, and all about them were duney hillocks and stunted pines, and ahead could be seen a straight, silvery line that was the sea. Far away, across the water, a lighthouse blinked, a pinprick in the darkness. Then ahead, the glow of street-lights, and houses with windows lit behind drawn curtains. A street of stone houses, like a terrace, but each house a different shape and height from its neighbour. She saw the church looming, the lighted clock like a round lantern, high in its tower. The hands stood at seven o'clock. Now, larger, handsome houses, set back behind tall stone walls. Creagan. It seemed deserted. No one trod the streets; no cars. No sound, not even the cry of gulls. Another turning, another street. Oscar drew up at the pavement's edge. He turned off the engine. For a moment he was still. Elfrida waited. Then he laid his hand over hers.

He said, 'Dear girl, we're there.'

The Estate House. Elfrida saw it for the first time by the light of street-lamps: square and solid, set back from the road behind a wrought-iron railing and a forecourt of sea pebbles. The face of the house was a child's drawing, with a door and five windows. Above these, set in the slope of the slated roof, two dormers jutted. They got out of the car and Elfrida set Horace free. He had not forgotten the growls and howls of Major Billicliffe's hound and was, sensibly, wary. But, finally reassured, he leaped down into the road and began tentatively to sniff for unfamiliar smells.

Oscar unlatched the gate and went up the path. Elfrida and Horace followed him. With the key he opened the door. It swung inward and he felt for a light switch, found one and turned it on.

They entered, and Elfrida instantly felt the warmth and smelt the cleanliness of a place newly scrubbed and polished. Ahead a staircase rose to a half-landing and an uncurtained stair window. On either side doors stood closed, but at the end of the hall a third door was open, and Oscar went through this and turned on another light.

Elfrida closed the front door behind her, sealing away the chill of the winter evening. She followed Oscar and found him in a kitchen, where stood an old-fashioned painted dresser and a wooden table. Beneath the window was a clay sink, and at its side a capacious gas cooker, dating back, perhaps, forty years or more.

Oscar said, 'Hardly all-singing, all-dancing.' He sounded a bit apologetic.

'It's fine,' Elfrida assured him, and meant it. 'Someone has left us a letter.' It lay in the middle of the table, a sheet of lined paper, weighted down with a jam jar. Oscar removed the jam jar and handed the letter to Elfrida. She read it aloud.

'I have turned on boiler (oil) You will need
to order more oil. Beds made up in 2 rooms.
Bath water hot. Coal and wood in shed. Some
of the windows won't open. Milk in fridge
(scullery). Will pop in tomorrow to see you all
right. Yours J. Snead (Mrs)'

Oscar said, 'Mrs Snead.'

'Yes.'

'Elfrida, are you about to cry?'

'I might be.'

'Why?'

'Relief.'

That had all happened three weeks ago. It was December now, a Friday, and five o'clock on a dark midwinter afternoon. Oscar, who had set out after lunch with Horace at his heels, had still not returned. Elfrida blotted out images of him dead of a heart-attack, his body prone at the foot of a sand dune. He was simply taking his time, hopefully enjoying his first real expedition into the country, feeling better for the exercise and filling his lungs with restoring fresh air. The decision to go had been his alone, and she had been careful not to appear too enthusiastic, fearful of giving him the impression that she longed to be rid of him.

She stood in the kitchen at the gas stove while the kettle boiled. She made a mug of tea, with a teabag, added milk and took it upstairs to the sitting room. They called it the sitting room but, indeed, it was a drawing room, formal and spacious, with a huge bay window looking out over the street and the church. Hours could be wasted simply sitting on the window-seat and watching the world go by: cars coming and going, delivery-vans and grit lorries; shoppers, pausing on the pavement to chat, strings of chattering children, like sparrows, walking to and from school.

The room was furnished, as was all the house, with the bare minimum of furniture. A thick Turkey carpet. A sofa and two chairs. A table against the wall, a glass-fronted bookcase, in which a few old books leaned against each other. No pictures, no ornaments. No clue as to the interests and lives of previous occupants. In a way, Elfrida found this lack of decoration and clutter quite therapeutic. Without pictures, knick-knacks, small bits of silver and sets of decorative porcelain to divert the eye, it was possible to appreciate the lovely proportions of the room, the ornate cornice and the plaster rose in the centre of the ceiling from which depended a charming Victorian chandelier.

Arriving, unpacking, she had put her modest stamp upon the place. The David Wilkie now hung opposite the fireplace, above the heavy oak table Oscar used as a desk. The Staffordshire dogs and her clock occupied the empty marble mantelpiece. From Arthur Snead, Fruit and Vegetables, she had bought a bunch of chrysanthemums, found a yellow jug and created a not very ambitious arrangement. Her half-done tapestry lay across the seat of a chair. Earlier on, she had lit the fire. Now, she fed it with coal and logs then went to the window to sit and watch for Oscar. But no sooner had she settled herself, her mug between her hands, than the telephone rang. This was startling because it had scarcely rung since they had taken up residence. Elfrida hoped it was not Major Billicliffe. She set the mug on the floor and went to answer it. The telephone stood on the first-floor landing, on a small chest just outside the sitting-room door. She picked up the receiver. 'Hello.'

'Elfrida?'

'Yes.'

'It's Carrie. Carrie Sutton.'

'*Carrie*. Where are *you*?'

'In London. How are you?'

'All right.'

'Jeffrey told me you were in Scotland. Gave me your number. Elfrida, I've got something to ask you. It's a favour. It's a huge favour.'

'Ask away.'

'It's about Christmas.'

It was, necessarily, a very long telephone call. Finally they were finished. Elfrida replaced the receiver; at the same moment she heard the front door open and close and knew that Oscar and Horace were home. She leaned over the banister and called, 'Are you safely back?'

'Yes. We're here.'

She went downstairs. In the hall, he was shedding jacket and hat, hanging them on the bentwood hat-stand. Horace had already headed for the kitchen, his water-bowl and his warm basket. 'You've been ages.'

'We went for miles. The other end of the links and back. I'd forgotten it was so far.' He put up a hand and ran it over his hair. He looked exhausted, she thought.

She said, 'A cup of tea?'

'I think I'm ready for something stronger.'

'A Scotch. Go upstairs. There's a fire. I'll bring it to you.'

In the kitchen, she poured his drink, then put the kettle on again and made herself another mug of tea because she knew that the first one would by now be cold. Horace was already asleep. She left him and went upstairs with the mug in one hand and the tumbler in the other. She found Oscar standing with a hand on the mantelpiece, gazing down into the fire. He turned his head as she came in and smiled gratefully. 'How good you are.'

He took the drink and lowered himself carefully into

one of the armchairs, stretching out his legs before him. Elfrida went to draw the curtains, shutting away the night. 'I didn't draw them before because I was sitting in the window watching for you. Doing a Sister Anne.'

'Did you think I was dead?'

'Imagination does terrible things.'

'I was delayed. Outside the golf club I met a man. We talked. He asked me into the club for a cup of tea, and I accepted, and he went to speak to an old man in a wheelchair. And I asked the waitress who he was, and he is called Peter Kennedy, and he is the minister.'

Elfrida waited. Finally, 'So, Oscar?'

'I thought of him knowing about what had happened. The crash. Gloria and Francesca, both dead. It occurred to me that perhaps Hector had forewarned him. I had thought him simply a friendly chap but I'm afraid he was being kind. Sorry for me. I don't want to be helped. I don't want to have to speak or to listen. I want to be left alone. So I didn't stay. I walked away. Came home.'

'Oh, Oscar.'

'I know. Rude and mannerless.'

'I'm sure he'll understand.'

'I hope so. I liked his face.'

'There's time. Give yourself time.'

He took a deep breath that sounded like a terrible sigh. He said, 'I hate myself.'

'Oh, my dear, never do that.'

'Do you reproach me?'

'No. *I* understand.' She drank some tea, scalding and comforting. She sat, facing him, in a little wide-lapped Victorian chair, upholstered in tartan. The firelight was warm on her shins. She said, 'Perhaps this isn't an

221

opportune moment but I have to ask you something. I have to tell you something.'

'Not, I hope, that you are about to leave me.'

'No, not that. I have had a telephone call. Jeffrey's daughter, Carrie Sutton. She has returned from Austria. She wants to come and spend Christmas with us.'

'But we are not having Christmas.'

'Oscar, I told her, a lamb chop for lunch and no tinsel. I told her that that was what you and I had agreed. She understands. It makes no difference to her. She says she's not interested in Christmas either.'

'Then let her come.'

Elfrida hesitated. 'There is a complication.'

'A man?'

'No. Jeffrey's grandchild. Carrie's niece. Lucy. If Carrie comes, then Lucy must come too.'

There was a very long silence. Oscar's eyes turned from Elfrida's face and gazed into the fire. For a moment he looked as old as his uncle had looked, that dreadful day when Elfrida had come unexpectedly upon the old man and thought for a frightening instant that he was Oscar. She said, 'I told Carrie I would have to ask you. I would have to tell you about the child.'

'How old is she?'

'Fourteen.'

'Why does she have to come?'

'Oh, I don't know.' Elfrida shrugged. 'Some story about her mother going to Florida for Christmas to stay with a friend and the daughter doesn't want to go with her. And Dodie, the grandmother, doesn't want the granddaughter. The sort of selfish muddle that was always happening in that particular family.' Oscar made no comment on this. Elfrida bit her lip. She said, 'I can ring Carrie and tell her no. I can tell her that it is too soon. A little girl around the place would be more than painful for you. It might be unbearable. I understand, and I shan't think any the less of you if you say no.'

He looked at her, his gentle features filled with affection. 'I love your directness, Elfrida.'

'It is the only way.'

'If they come . . .'

'I'll say. No Christmas.'

'But the child?'

'She will be with Carrie. They can do what they want. Go to church. Sing carols, give each other presents.'

'It sounds a little bleak for a youngster.'

'And for *you*, Oscar?'

'It can make no difference. It can change nothing. You want them to come, I think. Then tell them to come.'

'You're sure? You're certain?' He nodded. 'You are a dear, kind, brave man.'

'There's space for them?'

'The attics are empty. Perhaps we could buy a bed, and Lucy shall sleep up there.'

'We'll need to buy more than a bed.'

'Not very much more.'

'It's what you want. That's all that matters. Tell them they're welcome. Come whenever they want. They will be company for you. I'm afraid I am not very lively company.'

'Oscar, lively company was not the point of us coming here together.'

He drank a bit of his whisky, seemingly deep in thought. Then he said, 'Telephone Carrie now. If they take the train or come by aeroplane, we can send a taxi to meet them at Inverness. If they're driving, warn her about the snow.'

She was filled with gratitude for his generosity of spirit. To have him sitting there, mulling over such mundane details, made her feel a great deal better. He was being hostly, almost as though it was he who had issued the invitation and not had it dumped upon him. She finished her tea, and pulled herself to her feet. 'I'll ring her right away.' She made for the door, then turned back. 'Thank you, Oscar.'

Lucy

Lucy

Still Friday 8 December
I've already written down
all the wonderful things that
happened today, about Carrie
coming back and going out for lunch and
her saying maybe she and I can go away for
Christmas somewhere. The cinema was really
good, too. Well, now it is 10.30 and I'm just
going to bed, writing this in my dressing-gown.
What happened was I had a bath after supper
and washed my hair, and while it was drying
went into the kitchen to make a hot chocolate.
Then the phone rang, and Mum came to find me
and to say it was Carrie wanting to talk to me.
I think they'd already had a chat. I picked up
the kitchen telephone and waited till I'd heard
the click and knew Mum had put the other
phone down so wasn't going to listen. She does
sometimes.
And then Carrie told me. We are going
to Scotland for Christmas. Elfrida, Grandpa's

cousin, is staying there with a friend and they both want us to go. It's a place called Creagan, and they say the house is quite big. It is so exciting I could burst. Carrie says it's too far to drive in the middle of winter, so we're going to fly to Inverness and then a taxi will meet us and drive us the rest of the way. We're going on 15 December, and she's already booked seats.

Elfrida's friend is called Oscar, but Carrie doesn't know what he's like because she's never met him.

I said, had she told Mum and Gran, and she said no. And I said would I tell them, and she said no again, because Gran never much approved of Elfrida and it would be better if Carrie told them herself, so she's coming over some time tomorrow to break the news and calm Gran down if she starts being difficult. Mum won't say a word, because all she can think about is Randall and Florida.

I asked Carrie what I should pack, and she said fur coats and snow-shoes, but of course that was just a joke.

I can't believe I am going to Scotland.

I am already counting the days.

Carrie says it probably won't be very Christmassy on account of Oscar and Elfrida being so old. But compared with going away with Carrie, Christmas doesn't matter a bit, and I never liked Christmas pudding much anyway.

She says there is a beach and the North Sea.

I simply can't wait.

Elfrida

Elfrida

Now, Saturday morning, Elfrida was the first downstairs. She had dressed in thick corduroy trousers and two sweaters, and was glad of these when she opened the back door to let Horace out into the garden. During the night there had been a deep frost, all was iced and sparkling, and her footsteps left marks on the thick, crunchy grass of the little lawn. It was not yet light, and she and the dog emerged into the glow of a street-lamp, which lit the stepped lane that led up the hill.

Horace hated the cold, so she stayed with him, waiting while he nosed to and fro, shot up to the top of the garden where he smelt a rabbit, and took much time in finding exactly the right spot for his wee. Standing, freezing cold and trying to be patient, she looked up at the sky, and saw it sapphire blue and quite clear. In the east, over the sea, the glow of dawn was a streak of pink although the sun had yet to edge its way over the horizon. It was going to be a fine day, she decided, and was grateful. They had had enough of grey skies, howling winds and rain.

Finally Horace was done, and they scurried indoors to the warmth, and Elfrida shut the door. Then she put the kettle on, found the frying-pan and the bacon. She laid the table with a checked cloth, cups and saucers. She found eggs. Oscar enjoyed a cooked breakfast, and although Elfrida did not eat it with him, she relished the smell of bacon frying.

Cautiously, she made toast. In this old-fashioned kitchen, that was something of a hazard, because the toaster was elderly, past its best, and behaved accordingly. Sometimes it popped up two quite reasonable nicely browned slices. Other times, it regurgitated uncooked bread. But if, in a bad temper, it forgot to turn itself off, the kitchen was filled with dark smoke and the blackened crusts on offer were so disgusting that not even the seagulls would eat them.

Every now and then Elfrida told herself that they should buy a new toaster. There was a small shop in the high street, William G. Croft, Electrical Goods. The windows of this establishment were filled with microwaves, hair-dryers, steam irons and waffle-makers, along with a number of other gadgets that Elfrida could happily live without. But a toaster was essential. One day she had gone into Croft's but quailed at the expense and departed without having made a purchase.

It was all a bit difficult, because without the little income engendered by her home industry of stitching cushions she found herself chronically short of money: Mondays couldn't come around quickly enough, when she could go to the post office and collect her pension. She supposed that the sensible thing to do would be to find a tenant for Poulton's Row, and let it on a quarterly basis, thus ensuring a small trickle of cash. However, the logistics of organising this from Sutherland were too much for Elfrida, so the tentative idea was abandoned. As for Oscar, she had no idea whether or not he was in the same dilemma and was not about to ask. Probably he had a little bit put by, a stock or a share, but she knew that Gloria had footed the bills for the day-to-day expenses incurred by the lush and generous lifestyle of the Grange.

So, she struggled on with the inherited toaster, having decided that if she did find herself with a bit of spare cash, she preferred to spend it on books or flowers.

Today it was in a good mood, and the smell of bacon mingled with the scent of fresh toast and hot coffee. Coffee was most important. She was sitting at the table drinking her first cup when Oscar came downstairs to join her, and at once Elfrida noticed his appearance. Normally, he wore a thick shirt under a warm pullover. Very informal. No tie. But this morning he had put on not only one of his better shirts but a tie, a waistcoat and his good tweed jacket.

She eyed him in some astonishment. 'You're looking very smart.'

'Thank you. I'm pleased you noticed.'

'Why *are* you looking so smart?'

He retrieved his plate of bacon and eggs from the hotplate, where she had left it to keep warm. 'Because it's Saturday?'

'Not a good enough reason.'

'Because I must not allow myself to become a shabby, shambling old wreck.'

'Putting on a tie isn't going to make that much difference.'

He sat down, and she poured his coffee. 'Thank you.

No, you're quite right. I have made a small effort because I am going calling.'

Elfrida was surprised but took great pains not to show this. She was also intrigued. 'Who are you going to call on?'

'Rose Miller.'

'Who is Rose Miller?'

'A very old friend.'

'You've never mentioned her. Should I be mad with jealousy?'

'I don't think so. She must be eighty-five if she's a day. She was my grandmother's parlourmaid. She lives on the Corrydale estate in a very small cottage with a thatched roof. I am going to pay my respects.'

'Why have you suddenly decided to go and see your grandmother's parlourmaid? You've been keeping such a low profile anyone might think you're an escaped fugitive.'

'Do you mind?'

'Oh, dear Oscar, I'm absolutely delighted. But I don't entirely understand your change of heart.'

Oscar set down his coffee cup. When he spoke again, his voice was different, no longer bantering. He said, 'It was yesterday. Meeting that man. Peter Kennedy. The minister. Behaving so stupidly, so rudely. And there's another thing. During the last few weeks I've thought of myself as anonymous, but of course I'm not. If Peter Kennedy knows about me then so will many other people. They're just too polite and thoughtful and diffident to come banging on our door. This is a small place and news spreads like wildfire. By now Rose Miller is bound to have heard I've come back. And she will be intensely hurt if I don't get in touch with her. So I have decided to go. I shall buy her a bunch of flowers from Arthur Snead and together she and I will take a trip down Memory Lane. You don't need the car, do you?'

'No. That's the best of living here. I can walk across the square to the supermarket, I can walk down the street to the butcher, and on the way home I can go into the bookshop and browse. If I felt so inclined, I could have a little foray into the antiques shop and come back with a Victorian teapot. Or even have my hair tweaked.'

'Do you mean there's actually a hairdresser in Creagan?'

'Of course. Over the barber's shop. Where else?' She leaned across the table to remove his empty plate, and to pour herself her second cup of coffee. The gingham curtains were still drawn, so she pulled them back, and saw the lightening sky.

Suddenly she felt more cheerful than she had for a long time. Things, slowly, were looking up. The day would be fine. Icily cold but fine. Oscar was going calling, and next week Carrie and Lucy would be here. Thinking about it, she decided that perhaps yesterday had been the turning-point, although she had not recognised it as such.

'I shall go for a walk,' Oscar had announced. 'Stretch my legs. Get some fresh air. I shall take Horace with me.' Elfrida, clearly, was neither expected nor invited to join them. Which was just as well, because she had no wish to go out, tramping through the wind and the rain. Again, she managed not to show surprise, and simply told him to wrap up warmly against the bitter weather.

But, perhaps fortuitously, Oscar had met this man, this Peter Kennedy. The minister. And, for whatever reason, had been engaged in conversation, and treated with friendliness and hospitality. The fact that, like a dog biting the feeding hand, Oscar had panicked and walked out on him was probably of less consequence to Peter Kennedy than it was to Oscar who, clearly, had been much ashamed of his behaviour. Perhaps, during the night, he had lain awake filled with remorse. Perhaps going to visit the old parlourmaid, Rose Miller, was a way of reparation, his first voluntary step back into the company of others.

'What time will you go, Oscar?' She brought her cup back to the table. 'To keep your assignation with Rose?'

'It's not an assignation because she doesn't know I'm coming.'

'Yes, but *assignation* sounds so much more exciting.'

'I thought about half past ten. Would you consider that a suitable time?'

'Perfect. She'll be up and about, and she will give you a cup of tea and perhaps a biscuit.' She drank her coffee. 'Maybe, while you're at Corrydale, you should look in on Major Billicliffe.'

'I hoped you wouldn't say that.'

'Oh, Oscar, you are being feeble. He's a harmless old git, and probably dreadfully lonely. It's unkind to go on living here and just pretending he doesn't exist. After all, he was all ready with the key and a rather dim little drink.' Oscar, silent, did not look enthusiastic. 'You could just drop in casually to pass the time of day. Perhaps ask him along for a drink or something when Carrie and Lucy are here. You could say it was a party.'

Cunningly, Oscar steered the discussion off at a tangent. 'When are they coming?'

'Friday. I told you. They're flying to Inverness and I've asked the taxi man to go and get them.'

'I didn't know we had a taxi man.'

'Alec Dobbs.'

'I thought he was the undertaker.'

'He is, but he does taxis as well.'

'A man of many parts.'

Elfrida sipped her coffee. She had now forgotten about Major Billicliffe and was thinking instead about Carrie and Lucy's arrival. 'There isn't much time, is there? I'll have to get round to finding some furniture for the attic. There must be a second-hand shop around somewhere. I shall make enquiries.'

'Who will you ask?'

'The butcher?'

'Or the newsagent?'

'Or the undertaker?'

'Mrs Snead, of course. She will be bound to know.'

This fascinating discussion might have gone on for ever had they not been disturbed by the shrilling of the front-door bell, which caused Horace, startled out of his wits, to sit up in his basket and bark with agitation.

Elfrida shushed him, went out of the kitchen and down the hall. The doorbell had been the postman, and there were two letters on the mat. Which seemed, to Elfrida, another good omen because they had scarcely had any correspondence delivered since the day they arrived.

She stooped, picked up the letters and carried them back to Oscar.

'One is for you, typed and businesslike, probably from your bank manager. And the other is for me.'

'Now it's my turn to be jealous.'

'I don't think so.' She felt for her spectacles in the pocket of her sweater and put them on. 'Rather neat, spiky old writing.' She picked up a knife, slit the envelope and took out the letter. She turned the page over to find the signature, and smiled.

'Oscar, it's from Hector. That dear old man, writing to us.' She sat down and unfolded the thick blue paper. 'And a *cheque*! A cheque for five hundred pounds.'

Oscar's jaw fell. 'Five hundred pounds? Are you sure?'

'See for yourself. Made out to you.' She handed it over. He stared at it in some bewilderment, then said, 'Perhaps you'd better find out what it's all about.'

So, Elfrida read aloud:

My dear Oscar and Elfrida,
I have not written before, because I wanted to give you both time to settle in. I trust you had a safe journey and found the Estate House in good condition.
I have to confess that, after you left, I felt impelled to write a letter to Peter Kennedy, the minister of the parish church in Creagan. I know your desire for privacy and anonymity, to give you the opportunity to come to terms with the tragedy which you have suffered. But I could not help worrying about you, and Peter is a good man, and a good friend, and I knew I could trust him to keep your sad circumstances to himself. He was a regular visitor to Corrydale before I handed over to Hughie, and I much enjoyed his company and his keen mind. I expect he will be in touch, and would like you to accept his concern, and possible offer of comfort.
I hope you are not offended by my action.
I am also a little anxious in case the Estate House is under-furnished and under-equipped.

238

As you know, I have not seen it for years,
although, since the Cochranes departed, I
have arranged for its day-to-day upkeep. As
I feel responsible for persuading you to leave
Hampshire and take up residence in Creagan,
I would be happy to supply any extras that you
feel would make life more comfortable. So I am
enclosing a cheque for five hundred pounds which
I hope will be sufficient for your needs.
The weather in London is still grey and cold.
I do not go out very much, but observe it from
my window.
I hope you are both well. I would appreciate
a letter or a telephone call to set my mind at rest.
I saw in The Times *that the Grange is on the*
market. The boys have lost no time.
With my best wishes to you both,
Sincerely,
Hector

In silence, she folded the letter and put it back into its envelope. She said, 'I shall write this morning.'

'It's enormously generous. And we really don't need anything.'

'Oh, yes, we do,' Elfrida told him firmly.

'Like what?'

'Like a new toaster that doesn't burn the toast, or blow up or electrocute me. This one is archaic. And I've got to get a bed for Lucy, and it would be nice to have curtains on the stair window.'

'I never noticed any of these things,' said Oscar, looking a bit ashamed.

'Men never do.'

'Perhaps you could buy a dishwasher?'

'I don't want a dishwasher.'

'Or a microwave?'

'I don't want a microwave either.'

'Or a television set?'

'I never look at television. Did you?'

'Only the news. And *Songs of Praise*. And the Proms.'

'But aren't we lucky, Oscar, to have such simple needs?'

'We are certainly fortunate.' He picked up the cheque and eyed it. 'In more ways than one. I shall call in at the Bank of Scotland on Monday and open a joint account for the two of us. And you shall go mad buying furniture.'

'But the money's not for me.'

'It is for both of us.'

'And will the Bank of Scotland be so obliging?'

'I have banked with them since I was a boy. I can see no difficulties.'

'You are being dynamic, Oscar. And you won't forget the flowers for Rose?'

'No. I shall not forget.'

The day turned into one of dazzling brightness. The red sun rose in the eggshell blue sky, and there was not a breath of wind. Ladies, shopping, trod cautiously down the pavements, anxious not to slip or fall; they wore thick boots and were muffled up in woollen hats and gloves. But the cold did not stop them from pausing to gossip, their breath clouding like steam as they chattered away.

The church, behind the black lacework of bare trees, glowed golden in the sunlight. Over the spire the gulls wheeled, and jackdaws settled on the weathervane at its peak. Frost iced the grass of the ancient graveyard, and

cars, driven down from remote hill farms, wore blankets
of snow. One had a Christmas tree sticking out of the
open tailgate.

Having done a little cursory housework, made beds,
laid the fire and humped a basket of logs up from
the outdoor shed, Elfrida sat in her bay window and
observed all this seasonal activity. Oscar had departed,
having spent some effort on de-icing the windscreen and
getting the wipers to work. Elfrida hoped that Rose
Miller would be pleased to see him, and guessed that
she would.

She turned to the table, the thin sun warm on her
back, and started her letter to Hector.

The Estate House.
9 December

Dear Hector,
How very good of you to write, and thank you,
from Oscar and myself, for your very generous
cheque. It is more than welcome for a number of
reasons. We are a bit short of essentials, but have
managed very well without them. But now I have
a young cousin, Carrie Sutton, coming to stay for
Christmas, and she is bringing her niece, Lucy,
who is 14, so it will be good to be able to cheer
the place up a bit and make it more homely. We
do need a new toaster, but that's about all, but
I shall buy some furniture for Lucy's room (she's
going to sleep in the attic!) and your cheque will
come in very useful for that reason. I shall find a
second-hand shop.
Oscar is well. He has been very withdrawn
ever since we got here, and I have, from time

to time, become a little depressed about him, wondering if he ever would emerge from his cloud of grief and begin to go forward again. He did not want to see anybody, nor even speak to any person. Yesterday, however, he took Horace, my dog, for a long walk, and by the golf club was approached by Peter Kennedy. He liked him very much and said he had a nice face. He was invited into the clubhouse for tea, and went, but then realised that Peter Kennedy was the minister, took fright and fled.

He was terribly upset about this, but I think the incident brought him up short, and he realises he can't hide away for ever. So this morning he has gone in the car to pay a call on Rose Miller at Corrydale. It is his first voluntary step out into the world of other people, and I am filled with gratitude and hope that the Kennedys won't be far behind. Whatever happens, Oscar mustn't be goaded, but allowed to take it all at his own pace.

We are really all right, and the days pass peacefully. This is a very tranquil part of the world, and I take Horace for long walks on the beach, sometimes returning after the sun has set. We have no television, but really don't need one. Oscar brought his little radio with him, and we pass the long evenings playing canasta and listening to Classic FM.

We had a long drive up from Hampshire, and were . . .

So intent was she upon her letter, so unheeding of voices in the street below, that she did not hear the

wrought-iron gate open and shut, or the tread of footsteps up to the front door. When the doorbell rang
she was so startled that she dropped her pen. From
downstairs Horace, as usual, filled the house with panic-
stricken barking. She got up, went out of the room and
ran downstairs.

'Oh, Horace, be quiet!' Down the hall to open the
heavy door, swinging it wide to the sunshine, to the
penetrating cold, to an unknown and female figure.

'Sorry about the dog.'

'No matter.'

Her visitor was a woman, perhaps in her late thirties,
tall and slender and marvellously unconventional in her
appearance. She had very dark, almost raven-black hair
cut in a fringe and hanging loose and straight to her
shoulders. She wore a battered Barbour over a long
red woollen skirt and what looked like Doc Marten
boots. A tartan muffler was wound about her neck,
framing a face that was beautifully boned and innocent
of makeup. Her cheeks were tanned, rosy this morning
with cold, and her eyes deep set and dark as black
coffee. In one hand she carried a plastic shopping-
bag, and in the other a little rural basket containing eggs.

She smiled. 'Hello. You're Elfrida Phipps? I hope
I'm not disturbing you, but I'm Tabitha.' Elfrida was
no wiser, and puzzlement showed clearly on her face.
'Tabitha Kennedy. Peter Kennedy's wife.'

'Oh.' Elfrida made much effort not to appear too
astonished. She had never seen any one person in her
life less likely to be a minister's wife. 'How really nice
to meet you.' She stepped back inside, holding open the
door. 'Do come in.'

But Tabitha Kennedy hesitated. 'Not if you're busy. I just brought you some eggs. From my hens.'

'I'm not busy and fresh eggs are a real treat. Come on, I'll give you a cup of coffee.'

Tabitha stepped through the door, and Elfrida closed it behind her. 'Do you mind coming into the kitchen?' She led the way. 'I'll put the kettle on, and then we'll take our coffee upstairs. Or would you rather have tea?'

'I'd die for a cup of coffee. I'm frozen. Peter's got the car so I had to walk down the hill. I thought I was going to fall flat on my back, it's so icy.' She followed Elfrida into the kitchen, put the basket of eggs on the table and hung her plastic bag over a chair.

'Oscar's got the car, too. He's gone to Corrydale to call on someone called Rose Miller.'

'Goodness, there'll be a reunion. Rose always adored Oscar. Never stops talking about him. Do you know, I've never been in here? If I did come to the Estate House, it was very formal, straight up the stairs and into the big room. The Cochranes were a funny old couple, very reserved. Not, you might say, into entertaining. Once a year Peter and I were asked for tea and polite conversation. It was always a bit of an ordeal. How are you settling in?'

Elfrida, having filled the kettle and put it on to boil, began reaching for a tray, cups and saucers. 'We're fine.'

Tabitha looked about her. 'This kitchen reminds me of an exhibit in one of those National Heritage museums. My grandmother had one the same. I don't suppose the Cochranes went in for gadgets, but if they did Mrs Cochrane has certainly removed the lot. Have you got a dishwasher?'

'No. But I've never had one, so it doesn't matter.'

'How about a washing-machine?'

'There's an archaic one in the scullery. It takes hours, but it does work. And my dryer is the washing line at the top of the garden.'

'A scullery! Can I look?'

'Of course.'

'This door? Better and better. Tiled floors, clay sinks and wooden draining-boards. But you've got a fridge.'

'I hardly need one in this weather.'

Tabitha closed the scullery door, came back into the kitchen and pulled out a chair to sit at the table. 'Do you use the big upstairs sitting room?'

'All the time. A lot of running up and down stairs.'

'What about the ground-floor rooms?'

'One's a very gloomy Victorian dining room. Lots of heavy dark mahogany furniture, plush curtains and an upright piano with candle sconces. The other, I think, was the original estate office. I don't suppose the Cochranes ever used it. There's still an old roll-top desk and a table with special drawers for collecting rents. I'm afraid we've kept the doors shut on both of them. We either eat in here or by the fire.'

'Much simpler.'

'And Oscar doesn't seem to mind.'

Tabitha said, 'I'm glad Oscar's not here. One of the reasons I've come is to apologise, and now I shan't have to.'

'*Apologise?* For what?'

'Peter sent me. He's afraid he was rather crass and pushy yesterday afternoon. He hopes so much that he didn't upset Oscar.'

'I think Oscar feels he should apologise to Peter. It

was rude, just running away like that, but he panicked. He was filled with remorse. He knew he'd behaved badly.'

'Hector wrote and told us about his wife and his child dying in that appalling car accident. It takes a long while to move out of something like that and get back into life again.'

'It's called grieving.'

'I know. It can't have been easy for you.'

'As a matter of fact, it's been hellish.'

Elfrida heard herself come out with this and was amazed that the impulsive words had been spoken, because the moments of hellishness she had never acknowledged, or admitted, even to herself. 'I think frustration is the worst, because there is not a mortal thing one can do to help. And then impatience. And then guilt for feeling impatient. More than once I've had to bite my tongue. And another thing is, I'm quite a sociable animal. I don't mean endless parties but I like making friends and getting to know people. Because of Oscar I've had to keep a low profile. I've probably created a very snooty impression.'

'I'm sure not.'

'Mrs Snead has been my lifeline. We have long conversations over cups of tea.'

'I'm glad she's working for you.'

'Today ... today I have a feeling that the hellish time might just about be behind us. For Oscar's sake, I hope it is. He's such a sweet man, he didn't deserve what happened. Perhaps going to see Rose Miller is a step forward.'

'We were always there, Peter and I, but we decided you both needed a bit of time. It's sometimes difficult to gauge exactly the right moment.'

'Don't think about it. Please.'

'If Peter came to see Oscar, would that be a good idea? They could put things right between them.'

'I think it's a marvellous idea, but tell him to telephone first.'

'I'll do that.'

The coffee was made, the jug set on the tray. Elfrida picked it up. 'Let's go upstairs. It's more comfortable.'

She led the way and Tabitha followed. 'I'm always impressed by this beautiful staircase. It gives such a grand feel to your entrance. Peter says the banisters are made of Baltic pine, brought back as ballast on the herring boats.' She paused on the half-landing to gaze out at the garden. Still frosted and bleak with midwinter, it climbed the slope of the hill in a series of terraced lawns with a path and small flights of steps running up its centre. At the very top was a stand of pines filled with jackdaw nests. 'I'd forgotten how much land there is. You can't see it from the lane because of the high wall. I love a walled garden. Old Cochrane was a great gardener. He kept the Manse supplied with free lettuces.'

'Oscar gardens, but so far he's just swept up a few leaves.'

'In spring, there are daffodils and the terraces are purple with aubretia. And there's a lilac too.'

Elfrida, laden with the tray, went on upstairs. Behind her Tabitha continued her running commentary.

'It hasn't just got a grand feel, it really *is* imposing. The size is unexpected, like Dr Who's Tardis ... It all gets bigger and bigger ...' Low sun streamed through the open sitting-room door. '... and I always thought this drawing room one of the loveliest. Oh, look, you've been allowed to keep the chandelier. That must have come from Corrydale.' She looked around her at the empty walls, and spied the little painting Elfrida had brought with her from Dibton. 'Heavens, what a darling.' She moved to inspect it more closely. 'This wasn't here, was it?'

'No. It's mine.' Elfrida set the tray down on the table by the window.

'It's a David Wilkie. It has to be.'

Elfrida was impressed. 'Yes, it is. I've had it for years. I take it with me to every house I live in.'

'How did you come by such a precious possession?'

'It was given to me.'

Tabitha laughed. 'Someone must have liked you very much.'

'It looks a bit like a stamp on a blotting pad; too small for such an expanse of wall.'

'But enchanting.'

Elfrida went to put a match to the fire.

'Do we need a fire?' Tabitha asked. 'Everything feels so warm.'

'That's the best – an oil-fired boiler and central heating. When we came I was so afraid it would all be piercingly cold, but we're snug as bugs. The boiler does the water, too, so scalding baths.'

'And, of course, these old Victorian houses were so solidly and well built. Not a draught in the place.'

The fire kindled, snapped and crackled. Little flames leaped. Elfrida put on a chunk of coal, another log. 'Shall we sit by the window?'

'Let's. The sun is so gorgeous.' Tabitha unwound her muffler and unzipped her Barbour, which she took off and tossed on to a chair before coming to settle herself on the window-seat.

'Do you sit here and watch all the goings-on? Already you must know enough about us locals to write a book.'

'It is pretty fascinating.' Elfrida pushed aside the letter she had been writing to Hector. 'Have you lived here long?'

'About twenty years. We were married just before Peter came here as minister.'

'How old were you?'

'Twenty.' Tabitha made a face. 'Some of the parishioners didn't approve at all, but at the end of the day it all worked out. Both our children were born in the Manse.'

'How old are they?'

'Rory's eighteen. Just left school. We sent both of our offspring to the local academy. He's got his Highers and a place at Durham University, but he's not taking it up till next year. We're into his gap year, and goodness knows what he's going to do with himself. Peter says he doesn't care provided the boy is either earning or learning. Clodagh's twelve and, for some reason, mad on horses. We haven't worked out why she had to choose such an expensive hobby.'

'She might have gone for hang-gliding.'

Suddenly, they were both laughing and it was lovely to be gassing to a girlfriend, over a cup of coffee, discussing their men and children, as though they had known each other for ever.

She looked at Tabitha, sitting there in her black polo-necked sweater with her young girl's hair, and was filled with curiosity. 'Do you like being a minister's wife?'

'I adore being married to Peter. And I'm not totally a minister's wife because I teach art at the school. I'm a qualified teacher with all the right degrees. Five mornings a week.'

'Are you an artist?'

'Yes, I paint and draw, but I teach crafts as well – pottery and sewing. The senior girls stitched all the kneelers in the church. It was a huge project. And every mother in Creagan has a rather wobbly pot for her begonias.'

Elfrida said, 'I was an actress,' then felt a bit shy and wished she hadn't said it because it sounded as though she was capping Tabitha's talent.

But Tabitha was gratifyingly amazed. 'Were you really? Actually, I'm not a bit surprised. I can just see you on the stage. 'Were you famous?'

'No, not a bit. But I was always working, however humbly.'

'That's what matters, isn't it? Doing what you like and being paid for it. That's how I feel too. Really good for one's self-respect. Peter understands. It's one of the reasons I like him so much. I can't wait for you to meet him. I'd ask you up to the Manse, but perhaps we'd better wait until he and Oscar have sorted themselves out. Once they've done that I'll issue invitations. Which means a telephone call.'

'I can't think of anything I'd like more.'

'What are you doing for Christmas?'

'I don't think we're doing anything. I don't think Oscar wants to do anything. And I understand, because it can be a dreadfully emotive time. But it *is* tricky because I've got a cousin coming to stay next Saturday and she's bringing her niece with her. I've told them we won't be very festive, but they're coming anyway.'

'How old is she?'

'Carrie's thirty. But the niece is fourteen. She's called Lucy. I've never met her. I just hope she isn't too shy. Or too un-shy, for that matter. I – I also hope she won't be bored.'

'There's so much going on in Creagan at Christmas she'll have a wonderful time. All the local children get together—'

'She won't know the local children.'

'We'll introduce her to Rory and Clodagh and then she'll meet them all.'

Elfrida felt a bit doubtful about this. 'Won't they mind?'

'Mind? Why should they mind?'

'Well . . . a strange child. From London.'

'All the more reason to take care of her,' said Tabitha. Suddenly Elfrida caught a steely glimpse of the school teacher, keeping order, and the minister's wife, raising her children to true Christian standards. And knew that Tabitha Kennedy, for all her bohemian appearance and youthful attitudes, was a person to be reckoned with. Heightened respect made Elfrida like her even more.

A thought struck her. 'I've got to buy furniture. We're fairly short of everything here because the house has never been anything more than semi-furnished for a let. The bedroom for Carrie is all right, but I thought I'd put Lucy in the attic. It's lovely and light but there's . . .' She trailed off. 'Would you come up and look at it with me? Tell me what I have to get?'

'Of course. Nothing I'd like more.' Tabitha had finished her coffee, and now pushed back the cuff of her sweater to look at her watch. 'Then I must fly, Peter's got an early meeting in Buckly this afternoon and I must feed him soup before he goes.'

'If you haven't got time . . .'

'Of course I have. Come on, show me. I'm a dab hand at interior decoration.'

'On a shoestring.'

'I'm a minister's wife. What else?'

They climbed the stairs to the upper floor and the attics. One, windowless, contained three old trunks, a dressmaker's dummy and a lot of cobwebs. The other, with its huge skylight and combed ceiling, was filled only with pale winter sunlight.

Tabitha was enchanted. 'What a wonderful room. Any young girl would love to have this all to herself. Are you going to put down a carpet? The floorboards are lovely. And it's got a radiator too, cosy as anything. You'll need a bed, of course, and perhaps a chest of drawers. Or a little dressing-table. What about a television set?'

'We haven't got one.'

'Yes, but teenagers go all peculiar without something to goggle at! Rory's got an old one he doesn't use any more – I'll have a word with him about it. And a few lamps. And a blind for the skylight. Otherwise it might be a bit spooky.'

Elfrida said, 'I've got a bit of money – Hector sent it – but not much. I thought, a second-hand shop . . .'

'There's a marvellous market in Buckly.'

'I've never been to Buckly.'

'I'll take you. You can get everything there off stalls.'

'Beds?'

'Oh, marvellous beds. And sheets and pictures and *objets d'art*, and terrible old clothes and wardrobes and carpets. Next week. Some afternoon . . . Would Tuesday be all right?'

Elfrida, whose diary had been sadly blank for nearly a month, nodded.

'Could we go in your car? Peter's bound to need his.'

Elfrida nodded again.

'What fun we'll have. I can't wait.' She looked at her watch again. 'That's settled then. Now I simply must fly or Peter will fume.'

When Tabitha had gone, Elfrida returned to finish her letter to Hector.

> *. . . here by seven o'clock on the second day. This missive is taking a long time to write because I was interrupted by the arrival of Tabitha Kennedy, come to call. I am sure, very soon, Peter and Oscar will clear up their misunderstanding. Tabitha is lovely, and is going to take me to some market in Buckly to buy things for the house.*
>
> *Thank you again for your kindness and generosity. I hope you keep well, and that the weather will be kinder so that you can get out and about.*
>
> *With much love from us both,*
> *Elfrida*

She read this through, put it in an envelope, wrote the address and found a stamp. Then she went downstairs, and in the kitchen did a cursory inspection of the contents of the fridge. She decided all that was needed were vegetables and perhaps some fruit. Horace was sleeping in his basket and clearly did not wish to be disturbed, so she left him there, bundled herself up for the outdoors and stepped out of the front door. This, she did not lock: she had learned that in Creagan nobody locked doors.

The cold was deep freeze, but the low sun had melted away some of the frost and the pavements were black and wet. Even so, Elfrida trod as carefully as any of the other shopping ladies because right now she needed a broken leg like she needed a hole in the head.

She posted the letter, then crossed the street to Arthur Snead, Fruit and Vegetables. For once, the little shop was empty and Arthur Snead was leaning on his counter, reading the racing results. Seeing Elfrida, he straightened up and folded away the newspaper.

''Ullo, Mrs Phipps. 'Ow are you this fine morning?'

Arthur Snead was the other half of Mrs Snead, who always referred to him as Arfur. The Sneads had proved a comforting bonus when Elfrida first arrived in Creagan, not simply because Mrs Snead cleaned the Estate House and was a mine of useful information but because they were Cockneys, and Elfrida, having lived in London for so much of her life, relished the sound of their familiar voices, which somehow had helped her to feel a little less isolated. The Sneads had arrived in Creagan five years ago from Hackney. Elfrida had heard all about this unlikely move over several cups of tea with Mrs Snead. About how Arfur 'ad started life with a barrow in the North End Road, and finally managed to buy a little shop of 'is own. Then the council developers 'ad come, and slapped a compulsory purchase on 'im and 'e'd been so fed up, 'e'd seen this ad in a gardening magazine – 'e'd always taken that magazine because of 'is allotment, 'e grew wonderful marrows – and 'e'd said to Mrs Snead, ''Ow about it, old girl?' And Mrs Snead, loyal to the end, had said, 'OK, Arfur,' and they'd come, bought the shop and the little flat over it, and never looked back. A nice class of people they were, 'is customers, and 'e'd joined the bowling club and got 'ooked on sea fishing. As for Mrs Snead, she was now a member of the Church Guild, went on outings and sang, from time to time, in the choir.

Respected and accepted by the local community, they were still known, without malice, as White Settlers.

'You'll need to watch out, my darling, I've 'ad your man in this morning, buying chrysanths for another lady.'

'I know. Someone called Rose Miller, and I'm managing not to be jealous. Have you got any sprouts?'

'Nice bit of broccoli. Came in this morning. The lorry 'ad a really bad time getting over the 'ill. Says there's snow six inches deep up there. And there's Cyprus potatoes.'

She bought the broccoli and the potatoes, some tangerines in a net bag and two rather sad-looking grapefruit, which Arthur let her have half-price.

'Going straight 'ome, are you?'

'No.' Elfrida had made up her mind. 'I'm going to buy a new toaster. The one we've got is lethal.'

'Well, leave your bags 'ere, and I'll 'ump them across the road for you. Put them inside the front door.'

'You are kind. Why do potatoes have to be so heavy? Thank you, Arthur.'

And so, unburdened, on down the street to William G. Croft, Electrical Goods. The door gave a *ting* as she went inside, and Mr Croft, in his khaki overall, emerged from the open door of his back room where he spent most of his time mending vacuum cleaners or tinkering with television sets. He recognised her instantly from her previous visit.

'Good morning, Mrs Phipps, and so you're back again.'

'Yes. Toasters. But this time I'm going to buy one.'

'And did the other one blow up?'

'No. But it might at any moment.'

'Which was the model that you looked at?'

'The cheapest. But I think I'd like something a little more . . . modern.'

'I have the very thing.'

He fetched it in its box and unpacked it on the counter for Elfrida's inspection. It was extremely smart, streamlined and bright blue. He showed her how it worked, which wasn't very difficult, and how, if you turned a knob, you could have either very pale or very dark toast.

'And it has a year's guarantee,' Mr Croft finished, as though this made it irresistible. Which, of course, it was.

Elfrida said she would have it. 'The only thing is, I haven't enough money to pay for it right now. Would you keep it and I'll come back tomorrow or another day?'

'There's no need for that, Mrs Phipps. You take it with you now and pay for it the next time you're passing.'

'Are you sure?'

'I have no fears that you'll be running away with it.'

She took the toaster home, unpacked it, plugged it in and made herself two perfect pieces of toast, which she spread with Marmite and began to eat. She threw the old one in the bin and, as she did so, heard the front door open and shut and knew that Oscar had returned. Munching toast, she went out into the hall to meet him.

'You're back. How was Rose Miller?'

'In splendid form.' He took off his hat and hung it on the newel post at the foot of the banister. 'We had a great crack, and a glass of elderberry wine.'

'So much for cups of tea.'

'Why are you eating toast?'

'I bought a new toaster. Come and look.' She led him back into the kitchen. 'Isn't it smart? You told me I'd go mad buying things, so I did. Only thing is, I haven't paid for it yet. I said I'd go back tomorrow.'

'I'll come with you.' He took off his thick jacket, pulled out a chair and sat down. Elfrida eyed him. For a man who had just returned from sipping elderberry wine with an old admirer he looked tired and preoccupied. Perhaps the elderberry wine had been a bit too strong for eleven o'clock in the morning.

'Are you all right, Oscar?'

'Yes, I'm all right. I did what you told me, Elfrida. I went to see Major Billicliffe.'

'Oh, good man.'

'No. Not good. I don't feel good at all.'

'Why not? What happened?'

He told her.

Rose Miller's cottage at Corrydale was situated on the little road beyond the erstwhile factor's house, which he had passed on the way to pay his call. *Another day*, he had said to himself. *Billicliffe can wait until another day.* But then, primed with elderberry wine and on his way home, he had heard the dog howling. The sound was as arresting as a cry for help, and Oscar had been instantly rendered alert with concern. There could be no question of driving by. He had turned his car into the lane that led to the small stone house with its rural porch. When he turned off the engine, he had heard the dog howling once more.

Elfrida was aghast, already dreading the end of the story. 'What did you do?'

'Got out of the car and went to ring the bell. Nothing happened except the dog stopped howling and started barking. Then I tried the door and it was open. I went in and called out. But no answer.'

'Perhaps he'd forgotten to put his hearing-aids in.'

'No one there. And the dog had been shut in that same back place, hurling itself at the door, just as it did on our first evening.'

'You didn't let it loose?'

'Not then. I tried the other ground-floor room. The chaos there was even worse than it was in that sitting room. Drip-dry shirts hanging over the backs of chairs, old papers and boxes piled on a table, golf-clubs all over the floor. But there was a staircase, so I went up, opened the door at the top and peered in. And there was the old boy, in bed.'

'He wasn't dead?'

'For a moment I thought he was. Then I said his name and he stirred.'

'Thank heavens for that.'

He was not dead, but he looked ghastly and was clearly very unwell. However, realising that he had a visitor, he had tried to rally, pulled himself up on his pillows, put on a brave face. When Oscar drew up a chair, sat at his bedside and asked what was wrong, Major Billicliffe explained. He had been feeling pretty rotten for a month or two now, ghastly gripes in his stomach, a disinclination to eat. Yesterday his cleaning lady had turned up and been so concerned by his appearance that she had telephoned the Creagan GP, Dr Sinclair. The long and the short of it was that Dr Sinclair abandoned his morning surgery and drove immediately to Corrydale where, after a fairly thorough examination, he told Major Billicliffe that he thought it best if he went into hospital in Inverness, just for a few days for tests, in order to get to the root of his troubles. He had left sedatives and a pain-killer, and the district nurse would call in every day.

'When does he have to go to Inverness?'

'Monday. Dr Sinclair's booked him in.'

'And how will he get there?'

This, of course, was the problem. An ambulance would probably make the long journey from Inverness and pick the old boy up, but if the roads were impassable because of snow it would probably mean a helicopter. Here Major Billicliffe's weak voice had faltered, and Oscar realised that the old soldier was very frightened – not simply by the idea of being whisked away in a helicopter but by the prospect of hospitals, tests, doctors, illness, pain and a possible operation.

It was at this juncture that he had begun to feel responsible – there didn't seem to be anyone else – and had suggested to Major Billicliffe that he, Oscar, should drive him to the hospital and see him safely installed.

At the offer, Major Billicliffe had become quite emotional. 'But why?' he had asked, fumbling for a grubby handkerchief to wipe away the weak tears of an invalid. 'Why should you bother about a stupid old buffer like me?'

And Oscar had told him, 'Because I should like to. Because you are part of Corrydale. Because of my grandmother and Hector.' Major Billicliffe looked unconvinced. Oscar finished, 'Because you are my friend.'

Elfrida was much touched. 'You are sweet. And that was exactly the right thing to do. He won't be nearly so afraid if you're there.'

'I just hope to God we don't get stuck in a snow-storm.'

'Oh, cross that bridge when you get to it. What about the dog?'

'I went downstairs and let her loose in the garden. She was bursting for a pee. And not fierce at all – as he said, just a dear old Labrador needing a bit of attention. Her name, incidentally, is Brandy.'

'Interesting.'

'After she'd dealt with her little problem, I put her into the car, took her to Rose Miller and filled Rose in with all that had occurred. She was distressed that she'd had no idea of what was going on, that he'd been under the weather and that she hadn't been round to his house to see if there was anything she could do. By the time I left, she was already girding herself up to go and do a bit of tidying up and cooking for him. At eighty-five there's nothing she loves so much as a challenge. Funnily enough, she seems to be quite fond of old Billicliffe. She kept saying, "He's mad on the whisky, but he's a dear, good chentleman, and too proud to ask for help."'

'And what about the poor dog?'

'Rose is going to arrange for her nephew, Charlie, to look after her until Billicliffe comes back from hospital. He works on the estate, for the hotel people, and there's a shed for the dog to sleep in. Charlie will feed her and take her around with him.'

'You seem to have arranged everything.'

'I think he'll be all right. It's only two days and then he'll be in hospital.'

'Oh, Oscar, what a morning you've had.'

'But I'm glad I went.' He smiled. 'So that's it. How

about you? Besides buying a toaster, what else have you been up to?'

'I've had a lovely morning. Better than yours. I wrote to Hector, and Tabitha Kennedy came to see me. I've so much to tell you.'

'Then tell me over lunch. Let's treat ourselves. I need cheering up. Let's celebrate clear consciences and Hector's generosity. We'll go to the pub and have a sandwich, or perchance a pie, and I'll stand you a gin and tonic, and we'll drink to . . . us?'

Lunch. Out. 'Do you mean that?'

'Of course.'

'Oh, Oscar.' For a ridiculous moment, Elfrida felt a bit weepy, but instead came round the table, put her arms about him and hugged.

It was being a good day.

Oscar

Oscar

 After a late breakfast Oscar, bundled up as usual against the cold, walked down the street to the newsagent's to pick up the weekly wodge of Sunday papers. The little town was empty and quiet: no cars at this early hour, and only the sound of the gulls and the jackdaws, forever hovering and wheeling and settling on the church tower. It was another brilliant day, cloudless and with no breath of wind. All was petrified by frost, and his footsteps rang on the deserted pavements. He felt as isolated as an Arctic explorer.

Returning, he met Elfrida and Horace setting out for a good long walk along the beach. Elfrida wore a thick woollen hat, like a tea-cosy, pulled down over her ears, and her blanket coat, trimmed with fringe.

She said, 'Come with us,' but he declined her invitation because he wished to settle down with the arts section, and catch up with all that was happening in London. Galleries, operas and concerts. He also enjoyed reading the gardening articles. World news, for the moment, was going by the board.

'How long will you be?' he asked her.

'No idea, but home in time to grill your chop. And I've put a rice pudding in the oven.'

Oscar liked rice pudding. Elfrida had made him one before, and it had been splendid, creamy and rich and lightly spiced with lemon zest.

'Which way are you going?' he asked her.

'Along the dunes. Why?'

'If you're not back by dark I shall call up a posse and come searching.'

'I promised you, I shall tread carefully, like Agag.'

'Do that.'

They parted. He went indoors and up the stairs to their magnificent sitting room. Elfrida had laid the fire so he lit it, then went downstairs again and out to the shed to fill a second basket with logs. If the fire burned all day, one basket was not sufficient to last until bedtime. With the flames blazing nicely, he selected the arts section and settled down in considerable comfort to read.

The church bells disturbed him. The tower clock told him that it was half past ten. He dropped the paper, got to his feet, went over to the window-seat and sat there, half turned, so that he looked down on to the street. He found it fascinating, on Sunday mornings, how the empty town slowly but steadily began to fill up.

The church was coming to life, preparing itself for the weekly influx. The main doors had been opened, and vergers, elders, whatever they called them, in dark suits or kilts, strode up the path from the gate and disappeared inside. Oscar recognised Mr W.G. Croft, who had sold Elfrida their new toaster. Presently he heard, as though from very far away, the tones of the organ. 'Sheep May

Safely Graze'. The sound was muffled by stone-thick walls but recognisable to Oscar's professional ear as a good instrument, and competently played. So often, in country churches, an organist had to do his best with an aged, breathless piece of equipment, a creaky choir, and was obliged while pedalling to sing loudly to give the congregation some idea of the tune.

At first, Oscar had found it a little disconcerting to have the church so close a neighbour, a constant reminder, nudging at his shoulder, of all he had lost. Sitting now, watching the cars draw up and groups of people converging from street corners, stepping down the hill, he knew he had only to cross the road and he would be swept into the stream and, like a swimmer caught in a current, sucked through those imposing doors and into the soaring nave.

The windows of the church were tall, arched in Gothic style. From the outside, the colours and patterns of the stained glass were dimmed and he knew that to appreciate their jewel-like beauty one had to view them from the inside, with the light of day streaming through the colours and throwing lozenges of ruby, sapphire and emerald on to worn flagstones.

Perhaps this was symbolic. Perhaps, isolated from the church, there were other delights, pleasures, comforts that, because of his present state of mind, he deliberately denied himself.

It was an interesting supposition, but disturbing too, and one on which he did not wish to dwell. He left the window and went back to the fire and his newspaper. But when the congregation in the church across the street rose to their feet to sing their first hymn, he lowered the paper and listened, staring into the flames.

Hark, a thrilling voice is sounding,
Christ is nigh, it seems to say.
Cast away the dreams of darkness
O ye children of the day.

A good old classic Advent hymn. He remembered rehearsing the choir at the school where he had taught, imploring them to sing as though they truly believed the message of hope.

He thought, I must get in touch with Peter Kennedy.

But Sunday was the busiest day of a minister's week. Perhaps tomorrow. Or the next day.

Meantime . . . he settled his spectacles and endeavoured to concentrate on the *Sunday Times* and an erudite critique of Jonathan Miller's production of *Fidelio* at Covent Garden.

Monday was one of Mrs Snead's days. The other was Thursday. She came at nine on the dot while Elfrida and Oscar were still drinking the last of their breakfast coffee, her arrival heralded by the slam of the back door when she let herself in. Then a pause while, in the scullery, she divested herself of anorak, headscarf and boots, hanging the garments on her usual hook. She always carried a flowered plastic shopping-bag in which were stowed her working clothes: an apron and a trendy pair of trainers. Oscar and Elfrida waited. Then the door was flung open and bang! She was there.

'Morning, all.'

An entrance, thought Oscar, that any actress would be proud of.

'Morning, Mrs Snead.'

'Blimey, it's parky.' Rubbing her hands together to get her circulation going, Mrs Snead kicked the door shut behind her. 'There's a wind, goes through you like a knife.'

Elfrida put down her coffee cup. 'Have a cup of tea.'

'I wouldn't mind, before I get started in. Kettle's boiled, 'as it?' She caught sight of the new toaster. 'Well, just look what we've got 'ere. Love the colour. Been shopping, 'ave you? About time too – that other old thing was a killer. What did you do with it? Binned it, I 'ope.' She clattered around, finding a mug, a teabag and the milk carton. Her tea made, she pulled out a handy chair and sat to join them.

'What's this I'm 'earing about Major Billicliffe?'

They both stared at her. Then Oscar said, 'News travels fast.'

'Charlie Miller was in Arfur's yesterday evening, buying a cabbage. 'E told 'im. Says 'e's got to look after the dog. Say 'e's going to Inverness to the 'ospital. 'Ope it's nothing serious.'

'We hope so too, Mrs Snead. And Oscar's going to drive him over.'

'Charlie said something like that to Arfur.' She eyed Oscar. 'You up to it, Mr Blundell? It's a long way.'

'I think I'll manage, Mrs Snead.'

'At least it's not snowing. What time do you 'ave to be off?'

'As soon as I've finished breakfast.'

'Got a mobile phone, 'ave you? Ought to 'ave a mobile phone.'

'No, I haven't, but we shall be all right.'

'Well, let's 'ope so, anyway. No point in being pessimistic. Now, Mrs Phipps, before I forget Arfur says to ask you, do you want a Christmas tree, and if so 'e'll reserve one.'

'A Christmas tree?' Elfrida looked uncertain. 'Well ... I don't know.'

'You must 'ave a tree. Wouldn't be Christmas without a tree.'

'Yes. Perhaps. But we thought we wouldn't bother.'

'A tree's no bother. It's fun. Decorating and all that.'

Elfrida appealed to Oscar. 'What do you think?'

He decided it was time to put her out of her misery. 'That's very thoughtful of you, Mrs Snead, but we're getting our Christmas tree from Corrydale.'

Elfrida's jaw dropped. And for once in her life, she was quite cross with him.

'We're getting one from *Corrydale*? Why didn't you say? Here I am telling Mrs Snead we don't want a tree, and the next thing you're telling me you've already booked one. You are impossible.'

'I'm sorry.'

'When did you organise all this?'

'On Saturday when I went to see Rose. I told you, Charlie works in the gardens there. They've got a whole plantation of Christmas trees and Rose said she'd speak to him and he'd cut us a good one.'

'You should have said.'

'There was so much else to tell you I forgot. I thought it would be nice for Carrie and Lucy.'

Elfrida stopped being cross. 'That was a lovely idea. When is it coming?'

'We have to telephone Charlie, then go and fetch it.'

By now Mrs Snead had pricked up her ears.

She was a small, spare lady with tightly permed grey hair, and always wore sparkling dangly earrings.

Sitting there, with her head cocked and her bright eyes not missing a trick, she reminded Oscar of a cheeky sparrow.

''Aving visitors, are you?'

'I haven't had time to tell you yet, Mrs Snead, but my cousin and her niece are coming for Christmas. Lucy's the niece. She's fourteen.'

Mrs Snead was highly delighted. 'That's really lovely. That'll cheer you up, 'aving young people around the place. When are they coming? And where do you want them to sleep? We'll need to get the rooms cleaned up and polished.'

'I thought I'd put Lucy up in the attic.'

'But there's not a stick of furniture up there.'

'There will be after tomorrow. Tabitha Kennedy's going to take me to the market in Buckly. She says we can buy anything there.'

Mrs Snead sniffed. 'It's not new stuff,' she warned. 'All second-'and.'

'It'll be good enough, I'm sure.'

'I'd 'ave thought you'd 'ave liked a nice suite.' She was clearly disappointed in Elfrida's lowly taste. 'Saw one in Inverness last time I was there. Lovely, it was. Walnut veneer with filigree brass 'andles. And the bed 'ad a peach satin 'eadboard and valance.'

'It sounds very pretty, Mrs Snead, but a bit grand. And I don't want to have to drive all the way to Inverness.'

Mrs Snead, pondering this new domestic situation, sipped her tea. She said, 'We're a bit short of sheets and stuff. You don't want to buy *them* second-'and. Never liked the thought of a used blanket. There's a draper in Buckly, not much good for clothes but they run a line in soft furnishings. You could 'ave a word with Mrs Kennedy and pop in there.'

'I'll do that.'

'Oh, well.' Mrs Snead finished her tea, and sprang up to fling the dregs of her tea into the sink. 'Sitting 'ere chatting won't get the baby bathed. Where'd you want me to start, Mrs Phipps?'

'Let's get going on the attic. Get it swept and scrubbed and the skylight cleaned, and then when any furniture arrives it can be carried straight upstairs and put into place.'

''Oo's going to do the carrying, I'd like to know?' Mrs Snead could be quite protective and fierce. 'Not you and Mr Blundell, I 'ope. You'll give yourselves 'ernias.'

'I shall organise a van with removal men.'

'You can borrow Arfur if you like.'

'That's very kind.'

''E's 'andy with a screwdriver. I will say that for 'im.' With this parting shot, Mrs Snead collected brooms, dusters and her tin of polish, and set off up the stairs. A moment or two later the roaring of the ancient Hoover could be heard, accompanied by Mrs Snead's voice. '*I want to be Bobby's girl*,' she sang.

Elfrida stifled a giggle. Oscar said, 'Not only does Mrs Snead dust for us but brings with her music that takes me back over the years. She is indeed a remarkable lady.'

'What memory does her singing evoke for you, Oscar?'

'Schoolboys' studies, smelling of sweaty gym shoes and throbbing with pop.'

'That's not very romantic.'

'I was a bachelor schoolmaster. Romance did not

272

fly my way.' He looked at his watch. 'Elfrida, I must
be going.'

'You will take care, won't you?'

'I shall endeavour to.'

'It's beside the point but I think you're a saint.'

'I shall ask Mrs Snead to polish my halo.'

'Oscar . . .'

'What is it?'

'Good luck.'

That night the wind veered around to the east, and in the
early hours of the morning Oscar awoke to the whining,
piping sound of an imminent gale and the rattle of rain
flung at windowpanes. He lay awake for a long time,
thinking about Godfrey Billicliffe. At last he knew his
Christian name, because he had learned it in the course
of helping the ward sister to fill in countless forms before
leaving the sick old man to her tender mercies.

The undertaking had not been as demanding as he
had feared. The drive to Inverness had gone smoothly
and old Billicliffe, encouraged by caring attention, had
talked non-stop the entire way over. Oscar had learned
much about his life: his career in the Army, his spell in
Germany with the British Army of The Rhine, how he
had met his wife in Osnabrück, how they had married,
in Colchester, how they had never been blessed with
children. Oscar, at the wheel of his car, was thankfully
not expected to make much response to this stream of
reminiscence. All that was required, from time to time,
was a casual agreement, or a nod, whereupon Godfrey
Billicliffe bumbled on.

It was not until they were speeding down the motorway across the Black Isle and Inverness was in view across

the water that Major Billicliffe fell silent. For a moment Oscar wondered if he had fallen asleep but glancing sideways saw that he had not. Perhaps he was simply brooding. After a bit he started talking again, although now it was not about the past that he spoke but his present and his future.

'Been thinking, Oscar . . .'

'What have you been thinking about?'

'What's going to happen . . . Turning my toes up . . .'

'You're not going to turn your toes up,' Oscar assured him, hoping that he sounded robust.

'Never know . . . Not as young . . . Have to be prepared. Ready and prepared for all contingencies. Learned that in the Army. Prepare for the worst and hope for the best.' Another long pause. 'Wondered . . . up to you, of course . . . if you'd agree to be my executor. Good to know . . . Capable hands . . .'

'I'm not so sure my hands are capable.'

'Rubbish. Hector McLellan's nephew. Not that his son was great shakes . . . You . . . Different kettle of fish. Friends all dead. Thought you might . . . Appreciate it . . .'

Oscar found his unfinished sentences maddening. He said, as calmly as he could, 'If you want. If it would set your mind at rest, I'd be happy to be your executor. But—'

'Splendid. All settled. Tell my lawyer. Nice feller. Did all the conveyancing when I bought my house from the Corrydale estate. Keen fisherman. Liked the cut of his jib.'

'Has he got a name?'

Major Billicliffe gave a snort, which perhaps was meant to be laughter at Oscar's quirky question. 'Course

274

he's got a name. Murdo McKenzie. Firm's McKenzie & Stout. South Street, Inverness.'

'Murdo McKenzie.'

'I must tell him you're my executor. Settled ... Ring him up.' He thought about this. 'Suppose I can ring up from the hospital? They'll have telephones ... won't they?' he finished doubtfully.

'Of course. The nurse, I am sure, will bring one to your bedside.'

'Bit different from the old days,' said Major Billicliffe, as though he had once languished in the military hospital at Scutari. 'Medical officers' rounds and bedpans. And a matron like a sergeant major. No telephones then.' Remembering, he fell silent once more and did not speak again until they had reached their destination.

The hospital was the Royal Western. Oscar found it without too much difficulty, and once they had arrived matters were taken out of his hands. All he had to do was accompany Major Billicliffe on his way. A porter appeared with a wheelchair, and took over the new arrival, while Oscar walked alongside, carrying the necessary suitcase: an enormously heavy and battered piece of equipment, fashioned from what looked like elephant hide. They went upstairs in a huge lift, then down long corridors of polished linoleum, and finally into Ward Fourteen. The ward sister was ready and waiting for admission, with her clipboard and her forms. All went smoothly until she came to next-of-kin.

'Next-of-kin, Major Billicliffe?'

Suddenly, he looked bewildered. 'Sorry?'

'Next-of-kin. You know, wife, children, brothers or sisters.'

He shook his head. 'I have none. I have no one.'

'Oh, come along, there has to be someone.'

Oscar could not bear it. 'Me,' he said firmly. 'I am Major Billicliffe's next-of-kin. Oscar Blundell. You can write it down. The Estate House. Creagan.'

Sister did so. 'Have you got a telephone number.'

Oscar gave it to her.

Finally, all was written, recorded and signed. And it was time for Oscar to leave. He said goodbye.

'You'll come again?'

'Of course. Provided we don't get snowed in.'

'Thank you for bringing me. Obliged.'

'Not at all.'

And he walked away from the old man and his suitcase, and told himself that it wasn't his fault. There was no reason to feel as shifty as a traitor.

He could have done no more. Later, when there was news of the invalid, he and Elfrida would set out on the long drive once more and go to visit Godfrey Billicliffe. Elfrida, if anybody, would cheer him up. She would probably take him grapes.

A clout of wind struck the house. Oscar turned into the pillows and closed his eyes, and all at once found himself thinking about Francesca. This often happened in the dark hours of a restless night and he dreaded the inevitable aftermath, a torment of rekindled, anguished loss. Francesca. Soundlessly, his lips formed her name. Francesca. He slid his hand beneath his pillow to fumble for his handkerchief, knowing that he would probably weep. But instead of weeping he became aware of a sort of quiet, as though he were more at ease with himself than he had felt for weeks. Francesca. He saw her running towards him across the sunlit lawns of the Grange. And the image stayed, poignant but especially sweet.

Holding it close, he slept.

The next morning dawned to dismal weather. The sparkle of the big freeze was drowned in showers of sleety rain, driven in from the sea, and the street was filled with bobbing wet umbrellas. At midday the huge gritting lorry appeared, trundling back to its depot with snow crusted beneath its mudguards and windscreen wipers going full tilt.

Elfrida had bought herself a notebook and over lunch, which was soup and some Stilton she had found in the supermarket, she made lists. 'I've got to think of everything,' she told Oscar importantly. 'There isn't time for forgetting. They'll be here on Friday. Do you think Lucy will want a dressing-table?'

Oscar, who was trying to do *The Times* crossword puzzle, set it aside nobly and removed his spectacles, as though the better to think.

But 'I have no idea,' was all he could come up with.

'And a bed, of course.'

With some effort, he applied himself to the problem. 'A wardrobe?'

'We'd never get a wardrobe under those combed ceilings. Some hooks on the wall would do. And coathangers.' She wrote in her notebook.

Oscar sat back in his chair and watched her with amusement. He had never seen Elfrida so focused and organised. For a moment she reminded him, in the nicest possible way, of Gloria: planning and plotting and writing lists and making things happen.

'When does Mrs Kennedy come?'

277

'Half past two, she said she'd be here. I said I'd drive her in your car. You don't need it, do you?'

'No.'

'If you felt frightfully energetic you could take Horace for a walk.'

Oscar, hedging, said, 'I'll see,' and went back to his crossword.

When Tabitha Kennedy arrived, Elfrida was at the top of the garden, unpegging a line of wet washing that should never have been put out in the first place. So when the bell rang it was Oscar who went downstairs to open the door.

She was booted and raincoated, but her head was bare and her dark hair blew in the wind. She put up a hand to push a strand from her cheek. 'Hello. I'm Tabitha.'

'Of course. Come in out of the wet. Elfrida won't be a moment, she's getting a lot of wet clothes off the line. I'm Oscar Blundell.'

'I know.' She had a lovely smile. 'How do you do?' They shook hands. 'I hope I'm not too early.'

'Not at all. Come upstairs, it's more comfortable than standing around here.'

He led the way, and she followed, chatting as though she had known him for ever. 'Isn't it disappointing, the rain, after all that lovely frosty weather? There've been burst pipes all over the place and the plumber's run off his feet.' In the sitting room the fire burned brightly, and a pot of Arthur Snead's forced hyacinths filled the air with their fragrance. 'Oh, aren't they heaven! They really smell of spring, don't they? I said to Elfrida we'd have to go in your car but Peter's at home today so he let me bring ours. Anything rather than come shopping with me.'

'I sympathise. It's very good of you to help Elfrida out.'

'I'll love it. I adore spending other people's money. We'll probably be quite late back. The market won't close till five, and by then we'll both be ready for a restoring cup of tea.'

Downstairs, a door slammed and Elfrida's footsteps came running up the stairs. She appeared at the door in her blanket coat and her tea-cosy hat. 'Tabitha, I am sorry, have you been waiting? It's on days like this that I long for an electric dryer. But only on days like this. Now, I just have to get my bag and my list and the car keys.'

'You don't need them,' Tabitha told her. 'I'm driving you.'

They departed at last in some excitement, reminding Oscar of a couple of young girls setting off to enjoy themselves. He stood at the window and watched them go, getting into the well-worn estate car, fixing seat-belts, moving away across the square and out of sight.

He was alone. Horace slept by the fire. Aware of his own procrastination, Oscar made another attempt to finish the crossword but was defeated and laid the newspaper aside. There were other things, he knew, that he had to do. He pulled himself out of his chair and went across the room to the heavy oak table that stood against the wall opposite the fireplace and which he used as a desk. He made space, pushing aside a file or two and his briefcase, then settled down to write two long overdue letters. One was to Hector McLellan, thanking him for his generosity, and doing his best to sound positive and reassuring. The second was to Mrs Muswell, whom he had abandoned so abruptly. The memory of her standing, weeping, at the door of the Grange as he and Elfrida drove away had been pricking his conscience ever since. Now he assured her that he was well, thanked her for her loyalty and said that he hoped she had found other congenial employment. He sent his best wishes. He signed his name.

He folded the letters, addressed envelopes, found stamps. They were ready for posting.

Peter's at home today.

Now.

He went out of the room to where the telephone stood on the landing. He found the phone book, looked up the number, memorised it and punched the digits. He heard the ringing tone but only once, as though the instrument stood on a desk at a man's elbow, ready for instant response.

'Creagan Manse.' The warm familiar voice. 'Peter Kennedy.'

At half past five Oscar, bundled up and hatted, let himself out of the Estate House and set off along the stepped lane that led up the hill. Elfrida and Tabitha had not yet returned so he left the light burning in the hall as a welcome for when they eventually came home and a note for Elfrida on the kitchen table. 'Gone out for a while. I shan't be late.' He left Horace as well, having done his duty and taken the dog for a walk, then fed him his biscuits and lambs' hearts. Lambs' hearts, for Horace, was the treat of all time; he had guzzled the lot, then retired to his basket for a snooze.

Oscar walked between high walls and garden trees. It was very dark, an overcast evening, but the wind had dropped and a drizzling rain fell. At the top of the lane, a steepish climb, he paused to get his breath then continued on his way along the footpath that leaned up against the slope of the hill. The town dropped below him. He looked down on other gardens, roof-tops, the lines of the streets marked with lamps. In the tower of the church, the clock face shone like a full moon.

A little further on – by now, his eyes adjusted to the darkness – he could make out the long line of the distant coast, stretched, like an arm, out to sea and holding in its fingers the intermittent pinprick signal of the lighthouse. There were no stars.

A gate led out into a wide road, lined on the right-hand side by large, stone-built Victorian houses set in spacious gardens. The first house was the Manse. Oscar remembered its location from sixty years ago, when he was sometimes brought for tea by his grandmother and to play with the then incumbent's children. He remembered the house and the family who lived there but had forgotten their names.

A light burned over the door. He opened the gate, shut it behind him and went up the path, sea pebbles crunching beneath the soles of his boots. The front door had been painted bright blue. He pressed the bell.

Suddenly he shivered. He told himself that it was because of the cold and the damp.

He heard the inner door open, then the blue door was flung wide and he was dazzled by light. Peter Kennedy stood there, warm with welcome. He wore a thick polo-necked sweater and a pair of worn corduroys, and looked comfortingly unchurchly. 'Oscar! Come away in.' He looked over Oscar's shoulder. 'Did you not bring your car?'

'No. I walked.'

'Good man.'

He went indoors, into the hall. Saw the Turkey carpet, the fumed-oak hall stand, the antique kist on which stood a neat stack of parish magazines. A riding hat had been dumped on the newel post of the banister, and on the bottom stair stood a pair of football boots and a stack of clean, folded laundry. All left there, Oscar guessed, until the next obliging person would collect them, and bear them upstairs.

'Take your coat off. The children are both out, so we've got the place to ourselves. I've a fire going in my study. I've had an afternoon of it, catching up on paperwork and writing a long-overdue article for the *Sutherland Times*.' Oscar divested himself of gloves, jacket and hat, and Peter Kennedy took them from him and laid them on an impressive oak chair, which looked as though it might, at one time, have seated a bishop. 'Now, come along in.'

He led the way into his study, a bow-windowed front room that had probably been intended as the dining room of the original house. It was thickly curtained against the dreich evening and softly lit by three lamps, one on the huge, littered desk and two more burning on either side of the fire, where stood two ancient leather armchairs. The walls held shelves of books, and after the airy emptiness of the Estate House, it felt safe and dark and warm. A bit like going back to the womb.

Also there was a marvellous smell, which Oscar finally traced to the chunks of carefully stacked peat, smouldering in the fire basket. He said, 'A peat fire. I'd forgotten about peat. Sometimes, when I put the dog out at night, I can smell the smoke from chimneys. I must try and get hold of some just for that smell.'

'I'm very fortunate. One of my parishioners has his

own peat-patch and he keeps me supplied. Now come and sit down and make yourself comfortable. Would you like a cup of coffee?' Oscar did not immediately reply and Peter looked at his watch. 'A quarter to six. We could jump the gun and enjoy a glass of Laphroaig. I keep it, but only for special occasions.'

Malt whisky. Laphroaig. Irresistible. 'I think I'd like that more than anything.'

'I thought you might so I am prepared.' And Oscar saw on the desk – along with a word processor, a stack of books, papers in some disarray and the telephone – a small tray neatly set with the bottle of Laphroaig, two small tumblers and a jug of water. So much for the coffee. He was touched. 'The girls aren't back yet?'

'No.' Oscar lowered himself into one of the chairs, which was surprisingly soft and comfortable. Above him, in the centre of the mantelpiece, stood a clock, the sort that is presented to retiring ministers or schoolmasters after forty years of loyal service. It had a soft, solid tick, smooth and sweet as a carefully set metronome. 'I think they planned on treating themselves to a tea party once they'd finished their shopping.'

'I'm sure. I hope they were successful.' Carrying the two glasses, Peter handed Oscar his drink then settled down in the other armchair, facing his visitor. He raised his glass. '*Slàinte.*'

'Good health.'

The Laphroaig was like nectar, clean, delicious, slipping down his throat, warming.

Peter went on, 'Buckly's rather a depressing town at the moment. Most of the people are unemployed. The woollen mill went to the wall, and for skilled weavers and spinners there is little alternative work.'

Oscar frowned. 'The woollen mill? Not McTaggart's?'

'Yes. McTaggart's.'

'Gone bust? I had no idea. Astonishing. It's like being told the Rock of Gibraltar has crumbled. What happened?'

Peter told him. 'The old man died, the sons weren't interested. The workforce got a bit of financial help, a grant, and took it over themselves. They were doing all right and then we had a spell of dreadful weather. The river burst its banks and the place was flooded. Everything lost, destroyed.'

Oscar was appalled. 'Is that the end of it, then?'

'There's some word of a takeover – one of those big textile conglomerates, Sturrock & Swinfield, from London – but so far nothing very much seems to have happened and the people in Buckly are beginning to fear the worst. Which is that nothing is *ever* going to happen.'

'What a tragedy.' Oscar frowned. 'I can't think why I haven't heard about this before. I suppose . . . just now . . . I don't read the newspapers properly, and certainly not the City pages. And here, I only take *The Times* and the *Telegraph*, so I don't get the local news. And I haven't talked to many people except Mrs Snead. That, of course, is why I am here. To apologise to you. I should have come before but I didn't.'

'Please. Don't feel badly. I realised that I had taken you unawares and I should have waited for a more suitable occasion to make myself known to you. I hope you weren't too upset.'

'I don't know what came over me. It was ridiculous.'

'Please, think no more of it. No harm has been done. Another time you must join me there for tea or for a drink, or whatever you want. The best would be if you felt like joining the club and then, when the good weather starts again, we could have a game. You do play?'

'I used to play with my grandmother when I was a boy, but I was never much good, even then.'

'I'd be delighted to give you a game.'

'I have no clubs.'

'We'll borrow some from the pro. It's such a splendid course, it would be sad to live here and not experience at least one round. Your grandmother was a good golfer. When I came here, I heard a lot about her prowess. She was lady champion two years running. One way and another she must have been an exceptional lady.'

'Yes, she was.'

'And musical, too.'

'Yes. And an inspired gardener. She was extremely accomplished.' Oscar took another sip of the Laphroaig then set the glass down on the table beside him, where it glowed like a jewel in the soft light of the lamp. He said, 'Godfrey Billicliffe also invited me to join the golf club but I'm afraid, at that particular moment, we were in the throes of a rather traumatic encounter. Both Elfrida and I were exhausted after our long journey. All we wanted was to get the key of our house and escape. I'm afraid we were very offhand.'

'He can be daunting. I understand. I understand, as well, that you drove him to hospital yesterday morning.'

'How did you know that?'

Peter Kennedy smiled. 'There are few secrets in this small community. No, don't worry, it wasn't idle gossip. Dr Sinclair rang to put me in the picture. It was very good of you.'

'Did you know he was ill?'

'No. I don't think anybody knew. He's been something of a problem ever since his wife died – gone downhill at a frightening pace. Lonely, I think, but too proud to admit it, and not one of us had the nerve to suggest that he sold up and moved into the old people's home.'

'My stepsons exhorted me to go into a retirement home in Hampshire, but that was because they had inherited their mother's house and wanted me out of the way so that they could put it up for sale. I found the notion dire. Like the beginning of the end.'

'How did *you* guess something was amiss?'

'I went to see Rose Miller. On the way home I heard Billicliffe's dog howling. So I called in. To set my mind at rest, I suppose. Both Elfrida and I had been feeling rather badly about the old boy. And I found him upstairs in bed, obviously very poorly. He was frightened, too, of the prospect of ambulances or helicopters. He seemed so dreadfully alone. Saying I'd drive him to Inverness in my car was the least I could do.'

'I have to go to Inverness on Friday for a meeting with the Moderator. I'll pop into the hospital and pay a visit. See how he's getting on.'

'I said I would stand as his next-of-kin so my name and telephone number are on all the countless forms we had to fill in. I imagine that if there is any news I shall be informed.'

'Well, keep me in touch.'

'Of course.'

'Now, tell me about your uncle. How is Hector?'

'Growing older. Living in London. He came down to see me after – after the funeral. He didn't come to the funeral because he'd had flu and his doctor, rightly, forbade him. It was Hector who suggested that I left Hampshire and came back here.'

'I know, Oscar. He wrote me a long letter. I was so dreadfully sorry. I wanted to come right away to talk with you and to let you know that if there was anything I could do or say ... but my instinct told me that for the time being you needed to be on your own. I hope you didn't get the impression that I was either uncaring or inattentive.'

'No. I didn't think that.'

'Sometimes ... just to talk, to a stranger, a person disassociated, is easier.'

'Like confiding in a man met on a train journey, whom you know you will never see again.'

'Not entirely,' Peter smiled, 'because I hope you will see me again.'

'It's difficult to know where to start. It all seems to go a long way back.'

'Life tends to.'

'I never thought I should be married. I thought, always, that I would remain a bachelor all my life. I had my work as a schoolmaster, teaching piano and training the choir. For company other masters and their wives. My passion was music. The school was Glastonbury, a lesser-known public school but excellent for all that. I was very happy there. And then I grew older, and the Headmaster retired, and a new, younger man came to take his place. The Head had always been a close friend, and although his replacement was perfectly competent, pleasant and traditional, I decided after a year that the time had come for a change. I had been offered the post as organist and choir-master at St Biddulph's in London. I thought about it for a bit, but not very long.

The music at St Biddulph's had always been renowned for its excellence, and the choir was secure, funded by an enormously generous endowment that had been made by a grateful parishioner some years before. So I changed direction and moved to London. I lived in a comfortable, spacious flat on the second floor of an old terraced house only five minutes or so from the church, and the ladies of the parish made certain that I had a competent housekeeper and was well cared for.

'They were halcyon days. I suppose, the peak of my fairly modest career. Two of the choristers were professional concert singers, there was enthusiasm from the public, and we were able to enlarge our repertoire and perform, on special occasions, some ambitious chorales. Palestrina's "*Salvete Flores Martyrum*", Schubert's setting of the twenty-third psalm, Fauré's "*Requiem*". Glorious stuff.

'I met the Bellamys soon after my arrival at St Biddulph's. They lived in some style in a house in Elm Park Gardens, and from the first were enormously hospitable and kind to me. When George Bellamy became ill I used to go to their house to keep him company, play backgammon with him. When he died I arranged the music for his considerably important funeral.

'After the funeral, I thought that Gloria would no longer want me coming and going, that the reason for my visits had gone. But she continued to invite me to various small social affairs – a drinks party, or dinner, or Sunday luncheon. Sometimes we went to the cinema together, or spent a day at Kew. I thought little of it but much enjoyed her company. And then, one day, in a quite matter-of-fact fashion, she said that she thought it would be a good idea if we married. She explained that she did not enjoy living without a man, and she felt that I, in my advancing years, would be glad of a wife to take care of me. It all sounds, I know, a little cold-blooded, but the truth is that I was extremely fond of her and she, I think, of me. We were neither of us in our first flush of youth, so old enough to make a success of what others saw simply as a marriage of convenience.

'She was a wonderful wife, warm, generous and kind-hearted. I had never, since I was a boy coming to Corrydale, known such material comforts, such ease of living. She and George had sons, Giles and Crawford, but now they were adult, had fled the nest and set up establishments of their own. And Gloria was still a comparatively young woman, brimming with physical vitality. When she told me she was pregnant, I was quite ridiculously incredulous. I had never in all my life imagined that I would become a father. And when Francesca was born, that tiny child, I was filled with a wonder I don't suppose I shall ever experience again. It was as though a miracle had occurred. And she never stopped being a miracle.

'Sometimes, as she grew older, and was running about and talking nineteen to the dozen and generally making the usual din that all children make, I would watch her and still find it unbelievable that she was actually mine, that I had helped to create this beguiling, beautiful, miniature human being.

'Then Gloria was left this house in the country, in Hampshire, and we moved from London and started our new life in Dibton. I have to admit that I missed St Biddulph's, but music was still part of my life. I taught a little, and from time to time played the organ for morning service in the village church.'

Here, Oscar paused, to reach for his glass and to take another sip of the Laphroaig. A glowing lump of peat slipped, with a whisper, into the bed of the fire. The clock ticked on.

Peter spoke. 'Your friend, Elfrida, have you known her always?'

'No. We didn't meet until she came to live in our village. She was alone and Gloria made friends with her, generally took Elfrida under her wing. She was amusing, full of life, and we all enjoyed her company. Francesca was forever bicycling off to visit her in her little cottage. She made Francesca laugh. She was in Cornwall, staying with a cousin, at the time of the accident. She returned after the funeral with no idea at all of what had happened. When Hector suggested I left Hampshire and returned to Creagan, I knew I couldn't do it on my own. The journey seemed too arduous, and I dreaded being alone. so I asked Elfrida to come with me. It is a measure of her generous heart that she agreed. She is company for me, and in the blackest moments has always been able to make me smile. When I first met Elfrida, she asked me if I was religious. I told her that it is hard *not* to believe when you have been steeped in the liturgies and traditions of the Anglican Church for most of your life. And that I felt I needed some being to thank.

'Because I was fortunate. I was content. The marriage of convenience was working well, and because of Francesca I could have no regrets. But Gloria was very strong, a forceful character. And her considerable wealth was her own. At times she had to be handled with enormous tact. She loved company, people, parties, and sometimes she drank too much. I don't mean that she was an alcoholic – far from it – simply a serious social drinker.

Often, after an evening out, I would drive her home in her own powerful car, and she resented that and would be sullen-faced the next morning. I feel disloyal to her even talking about this. But I knew her weakness, just as I knew her many strengths.

'The day of the bonfire and the Guy Fawkes party she said she was taking Francesca and it occurred to me that I should go too. But I had a man coming to see me about building a new fence for the paddock. It was a job I had been wanting to see done and finished and I didn't feel inclined to put him off. Besides, it was simply a children's party. A big tea and fireworks. They would be home by seven at the latest.

'And, of course, it *was* a children's party. But adults were there too, most of them Gloria's friends. And after the fireworks were over, and the children were still running about in the garden, waving sparklers and working off their excitement, the adults went indoors for a drink.

'I don't know how much she had. There wasn't, thank God, an autopsy. Driving conditions were appalling, sudden heavy rain, the roads running with water. There had been some repair on the roundabout and lights had been left flashing to warn of this. Perhaps they confused her. We'll never know. The lorry driver said that her car had driven out at some speed straight into his path as he swung round from the right. It was, of course, his right of way. There was not a mortal thing he could do. A split second and Gloria's car was destroyed, unrecognisable, and Gloria and Francesca were both dead.

'The news was broken to me by the police. A nice young sergeant. Poor boy. I cannot describe my reaction because I felt nothing. Numb. Empty. Devoid of any emotion. And then, gradually, the void filled with a bitter rage and resentment against whoever, or whatever, had allowed this thing to happen to me. The world, I know, is filled with horror and one becomes hardened. Horrified but hardened by watching television images of destroyed villages, starving children, monumental natural disasters. But this was *me*. This was *my* life, my being. My wife. My child. If a God was there – and I had never been totally certain that He was – I didn't want to have any part of Him.

'Our cleric in Dibton called to comfort. He told me that God sends people only what they are strong enough to bear. And I rounded on him and said that I wished I were as weak as water and still had my child. And then I sent him away. We never got round to the guilt. I knew Gloria's weakness. I should have been with them. I should have been behind the wheel of the car. If only. If only is my nightmare.'

'If only is like hindsight. A useless exercise. The accident seems to me to have been one composed of several tragic circumstances. Who knows? Perhaps you would have died too, Oscar, and then an even larger hole would have been left in the lives of those who knew and loved you all ... As for God, I frankly admit that I find it easier to live with the age-old questions about suffering than with many of the easy or pious explanations offered from time to time, some of which seem to verge on blasphemy. I hope so much that no one has sought to try to comfort you by saying that God must have needed Francesca more than you. I would find it impossible to worship a God who deliberately stole my child from me. Such a God would be a moral monster.'

Oscar was astounded. 'Is that', he asked, at last, 'what you really believe?'

Peter nodded. 'It is what I truly believe. Thirty years in the ministry has taught me that the one thing we should never say when a young person dies is "It is the will of God." We simply don't know enough to say that. I am convinced, in fact, that when Francesca died in that terrible accident God's was the first heart to break.'

'I want to move on, to go on living, to be able to accept – to be able to give again. I don't like taking all the time. I've never been that sort of person.'

'Oh, Oscar, it will be all right. Because of your profession the Church has been so much part of your life for so many years that you will be as familiar as I am with the great biblical promises about life and death. The problem is that traumatic grief can often render them unreal. For a while what you are probably going to need most is not people who will quote the Bible to you but close friends who will continue to hold your hand and lend you a listening ear when you want to speak about Francesca.'

Oscar thought about Elfrida, and Peter paused for a moment, as though to give him time to argue this new conception. But Oscar did not say anything.

'Life is sweet,' Peter went on. 'Beyond the pain, life continues to be sweet. The basics are still there. Beauty, food and friendship, reservoirs of love and understanding. Later, possibly not yet, you are going to need others who will encourage you to make new beginnings. Welcome them. They will help you move on, to cherish happy memories and confront the painful ones with more than bitterness and anger.'

Oscar remembered the dark night, and the image of

Francesca, and how, for the first time, it had not reduced him to the painful tears of loss but had filled him with a peaceful comfort. Perhaps that had been the start of his recovery. Perhaps this conversation, this interview, whatever one called it, was the continuance. He did not know. He only knew that he felt better, stronger, not so useless. Perhaps, after all, he hadn't done so badly.

He said, 'Thank you.'

'Oh, my friend, I wish I could give you so much more.'

'No. Don't wish that. You have given me enough.'

Lucy

Lucy

 Lucy had flown only twice in her life: once to France, where she had been invited for a summer holiday with the family of a school friend, and the second trip had been to the Channel Islands with her mother and her grandmother. That was during Easter, and they had stayed in the sort of hotel where you had to change for dinner. Both times she had found it tremendously exciting, but today she made an effort to be consciously casual about the whole business so that any person who happened to look her way would get the impression that she was a seasoned, vastly experienced traveller.

Her clothes helped: her mother, perhaps to assuage unadmitted stirrings of guilt, had taken Lucy to Gap and there bought her daughter a number of delectable things. Now she was wearing the new jeans, warm ones lined in red brushed cotton. Her boots were pale suede with thick rubber soles, and her jacket scarlet, quilted and padded, a bit like being bundled up in an eiderdown. They had also bought two thick polo-necked sweaters, one navy and one white, a black mini-skirt and two pairs of thick black tights. The final item was her rucksack, navy blue canvas piped in red, in which Lucy had packed her diary, her purse, her brush and comb and a bar of chocolate. Last night she had washed her hair, and this morning brushed it back into a long pony-tail, secured with a cotton scrunchie. She felt sleek and neat. A credit to Carrie.

Carrie looked, as always, immensely elegant in her long boots, her loden coat, and a black fox fur hat. Lucy was very aware of heads turning to watch as Carrie walked by, pushing the trolley with their luggage. The only thing was, poor Carrie had a bit of a cold. It wasn't the sort of cold that made her look ugly, simply a bit frail. She said she had started feeling rough a day or so ago – there was a lot of flu going about – but it was only a cold and she had dosed herself with medicaments and would be fine once she started breathing the clean, cold Scottish air.

They checked in, went through security and, waiting for their flight to be called, Lucy began to feel safe. Ever since the plans had been laid for Christmas she had not only been counting the days but had fallen prey to a number of nervous forebodings. Something, she was sure, was bound to put a stop to her going with Carrie. Somebody would fall ill or Gran would decide all at once that Lucy should not stay with Elfrida Phipps, of whom she did not approve, and whom Lucy was longing to meet. Perhaps, in America, Randall Fischer would have a heart-attack, or die, and the phone would ring in London to tell Mummy that she was not to come.

But disaster did not strike, and at last they were in the plane winging their way north, and unless the aircraft actually fell out of the sky Lucy knew that nothing now could stop them. She sat with her forehead pressed against the little window, staring down at an England spread out below like a greenish-grey quilt and patterned with slow-moving cloud shadows.

Extraordinarily enough, it was a lovely peaceful morning, cold but not raining, and with no wind-chill to freeze the bones. Above the clouds the sky was a pure pale blue, the horizon hazy. Lucy thought about people on the ground looking up and seeing their jetstream, perhaps wondering where the plane was heading. Just as she looked down on what appeared to be stretches of uninhabited country, the only clue to any sort of industry being a tiny puff of smoke from a group of cooling towers. She wondered which was the real life, who were the real people.

The stewardess came around with little trays of food: rolls and butter, marmalade, a sliver of bacon, a tiny bunch of green grapes. There was coffee or tea, and both Carrie and Lucy had coffee. Everything was teeny, doll size, all fitted neatly on to a little plastic tray. Lucy was hungry and ate everything, and when Carrie didn't eat her roll, Lucy ate it as well. After the trays had been taken away, Carrie read the paper and Lucy turned back to gaze out of the window because she didn't want to miss a single inch of Scotland.

She thought perhaps when they got there it would be raining, or even snowing, but the skies remained wonderfully clear. When the plane began to lose height, the terrain below them slowly took shape and she saw snow on the tops of mountains and a lot of dark fur, which turned into plantations of conifer, then the blue gleam of the sea, boats, and a bridge over a wide firth. The plane banked and turned before coming in to land, and to the west stood bastions of snow-covered mountains, all glittering in the pale sunshine. Lucy knew that they could not have looked more beautiful and told herself that this had to be a good omen.

Carrie folded her paper and stowed it away. They smiled at each other. 'All right?' Carrie asked. Lucy nodded.

They landed, huge tyres thumping on tarmac. She saw the terminal building, which looked a bit like a large golf clubhouse, and there were flags flying in a brisk breeze.

'We are going to be met,' Carrie had told her.

'Who by?'

'A taxi from Creagan. The driver's called Alec Dobbs.'

'How shall we know him?'

'He'll be holding a board with Sutton written on it.'

And, once they had reclaimed their suitcases from the carousel, he was there in the arrivals hall: a solid-looking man in a padded windcheater, with a faded tweed cap pulled down over his brow. A number of other fascinating individuals stood about: a lanky old man in a deerstalker; a trousered lady, with wild white hair and weatherbeaten cheeks, and, best of all, a man in a faded, tattered kilt. Lucy could not help staring because his blue knees looked so cold.

'Well, and it is good to see you,' Alec Dobbs was saying. 'And did you have a good flight?' Not a bit like the usual run of taxi drivers, more like an old friend. He shook hands with them, then gathered up their suitcases, as though they weighed nothing and led the way out. The sun, low in the sky, was shining palely but it felt considerably colder than London, and there was still an edging of old snow around the border of the car park. The air smelled of pine, and when Lucy breathed it in the inside

300

of her nose felt so cold that she sneezed. She had never been to Switzerland but decided that this was probably how Switzerland felt, with the sunshine and the snow and the pine trees, all arched by a pristine, cloudless sky.

Alec's car was a four-wheel-drive Subaru. Loading their luggage into the back, he explained, 'I have another car, a big Rover, which would be more comfortable for you, but we have high ground to cross on the Black Isle and the snow is still lying.'

Carrie got into the back of the car and Lucy sat beside Alec.

'Is there a lot of snow?' she asked him, because she had never experienced a white Christmas, and longed to do so. A white Christmas truly would be the icing on the cake.

'Not a great deal, but it stays, which means there is more to come.' He had a soft voice, precise and gentle. It was the first time Lucy had heard the voice of Sutherland.

'How long a drive is it to Creagan?'

'An hour and a quarter, perhaps. No more.' Lucy looked at her watch. It was eleven fifteen. They would be there probably at about half past twelve. In time for lunch. She hoped it would be something hot and robust. Despite the two rolls, she was beginning to be hungry again. 'Is this the first time you have come to Creagan?'

'I've never been to Scotland before.'

'Well, well, you have treats in store. And you will be staying in a fine house. It stood empty for too long. It is good to have people living there again.'

Carrie leaned forward. 'How is Elfrida?' she asked. 'Mrs Phipps?'

'She is fine. I see her about the place, doing her shopping, walking her dog. It was she who came in to order the car for you. She telephoned this morning to be certain that I had not forgotten you.'

'Do you live in Creagan?' Lucy asked him.

'All my life. I was born there and my father before me. When he retired I took over his business.'

'Driving taxis?'

'It is not only taxis I drive.'

Lucy frowned. 'What else?'

'Hearses,' he told her, and there was an edge of laughter in his voice. 'I'm the undertaker.'

Lucy was momentarily silenced.

It was a spectacular drive. The road led through farmlands and over bridges, and on the high ground the tyres of the Subaru scrunched over snow. It followed the shores of a long tidal sea loch and ran through small villages with grey stone cottages flush on the pavement, and pubs and shops and sturdy no-nonsense churches surrounded by old graveyards filled with lichened, leaning headstones. Then, the last bridge, over another firth, stretching like a long arm of blue water up into the folds of the western hills.

Alec spoke. 'Only another ten minutes now,' he told them, 'and we'll be there.'

All at once some of the excitement died and Lucy began to feel a bit nervous. It wasn't just arriving in an unknown place and at a strange house, but the prospect of finally meeting her hosts, Elfrida and Oscar. She wasn't so worried about Elfrida, because Carrie had spoken so much about her and she sounded as though she were ageless and tremendous fun. But Oscar Blundell, Elfrida's friend, was a different prospect altogether. To start with he was a man, and Lucy was not used to the company of men.

But that was not all. Because Carrie had told her all about Oscar, and why Elfrida had come with him to this little northern town to keep him company. His wife and his daughter, aged twelve and called Francesca, had both been killed in a terrible motor smash. Carrie had not enlarged on this catastrophe and had turned away Lucy's horrified questioning. She had simply said that it had been an accident, nobody was to blame, but Oscar was still in the throes of coming to terms with what had happened.

Francesca had been twelve. Lucy was fourteen. 'Will he want me?' she had asked. 'Won't it be awful for him, having a person of my age around the place? Do you think he will hate me?'

Carrie had smiled and given her a hug. 'I said that to Elfrida on the telephone. And she spoke to Oscar about it and he was quite adamant that we have to go for Christmas. And it's his house we're going to stay in so he is our host and he has invited us. And nobody *ever* could hate you.'

But still, it was all a bit complicated and daunting. Right now, Lucy could do without complications. She had enough of them in London.

Now, quite suddenly, there was a feeling of the seaside: duney hillocks on either side of the road where stunted pines and clumps of heather grew, and a certain light, reflected off the sea. She rolled down the window and caught the smell of salt. The road ran downhill and ahead of them was the little town, and they were in the main street almost before she realised it. It wasn't grey and sombre like the other villages they had come through but built of golden sandstone that seemed to reflect the glow of the thin winter sunshine. Houses on

303

either side stood back behind walled gardens, and there were handsome buildings and trees, and an unexpected impression of prosperity and space.

Carrie hadn't said much during the course of the drive, but now she spoke. 'How extraordinary. It's like the Cotswolds. Like a Cotswolds town.'

Alec smiled. 'A lot of visitors make that observation, but I have never been to the Cotswolds.'

'Golden stone. Wide streets. And the gardens . . .'

'What many people do not realise is that because of the Gulf Stream we have a climate similar to Eastbourne. There can be rainstorms boiling in the hills and we play golf or walk on the beach in the sunshine.'

Lucy said, 'A sort of mini-climate.'

'Exactly so.'

The street widened out into a square, in the middle of which stood a large, lovely church and an old graveyard, all enclosed by a stone wall. The church had a tower, crested by a golden weathercock, and gulls and jackdaws wheeled about overhead. The gulls made a noise like summer holidays. The tower clock pointed to twenty-five minutes past twelve.

'We have made good time,' Alec observed. He drove, at a stately pace, right around the churchyard wall and drew up at the pavement's edge.

'Is this it?' Lucy asked.

He switched off his engine. 'This is it.'

They got out of the Subaru, but before Alec could even unlatch the gate there came the sound of frantic barking, and the next moment the front door of the house was flung open. Down the path came Elfrida Phipps and her vociferous dog.

'Carrie! Oh, my darling girl.' She flung her arms

around Carrie and they hugged enormously. 'You're here, you're here. I've been so looking forward – so excited – could hardly wait!'

Standing aside, Lucy watched. Elfrida was very tall and very thin, and she had a lot of rather wild hair the colour of marmalade. She wore trousers of some particularly garish tartan and a huge, thick grey sweater. Her eyelids were very blue and she wore a lot of lipstick. Lucy could understand instantly why Gran didn't approve. Kissing, she had left lipstick on Carrie's cheek.

Carrie said, 'Elfrida, you look wonderful. Scotland clearly agrees with you.'

'Darling, it's bliss. Bitterly cold, but bliss.'

'You have to meet Lucy.'

'But of course.' She laughed. 'Isn't this ridiculous, Lucy? We're relations and we've never set eyes on each other. But your grandfather was my most favourite cousin and we used to have wonderful, wild times together.' She put her hands on Lucy's shoulders. 'Let me look at you. Yes, I thought so. Pretty as paint. This is my dog Horace who, I am pleased to say, has stopped barking. He's been looking forward to meeting you because he hopes you'll take him for long walks on the beach. Oh, Alec, you've got the suitcases. Is that all? Would you be a saint and carry them upstairs for us? Come along, everybody, and we'll go into the house out of the cold and you can meet Oscar.'

They all streamed up the path and into the house in single file, Elfrida leading the way, then the dog, then Carrie, Lucy, and finally Alec laden with luggage. He kicked the front door shut behind them, and they went down a long hall then up a wide staircase. Lucy liked the feeling of the house: solid and secure, with

305

sturdy banisters and a thick stair carpet. And the smell of old polished wood and well-worn furniture, and the faint suggestion of something delicious cooking in the kitchen.

Elfrida was still talking. 'How was the flight? Not too bumpy? Thank goodness there isn't a howling gale.'

They had reached the first-floor landing. The pleasing staircase rose on to the upper floor. On the far side of the landing a shaft of sunlight streamed through an open door.

Elfrida raised her voice to call. 'Oscar! Here they are!' And then, in her ordinary voice again, 'He's in the sitting room. You two go and say hello, and I'll show Alec where to put the suitcases. Carrie's in here, Alec, and Lucy's upstairs. Can you deal with another climb?'

Carrie looked at Lucy and smiled reassuringly. She took Lucy's hand in hers, which was comforting, and they went through the open, sunlit door into a beautiful sitting room, white-walled, not over-furnished but filled with light. A little fire was burning in the grate, and a tall bow window faced out across the street: the church was so close you felt you could reach out a hand and touch it.

He was waiting for them, standing with his back to the fireplace. He was as tall as Elfrida but not so thin as she, and he had a fine head of silvery hair, and a quiet, kindly face, not rugged but strangely unlined. His eyes were hooded, and drooped at the corners. He wore a checked shirt and a woollen tie, and over these a blue Shetland sweater.

Carrie said, 'Oscar. How do you do? I'm Carrie Sutton.'

'My dear . . .' He came forward to greet them, and

Lucy thought he must find himself a little astonished to be welcoming a guest as sensationally glamorous as Carrie. But pleased, too. 'How good to see you. Have you had a peaceful journey?' They shook hands.

'Perfect,' Carrie told him. 'No problems.'

'And Alec found you all right? Elfrida's been mad with excitement all morning, rushing to the window to see if you had come.'

'It's so good of you to have us.' Carrie looked about her. 'And what a marvellous house you have.'

'I own only half.'

'That doesn't make it any less special.' She let go of Lucy's hand, and put an arm around her shoulder. 'This is my niece, Lucy Wesley.'

Lucy swallowed her nervousness. She said, 'How do you do?' He looked down at her and she willed herself to meet his eyes. For what seemed a long time he said nothing. She knew that he must be thinking of his own daughter, twelve years old and now dead. She knew that he must be comparing her with Francesca and was probably swamped by mixed emotions, including pain. She hoped that she compared favourably. There wasn't much else she could do. And then he smiled at her, and took her hand between his own, and his clasp was warm and friendly and after that she wasn't nervous any longer.

'So you are Lucy.'

'Yes.'

'And you are going to have to sleep in the attic.'

Carrie laughed. 'Oscar, you don't make it sound very tempting.'

'Attics never do sound tempting. Old trunks and the heads of defunct moose. Don't worry, Lucy, Elfrida has made it entrancing for you.

'Now,' he let go of Lucy's hand, and looked out of the window at the clock on the church tower, 'it's half past twelve. Why don't you both go and find your rooms and get settled? Then we'll have a drink, and then we'll have lunch. Elfrida has spent much of the morning concocting a shepherd's pie. She thought you would need something heartening to eat after your long journey.'

Lucy's spirits rose. The worst – the initial encounters – was over. Elfrida was funny, and Oscar was kind. And Elfrida had said she was as pretty as paint. And they were going to eat shepherd's pie for lunch.

They had lunch in the kitchen. 'We've got a dining room,' Elfrida explained, 'but it's so dark and gloomy we never eat there. And there isn't a hatch through from the kitchen and I should spend my time scuttling to and fro with dishes.'

'Much nicer in here,' said Carrie, and Lucy agreed with her. A long table, a gingham cloth, unmatched wooden chairs, all comfortably informal. It wasn't a smart kitchen. Dodie, Lucy knew, would die if she was asked to do anything under such old-fashioned conditions: for one thing, it was rather dark, facing out on to the wall of the neighbouring garden. And there were bars on the windows to keep out intruders, or possibly to stop overworked cooks and kitchenmaids escaping. And yet, like the rest of the house, it had a pleasant, settled feel about it, and there was a big sideboard, painted dark green, with an assortment of china displayed, and hooks for jugs and mugs and cups.

They ate the shepherd's pie, which was delicious, then a pudding made of stewed apples and meringue, with a jug of cream, and after that Carrie and Elfrida had coffee.

But Oscar did not want coffee. Instead, he looked at his watch and said, 'If Horace and I do not set out for a walk *now*, we won't be home before darkness falls.' He looked down the length of the table at Lucy. 'Would you like to come with us?'

'For a walk?'

'We could go on the beach. And then you will know the way.'

She felt very gratified to be invited. 'Yes, I'd love to.'

'Perhaps, Oscar,' said Elfrida, 'you could wheel her round the town first and show her where the shops are, it won't take more than five minutes, and then you can head for the dunes.'

'Certainly, if that's what she'd like. Have you got a warm coat, Lucy?'

'I've got my new jacket.'

'And a warm hat. The sea wind can freeze your ears off.'

'Yes, I've got that too.'

'Then go and get ready, and we'll set off together.'

'Shall I help to clear the table?' Lucy asked.

Elfrida laughed. 'How well brought up you are. Of course not. Carrie and I will do that when we've finished our coffee. Off you go with Oscar before it gets too cold.'

Five minutes later, they set off together, the elderly man, the girl and the dog. Horace wore his lead and Lucy held its other end in her gloved hand. She had pulled a thick woollen hat down over her ears and zipped herself into her new jacket. Oscar wore a heavy windproof jacket with a checked lining, and a tweed hat which she thought suited him and made him look distinguished and handsome.

As they went through the gate, he said, 'We'll do the town first,' so they did: down the street, all around the church wall, the gift shop, the chemist, the bookshop, the butcher, the newsagent. 'This is where I come to pick up the morning papers. If I want to be lazy and lie in my bed, you can do it for me.' The petrol pumps, a shop full of knitted sweaters, a small hotel, a window of beach toys, the supermarket. Beneath a leafless tree, Lucy paused to look through a wrought-iron gate up a flagged path to where a side door of the church stood open.

For some reason she longed to go inside. She could see a porch, stoutly doormatted, then an inner, closed door.

'Is the church open?' she asked.

'Always. Just this side door. For visitors, I suppose.'

'What's it like inside?'

'I don't know, Lucy. I have never been.'

'Can we go now? Just for a moment?'

He hesitated. 'I . . .'

'Oh, do let's. Churches are so nice when they're empty. Like empty streets. You can see their shape. Just for a moment.'

He took a deep breath, and she thought he was going to refuse; to say, 'There's not time,' or 'Another day.' But he let it all out in what sounded like a deep sigh. 'All right,' he said.

Lucy opened the gate, which squeaked on its hinges, and they went up the path. Inside the porch, they found a notice.

VISITORS WELCOME, BUT PLEASE,
NO DOGS.

They tied the end of Horace's lead to the handle of

the outer door and left him sitting on the doormat. He did not look pleased.

Inside, the church was empty. Their footsteps rang on the flagged floor and echoed up into the roof. Sunlight poured through the stained-glass windows. Three of the arms of the cruciform shape were lined with pews, all facing the central aisle so that it was a little like three churches. The walls were stone, and the arched ceiling soared upwards, high above them, the plaster between the curved beams painted the blue of a summer sky.

Lucy wandered off to investigate. She read the words on old memorial slabs, about people from another age who had been true servants of God and regular worshippers. There were a lot of noble and titled names, as well as ordinary ones. It was all much larger than she had thought it would be, and by the time she had inspected everything, from the ornate font to the kneelers, each handsomely upholstered in hand-stitched needlepoint, Oscar had tired of standing and was settled comfortably in the front pew, waiting for her.

She felt a bit guilty and went to sit beside him. 'I'm sorry.'

'Why?'

'For being so long.'

'I'm pleased that you are interested in such things.'

'Carrie told me that you were an organist. That you taught music.'

'That's true. I was choir-master as well.' He looked down at her. 'Do you play the piano?'

'No. I've never started to learn. Mummy said it would take too much time out of lessons and games and homework and things. Anyway, there isn't a piano in my grandmother's flat.'

'Would you like to play?'

'Yes, I think I would.'

'It's never too late to start. Do you listen to music?'

Lucy shrugged. 'Only pop and such.' She thought about this. 'Except sometimes at school we get taken to concerts. We went to an open-air concert in Regent's Park this summer. There was a huge stage and a proper orchestra.'

Oscar smiled. 'Did it rain?'

'No, it was a fine evening. And at the end of the concert they played the *Music for the Royal Fireworks*, and there was a firework display at the same time. I really loved that. The music and the bangs and the lights and the rockets all went along together and made everything doubly exciting. Now, if I hear the music again, I can see fireworks as well, and the night sky, all filled with every sort of star.'

'An experience.'

'Yes. It was lovely.' She sank her chin into her new jacket and gazed up at the tall stained-glass window that faced them. Mary with the baby Jesus. She said, 'I wouldn't want a birthday in the middle of winter. I wouldn't want to be born on Christmas Day.'

'Why not?'

'Well, for one thing you'd probably only get one present. And for another it's usually rather dark and gloomy weather.'

'When is your birthday?'

'July. Much better. Only thing is, I'm usually at school.'

'Still, it's summer.'

'Yes.'

Oscar thought for a moment, and then he said,

312

'Actually, I don't think Christ was born in wintertime. I think he was probably born in the spring.'

'Really? Why do you say that?'

'Well, the shepherds were guarding their flocks, which probably meant that it was lambing time and they were watching out for the wolves, in case they came and ate the babies. And another thing: scientific evidence tells us that there was a strangely bright star at that time, two thousand years ago, and in that place.'

'Then why don't we have Christmas in the spring?'

'I think the early Christians were a cunning lot. They simply adapted what was left to them by the pagan inhabitants of the countries they converted. There had always been the celebration of the winter solstice, the shortest day of the year. I suppose to cheer themselves up those pre-Christians had something of a party, lit fires, caroused, burned candles, plucked mistletoe, baked cakes.' Oscar smiled. 'Got drunk, indulged in lustful practices.'

'So the early Christians just used the same party?'

'Something like that.'

'But added other bits as well.'

'Their belief in the Son of God.'

'I see.' Considered, it seemed a very practical arrangement. 'What about Christmas trees?'

'They came from Germany. Brought by Albert, Victoria's prince consort.'

'And turkeys?'

'Turkeys came from America. Before that goose was the traditional bird.'

'And carols?'

'Some old, some new.'

'And wassailing? What does wassailing mean? I've never known.'

'Just boozing. A wassail was a drink of spiced ale.'

'And stockings?'

'I don't think I know where stockings are from.'

Lucy was silent for a moment. Then she said, 'Do you like Christmas?'

'Parts of it,' Oscar told her, sounding cautious.

'I don't really like it much. There's such a build-up and then it's sort of ... disappointing.'

'Which proves that we should never expect too much.' High above them, the church clock struck half past two. The chimes were distant, melodious, muffled. Oscar said, 'Perhaps we have lingered long enough.'

Lucy fell silent. The church was very quiet. From what seemed like far away, other sounds impinged: a passing car, a man's voice calling out, the long cry of a wheeling seagull high above the clock tower. She looked upwards, and noticed, for the first time, the discreet uplighters, high above, fitted within the lip of the carved stone cornice. They were not lit now, which was why she had not seen them before but ...

She said, 'It must be lovely in here when all those lights are on. Like floodlights, like sunshine, shining on the blue ceiling.'

'I expect they turn them on on Sundays for morning service.'

'I'd like to see that.'

He said, quietly, 'If you want to, you can.' And then he got to his feet. 'Come along. We're meant to be having a walk. We have to get as far as the beach, and before very long it will be dark.'

Carrie

Carrie

Oscar, Lucy and Horace were gone, off for their walk. The heavy front door of the Estate House slammed behind them and Carrie and Elfrida were left alone, still sitting at the kitchen table with the remains of lunch and their coffee. They smiled at each other. Two women of different generations but old friends, who had not been alone together for too long, and now relished their peaceful privacy.

Carrie said, 'What a perfectly sweet man.'

Elfrida, she thought, for all her sixty-two years, looked vital and energetic as a young girl. Her slenderness became her; the uncompromising blaze of suspect hair, the eccentric clothes, the slash of lipstick all declaimed a healthy denial of advancing years. Her very presence was like a shot in the arm.

'Isn't he?' she said, with satisfaction.

'I'm so pleased they've made friends. Lucy was apprehensive. I told her, of course, about his wife and daughter, and she was afraid that Oscar mightn't want her about the place, reminding him of Francesca. She thought he might find her presence distressing. Even that he might hate her.'

Elfrida was sympathetic. 'Poor little thing, but perceptive, too. And I don't think Oscar *knows* how to hate any person. And if he did he would never say so, nor ever show it. We had a slight hiccup when we arrived here in the shape of a rather sad old bore from whom we had to collect the key of the house. I must say, he was rather disquieting – kept telling Oscar that he'd put him up for the golf club, and they would meet over a drink. Oscar was terrified. He spent the first couple of weeks cowering indoors or scuttling across the road to the supermarket with his hat pulled over his eyes, like a criminal, in mortal fear of meeting Major Billicliffe and having to ask him back for a gin. But then he discovered the old chap was actually quite ill. He found him languishing in his bed, under the doctor, as they say. And the next thing was he'd offered to drive him over to the hospital in Inverness because he felt so sorry for him. Major Billicliffe's a widower and all alone. So, you see, Oscar's not very good at hating. You could never call him one of your consistent, paid-up, professional haters.'

'I think he's a darling. I just hope it's not going to be too much for you both having us here.'

'It's brilliant, just what we need.'

'It doesn't have to be an all-singing, all-dancing Christmas. Lucy and I both have a fairly low expectation of what is known as the Festive Season.'

'Us, too. Though once he knew you were coming Oscar did, privately, order a Christmas tree.'

'Lucy will love that. She can decorate it. Poor child, my mother was never much good at creating a magic atmosphere and Nicola's too idle. But I truly think Ma's grateful to you because now she can go and spend her giddy holiday in Bournemouth with a clear conscience.'

'How is she?'

'Just the same.' No more needed to be said.

'And Nicola?'

'Ditto. Unlike wine, they do not improve with age.'

'And your father?'

'Haven't seen him, but spoke to him on the telephone.'

'I had such a wonderful month with them all at Emblo in October. And then I got home to hear of this terrible thing that had happened to Oscar. It was like moving out of one world and into another. Life can change with such shocking abruptness.'

'I know.' Carrie thought about Andreas, then didn't think about him. She said again, 'I know.'

A silence fell. Carrie finished her coffee and set down the little cup. She knew what was coming next, which it did.

'And *you*, Carrie?'

'Me? I'm fine.'

'I don't think you are. For one thing you look tired and pale. And dreadfully thin.'

'Look who's talking. Admit, Elfrida, we'd neither of us ever have won a prize for the most voluptuous.'

'Why did you suddenly come back from Austria?'

Carrie shrugged. 'Oh, reasons. Whims.'

'I don't believe that.'

'Some time I'll tell you, I promise. But not just at this moment.'

'You're not ill?'

'No. I'm fighting a cold and I'm a bit tired, but I'm not ill.'

'Did you chuck up your job?'

'Yes.'

'Will you get another?'

'I think so. In fact, the travel company I worked for overseas telephoned the other evening, and the next day I went along and saw them. I've been offered a job – a good one – in the London office. I haven't accepted yet but I probably will when I go back after Christmas.'

'And your house?'

'Let till February. Until then I can camp with friends or rent.'

'I feel you're unhappy. I wish I could help.'

'You are helping. By having us here.'

'Not very exciting.'

'I don't want excitement.'

Elfrida was silenced. She finished her coffee, then sighed and ran a hand through her unruly, fiery hair. 'In that case, I will say no more. Now,' her manner changed, she became cheerful, in charge, once more, 'what would you like to do this afternoon? Perhaps a nap. I'll find a hot-water bottle.'

Bed and a hot-water bottle. Carrie could not remember how long it was since some other person had cherished her. Had said, 'You look tired.' And 'How about a little rest?' She had spent too many years being strong, looking after others and their problems: cancelled reservations, faulty ski-tows, unsuitable bedrooms, trains and buses that ran, through no fault of their own, late; the lack of snow, or the fact that there was too much of it; a band, playing too loudly into the early hours of the morning; lost passports, money, hairdryers . . . And then returning to London to be faced with another set of family problems that needed to be surmounted.

She realised that she was tired of being strong. Tired of being the sturdy pillar against which everybody leaned. Upstairs was her bedroom, her suitcase already in possession. She had gone there to shed her coat and comb her hair before lunch, and had seen, with some satisfaction, the enormous double bed, downy and soft, with its white cover, and great brass bedstead like the polished rails of some well-kept ship. She had longed right then and there to climb beneath the blankets and sleep.

Perhaps a nap. She was filled with grateful love for Elfrida. She said, 'I don't think there's anything I'd like more. But first can I be shown your house so that I know my way around? It seems so enormous, I might get lost. I'd imagined the two of you domiciled in some little cottage, and here you are in a veritable mansion.'

'Of course.' Elfrida got to her feet.

'What about the washing-up?'

'I'll do it later. We haven't got a dishwasher, but I've never had one so it doesn't matter. And I rather like splashing around in time-honoured fashion with lots of suds. Come along . . .'

She led the way out of the kitchen, and Carrie followed her down the hall to the two ground-floor rooms. 'It all used to belong to the Corrydale estate,' Elfrida explained, sounding a bit like a tour guide. 'The factor and his family lived here, so that's why it's so huge. We inherited only the most essential bits of furniture, and there's no point cluttering ourselves up with possessions.' She opened a door. 'This was the estate office and, as you can see, is totally uninhabitable. Like a junk shop. And *this* is our dining room. Utter gloom.'

It was indeed daunting, redolent of long, dull meals.

'But I love the table,' said Carrie. 'And a sideboard built for massive haunches of venison. And a piano! Shall we have concerts?'

'I shouldn't think so. God knows when it was last tuned.'

'But Oscar plays.'

'Not just now. Just now, he listens to music, he doesn't make it.'

They went upstairs. 'Lucy's in the attic. I did it all up for her, but I'm sure she'll want to show you herself. And you've seen the sitting room, and the bathrooms, and this,' she opened another door, 'is the second spare bedroom. I could have put Lucy in here, but it's very small and a bit drear. The attic seemed to me a much more attractive space for her, and I had all the fun of putting it together.'

Carrie peered into the small and undistinguished room, almost totally taken up with another enormous bed. It was, clearly, unoccupied, and for the first time she began to feel a bit uncomfortable, not knowing, but suspecting, what was going to happen next. Her interest in seeing over the house had been just that. Interest. Not curiosity. But her innocent request felt now a bit like taking the lid off Pandora's box.

'Elfrida . . .'

Elfrida either didn't hear or took no notice. Instead, she opened the final door with a flourish that had a touch of defiance about it. 'And this,' she said, 'is us.'

It was a spacious and important room, the master bedroom of the original house, with tall windows facing out over the light of the dying afternoon, the street and the church. In it stood a looming Victorian wardrobe, a pretty Victorian dressing-table and a chest of drawers.

And an enormously high, wide bed. Over this was spread Elfrida's scarlet silk shawl, the embroidery faded, the fringe beginning to fray, but still marvellously opulent and recognisable from the old days and Elfrida's house in Putney.

And other possessions. A man's ivory brushes on the chest of drawers, a pair of brogues placed neatly beneath a chair, dark blue pyjamas folded on a pillow. And a pleasant, masculine smell, compounded of polished leather and bay rum.

There fell a small silence. Then Carrie looked at Elfrida and caught on her face a faintly abashed expression. She was amused because Elfrida had never betrayed the smallest sense of shame about her many and varied sexual encounters.

Now she said, 'You're not shocked?'

'Elfrida, I'm me. I'm not Dodie.'

'I know you're not.'

'You're sleeping together?'

Elfrida nodded.

'You're lovers?'

'We are.'

Carrie thought of that charming, distinguished man, with his thick white hair and gentle face. She said, 'I'm glad.'

'I'm glad you're glad. But I have to tell you. Explain.'

'You don't have to explain to me.'

'No, but I want to.'

'We travelled together from Dibton to Scotland. I drove most of the way, the conditions were horrible and the A1 heavy with traffic. It had been a traumatic few days before we left, saying goodbyes and making arrangements, and

I think we were both exhausted. Oscar scarcely spoke at all. By the time it was dark we'd had enough of the motorway so we got off it at some junction and drove into Northumberland. Oscar said there was some little town he remembered with an old hotel in the main street, and by some miracle we found the town, and the hotel was still there. I sat in the car with Horace, and Oscar went in to see if they had rooms for us.

'After a bit he came out and said that they didn't mind about the dog, but they only had one room with a double bed. By then I was so tired I'd have slept in a cupboard so I told Oscar to go in and book it, and we wrote Mr and Mrs Oscar Blundell in the register. I felt like a giddy girl, sneaking off for the weekend with her boyfriend.

'We had baths and a drink and dinner. Then, because we had an early start the next morning, we went upstairs. There took place a ridiculous conversation, with Oscar saying he would curl up on the sofa, and me saying I would sleep on the floor with Horace. And then, suddenly, we were too tired to argue and we just got into bed together and fell fast asleep.

'But what I didn't know was that Oscar was having these terrible nightmares. He told me later that he'd been having them ever since the crash, that he put off going to bed at night because he was so filled with dread, so afraid. That night he woke me with his screams, and for a moment I was terrified. Then I knew I had to wake him. So I did, and he was weeping – it was so awful for him – and I gave him a drink of water and calmed him down, and I put my arms around him and held him close and after a bit he went back to sleep again. After that I would never let him be alone during the night.

When we came here, he was a bit worried at first about what people would think, what they would say. We have a sweet woman who comes and cleans for us, Mrs Snead. He was afraid she would gossip, and that there would be disapproval and bad feeling. And I said I didn't care if there was, I wasn't going to leave him.

'I think, Carrie darling, that all this might sound a little suspect. Opportunist. As though the moment Gloria was dead I crashed into Oscar's life, leaped into bed with him. But truly it wasn't like that. I'd always liked him immensely, but he was Gloria's husband and I liked her too, though perhaps not quite as much as I liked Oscar. It's rather difficult to explain. But everything I have done, every choice I have made, was only with the best of intentions in mind. He asked me to come to Scotland with him, and because he was a man on the verge of desperation I agreed.

'It might have been a disaster but instead we have a relationship which I think is a comfort to both of us. We first made love about a week after we got here. It was inevitable, of course. He is a very attractive man, and for some reason he seems to find battered old me attractive too. Since then the terrible dreams have begun to fade, and sometimes he sleeps through till morning. There are still nightmares, but not nearly so frequent. And if you do hear shouts in the middle of the night, don't be alarmed because I am with Oscar.

'I've kept nothing secret, told no lies. I confided in Mrs Snead privately, at the first opportunity, the circumstances of our design for living. Mrs Snead is a Londoner and quite unshockable, as well as being a good friend and a mine of useful information. When I had finished explaining, all she said was, "I think, Mrs

Phipps, it would be a cruel thing to let that man suffer if you can give 'im a spot of comfort in 'is hour of need.' So that was that. And now *you* know.'

For a moment neither of them said anything. Then Carrie sighed. 'Poor Oscar. But how much poorer he would be without you.'

'And Lucy? What shall we do about Lucy? She doesn't look a stupid child. Ought you to tell her?'

'Let's not make an issue of it. If she asks questions, I shall tell her the truth.'

'We're so old, she'll be astonished.'

'I don't think so. Her own grandfather has a very young wife and a couple of little children. Nothing's new to Lucy. She's clearly taken a shine to Oscar and she'll be as thrilled as I am.' Carrie put her arms around Elfrida's skinny shoulders and hugged her. 'It's all so sweet, needing each other and finding each other.'

'Oscar's not out of the wood yet, by any means. He still has a long way to go. Some days he's so depressed that he scarcely speaks. But I've learned to leave him alone. He has to deal with his grief in his own way.'

'It can't have been easy.'

'Oh, darling Carrie, nothing is. And now, we must waste no more time, otherwise the day will have died. I shall find you a hot-water bottle, and you shall go to sleep.'

Lucy

Lucy

Friday 15 December
We are here, and it is now
ten o'clock at night and it
has been a long day. Carrie
came to Gran's flat about half past eight in
the morning, and she had a taxi waiting, and
then we drove on to Heathrow. Mummy and
Gran were still at the flat. Mummy doesn't
fly to Florida till Tuesday. They were still in
their dressing-gowns and being very kind. I
think they both felt a bit guilty about all
the discussions and crossness. They gave me
Christmas presents, all wrapped, and I put
them in my suitcase. And Mummy gave me a
hundred and fifty pounds and Gran gave me
fifty pounds for spending money. I have never
felt so rich and am frightened of losing my
purse, but it's all right, quite safe in my new
rucksack.
The flight was all right and not bumpy and
we had a sort of breakfast on the plane. At

Inverness a nice man called Alec was there to meet us and drove us here. There was snow on a hill and it took about an hour and a quarter.

Creagan is very old and pretty and full of quite large houses and a huge church. This is an amazing house, it is much bigger than it looks and is on three storeys. It was rented out, and a lot of the furniture, Oscar told me, came from Corrydale, the big house he used to stay in when he was a boy and had a grandmother there. I say a lot of furniture, but in fact, there isn't much, and no pictures or anything. The sitting room and bedrooms are on the first floor, but I am up again, and in an attic, which Elfrida has done up especially for me. She didn't have to paint it as it's all white and quite fresh, but she has had to buy furniture which was very kind of her.

So. My room. It has a sloping ceiling and a skylight (no window) and a striped blind on the skylight, but I don't suppose I shall ever pull it down, as I am able to lie in bed and look up at the sky. Like being out of doors.

The bed is dark wood, and there is a blue and white striped duvet and a tartan rug in case I feel cold. There is a white dressing-table, with a swing mirror and little drawers, and a chest of drawers as well. Then, a bedside table, and a lamp, and a very useful table against one of the non-sloping walls. I think it must once have been a kitchen table, as it's a bit battered, but just right for writing my diary or

writing letters, etc. Then there are two chairs
and some hooks on the wall for me to hang
my clothes. I haven't brought very many. The
floor is scrubbed floorboards and in the middle
is a wonderful thick rug with lots of bright
colours, and by my bedside there is a sheepskin
for stepping out on to on cold mornings. I find
it all so different and romantic.

Elfrida and Oscar are really nice. I thought
they would be terribly old. They are old, but
don't look it or talk like it. Elfrida is very tall
and thin with orangey hair, and Oscar is also
tall, but not quite so thin. And he has a lot
of white hair and a very soft voice, and gentle
eyes. Before we left London, Carrie told me
about his wife and his daughter Francesca
being killed in a terrible car smash. And their
dogs as well. I was rather dreading meeting
him, because it is difficult sometimes to know
what to say to someone who has suffered
something so awful. But he is really nice and
didn't seem at all upset when he saw me and
Carrie. We had lunch, and then he asked me
to go out for a walk with him and Horace.
Horace is Elfrida's dog. So we went, and it
wasn't too cold, and we looked at shops and
sat in the church for a bit, and then we went
out again, and crossed the golf links and went
to the beach. The beach is lovely, long and
clean with no plastic bottles or rubbish. Lots of
shells. I picked up two scallops. I shall go again
and take Horace with me.

I am really happy. I've never lived in

such a big house, but it has a nice feel, as though well-to-do and cheerful people had always lived here. It has a big garden, too, at the back, but not much growing there at this time of year.

Tomorrow I shall explore.

Oscar

Oscar

Rather to his surprise, Oscar was having a bonfire.

At Dibton, at the Grange, he had become an enthusiastic gardener, mostly because he was retired, and a little piano teaching and the occasional Sunday-morning duty in the village church left him with time on his hands. To begin with he was totally inexperienced, had never even watered a window-box. But, starting up, long-forgotten wisdoms came floating up from his subconscious, wisdoms left over from the holidays he had spent at Corrydale with his grandmother, a natural gardener so experienced and accomplished that others came to view the glories of Corrydale and seek her advice.

The practical aspects he taught himself, by trial and error and by intensive study of huge gardening tomes. He also had the help of the two local men who came in to cut grass, do a bit of forestry and deal with the heavy digging. Before long, his new hobby had absorbed him and he enjoyed the physical exercise, the pleasures of planning and planting, and the simple satisfaction of being out of doors.

Coming to Creagan in the middle of winter, there wasn't much he could do about the steep terraced garden that climbed the slope behind the Estate House. He had swept up a number of dead leaves and cleared blocked drains, but that was all. This morning, however, at breakfast, Elfrida had complained about an overgrown lilac bush that spilled out over the path, and got in her way when she went up to the washing line with her basket of wet laundry.

Oscar said that he would deal with it.

After breakfast he took down the key of the potting-shed from its hook on the dresser and went out to investigate. It was a strange sort of day, overcast and with only a slight movement of chill air. From time to time the clouds parted to reveal a scrap of blue sky but he could still see snow lying on the hills, which meant there was more to come.

He managed to turn the rusty key and tug open the warped wooden door to reveal a dark and musty interior, scarcely lit by a small cobwebby window. There was a potting-table, on which lay a lot of earth, some broken flower-pots, a stack of yellowed newspapers and a few archaic tools, like dibbers and billhooks. There was no mower or Strimmer, or any piece of modern equipment, but around the walls, on huge masonry nails, hung heavy old forks and spades. There was also a rake, a hoe, a rusted saw, a formidable scythe. All were in dire need of care and attention, and he thought he would clean and oil them all, but could find no oil-can amongst the chaos and decided that that particular job must wait.

In a box filled with nuts, bolts and rusted spanners,

he found a pair of secateurs, ancient but more or less workable. Using these, he dealt with the lilac, which left him with a pile of branches in need of disposal. There was no wheelbarrow, and indeed a wheelbarrow would have been useless in this precipitous plot, so he found a ragged potato sack, stuffed the branches into it and lugged it up to the top of the garden where, behind an old plum tree, were the blackened remains of some previous bonfire.

He decided, then, to clear out the potting-shed, and as it was a dry, still day, burn all the rubbish while he was in the mood.

There was a great deal of it, and it took several journeys up and down the path to get it all collected. He made spills out of the newspaper, chopped up some rotted wooden seed-boxes and got his fire started. Soon it was blazing nicely, and he was raking up leaves and getting quite warm. He took off his jacket, hung it on the plum tree and worked in his sweater. The thick smoke rose, billowed and made everything smell of autumn. Then he started on some smothering ivy, cutting and tearing it back off the old stone wall. So intent was he on this labour that he did not hear the back gate open and shut, and he did not see the man who walked up the path behind him.

'Oscar.'

Startled, Oscar swung round to face Peter Kennedy, who was dressed for golf in his red jacket with his long-peaked baseball cap pulled down over his brow.

'Heavens, I never heard you.'

'I didn't mean to sneak up on you. I'm on my way to the golf club – I'm playing at half past ten. I saw the smoke from the fire, and guessed I'd find you here.'

'What can I do for you?'

'Nothing, really. But I wanted to tell you that I was in Inverness yesterday and I dropped in at the hospital to see Godfrey Billicliffe.'

'That was good of you. How is he?'

Peter shook his head. 'Not good news, I'm afraid. He's very ill. He has cancer.'

Cancer. Oscar said, 'Oh, God.'

'I think he already had his own suspicions, fears, but never said a word to anybody. He told me he'd been feeling unwell for a long time but had never gone to see the doctor, just dosed himself with pain-killers and whisky. He didn't want to be told – he was frightened of the truth.'

'He was frightened that day I found him in his bed.'

'I know.'

Oscar thought about the sick old man, remembered the weak tears that had brimmed in his rheumy eyes. 'Does he know?' he asked.

'Yes. He persuaded the young consultant to tell him.'

'How long has he got?'

'A little time. He's dying, but he's comfortable and quite peaceful, I think, rather enjoying all the attention and the nurses taking care of him. It will be a relief.'

'I must go and see him.'

'No. He asked me to tell you no. He's doped and frail, and already has the look of a man on his way out of this world. But he asked me to send you his regards and to say how grateful he was for your kindness.'

'I didn't do anything.'

'You did. And you were there when he most needed a friend.'

Oscar kicked a smouldering twig into the heart of his

fire. For a moment, remembering his reluctance to even speak to old Billicliffe, dodging around street corners in mortal dread of meeting him, he hated himself. He said, 'Did you speak to the doctor in the hospital?'

'Yes. When I'd said goodbye, I tracked down the consultant, who confirmed what I already knew.'

'What can I do?'

'Little, really. Perhaps write him a note. Send him a card. He'd like that.'

'It seems a bit tame.'

'He really is quite peaceful. Not struggling, not distressed. Sleeps most of the time, but when he did open his eyes, he recognised me and we spoke and he was perfectly lucid. I think, accepting.'

Oscar sighed hugely. 'Well, I suppose that's it, then.' He thought of practicalities. 'I'm down as his next-of-kin.'

'They'll let you know, or me. We'll keep in touch.'

'Thank you for telling me.'

'I knew you would want to know. Now, I must be off and leave you to your bonfire.'

Oscar laid down his rake. 'I'll come with you to the gate.'

They walked down the path, in single file. At the gate, Peter paused. 'There's something else. It occurred to me that perhaps you might be missing your music.' He felt in the pocket of his red golf jacket and produced a small brass key. 'The church is always open but the organ is locked. I have discussed it with Alistair Heggie, our organist, and he is happy for you to use it any time you feel so inclined. Here . . .' Before Oscar could protest Peter had taken his wrist and pressed the key into his outstretched palm, closing his fingers about it.

Oscar said, 'Oh, no . . .'

'You don't have to. You might not even want to. But I like to think that you can, if the impulse takes you and if you feel it would help.'

'You are too kind.'

'Just put it somewhere safe.' Peter grinned. 'It's our only spare.' He made as if to go, then turned back again, 'I think my brain's going soft. I very nearly forgot. Another of the reasons I came in search of you. Tabitha says would you all like to come up to the Manse for a drink and a mince-pie on Tuesday evening? Everybody's welcome. Nothing formal. Don't dress up. Our children will probably be around.'

'Tuesday.' Oscar, still holding the key, made a mental note. He must not forget to tell Elfrida. 'Tuesday at six. I think we'd like that very much.'

'Splendid.' Peter went through the gate, and latched it behind him. 'We'll see you then.'

'Have a good round. And thank you for coming.'

Lucy

Lucy

 On Monday morning, when Lucy descended from her eyrie in the attic, she saw, on the first-floor landing, that Carrie's bedroom door was closed. Her first thought was that perhaps Carrie had overslept, and she wondered if she should wake her. Then, fortuitously, she decided against it.

Downstairs she found Oscar and Elfrida in the throes of breakfast. This morning Oscar was eating sausages, and Lucy hoped there would be some for her. Sausages for breakfast was one of her ideas of heaven.

'Lucy.' As she appeared through the door, he laid down his knife and fork and stretched out an arm to greet her, pulling her close for a friendly hug. 'How are you this morning?'

'I'm fine, but where's Carrie?'

'Carrie's really not well.' Elfrida got up from the table to collect Lucy's sausages from the hotplate. 'I don't think she's got flu but she certainly isn't throwing this horrible cold off. Two sausages or three?'

'Three, please, if there's enough. Is she still in bed?'

'Yes, I looked in to see her, and she said she'd coughed all night and hadn't been able to sleep and was feeling thoroughly fed up with herself. I took her up a cup of tea, but she doesn't want anything to eat. When the health centre opens at nine I'm going to ring Dr Sinclair and ask if he'll come round and have a look at her.'

'Does he make house calls?'

'The health centre's only across the road.'

Lucy sat down to her sausages. 'In London doctors never do house calls. You have to go and sit in the waiting room with all the other sick people. Gran always says you come out with more things wrong with you than when you went in. Do you think she's going to be all right? Carrie, I mean. She must be all right for Christmas.'

'We'll see what Dr Sinclair says.'

'Can I go and see her?'

'I shouldn't until we know what's wrong. It might be frightfully contagious and then you'd come out in spots. Or running sores. Like poor Job.'

Lucy started on her sausages, which were delicious, and Elfrida poured her a cup of coffee. She said, 'It's really disappointing, because we'd planned a long walk on the beach this morning with Horace.'

'No reason why you shouldn't go.'

'Will *you* come, Oscar?'

'I can't this morning. I've got a lot of letters to write, and then I'm going to get my hair cut, and then I'm going to the bookshop to order two books, and then I'm going to pick up the meat from the butcher.'

'Oh, I see.' It was hard not to sound downcast.

He smiled. 'You can go on your own. Take Horace. He will guard you. You can be a lone explorer.'

Lucy brightened. 'Can I?'

'Of course.'

She mulled over this new prospect of freedom while she ate her sausages, and found that she was rather taken with the idea of setting out with the dog by herself. For obvious reasons she was not allowed to go for long, solitary walks on her own in London, and if she made some arrangement with Emma, her mother always had to know where she was going and when she would be back. But here, in Creagan, it was obvious that such precautions were not necessary. Elfrida and Oscar didn't even lock their front door. In the town cars and lorries drove very slowly, and shoppers quite often walked in the middle of the road, stopping from time to time to chat, and on the streets and pavements there always seemed to be unaccompanied children, skateboarding or otherwise flocking around in gangs. The day that Oscar had taken her as far as the beach, she had seen youngsters climbing rocks, riding bicycles and not an adult in view. As for sinister men in raincoats, drunks or drug addicts, they didn't seem to exist in this wholesome climate. Perhaps, like germs and mildew, they did not flourish in the cold.

The back door opened and banged shut.

'Mrs Snead,' said Oscar and, in a moment, she was with them, bursting into the kitchen wearing a pink tracksuit and a dashing pair of trainers.

'Oh, it's 'orrible again,' she told them. 'Black clouds. Looks like snow to me.' She saw Lucy. ''Ullo, what are you doing 'ere? Come to stay? Where's your auntie?'

She had a head of tight grey curls and wore pink glass earrings to match her tracksuit.

'She's in bed. She's not well.'

'Oh, that's too bad. Seen the doctor, 'as she?'

'Elfrida's going to ring him up and ask him to come.'

'Well.' Mrs Snead gazed at Elfrida. 'What a turn-up for the books. I mean, 'aving an invalid, and only just got 'ere. That's bad luck. Your name's Lucy, isn't it? Mrs Phipps told me about you. What do you think of your room? We 'ad a lovely time doing it all up for you. It was just an empty old attic before.'

'Have a cup of tea, Mrs Snead,' said Elfrida, and Mrs Snead said that would be very nice, and proceeded to make herself a mug, then settled down at the table to drink it.

Lucy knew that Gran would disapprove violently of such familiar carryings-on and, perversely, liked Mrs Snead all the more.

The morning progressed. Mrs Snead hoovered, Lucy and Oscar washed up the breakfast dishes, and Elfrida went off to telephone the doctor. At ten o'clock the front-door bell rang, and Lucy ran downstairs to let him in, but he had already done so himself, and she found him wiping his boots on the mat.

'Hello there,' he said, when he saw her. He had a very Highland voice, but he was quite young, with a wind-burned face and gingery eyebrows, like caterpillars. 'Who are you?'

'I'm Lucy Wesley. I'm staying here.'

'That's nice. Now, where's the invalid?'

'She's upstairs.'

Elfrida was hanging over the banister. 'Dr Sinclair, you are a saint to come.' He climbed the stairs, but Lucy did not follow him. Instead, she went back into the kitchen where Mrs Snead was sorting laundry for the washing-machine.

'That the doctor come? I 'ope it's not serious.'

'I thought it was just a cold. She felt rotten flying up, I know. It's so miserable for her.'

'Oh, cheer up, she'll be all right. Now, would you like to do something for me? 'Op upstairs and bring down the towels in Mrs Phipps's bathroom. Then I'll give you the clean ones to put in their place.'

Dr Sinclair did not take long. He and Elfrida went into Carrie's room and Lucy, collecting towels, heard their voices behind the closed door. It was reassuring to have him here but she hoped that he would not diagnose some sinister bug, an illness that would demand antibiotics and two weeks in bed. When he had finished with Carrie, he did not at once come downstairs but went into the drawing room to talk to Oscar.

Lucy, having finished her laundry duties, hung about for a bit in the hall, then could wait no longer and went to join them. The three were sitting on the window-seat, talking about somebody called Major Billicliffe. Major Billicliffe, it seemed, was in hospital in Inverness and very ill. They all wore rather long faces. Then Elfrida turned, saw her standing in the open door and smiled.

'Don't look so worried, Lucy.'

The doctor got to his feet. 'Is Carrie all right?' Lucy asked him.

'Yes, she'll be fine. All she needs is a bit of rest and lots of drinks – and I've left a prescription for that cough. Leave her in peace, and she'll be up and about in a couple of days.'

Lucy was much relieved. 'Can I go and see her?'

'I'd leave her for a moment.'

Elfrida said, 'Why don't you take Horace for his exploring walk?'

'Where are you going, Lucy?' the doctor asked.

'I thought along the beach.'

'Are you interested in birds?'

'I don't know their names.'

'There are beautiful birds on the beach. I'm calling in tomorrow to see your aunt, so I'll bring my bird book with me and you can look them up.'

'Thank you.'

'Not at all. Not at all. Well, I must be off. We'll be in touch, Mr Blundell. Goodbye, Mrs Phipps.'

And he was away, running downstairs, letting himself out, slamming the front door behind him. Looking from the window, Lucy saw him get into his car and drive off to his next call. There was a dog on the passenger seat, gazing from the window, a big springer spaniel with floppy ears. She decided it must be nice being a country GP and having a dog in your car.

Mrs Snead was right. It was a daunting sort of day, though not actually raining, which was odd because the weekend had been so soft and still and Oscar had been able to have his bonfire. With Horace on his lead, Lucy let herself out of the Estate House, went through the gate, across the square, then turned up the road that led to the golf club. There were not very many golfers around and only a few cars parked. The right-of-way led across the links, curving up and over the natural undulations of the land, and when she reached a shallow summit she saw the whole horizon, cold and still as steel, and a great arc of sky, grey with low cloud. It was half tide, and small waves washed up on to the shining wet sand. Far away, she could see the lighthouse, and when she reached the little car park flocks of gulls were pecking over the rubbish bins, as though expecting crusts or stale sandwiches. When Horace saw them he barked, and they all fluttered off, flew around for a moment then settled down again to their scavenging.

Lucy unclipped Horace's lead, and he ran ahead of her, down the ramp and on to the sand. In the shelter of the dunes it was deep and soft and difficult for walking, so she went out on to the wet, hard sand and, looking back, saw her own footsteps with Horace's pawmarks circling them, like a line of stitching.

There were rocks and small rock pools at the point, and then the big beach, curving northwards. Ahead, a long way off, the hills folded in on each other, grey and forbidding, dusted with snow. The sky beyond them was dark as a purple bruise, and she felt the light, freezing wind on her face.

She was alone. Not another soul, not another dog on the beach. Only birds skimming over the shallow breakers.

In this enormous, empty, airy world, she saw herself tiny as an ant, reduced to total unimportance by the sweep and size of nature. A nonentity. She rather liked the feeling of being without identity, of knowing that nobody knew *exactly* where she was, and that if she met somebody they wouldn't know *who* she was. So, she belonged to nobody but herself. She walked hard, keeping warm, pausing only every now and then to pick up a scallop shell or a particularly eye-catching pebble or shard of glass worn smooth by the sea. She put these treasures in her pocket. Then Horace found a long piece of seaweed, which he carried in his mouth like a trophy. Lucy tried to get it from him, and it turned into a game, Horace running and Lucy chasing. She found a stick and flung it into the waves, and Horace forgot about the seaweed, dropped it and went galloping into the water, only to discover that it was too cold for comfort before beating a startled retreat.

The beach ended at another outcrop of rocks, with pools and crannies of pebbles; there was a strong reek of seaweed. Lucy paused to get her bearings. Hillocky dunes separated the beach from the golf links, and as she hesitated, trying to decide which way to go next, she heard the sound of a motor and saw, above the rocks, a tractor trundling towards her over a rise. It was pulling a bogie so it wasn't moving very fast. Clearly, there had to be a sort of road. She decided that she would walk home that way, and with some difficulty hauled her way up a sandy cliff and into the dunes. Horace bounded ahead of her and out of sight. The dunes made a little hill, thick with rough grass and rushes, and on reaching the summit she saw the track.

Horace was already down there, waiting for her but not looking her way. He had, it was obvious, sensed strangers. He stood, ears pricked, and his plumy tail up like a flag. He was very still, watching. Lucy looked, and saw, coming up the slope from the direction of the town, another dog-walker striding out purposefully. She was dressed in boots, thick trousers and a sheepskin coat, and wore a tam o' shanter slanted at a cocky angle over cropped grey hair. Her dog, running free, spied Horace and stopped dead. The two animals eyed each other for a long moment. Lucy was petrified with dread: the other dog was a Rottweiler.

'Horace.' She had meant to call him but her mouth was dry and his name came out in an agonised whisper.

Horace either didn't hear her or pretended not to.

And then, stupid mutt that he was, he began to bark. The Rottweiler moved forward slowly, his shining body tense, muscles flexed. A snarling sound came from deep in his throat and his dark lips rolled back from his teeth. Horace, holding his ground, gave another timid bark, and with that the Rottweiler pounced.

Lucy screamed. Horace screamed as well, a dog-scream that sounded like a howl for help. He was being flattened, bitten and bruised, and however he struggled, he could not escape.

The dog's owner was of no use at all. She had a chain leash in her hand, but it was obvious that she was too wary to start manhandling her pet while he was in this frame of mind. Instead she produced a pea whistle, which she blew sharply, and proceeded to shout orders, like a sergeant major.

'*Brutus! Brutus! Down, boy! Down! To heel!*'

The Rottweiler took no notice.

'*Brutus!*'

'Get *hold* of him,' Lucy wailed, hysterical with horror. Horace, Elfrida's darling dog, was about to be murdered. 'Do something! *Stop* him!'

She had forgotten about the approaching tractor. Now, like the cavalry in some old western, it trundled into view in the nick of time; the door was flung open, the driver jumped down, sprinted the last few yards and, without showing the slightest fear or hesitation, went straight into action, landing his heavy boot into the muscled backside of the Rottweiler. 'Get off, you bloody brute!' The startled Rottweiler abandoned Horace, and turned to attack this new enemy, but the young man grabbed his studded collar and, with some strength, hauled him away from his prey.

In a thousand years, Lucy could never have imagined anyone being so level-headed, strong and brave.

'What the bloody hell do you think you're doing?' he demanded of the dog's owner, grabbing the chain leash from her hand and somehow clipping it to the collar of the snarling, struggling beast. He dragged the animal towards her, and she took the leather loop in both her hands.

There followed the most stupendous row.

'Don't you swear at me!'

'Why didn't you keep the dog on its chain?'

'He was *attacked*.' Now that the danger was over, she became belligerent. Her voice was not of Sutherland: she sounded as though she came from Liverpool or Manchester.

'He was no such thing. I saw it all!'

'There's no harm in Brutus unless he's *attacked*.' She was having a terrible time trying to control her dog and became quite red in the face with effort.

'He's a monster!'

'*Roobish!*'

'Where do you live?'

'And what's that got to do with you, young man?'

'Because if you lived here you'd know better than to walk a savage dog on a public footpath.'

'I do *not* live here,' said the woman, as though this was something to be proud of. 'I'm a visitor, staying with my sister in her caravan.'

'Well, go back to her caravan, and take your dog and shut him up.'

'Don't speak to me in that tone of voice.'

'I'll speak to you any way I like. I work for the golf club, I'm one of the staff.'

'Oh, hoity-toity, are you?'

'Take that dog and go. Just go. If I see him running free again, I'll report you to the police.'

'And I shall complain of impudence!'

But at this point, Brutus took charge. He had spied two innocent golfers striding down the fairway: with his blood up, and feeling a desperate need to sink his teeth into some other throat, he set off on the hunt. His owner, willy-nilly, went too, dragged in his wake, her short, trousered legs going like pistons.

'Never been so insulted,' she threw back over her shoulder. Clearly a woman who liked to have the last word. 'I'm not forgetting this . . .'

They heard no more. She was out of earshot, and her voice blown away by the wind. She was gone.

By now, Lucy was sitting on the wet, prickly grass with Horace gathered up in her arms, his head pressed against the front of her new red jacket. The young man came to kneel beside her. She saw that he was very young, his face wind-burned, his eyes blue. He had short yellow hair, which looked as though he had dyed it, and there was a gold ring in his left ear.

He said, 'Are you all right?'

Lucy, to her eternal shame, burst into tears. 'Yes, but Horace . . .'

'Here.' Gently, he loosened Horace from her clutches, touched and examined him, stroked the long hair off his face, making comforting, murmuring noises as he did so. 'I think he'll be all right. Just superficial cuts and bruises.'

'He only *barked*.' Lucy sobbed. 'He *always* barks. He's so stupid. I thought he was going to be *dead*.'

'Lucky he isn't.'

Lucy sniffed. She couldn't find a handkerchief. She wiped her nose on the back of her hand. 'He's not even my dog. He's Elfrida's. We just came for a walk.'

'Where from?'

'Creagan.'

'I'll take you back in the tractor. I can get you as far as the clubhouse. Can you walk from there?'

'Yes. I think so.'

'Well done. Come along.'

He helped her to her feet, then stooped to lift Horace and carried him over to the tractor. This he had abandoned with the doors open, the engine throbbing. Lucy clambered up into the cab. There was only one seat but she perched herself on its edge. Horace was placed at her feet, where he sat and leaned heavily against her knee. Then the young man jumped up beside her and put the tractor in gear. Lurching over the bumps and with the bogie rattling away behind them, they moved forward.

Lucy had stopped crying. Tentatively, she asked, 'Do you think Horace will be all right?'

'When you get home, give him a bath with disinfectant. You'll be able to gauge the damage then. If there are any really bad bites, he might need stitches – might need to go to the vet. He'll be bruised, that's for sure, and stiff for a couple of days.'

'I feel so guilty. I should have looked after him better.'

'Not a thing you could do. I think that female must be barmy. If I see her hellish animal again, I'll shoot it.'

'He's called Brutus.'

'Brutus the Brute.'

Despite everything, Lucy found herself smiling. She said, 'Thank you so much for helping.'

'You're staying at the Estate House, aren't you, with Oscar Blundell?'

'Do you know him?'

'No, but my father does. My father's Peter Kennedy, the minister. I'm Rory Kennedy.'

'I'm Lucy Wesley.'

'That's a pretty name.'

'I think it's horrible.' It was rather snug, sitting high up in the cabin of the tractor, sharing a single seat with this brave, kind young man. She liked the feel of his sturdy body pressed against her own, the oily smell of his thick jacket, the warmth of unaccustomed physical contact. 'It sounds like a missionary.'

'Well, there are worse things. I've got a small sister called Clodagh. She doesn't like her name either. She wants to be called Tracey Charlene.'

This time Lucy laughed.

'Didn't I see you in church yesterday?' he asked.

'Yes, but I didn't see you, I suppose because there were so many people. I wanted to see the lights turned on, shining on the ceiling. It's beautiful. Elfrida came with me. Carrie would have come too – she's my aunt – but she's had this cold and she stayed indoors. This morning the doctor came and she's got to stay in bed. There's nothing awful wrong with her, she just has to rest. Otherwise she'd have been with me, and probably that dog-fight would never have happened.'

'Nothing worse than a dog-fight. But not a thing you could have done to stop it.'

This was comforting. 'Do you work on the golf course?'

'Yes, for the time being. This is the start of my gap year. I finished Highers in July, and next year I go to

Durham University. I caddied for Americans all summer. That was really lucrative but they've all gone home so I'm helping out the head greenkeeper.'

'What are you going to do then?'

'I want to go to Nepal. I can get a job there, teaching in a school.'

Lucy was impressed. 'What will you teach?'

'Reading and writing, I suppose. Just little kids. And sums. And football.'

She thought about this. She said, 'I'm rather dreading my gap year.'

'How old are you?'

'Fourteen.'

'You've time enough to make plans.'

'The thing is, I don't want to go somewhere strange and scary. All by myself.'

'Scary?'

'You know. Crocodiles and revolutions.'

He grinned. He said, 'You've been watching too much television.'

'Perhaps I'll just stay at home.'

'Where do you live?'

'London.'

'Do you go to school there?'

'Yes. A day-school.'

'Up here for Christmas?'

'I came with Carrie. I live with my mother and my grandmother. My mother is going to America for Christmas. In fact, she's flying out tomorrow. And my grandmother is going to Bournemouth. So Carrie and I came here.'

'What about your father?'

'They're divorced. I don't see him much.'

'That's rough.'

Lucy shrugged. 'It's all right.'

'My mother told me I have to lend you my old TV. Do you want it?'

'Have you got one?'

'Sure.'

'Well, it would be kind of you but I'm managing very well without one.'

'I'll look it out.' For a bit they thumped along in silence, up and over the bumpy track. Then he said, 'I believe you're all coming up to the Manse for a drink tomorrow evening. There's a hooley in the school hall at seven o'clock. Clodagh and I are going. Do you want to come with us?'

'What's a hooley?'

'A dance.'

At once Lucy was filled with anxiety. She hated dancing, could never remember which was right and which was left. She had been to parties, but never a dance. And at parties she was usually consumed and silenced by shyness.

She said, 'I don't know.'

'What don't you know?'

'If I want to come to a dance.'

'Why not? It's just the schoolkids practising reels for the Hogmanay parties. Good fun.'

Reels. 'I don't know how to do reels. I don't know the steps.'

'So it's high time you learned.' Still, she hesitated, but then he turned his head to smile down at her, in a friendly and encouraging manner, and rather to her own surprise she found herself saying, 'All right. Yes. Thank you. Do – do I have to dress up?'

357

'Heaven forbid. Jeans and trainers.'

All the time they had been talking it had been growing threateningly dark. It was now that the first large white flakes of snow began to fall. They drifted from the leaden sky, lay on the front of the tractor and gathered against the windscreen. Rory turned on the wipers. He said, 'I wondered when that would start. You could see the snowclouds coming down from the north. I heard the weather forecast this morning and they said we're in for some heavy falls.'

'Is it going to be a white Christmas?'

'Would you like that?'

'I've never had a white Christmas.'

'Good for sledging. Hard work for the roadmen and the snowploughs.'

By now they were near the end of their journey, grinding up the slope that led to the clubhouse. Rory turned the tractor into the car park, killed the engine, opened the door and climbed down.

'Will you be all right, now?'

Snow settled on his hair and the shoulders of his thick donkey jacket. Lucy clambered down behind him, then he reached into the cab, lifted Horace down and set him on his feet. Horace gave himself a shake, and even wagged his plumy tail. The snow drifted and swirled all about them, and the ground beneath their feet was already iced with crunchy flakes. Lucy felt one settle on her nose and brushed it away. She took the lead from her pocket and Rory clipped it to Horace's collar.

'That's it, then.' He grinned down at her. 'You get home now.'

'Thank you so much.'

'See you tomorrow evening.'

'Yes.'

She walked away from him, down the hill into the falling snow. Bravely, Horace limped along beside her. A disinfectant bath, Rory had told her, and then, perhaps, a visit to the vet. She hoped Elfrida would not be too upset, but was pretty sure that she wouldn't. She would be sympathetic and would understand that none of it had been Lucy's fault. Behind her, she heard the tractor start up, and turned back to wave, but there was too much falling snow in the way for Rory to see.

She trudged on, quite shattered by emotion and excitement. It had been a momentous outing. A long walk, a dog-fight, a tractor ride, a snowstorm and an invitation to a dance. She could scarcely wait to get home and tell Oscar and Elfrida all about it.

Elfrida

Elfrida

It was an enormous relief to Elfrida when she heard the front door open and Lucy's voice calling. It was now nearly midday, but dark as evening, and the world beyond the kitchen window was blanketed with falling snow. Ever since the snow had started, drifting down from a granite sky, she had been worrying about Lucy, blaming herself for being irresponsible and letting the child go off on her own, imagining every sort of horror. Oscar, upstairs by the fire, was not nearly so concerned. He read his newspaper and assured Elfrida, each time she rushed to gaze from the window, that the girl was sensible, she had the dog with her, she couldn't be mollycoddled for the rest of her life. All of which Elfrida knew was true.

She returned to the kitchen to do something about lunch, peeling potatoes but keeping her ear cocked, like a dog. When she heard Lucy in the hall, she abandoned the potatoes and rushed out to meet her, wiping her hands on her apron. Lucy and Horace stood on the doormat, both encrusted in snow, with a terrible story to tell.

It was told in the warm kitchen, while Lucy shed her coat and hat and pulled off her boots. 'This horrible dog, it was a Rottweiler and it didn't have a lead and it went for Horace and bit him, and then there was a tractor – Rory Kennedy, and he was frightfully brave and had a dreadful row with the Rottweiler lady, both shouting at each other. She stumped off and Rory brought us back to the golf club in his tractor and then it snowed. And, oh, Elfrida, I am sorry, but I *couldn't* stop it. And poor Horace has got bites and bruises. Rory said we had to give him a disinfectant bath and maybe take him to the vet. Have we got any disinfectant? Because if not I can go down to the chemist and get some . . . It was *so* frightening. I thought he might have killed Horace.'

She was clearly upset by the whole incident but, in an extraordinary way, excited as well, having come through the entire adventure and brought Horace home alive. Her cheeks were pink and her eyes bright, and she looked more lively and vital than Elfrida had seen her. She was a sweet child, of course, but serious-minded, and docility did not suit a fourteen year old. This metamorphosis was hopeful, and Elfrida forgot about all her anxieties and knew that by sending Lucy off on her own she had done exactly the right thing.

Horace sat on the floor and looked sorry for himself.

'What happened, Horace?' Elfrida asked him. 'Were you attacked by a savage hound?'

'He did bark,' Lucy had to admit, 'but not very much.'

'Only stupid dogs bark at Rottweilers.'

Elfrida went upstairs for a bottle of Dettol, and Lucy filled the big clay sink in the scullery with warm water.

They lifted Horace into it, and all the snow that was stuck to his paws and his chest melted away. There wasn't a shower, but Elfrida found an old jug and used this to pour the hospital-smelling water over his back, his legs and his neck. He sat in sodden, suffering silence, but by the end of his bath Elfrida had discovered no serious wounds, simply a series of nips and punctures that would in time heal themselves. His stomach was badly bruised and one of his ears a bit torn but, by and large, he appeared to have emerged from his battering with little lasting harm.

Lucy sighed with relief. 'So we won't have to take him to the vet?'

'I don't think so. Just as well – I don't know where the nearest vet is, and in this snow we couldn't drive anywhere.' She let the water out, lifted Horace out of the sink and carried him into the kitchen, wrapped like a Bedouin in a thick clean bath-towel. Gently, she patted him dry. 'Now we've got two invalids. Perhaps we should put up a notice, saying "Estate House Nursing Home".'

Lucy was struck by guilt. 'How awful. I forgot about Carrie. Is she still asleep?'

'I expect so. I haven't heard a sound.'

'Where's Oscar?'

'In the sitting room.'

'I must go and tell him everything that's happened.'

'He'll be enthralled but, darling, your jeans are soaked. I think first you should go and get some dry clothes on. Bring the wet things down and we'll string them up on the pulley.'

'All right.' Lucy started to go, but at the open door turned back. 'Elfrida.'

'What is it, duck?'

'Rory Kennedy's terribly nice. And he's got dyed hair.'

'Dyed hair?' Elfrida put on an expression of horror. 'What *would* your grandmother say?'

Lucy told her, in Dodie's voice. ' "Dis-gusting"!' She grinned and was gone, and Elfrida heard her running up the stairs, two at a time, to her attic bedroom.

It was three o'clock that afternoon before Elfrida went to check on Carrie. The snow had stopped but the dark day was already dropping into evening, and she had had to turn on lights and draw curtains. She tapped gently on Carrie's door and opened it.

'Carrie?'

'I'm awake.'

In the half-light, Elfrida saw her head turn on the white pillow. She moved forward to switch on the little bedside light. Carrie stretched, then smiled at her. 'What time is it?'

'Three o'clock.'

'It's like night.'

'I know. It's been snowing and we've had about four inches, but it's stopped for the moment.' She went to close the window and draw the thick curtains, and the small bedroom at once became enclosed and cosy, with the single light burning and the corners thick with shadow. Elfrida perched herself on the edge of the huge bed. 'How do you feel?'

'Stunned. How could I sleep so long?'

'You were tired out. Would you like something to eat? Or a cup of tea or something?'

Carrie thought about this. 'I'd adore a cup of tea. And I've got to go to the loo.'

She climbed out of bed; long thin arms and legs and a lawn nightdress. She reached for her dressing-gown and wrapped herself in it, tying the sash tightly about her narrow waist. Elfrida left her and went downstairs to boil a kettle. She set a tray for the two of them, and found some very delicious and expensive biscuits that Oscar, on one of his shopping expeditions, had been impelled to buy. She carried the tray upstairs and found Carrie back in bed, having washed her face, cleaned her teeth and combed her dark hair. She had put on scent too, her own special perfume, and clearly felt much more presentable.

'Elfrida, you are an angel. I am sorry. So much trouble.'

'No trouble at all. I'm just so happy you were able to have a rest.'

'It's so quiet. Where is everybody?'

'Once the snow stopped Oscar and Lucy decided to go shopping in the town. They've gone to look for decorations for the Christmas tree.'

'Where will they find them?'

'No idea. Probably the ironmonger. Lucy took Horace for his walk and had a tremendous adventure ...' She told Carrie the saga of Horace and the Rottweiler, and Carrie was suitably horrified but impressed, too, by Lucy's composure and the manner in which she had conducted herself.

'What an adventure! Quite frightening, but probably just what she needs. She leads such a dull life in London with Dodie and Nicola. They're both so selfish and neither has a scrap of imagination. I can't imagine what my life at Lucy's age would have been like if it hadn't been for Jeffrey. And, of course, she hasn't got a Jeffrey and she hasn't got a proper father. Dodie and Nicola have such terribly limited horizons, there can be no stimulation at all. All they talk about is other people – mostly bitching – or clothes.'

'What does the poor child do all day?'

'Most of the time she's at school. She's got a nice little room of her own in the flat and a friend called Emma . . .'

'I suppose she never sees a man. Or a boy.'

'The school is all girls, and if she does visit her father, the dreaded Marilyn is always much in evidence. Jealous, probably, stupid cow.'

'I think she was rather taken by Rory Kennedy. Quite apart from being immensely brave and rescuing Horace, he has dyed hair. And an earring.'

'How exciting.'

'We've all been asked up to the Manse tomorrow evening for a drink with the Kennedys. I'd love you to be able to come because I want you to meet Tabitha, but perhaps you aren't feeling up to such wild sociality.'

'I'll see.'

'And then, apparently, there's some shindig on in the school hall – all the children are going to dance reels. Rory asked Lucy if she'd go with him and his sister, and she's all bright-eyed and bushy-tailed about that and says she's going to wash her hair tonight.'

Carrie drank her tea, which was scalding hot and smoky-tasting because Elfrida had made it with Lapsang Souchong teabags. She said, rather sadly, 'I have an awful feeling that when the time comes to go back to London we're going to have terrible sadness and tears.'

'Don't say it. I can't bear to think about it.'

'I've been thinking about this job with the travel

company in London. I've decided I'll take it. Maybe just for a year. Then I can be around for Lucy, try to brighten things up for her a bit. I'll bludgeon Dodie into submission, force her to let me take Lucy to Cornwall to stay with Jeffrey and Serena. You know, she's never seen Jeffrey. She was just a baby when they divorced, and Dodie's resentment and grudges show no signs of abating.'

'Poor woman.'

'Why do you say that?'

'Because she has nothing else to think about. More tea?' Carrie held out her empty cup and Elfrida refilled it.

'Did Nicola ring today?'

'Nicola? Were you expecting a call?'

'No. But tomorrow she's flying to Florida. I thought she might have called to say goodbye to Lucy. But she obviously hasn't.'

'Lucy never spoke about it. To be truthful, I think she's too preoccupied with doggy adventures, Rory Kennedy and buying Christmas-tree decorations with Oscar.'

'Good for Lucy.'

They fell silent, sipping tea, companionable. The house was very quiet. Elfrida said, as casually as she could, 'Is this a good time to talk?'

Carrie raised her head, and her beautiful dark eyes gazed into Elfrida's face. 'Talk?'

'You said you would tell me. Some time. Later. Why you left Austria. Why you came home so precipitantly. Why you are taking this job in London. Perhaps now, with no one to interrupt, is as good a time as any. I'm not prying, I just want to know. Not so much about Austria as why you are so worn out and sad-looking.'

'Is that how I look?'

'But no less beautiful.'

'Oh, Elfrida, what a star you are. I don't feel beautiful. I feel old and finished. I'm nearly thirty now. It's like a watershed. And I don't know what's waiting for me on the other side of the hill. Since I last saw you the years have gone so fast. Thirty once seemed an age away. Now, before I know it, I shall be forty then fifty and I have to make something of my life. But the simple prospect of decisions and meeting new people and finding old friends drains me of all energy.'

'That's probably why you caught this horrible cold and why it has laid you so low.'

'Psychosomatic, you mean?'

'No, I don't mean that, I mean physically vulnerable.'

'Vulnerable. I never thought any person would use that word about me.'

'Everybody is vulnerable.'

'I thought I was strong.' Carrie had finished her tea, and Elfrida took the empty cup, set it on the tray and got off the bed to put the tray on the floor. Then she went back to the bed, and made herself comfortable, leaning her back against the brass footrail.

'What happened, Carrie?'

'I'd been in Oberbeuren for about a year, done a winter season and a summer season. The pay was substantial and I'd found an apartment of my own, and I was doing what I liked doing better than anything else in the world. It was a good time. And then I met Andreas. He arrived with the first of the snow – he came with a party of men friends. It was a yearly date they'd kept, a sort of stag-party that had started when they were all at university. They stayed in the big hotel, and I met him then. He was a banker from Frankfurt, in a prestigious family business of which his father was head. He was married with two children. I knew from the beginning that he was married, but I wasn't a young innocent any longer and I told myself I could handle it. I didn't mean to fall in love with him, and I don't think he intended to fall in love either, but it happened. It just happened.

'He was the most attractive man I had ever met, and the most generous and amusing of companions, a brilliant skier, blissful in bed. He wasn't Germanic-looking at all, not fair or blue-eyed. In fact, he was very dark, tall and thin, rather intellectual in appearance. He could have been a writer or a professor. But he wasn't. He was a banker.

'He came to Oberbeuren quite often that first winter. He flew into Munich in the company plane and drove from there up into the mountains. Then he didn't stay in the hotel but with me. And it was like a private world that nobody else could enter. I thought, when the snow melted, that he would go too but he loved the mountains in summer just as much as wintertime and we walked, whole days on end, and swam in icy lakes and slept in remote inns. And we'd wake, in some goosefeather bed, and hear the cowbells as the herds came in for the morning milking.

'He travelled all over Europe on business, and sometimes I would join him, in Vienna or Luxembourg or Munich. In Vienna it was winter and we walked to the Christmas market, and bought gingerbread biscuits and sparkly stars and little painted wooden decorations. And we went to the opera that night, and listened to *Der Rosenkavalier*, and afterwards had dinner at the Three Hussars.

'Then, about six months ago, he came again to Oberbeuren. He looked tired and a bit preoccupied. When I asked him if anything was wrong, he told me that he had asked his wife if she would divorce him. Because he wanted to marry me. I felt torn in all directions. I remembered Jeffrey and Serena; I told myself how happy they were together. But I remembered, too, the acrimony and bitterness of that particular divorce. I didn't know his wife, except that she was called Inga. I couldn't imagine any woman not being totally in love with a man like Andreas. So I felt guilty and ecstatic at the same time. But I didn't look ahead because there was no point. I'd lived with Andreas from day to day for so long. I could scarcely remember the time when he had not been there, the most important thing in my life.

'He didn't talk about the divorce again. He came to the mountains and we were together, and sometimes he would say things like, "When we are married, we shall build a house here and come every weekend, and I shall bring my children. You shall meet my children!' "

'But I never made any sort of reply because I was afraid: it seemed like tempting providence.

'Then he said he had seen a lawyer. Later, that he had told his parents his marriage was over and he was going to get a divorce.

'I think there must have been a monumental row. Andreas's family were important in Frankfurt, rich, well-connected, influential. They were Catholic too. I can imagine how it must have been for him. And yet I can't. I only knew that I didn't have the strength to be the one to say goodbye. So what happened to me was up to him. Andreas. It was his decision.

'He held out for about three months, and he was so

strong and so sure and so reassuring that I truly believed he would see it through, stick to his guns and tear himself loose. But I think at the end of the day the pressure was too much. He was obviously deeply fond of his wife and adored his children. He respected his parents and relished his lifestyle. I think he had probably been told that if he tore the family apart he was finished. Out on his ear.

'It's all so banal, isn't it? One has heard it all before. A story out of an old melodrama or a Victorian opera. By the time Andreas told me that it had to end, our love, and that he was going back to Frankfurt and Inga and the children, I had steeled myself to accept his decision. But when the time came to say goodbye, and I knew I would never see him again, I felt as though all life was draining from my body, like bleeding to death, or something ghastly like that.

'I thought I could stay in Oberbeuren and try to get on with my work, but I couldn't. I couldn't keep my mind on anything, and the job was too demanding and important to be done at half-cock. So I went to my boss and told him I was lighting out, going back to London. I stayed long enough for them to find a replacement – an efficient girl who'd worked under me – and then I flew home.

'I have dreams about Andreas still. Sometimes they're frightening, other times he's there to tell me it was all a mistake and that Inga didn't want him any more and we can be together again. Those times I wake up feeling so happy . . .'

There was a long silence, and then Carrie stirred and smiled. She said, 'So that's it.'

'My darling girl, thank you for telling me.'

'Boring, really. Like I said, banal.'

'Not a bit.'

'I'll recover. I'll recover from Andreas and I'll recover from my little cold in the head. Life goes on. I'm here, with you. I shall pull myself together and do my best to be cheerful.'

'You don't have to pretend anything.'

'Will you tell Oscar?'

'If you want me to.'

'Just a quick précis. I'd like him to know. It will make things easier for both of us.'

'All right.' Elfrida sighed deeply. 'Carrie, you mustn't think this is the end of laughter and loving. Life is so extraordinary. Wonderful surprises are just around the most unexpected corners. From where you're standing it may seem a bit bleak and empty, but look at me! I thought I was alone for the rest of my life, in my little geriatric bolt-hole in Hampshire, and the next thing I'm in the north of Scotland living with Oscar Blundell.'

'Oscar's not married.'

'No.' Elfrida thought of Jimbo and sighed again, confused by the twists and turns of fate. She said, 'The world is full of married men.'

'Not for me, Elfrida. Never again.'

From downstairs there came the sound of the heavy front door being opened and shut, and the cheerful voices of Oscar and Lucy, returning from their shopping.

Elfrida pulled herself together and climbed off the high bed. 'I must go and make fresh tea for Oscar. Shall I tell Lucy to come and see you?'

'Yes, do. I want to hear the adventure of the dog-fight from her own lips – and to be told about her new friend.'

'You won't tease?'

'Oh, Elfrida. As if I would. I can still remember exactly how it felt to be fourteen.'

Sam

Sam

They stood at the bar of the Duke's Arms in Buckly, an austere little pub that had made no concessions to either the tourist trade or trendy décor. The walls were pitch pine tongue-and-groove, the lighting bleak, the floor worn dark-brown linoleum. The owner stood behind the bar and did not appear to be enjoying his job. Around the place were small round tables and uninviting chairs, and in a tiny grate a peat fire smouldered. Above it an enormous stuffed fish with cold eyes hovered in its glass case, and all smelled of old beer and whisky.

Fergus Skinner said, 'What'll it be?'

'A half of lager, please.'

'Will you not take a dram?'

'I'm driving.'

Fergus had brought Sam here, crossing the snowy road from the church hall after the meeting. It was his customary haunt, he told Sam, unfrequented by stray women, a place where a man could sit and enjoy a peaceful dram without some person approaching and engaging him in conversation.

'Yes, yes,' he said now, acknowledging Sam's situation. 'Well, that is a pity but it cannot be helped,' and he ordered a large Bell's for himself. 'I'm walking.' But if this was meant to be funny there was not a gleam of humour in his eye.

He was a tall man, in his early forties but looking older, with the dark hair and pale skin of a true Highlander. His features were strong – deep-set eyes, a beak of a nose, a long, lantern jaw – and his expression sombre.

But his appearance belied him. Fergus Skinner had been foreman at the mill in the old days, and when the McTaggart family broke up, it was he who had rallied the workforce, approached the Local Enterprise Company and organised the buy-out. Almost unanimously, he had been voted in as manager of the venture, and the demise of the business had been harder on him than anyone else.

But he remained undefeated because, probably, the only alternative was to go under and he was too strong a man for that. When Sam rang him from London, from the offices of Sturrock & Swinfield, asking him to set up some sort of a meeting with the workforce, Fergus Skinner had done his stuff: he put up notices alerting the public, and inserted various announcements in the local papers. Because of this the meeting had been well attended, so much so that latecomers found standing room only.

Now they carried their drinks to a wobbly table by the fireside. The only other customer was a very old man, who sat in a corner brooding over his glass and a drooping cigarette. He seemed uninterested in either of them. On the wall, a round clock, standing at half past five, ticked solidly. The barman, polishing a glass, gazed at a small black and white television set, the sound so low it was scarcely audible.

A lump of glowing peat slipped into the embers of the fire. Fergus raised his glass. 'Your good health.'

'And the future.' The lager tasted warm.

'The future.'

It had been a good meeting, held in the Buckly church hall because the mill was still in a state of desolation and disrepair, damp and chillingly cold. Sam and Fergus had sat upon the raised platform, and Sam had seen not only men but women as well, and here and there the odd child, too small to be left alone at home.

To begin with, the atmosphere had been cautious and not exactly friendly. These people, out of work for too long, were not going to take for granted any rosy promises. Sam had started by introducing himself as the new general manager of McTaggart's, the one who would be taking overall charge of the reconstruction of the ruined mill and the restart of the business. The response to this was silence, and he knew they probably regarded him as simply a money man, sent from London by Sturrock & Swinfield. So he told them a bit about his background: a Yorkshire boy, born and bred to the woollen industry and a family mill very like McTaggart's of Buckly. How they, too, had been faced with financial difficulties and rescued by Sturrock & Swinfield, which was why he, Sam, was here today.

The atmosphere relaxed a little. People shifted, settled down in their chairs.

He carried on.

It took a long time. He went through the whole process. The feasibility study, and the restructuring. A business built on tradition and goodwill but moving forward. So, new products, new markets, new machinery.

At the start of the meeting, he had asked for questions. Now hands were held up. 'Will that mean retraining?'

He told them yes. Other questions came thick and fast. 'Would there be redundancies?'

He said yes, there would be, to begin with, but once the new mill was up and going there would come gradual expansion and job creation.

A woman rose to her feet and asked if there would be work for her, a hand finisher, or would it all be done with this sophisticated new machinery? Sam told her that always, with the luxury goods they intended manufacturing, there would be work for hand finishers.

The most vital question was, when? How soon would they get back to work?

At the soonest nine months. At the latest a year.

Why so long?

There was a great deal to be done. If any one person wanted proof of this, plans were already drawn up and the blueprints on display boards at the back of the hall.

The outward appearance of the old mill would remain the same. Inside, it would be gutted and rebuilt. There would be a shop to attract tourists, and the architect had made provision for a small teashop and refreshment bar, both of which would offer employment.

And who would get the building contracts?

Sam explained that Sir David Swinfield was anxious that all tradesmen should come from hereabouts, and that all local builders, plumbers, electricians and joiners should be approached. After New Year tenders would be sent out and subsequent estimates considered.

Finally, it all became something of a general discussion, which was exactly the way Sam had wanted it to be. Before the meeting wound up he came down off the platform to be amongst them all; to clarify the blueprints, listen to problems and try to reassure. By the end he felt that he hadn't exactly made a lot of friends but that he had won some trust and, hopefully, co-operation.

It was a better start than he had expected, and no worse than he had feared.

Fergus stooped to place another lump of peat on the dying fire. 'And when,' he asked, 'will you be coming up to Buckly to live?'

'I'm here now, Fergus.'

'But you will be going back to London?'

'Yes, of course. I'll probably be up and down like a yo-yo but I'm based here now.'

'And where are you staying?'

'At the moment in Inverness in a hotel.'

'But you will be going home for Christmas?'

Sam hesitated. He was going to be working closely with Fergus and decided that it was best to be brutally frank with the man and put all his personal cards on the table. That way, nothing would be muddled or misconstrued. 'You know, at the moment, I don't have a home. My home was in New York. I don't even have a family. My wife and I are separated. She's still in the United States.'

Fergus said, 'That is a terrible thing. To have no home.'

Sam grinned. 'It's not so bad. Anyway, with the mill I've so much to occupy my time and my mind that I haven't even thought about Christmas. I could go back to London and be with friends, but at the moment I'd rather just concentrate on the job.'

'You can hardly drive to and from Inverness every day. Even with the new bridges it's a long journey.'

'I'll find something here. I'll rent or lodge. I'll be fine.'

'You would be very welcome in my house. My wife would be delighted and we have space.'

'You're more than kind but I'm better on my own.' He had finished his modest drink. He glanced up at the clock. 'I think I should be off. Like you said, it's a long drive.'

'But you have a good car. A Land Rover Discovery. And a new one too, it looks to me.'

'Yes, it's new. I bought it in London when I knew I would be living up here. I drove it north three days ago. It's a great vehicle.'

'Yes, yes, indeed. My son has a Land Rover.'

'What is your son's job?'

'He is a gamekeeper. He was not interested in the woollen trade, preferred to be out of doors. He was always mad on nature. As a boy he brought home wounded birds and sick squirrels, kept them in cages and nursed them back to health. There was always some poor wild animal in the corner of our kitchen. My wife once remarked to me that it was a good thing we didn't live in Kenya.'

As he said this so seriously, it took an instant for Sam to realise he was making a joke.

They went outside, and it was snowing again. Across the road, outside the church hall, Sam's dark green Discovery was coated in an inch of white.

Fergus said, 'I think before you set off for Inverness

you should telephone the AA. Get a check on conditions. The Black Isle can be a hazard on such a night as this.'

'Maybe. I'll see how I go.'

'Will I be seeing you before the New Year?'

'Bound to. I'll call you. Keep in touch.'

'It has been a pleasure to meet you.'

'The pleasure's mine, Fergus.'

They said goodbye, shaking hands. Fergus walked away, down the long narrow street, blanketed in heavy snowflakes and leaving a line of fresh footprints behind him. Sam saw him go, then climbed up into the big car, reached into his coat pocket and brought out two keys: the key of his car and the big old-fashioned key to Hughie McLellan's Estate House, attached to its label with a knot of string.

For a moment, Sam debated. The meeting had been something of an ordeal, taking much of his energy, but it was safely over and he felt elated rather than tired. It would be good to get back to base, to a bath, a drink in the bar and dinner. But on the other hand, surely, while he was so close to Creagan it would be worthwhile taking the short detour to the town and casting his eye over the place; orientating himself, locating Hughie's house. No need to go inside, just discover how it looked, assess its possibilities, decide if it would be worth returning to inspect with an eye to buying.

For a bit he sat and vacillated, then decided to toss a coin. Heads he would go straight to Inverness. Tails he would call in at Creagan. He found a tenpence piece and tossed it, took his hand away. Tails. He stowed the coin and the Estate House key in the cubby-hole on the dashboard, started up the engine and switched on the lights.

The strong, long beams danced with falling snow-flakes.

He felt adventurous.

Creagan, here I come.

Oddly enough, there was quite a lot of traffic on the road. Heavy transport, driving north, churning along through the snow with windscreen wipers going full tilt. Huge lorries, stacked with timber, oil tankers and cattle trucks. Cars returning home from work at the end of the day; a tractor, its warning light blinking like a star. Sam got stuck behind this for half a mile or more until it turned into a farmyard and he was able to pick up speed again.

The snowfall ceased abruptly, the shower blown away. A scrap of clear sky showed the curve of a crescent moon. He crossed a long bridge over a firth, and a couple of miles after that, his headlights touched the luminous road sign: TOURIST ROUTE. CREAGAN. 2 MILES.

He took the turning, and the single-track road wound alongside the shores of the sea loch. It was half tide, and he saw the black gleam of water. The mudflats were white with snow, and the impression was surreal, dreamlike. Far away, a prick of light showed from a small house on the further shore. After a bit, the road swung right, and he topped a hill of conifers, then there was open country beyond and in the distance the lights of a little town.

The sky darkened and it snowed again. He came into the town by way of a tree-lined road and, in the light of street-lamps, saw the church and the square and the old walled graveyard. He thought of Christmas cards. All that was missing was a crinolined lady carrying festive packages. He drove very slowly around the church, trying to get his bearings, wondering which was the empty, untenanted house that belonged to Hughie McLellan. Having accomplished a complete circuit without any satisfaction, he decided to ask for directions and drew in at the pavement edge. A couple was walking towards him, arm in arm, and clutching a number of carrier-bags and baskets. He rolled down the window. 'Excuse me.'

They stopped. 'Yes?' the man asked, obligingly.

'I'm looking for the Estate House.'

'You're there.' The man, amused, grinned. 'You're here.' He jerked his head, indicating the house behind him.

'Oh. I see. Thank you.'

'You're welcome.' They set off on their way.

'Goodnight,' Sam called.

'Cheerio.'

They had gone, and he sat in his car and stared at the house, which he had noticed but passed by because he knew it could not possibly be Hughie's. Hughie's house was empty, untenanted. Hughie had said so. And this house had windows which, behind carefully drawn curtains, were filled with light.

It was occupied, lived in. Sam told himself that he should simply drive on. Leave it. A busted duck. But he did not like mysteries, and knew that this one would niggle at him unless he found out what was going on. He reached into the cubby-hole for the key, turned off his lights and climbed down from the Discovery into the falling snow. He crossed the pavement, opened the heavy wrought-iron gate and closed it behind him. He walked up to the front door. There was a bell. He pressed it and heard it buzzing somewhere inside the house.

He waited for a bit, with snow seeping down the back of his collar, then pressed it again. All at once an outside light came on, and he stood there, as though caught in a searchlight. Then there were footsteps and the door was opened.

He was not quite sure who or what he had expected. An elderly, pinafored lady perhaps. Or a man in a V-necked pullover and bedroom slippers, resentful because some caller was disturbing his favourite television programme. What he didn't expect was a tall dark girl in jeans and a thick pullover. A sensationally good-looking girl who would have turned heads on Fifth Avenue.

They stared at each other. Then she said, without much enthusiasm, 'Yes?'

'I'm sorry, but is this the Estate House?'

'Yes.'

'Hughie McLellan's Estate House?'

'No. Oscar Blundell's Estate House.'

Spotlighted, drowned in snowflakes, wet and cold, Sam held up the labelled key. He said, 'Perhaps I have made a mistake.'

She stared at the key. Then she stepped back, opening the door. 'I think,' she said, 'you had better come in.'

Carrie

Carrie

That morning, the doctor popped into the Estate House, as he had promised, his face red with cold and his thick Harris tweed overcoat damp with freshly fallen snow and smelling of peat. He brought the bird book for Lucy, delivered it to her, then was upstairs, two at a time – a man with not a moment to waste – to check on the invalid. Carrie told him from her pillows that she was much better, had had a good night's sleep and felt a different person. But, with native caution, he suggested that she stay in bed for another day, and Carrie knew that if she refused it would mean an argument with Elfrida so she gave in gracefully.

When the doctor had gone, as abruptly as he had arrived, Elfrida came upstairs and put her head around the door. 'What did he say?'

'I'm all right but I have to stay here for another day. I'm sorry.'

'Why sorry?'

'Such a nuisance.'

'Don't be so silly. Not a nuisance. Do you want a hot-water bottle?'

'No, thanks. Warm as toast.'

'Rather a shame you'll miss our little party tonight with the Kennedy family, but you can meet them another time. I'm rather excited about it. Too stupid, but this is the first time Oscar and I have been out anywhere. We did have lunch in the pub one day, but that's the sum of it.'

'I shall stay here and oversee your supper.'

'It doesn't need much overseeing. I made a kedgeree, which I shall put in the oven, and if we don't eat it tonight we can have it tomorrow for lunch. Kedgeree is an accommodating dish.'

'Elfrida, you've been reading too many cookbooks.'

'Heaven forbid.'

The day progressed, and through her window Carrie watched the weather and was glad she did not have to be out in it. Snow showers came and went; the sky was grey. From time to time she heard the faint keening of wind whining around the old house. It was all rather cosy. She remembered, as a child, being ill and in bed and aware of others getting on with the business of day-to-day life without oneself having to participate. The telephone rang, and someone else hurried to answer it. Footsteps came and went; voices called and answered. Doors opened and shut. She heard Oscar stumping upstairs and down again, and knew that he was filling fireside baskets with logs. Towards noon there came smells of cooking – onions frying or perhaps a pot of soup on the boil. The luxuries of self-indulgence, idleness and total irresponsibility were all things that Carrie had long forgotten.

Lucy was a frequent visitor.

'Carrie, do look. Isn't Dr Sinclair kind? He's lent me his bird book so that I'll know the names next time I'm on the beach.'

'How thoughtful of him.'

'I wouldn't mind having a doctor like him in London. Ours is so unfriendly and we have to wait for ages.' She put the book aside. 'Carrie, I don't know what to wear tonight for this dance thing.' At the moment she was obviously more preoccupied with what was going to happen this evening than with the names of sea birds.

'What are the choices?'

'Well, I've got my new jeans but they might be a bit hot for dancing. I've got my old ones and they're clean and Elfrida ironed them for me. Or do you think I should wear my new mini-skirt and the black tights?'

'Did Rory say anything about what to wear?'

'He said jeans and trainers.'

'Then wear jeans and trainers. Your old ones and that red and white striped cotton sweater. I love you in that. It's so French. And it's always better to be underdressed rather than overdressed. I'd keep your mini-skirt for Christmas.'

'Christmas. It's so queer, I haven't thought much about it and it's only six days away. Nobody seems in the least bit worried, or preparing. By this stage, Gran usually gets a migraine – she says there's so much to see to.'

'Well, Oscar's ordered a tree and you've bought the decorations.'

'I know, but I *must* go and get some presents. For him and Elfrida. I don't know what to get. And there's other things. Food. Do you think we're even going to *have* a Christmas dinner?'

'Your guess is as good as mine, but I think, yes. Probably. It's just that Elfrida's always been very laid-back. It'll all be accomplished at the last moment.'

'What about stockings?'

'I think we'll probably give stockings a miss. Would you mind? It's not as though you still believed in Father Christmas and coming down the chimney and all that.'

'No, of course I don't. And, anyway, I think stockings are a bit silly. Except the tangerine and the bag of golden chocolate pennies.'

'I'll hang those on the tree for you.'

'Will you, Carrie? You know, it's rather nice, isn't it, having a different Christmas? Not knowing what it's going to be like.'

'I hope it will be fun for you ... with three old grown-ups.'

'I shall be grown-up too. That's what's so special.'

At a quarter to six Oscar, Elfrida and Lucy finally departed for the little party at the Manse. The snow showers had not stopped all day, and by now the roads were thick with it and quite hazardous.

As neither Oscar nor Elfrida relished the prospect of driving up to the Manse by way of the road, fearful of skids or drifts, they decided to walk up the hill by the lane. All muffled, hatted and booted, they came one by one to say goodbye, and Carrie told them to have a wonderful time and she would hear all about it when they returned.

'I don't suppose we'll have an awful lot to tell,' Elfrida admitted, 'unless they've asked other guests and one of them gets drunk.'

'You can always hope.'

Lucy was the last. Carrie thought she looked extremely pretty, with her bright eyes and her excited smile. She wore her new red padded jacket and her boots and her big woollen hat, and had her little rucksack slung over her shoulder.

'What's in that?'

'My trainers and a comb. And a bar of chocolate.'

'You'll have such fun.'

'I don't know when I'll be home.'

'It doesn't matter. Nothing matters. Rory will probably deliver you. If you want, you can ask him in for a beer or something. Whatever you like. Someone will be around.'

'Can I really? Well . . .' She debated this. 'I'll see.'

'You do that. Now, off you go.'

' 'Bye, Carrie.'

'Goodbye, darling.' They hugged and Lucy kissed her. 'Have a great time.'

They went at last, and Carrie heard the back door slam behind them. She waited five minutes or so, just in case something had been forgotten and they all trooped back again, but this didn't happen, so she got out of bed and ran a bath, soaked for ages, then put on jeans and her thickest sweater, did her hair, splashed on some scent and at once felt a great deal better. *I am recovered,* she told her reflection in the mirror.

She went out of her room and downstairs to check on the kedgeree and Horace. Both seemed in good health, although Horace was quiet and suffering from his bruises. To make up for his injuries he was being fed like a prince, on lambs' hearts and gravy, and was not required to venture forth further than just outside the back door.

Carrie stooped to fondle his head. 'Do you want to come upstairs by the fire?' she asked him, but Horace did not. He closed his eyes and went back to sleep, warm in his basket with his tartan rug.

She found a half-full bottle of wine, poured herself a glass and went back to the sitting room. Here, the curtains were drawn, the fire blazing, and a single lamp left burning by one of the fireside chairs. She put another log on the pyre, and settled down with Oscar's morning newspaper.

Outside in the street a few cars swished slowly to and fro, but the snow deadened all sound and most people by now were safely at home. She was reading a feature article about a well-known elderly actress, who had done a television series in London; it had become enormously popular and she had found herself basking in global fame. Carrie had just got to the Hollywood bit when, causing her almost to jump out of her skin, the fearsome buzz of the front-door bell drilled through the house.

Under normal circumstances, this would have been followed up by Horace's manic barking. But he had not forgotten yesterday's salutary experience with the Rottweiler and this did not happen.

Carrie said, 'Damn.' She lowered the paper and waited. Perhaps it was someone whose car had broken down, who now wanted to use a telephone. Or a local tradesman, delivering a bill or a Christmas card. Or three small children in a row, all set to sing 'Away in a Manger'.

Perhaps, if she did nothing, they would go away.

The bell shrilled again. No use, she'd have to go. In some exasperation she tossed the paper aside, sprang to her feet and ran downstairs, flicking switches as she went so that the hall was a blaze of light. The big door was unlocked and she flung it open to the snow and the cold and the solitary man who stood there, with the beam of the outside light streaming down upon him. He had dark, very short hair, and wore a thick navy blue overcoat, the collar turned up around his ears. His hair and his coat were all liberally sprinkled in snowflakes, as though somebody had dusted him with icing sugar.

She glanced over his shoulder, and saw the large, prestigious vehicle parked in the road. So this was neither a man seeking help, nor a tradesman, nor a carol singer.

She said, 'Yes?'

'I'm sorry, but is this the Estate House?'

His voice was pleasant, his accent – more of an intonation than an accent – familiar. American?

'Yes.'

'Hughie McLellan's Estate House?'

Carrie frowned. She had never heard of anyone called Hughie McLellan. 'No. Oscar Blundell's Estate House.'

It was his turn to hesitate. And then he held up in his gloved hand a large key, with a label knotted to it with string. On the label was written, in large black capitals with a waterproof pen, ESTATE HOUSE. As unsubtle as a clue in an old-fashioned mystery film. But how had he . . . ?

There must be explanations, of course, but it was too cold to stand here on the doorstep and listen to them. Carrie stepped back, opening the door wide. 'I think,' she said, 'you'd better come in.'

But he hesitated. 'Are you sure?'

'Of course. Come on.'

He went past her into the house and she closed the door against the cold, then turned to face him.

He looked a bit embarrassed. 'I'm really sorry. I hope I didn't disturb you.'

'Not at all. Hadn't you better take your coat off? We'll hang it here – there's a radiator and it'll dry.'

He had put the key back into his pocket and now removed his leather gloves, unbuttoned his overcoat and shucked it off. She saw that he was conventionally, even formally, dressed, in a dark grey flannel suit and a tie. She took the heavy coat from him and hung it on the old bentwood hat-stand.

'Perhaps,' he said, 'I should introduce myself. Sam Howard.'

'Carrie Sutton.' They did not shake hands. 'Come up to the sitting room. There's a fire and it's more comfortable there than standing in the hall.'

She led the way, and he followed behind her: up the stairs, across the landing and into the huge sitting room. Entering, he observed, as newcomers invariably did, 'What an amazing room.'

'It's unexpected, isn't it?' She went to pick up the abandoned newspaper. 'And lovely during daytime because it's always full of light.' She laid the paper on the table by her chair. 'Would – would you like a drink or something?'

'You're more than kind. I'd love one but I'm driving.'

'Where to?'

'Inverness.'

'*Inverness?* Right *now*? In this weather?'

'I'll be OK.'

Carrie doubted this, but gave a mental shrug. It was no business of hers. She said, 'Then why don't we both sit down and you can tell me why you have the key to Oscar's house?'

His expression was rueful. 'To be honest, I'm not quite sure.' But he came and settled himself in Oscar's chair and at once looked quite relaxed and at home, not at all as though he had just walked in out of the snow, unexpected and unasked. She thought he had an interesting face, neither handsome nor homely. Unremarkable.

But interesting. His eyes, deeply set, were unusual. He leaned back in the chair, his long legs crossed at the ankle. 'But I'm sure we can clear up the confusion. Tell me, did Mr Blundell once live in Hampshire?'

'Yes, he did.'

'And does he have an elderly uncle living in London?'

'I've no idea.'

'And a cousin called Hughie McLellan?'

'I'm afraid you're asking the wrong person. I'm simply staying here. A guest. I don't really know anything about Oscar's family. This is the first time I've met him, and I've had flu and I've been in bed, so there hasn't been much opportunity for finding things out about each other.'

'I see.'

'And Oscar and Elfrida – she's a sort of cousin of mine, and Oscar's friend – they're out. They won't be back till about eight o'clock.' She glanced at the little clock in the middle of the mantelpiece. 'It's nearly seven now. If you wanted to wait . . .'

'No, I can't wait. I must be on my way.'

'But I still don't know why you have a key to this house.'

'I was given it by Hughie. He wants to put the property on the market. Put it up for sale.'

Carrie stared at him. 'For *sale*?' She could feel her jaw drop. 'But it's *Oscar's* house.'

'I think they're joint owners, if I've done my sums right.'

'I know they're joint owners. Oscar told me. But even so, Hughie McLellan, whoever he is, has no right to put a house up for sale when he doesn't even own it.'

'Yes.' He agreed with her. 'It does seem a bit suspect.'

'And why would you want to come and look at it anyway? Do you want to buy it?'

He said, cautiously, 'I thought I might.'

'What for?'

'To live in. I have a new job in Buckly. Getting McTaggart's, the woollen mill, back on its feet again. I shall be based here, and I shall need somewhere to live.'

'Where's Buckly?'

'About twelve miles north. I've just come from there. Spent the afternoon having a meeting with the workforce.'

'Wouldn't you be better to live in Buckly?'

'The mill accommodation has all been sold off. It probably would be more convenient, but I was told about this place, given the key, and thought I'd come and, just quickly, drive around, have a look at the town. To be truthful, I thought the house would be empty. But then I saw the lights on and decided to ring the bell and solve the mystery.'

'But we haven't solved it.'

'No, not really, and we won't until I speak to Mr Blundell. And I'm afraid there's not time for that. Maybe another day. Right now, I think I should make tracks.'

'And *I* think it's important that you see Oscar. It's only fair on him that he should know what has happened – what is happening.'

'I really must . . .' He was on his feet. Carrie stood, too, and went to the big bay window, and drew back the heavy curtain. Outside lay a wintry scene. Snow fell heavily, steadily, and his Discovery, parked at the pavement's edge, was already blanketed. No cars moved, and no one trod the streets. She thought of the road to Inverness, the long miles, the hill that climbed the Black Isle from the bridge over the Cromarty Firth.

She, unlike Elfrida and Oscar, was not nervous of driving in snow. She had spent three winters in the mountains of Austria and after that nothing much fazed her. But this, obscurely, was different. There was a relentlessness to this weather. This snow was not going to stop, or be blown away. This was in for the night.

She turned. He had stayed by the fireside. She said, 'I don't think you should go.'

'You don't?'

'Come and look.'

He joined her, and together they gazed out at the deteriorating conditions. At first he didn't say anything, and Carrie felt a bit sorry for him.

'It really is bad,' she said.

'Yeah. Fergus Skinner, the manager at the mill, he said I should phone the AA and get a report. I didn't think it was necessary at the time but perhaps I was mistaken.'

'I would say that would be a good idea.'

'I have my mobile but no number.'

'I'll find it for you.'

She went out on to the landing, came back with the phone book and looked up the emergency number. 'Here it is. Do you want to write it down?'

He produced a pen, she read it out and he wrote it on the margin of the phone book, then took his mobile from his pocket.

She left him to it, sitting by the window with the opened curtain and a backdrop like a stage setting. She put another log on the fire, and stood, watching the fresh flames.

He got through almost at once, enquired about road

conditions, the A9 to Inverness. There was a long silence as he listened. Then, 'How about tomorrow?' Another pause. 'OK. I get the picture. Thank you. Goodbye.'

Across the room they looked at each other. She didn't say anything but knew that the news was the worst. He confirmed this. 'You were quite right. The road is impassable. I had no idea it would be so bad.'

'I'm sorry.'

'I . . .' He was stowing away his mobile. 'I think I'd better be off. Get out of your way.'

'Where?'

'Sorry?'

'Where will you be off to?'

'There'll be some guesthouse, hotel . . . I'll check in there.'

'There is no hotel or guesthouse open in Creagan at this time of year. Everything closes down for the winter. You'll find nothing.'

'But surely . . .'

She said, 'You'll have to stay here. With us.'

'*Here?* But I can't do that!'

'Why not?'

'You don't know me. I'm a stranger. I can't just come and—'

'Of course you can. Anyway, there doesn't seem to be an alternative. There's an empty bedroom, I know. An empty bed. It would be ridiculous not to use it.'

'But . . .'

Carrie smiled. Now that matters were settled and she had won her point, she was rather enjoying his discomfiture. 'What do they say? Any port in a storm.'

'But Mr Blundell . . .'

'He will be delighted to have another guest. And

400

most interested in what you have to tell him. Elfrida will be over the moon with joy. Nothing she likes better than unexpected arrivals and impromptu house parties. You don't even have to worry about dinner. There is a kedgeree in the oven, and plenty of hot bath water. All mod cons. What more could any man want?'

He shook his head, defeated by her insistence. 'Nothing, I guess.'

'A toothbrush?'

'I have one in the car, and my electric razor.'

'And you probably don't wear pyjamas, anyway. So there are no more problems.'

'No.' He thought about this. 'But, if it's all right by you, I should make another call.'

'Feel free.' (He obviously needed to ring home, wherever that was; explain to his wife what had happened.) 'You don't want anybody worrying.'

He took out his mobile once more and punched the numbers. Carrie wondered if she should make some excuse and go from the room, not wishing to overhear a private and personal conversation; loving words; messages for the children. But before she could do this, he had got through and was speaking to the receptionist at some hotel in Inverness. 'Just to let you know I shan't be back tonight. I'm stuck here, in Creagan, in a snowstorm. I'm all right. Staying with friends. Maybe back tomorrow. Just keep the room. Thanks. 'Bye.'

Call finished.

'Is that all?' Carrie asked.

'That's it.'

'No more calls?'

He slipped his mobile back into his jacket pocket and shook his head. 'Nope.'

'Right. Well, in that case, why don't you have that drink?'

'That would be great.'

'I shall have to go down to the kitchen and bring something up for you. We don't keep a drinks tray up here because there isn't a drinks table. Oscar's wine cellar is a slate shelf in the scullery.'

'Let me come and help.'

'No, you stay here and make yourself comfortable. What would you like? There's everything.'

'Scotch?'

'Soda, water or ice?'

'On the rocks.'

'Fine. I shan't be a moment.'

She ran downstairs, and in the scullery found a tray on which she loaded the whisky bottle, the filled ice bucket, a glass, and the wine bottle. She carried the tray upstairs, and found her visitor, not by the fire but on the other side of the room, gazing intently at Elfrida's little picture. In order to do this he had put on a pair of horn-rimmed spectacles, which made him look rather scholarly.

When Carrie appeared, he took these off. 'What a dear little painting.'

'Yes. It belongs to Elfrida. She brought it with her from Hampshire. She's had it for years. It's a David Wilkie. She says it's her insurance policy against the day when she runs out of money and doesn't want to become a bag-lady. As you can see, there are no other pictures in this room so it looks a bit lost.'

'It's certainly a treasure— Here, let me have that.' He took the tray and held it while Carrie made space on Oscar's table, shunting aside a few files and papers. She said, 'I'll let you do your own drink.'

'How about you?'

'I'm on wine.'

'Can I refill your glass?'

'Certainly, if you'd like to.'

She went back to her chair by the fire and watched him, liking the neat movements of his hands. Intrigued, in an objective sort of way, because his appearance at the Estate House, his reason for being here, and his reason for staying on (bad weather) all seemed like a sort of contrivance. The plot of a play, perhaps. The start of a film that might turn out to be disturbing.

He came across the room, with her wine and his whisky, and handed her her glass, then sat again where he had sat before.

He said, 'Good health.'

'And to you, too.'

'You said you'd just had flu?'

'Not very badly. I slept it off.'

'And you don't live here?'

'I told you, I'm a guest. I live in London. I have a young niece. I brought her with me. We're staying for Christmas and New Year.'

'Has she gone to the drinks party too?'

'Yes, and then she's going on to some sort of reel party with all the other children of the town. Goodness knows when she'll be home. Do you know this part of the world well?'

'No. I don't know it at all. I come from Yorkshire. Then I was based in London for a bit, and then New York for six years.'

Carrie smiled to herself because she had been right about the accent. 'Hence the Scotch on the rocks.'

'Exactly so.'

'What is your job?'

'I'm basically a wool-broker – I work for Sturrock & Swinfield.'

She was impressed. 'Goodness.'

'They bought out my father's woollen mill in Yorkshire some years ago, and I've been with them ever since.'

'New York and all?'

'New York and all.'

'This is going to be a bit of a culture change, isn't it, working up here?'

'Yes,' he agreed, 'a bit.'

'What did you say the mill was called?'

'McTaggart's of Buckly.'

'Is it a going concern?'

He said, bluntly, 'No,' then briefly enlarged on this. Explained the chain of events that had brought it down. Despite the heroic efforts of the workforce, it seemed that an act of God, in the shape of a flood, had finished the business off.

'And is this what you are expected to take on?'

'Not entirely on my own.'

'You mean you have Sturrock & Swinfield behind you?'

'That's right. And capital and expertise. Prestigious architects and designers.'

'And when it's all up and going, what will you produce?'

'Everything. A very wide scope. Traditional tweeds and tartans, but as well we'll head for new markets. The fashion trade. Luxury woollens.'

'When will you be in production?'

'The mill has to be gutted and rebuilt. So, maybe nine months. A year.'

'Why don't you just bulldoze it away and start afresh?'

'Because it's a particularly beautiful old building. Stone, with steep gables and long arched windows. It's over a hundred and fifty years old, part of the little town. It would be vandalism to destroy it.'

'And *you* have to have some place to live?'

'Yes.' He smiled. 'But I can't sort that one out until I've spoken to your host.'

'Did Hughie McLellan, whoever he is, did he mention a price?'

'Yes.'

'Am I allowed to be told?'

'A hundred and fifty thousand between the cousins – the two owners.'

'So if Oscar gave Hughie seventy-five thousand, he could buy him out.'

'He could.'

'It's not that much money, is it?'

'By today's standards, no.'

'But Oscar mightn't have seventy-five thousand. In fact, I'm pretty sure he hasn't. And he's so unworldly he wouldn't know where to lay his hands on such a sum. Anyway,' she shrugged, 'it's absolutely none of my business. I just think it would be nice if he could stay here.'

'I promise you I'm not going to throw him out.'

'You couldn't. It's his house.'

'Half house.'

'Sitter's rights. The security of his own bricks and mortar.'

Suddenly, defusing a small tension, he laughed. 'You're so right about that. I bought my first flat, freehold, when I went to work in London. It was a great feeling. That's some years ago now.'

'Where was your flat?'

'Eel Park Common.'

'How funny.'

'Why funny?'

'I've got a little house in Ranfurly Road. That's only about half a mile away.'

'Is that where you live?'

'I will, in February, when I get the tenants out.' Sam looked a bit confused, and Carrie suddenly felt sorry for him because, perhaps, she had not been particularly forthcoming. The thing was, she didn't really want to talk about herself. 'I've been in Austria for three years, in Oberbeuren, working for a travel firm called Overseas. That's why I let my house. But now I'm back, based in London again. I'm still with the firm but I've been offered a job in their head office, in Bruton Street.'

'Are you going to take it?'

'Yes. Why not?'

'You'll miss Austria and the mountains.'

Carrie said, 'Yes.' For a moment, neither of them spoke, and the silence was fraught with unsaid words. Then she moved in her chair and looked across at him. 'Your glass is empty. Would you like another drink?'

Elfrida

Elfrida

Oscar and Elfrida, arm in arm, making their way with tremendous caution, walked home. It was nearly eight o'clock, very dark, and snow was falling thickly, but there were street-lamps all the way so no need for the torch that Oscar, with some forethought, had tucked into his pocket. As they proceeded along the footpath that led along the top of the hill, the town was spread below them and they could see, beyond the topmost leafless branches of other people's trees, the round lighted face of the clock tower. All looked so transformed, so magical, that Elfrida was compelled to stop and gaze.

She said, 'Oscar, I do wish I could paint.'

As she had a firm hold of his arm, he had to stop too. But he enquired, 'Is this an appropriate moment to dwell on the might-have-been?'

'Why not?'

'I have snow trickling down the back of my neck.'

'But wouldn't it be lovely to be able to capture such a scene? To pin it down for ever? The snow falling into the light of street-lamps and bright windows. And the clock, like a constant moon. The only thing one couldn't paint would be the smell of peat smoke.'

'It would, I agree, be a satisfying exercise. But, please, let us go home.'

The lane sloped steeply down alongside the wall of Oscar's garden. There was a handrail here and they descended in single file holding on to it, like passengers leaving an aircraft. At the bottom, they could see their back gate and the bright light suspended over their back door.

They were safely home.

In the scullery, emulating Mrs Snead, they shed wet coats, snow-encrusted boots and sodden hats, and hung them about the place to dry. Elfrida said something about supper, but Oscar wanted to wait for a bit. He was full of smoked-salmon sandwiches and mince-pies. Also, he had been prudently abstemious because of the walk home, and wanted a large whisky before settling down to yet more food.

Elfrida went ahead of him, and in the kitchen greeted her dog with loving words. She was opening the oven door to peer at the good-tempered kedgeree when she heard him say, 'My whisky has gone.'

'Are you sure?'

He joined her as she closed the oven door, looking a bit put out. 'It's walked.'

'Perhaps Carrie felt like a tot.'

'I thought she was meant to be still in bed.'

'You can still be in bed and feel like a tot. Haven't you got another bottle?'

'Yes, but *that* one was open.'

'Let's investigate.'

They went out of the kitchen and upstairs. On the landing Elfrida paused. From behind the closed door of the sitting room she heard the low murmur of voices. Oscar heard them too. They looked at each other in some mystification. Oscar said, 'I think I know where my bottle is.'

'Ssh.' Silently, Elfrida tiptoed to Carrie's half-open bedroom door. She peered in, then returned to Oscar's side.

'Not there,' she told him, in a dramatic whisper. 'Empty bed.'

Oscar, joining in gamely, also dropped his voice. 'And she has a visitor.'

'Who can it be?'

'A mystery. Why don't we go and find out?'

Which they did.

Opening the sitting-room door, they came upon a peaceful, companionable scene: the lovely room, curtained and softly lighted, the fire blazing, the two most comfortable chairs drawn up to its warmth, and in them, looking as though they had known each other for ever, Carrie and a strange man. Possibilities instantly flashed through Elfrida's mind: an old acquaintance of Carrie's, perhaps, come in search of her; a long-time admirer, staunchly constant . . .

Carrie turned her head, saw them and at once rose to her feet. 'Elfrida, you're back. We didn't hear you. Did you have a good party?'

'Yes, it was splendid. But you're not meant to be out of bed.'

'I got bored.'

By now the unknown man was also on his feet, standing in front of the fire and waiting to be introduced.

411

Elfrida's first impression of this stranger was one of businesslike formality, in his beautifully cut dark-grey suit, his neat tie, and with his closely barbered hair. He was tall and long-legged, with a tanned complexion that accentuated his light hazel eyes. Despite her sixty-two years, she knew a frisson of physical attraction that dimmed in no way her affection for Oscar. It was just a sort of recognition, an ardent memory of how things, once, had been for her.

'Elfrida, this is Sam Howard. Elfrida Phipps. And my host, Oscar Blundell.'

'How do you do?' They all shook hands.

Sam Howard said, 'I'm really sorry about this intrusion.'

'Why is it an intrusion?'

'Because I'm in your house, unasked.'

At this juncture, Oscar spied his whisky bottle. 'There it is! I wondered where it had gone.'

Carrie laughed. 'Did you think I was boozing secretly? I am sorry. I brought it up to give Sam a drink. Do you want one?'

'Badly. I purposely had an abstemious evening so that I would be fit to walk Elfrida home through the snow.'

'In that case,' said Carrie, 'I shall give you one. But I'll need to go down and get some more glasses. What about you, Elfrida? I'm having a glass of wine . . .'

'I'll join you.' Suddenly Elfrida felt tired. She sat, with some relief, in the middle of the sofa, her long legs stretched out in front of her. 'I've been standing for two hours, eating sandwiches and mince-pies.'

'Anyone else there?'

'Oh, yes, a proper party. Three other couples, all so chatty and welcoming.'

'How about Lucy?'

'She disappeared with the Kennedy children to some other room, and hasn't been seen since. They'd gone to the reeling by the time we left. Just the way it should be.'

'That's good. I'll get those glasses and another bottle of wine. And soda for Oscar.'

She left them, and Elfrida heard her running downstairs. By now Oscar had sat down in his own armchair and they were left with the strange man. Oscar, Elfrida knew, had no idea what to say to him so she came to his rescue. She did this by smiling in her most friendly fashion and saying, 'Now tell us exactly who you are and why you're here. You must be an old friend of Carrie's.'

'Actually, I'm not.'

He reached for a chair and pulled it up to sit near Elfrida, leaning forward to speak to her with his hands clasped between his knees. 'I'd never met her before this evening.'

'Goodness,' said Elfrida, faintly.

He began to explain, and they listened. He was Sam Howard. He worked for Sturrock & Swinfield, the textile conglomerate that had taken over the defunct woollen mill in Buckly. McTaggart's. He was coming here to work as managing director.

Elfrida was none the wiser, but Oscar picked it up at once.

'Peter Kennedy told me about McTaggart's being taken over, but I didn't realise that things were already moving.'

'They aren't exactly moving yet but we're on our way.'

'That's splendid news.'

'I hope so.'

'When does it all get going again?'

'We have to rebuild the place first.'

Elfrida interrupted, 'What happened?'

'There was a long series of misadventures,' Oscar told her, 'and then a flood that destroyed everything.' He turned back to Sam. 'Have you been in this business for a long time?'

'All my life, really. My father owned a small mill in Yorkshire.'

'Well, bless my soul. Where are you based? In London?'

'I have been, but I've been working in New York for the last six years. Then, in November, I got called back to London to take this project over.'

'Does this mean you're going to be living up here?'

Now Carrie reappeared, with a second tray bearing bottles and glasses. Sam sprang to his feet and went to relieve her of it, and they spent a moment or two juggling for space on Oscar's table, shifting the ice bucket and setting out the glasses. The wine bottle was still frosted from the fridge, and Sam drew the cork neatly, poured wine for Elfrida and brought it over to her.

'How about you, sir?'

'Oh . . .' Oscar looked gratified. It was pleasant to sit by the fire and have some other man deal with hostly duties. 'A whisky and soda would be splendid. No ice.'

Sam poured the drink for him. 'Does that look about right?'

'Perfect.'

He topped up Carrie's glass. 'What about you?' Elfrida asked him, but he said he was all right, he hadn't finished his second drink. He rescued it from the little table by the fire and returned to his chair at her side.

Carrie said, 'How far have you got?'

'Sorry?'

'Explanations.'

'We've heard all about the woollen mill,' Elfrida told her. 'Surely there's not more excitement to come.'

'You'd be surprised, Elfrida.' She was back in her chair, curled up like a cat.

Elfrida waited. 'Surprise me, then.'

Sam took over again. 'This is all rather personal and very complicated. Just before I came up here, after I got back from New York, I was staying in London with old friends – Janey and Neil Philip. They have a house in Wandsworth. One evening, an old acquaintance of Janey's parents came for dinner. He was called Hughie McLellan.'

He paused, perhaps deliberately, giving time for this bombshell to sink in. Which seemed, to Elfrida, for ever. Then Oscar spoke. '*Hughie!* You wouldn't be talking about my cousin Hughie?'

'Yes, I think I probably am.'

'But Hughie's in Barbados.'

'No, he was back in London to see friends and deal with various business matters, I guess. Then he was going off to spend Christmas and the New Year with somebody called Maudie Peabody in the South of France.'

'What an extraordinary coincidence.'

'We talked for a bit, and then he learned – I think Janey told him – that I was coming up here to Buckly to take over at McTaggart's. And he asked me where I was going to live. And I said I didn't have any place to live but that I'd have to find somewhere. He produced from his pocket the key of this house. He said he owned half of it and that his cousin owned the other half, but that he wanted to sell.'

Oscar said, 'Well, I'll be buggered,' and Elfrida decided that his bad language, under the circumstances, was really very mild. 'What a little shyster he is. Always was. Why the hell didn't he get in touch with me?'

'To give him his due, I think he did try to telephone. You lived in Hampshire, I believe. He rang there but got no reply.'

'His father – Hector – knew where I was, that I'd come here, back to Creagan. Why didn't he tell him?'

'I think he hadn't seen his father, and didn't plan to get in touch until he came back from France, before he returned to Barbados.'

'Well, what a turn-up for the books.' Oscar, shattered at the perfidy of his cousin, took an enormous slug of his whisky and brooded a bit over the monstrousness of the situation. 'Why did he suddenly decide to sell this place? We've boxed along for so many years, sharing the trickle of rent, I never imagined he'd want to put it on the market. And certainly not without discussing it with me.'

'My guess is that he needs a bit of ready cash.'

'Not surprised. Alimony for three ex-wives must cost a bomb. But, then, he always went through money like a hot knife through butter.' He thought of something else. 'Did you come to this arrangement through an agent?'

'No. He intended going to Hurst & Fieldmore the day after I met him but decided that a private sale would be more satisfactory on all sides.'

'And what did you say?'

'I said nothing could possibly be arranged until you, his cousin, had been consulted.'

'So what are you doing here?'

'He had the key with him. He said, as I was coming north, why not have a look at the house? He told me it was empty, that an old couple had been living here, renting it, but that the husband had died and the wife gone elsewhere to live. With that, he simply took the key out of his pocket and handed it over to me.'

'Wasn't that rather trusting?'

'Very. But under the circumstances I suppose he reckoned I was as good a bet as any.'

'And a straight sale would save agents' fees?'

'Precisely.'

'Did he mention a sum?'

All the time they were talking, Sam had not moved in his rather inadequate and upright chair. His stillness was remarkable, and across the space that lay between them, his eyes stayed on Oscar, his regard intent. Now, down to the nitty-gritty, he did not blink, showed no sign of discomfiture. He said, 'A hundred and fifty thousand.'

'Would you be prepared to pay that?'

'I haven't seen over the house yet.'

'But if you wanted to buy it . . . ?'

'Of course.'

'Split down the middle, seventy-five thousand?'

'That's right.'

'Suppose I wanted more?'

'It's negotiable. I'm simply quoting your cousin.'

'I see.' Oscar finished his drink, and without saying anything, Sam Howard got to his feet, went to get the empty glass and took it over to refill it. He brought it back and handed it to Oscar. He said, 'Now that you know how it all came about, I really have to apologise to you both. I'll give you Hughie's key and we'll forget the entire business. It's just that I had to tell you the whole story so that you understand.'

'Of course.' Oscar looked at the fresh drink in his hand. 'Thank you,' he said, and set it on the table beside him.

Elfrida, who had managed with some difficulty to keep silent, now felt that the time had come to get her word in.

'You've made everything extremely clear, Mr Howard.'

'Sam.'

'All right. You've made everything extremely clear, Sam, but I still haven't worked out how you got here.'

'I drove north a couple of days ago.'

'Is this your first visit to the mill?' Oscar asked.

'Yes.'

'You said you were called back from New York in November. And now it's nearly Christmas. Sounds as though Sturrock & Swinfield have been dragging their feet a bit.'

Sam grinned, acknowledging this. 'I expect it does. But I went with the chairman to Switzerland to cost the new machinery we're going to buy. We were there for a good week.'

Elfrida asked, 'Are you staying in Buckly?'

'No. At an hotel in Inverness. This afternoon was my first meeting with the workforce. There was a good deal to be thrashed out. When it was over, and I'd had a beer with Fergus Skinner – he's the mill manager, who'd organised it all – I started back to Inverness, then had this idea that I'd make the diversion to Creagan, come and case the joint, as it were. A passer-by told me that

418

this was the Estate House, and it was so obviously lived in and tenanted that my curiosity was aroused. I got out of the car and rang the bell. I was never much good at unsolved mysteries.'

'I see.' Elfrida decided it was all very exciting. She could picture it. The handsome stranger, the ring of the doorbell, and ... Carrie. Going downstairs to open the door and let him in.

She looked at Carrie, curled up in the other arm-chair. She had not said a single word. Sometimes it was impossible to guess what she was thinking, and this was one of them.

She said, 'Carrie, I hope you've asked Sam to stay for dinner.'

Carrie began to laugh. She turned her head and a glance passed between her and Sam that Elfrida decided was almost conspiratorial. As though, already, they had an amusing secret to share. And then he smiled, and all at once looked much younger, less serious and responsible.

He said, 'More confessions.'

What on earth had they been up to? 'More con-fusion,' Elfrida remarked, quite sharply, and Carrie took pity on her.

'Elfrida, Sam is staying the night with us. I've asked him and he has to. All the roads to Inverness are blocked with snow. We rang the AA and they told us. As you know, there is not an hotel or a guesthouse open. I'm sorry. Do you mind very much?'

Elfrida said, 'I can't think of anything I would like more,' and could not keep the pleasure out of her voice.

It was nearly midnight. Elfrida lay in bed, and beside her

Oscar read his book, *Love In the Time of Cholera.* The lamp on his side of the bed was the only illumination, and the rest of the room was shadowed. The thick curtains had been opened a little, no more than a chink, allowing a shaft of light to penetrate from the street below and a draught of icy air from their slightly opened window. Fortunately Oscar and Elfrida agreed on such small matters, and neither could sleep in stuffy darkness.

The shaft of light fell across the brass rail at the foot of the bed, making it gleam like gold. The vast mahogany wardrobe, polished weekly by Mrs Snead, loomed against the wall, and on the old-fashioned dressing-table stood Elfrida's silver-framed photographs, her ivory-backed hand mirror, her bottle of scent. It was her room. Their room. Oscar's house.

She thought back over the many events of the evening, most of them unexpected. She, Oscar, Sam and Carrie had finally sat down to their supper in the kitchen at nine o'clock, by which time the kedgeree was a bit dried out but nobody seemed to mind too much and certainly nobody complained. With the kedgeree they had eaten peas (frozen, from the top of the old fridge), then peaches and cream, and Oscar had opened a bottle of white wine and, when that was done, another bottle. They were on to coffee when Lucy and Rory Kennedy returned from their dancing, both looking red-cheeked from leaping about, or perhaps the cold walk home from the school hall.

Lucy looked a bit surprised to see another person at the table, but was introduced to Sam, and the circumstances of his presence were explained to her. She was much impressed.

'Do you mean you're *snowed in*?' she asked incredulously.

'Seems so,' said Sam.

'It's so exciting. Like a book, an Agatha Christie. By tomorrow one of us may have been murdered.'

'Not by me.'

'Oscar, then. Oscar, you'll have to be the villain. You creep around at night with a knife, or a rope to strangle people with. And in the morning nobody will know it's you, and the police will come, and a frightfully clever detective.'

'Why do I have to be the villain?' Oscar protested.

'Because you're the nicest of all of us, and it's always the most unlikely person. It's got to be you.'

Oscar then asked about the reel party in the school hall, and it seemed that Lucy had had the most marvellous time, and done all the dances except a terribly difficult one called the Duke and Duchess of Edinburgh, which you had to learn. There had been a proper band, and lemonade to drink when you got really hot and thirsty.

Carrie was amused. 'Rory, who organised all this?'

'The headmaster, and one or two of the senior boys. It was good. Everybody came. Even the little kids.'

Oscar offered Rory a beer, but he said he'd rather have hot chocolate, and Lucy said she wanted hot chocolate too and that she would make it for both of them. Space was made at the table, and they pulled up chairs and joined the party, drinking hot chocolate and eating biscuits out of Elfrida's tin.

Finally Rory said it was time he went home. He got to his feet, and Sam asked, 'What's the weather doing?'

'Well, it's stopped snowing but that's about all you can

421

say for it. I'll tell my dad I met you, and about McTaggart's and things starting up again. He'll be delighted.'

'Don't let him be too delighted. It's going to take a bit of time.'

'Well,' said Rory, philosophically, 'you've got to start somewhere. Lucy, I'll try to get that television set down tomorrow afternoon. It all depends on what's going on at the golf course. Not much, I should think. There might be a bit of sledging, but if there is, I'll let you know. Give you a buzz.'

He departed by way of the back door because it was handier for home, and Lucy saw him off. She came back into the kitchen, smiling, and then the smile was almost at once lost in an enormous yawn.

Carrie put out an arm and drew her close. 'You're tired. Go to bed.'

'Can I have a hot bath first?'

'Of course. You had fun?'

Lucy kissed her. 'It was the best.'

While Oscar and Sam sat over their coffee, and the brandy that Oscar, surprisingly, had produced from his slate shelf wine cellar, Carrie and Elfrida washed up the dishes then went upstairs to raid Mrs Snead's linen cupboard and make up the last spare bed for Sam. They found sheets and pillowcases, a bath towel, and an extra blanket in case he felt cold. Carrie inspected the wardrobe, which was empty, save for two coathangers, and emanated a strong smell of mothballs. Elfrida went back to the cupboard, and returned with a duster and a lace-trimmed linen runner. After she had done a swift clean-up, she placed the runner on top of the chest of drawers. Carrie set and wound the bedside clock.

'What more,' asked Elfrida, 'could any man need?'

'Fresh flowers? Tissues? A mini-bar?'

'By the time Oscar's finished with him the last thing he'll need is a mini-bar. I haven't even got a spare toothbrush.'

'He's got one. He told me. And a razor. He'll be fine.'

'Jimmy-jams?'

'He probably sleeps in the buff anyway.'

'And how do you know?'

'Instinct, Elfrida. Feminine instinct.'

Suddenly, they were both laughing. Carrie said, 'You're a saint. I had to ask him to stay but the best was knowing you wouldn't mind.'

'I've always loved a full house, and this is a house for parties and people. Oscar and I have been rattling around in it for too long. Now it's full.' She said this in tones of the greatest satisfaction. 'Stretched to its limits. A family house. Just the way it should be.'

A family house. Elfrida lay in bed, and felt the house around her, like a shield, a carapace, a refuge. It was a house she had liked from the very start and had come to love. Filled with friends, it had become a home. Oscar's home. But Hughie wanted to sell it, and somehow the very thought of Oscar having to go along with Hughie's plans and leave the only place that had ever belonged to him was almost more than Elfrida could bear.

Oscar had come to the end of his chapter. He marked his book, closed it and laid it down on the bedside table.

'Are you still awake?' he asked.

'Yes.'

'I'm sorry.'

'I'm just awake.'

He turned off the light, but it was not dark because of the chink in the curtains.

She said, 'Oscar.'

'What is it?'

'If Hughie wants to sell his half of this house, couldn't you buy him out and then it would all be yours? For always.'

'Seventy-five thousand.'

'You . . . you don't have seventy-five thousand?'

'If I sold everything I owned, I might scrape up twenty.'

'You could get a mortgage.'

'Not for that amount. Not at my age. And I've always had a horror of mortgages. People say "get a mortgage", but what they really mean is "borrow money". It frightens me. I've never had much, but I've never been in debt. I couldn't start now.'

'If I had seventy-five thousand, would that help?'

'If you had seventy-five thousand, it would belong to you. It wouldn't be to bail me out.'

'I love this house so much.'

'Do you, dear girl?'

'It is so strong, so unpretentious, so . . . adaptable. Can't you feel it, like a heartbeat, keeping us all going, sheltering, taking care of us all?'

'I think I'm not as fanciful as you.'

'You can't lose it, Oscar.'

'Hughie can't sell it without my consent.'

'But he needs the money.' She lay silent, carefully framing in her mind what she was going to say. 'Oscar. Listen to me. If I sold my little picture, my David Wilkie, how much do you think that would fetch?'

'That is your treasure.'

'No, it is my insurance. And perhaps now is the time to release it.'

'It's your insurance, not mine.'

'Oscar, we're together. We're too old to prevaricate about such small details.'

'Seventy-five thousand is not a small detail. It is a lot of money.'

'If it is worth what I think it is, then we should sell it. If we don't get the seventy-five thousand for it, then we can fill in the gap with a mortgage. It's sense. Why keep a little picture if you can buy security? If you could buy this house? If you could live here for the rest of your days? You'd like that, wouldn't you? You'd like to be here for always? I can't bear to think of this darling place going to other people. I want you to have it. I want you to be here.'

For a long time, Oscar did not say anything. Then he reached for her hand, and took it in his own. His hand felt warm and she was close to him.

He said, 'You are the dearest person.'

'Go to sleep.'

'You are the most generous.'

'We'll talk about it,' she told him, 'in the morning.'

Lucy

Lucy

Wednesday 20 December
It is half past eight in the
morning, and I am writing my
diary. I should have written it
last night, but I was so tired I just had a bath
and went to bed, so got up early this morning to
write it down before I forget.
It was fabulous.
We walked up to the Kennedys' house
because Oscar didn't want to drive the car in
the thick snow. I have never seen such snow
except in photographs. It didn't take very long
because we took a short-cut. The Kennedys'
house is called the Manse because Peter Kennedy
is the minister. It is a big old house, not unlike
this one, but very furnished and with things
everywhere.
Carrie didn't come with us because of
her cold.
When we got there, other people were there
as well. We were all introduced. Mrs Kennedy

is called Tabitha, and is very pretty and young-looking, and unusual. Rory told me she teaches art at the school. Then we left all the grown-ups in the sitting room and went into the kitchen, and there were three other boys there, friends of Rory's from school, and his sister Clodagh who is twelve, and very skinny and sharp with bright blue eyes and fair pigtails. We all sat around and drank Coke, and Clodagh was very flirty. The table was already laid, and we had a sort of high tea there, an enormous macaroni cheese and salads, then a very rich chocolate cake and ice-cream. When that was finished, we all got ready again and walked down the hill and along the road to the school, about half a mile. The school is old, but has lots of new buildings around it, and the gym was one of them. They call it the hall but it's a gym as well.

There were lots and lots of children of all ages from about seven to grown-up. The headmaster is called Mr McIntosh and they all call him Waterproof behind his back, but I bet he knows about this. He was quite young and very nice. There was a platform at one end of the hall and a proper band. An accordionist, a drummer and a fiddler. There was a terrible din, and everybody was larking around, and then Mr McIntosh told everybody to be quiet, in quite a soft voice, and they were. He said it was time to get started and we were going to do Strip the Willow because it wasn't too difficult for little ones and learners (me).

Rory and the others who had been with us

helped get everyone into line, with partners and things. It didn't seem to matter who your partner was. Boys danced with boys, and girls with girls, if they wanted, which seems to me a very sensible arrangement. Two boys wanted to dance with Clodagh, but Rory said he would do it with me.

We stood about half-way up the line so I could see roughly what it was all about. The music was very lively and jiggy and made you feel you couldn't stand still, with a tremendous beat from the drum. It wasn't a very difficult dance, just spinning round and round with your partner, or some other person in the line, and then coming all the way back again. Sometimes you were armed by a huge boy who pulled you just about off your feet, and then the next one would be tiny, and you'd have to be careful not to spin him off his feet.

By the end we were all hot and breathless, but there was lemonade and then we started again.

We did an eightsome reel, but with sixteen people which makes it all the more complicated. And then something called Hamilton House, which was fun because you set to one boy and then spin with another. And then the Dashing White Sergeant when you go all round the room in threes, the lines in opposite directions, so by the end you have met absolutely everybody. Then the Gay Gordons, but Rory said that was a silly dance so we didn't do it but drank lemonade. I didn't dance with him all the time, but with lots of other people, who were friendly even though

*I didn't know their names, and came and asked
me. Most people were in jeans and old clothes,
but some boys wore their kilts, with rugby shirts,
or old tweed waistcoats.*

*The time absolutely flew, and it was so
strange, because however breathless and hot you
felt, as soon as the music struck up again, you
simply didn't want to stay off the floor.*

*It all ended at about ten o'clock, and nobody
wanted to go home, but once the band had gone,
there wasn't much point so we all went out to the
cloakroom and found our things again, and put
them on. Clodagh and the others went back to
the Manse. One of the boys had a sledge and they
took turns dragging each other along the road
and up the hill. But Rory walked back to Oscar's
house with me. It was such a beautiful night,
with the snow still falling softly, and everything
smothered in it.*

*Carrie had said to ask him in for a beer, so
I did, and he came in. And then, more surprises.
They were all in the kitchen, finishing supper.
And Carrie was up and about, and a strange
man was there too. He is called Sam Howard
and is going to live up here, and run some old
woollen mill in Buckly. Very nice-looking and I
should say just about the right age for Carrie.*

*I thought perhaps he was an old friend but it
seemed he'd been snowed in, couldn't get back to
Inverness and was staying the night. We'd seen
a rather handsome Range Rover thing outside in
the street, but hadn't put two and two together.*

Anyway, we had hot chocolate and some

432

biscuits with them, and then Rory went home. But he says he is coming today with the television set for my room. Not that I need one because so many things are happening here all the time that I don't think I shall have time to watch it.

The best is knowing that things are going to go on happening. I've never felt like this before. In London a treat is over and there aren't any more, but being here there are unexpected treats every single day.

Now I suppose I had better get dressed and go down and eat breakfast. There is a smell of bacon drifting up which is very appetising.

Elfrida

Elfrida

 As usual, Elfrida was the first downstairs. At the turn of the stairs she drew back the curtains (a marvellously grand, threadbare pair she had bought at the market in Buckly) and gazed out at the day. Actually, it was the night because it was still dark, but it had stopped snowing and by the light of the street-lamp she could see the garden, all shape and form obliterated. Bushes and trees drooped beneath the weight of the snow, and shrubs, pillowed, had lost all identity. It was very still and quiet.

She went on downstairs and into the kitchen. Horace, it seemed, was beginning to recover. As she opened the door he clambered out of his basket and came to greet her, plumy tail waving. She stroked and patted him, and they held a small conversation. Then she opened the back door and he stepped out. When he came indoors again, his face wore an expression of indignation. He had not expected such inconvenience, especially in his present delicate state of health.

He returned to his basket and sulked.

Elfrida dealt with breakfast: laid the table, made coffee, found bacon. It was the last of the bacon and they would have to buy more. In fact, she was going to have to start thinking about Christmas food: she had been putting it off from day to day, but now there was so little time left that probably all the shops would be denuded and she wouldn't be able to buy so much as a mince-pie. She found an old envelope and a pencil, and as she stood by the cooker, frying the bacon, she started on a tentative list. She wrote 'bacon', then 'tangerines', and decided not to write anything else until she had had her first cup of coffee.

She was drinking this when the kitchen door opened and Sam appeared. Elfrida was wearing her tartan trousers and a dark blue sweater with knitted sheep grazing all over it, but Sam was still in his suit because, of course, he had nothing else to wear. He looked a bit out of place, and Elfrida's first thought was for his comfort.

She said, 'I shall lend you a sweater.'

'I clearly look as peculiar as I feel. Overdressed.'

'Not at all. You look very nice, but a bit like a chairman about to make a speech. How did you sleep?'

'In great comfort. I remember beds like that in my mother's house.'

'I have cooked bacon for breakfast.'

'I smelt it wafting up the stairs.'

'I'll fry you an egg.'

'I can do that. I'm extremely handy.'

'Not in your best jacket. It will smell of cooking. I shall go now, and find you something a little less formal.'

She went upstairs. Oscar was in the bathroom shaving so she raided his chest of drawers and unearthed a pleasing blue Shetland jersey with a polo-neck. Back in the kitchen, she found Sam in his shirt-sleeves, neatly frying his egg. She tossed him the sweater. 'Too cold for shirt-sleeves.' He caught it and pulled it on, his head emerging from the ribbed collar like a swimmer's rising from the deep.

'That's much better,' Elfrida told him. 'Now you can relax.'

He flipped the egg on to a plate, and added a couple of rashers of bacon. Elfrida put more bread into her new toaster, then filled his coffee cup. They sat at the table together, and it felt companionable.

'The snow has stopped—'

'I feel so badly about last night—'

They both spoke at the same instant, then stopped, waiting for the other to carry on.

Elfrida said, 'Why do you feel badly? It was no trouble at all. All we did was feed you on some rather dried-up kedgeree and put a pair of sheets on a bed.'

'I didn't actually mean that. Although it was enormously kind of you. I meant barging in, clutching the key of your house and saying I'd come to buy it. I lay awake last night and went quite cold with embarrassment at the thought. I just hope I didn't offend Oscar, or upset him.'

'Oscar's not that sort of a man. For a moment he was a bit cross, but with Hughie, not you. And I must agree, I think Hughie has behaved shabbily. But according to Oscar he's never done anything else. However, I can't pronounce because I've never met him. Did *you* like him? Hughie, I mean.'

'Not enormously. Very smooth. Rather *passé*. Kept fondling his tie.'

Elfrida recognised the tiresome habit at once. 'Oh, I hate men who do that. I can just *see* him.'

'The key's still in my coat pocket. I'll give it to Oscar.'

'He's not that worried.'

'I . . .' Sam set down his knife and fork and reached for his coffee cup. 'I . . . suppose Oscar wouldn't think of buying Hughie out?'

'We talked about it in bed last night. You have to understand, Oscar and I haven't known each other for all that long. At the beginning of November his wife and child were killed in a terrible car crash and he had to leave Hampshire. I came with him. We share a bedroom and a bed but we have no certain future together. I am not, as yet, permanently part of his life. I am simply a sort of spare wheel to keep the car going until he's sorted himself out. So it is difficult for me either to press him into some sort of action or even to make suggestions.'

'Will he go back to Hampshire?'

'No. The house he lived in with Gloria is already on the market.'

'Is this his only property?'

'Yes. And it's half a property.'

'But wouldn't it be sensible for him to buy Hughie out?'

'Yes. Sensible, but not financially possible. I have only just found this out.'

'You mean he doesn't have the wherewithal?'

'Exactly that.'

'A mortgage?'

'Won't think about it.'

'I see.' Sam returned to his bacon and eggs, but his presence was so strong and sympathetic that Elfrida went on, confiding in him as she felt she could confide in no one else.

440

'As I said, we talked about it last night. He told me that if he sold everything he owned, he couldn't raise more than twenty thousand. And I said, "Oscar, I have my little picture."'

He looked up, and across the breakfast table their eyes met and held. Elfrida guessed that this possibility had already occurred to him.

'You're talking about your David Wilkie?'

'Exactly. It was given to me years ago as an authentic original. I've never had it valued because I've never insured it. But, like any old woman living on her own, I have always allowed myself to believe it is worth a lot of money. My back-up, in possible times of penury and trouble.'

'Would you sell it?'

'For Oscar I would do anything – short of leaping off a cliff or shooting myself. And, after all, what is a little picture? It's given me pleasure for many years but we have to keep some sense of proportion. Surely to be able to own such a lovely house as this is of more importance.'

'I agree with you,' said Sam. 'You've no idea how much it's worth?'

'Not really. And this is scarcely the time or the place to start getting it appraised. I am a stranger in this part of the world. I have no connections of any sort. I wouldn't know where to start. There's an antiques shop across the road but that's about as far as I can go.'

Sam was silent for a bit. And then he said, 'Janey Philip ... she's married to my oldest friend. As you know, I was staying with them in London when I met Hughie. Janey used to work for Boothby's, the fine-art dealers. I could ring her. I'm sure she'd have some bright suggestions.'

'It's a bit close to Christmas to start trying to sell pictures.'

'We don't have to do it right away.'

'And the snow precludes everything. Are you still snowed in with us, Sam? I hope so.' He put down his coffee cup, and started laughing. She frowned. 'What's so funny?'

'You. Most people would be desperate to get rid of the stranger.'

'I don't feel you're a stranger, but I suppose it was a stupid thing to say. You obviously want to get back to Inverness. Get home.'

'Elfrida, I'm going no further than Inverness.'

'But home?'

'At this precise moment I haven't got a home. Except an apartment in New York. That's where I lived for six years, but my wife and I separated, and then I had to come back to the UK to do this job in Buckly.'

'Oh, Sam, I'm sorry.'

'Why sorry?'

'Your wife . . . I didn't know.'

'Just one of those things.'

Separated. 'So you're still married?'

'Yes.'

'Children?'

'No.'

'Parents?' Elfrida persisted, beginning even to herself to sound a bit desperate.

'My parents are both dead. Our old Yorkshire home sold up.'

'So what will you do for Christmas?'

'I haven't thought about it. Christmas, at the moment, is a non-starter. I'll probably just stay in Inverness until the orgies of Hogmanay are over, then get back to Buckly and start getting the show on the road. At the moment, to be truthful, that's all-important. I'm giving family and celebrations a miss this year.'

'You must spend Christmas with us.'

'Elfrida . . .'

'No, I mean it. I couldn't bear you to be sitting in an hotel lounge in Inverness, wearing a paper hat and being all alone. It's ludicrous. Oscar and I didn't mean to have Christmas either. We thought we'd go pagan and celebrate the winter solstice with a lamb chop. But then Carrie and Lucy asked themselves, and Oscar went out and ordered a Christmas tree, and he and Lucy bought some decorations. And I'm just sitting here, thinking about food. I'm useless at this sort of thing and all I've written down is bacon and tangerines. But we could gather a bit of holly and go and shoot a turkey, or whatever one does. And, anyway, it's the people who count, isn't it? The friends you spend Christmas with. Don't go. It would be such fun for all of us to be together.'

She finished and he was silent, and she wondered if, as usual, she had overdone it and made a fool of herself. 'Oh, Sam, you do what you want to do. That's all that's important.'

He said, 'You're the most hospitable, generous person I think I've ever met. But I tell you what I'll do. I'll ring the AA and see what's happening on the roads. If they're clear then I'll go back to Inverness and get out of your hair. I really have a hell of a lot of work to do. If they're still impassable then I'll accept, with much gratitude, your invitation.'

'Oh, good. I'll pray for blizzards – do my snow dance.'

'What will Oscar say?'

'He'll say *splendid*, and go and read his newspaper.'

Sam pushed back the cuff of Oscar's sweater, and looked at his beautiful Rolex watch. He said, 'It's nearly nine o'clock. If you don't mind, I shall go now to incarcerate myself in my bedroom with my mobile phone and start making calls.'

'Why don't you do that? But, first, have another cup of coffee.'

Carrie was the next to appear. 'Where is everyone? I thought I heard voices.'

'You did. It was Sam, but he's gone back to his room to do telephoning.'

'There's still the most dreadful lot of snow.' Carrie poured coffee and put another bit of bread in the toaster. She took a rasher of bacon and ate it in her fingers. Then she sat down and saw the old envelope with the start of Elfrida's shopping list. 'What's this? Bacon and tangerines. We *are* going to have an orgy.'

'I was trying to start on Christmas. I simply must pull myself together and try to make a plan or two. I've been procrastinating and now we've only got four days.'

'Why don't you let me take over? I'm a professional organiser and there's nothing I like more than making lists. Where can I go and do a mammoth shop?'

'There's an enormous supermarket across the bridge at Kingsferry. You'd have passed it on your way here from the airport. It's called PriceRite. The only thing is, I'm not sure if you'll get there in this snow. It depends whether the road's been cleared. But when Sam's spoken to the AA we'll know.'

'PriceRite. Sounds hopeful.'

'You can buy everything from dog biscuits to rose

manure. I've only been there once because with just the two of us we didn't seem to need an enormous amount of food. But we do now.'

'Is Sam going back to Inverness?'

'Depends. If he's marooned then I've asked him to stay over the festive season.'

Carrie's face showed no expression. She simply said, 'In that case we'll be five in the house . . .' drew the envelope towards her and picked up the pencil. 'Now. Are we going to have a Christmas feast?'

'Yes. I suppose. Christmas Day lunch or dinner?'

'Oh, dinner, much more festive.'

'We'll never get a turkey into that little oven.'

'Then we'll have chickens. Two chickens.'

Carrie wrote furiously. Chickens. Brussels sprouts. Potatoes. Cloves for bread sauce. Frozen peas. Carrots. Masses of fruit. Butter. French bread. Cranberry sauce. Cinnamon sticks. 'How about crackers?' she asked.

'Yes, we must have crackers.'

'And the wine?'

'Oscar will want to deal with that.'

'Smoked salmon?'

'My favourite.'

'And nuts and stuff. Mince-pies?'

'Could you buy them? I'm useless at pastry. We can cheat and soak them inside with brandy. Christmas cake. I'll make that. Christmas pudding.'

'Should we have a cold ham? Terribly useful for Boxing Day and sandwiches.'

'Brilliant. And a big pot of soup.'

'I'll make the soup.' For once, Elfrida felt competent and efficient. Soup was her speciality, chicken stock and any handy vegetable. She called it Garbage Broth. 'And perhaps crisps and dips in case we decide to have a party.'

'A party?'

'Shouldn't we?'

'Who would we ask?'

'Well . . .' Elfrida considered the options, which were not many '. . . the Kennedy family. The doctor and his wife – and the nice bookshop man and *his* wife. They were at the Manse yesterday, and he and Oscar got on like a house on fire.'

Oscar, on cue, came through the door. 'With whom did I get on like a house on fire?'

'The bookshop man.'

'He's called Rutley, Stephen Rutley, and his wife is Anne.'

'How clever you are to remember. Oscar, we're going to have a little party so we shall ask them.'

'When shall we have a little party?'

Carrie and Elfrida looked at each other, because this had not been decided. Then Carrie said, 'Saturday night is party night.'

'The day before Christmas Eve.'

Oscar said, 'I shall have to buy some drink.'

'If the bridge is open Carrie's going to PriceRite in Kingsferry to do all the shopping. Perhaps you could go with her.'

'Yes, perhaps I could. Elfrida, somebody seems to have finished the bacon.'

'Oh, Oscar, I'm sorry. That was me,' Carrie admitted. 'I ate the last bit. I'll fry you some more.'

'There isn't any more,' Elfrida told her.

But it didn't matter because there were sausages in the fridge, and Carrie cooked those instead, then Lucy appeared and Elfrida left them at it and went upstairs, feeling much happier now that a few plans had been made and she was spared the ordeal of an hour or more in PriceRite, pushing a trolley down the crowded Christmas aisles, searching hopelessly for ground coffee.

In her bedroom, she did a little desultory tidying, making the bed and spreading upon it her red silk shawl. She folded clothes and put them away, then sorted the contents of the linen basket in the hope of doing a wash and hanging it out on the line to dry. Which perhaps it would because the sun was creeping up into a clear sky, and all the snow sparkled where the light touched it and the shadows were a wonderful smoky blue. Below, in the street, the morning was on its way: the first of the shopping ladies, slow-moving cars, a man at the wheel of a parked van eating a restorative ham roll. A girl came out of the bakery with a broom and started brushing the pavement. She wore her overall and a stout pair of rubber boots. Overhead, the seagulls wheeled and perched on the church weathervane, preening their feathers in the fine morning.

She tore herself away from the lovely sight, gathered up the laundry and dumped it on the bathroom floor. Later she would take it downstairs. She went into the sitting room, still dim and shrouded from last night, and drew back the curtains. The low sun flooded in and filled it with light. The detritus of the previous evening stood about: empty glasses, Oscar's whisky bottle, cushions squashed, chairs in disarray. She collected glasses and tidied up a bit, then knelt to deal with the remains of last night's fire – her least favourite task but one that had to be tackled each morning. Oscar always said to leave it for him to do but *his* job was humping logs and

447

it seemed a bit unfair to let him cope with a bucket full of ashes as well.

She was brushing the hearth when, from behind her, she heard Sam speak. 'Elfrida. I'll do that.'

'Oh.' She turned and he was standing in the open doorway. He closed the door behind him, and she abandoned the hearth brush and stood up, dusting her hands on the seat of her tartan trousers. 'Don't worry. I do it every morning. I'll finish it later. What's the news?'

He looked rueful. 'I'm afraid you've got me for Christmas.'

'Wonderful.' She made no attempt to keep the pleasure out of her voice, then thought it might be tactful to be a bit sorry for him. 'Poor Sam. You're stuck. You have no choice. Come and tell me.'

She went to the window-seat, and he came and sat beside her. Through the glass the thin sun felt almost warm.

'The roads are passable until the Cromarty Bridge, but the Black Isle is a no-go area, and Inverness is totally snowed up. No traffic in, no traffic out.'

'They must have had much more snow than us.'

'Yes. It seems they did.'

'Carrie and Oscar are planning a huge shopping expedition to PriceRite. That's across our bridge. Do you think they'll be able to make it?'

'They'll get that far, no problem. The snowploughs have been out. It's just further south that the trouble starts.'

'Have you telephoned your hotel?'

'Yes, I've done that, and I've spoken to my chairman, David Swinfield, in London, and Janey too.'

'Janey?' Elfrida frowned. She had already forgotten who Janey was.

'Janey Philip. I told you. Neil's wife.'

'Oh, yes, of course. Sorry. The one who used to work for Boothby's.'

'That's right. She was hugely helpful. She went off and found one of the current Boothby catalogues and did a bit of research. There's a Boothby's local representative for this part of the world. He lives at Kingsferry House and he's called Sir James Erskine-Earle.'

'Heavens.' Elfrida was much impressed. 'How frightfully grand.'

'She gave me his phone number but I haven't rung him yet. I thought I'd better have a word with you first. Just be sure that you really *do* want to sell your picture . . . or at least have it appraised.'

'I've barely mentioned it to Oscar.'

'Do you want to talk it over with him?'

Elfrida thought about this, then said, 'No, because he might try to persuade me not to.'

'An appraisal doesn't mean you have to sell. And, whatever, you really should insure it.'

'I don't suppose I'd be able to afford the premiums.'

'So what do you say? Shall I give him a ring?'

'Yes. Do that. See what he says.'

'I've left my mobile in my room. I'll go and do it there.'

He left her, and Elfrida stayed where she was, gazing across the room to where her little treasure hung, lonely in the middle of a large, empty expanse of wall. It had been part of her life for so long – the old couple sitting at the table with their family Bible, he so sombrely attired, she proud in her red dress and her daffodil-yellow silk

449

shawl, their faces watchful, wise and kind, their stillness emanating a certain dignity, a repose. They had been comforting companions for a number of years, and seen her through a number of distraught, desolate days. She was fond of them.

But they were not as important as Oscar.

Five minutes later, Sam was back, looking pleased with himself. 'All fixed.' He settled himself beside her once more.

'You spoke to him? Sir James Erskine-Earle?'

'Yes. No trouble. He answered the phone himself. He's coming over to Creagan this afternoon. It's to do with the war memorial – he's on some committee or other. He's going to drop in about four o'clock and cast his eye over your painting. He sounded rather interested.'

'Oh, Sam.' All at once Elfrida felt a bit nervous. 'I'm not sure if I can wait that long.'

'You'll have to.'

'We'll give him a cup of tea. I'll buy a scone or something. Did he sound nice?'

'Perfectly amenable.'

'It . . . it's rather exciting, isn't it?'

'It could be.'

'Shall I tell Oscar?'

'I would, if I were you. You don't want to start feeling underhand.'

'No. You're quite right. Thank you, Sam, for your trouble.'

'My pleasure. The least I can do. Now, you said Carrie and Oscar were going over to Kingsferry to shop. Instead, why don't I take her? Then I can help loading trolleys and carting everything home.'

Elfrida thought this a marvellous idea, and for more reasons than one.

'Brilliant. How kind you are. Oscar will be delighted. He loathes shopping.'

'I have ulterior motives.' Better and better. 'Because I must buy clothes. I can't go round looking like a tailor's dummy for the next five days. Do you think Kingsferry would rise to a gents' outfitter? And a chemist, because I haven't got any toothpaste.'

Elfrida said, brightly, 'Of course,' but felt slightly let down because she had hoped his ulterior motive was getting Carrie to himself.

'And I should like to buy some wine for Oscar ... Perhaps I should have a word with him before I go.'

'That would be a good idea. About wine Oscar has strong opinions.'

'And rightly so.'

Outside, in the brightening morning, the seagulls clamoured, perched on the ridge of the high roof, floating and circling around the tower, relishing the clear air. Elfrida turned her head to watch them. She said, 'In a strange way I should like you to have this house. It has such dignity and solidity, just right for the important head of a company.' She looked at him, sitting there in Oscar's blue sweater, and it already felt as though he had been with them all for ever. 'It's strange, isn't it, the way things happen? You with your key, and then the snow tumbling down. And here we all are. And it is very satisfactory having competent young people around us again. Carrie organising everything, and you making decisions that I could never make. I've always been useless at decisions. I've always worked on impulse and some have been disastrous. Oscar and I have been two old things for too long. Mrs Snead said visitors would cheer us up, but it's more than that. And I know that, without actually talking about it, we've both been dreading Christmas. Under the circumstances I felt it could be nothing but a bitter and sad time. But now, with you and Lucy and Carrie with us, it *can't* be as emotive as we had feared.' She thought about this, then smiled. 'Whatever, there's nothing we can do to stop it happening so we might as well make it fun. Perhaps it will be like one of those parties one longs not to have to go to that turns out to be one of the most memorable and the best. Do you know what I mean?'

Sam said he knew exactly what she meant.

Lucy

Lucy

Half past ten in the morning, and everyone was occupied.

Sam and Carrie had departed, in
Sam's impressive Discovery, for Kings-
ferry and PriceRite. Before they could go, however, a
certain amount of physical labour had been necessary.
Sam had found a shovel in Oscar's shed, and cleared
the snow from the path that led from front door to
gate, then a broom, with which he had brushed piled
snow from his car. Then he had squirted anti-freeze on
his windscreen. Finally Carrie joined him and they set off
on their shopping expedition, armed with a list that went
on for ever and which had taken a great deal of time and
communal thought to compose. Carrie wore her loden
coat and her black fur hat, and Sam was buttoned into
his handsome navy blue overcoat that made him look
very successful, which he probably was. Driving away
they left an opulent impression.

Having hung her washing out in the still, cold air,
Elfrida had taken Horace for a short walk, just up the
hill to the closed and shuttered hotel then home by the

station. Otherwise, she said, his muscles would atrophy and he would never move from his basket again. Oscar was by the fire in the sitting room, reading his newspaper. He had clearly been much relieved when told he didn't have to go shopping.

Lucy sat at the table in her bedroom and made her own plans. She would go out and buy her Christmas presents this morning. She had given Mummy and Gran theirs before she left London but there were still a lot more to go. Having her holiday money made everything much easier because it meant she wouldn't have to penny-pinch.

Elfrida, Oscar, Carrie. Now she added Sam. And Mrs Snead. And Rory. And, perhaps, Clodagh too, otherwise it might look a bit odd.

She couldn't think of anybody else.

She found her rucksack, put the list into it and checked her purse, which bulged satisfactorily. She put on her padded jacket and her boots, and went downstairs. On the way, she looked round the open sitting-room door. 'Oscar.'

'Yes, darling?'

'I'm going out to do some shopping.'

'Right.'

'When Elfrida gets back, will you tell her?'

'I shall do that.'

She left him and went on downstairs. Christmas was becoming real. Over breakfast plans had been laid and Lucy was told that they were going to have Christmas dinner in the evening, a proper grown-up party. In London, where Christmas was usually a fairly tame affair, the great feast always took place at lunchtime, but a party in the evening meant that there would be something to look forward to all day and Lucy could wear her new black mini-skirt and her white sweater. Going down the long hall, thinking about this, she paused, and then on an impulse opened the door of the desolate, disused dining room. It was dark and gloomy and in dire need of a good dust and polish, but in her imagination she saw it lit by firelight and candles and groaning with delicious food – things like crystallised fruits and a pudding, aflame with brandy, goblets of wine, silver dishes filled with nuts and chocolates, and the sparkle of crackers.

An idea took shape but there wasn't time, right now, to think it through so she closed the door, then let herself out into the cold, sweet morning and the dazzle of snow. Across the street stood a big council lorry with an extending ladder and two burly men were occupied in draping strings of fairy-lights around and over the branches of the bare trees that stood within the churchyard wall.

She started off down the pavement to do the rounds of the modest shops. They, too, were in the festive spirit, with mock snow sprayed on windows and displays arranged with red satin bows and plastic holly. In the ironmonger's window a chainsaw wore a tinsel ribbon and a card saying 'SUITABLE FOR CHRISTMAS GIFTING'.

Lucy wondered who would fall for that one.

She came to the jersey shop, went inside and found every sort of pullover, cardigan, tam o'shanter, sock and glove. There were knitted thistles on the front of some sweaters, and ethnic patterns that looked as though they had been designed by a mad Peruvian. In the end she unearthed a red cashmere scarf, very fine and very long, which she knew would look quite perfect wound around Carrie's elegant neck. And it would keep her cosy as well.

Next was the bookshop. And there, to serve her, was Mr Rutley, who ran the place and whom she had already met at the Manse. He greeted Lucy like an old friend, and was immensely helpful. After a bit of browsing, discussion and changing her mind, she chose a book for Oscar, a coffee-table book, filled with full-page colour photographs of old Scottish country houses, castles and gardens. She was sure he would love it. Mr Rutley said that if he didn't he could change it, but Lucy knew that Oscar wouldn't dream of doing that because he was the sort of person who would rather fall down dead than hurt a feeling.

For Sam, at Mr Rutley's suggestion, she got an Ordnance Survey map of Creagan and the surrounding district that included Buckly. It seemed a bit dull but, on the other hand, was probably the most useful thing he could own, since he was coming to live and work in the neighbourhood. It was quite expensive too, so Lucy bought it, and some cards, wrapping paper with holly and some glittery string. Mr Rutley put it all into a carrier-bag and took her money. 'I hope we'll see you all again over Christmas, Lucy.'

'Yes, I do too. Thank you.'

'Have fun.'

The chemist was next. That was much quicker. Some lavender soap for Mrs Snead, and for Clodagh, little hair ornaments that she could clip to the end of her pigtails. Rory was a bit difficult because Lucy hadn't the faintest idea what he would really like. It would be easier to choose if she had a brother of her own, or even a friend who was a boy. Then she saw a big bottle of Badedas. Her father had always used Badedas, in the safe old days when she was a little girl before the divorce. He would soak in his bath and the scented steam, smelling of chestnut oil, would fill the upstairs half of their house. Perhaps Rory would like to soak in Badedas after a long day's stint on the golf course. She wavered for a moment or two, and then, unable to come up with a better idea, bought it.

Elfrida was the most difficult. What could one give to Elfrida that would begin to pay her back for all the laughs and the spontaneous affection she had given Lucy? There was no inspiration in the chemist's, so she went out and walked on down the street, past Arthur Snead, Fruit and Vegetables. Then, struck by a brilliant idea, she retraced her steps and went through the door, which went *ping* when she shut it.

'Mr Snead?'

' 'Ullo there.'

'I'm Lucy Wesley. I'm staying at the Estate House. Mrs Snead is a friend of mine.'

'Oh, yes. She told me about you.'

'If I ordered some special flowers for Elfrida, would you be able to deliver them on Christmas Eve?'

He looked a bit doubtful, pursing his lips. 'Christmas Eve's a Sunday, darling.'

'Well, Saturday, then. Saturday would be better, actually, because they're going to have a little party.'

'The truth is, darling, it's dicey just now, with the snow. Nothing's getting through from Inverness and that's where all my regular stuff comes from. What were you thinking of? Chrysanths? Carnations?'

Lucy screwed up her nose. 'Not really.'

'I've got Stargazer lilies in the back, delivered yesterday when the roads were still open. But they're pricey.'

'Stargazers?'

'Lovely tight buds, and in the cool. Should just be starting to open in a day or two.'

'Could I see one?'

'Course you can.'

He disappeared through a door at the back of his shop and reappeared holding a single stem of creamy, elliptical, tightly closed buds. They looked just the same as the ones Gran bought from the flower-seller on the street corner in Fulham, and they sometimes lasted as long as two weeks.

'How many have you got?'

'A dozen but, like I said, they're pricey. Three pounds a stem.'

Three by six was eighteen. Eighteen pounds. But they would look so beautiful in Elfrida's sitting room. They would open slowly, spreading out into pale pink petals, and fill the whole house with their heady fragrance. She said, 'I'll have six and pay you now, but would you keep them here until Saturday and then bring them over?'

''Course I will. And tell you what, I'll wrap them in special paper and put a big pink bow on.'

'I've got a card. I bought it in the bookshop. If I write the card, could you put it in with the flowers?'

'I'll do that very thing.'

He lent her a pen and she wrote, 'Elfrida – Happy Christmas and lots of love from Lucy.'

She put it into its envelope, wrote 'Elfrida Phipps', struck down the flap and gave it to Mr Snead, then handed over the eighteen pounds. A terrible lot to spend on flowers, but worth it.

Mr Snead rang up his till. 'If you're wanting mistletoe, let me know. I've got a branch or two but it sells like hot cakes.'

Mistletoe was synonymous with kissing.

'I'll see,' said Lucy, cautiously.

She said goodbye and set off for home, laden with purchases and feeling tremendously Christmassy. Once back, she would go straight upstairs to her bedroom, close the door and settle down to wrapping all her presents in holly paper, tying them up with glittery string, then hiding them in her bottom drawer. As she crossed the square, she saw a car parked outside Oscar's house, an old estate car with its tailgate open, but thought nothing of it: in Creagan people parked their cars all over the place wherever they could find space. However, as she pushed the front door open she heard voices from the kitchen. Investigating, she found Elfrida stirring a pot on the cooker, and Rory Kennedy. On the kitchen table stood the television set, and a small black plastic trolley with wheels.

When she appeared in the open doorway, laden with shopping-bags, they stopped talking and turned to smile. Rory said, 'Hi.' He was wearing a grey fleecy jacket and rubber boots, and looked very masculine. Because his presence was so unexpected, Lucy was lost for words, yet delighted at the same time.

'Hello. I – I thought you were coming later on. Like tea-time. I thought you'd be working.'

'Not much to do on the golf course in weather like this. The greenkeeper sent us all home so I borrowed Dad's car and brought the set down for you.'

Lucy looked at it. It seemed much more sophisticated than the one she had in London. 'I thought it would be old. It doesn't look old at all.'

'I just got myself a bigger one. I brought the stand as well, in case you didn't have anywhere to put it.'

461

Elfrida lifted her pot off the cooker and put it down on an iron trivet. She said, 'I think it's amazing. We'll all be coming up to the attic to sit and goggle. Lucy, perhaps you'd better show Rory where it's got to go in your bedroom.'

'It's four flights of stairs,' Lucy told Rory.

He grinned. 'I think I can just about manage.'

She led the way, her carrier-bags bumping against her legs. 'You been shopping?' Rory asked, from behind her. She thought that only he would be able to carry something very heavy up so many stairs and still have breath for conversation.

'Yes. Christmas presents. I didn't have time in London.'

They reached the top landing and the door that led into her room. She went through and dumped the carrier-bags on her bed. Rory followed her and set down the television set carefully on the floor. Straightening, he looked appreciatively about him. 'Hey, this is a cool room. And lots of space. Do you always keep it as tidy as this?'

'Sort of,' Lucy told him casually, not wanting him to think her pernickety.

'Clodagh's room's a perpetual tip. Ma's always getting at her to put her things away. I'll nip down, get the table and then we'll get it set up.'

When he had gone, pounding down the stairs again, she quickly bundled all the carrier-bags into an empty bottom drawer and shut it firmly. It would be a shame if he guessed about the Badedas.

In a moment he was back with the little trolley. They found a suitable power socket, and Rory put the set on the trolley, and plugged it in. The set had its own aerial, and Rory switched it on, then fiddled until the picture stopped being fuzzy and became quite clear.

'It's really good,' Lucy marvelled.

'I can get it better.' He was sitting cross-legged on the rug, intent on what he was doing. He punched knobs, switched channels. Superman was on for children, and then an old black-and-white film. Then a lady showing them how to make Christmas cards, decorated with cut-outs from a seed catalogue. Rory checked the sound, gave the aerial another tweak. Lucy settled herself on the floor beside him.

'. . . and then you finish it off with a little bow of pretty ribbon. Like this. I think you'll agree any person would be delighted to receive such a personal card.'

Rory said, 'Not me,' and punched another button. An announcer was telling them about the weather in broad Scottish, which, in the foreseeable future, was not conducive to hill-walking or climbing.

'Do you want me to leave it on?' Rory asked.

'No. I know how to work it now.'

He switched it off. 'Just don't touch the aerial. I think I've got it as good as it gets.'

'It's really kind of you to let me borrow it – and to bring it.'

'No problem. Finishes everything off.' He looked about him once more admiringly. 'Is this all the stuff my mother helped buy? It's great. She loves going to the Buckly market more than anything – she always comes back with some bargain. A tatty old linen pillowcase or a china fairing or something useless. Our house is full of junk, but there always seems to be room for more. At home in London, do you have a room like this?'

'No. It's not nearly so big and it hasn't any sort of

view from the window. But it's pretty. And at least I don't have to share it with anybody. I've got my books there, and my computer. My things.'

'What's it like, living in a city?'

'It's all right.'

'Must be great, all those museums and exhibitions and concerts and plays. I've only been once. My dad took me when he had to attend some conference and we stayed in an hotel and went to a theatre every night. It was hot weather and we used to have our meals in pubs, sitting out on the pavement and watching all the weirdos wandering past. It was good. More exciting than Creagan.'

'It's different if you live there all the time.'

'Suppose so.'

'It can be quite nice if you've got a proper house with a garden. When I was little we had a house in Kensington with a proper garden, and that didn't feel like living in a city because there was always a bit of grass and trees and flowers and things. But then my parents divorced and now we live in a flat, me and my mother and my grandmother. It's near the river and it's got a balcony and a nice view, but there's nowhere to *be*. To go and lie on a bit of lawn and read a book. My friend Emma – she's at school with me – she lives in a proper house and sometimes we have a barbecue in the garden.'

She couldn't think of anything else to tell him, and was painfully aware that it all sounded very dull.

After a bit, he asked, 'Are you homesick?'

She looked at him in astonishment. *'Homesick?'*

'Well, you know, missing your mother. Your things. Everything. Clodagh's hopeless. She won't even go away for a night, bawls like a baby.'

'No.' Lucy heard her own voice, all at once surprisingly sharp and strong. 'No, I'm *not* homesick. I'm not even thinking about going back to London. I'm simply putting it out of my mind.'

'But . . .'

'You don't understand. It's not like here. It's not like this house, like your house, full of people and friends your own age coming and going. It's my grandmother's flat and she doesn't want my friends around the place. She gets headaches, she says. Sometimes Emma comes but Gran doesn't really like her much, and it's always a bit tense. We spend most of the time in my room. Once she came and both Mummy and Gran were out so we spent the whole afternoon in the bath washing our hair and putting on scent and painting our toenails with silver polish. When I'm in Emma's house, it doesn't seem to matter what we do. Her mother's out most of the time, working. She edits a magazine. And the au pair is usually quite fun and lets us cook and make disgusting puddings.'

She stopped, giving Rory opportunity to comment in some way on this flood of confidence but he said nothing. After a bit, Lucy went on. 'It's so different here. You can do anything, and if there's nothing to do, you can go out and shop and walk about, or go to the beach, or go exploring, or go out at night and nobody stops you. And here they all call me duck or darling, but at the same time they treat me like a grown-up. As though I were a person, not a child. Gran and Mummy call me Lucy. Just that. But I never feel I'm a proper person. I'm fourteen now, and sometimes I feel I've done nothing except go to school. It wouldn't be so bad if I had a brother or a sister. Specially a brother. Because just being with women

465

all the time can be dreadfully lowering. They talk about such unimportant things, like clothes, or restaurants or other people . . .'

'Where do you go to school?'

'It's called Stanbrook. Quite near where we live. I get the tube. It's only two stops. I really like it, and the teachers and the Head, and I met Emma there. And we do things like go to concerts and art exhibitions, and we go swimming and do games in the park. But it's all girls, and sometimes I think it would be really fun to go to a comprehensive. You'd meet so many different people.'

Rory said, 'How about your father?'

'I don't see him much because Mummy doesn't like me seeing him and, anyway, he's got a new wife and she doesn't want me around much either. I've got a grandfather, called Jeffrey Sutton. He's Carrie's father. But he lives in Cornwall with a new young wife and two little children.'

'Can't you go and stay there?'

'Yes, I could, but Gran's bitter about him and unforgiving, and his name is scarcely ever mentioned. One day I'll be really brave and strong and say I want to go and stay. But I suppose I'll have to wait until I'm a bit older to do that.'

'You don't have to wait. You have to do it *now*.'

'I think,' said Lucy sadly, 'I haven't the nerve. I simply hate rows and asserting myself. I did have one row with Mummy and Gran about having my ears pierced. Everyone at school has got pierced ears but they wouldn't let me. It's such a little thing, but the row went on for days and I couldn't bear it so I just caved in. I'm dreadfully feeble about things like that.'

Rory said, 'I think you'd look good with pierced

ears. You could have gold rings.' He grinned. 'Like me.'

'I wouldn't just have one. I'd have two.'

'Get them done here. There's a jeweller in Kingsferry.'

'My mother would die.'

'Your mother's in America.'

'How did you know that?'

'Elfrida told Ma and she told me.'

'She's got a boyfriend. He's called Randall Fischer. She's in Florida with him. She went for Christmas. That's why I came here with Carrie. I was asked too, but I didn't want to go. I'd just have been in the way. Besides,' she added, 'I don't really like him much.'

He said nothing to this, and it occurred to Lucy that he was very good at listening. She wondered if this gift came naturally to him, or whether his father had taught him the importance of silence at the appropriate time. And she remembered that day in London, when Carrie had suddenly appeared, just when Lucy was yearning for a confidante. She had thought that she could talk to Carrie, could open her heart to her, but Carrie, returning from Austria, had been obscurely different and clearly in no mood for confidences. Withdrawn, perhaps, was the word, as though some part of her had stayed in another place. But Rory Kennedy was different. Rory had time to listen and was sympathetic. Lucy found herself filled with grateful affection.

She said, 'I'm sorry. I didn't mean to say all this. It's just that it's all been so much fun. Being with Elfrida and Oscar, and going to do reels, and all the other people of my own age. And thinking that Christmas this year is going to be a real one, and not just eating roast pheasant with Mummy and Gran, or even going out to some boring restaurant because they can't be bothered to cook. And the snow and everything. And the church. And the fairy-lights going up . . .'

Her voice trailed away. She was finished. There was nothing more to say. She thought of the flat, and London, then stuffed away the image at the back of her mind and slammed down an imaginary lid. There was no point in remembering. No point in thinking about having to return. No point in spoiling this moment, this hour, this day. Now.

He was watching her. She met his eyes and smiled. He said, 'Do you want to come sledging this afternoon?'

'Are you going?'

'Why not? I'll ring up some of the others. We'll go to the golf course – there are some really good slopes.' He glanced at his watch. 'It's nearly twelve. We'll need to get off early before it gets dark. How about you come back home with me now and we'll get my ma to give us some food and get hold of the others?'

Lucy said, 'I haven't got a sledge.'

'We've got three or four in the garage. You can borrow one of those.' He pulled himself to his feet. 'Come on.'

'But won't your mother . . . ?'

'*No*, she won't mind, and there'll be enough food to feed an army. There always is.' He reached down, took Lucy's arm and hauled her to her feet. 'Stop being so worried,' he told her. 'Stop putting difficulties in your own way.'

'Is that what I'm doing?'

'Not any more.'

Elfrida

Elfrida

 The Kingsferry shopping expedition had been highly successful: not only had Sam and Carrie brought back with them a load of cardboard boxes stuffed with food – vegetables, cereal, fruit and Christmas goodies – but boxes of wine, crates of beer, mixers, Coke and six bottles of Famous Grouse whisky. Moreover, they had managed to run down the whereabouts of the gents' outfitter, where Sam had kitted himself out with a wardrobe of country clothes: corduroy trousers, warm shirts, a thick ribbed sweater, a pair of Timberland boots and a Barbour jacket. As well, no doubt – but Elfrida was too discreet to enquire – underclothes, socks, and the basic essentials necessary for shaving, washing, cleaning his teeth and generally rendering himself sweet-smelling and presentable.

Sam put on his new clothes for lunch, and they all admired his suave, casual appearance. After lunch, he shrugged himself into his Barbour, and he and Oscar set off to walk to the golf club, where Sam had made an appointment with the secretary because he wished to talk about the possibility of becoming a member. Elfrida, watching them stride side by side down the snowy pavement, thought it was good for Oscar to have a bit of masculine company.

She and Carrie were left to prepare for the arrival, at four o'clock, of Sir James Erskine-Earle. The first thing to decide was where they should give him tea. Elfrida thought the kitchen – no point in standing on ceremony – but Carrie said that that was all right for someone you *knew*, but perhaps Sir James would be a bit put out if asked to put his knees under the kitchen table and drink his tea from a mug.

Elfrida saw her point. 'Then we'll have it in the sitting room.'

'What? All perched around the fireside?'

'Why not?'

'Men hate perching, unless they're trained to it like vicars. They can't manage cups, saucers and fairy-cakes all at the same time. Let's have it on the table in the bay window – all laid out and proper, like Mother used to do.'

'I shall have to find a dainty tablecloth.'

'Bet there's one lurking in Mrs Snead's cupboard. Shall I make some scones?'

'*Can* you?' Elfrida was impressed.

'Of course. And you can go and buy iced fancies from the baker.'

Elfrida put on her blanket coat and went. The baker didn't sell iced fancies, but had gingerbread instead, so she bought one and a jar of homemade bramble jelly.

'Are you having a party, Mrs Phipps?' asked the girl, giving Elfrida her change. And Elfrida said, no, not exactly, just somebody coming for afternoon tea.

Back at the Estate House, Carrie's scones were already in the oven and smelling delicious. Elfrida produced the gingerbread and the jam, found a tray and stacked it with the best, if mismatched, plates, cups and saucers. She found a sugar bowl and a butter dish, even a butter knife.

'We're going to be very genteel,' she said. She found teaspoons, and gave the inside of the teapot a good scour.

Upstairs, she unearthed a tablecloth from the linen cupboard. Starched and ironed, it looked quite festive spread upon the old table. She laid out five plates and small knives, the cups and saucers, the butter dish and the jam jar. There weren't any flowers, but perhaps Sir James Erskine-Earle wouldn't mind too much about that.

She turned from the table with the empty tray in her hand, and looked across the room at her little picture, which, perhaps, after today, would be gone for ever. It was hanging very slightly crooked so she went over to set it straight, giving it a loving pat, as though it were a child encouraged to be on its best behaviour.

'If I don't have time to say goodbye,' she told it, 'I'll say goodbye now. It's been lovely having you.'

Oscar and Sam returned from the golf club in good time and good heart. The interview with the club secretary had been satisfactory. Sam had been told that there was a waiting list for membership, but as he was going to be a resident of Buckly it would probably be possible to jump the queue. They had been introduced to the captain and a few other members, had admired portraits and trophies, then walked home.

Oscar had clearly enjoyed his outing. Recalling his only other visit to the golf club, which had ended so disastrously with a panic-stricken escape, Elfrida gave silent thanks and wanted to hug him. Instead, she went upstairs to comb her flaming hair and put on another layer of lipstick.

When he came, on the dot of four o'clock, Sir James Erskine-Earle was something of a surprise. The front-door bell shrilled and Elfrida ran down to let him in. She was a little taken aback to be faced by a man so young, and although he had come straight from the meeting about the war memorial he was attired as though for gardening, in elderly tweed knickerbockers and a jacket that seemed to have lost most of its buttons. His shirt collar was frayed and his V-necked pullover had a small hole in it. When she opened the door, he removed his tweed cap and she saw that his mousy hair was cut like a schoolboy's.

'Mrs Phipps?'

'Yes. Sir James.' They shook hands. 'Please come in.' Leading him upstairs, she said, 'It is so good of you to come at such short notice.'

'Not at all.' He had a charming voice and an ingenuous smile. 'I always enjoy occasions when I am asked to cast my eye over something special.'

She led him into the sitting room and introduced him to the others, who were all standing about looking ill at ease, as though it were they whom Sir James Erskine-Earle had come to appraise. 'Oscar Blundell. Carrie Sutton, my niece, and Sam Howard, who is coming to run the old woollen mill in Buckly.'

'We spoke on the phone. How splendid to meet you. You're with Sturrock & Swinfield? I was at Eton with one of the Swinfields, but I think not your chairman.' He looked about him. 'This is a most surprising house.

From the outside one has no idea of its splendour. It was part of Corrydale, I understand.'

'Yes, but hasn't been for some years,' Oscar told him. 'Perhaps you knew my uncle, Hector McLellan?'

'Not well. I was working in London for some years. I didn't come north until my father died and we all came to live at Kingsferry. Bit of a culture shock for my family but they seem to have taken it in their stride.' He moved, inevitably, over to the window, as newcomers always did. It was dark but Elfrida had not drawn the curtains, and across the street the twinkling Christmas fairy-lights shone like jewels against the old stone face of the church. 'What an outlook. And so close to the church. You must be able to hear the organ from here. Marvellous instrument. We're so fortunate.' He turned back to face them all. 'But I mustn't waste your time rubber-necking. Where is this picture you want me to see?'

'It's . . .' Elfrida cleared her throat. 'It's here.'

'I see. In solitary state.'

'We have no other pictures.'

'May I take it down?'

'But of course.'

He crossed the room, gently took the frame in his hands and lifted it down, holding it as delicately as if it were a piece of the finest porcelain. 'What a lovely thing.' He tilted it beneath the light of the lamp that stood on Oscar's table. 'Sir David Wilkie.'

'Yes. I've always believed so.'

'A portrait of his parents. Did you know that? Painted, I suppose, about 1835.'

'I didn't know it was his parents. I thought just a sweet elderly couple.'

A silence fell. All faintly unnerved, they waited for

his verdict. Sir James Erskine-Earle took his time, first reaching into the pocket of his reprehensible jacket to bring out a pair of rimless spectacles. When he put them on, he resembled a penniless young student. Perhaps a medical student, for his hands were as sensitive as a surgeon's. Peering, he examined, touched with his fingertips, turned the painting over and closely inspected the back.

Finally, he laid the picture carefully down on Oscar's table. 'How did you come by it, Mrs Phipps?'

'It was a present. A long time ago – thirty years – from a friend.'

'And do you know where he bought it?'

'I think in a junk shop in Chichester.'

'Yes.' He nodded. 'That figures.'

'I've . . . I've always believed – been led to believe – that it's an original. But I've never had it appraised or insured.'

He looked at her, the reflected light from the lamp flashing from his spectacles, and he smiled. That engaging, youthful smile. He turned to lean against the table and took off his spectacles. He said, 'I am really sorry, but it's not the original. It's a copy.'

The stunned silence that followed was because nobody could think of anything to say.

'It is a most charming and beautifully executed work, but it isn't the original.'

Oscar found his voice. 'How can you know?'

'For one thing, it's not signed. The style, the subject, I agree, are unmistakably Wilkie's, but there is no signature. The other reason I know that it is a copy is that, oddly enough, the original passed through the Boothby's saleroom in Bond Street only about a year ago. It went to a dealer from the United States who was bidding for some museum or other. It was larger than your little painting, Mrs Phipps, which leads me to believe that this copy was never intended as a forgery, but more as a work of respect and admiration. A student, perhaps, wishing to emulate the master's style. It is certainly an extraordinary simulation – the brushwork, the colour, the light. A beautiful piece of art. If imitation is the sincerest form of flattery, one wonders who set himself to embark upon such a painstaking task.'

Again, silence fell upon the room. Finally, Elfrida made herself ask the dreaded question. 'What is it worth, Sir James?'

'Please. Jamie.'

'Well – Jamie – what do you think it is worth?'

'If it had been the original, I should have said in the region of eighty-five thousand pounds. I can't remember the *exact* sum it went for, but something like that.'

'And as it is only a copy?'

'A thousand? Maybe more, maybe less. It would depend on the market. Nothing is worth anything unless somebody wants it.'

A thousand. A copy, and worth only a thousand. Elfrida's little nest egg, her insurance against an impoverished and lonely future. A thousand. In a funny way, for herself, she didn't particularly mind. There was no point in selling it, so she could go on enjoying it for the rest of her life. But for Oscar she knew an agonising disappointment. All her plans for buying Hughie out and ensuring Oscar's security were to come to nothing. All her dreams reduced to dust, to rubbish. She saw them as though being swept away, out of reach, so much flotsam in a swift-flowing river. Gone.

For a dreadful moment she thought she might be about to burst into tears. In some despair she turned to Carrie, and Carrie's beautiful dark eyes were upon her, warm with sympathy and understanding. Elfrida opened her mouth to say something, but there were no words, and Carrie came to her rescue.

'I think,' said Carrie, 'that I shall go downstairs and boil a kettle, and we'll all have a restoring cup of tea.'

And then Sam spoke, for the first time since he had been introduced to Jamie Erskine-Earle. 'I'll come with you, lend you a hand.'

Elfrida knew perfectly well that it didn't take two people to boil a kettle but she was grateful to Sam for his tact in removing his presence from a difficult situation. She found herself wishing that Sir James Erskine-Earle would remove himself too. Asked, he had come to appraise her little painting, and she knew that it wasn't his fault it was a fake, but his knowledge and expertise had spoiled so much, and now Oscar would have no alternative but to sell his half of the house. She didn't mind so much about Sam having it. But she minded dreadfully about Oscar *not* having it.

When the others had gone, there was a pregnant silence. Perhaps Jamie sensed Elfrida's disappointment for he said, again, 'I am so sorry.'

She knew impatience; with herself and with him. 'Oh, for goodness' sake. It's not your fault.'

Carefully, precisely, he rehung the little picture. The old lady in her yellow shawl gazed benevolently down at him, as Elfrida found herself incapable of doing. He said, 'At least . . . it will continue to give you joy.'

'It will never be quite the same as before.'

Oscar, sensing tension, moved into the conversation.

'It is very precious to Elfrida, nevertheless. I am relieved that she has no reason to let it go.'

'Oh, Oscar, I have *every* reason. It's simply a *picture*. But not for a thousand. That sort of money is laughable.'

'Elfrida. It will be all right.'

She turned her back on both of them and went to the fire, in need of something to do that might assuage her disappointment. She took a log from the basket and hurled it on to the flames. She stood, watching it catch and flare up.

And then, behind her, Jamie spoke again. 'I'm sorry, I do hope you don't think I'm being curious, but who is the owner of that interesting little clock?'

For an instant, Elfrida thought that she had misheard. She turned to frown at him in puzzlement. 'The *clock?*'

'It caught my eye. So unusual . . .'

Oscar told him, 'It is Elfrida's.'

'I wonder, may I look?'

Elfrida nodded. She moved aside. Jamie put on his spectacles again, came to her side and took the little clock down from its place in the middle of the mantelshelf. For the second time, she and Oscar watched in silence while he examined it with minute care. Elfrida decided that if he told her it was a worthless bibelot, no more, she would brain him with the coal shovel.

He said, 'A travelling chronometer. Marvellous. How did you come by this little treasure?'

'Do you mean treasure as sentimental or treasure as in trove?'

He answered, politely, 'I'm not sure.'

Brusquely, she told him, 'It was left to me by an elderly godfather. An old sea-faring man.' And then, knowing that she sounded thoroughly cross, relented a little. 'You can see, one dial is for hours, one for minutes and one for seconds. I have to wind it every day. I suppose I could get it fitted with a battery, but it seems—'

'Heaven forbid. It's far too rare.'

'Rare? Surely it's just an old-fashioned sea-going clock?'

'Practical. But handsome, too.'

She looked at it, in his hands, and all at once the clock took on a new lustre, as everyday and familiar objects sometimes do when admired by another. The outside leather was worn, but inside still rich and dark; and the lid, which folded across like the cover of a book, was lined with a bruised pad of velvet, the colour of coral. Around the circular face, which contained the dials, the leather was decorated with a wreath of miniature golden leaves, and this pattern was repeated around the edge of the frame. The key, the hinges, the tiny locks were brass.

She said, 'I don't even know how old it is. Perhaps you can tell me.'

'Alas, I'm not a clock expert. But,' he added, 'I have a colleague who *is*. If you want – if you will let me – I can show it to him.'

'Why?'

'Because I think it is special.'

'How special?'

'We used the word treasure.'

'You mean, you think it's worth something?'

'I would rather not say. I'm not sufficiently special-ised.'

'It wouldn't be worth seventy-five thousand pounds, would it?' she asked bluntly, expecting a rueful shake of the head or, even, derisive laughter.

But Jamie Erskine-Earle did not laugh. He said, 'I really don't know. Mrs Phipps, would you – would you let me take it away with me? If I can't get hold of my colleague I can speak to him on the telephone, or send him a photograph of the clock. I shall, of course, give you a receipt for it, and will keep it under lock and key.'

Suddenly it was ludicrous. 'In Hampshire,' she told him, 'in my little cottage in Dibton, it sat on the mantel-piece in my downstairs sitting room and I never even locked the door.'

'Then may I congratulate you on your good luck. It's not insured,' he added, and he was stating a fact, not asking a question.

'No, of course it's not. It's just a little thing I've had for years and take everywhere with me.'

'If I may reiterate, a very special little thing. May I take it with me?'

'Of course.'

'If I could have a box – or something to wrap it in? My handkerchief is not exactly suitable.'

Oscar went to his table, pulled out a drawer and unearthed a sheet of bubble wrap, which he had salvaged from a parcel of new books.

'Will this do?'

'Perfect. And a sheet of writing paper for a receipt? I usually carry a pad of official forms but, of course, today I have left them at home.'

He gave Oscar the clock, which Oscar wrapped into a bulbous bundle, and Jamie Erskine-Earle sat at the desk and wrote out his receipt. 'I had better keep that,' Oscar told him. 'Elfrida is inclined to lose things.' And he stowed it away in the top pocket of his jacket.

'There's just one thing,' said Elfrida.

'Yes, Mrs Phipps?'

'Don't let's talk much about the clock when Sam and Carrie come back. We all got too worked up about the David Wilkie, and I couldn't bear raised and dashed hopes again. Can we just say that you think I should insure it, and you're going to give me a valuation?'

'Of course. A splendid explanation. And one, moreover, that happens to be true.'

That evening, trying to do something about supper, Elfrida felt that she had spent the entire afternoon on a roller coaster. And because of all the excitement, disappointment and rekindled expectations, she had clean forgotten about Lucy. She was stirring a bolognese sauce distractedly, when Lucy turned up, coming into the kitchen by way of the back door.

Elfrida glanced at the old kitchen clock. It was nearly seven o'clock. She stared at Lucy, trying to remember what the child had been doing all day.

Lucy said, 'Yes, it's me.'

'Oh, darling, I'm sorry.'

'You look as though I was the *very* last person you expected to see.'

'I'm doing my preoccupied act. So much has been happening here and you just floated out of my mind. But now you've floated in again, which is delightful.'

'What's been happening?' Lucy pulled off her woollen hat, then began to undo the fastenings of her jacket. 'Have I missed something?'

'Not really. Just a nice man came for tea. Carrie made scones. I think he ate most of them.'

'Who was the nice man?'

'He's called Sir James Erskine-Earle. He lives at Kingsferry House.'

Lucy said, 'I've just been to Kingsferry. With Rory.'

'I thought you'd gone sledging.'

'Yes, we did, but then it got dark so we went back to the Manse for tea; and then Rory and I went to Kingsferry.'

'Have you been shopping again?'

'No. Not exactly.'

Elfrida, her attention caught, became intrigued. Lucy's expression was secret, teasing. As though she couldn't stop smiling.

'You look like the Cheshire Cat. What have you been up to?'

Lucy put up a hand and tossed her long hair back from her neck. Elfrida saw the gleam of gold.

'I've had my ears pierced. The jeweller in Kingsferry did it for me. Rory took me. And he bought me the sleepers for Christmas. Real jewellery. Earrings.'

'Oh, darling . . .'

'I've been wanting them for ages.'

'Let me look.'

'But Mummy wouldn't let me.'

'They're wonderful. So grown-up. They make you look so grown-up. What a generous present.'

'I don't think,' said Lucy, 'I've ever been given anything I wanted more.'

Lucy

Lucy

Still Wednesday 20 December
I think this has been one of the
best days of my life. Lots and
lots of snow everywhere and it
all looks so pretty. This morning I did Christmas
shopping, and then when I got back Rory was
here, talking to Elfrida, with the television set he
is going to lend me. He carried it up to my room,
and made it work and then we sat and talked,
and somehow he was so easy to talk to that I
just told him everything; about boring London
and having to live in the flat, and Mummy and
Gran and Randall Fischer. And about Dad and
Marilyn, and about the family in Cornwall. It
was so wonderful having someone listen and
not interrupt and keep trying to cheer me up
or jolly me along, or even to say I was talking
a lot of rubbish. Or didn't know what I was
talking about.*
He just listened.
When I'd run out of things to say, we drove

back to the Manse and Mrs Kennedy made us
beefburgers and Rory rang some friends and
we all went sledging on the golf course, which
was tremendous fun and totally exhausting. We
sledged till it got dark and then went back to the
Manse for tea, and then Rory asked his father if
we could borrow the car again, and Mr Kennedy
said yes, and Rory took me to Kingsferry. It is a
very old and unexpected sort of town, with lots
of shops, and we parked the car and went to the
jeweller, and the man there pierced my ears, in
a moment, and it didn't hurt a bit, and fixed in
little gold rings called sleepers.

I had told Rory that I wasn't allowed to
have them at home, and he said I wasn't at
home now, I was with him, and he paid for
the piercing and the rings and said it is his
Christmas present for me.

On the way back in the car we talked some
more, and I feel as though I have reached a
turning-point or a watershed. Rory says I have
to remember a number of things. These are
the things.

I get good marks at school, so I am
not stupid.

If I don't assert myself a bit, nobody else is
going to.

I have to assert myself by reasoned
conversation, not sulks.

If I want to go to Cornwall to see my
grandfather and Serena and Amy and Ben,
then I should go. There is absolutely nothing
to stop me. I can make my own arrangements,

get my grandfather to invite me and
simply go.

I must be more enterprising. I can take care
of myself. I know about things like Ecstasy tablets
at parties; and about drunks and druggies and
flashers and sex maniacs and lonely old men who
come and talk to you at bus stations.

Perhaps I should think about going to a
co-educational boarding-school to do my A levels.
Last two years of school. I'd never thought of
that. I shall put the idea into Mummy's head
and make her talk it through. I shall get Miss
Maxwell-Brown on my side. And that would only
be two years away.

Just having something new to plan and look
forward to makes me feel much more determined.

I wish I had a brother like Rory.

No, I don't. Because if he was my brother it
wouldn't be the same.

My earrings don't hurt. When Gran and
Mummy see them they will know that I have
changed. That I am doing what I want. That I
can make my own decisions. I'm not a little child
any more.

They had someone for tea here called Sir
James Erskine-Earle. He has taken Elfrida's clock
to value it for insurance. Carrie said he ate
six scones.

Tomorrow is the first day of the rest
of my life.

Sam

Sam

Sam opened his eyes to darkness and bitter cold. It was the cold that had woken him and he realised that his eiderdown had slipped off the bed, and that he was shivering beneath the inadequate comfort of two blankets and an icy, monogrammed linen sheet. The curtains at his window were, as always, drawn back, and the window open – though not very wide – and a blast of air assailed him, chill as the sensation on opening a deep freeze. During the night the temperature had dropped to an uncomfortable low.

He heaved himself over, reached down for the quilt and dragged it back into place. He was still cold, but its soft, downy weight was a comfort. Waiting for warmth, he reached out a hand, turned on his bedside light and looked at his watch. Half past seven in the morning.

His room, familiar now, lay about him, the corners deep in shadow. There was not much furniture: a huge wardrobe, which contained all he possessed for the moment, and a Victorian washstand doing duty as a dressing-table – it had a liver-coloured marble top and on it stood a large, flowered bowl and a ewer for water. The only mirror was inside the wardrobe door, and there was one small, ornate chair. Not a room for working in, or a room for sitting in, but perfectly adequate for the business of sleeping.

And making businesslike calls on his mobile phone.

He lay, thawing slowly, and wondered why it all rendered him such satisfaction. He decided that the proportions of the room were exactly right, the empty walls undemanding, the threadbare curtains of faded cretonne, long enough to lie in festoons upon the worn carpet, reminiscent of his mother's curtains in the old house at Radley Hill. They were hung by brass rings upon a brass pole with pineapple finials, and when drawn made a satisfactory clatter.

This sound brought back his mother's voice. 'Darling, wake up. It's nearly time for breakfast.'

Nostalgia, perhaps, but at its best.

The whole house was the same. The spaciousness, the handsome half-empty rooms, with their elaborate cornices and tall panelled doors. The shallow-stepped staircase, rising in flights to the attics, with its banister of polished Baltic pine, the old-fashioned, but perfectly recognisable kitchen; the bathrooms, panelled in white-painted tongue-and-groove, complete with original Victorian fittings, and lavatory cisterns whose chains and handles had PULL written on them.

It had all felt, from that first embarrassing evening, a bit like coming home.

From the first moment, the house had appealed to Sam. It had spoken to him, welcomed him. He thought back over the extraordinarily coincidental chain of events that had brought him here, and at this particular time, then left him marooned so that he had no choice but to stay. With hindsight, it seemed as though it had all been carefully mapped out by fate. Some – hopefully benign – being; the influence of his star sign, perhaps, or the incomprehensible magnetism of ancient ley lines.

Meeting Hughie McLellan in London had been the first link in the chain. Being handed the key of Hughie's house in Creagan. Tossing a coin as he had sat in his car outside the church hall in Buckly. If it had come up heads, he would have driven straight back to Inverness and, in all likelihood, would have been able to traverse the road across the Black Isle before the snow rendered it impassable. But, instead, it had come up tails, and he had diverted to drive to Creagan.

If Sam had found the house shuttered and unoccupied, as he had expected it to be, he would not have dallied. Simply locating the place was all he had had in mind, and its position, size and air of solid Victorian dignity would have been enough to ensure that he returned for a more detailed viewing. But it hadn't been empty. Lights had blazed from upstairs windows and, curiosity aroused, he had left his car by the pavement's edge, walked up the path and rung the bell.

After that he was caught, and there was no going back.

Now, he had lived here for two days, in the company of four other remotely connected people, and would be staying until Christmas was a thing of the past. He had intended spending this time sorting out his own private priorities for the mill, working with laptop and calculator, but idleness was forced upon him because laptop, calculator, files, essential telephone numbers and papers had been left in his hotel bedroom in Inverness.

All he had brought to the meeting in Buckly were his mobile phone, a slim briefcase and the key to the Estate House.

Because work was impossible he had found it extraordinarily easy to switch off and slow down into a state of mind he had not experienced for years. Horizons shrank. Priorities altered. It felt a little like being on board a ship, isolated from the rest of the world but intensely involved with the other passengers. Strangers, who were slowly becoming as close as the family he no longer possessed. The house, like that ship, contained them all, and did so with a certain grace, as though content to have the spacious rooms filled once more, doors standing open, fires lit, voices calling, footsteps on the stairs.

A good house, and Sam wanted it. That was the problem. He wished to buy it from Hughie and Oscar, and have it for his own. Its location was perfect – it would take him only twenty minutes, no more, to drive the empty roads to the mill each morning and home again at the end of the day's work. He could step out of the front door and walk to the golf club. Short of a can of beer, a loaf of bread or a pint of milk, he had only to cross the square to the little supermarket.

As well, it would be a house with a future. His future. Owning it, Sam would never have to leave. Unlike a tiny terrace house, or a picturesque, rose-smothered cottage, it was capable of accommodating anything he chose to throw at it. It was this awareness of longevity that most attracted him. He would soon be forty. He didn't want to go on moving, buying and selling, starting anew. He wanted this to be the last start. He wanted to stay. Here.

But half of it belonged to Oscar Blundell, and this

was where he and Elfrida lived. It and each other seemed to be all they had. A dull fellow, Hughie had told Sam. My cousin is a dull fellow. But Sam didn't think Oscar was dull in the least. He liked him enormously and this made nothing easier.

If Sam had been Hughie he would have kept his mouth shut about Elfrida's little picture. He would never have taken the trouble to telephone Janey in London and find out the whereabouts of the local Boothby's representative, Sir James Erskine-Earle. The thought of selling the painting had occurred to Elfrida, but she was so vaguely unworldly about practical matters that she would never have got round to doing anything dynamic on her own. At the end of the day, the visit from James Erskine-Earle had solved nothing because the painting was a fake anyway. So they were all back where they had started. In a way Sam wished the David Wilkie had been rare, authentic and worth a million so that he could put away his own pipe-dreams and go off and look for somewhere else to live.

And yet ... he couldn't get rid of the feeling that here, in this square, unadorned, solid Victorian town house, was where he was destined to settle and spend the rest of his days.

Useless reflections. With some effort he put them out of his mind, got out of bed and went to close the window. His room was at the back of the Estate House, and in the light of the street-lamp that stood by the wooden gate he saw the terraced garden climbing up to the stand of pines, all petrified with cold, glittering with frost. There was not a breath of wind. No sound.

As a boy in Yorkshire, he had, from time to time, risen very early and gone out for a long hike up into

497

the moors to some elevated crag from which he could watch the sun rise. No dawn was quite the same as another, and the filling of the sky with light had always seemed a miracle. He remembered returning home, after these early expeditions, running down grassy paths and leaping streams, bursting with high spirits and energy, aware that much of his happiness came of knowing that a huge breakfast would be waiting for him when he finally got home.

It was a long time since he had watched a sunrise. Today, the shortest day of the year, was perhaps as good a morning as any to repeat the experience. He dressed, laced his boots, pulled on his Barbour, felt in the pockets for his thick leather driving gloves. He went quietly out of his room, closing the door behind him with elaborate care, then downstairs. In the empty kitchen, he found Horace snoozing in his basket.

'Want a walk?'

Recovered from his encounter with the Rottweiler, Horace did. Sam found Elfrida's shopping list, scribbled a note to her then went down the hall and took from the coatstand his tweed cap and a muffler which did not belong to him but felt comforting knotted around his neck. He turned the key of the front door, opened it and stepped out into the still, dark, paralysing cold of the morning. Iced snow crunched beneath his boots. As he opened the gate, he heard the sound of an engine and saw the great gritting lorry, headlights beaming, snowplough secured, set off across the square and down the street towards the main road.

Sam and the dog set off in the other direction.

They went by way of the golf club and the beach, leaving the street-lamps of the town behind them. The sky was clear, and a single star hung in the dark heavens, but mist lay along the distant margins of the sea. The tide was far out, the sand frozen and shallow rock pools hard as iron. The wind, stirring from the north, had an edge to it like a knife, and he pulled the soft folds of his muffler up and around his chin. He thought of other lands on this latitude, only a bit south of sixty degrees. To the west, beyond the Atlantic, Labrador, the Hudson Bay, Alaska. To the east, Scandinavia and the wastes of Siberia. There, a man stepping out of doors for five minutes in midwinter would probably freeze to death. And yet here he was, striding like any holiday-maker down a beach with a dog at his heels, not unduly perturbed by the cold.

The Gulf Stream was, indeed, a marvellous invention.

At a brisk pace he covered the length of the beach, then turned inland. He climbed over the dunes, crossed the track, the two fairways of the golf course, then strode up the steep slope that lay beyond, a winding path that rose uphill between thick clumps of gorse. By the time he reached the top he was warm with exertion, and Horace was panting furiously. He came to a fence and a stile. By now the dark of the sky had paled to grey, and the star was gone. He leaned against the stile, sheltered from the north by the thick windbreak of the gorse, and turned to face the sea. He saw the long line of the horizon, the bay sweeping out to the point where the lighthouse still blinked. Beyond it, to the south-east, the sky was stained with pink, the coming light diffused by mist. It was as good a viewpoint as any. He looked at his watch, and saw that it was eight forty. He sat on the wooden step of the stile and waited.

The dog sat at his knee. Sam pulled off his glove, laid

his hand on the dog's head and stroked the soft, silky fur, the velvety ears. The world, the empty universe, belonged at that moment to just the two of them. From this small elevation, it seemed limitless, new-minted, pristine, as though only yesterday had been the day of the Creation.

He remembered, for no particular reason, that afternoon in London when he had walked down the King's Road in the wet dusk, the streets clogged with shoppers and traffic, and told himself that there was no person in the world who would expect a Christmas present from him. So, he had arrived in Creagan totally unprepared. But now he must get busy so that on Christmas morning he would have packages to hand out. Four of them. There were four. Or maybe five, including the mysterious Mrs Snead whom he had not yet encountered. Oscar, Elfrida, Lucy. Carrie.

Carrie.

Losing Deborah, closing up the apartment, leaving New York and returning to London and his new job, the last thing on his mind had been the possibility of another woman coming into his life. Right now he needed an emotional involvement like he needed a hole in the head. But Carrie had been waiting for him, the last link in that extraordinary chain of coincidence, compounding the sensation that he was a helpless pawn in some other person's game. He had walked in the snow through the gate of the Estate House, up the path and pressed the bell. And it was Carrie who, eventually, had opened the door to him.

Carrie, with her smooth cap of chestnut hair, her dark and expressive eyes, her slenderness, her long neck. Her slanting eyebrows, the fascinating mole at one end of her mouth. Her voice, deep-toned, with an underlying suggestion of laughter so that he could never be sure when she teased or when she was serious. Her wrists were narrow, her hands long-fingered and capable, with unpainted nails, and she wore on her right hand a sapphire and diamond ring that looked as though it might have once been pressed upon her by some besotted man, mad to marry her. Or perhaps left, as a bequest, by an adoring elderly relation.

She was totally without artifice. If she had nothing to say, she said nothing. If she aired an opinion, it was deliberate, considered, intelligent. She did not seem to know the meaning of small-talk, and while others chatted over meals or an evening drink she was always attentive but often silent. Her relationship with Elfrida and Lucy, however, was deeply affectionate and caring. With the girl, Carrie was protective but not smothering. Lucy came and went, but always there were endearments for her, casual hugs, a listening ear. Laughter.

As for Sam, he found it impossible to guess what Carrie thought of him. She was totally at ease, in charge of the situation, but at the same time reserved to the point of withdrawal. The one time he had had her to himself for more than five minutes – when they had driven to Kingsferry to do the huge supermarket shop – he had thought that he could break through this barrier, but every time the conversation veered to Carrie and her private life she had fallen silent, then turned it in a different direction. When Sam, with some difficulty, had run to earth the gents' outfitter in Kingsferry, where he had to buy himself a capsule country wardrobe, he had expected that she would come into the shop with him, make suggestions, even joke about his choice of boxer shorts and pyjamas (which the gents' outfitter called Intimate Apparel) or insist on choosing Sam some dreadful and unsuitable tie. But she did none of these things. Instead, she crossed the road to the ironmonger where she had to buy Elfrida a new baking dish and a pudding bowl. So Sam did his intimate shopping on his own, and when he got back to the car she was waiting for him, reading *The Times* and not overly interested in his purchases.

He found himself wondering if she had once been married, but knew that he could never pluck up the nerve to ask such a question. It was, after all, nothing to do with him. That first evening, while they sat and waited for Oscar and Elfrida to return from their party, she had imparted a little casual information about herself. She enlarged on nothing, volunteered no gratuitous information, and he was left with the sense of a strong door firmly shut between them and that nothing was going to persuade Carrie to open it.

About Lucy, she was more open.

She had spoken, as well, about her own father, when her voice warmed, her lovely eyes shone and she became quite animated and informative. Her father was called Jeffrey and lived, with his second and much younger wife, in Cornwall. 'He's an amazing man,' Carrie had said. 'The most giving of men. He stayed with my mother, in some unhappiness, until Nicola and I were both adult and on our own, and only then did he light out and leave us all, and go off with Serena. If Lucy had had a father like Jeffrey things would be so different for her. He wasn't just my father, he was my best friend. He opened every door, never stopped praising and encouraging. With a man like that behind me, I always believed I could do anything.'

Anything. But sometime, somewhere along the line, something had gone wrong. And Carrie was not about to confide in Sam.

The less she spoke, the less she gave away, the more he longed to know. He wondered if this obsession was the beginning of falling in love with her. Otherwise why should it matter so much? And what was the point of falling in love with a woman already deeply committed to her career and her ill-assorted family; who would never, in a thousand years, jettison the lot and come to live in the north of Scotland with Sam Howard. Quite apart from the fact that he was still married to Deborah.

Horace shifted and whined: he was growing cold. Sam was cold too, but did not move. For when he looked again he saw that the faint shell pink had exploded into an aureole of red and yellow; vaporous streaks like flames. And over the shallow hills of the distant headland inched the first sliver of an orange sun. The curved rim of dazzling light touched the shifting sea, smudged shadows on the undulations of the sands and drained darkness from the sky so that gradually it was no longer sapphire blue, but faded to the colour of aquamarines.

He watched, and lost all sense of time as the orange orb sailed up, out from behind the far side of the world. And it was the same fresh miracle that it had always been, and he forgot about being cold. The pinprick blink from the lighthouse, all at once, ceased. The new day had begun, and after today the days would start to grow longer, and then it would be another year, and Sam, thinking about it, found himself unable to imagine what it might hold in store for him.

He walked back to Creagan at a brisk pace, following the

narrow path that led along the top of the snow-covered links. The mist was dissolving and the sky, a pale, pure blue, quite cloudless. By the time he reached the first of the houses, he saw that the morning was already on its way: cars came and went, shops were open, the first of the shoppers out with their baskets and plastic bags. The butcher was sweeping snow from his front step, and a young mother pulled her bundled baby along in a little wooden sledge.

He was ravenously hungry.

Letting himself into the house, he realised that it, too, was a hive of busy activity. From upstairs came the drone of a Hoover, and a female voice singing her version of an old Beatles song:

'*I love you, yeah yeah yeah . . .*'

The redoubtable Mrs Snead, no doubt, come to muck them all out.

From the open kitchen door flooded light, and the mouthwatering smells of bacon and coffee. He unclipped Horace's lead, took off his outer clothes and went through the open door. There he found only Carrie, sitting surrounded by the detritus of other people's breakfast. She was drinking coffee and reading *The Times*, but looked up and saw him and said, 'Good morning.'

That first evening, a mere two days ago, when he had so gracelessly barged in out of the dark and the snow, clutching Hughie McLellan's key, he had been knocked sideways by the unexpected glamour of the girl who had opened the door to him. She had only just risen from a bed of sickness and because of this had looked pale, frail and intensely vulnerable. He had still thought her sensational. But now the flu was a thing of the past, cast off by the resilience of youth. She wore this morning a red cashmere sweater, whose bright colour rendered her vital, radiant and more attractive than ever. In his present mood of well-being, he knew a physical urge to touch her, to sweep her up into his arms, embrace her, breaking down imagined barriers and starting to talk.

'Did you have a good walk?'

Mad impulses, prudently, retreated.

'Too far, perhaps. Horace is exhausted.' Horace, slopping the water on the floor, was treating himself to a noisy drink.

'You must be frozen.'

'No. I'm warm from exertion. But starving.'

'There's bacon.' She laid the newspaper down and got to her feet.

'I guessed.'

'I'll make fresh coffee.'

'Carrie, I can do that.'

'No.' A plate sat on the warmer, covered by another plate. With oven-gloved hands, she lifted it, set it down on the table and, with a certain flourish, removed the top plate. He saw not only bacon but eggs, a sausage and a fried tomato. Everything sizzled. 'I can. You start eating.'

He looked at the feast in some amazement. 'Who cooked all this?'

'I did. I reckoned you'd be hungry.'

He felt much touched. 'You are sweet.'

'No problem.'

He sat, and buttered a slice of toast. 'Where is everybody?'

Carrie filled the kettle and plugged it in.

'Oh, around and about. They've all finished breakfast. Mrs Snead has come, and I think Elfrida's making beds. Oscar's telephoning. We have to go and fetch the Christmas tree this morning. He wondered if you would do that in your car – easier to load trees in, and Oscar's a bit nervous of driving in snow.'

'Where do I have to fetch it from?'

'The Corrydale estate. That's who he's phoning now. Some man called Charlie Miller. It's all ordered and everything but he just wanted to be sure that Charlie was around when we went.'

'We? Are you coming with me?'

'Oscar's drawn a map. I shall have to come to be your navigator. Besides, I want to go to Corrydale. Oscar's told me all about it. How his grandmother used to live there, and then his uncle, and then Hughie. And Oscar used to spend holidays there when he was a little boy. He says the grounds and the garden used to be amazing, but of course it's different now because it's an hotel. Anyway, I'd like to see it. The hotel's empty so, if Charlie Miller says we can, we could have a nose around.'

Sam, eating bacon, was filled with a silent satisfaction. He could think of no better way to spend this fine morning than driving Carrie to Corrydale, collecting the Christmas tree and having a nose around. It would be interesting to see what Hughie McLellan had once owned and squandered. But he only said, 'Right,' and went on eating, because he didn't want Carrie to sense his pleasure and start backing off.

She spooned the ground coffee into the jug and poured on the boiling water. 'Shall I make more toast?'

'That would be kind.'

She made toast, then poured coffee for him, refilled her own cup and returned to her chair. Sam wondered if they were about to spend a few companionable moments together, but inevitably they were interrupted by Lucy, running downstairs and bursting in upon them.

'Carrie, Mrs Snead says she's going to do a white wash and do you want anything done? Hello, Sam. Did you and Horace have a lovely walk?'

'We certainly did.'

'When did you go?'

'About eight. It was still dark. We saw the sun rise.'

'Oh, how lovely. I wish you'd taken me. I've never seen a proper sunrise. It must have been pretty with all the snow on the golf course. Like Switzerland or somewhere.'

Carrie said, 'Sam and I are going to Corrydale to fetch the Christmas tree. Do you want to come with us?'

'Oh . . .' Lucy made an agonised face. 'Oh, I would *love* to, but I've promised Mrs Snead I'd help her do something. So I can't. And I really *want* to go and look at Corrydale.'

Sam, loving Lucy for not coming, said, 'I'll take you another time.'

'Will you? Is that a promise? Oscar says it's the most wonderful place in the world, and that his grandmother used to have the most beautiful azaleas in every single colour. And the grounds go down to the water, too, and he used to have a boat.'

From upstairs, Mrs Snead screeched, '*Lucy!* What about that laundry? I want to get it all collected . . .'

Carrie made a comic face. 'We'd better do what we're told, otherwise we'll be in trouble. Come on, Lucy . . .'

And Sam, left on his own, drank hot fresh coffee and felt contented as a well-fed schoolboy with a treat in the offing.

*   *   *

Oscar's little map of directions to Corrydale proved to be a meticulous plan of all that lay within the protection of the boundary wall. It appeared to be a small maze of roads and drives, stands of woodland and a long shoreline. Each estate worker's house had been drawn in some detail and named: Billicliffe's house; Rose Miller's house; gamekeeper's house; Home Farm (Mains of Corrydale). The last was the gardener's house (Charlie Miller), alongside the walled garden and the tractor shed. A little way off, along another winding driveway that ran parallel to the water, and standing in some grandeur all on its own, he had drawn Corrydale House, surrounded by formal gardens and with stepped terraces leading down to the meadows on the fringe of the firth.

The map reminded Sam of the endpapers of a Winnie-the-Pooh book, but Carrie said it was a work of art and should be framed.

The road they followed took Sam and Carrie into territory where neither had ventured before. Instead of crossing the bridge to Kingsferry, they forked right before reaching this, and went by way of the old road, which headed west, winding through farmland, dipping and climbing, tunnelling down tall avenues of skeletal beech trees. All was thick with snow, but the morning had kept its promise and the sky was cloudless, the air sparkling with cold. There was little traffic, and few people were about: a tractor, chuntering across a field with a load of hay for a huddle of sheep; a woman, hanging washing out in the still, freezing air; a red post van, making its way up a rutted farm lane.

On their left lay the great sea loch, penetrating inland for fifteen miles or more. The tide was at half flood, and the water blue as summer. On the far shore, massive hills reared up into the sky, all blindingly white save where dark rock stood sheer, or corries of scree tumbled, like waterfalls of stone.

Carrie said, 'It's all huge, isn't it? Even the sky seems twice as big as it does anywhere else.' She wore a black padded parka and her fur hat, and had put on dark glasses against the glare.

'No fog or pollution, I suppose. A clarity of air. Did you know that five of the finest salmon rivers in Scotland flow into this loch?'

'Who told you that?'

'Oscar.'

'I supposed he fished them as a boy.'

'Lucky boy.'

Carrie scrutinised Oscar's map. 'I think, quite soon, we'll be there. We come to the wall first, and then the main gate's about a quarter of a mile . . .'

The boundary wall appeared, almost at once, on the left-hand side of the road. Beyond this could be seen handsome trees, carefully positioned, suggesting parkland. The main gate, when they came to it, was flanked by two towering Wellingtonias. A small lodge blew a plume of smoke into the air; there was a line of washing out in the little garden and a child's plastic tractor abandoned on the front-door step.

They saw the notice.

CORRYDALE COUNTRY
HOUSE HOTEL
AA
RAC
****

Carrie said, 'Here we go.'

Sam turned in through the gates, and the formal drive led downhill between an avenue of huge oak trees. It was ridged with the tracks of other vehicles recently come this way, and the snow barred with the blue shadows of the trees. After about a quarter of a mile, the road forked, and here stood a wooden signpost. To the right, HOTEL VISITORS. This track, unused, was white with virgin snow. Ahead, HOME FARM AND SAWMILL, so they continued on their way. Carrie scanned Oscar's map. 'Next, we come to another fork and we go left again and we see Billicliffe's house.'

'And who is Billicliffe?'

'He used to be the factor here. Elfrida and Oscar had to go and call on him to get *their* key. Elfrida told me he was a bit of an old bore and his house was a tip, and they were both a little unkind about him. And then he confounded everybody by becoming extremely ill and Oscar had to drive him to hospital. Where he is now. Here's the fork in the road so we go left.'

The tyre tracks continued. It was clearly a well-used access. There then was revealed, set back from the verge, the first of the estate workers' cottages.

'Here,' said Carrie, 'is where Major Billicliffe lives.'

Sam, curious, slowed down to take a look at it. A small, stone-built house, soundly constructed, with a rural porch and two dormer windows set in the slated roof. A short driveway led from gate to door, where wearing at least ten inches of snow, an elderly Vauxhall stood rusted, sad and abandoned. The windows of the house were tightly closed, no light showed and no smoke rose from the chimney.

'What a gloomy little place,' Carrie remarked.

'Nothing's at its best when it's desolate.'

They moved on slowly, tyres crunching in icy ruts, exploring. The road twisted and turned in charmingly random fashion. Another corner, and now Rose Miller's cottage was there, a different kettle of fish altogether: snug and trim, with lace curtains at the windows and a few cheerful hens clucking around the small garden. She had lit her fire and peat smoke filled the air with its delicious smell.

They meandered on, past the farmhouse and a farm-yard reeking with the good smell of manure, a field of sheep, then another little cottage, the gamekeeper's, with kennels and a run at the back of the house from which two spaniels appeared, barking their heads off. 'Good thing we didn't bring Horace with us,' said Carrie. 'He'd have had a heart-attack and died.'

By now the loch was in view again, with fields running down to the water. More trees, another cottage, and then the north wall of the enclosed garden, a handsome stone edifice with double wrought-iron gates set in the middle. The big wooden tractor shed stood at the back of this, wide doors standing open, and alongside it a venerable mud-spattered Land Rover. Sam drew up alongside, and they climbed out of the car. As they did so, a young man appeared from the shed with an old yellow Labrador at his heels. The young man wore a boiler suit, rubber boots and a deerstalker, the peak tipped forward over his nose.

'Charlie Miller?'

'Yes, that's me. Now, stay down, Brandy, and don't jump up on the lady. You're a stupid old bitch with no manners.'

'I don't mind.' Carrie smiled.

511

'You would if she covered you with pawmarks.' He turned to Sam. 'You'll be Sam Howard.'

'That's right. And this is Carrie Sutton.'

Charlie Miller said, 'Pleased to meet you,' and he and Carrie shook hands. 'Oscar phoned me. You've come for the tree – it's in the shed, if you'd like to come away in.'

They followed him into the dim interior of the shed, which clearly accommodated a number of functions. Sam saw a pile of potato pallets, a stack of sawn logs, a number of old fruit boxes, turnips bagged in netted sacks. There was a good smell of earth, sawdust and engine oil. Leaning against an aged Ferguson tractor was their tree.

'Oscar said six foot would be tall enough so I picked this one out. It's a good shape, and no broken branches.'

'Looks fine to me.'

'Two pounds a foot. Twelve pounds. Have you got a stand for it?'

'I really wouldn't know. Oscar didn't say.'

'I've this.' Charlie produced, from some corner, a rough wooden contraption knocked together with masonry nails. 'The farmer's boy made them, selling at two fifty each.'

Sam eyed it doubtfully. 'Is it going to work?'

'Oh, yes, it'll work all right.

'Right.' Charlie set it down by the tree. 'So that's fourteen fifty you owe me.' He was obviously not a man to beat about the bush.

Sam dug out his wallet and handed over fifteen pounds. 'Tell the farmer's son to keep the change. He deserves it, if only for enterprise.'

'I'll tell him,' said Charlie, and the notes disappeared

into the pocket of the boiler suit. 'Will I load the tree for you?'

'If you would, that would be more than kind. I've put the back seats down so there should be enough space.'

'No problem.'

Carrie now spoke. 'Charlie, do you think it would be all right if we went for a walk? We've never been to Corrydale before and we wanted to look around, see the house. But if it's private or we're not allowed . . .'

'You're allowed, all right. Go anywhere you please. The hotel is closed anyway and there's not much to look at in the gardens.'

'We don't mind. Which is the best way to go?'

'Back the road you came and at Major Billicliffe's house take the left fork. That will bring you to the gardens and the house. There's a path from there down through the trees to the water, and a track leads back to here along the shore. While you're walking, I'll net the tree and load it, and if I'm not here when you're back I'll be away for my dinner.'

'Thank you.'

'No trouble. Have a good walk, now.'

They set off, footsteps scrunching on frozen ruts, the air sweet as chilled wine, the thin sunshine warming their backs and causing flurries of melted snow to drift down from the upper branches of trees. These, leafless, made patterns like black lace against the brilliant blue of the sky. They went by the farm and the gamekeeper's house; by the garden gate of Rose Miller's delectable dwelling.

'It's the sort of place,' Carrie observed, 'you feel you could happily snug up into and spend the rest of your life.'

After Major Billicliffe's deserted cottage they left the

road and took the path that led towards the main house. It was heavy walking because now the snow was virgin, untouched and quite deep.

Carrie said, 'There must once have been a lot of money. This is a huge establishment, with all those estate cottages and the farm and the walled garden and everything. I wonder where it all came from. The wealth, I mean.'

'Industry, probably. Shipbuilding, steel, that sort of thing. Or Far Eastern connections. Shipping, tea, teak. I don't know. We'll have to ask Oscar.'

'Oscar doesn't seem to have *anything*.'

'No. I don't think he does have much.'

'What's happened to it all? The money, I mean.'

'What's happened everywhere. Old people died and death duties claimed enormous chunks of the estate. The cost of living soared. The war changed everything. After the war there was a gradual decline. Then chaps like Hughie McLellan took possession, squandered the last of the capital and finally sold up. In the south of England, all this land would probably be littered with bijou bungalows and private building estates. But here, because of its remoteness and the fact that the hotel chain took over the house, it's managed to stay looking – at least – the way it always has done.'

'Why didn't Oscar inherit? He would have made a lovely laird.'

'I suppose he didn't qualify. Hughie was the son of the eldest son. Primogeniture. Just bad luck on everyone he proved to be such a shit.'

'It seems unfair, doesn't it?'

'Carrie, life is unfair.'

'I'm so sorry for Oscar. He deserves better, he and

Elfrida. They deserve some place to live together that they can call their own and know that they don't have to leave. I would like to be rich so that I could take care of them both – buy them a desirable residence and settle them for life. I wish we hadn't been there when they were told that the David Wilkie was a fake and worth so little. Elfrida was so filled with hope. And so certain that she owned a little treasure that would get them through and give them security. It was painful to see her so destroyed and downcast. I was embarrassed.'

'I was too,' Sam reminded her.

'But it's different for you.'

'Why different?'

'Because if they have no money then Oscar will be forced to sell you his half of the Estate House, and then you will have what you came for.'

'Do you think I'm that sort of a monster?'

'I don't know. I don't know you well enough. I don't know how you think.'

He let this pass. There was no point in precipitating a row so early on their expedition. Instead, 'Will they stay together, do you think?' he asked.

'Your guess is as good as mine. I think they probably will. Neither of them has anybody else. But where will they live?'

'Where they are. If Oscar doesn't want to sell, then Hughie can't.'

'So what will you do?'

'Look for someplace else.'

'In Buckly?'

'I don't know. So far I've hardly seen the neighbourhood in daylight, let alone investigated property for sale.'

For a bit Carrie said nothing to this. They were walking at a brisk pace, her long legs keeping up with his own as they trudged through the snow. To their left, the snowfields swept down to the water of the loch, and on their right a small wood of ancient beeches revealed dells and paths between the massive tree trunks, and the snow was patterned with the tracks of rabbits and birds. Overhead, rooks cawed, and from the empty shores came the long bubbling cry of a curlew.

She said abruptly, 'I would like to see your mill.'

Sam had never imagined her being remotely interested, and found himself taken aback by this suggestion. '*Would* you?'

'You sound disbelieving.'

'It's just that there's not much to see. Large, empty, damp spaces, some dye vats and a few bits of salvaged machinery.'

'But you told me it was a listed building. That in itself would be interesting. Can you get access? Have you got a key?' She was serious.

'Of course.'

'Shall we go one day?'

'If you want.'

'I like seeing buildings and houses stripped down. Empty places, bare walls. I like imagining how they were and trying to visualise what they could become. You must feel rather excited about it all, longing to get your teeth into the challenge. Putting it together, and getting it going again.'

'Yes.' He thought about it, and the seemingly insurmountable problems that had yet to be addressed. 'I am. But, at the same time, it's a fairly daunting prospect. Every now and then I shall doubtless become frustrated, impatient and even violently angry, but difficulties can be stimulating, particularly if some other person believes you can solve them. And in Buckly I have a good man, Fergus Skinner, on my side. I've a lot of faith in him.'

'It's still a long stride from working in New York.'

'If I were a much younger man, I probably wouldn't have taken the job on. But I'm thirty-eight now. Been there, done that. And for me this is exactly the right time to change course. For all the high finance in the world, nothing is so satisfactory as going back to the grass roots of the business.'

'Down-grading.'

'In a sense, yes. But, you see, I was born and bred into the woollen trade, and I secretly believe that there is nothing so good-looking, so comfortable, so exactly right as a familiar, well-tailored tweed jacket. It'll stand up to anything the elements choose to hurl at it, and by evening be perfectly acceptable at anybody's dinner table. I love the smell and the feel of tweed. I love the sound of well-tuned cog-wheels, the clack of looms, the monstrous pistons of the carding machines. And I like the people who work them, the men and women who have spinning and weaving and dyeing in their blood, going back two or three generations. So, I'm in my own world.'

'I think you're fortunate.'

'Because of my job?'

'Not just.' Carrie stopped, her head thrown back to watch a buzzard floating high in the sky. 'Because of coming to live up here. In this enormous, clean, unsullied place.' She went on walking. 'Just think, you can play golf, shoot grouse and pheasants, and fish in one of those salmon rivers you told me about.' She thought about this. 'You do fish?'

'Yes. I used to fish with my father in Yorkshire when I was a boy. But for trout, not salmon. And I'm not overkeen on shooting.'

'Nor me. Darling little wild birds tumbling out of the sky. You eat them at the Savoy and they look about the size of canaries.'

By now, ahead, they could see the wall of the formal garden, topped by an ornate wrought-iron fence. The path led to a wrought-iron gate, flanked by gate-posts bearing stone armorial lions and entwined by thorny roses, blackened now in winter.

They reached the gate and paused there, gazing through the lattice of intricate curlicues at the garden that lay beyond: lawns, climbing in stepped terraces, drawing their eyes to the first sighting of Corrydale House. It was a Victorian mansion, gabled and turreted, built of red stone, some of which was smothered in Virginia creeper. It was large, and perhaps a little pretentious, but attractive in a prosperous, settled sort of way. The windows were all shuttered, but facing south; glass panes flashed and shone with reflected sunshine. There was a tall white flag-pole at one side of the top terrace, but no flag flew from its masthead.

'Nice,' said Carrie, after a bit. 'What good times Oscar must have had.'

Sam said, 'Would you like to live here?'

'Do you mean in this house? In this place?'

'No. I just mean *here*. In Creagan. In Sutherland.'

'I have a job. In London. I have to have a job. I have to earn my living.'

'Supposing you didn't have to? Would you be content? Could you bury yourself in such an environment?'

'I don't know. I think I'd need notice. To weigh up

all the pros and cons. And to leave London, I'd need to be free. No commitments. No responsibilities.'

'Aren't you free?'

'There's Lucy.'

'*Lucy?*'

'Yes, Lucy.' She unlatched the gate and opened it. Beyond was a wide path, straight as a rule, leading across the garden towards a distant stand of beech trees. In the middle of this path, in line with the flights of steps that climbed the terraces to the house, stood a stone sundial and a curved wooden seat. Another flight of steps led down to a parterre garden, sheltered by shrubberies of rhododendron and azalea. Its formal structure, radiating from a stone statue of some mythical goddess, was composed of curves, circles, ellipses, all edged in box; buried in snow, it resembled nothing so much as an artist's design, drawn on thick white paper with a stump of charcoal.

'Lucy is the main reason for taking this London job. Somebody has to be there for her. Somebody has to winkle her out of that dull, enclosed, totally female life she's forced to lead through no fault of her own. She doesn't really stand a chance. I have to try to give her one.'

Sam considered this. He said, tentatively, 'She seems to me to be quite well-adjusted. Happy, even.'

'That's because she *is* happy. Here. With Elfrida and Oscar and people coming and going. And, of course, Rory Kennedy. Going back to London is going to be a real let-down.'

Sam found himself resenting this maiden-aunt attitude. Carrie was too young, too beautiful, to start structuring her life simply for the sake of one niece.

'She'll probably be all right,' he said. 'She's young enough to be resilient. In time, she'll make her own escape.'

'No.' Carrie was adamant. 'You don't know her selfish mother. You can't say that.'

'So what will you do with Lucy?'

'Oh, I don't know. Just be around, on the end of the telephone. *There.* Perhaps at Easter I'll take her away again. To Cornwall to stay with Jeffrey. He is, after all, her grandfather. Or maybe we could go skiing. His children are old enough. Jeffrey took me skiing for the first time when I was about nine and I loved it so much it started a whole new passion.'

'Will you go back to Oberbeuren?'

'No.' She had said the word almost before he had finished asking the question. 'Not Oberbeuren. Somewhere else. Arosa, or Grindelwald, or Val d'Isère.'

'You could go to the States. Colorado or Vermont. Sounds a long way to travel but it would certainly be cheaper.'

'Vermont.' Carrie, with her hands in the pockets of her parka, strolled along beside him. 'Have you skied in Vermont?'

'Yes. A number of times. We used to drive up for weekends from the city.'

'We,' Carrie repeated. 'You and your wife, you mean?'

So this was it. The nub around which they had both been circling, the moment of truth, the point of no return. He said, 'Yes. With my wife. You know I'm married?'

'Yes, I know.' She sounded untroubled.

They walked on, still in step, as though nothing was happening; nothing had been said.

'Elfrida told you.'

'Of course. Did you think she wouldn't?'

'No. I thought she probably would. My wife and I are separated.'

'She told me that, too.'

'Do you want the gory details?'

'Not particularly.'

'I think they're important.'

'To you, I'm sure they are.'

'I think they're important because I want you to understand.'

'Understand? Did you behave so badly?'

'No. Yes. I didn't sleep around or have affairs with other women, but I did work too hard and I was away from home too much, and I never gave her enough of my time.'

'Does she have a name?'

'Deborah. Debbie. I always called her Deborah. I was working in New York. I went down to Easthampton for a weekend with a friend and we got asked to this party, and I met her then. Her grandfather had a great house down there; land, beach, horses, paddocks, swimming-pool, the lot. We were married on the lawn at Easthampton in front of her grandfather's house, and there were seven hundred guests and ten bridesmaids and ten ushers all dressed up like penguins. Deborah looked ravishing and I was happy to be swept along in a current I couldn't control or resist. And then we bought this apartment in the upper Seventies, and it was all done up regardless, and that kept her happy for a time, but when it was finished and the interior designer had finally departed, I think that's when she started to get bored and restless. I had to travel all over the States, and sometimes while

521

I was away she went back to Easthampton. Other times she simply occupied herself having a good time.'

'Children?'

'No. She didn't want babies. Not so soon. Someday, perhaps, she'd promise me, but not just now. Anyway, some time last summer she met this guy again. She'd known him when she was at college. Since those days he'd been married twice but was on the loose again. In New York. Rich, smooth, pretty stupid. Randy as a tom-cat. They started what is politely known these days as a relationship. I never guessed. I never knew until she told me she was leaving me because she wanted to be with him. And I was devastated. Not just because I was losing her but because I knew she had fallen for a shit. And I knew, too, that he was the sort of guy who, marrying his mistress, was simply creating another job vacancy.'

'But you're not divorced?'

'No. There's hardly been time. Six weeks after she departed I got a call from my chairman, David Swinfield, asking me to come back to London. And since then . . . well, I've just procrastinated. Let it slide. Had other business to occupy my mind. No doubt, sooner or later, I'll be on the receiving end of a lawyer's letter, and after that the ball will roll.'

'Will she be greedy and demand great wads of alimony?'

'I don't know. It depends on the lawyer. I don't think so. She was never that sort of a person. Anyway, the shit is loaded, and Deborah has money of her own. Too much, maybe. Perhaps that was one of our problems. My problems.'

'Are you still in love with her?'

'Oh, Carrie . . .'

'I know. But you feel responsible. You have anxieties about her future. You're afraid she's going to be hurt, to be dumped. You still feel protective.'

After a bit, 'Yeah,' Sam admitted. 'I suppose I do.'

'If she wanted . . . if she beckoned, demanded . . . would you go back to her?'

He thought about this. He said, 'No.'

'Why not?'

'Because my life has changed direction. Because Deborah is part of the past and I've left that behind. I'm here now. And this is where I'm staying, because I have a job to do.'

'She's still your wife.'

'What's that meant to mean?'

'That if you've been married to a person, they're part of you. You can never be free. You belong to them.'

She spoke with such bitterness that Sam knew all at once that he only had to push a bit further and the closed door, which had stood between them, would finally, creakily, open.

He turned to her. 'Carrie . . .'

But she strode on and he had to catch her up and take her by the arm and jerk her round to face him. The black orbs of her sunglasses stared up at him, and he put up a hand, took them off and saw, to his horror, that her dark eyes were shining with tears. 'Carrie. Tell me.'

'Why?' She was angry, blinking the tears away. 'Why should I tell you?'

'Because I've been honest with you.'

'I never made a deal. It's none of your business and I don't want to talk about it. It's not worth talking about. And you wouldn't understand.'

'I could try. And I think I would understand. I've

been through bad times myself. The worst was knowing that everybody was aware of what was going on except thickhead me. Taking one day at a time, and each day being like a treadmill and getting nowhere. Trying to come to terms with a total rejection.'

'I wasn't rejected,' Carrie shouted at him, and all at once her face creased up like a child's and she was in floods of tears. Furious with herself, she pushed at him, trying to escape his grip, but he held her shoulders between his hands and would not let go, because he felt that if he did she might fall to pieces, and his strength was the only thing that kept her whole. 'I wasn't rejected. I was loved. We were in love, and all we wanted was to be together. But the odds were too great. Stacked against us. Too many demands, responsibilities, traditions. His job, his family, his wife, his children, his religion, his money. I was simply his mistress. Living in the back-streets of his life. I didn't stand a chance. Never did. And what I really hate is that I always *knew*. I hate myself for shutting my eyes, burying my head in the sand like a stupid ostrich. Pretending everything would work out. I'm thirty, for God's sake. I thought I could handle it. And finally, when Andreas walked away from me, I went to bits. So now you know, Sam, and now you can stop trying to find out. And perhaps you can accept the fact that I'm really not very interested in married men. And if you start being sympathetic or sorry for me, I shall scream.'

He opened his mouth to protest, but at that moment, with a wrench of her body, she slid out of his hold and set off, at a run, away from him, stumbling in the snow, righting herself, carrying on. He went after her, and caught her once more. 'Oh, Carrie,' and this time she did not fight him. Perhaps she was too tired, too breathless with sobs. He took her into his arms and she leaned against him, her shoulders heaving, weeping into the front of his Barbour.

Holding her, having her in his arms, was something he had been wanting to do all day. She felt slender, weightless, and he told himself that he could feel the beating of her heart through all their combined layers of winter clothing. The fur of her hat tickled his cheek, and her skin smelt sweet and cool.

'Oh, Carrie.' It was shameful to feel so elated when she suffered from such desolation and wretchedness. Trying to comfort, 'It will be all right.'

'It *won't* be all right.'

So cold, so adamant was her voice, that he was suddenly wise, realising that it was hopeless to continue mouthing pointless platitudes. Standing there, with his arms about her, Sam found himself uncharacteristically confused and disorientated. Normally, his instincts did not let him down; instead told him how to deal with any situation, emotional or otherwise. But, right now, he knew all at once that he was totally at a loss. Carrie was beautiful, intelligent and desirable, but also complicated. And perhaps because of this, she remained an enigma. To truly understand her was going to take much patience and a lot of time.

He accepted this. He said again, 'It will be all right.'

'You don't know.'

Now, he had the confidence and the good sense not to argue. After a bit, her furious weeping calmed down. She made motions as though to pull herself together. Gently, Sam put her away from him, and watched as she wiped at tear-stained cheeks with her padded glove.

He said, 'I'm sorry.'

'What for?'

'Sorry, because this wasn't what I had planned, nor anticipated. I didn't mean to upset you so. This was simply an outing, to pick up a Christmas tree and go for a walk. No ulterior motives. It just went wrong.'

'Not your fault. So stupid . . .'

'I talked about Deborah, because sometimes I need to. I didn't mean to wind you up.'

'I know. Let's forget it. Pretend it never happened. Walk on, the way we'd planned.'

'We did talk. To talk is always good. I thought we never would.'

'Is talking so good? I'm not so sure.'

'Clears the air. Makes things easier to understand.'

'I don't know that I want to be understood. Just left alone. Perhaps right now I'm better off that way. Independent. Not belonging to any person.'

Sam said, 'Don't be too sure about that.' But he did not say it aloud.

Lucy

Lucy

Thursday 21 December
This morning Carrie and Sam
went and got the Christmas
tree. And Mrs Snead and I
spring-cleaned the dining room. It was dreadfully
dusty and deserted. We put a notice on the door
saying DO NOT DISTURB *so that nobody came in.*
Mrs Snead lit a bit of paper in the fire to be sure
that the chimney wasn't full of jackdaw nests,
but the smoke all went up and she said it was
quite clear so we shall be able to have a huge fire
which will make all the difference.

And there were a couple of big cardboard
crates which seemed to be filled with crumpled
newspaper, but we explored and found some
silver candlesticks, four of them, dreadfully
tarnished but very handsome. We took all the
rubbish across the hall, and added it to the
collection in the old office. There are very thick,
sort of tapestry curtains, which were a bit dusty,
so we found a step-ladder in the scullery and

took them down, and took them into the garden
to shake them, and then hung them up again. I
cleaned the window, and Mrs Snead washed all
the fireplace tiles, and then we moved the table
and Mrs Snead hoovered. Then we polished all
the furniture, and then we spread newspaper and
cleaned the candlesticks which took ages because
they are very ornate and patterned. Then, while
I went out and bought some candles (tall and
cream, a bit like church candles) Mrs Snead
went upstairs to look for tablecloths in her linen
cupboard. There weren't any, but she found an
old linen sheet which is just as good, and we put
a thick blanket underneath to protect the table.
That's as far as we got because she had to go
home and give Arthur his dinner, but with the
candlesticks and everything, and the fire all laid,
it really looks wonderfully festive.

I didn't want anybody to know about it, so
that it would be a surprise, but just before lunch
Carrie and Sam got back with the Christmas tree
and there was a great discussion as to where we
should put it. We thought the sitting room, but
Elfrida's having this party on Saturday and there
will be quite a lot of people, and she thought
it might take up too much space. Then Oscar
suggested the landing, but there's going to be a
table there for drinks, and it would get in the
way of people going up and down stairs. So then
I had to admit about the dining room, and they
all trooped downstairs to inspect what we had
been doing, and it was lovely because everybody
was thrilled, and it all smelt polishy, and Elfrida

said she had no idea the dining room could ever look so festive. And, of course, that *was exactly* the right place for the tree. So Sam went out and brought it in and he'd bought a sort of stand for it as well, so that made everything much easier. And Elfrida fetched her red silk shawl from her bed, and draped it around the stand to hide the raw wood and the nails, and it looked beautiful and is a lovely shape and size. I love the smell of trees coming indoors, it's like pine essence for the bath.

In the afternoon, Oscar collected all the decorations we'd bought and we tied them on the tree, and Sam fixed the lights and the star on the top branch. And Elfrida produced a whole roll of lovely tartan ribbon she'd bought for tying up her presents, but she said sticky tape would be just as good. So we cut it and made lovely bows and put them all over the tree, and with the tinsel and the lights turned on, it is the prettiest I think I've ever seen.

Carrie told me that Corrydale is lovely and that some time I have to go to see it all. She said there was snow everywhere and blue shadows and sunlight, and that there are gardens stretching right from the house down to the water, and lots of big old trees. In a way, I wish I had gone with them to get the tree, but I had to do the dining room while Mrs Snead was here because she'd promised to help.

Tomorrow we have to get started on the party. Elfrida has rung Mrs Kennedy and is going to borrow some glasses because we haven't got *enough. And Carrie is in charge of the food. This afternoon, after we'd dealt with the Christmas tree, we went to the baker's together and ordered sausage rolls and little quiches and pizzas. And then we ordered smoked salmon to put on brown bread. The party is to start at six and Mrs Snead and Arthur are going to come and help. I hadn't realised that throwing a party was quite so much hard work. Perhaps that's why Mummy and Gran never do in London.*

Rory has been asked, of course, and Clodagh. I shall wear my new black mini-skirt and my black tights and my white sweater. I would like to fix my hair up into a sort of knot so that my earrings will show.

Elfrida

Elfrida

In midwinter, waking to darkness in this cold northern country, Elfrida would open her eyes and have no clue as to the time. After a little, she would fumble for her watch and squint at its luminous face, and if it was two in the morning would probably clamber out of bed, put on her dressing-gown, and stumble off to the bathroom. Sometimes it was five a.m. Or eight in the morning and time to get up, but even then not a glimmer of light showed in the sky and all was black as midnight.

This morning, she reached out a hand, found her watch and it was half past seven. Beside her, Oscar still slept. She got quietly out of bed, so as not to disturb him, reached for her thick dressing-gown, pushed her feet into slippers and went to close the window. Outside, she saw it was snowing again, not heavily but sleety flakes driven in by a wind from the sea. These swirled and blew around the church, and through the black branches of the graveyard trees, the light of the street-lamps turned them to gold. The effect was so spectacular that Elfrida knew she had to share it with some other person. Oscar would not appreciate being woken so she left him, went out of the room, turned on lights and went downstairs to the kitchen where she boiled a kettle and made two cups of tea. Upstairs again to the sitting room, where she drew back the curtains, and set the two mugs on the table by the window. Then she went on up to the attic to wake Lucy.

Lucy slept, looking innocent as a small child, her hand tucked under the sweet curve of her cheek, her long hair tumbled around her neck. Her bed stood beneath the sloping window set into the roof. The blind was not drawn, the glass blanketed with wet snow. Elfrida switched on the bedside light.

'Lucy.'

Lucy stirred, turned, yawned, opened her eyes.

'Lucy.'

'Umm?'

'You awake?'

'I am now.'

'I want you to get up. I want to show you something. I've made a cup of tea for you.'

'What time is it?'

'Nearly a quarter to eight.'

Sleepily, Lucy sat up, rubbing her eyes. 'I thought it was the middle of the night.'

'No. Morning. And so beautiful. Everyone else is still sleeping, but I wanted to show you.'

Lucy, still fuddled with sleep, got out of bed and pulled on her camel-hair dressing-gown. She said, 'It's cold.'

'It's the wind. It's snowing again.'

They went downstairs, through the quiet house. The

536

sitting room was filled with light from out of doors. 'Look,' said Elfrida, led the way across the room and settled herself on the window-seat. 'It's so amazing I had to wake you and show you. I was afraid that the snow would have stopped and you wouldn't see it. But it's just like it was when I woke up.'

Lucy, staring, sat beside her. After a little, she said, 'It's like one of those glass balls I used to have. It was full of water, and it had a little church, and when you shook it there was a snowstorm.'

'That's just what I thought. But these flakes are golden because of the lights, like flecks of gold.'

Lucy said, 'It's the sort of thing people draw on Christmas cards and you think it could never be like that.'

'And the streets so clean! Not a footprint, not a car track. As though there was nobody else in the world except us.' She fell silent, then thought of something. 'I suppose there'll be blizzards and drifts on the main roads. I'm glad we don't have to go anywhere.' Lucy shivered. 'Here, have some tea.'

Lucy took it and drank gratefully, her fingers wrapped around the mug, savouring its warmth. In silence they both stared at the scene beyond the window. Then, a single car appeared, circling the church and heading off in the direction of the main road. It drove cautiously, grinding along in second gear, and left a pair of dark tracks in its wake.

When it was gone, Lucy asked, 'What time is it in Florida?'

Elfrida was taken aback. Lucy never talked about Florida, or about her mother, or about her mother's new friend. She said casually, 'I don't know. Five hours ago,

I suppose. About three in the morning. And I expect it's warm and humid. It's hard to imagine. I've never been to Florida. I've never been to America.' She waited for Lucy to enlarge on this, but Lucy said nothing. 'Wouldn't you like to be there?' Elfrida asked gently. 'Blue skies and palm trees and a swimming-pool?'

'No. I should hate it. That's why I didn't go.'

'But lovely for your mother. Like a wonderful holiday.'

'I don't like Randall Fischer much.'

'Why not?'

'He's sort of smooth. Creepy.'

'He's probably very nice and totally harmless.'

'Mummy thinks so, anyway.'

'Well. That's nice for her.'

'I'd rather be here a thousand times over than in Florida. This is *really* Christmas, isn't it? It's going to be a *real* one.'

'I hope so, Lucy. I'm not sure. We'll just have to wait and see.'

'Oscar.'

Oscar, settled by the fire, looked up from his newspaper.

'My dear.'

'I am about to leave you on your own.'

'For ever?'

'No. For about half an hour. I telephoned Tabitha Kennedy and I'm going up to the Manse to borrow some extra glasses for our party. She has spare boxes that she keeps for parish dos and she says we can have them.'

'That's very kind.'

'I shall have to use the car. I shall drive at five miles an hour and take every precaution.'

'Would you like me to come with you?'

'If you want.'

'I should prefer to stay here but am ready and willing to be of any service.'

'Perhaps, when I get back, you could help me unload the boot and bring it all indoors.'

'Of course, give me a shout.' He thought for a moment. 'It's very quiet. Where is everybody?'

'Sam and Carrie have gone to Buckly. And Lucy's incarcerated in her attic, tying up her Christmas presents. If you wanted you could both take Horace for a little walk. It's stopped snowing.'

Oscar did not look particularly delighted by this suggestion. He simply said, in a noncommittal way, 'Yes.'

Elfrida smiled, then stooped to kiss him. 'Take care,' she told him, but he had already resumed his reading.

Out of doors the wind was bitter and the snow treacherous. Elfrida, bundled up in boots, the blanket coat and woollen hat, emerged from the warmth of the house and paused to gaze upwards. She saw clouds wheeling in across a fitful sky, and gulls blown hither and thither in the freezing air. Oscar's car was covered in snow. Elfrida brushed the fresh fall from the windscreen with her gloved hand, but there was ice beneath it, so she got in, started the engine and turned on the heater. Presently the ice trickled away and she contrived two arcs of clear glass. Cautiously, she set off, chugging along down the street, then turning up the hill that led to the Manse. The gritting lorry had already passed this way and so, with some relief, she reached her destination without skid or other mishap.

She parked at the Manse gate, trod up the path of the front garden, knocked the snow from her boots, rang the bell, then stepped into the porch and opened the inner door. 'Tabitha.'

'I'm here. In the kitchen.'

Elfrida saw that the minister's house was already decked out for Christmas. A tree (not very large) stood at the foot of the stairs, strung with tinsel and stars, while rather worn-looking paper chains had been festooned overhead. Through the open door at the back of the hall Tabitha appeared, bundled up in an apron, her dark hair gathered back into a pony-tail. 'What a day! So lovely to see you. I've got coffee perking. Come in quickly and shut the door. You didn't walk up?'

Elfrida unbuttoned her coat and hung it on the newel post of the banister. 'No, I was intrepid and brought the car. Had to. I couldn't begin to carry two crates of glasses home. I'd have slipped on the lane, probably broken my leg and certainly broken the glasses.' She followed Tabitha back into the kitchen. 'Good smells.'

'I'm baking. Mince-pies, sausage rolls, two cakes and some shortbread biscuits. You know I like to cook, but Christmas is becoming beyond a joke. I've been at it all morning, and there's still stuffing to make and brandy butter. And the Christmas cake to ice and a ham to be boiled. The thing is, so many parishioners call round at this time of the year with cards, or presents for Peter, and they all have to be asked in and watered and fed if only out of appreciation.'

'I'm sorry. You're so busy and I'm interrupting.'

Tabitha poured coffee into a mug. 'Not at all. It's

540

an excuse to sit down for five minutes. Pull out a chair, make yourself comfortable.' She dumped the mug on the table. 'What I'd really like is to be out of doors. We should be walking on the beach or sledging on the golf course, shedding all responsibilities, instead of being slave-driven by the demands of the festive season. I'm sure it was never intended to be such labour. Every year I swear I'll simplify and all I ever do is complicate.'

Seduced by the fragrant smell of coffee, Elfrida did as she was told. The Manse kitchen was very nearly as old-fashioned as the kitchen at the Estate House but a great deal more cheerful, with Clodagh's art work stuck up on the panels of doors and an old desk piled with papers and family photographs. Clearly this was Tabitha's domain, where she not only cooked and fed her family but organised her busy life, did her telephoning and wrote letters. Now, she poured a mug of coffee for herself and settled down on the other side of the table.

'Tell me all the news. What's happening with you?'

'Nothing much. I left Oscar reading the paper, and Sam and Carrie have gone off to Buckly to look at the woollen mill.'

'Sam's the mysterious stranger who walked in out of the snow? He's still with you?'

'He's staying over Christmas. The weather's so awful and he doesn't seem to have anywhere else to go.'

'Goodness, how sad. Have he and Carrie made friends?'

'They seem to have,' said Elfrida, cautiously.

'Rather romantic.'

'Tabitha, he's married.'

'Then why isn't he with his wife?'

'She's in New York.'

'Are they non-speaks?'

'Separated, I think. Don't know the details.'

'Oh, well,' said Tabitha, sounding philosophical. 'It takes all sorts.'

'It's so odd to think you haven't even met him. It feels as though we've all been together for months but, really, it's only been a few days. Whatever, you'll meet both Sam and Carrie tomorrow evening. Drinks at the Estate House, six to eight.'

'I put the boxes out in the hall. Six wine glasses and six tumblers and a couple of jugs. Are you going to need plates?'

'I don't think so. We're not actually feeding people, just little snacky things. Carrie's doing those.'

'How many guests do you expect?'

'I think we're about seventeen. You four—'

'Clodagh probably won't come. She's been invited to a supper party and a sleepover with a schoolfriend. Do you mind?'

'Not a bit. Much more fun for her.'

'But Rory will definitely be there. Who else?'

'Jamie Erskine-Earle and his wife.'

'Jamie and Emma? I didn't know you'd met them.'

'He came to appraise my David Wilkie painting. But it's a sham and not a David Wilkie at all, so that's another pipe-dream down the drain.'

'Were you thinking of selling it?'

'I might have. But not now.'

'Isn't he a hoot? Jamie, I mean. Looks about fifteen, and is not only an expert in his field but the father of three lusty sons. Have you met Emma?'

'Only spoken to her on the phone when I invited them to come.'

'She's really nice, the most down-to-earth, outspoken creature you ever met. She breeds Shetland ponies, works dogs and oversees everything at Kingsferry. Jamie's far more interested in chasing up antiques, identifying prick candlesticks and unearthing forgotten portraits. Emma's the one who runs the farm, helps with the lambing and gets the roof mended. Who else have you asked?'

'The bookshop Rutleys.'

'Good.'

'And Dr Sinclair and his wife.'

'Good again.'

'I don't know their names.'

'Geordie and Janet.'

'And the Sneads.'

'Mrs Snead and Arfur?'

'Well, when she knew I was asking a few people in, Mrs Snead offered to come and hand round and wash glasses. But I couldn't bear to think of her being incarcerated in the kitchen all the time so I told her to come and join in and bring Arfur with her. She said Arfur could have a tray and hand round drinks.'

'Like a butler.'

'She's been such a friend to Oscar and me, I couldn't leave them out.'

'They'll be the life and soul of the party.'

Tabitha drank her coffee. Then she set down her mug, and across the table, their eyes met. Tabitha said, 'How is Oscar?'

'He's all right. He still likes being quiet, left alone with his newspaper and his crossword.'

'Peter gave him the spare key to the church organ. Did you know that?'

'No. Oscar never said.'

'Peter thought it might help, Oscar's music, that it would be a sort of therapy.'

'He's never used it. He's only been into the church once, and that was with Lucy because she wanted to look around. To my knowledge he's not been back.'

'I don't imagine it would afford him much comfort.'

'Comfort isn't what Oscar needs. He just wants to be left alone to get through the days at his own pace. As for all our houseguests, expected and unexpected, I think in a funny way he quite enjoys all the coming and going. He's very fond of Lucy. But, Tabitha, it still isn't right. Oscar and I are very close, yet I know that part of him is still withdrawn, even from me. As though that part of him was still in another place. Another country. Journeying, perhaps. Or in exile. Across a sea. And I can't be with him because I haven't got the right sort of passport.'

'Peter would say it's a question of patience.'

'Patience was never one of my virtues. Not that I ever had many.'

Tabitha laughed. 'Rubbish. They're just not the same as other people's. Have more coffee.'

'No. That was delicious.' Elfrida got to her feet. 'Now I must get out of your way. Thank you for the glasses and for being a listening ear.'

'I'll come and help you stow the boxes in the boot of your car. They're not very heavy, just awkward. And we'll all be with you tomorrow evening at six, dressed up in our Christmas bibs and tuckers. Very exciting. I can't wait.'

Oscar

Oscar

Elfrida had not been gone for more than ten minutes, when Oscar, busily breaking into *The Times* crossword, was interrupted by the appearance of Lucy. She wore her red padded jacket and her boots and was apparently on her way out.

'Oscar.'

'Hello there, duck.' He laid down the paper. 'I thought you were wrapping Christmas presents.'

'Yes, I am, but I've run out of ribbon. Oscar, where's Elfrida?'

'She's gone to the Manse to borrow things. She won't be long.'

'I just wondered if there was anything she wanted me to get in the shop.'

'I think all she wanted was for Horace to be taken for a walk.'

'Well, I'll go to the bookshop first, then take Horace down to the beach.'

'It's very snowy.'

'I don't mind. I've got my boots on.'

'Well, be sure not to get attacked by Rottweilers.'

Lucy made a hideous face. 'Don't even remind me.'

'I'll tell Elfrida you'll be back for lunch.'

Lucy went. In a moment, Oscar heard Horace's cheerful pre-walk barking, then the front door opened and slammed shut, and he was alone once more. He returned to his crossword. Six across. *Period by river for one producing picture.* He brooded over this. The telephone began to ring.

His immediate instinct was to leave it, to wait for someone else to answer the tiresome instrument. But then he remembered that he was the only one in the house, and so, in some irritation, he set down the paper, stowed his pen in his pocket, heaved himself out of his chair and went on to the landing.

'Estate House.'

'I wonder, is Mr Blundell there?' A female voice, very Scottish.

'Speaking.'

'Oh, Mr Blundell, this is Sister Thomson from the Royal Western in Inverness. I'm afraid it's sad news. Major Billicliffe died early this morning. I have your name as his next-of-kin.'

Old Billicliffe. Dead. Oscar found himself struggling to think of something to say. All he could come up with was, 'I see.'

'It was all very peaceful. He had a quiet end.'

'I'm pleased. Thank you very much for letting me know.'

'There are personal possessions you'll want to collect. If you could . . .'

Oscar said, 'Of course.'

'And any other arrangements . . .' Sister tactfully did

not finish her sentence. But Oscar knew exactly what she was driving at.

He said, again, 'Of course. Thank you. And for taking care of him. I'll be in touch.'

'Thank you, Mr Blundell. I'm very sorry. Goodbye.'

'Goodbye, Sister.'

He rang off, and because all at once he needed to sit down, he went and perched on the bottom of the stairs that led up to Lucy's attic. Billicliffe was dead, and Oscar was not only his next-of-kin but his executor. He found his head spinning with unworthy and pettish thoughts, and was grateful that Elfrida was not here, otherwise he might have voiced them aloud.

How typical of that old idiot to go and die *now*, of all times. A house full of people, Christmas upon them, and the roads to Inverness impassable. If he had planned it, Billicliffe could not have hit upon a more inconvenient moment to turn up his toes.

But then Oscar remembered leaving the old boy, stopped feeling resentful and instead felt sad because he had died alone, and Oscar and Elfrida, despite their best intentions, had been unable to get to the hospital to visit him, make amends for their unsocial behaviour and say goodbye.

He pondered for a bit as to what he should do next. The ball, it was obvious, was in his court and it was he who had to take the initiative, but he found himself with no idea of how to start. And it occurred to him, sitting like a beached whale at the foot of the stairs, that it was less than two months since that ghastly evening when he had been told that Gloria and Francesca were dead. He had little recollection of the stunned days that followed. There had been a funeral, of course, the Dibton church packed, the Vicar, who had never been much of a preacher, struggling for words, and Oscar in his good black overcoat standing in the front pew. But how he had got there he could not say, and had no memory at all of the considerable organisation that had preceded the occasion. He only knew that at some time Giles, Gloria's eldest son, had turned up and taken over while Oscar, rendered incapable by shock, had simply done what he was told. Giles, whom Oscar had never found the most engaging of young men, had nevertheless proved himself immensely efficient. All went on oiled wheels, and the entire nightmare process had slipped by, and away, and into the past.

When it was all over, Oscar felt that nothing of any importance would ever happen to him again, and he moved through the dead days like a zombie. Then Giles turned up once more at the Grange to inform him that he would have to move out as Gloria's house was going to be put up for sale. And Oscar felt no resentment. Giles was, once more, at the helm, and Oscar took the line of least resistance and simply went with the flow, agreeing to everything. It was only when the old folks' home was mentioned that he experienced the first stirrings of alarm.

But now things were different, and it was *his* turn to take over. How had he got himself into such a situation? He thought back to that cold morning when he had driven Major Billicliffe over the Black Isle to the hospital in Inverness. And how the old boy had talked, meandering on in an incomprehensible stream of reminiscence. Then, 'Prepare for the worst and hope for the best,' he had said, and asked Oscar to be his executor.

The lawyer. In his diary, Oscar had made a note of the man's name. He got up off the stair, went into the sitting room and found his diary on his makeshift desk. He turned the pages. Murdo McKenzie. It occurred to him that only Billicliffe would have a lawyer with such an outlandish name. Murdo McKenzie, McKenzie & Stout, South Street, Inverness.

There was no telephone number so he looked it up in the book, copied it into his diary and returned to the landing. He sat on the stairs again, lifted the telephone off the table, set it handily beside him, then punched the number.

He thought, There will have to be a funeral. A church. A wake. People will have to be told. I must tell Peter Kennedy. And an announcement in the newspaper. Just a few lines. But which paper? The national press, or the local . . .

'McKenzie & Stout.'

'Oh, good morning. I wonder, could I speak to Mr Murdo McKenzie?'

'Who shall I say is calling?'

'Oscar Blundell. From Creagan.'

'Hold on a moment, please.'

Oscar's heart sank. Others had spoken those words before and he had been forced to wait a great deal longer than a moment, listening to a tinkly rendering of 'Greensleeves' or some other soupy tune. But his fears were unfounded. Murdo McKenzie came on the line almost at once.

'Mr Blundell, good morning, Murdo McKenzie here. What can I do for you?'

A good Scottish voice, strong and capable-sounding. Oscar felt encouraged.

'Good morning. I'm sorry to bother you, but I've just heard from the hospital that Major Billicliffe died this morning. Major Godfrey Billicliffe,' he added, as though there could possibly be two.

'Oh, that's sad news. I am sorry.' (He really sounded sorry, too.) 'But perhaps not unexpected.'

'They called me first because they had my name as next-of-kin. And as well, of course, Major Billicliffe asked me to be his executor. There didn't seem to be anyone else.'

'No. He had no family. He told me about this arrangement and said that you had agreed to take on the duty.'

'That's why I'm calling. There will have to be a funeral, but where, when and how? He has friends in Creagan who will certainly want to be there, but as far as I know the roads are still impassable and there's no hope in hell of anybody getting to Inverness. To say nothing of the fact that Christmas is just about on us. And an undertaker will have to be approached, of course, and the bank notified, and the registrar . . .'

Murdo McKenzie smoothly intervened: 'Mr Blundell, why don't you leave all this to me? The first thing is that Major Billicliffe left instructions with my office that he wished to be cremated, so that precludes a good many headaches. As for an undertaker, I can deal with that. There's an excellent firm in Inverness who have a good reputation, and I know them well. How would it be if I get in touch with Mr Lugg and make all the necessary arrangements?'

'That's enormously kind of you . . . but when?'

'I would suggest the end of next week. Before New Year. By then the weather should have eased off a bit and you and any friends from Creagan should be able to make your way over the Black Isle to attend the ceremony.'

'But shouldn't we have some sort of get-together – a cup of tea somewhere? I should be more than willing to foot the bill for that.'

'Mr Lugg can see to that as well. Perhaps the lounge of an hotel, or the function room. It depends how many people will be there.'

'And all the other details, probate and the bank and such. Freezing his account.'

'We'll deal with all that.'

'And his personal possessions.' Oscar thought of Billicliffe's washed-out flannel pyjamas, his hearing-aids, his battered leather suitcase. All too pathetic and, to his horror, he felt a ridiculous lump grow in his throat. 'His possessions. They will have to be collected from the hospital.'

'I'll telephone and have a word with the ward sister. Do you remember the number of the ward?'

Rather to his surprise, Oscar did. 'Fifteen.'

'Fifteen.' A pause while Murdo McKenzie made a note or two. 'I'll get my secretary to see to that.'

'I really can't thank you enough. You've taken a great weight off my shoulders.'

'I know that Major Billicliffe did not want you to be inconvenienced in any way so I shall telephone Mr Lugg and get back to you when I know what arrangements he's been able to make. Have I got your telephone number?'

Oscar gave it to him.

'And you're at the Estate House in Creagan?'

'That's right.'

'No problems, then. And if any should arise I'll give you a ring.'

'It really is more than good of you. If you could keep in touch. Thank you again. And now I'll waste no more of—'

'Mr Blundell!'

'Yes?'

'Don't ring off. I have something else to say. I shall be writing to you, of course, but the post is a little unreliable at this time of the year and as we're talking now perhaps I should put you in the picture.'

Oscar frowned. 'Sorry, I don't understand.'

'Once he was settled in hospital, Major Billicliffe rang me and said that he wanted to see me. I live out on the Nairn road and pass the hospital on my way into the office, so I called in early last Monday morning. He was in bed, of course, and very frail, but perfectly lucid. He was worried about his will. Since his wife died he had not got round to making a new one and he wished to do this right away. He gave me instructions, the will was written that day, in my office, and he was able to sign it. You are his sole beneficiary, Mr Blundell. He was not a man of property or great wealth, but he wanted you to have his house at Corrydale, his car and his dog. I'm afraid neither the car nor the dog are bequests you would have chosen, but those were his wishes. As for his money, he lived, very frugally, on his pension, which, of course, stops on his death. But he had, as well, some savings, which, once all the funeral expenses have been settled and any outstanding bills, should come to about two thousand five hundred pounds.'

Oscar sat on his stair, with the telephone to his ear, and could not think of a single thing to say.

'Mr Blundell?'

'Yes, I'm still here.'

'I thought maybe the line had gone dead.'

'No. I'm here.'

'It's not a substantial legacy, I'm afraid, but Major Billicliffe was anxious that you should know how much he appreciated your kindness to him.'

Oscar said, 'I wasn't kind.' But if the lawyer heard this, he ignored it.

'I don't know if you know the house?'

'I went there a couple of times. But of course I knew it in the old days, when it was the forester's cottage and my grandmother was living at Corrydale.'

'I did the conveyancing when Major Billicliffe bought it from the estate. It is quite a modest establishment but I would say with distinct possibilities.'

'Yes. Yes, of course. I am sorry to be so uncommunicative but I am truly lost for words.'

'I understand.'

'I never thought ... expected ...'

'I'll put it all down in writing in a letter to you, then you can decide what you do next. And don't worry about arrangements over this side. I'll speak to Mr Lugg and put everything into his capable hands.'

'Thank you.' Oscar felt something more was expected of him. 'Thank you so very much.'

'A pleasure, Mr Blundell. Goodbye. And have a good Christmas.'

He rang off. Slowly Oscar replaced the receiver. At the end of the day old Billicliffe had come up trumps. Oscar ran a hand over his bewildered head. He said aloud to the empty house, 'Well, I'll be buggered.'

He thought for a long time about the little house on the Corrydale estate, not during the Billicliffe time but years ago, when the head forester and his homely wife had lived there. Then it had been a hive of activity, with four children underfoot, three dogs, a cage with ferrets by the back door and strings of washing flapping on the line. There had always been a good peat fire in the hearth, a vociferous welcome for a small boy and a hot plate of drop scones, dripping in butter. Oscar tried to remember the layout of the place, but in those days he had never gone further than the living room, with its smell of paraffin lamps and baking bread.

Now it belonged to him.

Oscar looked at his watch. It was five minutes past noon, and all at once, he longed for a drink. Usually, he never drank in the middle of the day, and if he did, only a glass of lager. But now, he needed – he really needed – a sophisticated and restoring gin and tonic, to settle himself and give him the necessary Dutch courage to deal with this new, and unexpected, turn of events.

He pulled himself to his feet, went downstairs and through the kitchen to his slate shelf wine cellar. There he found half a bottle of Gordon's, a bottle of tonic, and took them back into the kitchen, got a glass and poured himself a restoring slug.

The front door opened. 'Oscar!' Elfrida, returned.

'I'm here.'

'Can you come and help me?'

He went out to greet her, bearing his glass. He said, 'I am secretly drinking. I have become a secret drinker.'

Elfrida did not look greatly disturbed. 'Oh. Well done. I've got two huge boxes in the back of the car.'

She had left the front door open behind her. He put a hand over her shoulder and pushed it shut. He said, 'Later.'

'But—'

'We'll bring them in later. Come. I want to talk to you. I have something to tell you.'

Her eyes went wide. 'Is it dire?'

'Not dire at all. Take off your coat and come into the kitchen where we can sit and be peaceful.'

'Where's Lucy?'

'She has taken Horace shopping – to buy ribbon – and then for a walk. And Sam and Carrie are not yet back. So, for once, we are on our own. Let us not waste a bit of peace. Do you want a gin and tonic?'

'If we've really started lunchtime boozing I'd prefer a glass of sherry.' Elfrida unbuttoned her coat, slung it on the end of the banister and followed him into the kitchen. 'Oscar, you're looking quite flushed and excited. What *has* been going on?'

'I shall tell you.'

She sat at the table and he brought her her sherry, then sat too. 'Cheers, my dear girl.'

'And to you, Oscar.'

The gin and tonic was pretty strong, but delicious and exactly what his stomach needed. He set down the glass and said, 'If I tell you, quite slowly, because it's rather complicated, will you listen and not ask questions until I've got to the end? Otherwise I shall become confused.'

'I'll try.'

'Right. The first is that Major Billicliffe died this morning. I had a phone call from the hospital.'

Elfrida put her hand over her mouth. 'Oh, *Oscar.*'

'I know. We never got to see him. We never sat at his bedside and fed him grapes. But truly, with the roads the way they are, we could never have made the journey.'

'It's not *that* so much. It's just so sad. To be all alone and dying ...'

'He wasn't alone. He was in a ward with kindly nurses and people around him all the time. Not nearly so alone as he's been since his wife died.'

'I suppose so.' Elfrida thought about this, then sighed. 'What a complication. And you were his next-of-kin ... Does that mean ... ?'

He said, 'Now. Listen.'

And so he told her. About telephoning the lawyer, Murdo McKenzie, and having all responsibility removed from his shoulders by a man clearly experienced in such matters. He told her about the Inverness undertaker, Mr Lugg, in whom Murdo McKenzie had such touching faith, and how Mr Lugg would be the right person to see to everything, from crematorium to function rooms.

'But when will the funeral be?' Elfrida asked.

'The end of next week, we thought. By then all the Creagan people should be able, with a bit of luck, to get there. The snow can't lie for ever. Sooner or later there must come a thaw.'

'We should put an announcement in some paper.'

'Mr McKenzie has taken that on as well.'

'And let the local people know.'

'I'll ring Peter Kennedy.'

'Oh dear. What a terribly inconvenient time to die.'

'Exactly what I thought, and then had to pull myself together and stop being unchristian.'

'Oh, well. I suppose that's it.'

'No, Elfrida. That's not the end.'

'More?'

'Billicliffe's will was out of date. His wife had died and he had to make a new one. He has made me his sole beneficiary. No, don't say a word till I've finished. It means he has left me his house, his motor car, his dog and his fortune. His fortune, all bills and expenses paid, is in the region of two thousand five hundred pounds. All his savings. He has been living on his pension.'

'His house? He's left you his house? How terribly touching. Sweet. So kind. Did he really have no other family? No relation?'

'Nobody.'

'Poor lonely man. Oh, Oscar, and we were so horrid about him.'

'Just between ourselves.'

'Hiding behind the sofa in case he called.'

'Don't remind me.'

'What will you do with the house?'

'I don't know. I haven't had time to think. Sell it, I suppose. But it would have to be emptied of Billicliffe clobber first and probably fumigated.'

'What's it like?'

'You know. You saw. A tip.'

'No, I mean, how many rooms? Is there a kitchen? A bathroom?'

'I suppose, in estate-agent jargon, you'd say two up, two down, kitchen and bathroom probably added on after the war, sticking out at the back.'

'Which way does it face?'

Oscar had to work this one out. 'North at the front door, south on the other side.'

'And a garden?'

'Yes, I suppose a bit of land. I can't really remember. Mrs Ferguson, the forester's wife, used to grow potatoes and leeks. And there was an apple tree . . .'

Elfrida was silent for a moment, chewing this information over. And then, astonishingly, she said, 'Why don't you go and live there?'

Oscar stared at her in total disbelief. 'Live there? All on my own?'

'No, stupid, I'll come with you.'

'But you thought the house was horrible.'

'No house is impossible. There's no such thing as a place that cannot be improved, enlarged, redecorated. I'm sure when the forester lived there it was a dear little place. It was hearing-aids and dog-hair and brimming ashtrays and smeary glasses that made it all so disgusting. Nothing to do with the bricks and mortar.'

'But I have a house. I have this house.'

'You only own half a share. That's not very secure. You could sell your half and then you'd have seventy-five thousand pounds and you could spend that on Major Billicliffe's house and live happily ever after.'

'You mean, sell up here? Leave Creagan?'

'Oh, Oscar, don't sound so horrified. It's really quite a good idea. Sam Howard wants it, and Hughie McLellan is obviously agog to get rid of his half. I know you love it here, and I do too, but admit, it is big and faintly unfurnished and when Sam and Carrie and Lucy have gone we're going to be alone again, rattling around like a pair of peas in a drum. And another thing, I always think of *here* as a family house. It's not meant for a couple of old dears like us. It should have young people and children growing up . . .'

'Sam hasn't got any children.'

'No, but he's bound to get married again . . .' Elfrida did not finish her sentence. In the silence which followed, with some reluctance, she looked Oscar in the eye.

He said, 'Not Carrie.'

'Why not Carrie?'

'You mustn't matchmake.'

'It's impossible not to. They're so perfect together.'

'They're not perfect at all. He never stops being amiable while Carrie is remote and prickly as a gorse bush.'

'She's vulnerable just now. And yesterday they were away for ages, getting the Christmas tree. Carrie said they were exploring Corrydale, but I can't believe that they paced along for two hours without some exchange of words.'

'All that's happened is that they have been flung together by circumstances.'

'Maybe so.' Elfrida sighed. 'You're probably right. But, discounting Carrie, this is exactly the right establishment for a man like Sam Howard. The businessman, the manager of the resuscitated woollen mill, an important member of the community. I can just see him entertaining business colleagues from Japan and Germany, giving his chairman a weekend of golf. Besides – and this is the most important thing – Sam really wants this house. I think he feels *right* here, he feels at home. And wouldn't it be better to sell it to him than some stranger? And have seventy-five thousand pounds to put in your pocket?'

'Elfrida, I am not a man of means. If I did sell the Estate House, that money would have to be squirrelled away for old age and senility. I couldn't be mad enough to sink the lot into Major Billicliffe's cottage and leave myself with nothing put by.'

'We don't know how much we'd have to spend – on tidying things up, I mean.'

Oscar said, 'A lot.'

But Elfrida would not be put off. 'Then supposing

I sell my house in Hampshire, and we use *that* money for—'

Oscar, quite firmly for him, said, 'No.'

'Why not?'

'Because that is *your* house. It's about all you own, and you must under no circumstances sell it. Rent it out if you can find someone who wants to live there, but you must never sell.'

'Oh, well.' She became resigned and Oscar felt a brute. 'It was a good idea while it lasted, but I suppose you're right.' Then she perked up again. 'Whatever, it's all terribly exciting and no wonder you're looking flushed. One thing is certain, we must go and look round the poor little place, inspect it from attic to cellar. And rescue the car before it dies of cold in the snow. And the dog. What shall we do with the dog?' Suddenly she was laughing. 'What shall we do with our Baskerville hound, baying in the night and flinging its weight against locked and bolted doors?'

'To be honest, I prefer Horace. Perhaps I can bribe Charlie Miller to keep the dog. I'll have a word with Rose . . .'

Upstairs, on the landing, the telephone began to ring. Elfrida said, 'Damn. Why are phones so intrusive?'

'Leave it. Pretend we're out.'

'I wish I had the strength of mind. But I haven't.' She pulled herself to her feet and went out of the room. Oscar heard her running upstairs and, almost at once, the insistent ringing ceased. From the upper floor, faintly, Elfrida's voice floated. 'Hello.'

Oscar sat on, waiting patiently for her to return to him, mulling over her wild ideas and wishing he could go along with them. But if he did sell the Estate House to Sam, then the sum released would be his only capital, his buffer against an impoverished old age. They would certainly go and look at Billicliffe's house, that was only sensible. Perhaps cleaned and painted up a bit it wouldn't be so bad. But still, a poky, dark place in which to live after the spacious grandeur of the Estate House. He would miss, unbearably, the airy, sunny rooms, the sense of space, the good, solid feel of security. It would, indeed, be painful to sell up – even to a friend like Sam Howard – and leave it for ever.

Upstairs Elfrida still talked. He could hear the murmur of her voice but not the words she spoke. Every now and then she fell silent for some time then spoke again. He could not imagine who was at the other end of the line. He hoped that it was not sinister or disturbing news.

He had finished his gin and tonic. Standing up to rinse out the glass under the tap, he remembered the two boxes of borrowed glasses still in the boot of the car. He went out of the kitchen, down the hall and out through the front door into the piercing cold. He trod down the snowy path and through the gate to where his old car stood parked, and opened the boot. The boxes were unwieldy and heavy, and he had to make two journeys, carrying them one at a time. He put the second down on the kitchen table, then went back to shut the front door. As he did this, he heard the *ting* of the telephone, which it always made when one replaced the receiver. He stood at the foot of the stairs, his face upturned, waiting for her to appear. When she didn't, he called her name. 'Elfrida.'

She did not say anything. She simply came down the stairs, with an expression on her face that he could not fathom. He knew only that he had never seen her eyes so bright, had never seen her look so young, with a radiance about her that had nothing to do with the noonday light shining through her flaming shock of hair.

'My dear . . .'

'Oscar.' She reached him, standing on a stair above him, put her arms around him and pressed her cheek against his own. 'Something simply, utterly wonderful has happened to me.'

'Do you want to tell me about it?'

'Yes, but I think we both must be sitting down.'

So he took her hand and led her back into the kitchen, and they sat once more facing each other across the table.

'That was Jamie Erskine-Earle. About my little clock. You know he said he was going to show it to a colleague in Boothby's? Well, the colleague is in London and in this weather there was no way Jamie could get it south. But he sent him a fax, with a detailed description of the clock and some photographs. And the colleague, whoever he is, telephoned back from London this morning. And he said the clock was a very special item. A very rare timepiece. It's French, and it was made by one J. F. Houriet, about 1830. Its official description is a silver chronometer tourbillon. Just imagine, Oscar, all these years I've owned a silver tourbillon, and never had the faintest suspicion. And then he wanted to know how I had come by it, and Jamie told him that I'd inherited it from an elderly sea-faring godfather, but of course I've never had any idea of how it came into *his* possession. Anyway, Jamie said that it really is something of a treasure, and I should certainly have it well insured. So I plucked up my courage and said, "Is it valuable?" And he said "Yes." And I asked what

564

it was worth, and he said at auction ... possibly ... Guess, Oscar!'

'Impossible. Put me out of my misery. Tell me.'

'Seventy to eighty thousand pounds,' Elfrida gleefully shouted at him.

'I have misheard you. It can't be true.'

'You haven't misheard me and it is true. Jamie said his colleague said that it's a very serious piece to any collector. Don't you adore the word *serious*? Get it into a Boothby's sale of important clocks, watches and marine chronometers, and the figure might rise even higher.'

'I am left without words.'

'And all this time I told myself it was my little painting that would be my insurance and keep me out of the poorhouse. But instead my true treasure was my clock. Isn't it a lucky thing that nobody nicked it off the mantelpiece at Poulton's Row?'

'I might put it more strongly than that. Especially as you never locked your front door. It was always a lovely thing to own. You aren't thinking of selling it? You mustn't sell it.'

'Oh, Oscar, for goodness' sake, of course I'm going to sell it. Don't you see? With that money we can really transform Billicliffe Villa into the most desirable of residences. Build a conservatory. Fling out a ballroom wing ...'

'Elfrida.'

'... and buy a microwave.'

'Elfrida, listen. That money, if you sell the clock, belongs to you.'

'Oscar, listen. It belongs to *us*. And we'll end our days in a charming little cottage filled with sunlight, just the way this house always is. And we shall grow potatoes and leeks, if you want, and we shall have Rose Miller for a neighbour and a four-star country-house hotel in the garden. Who could ask for more? It's so exciting. Isn't it tremendously, wonderfully exciting?'

'Of course it is. But, dear girl, we must be practical. We must be sensible.'

'I hate being sensible. I want to go out and dance in the street. Shout our good news from the rooftops.'

Oscar considered this, as though it were a perfectly viable suggestion. And then he said, 'No.'

'No?'

'Just for the moment. What I would like is for nothing to be said about *anything* until I've had a chance to get Sam on his own and explain the situation. He must know that we're thinking of selling up here because I'm certain he'll want first refusal. Not having to start searching for another property will be a great weight off his mind. He has, at the moment, quite enough to think about without wondering where he's going to live. He's not going to be with us for ever, so we should put him in the picture before he leaves us and we don't see him again. He may need time to think it all through, perhaps raise the cash. We don't know. But I feel he must be our first consideration.'

'Yes. You're absolutely right. When will you tell him?'

'I shall take him down to the pub this evening.'

'And the others? Carrie and Lucy?'

'After I've spoken to Sam.'

'What if Billicliffe's house proves to be a total disaster?'

'Then we shall have to think again.'

'I can't wait to go and look at it. You and I. But we

can't go this afternoon because of the snow. The roads are horribly skiddy. And we can't go tomorrow because of getting ready for the party.'

'Sunday?

'Christmas Eve!'

'As good a day as any. Sunday morning.'

'All right. We'll go then. Perhaps we should ask Sam to drive us in his car. That should preclude us ending up in a ditch.' She thought about this, then came up with an even brighter idea. 'I know. We'll all go, Carrie and Lucy too.'

Oscar was wary. 'That will entail five different people all coming up with their own opinions and ideas.'

'All the better. I'm sure Sam will be wonderfully practical. He'll talk about things like soffits and rap walls and be knowledgeable about rising damp. And I've had another brilliant idea. If we went to Corrydale in the morning, and it wasn't raining or snowing, we could take a lunch picnic. A winter picnic. I shall make a pot of my Garbage Broth. Oscar, have we got a key for Major Billicliffe's house?'

Oscar had not thought about a key. 'No.'

'Then how shall we get in?'

'Rose Miller will have a key, or know some person who has. I'll telephone her. I should let her know that the old boy has died, anyway, though she's probably heard by now. And I must call Peter Kennedy.'

Carrie

Carrie

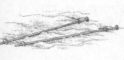They drove to Buckly by way of the narrow back road that wound along the coast. The prospects about them could not have been more wintry: white hills, grey skies running with cloud driven on a wind that blew from the Arctic seas, and across great tracts of snow-covered moors. The car crested a shallow hill, and Carrie saw below them the sea loch, at half tide, the dark conifer forests on the further shore, and the huddle of white cottages above a disused, ruined pier.

She had never been this way before. 'What is the loch called?' she asked.

'Loch Fhada. It's a bird sanctuary,' Sam told her.

They turned along the shore road. The beach was rocky and inhospitable. The sea, racing in on the flood, was grey as the skies above and flecked with spray. Far out, on a sandbank, a number of seals rested and, as she watched, a flight of duck moved in from the east to land on an isolated pool, not yet drowned by the running tide.

At the far end of the loch, a road bridge spanned the

water, and beyond this was wild country, a glen of scrub and bracken and dead water, edging up into the hills. At the main road they turned north; the gritters had been out, and the snow was dirtied by the mud thrown up by lorries and tractors. Between the road and the sea lay farmland; sheep huddled in the lee of drystone dykes, small farmsteads with bravely smoking chimney-pots, reeking of peat. A tractor was crossing a field, trailing a bogie laden with hay, and a woman emerged from a door to throw crusts to her flock of gobbling geese. Further on they came upon a man trudging along the side of the road, a solitary figure, head down against the weather; he held a long crook and his sheepdog ran at his heels. As they approached, he paused to let them by and raised a mittened hand in greeting.

'He looks,' said Carrie, 'as though he had been painted by Breughel.'

She remembered farms in the south of England, so bosky and green, and her father's smallholding in Cornwall where the milk cows grazed out of doors all winter. She said, 'I can't imagine working a farm in weather like this. It seems a question of survival rather than anything else.'

'They're always prepared for bad weather. Winters have always been harsh. And they're a tough breed.'

'They'd need to be.'

They were on their way to view the woollen mill, which was to be Sam Howard's future. Now Carrie wished that she had never come up with that suggestion, so casually made. 'I should like to see your mill,' she had said, with no idea that he would be so enthusiastic about the prospect of showing her around. That had been before all that happened later, and this morning, of course, it was too late to back out, to make some excuse, to pretend that she wasn't particularly interested after all.

Too late. Too late to blot out that outburst of passionate honesty, the truth that she had been so careful to keep to herself, concealed and hopefully unsuspected. She told herself that she couldn't conceive of how it had all come about, knowing perfectly well what had precipitated the breakdown of defences, the opening up of her own unhappy heart.

It was Corrydale. The place. The sunlit snow, the aromatic scent of pine trees, the dark blue skies, the mountains on the far side of the glittering firth. The warmth of the low sun, seeping through the padding of her jacket, the crunch of fresh snow underfoot, the dazzle, the pleasure of breathing pure cold air down into her lungs. Austria. Oberbeuren. And Andreas: the place and the man, indivisible. Andreas, here, now, walking beside her, talking incessantly, his voice always with that undertone of laughter. Andreas. Making plans, making love. So strong was the illusion that she thought she could smell the cool fresh lemony scent of his aftershave. And even as she felt his presence so strongly she had known that it was simply a figment of her own heightened imagination. Because Andreas was gone. Back to Inga and his children, leaving Carrie with such a devastating sense of pain and loss that all at once it was no longer possible to remain cool and rational.

Sam, talking about his wife, his broken marriage and the end of his job in New York, had simply compounded her misery, and when he had come out with that horrible word 'rejected', she had turned on him in the sort of rage of which she had never believed herself capable, and the furious words had broken free, and it was only tears that stemmed the outburst. A flood of tears that left her ashamed and humiliated, and when she had tried to run away from her own humiliation, Sam had pulled her back and taken her into his arms and held her close, as he might have held an inconsolable child.

She thought now that in a book, in a film, that moment would have been the end. The final embrace, after reels of antagonism and misunderstanding, the camera backing off into a long shot, panning up to the sky, a skein of home-flying geese or some other meaningful symbol, throbbing theme music, the credits rolling, and the good sensation of a happy ending.

But life didn't stop at the end of the story. It moved on. Sam's embrace, his arms around her, the physical contact, the closeness had comforted her, but not melted her own coldness. She was not changed. She was still Carrie, thirty years old, with the love of her life gone for ever. Perhaps that was the way she wanted to be, with a heart frozen as the winter landscape all about them. Perhaps that was the way she wanted to stay.

Elfrida had said, so sadly, 'The world is full of married men.' It was better not to get too close to another person. The closer you got, the more likely you were to get hurt.

McTaggart's of Buckly.

The mill stood on the outskirts of the small town, set back from the road behind a stone wall and an imposing wrought-iron double gateway, wide enough to allow the passage of a horse and cart. Overhead curved a decorative archway, crowned by an ornate device, vaguely heraldic in appearance.

The gate, this morning, stood open, and beyond was a spacious area set about with circular raised flower-beds, contained by walls of cobblestones. All lay under snow, and the flower-beds were empty, but Carrie guessed that in summertime there would be a fine show of geraniums, lobelia, aubretia and other municipally approved planting.

The snow was unmarked by footprints or tyre tracks. They were, it was clear, the first and only visitors of the day. Passing beneath the gateway, Carrie had her first sighting of the mill, through the windscreen, and could at once understand why the environmental authorities had deemed it worthy of being listed. There was an industrial chimney, of course, rearing up beyond the pitched roof, and other more utilitarian sheds and store-houses set about, but the main building was both impressive and good-looking.

Built of local stone, its façade was long and pleasingly symmetrical. A central pediment was topped by a clock tower. Beneath this, there was a single window on the first floor, and then, below again, an important double door over which arched an elegant glass fanlight. On either side of the pediment the two wings were set with a double row of windows, all formally fenestrated. The sloping roof was slate, pierced by skylights, and here and there the stonework was softened by the dark, glossy green of climbing ivy.

Sam drew up in front of the big door, and they stepped down into the snow. Carrie stood for a moment, looking around her, and Sam came to stand at her side, his hands deep in the pockets of his Barbour. After a bit he asked, 'What do you think?'

'I think it's very handsome.'

'I told you, no question of bulldozing the lot and starting anew.'

'I was expecting a dark, satanic mill. Or a factory. This looks more like a well-established public school. All that's missing are a few playing-fields with goal-posts.'

'The original mill buildings are round at the back, nearer to the river. This block was put up in eighteen sixty five so it's relatively new. It was conceived as a form of window-dressing. Offices, sale rooms, conference rooms, that sort of thing. There was even a reading room incorporated for the employees – a good example of Victorian paternalism. On the first floor, the space was for finished goods, and above again, in the lofts, wool stores. You have to remember that the business has been going since the middle of the eighteenth century. The river, of course, was the reason that the original mill was sited in this particular spot.'

Carrie said, 'It all looks in such good order. Hard to believe it's suffered a fatal flood.'

'Well, brace yourself. You're in for a shock.'

He produced from his pocket a considerable key, fitted it into the brass lock, turned it and pushed open the door. He stood aside, and Carrie went past him and into a square, high-ceilinged hallway.

And devastation.

It was empty. The high-tide mark of the floodwater reached to nearly five feet. Above this, handsome flock wallpaper had survived, but, below, all colour had been soaked away and it peeled from the wall in ruined tatters. The floor, too, bare boards, was much damaged: old planks rotted and broken; gaping holes revealing original joists and the dark cavities of deep foundations.

There hung over all the pervading and depressing smell of mould and damp.

'This was the reception area for visitors, or new customers, an important first impression. I believe it was all furnished and carpeted in some style, with portraits of various McTaggart founders glowering down from the walls. You can see that the plaster cornice survived, but the flood rendered everything else beyond repair and it all had to be jettisoned.'

'How long did it take for the water to go down?'

'About a week. As soon as possible, industrial blowers were installed to try to dry things out but too late to save anything in here.'

'Has the river ever flooded before?'

'Once. About fifty years ago. After that a dam and a sluice were constructed to control the level of the water. But this time the rain was relentless, and to make matters worse there was a very high tide, and the river simply burst its banks.'

'It's almost impossible to imagine.'

'I know. Come and see – careful where you walk, I don't want you falling through the floorboards.'

Another door stood at the back of the hallway and Sam opened this. Carrie followed him. It was a bit like going through the green baize door of a large house with servants' quarters, for it led into a stone-floored space, big as a warehouse and glass-roofed for light. It was empty, echoing and piercingly cold. Here and there was evidence of past industry, like the mountings set into the flags where once had stood the weaving looms, and at the far side, an open-treaded wooden staircase led to an upper gallery.

It felt dead and sadly desolate.

'What went on here?' Carrie asked, and her voice rang back at her from the soaring roof and the empty, stained walls.

'This is a weaving shed. Fergus Skinner – he was the guy in charge of the mill at the time of the flood – told me some of what happened. That night, they went on working here until eleven o'clock, because even as the water trickled in they were still hoping that the flood would abate. But it didn't, and the rest of the night they spent lifting everything they could off the floor. A desperate but hopeless task. They salvaged what they could. The spinning frames, although they were badly damaged. Old wooden scouring machines survived, and the teazle-raising machines. Financially the worst disaster was the ruin of all the finished goods, orders worth thousands, packed and ready for delivery. It was that loss, really, that finally finished off McTaggart's.'

'Was the office on the ground floor?'

'Unfortunately, yes. Fergus told me that he waded in there to see if he could salvage anything, but the water was waist level by then, the computers drowned, and letters of credit floating towards him down the aisle . . .'

'What happened the next day? The workforce?'

'All laid off. No alternative. But as soon as the waters subsided, about a hundred men turned up to save what they could. Half of the machinery had to be scrapped, including the German electronic shuttle looms that had only recently been installed. So much for modern, and extremely expensive, technology. What did survive was some of the older, less sophisticated machinery, looms which had been bought in second-hand and were already forty or fifty years old. The engineers stripped down the carding machine and cleaned it off before the rust set in, so that can be set up again. And there was some specialist machinery from Italy. That's in store right now and we plan to send it back to Milan for refurbishment and re-use.'

Carrie, fascinated and attentive, was nevertheless starting to feel tremendously cold. Damp chill crept up through the thick soles of her boots and she shivered. Sam saw this and was remorseful. 'Carrie, I'm sorry. Once I start expounding I forget everything else. Do you want to go? Have you had enough?'

'No. I want to see it all. I want you to show it *all* to me and tell me what you're going to do, and the new plans, and where everything's going to be. At the moment, I'm completely bewildered by the prospect of doing anything at all. Its mind-boggling. Like being given a totally impossible task.'

'Nothing is impossible.'

'But still . . . being the guy in charge.'

'Yes, but with the resources of a huge conglomerate behind me. That makes the hell of a difference.'

'Even so. They chose *you* to take on the job. I wonder why?'

Sam grinned, and all at once looked not simply boyish but bursting with eager confidence. He knew what he was talking about. He was on his home ground.

He said, 'I suppose because, basically, I'm a Yorkshire boy. And where there's muck there's brass. Now, come, before you freeze, and I'll show you the rest . . .'

By the time the tour was finished and they stepped once more into the outdoors, Carrie was chilled to the bone. She stood in the snow while Sam closed and locked the door behind him. Then he turned and saw her, hunched into her thick grey loden coat, with her hands dug deep into the pockets. 'You look frozen, Carrie.'

'I am.'

'I'm sorry. I shouldn't have kept you so long.'

'I liked it. It's just that my feet are frozen.'

'I hope you weren't bored.'

'Not at all. Fascinated.'

He looked at his watch. 'It's half past eleven. Shall we go back to Creagan, or would you like a heartening drink? From the look of you, a Whisky Mac might be the best thing.'

'Coffee would do the trick.'

'Whatever. Come along, get back into the car and we'll warm you up.'

So they drove away from the deserted mill, over the cobbles, under the handsome gateway, then turned right and went on down the road into Buckly, making their way along narrow, winding streets, and across a small square past the war memorial. There weren't many people about, but little shops had their lights on and brave Christmas decorations in the windows. Then, a stone bridge spanned the ravine of a river in spate, and beyond this, Sam drew up by the pavement outside a gloomy-looking establishment with the DUKE'S ARMS written in curly gold capitals above the door. Carrie eyed it without much enthusiasm.

'I'm sure,' Sam told her, 'that in Buckly there are more lively spots, but this happens to be the only one I know. And it is, in its own way, unique.'

'It doesn't look a riot of fun.'

'We shall make it so.'

They got out of the car, crossed the pavement and

Sam pushed open the door, letting loose a warm, beery smell. Carrie followed gingerly. Inside, it was dark and seedy, but gloriously overheated. A coal fire glowed and flickered in the old-fashioned hearth, and over the mantelpiece hung an enormous fish in a glass case. Small wobbly tables held brewery beermats and ashtrays, and there seemed to be only two other customers, both silent, male and very old. Behind the bar, the proprietor was intent on a small black-and-white television set, with the sound turned down to a murmur. A clock ticked, and a bit of coal collapsed in the fire with a whisper. The atmosphere was so dour that Carrie wondered if they should simply turn round and tiptoe away again.

But Sam had other ideas. 'Come on,' he said, and his voice rang round the room in an off-putting way. 'Sit here, close to the fire.' He pulled a chair away from a table. 'I'm sure you'll get a cup of coffee if you really want one, but would you try a Whisky Mac? It's the most warming drink in the world.'

It sounded more tempting than coffee. 'All right.'

She sat and pulled off her gloves, unbuttoned her coat and spread her hands to the heat of the fire. Sam went over to the bar, where the man dragged himself away from the television set and took his order. After that, in the way of all countrymen in pubs, they fell into conversation, their voices low, as though they spoke secrets.

Carrie pulled off her fur hat and laid it on the chair beside her, ran her fingers through her hair and caught the eye of the old man who sat beneath the window. It was a rheumy eye, and blazed with disapproval, and Carrie guessed that the Duke's Arms was not an establishment frequented by women. She tried smiling at him, but he only munched on his dentures, and returned his attention to his beer.

The exchange at the bar continued. Sam stood with his back to her, in the classic attitude of a man at ease in his pub, with one foot on the brass rail and an elbow on the polished counter. Very slowly, as they talked, the barman assembled Sam's order, pausing every now and then to check up on what the television set had to say.

Carrie leaned against the hard chairback, stretched out her legs and watched them. She thought that this morning she had seen, for the first time, the other side of Sam, the man who had walked in out of the snow only three or four days ago, who had been forced by the vile weather to stay and had become, with no apparent effort or forced bonhomie, an integral part of an ill-assorted household. Absorbed as easily as an accomplished and experienced house guest.

She thought of him dealing, unasked, with a number of not very exciting day-to-day tasks, like humping great baskets of logs, filling the coal bucket, walking the dog, carving a roast pheasant and even gutting the salmon that Elfrida, in a mad moment, had been impelled to buy from the man who sold fresh fish from the back of his van. Uncomplaining, Sam had shovelled snow, pushed trolleys around the supermarket, stocked up Oscar's wine cellar and brought home the Christmas tree. Even better, he had set it up on its dicey-looking wooden stand, then managed to unravel and get working the annual headache of the Christmas-tree lights.

For this noble effort, Oscar had been particularly grateful.

On another level altogether, he had proved to be

something of an asset when Elfrida decided to sell her picture, producing Sir James Erskine-Earle out of nowhere, like a rabbit out of a hat. The fact that that particular project had come to nothing, and the picture was pronounced a fake, had upset Sam considerably, as though the worthlessness of the painting was somehow all his fault.

He was a man hard to dislike. He and Oscar (nobody's fool) had slipped at once into a companionable friendship that belied the years that lay between them. Left alone together they never ran out of things to talk about because Oscar enjoyed sharing memories of the days when he was a boy and travelled to spend summers with his grandmother at Corrydale. Because of his local knowledge, not only of the people but the countryside, he was able to fill Sam in with much information, and a great many anecdotes, about the district in which Sam was coming to live and work.

On Oscar's part, he clearly enjoyed the company of another man, a stranger maybe but one to whom he had taken instantly. He was fascinated by the progress of Sam's career, the boyhood in Yorkshire, the years in London and New York, and now the challenge of getting a defunct business on its feet again. Remembering the old McTaggart's and the sturdy tweeds that had come from its looms, he was amazed by the exciting plans that had already been drawn up by Sturrock & Swinfield, the expensive machinery ordered from Switzerland, the marvels of modern technology, the marketing prospects for new luxury products, and the programme for retraining the workforce – McTaggart's most valuable asset.

From time to time, with the world set to rights, they had ambled off together to visit the golf club or drop into the Creagan pub for a peaceful, manly dram.

Elfrida, as well, was entranced by her visitor. But, then, she had never been able to resist the charms of an attractive man, especially one who laughed at her dotty remarks, and was capable of concocting a perfect dry martini. As for Lucy, she had confided to Carrie one night, when Carrie had gone up to the attic to kiss her goodnight, that she thought Sam was almost as good-looking as Mel Gibson.

Amused, Carrie had asked, 'You like him then?'

'Yes. He's gorgeous and he's comfortable. I usually feel a bit shy with men, like other girls' fathers, but Sam's like the sort of uncle you've known for ever or somebody's oldest friend.'

And that was how it had been. And that was how, for Carrie, it might have stayed, had it not been for the traumatic events of yesterday.

And this morning.

Nothing, *really*, had happened. It was just that following Sam through the cold and lofty spaces of the mill, the echoing passages, the deserted stores and dye-sheds, Carrie was made aware for the first time of his *alter ego*. Before her eyes, he seemed to change. He grew in stature, spoke with confidence and authority as he described to her the devastation of the flood, explained the plans for the future, quoting figures that made her head reel. Once or twice he had tried to make clear to her the details of some technicality of spinning or weaving, which she could scarcely understand, because it was a bit as though he was talking in a foreign language. Irritated by her own stupidity, she felt diminished and also confused because Sam, back in his own world, was strangely transformed:

no longer the amiable house guest of the last few days but a man in charge, a man to be reckoned with and, at the end of the day, a man you would not choose to cross.

He returned to her at last, bearing their drinks and two packets of peanuts. 'Sorry.' He set these down on the table and drew up a chair. 'Conversation.'

'What were you talking about?'

'Football. Fishing. The weather. What else?' He had bought himself a pint of bitter. He raised the tall glass. Across the table their eyes met. '*Slàinte.*'

'I don't speak the language.'

'It's Gaelic for down the hatch.'

Carrie took a mouthful of her drink and hastily set down the glass. 'Heavens, that's strong.'

'The classic warmer when you're out on a winter hill. That, or cherry brandy.'

'What's the weather going to do?'

'There's a thaw on the way. That's why our friend is glued to the box. The wind is moving around to the south-west and milder airstreams are *en route.*'

'No white Christmas?'

'Wet white rather than freezing white. And the road to Inverness is open again.'

'Does that mean you're going to disappear instantly?'

'No.' He shook his head. 'I've been asked for Christmas so I'm staying. Anyway, I've nowhere else to go. But on Boxing Day I must come down to earth with a bang, pack my bags and leave.' His smile was wry. 'It's going to feel a bit like the end of the holidays and having to go back to school.'

'Never mind. Lots of fun and games in the pipeline. Elfrida's party for one.'

'I have to be here for *that*. I've promised to fix the dry martini.'

'Don't make it too strong. We don't want any untoward behaviour – like Lady Erskine-Earle and Arfur Snead dancing Highland Flings together.'

'That would be disastrous.'

'When – when you get to Inverness, will you stay there?'

'No. I have to be in London next week. The head office is open for a couple of days before New Year and David Swinfield's set up a meeting. Then, I think, Switzerland again. I shan't be back here until about the twelfth of January.'

'Lucy and I go on the third. We're booked on the morning flight.' She bit her lip, thinking about this. 'I'm not looking forward to it. I think Lucy is going to be desolate and I don't know what I'm going to say to cheer her up. I only know I wouldn't want to be her, leaving all the fun and freedom behind and going back to that dull flat, and a mother who won't be particularly delighted to see her.'

'It can't be as bad as that.'

'Sam, it is.'

'I'm sorry. I shall buy her a splendid Christmas present. What do you think she would like?'

Carrie was amused. 'Have you still not done your shopping?'

'You must admit, I've scarcely had time. I shall go to Kingsferry tomorrow morning and get the lot.'

'Tomorrow? It'll be a nightmare. Crowds on the pavements, queues in the shops.'

'In Kingsferry? I think not. Besides, I'm accustomed to buying presents in Regent Street or Fifth Avenue on

586

Christmas Eve. I rather enjoy the buzz and the din. "I Saw Mommy Kissing Santa Claus" blaring out over the Tannoy. And there'll be no time for dithering.'

Carrie laughed. 'It's my idea of a bad dream but I see your point. And, after all your years of experience, Kingsferry's high street will not seem in the least alarming. You will shoulder your way bravely through the throng.'

'You still haven't told me what to get for Lucy.'

Carrie considered this. 'How about little gold studs for her ears? Something pretty but not too over-the-top for when she can take her sleepers out.'

'Rory gave her those. I don't suppose she'll ever want to take them out.'

'Still. Nice to know you've got another pair.'

'I'll see.'

He fell silent. The quiet lay between them and felt companionable. Outside in the street a car passed by, and somewhere a herring gull was screaming its heart out from a windy chimney-pot. Sam reached for one of the packets of peanuts and opened it with great neatness and dexterity, shook a few out into the palm of his hand, and offered them to Carrie.

She said, 'I don't really like peanuts.'

He ate a couple, and tossed the packet back on to the table. He said, 'I sympathise with Lucy. I decided the other morning that life at the Estate House is a bit like being on a cruise with just a few other passengers, marvellously removed from all the stresses and strains of everyday life. I have a sinister feeling I could happily jog along in low gear for weeks, achieving nothing.'

'I suppose, if you think about it, it's all been a bit of a waste of time for you.'

He frowned. 'A waste of time?'

'Well, the whole point of your coming to Creagan was to inspect Hughie McLellan's house, perhaps to buy it. And that all fell through. A busted flush. So now you're going to have to find some other place to live.'

'That's the least of my problems.'

'I'm not on anybody's side. Half of me relishes the idea of Mr Howard, the director of the mill, living at the Estate House, a suitably dignified environment for an important man. On the other hand, at the moment, it seems to be Oscar and Elfrida's only home where they are happily settled for their twilight years.'

'I don't think of Elfrida as twilight. More high noon. And it all boils down, as most things do, to the distasteful question of hard cash. A busted flush, maybe, but never a waste of time. Never think that.'

Carrie reached for her glass, and took another mouthful of her fiery, reviving drink. She put the glass down on the scarred wooden surface of the table and looked up into Sam's face. *Never a waste of time.* And an extraordinary thing happened, because all at once it was as though she had never truly seen him before, and now all she knew for certain was that her recognition of him was too late, because he would go away, and it would be all over, and she would probably never see him again.

Perhaps it was the warmth of the fire, or the effect of the Whisky Mac, but suddenly she felt dangerously emotional and quite unsure of herself. She thought of how injured victims, devastated by some dreadful accident, lay on hospital beds in comas, wired up to every sort of tube and machine while loved ones sat by them, holding hands, talking, hoping against hope for some flicker of recognition or other sign. And then the miracle. The twitching eyelid, the nod. The start of recovery.

Yesterday, at Corrydale, after her outburst of words and her angry weeping, Sam had taken her in his arms and held her until the tears ceased. And she had felt no warmth for him, no physical reaction to his closeness, only a grudging gratitude for his comfort, and shame for herself for behaving like a fool.

But now . . . the beginning of recovery, perhaps. The melting of the coldness that had been her only armour. To love. To be loved again . . .

'Carrie.'

'What is it?'

'Can we talk?'

'What about?'

'You and me. Us.' Carrie said nothing. After a bit, perhaps encouraged by her silence, he went on, 'It seems to me that we've met each other, got to know each other, at a bad time. We're both, as it were, in something of a state of limbo. Perhaps we both need a bit of space to get our various houses in order. Also, neither of us is free. You've taken on the moral responsibility for Lucy and I'm still married to Deborah.'

He watched for her reaction to all this, and his expression was both anxious and very serious. Carrie's response was clearly of great importance to him.

'What are you telling me, Sam?'

'Just that perhaps we should give ourselves a bit of time. You go back to London, repossess your house, get on top of your new job. And I shall get in touch with New York and Deborah's lawyer. I'm pretty certain that by now she'll have started proceedings. I don't know how long it will take but as we had no children there should be

589

no hang-ups, no serious complications. Simply material matters. The apartment, the car, the money.'

'Is that what you really want? Divorce?'

'No.' He was bluntly honest. 'I don't want it. Any more than I would choose to have a surgical amputation. But I have to sort out the past before I can embark on a new future. Get rid of a lot of emotional clobber.'

'Will Deborah be all right?'

'I hope so. And I hope she'll be happy. She has the backing of a loving and devoted family.'

'Will you have to go to New York?'

'Probably.'

'Is it going to be painful?'

'Ending something that was once good is bound to be painful. But, done and over, the hurting stops.'

Carrie said, 'I know what you mean.'

He went on, 'I shall be living and working here in Buckly. You'll be in London. Hundred of miles apart. But I know I shall be flying up and down to London like a yo-yo, for meetings and conferences and such. I thought perhaps . . . we could see each other again. Go to a concert, out to dinner. Start over. Afresh. As though none of this time had ever happened.'

Start over. Afresh. The two of them. Carrie said, '*I* wouldn't want this time not to have happened.'

'I'm glad. It's been extraordinary, hasn't it? Magic. Like days stolen from another life, another world. When it is over, and I am gone, I shall wallow in nostalgia.' Carrie's hand lay on the table between them, and the firelight was reflected and sparked facets of light from her sapphire and diamond ring. Without curiosity, he asked, 'Who gave you your ring?'

'Andreas.'

'I hoped it might have been bequeathed to you by an elderly but devoted aunt.'

'No. It was Andreas. We were in Munich together. He saw it on a velvet tray in the window of an antique shop and he went in and bought it for me.'

'You must wear it always,' Sam told her. 'It's so lovely on your hand. How shall I find you in London, Carrie?'

'Overseas. Bruton Street. It's in the phone book. And I'll be back in Ranfurly Road in February.'

'I haven't been to Fulham since I sold my house in Eel Park Common and left for New York. Perhaps I shall come. Take a trip down Memory Lane. And you shall show me where you live.'

'Do that. I'll cook you dinner.'

'No promises. No commitments.'

'No promises.'

'So we leave it like that?'

'We leave it like that.'

Sam said, 'Good.' And, as though he were sealing their agreement he covered her hand with his own, and she turned up her palm, and wrapped her fingers around his wrist. Their drinks finished, the peanuts left abandoned, it was perhaps time to leave, but both were reluctant to go. So they stayed while the barman, slowly polishing glasses with a tea-towel, gazed at some quiz show. And the two old men, heads sunk into the collars of their worn overcoats, sat on, ancient and silent as a pair of hibernating tortoises. They seemed unaware that, as they whiled away the last of the morning, the whole world had changed.

Sam

Sam

That evening, at six thirty, Sam found himself once more in a pub, but now it was Creagan and he was with Oscar.

'Let's go and have a drink,' Oscar had suggested. They were alone in the sitting room of the Estate House. Others were occupied elsewhere; Carrie and Elfrida clashing about in the kitchen together, concocting dinner, food for the party tomorrow and starting on the long-term preparations for the Christmas feast. During the course of the afternoon, Rory Kennedy had appeared, with large bunches of berried holly, and he and Lucy had set to, decorating, and were still at it. They had gone up to the top of the garden and torn away from the wall long strands of dark green ivy, and it was taking them much concentration and effort to twine this down the whole length of the banister, from attic to hall. Rory had been invited for supper, and accepted, which was just as well because it all seemed to be taking a very long time.

The Creagan pub was a great deal more cheerful than the Duke's Arms in Buckly, although Sam guessed that he would always remember that charmless spot with much affection and a certain amount of sentiment. Here seasonal festivities seemed to have started, and there were unknown faces at the bar. In one corner a noisy party was already well under way: young men in elegantly battered tweeds and their trendy girlfriends with London voices. They had doubtless driven down the glen from some remote family shooting lodge, opened up for Christmas and the New Year, and filled with house guests. They were, thought Sam – conveniently forgetting that, once, he had behaved just as boisterously – making an unnecessary and embarrassing din.

But it all felt very lively. Open fires burned and decorations were festooned all about the place, tastefully entwined with holly and cardboard Bambis and Father Christmases twinkling with glitter.

It took a bit of time to shoulder up to the bar and then to catch the attention of the frantic barman, but finally Oscar had ordered two Famous Grouses, one for Sam, on the rocks, and one for himself, with tap water. Then they had something of a search for a place to sit, and ended up at a small, unoccupied table in a dark corner away from the fire. It didn't matter. It was quite warm enough.

Oscar said, 'Cheers,' took a mouthful of his drink and got straight down to business. 'I thought it would be easier to talk here than at home. The telephone is inclined to ring or someone comes flying in with questions on their lips. I didn't want us to be disturbed.'

'Oscar, this all sounds very sinister.'

'Not sinister at all, dear boy, but slightly complicated. And I wanted to talk to you on my own.'

'What's happened?'

'What has happened is that Major Billicliffe has died. You have heard, maybe – You know about Major Billicliffe?'

'The old factor who was in hospital.'

'Exactly so.'

'I'm sorry.'

'We are all sorry, for different reasons. Whatever, he has died. I think he had been ill for a long time, far longer than any of us suspected. To cut a long story short, Sam, he has left me his house at Corrydale.'

'But that's wonderful news.'

'I am not so sure. It's in a fairly neglected state.'

'Carrie and I looked at it when we went to get the Christmas tree. A bit desolate, perhaps, and completely snowed up, but I would have thought a good little property. And, of course, that marvellous view down the fields and the trees to the water.'

'As well,' Oscar went on, sounding like a man determined to make a clean breast of things, 'he has left me his car *and* his Labrador, and a small amount of money.'

Sam made a face. 'I can't be too enthusiastic about the car. It looked to me as though it would never start again. As for the dog, I think that's the one Charlie Miller had with him. Perhaps he can be persuaded to keep it.'

'Yes.'

'Oscar, this is really good news. What will you do with the cottage? Put it on the market? Or you could turn it into a holiday let, a nice little earner, as they say.'

'Yes,' said Oscar. 'I could. But Elfrida and I think that we might go and live there. I know it sounds a little outlandish, and it all depends on Elfrida's reaction when she actually gets to see over the place. You see, she's never been to Corrydale. Before you all came we didn't do very much, I'm afraid. Kept a bit of a low profile. And she knew that, in a strange way, I rather dreaded going back to a place where once, long ago, I had been so happy.'

'I understand.'

'We did drop in, of course, on our first night, because we had to collect the key to the Estate House, but it was dark and cold and we were tired, and old Billicliffe was not the neatest of housekeepers and we couldn't wait to get away. When he was ill and I went to see him in bed it looked even worse, and our impressions of the place are so dismal that we shall have to think deeply before we make up our minds and do a total assessment of the situation.'

'Would you like to live there?' Sam asked. 'Is it not very remote?'

'Not really. A bit off the road, but neighbours all about. The home farm, the Millers, and Rose who was my grandmother's parlourmaid. A little community. The house will probably need a bit spent on it, and we'll have to try to work that out, but the idea does have possibilities.'

Sam said, 'It did seem a bit neglected, but the roof wasn't fallen in or windows broken. How much space would you have?'

'All the estate houses were the same design, two up and two down originally. Little kitchens and bathrooms were added on after the war.'

'Would that be big enough for you both?'

'I think so. Between us, we have few possessions.'

'And the Estate House?'

'That's why I want to talk to you. If we go to Corrydale, Elfrida and I want you to have my share of the Estate House. That means that you can get in touch with Hughie and tell him that you wish to buy us both out.'

'*If* you move to Corrydale?'

'Yes.'

'What if Elfrida decides against living there? What if you both have second thoughts once you've really looked at the place?'

'Then we shall all have to think again. But somehow I don't think that will happen. It will doubtless need a certain amount of money spent on it to make it sound, dry and warm. Painting and such, probably new window-sashes. That sort of thing. But between us, we could manage. And if I get seventy-five thousand for my share of the Estate House then we should have no problems, financially speaking.'

'Seventy-five thousand, Oscar?'

'That was the sum you mentioned.'

'No. That was the sum *Hughie* mentioned. What you have just told me changes everything.'

'I don't understand.'

'Your cousin Hughie, I think, is strapped for cash. And he needs it quickly. That was why he was so keen to press his door-key into my hand, and so anxious to avoid the added expense of an estate-agent's cut. Personally, I think the Estate House is worth a great deal more than a hundred and fifty thousand. So you must be hard-headed, Oscar. Before we talk any more you must get a surveyor in, and have an independent valuation made. Willing seller, willing buyer. After that, consult a lawyer to deal with the conveyancing of the property. You may be told – I think you will – that the house is worth a good deal more than a hundred and fifty thousand. Personally I should add another fifty thousand. Possibly more.'

Oscar gaped. 'Two hundred thousand?'

'At least. Another thing, Oscar. You may decide to put it on the open market.'

'No. I want to sell it to *you*.'

'A private deal?'

'Yes.'

'In that case, by law I should have to make an offer well

over the valuation price.' Sam smiled. 'So it seems, Oscar, that you might do rather well.'

'I am bewildered. Whose side are you on?'

'Yours and Elfrida's. You have a wonderful property here, and I want desperately to buy it from you. But I couldn't look myself in the eye if it wasn't all accomplished in a totally businesslike fashion.'

'Do you have that sort of money?'

'Yes. And if I didn't I have Sturrock & Swinfield, solid as a rock, behind me. There are some advantages in working for an enormous conglomerate.'

Oscar shook his head, quite bemused by the turn of events. He said, 'Well, I'll be buggered.'

Sam laughed. 'Don't get over-excited. Not until you've fully inspected your other piece of property.'

'Billicliffe's place, you mean. Elfrida thought we might all go over on Sunday morning and take a look at it. Make a bit of an occasion. Take a picnic lunch. If it buckets with rain or snow we'll have a picnic indoors. I must find out who has the key. I'll ring Rose. She'll know.'

'Are you sure you want all of us there? You mustn't be influenced. You and Elfrida must make up your own minds. You owe that much to yourselves.'

'Of course you must all come. Elfrida needs you to tap walls and check out for death-watch beetle.'

'That's putting temptation in my way. I might pretend not to find it.'

'I don't think you'd do that.' Oscar gave a crack of his head. 'You're a good man, Sam.'

'A saint. And to prove it, and seal the bargain, let me get you the other half. It would seem we're both men of property and deserve to toast one another.'

Lucy

Lucy

Friday 22 December
Why I love it here so much is
because things that you want
to happen, happen absolutely
on time. Today was absolutely filled with
unexpected events. It's still dreadfully cold, and
windy too, which makes it even more cold, but
somehow it's all part of everything that's going
on. It hasn't snowed any more, but there's still
snow everywhere, and the streets are half slush
and half frozen stuff. Going shopping, you have
to walk in the middle of the street.
     Anyway, this morning, I packed up all
my Christmas parcels, ran out of ribbon but
got more and took Horace for a walk at the
same time. We went to the beach, and we
were both jolly glad to get home and into the
warm. In the afternoon, Rory turned up with
lots of holly that he'd nicked from the hotel
garden (the hotel is closed), and all afternoon
he helped me decorate. We put the holly over

pictures (what pictures there are) and in a
big jug on the landing. And then we got ivy,
and found some green string, and we twined
the ivy down the banisters from the top of the
house to the bottom. There were a few little
bugs in the ivy, but they disappeared after a
bit, probably to make cosy little dens all over
the place. The ivy smells very strongly but it's
a nice Christmassy smell. It took us a long
time; so long, that Elfrida asked Rory to stay
for supper so that we could finish it all. While
we were doing this, Elfrida and Carrie were
cooking in the kitchen and getting everything
ready for the next couple of days. For tea,
there were hot scones, which Carrie had made.

About six, while they were still cooking
supper, Oscar and Sam went off to the pub for
a drink, and when they got back, Rory and I
had finished all the ivy and holly and Oscar
said he thought it all looked very beautiful.

Sam said it needed a long, long string of
fairy-lights, twined over the ivy, but of course
we hadn't got that so he said he's going
shopping in Kingsferry tomorrow and that he'll
buy some for us and bring them home.

I think he is a most thoughtful and
generous person.

Supper was spaghetti and bolognese sauce
and cheese, and then mince-pies and cream.
And over supper, when we were all talking
away, Oscar told us to stop talking and listen.
So we did.

He told us that he has got another house.

Major Billicliffe, who was the factor at Corrydale, has died in hospital in Inverness and he has made a will and left all he owns to Oscar, which includes this little cottage on the Corrydale estate.

I've never been there, but of course Sam and Carrie have and they saw it the day they went to get the tree. And Elfrida has been there, but only once, in the dark.

Anyway, what Oscar wants to do is to sell his share of this house to Sam, who wants it, and he and Elfrida will go and live in this other little place. I can't bear to think of them not being here, but Elfrida says it is a bit big for them, and I can understand that because when we go it will be very empty for them. She says that between them they have got enough money to make Major Billicliffe's little house very nice, and they have got neighbours so won't be alone in time of emergency.

But nothing can be cut and dried until we have all gone to Corrydale to look it over. So we are going on Sunday morning, and Sam is going to drive us in the Range Rover and we are going to take a picnic. I said could Rory come too, and Elfrida said, 'But of course.' We are going in the morning, so that we can get home before it gets dark, and with a bit of luck the sun will shine and it will be a real picnic.

Now it is ten o'clock at night, and I am really tired.

I do hope we all like the new cottage. In a

way, I think it would be lovely for Oscar and
Elfrida to live in the country. And it means
that he will return to Corrydale, which was
his grandmother's house when he was small.
Like a wheel, going full circle. He is so darling,
I really want the little cottage to be perfect so
that when I am back in London I can think of
them both there, together.

My presents look really festive, all wrapped
up. When I had finished them, I put them
under the tree in the dining room. And
I found some parcels there already, and I
had a good look, and they were for all of us
from Carrie. With a bit of luck, there'll be
lots more.

Elfrida's Party

Elfrida's Party

That morning, Sam was the first downstairs. Eight o'clock and the rest of the household still slept. In the kitchen, he put a kettle on to boil, then opened the back door and let Horace out into the garden. The weather was totally changed. The barman at the Duke's Arms had been right – or at least, his television set had been – and the dark morning air had lost its freezing bite. During the night the north wind had dropped and moved round to the west, and at the top of the garden, the pines soughed in this gentler breeze. By the light of the street-lamp, Sam saw that in places the snow had seeped away, revealing patches of rough, tufty grass, and there was the fresh smell of moss and damp earth.

When Horace finally returned to him, he went back indoors and there found Lucy, fully dressed and making toast.

'Hello. What are you doing?'

'I've been awake since seven. I was reading, and then I heard someone go downstairs so I got up. Are you going to Kingsferry?'

'Yes. Do you want to come? I'm going to do Christmas shopping before all the crowds move in. You can come and help me carry parcels.'

The roads were wet but the hard ice had gone; and the overcast sky, gradually, was lightening. Crossing the bridge, over a flood tide, they saw the deep waters of the firth, the colour of dark slate, penetrating westward into hills that still had not yet shed their snow and probably would not until the end of winter. To the east, the sea was tossed into rough little waves by the offshore wind, and a pair of curlews flew low over the scrubby seafields where the Highland cattle grazed.

'It's a bit like an old painting, isn't it?' Lucy observed. 'You know, the sort that people with huge houses have hanging in their dining rooms.'

'I know exactly what you mean. Not exactly cheerful but impressive.'

'Are you looking forward to living up here in Scotland?'

'I think so. I think I'm going to like it very much.'

'I'd like to come in summer. See it then. Rory says it's really good fun. They go windsurfing. And Tabitha told me that there are incredible wild flowers on the dunes, and all the gardens in Creagan are filled with roses.'

'Hard to imagine at this time of year.'

'Are you really going to live in the Estate House?'

'If Oscar wants to sell it to me.'

'It's pretty big for one person.'

'Perhaps I shall use all the rooms in rotation.'

'Will you change it all, and make it frightfully new and convenient?'

'I don't know, Lucy.' He remembered the apartment in New York, unrecognisable by the time Deborah and her interior designer had finished with it. 'I rather like it just the way it is.'

'My grandmother loves what she calls doing rooms over. The sitting room in her flat is all pinks and blues and lots of little bits of china.'

'Is it a big flat?'

'Yes, it is. Quite big. And it has a nice view over the river. But my room's at the back and I look out over the well so I don't have a view.' And then as though fearful of sounding complaining, she added, 'But I *do* like it, and it's all mine.'

'It's good to have your own space.'

'Yes.' She was quiet for a moment, then said, 'Actually, I'm not thinking about London just now. Usually I'm quite pleased to be going back to school and seeing friends again. But this time I'm not looking forward to it one little *bit*.'

'I feel the same. Boxing Day, and I head back to Inverness to get my nose to the grindstone again.'

'But *you*'re coming back. To live for ever.'

'You can come back too,' he reminded her. 'Stay with Elfrida and Oscar.'

'But it won't be the Estate House. And the cottage, if they do go and live there, mightn't have a spare bedroom.'

'I don't think a small detail like that would faze Elfrida. She'd put you in the bath, or on the sofa, or in a tent in the garden.'

'In the summer that might be rather fun.'

Now, ahead of them, lay the lights of Kingsferry, the church spire and the tower of the town hall.

'Do you know what you're going to give everybody?' Lucy asked.

611

'No idea,' Sam admitted. 'I hope to be inspired.'

They drove into the high street as the town hall clock struck nine, and saw that already the morning was well under way. Shops had opened, cars swept slushily by, people bought morning rolls and newspapers, and a parked van was unloading crates of fruit and vegetables, bundles of holly and tiny Christmas trees. The car park behind the church was already half full, but Sam found a slot, paid for his ticket and they set off together on foot.

Shopping was not one of Lucy's favourite occupations. Sometimes, in London, she went with her mother and started out quite enthusiastically, but after two hours of trailing around overheated stores, waiting for Nicola to make up her mind about which pair of shoes to buy or what colour lipstick, she became bored, complained of the heat and demanded to be allowed to go home.

But shopping with Sam wasn't like that. It was a revelation, in fact. In and out of shops they went, like a dose of salts – as Mrs Snead would say – making snap decisions and never asking the price of anything. Sam paid all the bills with his credit card, and Lucy began to suspect that he must be frightfully rich.

The goodies piled up, bundled into plastic carrier-bags. A sea-green cashmere cardigan for Elfrida, fur-lined gloves for Mrs Snead. In the stationer he chose a Mont Blanc fountain pen for Oscar and a desk diary of the finest Italian leather.

Lucy spied some rolls of gold paper. She said, 'Have you got stuff for wrapping up all your presents?'

'No.'

'Shall we get some? And ribbon and cards?'

'You choose it. In New York, if you buy something,

the girl says, "Do you want it gift-wrapped?" and you say, "Yes," and she goes away and does it for you. I haven't wrapped a present for years, and I'm very bad at it.'

'I shall do it for you,' Lucy announced, 'but *you*'ll have to write the messages.' She went off and returned with six rolls of paper, some packets of red labels with holly on them, and a ball of red and gold ribbon.

By now there was quite a lot to carry, but Sam was by no means finished. In an old-fashioned grocery store, which smelt a bit like the ground floor of Fortnum & Mason and had ITALIAN WAREHOUSEMAN written in gold above the door, he spent much time choosing all sorts of delicious treats. Smoked salmon and quails' eggs, and a jar of caviar; huge boxes of Bendick's chocolates and a Stilton cheese in an earthenware pot. By now, the man behind the counter, recognising a good customer when he saw one, had become Sam's best friend. Between the two of them, after some discussion, they decided on a dozen bottles of special claret, four bottles of champagne and a bottle of Cognac.

All of this, gathered together on the counter, made an impressive show. 'How are we going to get all *this* home?' Lucy asked, but the grocer said he would deliver it in his van. So Sam gave him his name and the address of the Estate House, and produced his credit card once more. When all was accomplished, the grocer came out from behind his counter to open the door for them, which he did with something of a flourish, wishing them both a happy Christmas.

'That,' said Lucy, 'was much nicer than trudging round a supermarket. Who's left now? You simply must have bought a present for everybody.'

'Carrie?'

'I thought the chocolates were for her.'

'I don't think chocs are a very exciting present, do you?'

'How about a precious jewel? There's a jeweller's a bit further down the street. I know because Rory took me there to have my ears pierced and buy my sleepers.'

'Show me.'

But before they had reached the jeweller's, Sam spied the little art gallery, which stood across the road. 'Let's go and look,' he said, so they crossed the road, to stand on the pavement and gaze through the window. Lucy did not think there was all that much to gaze at. A blue and white jug with twigs in it, and a small painting, gold-framed, on a little easel. The picture was of roses in a silver jug. Three pink roses and one white one. And there was a sort of scarf lying on the table, and a bit of curtain.

For quite a long time, Sam didn't say anything. Lucy looked at him and realised that, for some reason, his attention had been captured by the little still-life. She said, 'Do you like it?'

'Um? What? Yes, I do. It's a Peploe.'

'A what?'

'Samuel Peploe. A Scottish painter. Let's go in.'

He opened the door, and Lucy followed. Inside, they found themselves in a surprisingly spacious room, the walls covered with pictures. A number of other objects stood about: rather strange sculptures and hand-thrown pots, which looked as if they might leak when filled with water. In the corner of the room was a desk behind which sat a young man of amazing thinness, wearing a huge, baggy hand-knitted sweater. He had a lot of flowing hair and a stubbly chin, and as they appeared, he hauled himself, in a fatigued sort of way, to his feet.

'Hi.'

Sam said, 'Good morning. The painting in your window . . .'

'Oh, yes, the Peploe.'

'An original?'

'But of course. I don't deal in prints.'

Sam kept his cool. 'May I see it?'

'If you want to.'

He went to the window, reached in, lifted the picture off its easel and brought it back to where Sam stood, holding it out beneath the overhead lights.

Sam set down his burden of plastic carrier-bags. 'May I?' he asked, and gently took the heavy frame. A silence fell while he inspected it, and the young man, apparently too exhausted to stand for a moment longer, leaned against the edge of the desk, and folded his arms.

Nothing much happened after that. Lucy, bored with hanging around, wandered off to look at the other pictures on the walls (mostly abstracts), and bits of pottery and sculpture. There was one sculpture which was called *Rationality Two*, and consisted of two pieces of driftwood tied together with rusted wire. She saw that it cost five hundred pounds, and decided that if ever she needed to make a quick bit of cash, this would be as good a way as any.

Now the two men were talking.

'Where did this come from?' Sam asked.

'An old house. Local. A sale. The old lady died. She had been a friend of Peploe when he was alive. I'm not sure the picture wasn't a wedding gift.'

'You were astute to buy it.'

'I didn't. I bought it off a dealer. You're an admirer of Peploe?'

'My mother had one. I own it now. It's in store in London.'

'In that case . . .'

'This isn't for me.'

Lucy, chipping in, said, 'Who's it for, Sam?'

Sam had apparently forgotten about her, but now, reminded of her presence, laid the picture on the desk. 'Lucy, this is going to take a bit of time. You don't want to hang around.' He felt in his back pocket for his wallet, took it out and peeled off three ten-pound notes, which he pressed into her hand. 'We still haven't bought the fairy-lights for the banisters. There's an electrical store next to the grocer's. You nip along and buy as many as you think you'll need, then come back here when you've got them. Leave all the shopping behind – you don't want to have to lug it with you. And if you see anything else you think we might need, get that too. OK?'

'OK,' said Lucy. She pocketed the money (thirty pounds!) dumped the carrier-bags under a chair and went. She had a pretty good idea that Sam wanted to get rid of her for two reasons. He didn't want her to know how much the picture was going to cost, and he still hadn't bought a present for *her*, and of course he couldn't do that with Lucy watching.

She set off, back down the street, the way they had come. She hoped Sam would not buy her a wobbly jug, but was pretty sure that he wouldn't. She wondered if the Samuel Peploe was to be a present for Carrie. And thirty pounds would buy *yards* of fairy-lights.

After some discussion and a certain amount of haggling, Sam and the hairy young man came to an agreement, which ended up with Sam buying the Peploe. While it was being wrapped up, and the necessary paperwork done, he went out, crossed the road and found, without much difficulty, the jeweller's shop, its window filled with silver photograph frames and small ornate clocks. Inside, he was shown a selection of earrings, and chose a pair of gold studs, fashioned like daisy heads. The girl who had served him put them into a box and a gold envelope, and he paid her, stuffed the box into his pocket, and went back to the art gallery, where all had been accomplished. The only problem was that the young man didn't handle credit cards, so Sam had to write a cheque.

'Who shall I make it out to?'

'Me.'

'Do you have a name?'

'Yes.' He produced a card. 'Tristram Nightingale.'

And Sam, writing the cheque, felt quite sorry for him. Lumbered with a handle like that, a man was allowed to be a bit charmless. As he signed his own name, Lucy reappeared with yet another box to lug back to the car.

'Did you get them?' he asked.

'Yes. Four strings. I think that should be enough, don't you?'

'Ample. We'll get Rory to help us set them up.' He handed over the cheque and picked up the strongly wrapped parcel. 'Thank you very much.'

Tristram Nightingale laid the cheque on his desk, and then, as they gathered up their packages, he loped to the door and opened it for them. 'Have a good Christmas,' he said, as they went out.

'And the same to you,' said Sam, but as soon as they were out of earshot, he added, 'with knobs on, Mr Nightingale.'

'Mr *Who*?'

'He's called Tristram Nightingale. His parents must have been sadists. No wonder he hates the world.'

'What a dreadful name. Except you'd have thought that by now he'd have got used to it. Sam, who's the picture for?'

'Carrie. Don't tell her.'

'Of course I won't. Was it frightfully expensive?'

'Yes, it was, but when things are as expensive as that you don't call it expensive. You call it a Good Investment.'

'I think that's a lovely present. And when she goes back to live in Ranfurly Road, she can hang it on her sitting-room wall.'

'That's what I thought.'

'And she'll remember Scotland and Creagan and everything.'

'I thought that, too.'

'Will you ever see her again?'

'I don't know.' Sam smiled down at Lucy. 'I hope so.'

'I hope so, too,' said Lucy. After a bit, 'It's been a good morning. Thank you for letting me come with you.'

'Thank you for coming. You were a tremendous help.'

By half past five that evening, the Estate House stood ready for Elfrida's party.

The front door wore a wreath of holly, and the overhead light clearly illuminated a thumb-tacked cardboard notice that read PLEASE WALK IN. This, Elfrida hoped, would preclude the hassle of ringing the bell, Horace barking and the repetitive running up and downstairs to greet the guests. Once through the door, the dining-room

Christmas tree was revealed in all its glory, lit up and standing knee deep in packages. At the far end of the hall, the staircase rose, entangled with holly and ivy and sparkling with white fairy-lights.

Above, the landing had been turned into a bar, where the big table from the sitting-room bay window – shunted to its new location by Oscar and Sam – was spread with a white cloth, one of Mrs Snead's best linen sheets, and neatly set out with bottles, ice bucket and rows of polished glasses.

All of this had taken some time and effort, and when the Sneads arrived to take charge of the last-minute prep-arations, like heating up the tiny pizzas and spearing hot sausages with cocktail sticks, everyone had disappeared to shave, bath, change and generally doll themselves up for the evening ahead. From behind closed doors came sounds of running taps, the buzz of electric razors and the steamy fragrance of bath oil.

Horace, sneaking upstairs for a bit of company that wasn't the Sneads, found nobody around so made his way into the sitting room and there settled down comfortably in front of the blazing fire.

Oscar was the first to emerge. He closed the bed-room door behind him, and stood alone for a moment to savour the Christmas transformation of his house, prepared and ready for an influx of guests. He saw the neat arrangement of polished glasses, like so many soap bubbles, the green and gold of champagne bottles jammed into a bucket of ice, the crisp white linen of napkin and tablecloth. The drawn stair curtains shut away the night, and the stairwell, all three flights of it, was entwined with dark ropes of greenery, red-berried holly and starry lights. So much, he thought wryly, for the bleak winter solstice, which was all he had promised Elfrida. And he decided that the Estate House, normally so minimal and austere but now dressed and adorned to the nines, was a bit like a strait-laced, elderly but much loved aunt, who had put on her best finery and precious jewels for some special occasion and ended up looking not bad at all.

Oscar, too, had made an effort and wore a favourite old smoking jacket and his best silk shirt. Elfrida had chosen his tie, and insisted he wore his gold-embroidered black velvet slippers. He could scarcely remember when he had last dressed up, but the silk shirt felt luxurious against his skin and he had slapped on some bay rum and sleeked down his thick white hair.

Elfrida, whom he had left at her mirror, still in her dressing-gown and screwing in her earrings, had told him he looked toothsome.

From the kitchen came Snead voices and other sounds of culinary activity. Mrs Snead had arrived, not in her tracksuit but in her best black dress with sequins twinkling from the bodice. She had also had her hair done for the occasion, and decorated this new coiffure with a black satin bow.

As he had bathed, shaved, dressed, chatting the while to Elfrida, Oscar had not allowed himself to think back to his last Christmas at the Grange, the lavishness of that time and the hospitality on a scale that beggared belief – huge meals, too many guests, too many presents, too huge a tree. Somehow Gloria had got away with it all, the sheer size of everything tempered by her enjoyment, her generosity of spirit.

He had not allowed himself to think back, but now, in a rare moment of solitude, he did. And it all seemed so long ago – he could scarcely realise it was only twelve months – and it felt a bit like recalling a time out of another existence. He thought of Francesca, remembered her running down the great staircase at the Grange with her hair flying loose, wearing a black velvet dress that was a present from her mother. She had always seemed to be running, as though time was so precious there was not a moment to be wasted.

Only a short while ago this memory would have shattered him with grief, but now Oscar simply felt grateful because Francesca would always be part of his life, part of his being. And because, after all that had happened, he had somehow survived. And, more, found himself surrounded and sustained by friends.

Below, he heard the kitchen door open and Mrs Snead's voice giving Arthur his orders. Then Arthur appeared up the staircase, bearing a tray of what Mrs Snead called canaypes: nuts and small biscuits spread with pâté and such. Arthur wore his best grey flannel trousers and his bowling-club blazer, emblazoned with a gold emblem on the breast pocket.

Climbing the last flight, he spied Oscar. 'Well, there you are, Mr Blundell, and don't you look dressy? My wife said to bring these up and put them round the sitting room. 'Ot stuff's coming later. Only thing is, 'Orace sneaked off. Bet 'e's sitting by the fire. Don't want 'im eating this lot.'

'We'll put them out of his reach, Arthur.'

He led Arthur into the big room, which looked warm and welcoming and unnaturally neat and tidy. Every light and lamp had been turned on, and the fire blazed. Elfrida had filled jugs with holly and white chrysanthemums, but the best was the huge vase of Stargazer lilies that Lucy had given Elfrida for Christmas. Arthur had delivered them during the course of the morning, all wrapped in Cellophane and tied with a large pink bow, and Elfrida had nearly burst into tears, so touched and delighted had she been. They stood now on a small table by the sofa, their exotic petals slowly opening in the warmth of the room, exuding their heavy, almost tropical fragrance.

They set out the nuts and crisps, well out of reach of Horace, who lay by the fire, pretending to be fast asleep. Oscar wondered if he should boot the dog downstairs again, but left him where he was because he looked so comfortable. Once they had disposed of the little dishes at a safe height, Oscar and Arthur returned to the bar where they found Sam, looking sleek in his dark suit and an enviable blue and white striped shirt.

'You know Sam Howard, don't you, Arthur?'

'Don't think I've 'ad the pleasure. Pleased to meet you.'

'Arthur's going to be our barman, Sam.'

Sam said, 'I'm sure you know how to open a bottle of champagne, Arthur.'

'Well, I can't say I've 'ad that much practice, being a beer man myself. But on the telly, like the Grand Prix, it's all a bit of shaking and squirting each other, like a fire 'ose. Dreadful waste of good booze, I always thinks.'

Sam laughed. 'Good fun, but I agree with you. A terrible waste. Actually, it's no problem. You don't want any loud pops, corks hitting the ceiling or gallons of froth.' He took a bottle from the ice bucket. 'Just untwist the wire, and then the gentlest easing out of the cork . . . like this. And you don't turn the cork. You hold it and turn the bottle . . .' He demonstrated the subtle art and the cork slipped gently out with the softest of sounds, and the golden wine creamed into the waiting glass without a drop spilled.

'Well, that's very neat I must say,' said Arthur. 'I never knew it could be done so quiet.'

Elfrida, with the final eyelash tweaked into place, gazed at her reflection in the long mirror of the wardrobe. She had put on black silk trousers and a filmy little black blouse, over which she wore a loose green silk coat. Dangling earrings and long strings of beads were the same jade green as the coat, her eyelids were blue, her mouth scarlet, and her hair a freshly twinked blaze of flame.

She hoped that all her new friends in Creagan would not think she had gone over the top.

Emerging from her bedroom, she found Arthur Snead all ready for duty by the makeshift bar.

'Arthur! You look so handsome. Where's Mrs Snead?'

'Just finishing off the last of the mini kievs, Mrs Phipps. She'll be up in a mo. I 'ope you don't mind my saying so but you look very dashing. Would hardly 'ave recognised you, meeting you in the street.'

'Oh, thank you, Arthur. Is everybody present and ready?'

'All inside by the fire. Guests ought to be 'ere any moment now.'

'They're meant to walk in but, if they don't, could you be a saint and go down and open the door?'

'I'll do that, Mrs Phipps. And now 'ow about a nice glass of bubbly? The others are already at it. Dutch courage, Mr Blundell said. Not that I think 'e needs much courage on such an occasion of celebration.'

He poured her a glass and, carrying it, she went to join

the others. The room, and they, all looked wonderfully sophisticated and glamorous, like an illustration from some glossy magazine. Lucy had somehow put her hair up and, with her long black legs and her elegant neck and her earrings, looked about seventeen. As for Carrie, she was ravishingly beautiful, with a glow to her skin and a shine in her dark eyes that Elfrida had not seen for years. She had put on a sleeveless black dress, simple as a T-shirt, but with a skirt that flowed softly from her slender hips to her ankles. On her feet were sandals that were no more than a couple of sparkling straps, with very high heels, and her only jewellery was her sapphire ring and a pair of diamond earstuds.

Seeing her, Elfrida could not imagine how any man could stop himself falling in love with her, but Sam was playing his cards close to his chest and seemed to take Carrie's sensational appearance entirely for granted. Which, perhaps, was a hopeful sign. Elfrida wanted, above all else, for Carrie to be happy again, but Oscar was right. This was too soon for conjecture, too early for matchmaking. One just had to be content with what had happened so far. Which was that Sam had turned up out of nowhere in the first place. And that he and Carrie seemed, at last, to have made friends.

They were all talking but Oscar, standing by the fireplace, saw Elfrida as she came through the door. Their eyes met, and for an instant it was as though it was just the two of them, alone in the brilliantly lighted room. Then he set down his glass and came across to take her hand. 'You look *quite* wonderful,' he told her.

'*I* thought I looked a bit like a battered old actress. Which of course I am. But a happy one.' She kissed his cheek cautiously, so as not to leave a smudge of lipstick.

'And you, Oscar?' They understood each other very well. 'All right?'

He nodded. Downstairs, some person, mistakenly, rang the doorbell. Horace leaped to his feet, burst into a cacophony of barking, fled out of the room and down the stairs.

Elfrida began to laugh. 'So much,' she said, 'for my carefully laid plans.'

'I'll go,' said Lucy instantly. (Probably hoping it was the Kennedys and longing for Rory to be astonished by her new, grown-up image.) She disappeared after Horace, and the next moment there floated upwards the sound of voices. 'Are we the first? Are we too early?' And Lucy replying, 'Of course not. We're waiting for you. Let me take your coats. Everybody's upstairs.'

Elfrida's party, at last, was on its way.

A quarter past eight, and it was all over. Rutleys, Sinclairs and Erskine-Earles had departed to the sound of good-byes and thank-yous ringing down the deserted street. Only the Kennedys lingered, and that was because they had been late arriving in the first place, coming to the Estate House straight from the annual party at the old people's home. Peter, wearing his dog collar, announced himself awash with tea and buns, but that didn't stop him gratefully downing a dram and plunging enthusiastically into another room full of slightly less geriatric friends.

Now, a certain languor prevailed. Sam had built up the fire, and all had collapsed into chairs, grateful to get the weight off their feet. Rory and Lucy were down in the kitchen, helping Mrs Snead and Arthur with the last of the clearing-up. Cheerful noises and much laughter floated up, and it was obvious that the party continued below stairs.

Elfrida, sunk gratefully into cushions with her shoes off, said, 'I can't believe it's gone so quickly. We've been beavering away all day, and the next thing you know, it's eight o'clock and guests start looking at their watches and saying it's time to go.'

'That's the sign of a good party,' said Peter. And added, 'Time flies when you're enjoying yourself.' He sat in the wide lapped chair by the fireside, and his wife was on the hearthrug, leaning in comfort against his knees.

'I liked Lady Erskine-Earle,' said Carrie. 'She looked like a dear little Highland pony, all dressed up in cashmere and pearls.'

Tabitha laughed. 'Isn't she a star?'

'She and Mrs Snead chatted for hours.'

'That's because they're both on the fund-raising committee for the church. And the Women's Institute. Elfrida, asking the Sneads was a huge bonus. No fear of pregnant pauses with Mrs Snead and Arthur on the go.'

'Arthur was not a barrow-boy for nothing,' Oscar pointed out. 'He never misses a trick. When he wasn't being either butler or guest, he found time to do a little business as well. Orders for New Year's Eve. Chrysanthemums for Emma Erskine-Earle and six avocados for Janet Sinclair. Incidentally, I think Janet's charming. We hadn't met her before. Only the doctor when he came to see Carrie.'

'And what is more,' Carrie told Oscar, 'she's an architect. She works three days a week in a practice in Kingsferry.'

'And,' Peter added, 'she's extremely efficient. She

designed a new wing for the old people's home and did a good job. Only thing is, it makes the rest of the place look a bit gloomy.' He set down his glass, shifted slightly in his chair, as though his wife's weight against his knees might be giving him cramp, and looked at his watch. 'Tabitha, my love, we should be on our way.'

'Oh, don't go,' Elfrida begged, 'unless you have to. This is the best bit of a party. Talking it all over with the last of the friends. Stay, and we'll have kitchen supper. We'll finish up all the scraps and we've got some soup, and there's more smoked salmon. Sam gave it to us. And a delicious Stilton.'

'Are you sure?' Tabitha was clearly tempted. 'If we go back to the Manse it's only scrambled eggs.'

'Of course you must stay.'

Here, Carrie took over. 'In that case, *I* shall be in charge.' She got up from the sofa. 'I'll go and see what's happening in the kitchen and find something for us all to eat. No, Sam, you stay and chat, you've done your part for the evening.'

Elfrida was grateful. 'Darling, you are sweet. If you want any help, give me a shout.'

'I'll do that.'

She went out of the room, and closed the door behind her. On the landing, all that was left of Elfrida's party was the table with the white cloth. Bottles and glasses had all been cleared away. The Sneads, Rory and Lucy had clearly been hard at work.

The telephone began to ring. Carrie looked at it in some astonishment, because for some reason it was the last thing she expected to happen. She picked up the receiver. 'Hello.'

'Who's that?' The female voice was as clear as a

bell, but there was a tiny hiccup of hesitation on the line.

'It's Carrie.'

'Carrie. It's Nicola. From Florida.'

'For heaven's sake. How are you?'

'I'm great. Fine. What are you doing?'

'Just had a party. We're all sitting around recovering.'

'Is Lucy there?'

'Yes, she's downstairs, helping with the clearing up. She's been having the time of her life. How's Florida? Is the sun shining?'

'Non-stop. Everything's wonderful.'

'Hold on. I'll go and find Lucy.'

Carrie laid the receiver on the table and went downstairs. In the kitchen she saw that all the washing-up and putting-away had already been accomplished, and Mrs Snead was now pulling on her mock-Persian-lamb coat and fastening the silver buttons. Arthur was enjoying the last of a final beer, while Rory leaned against the sink and Lucy was sitting on the kitchen table.

Mrs Snead was still in full flow. 'Well, I must say, that was a really good do,' she was saying. She hiccupped slightly and Carrie saw that the bow on her coiffure had slipped a bit, giving her a rakish appearance. 'And here's Carrie. I was just saying, Carrie, that was a really good do. Nice company, too.'

'I certainly enjoyed it,' Carrie told her. 'Lucy, you must run upstairs quickly, your mother's on the telephone.'

Lucy's head jerked round. Her eyes met Carrie's, and Carrie saw in them an expression of alarm.

'Mummy?'

'Yes. From Florida. Go quickly, because it costs a bomb.'

Lucy slipped down from the table. She looked at Rory, then back at Carrie, went out of the kitchen and up the stairs.

Discreetly, Carrie closed the door behind her.

'Fancy that,' said Arthur. 'All the way from Florida.'

'It's still afternoon there. Five hours' difference, you know,' Mrs Snead informed them all, importantly. Having buttoned her coat, she took off her suede court shoes and pulled on stout boots in readiness for the short walk home. 'Lucy's been a real help, I must say. We got through it all like a dose of salts, didn't we, Rory? And Arfur's put the empties out in the scullery, and I put a few scraps of sausages on a plate for Horace. He can 'ave them for 'is dinner tomorrow.'

Carrie was grateful. 'You've both been marvellous. You *made* the party.'

Arthur drained his beer and set down the empty glass. 'I'd like to agree with my wife. A very nice bunch of customers. And tell your friend I'm grateful to know 'ow to open a bottle of champagne. A real little art that one is. Next time we 'ave a bowling-club party, I'll be able to demonstrate my skill.'

'Oh, Arfur, you are a *one*.'

'I always say, it's a good day when you learn something.'

Mrs Snead gathered up her possessions, her handbag and the plastic carrier into which she had put her good shoes. 'We'll say goodnight, then, Carrie.'

'Goodnight, Mrs Snead. And have a great Christmas.'

'Same to you. And tell Mrs Phipps I'll be in Thursday as usual.'

When they had gone, arm in arm, out into the night, and the back door had closed behind them, Rory said, 'What's Lucy's mother ringing about?'

'I don't know, Rory.' Carrie took Elfrida's apron from its hook, and tied it on over her black dress. 'Probably just to say happy Christmas.'

'It's not Christmas yet.'

'Perhaps she's just getting her word in early. Elfrida's asked you and your parents to stay for supper so I came down to try and get something organised.'

'Do you want me to help?'

'I think you've already done your share.'

'I don't mind. I'd rather do that than make small-talk.'

'It seemed to me you managed rather well.'

'It's not so bad if you *know* people. What do you want done?'

'Well, if you really mean it, perhaps you could lay the table. For eight of us. Knives and forks are in that drawer and the plates are in that cupboard. And there's smoked salmon in the fridge. I think it's all sliced. You could maybe put it on a plate, and then we'll have to butter some bread.'

She went into the icy scullery and returned to the kitchen bearing an enormous pot filled with Elfrida's latest brew of soup. She lit the gas ring on the cooker, turned the flame down low, and put the pot on top of this to heat through slowly.

Behind her, Rory said, 'Lucy talked to me.'

Carrie turned her head to look at him. 'Sorry?'

'Lucy.' At the table, he squared off a knife and fork.

'She talked to me. About London and everything. Her parents' divorce. Her grandmother. About not really wanting to go back.'

'Oh, *Rory*.' He did not look at her, simply went on with what he was doing. 'I'm sorry.'

'What have you got to be sorry about?'

'Because in a way I feel responsible. Guilty, perhaps, because I shouldn't have stayed away so long in Austria, and somehow lost touch with my family. Everybody was all right except Lucy. It wasn't until I got back that I realised how impossible life must be for her. It's not that anybody's *unkind* to her ... In a way, she has everything. But she misses her father. And she's never been encouraged to get in touch with her grandfather, my father. There's so much acrimony. It's not good to live with.'

'Couldn't she go to boarding-school? That, at least, would be a different environment.'

Carrie was surprised by such perception in a young man of only eighteen.

'Perhaps she should, Rory. But, you see, I am simply a maiden aunt. I don't dare make too many controversial suggestions in case I'm cast out into the wilderness as well.' She thought about this. 'And her school is *good*. She has a splendid headmistress whom she's really fond of.'

'But it's all girls.' Rory had now finished laying the table. He said, 'Where's the smoked salmon?'

'In the fridge, which is in the scullery.'

He went to get it. Carrie took a loaf of brown bread from the bread crock, then returned to the cooker to give the soup a stir. When he returned, she cleared a space for him and found a large oval meat dish on which to arrange the delicate rosy slices. Rory slit the Cellophane

631

with a knife, and began, neatly, to separate the slices of smoked salmon and lay them out in overlapping layers. Carrie took a couple of lemons from the fruit bowl and started cutting them into wedges.

Rory worked on, intent and businesslike, and Carrie watched him, saw his unlikely bright yellow hair, the ring in his ear, the blunt features, youthful but strong, well on his way to manhood. Helping the Sneads, probably washing-up, he had rolled up the sleeves of his dark blue cotton shirt, and his forearms were tanned, his hands strong and capable. Carrie could perfectly understand why Lucy liked him so much. She only prayed that her niece, at fourteen, had not fallen in love, because they were too young for love: Rory had his sights set on getting to Nepal and a teenage infatuation now was almost bound to result in a broken heart.

She said, 'You've been so kind to her, Rory. A lot of guys your age simply wouldn't have bothered.'

'I felt sorry for her.'

'I wonder why.'

'She seemed so lonely.'

'But sweet. She's a sweet kid.' She could not resist a small tease. 'And you bought sleepers for her ears.'

He looked at her and grinned. 'Oh, come on, Carrie, that was just giving the finger to her mum. Anyway, she wanted her ears pierced. So what? It's part of growing up.' He stood back to survey the plate of neatly arranged salmon. 'There, that's it. Is that going to be enough?'

'Have to be. We're keeping the other lot for Christmas Day.'

'Wonder how Lucy's getting on.'

'Perhaps I'd better go and see. You come too. You've worked hard enough.'

'No, I'll stay here, be the chef. I quite like cooking. I used to make gingerbread men with my mum. You go back to the others and I'll butter the bread. There are still some pizzas left over so I might put them in the oven. Do you want me to open a bottle of wine or anything like that?'

Finally, Carrie unwound herself from Elfrida's apron, hung it on a hook and left Rory to it. She went out of the kitchen and upstairs. The landing stood empty. The receiver back in the cradle. There was no sign of Lucy. She hesitated for a moment, experiencing a pang of unexplained disquiet. Then, just as before, the telephone rang.

Carrie picked up the receiver. 'Hello?'

'Who is that speaking? Is that the Estate House? I want Carrie.'

Unmistakable. Carrie's heart sank. 'Yes,' she said, 'I'm here. Hello, Ma.'

'It's you. Oh, thank heavens. My dear, has Nicola been on to you?'

'Yes. She rang from Florida about twenty minutes ago. But she wanted to talk to Lucy.'

'Did she tell you?'

'Tell me what?'

'Oh, my dear, she's married to Randall Fischer. This morning. They had some sort of a whirlwind ceremony in a church called the Wee Chapel of the Angels or something, and they're *married*. She didn't even let me know she'd got engaged, that they were planning this. I had simply no idea. Until I got this call from Florida.'

Carrie told herself that she had to keep calm or everything was going to go to bits. 'She rang you before she rang Lucy?'

'Yes. She wanted to make arrangements.'

'What sort of arrangements?'

'For Lucy, of course. What else do you think? When she's getting back from Scotland and that sort of thing.'

Oh, God, thought Carrie. Here we go again.

'She's talking about a honeymoon, not flying back to London until the end of the month. She's going to cancel her flight back. Postpone it. And she expects *me* to be in London so that I can get Lucy back to school. But I've planned to stay here in Bournemouth until the end of January and I cannot see why I should change all my arrangements. It's really too much, Carrie. I'm simply not up to it. I told her so. I said, "I'm not up to it, Nicola." But you know how selfish and unkind she can be if she doesn't get her own way. And now, of course, she's besotted with this man and *he's* all she's thinking about.'

'Is she going to spend the rest of her life in America?'

'I suppose so. If you marry an American, I suppose that's what you have to do.'

'What about Lucy?'

'Oh, Lucy will just have to do what she's told for once. The immediate problem is, who is going to look after her until her mother gets home?'

Carrie did not answer this question. She simply stood there holding the receiver, aware of a great wave of impatience and fury directed at both her mother and her sister. She had felt this way before, many times, and doubtless would again, but she could not remember ever having been so angry. She thought of Randall Fischer, and silently cursed him for his tactlessness, his lack of imagination, of feeling. Surely he could have persuaded Nicola to give her family some warning before he marched her off to the Wee Chapel of the Angels and stuck a wedding ring on her finger? He could not have caused more trouble if he had been a fox sneaking into a chicken coop, setting up a panic-stricken cackling and causing feathers to fly. She knew that if she made any remark it would be wrong, finally precipitating a useless slanging match that would solve nothing.

'Carrie?'

'Ma, I think it would be better if I rang you back.'

'Have you spoken to Lucy?'

'No, not yet. This is the first I've heard of the happy news.'

'Are you being sarcastic?'

'No.'

'You've got my number here in Bournemouth?'

'Yes. I'll call you.'

'When?'

'Sometime. Tomorrow, maybe.'

'Don't leave it too long. I'm worried sick.'

'I'm sure.'

'Oh, and, darling, you will have a lovely Christmas, won't you?'

'Lovely,' Carrie told her.

She put down the receiver and stood for a moment, giving herself time to cool down, gather her wits and face facts. Nicola was now Mrs Randall Fischer. She had married him in Florida, in the Wee Chapel of the Angels. Carrie tried to picture the ceremony: blue skies and palm trees, Randall Fischer in a white suit and Nicola in some little concoction suitable for such an occasion. Had there been friends to witness the marriage? Had some old chum of Randall's been wheeled in to give Nicola away? Had the old chum's wife stood in as matron-of-honour, wearing an ankle-length gown and a corsage of orchids? And after the ceremony had the four of them driven to the local country club, there to be fêted by anyone who happened to be around?

But it was all unimaginable. And how or when it had taken place didn't really matter because it was done and could not be undone, and there was so much emotional rubbish littered around, waiting to be picked up, that Carrie felt she scarcely knew where to start.

Lucy. Lucy was the first. Lucy had been given the joyous news over the telephone by her mother, put down the receiver and disappeared. But where? Lucy didn't much like Randall Fischer, and had uncharacteristically rebelled at the very suggestion that she might spend the two weeks of Christmas in his company and in Florida.

But this? If Nicola had her way, this would be permanent, for good. Lucy was fourteen, uprooted, transported to another country, another culture, a whole new and probably unwelcome life.

Suddenly Carrie was filled with apprehension. Where *was* Lucy? Had she slammed down the telephone, run silently downstairs, out of the front door and disappeared, heading for the sea, the beach, the dunes, the bitter cold? If there had been a cliff nearby, it would have been more than easy for Carrie to imagine the girl flinging herself from its edge and crashing to her death on rocks far below.

Trembling with anxiety, she pulled herself together, put such gruesome images out of her mind and became sensible. She took a deep breath and climbed the stairs to Lucy's attic. The landing light was on but the bedroom door firmly closed. Carrie knocked. No reply. Gently she opened the door. All was darkness. She reached for the light and switched it on. 'Lucy?' Her voice betrayed her anxiety.

A hump under the blue and white duvet did not move or answer, but Carrie felt quite weak with relief for at least she was *here* and safe, and hadn't fled from the house, out into the darkness . . .

'Lucy.' She went into the room, closed the door behind her, crossed over to the bed and sat on the edge of it. 'Lucy.'

'Go away.'

'Darling, it's Carrie.'

'I don't want to talk.'

'Darling, I know. Gran rang from Bournemouth. She told me.'

'I don't care if she told you or not. It doesn't make any difference. Everything's spoiled now. Everything. It always is. They always do.'

'Oh, Lucy . . .' Carrie laid her hand on the duvet, meaning to comfort, but Lucy jerked her shoulder and spurned the tentative touch.

'I wish you'd go away and leave me alone.' Her voice was choked. Filled with tears. She had been crying and now she was angry and resentful. Carrie understood, but still felt loath to leave her.

'To be truthful, I think your mother shouldn't have done this, and certainly she shouldn't have sprung it on you over the telephone, expecting you to be delighted. But I suppose we have to try to see her point of view . . .'

All at once, Lucy flung the duvet aside and turned up her face to Carrie's. It was swollen and stained with weeping, her hair, which she had put up so carefully, was tangled and in strands around her cheeks. She was ugly with anger and misery – and, Carrie realised with despair, the anger was directed not simply against her mother but Carrie too, because they were all adult and there was not a single adult who could be trusted.

'Of *course* you take her side,' Lucy shouted at Carrie. 'She's your *sister*. Well, I hate her. I hate her because of all this, and because I've never mattered. I matter even less now. And I won't go and live in America, or Florida or Cleveland or anywhere. And I hate Randall Fischer and I don't want to talk about it and I just want to be left alone. So *go away!*'

And she flung herself away from Carrie, pulled the duvet over her head and buried her face in an already sodden pillow. She was crying again, wailing and sobbing, inconsolable.

Feebly, Carrie tried again. 'The Kennedys are all staying for supper.'

'I don't care if they are,' scarcely audible from beneath the folds of duvet.

'I could bring your supper up here.'

'I don't want supper, I want you to *go away!*'

Impossible. Carrie stayed for a moment and then, knowing that it was hopeless to persist, got to her feet, went out of the room and closed the door once more.

She felt completely shattered, and without any idea of what to do next. She stood at the top of the stairs and heard the voices of the others in the sitting room, still gathered around the fire. A burst of carefree laughter. She went downstairs, and for the third time that evening as she reached the landing, the telephone rang.

Nothing could get much worse. She picked up the receiver.

'Hello?'

'Carrie. Is that Carrie?'

'Nicola.'

'Yes, it's me again.' She was high-pitched, furiously indignant. 'I've been trying to ring back for the last ten minutes. I couldn't get through. Lucy put the phone down on me. I was telling her—'

'I know what you were telling her.'

'She put the phone down on me. I couldn't finish what I was saying. I want to talk to her again. Go and get her. She has no right to ring off like that!'

'I think she has every right. She thought you were calling to say happy Christmas and all you do is blurt out that you've married Randall Fischer and expect her to be delighted.'

'So she should be. A lovely new father, a heavenly house, a heavenly place to live. If only she'd come with me she'd have seen it all for herself. Why does she have to be so against anything I do? I've done everything for her! Isn't it about time she started thinking about other people's happiness? Doesn't it mean anything to her that I'm so happy? At last—'

'Nicola—'

'Mother's the same. She even resents me staying on a bit longer so that we can have a honeymoon.'

'Nicola, *I* don't resent anything. I'm pleased for you. Honestly. But you have a child to consider, and she's not a baby. You can scarcely expect her to be over the moon when it seems that her whole life is going to be turned upside down.'

'I don't want to listen to this. I can't imagine what all the fuss is about. Just go and get her for me.'

'No, I won't. I can't. She's up in her room, bundled in her duvet and crying her heart out. I've tried to speak to her but she's too upset even to talk to me. And there are practicalities as well. We go back to London after the New Year and Lucy has to go back to school. Who's going to be there for her? Mother wants to stay in Bournemouth.'

'Can't you even do *that* for me?'

'I haven't got a house to live in.'

'Well, you can go to Mother's flat and be with Lucy there, get her back to school.'

'Nicola, I have a new job waiting for me.'

'Oh, your *career*, I suppose. Your great *career*. That was always more important than any of us. I should have thought just for once—'

'*I* should have thought, just for once, you'd think about other people and not yourself all the time.'

'That is *the* most unkind thing to say. This is the first time in years, since Miles walked out and left me, that I've thought about *myself*. At least Randall appreciates me. I have at last got someone in my life who appreciates me!'

Carrie stopped trying to be nice. 'Oh, don't talk such a load of codswallop.'

'I'm not going to listen!' Nicola's voice soared in righteous indignation, and Carrie relented.

'Nicola. Look. Sorry. This is getting us nowhere. I've got your number in Florida. I'll try and work something out and I'll ring back.'

'Tell Lucy to ring me.'

'I don't think there's much chance of that in the foreseeable future. But try not to get in too much of a state. And I *will* try to work something out.'

Finally, grudgingly, Nicola said, 'All right.'

'And have a good Christmas.'

But Nicola, as always, missed the irony. She said, 'Same to you,' and rang off.

What Carrie wanted, above all, was for it to be yesterday, and none of this to have happened. To be in the empty, deserted woollen mill, alone with Sam Howard; walking through the echoing sheds, following his tall figure up stairways, across catwalks. She wanted to be back in the Duke's Arms, with the hot fire and the warming drink and the two old men and the murmur of the barman's television. And no one to think about but herself and the man who sat across the table from her, talking about their tenuous and uncertain future.

But this was now, and everything was changed. She ran a hand through her hair, straightened her shoulders, turned and opened the sitting-room door. Beyond it, they were all still there, in the same chairs, the same positions, as though nothing untoward could possibly have taken place. They had been joined, she saw, by Rory who, finished with his chef's duties down in the kitchen, had come upstairs to find out what was happening and why nobody had appeared to partake of the informal makeshift meal. He sat now, opposite his mother, cross-legged on the hearthrug, with a glass of lager in his hand.

They were all talking peacefully amongst themselves, but when Carrie came through the door conversation drifted away and heads were turned as though her appearance was either long overdue or unexpected.

She said, 'Here I am,' which was banal, and closed the door behind her. 'Sorry to keep you all waiting.'

Elfrida said, 'Darling, what's been going on? So many telephone calls. Rory said Lucy's mother had phoned from Florida. Nothing wrong, I hope?'

'No. Nothing wrong.' Which was true but utterly untrue all at the same time. 'Just everything. Another family crisis, but it's my family so please don't be too concerned.'

'Carrie. It sounds dire. Tell us.'

Carrie said, 'I don't know where to start,' and Sam, who had been sitting at the far end of the room, got up from his chair and came over to her side. He said, 'Would you like a drink?'

She shook her head, wondering if she appeared either deathly pale or flushed with unbearable exertion. He reached for a chair and drew it forward, next to Elfrida. Carrie sat down with a grateful thump and felt Elfrida take her hand.

'Darling Carrie, tell us.'

So she did. 'Nicola's just been on the telephone. Lucy's mother,' she enlarged for the benefit of the Kennedys. 'My sister. She went out to Florida to stay with this man called Randall Fischer. And this morning they got married. It was the first we'd heard of it. She rang to speak to Lucy and she told Lucy then, and Lucy hung up on her in mid-flow, as it were, and is now in tears in her bedroom, swearing black and blue that she never liked Randall Fischer and she will never go to live in America. Then my mother telephoned to tell me the news. Apparently Nicola has postponed her flight home and is determined to have a honeymoon with Randall before she finally comes back to London. My mother is in hysterics about this because she wants to stay in Bournemouth until the end of the month and refuses to return just so that she can be with Lucy. Then Nicola got back on the phone again to tell me that Lucy had hung up on her. The upshot of *that* was that we had the usual sisterly difference of opinion and only just stopped short of a flaming row.'

Elfrida said, 'I can't bear it,' which, Carrie decided, was the understatement of the year.

She went on, 'So the crisis is immediate and also long-term. Immediate, because there is nobody in London to take care of Lucy and get her back to school. Except, of course, dogsbody me. And, of course, if necessary, I'll do it, and stay in my mother's flat until either she or Nicola gets back to London. But the long-term problem is a different kettle of fish altogether. The long-term problem is Lucy's future. Nicola's married an American and, quite naturally, will make her home out there. I think she relishes the prospect. Lucy, on the other hand, never wanted to go to America, even for a holiday. She doesn't particularly like Randall and, to be truthful, I don't think she's all that fond of her mother.'

They had all listened attentively, and with growing concern, but now, as Carrie fell silent, nobody said anything.

Then Tabitha spoke. 'Oh, *dear*,' she said, which was inadequate, but sympathetic.

'She doesn't *have* to go and live in America,' Elfrida ventured hopefully. 'How about going to her school as a boarder?'

'It's a day-school, Elfrida. And there are still holidays.'

'Your mother?'

'You know as well as I do, Ma would never cope on her own. Wouldn't even try.'

'Perhaps Lucy's father . . .'

'No way. Number-two wife would never consider it.'

'But—'

'This is all ridiculous.' A new voice broke into the

argument, or the discussion, or whatever it could be called. It was Rory Kennedy. In some surprise, Carrie turned her head to look at him, and saw that he was no longer sitting comfortably on the hearthrug but stood before them all, his back to the fire and his blue eyes blazing with indignation. Taken entirely by surprise, nobody interrupted him.

'It's ridiculous. You're all talking in circles, taking it for granted that Lucy will go back to London, just as though nothing had happened. But she can't go. She's miserable enough there, she told me so, and what's happened just now only makes everything more impossible for her. She has no friends, she has no proper home and she's never felt loved. What has made her really happy has been staying here with Elfrida and Oscar. In Creagan. She told me she'd never been so happy as she is here. She never wanted to go back to London in the first place. So don't send her back. Keep her here. She can stay with Elfrida and Oscar, and Mum and Dad will be around, and Clodagh, and she's made friends with our friends and she can go to day-school in Creagan. Dad can fix that with Mr McIntosh. He'll squeeze her in somehow. He'll find a place for her. That is what I believe you should all do. I think if you let her go back to London, without any sort of plan for the future, it would be criminal. Unhappy teenagers do terrible, stupid things. We all know that. Lucy belongs to you all far more than she belongs with her mother. So this is where she should be. I think you have a moral obligation to do the right thing for her. Which is to keep her here in Creagan.'

He stopped, red-cheeked from the warmth of the fire and the passion of his feeling. For a moment an astounded silence filled the room, as all the adults stared at him in speechless but respectful astonishment. Rory, perhaps feeling that he had gone too far, looked a bit sheepish, gave the hearthrug a kick and apologised.

'Sorry,' he said. 'I didn't mean to speak out of turn.'

Silence again. Then Peter Kennedy gently shifted Tabitha's weight from his knees and got up to stand beside his son. 'You didn't speak out of turn,' he told him, laying a hand on the boy's shoulder. 'I think you're right. Well said, Rory.'

Lucy lay and stared at the sloping ceiling of her bedroom, exhausted by weeping and beginning to feel remorseful about the way she had behaved to Carrie. She was not in the habit of having tantrums and was not quite sure about her next move. Nothing was going to be all right again until she told Carrie she was sorry, was hugged and forgiven, but she could not bring herself to get out of bed, comb her hair, wash her face and go downstairs to face everybody. The Kennedys were all still here, staying for supper, but that only made everything worse.

She felt headachy, drained, yet tremendously hungry. She thought about the satisfaction of slamming down the telephone on her mother's voice, all the way from the United States, telling her that she was now married to Randall Fischer, that she had a new father, that they were all going to be happy ever after, living in well-heeled style and with the blissful warmth of Gulf Stream Florida always there. Listening to her mother burbling on, lyrical with excitement and as insensitive to others' feelings as she had always been, had all at once become too much and Lucy, unable to listen to one more word, had simply put the receiver back on the cradle.

Now, alone and desolate, she told herself that she had

been a coward. She should, then and there, while they were still speaking, have unleashed upon her mother the full force of her indignation and shock. She should have let her know, at once, that she was terrified at the very thought of being uprooted, forced to move to a foreign country and accept that her entire existence was to be turned upside down.

But now it was too late.

She longed to be older, to be eighteen and an adult, with the weight of British law behind her. At eighteen, she could refuse to budge, could stay where she felt familiar and secure, make a life and a future for herself. But being fourteen was a hopeless age: too old to be uncomplainingly shunted around, like a brown paper parcel, and too young for independence. Things before had been bad enough. Now, they had become – or were about to become – impossible.

Above her bed, her head, was the skylight. Beyond the glass, the darkness was rendered opaque by the reflected glow of the street-lights below. But she could see a star, and imagined the skylight opening slowly to a gust of freezing, sea-smelling air, and herself being drawn, as though by some irresistible force, out of her bed, up, flying through the open hatchway, seeing the planet drop away beneath her, the stars grow larger every second ... Like a rocket, she would head for the moon and there would never be any coming back.

A sound. A step on the stair. Carrie. Perhaps it was Carrie. If it was Carrie, Lucy was very much afraid that, without wishing to, she would start bawling again, and hated the feeling that she seemed to have lost control of her emotions.

A tap on the door. She lay with her cheek on the sodden pillow and said nothing. The door opened.

'Lucy?'

It wasn't Carrie. It was Oscar. And Lucy was tremendously embarrassed that he should find her thus, all rumpled and fusty and untidy and tear-stained. Why had he come up? Why had they let *him* come to fetch her? Surely Carrie could have returned to her, or Elfrida?

She said nothing.

He said, 'Do you mind?' And then, when she still did not reply, he crossed the floor, leaving the door behind him ajar, and came to sit on the edge of her bed. His weight was strangely comforting, pulling the duvet tight around her body, and she shifted her position to make more space for him, drew a long, shuddering breath and said, 'No, I don't mind.'

He said, 'How are you feeling?' as though he were a kindly doctor and she had been ill for a long time.

She said, 'Awful.'

'Carrie came downstairs and told us what had happened.'

'I was horrible to her.'

'She didn't tell us that, just that you were upset. And who can wonder, having that bit of news sprung on you over the telephone? I always dislike being given news over the telephone. Somehow one feels so impotent and removed, simply because one can't see the other person's face.'

Lucy said, 'It wouldn't be so bad if I really liked him. Randall, I mean.'

'Perhaps you would get to like him.'

'No. I don't think so.' She looked at Oscar, saw the hooded eyes that always made him seem a bit sad, and the gentle expression on his face, and thought that you liked people instantly, just as she had always liked Oscar. And that all the time in the world would never render her as close to Randall Fischer as she had instantly felt to Oscar.

She said, 'I was so horrid to Carrie.' Her eyes filled again with tears, but it didn't matter now and it was important to tell him. 'I shouted at her and told her to go away, and she was being so sweet. I feel dreadful about her.'

She sniffed lustily and felt her mouth trembling like a baby's, but Oscar only reached into the breast pocket of his lovely velvet jacket and produced a much-laundered linen handkerchief that smelt of bay rum. He gave it to her, and she took it gratefully and blew her nose.

After that she felt a bit better. She said, 'I don't usually shout at people.'

'I know you don't. And the wicked thing is that when we're really upset we always take it out on the people who are closest and whom we love the most.'

'Do we?' She was amazed to be told this.

'Always.'

'I can't imagine you ever shouting at anybody.'

He smiled, his rare, warm smile that always seemed to change his whole demeanour. He said, 'You'd be surprised.'

'It was just that . . . I feel so awful, because I suppose I should be pleased. But it was . . .'

'I know. A shock.'

'If it was someone I really *knew*, who lived in England, then it wouldn't be so bad. But I don't want to have to go and live in America and go to school there and everything. London's not much, but at least I know where I am. And I can't stay with Gran because she always makes a fuss about everything, and wants to do her own thing, and go out and see her friends and have bridge parties. When she has bridge parties she doesn't even like me going into the room to say hello. And she hates it when Emma comes because she says we make so much noise. I couldn't be with her, Oscar.'

'No.'

His hand lay on the duvet. She gave him back his handkerchief and he took it, then took her hand in his own. It felt warm and safe over her fingers, a physical contact, a sort of lifeline that made it easier to talk. She said, 'I don't know what will happen. That's the worst. I don't know what I'm going to do. And I'm not old enough to do *anything*.'

He said, 'I don't think you have to do anything. I think others have to do it for you.'

'Who?'

'Like me.'

'You?'

'Now, just listen. Here's a suggestion. Downstairs we've all been having a little chat, and we've come up with an idea. Supposing, after the New Year, you don't go back to London with Carrie? You stay here with Elfrida. And *I* shall go back to London with Carrie and go to see your grandmother in Bournemouth.'

Lucy was alarmed. 'What are you going to say to her?'

'I am going to suggest that until your mother's new life is sorted out somewhat, you should remain in Creagan with Elfrida and myself. Just for the time being.'

'But what about school? I have to go back to school!'

'Yes, of course you do, but how about taking a term off from your school in London and going to school in Creagan instead? Peter Kennedy is a good friend of the headmaster, and he will have a word with him and see that you get a place in a suitable class. It's a very good school, and I am sure there would be no objections from your present headmistress.'

'Miss Maxwell-Brown?'

'Is that her name?'

'I can't simply *leave* school.'

'I'm not suggesting that. Just take a term off. Plenty of children do this sort of thing, if their parents are sent abroad or other circumstances dictate. I am sure Miss Maxwell-Brown would be perfectly amenable to letting you go for a single term, and keeping the options open for your return when this small crisis has settled down and we are all aware of what is expected of us.'

'You mean . . .' Lucy felt that she had to get the facts right because what Oscar was telling her sounded almost too good to be true. 'You mean, I wouldn't go back to London after the New Year?' Just stay on with you and Elfrida?'

'If you want to. Yours must be the decision.'

She was silent for a moment or two, mulling this over. It seemed to her that the whole situation was fraught with obstacles. One of them being Elfrida.

'Gran doesn't approve of Elfrida,' she told Oscar bluntly.

Oscar laughed. 'So I believe. But she will, I am sure, approve of *me*. I shall present myself as a schoolmaster and a church organist with an impeccable background and an unsullied reputation. Will she be able to resist that?'

Lucy said, with a quirk of humour, 'Not if it means getting rid of me.'

'And your mother?'

'She won't care either. She never did, much. She'll care even less now that she's got Randall.'

'So no objections from her?'

'I wouldn't think so.'

'Carrie's going to telephone them both tomorrow. She can outline our plans. It is, after all, just until Easter. After that we'll have to think again.'

'I won't change, Oscar. I won't ever want to go and live in America.'

'I don't see why you should have to. The odd visit, perhaps, would be interesting and educational; it's always good to see another country and learn how others live. But I believe that, basically, you should stay where you feel most happy.'

'I've never been so happy or at home as I have here.'

'Then why don't we go for that? Stay on, for as long as you wish, with Elfrida and me in Creagan. Go to the local school. Get your GCSEs. After that you should spread your wings a bit. Maybe a co-educational boarding-school where you could take your A levels. I know several splendid establishments where I am sure you would enjoy every moment. With my schoolmasterly connections, I could make enquiries and get prospectuses and we could all talk it over together. Go and inspect them. Let you make your own choice.'

'That's what Rory said when we talked about things. A co-educational boarding-school.'

'He's a wise lad. He is your champion. It was he who stirred us all to action when Carrie broke the news about your mother remarrying. "*You have to do something*," he told us. 'And of course he was quite right.'

'But, Oscar . . .'

'What now?'

'You and Elfrida don't want me living with you for *two years.*'

'Why not?'

'Because you're old. Like Gran. She always says she can't cope. Because she's a grandparent.'

Oscar laughed. 'Oh, Lucy, grandparents are wonderful inventions. All over the world, grandparents, for one reason or another, are bringing up their grandchildren, having a great time and doing a good job. I think it would be fun.'

'But would you *want* me? Really *want* me?'

'More than anything.'

'Wouldn't I be in the way?'

'Never.'

'Supposing you move to the cottage at Corrydale and sell this house to Sam?'

'Well?'

'You wouldn't have space for me.'

'We haven't seen the house yet. And, if necessary, we shall redesign it. And there will be a special apartment labelled LUCY'S ROOM.'

'Oscar, I don't know why you're so kind.'

'Because we love you. Perhaps we need you. Perhaps I'm being selfish, but I don't want to let you go. I need a young person about the place. I've got used to the sound of your voice, and footsteps on the stairs, and doors bursting open. And laughter. I shall hate it if you leave. Probably go into a decline.'

Lucy said, 'When I first came here, when Carrie and

I flew up from London and came here, to Creagan, I was terribly nervous because she had told me about your daughter ...'

'Francesca.'

'She had told me about Francesca, and I was afraid that I would upset you ... remind you of her and make you dreadfully sad again.'

'You remind me of her, but it doesn't make me sad.'

'What did she look like?'

'Like you, I suppose. Long fair hair and freckles on her nose. She had bands on her teeth. She was two years younger than you. She was always on the go, never still, except when she and I settled down in my armchair and read aloud to each other.'

'My dad and I used to do that. When I was little and we were all still together. We read *The Borrowers*. And when he wanted to tease, he called me Arietty. And he put Badedas in his bath and made the whole house smell piney. What else did Francesca like doing?'

'Everything. She had a little pony, and an old bicycle, and a guinea-pig in a hutch, and a bedroom full of books. On wet days she used to go into the kitchen and make biscuits, and they were always either burned or raw, and I used to have to eat them and swear they were delicious. And we listened to music together, and played duets on the piano ...'

'Was she good at the piano?'

'Not very.'

'Was she good at lessons?'

'Not very.'

'What was she really good at?'

'Living.'

Their eyes met, and they gazed at each other, both silenced by the enormity of what Oscar had just said. It was as though he had spoken without thought, and the word hung between them like a lie. Francesca had been good at living, but now she was dead, her young life ended with the brutal finality of a fatal car crash.

Lucy did not know what to say. To her horror she saw Oscar's eyes fill with tears, his mouth tremble. Then, in an abrupt movement, he covered his eyes with his hand. He tried to speak, but words did not come; instead, a sound was torn from deep in his chest, a sob of utter despair.

She had never before seen a grown-up weep, rendered incapable by an almost overwhelming grief. She stared at him, wondering what she could do to comfort, and saw him shake his head, denying his own weakness, somehow struggling for control of his unbearable emotion. After a bit, to her huge relief, he took his hand from his face, and reached into his breast pocket for his handkerchief. Then he blew his nose; made an effort to smile at her, reassuring. He said, 'Sorry.'

'It doesn't matter, Oscar. I don't mind. I understand.'

'Yes, I think you do. Death is part of living. I have to remember that, but from time to time the truth eludes me.'

'Living is important, isn't it? And remembering?'

'More important than anything else.' He stowed his handkerchief away once more. 'That first day, the day you arrived, you and I sat in the church and talked about Christmas and the winter solstice. It was then that I remembered Francesca, for the first time, without total desolation. I remembered having exactly the same conversation with her, a year or so ago. Trying to explain about the Christmas star and the scientist's theory of time. And she listened, but was not convinced. She didn't want to be convinced. She liked the story just as it was.

> *In the bleak midwinter*
> *Frosty wind made moan*
> *Earth stood hard as iron*
> *Water like a stone.*

That was the way she wanted Christmas to be, and for Francesca it wouldn't have been magic any other way. Because the carols and the darkness and the presents were all part of a time when life took flight and the whole world soared to the stars.'

Lucy said, 'That's how this Christmas is going to be.'

'Stay with us.'

'I do love you, Oscar.'

'There's a lot of love around. Don't ever forget that.'

'I won't.'

'Do you want to come downstairs now, and join the others, and have some supper? If they've left any for us.'

'I have to comb my hair and wash my face.'

'In that case . . .' He relinquished her hand with a little pat, got off the bed and went to the door. She watched him go. As he left the room, he turned back for a final reassuring smile. 'Don't be too long, my duck.'

Christmas Eve

Christmas Eve

Christmas Eve.

In this fickle northern climate, one woke each morning without any idea of what the elements were about to reveal, but today had dawned astonishingly pure and gentle, like a day stolen from spring. The thaw had melted the snow away from streets and fields, and only the hills still wore their white mantles, summits glittering in the light of the low sun, streaming down from a cloudless sky. A sun that, because there was no breath of wind, even managed to engender a faint warmth. Birds sang from leafless trees, and in the Estate House garden, a few early snowdrops pierced the rough, untended grass beneath the lilac bush.

At Corrydale, in Rose Miller's garden, stood a bird table, laden with scraps and crusts and with a bag of nuts dangling. Pigeons and starlings were out in full and greedy force, while tits and robins pecked at the nuts and the scraps of fat Rose had threaded on a piece of string. They hovered, and paused, then flew off into the safety of a nearby hawthorn bush whose twiggy branches trembled and swayed with fluttering wings and feathered activity.

Because of the fine day, and the fact that the roads were clear, Elfrida and Oscar had come to Corrydale on their own in Oscar's car. The others, Carrie, Sam, Lucy and Rory Kennedy, were driving over later, because Carrie reckoned that she had to wait until noon before getting on the telephone to her sister in Florida. She had already spoken to Dodie, holed up in her hotel bedroom in Bournemouth, and the conversation had gone more smoothly than any of them had dared to hope. Dodie was clearly much relieved to shed sole responsibility for Lucy, and even spoke quite warmly of Elfrida's kindness and hospitality, conveniently forgetting that, at one time, she had not had a good word to say for her ex-husband's raffish theatrical cousin.

'Oscar will come and see you in Bournemouth,' Carrie had promised. 'He says he would like to meet you and, if you want, talk things over.' Dodie had raised no objection to this suggestion either, and said that she would be pleased to stand him afternoon tea in the residents' lounge of the Palace Hotel.

Now there was only Nicola to be dealt with, to be told of the tentative plans for her daughter and encouraged to fall in with them. Having listened to Carrie speaking to Dodie, all sweetness and understanding, Elfrida was pretty sure she would do as good a job on Nicola. Objections, should there be any, would be token. Nicola wouldn't care much what happened to anybody, provided her own chosen path lay smooth and free of any sort of *angst*.

As well, Carrie had volunteered to assemble and bring the picnic. Elfrida had started making suggestions about hot soup and ham rolls, but Carrie and Sam had shooed her out of the kitchen and sent her and Oscar, feeling quite irresponsible and light-hearted, on their way.

Now, from the window of Rose Miller's sitting room, Elfrida watched the birds. Rose's garden was empty of flowers and vegetables, save for a few rotting Brussels sprouts, but beds were neatly dug and the earth raked, all ready for planting time. The garden ran, a long, narrow plot, down the slope of the hill. At its foot was a wooden fence and some gnarled beech trees, and beyond, the seafields of Corrydale sweeping down to the blue firth and the hills on the further shore. Elfrida was much interested in this prospect because she knew that the view from Major Billicliffe's house would be almost identical. Today, with the clear winter air, the colours so sharp and brilliant, the lacy branches of trees so black, she could not imagine any outlook more beautiful.

Behind her, Oscar and Rose sat on either side of Rose's fireplace, where a glowing stack of peat burned, and drank the coffee Rose had made for them. Rose was talking. She had not done much else since Oscar and Elfrida had arrived, as arranged, at half past eleven.

'. . . and, of course, the poor gentleman let the house get in a terrible state. Betty Cowper, she's the tractorman's wife, she did what she could for him after his wife died, but she has three children of her own and a man to care for and she swore it was an uphill task. Once we'd heard he'd passed on, she and I went along and did our best to clear the place up. Most of his clothes were in a terrible state, fit for nothing but a bonfire, but there's a few things that would maybe do for the charity shop and we packed them in suitcases. He didn't seem to own anything of value, but we left his ornaments and possessions and books and such where they were so you'll be able to do what you want with them.'

'That was good of you, Rose.'

'Betty gave the place as good a clean as possible, scrubbed the kitchen floor and the bathroom, which was in a terrible state. A disaster. Poor lonely man. It's sad to think of him dying alone, with no family. You said the funeral would maybe be at the end of the week? Will you let me know? I'd like to be there.'

'Of course . . . and it's going to be a cremation. But we'll take you with us to Inverness in the car.'

'It wasn't his fault the wee place fell into such disrepair. But no doubt you'll be altering things for yourself, and if you get the builders in, they'll tear the place apart and make a lot of dust.'

Oscar said, 'We haven't finally decided if we're going to take up residence.'

'And why should you not?' Rose sounded quite indignant. 'Major Billicliffe would never have left it to you in his will had he not thought that you would live there. Just imagine! The chance to come back and live at Corrydale again after all these years!'

'It might not be large enough, Rose. You see, we maybe have another young person coming to live with us.'

Rose let out a hoot of unexpectedly earthy laughter. 'Don't tell me you're having a wee baby!'

Oscar remained unfazed by this wild suggestion. 'No, Rose, not that. But you remember, I told you we were expecting visitors for Christmas. Lucy is fourteen, but her mother has just remarried, in America, and rather than send her back to London she's going to stay with Elfrida and me for a bit and go to the school in Creagan.'

'But that will be splendid. And good for us all to have another young person about the place. She can be friends with Betty Cowper's family. They're a bit younger, but a cheery bunch. And it's paradise for children here at Corrydale. They have the whole estate to themselves for bicycle riding and no fear of being knocked to kingdom come by some great lorry.'

Elfrida turned from watching the birds, and went to join Oscar and Rose, to sit in an antique wheelback chair and reach for her coffee cup.

She said, 'Perhaps we could make Major Billicliffe's house a little larger. Build on an extra room, or something. We'll have to see.'

'You'll need to get the planning permission,' Rose warned, sagely. For all her years, she was up to all the tricks of the local authorities. 'Tom Cowper put up a greenhouse without permission and as near as a whisker he just about had to tear it down again. And where is the child now?'

Elfrida explained, 'They're driving over later. Lucy and her aunt, Carrie, who's a cousin of mine. And Rory Kennedy. And Sam Howard. Sam was an unexpected guest. He called in at the Estate House, and then got stuck there by the snow. Couldn't get back to Inverness.'

'And who is *he*?'

'He's going to run McTaggart's in Buckly.'

'Well I never did! What a party you'll be for Christmas. When Oscar telephoned me to tell me you were coming today and bringing a picnic, I got the key from Betty and went along and laid a wee fire, in case the place was cold for you. But on a day like this you could eat a picnic in the garden. It's as though the good Lord wanted you to see it at its best.'

'Yes,' said Elfrida. 'It does seem a bit like that.'

Rose was old and tiny, but spry as a bird. She wore a tweed skirt, a blouse with a brooch at the collar and a red Shetland cardigan, and her bright, dark eyes seemed to see everything without the help of spectacles. Her hair, thin and white, was dragged back from her brow in a little bun, and the only apparent sign of ageing showed in her hands, which were worn and knuckled with arthritis. Her house was just as neat, colourful and confident as herself: polished tables stood awash with scraps of china, mementoes and snapshots, and over the fireplace was an enlarged photograph of her brother, in seaman's uniform, who had been drowned at sea when the *Ark Royal* was sunk during the Second World War. She had never married. Her whole life had been dedicated to Mrs McLellan and to Corrydale House. But she was not in the least sentimental, and the fact that the house was now an hotel and no longer belonged to the family was something she had taken entirely in her stride.

She said, 'And what will you all be doing tomorrow?'

Elfrida laughed. 'I'm not sure. Opening presents, I suppose. We've got the tree in the dining room, and we're going to have Christmas dinner in the evening.'

'Christmas dinner! I remember Christmas dinner parties at Corrydale in the old days, with the long table set with all the lace mats and the candlesticks. There was always a house party, friends and cousins and relations, and everybody dressed up in dinner jackets and evening gowns. Christmas Eve, it was the same. Very formal. And then after Christmas Eve dinner, all the house party would get into motors and drive to Creagan for midnight service in the church – and there was a car, too, for the staff and anyone who wanted to go. And what a sensation they created, walking into the church and down the aisle, all dressed up, and Mrs McLellan in black taffeta that swept the floor, and her mink coat, leading the way. People liked to see that. So elegant and festive. And the men in their good overcoats and their black ties. You won't remember that, Oscar.'

'No. I was never at Corrydale for Christmas.'

'When Hughie was here all the old traditions went out the door. I don't think he ever went to church, even on Christmas Eve. Sad, when you think about it. That he, such a fushionless creature, should be the one to take over the place and let it all slip through his fingers.' She shook her head and sighed at the iniquities of the hopeless Hughie. 'But that's all in the past now. And how about you, Oscar? Will you be going to the midnight service? No need for a car. Just step across the street.'

Elfrida did not look at Oscar. She had finished her coffee and now laid the empty cup and saucer down on the little table alongside her chair.

'No, Rose. I shan't be going. But maybe the others . . .'

Oh, Oscar, Elfrida thought sadly.

But she said nothing. His own apartness, his withdrawal, was his own problem, and one that only he could deal with. It was a bit, she decided, as though he had had a disagreement with an old friend. As though words had been spoken that might never be unspoken, and until one of them proffered the hand of friendship, the impasse remained. Perhaps by next year, she told herself. Another twelve months and he would feel himself strong enough to take this last hurdle.

She said, '*I* shall certainly go. The church at night is so beautiful and, as you say, it's just a step across the street. The others can do what they want, but I think Lucy will want to come and certainly Carrie. How about you, Rose? Will you be there?'

'I wouldn't miss it for anything. My nephew Charlie said he'd drive me into Creagan.'

'We'll see you, then.'

Oscar remembered something. Or perhaps he just wanted to change the subject. 'Rose, I had another small bequest from Major Billicliffe, about which I do not feel so enthusiastic. The dog.'

'Did he leave you Brandy?'

'I'm afraid so.'

'Do you not want her?'

'No, I don't think I do.'

'In that case Charlie will keep her. He likes the old girl, and she's company for him when he's working in the shed. And his children would be heartbroken to see her go.'

'Are you sure? Hadn't we better speak to Charlie first?'

'I'll speak to Charlie,' Rose told him, in tones which boded ill for nephew Charlie should he not fall in with her plans. 'He'll keep the dog, all right. And now, how about another cup of coffee?'

But it was time to leave. They all got to their feet, and Rose took the key from inside an old flowered teapot that stood on the mantelpiece. This she gave to Oscar. Then she came to the door to see them off. 'Why do you not leave your motor here and walk to Major Billicliffe's house? It's only a step, and there's not much parking space.'

'It won't be in your way?'

'And why should it be in my way?'

666

So they did as she suggested, only pausing to open the door of the car and let Horace out because while they had been chatting with Rose he had remained incarcerated, in case he chased a rabbit or put up a pheasant or otherwise misbehaved himself. He leaped down lightly, and was at once delighted by local smells.

'For a dog,' observed Elfrida, 'this must be a bit like being let loose in the perfume department of Harrods. *Eau d'autre chien.* He's going to buy a bottle and dab it behind his ears.'

High above, rooks cawed from empty branches and Elfrida, gazing skywards, saw the white, ruler-straight line of a jetstream being dragged across the blue sky by a four-engined passenger aeroplane. It was so high that she could scarcely see it, just the jetstream, but it was headed north-west, flying, she guessed, from Amsterdam.

'Do you ever think, Oscar, that in that tiny dot people are eating nuts and reading magazines and ordering gin and tonic?'

'In truth, it never occurred to me.'

'I wonder where they're going?'

'To California? Over the Pole?'

'Over the Pole for Christmas. I'm glad I'm not going to California for Christmas.'

'Are you?'

'I'd rather be going to Major Billicliffe's house for a picnic. We must find a new name for it. We can't go on calling it Major Billicliffe's house now that Major Billicliffe is no more.'

'It used to be the forester's house. But I believe that in the fullness of time it will simply become Oscar Blundell's house. Doesn't that make sense?'

'Oscar, everything you say makes sense.'

A few moments, and they had traversed the hundred yards or so that lay between the two cottages, and were there, standing in the open gateway of Oscar's new property. It was a twin of Rose's house, but not nearly so appealing, and the rusted car parked before the front door did nothing to enhance a first impression. Elfrida, with Oscar at her side, remembered that first dark evening when, exhausted after the long journey, they had finally run Major Billicliffe's abode to earth and come to collect the key of the Estate House. So much had taken place since then that she felt as though years had passed.

They walked up the driveway, the soles of their boots scrunching on sea pebbles, and Oscar put the key in the lock, turned it and then the brass knob. The door swung inwards, and she followed him, fingers crossed, indoors, and so into the little sitting room.

It felt very cold, and a bit dank, but not nearly as bad as Elfrida had remembered and feared. The window at the back of the room let in a flood of sunshine, and Betty Cowper and Rose, between them, had scoured, cleaned, emptied ashtrays, shaken rugs, polished furniture, dispatched much rubbish and scrubbed floors. Over all hung the smell of strong soap and carbolic disinfectant. The roll-topped desk had been closed, and the trolley, which Major Billicliffe had called his bar, cleared of old bottles and used glasses. Even the dingy cotton curtains had been washed and ironed, and in the fireplace were laid paper and sticks, all ready for kindling, and there was a polished brass bucket filled with coal, and a pile of dry logs on the hearth.

Oscar said, 'First things first,' removed his jacket, and knelt to set a match to the newspaper and to start the sticks crackling. At the back of the room stood the door against which poor Brandy, howling and frustrated, had flung herself, frightening Elfrida out of her wits. Now Elfrida went cautiously to open this, and found herself in a mean, chilly little kitchen, built of breeze block with utilitarian steel-framed windows. There was a clay sink, a wooden draining-board, a tiny refrigerator and a gas cooker. A small table was spread with an oilcloth, and worn linoleum covered the floor. Not much else. A half-glassed door to her left led out on to a bit of paving, where stood a broken wheelbarrow, a fork and a dried-out tub containing dead geraniums. There was no sign of a hot pipe or any sort of heating and it all felt cold as charity.

She went back to Oscar, who was piling coal on to flames. She watched him add a log or two. She said, 'How did Major Billicliffe keep himself warm?'

'Probably didn't. I don't know. We'll find out.' He pulled himself to his feet, dusting off his hands on the seat of his corduroys. 'Come. Let us go and explore.'

It did not take very long. They went through the small lobby into the other room; Major Billicliffe's dining room, where Oscar remembered the old man's drip-dry shirts draped over the backs of the chairs. But here, too, Betty and Rose had been busy, and all was cleaned and set to rights. The old cardboard boxes and piles of newspapers had disappeared, the table was decently polished and set about with four chairs.

From this room, stairs, very steep and narrow, led to the upper floor, and they ascended and inspected the two bedrooms. In Major Billicliffe's bedroom, only a couple of ancient leather suitcases, firmly closed, remained as evidence of the former occupant. They were packed,

Elfrida guessed, with his more respectable clothes. The bed was covered with a fresh cotton counterpane, and the rag rugs had been laundered.

'We could move in tomorrow,' Elfrida observed, and then, added hastily, in case Oscar should take her at her word, 'if we wanted to.'

'Dear girl, I don't think we want to do that.'

The second bedroom was smaller, and the bathroom, if not exactly the disaster that Rose had predicted, Spartan to a degree and not conducive to long soaks in scented water. The bath, which stood on feet, was stained and rusted, the basin cracked and the linoleum beginning to curl up at the corners. A clean threadbare towel hung on a wooden rail, and a bar of Lifebuoy soap sat on the basin.

The best thing about the bathroom, like the kitchen, was the view. Elfrida, with some difficulty, got the window open and hung out. It was very still and quiet, but she could hear the movements of the trees in some mysterious, unfelt breeze. And then two curlews flew by, headed for the water, calling their sad, lonely cry. Below her, the garden lay untended: rough grass, clumps of weed, two rusted washpoles with a bit of rope suspended between them. Nothing, it seemed, had been done for years, yet she did not feel either depressed or disheartened. The view, the same view that she had admired from Rose's window, was there. The sloping fields and the dazzling blue water and the distant hills. And she thought that for a house that was not exactly bursting with happy memories it had a good feel to it. It had been neglected but was not without hope. It simply needed, like any human being, a bit of laughter and some tender loving care, and it would leap into life again. The only thing was, they'd have to do something about keeping themselves warm.

From behind her Oscar spoke. 'I am going to go out of doors,' he told her, 'to inspect my policies.'

'You do that. You'll burst with pride when you see your ragwort.'

She heard him go downstairs, whistle for Horace. She waited. Presently he appeared beneath her, having let himself and the dog out of the kitchen door. She watched him, foreshortened, stand in the sunshine and look about him. Then, with Horace at his heels, he set out to walk down the length of his plot. When he came to the end, and the sagging fence that was his boundary, he leaned an elbow on one of the posts, and stood there, watching the seabirds on the shore of the firth.

Elfrida thought, I must buy him a pair of field-glasses. And then she thought that he looked comfortable and at ease with himself. A countryman who had finally come home.

She smiled, shut the window, went out of the bathroom and crossed the narrow passage into the smaller bedroom for a quick reassessment: this would have to be for Lucy. She eyed it professionally, trying to decide if there would be space to put a desk for homework. There would, if they replaced the enormous fumed oak double bed with a single divan. The only thing was, it faced north so was a bit lightless. Maybe something could be contrived on the western aspect . . .

She heard the sound of the approaching car and, peering through the window, saw Sam's Discovery bumping down the drive from the main road, swinging around the turn and drawing to a stop at the open gate. The back door opened and Lucy tumbled out.

'Elfrida!'

She sounded joyous, as though everything, for once in her life, was going to work out. Feeling ridiculously hopeful and happy, Elfrida turned and went from the room, ran down the narrow stairway to fling open the front door and hold wide her arms.

Lucy bolted into them and was already imparting information, in high excitement, before Elfrida could say a word. 'Oh, Elfrida, it's all right. Carrie got hold of Mummy, and she was frightfully surprised and had to have it all explained to her *twice* before she finally understood what we all want to do. And Carrie was marvellously persuasive and told her that she had to think about *herself* and *Randall*, and have a lovely honeymoon and take her time before coming back to England. And Mummy said that they want to go to Hawaii for their honeymoon, then go to Cleveland to see Randall's other house there so she'll need masses of time. And she said it was very, very kind of you to have me and I could stay with you.'

Elfrida, relieved and delighted as she was, managed to remain practical. 'What about school? School in London, I mean.'

'Oh, Mummy's going to see to all that. Ring Miss Maxwell-Brown and explain, and ask her to keep my place open for me next summer just in case I want to go back then. And she wanted to speak to you but Carrie said you were here, so Mummy said she'd ring back and speak to you another time. Elfrida, isn't this the sweetest house? What's the old car doing there?'

'Rusting.'

'Where's your car?'

'At Rose's.'

672

'We thought maybe you'd flogged it at a garage and bought that one instead.'

'You never thought any such thing.'

'Does it go?'

'I don't know.'

'Rory will get it started. Oh, and Elfrida, he's had a letter. He's going to Nepal in the middle of January. Isn't that exciting? The only thing is, he won't be here when I'm here, but he's coming back in August to be ready for university. Elfrida, is this the sitting room? And look, you've already lit a fire! It's so cosy. Where's Oscar?'

'Out in the garden.'

'How do I get to him?'

'Through the kitchen, out the door . . .'

With no hanging about, Lucy went galloping down the garden calling Oscar's name. Then Carrie appeared, staggering through the door with a huge shopping basket sprouting Thermos flasks and bottles slung over her arm.

'Here we all are. Sorry, I hope we haven't kept you waiting.' She dumped the basket on the floor. Then, straightening up, she raised a clenched fist as a sign of victory. 'Done it,' she told Elfrida. 'Got through to Nicola, talked her into a good mood and everything's OK. Parental approval has been bestowed. Lucy can stay and go to school in Creagan, and Nicola says she'll be in touch about contributing a bit of cash to the household for board and lodging.'

'I never thought of that,' Elfrida admitted.

'No, I don't suppose you did. And she will honour you with her presence next time she comes back to this country. I suppose that means driving north in some fantastic car, with Randall Fischer at the wheel, to flaunt her new-found riches and cast a beady eye over you and Oscar.'

'Carrie, don't be unkind.'

'She'll probably patronise.'

'It doesn't matter. We've got our way. Oh, well done.' They hugged in triumph. Then Carrie drew away, and her expression became serious. 'Elfrida, you promise, it's not going to be too much for you?'

Elfrida shook her head. 'I don't think so.'

'It's a lot you're taking on.'

'Don't say that. Ever.'

'What's the house like?'

'Cold. That's why we lit the fire.'

'Can I nose around?'

'Of course.'

'Is this the kitchen?'

'Isn't it gruesome?'

'But full of sunshine! Oh, look, there's Oscar ...' She drifted out into the garden by way of the kitchen door. '*Oscar!*'

Elfrida picked up the basket, humped it into the kitchen and set it down on the table. As she did this she was joined by Sam, hefting a grocery box close to his chest. It looked very heavy.

'Is this all picnic?' she asked, in some amazement.

'A feast. Where shall I put it?'

'Here, by the basket. Where's Rory?'

'Trying to deal with Major Billicliffe's old car. It looks dreadful standing there. Have we got the ignition key?'

'I've no idea.'

'We can take the brake off and shove it out of the way. It lowers the tone of your newly acquired property.' He went to the window and stood looking down the garden to where Oscar, Carrie and Lucy had started to walk back to the house. He said, 'What an amazing view. It's a good house, Elfrida. It's got a solid feel to it.'

And she felt warmed, like a mother whose child is praised for its beauty. 'That's what I think too.'

The Christmas Eve picnic at Corrydale, the first they ever had there, was something of a movable feast. It started with a glass of wine by the fireside, in the warmth of the blazing logs, but slowly progressed out of doors because the day was so beautiful that it seemed almost sacrilegious to be inside. Rory and Lucy were the first to make their way out into the garden, and the others joined them, one by one, to perch on kitchen chairs or cushions from the sofa, or the thick rug that Rory fetched from Sam's car. The air was cold but the sun beamed down upon them, and in the shelter of the house there was no breath of wind.

Carrie and Sam had done a splendid job. They had brought hot soup, laced with sherry and drunk from mugs, fresh rolls filled with thick slices of ham and English mustard, a bacon and egg quiche, chicken drumsticks, tomato salad, crisp green apples and chunks of Cheddar cheese. Finally there was a flask of boiling hot coffee.

Elfrida, sitting on a cushion with her back against the wall, turned her face up to the sun and closed her eyes. 'That was the best picnic ever. Thank you, Carrie. I feel quite stunned with wine. Maddened by drink. I could be in Majorca.'

Oscar laughed. 'Discount the fact that you're still wrapped up in your blanket coat.'

Rory and Lucy, having finished their picnic and

shared between them a large bag of potato crisps and a bar of chocolate, had disappeared indoors to inspect the layout of the little house. Now they appeared again.

'It's so nice, Oscar,' Lucy told him.

'The only thing is,' said Rory, bluntly, 'you're going to have to do something about the heating problem. It's Arctic.'

Carrie protested, 'Rory, it's been standing empty and there's been snow. Come on, it's December. Nothing's particularly warm in December.'

'No,' Oscar said firmly. 'Rory's right. Heating will be our first priority. Where are you two off to now?'

'We thought we'd take Horace for a walk down to the water and the beach.'

Oscar tipped back the last of his coffee. 'I shall come with you.' He had eaten his picnic sitting on the step of the kitchen door. Now he set down the mug and held out a hand to Rory, who took it and pulled him to his feet. 'After that feast, I need exercise. Who's coming with us?'

'I shall,' said Carrie.

'I shan't,' said Elfrida firmly. 'Why can't you sit around, just for a moment? It's all so blissfully peaceful.'

'If we do, it will be dark before we know it and too late for a walk. What about you, Sam?'

'I shall stay with Elfrida. I would like to do a building inspection.'

Showing Sam Howard around Major Billicliffe's house was quite different from looking at it with Oscar. With Oscar, Elfrida had simply gone from room to room and ended up grateful that it was neither as poky nor as decrepit as they had feared. But Sam was infinitely more practical and meticulous, just as she had suspected he would be. He tapped walls, turned taps, inspected window-frames and power points, and made no comment when she revealed to him the horrors of the breeze-block bathroom. Finally they were finished and back in the sitting room. The fire was dying so she put another couple of logs on the embers and stirred it up with a poker. Sam had said so little, made so few observations that she began to feel afraid that, mentally, he had condemned Oscar's inheritance and was about to break the news that, in his opinion, it was unfit for human habitation.

'What do you think, Sam?' she asked nervously.

'I think it has great possibilities. And the location is out of this world ... Hang on a moment, I just have to fetch something from the car. Is there electricity? Could we have a light or two on? It's beginning to get a bit dark in here.'

When he had gone, she turned on lights. A faint gleam emanated from an overhead shade. Was the bulb on its last legs, or was this simply another example of Major Billicliffe's parsimonious lifestyle? A lamp by the fireside, another on the desk. After that things looked a bit better. When Sam returned she saw that he had brought with him a yellow scratch pad and a ballpoint pen.

They sat together on the sofa. 'Now,' said Sam, reaching into his pocket for his spectacles and putting them on, 'let's talk turkey. Do you intend living in the place just as it is, or do you want to change a few things?'

'It depends,' said Elfrida, cautiously.

'On what?'

'How much it would cost.'

'Supposing . . .' He began to draw a plan on the scratch pad. 'Supposing to begin with, you demolished the existing kitchen and bathroom. They're ugly, impractical, and shut out the light from the south. And then, I think, you should demolish the wall dividing the two downstairs rooms – it's only plasterboard and doesn't seem to support anything. Then you'd have one big open-plan room. And my suggestion would be that you make the dining room into a kitchen, and maybe build a small dining area out to the south. The south and west walls could be glassed – you'd get all the view and every ray of sun. And it would give you a sheltered corner for sitting out. A little terrace. Good for warm summer evenings.'

'What would we do about the staircase?'

'Move it around to the back wall.'

'And things like fridges and washing-machines? Appliances, I think the word is.'

'Incorporate them into a fitted kitchen. There's a chimney there already so you could install an Aga or a Rayburn. Continual steady heat, winter and summer, and if you're visited by a heatwave, which isn't very likely in this part of the world, you just open all the doors and windows.'

'Would that do instead of central heating?'

'I would reckon so. This house is so well built, and of stone, that once you get it properly insulated it'll stay warm. And you've got this fire in your sitting room. As for the bedrooms, you could put in electric radiators and heat your water by electricity too. It's enormously efficient, and if you have a power-cut you've still got the Aga.'

'Bathroom?'

'A new one.' He sketched it in on his rough plan. 'Over the dining room.'

'Lucy would have to use it too.'

'No problem.'

'The small bedroom, where she would sleep, is terribly dark.'

'Once you've got rid of the old bathroom, and the passage, she'd have a southern wall for another window.'

Elfrida gazed at his simple suggestions, all drawn out for her on the yellow scratch pad, and was astonished that he had so quickly solved all dilemmas. And as for a single, open-plan living space, she rather liked it. She imagined herself and Oscar sitting, just as she was sitting now, by the fire, with the comfort of a modern kitchen at the far end of the room.

'The lobby?' she ventured.

'Get rid of it. It's simply a draught trap. But double glazing and a new front door will keep the cold out.'

Elfrida chewed her thumbnail. She said, 'How much will all this cost?'

'Honestly, I don't know.'

'Would it – would it cost more than eighty thousand pounds?'

He laughed, his face creasing up with amusement. 'No, Elfrida. I don't think it would cost as much as that. You're not, after all, rebuilding. Simply adapting. The roof seems to be sound, which is the most important thing. No sign of damp. But I think you should get a surveyor in. And you'd be better to have all the electricity rewired. Even so, eighty thousand should be more than adequate.' He took off his spectacles and looked at her. 'Have you *got* eighty thousand?'

'No, but I hope to have. Jamie Erskine-Earle is going to sell my little clock for me. We never told you but apparently it's very rare. A collector's piece. Worth a lot of money. So I told him to sell it.'

'Eighty thousand?'

'That's what he said. Top price eighty-five.'

'In that case you have no problems. I'm delighted for you! Go for it, Elfrida.'

'We'll have to get an architect – and planning permission and things like that.'

'How about the doctor's wife? Janet Sinclair – she's an architect. Give her the job. The bonus there is that she's local and she'll know all the best builders, joiners and plumbers.'

'How long will it take?'

'I suppose six months. I don't know.'

'We'll have to stay in the Estate House until it's ready for us to move in.'

'Of course.'

'But you, Sam? You want the Estate House.'

'I can wait. I'm certainly not about to throw you out on to the streets.'

'But you'll be working in Buckly so where will you live?'

'I'll be OK.'

A brilliant idea occurred to Elfrida and, in her impulsive way, she immediately shared it with him. 'You can live with us. At the Estate House. You and Lucy and Oscar and me. You've already got a room there. You might just as well stay.'

Again Sam laughed. 'Elfrida, these are the sort of suggestions you should think about very deeply.'

'Why?'

'Because you may change your mind. And you must talk it over with Oscar. He may not like the idea at all.'

'Oh, Oscar will love to have you. And so shall I. It will be a new job for me, letting lodgings. You know, I've been a lot of things in my time – an actress, albeit not a very good one, a waitress, when I wasn't working, a lady of not very respectable repute, a cushion stitcher. And now I shall become a landlady. Oh, please, say yes. I feel the Estate House is already yours, in a strange way, even though you don't own it yet. As though you were always meant to come and live there. And that's where you should be.'

'Thank you,' said Sam. 'In that case, I accept, subject of course to Oscar's approval.'

The sun was beginning to dip down out of the sky by the time the walkers returned. Oscar and Carrie were first, with Horace, badly in need of a cooling drink.

'How was it?' Elfrida asked, searching a cupboard for a suitable bowl for a dog.

'Perfect,' Carrie told her, unknotting her scarf. 'Such a heavenly place. And all the birds down on the shore! Ducks and cormorants and gulls. How did you and Sam get on?'

'Sam is *brilliant*. He's practically drawn the plans. You must come and look, Oscar. We hardly have to do anything. Just knock bits down and build other bits and get rid of a wall and find an Aga. Don't gape, Oscar, it's all very straightforward. And we'll ask Janet Sinclair to be our architect. And Sam says we must have it all surveyed and rewired, but he doesn't think there's a thing wrong *anywhere*. Come and see . . .'

It was half an hour before Rory and Lucy finally joined them, by which time Oscar had seen and listened to all Sam's ideas, been persuaded and given his consent. Carrie approved as well. 'You know, I've always loved the idea of an open-plan ground floor, specially in a small house. And with the new extension it means you'll get masses more light. Sam, you are clever. You actually are *very* clever. How did you learn so much about knocking down walls and drawing plans?'

'For the last two months I've been living with plans and projects and elevations and architects' blueprints. I'd be pretty dumb if I hadn't absorbed a bit of know-how . . .'

Now, the light was fading. Carrie looked at her watch and said that it was time to go back to Creagan. Lucy still had to finish laying the table for Christmas dinner, and Carrie was going to cook a large, satisfying dish that they could eat this evening. 'Are we going to midnight service, Elfrida?'

'I think so. Oscar doesn't want to come, but I'll go.'

'Me too. And Lucy and Sam are coming. We'll have a late meal, otherwise it's a very long evening.'

Oscar said, 'We'll play cards. I found some packs in the bottom drawer of the bookcase. Who knows how to play three-pack canasta?'

'Samba, you mean?' said Sam. '*I* know how. There was a great craze for it in New York when I was there.'

'I can't play,' said Lucy.

'Never mind,' he told her. 'You can play with me.'

Eventually, having packed up the remains of the picnic, found hats and gloves and generally sorted themselves out, the first party took their leave in Sam's car. Elfrida, Oscar and Horace were left behind to lock up and follow later, but they went out to see the others off.

By now, at only four o'clock, the blue dusk had crept

in, and a fine new moon, delicate as an eyelash, hung above them in the sapphire sky. The snowcapped hills became almost luminous in the strange half-light, and the ebbing tide was draining the firth, revealing sweeps of beach and sandbank. Curlews still flew, skimming the shore, but other birds were silent, their song finished for the day.

The big Discovery, tail-lights shining, disappeared up the drive. Oscar and Elfrida waited by the door until they could hear the sound of its engine no longer, then turned and went back inside.

Elfrida said, 'I don't want to go. I don't want to leave. I don't want today to end.'

'Then we'll stay for a little.'

'If I had any tea I'd make you a cup.'

'We'll have one when we get back.'

He sank tiredly down on the sofa, where, earlier, Sam had sat. He had walked, with the young ones, further than he intended and felt weary. Elfrida put the last bit of wood on the fire, then sat opposite him, stretching her cold fingers to the blaze.

She said, 'We will live here, won't we, Oscar?'

'If you want.'

'I want. But do you want?'

'Yes. I admit I had reservations, but now that I've seen it again, and Sam has come up with all these ideas and possibilities, I think it's exactly what we should do.'

'It's exciting. A new start. Architects and builders, and everything made new. One of my most favourite smells is that of wet plaster. And the next most favourite is the smell of fresh paint.'

'Furniture?'

'We can manage with what's here for the time being.

Maybe look around, pick up some pretty bits at auction. The first priority is to get the place the way we want it. Warm and light and airy. With an Aga and a good-looking kitchen. Warm is the most important. I can't imagine how Major Billicliffe lived here for so long without dying of hypothermia.'

'He was one of the old school. A thick tweed jacket, long woolly underfugs and no nonsense about feeling the cold.'

'You won't ever be like that, will you, Oscar? I couldn't bear it if you started wearing long woolly underfugs.'

'No. With a bit of luck I won't ever do that.'

The shadows lengthened. Beyond the window, the bare trees faded into the darkness. Elfrida sighed. 'I suppose we should go. I mustn't leave everything to Carrie . . .'

But Oscar said, 'Wait. I want to talk.'

'What about?'

'Us.'

'But . . .' She had been about to say, 'we've been talking about us all day,' but Oscar interrupted her.

'Just listen. Just listen to me.' And his voice sounded so serious and intent that she got up from her chair and went to sit beside him, close, on the old sofa, and he put out his hand and laid it upon her own. And she remembered his doing this once before as they sat at the kitchen table at the Grange, with Gloria and Francesca dead, and neither of them able to find words to comfort each other.

'I'm listening,' she told him.

'This is a new step we're going to take. Together. A real commitment. Doing up this house, spending serious money and coming to live here. As well, for the foreseeable future, Lucy is coming too. Don't you think perhaps the time has come for us to get married? To be man and wife? It's a formality, I know, because if we tried we could scarcely be more married than we already are. But it would put a seal on our union . . . not in a moral sense but an affirmation of our trust in the future.'

Elfrida realised that her stupid eyes were filling with tears. 'Oh, Oscar . . .' She drew away her hand and began to search for her handkerchief. 'Old people,' she had once told herself, 'look hideous when they cry.' '. . . you don't need to do this. It's only months since they died. So little time to grieve and recover. And you mustn't think of me because I'm not that sort of person. I will stay with you happily for the rest of my life, but I don't want you to feel you have to marry me.'

'I don't feel that. I love you and I honour you just the way things are, and I don't suppose either of us gives a jot what other people think or choose to say. All things being equal, I should happily settle for carrying on just the way things are. But we have Lucy, now, to consider.'

'What difference does she make to how we live our lives?'

'Oh, my dearest Elfrida, just think. So far the people of Creagan have accepted you and me with great kindness; even forebearance. No questions. Not a single soul has cast a stone, not even a tiny pebble. But for Lucy it is different. She is going to the local school. Children are not always very kind. Rumours can be started, and even in this day and age, their parents can be mean-spirited. I wouldn't want any of that sort of thing to rub off on Lucy. As well, we have Nicola's new husband to consider. We know nothing about him, and he's probably a perfectly decent chap, but he might turn out to be one of those high-minded individuals with a strong and ungiving moral code. Sometime, Nicola is bringing him to visit us. We don't want to give either of them a valid reason for spiriting Lucy off to Cleveland, Ohio against her will.'

'You mean, he wouldn't want to leave her with us, simply because we live in sin?'

'Exactly so.'

'So for her sake, we should be married.'

'Put baldly, yes.'

'But Gloria . . .'

'Gloria, of all women, would understand.'

'It's such a short time, Oscar.'

'I know.'

'You're sure?'

'Yes, I am sure. Because one thing is truly certain, and that is that you have helped me to start again, and it is you who have made a dark and painful time not only bearable and possible but even joyful as well. I think you carry joy around with you. We can't go back. Life, for both of us, can never be the same as it was, but it can be different, and you have proved to me that it can be good. I told you a long time ago that you could always make me laugh. And you have made me love you. Now I cannot imagine an existence without you. Please marry me. If I wasn't feeling so bloody stiff I'd get down on one knee.'

'I'd hate you to do that.' Elfrida, having at last found her handkerchief, now blew her nose. 'But I'd like to marry you very, very much. Thank you for asking me.' She put her handkerchief away, and once more he took her hand.

'So. We are betrothed. Shall we break the news or keep it to ourselves?'

'Let's keep it to ourselves. Secretly relish. Just for the time being.'

'You're right. There's so much going on. Let us get Christmas behind us, and then I shall take you to Kingsferry and buy you a diamond ring, and after that we can announce our happiness to the world.'

'I have to be truthful,' Elfrida admitted, 'I'm not all that mad on diamonds.'

'Then what would you like me to buy you?'

'Aquamarines?'

And Oscar laughed, and kissed her, and they might have sat on, in the gloaming, for the rest of the evening, but the last of the logs had burned out and the house, with the sun gone, grew cold again. It was time to leave. Outside the air, so quickly, had chilled and it was winter again. A wind stirred from the north, shivering the leafless branches of the big beech tree that stood opposite their gate.

Elfrida, her hands deep in the pockets of her coat, looked about her. The moon was rising, the first star pricked. 'We'll be back,' she said, to no one in particular.

'Of course.' Oscar locked his front door, took her arm and, with Horace at their heels, they walked, in the deep blue evening light, down the pebbled path.

Christmas Eve
It's nearly eight o'clock in the evening, and
there's still masses to do but must write
everything down otherwise it will be lost for
ever. So much has happened. The worst was

Mummy ringing yesterday in the middle of
Elfrida's party to say that she has married
Randall Fischer. I think it was the worst thing
that ever happened to me, because all I could
think about was having to go and live in
America and lose all my friends, or else have
to live with Gran in London on my own. And
not fit in or be wanted in either place. It was
really dire. I had horrible hysterics and made
myself feel quite ill and was beastly to Carrie,
but that's all over now.

Anyway, now it is all sorted out and I'm
going to stay here, in Creagan, with Elfrida
and Oscar, for the time being, anyway, and
go to day-school in Creagan. Rory was the
one who told everybody that I must do this,
and I am so pleased that he and I had time
to talk, when he was fixing the television,
so that he knew exactly how I felt, even if
nobody else did. I think he is really my best
friend. He is going to Nepal next month and is
tremendously excited about it. I shall miss him
but will see him again, I am sure, when he
gets back in August. Whatever has happened
by then, I shall make a point of seeing him,
and I shall be fifteen then. Fifteen sounds
much older than fourteen.

So this morning I woke up and knew that
everything was going to be all right, and it
was like having a huge weight off my mind.
Carrie rang Gran and told her about the
plans, and she went along with them, and
then later Carrie rang Mummy in Florida and

persuaded her too. Actually, it didn't take very
long. And then I had a chat with Mummy
and managed not to sound too delighted in
case she took offence and changed her mind.
  So then Rory appeared, and we got a
picnic together, and Sam drove us over to
Corrydale. I have always longed to go there
and see it all. It is beautiful and it was a
perfect day, with no clouds or wind and really
quite warm. Oscar's little house is sweet,
tucked away on the estate, with a few other
little houses in view, and great big trees, and
a long view of the water and other hills. It
was tremendously quiet; only birdsong, and no
sound of traffic or anything. The house isn't
very big and is fairly shabby and dreadfully
cold, but Oscar had lit a fire which made
it look cosy. There are only two bedrooms,
and the one I shall have is a bit gloomy, but
Elfrida says it will be better when they have
done a few alterations. Sam thought up lots of
clever ideas, and when it is finished it will look
really nice. It has a garden, but a bit weedy,
and a sort of little terrace where we all went
out and ate our picnic. Elfrida says there are
other children, called Cowper, who live nearby
at the farm, and they go to Creagan school
too, so maybe when term starts I can get a lift
in the mornings with them.
  We came back with Sam, left Rory at the
Manse, then came home. Carrie made a huge
dish called a tortilla for us to have for supper.
It had potatoes and leeks in it, and eggs and

bacon and heaps of other delicious things.
While she did this, I finished laying the table
for Christmas dinner, and put on the candles
and the crackers and dishes of chocolates, and
folded the napkins. There's a bowl of holly
in the middle of the table and it looks really
festive, and when we've lit the fire it will look
exactly right, like a Christmas card. Carrie
said all that was missing was a Jolly Cardinal.
Then we're going to play cards to fill in
the long evening, and then we're all going to
midnight service, except Oscar who says he
doesn't want to come.
I don't know how long it will be before
they are able to move to Corrydale because of
all the work that has to be done there. I would
love to be there in the summer, but Elfrida
says we'll have to see. Meantime, it's lovely
here. And Sam is going to come and be our
lodger until everything is sorted out.
I can't believe that I could be so miserable
and despairing one day, and so utterly happy
the next.
The next time I write in my diary,
Christmas will be over.

Elfrida endeavoured to fan out her enormous hand of
cards, and at the same time decide what she was going
to throw. She had run out of twos and threes, and was
now in the uncomfortable position of trying to work out
whether or not Carrie had a pair in her hand and, if
so, a pair of what? The discard pack was too large for
comfort, they were nearing the end of the game, and

if Carrie picked it up now, Elfrida and Sam would be defeated.

'Come along now, Elfrida.' Oscar was getting tired of the long wait. 'Be brave. Throw something you don't want.'

So she gritted her teeth and threw the eight of hearts, and waited anxiously for Carrie to let out a shout of glee and pounce. But Carrie shook her head, and Elfrida relaxed with a sigh of relief. 'I can't stand the nerves! If I wasn't going to church I should have another large drink.'

It was now ten past eleven, and they were on the last hand. So far, Sam and Elfrida were ahead on points but the tension would continue until the final card was turned. Elfrida had played samba, long ago, when Jimbo was still alive and they had sometimes whiled away the evening with a couple of friends. But she had forgotten some of the rules, and it was not until she started playing again that the old tricks and shibboleths came back to her. Oscar and Sam were both old hands and up to all the nuances of the game, but Carrie and Lucy were starters. Carrie quickly picked it up and Lucy played with Sam, who was kindly and patient about explaining, and by the end of the first hand was allowing her to make the choices of discard and not becoming annoyed when she made the wrong one.

Carrie picked up two cards, put them into her hand and was then able to finish a samba. Oscar let out a grunt of approval. She threw the four of spades. 'If you pick that up, Sam, I shall strangle you with my bare hands.'

'I can't.'

Lucy said, 'There are only four cards left.'

'When they're finished, the game's done,' Sam told her. 'Pick two up, Lucy, and see what we've got.'

From the landing, the telephone rang.

Oscar said, 'That damned telephone. Who's ringing us at this hour?'

Elfrida said, 'I'll go.'

But Oscar had already laid down his cards and was getting to his feet. He went out of the room, closing the door behind him. Elfrida heard him say, 'Estate House.'

And then silence as the caller spoke, then a murmured reply. The next moment, he was back with them, settling down in his place on the window-seat, picking up his cards again.

Elfrida was curious. 'Who was it?'

'Nothing much. A mistake.'

'You mean, wrong number?'

Oscar gazed at his cards.

Sam said, 'If you're the wrong number, why did you answer the phone?' and Lucy giggled at the old joke, sitting with her head on one side and trying to decide what she should throw.

In the end they ran out of cards and nobody won. But Sam pulled the score pad towards him, totted up all the figures and announced that he and Elfrida were the overall winners and that he hoped that Oscar was about to come up with a valuable prize.

'I am about to do no such thing,' Oscar informed him, with dignity. 'You were extremely lucky and held all the best cards, nothing to do with skill.' And with that he laid his cards on the table and got to his feet. He said, 'I'm going to take Horace for a walk.'

Elfrida stared at him in some astonishment. He often

took Horace out into the garden last thing at night but never for a walk.

'A walk? Where are you going? Down to the beach?'

'I don't know. I just feel in need of some fresh air and to stretch my legs. Horace might as well come with me. I may not be back by the time you set off for church, but leave the door open and I'll still be up when you all return. Have a good time. Sing nicely, Lucy.'

'I will,' she promised him.

He left them, closing the door behind him.

Elfrida's expression was puzzled. '*Funny*. You'd have thought he'd had enough exercise today to last him for a week.'

'Oh, leave him, Elfrida,' said Carrie, gathering up all the cards and starting to sort them out into three separate packs, one blue, one red and one flowered. 'Help me, Lucy. You can do the flowered ones. I think that's a marvellous game. There comes a subtle moment when you stop playing samba and start playing canasta. The scoring's a bit complicated, though. You'll have to write it down for me, Sam, so that I don't forget.'

'I'll do that.'

The cards were sorted, stacked and put away. Elfrida went around the room, puffing up cushions and picking up newspapers from the floor. The fire was low, but she left it and stood the guard in front of the smouldering wood ashes.

'We shouldn't be too long making our way, I think. There's bound to be a huge congregation and we want to be able to get a seat.'

'It's like going to the theatre,' said Lucy. 'Will it be cold in the church? Should I wear my red jacket?'

'Yes, definitely, and your warm boots.'

Alone in her bedroom, Elfrida combed her hair, put on a bit more lipstick and sprayed herself with scent. Then she took her blanket coat from the wardrobe, buttoned it up and put on her tea-cosy hat. She sat on the bed and pulled on her fur-lined boots. Some money for the collection, a handkerchief in case she felt emotionally touched by carols, and a pair of gloves.

All ready. She surveyed her reflection in the long mirror. Elfrida Phipps, soon to become Mrs Oscar Blundell. She thought that she looked terrific. *Here I come, God. And thanks.*

She went out of her room and downstairs to the kitchen to check that all was in order for Christmas morning and that she hadn't left the gas on or a kettle boiling itself dry, which she quite often did. And in the kitchen, in his basket, she found Horace.

She frowned, 'Horace, I thought Oscar had taken you for a walk.'

Horace gazed at her and thumped his tail.

'Did he leave you behind?'

Horace closed his eyes.

'Where's he gone?'

Horace did not tell her.

She went upstairs again and into the sitting room. 'Oscar?' But the sitting room was empty and all the lights switched off. No Oscar.

On the landing, she found Sam pulling on his navy blue overcoat. 'Oscar's disappeared.'

'He's walking Horace,' Sam reminded her.

'No, Horace is in the kitchen in his basket. It's a mystery!'

Sam grinned. 'Oscar's probably sneaked off to the pub.'

'What a suggestion.'

'Don't worry. He's a big boy now.'

'I'm not worrying.' And of course she wasn't. Just puzzled as to where Oscar could possibly have taken himself.

Lucy ran downstairs from her attic. 'All ready, Elfrida. Do we need collection?'

'Yes. Have you got any?'

'Fifty p. Is that enough?'

'Masses. Where's Carrie?'

'She's still getting ready.'

'Well, you and I will go, Lucy, and bag a pew for the four of us. Sam, will you wait for Carrie, and come over with her?'

'Of course.'

Elfrida and Lucy ran downstairs and, standing on the landing, Sam heard them open and slam shut the big front door.

He stood there on the landing, in the emptied house, and waited for Carrie. Soft sounds came from behind her closed bedroom door: drawers being opened, a cupboard door shut. He felt no sense of impatience. He had waited, during the course of his life, for countless women to appear, sitting at bars, standing around in the foyers of theatres, whiling away the time at the table of some small Italian restaurant. He had waited, more times than he could remember, for Deborah, who had never been punctual for anything. So now, in the house that would, one day, belong to him, he waited for Carrie.

'Oh, Sam.' She came out of her room, shut the door behind her, saw him there and looked a bit abashed. 'Are you waiting for me? I am sorry. I couldn't find my silk scarf.' She wore her loden coat, her fur hat, her long, shining boots. The errant scarf, all pinks and blues, was softly wound around her slender throat, and although all of this was by now dearly familiar to him, he knew that he had never seen her look more beautiful. 'Where are the others? Have they already gone?'

He said, 'Yes,' put his hands on her shoulders, drew her close and kissed her. Something he had been longing to do ever since that first night when she had opened the door to him and found him standing on the doorstep in the falling snow. So, now, it took a long time. When, at last, they drew apart, he saw that she was smiling, and her dark eyes had never seemed so lustrous.

He said, 'Happy Christmas.'

'Happy Christmas, Sam. Time to go.'

Elfrida and Lucy crossed the street. The square, lamplit, was already busy with cars arriving and people converging on the church. It was clear there was indeed going to be a huge congregation. Voices called out, country people greeting each other, falling into step as they made their way.

'Elfrida!'

They stopped and saw Tabitha, Rory and Clodagh behind them, having walked down the steep lane from the Manse.

'Hello! I thought we were early but it seems we're not. I've never seen so many people.'

'I know, it's fun, isn't it?' Tabitha wore a tartan coat, and had wound a red muffler around her neck. 'It's always like this. People come from miles away ... The only thing is, we've had a bit of a setback. Alistair Heggie, the organist, has got flu, so we won't have any proper music.'

Elfrida was horrified. 'You mean, we've got to sing carols unaccompanied? I can't *bear* it!'

'Not quite. Peter rang Bill Croft, the television man, and he's come to the rescue. He's set up a ghetto-blaster and we're going to use taped music. It's a bit of a come-down but better than nothing.'

'Oh, that is disappointing . . . poor Peter.'

'It can't be helped. Come on, with a bit of luck we'll get a pew to ourselves.'

They crossed the street to the wide gates and the path beyond, which led to the wide flight of stone steps and the double doors of the church. Tonight these had been flung wide open. Light from inside streamed out on to the cobbles, and Elfrida could hear the taped music from within the church. A choir. Singing carols.

> *God rest you merry, gentlemen,*
> *Let nothing you dismay.*

It sounded a bit mechanical and tinny. A bit, thought Elfrida, like a portable gramophone played on a picnic. Inappropriate and somehow inadequate.

> *For Jesus Christ our . . .*

Silence. Either the tape-player had broken down or someone had inadvertently switched off the electricity.

'Oh, no!' said Rory. 'Don't say the ghetto-blaster's got flu.'

And then it started. A great surge of sound from the organ. Huge chords and waves of music filled the church, overflowed out through the open doors, resounded up and out into the night.

Elfrida stopped dead. She looked at Tabitha, whose eyes were wide and innocent. For a long moment, neither of them spoke. Then Elfrida said, 'Did Peter ring Oscar? About a quarter past eleven?'

Tabitha shrugged. 'No idea. Come on, kids, see if we can find somewhere to sit.'

And she turned, and ran up the steps with her two children and Lucy at her heels.

After a moment, Elfrida followed. A nice man with a beard was waiting for her. He said, 'Good evening, Mrs Phipps,' and handed her a hymn book. She took it automatically, neither looking at him nor thanking him. She walked into the church, and saw that it was already nearly filled, the congregation shuffling into their places, leaning to chat to neighbours or others sitting behind them. The music thundered all about her, filling the huge void of the soaring arched ceiling, echoing down the long nave. She began to move down the centre aisle, which was paved in red and blue. Walking into the music was like stepping into a pounding sea of sound.

A hand touched her arm. She stopped. 'Elfrida. Here.' It was Lucy. 'We're keeping seats for you and Sam and Carrie.'

She took no notice. Did not move.

The Christmas tree, lavishly decorated and twinkling with lights, stood in the middle of the transept between the pulpit and the lectern. Beyond this, against the north wall of the church, the organ pipes soared. The organist's seat was enclosed by an oaken stall so that he was not visible to the seated assembly. But Elfrida was standing. And she was tall. An overhead spotlight shone down upon him, and she could clearly see his head, and his profile, and the thick white hair, rendered unruly by the unselfconscious exuberance of his own performance.

Beethoven. 'Song of Joy'.

And Oscar Blundell playing his heart out. Reconciled. Returned. Back where he belonged.

LEARN MORE
about your favourite author
in this enchanting account
of her Cornish childhood.

Two Mothers

by Rosamunde Pilcher

My mother was born in the Orkney Islands, one of eight children, the offspring of a hard-working farmer and his wife. When she was in her teens, they fell upon hard times; I suspect a drink problem on the part of my grandfather, but this was never confirmed. The farm was sold and the family moved to Glasgow. All the boys and one sister emigrated to the United States, so only three sisters were left. Davina married a doctor, domiciled in the wilds of the Western Highlands. The second sister, Nan, married a dear man who had been a Sergeant in the Argyll and Sutherland Highlanders during the First World War. His job was in Glasgow, and they lived in a wonderfully cosy tenement house, with a washing line in the communal yard, and a parlour kept for when the Minister came to call.

My mother, Helen, married my father, Charles Scott. He was in the Royal Navy, and I can only imagine they met while his ship was in port. No details were ever shared with us. Whatever, they became engaged, and my mother travelled alone to Hong Kong, where they were married in Hong Kong cathedral, and spent a two-day honeymoon in Kowloon. He left the Navy and they moved on to Australia, where he thought he would make his fortune farming. This did not happen, and they were forced to return home, my father selling his gun in order to pay for the passage. By now there were three of them, my older sister having been born in 1919 in Turramurra.

I think this was probably the first time my mother met her in-laws, and the encounter was not successful. His family considered, not perhaps without justification, that their eldest son had married beneath him, and were appalled that my sister, now aged five, spoke with a strong Australian accent. My mother never truly forgave them for this initial rejection, and there was always a certain frigidity in the air on the few occasions when they all got together. Much of this emanated from my mother, which was sad, because I only remember affection and welcome from these various aunts and uncles, and would have loved to see more of them, and spend time with my cousins.

Life was not easy after the First World War, and jobs hard to come by. Finally my father was offered employment, but it was in Burma, working with the Government. He was put in charge of the Irrawaddy dredging works in Rangoon harbour, keeping the river port open for the boats, laden with teak and rubies, that sailed down from Mandalay. It was a responsible job and he was housed, accordingly, in some style. My mother, pregnant with me, did not accompany him. Alone, she cast about for some place to live and to bring up two children. She settled for Cornwall, where once she had visited a girlfriend. Weighing up the pros and cons, she decided that if she was going to have to bring up two children on her own, she might as well do it in a pleasant place.

We ended up in Lelant, on the Hayle estuary and only three miles from St Ives. At first she stayed in a small boarding house, where I was born with the help of the village midwife, and then we took possession of a rented house. The Elms, where we remained until 1939 and the Second World War.

Being without a father was not unusual in those days. Most families seemed to have some male or other out in India, or Malaya, or Africa, planting rubber, or doing their bit to keep the British Empire ticking along, or serving in the Armed Forces. Having never known my father, I did not miss him, but it must have been very hard for my sister, Lalage. At five years old, she knew my father well, he was one half of her family. When he went to Burma, he virtually left for good, doing stints of three or four years before getting three months home leave. Air travel was in its infancy, and the P & O boats took three weeks to make the long journey through the Indian Ocean, the Suez Canal, and the Mediterranean. There was no telephone connection, and in an emergency the only form of contact was a telegram. He wrote to us every week, a letter each, neatly typed, and we wrote back, but for a small girl, missing him desperately, it must have been traumatic. Her reaction to this loss was to bury herself in books. She had learned to read very early, and losing herself in her book was her refuge from the day-to-day trials and disappointments of life. This escape route, like a drug, remained with her until the day she died, at 52, of cancer in Sausalito, California.

I suppose we were friends, but seldom played together. Sometimes on a wet morning, we would go up to the nursery and indulge in her favourite flight of fancy, dressing up in grown-up clothes and pretending that my father was coming home. The attic staircase was the train to London; the spare bedroom the docks; the landing was the gangway, where we waited for him to make his way down from the upper deck of the P & O liner.

Her other passion was dancing. We both went to dancing class, and my sister took to the occasions like a duck to water. She was forever pirouetting and doing arabesques, and tried hard to be the teacher and pass her passion on to me. I hated dancing. I have always been uncoordinated and singularly unsupple, and I galumphed miserably about in the beginners' class. Our teacher was called Miss Fildes. She had red hair and my sister was deeply in love with her.

What I really wanted was to be taught to play the piano. We had an old upright in our winter sitting room, and I was hugely frustrated by the knowledge that music lay behind the ebony black wood ... music that only needed a little knowledge to release it. I found an old book of Student Songs, and taught myself to pick out the tunes with one finger, but never progressed any further.

If my father had been around, I am sure he would have recognised my desire, cancelled out the dancing classes, and started me on piano lessons. But my mother could be very unperceptive, and maybe this was deliberate, because the hassle of dancing class, the expense, the logistics of actually getting us there, was just about all she could deal with.

Another void in the normal pattern of family life was created by the fact that my mother, for reasons that I have never understood, had decided, at some point, to embrace Christian Science. I would not recommend any parent to lumber his or her children with this arrogant doctrine. For us, it meant that we never went to the pretty, ancient village church, built on the edge of the golf course and within sight of the sea. I was christened there, but that was the only time I was taken formally through its doorway. And if we were ill, running temperatures, or choking with whooping cough, we were simply told to think beautiful thoughts. Christian Science dictated that we never experienced the kindly masculine presence of either local priest or family doctor, and it was seldom that a man of any sort came through our front door.

Because of this I was fascinated by men, and made friends with the most unlikely people. The coalman, delivering coal on his horse-drawn cart. And Willie, who had a little pony and a float, and brought trunks and suitcases up the hill from the station when there were guests from London, come to stay at one of the big houses. And if a workman turned up to fix a dripping tap, or do a bit of painting, I drove him mad with my constant companionship and endless questions.

Despite all this, I was perfectly happy. Because my sister was not very companionable, I learned contentment on my own, or else played with one of the boys next door. There were few restrictions. I played in the garden, and then opened the gate, and moved on, to the lane, and the little station, and the pinewood. And then, over the railway line and down to the shore of the estuary. The changing tides were an endless diversion.

As we grew older, we went to the big beach. My mother did not come. She disliked sand and chill sea breezes. But there was always a small group of beach goers gathered by the church, and we'd join up with them, a straggling cavalcade of babies in push chairs, visiting teenagers, dogs and Nannies and sometimes an intrepid parent or two. We took our own picnic tea in a basket, and it was at this time that I learned that sad truth: other people's picnics are always better than one's own.

Meanwhile, my mother lived her own life. She was an accomplished seamstress, and always busy creating a dress, or a pair of curtains, or cotton frocks for her two daughters. Up to a point, she was quite sociable. A tea party, perhaps, and a little sedate Mah Jongh. Her friends were inclined to be the village eccentrics, but there were ex-Burma colleagues as well, now retired and living nearby. Otherwise, she was not a great entertainer, although the boys next door and their friends and cousins always enjoyed coming to our house for tea. Because my mother loved to bake there were always piles of scones and pancakes and cakes for hungry boys to wolf down.

In summer time, friends would come to stay, or to rent out the house next door to us, while the neighbours took themselves off to London for a month, to enjoy hotel life and a little urban distraction. Our favourite family was the Gilberts, Irish and totally unpredictable. Henry Gilbert had been in the Navy with my father. He had four lively daughters and a Scottish wife, who never did anything but sit by the fire, write letters and eat peppermint creams. They were a noisy and demonstrative lot, and I loved it when they were around, because there was always laughter and huge, soft, hugs, and someone to give a piggy back if your legs were tired.

We seldom went away from home, because living in Cornwall was a bit like being on holiday all year round. Lovely things were all about us. The Atlantic Ocean, the white beaches, and the wind-blown dunes. The golf links, aromatic with the scent of thyme. The long summers; the short, gale-torn winters; the miraculously early springs. The train ride to St Ives, along the very rim of the cliffs, and then shopping in the steep, narrow streets of the town. The presence, everywhere, of artists, potters, writers, sculptors. The magic of surfing on belly boards on Porthmeor beach, or doing the cliff walk, all three miles of it, on cold grey winter afternoons. The moors inland, and Trencrom hill, where grew the earliest of the wild primroses. The green parkland of Trevethoe, where lived Jiffy Tyringhame, our squire, and where the church fête took place every summer. And our own little village, with its grocer, butcher, sweet shop, post office and pub. The smell of violets, the scent of flowering privet, and the spicy tang of escallonia. And always the salty freshness of the sea, and the dull thunder of distant rollers breaking up on the shore.

We went to school. I did lessons with the vicar's wife, and

my sister went to St Clare's in Penzance. When I was eight, I followed her there, and on my first day decided that I must have a special friend. I picked a sturdy little girl with dark bobbed hair and a fringe. We danced the polka together, accompanied by a tinny piano. At the end of the day, I caught the bus home, and burst into the house to tell my mother, 'I have a best friend.'

She laughed. She always thought me something of a joke.

'It's true,' I insisted.

'Just wait until tomorrow, and see if she still likes you.'

'She will.'

And she did. Sarah Trembath remained my friend, all my life, and until she died.

And her mother, Kitty Trembath, became my second mother.

Jim Trembath was the manager of Lloyds Bank in Penzance, that handsome domed building that stands, like some Florentine church at the top of Market Jew Street. The Trembaths were Cornish farmers who, at some time, had left Cornwall and moved to Gloucestershire. This move had involved a large herd of cattle, and all the Trembath menfolk, however young, had been involved in this massive drive. Jim was the second son, and so the Gloucestershire farm was destined for his older brother, and Jim was put to work with Lloyds Bank. He prospered, married, had his two little girls, and was working as Manager in a small town in Derbyshire, when he was offered the post in Penzance.

So he returned to his Cornwall. The family moved into a white stucco early Victorian villa between Penzance and Newlyn. It had spacious walled gardens sloping down the hill, and – give or take a tall terrace of dour houses smack in the way – a prospect of Mounts Bay.

Jim was a passionate gardener. His farming blood and his love of growing things was fulfilled by his garden, and every weekend, and every summer evening, he was out there, working in his old clothes; trimming and staking and weeding and watering. He grew peaches, trained up the high wall, and pollinated them with a rabbit's scut on a long pole. And there were pears as well, and a cucumber frame, and spectacular sweet peas. He had an old greenhouse which always smelled of freesia, and a noisy motor mower which he drove to and fro, cutting the grass on the extremely cramped tennis court, so that we could put up the net and have a game.

He had a car as well, an old Austin with a dickey, but this stayed in the garage (an old coach house) all week, for he always walked the mile or so to work, striding out, spare and trim, rain or shine, with his shoes polished and a flower in his buttonhole. On Summer Sundays, the car would come out and we would all pile in and go for picnics to Rinsey, or Prussia, or Porthcurno, or Treen. Or drive across the narrow width of the county to Porthkerris, the cove hidden far below the massive northern cliffs.

He read aloud better than anyone has ever done, putting on a different voices for all the characters, but always sounding as Cornish as he was. He read us *Tarka the Otter*, and we all blubbed, and he read *Treasure Island*, but we found Blind Pew so scarey that he had to stop and hide the book away.

At night, when we were asleep, he would come upstairs and leave us each a toffee by our beds, to be chewed and relished (bad for the teeth?) first thing in the morning.

Harriet, Sarah's sister, was two years older than Sarah and myself, but because of her sweet nature and natural friend-liness, there was never any friction among the three of us. She was a clever, diligent child, always top of her class, and good at everything. She even sang in the school choir. I was very fond of her, and wished that my own sister could be so cooperative, instead of constantly insisting that I was too stupid for words.

Their mother, Kitty Trembath, came from South Wales. When I first met her, she must have been in her late thirties, a sweet-faced woman with a smile that made her beautiful. She smiled a lot, and from our very first encounter, I was made to feel special, as though I was the one person she really wanted to see.

The house was her responsibility, with the considerable assistance of a live-in cook (Hilda) and a house parlourmaid (Eileen) Even in this modest set up, a Nanny would have been the norm, but Kitty loved her daughters too much to hand them over to another person.

Theirs was an old house, and nobody had ever thought to modernise it. Quite shabby and well worn, it smelled of floor polish, with a faint whiff of antique shops which I found delightful. Surprisingly, it had been built with a lavatory, complete with rose-patterned bowl, a cistern, and a chain, but no bathroom. It had however, a charming curved staircase which led to the upper floor, and some previous owner had hit upon the bright idea of building a bathroom onto the turn of this staircase, where once a large and ornate window would have let the light in. This bathroom was simply a wooden extension tacked on to the back wall, over the kitchen yard, and propped in position by a couple of sturdy posts. In winter it was very cold, and I always expected it, one day, to come away from its moorings and crash down onto the washing line.

But it never did.

Downstairs, there was a drawing room, a dining room, a morning room and the kitchen. The kitchen was wonderfully archaic, with a Cornish range for cooking and a huge scullery at the back. The morning room was given over to the children; not a nursery, but a sitting room with sagging sofas and books on shelves, and a fire, which in winter months, was always lit and blazing away by the time we had finished breakfast.

My first visit to the Trembaths was a Saturday in November, when I was invited by Sarah for lunch. I travelled to Penzance by bus, a bundle of nervous excitement. Would the Trembaths like me? What would I be given to eat, and what would I do if it was Brussels sprouts? Would I be shown, right away, the location of the lavatory? What would happen if I lost my return bus ticket?

But all was well. Mrs Trembath and Sarah were waiting to meet me at the last bus stop, and for a marvellous moment, I thought Mrs Trembath was going to embrace me. We walked to their house, and there was the gardener, digging in the vegetable patch.

The gardener turned out to be Sarah's father. Lunch was in the dining room, the table formally laid. It was mutton stew and cauliflower, so that was all right. And there was jelly for pudding.

We spent the afternoon out of doors and playing hide and seek.

I realised that there was space for every sort of game, and the bonus of a trellissed summerhouse smothered in prickly roses, and a huge chestnut tree. When it grew dark, we came indoors for tea, and it was time to go home again. Mr Trembath walked me to the bus stop and saw me on my way, and I travelled home in a bliss of remembrance, wondering how soon it would be before I was asked again.

By the time I got to Lelant, night had fallen. Alone, I walked home down the dark country road, unlit by street lamps, and the bare branches of November trees swayed in the wind high above me, and the wind smelt of salt. I began to run, because it was cold and I wanted to be safely home, and to tell my mother every single detail.

She was amused by my excitement.

'What a time you've had.'

'I hope they'll ask me again.'

'I shouldn't count on it.'

But I was sure they would. And they did.

Over the months, I became one of the Trembath family. Harriet and Sarah were the companionable sisters I had never known, and before long I was invited to call their parents Uncle Jim and Auntie Kitty. During the Easter term, when Cornwall is at its most glorious, I was asked to spend the half term holiday, all four days, from Thursday to Tuesday.

My excitement was unbounded. I had never been away to stay by myself before, but on the Thursday morning, set off for school with my satchel and my weekend bag, without a backward glance. As for my mother, she had new sitting room curtains to be stitched; a border to be weeded, and a Mah Jong tea party organised; she was probably quite pleased to have me out of the way. And as for my sister, she had become more involved than ever in her books and her school work and her dancing classes. A display was being organised by Miss Fildes, and my sister yearned to be given the part of Columbine in a little ballet, and when not lost in some book, could be found practising at the barre (the upstairs bannister) or sticking pictures of Irina Baranova up on her bedroom wall.

Living with the Trembaths, having my own bedroom, coming down to breakfast in the mornings, was a satisfying experience. The weather was spring-like, but even if it poured with rain, Auntie Kitty was a reliable source of entertaining ideas, and would produce a packet of transfers, or three new painting books, with promises of a prize for the best colourist. The prize was probably a toffee, or a little bar of Nestlés chocolate, but in the end, we all got one, because she was tender hearted and upset by disappointed faces.

Life was not lavish. There were no expensive treats, even at Christmas time, but Auntie Kitty had a flair of thinking up absorbing ploys, or making the dullest of walks into an exploration or an adventure. She had a total rapport with children, and I am convinced that she preferred our company to that of unsympathetic grown ups.

In the drawing room, there was a grand piano. She was not particularly accomplished, but quite capable of playing a tune for Musical Bumps, or accompanying the three of us, should we feel impelled to sing, rollicking choruses of 'Blow Away The Morning Dew', or 'Sweet Lass of Richmond Hill.'

As well, there was a wireless, which was more than we had at home, and we listened regularly to Henry Hall and his Orchestra, and *In Town Tonight*, which was one of the earliest chat shows. Sometimes, on Saturday evenings, there would be an Operetta to listen to 'The Merry Widow', or 'Wild Violets' and on these occasions Auntie Kitty made a little ceremony of it, turning down the lights, and pretending we were in the theatre, the firelight the footlights, and a small box of Cadbury's Milk Tray to hand round in the 'interval'.

She was a pious person and her Anglican Faith meant a great deal to her. She liked to go to church on Sunday mornings, and sometimes we went with her, walking the length of Penzance promenade and up the steep street to St Mary's. The services were very High – classic smells and bells – with Sung Eucharist and incense being flung about, and it was always a relief to get out into the fresh air again, and walk home to the cheerful prospect of Sunday lunch.

It was some time before my mother and Auntie Kitty met

each other. The encounter was not a rousing success, because my mother had become slightly jealous of my devotion to this unknown woman; and because Auntie Kitty found it impossible to forgive my mother for her Christian Science.

When I told her about this, innocently blurting it out, Auntie Kitty was deeply affected. She felt, with some justification, that my spiritual and physical needs were being neglected, and I think from that moment on her feelings for me were both altered and deepened. I was not simply a school friend of Sarah's, but vulnerable and needy, and she longed to keep me with her forever, and would my life into the ways that she felt my future should follow.

I was aware of this conflict between my two mothers, but chose to ignore it. Divided loyalties are difficult at the best of times and, at ten years old, impossible to deal with.

When I was twelve, my sister, at seventeen, left school, and my mother decided to take her out to Burma for a year, to grow up and to spend some time with my father in his house in Rangoon. I would be left on my own. At first it was decided that I should board at St Clare's and spend holidays with any person willing to have me. I did not think this at all a good idea, and neither did Auntie Kitty. She swallowed her pride, telephoned my mother and said, please, please, could I spend the year with the Trembaths. I could go to school each day with Sarah and Harriet, and we could all enjoy the holidays together, and Auntie Kitty and Uncle Jim promised that they would take the greatest care of me.

My mother bucked slightly at this scheme. Perhaps she felt that she was simply handing me over; giving me away to another family. And she had always hated decisions or control being taken out of her hands. At first, she declined the invitation, but then my father intervened, letters passed to and fro from Burma, and finally, to my enormous relief, my mother gave in and agreed to the plan.

Trunks were packed and passages booked. My mother's sewing machine became red hot, whizzing away at tropical dresses for the two of them. Then it was time to say goodbye, and they disappeared, borne away by the London train. Auntie Kitty was with me to see them off. When the train had disappeared, we walked from the platform, through the booking office and out onto the carpark where the old Trembath Austin waited for us.

That year, without my family, flew by, terms and holidays and seasons crowding in on each other. The three of us walked to school in the mornings, and home again at four o'clock, in time for tea and then to do our homework. Auntie Kitty was very firm about this, and believed that homework should be dealt with at once, so that we could lightheartedly enjoy what remained of the evening. Homework was always a hurdle, but Auntie Kitty was prepared to help, which my mother never would. She did not do the work for us, but was always there, producing a dictionary, or an encyclopedia if needed, or hearing our French verbs or testing History dates. She was useless, however, at Maths, and we all spent hours struggling over algebra and sadistic problems. Trying to divide four pounds, eight shillings and fourpence by one pound two shillings and sixpence, caused us all much grief and frustration, and although we got good marks for all our other work, Sarah and I both trailed miserably when it came to Maths.

In the Easter holidays, we went on primrose gathering expeditions, and if it was anything like warm enough, insisted on bathing in the sea. In and out of the breakers, just for a frozen moment, and then scurrying up the beach, blue with cold, to be bundled into warm sweaters, and given a ginger biscuit which was meant to alleviate the agony.

At one point, we all got measles together, and the doctor came to inspect our spots and take our temperatures, and cheer us on our way.

In summer, the garden baked in a heatwave, and the tennis court dried out and flowers blazed from the borders. We lay in the shade, in a grassy corner where Uncle Jim kept his roller, and read books until it was cool enough to walk down to the rocky little beach below the house and have an evening swim. One summer morning, we got up tremendously early and walked down to Newlyn to watch the French crabbers come into harbour and unload their catch. As the summer died, we picked blackberries for Hilda to make bramble jelly, and took picnics up onto the moors, where the bracken turned gold and heather bloomed in great cushions of purple.